C++

AN INTRODUCTION TO COMPUTING

C++

An Introduction to Computing

Third Edition

Joel Adams

Larry Nyhoff

Calvin College

Grand Rapids, Michigan

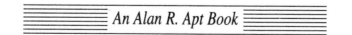

An Alan R. Apt Book

Prentice Hall

Pearson Education

Upper Saddle River, New Jersey 07458

Library of Congress Cataloging in Publication Data

Available on file

Vice President and Editorial Director, ECS: *Marcia J. Horton*
Publisher: *Alan R. Apt*
Associate Editor: *Toni D. Holm*
Development Editor: *Nick Murray*
Editorial Assistant: *Patrick Lindner*
Vice President and Director of Production and Manufacturing: *David W. Riccardi*
Executive Managing Editor: *Vince O'Brien*
Assistant Managing Editor: *Camille Trentacoste*
Production Editor: *Chirag Thakkar*
Creative Director: *Carole Anson*
Art Director: *Heather Scott*
Assistant Art Director: *John Christiana*
Interior Designer: *RepoCat Graphics & Editorial Services*
Cover Designer: *Heather Scott*
Cover Image: *Saguaro Cactus Sketch, Frank Lloyd Wright, courtesy Taliesen West*
Manufacturing Manager: *Trudy Pisciotti*
Manufacturing Buyer: *Lisa McDowell*
Marketing Manager: *Pamela Shaffer*
Marketing Assistant: *Barrie Reinhold*

Prentice Hall

Pearson Education, Inc.
Upper Saddle River, NJ 07458

Printed in the United States of America
10 9 8 7 6 5 4 3 2 1

ISBN 0-13-091426-6

Pearson Education Ltd., *London*
Pearson Education Australia Pty. Ltd., *Sydney*
Pearson Education Singapore, Pte. Ltd.
Pearson Education North Asia Ltd., *Hong Kong*
Pearson Education Canada, Inc., *Toronto*
Pearson Educacion de Mexico, S.A. de C.V.
Pearson Education–Japan, *Tokyo*
Pearson Education Malaysia, Pte. Ltd.
Pearson Education, Inc., *Upper Saddle River, New Jersey*

PREFACE

To properly introduce students to computing, we believe that the first computing course should accomplish two goals:

1. Introduce the methodologies and techniques of computer programming using a modern programming language, providing a (fairly) complete introduction to the language.
2. Introduce students to the breadth of the discipline of computing, so that they come to understand the role of programming in the broader context of computing.

The aim of previous editions and this new edition is to realize both of these goals.

Pedagogy

- A popular feature of the earlier editions and other texts we have written is to use a "real-world" problem at the beginning of each chapter to introduce the subject of that chapter (e.g., functions, `if` statements, loops, and so on). Seeing the *practice* of a new topic provides students with a framework in which the more general *concepts* that underlie that topic can be organized and understood.

- We continue the "use it, then build it" approach with respect to the more difficult topics for beginning programmers—a kind of *spiral* approach that revisits topics in increasingly greater detail. For example, predefined functions are used in Chapter 3 as components of expressions. Once students have experience using functions, Chapter 4 teaches them to build simple functions, and Chapters 6–8 show how to build increasingly sophisticated functions. Through this "use it, then build it" approach, students receive extensive exposure to the concepts underlying each of these constructs, reducing the learning curve when the time comes to actually build those constructs.

- A major pedagogical issue in a first programming course using C++ is where to present classes and objects—early, gradually, late, or not at all. In earlier editions and for the most part in this one, we use the spiral approach to introduce classes gradually. Thus, in Chapter 1 we introduce our design methodology, called *object-centered design*, a four-phase graduated methodology that novice programmers can use as an aid in designing software solutions. This methodology is used consistently to solve the problems presented throughout the remainder of the text. As the reader learns new language constructs in subsequent chapters, the methodology is expanded to incorporate these new constructs—for example, Chapter 5 introduces the student to the use of standard classes and methods; more practice follows in Chapters 7–10. Once students are firmly grounded in the use of (predefined, standard) classes, they learn to build classes in Chapter 11.

We realize, however, that a significant number of instructors prefer a classes/objects-early approach. We have made this possible by adding a special **optional** *OBJECTive Thinking* section to each chapter, beginning in Chapter 1, that introduces classes and objects. (The topics of these sections are listed later in this preface.)

New to this Edition

Thanks to constructive feedback from users of the first edition, this new edition incorporates a number of changes, including the following:

- Chapter objectives and end-of-chapter summaries consisting of key words and notes have been added to help students identify the main concepts of each chapter.
- The lengthy second chapter on types and expressions from the second edition has been split into two separate chapters.
- A new final chapter on data structures has been added.
- Case studies have been added in which a problem is presented, some ideas about how to solve it are given, and a complete solution, including both design and program code, is given on the book's Web site.
- As noted earlier, special optional *OBJECTive Thinking* sections have been added, one in each chapter, that present classes and objects, beginning already in Chapter 1. The approach here is a spiral one. The titles are as follows:
  - OBJECTive Thinking: Spheres as Objects
  - OBJECTive Thinking: Attribute Variables
  - OBJECTive Thinking: Initialization and Constructors
  - OBJECTive Thinking: Class Methods
  - OBJECTive Thinking: Instance Methods
  - OBJECTive Thinking: Mutator Methods
  - OBJECTivc Thinking: Code Reuse through Inheritance
  - OBJECTive Thinking: Class Variables, Instance Variables, and Scope
  - OBJECTive Thinking: Objects and Streams
  - OBJECTive Thinking: Objects and Sequences
  - OBJECTive Thinking: Operator Overloading and Friends
  - OBJECTive Thinking: Inheritance and Polymorphism
  - OBJECTive Thinking: The Matrix Class Revisited
  - OBJECTive Thinking: Pointers and Polymorphism

These sections can be omitted without loss of continuity. They might be used by students taking a course for honors credit or for independent study by students needing more challenging work.

- The history of computing section in Chapter 0 has been updated to include more events and photos, along with descriptions of more recent developments such as GUIs and networking.
- Ann Marchant of George Mason University has updated and expanded her superb presentation of the major ethical issues in computing in Chapter 1.

The Breadth of Computing

Introducing the students to the breadth of the discipline of computing grows out of an important theme of curriculum recommendations of the Association of Computing

Machinery (ACM) that an introductory course in computing should introduce the various knowledge areas of the discipline so that a solid base is established for later courses in computer science. To accomplish this, we have included *optional Part of the Picture* sections (some of which are introduced in the text with complete presentations on the book's Web site). They introduce the major areas of computer science, trying to capture the spirit of the curriculum guidelines in a natural, unobtrusive way. Several of them were written by experts in various areas of computing. They have been carefully selected to provide an overview of the discipline of computer science and to provide a foundation for further study in theoretical or applied computer science. Their titles include the following:

- What Is Computer Science?
- The History of Computing
- Introduction to Computer Systems
- Ethics and Issues (by Ann Marchant)
- Data Representation
- Computability Theory
- Simulation
- Boolean Logic and Digital Design
- Computer Architecture (by William Stallings)
- Introduction to Algorithm Analysis
- Numerical Methods
- Database Systems (by Keith Vander Linden)
- Component Programming
- Artificial Intelligence (by Keith Vander Linden)
- The C++ Type Hierarchy
- Algorithm Efficiency
- Expert Systems

Other Features

- The Web site `cs.calvin.edu/books/c++/intro/3e` will be maintained by the authors and will include corrections, additions, reference materials, and other supplementary materials such as solutions to case studies and some *Part of the Picture* sections.
- Optional sections (marked with asterisks) delve into more advanced topics, without requiring that they be covered in a normal introductory course.
- *Programming Pointers* at chapter ends highlight important points, including
  - proper techniques of design and style and
  - common programming pitfalls.
- Approximately 500 *Quick Quiz* questions provide a quick check of understanding of the material being studied. The answers to all of the Quick Quiz questions are given in Appendix E.

- Approximately 800 written exercises extend the Quick Quizzes and apply the material of the preceding section(s). No answers for these are provided in the text, therefore, they can be used for written assignments.
- The *Programming Problems* sections at the chapter ends contain more than 300 programming problems drawn from a wide range of application areas.
- A completely new design makes the text attractive and readable.
- Color is used to emphasize and highlight important features.
- Boxed displays make it easy to find descriptions of the basic C++ statements and constructs.
- Icons serve as markers to point out key parts of the text.

OBJECTive Thinking

Object-Centered Design

Object-Oriented Design

Note

Quick Quiz

Exercises

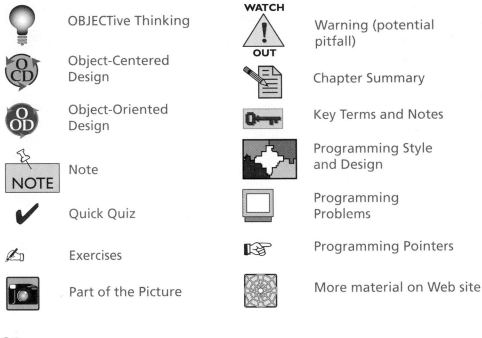

Part of the Picture

Warning (potential pitfall)

Chapter Summary

Key Terms and Notes

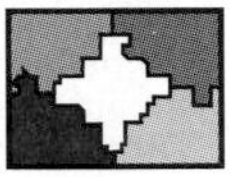
Programming Style and Design

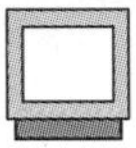
Programming Problems

Programming Pointers

More material on Web site

CS1 & CS2

This book is the first of a series of two, which together provide a thorough presentation of the C++ language. This first volume introduces the essential ideas of C++ programming and the breadth of the discipline of computing, making it ideal for a one-semester course in computer science. The second volume, *C++: An Introduction to Data Structures* by Larry Nyhoff, covers the more advanced features of C++ programming (e.g., recursion, inheritance, and polymorphism) and introduces topics that are traditionally taught in the second course (including elementary data structures, algorithms, and complexity) and how these three topics converge in the C++ Standard Template Library. Together, these two texts provide the beginning computer-science student with a complete introduction to C++ and a solid introduction to the discipline of computer science. If you choose to take advantage of the two-semester option, your local Prentice Hall Sales Representative can provide you with a discount on both volumes.

Supplementary Materials

- Web sites at `www.prenhall.com/adams` and `cs.calvin.edu/books/c++/intro/3e` will contain source code, an online study guide, color screen snaps of graphical output, and links to important sites that correspond to items in the text. Other enrichment materials are also planned for inclusion on these Web sites.
- The Instructors Resource CD-ROM contains most of the preceding items along with PowerPoint slides, as well as solutions to the exercises and many of the programming problems.
- A Lab Manual containing laboratory exercises and projects coordinated with the text is available in hardcopy with access to an on-line version. It can be used with GNU C++, Borland's C++ Builder, Metrowerks CodeWarrior C++, and Microsoft's Visual C++.
- Also available are software value pack options that include any of the following three software CD-ROM's: Borland's C++ Builder 6 Enterprise Trial Edition, CodeWarrior's Learning Edition Version 2.0, or Microsoft's Visual C++ 6.0.

Suggestions

The authors welcome feedback, both positive and negative. Your comments on features of the text and how the text could be improved are valuable to us in the preparation of subsequent editions. We would also appreciate notification of any errors. Such comments can be directed to either of the authors at `adams@calvin.edu` or `nyhl@calvin.edu` via the Internet or at the following U.S. mail address:

Department of Computer Science
Calvin College
3201 Burton SE
Grand Rapids, MI 49546
USA

Acknowledgments

We express our sincere appreciation to all who helped in the preparation of this text, especially Alan Apt, Toni Holm, Patrick Lindner, Nick Murray, Jake Warde, Chirag Thakkar, Camille Trentacoste, Heather Scott, and Sarah Burrows. We also appreciate the valuable comments and suggestions made by the following reviewers: David Barrentine (Johnson C.C.), Emily Crawford (Virginia Tech.), Lynn Kelly (New Mexico State Univ.), Mark McCullen (Michigan State Univ.), Bob Sompolski (Oakton C.C.), and David Spiegel (Wright State Univ.). In addition, we would like to thank Ann Marchant, William Stallings, and Keith Vander Linden for contributing *Part of the Picture* sections. And, of course, we must also thank our families—Barb, Roy, and Ian; Jeff, Dawn, Rebecca, Megan, Sara, Jim, Greg, Julie, Joshua, Derek, Lin, Tom, Joni, Abigail, and Micah—for encouraging and supporting us and for being understanding and patient when we slighted their needs and wants. Above all, we give thanks to God for giving us the opportunity, ability, and stamina to prepare this text.

Joel Adams
Larry Nyhoff

BRIEF CONTENTS

Contents

CHAPTER 3

CHAPTER 4

CHAPTER 5

CHAPTER 6

Selection 279

CHAPTER 7

CHAPTER 9

CHAPTER 10

CHAPTER 11

CHAPTER 12

CHAPTER 13

Multidimensional Arrays and Vectors 761

CHAPTER 14

CHAPTER 15

CHAPTER 0
Beginning Snapshots

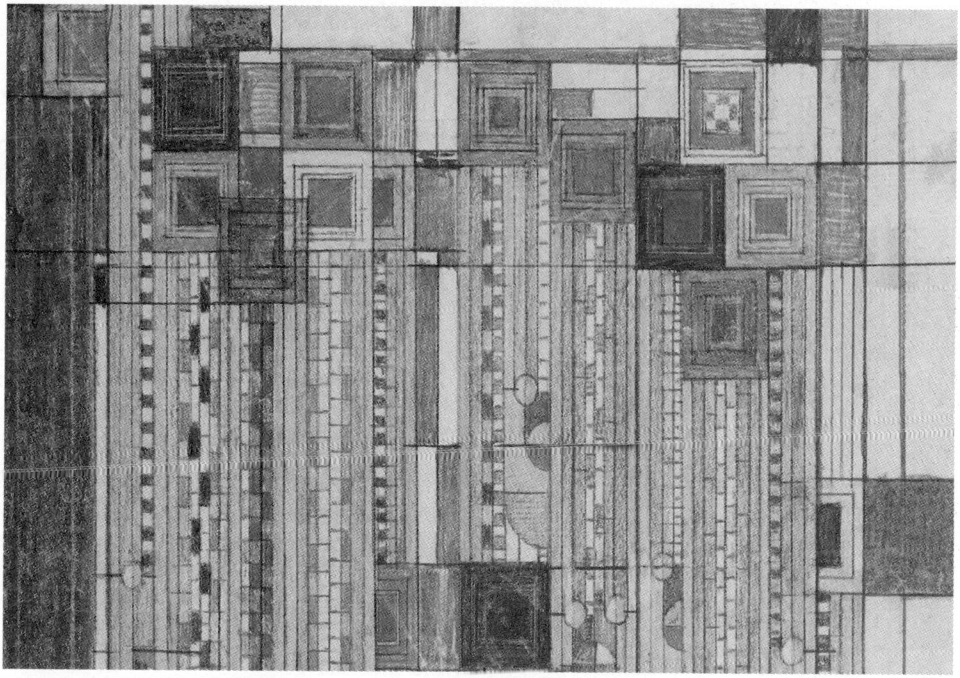

Is computer science a science? An engineering discipline? Or merely a technology, an inventor and purveyor of computing commodities? What is the intellectual substance of the discipline? Is it lasting, or will it fade within a generation?

-From the 1989 report of the Task Force on the Core of Computer Science

I wish these calculations had been executed by steam.

-Charles Babbage

Where a computer like the ENIAC is equipped with 18,000 vacuum tubes and weighs 30 tons, computers in the future may have only 1,000 vacuum tubes and weigh only 1 1/2 tons.

-Popular Mechanics, March 1949

640K ought to be enough for anyone.

-Bill Gates, 1981

So IBM has equipped all XTs with what it considers to be the minimum gear for a serious personal computer. Now the 10-megabyte disk and the 128K of memory are naturals for a serious machine.

-Peter Norton, 1983

Chapter Contents

Chapter Objectives

- (Optional) Give an overview of computer science to show its breadth.
- (Optional) Provide a context for many fundamental concepts of computing by pointing out some of the events from the past that have led to modern-day computing.
- (Optional) Describe basic components and organization of computer systems to better understand programming methods and features.

A first course in computing should help students develop an accurate and balanced picture of computer science as a discipline. This is important to students majoring in computer science, for whom this introduction to the discipline will be fleshed out in later courses, as well as to students majoring in other disciplines, for whom the portrayal of computing should be a realistic one. Thus, although most of this text is devoted to developing problem-solving and programming skills, we attempt to give a more complete picture of computer science by including special "Part of the Picture" sections throughout the text that introduce topics from various areas of computer science. They may be omitted without loss of continuity, but *we encourage you to read these Part of the Picture sections to better understand this young discipline called computer science.*

Part of the Picture: What Is Computer Science?

The term *computer science* has been a source of confusion. Although there are sciences called physics and biology, there are no disciplines called telescope science or microscope science. How can there be a computer science if a computer is simply another scientific tool or instrument?

Let us begin with what computer science is not. It is not simply writing computer programs. Although problem solving and programming are indeed the primary focus of this text, the discipline of computing consists of much more. The breadth of the discipline is evidenced by the following list of the main areas of computer science given in curriculum recommendations from the professional societies ACM (Association of Computing Machinery) and IEEE (Institute of Electrical and Electronics Engineers).[1] This list contains some terms that you may not understand, but most of them will be explained later. In our attempt to portray computer science as a discipline, the *Part of the Picture* sections that follow will focus on many of these areas and help you to better understand them.

---

[1] Allen B. Tucker, ed., *Computing Curricula 1991: Report of the ACM/IEEE-CS Joint Curriculm Task Force* (ACM Press and IEEE Computer Society Press, 1991).

Area of Computer Science	What This Area Deals with
Algorithms and Data Structures	Specific classes of problems and their efficient solutions
	Performance characteristics of algorithms
	Organization of data relative to different access requirements
Architecture	Methods of organizing efficient, reliable computing systems
	Implementation of processors, memory, communications, and software interfaces
	Design and control of large, reliable computational systems
Artificial Intelligence and Robotics	Basic models of behavior
	Building (virtual or actual) machines to simulate animal and human behavior
	Inference, deduction, pattern recognition, and knowledge representation
Database and Information Retrieval	Organizing information and designing algorithms for the efficient access and update of stored information
	Modeling data relationships
	Security and protection of information in a shared environment
	Characteristics of external storage devices
Human–Computer Communication	Efficient transfer of information between humans and machines
	Graphics
	Human factors that affect efficient interaction
	Organization and display of information for effective utilization by humans
Numerical and Symbolic Computation	General methods for efficiently and accurately using computers to solve equations from mathematical models
	Effectiveness and efficiency of various approaches to the solution of equations
	Development of high-quality mathematical software packages

Area of Computer Science	What This Area Deals with
Operating Systems	Control mechanisms that allow multiple resources to be efficiently coordinated during execution of programs
	Appropriate service of user requests
	Effective strategies for resource control
	Effective organization to support distributed computation
Programming Languages	Notations for defining virtual machines that execute algorithms
	Efficient translation from high-level languages to machine codes
	Extension mechanisms that can be provided in programming languages
Software Methodology and Engineering	Specification, design, and production of large software systems
	Principles of programming and software development, verification, and validation of software
	Specification and production of software systems that are safe, secure, reliable, and dependable
Social and Professional Context	Cultural, social, legal, and ethical issues related to computing

Because to some people the term *computer science* seems inadequate to describe such a broad range of areas, the Computing Curricula 1991 Report suggests that *computing* is a more appropriate term than *computer science*. However, we will use the two terms interchangeably throughout this text.

Part of the Picture: The History of Computing

The computer is one of the most important inventions in history. It has evolved into an essential component of many areas of human culture, including business, industry, government, science, and education; indeed, it has touched nearly every aspect of our lives. The impact of twentieth-century information technology has already been nearly as widespread as the impact of the printing press and the Industrial Revolution. As part of the picture of computing, it is necessary to be aware of some of the events that led to modern-day computing, not only for the purpose of contextualizing the present-day computer within its own history, but also because an examination of the history of the computer serves as a superb introduction to the fundamental concepts of computing.

Four important concepts have shaped the history of computing:

- the **mechanization of arithmetic;**
- the **stored program;**
- the **graphical user interface;**
- the computer **network**.

The following timeline of the history of computing shows some of the important events and devices that have implemented these concepts, especially the first two. Additional information about these and the other two important concepts follow the timeline.

MACHINES TO DO ARITHMETIC

The term *computer* dates back to the 1600s. However, until the 1950s, the term referred almost exclusively to a *human* who performed computations.

For human beings, the task of performing large amounts of computation is one that is laborious, time consuming, and error prone. Thus, the human desire to mechanize arithmetic is an ancient one. One of the earliest "personal calculators" was the **abacus**, with movable beads strung on rods to count and to do calculations. Although its exact origin is unknown, the abacus was used by the Chinese perhaps 3000 to 4000 years ago and is still used today throughout Asia. Early merchants used the abacus in trading transactions.

The ancient British stone monument **Stonehenge**, located near Salisbury, England, was built between 1900 and 1600 B.C. and, evidently, was used to predict the changes of the seasons.

In the twelfth century, a Persian teacher of mathematics in Baghdad, Muhammad ibn-Musa **al-Khowarizm**, developed some of the first step-by-step procedures for doing computations. The word **algorithm** used for such procedures is derived from his name.

In Western Europe, the Scottish mathematician John Napier (1550–1617) designed a set of ivory rods (called **Napier's bones**) to assist with doing multiplications. Napier also developed tables of logarithms and other multiplication machines.

The videotape series entitled "The Machine That Changed The World" is highly recommended by the authors. For information about it, see http://ei.cs.vt.edu/~history/TMTCTW.html. A Jacquard Loom, Hollerith's tabulator, the ENIAC, UNIVAC, early chips, and other computer artifacts can also be viewed at the National Museum of American History of the Smithsonian Institution in Washington, D.C.

EARLY CALCULATORS

3000 B.C. ABACUS

1900-1600 B.C. STONEHENGE

12TH CENTURY:
AL-KHOWARIZM

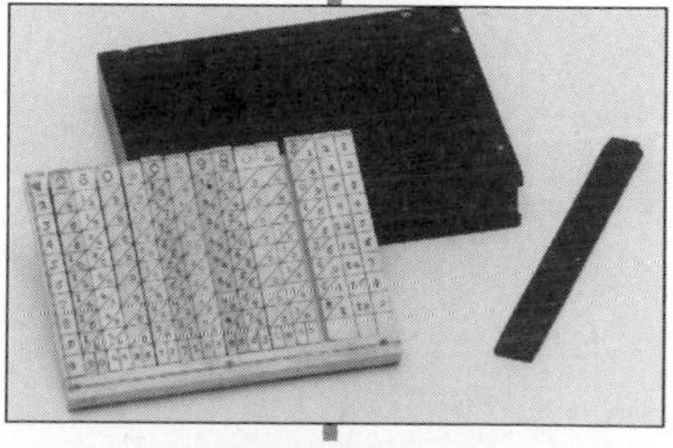

1612 NAPIER'S BONES

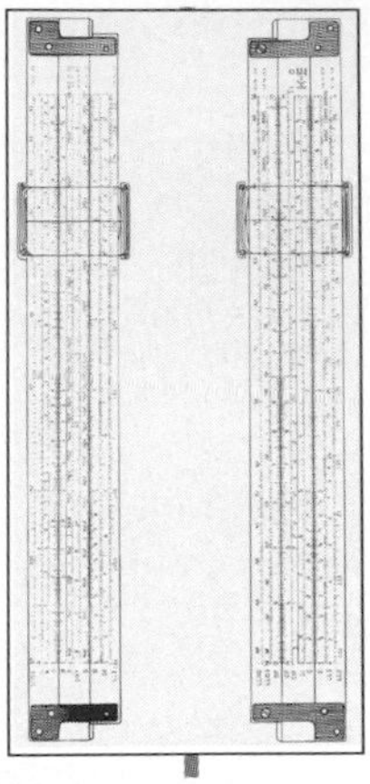

1630 SLIDE RULE

The English mathematician William Oughtred invented a circular **slide rule** in the early 1600s. Slide rules were based on Napier's logarithms, and more modern ones like that shown here were used by engineers and scientists through the 1950s and into the 1960s to do rapid approximate computations.

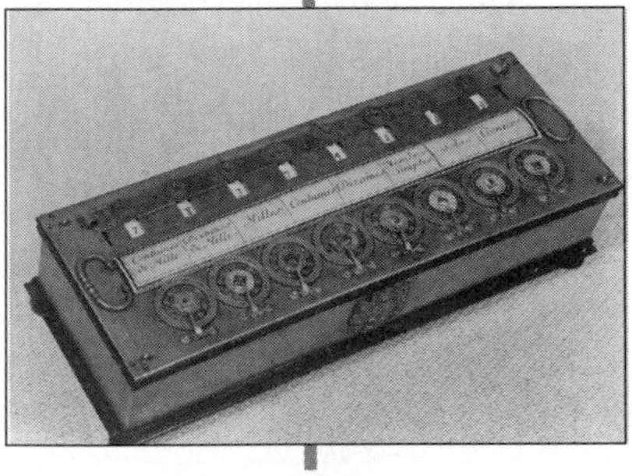

1642 PASCALINE

The young French mathematician **Blaise Pascal** (1623–1662) invented one of the first mechanical adding machines to help his father with calculating taxes. It used a series of eight ten-toothed wheels (one tooth for each decimal digit), which were connected so that numbers could be added or subtracted by moving the wheels.

The "Pascaline" was a **digital** calculator, because it represented numerical information as discrete digits, as opposed to a graduated scale like that used in *analog* instruments of measurement such as nondigital clocks and thermometers. Each digit was represented by a gear that had ten different positions (a *ten-state device*) so that it could "count" from 0 through 9 and, upon reaching 10, would reset to 0 and advance the gear in the next column so as to represent the action of "carrying" to the next digit.

Although Pascal built more than 50 of his adding machines, his commercial venture failed because the devices could not be built with sufficient precision for practical use. Nevertheless, Pascal is important in the history of computing because this was one of the first digital mechanical calculators. In the late 1960s a programming language was named Pascal in his honor.

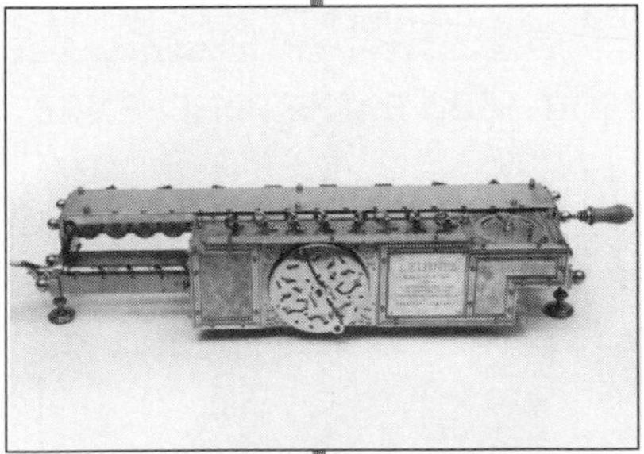

1673 LEIBNIZ' CALCULATOR

The German mathematician **Gottfried Wilhelm von Leibniz** invented an improved mechanical calculator that, like the Pascaline, used a system of gears and dials to do calculations. However, it was more reliable and accurate than the Pascaline and could perform all four of the basic arithmetic operations of addition, subtraction, multiplication, and division.

A number of other mechanical calculators followed that further refined Pascal's and Leibniz's designs, and by the end of the nineteenth century, these calculators had become important tools in science, business, and commerce.

THE STORED PROGRAM

The fundamental idea that distinguishes computers from calculators is the concept of a stored **program** that controls the computation. A program is a sequence of instructions that the computer follows to solve some problem. An income tax form is a good analogy. While a calculator can be a useful tool in the process, computing taxes involves much more than arithmetic. To produce the correct result, one must execute the form's precise sequence of steps of writing numbers down (storage), looking numbers up (retrieval), and computation to produce the correct result. Likewise, a computer program is a precise sequence of steps designed to accomplish some human task.

The stored program concept also gives the computer its amazing versatility. Unlike most other machines, which are engineered to mechanize a single task, a computer can be programmed to perform many different tasks—that is, the choice of task is deferred to the user. This is the fascinating paradox of the computer: Although its **hardware** is designed for a very specific task—the mechanization of arithmetic—computer software programs enable the computer to perform a dizzying array of human tasks, from navigational control of the space shuttle to word processing to musical composition. For this reason, the computer is sometimes called the **universal machine**.

An early example of a stored program automatically controlling a hardware device can be found in the weaving loom invented in 1801 by the Frenchman **Joseph Marie Jacquard**. Holes punched in metal cards directed the action of this loom: A hole punched in one of the cards would enable its corresponding thread to come through and be incorporated into the weave at a given point in the process; the absence of a hole would exclude an undesired thread. To change to a different weaving pattern, the operator of this loom would simply switch to another set of cards. Jacquard's loom is thus one of the first examples of a programmable machine, and many later computers would make similar use of punched cards.

The punched card's present-or-absent hole also marks the early occurrence of another key concept in the history of computing—the **two-state device**, which refers to any mechanism for which there are only two possible conditions. Within a decade, thousands of automated looms were being used in Europe, threatening the traditional weaver's way of life. In protest, English weavers who called themselves *Luddites* rioted and destroyed several of the new looms and cards. Some of the Luddites were hanged for their actions. (The term Luddite is still used today to refer to someone who is skeptical of new technology.)

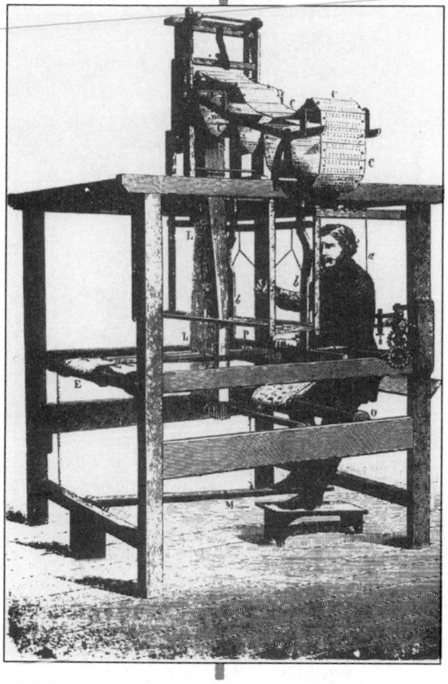

1801 JACQUARD LOOM

1822 BABBAGE'S DIFFERENCE ENGINE

1833 BABBAGE'S ANALYTICAL ENGINE

The two fundamental concepts of mechanized calculation and stored program control were combined by the English mathematician **Charles Babbage** (1792–1871). In Babbage's lifetime, humans involved in almost any form of computation relied heavily upon books of mathematical tables that contained the results of calculations that had already been performed by others. However, such mathematical tables took far too long for humans to produce and were typically rife with errors. Moreover, world travel, the Industrial Revolution, and other new scientific and economic realities had produced an explosion in the need for mathematical computations. It was clear to Babbage that "human computers" were simply not up to the task of supplying the demand.

In 1822, supported by the British government, Babbage began work on a machine that he called the **Difference Engine**. Comprised of a system of gears, the Difference Engine was designed to compute polynomials for preparing mathematical tables. Babbage continued this work until 1833, when he abandoned this effort having completed only part of the machine. According to Doron Swade, curator of the London Science Museum, the cantankerous Babbage argued with his engineer, ran out of money, and was beset by personal rivalry.

In 1833, Babbage began the design of a much more sophisticated machine that he called his **Analytical Engine**, which was to have over 50,000 components. The operation of this machine was to be far more versatile and fully automatic, controlled by programs stored on punched cards, an idea based on Jacquard's earlier work. In fact, as Babbage himself observed: "The analogy of the Analytical Engine with this well-known process is nearly perfect."

The basic design of Babbage's Analytical Engine corresponded remarkably to that of modern computers in that it involved the four primary operations of a computer system: **processing**, **storage**, **input**, and **output**. It included a mill for carrying out the arithmetic computations according to a sequence of instructions (like the central processing unit in modern machines); the store was the machine's memory for storing up to 1,000 50-digit numbers and intermediate results; input was to be by means of punched cards; output was to be printed; and other components were designed for the transfer of information between components. When completed, it would have been as large as a locomotive, been powered by steam, and able to calculate to six decimal places of accuracy very rapidly and print out results, all of which was to be controlled by a stored program!

Babbage's machine was not built during his lifetime, but it is nevertheless an important part of the history of computing because many of the concepts of its design are used in modern computers. For this reason, Babbage is sometimes called the "Father of Computing."

Ada Augusta, Lord Byron's daughter, was one of the few people other than Babbage who understood the Analytical Engine's design. This enabled her to develop "programs" for the machine, and for this reason she is sometimes called "the first programmer." She described the similarity of Jacquard's and Babbage's inventions: "The Analytical Engine weaves algebraic patterns just as the Jacquard loom weaves flowers and leaves." In the 1980s, the programming language Ada was named in her honor.

1842 ADA AUGUSTA

During the next 100 years, little progress was made in realizing Babbage's dream. About the only noteworthy event during this time was the invention by **Herman Hollerith** of an electric tabulating machine that could tally census statistics that had been stored on punched cards. There was a fear that, because of growing population, it would not be possible to complete processing of the 1890 census before the next one was to be taken. Hollerith's machine enabled the United States Census Bureau to complete the 1890 census in 2 1/2 years. The Hollerith Tabulating Company later merged with other companies to form the International Business Machines (IBM) Corporation.

ELECTROMECHANICAL COMPUTERS

1890 HOLLERITH'S TABULATING MACHINE

Much of Babbage's dream was finally realized in the "Z" series of computers developed by the young German engineer **Konrad Zuse** in the 1930s. Ingeniously, Zuse designed his computers to mechanize arithmetic of **binary** numbers rather than that of decimal numbers. Because there are only two binary digits, 0 and 1, Zuse could construct his machine from two-state devices instead of ten-state devices, thus greatly simplifying the engineering of his computer. The two-state device Zuse deployed was the electromechanical relay, a two-position switch that would either complete or break the circuit connecting two phone lines. This mechanism was in wide use in the telephone industry to automate connections previously managed by human operators.

However, Zuse ultimately grew dissatisfied with the slow speed at which the relay switched from one state to the other. His assistant, **Helmut Schreyer**, made the brilliant suggestion of using vacuum tubes, which could switch between states—on and off—electronically, thousands of times faster than any mechanical device involving moving parts. In the middle of World War II, however, Adolf Hitler was convinced that victory was near and refused to fund Zuse's proposal to build the first fully **electronic** computer.

1935-1938 KONRAD ZUSE

1937 ALAN TURING

1944 MARK I

EARLY ELECTRONIC COMPUTERS

1936-1939 ATANASOFF'S ELECTRONIC DIGITAL COMPUTER (ABC)

In addition to building electromechanical computers, Konrad Zuse in 1945 designed a high-level programming language that he named Plankalkül. Although Zuse wrote programs using this language, it was never actually implemented due to a lack of funding. As a result, it lay in obscurity until 1972 when Zuse's manuscripts were discovered. This language was amazingly sophisticated for its time—over 15 years passed before its features began to appear in other languages. Zuse designed programs to perform tasks as diverse as integer and floating-point arithmetic, sorting lists of numbers, and playing chess.

World War II also spurred the development of computing devices in the United States, Britain, and Europe. In Britain, **Alan Turing** developed the universal machine concept, forming the basis of **computability theory**. (See Chapter 4.) During World War II, he was part of a team whose task was to decrypt intercepted messages of the German forces. Several machines resulted from this British war effort, one of which was the Collosus, finished in 1943.

The best-known computer built before 1945 was the Harvard **Mark I** (whose full name was the Harvard–IBM Automatic Sequence Controlled Calculator). Like Zuse's "Z" machines, it was driven by electromechanical relay technology. Repeating much of the work of Babbage, Howard Aiken and others at IBM constructed this large, automatic, general-purpose, electromechanical calculator. It was sponsored by the U.S. Navy and (like Babbage's machines) was intended to compute mathematical and navigational tables.

The first fully electronic binary computer, the **ABC** (Atanasoff–Berry Computer), was developed by John **Atanasoff** and **Clifford Berry** at Iowa State University during 1937-1942. It introduced the ideas of binary arithmetic, regenerative memory, and logic circuits.

Unfortunately, because the ABC was never patented and because others failed at the time to see its utility, it took three decades before Atanasoff and Berry received recognition for this remarkable technology. Although the ENIAC (1943–1946) bore the title of the first fully electronic computer for many years, a historic 1973 court decision ruled that Atanasoff was the legal inventor of the first electronic digital computer.

Grace Murray Hopper (1907–1992) began work as a coder—what we today would call a programmer—for the Mark I in 1944. In the late 1950s, "Grandma COBOL," as she has affectionately been called, led the effort to develop the COBOL programming language for business applications.

1944 GRACE HOPPER

The actual physical components that make up a computer system are its **hardware**. Several generations of computers can be identified by their type of hardware. **First-generation** computers are characterized by their extensive use of vacuum tubes. Although they could do calculations much more rapidly than mechanical and electromechanical computers, the heat generated by large numbers of vacuum tubes and their short lifetimes led to frequent failures.

FIRST-GENERATION COMPUTERS

1945-1956 FIRST-GENERATION COMPUTERS—VACUUM TUBES

The ENIAC (Electronic Numerical Integrator and Computer) is arguably the best known of the early electronic computers (and long thought to be the first). It was designed by **J. Presper Eckert** and **John Mauchly**, who began work on it in 1943 at the Moore School of Engineering at the University of Pennsylvania. When it was completed in 1946, this 30-ton machine had 18,000 vacuum tubes, 70,000 resistors, and 5 million soldered joints and consumed 160 kilowatts of electrical power. Stories are told of how the lights in Philadelphia dimmed when the ENIAC was operating.

This extremely large machine could multiply numbers approximately 1000 times faster than the Mark I, but it was quite limited in its applications and was used primarily by the Army Ordnance Department to calculate firing tables and trajectories for various types of artillery shells. The instructions that controlled the ENIAC's operation were entered into the machine by rewiring some of the computer's circuits. This complicated process was very time consuming, sometimes taking a number of people several days; during this time, the computer was idle. In other early computers, the instructions were stored outside the machine on punched cards or some other medium and were transferred into the machine one at a time for interpretation and execution. Unfortunately, because of the relative slowness of the moving parts of mechanical input devices in comparison to the electronic parts of the computer dedicated to processing, such computers would always finish executing the instruction long before the next instruction was finished loading. Thus, again, the processing portion of the computer was sitting idle too much of the time.

1943-1946 ENIAC

1945 JOHN VON NEUMANN'S "FIRST DRAFT OF A REPORT ON THE EDVAC"

In 1945, John von Neumann wrote "First Draft of a Report on the EDVAC (Electronic Discrete Variable Automatic Computer)" in which he described a scheme that required program instructions to be stored internally before execution. This led to his being credited as the inventor of the stored-program concept. The architectural design he described is still known as the **von Neumann architecture** (although there is evidence that others including Eckert and Mauchly and Zuse had similar ideas several years before this).

The advantage of executing instructions from a computer's memory rather than directly from a mechanical input device is that it eliminates time that the computer must spend waiting for instructions. Instructions can be processed more rapidly and more importantly; they can be modified by the computer itself while computations are taking place. The introduction of this scheme to computer **architecture** was crucial to the development of general-purpose computers.

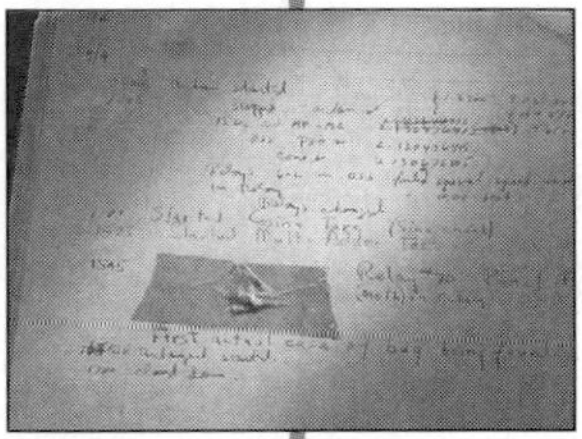

1945 COMPUTER BUG

While working on the Mark II computer, Grace Hopper found one of the first computer "**bugs**"—an actual bug stuck in one of the thousands of relays that has been preserved in the National Museum of American History of the Smithsonian Institution. She glued it into the logbook, and subsequent efforts to find the cause of machine stoppage were reported to Aiken as "debugging the computer."

1951 UNIVAC

Eckert and Mauchly left the University of Pennsylvania to form the Eckert–Mauchly Computer Corporation, which built the **UNIVAC** (Universal Automatic Computer). Started in 1946 and completed in 1951, it was the first commercially available computer designed for both scientific and business applications. The UNIVAC achieved instant fame partly due to its correct (albeit unbelieved) prediction on national television of the election of President Eisenhower in the 1952 U.S. presidential election, based upon 5% of the returns. UNIVAC soon became the common name for computers.

Soon afterward, because of various setbacks, Eckert and Mauchly sold their company to the Remington–Rand Corporation, who sold the first UNIVAC to the Census Bureau in 1951.

SECOND-GENERATION COMPUTERS

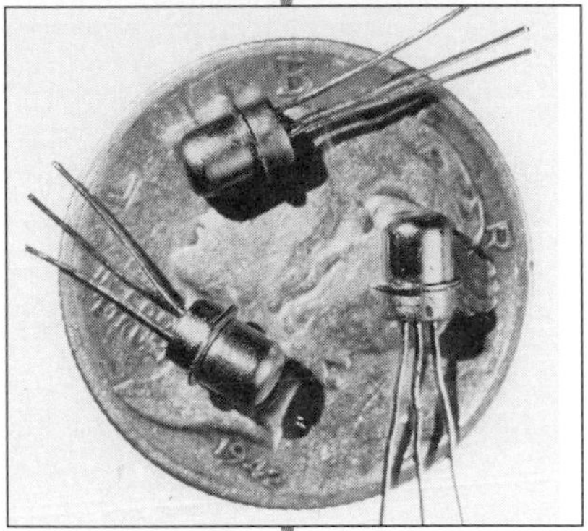

Second-generation computers, built between 1956 and 1963, used **transistors** in place of the large, cumbersome vacuum tubes, marking the beginning of the great computer shrinkage. These computers were smaller, faster, required less power, generated far less heat, and were more reliable than their predecessors. They were also less expensive.

Early computers were difficult to use because of the complex coding schemes used to represent programs and data. A key development during the late 1950s and early 1960s was the development of programming languages that made it much easier to develop programs.

1956–1963 SECOND GENERATION COMPUTERS—EARLY TRANSISTORS

In 1957, after three years of work, John Backus and his colleagues delivered the first **FORTRAN** (FORmula TRANslation) compiler for the IBM 704. Their first report commented that a programmer was able to write and debug in four to five hours a program that would have taken several days to complete before. FORTRAN has undergone several revisions and remains a powerful language for scientific computing.

1957 FORTRAN

In 1958, IBM introduced the first of the second-generation computers (the 7090 and other computers in their 7000 series), vaulting IBM from computer obscurity to first place in the computer industry.

1958 IBM 7090

Also in 1958, as part of his work in developing artificial intelligence, John McCarthy developed the programming language **LISP** (LISt Processing) for manipulating strings of symbols, a non-numeric processing language.

LISP

Since 1952, Grace Hopper had been developing a series of natural-language-like programming languages for use in business data processing. This culminated in 1960 with the development of **COBOL** (COmmon Business Oriented Language) by an industry-wide team. Since then, more programs have been written in COBOL than in any other programming language.

1960 COBOL

Another language that appeared in 1960 was **ALGOL 60** (ALGOrithmic Language), which became the basis of many programming languages that followed, such as **Pascal**.

ALGOL 60

THIRD-GENERATION COMPUTERS

1964-1971 THIRD-GENERATION COMPUTERS—CHIPS AND INTEGRATED CIRCUITS

Third-generation computers used **integrated circuits** (IC, chips), which first became commercially available from the Fairchild Corporation. These ICs were based on the pioneering work of **Jack Kilby** and **Robert Noyce**.

It was also during this period that, in addition to improved hardware, computer manufacturers began to develop collections of programs known as **system software**, which made computers easier to use. One of the more important advances in this area was the third-generation development of **operating systems**. Two important early operating systems still used today are Unix (1971) and MS-DOS (1981).

1964 THE IBM SYSTEM/360

The **IBM System/360,** introduced in 1964, is commonly accepted as the first of the third generation of computers. Orders for this family of mutually compatible computers and peripherals climbed to 1000 per month within two years

1965 PDP-8

In 1965, Digital Equipment Corporation introduced the **PDP-8,** the first commercially successful **minicomputer**. Because of its speed, small size, and reasonable cost— $18,000, less than 20% of the six-digit price tag for an IBM 360 mainframe—it became a popular computer in many scientific establishments, small businesses, and manufacturing plants.

In 1968, **Douglas Engelbart** and his research team worked at developing a more user-friendly form of computing, usable by average persons and for purposes other than numerical computation. Engelbart's inventions anticipated many of the attributes of personal computing, including the **mouse**, word processor, windowed interfaces, integrated "Help," and linked text that would later be termed "hypertext."

1968 DOUGLAS ENGELBART: COMPUTER MOUSE, TWO-DIMENSIONAL DISPLAY, EDITING, HYPERMEDIA

It was also in 1968 that Niklaus Wirth, a professor at the Swiss Federal Institute of Technology (ETH) in Zurich, began work on a new ALGOL-based programming language. It was named **Pascal**, in honor of Blaise Pascal, and became the language of choice for teaching computer programming through the 1980s.

PASCAL

Disillusioned by how work on the multiuser operating system Multics was proceeding, **Ken Thompson** of Bell Telephone Laboratories began work in 1969 on a simpler OS aimed at the single user. His first implementation of Unix was written in the assembly language of a spare Digital Equipment Corporation PDP-7 computer. In a pun on the name Multics, the new operating system was named **Unix**.

Unix is still undergoing development today and has become one of the most popular operating systems. It is the only operating system that has been implemented on computers ranging from microcomputers to supercomputers.

1969 KEN THOMPSON: UNIX

Another noteworthy event began in 1969 when the Advanced Research Projects Agency (ARPA) of the U.S. Department of Defense introduced the **ARPANET**, a network linking computers at some of the department's university research centers. Transmissions between the ARPANET computers traveled in the form of **packets**, each of which was addressed so that it could be routed to its destination. As more and more hosts were added to the ARPANET backbone, it became known as the **Internet**.

ARPANET—THE BEGINNING OF THE INTERNET

FOURTH-GENERATION COMPUTERS

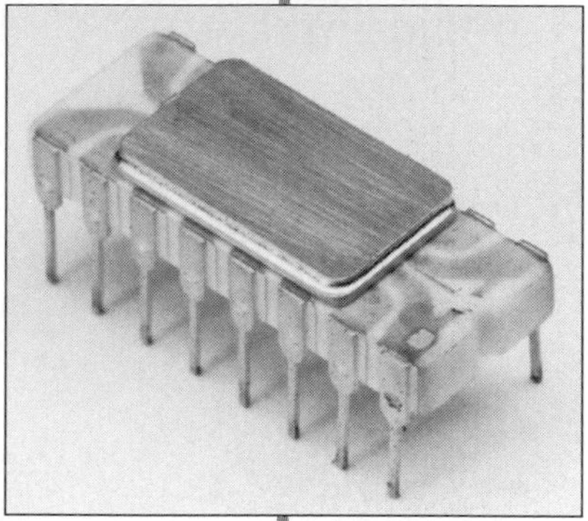

1971 INTEL 4004 CHIP

Computers from the 1980s on, commonly called **fourth-generation computers**, use very large-scale integrated (VLSI) circuits on silicon chips and other microelectronic advances to shrink their size and cost still more while enlarging their capabilities. A typical chip is equivalent to millions of transistors, is smaller than a baby's fingernail, weighs a small fraction of an ounce, requires only a trickle of power, and costs but a few dollars.

The first chip was the 4004 chip designed by Intel's **Ted Hoff**, giving birth to the microprocessor, which marked the beginning of the fourth generation of computers. This, along with the first use of an 8-inch floppy disk at IBM, ushered in the era of the personal computer.

Robert Noyce, one of the cofounders of the Intel Corporation (which introduced the 4004 microprocessor in 1971), contrasted microcomputers with the ENIAC as follows:

An individual integrated circuit on a chip perhaps a quarter of an inch square now can embrace more electronic elements than the most complex piece of electronic equipment that could be built in 1950. Today's microcomputer, at a cost of perhaps $300, has more computing capacity than the first electronic computer, ENIAC. It is twenty times faster, has a larger memory, consumes the power of a light bulb rather than that of a locomotive, occupies 1/30,000 the volume and costs 1/10,000 as much. It is available by mail order or at your local hobby shop.

1973 DENNIS RITCHIE: C

ETHERNET

HISTORIC COURT DECISION REGARDING FIRST ELECTRONIC COMPUTER

To simplify the task of transferring the Unix operating system to other computers, Ken Thompson began to search for a high-level language in which to rewrite Unix. None of the languages in existence at the time were appropriate; therefore, in 1970, Thompson began designing a new language called B. By 1972, it had become apparent that B was not adequate for implementing Unix. At that time, **Dennis Ritchie**, also at Bell Labs, designed a successor language to B that he called **C**, and approximately 90 percent of Unix was rewritten in C.

Other noteworthy events in 1973 included the following:

- **Ethernet**, the basis for LANs (Local Area Networks), was developed at Xerox PARC by Robert Metcalf
- A district court in Minneapolis ruled that John Atanasoff was the legal inventor of the first electronic digital computer, thus invalidating Eckert's and Mauchly's patent.

Noteworthy in 1974:

- The MITS **Altair 8800** hobby-kit computer was invented by Edward Roberts (who coined the term **personal computer**), William Yates, and Jim Bybee. It was driven by the 8-bit Intel **8080** chip, had 256 bytes of memory, but no keyboard, no display, and no external storage. It sold for $300–400.

- **Bill Gates** and **Paul Allen** wrote a BASIC compiler for the Altair.

- Working in a garage, Steven Jobs and Steve Wozniak developed the **Apple I**.

1974

ALTAIR

BASIC

JOBS & WOZNIAK: APPLE 1

One of the most popular early personal computers was the **Apple II**, introduced in 1976 by Steven Jobs and Steve Wozniak. Because of its affordability and the availability of basic software applications, it was an immediate success, especially in schools and colleges.

1976 APPLE II

The first **supercomputer** and the fastest machine of its day, the **Cray I**, developed by Seymour Cray, was also introduced in 1976. It was built in the shape of a C so components would be close together, reducing the time for electronic signals to travel between them.

CRAY 1

Also in 1976, **Apple** Corporation and **Microsoft** Corporation were founded.

APPLE CORP.
MICROSOFT CORP.

1981 IBM PC

In 1981, IBM entered the personal computer market with the IBM PC, originally called the Acorn. Driven by the Intel 8-bit 8088 chip, it used Microsoft's **DOS** operating system under an agreement that gave Microsoft all the profits in exchange for their having borne the development costs. MS-DOS thus became the most popular operating system for personal computers, and the PC established a microcomputer standard adopted by many other manufacturers of personal computers.

The IBM XT debuted the following year, sporting a 10-megabyte hard disk drive. The IBM AT followed in 1983, driven by the 16-bit Intel 80286 microprocessor, the first in the line of Intel's "80x86" chips.

1983 BJARNE STROUSTRUP: C++

By the late 1970s, a new approach to programming appeared on the scene—**object-oriented programming** (OOP)—that emphasized the modeling of objects through classes and inheritance. A research group at Xerox' Palo Alto Research Center (PARC) created the first truly object-oriented language, named **Smalltalk-80**.

Another Bell Labs researcher, **Bjarne Stroustrup**, began the work of extending C with object-oriented features. In 1983, the redesigned and extended programming language C With Classes was introduced with the new name **C++**.

Also in 1983

NOVELL ANNOUNCES NETWARE

- **Novell** Data Systems introduced NetWare, a network operating system (NOS), which made possible the construction of a **Local Area Network** (LAN) of IBM PC-compatible microcomputers.

TCP/IP

- **Transmission Control Protocol/Internet Protocol (TCP/IP)** became the official protocol governing transmitting and receiving of data via the ARPANET. Later that year, the University of California at Berkeley released a new version of BSD (also known as Berkeley Unix), which included TCP/IP, thus providing academic computing systems nationwide with the technology to tie into the ARPANET. Explosive growth in the ARPANET resulted.

Using a renowned Orwellian advertisement parodying the downtrodden masses subservient to the IBM PC, Apple announced in 1984 the **Macintosh**, a new personal computer driven by the 32-bit Motorola 68000 microprocessor. Inspired by Steve Jobs' visit to Xerox PARC in 1979, the "Mac" brought the graphical user interface (GUI) to personal computing.

1984 MACINTOSH

In 1985, Microsoft introduced **Windows 1.0**, its graphical user interface for IBM-PC compatibles. It was not until the release of Windows 3.0 in 1990, however, that it gained widespread acceptance.

1985 WINDOWS

In 1986, **Intel** released the 32-bit **80386 chip** (better known as the "386" chip), which became the best-selling microprocessor in history. It contained 275,000 transistors. The **80486**, released in 1989, had more than a million.

1986 INTEL 386 CHIP

In 1991, CERN (European Organization for Nuclear Research) introduced the **World Wide Web**, developed by **Tim Berners-Lee**.

1991 TIM BERNERS–LEE: WWW

In 1992, Linus Torvalds developed **Linux**, a free version of the Unix operating system for PCs.

1992 LINUX

1993 PENTIUM CHIPS

Several noteworthy things happened in 1993:

- Intel introduced the 64-bit Pentium chip containing more than 3 million transistors. The Pentium Pro released in 1995 had more than 5.5 million. The Pentium II followed in 1997 with 7.5 million transistors, and the Pentium III in 1999 with more than 10 million.

POWER PC CHIP

- Motorola shipped the first PowerPC chip.

MOSAIC

- The National Center for Supercomputing Applications (NCSA) at the University of Illinois released the first version of **Mosaic**, the first graphical Web browser.

APPLE NEWTON

- Apple introduced the Newton, the first "palmtop" computer.

1994 NETSCAPE NAVIGATOR 1.0

In 1994

- **Netscape Navigator 1.0** was released.

YAHOO!

- **Yahoo!,** the first major Web index, went online. It was started in April 1994 by Electrical Engineering Ph.D. candidates at Stanford University, David Filo and Jerry Yang, as a way to keep track of their personal interests on the Internet.

PALM COMPUTING

- **Jeff Hawkins** and **Donna Dubinsky** founded **Palm Computing**. The first Pilot was shipped in 1996.

1995 JAMES GOSLING: JAVA

In 1995, the new C++-based object-oriented programming language Oak, developed at Sun Microsystems by **James Gosling**, was renamed Java and burst onto the computer scene. Applications created in Java can be deployed without modification to any computing platform, thus making versions for different platforms unnecessary.

WINDOWS 95
INTERNET EXPLORER

Other important events in 1995

- Microsoft introduced **Windows 95.**
- Microsoft released **Microsoft Internet Explorer 1.0** to compete with the unforeseen popularity of Netscape.

INTERNET GOES COMMERCIAL

- The U.S. Government turned the maintenance of the Internet backbone over to commercial networking companies. Commercial traffic was now allowed on the Internet. America Online, Compuserve, and Prodigy brought the Internet to the public.

1998
WINDOWS 98

Important events in 1998

- Microsoft announced **Windows 98**

APPLE'S IMAC

- iMac Apple released the **iMac**.

MICROSOFT'S COURT CASE

- The U.S. Justice Department took Microsoft to court over alleged antitrust violations. In 1999, a federal judge found Microsoft to be monopolistic.

- In 1999 more than $300 billion was spent worldwide in the years leading up to Jan. 1, 2000 to solve the **Y2K** problem (also known as the millennium bug) —the inability of old hardware and software to recognize the century change because years were stored with only two digits.
- Apple released the **PowerMac G4**
- In 2000 Microsoft launched **Windows 2000**
- AMD's Athlon and Intel's Pentium III broke the **1GHz** barrier.
- In 2001 Apple released **MacOS X**
- Microsoft released **Windows XP**
- In 2002 IBM's Almaden Research Center unveiled a **quantum computer.**

1999
Y2K PROBLEM

POWERMAC G4

2000
WINDOWS 2000

1GHZ PROCESSORS

2001
MAC OS X
WINDOWS XP

2002
QUANTUM COMPUTER

This summary of the history of computing has dealt mainly with the first two important concepts that have shaped the history of computers: the mechanization of arithmetic and the stored program concept. Looking back, we marvel at the advances in technology that have, in barely 50 years, led from ENIAC to today's large array of computer systems, ranging from portable palmtop, laptop, and notebook computers to powerful desktop machines known as workstations, to supercomputers capable of performing billions of operations each second, and to massively parallel computers, which use thousands of microprocessors working together in parallel to solve large problems. Someone once noted that if progress in the automotive industry had been as rapid as in computer technology since 1960, today's automobile would have an engine that is less than 0.1 inch in length, would get 120,000 miles to a gallon of gas, have a top speed of 240,000 miles per hour, and would cost $4.

We have also seen how the stored program concept has led to the development of large collections of programs that make computers easier to use. Chief among these is the development of operating systems, such as Unix, Linux, MS-DOS, MacOS, and Windows, that allocate memory for programs and data and carry out many other supervisory functions. They also act as an interface between the user and the machine, interpreting commands given by the user from the keyboard, by a mouse click, or by a spoken command and then directing the appropriate system software and hardware to carry them out.

The Graphical User Interface

The third key concept that has produced revolutionary change in the evolution of the computer is the graphical user interface (GUI). A user interface is the portion of a software program that responds to commands from the user. User interfaces have evolved greatly in the past two decades, in direct correlation to equally dramatic changes in the typical computer user.

In the early 1980s, the personal computer burst onto the scene. However, at the outset, the personal computer did not suit the average person very well. The explosion in the amount of commercially available application software spared computer users the task of learning to program in order to compose their own software; for example, the mere availability of the Lotus 1-2-3 spreadsheet software was enough to convince many to buy a PC. Even so, using a computer still required learning many precise and cryptic commands, if not outright programming skills.

In the early 1980s, the Apple Corporation decided to take steps to remedy this situation. The Apple II, like its new competitor, the IBM PC, employed a command-line interface, requiring users to learn difficult commands. In the late 1970s, Steve Jobs had visited Xerox PARC and had viewed several technologies that amazed him: the laser printer, Ethernet, and the graphical user interface. It was the last of these that excited Jobs the most, for it offered the prospect of software that computer users could understand almost intuitively. In a 1995 interview he said, "I remember within ten minutes of seeing the graphical user interface stuff, just knowing that every computer would work this way some day."

Drawing upon child development theories, Xerox PARC had developed the graphical user interface for a prototype computer called the Alto that had been realized in 1972. The Alto featured a new device that had been dubbed a "mouse" by its inventor, PARC research scientist Douglas Engelbart. The mouse allowed the user to operate the computer by pointing to icons and selecting options from menus. At the time, however, the cost of the hardware the Alto required made it unfeasible to market, and the brilliant concept went unused. Steve Jobs saw, however, that the same remarkable change in the computer hardware market that had made the personal computer feasible also made the graphical user interface a reasonable possibility. In 1984, in a famous commercial first run during half-time of the Super Bowl, Apple introduced the first GUI personal computer to the world: the Macintosh. In 1985, Microsoft responded with a competing product, the Windows operating system, but until Windows version 3.0 was released in 1990, Macintosh reigned unchallenged in the world of GUI microcomputing. Researchers at the Massachusetts Institute of Technology also brought GUI to the Unix platform with the release of the X Window system in 1984.

The graphical user interface has made computers easy to use and has produced many new computer users. At the same time, it has greatly changed the character of computing: computers are now expected to be "user friendly." The personal computer, especially, must indeed be "personal" for the average person and not just for computer programmers.

Networks

The computer network is a fourth key concept that has greatly influenced the nature of modern computing. Defined simply, a computer network consists of two or more computers that have been connected in order to exchange resources. This could be hardware resources such as processing power, storage, or access to a printer; software resources such as a data file or access to a computer program; or messages between humans such as electronic mail or multimedia World Wide Web pages.

As computers became smaller, cheaper, more common, more versatile, and easier to use, computer use rose and with it, the number of computer users. Thus, computers had to be shared. In the early 1960s, timesharing was introduced, in which several persons make simultaneous use of a single computer called a *host* by way of a collection of terminals, each of which consists of a keyboard for input and either a printer or a monitor to display output. With a *modem* (short for "modulator/demodulator," because it both modulates binary digits into sounds that can travel over a phone line and, at the other end, demodulates such sounds back into bits), such a terminal connection could be over long distances.

Users, however, began to wish for the ability for one host computer to communicate with another. For example, transferring files from one host to another typically meant transporting tapes from one location to the other. In the late 1960s, the Department of Defense began exploring the development of a computer network by which its research centers at various universities could share their computer resources with each other. In 1969, the ARPANET began by connecting research center computers, enabling them to share software and data and to perform another kind of exchange that surprised everyone in terms of its popularity: electronic mail. Hosts were added to the ARPANET backbone in the 1970s, 1980s, and 1990s at an exponential rate, producing a global digital infrastructure that came to be known as the Internet.

Likewise, with the introduction of microcomputers in the late 1970s and early 1980s, users began to desire the ability for PCs to share resources. The invention of Ethernet network hardware and such network operating systems as Novell NetWare produced the Local Area Network, or LAN, enabling PC users to share printers and other peripherals, disk storage, software programs, and more. Microsoft also included networking capability as a major feature of its Windows NT.

The growth of computer connectivity continues today at a surprising rate. Computers are becoming more and more common, and they are used in isolation less and less. With the advent of affordable and widely available Internet Service Providers (ISPs), many home computers are now "wired" into a growing global digital infrastructure.

Exercises

1. What are four important concepts in the early history of computation?
2. Match each item in the first column with the associated item in the second column

_____ John von Neumann	A. early high-level language
_____ Charles Babbage	B. first commercially available computer
_____ Blaise Pascal	C. developed first fully electronic computer
_____ Herman Hollerith	D. stored program concept
_____ Grace Murray Hopper	E. Difference Engine
_____ Konrad Zuse	F. designer of FORTRAN language
_____ Alan Turing	G. Harvard Mark I
_____ Howard Aiken	H. an early electronic computer
_____ John Backus	I. integrated circuits (chips)
_____ Joseph Jacquard	J. vacuum tubes
_____ Ada Augusta	K. transistors
_____ John Atanasoff and Clifford Berry	L. Apple Computer
_____ Bjarne Stroustrup	M. automatic loom
_____ Steven Jobs and Steve Wozniak	N. developed the Unix operating system
_____ Ken Thompson	O. developed the World Wide Web

_____ Dennis Ritchie	P. developed the C language
_____ James Gosling	Q. developed the C++ language
_____ Tim Berners–Lee	R. developed the Java language
_____ FORTRAN	S. first programmer
_____ ARPANET	T. adding machine
_____ first-generation computers	U. punched card
_____ second-generation computers	V. minicomputer
_____ third-generation computers	W. universal machine concept
_____ ENIAC	X. precursor of the Internet
_____ PDP-8	Y. the first computer bug; COBOL
_____ UNIVAC	Z. developed pre-World-War-II computers that used binary arithmetic

For Questions 3–24: describe the importance of the person to the history of computing

3. al-Khowarizm
4. William Oughtred
5. Charles Babbage
6. Blaise Pascal
7. John von Neumann
8. Herman Hollerith
9. Joseph Jacquard
10. Gottfried Wilhelm von Leibniz
11. John Atanasoff
12. Steven Jobs and Steve Wozniak
13. Robert Noyce
14. J. Prespert Eckert
15. John Backus
16. Alan Turing
17. Konrad Zuse
18. Grace Murray Hopper
19. Ken Thompson
20. Dennis Ritchie
21. Bjarne Stroustrup
22. James Gosling
23. Tim Berners–Lee
24. Bill Gates

For Exercises 25–35: describe the importance of each item to the history of computing

25. ENIAC
26. Analytical Engine
27. Jacquard loom
28. UNIVAC
29. Mark I
30. MITS Altair 8800
31. Apple II
32. Cray I
33. DOS
34. ARPANET
35. Java

36. Distinguish the four different generations of computers.

0.3 Part of the Picture: Introduction to Computer Systems

Babbage's Analytical Engine (described in the history timeline of the preceding section) was a system of several separate subsystems, each with its own particular function: processing, storage, input, and output. This general scheme was incorporated in many later computers and is, in fact, a common feature of most modern computers. In this section we briefly describe the major components of a modern computing system and how program instructions and data are stored and processed. For a more complete description see the *Part of the Picture: Computer Architecture* in Chapter 6.

Processing

Most present-day computers exhibit a structure that is often referred to as the **von Neumann architecture** after Hungarian mathematician John von Neumann (see the entries for 1945 in the history timeline of the preceding section), whose theories defined many key features of the modern computer. According to the von Neumann architecture, the heart of the computing system is its **central processing unit (CPU)**. The CPU controls the operation of the entire system, performs the arithmetic and logic operations, and stores and retrieves instructions and data.

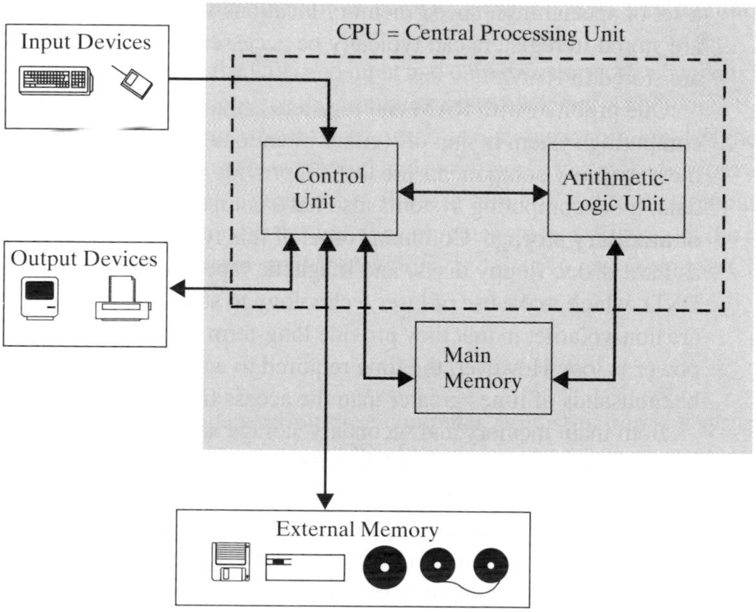

Fig.01. Major components of a computing system.

Programming

Program instructions for the CPU must be stored in memory. They must be instructions that the machine can execute, and they must be expressed in a form that the machine can understand—that is, they must be written in the **machine language** for that machine. These instructions consist of two parts: (1) a numeric **opcode**, which represents a basic machine operation, such as load, multiply, add, and store; and (2) the address of the **operand**. Like all information stored in memory, these instructions must be represented in a binary form.

As an example, suppose that values have been stored in three memory locations with addresses 1024, 1025, and 1026 and that we want to multiply the first two values, add the third, and store the result in a fourth memory location 1027. To perform this computation, the following instructions must be executed:

1. Fetch the contents of memory location 1024, and load it into a register in the ALU.
2. Fetch the contents of memory location 1025, and compute the product of this value and the value in the register.
3. Fetch the contents of memory location 1026, and add this value to the value in the register.
4. Store the contents of the register in memory location 1027.

If the opcodes for load, store, add, and multiply are 16, 17, 35, and 36, respectively, these four instructions might be written in machine language as follows[3]:

```
1. 00010000000000000000010000000000
2. 00100100000000000000010000000001
3. 00100011000000000000010000000010
4. 00010001000000000000010000000011
   \______/\______________________/
    opcode         operand
```

These instructions can then be stored in four (consecutive) memory locations. When the program is executed, the control unit will fetch each of these instructions, decode it to determine the operation and the address of the operand, fetch the operand, and then perform the required operation, using the ALU if necessary.

Programming in the machine language of an early computer was obviously a very difficult and time-consuming task in which errors were common. Only later did it become possible to write programs in **assembly language**, which uses mnemonics (names) in place of numeric opcodes and variable names in place of numeric addresses. For example, the preceding sequence of instructions might be written in assembly language as

```
1. LOAD A, ACC
2. MULT B, ACC
3. ADD C, ACC
4. STOR ACC, X
```

An **assembler**, which is part of the system software, translates such assembly language instructions into machine language.

---

[3] In binary notation, the opcodes 16, 17, 35, and 36 are 10000, 10001, 100011, and 100100, respectively, and the addresses 1024, 1025, 1026, and 1027 are 10000000000, 10000000001, 10000000010, and 10000000011, respectively. See the text's Web site for more information about nondecimal number systems, including methods for converting base-10 numbers to base-2 (binary) numbers.

Today, most programs are written in a **high-level languages** such as C++ and Java. Such programs are known as **source programs**. The instructions that make up a source program must be translated into machine language before they can be executed. For some languages (e.g., C++), this is carried out by a **compiler** that translates the source program into an **object program**. For example, for the preceding problem, a programmer might write the C++ statement

```
X = A * B + C;
```

which instructs the computer to multiply the values of `A` and `B`, add the value of `C`, and assign the value to `X`. A C++ compiler would translate this statement into a sequence of machine language instructions like those considered earlier. (For programs that use libraries, a **linker** will also be used to connect items that are defined outside of the object file with their definitions to produce an **executable program**.)

Exercises

1. Match each item in the first column with the associated item in the second column.

_____ peripheral devices	A. random access memory
_____ bit	B. central processing unit
_____ byte	C. 1024
_____ megabyte	D. terminals, scanners, printers
_____ object program	E. binary digit
_____ source program	F. group of binary digits
_____ CPU	G. 1024 K bytes
_____ K	H. written in machine language
_____ RAM	I. written in high-level language
_____ compiler	J. language translator

Briefly define each of the terms in Exercises 2-16:

2. ALU
3. CPU
4. peripheral devices
5. bit
6. byte
7. word
8. K
9. megabyte
10. source program
11. object program
12. machine language
13. assembly language
14. compiler
15. assembler
16. operating system

CHAPTER 1

Problem Solving and Software Engineering

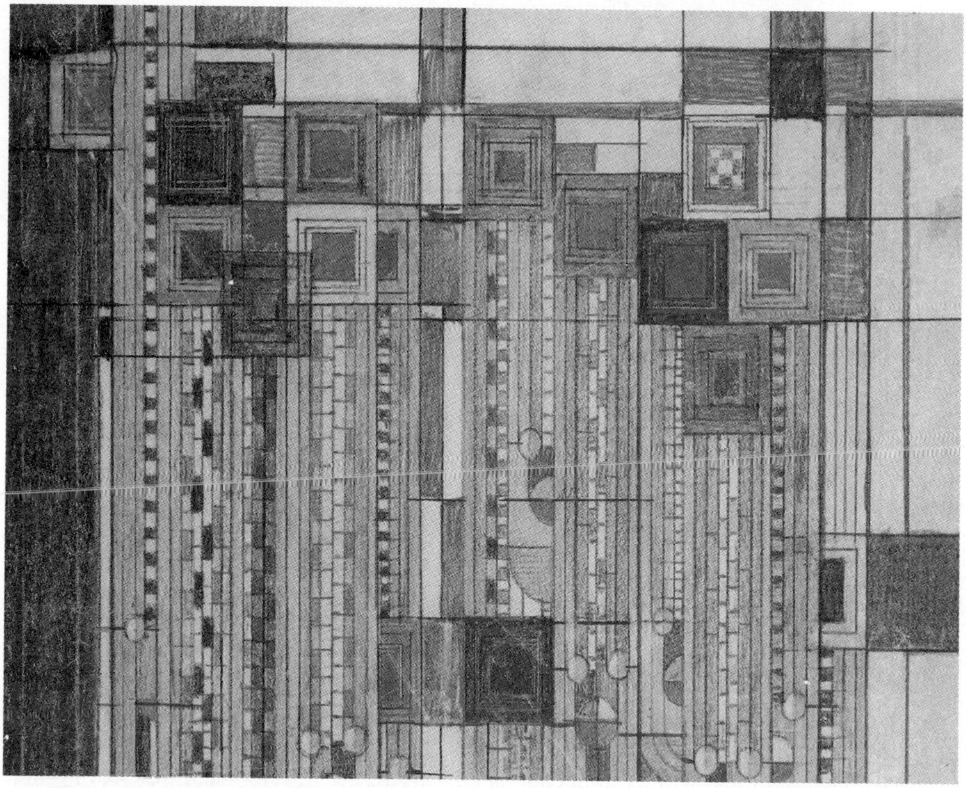

If we really understand the problem, the answer will come out of it, because the answer is not separate from the problem.

-Jiddu Krishnamurti

People always get what they ask for; the only trouble is that they never know, until they get it, what it actually is that they have asked for.

-Aldous Huxley

It's the only job I can think of where I get to be both an engineer and an artist. There's an incredible, rigorous, technical element to it, which I like because you have to do very precise thinking. On the other hand, it has a wildly creative side where the boundaries of imagination are the only real limitation.

-Andy Hertzfeld

Chapter Contents

Chapter Objectives

- Indicate the many and varied uses of computers
- Take a first look at a C++ program
- Illustrate the basic phases of the software life cycle, including object-centered design
- (Optional) Highlight issues that computing professionals face and give some ethical principles
- (Optional) Take a first look at classes and object-oriented design

We noted in the preceding chapter that the computer has become an indispensable tool in many areas. Its applications are far too many to enumerate; those in the following list and those pictured in Figure 1.1 are intended only to show some of the diverse uses of computers. These and many other applications all require the development of software, and the focus of this text is on how C++ can be used to write this software. Thus, in this chapter we see what a simple C++ program looks like and then illustrate how such programs to solve problems can be developed using Object-Centered Design (OCD). The first of several case studies in this text introduces a more substantial problem for the reader to attempt, with the complete solution including OCD given on the text's Web site. We also begin a series of optional *OBJECTive Thinking* sections provided for those who want a gradual introduction to classes from the beginning. The chapter closes with an introduction to the first of the *Part of the Picture* sections used throughout the text to introduce the reader to the major areas of computer science.

- Business and Finance
  - Mailing lists and billings
  - Inventory control
  - Word processing
  - Spreadsheets
  - ATMs (automatic teller machines)
  - Home banking
  - Processing of insurance claims
  - Payroll and accounting
  - Reservations systems (airlines, car, etc.)
  - Data management
  - EFT (electronic funds transfer)
  - Electronic mail
  - Financial planning

Fig. 1.1 (a) CAD design of an automobile. (b) Student and teacher finding information on the Internet. (c) Robot-controlled Chrysler automobile assembly plant. (d) National Weather Service satellite imagery. (e) Oil-drilling computerized tracking model. (f) Flight deck of the space shuttle Columbia. (g) Northern Arizona University observatory.

- Industry
  Robots in assembly lines
  CAD (computer-aided design)
  CIM (computer-integrated manufacturing)
  Project management and control
  Production scheduling
  CAM (computer-aided manufacturing)
  Market analysis
- Government
  Defense systems
  Compilation of census data
  State and local lotteries
  The FBI's NCIS (National Crime Information System)
  Weather forecasting by NOAA (National Oceanic and Atmospheric Administration)
  Space programs
  Automated traffic-control systems
- Medicine
  Monitoring life-support systems
  CAT (computerized axial tomography) scans
  Online access to patients' medical records
  Expert diagnosis systems
  MR (magnetic resonance) scans
- Entertainment
  Film animation
  Film colorization
  Film special effects
  Computer and video games
- Science
  Analysis of molecules
  Testing food quality
  Study of crystal structures
  Simulation of large dynamical systems
- Information Technology
  Digital libraries
  Multimedia reference works
  Online art galleries

Developing programs to solve problems is a complex process that is both an art and a science. It requires imagination, creativity, and ingenuity, but it also makes use of techniques and methodologies. Software engineering is the application of these techniques and methodologies to produce software solutions to problems. In this chapter, we describe some of these methodologies and phases of the software-development process and illustrate them with an example.

1.1 Welcome to the World of C++

A **program** is a collection of statements written in a programming language. Just as there are English *grammar rules* that specify how an English sentence is constructed, there are C++ grammar rules that determine how C++ statements are formed and how they are combined into more complex statements and into programs. Much of this text is devoted to learning how to write such statements and how to assemble them together into a program. In this section, we take a first look at a simple C++ program.

Figure 1.2 shows a C++ program that greets its user. It asks the user to enter his or her first name and then displays a message personally welcoming the user to the world of C++. In the sample run of the program, the information entered by the user (`Sarah`) is underlined to distinguish it from the output produced by the program. We will use this program to illustrate the basic structure of C++ programs.

Fig. 1.2 Greeting a user.

```
/* greeting.cpp greets its user.
 *
 * Input:  The name of the user
 * Output: A personalized greeting
 *********************************************************/

#include <iostream>                  // cin, cout, <<, >>
#include <string>                    // string
using namespace std;

int main()
{
   cout << "Please enter your first name: ";
   string firstName;
   cin >> firstName;

   cout << "\nWelcome to the world of C++, " << firstName << "!\n";
}
```

Sample run:

```
Please enter your first name: Sarah     <———— user input
Welcome to the world of C++, Sarah!
```

The first line of the program begins with the pair of characters `/*`, and the fifth line ends with the pair `*/`. In a C++ program, anything contained between these character pairs is a **comment.** The multiline comment in these opening lines of the program is **opening documentation** that describes what the program does, what is input to the program, and what output the program produces.

The two lines that follow begin with `#include` and are called **compiler directives.** They instruct the compiler to add to the program the items in the *library* `iostream` that are needed to perform input and output and the items in the library `string` that are needed to process character strings. (The items are listed in the comment following `//`.) We want these to be the standard libraries from the **namespace** named `std`.[1] The next line informs the compiler of this. Without it, we would have to qualify each library item (such as `cout`) with the prefix `std::`; for example,

```
std::cout << "Please enter your first name: ";
```

1. In 1997, the C++ ANSI standard specified new names for the standard libraries and stored all predefined identifiers in **namespaces**: logical containers for related names. The ANSI standard identifiers are stored in the `std` namespace. With non-ANSI-compliant compilers, it may be necessary to use the older library names—e.g., `iostream.h` instead of `iostream`, and `math.h` instead of `cmath`—and remove the `using namespace std;` line.

The rest of the program has the form

```
int main()
{
   A list of C++ statements
}
```

This is actually a function named `main` and is called the **main function** of the program. Here the word `int` preceding the word `main` is a C++ keyword that specifies the return type of the function and indicates that the main function will return an integer value to the operating system. Returning zero indicates normal termination. Some programmers use (and some compilers require— e.g., Microsoft's Visual C++—) a **return statement** `return 0;` as the last statement in the program. A nonzero return value is used to indicate abnormal termination.

Execution of a C++ program begins with the first of the statements enclosed between the curly braces ({ and }) in this main function and proceeds through the statements that follow it. Note that each statement ends with a semicolon.

In the program in Figure 1.2, the first statement uses the << operator to output a message to the screen (`cout`) that prompts the user to enter her or his first name:

```
cout << "Please enter your first name: ";
```

The next statement

```
string firstName;
```

declares a *variable* `firstName` to store a character string, and the statement

```
cin >> firstName;
```

uses the >> operator to read the character string entered by the user from the keyboard (`cin`) and stores it in variable `firstName`. The next statement

```
cout << "\nWelcome to the world of C++, " << firstName << "!\n";
```

then displays on the screen a personalized greeting consisting of

1. a special character (`\n`) that causes an advance to a new line followed by the string

   ```
   Welcome to the world of C++,
   ```

2. the character string that is stored in `firstName`
3. the character ! followed by the new-line character

1.2 Problem Solving through Software Engineering

As we noted in the introduction to this chapter, software engineering uses certain basic methodologies to obtain software solutions to problems. Although the problems themselves vary, several phases or steps are common in software development:

1. **Design:** The problem is analyzed and a solution is designed, resulting in an *algorithm* to solve the problem.

2. **Coding:** The solution is written in the syntax of a high-level language (e.g., C++), resulting in a *program.*
3. **Testing, Execution, and Debugging:** The program is rigorously tested and any errors (called *bugs*) are removed.
4. **Maintenance:** The program is updated and modified, as necessary, to meet the changing needs of its users.

In this section, we examine each of these stages in the **software life cycle** and illustrate them with an example. This is a rather simple example so that we can emphasize the main ideas in each stage without getting lost in a maze of details.

PROBLEM

The world's largest ball of twine is located in Cawker City, Kansas.[2] People in the area have been winding twine on the ball since 1953. At the time of this writing, the average radius of the ball was approximately 6∫ feet. Two common questions that tourists have are as follows:

1. How much does the ball weigh?
2. How many miles would the twine reach if it were unrolled?

We will design a program to answer the first question. The second question is left as an exercise. (See Exercise 4 at the end of this section.)

Fig. 1.3 The world's largest ball of twine.

2. The hometown of one of the authors. For more information, see `http://skyways.lib.ks.us/kansas/towns/Cawker/cawker.html`

Object-Centered Design

Problems to be solved are usually expressed in a natural language, such as English, and often are stated imprecisely, making it necessary to analyze the problem and formulate it more precisely. For the preceding problem, this is quite easy:

> *Given the radius of a spherical ball of twine, compute the weight of the ball.*

For many problems, however, this may be considerably more difficult, because the initial descriptions may be quite vague and imprecise. People who pose the problems often do not understand them well. Neither do they understand how to solve them nor what the computer's capabilities and limitations are.

We will call the approach we use in designing a software solution to a problem **object-centered design (OCD)**. In its simplest form, it consists of the following steps:

1. *Behavior:* State how you want the program to behave, as precisely as possible.
2. *Objects:* Identify the real-world objects in your problem description, and categorize them.
3. *Operations:* Identify the operations that are needed to solve the problem.
4. *Algorithm:* Arrange the problem's objects and the operations in an order that solves the problem.

The arrangement of a problem's objects and operations that results from Step 4 is called an **algorithm** for the problem, and this algorithm serves as a blueprint for writing the program.

Behavior. We begin by writing out exactly what we want our program to do (i.e., how we want it to behave). The remainder of our design depends on this step, so we must make it as precise as possible:

> *Behavior:* The program should display a prompt for the radius of a sphere on the screen. The user should enter this radius at the keyboard from which the program should read it. The program should then compute the weight of the sphere and display it on the screen.

Note that we have generalized the problem to calculating the weight of an arbitrary sphere. This **generalization** is an important aspect of analyzing a problem. The effort involved in later phases of solving a problem demands that the program eventually developed be sufficiently flexible to solve not only the given specific problem, but also any related problem of the same kind with little, if any, modification required.

Objects. Once we have decided exactly what should happen, we are ready for the next step, which is to identify the objects in the problem. One approach is to begin by identifying all of the *nouns* in our behavioral description, ignoring nouns like *user* and *program*:

> *Behavior:* The program should display a <u>prompt for the radius of a sphere</u> on the <u>screen</u>. The user should enter this <u>radius</u> at the <u>keyboard</u> from which the

program should read it. The program should then compute the weight of the sphere and display it on the screen.

This gives us the following list of objects:

Problem's Objects:

prompt for the radius of a sphere
screen
radius of a sphere
keyboard
weight of the ball

Real-world objects such as these must be represented in a programming language by *software objects* (sometimes called *entities*).[3] Software objects in C++ must have a specified *type* that tells what kind of values they can have. Some of these software objects will have values that vary; they are called **variables** and must be *named*. Those whose values remain constant may or may not be named. In our example, we can classify our objects as follows:

Problem Objects	Software Objects		
	Type	Kind	Name
prompt for the radius of a sphere	`string`	constant	none
screen	`ostream`	variable	`cout`
radius of a sphere	`double`	variable	*radius*
keyboard	`istream`	variable	`cin`
weight of the ball	`double`	variable	*weight*

We will not name the first software object in our problem, the prompt, because its value does not change during execution of the program and is unlikely to change in the future. Sequences of characters are called `string` values in C++, and within a program, string constants (also called *string literals*) must be surrounded by double quotes.

The second object, the screen (or window), has the predefined name `cout` in C++ and has the predefined type `ostream` (for *o*utput *stream*). Because the contents of the screen will change during program execution, its value varies.

We have chosen the name *radius* for the third software object, the radius of the sphere. Its value will vary, because the user enters that value from the keyboard. Numeric objects that can store real values (i.e., numbers with decimal points) are represented by the type `double` (or `float`) in C++.

The keyboard has the predefined name `cin` in C++ and its type is the predefined type `istream` (for *i*nput *stream*). Because values will be entered via the keyboard during program execution, the value of this object also varies.

---

3. The term *object* has a precise meaning in object-oriented languages; an object is an instance of a class. To avoid confusion, we will refer to objects (i.e., things) in a problem's description as *real-world objects* or as *problem objects* and use the term *software objects* for those things used to represent real-world objects in a programming language. The C++ standard uses the term *entities* for these software objects.

Finally, we have chosen the name *weight* for our last software object, the weight of the ball. Because it will store a real value, its type is `double`. It is a variable, because its value will be computed by the program.

Operations. Once we have identified and classified the objects in our program, we can proceed to the next step, which is to identify the operations needed to solve the problem. To identify the objects, we identified the nouns in our behavioral description; to identify the operations, we can begin by identifying the *verbs* that describe actions, of the program:

Behavior: The program should display a prompt for the radius of a sphere on the screen. The user should enter this radius at the keyboard from which the program should read it. The program should then compute the weight of the sphere and display it on the screen.

Using the objects we identified earlier, we can describe these operations as follows:

Operations:

Output a prompt for the radius of a sphere to `cout`
Input a real value from `cin` and store it in *radius*
Compute *weight*
Output *weight* to `cout`

C++ provides an output operator `<<` that can be used to insert string and numeric values into `cout`, which will display them on the screen. We can use this operator to display the prompt for the radius and to display the value of *weight*. Similarly, C++ provides an input operator `>>` that extracts values from `cin` (i.e., the keyboard) and stores them in variable objects. We can use this operator to input a real value from the keyboard and store it in *radius*.

Computing the weight of the ball requires some additional work. This is given by the formula

$$weight = density \times volume$$

The volume V of a sphere of radius r is given by

$$V = 4\pi\frac{r^3}{3}$$

Combining these two formulas gives the following formula for *weight*:

$$weight = density \times 4.0 \times \pi \times \frac{radius^3}{3.0}$$

This implies that we need to expand our list of operations:

Operations:

Output a prompt for the radius of a spherical ball to `cout`
Input a real value from `cin` and store it in *radius*

Output a prompt for the density of a spherical ball to `cout`
Input a real value from `cin` and store it in *density*

Compute *weight*
    Raise *radius* to the third power
    Multiply real values (three times)
    Divide real values

Output *weight* to `cout`

As in most languages, real values can be multiplied in C++ using the * operator and can be divided using the / operator. Although there is no exponentiation operator, the standard math library contains a function named `pow()` that performs exponentiation. Thus, all of the operations needed to solve our problem are readily available.

However, our formula for computing the weight of the ball adds six new objects to our list:

	Software Objects		
Problem Objects	**Type**	**Kind**	**Name**
prompt for the radius of a sphere	`string`	constant	none
screen	`ostream`	variable	`cout`
radius of a sphere	`double`	variable	*radius*
keyboard	`istream`	variable	`cin`
prompt for the density of a sphere	`string`	constant	none
density of a sphere	`double`	variable	*density*
weight of the sphere (in pounds)	`double`	variable	*weight*
4.0	`double`	constant	none
π	`double`	constant	*PI*
3	`integer`	constant	none
3.0	`double`	constant	none

We have decided to use a name for π, because this increases readability and will also make it easier to modify the program if more or less precision is needed.

Algorithm. Once we have identified all of the objects and operations, we are ready to arrange those operations into an algorithm. If we have done the preceding steps correctly, this is usually straightforward:

ALGORITHM

1. Initialize the constant *PI*.
2. Output a prompt for the radius of a sphere to `cout`.
3. Input a real value from `cin` and store it in *radius*.
4. Output a prompt for the density of a sphere to `cout`.
5. Input a real value from `cin` and store it in *density*.

6. Compute *weight* = *density* * 4.0 * *PI* * *radius*^{3} / 3.0.
7. Output *weight* to `cout`.

This sequence of instructions is sometimes called a *pseudocode algorithm*, because it is not written in any particular programming language, and yet it bears some similarity to a program's code. This algorithm becomes our blueprint for the next stage of the process.

CODING IN C++

Once we have designed an algorithm for our problem, we are ready to translate that algorithm into a high-level language like C++. We can do this a step at a time as follows:

- First, create a **program stub** that contains
  - opening documentation
  - compiler directives that add items in libraries needed for some of the objects and operations
  - an empty main function
- Convert each step of the algorithm into code. If it uses a software object that hasn't already been declared, add a *declaration statement* that specifies the object's type and name.

For our example, we might begin with the following program stub:

```
/* sphereWeight.cpp computes the weight of a sphere.
 *
 * Input:  The radius (feet) and
 *           the density (pounds/cubic foot) of a sphere
 * Output: The weight of the sphere (pounds)
 *********************************************************/

#include <iostream>                    // cin, cout, <<, >>
#include <cmath>                       // pow()
using namespace std;

int main()
{
}
```

We have used a `#include` directive for the libraries `iostream` and `cmath` that provide the objects and operations listed in the comments that follow these directives. This program stub is, in fact, a complete program that could be compiled and executed.

Now we convert each step of the algorithm into code, one line at a time. The first line of the algorithm

1. Initialize the constant *PI*.

is translated into the C++ statement

```
const double PI = 3.14159;
```

and added to the main function:

```
. . .
int main()
{
  const double PI = 3.14159;
}
```

The next step in the algorithm,

2. Output a prompt for the radius of a sphere to `cout`.

can be written in C++ as

```
cout << "Enter the sphere's radius (feet): ";
```

and so we add this statement to the main program:

```
. . .
int main()
{
   const double PI = 3.14159;

   cout << "Enter the sphere's radius (feet): ";
}
```

(We separated this statement from the constant declaration with a blank line for readability.)
The next step in the algorithm,

3. Input a real value from `cin` and store it in *radius*.

uses the two objects `cin` and *radius*. The first object, `cin`, is provided by the `iostream` library, which has already been added to our program by the first `#include` directive. For *radius*, however, we must add a **declaration** like the following that gives its type and name:

```
double radius;
```

Then we can add the statement that implements Step 3 of the algorithm:

```
. . .
int main()
{
   const double PI = 3.14159;

   cout << "Enter the sphere's radius (feet): ";
   double radius;
   cin >> radius;
}
```

We continue through the algorithm in this manner, translating it step by step into code. Figure 1.4 shows the final program that results. It also shows a sample run of the program with input values 6.5 for `radius` and 14.6 for `density`.

Fig. 1.4 Weight of a sphere.

```
/* sphereWeight.cpp computes the weight of a sphere.
 *
 * Input:  The radius (feet) and
 *           the density (pounds/cubic foot) of a sphere
 * Output: The weight of the sphere (pounds)
 ************************************************************/

#include <iostream>                  // cin, cout, <<, >>
#include <cmath>                     // pow()
using namespace std;

int main()
{
   const double PI = 3.14159;

   cout << "Enter the sphere's radius (feet): ";
   double radius;
   cin >> radius;
   cout << "Enter its density (pounds/cubic feet): ";
   double density;
   cin >> density;

   double weight = density * 4.0 * PI * pow(radius, 3) / 3.0;

   cout << "\nThe weight of the sphere is approximately "
        << weight << " pounds.\n";
}
```

Sample run:

```
Enter the sphere's radius (feet): 6.5
Enter its density (pounds/cubic feet): 14.6

The weight of the sphere is approximately 16795 pounds.
```

A software program called a *text editor* can be used to enter this program into a computer's memory.[4] The text editor is also used in the next stage of software development to correct any errors in the program.

4. In the Unix environment, common text editors include `vi`, `emacs`, and `xemacs`. Most microcomputer C++ implementations (e.g., C++ Builder, CodeWarrior, and Visual C++) have a built-in text-editing window.

TESTING, EXECUTION, AND DEBUGGING

There are a number of different points at which errors can be introduced into a program. Three of the most common are

1. violations of the grammar rules of the high-level language in which the program is written;
2. errors that occur during program execution; and
3. errors in the design of the algorithm on which the program is based.

The process of finding such errors is called **debugging** the program.

The first kind of error is called a **syntax error,** because the program violates the syntax (i.e., the grammar rules) of the language. A **compiler** is a program that translates a program written in a high-level language into a functionally equivalent program in the machine language of a given computer.[5] As it performs this translation, the compiler checks whether the program it is translating conforms to the syntax rules of the language. If the program violates any of these rules, the compiler generates an *error* (or *diagnostic*) message that explains the (apparent) problem. For example, if we forgot to type the semicolon at the end of the line

```
double radius;
```

in the program in Figure 1.4, and entered

```
double radius
```

instead, the compiler would display a diagnostic message like the following:

```
Error   : ';' expected
sphereWeight.cpp line 18  cin >> radius
```

A different compiler might display a less precise diagnostic for the same error such as

```
sphereWeight.cpp: In function 'int main()':
sphereWeight.cpp:18:  parse error before '>'
```

The compiler displayed the number of the line it was processing when it detected that something was wrong, which is the line following the line containing the error. The second diagnostic is also much less informative; it only indicates that the *parser* (a part of the compiler) encountered something unexpected. Learning to understand the messages that a particular compiler produces is an important skill.

The second kind of error, called a **run-time error**, is not detected until execution of the program has begun. Run-time errors include such things as attempting to divide by

---

5. Most microcomputer C++ implementations provide a menu whose choices include `Compile` (to translate your program into machine language) and `Link` (to link calls to library functions like `pow()` to their definitions). Such menus usually also have a `Make` or `Build` choice that performs both compilation and linking, although this usually requires the creation of a *project*. On Unix systems, users of g++ (the GNU C++ compiler) can compile a program from the command line by typing a line of the form

```
g++ progname.cpp -o progname
```

Users of the `emacs` text editor can compile from within the editor by using the `M-x compile` command. `emacs` will respond with `make -k`, which can be replaced with a compile command like the preceding.

zero in an arithmetic expression, attempting to compute the square root of a negative number, and generating some value that is outside a given range. Error messages describing the errors are usually displayed on the screen or can be found in user documentation. Once the cause of the error is found, the offending statements or expressions must be replaced with correct ones, and the modified program must be recompiled and reexecuted.

The third kind of error is called a **logic error**, because it represents programmer mistakes in the design of the algorithm. For example, the program in Figure 1.4 contains the statement

```
double weight = density * 4.0 * PI * pow(radius, 3) / 3.0;
```

But suppose that we misread the formula for the weight of the ball and typed a + in place of the first * operator:

```
double weight = density + 4.0 * PI * pow(radius, 3) / 3.0;
```

Because the resulting program violates none of the grammatical rules of C++, the compiler will not detect the error. It has no basis for identifying this statement as erroneous, because it is a valid C++ statement. Consequently, *the program will compile and execute, but it will produce incorrect values* because the formula used to compute the weight is not correct.

To determine whether a program contains a logic error, it must be run using sample data and the output produced checked for correctness. This **testing** of a program should be done several times using a variety of inputs, ideally prepared by people other than the programmer, who may be making nonobvious assumptions in the choice of test data. If *any* combination of inputs produces incorrect output, then the program contains a logic error.

Once it has been determined that a program contains a logic error, finding the error is one of the most difficult parts of programming. Execution must be traced step by step until the point at which a computed value differs from an expected value is located. To simplify this tracing, most implementations of C++ provide an integrated debugger[6] that allows a programmer to actually execute a program one line at a time, observing the effect(s) of each line's execution on the values produced. Once the error has been located, the text editor can be used to correct it.

Thorough testing of a program will increase one's confidence in its correctness, but it must be realized that it is almost never possible to test a program with every possible set of test data. There are cases in which apparently correct programs have been in use for more than ten years before a particular combination of inputs produced an incorrect output caused by a logic error. The particular data set that caused the program to execute the erroneous statement(s) had never been input in all that time!

As programs grow in size and complexity, the problem of testing them becomes increasingly more difficult. No matter how much testing is done, more could always be done. Testing is never finished; it is only stopped, and there is no guarantee that all the

---

6. On popular microcomputer C++ implementations, the debugger is integrated with the compiler and editor and can be enabled via a `Debug` menu (or a `Debug` choice on some other menu). In the GNU implementation of C++, the compiler `g++` and the debugger `gdb` can both be executed from within the text editor `emacs` (but the program must be compiled using the `-g` switch) providing the functional equivalent of an integrated environment. The debugger `insight` is available for free from *www.redhat.com*, which is `gdb` with a modern graphical user interface.

errors in a program have been found and corrected. Testing can only show the presence of errors, not their absence. It cannot prove that a program is correct; it can only show that it is incorrect.

MAINTENANCE

Student programs are often run once or twice and then discarded. By contrast, real-world programs often represent a significant investment of a company's resources and may be used for many years. During this time, it may be necessary to add new features or enhancements to the program. This process of upgrading a program is called **software maintenance.**

To illustrate, users of the program in Figure 1.4 might find it more informative to have the weight of the ball displayed in both pounds and tons. The program might be modified by making the changes (shown in color) in the program in Figure 1.5.

Fig. 1.5 Weight of a sphere—revised. (Part 1 of 2)

```
/* sphereWeight.cpp computes the weight of a sphere.
 *
 * Input:  The radius (feet) and
 *            the density (pounds/cubic foot) of a sphere
 * Output: The weight of the sphere (pounds and tons)
 ******************************************************************/

#include <iostream>                       // cin, cout, <<, >>
#include <cmath>                          // pow()
using namespace std;

int main()
{
   const double PI = 3.14159;

   cout << "Enter the sphere's radius (feet): ";
   double radius;
   cin >> radius;
   cout << "Enter its density (pounds/cubic feet): ";
   double density;
   cin >> density;
   double weight = density * 4.0 * PI * pow(radius, 3) / 3.0;

   cout << "\nThe weight of the sphere is approximately "
        << weight << " pounds, \nwhich is the same as "
        << weight / 2000.0 << " tons.\n";
}
```

Fig. 1.5 Weight of a sphere—revised. (Part 2 of 2)

Sample run:

```
Enter the sphere's radius (feet): 6.5
Enter its density (pounds/cubic feet): 14.6

The weight of the sphere is approximately 16795 pounds,
which is the same as 8.39752 tons.
```

In other problems, it may be necessary to compute values for spheres whose radii are measured very precisely. When we execute the program, we find that it produces imprecise answers. This imprecision might be caused by the fact that the value for `PI` (3.14159) only uses five decimal places of precision, so we might increase the precision:

```
const double PI = 3.14159265358979324;
```

✔ Quick Quiz 1.2

1. A(n) __________ is a collection of statements written in a programming language.
2. In a C++ program, anything contained between /* and */ is a(n) __________.
3. Execution of a C++ program begins with the first statement enclosed between __________ in the __________ function.
4. A(n) __________ statement causes execution of a program to terminate and return a value to the operating system.
5. Name the four stages of the software life cycle.
6. List the four steps in object-centered design.
7. The __________ in a problem can be identified by finding the nouns in the behavioral description of the problem.
8. The __________ in a problem can be identified by finding the verbs in the behavioral description of the problem.
9. Objects whose values will change are called __________.
10. The screen has the predefined name __________ in C++, and its type is __________.
11. The keyboard has the predefined name __________ in C++, and its type is __________.
12. __________ is the output operator in C++, and __________ is the input operator.
13. Finding the errors in a program is called __________.
14. What are three types of errors that can occur in developing a program?

Exercises 1.2

For each of the following problems, give a precise description of how a program to solve that problem must behave. Then describe the objects and operations needed to solve the problem, and design an algorithm for it.

1. Calculate and display the perimeter and the area of a square with a given side. (The perimeter of a square where the length of each side is s is $4s$ and the area is s^2.)
2. Calculate and display the diameter, circumference, and the area of a circle with a given radius. (The diameter is twice the radius. For radius r, the circumference is $2\pi r$, and the area is πr^2 where π is the mathematical constant pi whose value is approximately 3.14159.)
3. Two common temperature scales are the Fahrenheit and Celsius scales. The boiling point of water is 212° on the Fahrenheit scale and 100° on the Celsius scale. The freezing point of water is 32° on the Fahrenheit scale and 0° on the Celsius scale. Assuming that the relationship between these two temperature scales is $F = \frac{9}{5}C + 32$, convert a temperature on the Celsius scale to the corresponding Fahrenheit temperature.
4. Consider the program developed in this section to solve part of the ball-of-twine problem. We also stated a second part of the problem:

   How many miles would the twine reach if it were unrolled?

   a. Extend the behavior of the program to solve this problem also.
   b. Extend the list of objects as necessary for this problem.
   c. Extend the list of operations to include those needed to solve this problem. Assume that approximately 350 feet of the twine must be wound to form a ball that weighs 1 pound and that there are 5280 feet in a mile, so the total length of the twine in the ball is 350 **weight* / 5280 miles.
   d. Modify the algorithm so that it will also solve this problem.

1.3 Case Study: Revenue Calculation

In several chapters of this text, we have added case studies near the ends of the chapters. These are intended to provide more practice with applying what has been presented in the chapter and in some cases to present detailed solutions of somewhat more complex problems. To save space, we will usually give only brief introductions to these case studies in the written part of this text and suggest that you finish solving the problem. Complete solutions are provided on the book's Web site whose URL is given in the preface. Normally, these will include problem analysis and specification, object-centered design, source code, and testing.

Problem. Sam Splicer installs coaxial cable for the Metro Cable Company. For each installation, there is a basic service charge of $25.00 and an additional charge of $2.00 for each foot of cable. The president of the cable company would like a program to compute the revenue generated by Sam in any given month. For example, if during the month of January, Sam installs a total of 263 yards of cable at 27 different locations, he generates $2253.00 in revenue.

Object-Centered Design. Following the principles of object-centered design, you should begin with a description of the behavior of the program, then identify the objects and operations, and finally, write an algorithm. Here is one possible statement of the behavior to get you started.

> The program should display on the screen a prompt for the number of installations performed and the total number of yards of cable installed. The user should enter those values from the keyboard. The program should compute and display on the screen the total amount of revenue resulting from these installations.

From this statement of the program's behavior, identify the objects and operations and organize them into an algorithm. Then, following the examples of this chapter, see if you can translate your algorithm into code. If you have difficulty, see the text's Web site.

The output of monetary amounts by your program will probably not be in a standard format. In particular, some amounts may have fewer than two decimal places while others have more than two. This difficulty can be fixed using *I/O manipulators*. We will study these in detail in Chapter 5, but an introduction to them along with examples is part of the discussion of maintenance in the solution of this problem on the Web site.

1.4* OBJECTive Thinking: Spheres As Objects[7]

In Section 1.2, we wrote programs to compute the weight of any sphere, given its radius and density. These programs are *functionally correct*: given a sphere's radius and density, they compute that sphere's weight. However, one of the goals of **object-oriented design** is to design software that is *reusable*. The programs in Figures 1.4 and 1.5 do not achieve this goal; none of their code can be easily reused by another program.

To see how these programs could be improved, consider our behavioral description:

Behavior: The program should display a prompt for the radius of a sphere on the screen. The user should enter this radius at the keyboard, from which the program should read it. The program should then compute the weight of the sphere and display it on the screen.

From this description, it should be evident that the central "object" in the problem is a *sphere*. Yet the programs in Figures 1.4 and 1.5 do not use any *sphere* objects. Instead, these programs use *sphere attributes*, namely, *radius*, *density*, and *weight*. To keep things simple in our first look at design, we ignored *sphere*—the central noun in our behavioral description.

The difficulty is that there is no predefined `Sphere` type that can be used to define a *sphere* object. In such situations where there is no predefined software type to represent a problem object, an object-oriented programmer will build a new type by writing a piece of code called a **class**. A class provides two things:

- *space*, for storing the attributes of an object; and
- *operations*, for manipulating the object.

For the problem at hand, the object-oriented approach would be to build a `Sphere` class that can be used to represent sphere objects. Space consisting of three `double` values would be used to store a sphere's attributes—*radius*, *density*, and *weight*—and various sphere-related operations such as the following would be defined:

- *initialization*: set attributes to default values

7. *Objective Thinking* sections are starred to indicate that they are optional and can be omitted without loss of continuity. They are provided for those who want a gradual introduction to classes from Chapter 1 on. An alternative is to skip them until Chapter 11 is reached and then cover them before or in conjunction with Chapter 11.

- `readRadiusAndDensity(in)`: read *radius*, *density* from istream *in*; define *weight*
- `readRadiusAndWeight(in)`: read *radius*, *weight* from istream *in*; define *density*
- `readDensityAndWeight(in)`: read *density*, *weight* from istream *in*; define *radius*
- `print(out)`: display a sphere's attributes to ostream *out*
- `getRadius()`: retrieve a sphere's *radius*
- `getDensity()`: retrieve a sphere's *density*
- `getWeight()`: retrieve a sphere's *weight*
- ... other operations discussed in later chapters.

(There are three different input operations because the value of any attribute can be determined when values of the other two are known.)

Building such a class requires knowing more C++ than we have introduced in this chapter, but we will study how to do this in later chapters.

Objects. Suppose for now that such a `Sphere` class exists. The list of objects in our problem can then be simplified as follows:

Problem Objects	Software Objects		
	Type	Kind	Name
prompt for a sphere's radius and density	`string`	constant	none
screen	`ostream`	variable	`cout`
a sphere	`Sphere`	variable	*aSphere*
keyboard	`istream`	variable	`cin`

Because our `Sphere` class stores all of the attributes of a sphere (i.e., *radius*, *density*, and *weight*), we do not consider such attributes as distinct objects.

Operations. Given a `Sphere` class, we can also simplify the list of operations:

Operations:

Output a prompt for the radius and density of a sphere to `cout`
Input the radius and density of *aSphere* from `cin`
Access the weight of *aSphere*
Output a real value (the weight) to `cout`

Note that the two sphere-related operations are provided by the `Sphere` class: We can input the radius and density of *aSphere* using the `readRadiusAndDensity()` operation; and we can access the weight of *aSphere* using the `getWeight()` operation.

These four operations in the order given make up the revised algorithm for our problem, and so we will proceed directly to the coding of that algorithm.

Coding. Figure 1.6 presents a program that solves our problem using a `Sphere` class that is stored in a separate file named *Sphere.h*.

Fig. 1.6 sphereWeight using a `Sphere` class.

```
/* sphereWeight.cpp demonstrates the use of a Sphere class.
 *
 * Input:  A sphere's radius and density
 * Output: The sphere's weight
 ************************************************************/

#include <iostream>                      // cin, cout, <<, >>
#include "Sphere.h"                      // Sphere class
using namespace std;

int main()
{
   cout << "Enter the radius (feet) "
        << " and density (lbs/sq-ft) of the sphere: ";
   Sphere aSphere;
   aSphere.readRadiusAndDensity(cin);
   cout << "\nThe sphere weighs "
        << aSphere.getWeight() << " pounds.\n";
}
```

When executed, this program generates output similar to that of Figure 1.4.

Just as the types `int` and `double` let us represent integers and reals and perform arithmetic operations, the `Sphere` class declared in the file *Sphere.h* lets us represent *sphere* objects and perform *sphere*-related operations on them. The declaration

```
Sphere aSphere;
```

declares `aSphere` as the name of a `Sphere` object.

In Figure 1.6, we invoked the `readRadiusAndDensity()` operation on object `aSphere` by writing

```
aSphere.readRadiusAndDensity(cin);
```

In object-oriented terminology, this is called **sending a message** to the `Sphere` object `aSphere`, specifically, sending `aSphere` the `readRadiusAndDensity()` message. That is, we can think of this notation as having our main function call out to its `aSphere` object, *"Hey aSphere! Read your radius and density values from cin!"* Our `aSphere` object responds to this message by filling its *radius* and *density* attributes with the `double` values the user enters at the keyboard.

Similarly, when we want to know aSphere's weight, we send it the getWeight() message:

```
aSphere.getWeight();
```

We can think of this notation as having our main function say to aSphere, *"Hey aSphere, how much do you weigh?"* Being a well-behaved object, aSphere responds with the value of its weight attribute. As we shall see, much of object-oriented programming consists of sending messages to objects.

Like the programs in Figures 1.4 and 1.5, the program in Figure 1.6 solves the problem of computing a sphere's weight, given its radius and density. But unlike those earlier programs, the program in Figure 1.6 stores all of the sphere-related functionality in a class that other programs can reuse, rather than in a main function where it is not accessible to other programs. Building the Sphere class requires us to spend extra time designing and coding, but the result is code that we can reuse in other problems. As a simple example, if we wished to compute the density of our planet the Earth, we could write the program shown in Figure 1.7.

Fig. 1.7 sphereDensity using a Sphere class.

```
/* sphereDensity.cpp computes the density of a Sphere.
 *
 * Input:  A sphere's radius and weight
 * Output: The sphere's density
 ***************************************************************/

#include <iostream>                    // cin, cout, <<, >>
#include "Sphere.h"                    // Sphere class
using namespace std;

int main()
{
   cout << "Enter the radius (feet) "
        << " and weight (lbs) of the sphere: ";
   Sphere aSphere;
   aSphere.readRadiusAndWeight(cin);
   cout << "\nThe sphere's density is "
        << aSphere.getDensity() << " lbs/sq-ft\n";
}
```

Comparing Figures 1.6 and 1.7, you can see that in an object-oriented program, the primary role of a main function is often simply to coordinate input and output. The real work of the computation is performed by the program's object(s).

If using a Sphere class is the object-oriented way to solve the problem, you may be wondering why we didn't do so in the first place. Why introduce object-*centered* design instead of object-*oriented* design? The reason is that object-oriented design is a more complex endeavor than object-centered design. Just as a child learns to walk before it learns to run, we need to learn some of the more fundamental aspects of programming before we are ready to build classes. As we shall see, object-centered design will evolve in subsequent chapters to the point that it becomes object-oriented design in the *OBJECTive Thinking* section of Chapter 7.

In this first *OBJECTive Thinking* section our intent was to introduce you to the basic ideas and vocabulary of object-oriented programming. In the *OBJECTive Thinking* sections of the following chapters, we will gradually learn how to build classes like the `Sphere` class. In doing so, we will see how to design reusable software components.

✔ Quick Quiz 1.4

1. One of the goals of object-oriented programming is to design software that is __________.
2. When there is no predefined type to represent an object in a problem, an object-oriented programmer will build a new type by writing a(n) __________.
3. What two things does a class provide?
4. Invoking one of the operations of an object is referred to as sending a(n) _________ to the object.
5. (True or false) Object-oriented design is easier than object-centered design.

Part of the Picture

Ethics and Issues

by Anne Marchant, George Mason University

> To be good is noble, but to show others how to be good is nobler, and no trouble.
>
> *Mark Twain*

Professor Marchant has prepared a superb *Part of the Picture* dealing with computer ethics. It begins as follows:

ETHICS AND SOCIETY

What will the future bring? Will we live a life of leisure with all our tedious chores performed by intelligent machines? Perhaps we will live instead in an "information prison" with all the details of our lives recorded and analyzed by government or by corporations that exist solely to buy and sell information. To a large extent, the future will be driven by the choices we make now. Computers permeate every aspect of our lives. In addition to making businesses more productive, they also perform many life-critical tasks such as air-traffic control, medical diagnosis and treatment, and emergency communication. The field of computer science is largely unregulated. Programmers are not required to pass proficiency exams or obtain state licenses to practice their art. In an effort to protect society from the obvious dangers, the field is regulating itself. It does this by encouraging the study of ethics and by demanding the highest level of integrity from its members. Some companies are instituting ethics training for their employees and ethics Web sites are appearing where professionals can debate ethical concerns. Professional organizations such as the Association for Computing Machinery (ACM) and the IEEE (Institute of Electrical and Electronics Engineers) have adopted and instituted a Code of Ethics. Students are encouraged to join these organizations and familiarize themselves with these codes. Most colleges and universities also have policies governing the responsible use of computers. Students are encouraged to read these carefully and to develop their own personal standards.

Due to lack of space, we are cannot reproduce her entire essay here, but it is available on the text's Web site and you are strongly urged to read it. The following list of section titles shows how very relevant are the topics that she discusses:

- Ethics and Society
- Computer Crime and Security
- Health Concerns and the Environment
- Information Ownership
- "Netiquette" and Hoaxes
- Internet Content and Free Speech
- Privacy
- Quality Control and Risk Reduction
- The Future

CHAPTER SUMMARY

Key Terms & Notes

`#include`
algorithm
behavior
C++
`cin`
class
coding
comment (/*, */, //)
compiler
compiler directive
`cout`
curly braces ({ and })
debugger
debugging
declaration
design
execution
generalization
input (>>)
library
logic error
main function
maintenance
namespace
object-centered design (OCD)
object-oriented design
objects
opening documentation
operations
output (<<)
program
program stub
`return` statement
run-time error
sending a message
software engineering
software life cycle
software maintenance
`std`
syntax error
testing
variable

Programming Problems

Section 1.1

1. Enter and execute the following C++ program on your computer system:

```
/* This program adds the values of variables x and y.
 *
 * Output (screen):  The value x + y
 *************************************************************/

#include <iostream>
using namespace std;

int main()
{
   int x = 214,         // the first value
       y = 2057,        // the second value
       sum = x + y;

   // output the resulting value
   cout << "\nThe sum of " << x << " and " << y
        << " is " << sum << endl;
}
```

2. Make the following changes in the program in Exercise 1, and execute the modified program:
   - **a.** Change `214` to `1723` in the statement that gives `x` a value.
   - **b.** Change the variable names `x` and `y` to `alpha` and `beta` throughout.
   - **c.** Add the comment

     ```
     // find their sum
     ```

     following the declaration of `sum`.
   - **d.** Change the variable declaration to

     ```
     int alpha = 214,                  // the first value
         beta = 2057,                  // the second value
         difference = alpha - beta,    // find their difference
         sum = alpha + beta;           // find their sum
     ```

     and add the following statement after the output statement:

     ```
     cout << "\nThe difference of " << alpha << " and "
          << beta <<  " is  " << difference << endl;
     ```

3. Modify the program in Figure 1.2 so that it will also display the person's last name.
4. Modify the program in Problem 3 so that it will also display the current date.

Section 1.2

5. Using the programs in this chapter as a guide, write a C++ program to solve the problem in Exercise 1.
6. Using the programs in this chapter as a guide, write a C++ program to solve the problem in Exercise 2.
7. Modify the program in Figure 1.4 so that it will also solve the twine-ball problem in Exercise 4.
8. Extend the program in Problem 7 to calculate the length of the twine in both feet and miles.

Section 1.3

9. Execute the program in Figure 1.6. What happens if you enter a nonpositive value for its radius?
10. Execute the program in Figure 1.6. What happens if you enter a nonpositive value for its density?
11. Using the program in Figure 1.6 as a guide, write a C++ program that given a sphere's density and weight, computes its radius, using the `Sphere` class.

CHAPTER 2

Types

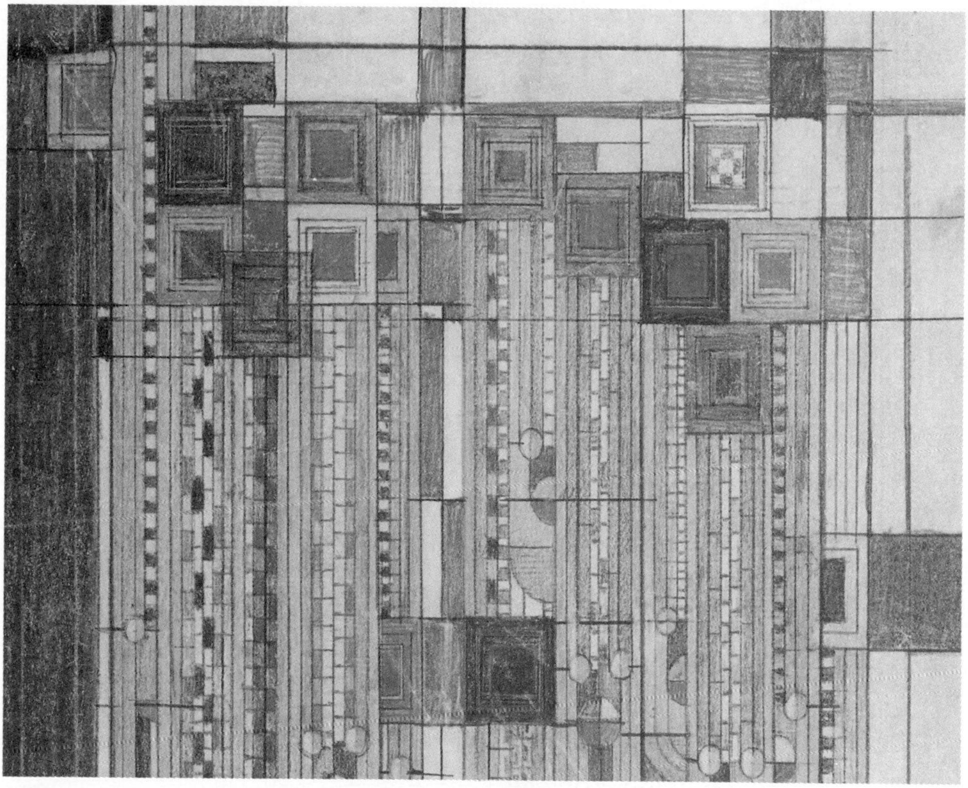

There are three types of people in this world: Those who can count, and those who can't.

-Seen on a bumper sticker

Kindly enter them in your notebook.
And, in order to refer to them conveniently,
let's call them A, B, and Z.

-The Tortoise in Lewis Carroll's
-"What the Tortoise Said to Achilles"

"'The name of the song is called 'Haddocks' Eyes.'"
"Oh, that's the name of the song, is it?" Alice said, trying to feel interested.
"No, you don't understand," the Knight said, looking a little vexed. "That's what the name is called. The name really is 'The Aged Aged Man.'"

"Then I ought to have said 'That's what the song is called'?" Alice corrected herself.
"No, you oughtn't: that's quite another thing! The song is called 'Ways and Means': but that's only what it's called, you know!"
"Well, what is the song, then?" said Alice, who was by this time completely bewildered.
"I was coming to that," the Knight said. "The song really is 'A-sitting on a Gate': and the tune's my own invention."

-Lewis Carroll

For, contrary to the unreasoned opinion of the ignorant, the choice of a system of numeration is a mere matter of convention.

-Blaise Pascal

Chapter Contents

Chapter Objectives

- See some of the types provided in C++ and some literals of these types.
- Explain C++'s syntax rules for forming identifiers and naming conventions for them.
- Study variables and constants—what they are, how they differ, how they are declared, and how they are used.
- (Optional) Investigate how values of the various fundamental types are represented internally in a computer and some of the advantages and limitations of these representations.
- (Optional) Take a first look at using attribute variables in classes.

An important part of using a computer to solve a problem is encoding the algorithm for solving that problem as a program. Whereas algorithms can be described somewhat informally in a pseudoprogramming language, the corresponding program must be written in strict compliance with the rules of some programming language. We now begin a detailed study of the language C++.

In 1989, the American National Standards Institute (ANSI) convened committee X3J16 to establish a standard for the C++ language. This committee was the major contributor to an international effort to standardize C++ under the auspices of the International Standards Organization (ISO) working group WG21. In 1995, a working draft was released for public comment and review. This along with later revised drafts were the principal references for the earlier printings of this text. In November 1997, a final draft was approved unanimously as the C++ standard. This document (ISO/IEC FDIS 14882) is the basis for this latest revision of this text.

In this chapter, we look at some of the data types that are provided in C++, focusing on the simplest ones, called *fundamental types*. The *Part of the Picture* section shows how values of these types are represented in such a way that they can be stored in memory. The optional *OBJECTive Thinking* section takes a first look at the internal structure of classes, which are types used for more complex objects.

2.1 Introductory Example: Computing Student Pay

PROBLEM

Suppose we are given the task of writing a program to help the payroll office compute the pay for student workers at Somewhere University. After meeting with SU's payroll office to discuss their needs, we learn that all students are paid the same hourly rate: $6.75 per hour. Our first attempt at such a program might proceed as follows.

Object-Centered Design

Behavior. The program should display on the screen a prompt for a student's name (last, first, middle initial), which the user should enter at the keyboard and the program should read. The program should also display a prompt for the student's id number, which the user should enter and the program read. The program should then display a prompt for the hours the student has worked this pay period, which the user should enter and the program read. After this, the program should compute the student's pay and then display the student's name, id number, and pay, along with meaningful labels.

Objects. From our behavioral description, we can identify the following objects:

	Software Objects		
Problem Objects	**Type**	**Kind**	**Name**
screen	`ostream`	varying	`cout`
various prompts	`string`	constant	none

Problem Objects	Software Objects		
	Type	Kind	Name
student's name			
– last name	`string`	varying	*lastName*
– first name	`string`	varying	*firstName*
– middle initial	`char`	varying	*middleInitial*
keyboard	`istream`	varying	`cin`
student's id number	`int`	varying	*idNumber*
student's hourly wage	`double`	constant	*HOURLY_WAGE*
student's hours worked this pay period	`double`	varying	*hoursWorked*
student's pay	`double`	varying	*pay*
descriptive label	`string`	constant	none

Operations. Again, from our behavioral description, we have the following operations:

i. Display a string (the prompts, descriptive labels, student's name)
ii. Read a string (*lastName, firstName*)
iii. Read a character (*middleInitial*)
iv. Read an integer (*idNumber*)
v. Read a real value (*hoursWorked*)
vi. Compute *pay* = *hoursWorked* * *HOURLY_WAGE*
vii. Display an integer (*idNumber*)
viii. Display a real value (*pay*)

Each of these operations is provided in C++.

Algorithm. Next we organize these objects and operations into an algorithm:

1. Declare the constant *HOURLY_WAGE*.
2. Display to `cout` a prompt for the student's name (last, first, middle initial).
3. Read two strings and a character from `cin` into *lastName, firstName, middleInitial*.
4. Display to `cout` a prompt for the student's id number.
5. Read an integer from `cin` into *idNumber*.
6. Display to `cout` a prompt for the student's hours.
7. Read a real value from `cin` into *hoursWorked*.
8. Compute *pay* = *hoursWorked* * *HOURLY_WAGE*.
9. Display *firstName*, *lastName*, *middleInitial*, *idNumber*, and *pay*, with descriptive labels.

Coding, Execution, and Testing. In the preceding chapter, we outlined a procedure you can follow to translate the algorithm into code:

1. Create a *program stub* that contains opening documentation, compiler directives that add items in libraries needed for some of the objects and operations, and an empty main function.
2. Convert each step of the algorithm into code. For those that use a software object not already declared, add a *declaration statement* that specifies the object's type and name.

Space restrictions prevent our going through this procedure one step at a time for each example in this text. Until coding becomes easier for you, however, you should follow this procedure to develop programs like the finished product shown in Figure 2.1. Also shown are two sample runs with test data for which the output can be easily verified and a third execution with "real" data.[1]

Fig. 2.1 Student pay computation. (Part 1 of 2)

```
/* studentPay.cpp computes a student worker's pay,
 *
 * Input: A student's name, id number, hourly wage, hours worked.
 * Precondition: hoursWorked >= 0.0 && hoursWorked <= 40 &&
 *                hourlyWage > 0.0 && idNumber > 0.
 * Output: The student's name, id number, and pay.
 ***************************************************************/

#include <iostream>          // cin, cout, <<, >>
#include <string>            // string
using namespace std;

int main()
{
  const double HOURLY_WAGE = 6.75;      // dollars/hour

  cout << "\nEnter the student's name (L, F, MI): ";
  string lastName, firstName;
  char middleInitial;
  cin >> lastName >> firstName >> middleInitial;
```

1. The monetary amounts are not displayed in a very nice format—one has two decimal places, the second has only one, and the third has three. The case study in Section 1.3 and our study of output expressions in the next chapter show how *format manipulators* can be used to improve the output; for example, changing the output statement as follows will cause the value of pay to be displayed with two decimal places:

```
cout << "\nName: "
     << firstName << ' ' << middleInitial << ". " << lastName
     << "\nId Number: " << idNumber
     << fixed << showpoint << setprecision(2)
     << "\nPay: $" << pay << '\n';
```

Fig. 2.1 Student pay computation. (Part 2 of 2)

```
   cout << "Enter their id number: ";
   int idNumber;
   cin >> idNumber;

   cout << "Enter their hours this pay period: ";
   double hours;
   cin >> hours;

   double pay = hours * HOURLY_WAGE;

   cout << "\nName: "
        << firstName << ' ' << middleInitial << ". " << lastName
        << "\nId Number: " << idNumber
        << "\nPay: $" << pay << '\n';
}
```

Sample runs:

```
Enter the student's name (L, F, MI): VanderDoe Van V
Enter their id number: 12345
Enter their hours this pay period: 1

Name: Van V. VanderDoe
Id Number: 12345
Pay: $6.75

Enter the student's name (L, F, MI): Smith John Q
Enter their id number: 98765
Enter their hours this pay period: 10

Name: John Q. Smith
Id Number: 98765
Pay: $67.5

Enter the student's name (L, F, MI): FoneBone Fran F
Enter their id number: 33234
Enter their hours this pay period: 38.5

Name: Fran F. FoneBone
Id Number: 33234
Pay: $259.
```

The program in Figure 2.1 uses several different C++ types. In the remainder of this chapter, we will explore the many predefined types available in C++ and how they can be used to represent objects.

2.2 Types and Declarations

As we discussed in Chapter 1, object-centered programming begins by identifying the objects involved in a problem. These real-world objects must be represented in a programming language by software objects. To allow the C++ compiler to check that these software objects are being used properly, C++ requires that their types be specified, or **declared,** before those objects are used. In this section, we examine the fundamental types provided in C++. The *Part of the Picture* section that follows shows how data values of these types are commonly stored in memory.

FUNDAMENTAL TYPES

The most important fundamental data types provided in C++ are as follows:[2]

- **integers:** whole numbers and their negatives: of type `int`
- **integer variations:** types `short`, `long`, and `unsigned`
- **reals:** fractional numbers: of type `float`, `double`, or `long double`
- **characters:** letters, digits, symbols, and punctuation: of type `char`
- **booleans:** logical values `true` and `false`: of type `bool`

A value of one of these types is called a **literal.**[3] For example, `123`, `0`, and `-15` are integer literals; `-45.678` and `3.14159` are real literals; `'A'`, `'a'`, `'0'`, and `'$'` are character literals; `true` and `false` are boolean literals. We now discuss these types in detail.

Integers. The amount of memory used to store an `int` value depends on the word size of the machine. Usually, a 16-bit machine will store `int` values using 16 bits, a 32-bit machine will use 32 bits, and a 64-bit machine will store `int` values using 64 bits. This can cause portability problems, because a program that uses `int` values may behave differently on different machines.

To deal with this problem, C++ allows `int` declarations to be modified with one of the key words `short` or `long`. These modifiers have the following effects:

- A `short int` (or just `short`) is usually a 16-bit value, ranging from -32768 ($= -2^{15}$) through 32767 ($= 2^{15} - 1$).
- A `long int` (or just `long`) is usually a 32-bit value,[4] ranging from -2147483648 ($= -2^{31}$) through 2147483647 ($= 2^{31} - 1$).

---

2. Other fundamental types are the `signed char` and `unsigned char` integer types, the wide character type `wchar_t`, `complex`, and the `void` type for an empty set of values (see Section 4.2).
3. The usage of the word *literal* in computing refers to any value typed in by the programmer that does not change during program execution—the string of characters you type is (literally) the value you get.
4. On machines whose word size is 64 bits, a `long` value may be stored in 64 bits instead of 32.

Programmers who are concerned with efficiency and portability can use `short` for integer data objects with relatively small values and `long` for those that may have larger values. In this text we will use `int` in most of our examples.

The internal representation of an integer typically uses one bit as a **sign bit,** so that the largest positive value of a 16-bit integer is $2^{15} - 1$ and not $2^{16} - 1$. (See the *Part Of The Picture* section that follows this section.) However, some data objects never have negative values. For example, in a program for processing student test scores, a score would (hopefully) never be negative. To avoid wasting the sign bit for integers whose values are never negative, C++ provides the modifier `unsigned`:

- An `unsigned int` (or just `unsigned`) is a nonnegative integer whose size usually is the word size of the particular machine being used.
- An `unsigned short` is usually a 16-bit value, ranging from 0 through 65535 ($= 2^{16} - 1$).
- An `unsigned long` is usually a 32-bit value, ranging from 0 through 4294967295 ($= 2^{32} - 1$).[5]

Integer literals are taken to be decimal integers unless they begin with 0. In this case:

- A sequence of digits that begins with `0` is interpreted as an **octal** integer (provided that the digits are octal digits 0, 1, . . . , 7).
- A sequence of digits preceded by `0x` is interpreted as a **hexadecimal** integer—the hexadecimal digits for ten, eleven, . . . , fifteen are `A`, `B`, . . . , `F`, respectively, or their lowercase equivalents `a`, `b`, . . . , `f`.
- Any other digit sequence is a decimal (base-ten) integer.

For example, the literal

```
12
```

has the decimal value $12_{10} = 1 \times 10^1 + 2 \times 10^0$. However, the literal

```
012
```

has the octal value $12_8 = 1 \times 8^1 + 2 \times 8^0 = 10_{10}$ and

```
0x12
```

has the hexadecimal value $12_{16} = 1 \times 16^1 + 2 \times 16^0 = 18_{10}$. Table 2.1 is a quick guide to the C++ representation of integer values in the three bases. (See the text's Web site described in the preface for additional details about binary, octal, and hexadecimal number systems.)

---

5. By default, whole numbers (e.g., `-30, 0, 1, 12, 365`) are treated as type `int` by the C++ compiler. To instruct the compiler to treat a literal value as an `unsigned` instead of as an `int`, the letter `U` or `u` can be appended to the literal (e.g., `0U, 1U, 12U, 365U`). Appending the letter `L` or `l` to a literal (e.g., `-30L, 0L, 1L, 12L, 365L`) instructs the compiler to treat a literal value as a `long` instead of as an `int`. Appending both of the suffixes `L` (or `l`) and `U` (or `u`) in either order causes a literal to be treated as `unsigned long`.

Table 2.1 C++ Integer Constants.

Decimal	Octal	Hexadecimal
0	0	0x0
1	01	0x1
2	02	0x2
3	03	0x3
4	04	0x4
5	05	0x5
6	06	0x6
7	07	0x7
8	010	0x8
9	011	0x9
10	012	0xA
11	013	0xB
12	014	0xC
13	015	0xD
14	016	0xE
15	017	0xF
16	020	0x10
17	021	0x11
18	022	0x12
19	023	0x13
20	024	0x14

Reals. C++ provides three types of real values:

- `float`, usually a 32-bit real value
- `double`, usually a 64-bit real value
- `long double`, typically a 96-bit or a 128-bit real value

The type chosen for an object should be determined by the degree of precision required for that data object. The range of values and the precision of each of these types is implementation dependent. These are defined in one of the standard libraries `cfloat` or `climits` (described later in this section) that C++ implementations provide.

Like most programming languages, C++ provides two ways to represent real values, fixed-point notation and floating-point notation. A **fixed-point** real literal has the form

m.n

where either the integer part *m* or the decimal part *n* (but not both) can be omitted. For example,

```
5.0
0.5
```

```
5.
.5
```

are all valid fixed-point real literals in C++.

Scientists often write very large or very small real numbers using a special notation called *exponential, scientific*, or *floating-point* notation. For example, a scientist might write the number 12 billion (12,000,000,000) as

$$0.12 \times 10^{11}$$

In C++, a **floating-point** real literal has one of the forms

`xEn` or `xen`,

where `x` is an integer or fixed-point real literal and `n` is an integer exponent (positive or negative). For example, 12 `billion` = 0.12×10^{11} can be written in any of the following forms:

```
0.12e11
1.2E10
12.0E9
12.e9
12E9
```

NOTE

C++ compilers treat all real literals (whether fixed- or floating-point) as being of type `double`.[6] This means that if a value is computed using real literals and assigned to a `float` variable, then the value stored in the variable does not have the precision of the computed value. For this reason, *many programmers never use the type* `float`, *and instead always use the type* `double` *for real values.*

Characters. The `char` type is used to represent *individual characters* in the machine's character set (commonly the ASCII character set shown in Appendix A). This includes the uppercase letters `A` through `Z`; lowercase letters `a` through `z`; common punctuation symbols such as the semicolon (`;`), comma (`,`), and period (`.`); and special symbols such as +, =, and >.

Characters are represented in memory by numeric codes, and in C++, values of type `char` are stored using these integer codes. (See the next section for a description. Also, see Potential Pitfall 2 at the end of this chapter to see how this can lead to confusion.) *Character literals* are usually written in C++ as single character symbols enclosed in apostrophes (or single quotes).[7] For example,

```
'A', '@', '3', '+'
```

---

6. To instruct the compiler to process a real literal as a `float`, an `F` or `f` can be appended to it (e.g., `1.0F`, `3.1316F`, `2.998e8F`). Similarly, appending an `L` or `l` to a real literal instructs the compiler to treat it as a long double (e.g., `1.0L`, `0.1E1L`).
7. Character literals of the form `L'x'` where `x` consists of one or more characters are *wide-character literals* and are used to represent alternate character sets. They are of type `wchar_t` and have implementation-dependent values.

are all examples of C++ character literals. The C++ compiler stores these values using their numeric codes, which in ASCII are

65, 43, 51, and 124

respectively.

Using an apostrophe as a delimiter raises the question, What is the character literal for an apostrophe? A similar question arises for characters such as the newline character, for which there is no corresponding symbol. For such characters that have a special purpose and cannot be described using the normal approach, C++ provides **escape sequences.** For example, the character literal for an apostrophe can be written as

```
'\''
```

and the newline character as

```
'\n'
```

Table 2.2 lists the escape sequences provided in C++.

Strings. A different, but related, type of literal is the *string literal*, which consists of a sequence of characters enclosed in double quotes.[8] For example,

```
"Hello, there"
"Enter id number on one line\n\tand your name on the next.\n "
"\nThe revenue = $"
"Hamlet said, \"To be or not to be ... \""
```

Table 2.2 C++ Character Escape Sequences.

Character	C++ Escape Sequence
Newline (NL or LF)	`\n`
Horizontal tab (HT)	`\t`
Vertical tab (VT)	`\v`
Backspace (BS)	`\b`
Carriage return (CR)	`\r`
Form feed (FF)	`\f`
Alert (BEL)	`\a`
Backslash (`\`)	`\\`
Question mark (`?`)	`\?`
Apostrophe (single quote, `'`)	`\'`
Double quote (`"`)	`\"`
With numeric octal code *ooo*	`\`*ooo*
With numeric hexadecimal code *hhh*	`\x`*hhh*

8. String literals of the form `L"..."` are wide string literals; they may contain wide characters.

are all string literals. Note that escape sequences can be used within string literals. Note also that *string literals containing a single character are not* `char` *literals;* for example,

WATCH OUT

`"A"` is a string literal

`'A'` is a `char` literal

These two kinds of literals are not interchangeable.

The double newline character string literal

```
"\n\n"
```

can be used to separate lines of output with blank lines, making the output more readable. For example, consider the output of a string literal of the form

```
"One line\n\nAnother line"
```

The first newline (shown as ↵ in the following output) ends the line on which `One line` appears, and the second newline makes the next line a blank line, after which `Another line` appears:

```
One line↵
↵
Another line
```

Inserting blank lines into output is an easy way to increase its readability.

Two string literals that are consecutive or are separated only by **white space** (spaces, tabs, and end-of-lines) are automatically concatenated to form a single literal. For example, for

```
"John " "Doe"
```

or

```
"John "
"Doe"
```

the two string literals will be combined to form the single literal

```
"John Doe"
```

IDENTIFIERS

We have given *names* to most of the software objects used in the programs considered thus far. These names are called **identifiers.** They may not be C++ **keywords** (e.g., `int`, `const`, `double`, etc.), which are words that have predefined meanings. A complete list of the C++ keywords is given in Appendix B.

In C++, an identifier should begin with a letter, which may be followed by any number of letters, digits, or underscores.[9] This allows the user to give an object a meaningful name that describes what that object represents. For example, the identifier

```
hoursWorked
```

9. Identifiers that begin with an underscore (_) followed by an uppercase letter or that contain two *consecutive* underscores (_ _) are reserved for special use and should be avoided.

is more meaningful than the shortened identifier

```
h
```

NOTE

which could represent *height, hard-drive, henrys, hertz,* or *hackers*, or anything else beginning with the letter 'h'. One should resist the temptation to use a short identifier just to save a few keystrokes. *Complete words are preferable to abbreviations. It is good programming practice to use meaningful identifiers that suggest what they represent, because such names make programs easier to read and understand. They serve, therefore, as part of the program's documentation and thus facilitate program maintenance.*

NOTE

It is important to remember that *C++ is case sensitive—that is, it distinguishes between uppercase and lowercase*. For example, `firstName` and `firstname` are different identifiers in C++. Similarly, the main function must be named `main`, not `Main`. One must be careful to use the same names consistently.

The primary goal in choosing identifiers is to enhance the program's readability. Although different programmers may use different naming conventions, one of the most common is the following:

Constants: Names are given in uppercase. If a name consists of several words, these words are separated by underscore (_) characters. Some examples are `PI`, `HOURLY_WAGE`, and `SPEED_OF_LIGHT`

Variables: Names are in lowercase, except that if a name consists of several words, the first letter of the second and each following word is capitalized. Some examples are `hours`, `pay`, `firstName`, and `myLastName`

This naming convention makes it easy to distinguish names for values that are constant from those that can vary.

To use an identifier in a program, we must inform the compiler of the meaning of that identifier before its first use. This is accomplished by using a **declaration statement.** Thus far we have seen two kinds of identifiers, those for variables and those for constants, and we now describe their declarations in greater detail.

CONSTANTS

We have seen that C++ permits the declaration of software objects whose values remain constant. For example, the program in Figure 2.1 contains the constant declaration

```
const double HOURLY_WAGE = 6.75;   // dollars/hour
```

The ability to define constant objects is especially useful when a program uses universal constants, such as the speed of light c or the geometric constant π,

```
const double SPEED_OF_LIGHT = 2.997925e8;   // meters/sec
const double PI = 3.14159;
```

but it can also be used to associate names with other constants to be used in a program:

```
const int ZIP_CODE = 99999,
          UPPER_LIMIT = 1000;
```

```
const char
      DOLLAR_SIGN = '$',   // using a normal character
      SPACE = ' ',         // using a white space char
      FORM_FEED = '\f',    // using an escape sequence
      BELL = '\007';       // using an octal (ASCII) code
```

For objects of type `string`, we must use a `#include` directive to include the `string` library prior to their declarations; for example,

```
#include <string>
using namespace std;
...
const string UNIVERSITY = "Somewhere University";
```

In general, a **constant declaration** has the following form:

Constant Declaration

Form:

```
const type CONSTANT_NAME = expression;
```

where

`const` is a C++ keyword;

`type` may be any type that is known to the compiler;

`CONSTANT_NAME` is a valid C++ identifier; and

`expression` is any valid expression (as described in later sections) whose value is of type *`type`*.

Purpose: Declares and provides a value for a named constant. Any attempt to change this value within a program is an error.

NOTE

There are two important reasons for using constants instead of the literals they represent. One reason is *improved readability*. To illustrate, consider which of the following statements is more readable:

```
populationChange = (0.1758 - 0.1257) * population;
```

or

```
populationChange = (BIRTH_RATE - DEATH_RATE) * population;
```

If we define the constants `BIRTH_RATE` and `DEATH_RATE` by

```
const double
      BIRTH_RATE = 0.1758, // rate at which people are born
      DEATH_RATE = 0.1257; // rate at which people die
```

we can use the second statement, and that part of our program becomes much easier to understand.

NOTE

A second benefit of using constants is that they *facilitate program modification*. To illustrate, suppose that you are solving a population-related problem and that you use the birth rate and death rate literals `0.1758` and `0.1257` throughout your program. Suppose further that new values are published for the birth and death rates of the population you are studying. To modify your program to use these new values, you must find each occurrence of the old values and replace them with the new values.

If you had instead declared constants `BIRTH_RATE` and `DEATH_RATE` and used them throughout the program, you could simply change their declarations:

```
const double
      BIRTH_RATE = 0.1761, // rate at which people are born
      DEATH_RATE = 0.1252; // rate at which people die
```

Changing the values of `BIRTH_RATE` and `DEATH_RATE` in these declarations will change their values throughout the program without any further effort on your part.

NOTE

It is considered good programming practice to *place all declarations of constants at the beginning of the function in which they are used*. This makes it easy to locate these declarations when it is necessary to modify the value of a constant.

In addition to programmer-defined constants, C++ provides many predefined constants in its various libraries. For example, the library `climits` contains

`SHORT_MIN`	minimum `short int` value
`SHORT_MAX`	maximum `short int` value
`INT_MIN`	minimum `int` value
`INT_MAX`	maximum `int` value
`UINT_MIN`	minimum `unsigned int` value
`UINT_MAX`	maximum `unsigned int` value
`LONG_MIN`	minimum `long int` value
`LONG_MAX`	maximum `long int` value

and the library `cfloat` contains

`FLT_MIN`	minimum `float` value
`FLT_MAX`	maximum `float` value
`DBL_MIN`	minimum `double` value
`DBL_MAX`	maximum `double` value
`LDBL_MIN`	minimum `long double` value
`LDBL_MAX`	maximum `long double` value

These lists are by no means exhaustive; for example, in addition to the minimum and maximum of each of the real types, `cfloat` contains constants for the precision of each real type, the minimum and maximum exponent permitted in scientific notation, and so on.

VARIABLES

When designing a solution to a problem, we often discover relationships that exist between the objects in the problem and that can often be expressed by *formulas*. For example, the program in Figure 2.1 makes use of the formula

$$p = r \times h$$

which describes the relationship between a worker's pay, hourly rate, and the hours worked. These symbolic names—*p*, *r*, and *h*—are called *variables*. If specific values are substituted for *r* and *h*, then this formula can be used to calculate the pay *p*.

When a variable is declared in a program, the compiler associates its name with a particular memory location. The value of a variable at any time is the value stored in its associated memory location at that time. In computing, therefore, the term **variable** refers to a memory location in which values can be stored (thus changing the variable's value) and whose contents can be retrieved and processed. Variable names are identifiers and thus must follow the rules for valid identifiers.

As discussed previously, a **variable declaration** indicates to the compiler the kind of data that a variable object is to contain by associating a type with that variable. It has the following form:

Variable Declaration

Forms:

```
type variable_name;
type variable_name = initializer_expression;
```

where

`type` may be any type that is known to the compiler; and

`variable_name` is a valid C++ identifier.

Purpose: Instructs the C++ compiler to reserve sufficient memory to store a value of type `type` and associates that memory with the name `variable_name`. In the second form, the value of `initializer_expression` will be stored in this memory location; for the first form, the value of `variable_name` is *undefined* (or *indeterminate*).

The type specified for a variable enables the compiler to associate the proper amount of memory with the variable. For example, it would be wasteful to use 4 bytes to store a character when a single byte is sufficient or 8 bytes to store a small integer when 2 are sufficient. Consequently, the type of a C++ variable must be one of the fundamental data types described previously (or one of the other data types to be discussed later).

The following declarations from the program in Figure 2.1 illustrate the first form of variable declarations:

```
int idNumber;
double hours;
char middleInitial;
string firstName, lastName;
```

For each of these a memory location of appropriate size will be associated with the variable. For example, for the `double` variable `hours`, a memory location of appropriate size for `doubles` (typically, 8 bytes) will be allocated. We might picture this as follows:

WATCH OUT

The question mark indicates that this variable is **undefined** (sometimes also said to be **indeterminate**). The actual value of `hours` is implementation dependent; some versions of C++ may initialize numeric variables to 0 while others may simply let their initial values be whatever value corresponds to the string of bits in that memory location allocated for it—commonly referred to as **garbage values.** *You should not assume that uninitialized variables will have a specific value.*

If the declaration of `hours` were changed to

```
double hours = 40.0;
```

40.0 would be used as the initial value:

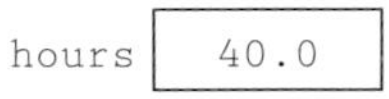

For either of the preceding declarations of `hours`, if the value 37.5 were entered in response to the input statement

```
cin >> hours;
```

the value stored in `hours` would change to 37.5:

Similarly, the declaration

```
string lastName = "Doe";
```

would use “Doe” as the initial value for `lastName`:[10]

---

10. A description of the relationship between a variable, its name, its memory location, and its value sounds something like a modern-day version of the second Lewis Carroll quote at the beginning of this chapter:
“The student’s last name is called `lastName`.”
“Oh, that’s her last name, is it?” Alice said, trying to feel interested.
“No, you don’t understand,” the Knight said, looking a little vexed. “That’s what it’s called. `lastName` is the name of a variable whose value is her last name.”
“Then I ought to have said 'The student’s last name is a variable’?” Alice corrected herself.
“No, you oughtn’t: that’s quite another thing! The variable is memory location 0x123abc: but that’s only what it’s called, you know!”
“Well, what is her last name, then?” said Alice, who was by this time completely bewildered.
“I was coming to that,” the Knight said. “Her name really is ‘Doe’ and it’s my own initialization.”

C++ allows variable declarations to be placed (almost) anywhere before their first use in a function body. For example, in the main function in Figure 2.1,

```
int main()
{
   const double HOURLY_WAGE = 6.75;      // dollars/hour

   .
   .
   .

   cout << "Enter their hours this pay period: ";
   double hours;
   cin >> hours;

   double pay = hours * HOURLY_WAGE;

   .
   .
   .
}
```

program statements and the declarations of HOURLY_WAGE, hours, and pay are intermixed.

Of course, C++ does not prohibit declaring all variables at the beginning of the function, and some programmers prefer this style, to keep all the declarations together. To illustrate, we could have written the preceding main function as follows:

```
int main()
{
   const double HOURLY_WAGE = 6.75; // dollars/hour
   double hours;
   double pay;

   .
   .
   .

   cout << "Enter their hours this pay period: ";
   cin >> hours;

   pay = hours * HOURLY_WAGE;

   .
   .
   .
}
```

NOTE

Where variable declarations are placed is largely a matter of programming style. In this text, we usually declare variables just prior to their first use rather than at the beginning of a function, because declaring a variable near its first use makes it easier to ensure that the variable is used in a manner consistent with its type.

Quick Quiz 2.2

1. List the fundamental data types provided in C++.
2. List the three integer type variations.

3. List the three real types.
4. A constant of a particular type is called a(n) ________.
5. (True or false) `0123` and `123` represent the same integer value.
6. (True or false) `0xA` and `10` represent the same integer value.
7. (True or false) All real literals are treated as being of type `double`.
8. Character literals must be enclosed in ________.
9. (True or false) `'1/n'` is a valid character literal.
10. (True or false) `'\n'` is a valid character literal.
11. `'\n'` is an example of a(n) ________ sequence.
12. String constants must be enclosed in ________.

For Questions 13–16, tell whether each is a legal identifier. If is it not legal, indicate the reason.

13. `55MPH`
14. `W_D_4_0`
15. `N/4`
16. `First Name`

For Questions 17–24, tell whether each is an integer literal, a real literal, or neither.

17. `1234`
18. `1,234`
19. `1.234`
20. `123e4`
21. `123-4`
22. `0.123E-4`
23. `0x123E4`
24. `0199`

For Questions 25–32, tell whether each is a character literal, a string literal, or neither.

25. `'A'`
26. `'AB'`
27. `"ABC"`
28. `"@#'%&"`
29. `'/'`
30. `'\\'`
31. `'\123'`
32. `"John Doe'`
33. Write a constant declaration to associate `GRAVITY` with the integer 32.
34. Write constant declarations to associate `EARTH` with 1.5E10 and `MARS` with 1.2E12.
35. Write a declaration for a variable `distanceTraveled` of type `int`.
36. Write declarations for variables `idNumber` of type `unsigned`, `salary` of type `float`, and `employeeCode` of type `char`.
37. Repeat Question 35, but initialize `distanceTraveled` to zero.
38. Repeat Question 36, but initialize `idNumber` to 9999, `salary` to zero, `employeeCode` to a blank.

Exercises 2.2

For Exercises 1–16, determine if each is a valid C++ identifier. If it is not, give a reason.

1. `XRay`
2. `X-Ray`
3. `Jeremiah`
4. `R2_D2`
5. `3M`
6. `PDQ123`
7. `PS.175`
8. `x`
9. `4`
10. `N/4`
11. `$M`
12. `Z_Z_Z_Z_Z_Z`
13. `night`
14. `ngiht`
15. `nite`
16. `to day`

For Exercises 17–36, classify each as an integer literal, a real literal, or neither. If it is neither, give a reason.

17. `12`
18. `12.`
19. `12.0`
20. `"12"`
21. `8 + 4`
22. `-3.7`
23. `3.7-`
24. `1,024`
25. `+1`
26. `$3.98`
27. `0.357E4`
28. `24E0`
29. `E3`
30. `five`
31. `3E.5`
32. `.000001`
33. `1.2 × 10`
34. `-(-1)`
35. `0E0`
36. `1/2`

For Exercises 37–48, determine if each is a valid string literal. If it is not, give a reason.

37. `"X"`
38. `"123"`
39. `IS"`
40. `"too yet"`
41. `"Say \"AH\""`
42. `"isn't"`
43. `"constant"`
44. `"$1.98"`
45. `"DON\'T"`
46. `"12 + 34"`
47. `"\'twas"`
48. `"\"A\"\"B\"\"C\""`

For Exercises 49–52, write constant declarations to associate each name with the specified literal.

49. `1.25` with the name `RATE`
50. `40.0` with the name `REGULAR_HOURS` and `1.5` with the name `OVERTIME_FACTOR`
51. `1776` with the name `YEAR`, the letter `F` with `FEMALE`, and a blank character with `BLANK`
52. `0` with `ZERO`, `*` with `ASTERISK`, and an apostrophe with `APOSTROPHE`

For Exercises 53–56, write declarations for each variable.

53. `item`, `number`, and `job` of type `double`
54. `shoeSize` of type `int`
55. `mileage` of type `double`, `cost` and `distance` of type `unsigned`
56. `alpha` and `beta` of type `long`, `code` of type `char`, and `root` of type `double`

For Exercises 57–58, write declarations to declare each variable to have the specified type and initial value.

57. `numberOfDeposits` and `numberOfChecks` to be of type `int`, each with an initial value of `0`; `totalDeposits` and `totalChecks` to be of type `double`, each with an initial value of `0.0`; and `serviceCharge` to be of type `double` with an initial value of `0.25`
58. `symbol_1` and `symbol_2` to be of type `char` and with a blank character and a semicolon for initial value, respectively; and `debug` to be of type `char` with an initial value of `T`
59. Write constant declarations that associate the current year with the name `YEAR` and 99999.99 with `MAXIMUM_SALARY` and variable declarations that declare `number` and `prime` to be of type `int` and `initial` to be of type `char`.

Part of the Picture

Data Representation

The third *Part Of The Picture* section in Chapter 0—Introduction to Computer Systems—noted that a binary scheme having only the two binary digits 0 and 1 is used to represent information in a computer. It also described how instructions can be represented in base two and stored in memory. We now look at how literals of the various data types can be represented and stored in binary.

INTEGERS

When an integer value must be stored in the computer's memory, the binary representation of that value is typically stored in one word of memory. To illustrate, consider a computer whose word size is 32 and suppose that the integer value 58 is to be stored. The base-two representation of 58 is

$$58 = 111010_2$$

If 58 is being used as an `unsigned` literal, all 32 bits are used for the binary digits of the value. The six bits in the binary representation of 58 can be stored in the rightmost bits of the memory word and the remaining bits filled with zeros:

0	0	0	0	0	0	0	0	0	0	0	0	0	0	0	0	0	0	0	0	0	0	0	0	0	0	1	1	1	0	1	0

Unlike `unsigned` values, which are always nonnegative, `int` values may be negative and so they must be stored in a binary form in which the sign of the integer is part of the representation. There are several ways to do this, but one of the most common methods is the **two's complement** representation. In this scheme, positive integers are represented in binary form, as just described, with the leftmost bit set to 0 to indicate that the value is positive. Thus, if 58 is being used as an `int` literal, 31 bits are used for the binary digits of the value and one bit for the sign:

sign
↓

0	0	0	0	0	0	0	0	0	0	0	0	0	0	0	0	0	0	0	0	0	0	0	0	0	0	1	1	1	0	1	0

The two's complement representation of a negative integer $-n$ is obtained by first finding the binary representation of n, complementing it—that is, changing each 0 to 1 and each 1 to 0—and then adding 1 to the result. For example, the two's complement representation of –58 using a string of 32 bits is obtained as follows:

1. Represent 58 by a 32-bit binary numeral:

00000000000000000000000000111010

2. Complement this bit string:

11111111111111111111111111000101

3. Add 1:

11111111111111111111111111000110

This string of bits is then stored:

sign
↓

1	1	1	1	1	1	1	1	1	1	1	1	1	1	1	1	1	1	1	1	1	1	1	1	1	1	0	0	0	1	1	0

Note that the sign bit in this two's complement representation of a negative integer is always 1, indicating that the number is negative.

The number of bits used to store an integer value determines the range of the integers that can be stored internally. For example, the largest `unsigned` value that can be stored in 32 bits is

$$11111111111111111111111111111111_2 = 2^{32} = 4294967296$$

The range of integers that can be represented using 32 bits is

$$10000000000000000000000000000000_2 = -2^{31} = -2147483648$$

through

$$01111111111111111111111111111111_2 = 2^{31} - 1 = 2147483647$$

Representation of an integer outside the allowed range would require more bits than can be stored, a phenomenon known as **overflow.** Using more bits to store an integer will enlarge the range of integers that can be stored, but it does not solve the problem of overflow; the range of representable integers is still finite.

REALS

Digits to the left of the binary point in the binary representation of a real number are coefficients of nonnegative powers of two, and those to the right are coefficients of negative powers of two. For example, the expanded form of 10110.101_2 is

$$(1 \times 2^4) + (0 \times 2^3) + (1 \times 2^2) + (1 \times 2^1) + (0 \times 2^0)$$
$$+ (1 \times 2^{-1}) + (0 \times 2^{-2}) + (1 \times 2^{-3})$$

which has the decimal value

$$16 + 0 + 4 + 2 + 0 + \frac{1}{2} + 0 + \frac{1}{8} = 22.625$$

There is some variation in the schemes used for storing real numbers in computer memory, but one floating-point representation was standardized in 1985 by the Institute for Electrical and Electronic Engineers (IEEE) and has become almost universal. This **IEEE Floating Point Format** specifies how reals can be represented in two formats: *single precision,* which uses 32 bits, and *double precision,* which uses 64 bits. The double-precision format is simply a wider version of the single-precision format, so we will consider only single precision.

We begin by writing the binary representation of the number in **floating-point form,** which is like scientific notation except that the base is two rather than ten:

$$b_1 \cdot b_2 b_3 \cdots \times 2^k$$

where each b_i is 0 or 1 and $b_1 = 1$ (unless the number is 0). $b_1.b_2b_3\ldots$ is called the **mantissa** (or **fractional part** or **significand**) and k is the **exponent** (or **characteristic**). To illustrate it, consider the real number 22.625, which we have seen can be written in binary as

$$10110.101_2$$

Rewriting this in floating-point form,

$$1.0110101_2 \times 2^4$$

is easy since multiplying (dividing) a base-two number by 2 is the same as moving the binary point to the right (left). 1.0110101_2 is the mantissa and 4 is the exponent.

In the IEEE format for single precision real values,

- the leftmost bit stores the sign of the mantissa, 0 for positive, 1 for negative;
- the next 8 bits store the binary representation of the exponent + 127; 127 is called a **bias**;
- the rightmost 23 bits store the bits to the right of the binary point in the mantissa. (The bit to the left need not be stored since it is always 1.)

For 22.625, the stored exponent would be 4 + 127 = 10000011_2 and the stored mantissa would be $01101010000000000000000_2$:

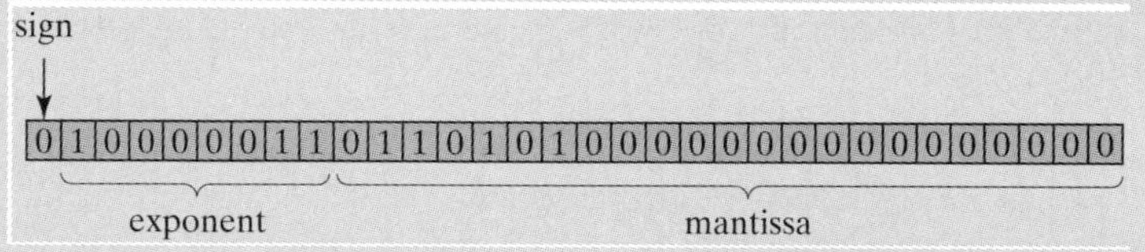

The IEEE representation for double precision uses an 11-bit exponent with a bias of 1023 and 53 bits for the signed mantissa.

Because the binary representation of the exponent may require more than the available number of bits, we see that the **overflow** problem discussed in connection with integers also occurs in storing a real number whose exponent is too large. An 8-bit exponent restricts the range of real values to approximately -10^{38} to 10^{38}, and overflow occurs for values outside this range. A negative exponent that is too small to be stored causes an **underflow.** Real values represented using an 8-bit exponent must be greater than approximately 10^{-38} or less than -10^{-38}, and underflow occurs between these values:

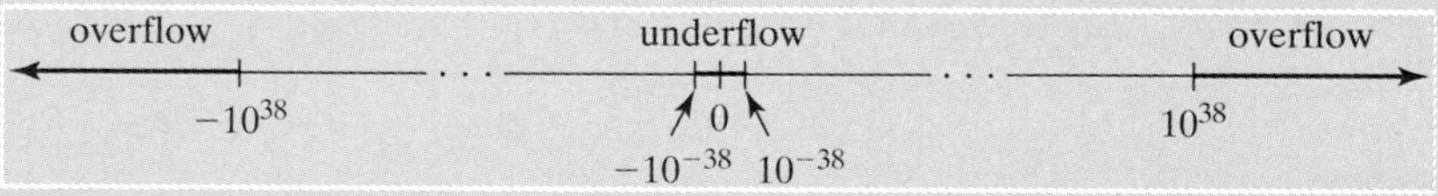

Also, there obviously are some real numbers whose mantissas have more than the allotted number of bits; consequently, some of these bits will be lost when such numbers are stored. In fact, most real numbers do not have finite binary representations and thus cannot be stored exactly in any computer. For example, the binary representation of the real number 0.7 is

$$(0.101100110011001100110011001100110\ldots)_2$$

where the block 0110 is repeated indefinitely. Because only a finite number of these bits can be stored, the stored representation of 0.7 will not be exact (e.g., 0.6999999284744263). This error in the stored representation of a real value, called **roundoff error**, can be reduced, but not eliminated, by storing a larger number of bits. A 24-bit mantissa gives approximately 7 significant decimal digits for real values and a 48-bit mantissa gives approximately 14 significant digits.

CHARACTERS AND STRINGS

The schemes used for the internal representation of character data are based on the assignment of a numeric code to each of the characters in the character set. Several standard coding schemes have been developed, such as ASCII (American Standard Code for Information Interchange), EBCDIC (Extended Binary Coded Decimal Interchange Code), and Unicode.*

Characters are represented internally using these binary codes. For example, the ASCII code of `c` is 99 = 01100011_2, which can be stored in one 8-bit byte,

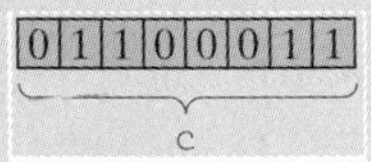

and the character string `code` can be stored in a 32-bit word with the code for `c` in the first byte, the code for `o` in the second byte, and so on:

Character strings whose lengths exceed the number of bytes in a word are usually stored in adjacent memory words.

Unicode is designed for use with most of the written languages of the world and must therefore provide codes for many characters. Whereas ASCII can encode only 128 characters, Unicode provides codes for more than 65,000 characters. To accomplish this it uses 16-bit codes. For example, the code for `c` (99—same as in ASCII) would be stored in two bytes:

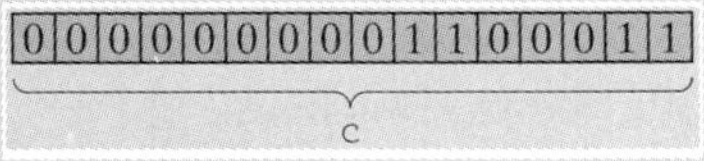

The code for the non-ASCII character π (Greek pi) is 960 = 0000001111000000_2 and can also be stored in two bytes:

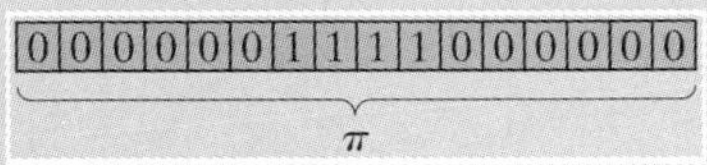

BOOLEANS

There are only two boolean values: `false` and `true`. If `false` is encoded as 0 and `true` as 1, then a single bit is all that is needed to store a `boolean` value. Usually, however, an entire word or byte is used with all bits set to 0 for `false` and any other bit string representing `true`.

* See Appendix A for a table of ASCII codes for all characters.

2.3* OBJECTive Thinking: Attribute Variables

We have seen how to declare variables and constants whose values are of one of the C++ predefined types—`boolean`, `char`, `int`, `double`, `string`, and so on. These predefined types are sufficient to perform a wide variety of useful computations and can be used to solve many different problems.

However, many computational problems involve more complicated objects—objects whose values cannot be directly represented using one of the predefined C++ types. For example, the *windows* and *buttons* in the graphical user interface of a modern computer are objects that cannot be directly represented using a predefined C++ type. Likewise, objects like a *student* or a *sphere* cannot be directly represented using the predefined types.

Representing complicated objects in a program is a two-step process:

1. We design and build a **class** that creates a new type.
2. We use the new class type to declare the object(s).

We can then perform a computation by sending messages to the object(s).

As we saw in Section 2.2, if we are given a class that creates a new type, we can declare an object of this type with a statement of the form

```
typeName objectName;
```

where *`typeName`* is the name of the class. In this section, we take a first look at the more challenging task of designing and building a class.

In order to provide an accurate model of its objects, a class must specify the *attributes* of its objects along with the *operations* that will be applied to them. In this section, we will see how a class reserves space for an object's attributes and will look at operations in later *OBJECTive Thinking* sections.

CLASS STRUCTURE

A class declaration creates a new type that we can use to declare objects. For example, in Section 1.4, we saw how a `Sphere` class provided us with a `Sphere` type, which we used to declare a variable object named `aSphere`. A simplified pattern for the structure of a class is as follows:

Simple Class Declaration

Form:

```
class ClassName
{
 public:
   ... declarations of operations
 private:
   ... declarations of attributes
};
```

where

ClassName is a valid C++ identifier naming the new type that is being created; and

class, public, and private are C++ keywords.

Purpose: Instructs the C++ compiler to create a new type named *ClassName* so that objects of that type can be sent the messages declared between public: and private: and which will have the attributes declared below private:.*

* This is a common structure for a class. A class can actually have multiple public: and private: sections. It can also name one or more parent classes, as we'll see in Chapter 7.

For example, to make a Sphere class, we would begin by writing

```
class Sphere
{
 public:
   ... Sphere-operation declarations go here
 private:
   ... Sphere-attribute declarations go here
};
```

In Section 2.1, we saw that although we can represent the individual pieces of a person's name as strings, there is no predefined type to represent a person's entire name. We might thus declare a Name class as follows:

```
class Name
{
 public:
   ... Name-operation declarations go here
 private:
   ... Name-attribute declarations go here
};
```

We also saw in Section 2.1 that we can represent the individual attributes of a student using existing C++ types, but C++ provides no predefined type for representing a student. We might therefore declare a Student class:

```
class Student
{
 public:
   ... Student-operation declarations go here
 private:
   ... Student-attribute declarations go here
};
```

To make it easy to reuse a class declaration, it is usually placed in a separate file called a **header file** (or **include file**, or **.h file**). The name of a programmer-defined header file is usually the name of the class followed by the *.h* extension. Thus, we would store our

`Sphere` class declaration in a file named *Sphere.h*, our `Name` class declaration in a file named *Name.h*, and a `Student` class declaration in a file named *Student.h*. To use one of these classes to declare variables (or constants) in a program, we need only include (using the `#include` directive) the header file for that class. For example, to declare `Sphere` variables, we could use

```
#include "Sphere.h"
int main()
{
   ...
   Sphere oneSphere, anotherSphere;
   ...
}
```

Including *Name.h* makes it possible to declare `Name` variables:

```
#include "Name.h"
int main()
{
   ...
   Name myName, yourName;
   ...
}
```

Similarly, to declare `Student` variables we could use

```
#include "Student.h"
int main()
{
   ...
   Student firstStudent, lastStudent;
   ...
}
```

At this point, our classes don't do much beyond create a new type. We will now see how to declare the attributes of a class.

ATTRIBUTE VARIABLES

Often an object in a problem has multiple attributes that cannot be represented using a single predefined type. A class declaration is what is needed because it accomplishes two things:

- It lets us "wrap" the multiple attributes of an object within a single structure.
- It creates a new type, for which objects of that type will have storage for all attributes specified by the class declaration.

To illustrate, we saw in Section 1.4 that a sphere has three attributes: *radius*, *density*, and *weight*. While we could represent any one of these attributes *individually* using a `double`, we cannot use one `double` to represent all three values that define a sphere. A `Sphere` class declaration, however, lets us wrap the three sphere attributes within a single entity (the `Sphere` class) and it declares the name `Sphere` as a new type.

To wrap the sphere attributes within a `Sphere` class, we simply declare those attributes inside the class' private section like normal variables:

```
class Sphere
{
 public:
   ... Sphere-operation declarations go here
 private:
   double myRadius,
          myDensity,
          myWeight;
};
```

To distinguish these **attribute variables** from "normal" variables, it is our convention to name them with the prefix "my" followed by the name of the attribute. As we shall see later, this convention can help make the operations of a class more readable as well as help us design and code them from the perspective of an object that receives a message.

With this modified `Sphere` declaration in the file *Sphere.h*, a programmer can now write

```
#include "Sphere.h"
int main()
{
   Sphere oneSphere, anotherSphere;
}
```

and the two objects `oneSphere` and `anotherSphere` will each have space within them for the three sphere attributes:

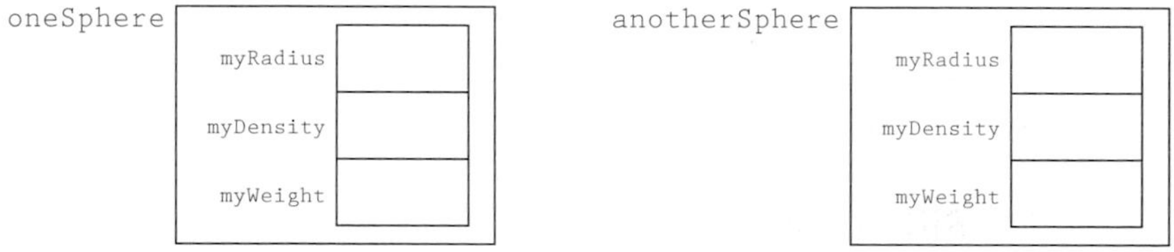

Just as a sphere has three attributes, a person's name is defined by three attributes: first name, middle name, and last name. Each of these can be represented by strings. We can thus wrap these three attributes inside our `Name` class:

```
#include <string>       // the string class
using namespace std;
class Name
{
 public:
   ... Name-operation declarations go here
```

```
 private:
    string myFirstName,
           myMiddleName,
           myLastName;
};
```

If such a declaration is saved in a file *Name.h*, a programmer can write

```
#include "Name.h"
int main()
{
   Name myName, yourName;
}
```

and the two `Name` objects `myName` and `yourName` will each have their own distinct spaces for their attributes:

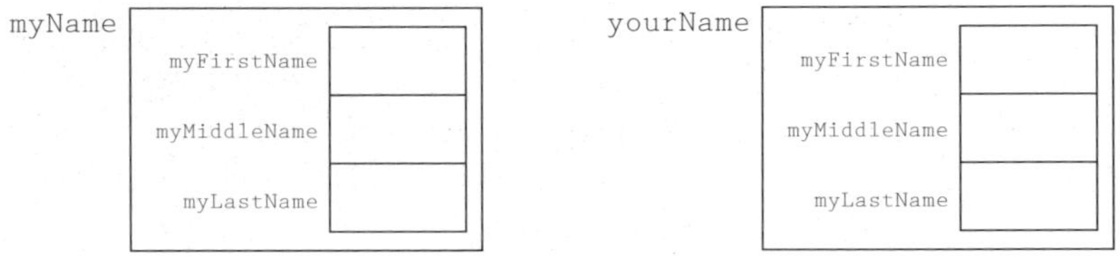

As a final example, student workers have many attributes, including their name, id number, hourly wage, and hours worked in a given pay period. We can wrap these attributes inside our `Student` class declaration:

```
#include "Name.h"
class Student
{
 public:
   ... Student-operation declarations go here
 private:
   Name   myName;
   int    myIdNumber;
   double myHourlyWage,
          myHoursWorked;
};
```

If this declaration is saved in the file *Student.h*, a programmer can write

```
#include "Student.h"
int main()
{
   Student firstStudent, lastStudent;
}
```

and the `Student` objects `firstStudent` and `lastStudent` will each have their own distinct spaces for their attributes:

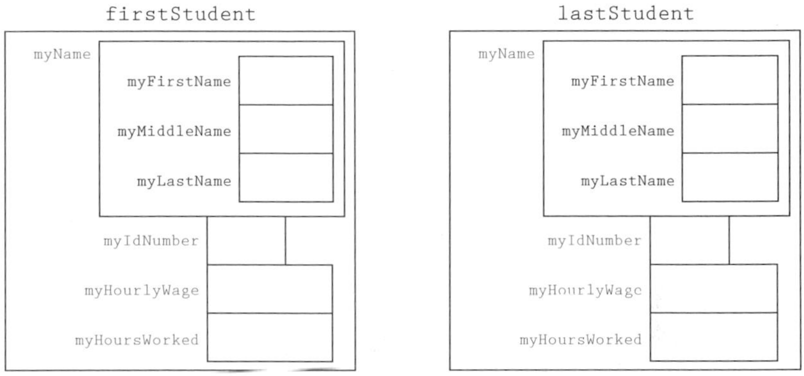

Attribute variables thus allow each object to store the attributes that distinguish it from other objects of the same class. Because an object is sometimes called an *instance of a class*, such attribute variables (for which each object has its own storage) are commonly known as **instance variables** or **data members**.

This concludes our introduction to classes and attribute variables. In the *OBJECTive Thinking* section of the next four chapters, we will see how to define methods that allow an object to respond to messages.

✔ Quick Quiz 2.3

1. A class declaration contains declarations of the ________ of objects along with the ________ applied to those objects.
2. A class declaration is usually placed in a ________ file so it will be easy to reuse.
3. ________ variables are used in a class declaration to store the attributes of objects.
4. The variables in Question 3 are stored in a section of a class declaration that begins with the keyword ________.
5. The variables in Question 3 are also known as ________ variables or ________.

Exercises 2.3

For the following exercises, write (partial) class declarations similar to those in this section—that is, which contain attribute variables, but no operations—to represent the given real-world objects.

1. Temperature measured in degrees and a scale (Fahrenheit or Celsius)
2. Time measured in hours, minutes, and seconds
3. Dates consisting of a month name, day number, and year
4. A telephone number (e.g., 616-957-6000) consisting of an area code (616), an exchange (957), and a local number (6000)
5. Student information consisting of a student number (an integer), name (use the type `Name` in this section), credits earned (a real number), and grade point average (a real number)

CHAPTER SUMMARY

Key Terms & Notes

#include directive
.h file
attribute variable
bool
char
class
class declaration
compiler directive
const modifier
constant declaration
data member
declaration statement
declare
double
escape sequence
exponent
false
fixed-point
float
floating-point
fractional part
fundamental type
garbage value
header file
hexadecimal
identifier
IEEE Floating Point Format
include file
instance variable
indeterminate
int
keyword
library
literal
long double
long int
mantissa
octal
overflow
return statement
roundoff error
short int
sign bit
string
true
two's complement
type
undefined
underflow
unsigned
variable
variable declaration
white space

- In a C++ program, types of objects must be declared before those objects are used.
- The fundamental types in C++ include `short`, `int`, and `long` for integers; `unsigned` for nonnegative integers; `float` and `double` for real values; `boolean` for logical values; and `char` for individual characters.
- C++ compilers treat all real literals as being of type `double`. Thus, most programmers use `double` for real objects and seldom use `float`.
- The `char` type is used to represent single characters.
- `char` literals must be enclosed in single quotes.
- Escape sequences such as `\n` (new line) and `\t` (tab) are used for characters that have a special purpose.

- The string type is provided for processing strings of characters. The <string> library must be included before string objects can be declared.
- An identifier may begin with a letter or _ (underscore), which may be followed by any number of these characters or digits; it may not be a C++ keyword.
- Using meaningful identifiers that suggest what they represent makes programs easier to read and understand.
- C++ is case sensitive.
- Any name in a program that is not a C++ keyword is an identifier and must be declared before it can be used.
- The const modifier is used to declare constants, which are values that cannot be changed during program execution.
- Using named constants instead of the literals they represent improves code readability and facilitates program maintenance.
- Placing constant declarations at the beginning of the class or method in which they are used is good programming practice because it makes it easy to locate them when modifications are necessary.
- If no initial value is specified in a variable declaration, its value is undefined (or indeterminate).
- The form of a class is

```
class ClassName
{
 public:
   ... declarations of operations
 private:
   ... declarations of attributes
}
```

- A class declaration
  - can be used to "wrap" multiple attributes of an object within a single structure;
  - creates a new type. (Objects of that type will have space to store these attributes.)
- Class declarations are usually placed in a header file of the form *ClassName.h*. Using a compiler directive of the form #include "*ClassName.h*" makes it possible thereafter in the program to declare objects of type *ClassName*.

Programming Pointers

In this section, we consider some aspects of program design and suggest guidelines for good programming style. We also point out some errors that may occur in writing C++ programs.

Program Style and Design

1. In the examples in this text, we adopt certain stylistic guidelines for C++ programs, and you should write your program in a similar style. In this text, we use the following standards; others are described in the Programming Pointers of subsequent chapters:
   - *Put each statement of the program on a separate line.*

- *Use uppercase and lowercase letters in a way that contributes to program readability;* for example, put identifiers in lowercase, capitalizing the first letter of each word after the first.
- *Put each* { and } *on a separate line.*
- *Align each* { and *its corresponding* }. *Indent the statements enclosed by* { and }.
- *When a statement is continued from one line to another, indent the continued line(s).*
- *Align the identifiers in each constant and variable declaration, placing each on a separate line;* for example,

```
const double taxRate = 0.1963,
             interestRate = 0.185;

int empNumber;

double hours,
       rate,
       wages;
```

- *Insert blank lines between declarations and statements and between blocks of statements to make clear the structure of the program.*
- *Separate the operators and operands in an expression with spaces to make the expression easy to read.*

2. *Declare constants at the beginning of a function and declare variables near their first use.* This makes it easy to find constants when they must be modified. It also reduces the tendency to declare unused variables, since declarations are deferred until they are needed.
3. *Programs cannot be considered to be correct if they have not been tested.* Test all programs with data for which the results are known or can be checked by hand calculations.
4. *Programs should be readable and understandable.*

- *Use meaningful identifiers.* For example,

```
wages = hours * rate;
```

is more meaningful than

```
w = h * r;
```

or

```
z7 = alpha * x;
```

Also, avoid "cute" identifiers, as in

```
baconBroughtHome = hoursWasted * pittance;
```

- *Use comments to describe the purpose of a program or other key program segments.* However, do not clutter the program with needless comments; for example, the comment in the statement

```
int counter;      // a counter
```

is not helpful and should not be used.

- *Label all output produced by a program.* For example,

```
cout << "Employee # " << empNumber
     << " Wages = $" << wages;
```

produces more informative output than

```
cout << empNumber << wages;
```

5. *Programs should be general and flexible.* They should solve a class of problems rather than one specific problem. It should be relatively easy to modify a program to solve a related problem without changing much of the program. Using named constants instead of "magic numbers" as described in Section 2.2 is helpful in this regard.
6. *Identify any preconditions a program has.* Preconditions are assumptions made in a program, often one or more restrictions on what comprises a valid input value. State all preconditions in a program's opening documentation.

WATCH OUT

Potential Pitfalls

1. *Character constants must be enclosed in single quotes. In particular,* `string` *literals cannot be assigned to variables of type* `char`. For example, the declaration

   ```
   char ch = "x";
   ```

   is not valid.
2. *Values of type* `char` *are stored as their (integer) numeric codes.* This can be confusing, since strange things like the following are allowed in C++:

   ```
   char letterGrade = 65;
   ```

   On machines using the ASCII character set, this causes `letterGrade` to have exactly the same value as if it had been initialized to `'A'` (since 65 is the decimal ASCII code for `'A'`). Such mixing of integer and character values within an expression should normally be avoided.
3. *Character string constants must be enclosed within double quotes.* If either the beginning or the ending double quote is missing, an error will result. Escape sequences—`\"`, `\'`, `\t`, `\n`, . . .—can be used to represent double quotes, single quotes, tabs, newlines, etc.
4. *Comments are enclosed within* `/*` *and* `*/` *or between* `//` *and the end of the line.* Be sure of the following:
   - *Each beginning delimiter* `/*` *has a matching end delimiter* `*/`. *Failure to use these in pairs can produce strange results. For example, in the program segment*

     ```
     /* Read employee data
     cin >> empNumber >> hours >> rate;
     /* Calculate wages */
     wages = hours * rate;
     ```

     everything from "Read employee data . . ." through "Calculate wages," including the input statement, is a single comment. No values are read for `empNumber`, `hours`, and `rate`, and so `hours` and `rate` are undefined when the statement `wages = hours * rate;` is executed.
   - *There is no space between the* `/` *and the* `*` *or between the two slashes.* Otherwise these pairs will not be considered to be comment delimiters.
5. *Every* `{` *must be matched by a* `}`. Failure to include either one produces a compilation error.
6. *All identifiers must be declared.* Attempting to use an identifier that has not been declared will produce a compilation error. In this connection, remember that *C++ distinguishes between uppercase and lowercase letters.* For example, declaring

   ```
   double sumOfXValues;
   ```

   and then later in the program writing

   ```
   SumOfXValues += X;
   ```

   causes a compile-time error since the identifier `SumOfXValues` has not been declared.

7. *Variables should be initialized at their declarations, unless they are going to be immediately changed by an input or assignment statement;* in this case, there is little point in giving them initial values since those values will be overwritten by the input or assigned values. Other variables should be initialized appropriately since the value of an uninitialized variable is *undefined.* This means that it is not possible to predict the contents of the memory location associated with a variable until a value has been explicitly assigned to that variable. For example, the statements

```
int x, y;
   ...
y = x + 1;
```

will produce a "garbage" value for *y*, since x has not previously been initialized or assigned a value, as in

```
int x = 0, y;
   ...
y = x + 1;
```

8. *Keywords, identifiers, and constants may not be broken at the end of a line, nor may they contain blanks (except, of course, a string constant may contain blanks).* Thus, the statements

```
empNumber = 12345;
cout << "The number of the current employee is "
     << empNumber;
```

are valid, whereas the statements

```
empNumber = 12 345;
cout << "The number of the current employee
        is " << empNumber;
```

are not valid. If it is necessary to split a string over two lines, as in the second statement, the string should be split into two separate strings, each enclosed in double quotes, and placed as consecutive items in the output list,

```
cout << "The number of the current employee "
        "is " << empNumber;
```

or separated by the output operator,

```
cout << "The number of the current employee "
     << "is " << empNumber;
```

or placed in separate output statements:

```
cout << "The number of the current employee ";
cout << "is " << empNumber;
```

Programming Problems

Section 2.2

1. Write a program to convert a measurement given in feet to the equivalent number of (**a**) yards, (**b**) inches, (**c**) centimeters, and (**d**) meters (1 ft = 12 in. 1 yd = 3 ft, 1 in. = 2.54 cm, 1 m = 100 cm).
2. Write a program to convert a weight given in ounces to the equivalent number of (**a**) pounds, (**b**) tons, (**c**) grams, and (**d**) kilograms (1 lb = 16 oz, 1 ton = 2000 lb, 1 oz = 28.349523 g, 1 kg = 1000 g).

3. Write a program to read a student's number, his or her old grade point average, and the old number of course credits (e.g., 31479, 3.25, 66), and to then print these with appropriate labels. Next, read the course credit and grade for each of four courses—for example, `course1Credits` = 5.0, `course1Grade` = 3.7, `course2Credits` = 3.0, `course2Grade` = 4.0, and so on. Calculate

   old # of honor points = (old # of course credits) * (old GPA)

   new # of honor points = `course1Credits * course1Grade + course2Credits * course2Grade + ...`

   total # of new course credits = `course1Credits + course2Credits + ...`

   $$\text{current GPA} = \frac{\text{\# of new honor points}}{\text{\# of new course credits}}$$

   Print the current GPA with an appropriate label. Finally, calculate

   $$\texttt{cumulativeGPA} = \frac{(\text{\# of old honor points}) + (\text{\# of new honor points})}{(\text{\# of old course credits}) + (\text{\# of new course credits})}$$

   and display this with a label.

4. Write a program that finds the resistance of an electronic circuit with three parallel resistors *resistor1*, *resistor2*, and *resistor3*. The resistance can be computed using the following formula:

   $$\text{resistance} = \frac{1}{\dfrac{1}{resistor1} + \dfrac{1}{resistor2} + \dfrac{1}{resistor3}}$$

5. Write a program that, given the amount of a purchase and the amount received in payment, computes the change in dollars, half-dollars, quarters, dimes, nickels, and pennies.

6. The shipping clerk at the Rinky Dooflingy Company is faced with the following problem: Dooflingies are very delicate and must be shipped in special containers. These containers are available in the four sizes huge, large, medium, and small, which can hold 50, 20, 5, and 1 dooflingy, respectively. Write a program that reads the number of dooflingies to be shipped and displays the number of huge, large, medium, and small containers needed to send the shipment in the minimum number of containers and with the minimum amount of wasted space. Use constant definitions for the number of dooflingies each type of container can hold. The output should be similar to the following:

```
Container  Number
=========  ======
  Huge       21
  Large       2
  Medium      1
  Small       3
```

   Execute the program for 3, 18, 48, 78, and 10598 dooflingies.

Section 2.3

7. Write a program to test the temperature class of Exercise 1. It should `#include` your temperature class library and the `iostream` library and its main function should contain the following:

   a. a declaration of an object of this temperature type, and

b. a statement of the form

```
cout << object.data_member;
```

that tries to output the value of one of the private data members, check that an error occurs when you try to compile and execute the program.

c. Now add the declaration

```
double pubDataMember;
```

to the public section of your temperature class and replace the `data_member` part of the statement from part (b) with `pubDataMember`. See what happens now when you try to compile and execute the program.

8. Proceed as in Problem 7 for the time class of Exercise 2.
9. Proceed as in Problem 7 for the date class of Exercise 3.
10. Proceed as in Problem 7 for the telephone-number class of Exercise 4.
11. Proceed as in Problem 7 for the student-information class of Exercise 5.

CHAPTER 3
Operations and Expressions

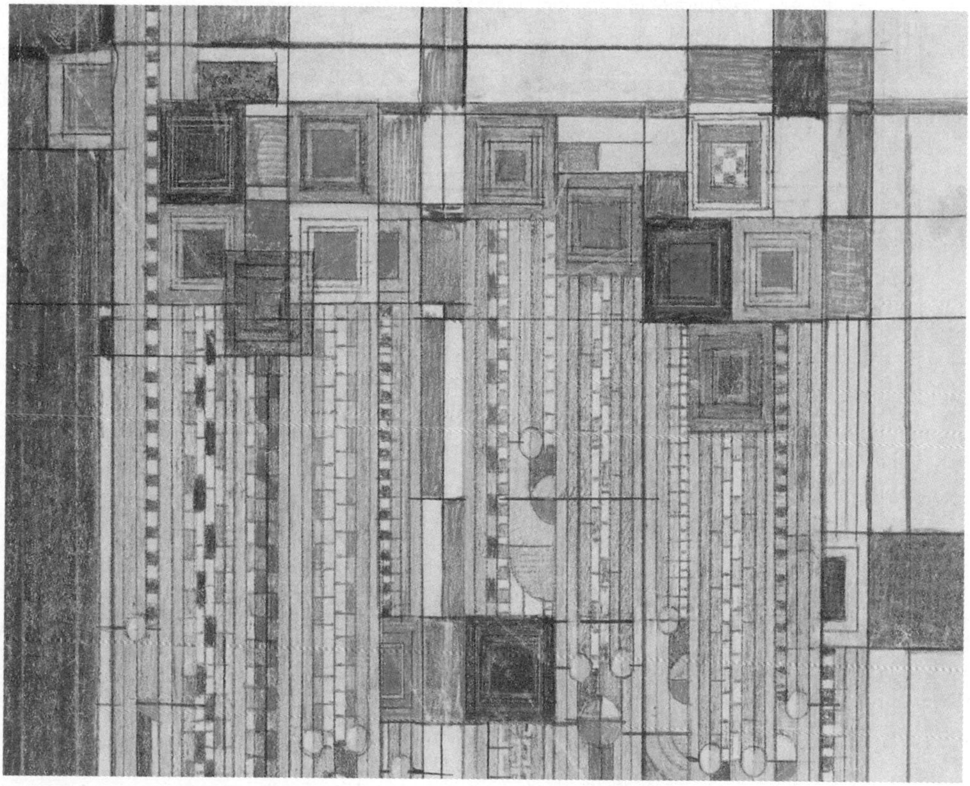

```
<>!*''#
^"`$$-
!*=@$_
%*<>~#4
&[]../
|{,,SYSTEM HALTED
```

-The WakaWaka Poem
-Fred Bremmer and Steve Kroeze
*(while students at Calvin College)**

Arithmetic is being able to count up to twenty without taking off your shoes.

-Mickey Mouse

A little inaccuracy sometimes saves tons of explanation.

-Saki (H.H. Munroe)

* Several years ago, a magazine poll established "waka" as the proper pronunciation for the angle-bracket characters < and >. Here is a phonetic version of this poem:

Waka waka bang splat tick tick hash,
Caret quote back-tick dollar dollar dash,
Bang splat equal at dollar underscore,
Percent splat waka waka tilde number four,
Ampersand bracket bracket dot dot slash,
Vertical-bar curly-bracket comma comma CRASH.

Chapter Contents

Chapter Objectives

- Study another example of software development using OCD.
- Take a detailed look at numeric types—both integer and real—together with operations and predefined functions for these types.
- Examine the `bool` data type and operators for building logical expressions—both simple and compound—along with short-circuit evaluation of these expressions.
- Look at the `char` data type for processing individual characters and some of the predefined functions provided in C++ for processing character data.

- Study the assignment operator and the related increment and decrement operators along with the shortcut assignment operators.
- Take a first look at input and output operators along with format manipulators.
- (Optional) Take a first look at class constructors—default and explicit-value—and how they are used to initialize instance variables.

The main aspects of object-centered design (OCD) are as follows:

- Identify the real-world *objects* in the problem.
- Identify the *operations* needed to solve the problem.
- Arrange these in an *algorithm.*

This algorithm must then be encoded in some programming language such as C++. This program must be written carefully, following the syntax rules for that language.

The preceding chapter focused on how to represent the problem objects as *software objects* (also called *program entities*). We studied some of the types provided in C++ for these software objects and the statements used to declare them. This chapter focuses on the operations. We study in detail the operations provided in C++ to implement the operations needed to solve a problem and how they are used to form expressions of various kinds—numeric, boolean, character, assignment, input, and output. The optional *OBJECTive Thinking* section introduces the first and most basic operations that a class provides—constructors.

3.1 Introductory Example: Einstein's Equation

PROBLEM

For his physics course, Albert Onemug has a large problem set that is due by the next class meeting. Many of the problems require (among other things) using Einstein's equation to calculate the amount of energy released by a quantity of matter for a mass given in the problem. Because the deadline is near, Albert asks for our help. Our task, therefore, is to write a program to do these calculations.

Object-Centered Design

Behavior. The program should display on the screen a prompt for the quantity of matter (i.e., its mass). The user will enter a nonnegative real value at the keyboard. The program should read this number and use Einstein's equation to compute the energy that can be produced by that quantity of matter. It should display this amount of energy along with a descriptive label.

Objects. From our behavioral description, we can identify the following objects in the problem:

Problem Objects	Software Objects		
	Type	Kind	Name
screen	`ostream`	varying	`cout`
prompt	`string`	constant	none
quantity of matter	`double`	varying	*mass*
keyboard	`istream`	varying	`cin`
quantity of energy	`double`	varying	*energy*
descriptive label	`string`	constant	none

Operations. From our behavioral description, we see that the following operations will be needed:

i. Display a string (the prompt) on the screen
ii. Read a nonnegative number (*mass*) from the keyboard
iii. Compute *energy* from *mass*
iv. Display a number (*energy*) and a string on the screen

Each of these operations is provided for us by C++, with the exception of Operation iii. It requires the use of Einstein's equation

$$e = m \times c^2$$

where m is the mass, c is the speed-of-light constant, and e is the energy produced. Performing this operation thus requires the following operations:

Exponentiation (c^2)

Multiplication of reals $\left(m \times c^2\right)$

Storage of a real $\left(e = m \times c^2\right)$

This refinement to Operation iii adds two additional objects to our object list:

Problem Objects	Software Objects		
	Type	Kind	Name
screen	`ostream`	varying	`cout`
prompt	`string`	constant	none
quantity of matter	`double`	varying	*mass*
keyboard	`istream`	varying	`cin`
quantity of energy	`double`	varying	*energy*
descriptive label	`string`	constant	none
speed of light	`double`	constant	*SPEED_OF_LIGHT*
2	`int`	constant	none

Algorithm. We now organize these objects and operations into an algorithm:

1. Declare the constant *SPEED_OF_LIGHT.*
2. Display to `cout` a prompt for the mass to be converted into energy.
3. Read a nonnegative number from `cin` into *mass.*
4. Compute $energy = mass \times SPEED\_OF\_LIGHT^2$.
5. Display to `cout` a descriptive label and *energy.*

Coding, Execution, and Testing. Figure 3.1 shows one way to implement the preceding algorithm as a program.[1] Also shown are two sample runs with test data for which the output can be easily verified and a third execution with "real" data.

Fig. 3.1 Mass-to-energy conversion. (Part 1 of 2)

```
/* mass2energy.cpp computes energy from a given mass using
 *    Einstein's mass-to-energy conversion equation.
 *
 * Input:         The mass (in kilograms) being converted to energy
 * Precondition: mass >= 0
 * Output:        The amount of energy (in kilojoules) corresponding
 *                  to mass
 ******************************************************************/

#include <iostream>                         // cin, cout, <<, >>
#include <cassert>                          // assert()
#include <cmath>                            // pow()
using namespace std;

int main()
{
   const double SPEED_OF_LIGHT = 2.997925e8; // meters/sec

   cout << "To find the amount of energy obtained from a given mass,\n"
           "enter a mass (in kilograms): ";
   double mass;
   cin >> mass;                             // get mass
   assert(mass >= 0);                       // make sure it's nonnegative
                                            // compute energy
   double energy = mass * pow(SPEED_OF_LIGHT, 2);
```

1. C++ libraries whose names take the form `<cxxxxx>` are actually **C libraries**. With compilers that are not fully ANSI compliant, it may be necessary to use the older C names `<xxxxx.h>`—for example `<assert.h>` instead of `<cassert>`—and to make other changes as described in Footnote 1 of Chapter 1.

Fig. 3.1 Mass-to-energy conversion. (Part 2 of 2)

```
                                    // display energy
   cout << mass << " kilograms of matter will release "
        << energy << " kilojoules of energy.\n";
}
```

Sample runs:

```
To find the amount of energy obtained from a given mass,
enter a mass (in kilograms): 1
1 kilograms of matter will release 8.98755e+16 kilojoules of energy.

To find the amount of energy obtained from a given mass,
enter a mass (in kilograms): 2
2 kilograms of matter will release 1.79751e+17 kilojoules of energy.

To find the amount of energy obtained from a given mass,
enter a mass (in kilograms): 125.5
125.5 kilograms of matter will release 1.12794e+19 kilojoules of energy.
```

This program uses several different kinds of expressions. In the remainder of this chapter, we will explore the rich variety of expressions available in C++.

3.2 Numeric Expressions

A C++ **expression** is a sequence of one or more data values called *operands* and zero or more *operators* that combine to produce a value. For example,

```
12
```

is an expression that consists of one integer value (`12`) and no operators; it produces the integer value 12. Similarly,

```
2.2 + 3.3
```

is an expression that consists of two operands (`2.2` and `3.3`) and one operator (+) and produces the real value 5.5. The type of the value produced by an expression is called the type of the expression. Expressions that produce an `int` value are called `int` expressions, expressions that produce a `double` value are called `double` expressions, and so on.

In this section, we examine the arithmetic operators and functions that are used in writing numeric expressions in C++ programs.

OPERATORS

In C++, addition and subtraction are denoted by the usual plus (+) and minus (-) signs. Multiplication is denoted by an asterisk (*), which must be used to denote every multiplication. That is, to multiply n by 2, we can write 2*n or n*2, but not 2n. Division is denoted by a slash (/), which is used for both real and integer division. Another operation closely related to integer division is the **modulus** or **remainder** operation, denoted by percent (%), which gives the remainder in an integer division. The following table summarizes these operators.

Operator	Operation
+	addition, unary plus
-	subtraction, unary minus
*	multiplication
/	real and integer division
%	modulus (remainder in integer division)

For the operators +, -, *, and /, the operands may be of either integer or real type. If both are integers, the result is integer; but if either is real, the result is real. For example,

```
2 + 3 → 5                 2 + 3.0 → 5.0
2.0 + 3 → 5.0             2.0 + 3.0 → 5.0
7.0 / 2.0 → 3.5           7 / 2 → 3
```

It is important to understand the difference between integer and real division. Consider the two expressions

```
3 / 4
```

and

```
3.0 / 4
```

Since both operands in the first expression, 3 and 4, are integers, integer division is performed, producing the integer quotient 0. By contrast, the second expression has a real operand, 3.0, and so real division is performed, producing the real result 0.75. One of the common difficulties for beginning programmers is to remember that the value of

```
1/n
```

is 0 if n is an integer different from –1, 0, or 1.

Integer division produces both a quotient and a remainder, and C++ provides one operator (/) that gives the integer quotient and another operator (%) that gives the remainder from an integer division.[1] The following are some examples:

```
  9 / 3 →3                  9 %  3 → 0
 86 / 10 → 8               86 % 10 → 6
197 / 10 → 19             197 % 10 → 7
```

1. Neither i / j nor i % j is defined if j is zero. A run-time error will occur if such an expression is encountered.

Type Conversions. We just saw that the division operation in the expression

```
3.0 / 4
```

performs real division and produces a real value as its result, even though only one of the operands is a real value. Some languages do not allow integer and real values to be intermixed within an expression in this manner. In such mixed-type expressions, C++ will automatically convert *narrower values to wider values*; that is, the value in such an expression that is stored in the smaller number of bits will be converted to the type that occupies the larger number of bits. For example, suppose that in the expression

```
3.0 / 4
```

the `double` value `3.0` is stored in 64 bits and the `int` value `4` is stored in 32 bits. C++ will convert the narrower value (`4`) to a 64-bit `double` value, so that the division can be performed on two 64-bit `doubles`, producing a 64-bit `double` value as the result. No information or precision is lost, as would happen if the wider value were narrowed to the size of the narrower value.

This automatic widening of a narrower value to the size of a wider value in an expression is often described as **promotion** of the narrower value. Promotion is what permits `short`, `unsigned`, `int`, and `long` integer values to be freely intermixed in C++ expressions; and integer values will be promoted to real values when necessary. Two values are said to be **compatible** if one of the following is true:

- They are both of the same type.
- The type of one value can be promoted to the type of the other value.
- The types of both can be promoted to the same type.

For example, `char` and `int` are compatible, since `char` can be promoted to `int`.

Operator Precedence. The arithmetic operators can be grouped into two groups: the **additive** operators (`+` and `-`) and the **multiplicative** operators (`*`, `/`, and `%`). These groupings are important because they determine the order in which operators in an expression are applied. The order of evaluation in an expression is determined by a characteristic known as **operator precedence** (or **priority**):

NOTE

In an expression involving several operators, the multiplicative operators have higher precedence than (i.e., are applied before) the additive operators.

Thus, in the expression

```
2 + 3 * 5
```

`*` has higher precedence than `+`, so the multiplication is performed before the addition; therefore, the value of the expression is 17.

Operator Associativity. In C++, the operators `+`, `-`, `*`, `/`, and `%` are all **left-associative** operators, which means that in an expression having two operators that have the same priority, the left operator is applied first. Thus,

```
9 - 5 - 1
```

is evaluated as

```
(9 - 5) - 1 → 4 - 1 → 3
```

In a later section, we will see that some C++ operators are **right associative**.

Associativity is also used in more complex expressions containing different operators of the same priority. For example, consider

```
7 * 10 - 5 % 3 * 4 + 9
```

There are three high-priority operations, `*`, `%`, and `*`, and so the leftmost multiplication is performed first, giving the intermediate result

```
70 - 5 % 3 * 4 + 9
```

Because of left associativity, `%` is performed next, giving

```
70 - 2 * 4 + 9
```

and the second multiplication is performed last, yielding

```
70 - 8 + 9
```

The two remaining operations, `-` and `+`, are equal in priority, and so left associativity causes the subtraction to be performed first, giving

```
62 + 9
```

and then the addition is carried out, giving the final result

```
71
```

Using Parentheses. Parentheses can be used to change the usual order of evaluation of an expression as determined by precedence and associativity. Parenthesized subexpressions are first evaluated in the standard manner, and the results are then combined to evaluate the complete expression. If the parentheses are "nested"—that is, if one set of parentheses is contained within another—the computations in the innermost parentheses are performed first.

For example, consider the expression

```
(7 * (10 - 5) % 3) * 4 + 9
```

The subexpression `(10 - 5)` is evaluated first, producing

```
(7 * 5 % 3) * 4 + 9
```

Next, the subexpression `(7 * 5 % 3)` is evaluated left to right, giving

```
(35 % 3) * 4 + 9
```

followed by

```
2 * 4 + 9
```

Now the multiplication is performed, giving

```
8 + 9
```

and the addition produces the final result

```
17
```

WATCH OUT

Care must be taken in writing expressions containing two or more operations to ensure that they are evaluated in the order intended. Even though parentheses may not be required, they should be used freely to clarify the intended order of evaluation and to write complicated expressions in terms of simpler expressions. It is important, however, that the parentheses balance—for each left parenthesis, a matching right parenthesis must appear later in the expression—since an unpaired parenthesis will result in a compilation error.

Unary Operators. The operators + and - can also be used as **unary operators** (i.e., they can be applied to a single operand); for example, `-x` and `+34` are allowed. Similarly, the expression `3 * -4` is a valid C++ expression, producing the value `-12`. Unary operations have higher priority than the binary operations +, -, *, /, and %.

Summary. In summary, the following rules govern the evaluation of arithmetic expressions.

Precedence Rules

Higher: unary +, unary -
*, /, and %
Lower: binary +, binary -

1. Higher-priority operations are performed before lower-priority operations.
2. Operators having the same priority are applied according to their associativity.
3. If an expression contains subexpressions enclosed within parentheses, these are evaluated first, using the standard order specified in Rules 1 and 2. If there are nested parentheses, the innermost subexpressions are evaluated first.

Bitwise Operators. C++ also provides other numeric operators, including operations that can be applied to integer data at the individual bit level: ~ (negation), & (bitwise and), | (bitwise or), ^ (bitwise exclusive or), << (bitshift left), and >> (bitshift right). In practice, such operations are used in programs that must inspect memory or interact directly with a computer's hardware, such as low-level graphics methods or operating-system methods. See the text's Web site for more information about these bitwise operators.

NUMERIC FUNCTIONS

In the program in Figure 3.1, we computed the value of `energy` using the following statement:

```
energy = mass * pow(SPEED_OF_LIGHT, 2);
```

Here we see that in addition to simple objects like literals, constants, and variables, an operand may also be a value returned by a function. In this case, we used the standard math library function `pow()`, which provides the exponentiation operation in C++.

Many languages provide standard functions, such as square root, logarithm, and absolute value, as part of the language. This is convenient because a program can simply call such functions when they are needed. The problem is that these functions may add to the size of the compiled program, regardless of whether the program uses them. This is a significant price (in terms of space) to pay for the convenience of built-in functions.

C++ provides so many predefined functions that even a simple program (such as that in Figure 3.1) would be huge if all of the predefined functions were added to the program. Instead, C++ stores its predefined functions in various **libraries.**

As the name implies, a library is a place where functions (and other things such as constant declarations) can be stored, so that a program can "borrow" them when necessary. For example, the iostream **library** <iostream> is where declarations of the stream objects cin and cout are stored along with input (>>) and output (<<) functions. Similarly, the **C math library** <cmath> stores pow(), sqrt(), and other math-related functions. The **C standard library** <cstdlib> contains many other commonly used functions such as the absolute-value function abs() for integers and exit(), which can be used to terminate program execution if an error occurs. Becoming familiar with the functions available in these libraries is an important part of learning to program in C++, because they provide many commonly needed operations.

To use objects and functions stored in a library, a program must use the #include directive to insert that library's **header file**—a special file containing the declarations of the library's objects and functions. Thus, since the program in Figure 3.1 uses the pow() function, which is stored in the math library, the program must contain the directive

```
#include <cmath>              // pow()
```

to make the contents of the math library available to the program. It is good programming practice to follow a #include directive with a comment like that shown, which lists the items from the library that are being used.[1]

Since the program in Figure 3.1 reads numeric values from the keyboard via cin,

```
cin >> mass;
```

and writes values to the screen via cout,

```
cout << mass << " kilograms of matter will release "
     << energy << " kilojoules of energy.\n";
```

and since the objects cin and cout and their operations are stored in the iostream library, the program must contain the directive

```
#include <iostream>        // cin, cout, <<, >>
```

The iostream library is discussed in greater detail in Section 5.3.

Finally, because the program uses assert(), which is declared in the **C assert library** <cassert>, the program contains the directive

```
#include <cassert>            // assert()
```

When the C++ compiler processes a #include directive, the contents of that file are *inserted* into the program. The angle brackets (< and >) around the name of the header

---

1. As noted earlier, some C++ compilers that are not ISO/ANSI-compliant may use old names for the libraries—for example, iostream.h, math.h, assert.h, and stdlib.h, instead of iostream, cmath, cassert, and cstlib, respectively.

file tell the compiler to look for that file in a special system *include directory* that contains the header files of most of the standard C++ libraries.[1]

To *call* any of the functions from a library whose header file has been included, we simply give the function name, followed by any **arguments** it requires—constants, variables, or expressions to which the function is to be applied—enclosed within parentheses. For example, the program in Figure 3.1 uses the call

```
pow(SPEED_OF_LIGHT, 2)
```

Computing x^n requires two operands, x and n, so the `pow()` function requires two arguments. By contrast, if we wanted to find the absolute value of an integer value, we could use the standard library function `abs()`, which takes a single argument,

```
positiveValue = abs(intValue);
```

but to do so, we must first have included the header file of the standard C library `cstdlib`:

```
#include <cstdlib>
```

Table 3.1 lists several of the functions provided by the C math library. Each of these functions takes one or more arguments of type `double` and returns a value of type `double`. Thus, to calculate the square root of `5`, we can write

```
sqrt(5.0)
```

Most implementations will also allow

```
sqrt(5)
```

since the `int` value `5` can be promoted to the `double` value `5.0`.

Table 3.1 Math Library Functions.

Function	Description
`abs(x)`	Absolute value of real value x
`pow(x, y)`	x raised to power y
`sqrt(x)`	Square root of x
`ceil(x)`	Least integer greater than or equal to x
`floor(x)`	Greatest integer less than or equal to x
`exp(x)`	Exponential function e^x
`log(x)`	Natural logarithm of x
`log10(x)`	Base-10 logarithm of x
`sin(x)`	Sine of x (in radians)
`cos(x)`	Cosine of x (in radians)
`tan(x)`	Tangent of x (in radians)
`asin(x)`	Inverse sine of x

1. Different platforms store the include directory in different places. See your instructor or system manuals for the location of the include directory for your particular system.

Table 3.1 Math Library Functions. (Continued)

Function	Description
`acos(x)`	Inverse cosine of *x*
`atan(x)`	Inverse tangent of *x*
`sinh(x)`	Hyperbolic sine of *x*
`cosh(x)`	Hyperbolic cosine of *x*
`tanh(x)`	Hyperbolic tangent of *x*

As a more complicated example, if we wish to calculate $\sqrt{b^2 - 4ac}$, we could write

```
sqrt(pow(b, 2) - 4.0 * a * c)
```

Note that if the value of the expression

```
pow(b, 2) - 4.0 * a * c
```

is negative, then an error results because the square root of a negative number is not defined.

Type Conversions. If `intVal` is an integer variable and `doubleVal` is a `double` variable, then the expression

```
double(intVal)
```

produces the `double` value equivalent to `intVal`. Similarly, the expression

```
int(doubleVal)
```

will truncate the fractional part and produce the integer part of `doubleVal` as its value. More generally, the type of an expression can be explicitly converted to a different type as follows:[1]

Explicit Type Conversion

Forms:

`type(expression)`

or

`(type) expression`

1. The C++ standard added new type-conversion operators: `const_cast`, `dynamic_cast`, `reinterpret_cast`, and `static_cast`. The examples given could also be written `static_cast<double> intVal` and `static_cast<int> doubleVal`. Some C++ compilers that are not fully ISO/ANSI-compliant may not support these conversions.

where

type is a valid C++ type; and

expression is any C++ expression.

Purpose: The type of the value produced by *expression* is converted to *type* (if possible). The first form is sometimes referred to as *functional notation* and the last form as (C-style) *cast notation*.

✔ Quick Quiz 3.2

Find the value of each of the expressions in Questions 1–12, or explain why it is not a valid expression.

1. `3 - 2 - 1`
2. `2.0 + 3.0 / 5.0`
3. `2 + 3 / 5`
4. `5 / 2 + 3`
5. `7 + 6 % 5`
6. `(7 + 6) % 5`
7. `(2 + 3 * 4) / (8 - 2 + 1)`
8. `12.0 / 1.0 * 3.0`
9. `sqrt(6.0 + 3.0)`
10. `pow(2.0, 3)`
11. `floor(2.34)`
12. `ceil(2.34)`

Questions 13–20 assume that `two`, `three`, and `four` are reals with values 2.0, 3.0, and 4.0, respectively, and `intEight` and `intFive` are integers with values 8 and 5, respectively. Find the value of each expression.

13. `two + three * three`
14. `intFive / 3`
15. `(three + two / four) * 2`
16. `intEight / intFive * 5.1`
17. `four * 2 / two * 2`
18. `intFive * 2 / two * 2`
19. `sqrt(two + three + four)`
20. `pow(two, intFive)`
21. Write a C++ expression equivalent to $10 + 5B - 4AC$.
22. Write a C++ expression equivalent to the square root of $A + 3B^2$.

Exercises 3.2

Find the value of each of the expressions in Exercises 1–24, or explain why it is not a valid expression.

1. `9 - 5 - 3`
2. `2 / 3 + 3 / 5`
3. `9.0 / 2 / 5`
4. `9 / 2 / 5`
5. `2.0 / 4`
6. `(2 + 3) % 2`
7. `7 % 5 % 3`
8. `(7 % 5) % 3`
9. `7 % (5 % 3)`
10. `(7 % 5 % 3)`
11. `25 * 1 / 2`
12. `25 * 1.0 / 2`
13. `25 * (1 / 2)`
14. `-3.0 * 5.0`
15. `5.0 * -3.0`
16. `12 / 2 * 3`
17. `((12 + 3) / 2) / (8 - (5 + 1))`
18. `((12 + 3) / 2) / (8 - 5 + 1)`
19. `(12 + 3 / 2) / (8 - 5 + 1)`
20. `sqrt(pow(4.0,2))`
21. `sqrt(pow(-4.0,2))`
22. `pow(sqrt(-4.0),2)`
23. `ceil(8.0 / 5.0)`
24. `floor(8.0 / 5.0)`

Exercises 25–32 assume that `r1` and `r2` are reals with values 2.0 and 3.0, respectively, and `i1`, `i2`, and `i3` are integers with values 4, 5, and 8, respectively. Find the value of each expression.

25. `r1 + r2 + r2`
26. `i3 / 3`
27. `i3 / 3.0`
28. `(r2 + r1) * i1`
29. `i3 / i2 * 5.1`
30. `pow(i1,2) / pow(r1,2)`
31. `pow(i2,2) / pow(r1,2)`
32. `sqrt(r1 + r2 + i1)`

Write C++ expressions to compute each of the quantities in Exercises 33–39.

33. $10 + 5B - 4AC$
34. Three times the difference $4 - n$ divided by twice the *quantity* $m^2 + n^2$
35. The square root of $a + 3b^2$

36. The square root of the average of *m* and *n*
37. $|A / (m + n)|$ (where $|x|$ denotes the absolute value of *x*)
38. a^x, computed as $e^{x \ln a}$ (where ln is the natural logarithm function)
39. The real quantity *amount* rounded to the nearest hundredth
40. Using the given values of `cost`, verify that the statement

```
cost = double(int(cost*100.0 + 0.5)) / 100.0;
```

can be used to convert a real value `cost` to dollars, rounded to the nearest cent.

   a. 12.342
   b. 12.348
   c. 12.345
   d. 12.340
   e. 13.0

41. Write an expression similar to that in Exercise 40 that rounds a real amount `x` to the nearest tenth.
42. Write an expression similar to that in Exercise 40 that rounds a real amount `x` to the nearest thousandth.

3.3 Boolean Expressions

In the mid-1800s, a self-taught British mathematician George Boole (1815–1864) developed an algebra of logic in which expressions could be formed to process logical values. Such logical expressions, which produce either the value *true* or the value *false*, have thus come to be known as **boolean expressions**. They are also often called **conditions**, and we will use the two terms interchangeably.

Every modern programming language provides some means for constructing boolean expressions, and in this section we consider how they are constructed in C++. We look first at simple boolean expressions and then at how logical operators can be used to combine boolean expressions to form compound expressions.

SIMPLE BOOLEAN EXPRESSIONS

In C++, the type `bool` has two literals: `false` and `true`.[1] A boolean expression is thus a sequence of operands and operators that combine to produce one of the boolean values, `true` or `false`.

The operators that are used in the simplest boolean expressions test some *relationship* between their operands. For example, the program in Figure 3.1 contains the boolean expression

```
mass >= 0
```

which compares the operands `mass` and `0` using the *greater-than-or-equal-to* relationship, and produces the value `true` if the value of `mass` is nonnegative, and produces the value `false` if the value of `mass` is negative. Similarly, the C++ boolean expression

```
count == 5
```

---

1. For upward compatibility with C, C++ also allows integers to be used as boolean values: 0 in place of `false`, and any nonzero value can be used for `true`, with 1 being the most commonly used nonzero value.

tests the *equality* relationship between the (variable) operand `count` and the (literal) operand `5`, producing the value `true` if the value of `count` is `5` and the value `false` otherwise.

WATCH OUT

Note: *Be sure to use the == operator for equality comparisons, and not = (assignment) since an error will almost surely result otherwise. (See Potential Pitfall 9 at the end of the chapter to see why.)*

Operators like >= and == that test a relationship between two operands are called **relational operators**, and they are used in boolean expressions of the form

$expression_1$ *relational_operator* $expression_2$

where $expression_1$ and $expression_2$ are two C++ compatible expressions and the *relational_operator* may be any of the following:

Relational Operator	Relation Tested
<	Is less than
>	Is greater than
==	Is equal to
!=	Is not equal to
<=	Is less than or equal to
>=	Is greater than or equal to

These relational operators may be applied to operands of any of the standard data types: `char`, `int`, `float`, `double`, and so on. For example, if `x`, `a`, `b`, and `c` are of type `double`, `number` is `int`, and `initial` is of type `char`, then the following are valid boolean expressions formed using these relational operators:

```
x < 5.2
b * b >= 4.0 * a * c
number == 500
initial != 'Q'
```

For numeric data, the relational operators are commonly used to compare numbers. Thus, if `x` has the value 4.5, then the expression

```
x < 5.2
```

produces the value `true`. Similarly, if `number` has the value 17, then the expression

```
number == 500
```

produces the value `false`.

COMPOUND BOOLEAN EXPRESSIONS

Many relationships are too complicated to be expressed using only the relational operators. For example, a typical test score is governed by the mathematical relationship

$$0 \leq \text{test score} \leq 100$$

which is true if the test score is between 0 and 100 (inclusive) and is false otherwise. However, this relationship *cannot* be correctly represented in C++ by the expression

```
0 <= testScore <= 100
```

To see why, suppose that `testScore` has the value 101, which would mean that the expression should be false. Because these relational operators are left associative, the preceding expression is processed as

```
(0 <= 101) <= 100
```

The subexpression

```
(0 <= 101)
```

is evaluated first, producing the value `true`, which is treated in C++ as the `int` value 1. This 1 is then used as an operand for the second <= operator, so that the expression

```
(1 <= 100)
```

is evaluated. This, of course, is `true`, which is not the value of the original mathematical expression.

To avoid this difficulty, we must rewrite the mathematical expression

$$0 \le \text{test score} \le 100$$

in the form

$$(0 \le \text{test score}) \text{ and } (\text{test score} \le 100)$$

This expression can be correctly coded in C++, because C++ provides **logical operators** that combine boolean expressions to form **compound boolean expressions**. These operators are defined as follows:

Logical Operator	Logical Expression	Name of Operation	Description
!	`!p`	*Not (Negation)*	`!p` is false if `p` is true; `!p` is true if `p` is false.
&&	`p && q`	*And (Conjunction)*	`p && q` is true if both `p` and `q` are true; it is false otherwise.
||	`p || q`	*Or (Disjunction)*	`p || q` is true if either `p` or `q` or both are true; it is false otherwise.

These definitions are summarized by the following **truth tables**, which display all possible values for two conditions `p` and `q` and the corresponding values of the logical expression:

p	!*p*
true	false
false	true

<table>
<tr><th>p</th><th>q</th><th>p && q</th><th>p || q</th></tr>
<tr><td>true</td><td>true</td><td>true</td><td>true</td></tr>
<tr><td>true</td><td>false</td><td>false</td><td>true</td></tr>
<tr><td>false</td><td>true</td><td>false</td><td>true</td></tr>
<tr><td>false</td><td>false</td><td>false</td><td>false</td></tr>
</table>

We can thus use the `&&` operator to represent the mathematical expression

$$(0 \leq \text{test score}) \text{ and } (\text{test score} \leq 100)$$

by the compound boolean expression

```
(0 <= testScore) && (testScore <= 100)
```

This expression will correctly evaluate the relationship between `testScore` and the integers `0` and `100`, for all possible values of `testScore`.

WATCH OUT

Note: *Be sure to use the* `&&` *and* `||` *operators for logical operations, and not* `&` *and* `|` *(bitwise operators) since an error will almost surely result otherwise. (See Potential Pitfall 10 at the end of the chapter to see why.)*

OPERATOR PRECEDENCE

A boolean expression that contains an assortment of arithmetic operators, boolean operators, and relational operators is evaluated using the following precedence (or priority) and associativity rules:

<table>
<tr><th>Operator</th><th>Priority</th><th>Associativity</th></tr>
<tr><td>!, unary +, unary -</td><td>highest</td><td>Right</td></tr>
<tr><td>/, *, %</td><td></td><td>Left</td></tr>
<tr><td>+, -</td><td></td><td>Left</td></tr>
<tr><td><, >, <=, >=</td><td></td><td>Left</td></tr>
<tr><td>==, !=</td><td></td><td>Left</td></tr>
<tr><td>&&</td><td></td><td>Left</td></tr>
<tr><td>||</td><td></td><td>Left</td></tr>
<tr><td>=, +=, *=, . . .</td><td>lowest</td><td>Right</td></tr>
</table>

An operator with a higher priority is applied before an operator with a lower priority.

To illustrate, consider the boolean expression

```
x < y/2 && x != 0
```

The / operator has highest priority, and so this operator is applied first, producing an intermediate real value `r` and the expression

```
x < r && x != 0
```

Of the remaining operators, < has the highest priority, so that operator is applied next, producing an intermediate boolean value `b1` and the expression

```
b1 && x != 0
```

Of the remaining two operators, != has the higher priority, so that operator is applied next, producing an intermediate boolean value `b2` and the expression

```
b1 && b2
```

Finally, the `&&` operator is applied to the two boolean values `b1` and `b2` to produce the value of the expression.

Because it is difficult to remember so many precedence levels, it is helpful to remember the following:

- ! is the highest-precedence operator (that we have seen so far).
- `*`, `/`, and `%` have higher precedence than + and `-`.
- Every numeric operator has higher precedence than every relational logical operator (except !).
- Every relational operator has higher precedence than the logical operators `&&` and `||`.
- Use parentheses for all the other operators to clarify the order in which they are applied.

SHORT-CIRCUIT EVALUATION

An important feature of the `&&` and `||` operators is that they do not always evaluate their second operand. For example, if `p` is false, then the condition

```
p && q
```

is false, regardless of the value of `q`, and so C++ does not evaluate `q`. Similarly, if `p` is true, then the condition

```
p || q
```

is true, regardless of the value of `q`, and so C++ does not evaluate `q`. This approach is called **short-circuit evaluation** and has two important benefits:

1. One boolean expression can be used to *guard* a potentially unsafe operation in a second boolean expression.
2. A considerable amount of time can be saved in the evaluation of complex conditions.

As an illustration of the first benefit, consider the boolean expression

```
(n != 0) && (x < 1.0 / n)
```

No division-by-zero error can occur in evaluating this expression, because if `n` is 0, then the first expression

```
(n != 0)
```

is false and the second expression

```
(x < 1.0 / n)
```

is not evaluated. Similarly, no division-by-zero error will occur in evaluating the condition

```
(n == 0) || (x >= 1.0 / n)
```

because if `n` is 0, the first expression

```
(n == 0)
```

is true and the second expression is not evaluated.

PRECONDITIONS AND THE `assert()` MECHANISM

In many problems, the set of possible input values is much larger than the set of input values for which the program is designed. This creates a potential problem: If the user inputs an invalid value, the program will not compute the correct result. For example, in the mass-to-energy conversion problem we considered in Section 3.1, the problem is only defined for nonnegative masses. If the user should enter a negative value for `mass`, the result produced by the program will not be correct.

In problems like this, a restriction imposed on the set of valid input values is called a **precondition**—a condition that must be true before the computation can proceed correctly. For example, the mass-to-energy problem has the following precondition:

mass must be nonnegative.

Boolean expressions can be used to construct expressions to represent such preconditions. For example, the preceding precondition can be represented by the boolean expression

```
mass >= 0
```

C++ also provides the `assert()` mechanism (defined in the C assert library `cassert`) as a convenient way to check that a precondition is `true`. For example, the program in Figure 3.1 contains the statement

```
assert(mass >= 0);
```

When this statement is executed, the boolean expression `mass >= 0` is evaluated. If it is true, then execution proceeds normally. However, if the expression is false, execution of the program will be terminated and a diagnostic message such as

```
failed assertion: mass >= 0
```

will be displayed to inform the user that the value entered for `mass` did not satisfy the program's precondition. The program is thus prevented from processing invalid inputs.

In general, the `assert()` mechanism can be described as follows:

The `assert()` Mechanism

Form:

`assert(`*`boolean_expression`*`);`

where

boolean_expression is any valid expression evaluating to true or false.

Purpose: Checks a condition that must be true at a given point in a program.

If *boolean_expression* is true, then execution proceeds normally. If it is false, the program is terminated and a diagnostic message is displayed.

✔ Quick Quiz 3.3

1. The two `bool` literals are ________ and ________.
2. List the six relational operators.
3. List the three logical operators.

For Questions 4–8, assume that `p`, `q`, and `r` are boolean expressions with the values `true`, `true`, and `false`, respectively. Find the value of each boolean expression.

4. `p && !q`
5. `p && q || !r`
6. `p && !(q || r)`
7. `!p && q`
8. `p || q && r`

For Questions 9–13, assume that `number`, `count`, and `sum` are integer variables with values 3, 4, and 5, respectively. Find the value of each boolean expression, or indicate why it is not valid.

9. `sum - number <= 4`
10. `number*number + count*count == sum*sum`
11. `number < count || count < sum`
12. `0 <= count <= 2`
13. `(number + 1 < sum) && !(count + 1 < sum)`
14. Write a boolean expression to express that `x` is nonzero.
15. Write a boolean expression to express that `x` is strictly between –10 and 10.
16. Write a boolean expression to express that both `x` and `y` are positive or both `x` and `y` are negative.

Exercises 3.3

For Exercises 1–10, assume that `m` and `n` are integer variables with the values –5 and 8, respectively, and that `x`, `y`, and `z` are real variables with the values –3.56, 0.0, and 44.7, respectively. Find the value of the boolean expression.

1. `m <= n`
2. `2 * abs(m) <= 8`
3. `x * x < sqrt(z)`
4. `int(z) == (6 * n - 4)`

5. `(x <= y) && (y <= z)`
6. `!(x < y)`
7. `!((m <= n) && (x + z > y))`
8. `!(m <= n) || !(x + z > y)`
9. `!((m <= n) || (x + z > y))`
10. `!((m > n) && !(x < z))`

For Exercises 11–16, use truth tables to display the values of the boolean expression for all possible (boolean) values of a, b, and c.

11. `a || !b`
12. `!(a && b)`
13. `!a || !b`
14. `(a && b) || c`
15. `a && (b || c)`
16. `(a && b) || (a && c)`

For Exercises 17–25, write C++ boolean expressions to express the condition.

17. x is greater than 3.
18. y is strictly between 2 and 5.
19. r is negative and z is positive.
20. Both alpha and beta are positive.
21. alpha and beta have the same sign. (Both are negative or both are positive.)
22. $-5 < x < 5$.
23. a is less than 6 or is greater than 10.
24. p is equal to q, which is equal to r.
25. x is less than 3, or y is less than 3, but not both.

Exercises 26–28 assume that a, b, and c are boolean values.

26. Write a C++ boolean expression that is true if and only if a and b are true and c is false.
27. Write a C++ boolean expression that is true if and only if a is true and at least one of b or c is true.
28. Write a C++ boolean expression that is true if and only if exactly one of a and b is true.

3.4 Character Expressions

As mentioned in Section 2.2, C++ provides the char type for representing character values (and wchar_t for wide characters; see Footnotes 7 and 8 of Chapter 2); also, a char literal consists of a character surrounded by single quotes; and objects of type char can be defined and initialized in a manner similar to int and double objects; for example,

```
char myMiddleInitial = 'C';
const char DIRECTION = 'N';    // N, S, E or W
```

Character values can be assigned in the usual manner,

```
myMiddleInitial = 'R';
```

can be read from the keyboard via `cin`,

```
cin >> myMiddleInitial;
```

and can be written to the screen via `cout`:

```
cout << myMiddleInitial;
```

C++ allows `char` values to be compared using the relational operators. For example, suppose that we are solving a problem with the precondition that a character variable *letter* must have an uppercase value. This precondition can be expressed in C++ using a compound boolean expression:

```
('A' <= letter) && (letter <= 'Z')
```

We can thus use the `assert()` mechanism as follows to test this precondition:

```
assert('A' <= letter && letter <= 'Z');
```

Characters are compared using their numeric codes, commonly ASCII. (See Appendix A.) Thus,

```
'A' < 'B'
```

is a true boolean expression because the code of `A` (65) is less than the code of `B` (66). This expression thus produces the value `true`. Similarly, the expression

```
'a' < 'b'
```

produces the value `true`, because the code of `a` (97) is less than the code of `b` (98). The boolean expression

```
'a' < 'A'
```

is `false`, because the code of `a` (97) is not less than the code of `A` (65).[1]

CHARACTER-PROCESSING OPERATIONS

In addition to the operations just mentioned, the **C `char`-type library** `cctype` provides a number of functions for performing commonly needed operations on character values. The most useful of these character-processing functions are shown in Table 3.2. These functions provide the programmer with a variety of "off-the-shelf" solutions to common problems that involve character values. For example, an alternative way to write the earlier assertion that `letter` is an uppercase letter is

```
assert( isupper(letter) );
```

---

1. Most versions of C++ use ASCII. In EBCDIC representation of characters, the boolean expressions `'A' < 'B'` and `'a' < 'b'` would both be true. However, the expression `'a' < 'A'` would also evaluate to `true`, because the EBCDIC code for `a` (129) is less than the EBCDIC code for `A` (193). In Unicode, these comparisons would be the same as for ASCII.

Table 3.2 Character Operation in `cctype`.

Operation	Description
`isalnum(ch)`	`true` if *ch* is a letter or a digit, `false` otherwise
`isalpha(ch)`	`true` if *ch* is a letter, `false` otherwise
`iscntrl(ch)`	`true` if *ch* is a control character, `false` otherwise
`isdigit(ch)`	`true` if *ch* is a decimal digit, `false` otherwise
`isgraph(ch)`	`true` if *ch* is a printing character except space, `false` otherwise
`islower(ch)`	`true` if *ch* is lower case, `false` otherwise
`isprint(ch)`	`true` if *ch* is a printing character, including space, `false` otherwise
`ispunct(ch)`	`true` if *ch* is a punctuation character (not a space, an alphabetic character, or a digit), `false` otherwise
`isspace(ch)`	`true` if `ch` is a white-space character (space, `'\f'`, `'\n'`, `'\r'`, `'\t'`, or `'\v'`), `false` otherwise
`isupper(ch)`	`true` if *ch* is uppercase, `false` otherwise
`isxdigit(ch)`	`true` if *ch* is a hexadecimal digit, `false` otherwise
`toupper(ch)`	returns the uppercase equivalent of *ch* (if *ch* is lowercase)
`tolower(ch)`	returns the lowercase equivalent of *ch* (if *ch* is uppercase)

✔ Quick Quiz 3.4

1. A character literal must be enclosed in ________.
2. (True or false) `char x = '1/2';` is a valid declaration.
3. (True or false) `char x = '\12';` is a valid declaration.
4. Using relational operators, write an `assert` statement to test the condition that the value of the `char` variable `c` is one of the digits `'0'`, `'1'`, `'2'`, `...`, `'9'`.
5. Repeat Question 4, but use a function from `cctype`.
6. Write a statement that checks if the value of the `char` variable `c` is an uppercase or lowercase vowel.

3.5 Assignment Expressions

An **assignment expression** uses the assignment operator (=) to assign a value to a variable.

Assignment Expression

Form:

```
variable = expression
```

where

variable is a valid C++ identifier, declared as a variable;

expression may be a constant, another variable to which a value has previously been assigned, or a formula to be evaluated.

Behavior:

1. `expression` is evaluated, producing a value *v* (which is converted to the type of `variable` if this is necessary and is possible).
2. The value of `variable` is changed to *v*.
3. The = operator produces the value *v*.

For example, suppose that `xCoord` and `yCoord` are real variables, `number` and `position` are integer variables, `code` is a character variable, and `isOkay` is a boolean variable, declared as follows:

```
double xCoord, yCoord;
int number, position;
char code;
boolean isOkay;
```

These declarations associate memory locations with the six variables as described in Section 2.2. This might be pictured as follows, with the question marks indicating that these variables are initially undefined (or indeterminate), so the content of the memory locations is uncertain:

xCoord	?
yCoord	?
number	?
position	?
code	?
isOkay	?

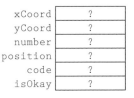

Now consider the following assignment statements:

```
xCoord = 5.23;
yCoord = sqrt(25.0);
number = 17;
code = 'M';
isOkay = true;
```

Note that the value of a variable of type `char` is a single character and not a string of characters.

The first assignment statement assigns the real constant `5.23` to the real variable `xCoord`, and the second assigns the real constant `5.0` to the real variable `yCoord`. The next assignment statements assign the integer constant `17` to the integer variable `number`, the character `M` to the character variable `code`, and the boolean constant `true` to the boolean variable `isOkay`. More precisely, when these assignment statements are executed, the values `5.23`, `5.0`, and `17`, the numeric code for `M`, and the integer `1` or some other nonzero integer (representing `true`) are stored in the memory locations associated with the variables `xCoord`, `yCoord`, `number`, `code`, and `isOkay`, respectively. The variable `position` is still undefined.

xCoord	5.23
yCoord	5.0
number	17
position	?
code	M (77)
isOkay	true(1)

These values are substituted for the variables in any subsequent expression containing these variables. Thus, in the assignment statement

```
position = number / 3 + 2;
```

the expression `number / 3 + 2` is evaluated (with the value `17` substituted for the variable `number`) yielding `7`. This value is then assigned to the integer variable `position`; the value of `number` remains unchanged.

xCoord	5.23
yCoord	5.0
number	17
position	7
code	M (77)
isOkay	true(1)

Compare this with the assignment statement

```
xCoord = 2.0 * xCoord;
```

in which the variable `xCoord` appears on both sides of the assignment operator (=). In this case, the current value `5.23` for `xCoord` is used in evaluating the expression `2.0 * xCoord`, yielding the value `10.46`; this value is then assigned to `xCoord`. The old value `5.23` is lost because it has been replaced with the new value `10.46`.

xCoord	10.46
yCoord	5.0
number	17
position	7
code	M (77)
isOkay	true(1)

WATCH OUT

In every assignment statement, the variable whose value is to be changed must appear on the left of the assignment operator (=), a valid expression must appear on the right, and both the variable and the expression should be of the same type. Although mixing of numeric types is permitted in C++, the practice should be used with caution because significant information can be lost. To illustrate, consider the assignment statement

```
number = 4 / yCoord;
```

Here, the expression `4 / yCoord` will be evaluated and since `yCoord` is of type `double`, the result will be the real value `0.8`. However, assigning a real value to an integer variable truncates the real value (i.e., discards its fractional part). In this example, therefore, the fractional part `.8` is truncated and only the integer portion `0` is assigned to `number`.

WATCH OUT

An unusual feature of C++ we have noted is that it treats characters as integers. This means that assignments like

```
code = 65 + 1;
```

or

```
number = 'A' + 'B';
```

are allowed in C++. Assuming ASCII, the first statement will assign the value `66` (the numeric code for `'B'`) to `code` and the second will assign the value `131 (65 + 66)` to `number`. Such statements are poor programming style and should normally be avoided. *Assign character values to character variables, integer values to integer variables, and real values to real variables.*

The following are examples of *invalid* C++ assignment statements. A reason is given for each to explain why it is not valid. The variables in these statements are assumed to have the types specified earlier.

Statement	Error
`5 = number;`	A variable must appear on the left of the assignment operator.
`xCoord + 3.5 = 2.7;`	Arithmetic expressions may not appear on the left of the assignment operator.
`code = "ABC";`	The value of a `char` variable is a single character.
`number = "12" + "34";`	`"12" + "34"` is not a valid integer expression.

WATCH OUT

It is important to remember that *the assignment statement is a replacement statement.* Some beginning programmers forget this and write an assignment statement like

```
a = b;
```

when the statement

```
b = a;
```

is intended. These two statements produce very different results: The first assigns the value of `b` to `a`, leaving `b` unchanged, and the second assigns the value of `a` to `b`, leaving `a` unchanged.

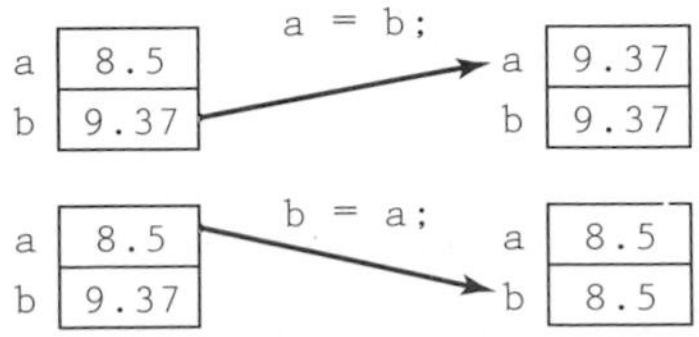

To illustrate further the replacement property of an assignment, suppose that the integer variables `alpha` and `beta` have values `357` and `59`, respectively, and that we wish to interchange these values. For this, we use an auxiliary integer variable `temp` to store the value of `alpha` while we assign `beta`'s value to `alpha`; then we can assign this stored value to `beta`:

```
temp = alpha;
alpha = beta;
beta = temp;
```

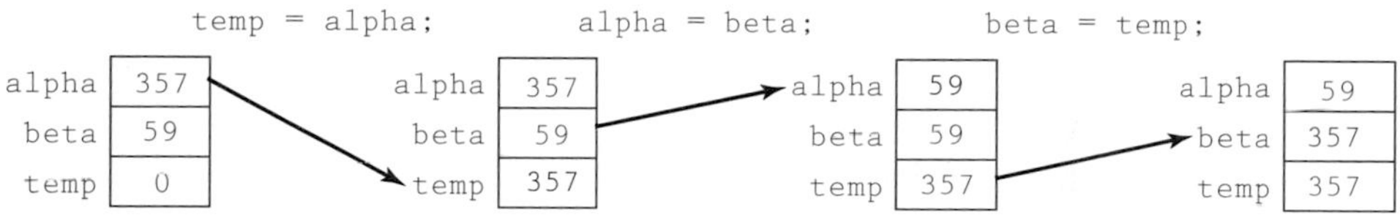

ASSIGNMENT AS AN OPERATION

We have seen that an assignment

```
variable = expression
```

produces three actions:

1. *`expression`* is evaluated, producing a value *v*.
2. The value of *`variable`* is changed to *v*.
3. The = operator produces the value *v*.

Thus far in our discussion, we have concentrated on Actions 1 and 2, but we now turn our attention to Action 3 in this description.

Just as the expression

```
2 + 2
```

produces the value `4`, the assignment

```
number = 4
```

is an expression that produces the value `4`. The assignment operator = *is a binary operator whose result is the value assigned to the left operand.* For example, if the value of `number` is `4`, then in the expression

```
number = number * 2
```

the `*` is applied first (the precedence of the = operator is lower than almost all other C++ operators),

```
number = (number * 2)
```

producing the result `8`. That value is then assigned to `number`,

```
number = 8
```

NOTE

which changes the value of `number` to `8`, after which the = operator produces the result `8`. *It is important to remember that* = *is a value-producing operator.*

CHAINING ASSIGNMENT OPERATORS

Because = is a value-producing operator, several assignment operators may be chained together in a single statement such as

```
xCoord = yCoord = 2.5;
```

which is equivalent to the two separate statements

```
yCoord = 2.5;
xCoord = yCoord;
```

Unlike the arithmetic operators we have seen thus far, the assignment operator = is **right associative,** which means that in the statement

```
xCoord = yCoord = 2.5;
```

the rightmost = is applied first; that is,

```
xCoord = (yCoord = 2.5);
```

which changes the value of `yCoord` to `2.5`, and because this = operator produces the value assigned to `yCoord` (i.e., `2.5`), the leftmost = is then applied using this value:

```
xCoord = 2.5
```

This changes the value of `xCoord` to `2.5`, after which this = produces the assigned value `2.5` as its result.

Chained assignment operators can be used to assign a group of variables the same value; for example,

```
a = b = c = d = 1;
```

will set `d` to `1`, `c` to `1`, `b` to `1`, and finally, `a` to `1`. Similarly, in the statement

```
area = (length = 2.0) * (width = 2.5);
```

`length` is set to `2.0`, `width` is set to `2.5`, and `area` is set to the product (`5.0`) of the values produced by these assignments.

ASSIGNMENT SHORTCUTS

One kind of assignment that occurs often is one that changes the value of a variable by operating on it with some other value. For example, the pseudocode statement

"Add *counter* to *sum*"

implicitly changes the value of *sum* to the value of *sum* + *counter*. This can be encoded in C++ as

```
sum = sum + counter;
```

The following diagram illustrates this for the case in which the integer variables `sum` and `counter` have the values `120` and `16`, respectively:

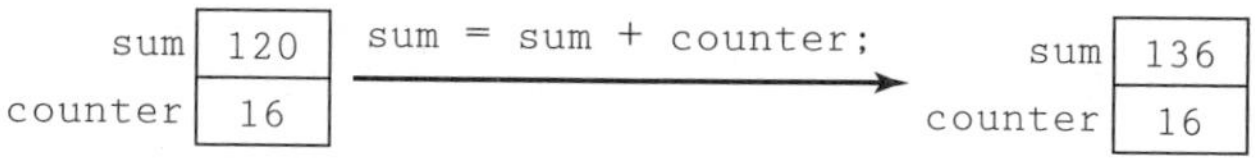

This operation occurs so frequently that C++ provides special operators for it. Instead of writing

```
sum = sum + counter;
```

we can write

```
sum += counter;
```

to accomplish the same thing.

Each of the arithmetic operators can be used in this way. For example, the statement

```
number = number / 2;
```

can be written

```
number /= 2;
```

In general, a statement of the form

```
alpha = alpha Δ beta;
```

can be written

```
alpha Δ= beta;
```

where Δ is any of the operators +, -, *, /, or %. Each of the following is, therefore, an acceptable variation of the assignment operator:[1]

+=, -=, *=, /=, %=

Like the regular assignment operator, each of these is right associative and produces the value assigned as its result, which means that they can be chained together. This is not good programming practice, however, because it produces expressions for which it can be difficult to follow how they are evaluated. For example, if `xCoord` has the value `4.0` and `yCoord` the value `2.5`, then the statement

```
xCoord *= yCoord += 0.5;
```

has the effect of

1. assigning `yCoord` the value `2.5 + 0.5 = 3.0`, and then
2. assigning `xCoord` the value `4.0 * 3.0 = 12.0`.

NOTE

Chaining such operators together should normally be avoided so that the readability of the program does not suffer. Programs that are cleverly written but are difficult to read are of little use because they are too costly to maintain.

---

1. In addition to those listed here, the bitwise operators can be applied in this manner: <<=, >>=, &=, |=, and ^=.

THE INCREMENT AND DECREMENT OPERATIONS

Algorithms often contain instructions of the form

"Increment *counter* by 1."

One way to encode this instruction in C++ is

```
counter = counter + 1;
```

Such a statement, in which the same variable appears on both sides of the assignment operator often confuses beginning programmers. Although we read English sentences from left to right, execution of this statement *begins to the right of the assignment operator*, so that

1. the expression `counter + 1` is evaluated, and
2. the resulting value is assigned to `counter` (overwriting its previous value).

For example, if `counter` has the value `16`, then

1. the value of `counter + 1`, `16 + 1` = `17`, is computed, and
2. this value is assigned as the new value for `counter`:

As we have seen, the old value of the variable is lost because it was replaced with a new value.

We could rewrite the assignment statement using a shortcut assignment,

```
counter += 1;
```

which is an improvement. However, this particular kind of assignment (i.e., incrementing a variable) occurs so often that C++ provides a special unary **increment operator ++** for this operation.[1] It can be used as a postfix operator,

`variableName``++`

or as a prefix operator,

`++`*`variableName`*

where *`variableName`* is an integer variable whose value is to be incremented by 1. Thus, the assignment statement

```
counter = counter + 1;       // or counter += 1;
```

can also be written

```
counter++;
```

or

```
++counter;
```

1. The name C++ stems from this increment operator—C++ is C that has been incrementally improved.

The difference between the postfix and prefix use of the operator is subtle. To explain it, consider the following program segments where `counter`, `number1`, and `number2` are `int` variables:

	Output
`//POSTFIX:  Use first, then increment`	
`counter = 10;`	
`cout << "counter = " << counter << '\n';`	`counter = 10`
`number1 = counter++;`	
`cout << "number1 = " << number1 << '\n';`	`number1 = 10`
`cout << "counter = " << counter << '\n';`	`counter = 11`

and

	Output
`//PREFIX:  Increment first, then use`	
`counter = 10;`	
`cout << "counter = " << counter << '\n';`	`counter = 10`
`number2 = ++counter;`	
`cout << " number2 = " << number2 << '\n';`	`number2 = 11`
`cout << "counter = " << counter << '\n';`	`counter = 11`

Note that after execution of both sets of statements, the value of `counter` is `11`. However, in the first set of assignments, the value assigned to `number1` is `10`, whereas in the second set of assignments, the value assigned to `number2` is `11`.

To understand this difference, we must remember that these increment expressions are assignment expressions and thus produce values. If `counter` has the value `10`, then in the *prefix* expression

```
++counter
```

`counter` is incremented (to `11`), and *the value produced by the expression is the incremented value* (`11`). By contrast, if `counter` again has the value `10`, then in the *postfix* expression

```
counter++
```

`counter` is still incremented (to `11`), but *the value produced by the expression is the original value* (`10`). That is, the assignment

```
number2 = ++counter;
```

is equivalent to

```
counter = counter + 1;
number2 = counter;
```

By contrast, the assignment

```
number1 = counter++;
```

is equivalent to

```
number1 = counter;
counter = counter + 1;
```

It does not matter whether the prefix or postfix form is used if the increment operator is being used simply to increment a variable as a stand-alone statement:

```
counter++;
```

or

```
++counter;
```

Both of these statements produce exactly the same result; namely, the value of `counter` is incremented by 1.

Just as you can increment a variable's value with the ++ operator, you can decrement the value of a variable (i.e., subtract 1 from it) using the **decrement operator** (`--`), For example, the assignment statement

```
counter = counter - 1;
```

can be written more compactly as

```
counter--;
```

or

```
--counter;
```

The prefix and postfix versions of the decrement operator behave in a manner similar to the prefix and postfix versions of the increment operator.

TRANSFORMING EXPRESSIONS INTO STATEMENTS—SEMICOLONS

We are finally ready to understand the significance of the semicolon in C++. *An expression followed by a semicolon becomes an* **expression statement.** For example, in the statement

```
number = 2 + 2;
```

the following actions occur:

1. The expression `2 + 2` is evaluated, producing the value `4`.
2. The expression `number = 4` is evaluated, which
   a. changes the value of `number` to `4` and
   b. produces the value `4`.
3. The semicolon terminates the statement, causing the value `4` (produced by the assignment operator) to be discarded.

The semicolon can thus be thought of as an operator that causes the expression to its left to be evaluated and then discards the result of that expression.

Any C++ expression can become a statement simply by appending a semicolon. Thus,

```
'A';
```

and

```
sqrt(1.234);
```

and even

```
;
```

(where the expression is empty) are valid C++ statements; they just don't accomplish any useful work the way an assignment expression does.

Thinking of the semicolon this way gives a different insight into the behavior of an assignment statement:

```
variable = expression;
```

Such an assignment is really an expression that returns the value of `expression` and has the **side effect** of changing the value of `variable`.

✔ Quick Quiz 3.5

Questions 1–15 assume that the following declarations have been made:

```
int m, n;
double pi;
char c;
```

Tell whether each is a valid C++ statement. If it is not valid, explain why it is not.

1. `pi = 3.0;`
2. `0 = n;`
3. `n = n + n;`
4. `n+n = n;`
5. `m = 1;`
6. `m = "1";`
7. `m = n = 1;`
8. `c = '65';`
9. `c = 65;`
10. `m = m;`
11. `pi = m;`
12. `m = pi;`
13. `m++;`
14. `m + n;`
15. `++pi;`

For Questions 16–25, assume that the following declarations have been made:

```
int intEight = 8, intFive1 = 5, intFive2 = 5, jobId;
double two = 2.0, three = 3.0, four = 4.0, xValue;
char code = 'A', letter;
bool check;
```

Find the value assigned to the given variable or indicate why the statement is not valid.

16. `xValue = three + two / four;`
17. `xValue = intEight / intFive1 + 5.1;`
18. `jobId = intEight / intFive1 + 5.1;`
19. `xValue = sqrt(three * three + four * four);`
20. `jobId = abs(three - 4.5);`

21. `jobId = intFive1++;`
22. `jobId = ++intFive2;`
23. `intEight *= 8;`
24. `letter = tolower(code);`
25. `check = isupper(code);`

For each of Questions 26–27, write a C++ assignment statement that calculates the given expression and assigns the result to the specified variable.

26. *rate* times *time* to *distance*
27. $\sqrt{a^2 + b^2}$ to c
28. Assuming that x is an integer variable, write four different statements that increment x by 1.

Exercises 3.5

Exercises 1–16 assume that `number` is an integer variable, `xValue` and `yValue` are real variables, and `grade` is a character variable. Tell whether each is a valid C++ statement. If it is not valid, explain why it is not.

1. `xValue = 2.71828;`
2. `3 = number;`
3. `grade = 'B+';`
4. `number = number + number;`
5. `xValue = 1;`
6. `grade = A;`
7. `number + 1 = number;`
8. `xValue = '1';`
9. `xValue = yValue = 3.2;`
10. `yValue = yValue;`
11. `xValue = 'A';`
12. `grade = grade + 10;`
13. `xValue /= yValue;`
14. `xValue = number;`
15. `number = yValue;`
16. `xValue = yValue++;`

For Exercises 17–36, assume that the following declarations have been made:

```
int int1 = 16, int2 = 10, int3;
double real1 = 4.0, real2 = 6.0, real3 = 8.0, xCoord;
char numeral = '2', symbol;
bool check;
```

Find the value assigned to the given variable or indicate why the statement is not valid.

17. `xCoord = (real1 + real2) * real2;`
18. `xCoord = (real2 + real1 / real3) * 2;`
19. `xCoord = int1 / int2 + 5;`

20. `int3 = int1 / int2 + 5;`
21. `xCoord = pow(int2,2) / pow(int1,2);`
22. `int3 = pow(int2,2) / pow(int1,2);`
23. `symbol = 4;`
24. `symbol = numeral;`
25. `symbol = '4';`
26. `symbol = real3;`
27. `real1 = 2;`
28. `real1 = '2';`
29. `real1 = numeral;`
30. `int1 = int1 + 2;`
31. `int3 = 1 + numeral;`
32. `int3 = ceil(pow(int1 % int2, 2) / real3);`
33. `check = isdigit(numeral);`
34. `check = (int1 == 16);`
35. `check = (1 < int1 < 20);`
36. `check = (real1 > 5) || (real2 > 5);`

For each of Exercises 37–41, write an assignment statement that changes the value of the integer variable `number` by the specified amount.

37. Increment `number` by 77.
38. Decrement `number` by 3.
39. Increment `number` by twice its value.
40. Add the rightmost digit of `number` to `number`.
41. Decrement `number` by the integer part of the real value `xCoord`.

For each of Exercises 42–47, write a C++ assignment statement that calculates the given expression and assigns the result to the specified variable. Assume that all variables are of type `double`, except where otherwise noted.

42. `rate` times `time` to `distance`
43. `xCoord` incremented by an amount `deltaX` to `xCoord`
44. $\dfrac{1}{\dfrac{1}{\mathtt{res1}} + \dfrac{1}{\mathtt{res2}} + \dfrac{1}{\mathtt{res3}}}$ to `resistance`
45. Area of a triangle with a given `base` and `height` (one-half base times height) to `area`
46. The last three digits of the integer `stockNumber` with a decimal point before the last two digits to `price` (e.g., if `stockNumber` is 1758316, `price` is assigned the value 3.16)
47. `tax` rounded to the nearest dollar to `tax`.

For each of Exercises 48–50, give values for the integer variables `a`, `b`, and `c` for which the two given expressions have different values:

48. `a * (b / c)` and `a * b / c`

49. `a / b` and `a * (1 / b)`
50. `(a + b) / c` and `a / c + b / c`

3.6 Input/Output Expressions

In many high-level languages, values are input to a program by using an input statement, often some kind of *Read* statement; and values are output by using some kind of *Print or Write* statement or some other output statement. In C++, however, input and output are carried out using special input and output *operators*. Thus, to perform input, we write an input expression; to perform output, we write an output expression. In this section, we will take a first look at input/output; a more complete discussion is given in Chapters 5 and 9.

I/O STREAMS

C++ avoids the nitty-gritty details about how I/O is actually carried out on any particular machine by dealing with **streams,** which connect an executing program with an input/output device. When characters are entered from the keyboard, they enter an input stream called an `istream` that transmits the characters from the keyboard to the program. Similarly, when output is to be displayed by a program on the screen, the output characters are placed in an output stream called an `ostream` that transmits the characters to the monitor.[1]

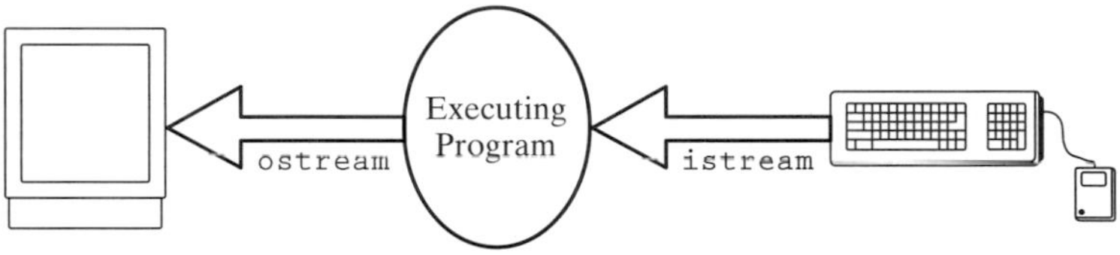

C++ has no input or output facilities built into the language. Instead, `istreams` and `ostreams` are provided by a special library `iostream`. This library defines three important data objects:

- An `istream` object named `cin`, which is associated with the *keyboard*
- An `ostream` object named `cout`, which is associated with the *screen*
- An `ostream` object named `cerr`, which is associated with the *screen* and is used to display error messages[2]

Input and output are operations on these data objects.

---

1. The names `istream` and `ostream` are the names of two *classes* (see Section 5.3). The ability to develop an entire I/O system using classes provides some indication of their powerful capabilities. The class `iostream` has also been added to C++ to define streams that can be used for both input and output. Other I/O classes are `ifstream`, `ofstream`, and `fstream` for streams connecting to files (see Chapter 9), and `istringstream`, `ostringstream`, and `stringstream` for streams connected to strings (see Section 9.4).
2. One of the differences between and `cout` and `cerr` is that `cout` is *buffered*, but `cerr` is not. This means that output to `cerr` goes directly to the screen, whereas output to `cout` goes into a section of memory called an *output buffer* and appears on the screen only when this buffer is emptied, for example, by `endl`. More details about streams appear in Chapters 5 and 9.

INPUT EXPRESSIONS

The program in Figure 3.1 contains the input statement

```
cin >> mass;
```

where `mass` is a real variable. We have seen that `cin` is the name of the `istream` data object defined in `iostream`, but what is the purpose of the `>>`? The answer is that `>>` is the operator that performs the input operation. Just as the expression

```
x + 2
```

consists of the *addition* operator (+) and two operands (`x` and `2`), and

```
y = 1
```

consists of the *assignment* operator (=) and two operands (`y` and `1`), the expression

```
cin >> mass
```

is an input expression in which the **input** (or **extraction**) **operator** `>>` is applied to the two operands `cin` and `mass`. That is, the `>>` symbol is a binary operator that acts as follows:

Input Expression

Form:

`input_stream >> variable`

where

`input_stream` is the name of any declared C++ input stream; and

`variable` is any C++ variable for which the input operator `>>` is defined.

Behavior:

1. A value *v* is read from *`input_stream`*. (If there is none, program execution is suspended until one is entered.)
2. The value *v* is shifted from *`input_stream`* into *`variable`*.
3. The >> operator produces the value *`input_stream`* as its result.

The >> operator is *left associative,* which, along with Part 3 of its behavior, allows input expressions to be chained together. For example,

```
cin >> x >> y;
```

is evaluated as

```
(cin >> x) >> y;
```

in the following manner:

1. The next value is read from `cin` (if none is present, program execution is suspended until a value is entered), removed from `cin`, and assigned to `x`, and the `>>` operator produces the value `cin`, giving

```
cin >> y;
```

2. The next value is read from this modified `cin` (if none is present, program execution is suspended until a value is entered), removed from `cin`, and assigned to `y`, and the `>>` operator produces the value `cin`, giving

```
cin;
```

3. This last expression, which consists only of the modified `cin`, is evaluated and discarded by the semicolon.

Note that just as a semicolon serves to make an assignment expression into an assignment statement, a semicolon serves to make an input expression into an input statement. We can thus describe a typical C++ (interactive) input statement as follows:

C++ Interactive Input Statement

Form:

`cin >>` $variable_1$ `>>` $variable_2$ `>> ... >>` $variable_n$`;`

where

`cin` is the `istream` declared in `iostream`;

`>>` is the input operator; and

each $variable_i$ is a variable for which `>>` is defined.

Purpose: Execution of an input statement reads a sequence of n values from the input device with which `cin` is associated, storing them in $variable_1$, $variable_2$, . . ., $variable_n$, and removing them from the `istream cin`.

Note that the user must enter a value (of the appropriate type) for each variable in the statement before execution of the program will resume. Thus, if `side1`, `side2`, and `side3` are real variables, the statement

```
cin >> side1 >> side2 >> side3;
```

is executed, and the user enters the values

```
2.0 3.0
```

Then execution will not resume until the user enters a third value:

```
4.0
```

The first value is stored in the first variable, the second value in the second variable, and so on. In our example, the value of `side1` will be 2.0, the value of `side2` will be 3.0, and the value of `side3` will be 4.0. Program execution then resumes. Any **white space** (spaces, tabs, or newlines) can be used to separate input values. For example, the user could separate the values with newlines by entering each data item on a separate line,

```
2.0
3.0
4.0
```

and produce the same result.

NOTE

Because execution is suspended and because the correct number and types of values must be entered before execution can resume, *it is good practice to provide an informative message to prompt the user whenever it is necessary to enter data values.* This is accomplished by preceding input statements with output statements that display appropriate prompts; for example,

```
cout << "Enter the three sides of the triangle: ";
```

We turn now to a study of such output statements.

OUTPUT EXPRESSIONS

There is a natural symmetry between C++ input and output statements. To illustrate, consider the input statement

```
cin >> mass;
```

and the output statement

```
cout << "Enter a mass (in kilograms): ";
```

Just as `cin` is the name of an `istream` data object, `cout` is the name of an `ostream` data object defined in `iostream`. Just as `>>` is the `istream` input (or extraction) operator, `<<` is the `ostream` **output** (or **insertion**) **operator.** And, just as the expression

```
cin >> mass
```

performs the *input* operation (`>>`) using two operands (`cin` and `mass`), the expression

```
cout << "Enter a mass (in kilograms): "
```

performs the *output* operation (`<<`) using two operands—`cout` and `"Enter a mass (in kilograms): "`. The `<<` symbol is a binary operator that behaves as follows:

Output Expression

Form:

output_stream << *expression*

where

output_stream is the name of any declared C++ output stream, and expression is any C++ *expression* for which << is defined.

Behavior:

1. *expression* is evaluated, producing a value *v*.
2. The value of *v* is inserted into *output_stream*.
3. The << operator produces the value *output_stream* as its result.

Like >>, the << operator is *left associative*, which, along with Part 3 of its behavior, allows output expressions to be chained together. Thus,

```
cout << "Perimeter = " << side1 + side2 + side3 << endl;
```

is evaluated as

```
((cout << "Perimeter = ") << side1 + side2 + side3) << endl;
```

and its behavior is as follows:

1. The expression `"Perimeter = "` is evaluated and inserted into `cout`, and the << operator produces the value `cout`, giving

   ```
   cout << side1 + side2 + side3 << endl;
   ```

2. The expression `side1 + side2 + side3` is evaluated and shifted onto `cout`, and the << operator produces the value `cout`, giving

   ```
   cout << endl;
   ```

3. The expression `endl` is evaluated, which inserts a newline character (`'\n'`) into `cout` and then *flushes* it, causing output to appear on the screen (see Footnote 11). The << operator produces the value `cout`, giving

   ```
   cout;
   ```

4. The expression `cout` is evaluated and discarded by the semicolon.

We can thus describe a typical C++ (interactive) output statement as follows:

C++ Interactive Output Statement

Form:

`cout <<` $expr_1$ `<<` $expr_2$ `<< ... <<` $expr_n$`;`

where

`cout` is the `ostream` declared in `iostream`;

<< is the output operator; and

each $expr_i$ is a C++ expression for which << is defined.

Purpose: Execution of an output statement inserts the values of $expr_1$, $expr_2$, . . ., $expr_n$ into the `ostream` `cout` so they will be displayed on the output device with which `cout` is associated.

For example, the statement

```
cout << side1 << ' ' << side2 << '\n' << side3 << endl;
```

displays the values of `side1` and `side2` on one line and the value of `side3` on the next line. Subsequent output would begin on yet another line.

WATCH OUT

Note that if white space is to appear in the output, it must be specified explicitly. For example, if the values of the integer variables `a` and `b` are 2 and 3, respectively, then the output statement

```
cout << "The sum of" << a << "and" << b
     << "is" << a + b;
```

will display the output

```
The sum of2and3is5
```

whereas the output statement

```
cout << "The sum of " << a << " and " << b
     << " is " << a + b;
```

will display

```
The sum of 2 and 3 is 5
```

Newline escape sequences must be used to cause values being displayed to appear on separate lines. For example, the output statement

```
cout << "Rats\nSnails\n\nPuppy Dog Tails\n";
```

will display the output

```
Rats
Snails

Puppy Dog Tails
```

As we noted earlier, `endl` can be used in an output list to insert a newline character; it also flushes the stream so that its contents are transferred to the screen.

OUTPUT FORMATTING

As we have seen previously (e.g., see Figure 2.1), the default output format for real values is not really satisfactory for monetary values. This and many similar formatting problems can be remedied by inserting **format manipulators** into an output list, to specify the appearance of the output. A few manipulators are given here; a more complete description of the capabilities provided by the `iostream` and `iomanip` libraries can be found in Section 5.3 and in Chapter 9.[1]

Format Manipulators

Manipulators: Description:

From `iostream`:

`showpoint`	Display decimal point and trailing zeros for all real numbers.
`noshowpoint`	Hide decimal point and trailing zeros for whole real numbers (default).
`fixed`	Use fixed-point notation for real values.
`scientific`	Use scientific notation for real values.
`boolalpha`	Display boolean values as strings "true" and "false".
`left`	Display values left justified within a field.
`right`	Display values right justified within a field (default).

From `iomanip`:

`setw(`*`w`*`)`	Display the next value in a field of size *w* (default 1).
`setprecision(`*`p`*`)`	Display *p* fractional digits for all subsequent output of real values (common default is 6).

Purpose: When inserted into an output list, these format manipulators specify the appearance of the output (i.e., its format) of subsequent items in the list.

Note: `setw()` applies to only the next output item; the other format manipulators apply to all subsequent items in output statements.

To illustrate the use of format manipulators, consider the statements

```
double alpha = 8.0 / 3.0,
       beta = 9.0 / 3.0;
cout << '(' << alpha << ")\n" << '(' << beta << ")\n";
```

1. Compilers that are not fully ISO/ANSI-C++ compliant may not support the use of format manipulators from `iostream` as described here. The `boolalpha` manipulator may not be provided, and it may be necessary to include `<iomanip>` or `<iomanip.h>` and use `setiosflags(`*flag*$_1$ `|` *flag*$_2$ `|` ...`)` in the output statement where each *flag*$_i$ is one of `ios::fixed`, `ios::showpoint`, `ios::right`, and so on. For example,

```
cout << setiosflags(ios::showpoint | ios::fixed | ios::right) << ...
```

You may also have to use `resetiosflags(`*flag*$_i$`)` to reset the `ostream` to a value. See Chapter 5 for more details.

While the default format depends on the particular C++ implementation, the output displayed by these statements might appear as

```
(2.666667)
(3)
```

Using the `showpoint` manipulator will cause the decimal point and trailing zeros of `beta` to be displayed, and using the `fixed` manipulator will ensure that values are displayed in fixed-point (rather than scientific) form; thus,

```
cout << showpoint << fixed
     << '(' << alpha << ") \n" << '(' << beta << ")\n";
```

will cause the output to appear as

```
(2.66667)
(3.00000)
```

If we wish to alter the precision to display only three decimal places, we can insert the `setprecision()` manipulator from the `iomanip` library,

```
cout << showpoint << fixed
     << setprecision(3)
     << '(' << alpha << ")\n" << '(' << beta << ")\n";
```

which will alter the output as follows:

```
(2.667)
(3.000)
```

Similarly, we can use the `setw()` manipulator from `iomanip` to change the width of the field in which an output value appears:

```
cout << showpoint << fixed
     << setprecision(3)
     << '(' << setw(10) << alpha << ")\n"
     << '(' << beta << ")\n";
```

Here, the number of positions (5) required to display the value of `alpha` is now smaller than the width of the field (10) being used to display it. If values are left justified in their fields, the output will appear as

```
(2.667     )
(3.000)
```

and if they are right justified, it will be

```
(     2.667)
(3.000)
```

To specify the justification, we can use the `left` and `right` manipulators. For example,

```
cout << showpoint << fixed << right
     << setprecision(3)
     << '(' << setw(10) << alpha << ")\n"
     << '(' << beta << ")\n";
```

will produce the latter output.

The `setw()` and `right` manipulators can be used to align right-justified values in a column. For example, inserting another `setw()` before outputting `beta`

```
cout << showpoint << fixed << right
     << setprecision(3)
     << '(' << setw(10) << alpha << ")\n"
     << '(' << setw(10) << beta << ")\n";
```

changes the output to

```
(     2.667)
(     3.000)
```

WATCH OUT

It is important that you note the difference between `setw()` and the other manipulators. `setw()` *affects the format of only the next value to be displayed, whereas the other manipulators affect the appearances of all values that follow.*

3.7 Example: Truck Fleet Accounting

PROBLEM

Suppose that a manufacturing company maintains a fleet of trucks to deliver its products. On each trip, the driver records the distance traveled in miles, the number of gallons of fuel used, the cost of the fuel, and other costs of operating the truck. As part of the accounting process, the controller needs to calculate and record for each truck and for each trip the miles per gallon, the total cost of that trip, and the cost per mile. A simple program is to be designed to assist the controller in performing these calculations for a given trip.

Object-Centered Design

Behavior. The program should display on the screen a prompt for the distance traveled in miles, the number of gallons of fuel used, the cost per gallon of the fuel, and the per-mile cost of operating the truck. The program should read these values from the keyboard. The program should then calculate and display the truck's mileage (in miles per gallon), the total cost of the trip, and the cost per mile.

Objects. From the behavioral description, we can identify the following objects in this problem:

	Software Objects		
Problem Objects	**Type**	**Kind**	**Name**
screen	`ostream`	variable	`cout`
total miles traveled	`double`	variable	*miles*
total gallons of fuel used	`double`	variable	*gallonsOfFuel*
cost per gallon of fuel	`double`	variable	*unitFuelCost*

Problem Objects	Software Objects		
	Type	Kind	Name
operating cost per mile	`double`	variable	*unitOperatingCost*
keyboard	`istream`	variable	`cin`
miles per gallon	`double`	variable	*milesPerGallon*
total cost of the trip	`double`	variable	*totalTripCost*
cost per mile	`double`	variable	*costPerMile*

Operations. From the behavioral description, we can identify the following operations:

i. Display a prompt for input on the screen
ii. Read a sequence of four real values from the keyboard
iii. Compute the number of miles driven per gallon
— Divide the number of miles traveled by the number of gallons of fuel used
iv. Compute the total cost of the trip: add the following two values:
— The cost of fuel: multiply gallons used by price per gallon
— The operating costs: multiply miles driven by cost per mile
v. Compute the cost of the trip per mile
— Divide the total cost of the trip by the number of miles traveled
vi. Output three real values

Solving this problem thus requires only the standard C++ arithmetic and I/O operations. Note that the problem assumes that all of the input values are positive, making this a *precondition* for the problem.

Algorithm. Organizing these operations into an algorithm gives the following. Note that we have used two new objects, *fuelCost* and *operatingCost* in calculating *totalTripCost*.

Algorithm for Truck Cost Problem

1. Display a prompt via `cout` for *miles*, *gallonsOfFuel*, *unitFuelCost*, and *unitOperatingCost*.
2. Read values from `cin` into *miles*, *gallonsOfFuel*, *unitFuelCost*, and *unitOperatingCost*.
3. Check that each of these values is positive.
4. Compute *milesPerGallon = miles / gallonsOfFuel.*
5. Compute *fuelCost = gallonsOfFuel * unitFuelCost.*
6. Compute *operatingCost = unitOperatingCost * miles.*
7. Compute *totalTripCost = fuelCost + operatingCost.*
8. Compute *costPerMile = totalTripCost / miles.*
9. Via `cout`, display *milesPerGallon, totalTripCost* and *costPerMile*, with descriptive labels.

Coding and Testing. A C++ implementation of this algorithm and two sample runs are shown in Figure 3.2:

Fig. 3.2 Trip costs. (Part 1 of 2)

```
/* tripCost.cpp calculates the total cost and miles per gallon
 * of a vehicle, based on the miles traveled, fuel consumed,
 * cost per gallon of fuel, and operating cost per mile.
 *
 * Input: The total miles traveled, total fuel consumed,
 *         unit cost of the fuel, and operating cost per mile.
 * Precondition: miles, gallonsOfFuel, unitFuelCost and
 *         unitOperatingCost are all positive.
 * Output: The miles per gallon, total cost of the trip
 *         and the cost per mile.
 *************************************************************/

#include <iostream>          // cin, cout, <<, >>, fixed, showpoint
#include <iomanip>           // setw(), setprecision()
#include <cassert>
using namespace std;

int main()
{
   const int WIDTH = 7;                        // width of output field

   cout << "Enter:\n\ttotal miles traveled,"
        << "\n\tgallons of fuel used,"
        << "\n\ttotal cost per gallon of the fuel, and"
        << "\n\toperating cost per mile."
        << "\n\t---> ";
   double miles,                               // total miles traveled
          gallonsOfFuel,                       // total gallons used
          unitFuelCost,                        // fuel cost per gallon
          unitOperatingCost;                   // operating cost per mile
   cin >> miles >> gallonsOfFuel
       >> unitFuelCost >> unitOperatingCost;

   assert(miles > 0 && gallonsOfFuel > 0 &&
          unitFuelCost > 0 && unitOperatingCost > 0);

   double milesPerGallon = miles / gallonsOfFuel,
          fuelCost = unitFuelCost * gallonsOfFuel,
          operatingCost = unitOperatingCost * miles,
          totalTripCost = fuelCost + operatingCost,
          costPerMile = totalTripCost / miles;
```

Fig. 3.2 Trip costs. (Part 2 of 2)

```
   cout << showpoint << fixed << setprecision(2)
        << "\n\tMiles per gallon: " << setw(WIDTH) << milesPerGallon
        << "\n\tTotal cost:       $" << setw(WIDTH) << totalTripCost
        << "\n\tCost per mile:    $" << setw(WIDTH) << costPerMile
        << endl << endl;
}
```

Sample runs:

```
Enter:
   total miles traveled,
   gallons of fuel used,
   total cost per gallon of the fuel, and
   operating cost per mile.
   ---> 10 1 1.50 3.50

   Miles per gallon:    10.00
   Total cost:       $  36.50
   Cost per mile:    $   3.50

Enter:
   the total miles traveled,
   the gallons of fuel used,
   the total cost per gallon of the fuel, and
   the operating cost per mile.
   ---> 100 10 15 10

Miles per gallon:    10.00
Total cost:       $1150.00
Cost per mile:    $  11.50
```

✔ Quick Quiz 3.7

1. In C++, input and output are carried out using ________, which connect an executing program with an input/output device.
2. (True or false) C++ has no input or output facilities built into the language.
3. ________ is the stream object associated with the keyboard; its type is ________.
4. ________ and ________ are stream objects associated with the screen; their type is ________.
5. The input operator is ________.
6. The output operator is ________.

7. The value produced by the input expression `cin >> x` is _________.
8. The value produced by the output expression `cout << x` is _________.
9. The input and output operators are (left or right) _________ associative.
10. _________ can be inserted into an output list to format the output of items.

Questions 11–13 assume the declarations

```
int number = 123;
double rate = 23.45678;
```

For each, show precisely the output that the set of statements produces, indicating blanks with ␣, or explain why an error occurs.

11.
```
cout << number << rate << endl;
```

12.
```
cout << '\n' << setw(5) << number << number + 1
     << setw(5) << number + 2
     << setw(1) << number + 4 << endl;
```

13.
```
cout << showpoint << fixed
     << setw(8) << setprecision(0) << rate << endl
     << setw(8) << setprecision(1) << rate << endl
     << setw(8) << setprecision(2) << rate << endl
     << setw(8) << rate << endl
     << setprecision(1) << rate << endl;
```

Questions 14–17 assume the declarations

```
int number1, number2, number3;
double real1, real2, real3;
```

For each, tell what value, if any, will be assigned to each variable, or explain why an error occurs when the statement is executed with the given input data:

14.
```
cin >> number1 >> number2 >> number3;
```
Input:
```
11  22
33  44
```

15.
```
cin >> real1 >> real2 >> real3;
```
Input:
```
1.1 2 3.3 4
```

16.
```
cin >> number1 >> number2 >> number3;
```
Input:
```
1.1 2 3.3 4
```

17.
```
cin >> number1 >> real1 >> number3;
    >> real2 >> number3 >> real3;
```
Input:
```
1.1 2
3.3 4
5.5 6
```

Exercises 3.7

Exercises 1–8 assume the declarations

```
double alpha = -567.392, beta = 0.0004;
int rho = 436;
```

For each, show precisely the output that each of the statements produces, indicating blanks with ␣, or explain why an error occurs.

1.
```
cout << rho << rho + 1 << rho + 2;
```

2.
```
cout << "alpha ="
     << setw(9) << setprecision(3) << alpha << endl
     << setw(10) << setprecision(5) <<  beta << endl
     << setw(7) << setprecision(4) <<  beta << endl;
```

3.
```
cout << setprecision(1) << setw(8) << alpha << endl
     << setw(5) << rho << endl
     << "Tolerance:"
     << setw(8) << setprecision(5) << beta << endl;
```

4.
```
cout << "alpha =" << setw(12) << setprecision(5)
     << alpha << endl
     << "beta =" << setw(6) << setprecision(2)
     << beta << endl
     << "rho =" << setw(6) << rho << endl
     << setw(15) << setprecision(3)
     << alpha + 4.0 + rho << endl;
```

5.
```
cout << "Tolerance =" << setw(5)
     << setprecision(3) <<  beta;
cout << setw(2) << rho << setw(4) << alpha;
```

6.
```
cout << setw(8) << setprecision(1) << 10 * alpha
     << setw(8) << ceil(10 * alpha);
cout << setprecision(3) << setw(5) << pow(rho / 100, 2.0)
     << setw(5) << sqrt(rho / 100);
```

7.
```
cout << "rho =" << setw(8) << setprecision(2) << rho
     << "*****";
```

8.
```
cout << setw(10) << alpha << setw(10) <<  beta;
```

For Exercises 9 and 10, assume the declarations

```
int i = 15, j = 8;
char c = 'c', d = '-';
double x = 2559.50, y = 8.015;
```

Show precisely the output that each of the statements produces; indicate blanks with ␣.

9.
```
cout << setw(j) << setprecision(2) <<  "new balance ="
     << x << ' ' <<  setw(i % 10) << c
     << setw(j) << setprecision(j-6) << y;
```

10.
```
cout << "i =" << setw(i) << i
     << "j =" << setw(j) << setprecision(j) << j << endl
     << setw(j) << i << ' '
     << setw(i) << j;
```

For Exercises 11–14, assume the declarations

```
int n1 = 39, n2 = -5117;
char c = 'F';
double r1 = 56.7173, r2 = -0.00247;
```

For each exercise, write output statements that use these variables to produce the given output. (The underlining dashes are shown here only to help you determine the spacing.)

11.
```
  56.7173   F   39
------------------

-5117PDQ-0.00247
------------------
```

12.
```
 56.717    -0.0025***39  F
---------------------------

   56.72  39-5117
---------------------------
```

13.
```
Roots are  56.717 and -0.00247
------------------------------
```

14.
```
Approximate angles:  56.7 and -0.0
----------------------------------

Magnitudes are     39 and  5117
----------------------------------
```

For Exercises 15–21, assume that a, b, and c are integer variables and x, y, and z are real variables. Tell what value, if any, will be assigned to each of these variables, or explain why an error occurs when the input statements are executed with the given input data:

15.
```
cin >> a >> b >> c                    Input:  1   2   3
    >> x >> y >> z;                           4 5.5 6.6
```

16.
```
cin >> a >> b >> c;                   Input:  1
cin >> x >> y >> z;                           2
                                              3
                                              4
                                              5
                                              6
```

17.
```
cin >> a >> x;                        Input:  1 2.2
cin >> b >> y;                                3 4.4
cin >> c >> z;                                5 6.6
```

18.
```
cin >> a >> b >> c;                   Input:  1 2.2
cin >> x >> y >> z;                           3 4.4
                                              5 6.6
```

19.
```
cin >> a;                             Input:  1   2   3
cin >> b >> c;                                4 5.5 6.6
cin >> x >> y;
cin >> z;
```

20.
```
cin >> a                              Input:  1   2   3
    >> b >> c                                 4 5.5 6.6
    >> x >> y
    >> z;
```

21.
```
cin >> a >> b;                        Input:  1    2     3
cin >> c >> x >> y >> z;                      4    5.5   6.6
                                              7    8.8   9.9
                                              10   11.11 12.12
                                              13   14.14 15.15
```

3.8* OBJECTive Thinking: Initialization and Constructors

In the *OBJECTive Thinking* section of the preceding chapter, we saw how to declare the *instance variables* (also called *attribute variables* or *data members*) needed by a class to represent attributes of objects being modeled by that class. In this *OBJECTive Thinking* section, we will examine how such instance variables can be initialized.

To initialize the instance variables of a class, C++ provides a special mechanism called a **constructor**. Since the best way to understand a new idea is to see some examples of it, we will show how to write constructors for the `Sphere`, `Name`, and `Student` classes described in the preceding *OBJECTive Thinking* section. Using these as examples, we will then discuss constructors in general.

A `Sphere` CONSTRUCTOR

The role of the constructor is to initialize the instance variables of an object. As such, it typically uses assignment statements to assign values to those instance variables. The simplest kind of constructor is a **default-value constructor**, that assigns *default values* when the programmer supplies none.

Most classes need a default-value constructor for declarations of objects when no initial values are provided:

```
className objectName;
```

The highlighted parts of the following code present a default-value constructor for our `Sphere` class that assigns a default value of zero to each of the instance variables:

```
class Sphere
{
 public:
   Sphere();
   ... other Sphere-operation declarations go here
 private:
   double myRadius,
          myDensity,
          myWeight;
};

inline Sphere::Sphere()
{
   myRadius = myDensity = myWeight = 0.0;
}
```

What does all of this mean? Let's look at it step-by-step:

1. The name of a constructor is always the same as the name of the class, so the name of our constructor must be `Sphere`.
2. Inside a class, we must declare any operation we want the class to provide. Since a constructor is an operation, we must declare it within the class. The

empty parentheses after the name tell the compiler that this is a default-value constructor.

3. Operations declared inside a class are (usually) defined outside the class. For simple operations like this constructor, we can define the operation in the header file, after the class declaration.
   a. This definition begins with the keyword `inline`. This tells the compiler to optimize calls to this operation.
   b. Next is the name of the class (`Sphere`), followed by a special **scope operator** (`::`), followed by the name of the operation (`Sphere()`) being defined. This tells the compiler that what follows is the definition of the operation we declared in Step 2 inside class `Sphere`.
   c. Last is a pair of curly braces containing the statements that initialize the instance variables. In this case, all of our instance variables are being initialized to the same default value (0.0), so we chain the assignments together into one statement.

Given such a constructor in *Sphere.h*, a programmer may write

```
#include "Sphere.h"
int main()
{
   Sphere oneSphere, anotherSphere;
}
```

and the instance variables of the two objects `oneSphere` and `anotherSphere` will each automatically be initialized to the default values we specified in our constructor:

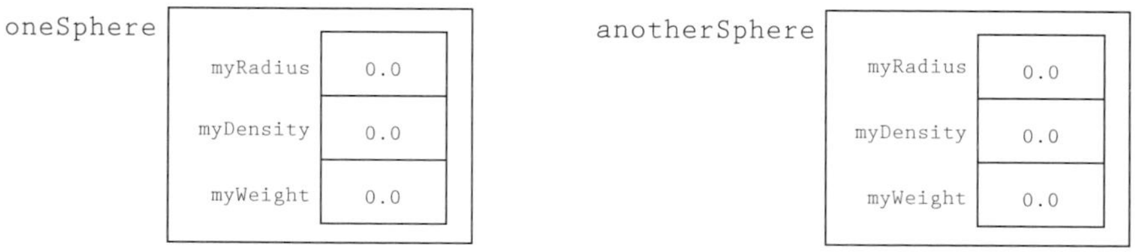

`Name` CONSTRUCTORS

A default-value constructor provides for the initialization of instance variables to default values. For our `Name` class, we might build such a constructor as follows:

```
#include <string>        // the string class
using namespace std;
class Name
{
 public:
   Name();
   ... other Name-operation declarations go here
```

```
 private:
   string myFirstName,
          myMiddleName,
          myLastName;
};

inline Name::Name()
{
   myFirstName = myMiddleName = myLastName = "";
}
```

Given this definition in *Name.h*, a programmer can now write

```
#include "Name.h"
int main()
{
   Name myName, yourName;
}
```

and the instance variables of the two `Name` objects `myName` and `yourName` will each be initialized to the empty string:

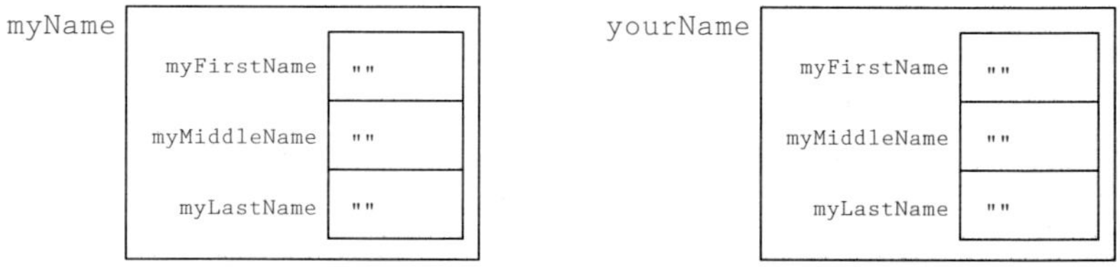

But now suppose we want to initialize these names to nondefault values. In this case, a default-value constructor is of no use. Instead, we need an **explicit-value constructor** that lets us specify the initial values for each instance variable. The highlighted segments of the following code present an explicit-value constructor for our `Name` class:

```
#include <string>       // the string class
using namespace std;
class Name
{
 public:
   Name();
   Name(string first, string middle, string last);
   ... other Name-operation declarations go here
 private:
   string myFirstName,
          myMiddleName,
          myLastName;
};

inline Name::Name()
{
   myFirstName = myMiddleName = myLastName = "";
}
```

```
inline Name::Name(string first, string middle, string last)
{
   myFirstName = first;
   myMiddleName = middle;
   myLastName = last;
}
```

As before, we must both declare and define the explicit-value constructor operation. However, this version of the constructor requires three variables (that we have named `first`, `middle`, and `last`) by which the initial values can be communicated to the operation. These variables are called **parameters** and are declared within the parentheses that tell the compiler this is the constructor operation. *The type of a parameter should always match the type of value it is to store*, so each of these three parameters has the type `string`.[1]

Note that we now have *two* constructor operations: a default-value constructor with no parameters and an explicit-value constructor with a parameter for each instance variable. It is not uncommon for a class to provide multiple constructors: one for each different way that an object might be initialized. The compiler uses the types of each constructor's parameters to distinguish it from other constructors, so *each constructor's parameter types must be unique.*[2]

Given such a definition in *Name.h*, a programmer can now write

```
#include "Name.h"
int main()
{
   Name hisName("John", "Paul", "Jones"),
        herName("Mary", "Anne", "Smith"),
        itsName;
}
```

---

1. In our `Sphere` class, we could supply an explicit-value constructor with three `double` parameters (*radius*, *density*, and *weight*), but doing so would require that a programmer know in advance all three attributes. Since the purpose of the `Sphere` class is to compute one attribute given the other two, we chose not to provide such a constructor.
2. In our `Sphere` class, we *could* supply an explicit-value constructor with two `double` parameters for two of the instance variables that would compute and initialize the third, e.g., `Sphere(`*`radius, density`*`)`:

```
inline Sphere::Sphere(double radius, double density)
{
   assert(radius > 0.0 && density > 0.0);
   myRadius = radius; myDensity = density;
   myWeight = density * 4.0 * PI * pow(radius, 3.0) / 3.0;
}
```

But we *could not* then provide explicit-value constructors `Sphere(`*`radius, weight`*`)` or `Sphere(`*`density, weight`*`)` because the parameter types of each of these constructors would be the same as the preceding one, producing a compilation error. Rather than supply just one of these three constructors, we elected to use a different approach as described in Section 1.4.

and the instance variables of the two `Name` objects `hisName` and `herName` will each be initialized to the specified values using the explicit-value constructor, while the `Name` object `itsName` will be initialized using the default-value constructor:

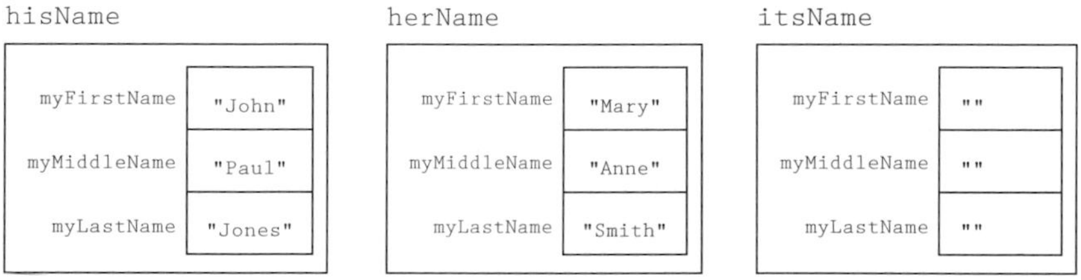

The values we specify as initial values within the parentheses (e.g., `"John"`, `"Paul"`, and `"Smith"`) are known as **arguments**. When the compiler processes a declaration statement, it uses the types of the arguments to determine which constructor operation to use. Thus, in the declarations of `hisName` and `herName`, the compiler sees three `string` arguments and so invokes the explicit-value constructor that has three `string` parameters. When the compiler processes `itsName`, it sees no arguments, and so it invokes the default-value constructor.

`Student` CONSTRUCTORS

We will finish this section by showing some of the constructors we might write for our `Student` class:

```
#include "Name.h"
class Student
{
 public:
   Student();
   Student(string first, string middle, string last,
           int id);
   Student(string first, string middle, string last,
           int id, double wage, double hours);
   ... other Student-operation declarations go here
 private:
   Name   myName;
   int    myIdNumber;
   double myHourlyWage,
          myHoursWorked;
};

inline Student::Student()
{
   myIdNumber = 0;
   myHourlyWage = 0.0;
   myHoursWorked = 0.0;
}
```

```
inline Student::Student(string first, string middle,
                        string last, int id)
{
   myName = Name(first, middle, last);
   myIdNumber = id;
   myHourlyWage = 0.0;
   myHoursWorked = 0.0;
}

inline Student::Student(string first, string middle,
                        string last, int id, double wage,
                        double hours)
{
   myName = Name(first, middle, last);
   myIdNumber = id;
   myHourlyWage = wage;
   myHoursWorked = hours;
}
```

Here, we create three constructors: a default-value constructor, an explicit-value constructor for unemployed students, and an explicit-value constructor for employed students. Note that we need not initialize the `Name` instance variables in our default-value constructor, because the `Name` default-value constructor automatically does this for us. Note also that we explicitly invoke the explicit-value `Name` constructor in the latter two definitions.[1]

Given these definitions in the file *Student.h*, a programmer can now write

```
#include "Student.h"
int main()
{
   Student firstStudent("John", "Jay", "Doe", 1, 7.25, 20.0),
           secondStudent("Jane", "Ann", "Smith", 35);
}
```

and the `Student` objects `firstStudent` and `secondStudent` will each appear as follows:

---

1. The careful reader will note that the two explicit-value `Student` constructors are very similar. In such situations, C++ lets us avoid redundant coding by invoking the constructor with more parameters from the one with fewer parameters, as follows:

```
inline Student::Student(string first, string middle,
                        string last, int id)
{
   Student(first, middle, last, id, 0.0, 0.0);
}
```

Such a call to a constructor from within a constructor must be the first statement in the constructor.

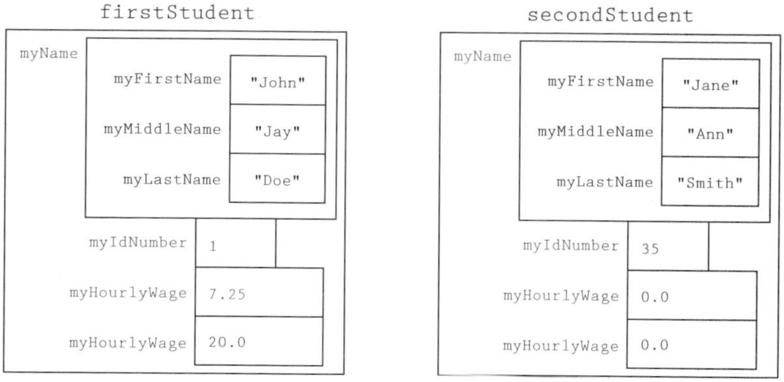

As should be evident, the compiler notes the six arguments in the declaration of `firstStudent` and invokes the explicit-value `Student` constructor that has six matching parameters. Likewise, the compiler notes that the declaration of `secondStudent` has four arguments and invokes the explicit-value `Student` constructor that has four matching parameters. C++ *declarations* are thus actually *expressions*, which become *expression-statements* when a semicolon is appended (just like the other expressions we have seen in this chapter).

We have now seen how a constructor lets us initialize the instance variables of an object. In the *OBJECTive Thinking* section of the next chapter, we will see how to build other operations that access an object's attributes.

Quick Quiz 3.8

1. A(n) ________ is used to initialize the instance variables in a class.
2. The simplest kind of constructor is a(n) ________-value constructor.
3. (True or false) Operations provided by a class are usually declared outside the class.
4. (True or false) Operations provided by a class are usually defined outside the class.
5. The ________ operator, denoted by ________, is used to attach the name of a class to the name of an operation being defined.
6. A(n) ________-value constructor allows a user to specify initial values for instance variables.
7. A constructor like that in Question 6 uses variables called ________ to store the initial values communicated to it.
8. The initial values specified within parentheses in an object's declaration, which has a constructor like that in Question 6, are called ________.

Exercises 3.8

For Exercises 1–5, add to the class declarations in the exercises of Section 2.3 declarations and definitions of the specified kind of default-value constructor.

1. The temperature class in Exercise 1 of Section 2.3 so the instance variables represent 0°C
2. The time class in Exercise 2 of Section 2.3 so the instance variables represent midnight (12:00 AM)

3. The date class in Exercise 3 of Section 2.3 so the instance variables represent a date of your choosing
4. The telephone-number class in Exercise 4 of Section 2.3 so the instance variables represent some phone number of your choosing
5. The student-information class in Exercise 5 of Section 2.3 so the student's id number is 0, the first, middle, and last names are empty strings, and the credits and GPA are both zero

For Exercises 6–10, proceed as with Exercises 1–5, but with explicit-value constructors.

6. The temperature class in Exercise 1
7. The time class in Exercise 2
8. The date class in Exercise 3
9. The telephone-number class in Exercise 4
10. The student-information class in Exercise 5

For Exercises 11–15, write declarations for the following objects that could appear in a main program.

11. For the temperature class in Exercises 1 and 6, objects `freezing` with default initial value and `boiling` with initial value 212°F
12. For the time class in Exercises 2 and 7, objects `midnight` with default initial value and `noon` with initial value 12:00 PM
13. For the date class in Exercises 3 and 8, objects `someYear` with default initial value and `birthday` with your birthdate as initial value
14. For the telephone-number class in Exercises 4 and 9, objects `number1` with default initial value and `number2` initialized with your telephone number (or someone else if you don't have a phone number)
15. For the student-information class in Exercises 5 and 10, objects `student1` with default initial value and `student2` initialized with information about you

CHAPTER SUMMARY

Key Terms & Notes

`#include` directive
additive operator
argument
assignment expression
assignment operator (=)
attribute variables
bitwise operators
boolean expression
C assert library (`cassert`)
C `char`-type library (`cctype`}
C math library (`cmath`)
C standard library (`cstdlib`)
`cerr`
`cin`
compatible
compound boolean expression
condition
constructor
`cout`
data members
decrement operator (--)
default-value constructor
`endl`
escape sequence
explicit-value constructor
expression

expression statement
extraction operator
fixed-point
floating-point
format manipulator
header file
increment operator (++)
input operator (>>)
insertion operator
instance variables
`iostream` library
`istream`
left-associative
library
logical operator
modulus operator (%)
multiplicative operator
operand
operator
operator precedence
operator priority
`ostream`
output operator (<<)
parameter
precedence rules
precondition
priority
promotion
relational operator
remainder
right-associative
scope operator (::)
short-circuit evaluation
short-cut assignment operations
side effect
stream
truth table
type conversion
unary operator
white space

- It is important to understand the difference between integer and real division. If `a` and `b` are both integers with $b \neq 0$, `a / b` gives the integer quotient when `a` is divided by `b`, and `a % b` gives the remainder. If `a` or `b` is real, real division is used for `a / b` and `a % b` results in an error.
- Promotion is the automatic widening of a narrower value to the size of a wider value. It is used in mixed-type expressions to convert a narrower value to the type of a wider value in the expression.
- Two values are compatible if one of the following is true:
  - They are both of the same type.
  - The type of one value can be promoted to the type of the other value.
  - The types of both can be promoted to the same type.
- In an expression, multiplicative operators have higher precedence than additive operators.
- Associativity determines whether equal-priority operators are applied from left to right or from right to left.
- Parentheses can be used to change the usual order of evaluation in an expression.
- A directive of the form `#include <lib>` must be used to insert the contents of a C/C++ library before the functions in that library can be used.
- Expressions of the form `type(exp)` or `(type) exp` can be used to convert the value of `exp` to the specified `type`.
- Be sure to use the == operator for equality comparisons, and not = (assignment).
- Be sure to use the `&&` and `||` operators for logical operations, and not `&` and `|` (bitwise operators).

- The `assert()` mechanism is useful for checking a condition that must be true at a given point in a program.
- The C `char`-type library `cctype` contains useful functions for performing common operations on `char` values such as checking case and changing case.
- An assignment statement is a replacement statement: `a = b;` replaces the value of `a` with the value of `b`.
- Assignment is a value-producing operator that returns the value being assigned. This together with right associativity makes it possible to chain assignments; for example, `a = b = c = d;`.
- An assignment statement of the form `alpha = alpha Δ beta;` can be written more compactly as `alpha Δ= beta;`.
- The increment (++) and decrement (--) operations are useful for incrementing/decrementing an integer variable by 1.
- An expression followed by a semicolon becomes a statement.
- I/O is carried out in C++ by operators acting on streams (`istreams` for input and `ostreams` for output), which connect an executing program with an input/output device.
- Input statements of the form

  $\texttt{an\_istream >> variable}_1\texttt{ >> variable}_2\texttt{ >> ... >> variable}_n\texttt{;}$

  are used to input values for variables; `cin` is the `istream` associated with the keyboard. White space (spaces, tabs, or newlines) is used to separate input values. Leading white space will be ignored when reading a value for a variable.
- It is good practice to prompt the user with an informative message when data values are to be entered.
- Output statements of the form

  $\texttt{an\_ostream >> expr}_1\texttt{ >> expr}_2\texttt{ >> ... >> expr}_n\texttt{;}$

  are used to output values of expressions; `cout` and `cerr` are `ostreams` associated with the screen.
- The format of output is controlled by inserting format manipulators into output lists.
- Classes have special methods called *constructors* used to initialize the data members of objects. *Default-value constructors* are used for objects whose declarations provide no initial values. *Explicit-value constructors* are used when initial values are specified.
- The name of a constructor is always the same as the name of the class.
- Any operation to be provided by a class must be declared within the class and is usually defined outside the class. For a simple operation, this definition is usually placed in the header file, after the class declaration. It begins with the keyword `inline`, and its name must have the name of the class attached with the scope operator (`::`).
- Initial values for data members are passed to explicit-value constructors via special variables called *parameters*. The values are specified in declarations of the form

  ```
  ClassName objectName(list_of_initial_values);
  ```

  and are known as *arguments*.

Programming Pointers

Program Style and Design

1. In the examples in this text, we adopt certain stylistic guidelines for C++ programs, and you should write your program in a similar style. In this text, we use the following standards; others are described in the Programming Pointers of subsequent chapters:
   - *Insert blank lines between blocks of related statements to make clear the structure of the program.*
   - *Separate the operators and operands in an expression with spaces to make the expression easy to read.*
   - *Label all output produced by a program.* For example,

     ```
     cout << "Employee # " << empNumber
          << "  Wages = $" << wages;
     ```

     produces more informative output than

     ```
     cout << empNumber << wages;
     ```

2. *Identify any preconditions a program has, and check them using the* assert() *mechanism.* Preconditions are assumptions made in a program, often one or more restrictions on what comprises a valid input value. The `assert()` mechanism evaluates a boolean expression and terminates the program if it is false. Identify the preconditions in a problem, and use `assert()` to check them.

WATCH OUT

Potential Pitfalls

1. *The type of value stored in a variable should be the same as or promotable to the type of that variable.*
2. *If an integer value is to be stored in a real variable, the integer will be promoted to a real type. By contrast, if a real value is to be stored in an integer variable, then the real value is truncated, possibly resulting in the loss of information.*
3. *Parentheses in expressions must be paired.* That is, for each left parenthesis, there must be exactly one matching right parenthesis that occurs later in the expression.
4. *Both real and integer division are denoted by /; which operation is performed is determined by the type of the operands.* Thus, `8 / 5 = 1`, but `8.0 / 5.0 = 1.6`.
5. *All multiplications must be indicated by* `*`. For example, `2*n` is valid, but `2n` is not.
6. *A semicolon must appear at the end of each expression (assignments, input, output, etc.) that is meant to be a programming statement.*
7. *Use parentheses in complex expressions to indicate those subexpressions that are to be evaluated first.* The precedence of the operators used thus far is as follows:

!, unary+, unary-, ++, --	Highest (performed first)
/, *, %	
+, -	
<, >, <=, >=	
==, !=	
&&	
||	
=, +=, *=, etc.	Lowest (performed last)

However, there are so many operators in C++ (see Appendix C) that remembering their precedence levels is difficult. For this reason, we recommend using parentheses in complex expressions to specify clearly the order in which the operators are to be applied.

8. *When real quantities that are algebraically equal are compared with ==, the result may be a false boolean expression, because most real numbers are not stored exactly.* For example, even though the two real expressions `x * (1/x)` and `1.0` are algebraically equal, the boolean expression `x * (1/x) == 1.0` may be false for some real numbers `x`.
9. *One of the most common errors in writing boolean expressions is to use an assignment operator (=) when an equality operator (==) is intended.* For example, if `x` is an integer variable, the statements

```
cin >> x;
bool isOne = (x = 1);        // should be (x == 1)
```

will assign `true` to `isOne` regardless of what value is input for `x`, because `x = 1` assigns 1 to `x` and produces the value 1, which is interpreted as true.

10. *Be careful in writing compound boolean expressions to use the logical operators* `&&` *and* == *and not the bitwise operators* `&` *and* `|`. For example, suppose that `x` is an integer variable with value 3, and consider the statement

```
bool ok = (x > 1) & (x < 4); // should be (x > 1) && (x < 4)
```

The value (true or false) of the condition `x > 1` might be represented by the value of `x - 1` if it is positive (since nonzero values represent true) and 0 otherwise; in our case, this difference is 2. Similarly, the value of the condition `x < 4` might be represented by the value of `4 - x` if it is positive and 0 otherwise; in our case, this difference is 1. The value of `(x > 1) & (x < 4)` thus is `2 & 1` which is 0, which means that `ok` is assigned the value `false`.[1] The value of `(x > 1) && (x < 4)`, however, would be `true`.

Programming Problems

1. Write a program that reads two three-digit integers and then calculates and displays their product and the quotient and the remainder that result when the first is divided by the second. The output should be formatted to appear as follows:

```
  739              61 R 7
x  12             -----
-----          12) 739
 8868
```

2. Write a program to read the lengths of the two legs of a right triangle and to calculate and display the area of the triangle (one-half the product of the legs) and the length of the hypotenuse (square root of the sum of the squares of the legs).
3. Write a program to read values for the coefficients a, b, and c of the quadratic equation $ax^2 + bx + c = 0$ and then find the two roots of this equation by using the quadratic formula

$$\frac{-b \pm \sqrt{b^2 - 4ac}}{2a}$$

Execute the program with several values of a, b, and c for which the quantity $b^2 - 4ac$ is nonnegative, including $a = 4$, $b = 0$, $c = -36$; $a = 1$, $b = 5$, $c = -36$; and $a = 2$, $b = 7.5$, $c = 6.25$.

---

1. See the descriptions of the bitwise operators on the text's Web site.

4. Write a program that reads the amount of a purchase and the amount received in payment (both amounts in cents) and then computes and displays the change in dollars, half-dollars, quarters, dimes, nickels, and pennies.

5. Angles are often measured in degrees (°), minutes ('), and seconds ("). There are 360 degrees in a circle, 60 minutes in one degree, and 60 seconds in one minute. Write a program that reads two angular measurements given in degrees, minutes, and seconds and then calculates and displays their sum. Use the program to verify each of the following:

74°29'13" + 105°8'16" = 179°37'29"

7°14'55" + 5°24'55" = 12°39'50"

20°31'19" + 0°31'30" = 21°2'49"

122°17'48" + 237°42'12" = 0°0'0"

6. Write a program that reads two three-digit integers and then displays their product in the following format:

```
      749
 x    381
 -------
      749
    5992
   2247
 -------
  285369
```

Execute the program with the following values: 749 and 381; –749 and 381; 749 and –381; –749 and –381; 999 and 999.

7. In a certain region, pesticide can be sprayed from an airplane only if the temperature is at least 70°, the relative humidity is between 15 and 35%, and the wind speed is at most 10 miles per hour. Write a program that accepts three numbers representing temperature, relative humidity, and wind speed; assigns the value true or false to the boolean variable `okToSpray` according to these criteria; and displays this value.

8. A certain credit company will approve a loan application if the applicant's income is at least $25,000 or the value of his or her assets is at least $100,000; in addition, the applicant's total liabilities must be less than $50,000. Write a program that accepts three numbers representing income, assets, and liabilities; assigns the value true or false to the boolean variable `creditOK` according to these criteria; and displays this value.

9. Write a program that reads three real numbers, assigns the appropriate boolean value to the following boolean variables, and displays the associated values.

`triangle`: true if the real numbers can represent lengths of the sides of a triangle (the sum of any two of the numbers must be greater than the third); false otherwise.

`equilateral`: true if `triangle` is true and the triangle is equilateral (the three sides are equal); false otherwise.

`isosceles`: true if `triangle` is true and the triangle is isosceles (at least two sides are equal); false otherwise.

`scalene`: true if `triangle` is true and the triangle is scalene (no two sides are equal); false otherwise.

CHAPTER 4

Functions

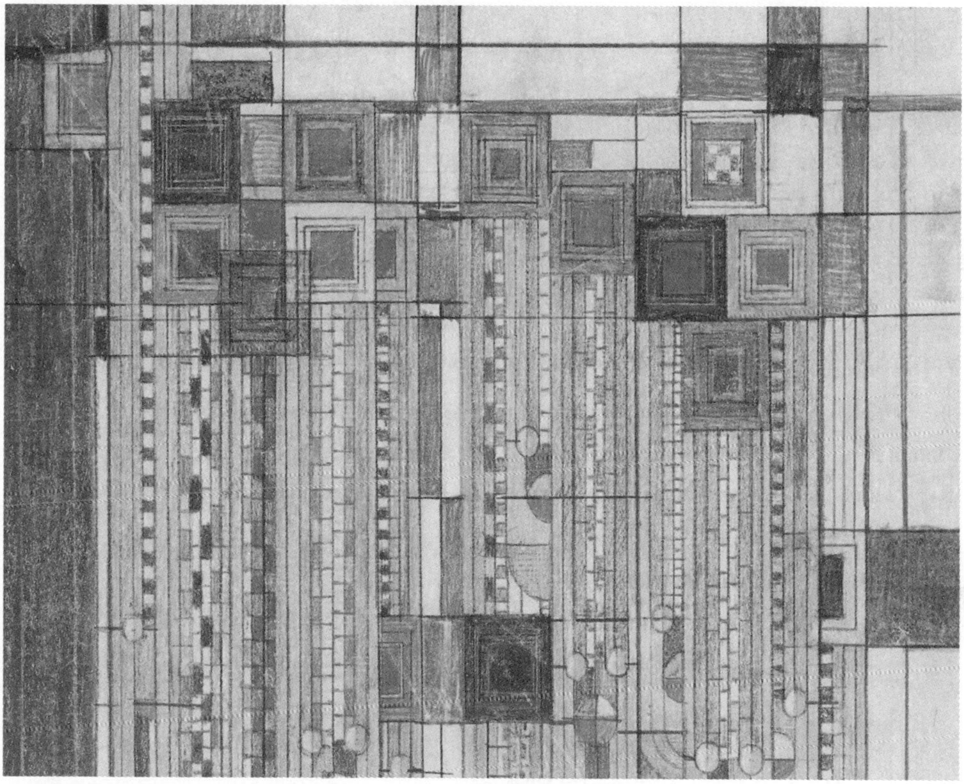

Great things can be reduced to small things, and small things can be reduced to nothing.

-Chinese Proverb

If you can keep your head, when all around are losing theirs.

-Rudyard Kipling

Those who do not learn from history are doomed to repeat its mistakes.

-Unknown

I never met a library I didn't like.

-V. Orehck III (fictitious)

Chapter Contents

Chapter Objectives

- Study another example of software development using OCD.
- Take a first look at how to build functions.
- Study how a function is called, how arguments and parameters are used to pass values to the function, and how the function can return a value to the calling function.
- Investigate how a function is executed and how execution returns to the calling function.
- Show how the design process for functions is virtually identical to that for programs.
- Take a first quick look at the three basic control structures—sequential, selection, and repetition—and give examples of problems whose solutions use these control structures.
- Introduce briefly one of C++'s statements used to implement selective execution—the `if` statement.
- Introduce briefly two of C++'s statements used to implement repetitive execution—the `for` and `while` statements.
- Study libraries, and see how they can be used to reuse items in different programs.
- (Optional) Give a brief indication of the area of computability theory.
- (Optional) Take a first look at class methods.

Most people dislike unnecessary work, and the theme of this chapter is to show how to avoid it in programming by writing code that is *reusable*. We will first describe reusability on a "local" level in which segments of code are *encapsulated in a function* that is separate from the program. Such a function can then be used anywhere in the program, and because it is separate from the program, it is easy to copy and paste it for use with other programs.

A better way to facilitate such reusability on a larger scale, however, is to store such functions in a *library*. Any program can then retrieve functions from the library and use them, just as the program in Figure 3.1 used the function `pow()` from the `cmath` library.

In this chapter, we will first look at functions in some detail and give several examples, because understanding how to construct and use functions is fundamental to writing reusable code. In the last section, we will show how libraries are constructed. It must be realized, however, that this first look at functions and libraries is only an introduction. Many more features and uses will be given in the chapters that follow. The optional *OBJECTive Thinking* section introduces one way that functions are used as class methods to carry out class operations.

4.1 Introductory Example: Temperature Conversion with Expressions

There are many problems whose solutions involve the use of one or more formulas, such as the problem in Figure 3.1 of computing the amount of energy released by a quantity of matter that was solved using Einstein's equation $e = m \times c^2$. Writing programs to solve such problems is usually straightforward if we know how to write C++ expressions for the formulas. Another example, which we will use throughout this chapter, is the following temperature-conversion problem.

PROBLEM: TEMPERATURE CONVERSION

Two scales used to measure temperature are the Fahrenheit and Celsius scales. A program is needed to convert temperatures in Fahrenheit to the equivalent Celsius temperatures.

Object-Centered Design

Behavior. The program will display on the screen a prompt for a Fahrenheit temperature. The user will enter a numeric value from the keyboard, which the program will read. The program will compute the Celsius temperature equivalent to that Fahrenheit temperature and display this Celsius temperature on the screen along with descriptive text.

Objects. From the statement of the desired behavior, we can identify the following objects:

	Software Objects		
Problem Objects	**Type**	**Kind**	**Name**
screen	`ostream`	varying	`cout`
prompt	`string`	constant	none
Fahrenheit temperature	`double`	varying	*tempFahrenheit*

Problem Objects	Software Objects		
	Type	Kind	Name
keyboard	`istream`	varying	`cin`
Celsius temperature	`double`	varying	*tempCelsius*
descriptive text	`string`	constant	none

Operations. The formula for converting temperature measured in Fahrenheit to Celsius is

$$C = \frac{F - 32.0}{1.8}$$

where F is the Fahrenheit temperature and C is the corresponding Celsius temperature. This gives two additional data objects—the numeric values 32.0 and 1.8. We will not include in our object list constant values such as these that are unlikely to change in the foreseeable future.

From this formula and our statement of the desired behavior, we can identify these operations:

i. Display a string on the screen
ii. Read a number from the keyboard
iii. Compute the Celsius equivalent of a Fahrenheit temperature
   a. Perform real subtraction
   b. Perform real division
iv. Display a number on the screen

Algorithm. As in all of our programs thus far, each of these operations is provided in C++, so we can organize them into an algorithm, as follows:

1. Output a prompt for a Fahrenheit temperature to `cout`.
2. Input *tempFahrenheit* from `cin`.
3. Calculate *tempCelsius* = (*tempFahrenheit* – 32.0) / 1.8.
4. Output *tempCelsius* (and descriptive text) to `cout`.

Coding and Testing. A C++ program that solves this problem is given in Figure 4.1.[1]

Fig. 4.1 Converting a temperature—version 1. (Part 1 of 2)

```
/* f2c.cpp converts a temperature from Fahrenheit to Celsius,
 * using the standard Fahrenheit-to-Celsius conversion formula.
 *
 * Input:   tempFahrenheit
 * Output:  tempCelsius
************************************************************************/
```

1. As we noted previously, with some C++ compilers that are not ISO/ANSI compliant, it may be necessary to use the old names for the libraries—for example, `iostream.h` instead of `iostream`—and to remove the `using namespace std;` line.

Fig. 4.1 Converting a temperature—version 1. (Part 2 of 2)

```
#include <iostream>
using namespace std;

int main()
{
   cout << "This program converts a temperature\n"
           "from Fahrenheit to Celsius.\n";

   cout <<"\nEnter a Fahrenheit temperature: ";
   double tempFahrenheit;
   cin >> tempFahrenheit;

   double tempCelsius = (tempFahrenheit - 32.0) / 1.8;

   cout << tempFahrenheit << " degrees Fahrenheit is equivalent to "
        << tempCelsius << " degrees Celsius\n";
}
```

Sample runs:

```
This program converts a temperature
from Fahrenheit to Celsius.

Enter a Fahrenheit temperature: 212
212 degrees Fahrenheit is equivalent to 100 degrees Celsius
This program converts a temperature
from Fahrenheit to Celsius.

Please enter a Fahrenheit temperature: 32
32 degrees Fahrenheit is equivalent to 0 degrees Celsius
```

4.2 Introductory Example: Temperature Conversion with Functions

Before writing a program like that in Figure 4.1, we should ask whether we (or someone else) might someday need to expand this program or perhaps write new programs that will use the same conversions. If so, we should construct a function that *encapsulates* the code used to carry out the conversion as illustrated in the program in Figure 4.2, rather than build the conversion into our program, like we did in Figure 4.1.

Fig. 4.2 Converting a temperature—version 2.

```
/* f2c.cpp converts a temperature from Fahrenheit to Celsius,
 * using a conversion function named fahrToCelsius().
 *
 *  Input:  tempFahrenheit
 *  Output: tempCelsius
 *********************************************************************/

#include <iostream>
using namespace std;

double fahrToCelsius(double tempFahr);          // function prototype

int main()
{
   cout << "This program converts a temperature\n"
           "from Fahrenheit to Celsius.\n";

   cout << "\nEnter a Fahrenheit temperature: ";
   double tempFahrenheit;
   cin >> tempFahrenheit;

   double tempCelsius = fahrToCelsius(tempFahrenheit);

   cout << tempFahrenheit << " degrees Fahrenheit is equivalent to "
        << tempCelsius << " degrees Celsius\n";
}

/* fahrToCelsius converts a temperature from Fahrenheit to Celsius.
 *
 * Receive: tempFahr, a (double) Fahrenheit temperature
 * Return:  the equivalent Celsius temperature
 *********************************************************************/

double fahrToCelsius(double tempFahr)          // function definition
{
   return (tempFahr - 32.0) / 1.8;
}
```

The program in Figure 4.2 produces exactly the same output as that in Figure 4.1, but the flow of execution is very different. Here the Fahrenheit-to-Celsius conversion is performed using a function that is defined following the main function. The following diagram illustrates the flow of control in this new program.

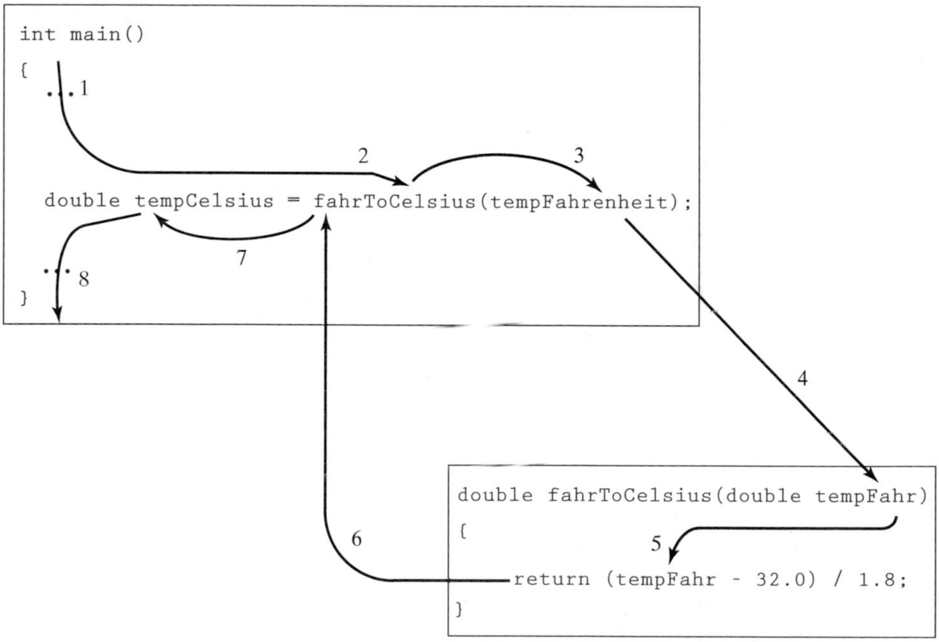

When the program is run, execution proceeds from the beginning of the program in the usual manner (1), until the assignment statement containing the **call** to function `fahrToCelsius()` is reached (2).[2] At that time, the function's **argument** `tempFahrenheit` is evaluated (3) and copied into the **parameter** `tempFahr` in the function `fahrToCelsius()` (4). Control is transferred from the main function to the function `fahrToCelsius()`, which begins execution (5). The expression

```
(tempFahr - 32.0) / 1.8
```

is evaluated, and since `tempFahr` contains a copy of the value of `tempFahrenheit`, the resulting value is the Celsius equivalent of the value of `tempFahrenheit`. The `return` statement makes this value the **return value** of `fahrToCelsius()` and transfers execution back to the main function (6). There, the return value of `fahrToCelsius()` is assigned to `tempCelsius` (7), and execution proceeds normally through the rest of the main function (8).

We now describe how such C++ functions are constructed, using the program in Figure 4.2 to illustrate the discussion.

---

2. We will use notation of the form *`functionName`*`()` for function names, with the parentheses used to distinguish them from identifiers that do not represent functions.

DEFINING A FUNCTION

A C++ function definition can be described as follows:

C++ Function Definition

Form:

```
return_type function_name (parameter_declaration_list )
{
   statement_list
}
```

where

return_type is the type of value returned by the function or the keyword `void` if the function does not return a value;

function_name is an identifier that names the function;

parameter_declaration_list is a list of declarations of the function's parameters, separated by commas—it is omitted if there are no parameters;

statement_list is a sequence of statements that describe the behavior of the function.

Purpose: Defines a function. A call to the function causes execution of the statements in the statement list and a return to the calling program unit after execution of the function is terminated, usually by encountering a `return` statement.

Thus, in the program in Figure 4.2, the lines

```
double fahrToCelsius(double tempFahr)
{
   return (tempFahr - 32.0) / 1.8;
}
```

constitute the definition of the function `fahrToCelsius()`. The first occurrence of `double` specifies the return type of the function; `fahrToCelsius` is the identifier naming the function, and inside the parentheses that follow the function name, the parameter declaration list declares a single parameter whose type is `double` and whose name is `tempFahr`. The **body** of the function consists of a pair of curly braces surrounding a `return` statement, whose syntax is

```
return expression;
```

where the type of *expression* matches the return type of the function.

Functions are often called **subprograms,** because defining a function is similar to defining a program. The same steps used to design a program can be used to design a function:

1. Behavior
2. Objects

3. Operations
4. Algorithm
5. Coding
6. Testing, execution, and debugging
7. Maintenance

Behavior. In addition to input from the keyboard or output to the screen, the behavior of a function typically describes things that the function must

- **receive** from the calling function
- **return** to the calling function.

For example, we might describe the behavior of `fahrToCelsius()` as follows: The function should receive from its caller a Fahrenheit temperature to be converted to Celsius. The function should return to its caller the Celsius temperature equivalent to this Fahrenheit temperature.

Objects. It is especially important for a function's behavior to specify each value that the function must receive or return to solve its problem. This receive or return information is often described as the function's **specification**, because it specifies the behavior of the function. Since received values can be thought of as flowing from the caller *into* the function, and returned values as flowing from the function *out* to the caller, we call this characteristic the **movement** of the objects with respect to the function and note it in the object list for the function:

	Software Objects			
Problem Objects	**Type**	**Kind**	**Movement**	**Name**
a Fahrenheit temperature	`double`	varying	received (in)	*tempFahr*
the equivalent Celsius temperature	`double`	varying	returned (out)	none

Function Design. Besides the name of the function, the **heading** in a function definition must include the following:

1. **Parameters**—variables declared within the function heading's parentheses—to hold the values that are received. If no values are *received*, no parameters are required.
2. The *return type* of the function is the type of the value returned by the function. If the function does not return a value, then its return type is indicated by the **keyword** `void`—the absence of any type.

The specification of the function provides this information. For example, the specification for `fahrToCelsius()` tells us that

1. `fahrToCelsius()` requires one parameter of type `double`;
2. the return type of `fahrToCelsius()` is `double`.

Once we have this information, we can begin defining the function. If we choose the name `tempFahr` for the parameter, we can construct the following **function stub** for `fahrToCelsius()`:

```
double fahrToCelsius(double tempFahr)
{
}
```

A function stub is a function definition consisting of a function heading plus a function body (a pair of curly braces) containing no statements. Once we have written such a stub, all that remains is to design an algorithm that solves the problem and then encode that algorithm within the body of the function stub.

Designing the algorithm for a function is almost the same as designing the algorithm for a program. The only differences are as follows:

Algorithm for a Program	Algorithm for a Function
Usually includes a step to *input* the data values required in solution of the problem	Usually the *parameters already contain the data values* because values of the arguments are copied into the function's parameters when the function is called
Usually includes a step to *output* data values	Usually contains a step to *return* a data value to the function that calls it

Thus, when the function `fahrToCelsius()` begins execution, we can assume that parameter `tempFahr` already contains the Fahrenheit temperature to be converted. This leaves the following operations to be performed:

Operations:

Real subtraction (`tempFahr - 32.0`)
Real division (`(tempFahr - 32.0) / 1.8`)
Return a real value

These operations can be organized into the following simple algorithm for function `fahrToCelsius()`:

Algorithm for Fahrenheit-to-Celsius Conversion Function

1. Return (*tempFahr* – 32.0) / 1.8.

Coding a Function. Given a C++ function stub and a pseudocode algorithm, this algorithm is encoded in C++ by inserting appropriate C++ statements into the stub. In our example, the `return` statement and predefined C++ operations can be used to code the single instruction in the algorithm:

```
double fahrToCelsius(double tempFahr)
{
   return (tempFahr - 32.0) / 1.8;
}
```

As this example illustrates, the specification of a function determines the form of a function's heading, and its algorithm determines the content of the function's body:

Design Component	Determines
Specification	The form of the function heading
Algorithm	The content of the function body

For a simple function like `fahrToCelsius()`, the specification and design steps may seem like extra work, but they are absolutely essential for more complicated problems. A well-defined specification makes the process of constructing the function heading almost mechanical, and a well-defined algorithm can make the process of coding the body of the function similarly straightforward.

Testing, Execution, and Debugging. Just as a program must be tested to verify its correctness, a function should also be rigorously tested to ensure that it is correct. Functions written for real-world software projects are often large and complex, and they must be thoroughly checked for logical errors before they are incorporated into the project.

To test a function, we can write a program that calls the function with specific values and displays the values returned by the function. Such a program is called a **driver program** because it "test drives" the function. Figure 4.3 shows a simple driver program for `fahrToCelsius()`. The sample run indicates that `fahrToCelsius()` is performing correctly for the test values we have chosen.

Fig. 4.3 A sample driver program. (Part 1 of 2)

```
#include <iostream>                  // cin, cout, <<, >>
using namespace std;

double fahrToCelsius(double tempFahr);    // function prototype

int main()
{
   cout << "212F => " << fahrToCelsius(212)
        << "C\n 32F => " << fahrToCelsius(32)
        << "C\n";
}

double fahrToCelsius(double tempFahr)      // function definition
{
   return (tempFahr - 32.0) / 1.8;
}
```

Fig. 4.3 A sample driver program. (Part 2 of 2)

Sample run:

```
212F => 100c
32F => 0c
```

FUNCTION PROTOTYPES

The programs in Figures 4.2 and 4.3 each contain the line

```
double fahrToCelsius(double tempFahr);
```

before the main function. This is called the **prototype**, or **declaration**, of the function `fahrToCelsius()`.[3] A general rule in C++ is that things must be declared before they are used so that the compiler can check whether each is being used in a manner consistent with its type. This principle applies to functions also; the compiler must be able to check whether they are being called correctly. The information about the function needed by the compiler to do this is supplied by the function's prototype:

- The *return type* of the function
- The function's *name*
- The *number of parameters* for the function
- The *type* of each parameter

The (simplified) syntax of a function prototype is as follows:

C++ Function Prototype

Form:

```
return_type function_name (parameter_declaration_list );
```

where

`return_type` is the type of value returned by the function or the keyword `void` if the function does not return a value;

`function_name` is the name of the function;

`parameter_declaration_list` is a list of declarations of the function's parameters, separated by commas. (Parameter names are optional, but it is good practice to include them to indicate what the parameters represent.)

Purpose: Declares a function. Provides sufficient information for the compiler to check that the function is being called correctly, with respect to the number and types of the parameters and the return type of the function.

3. We will use the term *prototype* because beginning programmers often confuse the words "declaration" and "definition."

> Note that as with other declarations, a semicolon is placed at the end of a function prototype to make it a statement.

NOTE

A function prototype can thus be the same as the heading in a function definition followed by a semicolon. For example, to prototype `fahrToCelsius()` in Figures 3.2 and 3-3, we wrote

```
double fahrToCelsius(double tempFahr);
```

This is sufficient to inform the compiler that the return type of the function is `double`, that its name is `fahrToCelsius`, that it has one parameter, and that the type of that parameter is `double`. Thus, if we should call the function incorrectly, such as passing it two arguments as in

```
double tempCelsius = fahrToCelsius(32.0, 'F');
```

the compiler can generate an error message to inform us of the mistake.

Although C++ allows functions to be declared inside a calling function, in this text we will declare them outside, because this is consistent with the use of libraries (see Section 4.6). It also improves readability, because placing function prototypes inside calling functions tends to clutter and obscure the structure of these functions.

CALLING A FUNCTION

Since a function call returns a value, it is a kind of expression, which means that a function can be called at any point where an expression whose type matches the function's return type is permitted. Thus, because the return type of `fahrToCelsius()` is `double`, a call to `fahrToCelsius()` can be used to initialize a variable of type `double` such as `tempCelsius` in the program in Figure 4.2:

```
double tempCelsius = fahrToCelsius(tempFahrenheit);
```

Similarly, the output statement in the driver program in Figure 4.3,

```
cout << "212F => " << fahrToCelsius(212)
     << "C\n 32F => " << fahrToCelsius(32)
     << "C\n";
```

which contains two calls to `fahrToCelsius()`, is a valid statement, since the `<<` operator can be used to output the value of a `double` expression to `cout`.

LOCAL VARIABLES

The only variable used by the function `fahrToCelsius()` is the parameter `tempFahr`. Many functions, however, use other variables or constants in computing their return values. For example, one of the formulas for computing the wind chill index is given by the rather complicated formula

$$\text{wind chill} = 35.74 + 0.6215 \times t - 35.75 \times v^{0.16} + 0.4275 \times t \times v^{0.16}$$

where v is the wind speed in miles per hour and t is the temperature in degrees Fahrenheit.[4] The function `windChill()` in Figure 4.4 uses this formula to compute the wind chill index, but it breaks it up into two steps to simplify the computation:

1. Compute $vPart = -35.75 \times 0.4275 \times t$.
2. Compute wind chill $= 35.74 + 0.6215 \times t + vPart \times v^{0.16}$.

The variable `vPart` is used to store the result computed in Step 1. Figure 4.4 also shows a simple driver program to test `windChill()`.

Fig. 4.4 Computing wind chill. (Part 1 of 2)

```
/* This is a driver program to test the windChill() function.
 *************************************************************/

#include <iostream>                // cin, cout, <<, >>
using namespace std;

double windChill(double tempFahr, double windSpeed); // prototype

int main()
{
   double temp,                    // Fahrenheit temperature
          wind;                    // wind speed (mph)

   cout << "Enter Fahrenheit temperature and wind speed (mph): ";
   cin >> temp >> wind;
   cout << "Wind chill index is " << windChill(temp, wind) << endl;
}

/* windChill computes wind chill.
 *
 * Receive: tempFahr, a Fahrenheit temperature
 *          windSpeed, in miles per hour
 *
 * Return:  the wind chill
 *************************************************************/

#include <cmath>                   // pow()
using namespace std;
```

4. This formula, announced by the National Weather Service in August 2001, replaces the formula

$$\text{wind chill} = 91.4 - (0.474677 - 0.020425) \times v + 0.303107 \times \sqrt{v} \times (91.4 - t)$$

used for several years. (See `http://www.nws.noaa.gov/iln/tables.htm`.)

Fig. 4.4 Computing wind chill. (Part 2 of 2)

```
double windChill(double tempFahr, double windSpeed)   // definition
{
   double v_part = -35.75 + 0.4275 * tempFahr;
   return 35.74 + 0.6215 * tempFahr + v_part * pow(windSpeed, 0.16);
}
```

Sample runs:

```
Enter Fahrenheit temperature and wind speed (mph): 10 5
Wind chill index is 1.23564

Enter Fahrenheit temperature and wind speed (mph): 0 20
Wind chill index is  21.9952

Enter Fahrenheit temperature and wind speed (mph): -10 45
Wind chill index is -44.0695
```

Variables such as `v_part`, constants, and parameters that are declared within a function are said to be **local** to that function because they are *defined only while the function is executing;* they are undefined both before and after its execution.[5] (See Potential Problem 2 in the Programming Pointers at the end of the chapter.) This means that they can be accessed only within the function; any attempt to use them outside the function is an error. It also means that the name of a local variable, constant, or parameter may be used outside the function for some other purpose without conflict.

FUNCTIONS THAT RETURN NOTHING

In applying object-centered design, one sometimes encounters an operation that returns nothing to its caller. For example, in a problem that involves monetary calculations, we might need to display a dollar amount, formatted as a monetary value. Because there is no one predefined C++ operation that performs this operation, we would probably use the output operator and several format manipulators[6]

```
int main()
{
   // ...
```

5. These are also called **automatic** objects because they automatically begin to exist when the function begins executing and automatically cease to exist when it is finished. Prepending the keyword `static` to a local object's declaration makes it a **static** object, which will retain its value from one function call to the next.

6. As noted earlier, if your compiler is not fully ISO/ANSI-C++ compliant, you may have to use the `setiosflags` manipulator from `<iomanip.h>` to do some of the formatting. See Chapter 5 for more details.

```
   cout << fixed << showpoint
        << right << setprecision(2)
        << '$' << dollarAmount;
}
```

to display a dollar amount in a nice format like

```
$4.95
```

Putting such details in a main function, however, can make a program messy and cluttered, especially when they must be used at several different places. It would be much better if we could simply write a single statement such as

```
int main()
{
   // ...
   printAsMoney(dollarAmount);
}
```

In some languages, subprograms like `printAsMoney()` are called *procedures* or *subroutines* and have a syntax that is different from that for functions. In C++, however, the *only subprograms are functions*. This means that we will have to write a function named `printAsMoney()`. A specification for this function is

Receive: `dollars`, a `double`

Output: `dollars`, appropriately formatted as a monetary value

Note how this specification clarifies the problem. It does not require the function to return anything to its caller, but instead it performs output for its caller.

From this specification, we see that the function `printAsMoney()` will have a `double` parameter named `dollars`, but what do we use as the return type of a function that returns nothing to its caller? For such situations, C++ provides the keyword `void` to denote the absence of any type. Because function `printAsMoney()` returns nothing to its caller, its return type should be given as `void`:

```
void printAsMoney(double dollars);
```

Void functions in C++ are, therefore, the counterparts of procedures and subroutines in other programming languages.

Since `void` functions do not return values, they cannot be called in the same way as the functions we have considered up to now. They are not used in expressions, but rather are called in statements of the form

```
function_Name(argument_list);
```

For example, the statement

```
printAsMoney(dollarAmount);
```

can be used to display the value of `dollarAmount`. Attempting to use such function calls in expressions such as

```
cout << "Amount due: "
     << printAsMoney(dollarAmount)   // ERROR!
     << endl;
```

is an error, because `printAsMoney(dollarAmount)` returns no value.

Figure 4.5 gives the complete definition of `printAsMoney()`. It also shows a program that inputs the amount of a purchase and the amount received and uses `printAsMoney()` to display the amount returned to the customer.

Fig. 4.5 Monetary transactions. (Part 1 of 2)

```
/* transaction.cpp computes the amount to be returned for a purchase.
 *
 * Input:  purchase, payment
 * Output: amount returned to customer (via printAsMoney())
 ********************************************************************/

#include <iostream>      // cin, cout, <<, >>, ...
#include <iomanip>       // setprecision, ...
using namespace std;

void printAsMoney(double dollars);          // prototype

int main()
{
   double purchase,                         // amount of purchase
          payment;                          // amount paid
   cout << "Enter amount of purchase: ";
   cin >> purchase;
   cout << "Enter amount paid (>= purchase): ";
   cin >> payment;
   cout << "Amount to return is: ";
   printAsMoney(payment - purchase);
   cout << endl;
}

/* printAsMoney displays an amount in monetary format.
 *
 * Receive: dollars, the double value to be displayed
 * Output:  dollars in monetary format
 ******************************************************************/

void printAsMoney(double dollars)
{
   cout << fixed << showpoint
        << setprecision(2)
        << '$' << dollars;
}
```

Fig. 4.5 Monetary transactions. (Part 2 of 2)

Sample runs:

```
Enter amount of purchase: 4.01
Enter amount paid (>= purchase): 5.00
Amount to return is: $0.99

Enter amount of purchase: 9.00
Enter amount paid (>= purchase): 20.00
Amount to return is: $11.00
```

The effect of shifting details from `main()` to `printAsMoney()` is to "clean up" the main function by hiding the money-format details in a function, which makes the main function easier to read. In computer science, such detail hiding is called an **abstraction.** An abstraction is a view of something that simplifies it by hiding some of its details. Our `printAsMoney()` function is therefore an abstraction of the display-a-monetary-value operation, because it "hides" the details of how the operation is accomplished (at least as far as readers of the main function are concerned).

SUMMARY

Functions are an essential part of C++, because they are used to write program components that are reusable. Because they are so fundamental to C++ programming, we review some of the important ideas about functions that have emerged thus far:

- For each value that a function must receive from its caller, a *variable* to hold that value must be declared within the parentheses of the function heading. Such variables are called the *parameters* of the function. For example, in the definition of the function `fahrToCelsius()`,

  ```
  double fahrToCelsius(double tempFahr)
  {
    return (tempFahr - 32.0) / 1.8;
  }
  ```

  the variable `tempFahr` is a parameter of `fahrToCelsius()`.

- A *value* that is supplied to a function when it is called is an *argument* to that function call. For example, in the function call

  ```
  double tempCelsius = fahrToCelsius(tempFahrenheit);
  ```

  `tempFahrenheit` is an argument to the function `fahrToCelsius()`. When execution reaches this call, the value of the argument `tempFahrenheit` is *passed* (i.e., copied) from the main function to the parameter `tempFahr` in function `fahrToCelsius()`.[7]

- When one function `f()` calls another function `g()`, the flow of execution is from `f()` to `g()` and then back to `f()`. To illustrate, consider again the main function's call of function `fahrToCelsius()` in Figure 4.2:

```
//...
int main()
{
    //...
    double tempCelsius = fahrToCelsius(tempFahrenheit);
    //...
}
```

  When the call to `fahrToCelsius()` is encountered, execution proceeds as follows:

  1. The value of the argument `tempFahrenheit` is determined.
  2. This value is passed from the main function to `fahrToCelsius()` and copied into the parameter `tempFahr`.
  3. Control is then transferred from the line containing the function call (in `main()`) to the first statement of `fahrToCelsius()`, which begins execution using the value of its parameter.
  4. When a `return` statement (or the final statement of the function) is executed, control is transferred back to the caller (i.e., the main function), and execution of the caller resumes.

- *Local variables, constants, and parameters are defined only while the function containing them is executing.* They can be accessed only within the function, and any attempt to use them outside the function is an error.
- `void` is used to specify the return type of a function that returns no values. Such functions are called with statements of the form *`function_Name(argument_list)`*`;`

The ability to define functions is a powerful tool in object-oriented programming. If the solution of some problem requires that an operation not provided in C++ (as an operator or as a predefined function) be applied to some item in that problem, we can simply

1. define a function to perform that operation and
2. apply that function to the item

as we did with the temperature-conversion operation `fahrToCelsius()`. As we shall see in Section 4.6, such functions can then be stored in a library, from which they can be retrieved when needed.

---

7. In Chapter 8, we will see that there also is a different kind of parameter called a *reference parameter* that shares the same memory location as the corresponding argument. This means that the value of the argument is not copied to the parameter because they refer to the same memory location and thus have the same value. It also means that modifying the parameter in the function will also modify the corresponding argument.

✔ Quick Quiz 4.2

1. In addition to input and output objects, what two other kinds of objects are usually included in the description of a function's behavior?
2. In the function heading `double sum(int a, char b)`, a and b are called ________.
3. For a function whose heading is `double sum(int a, char b)`, the type of the value returned by the function is ________.
4. The keyword ________ is used to indicate the return type of a function that returns no value.
5. A function stub is a function definition in which the function's body contains ________.

Questions 6–10 deal with the following function definition:

```
int what(int n)
{
   return (n * (n + 1)) / 2;
}
```

6. If the statement `number1 = what(number2);` appears in the main function, `number2` is called a(n)________ in this function call.
7. If the statement `int number = what(3);` appears in the main function, the value assigned to `number` will be ________.
8. (True or false) The value assigned to `number` by the statement `int number = what(2+3);` in the main function will be 15.
9. (True or false) The value assigned to `number` by the statement `int number = what(1, 5);` in the main function will be 3.
10. Write a prototype for function `what()`.
11. Write a function definition that calculates values of $x^2 + \sqrt{x}$.
12. Write a function definition that calculates the integer average of two integers.
13. Write a function definition that displays three integers on three lines separated by two blank lines.

Exercises 4.2

The following exercises ask you to write functions to compute various quantities. To test these functions, you should write driver programs as instructed in Programming Problems 1–12 at the end of this chapter.

1. Write a function `celsiusToFahr()` that returns the Fahrenheit equivalent of a Celsius temperature.
2. U.S. dollars are typically converted to another country's currency by multiplying the U.S. dollars by an *exchange rate*, which varies over time. For example, if on a given day, the U.S.-to-Canada exchange rate is 1.22, then $10.00 in U.S. currency can be exchanged for $12.20 in Canadian currency. Write a function `US_to_Canadian()` that, given a dollar amount in U.S. currency and the exchange rate, returns the equivalent number of dollars in Canadian currency.
3. Proceed as in Exercise 2, but write a function `Canadian_to_US()` that, given a dollar amount in Canadian currency and the exchange rate, returns the equivalent number of dollars in U.S. currency.

4. Write a function `range()` that, given two integers, returns the range between them—that is, the absolute value of their difference.

5. Write a function `wages()` that, given the number of hours worked and an hourly pay rate, returns the wages earned.

6. Write a function that, given the radius of a circle, returns its circumference. ($C = 2\pi r$)

7. Write a function that, given the radius of a circle, returns its area. $\left(A = \pi r^2\right)$

8. Write a function that, given the lengths of the sides of a rectangle, returns its perimeter. ($P = 2l + 2w$)

9. Write a function that, given the lengths of the sides of a square, returns its area. $\left(A = s^2\right)$

10. Write a function that, given the lengths of the three sides of a triangle, returns its perimeter. ($P = s_1 + s_2 + s_3$)

11. Write a function that, given the lengths of the three sides of a triangle, returns its area. (The area of a triangle can be found by using *Hero's formula*

$$\sqrt{s(s-a)(s-b)(s-c)}$$

where a, b, and c are the lengths of the sides and s is one half of the perimeter.)

12. The number of bacteria in a culture can be estimated by $N \cdot e^{kt}$, where N is the initial population, k is a rate constant, and t is time. Write a function to calculate the number of bacteria present for given values of N, k, and t.

13. Write a function that, given a number of seconds, returns the equivalent number of minutes.

14. Write a function that, given a number of minutes, returns the equivalent number of hours.

15. Write a function that, given a number of hours, returns the equivalent number of days.

16. Using the functions from Exercises 13–15, write a function that, given a number of seconds, returns the equivalent number of days.

17. Write a function that accepts a seven-digit integer representing a phone number and displays it in the format *abc-defg*.

18. The wind chill index, described in the text, was developed in 1941, with the latest revision of the formula for it published in 2001. It is a measure of discomfort due to the combined cold and wind and is based on the rate of heat loss due to various combinations of temperature and wind. The *heat index*, developed in 1979, is a measure of discomfort due to the combination of heat and high humidity and is based on studies of evaporative skin cooling for combinations of temperature and humidity. It is computed using the formula

$$\begin{aligned}\texttt{heat index} = {} & -42.379 + 2.04901523 \times t + 10.14333127 \times r \\ & - 0.22475541 \times t \times r - (6.83783\text{E}{-3}) \times t^2 \\ & - (5.48171\text{E}{-2}) \times r^2 + (1.22874\text{E}{-3}) \times t^2 \times r \\ & + (8.5282\text{E}{-4}) \times t \times r^2 - (1.99\text{E}{-6}) \times t^2 \times r^2\end{aligned}$$

where t is the temperature in degrees Fahrenheit and r is the relative humidity. Write a function to compute the heat index.

19. Write four functions `printZero()`, `printOne()`, `printTwo()`, and `printThree()` to produce "stick numbers" like those on a calculator display, for the digits 0, 1, 2, and 3, respectively:

```
 - - -          |          - - -         - - -
|     |         |               |             |
|     |         |          - - -         - - -
|     |         |         |                   |
 - - -          |          - - -         - - -
```

4.3 Functions That Use Selection[8]

Although the C++ language features we have studied thus far are sufficient to write functions that encode a variety of formulas, there are many problems whose solutions require more. To see this, consider the following problem:

PROBLEM: FINDING A MINIMUM OF TWO VALUES

Write a function that, given two real values, returns the minimum of the two values.

Object-Centered Design

Behavior. Our function should receive two real values from its caller. If the first is less than the second, the function should return the first value; otherwise, it should return the second value.

Objects. From the behavioral description, we can identify the following objects in the problem:

	Software Objects			
Problem Objects	**Type**	**Kind**	**Movement**	**Name**
The first value	`double`	variable	received	*first*
The second value	`double`	variable	received	*second*
The minimum value	`double`	variable	returned	none

We can thus specify this problem as follows:

Receive: *first* and *second*, two real values

Return: the minimum of *first* and *second*

From this information, we can write the following stub for our function:

```
double minimum(double first, double second)
{
}
```

To fill in the body of the stub, we must look at what operations are needed to solve the problem.

---

8. This section provides only an introduction to the `if` statement. This material is used only in the *Case Study* sections of this chapter and the next and in a few examples and exercises in Section 5.4 so that it is possible to defer its study until Chapter 6 if one prefers to study all selection structures together.

Operations. Again, from our behavioral description, we can identify the following operations:

i. Receive two real values from the function's caller
ii. Compare two real values to see if one is less than the other
iii. Return the first value
iv. Return the second value
v. Select either iii or iv (but not both), based on the result of ii

The first operation will occur automatically through the normal function-call mechanism, because we are providing two parameters to hold the values received:

```
double minimum(double first, double second)
```

The second operation can be performed using the relational operator < described in Section 3.3:

```
first < second
```

We have also seen that `return` statements can be used to perform the third and fourth operations:

```
iii. return first;
iv. return second;
```

Our difficulty is with the last operation. How can we select one and only one of these two `return` statements? The answer is to use a new C++ statement called the `if` **statement,** which allows the selection of either of a pair of statements.

Algorithm. We can use a pseudocode version of an `if` statement to express the logic of our solution as follows:

Algorithm for Minimum of Two Numbers

If *first* < *second*
    return *first*;
otherwise
    return *second*.

Coding. In the syntax of C++, this algorithm can be expressed as shown in Figure 4.6.

Fig. 4.6 Function `minimum()`. (Part 1 of 2)

```
/* minimum finds the minimum of two doubles.
 *
 * Receive:   first and second
 * Return:    the smaller of first and second
*********************************************/
```

Fig. 4.6 Function `minimum()`. (Part 2 of 2)

```
double minimum(double first, double second)
{
   if (first < second)
      return first;
   else
      return second;
}
```

Testing. To verify that our function is correct, we can test it with a simple driver program like that in Figure 4.7 that calls the function, using a variety of input combinations to "exercise" it. Once we have verified that `minimum()` behaves correctly, it could be moved to a library as described in Section 4.6 for convenient reuse by any program needing its functionality.

Fig. 4.7 Driver for `minimum()`. (Part 1 of 2)

```
/* driver.cpp is a driver program to test the minimum function.
 ******************************************************************/

#include <iostream> // cin, cout, <<, >>
using namespace std;

double minimum(double first, double second);

int main()
{
   double num1, num2;
   cout << "Enter two numbers: ";
   cin >> num1 >> num2;
   cout << "Minimum is " << minimum(num1, num2) << endl;
}

/*** Insert the definition of function Minimum()
     from Figure 4.6 here. ***/
```

Sample runs:

```
Enter two numbers: -2 -5
Minimum is -5

Enter two numbers: -2 3
Minimum is -2
```

Fig. 4.7 Driver for `minimum()`. (Part 2 of 2)

```
Enter two numbers: 3 3
Minimum is 3

Enter two numbers: 3 5
Minimum is 3
```

SEQUENTIAL EXECUTION

If we think of the flow of execution through a program as traveling along a roadway, then **sequential execution** is like traveling down a straight road from one place to another:

A **flow diagram** is a chart that uses arrows to indicate the order in which the statements in the diagram are executed. The flow diagram that follows shows the straight line pattern of execution that characterizes sequential execution:

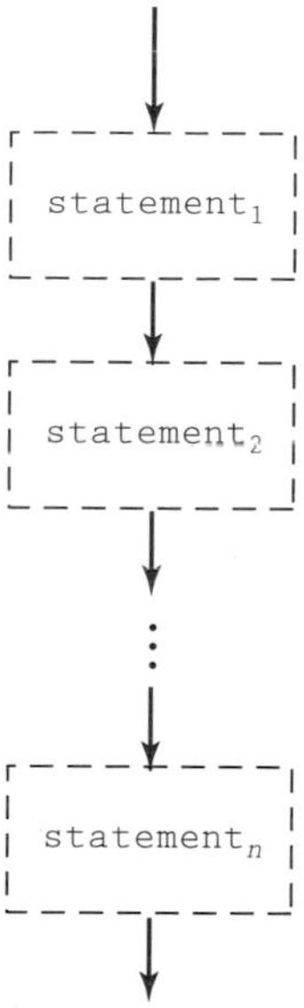

Some programmers prefer to use box diagrams instead of flow diagrams. A **box diagram** for sequential flow has the following form:

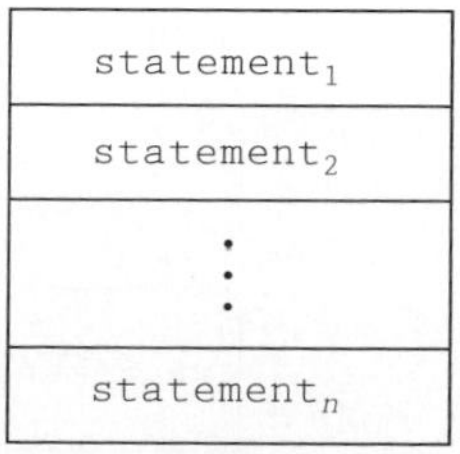

As these diagrams indicate, sequential execution refers to the execution of a sequence of statements in the order in which they are given, so that each statement is executed exactly once. All of the methods of earlier chapters and sections were methods that used only sequential control.

SELECTIVE EXECUTION

For situations where statements must be executed **selectively**, C++ provides the `if` **statement** (and other selection statements described in Chapter 6). If we think of the flow of execution through a program as traveling along a roadway, we might visualize an if statement as a fork in the road:

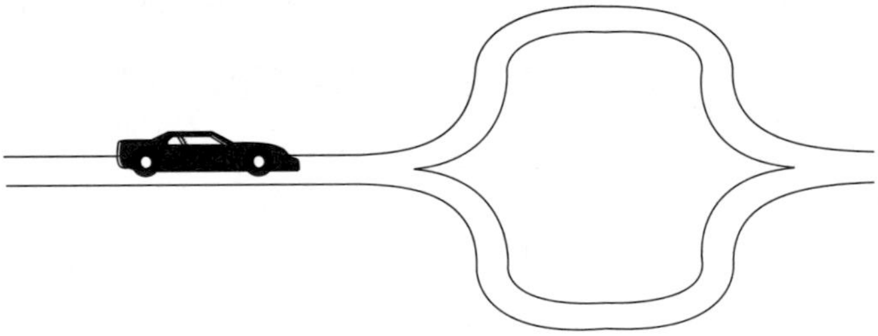

In a flow diagram, the fork is usually indicated by a diamond-shaped box that contains the boolean expression with one corner labeled true and one labeled false:

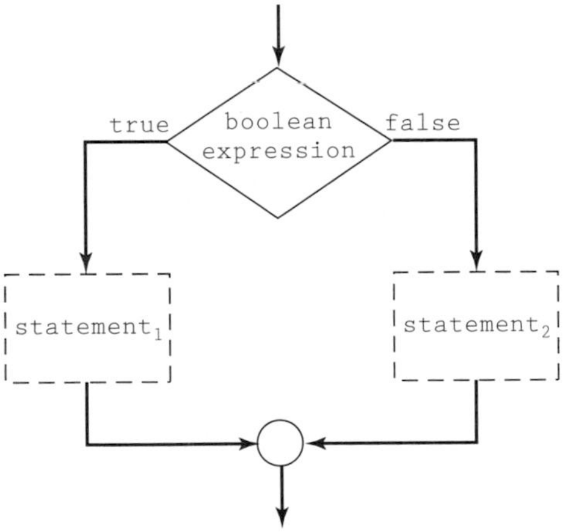

Based on the value of a boolean expression, execution will pass through *statement*$_1$ or through *statement*$_2$, *but not both*, before proceeding to the next statement. The corresponding box diagram for selection is

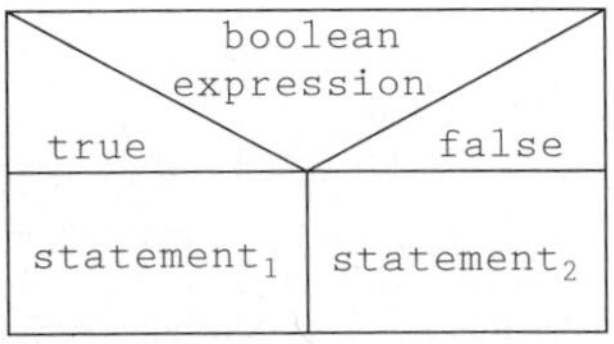

When execution reaches an `if` statement, the boolean expression is evaluated:

```
if (first < second)
   return first;
else
   return second;
```

If the expression is `true`, then the first statement is executed, and the trailing `else` and its statement are skipped:

```
if (true)
   return first;
else
   return second;
```

However, if the boolean expression evaluates to `false`, then the first statement is skipped, and the statement in the `else` part is executed:

```
if (false)
   return first;
else
   return second;
```

In general, the form of the `if` statement can be summarized as follows:

`if` Statement

Forms:

```
if (boolean_expression)
   statement

if (boolean_expression)
   statement_1
else
   statement_2

if (boolean_expression_1)
   statement_1
else if (boolean_expression_2)
   statement_2
     .
     .
     .
else if (boolean_expression_n)
   statement_n
else
   statement_n+1
```

where

`if` and `else` are keywords;

each *statement*, $statement_1$, $statement_2$, . . . is a C++ statement (and may be compound).

Purpose: In the first form, if the *boolean_expression* is true, then *statement* is executed; otherwise *statement* is bypassed.

In the second form, if the *boolean_expression* is true, $statement_1$ is executed and $statement_2$ is bypassed; otherwise $statement_1$ is bypassed and $statement_2$ is executed.

In the last form, if $boolean\_expression_1$ is true, $statement_1$ is executed and the remainder of the statement is bypassed; otherwise if $boolean\_expression_2$ is true, $statement_2$ is executed and the remainder of the statement is bypassed; and so on. If none of the $boolean\_expression_i$ is true, $statement_{n+1}$ (if present) is executed.

BLOCKS

When a group of statements must be selected for execution, we enclose them between curly braces { and } to form a single statement. This is called a **block** or a **compound statement**:

Block (Compound Statement)

Form:

```
{
    statement1
    statement2
        .
        .
        .
    statementn
}
```

where

each $statement_i$ is a C++ statement.

Purpose: The sequence of statements is treated as a single statement, in which $statement_1$, $statement_2$, . . ., $statement_n$ are executed in order, with each statement being executed exactly once.

Note that the block does not require a semicolon after the final curly brace; a block is a complete statement by itself.

We have already seen examples of blocks—the body of a function is a block. Thus, the general form of a function definition can be described by

```
return_type function_name(parameter_declaration_list)
block
```

A block is also used when more than one statement must be selected in an `if` statement; for example,

```
if (hoursWorked > 40.0)
{
   overtime = hours - 40.0;
   overtimePay = 1.5 * overtime * rate;
   regularPay = 40.0 * rate;
}
else
{
   regularPay = hours * rate;
   overtimePay = 0.0;
}
totalPay = regularPay + overtimePay;
```

If the value of `hoursWorked` is more than 40.0, the three statements in the first block are executed and the second block is bypassed. If the value of `hoursWorked` is 40.0 or less, the first block is bypassed and the second block is executed.

STYLE

There are a variety of styles used by programmers to write `if` statements. They differ in the placement of the statements with respect to the `if` and `else` keywords, the location of a block's curly braces, and so on. In our opinion, the key issue is *readability:*

Use a form that is easy to read.

Accordingly, we will

1. align the `if` and the `else` and
2. use white space and indentation to clearly mark the statements that are being selected by the `if` and `else`.

When a single statement is being selected, we will usually indent that statement on the line below the `if` or the `else`; for example,

```
if (first < second)
   return first;
else
   return second;
```

When a block of statements is involved, we will place the curly braces on separate lines, aligned with the `if` and `else`, and indent the statements they enclose; for example,

```
if (hours > 40.0)
{
   regularPay = 40.0 * rate;
   overtime = hours - 40.0;
   overtimePay = 1.5 * overtime * rate;
}
else
{
   regularPay = hours * rate;
   overtimePay = 0.0;
}
```

Another common style is to put the opening curly brace on the same line as the `if` (or the `else`) and align the closing curly brace with the `if` (or the `else`).

When writing `if-else-if` statements (the third form), we will place the `else` and the following `if` on the same line and indent the statements in each part; for example,

```
if (percentage >= 90)
   grade = 'A';
else if (percentage >= 80)
   grade = 'B';
else if (percentage >= 70)
   grade = 'C';
elsc if (percentage >= 60)
   grade = 'D';
else
   grade = 'F';
```

NESTED `if`s

The statements selected by `if` and `else` may be any C++ statements; in particular, they may be other `if` statements. In this case, an inner `if` statement is said to be **nested** within the outer `if` statement.

When one `if` statement is nested within another, it may not be clear with which `if` an `else` is associated. (See Potential Pitfall 7 in the Programming Pointers at the end of this chapter.) This ambiguity is resolved in C++ by the following important rule:

> *In a nested* `if` *statement, an* `else` *is matched with the nearest preceding unmatched* `if`.

Aligning each `else` with its corresponding `if` helps make this clear.

It should be noted that the `if-else  if` form we considered earlier is really a nested `if` statement. We are simply writing

```
if (boolean_expression1)
   statement1
else statement
```

where *statement* happens to be an `if` statement that begins on the same line:

```
if (boolean_expression1)
   statement1
else if (boolean_expression2)
   statement2
else
   statement
```

and so on. Each `if` in an `else if` clause is actually a new `if` statement that is only executed if the conditions in all of the preceding `if` statements are false. Similarly, each `else` in an `else if` clause is actually associated with the `if` of the preceding `else if` clause (or the first `if`), as shown by the arrows in the following diagram:

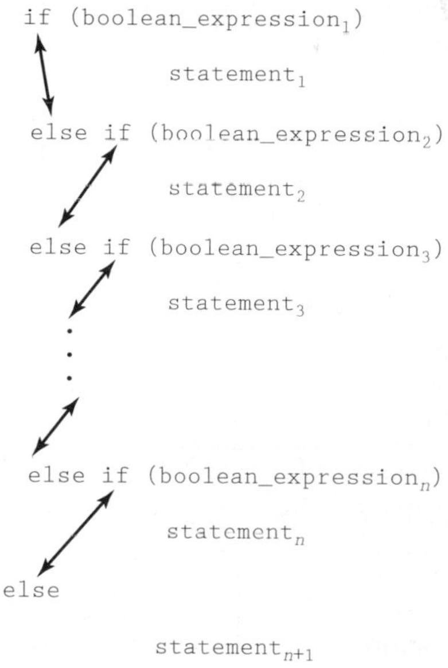

Quick Quiz 4.3

Questions 1–3 refer to the following `if` statement:

```
if (x >= y)
   cout << x;
else
   cout << y;
```

1. Describe the output produced if x is 6 and y is 5.
2. Describe the output produced if x is 5 and y is 5.
3. Describe the output produced if x is 5 and y is 6.

Questions 4–6 refer to the following `if` statement:

```
if (x >= 0)
   if (y >= 0)
      cout << x + y;
   else
      cout << x - y;
else
   cout << y - x;
```

4. Describe the output produced if `x` is 5 and `y` is 5.
5. Describe the output produced if `x` is 5 and `y` is –5.
6. Describe the output produced if `x` is –5 and `y` is 5.

Questions 7–11 refer to the following `if` statement:

```
if (n >= 90)
   cout << "excellent\n";
else if (n >= 80)
   cout << "good\n";
else if (n >= 70)
   cout << "fair\n";
else
   cout << "bad\n";
```

7. Describe the output produced if `n` is 100.
8. Describe the output produced if `n` is 90.
9. Describe the output produced if `n` is 89.
10. Describe the output produced if `n` is 70.
11. Describe the output produced if `n` is 0.
12. Write a statement that displays `"Out of range"` if `number` is negative or is greater than 100.
13. Write an efficient `if` statement to assign `n` the value 1 if $x \le 1.5$, 2 if $1.5 < x < 2.5$, and 3 otherwise.

Exercises 4.3

Exercises 1–4 refer to the following `if` statement:

```
if (x * y >= 0)
   cout << "yes\n";
else
   cout << "no\n";
```

1. Describe the output produced if `x` is 5 and `y` is 6.
2. Describe the output produced if `x` is 5 and `y` is –6.

3. Describe the output produced if x is –5 and y is 6.
4. Describe the output produced if x is –5 and y is –6.

Exercises 5–7 refer to the following `if` statement:

```
if (abs(n) <= 4)
   if (n > 0)
      cout << 2*n + 1;
   else
      cout << 2*n;
else
   cout << n << " out of range";
```

5. Describe the output produced if n is 2.
6. Describe the output produced if n is –7.
7. Describe the output produced if n is 0.

For Exercises 8–10, write `if` statements that will do what is required.

8. If `taxCode` is `'T'`, increase `price` by adding `taxRate` percentage of `price` to it.
9. If `code` is 1, input values for `x` and `y`, and calculate and display the sum of `x` and `y`.
10. If a is strictly between 0 and 5, set b equal to $1/a^2$; otherwise set b equal to a^2.

For Exercises 11–14, write functions that will do what is required. To test these functions, you should write driver programs as instructed in Programming Problems 14–18 at the end of this chapter.

11. Given a distance, return a cost, according to the following table:

Distance	Cost
0 through 100	5.00
More than 100, but not more than 500	8.00
More than 500, but less than 1000	10.00
1000 or more	12.00

12. A quadratic equation of the form $Ax^2 + Bx + C = 0$ has real roots if the discriminant $B^2 - 4AC$ is nonnegative. Write a function that receives the coefficients *A*, *B*, and *C* of a quadratic equation and returns true if the equation has real roots and false otherwise.
13. A certain city classifies a pollution index less than 35 as "pleasant," 35 through 60 as "unpleasant," and above 60 as "hazardous." Write a function that displays the appropriate classification for a pollution index.
14. A wind chill of 10° F or above is not considered dangerous or unpleasant; a wind chill of –10° F or higher, but less than 10° F is considered unpleasant; if it is –30° F or above, but less than –10° F, frostbite is possible; if it is –70° F or higher, but below –30° F, frostbite is likely and outdoor activity becomes dangerous; if the wind chill is less than –70° F, exposed

flesh will usually freeze within half a minute. Write a function that displays the appropriate weather condition for a wind chill index.

4.4 Functions That Use Repetition[9]

The problems we considered in the preceding chapters and those at the beginning of this chapter required only *sequential* processing of instructions for their solution. In the last section, we saw that there are problems whose solutions require *selection*. In this section, we introduce *repetition*, a form of control that is needed to solve many problems.

PROBLEM: COMPUTING FACTORIALS

The **factorial** of a nonnegative integer n, denoted by $\boldsymbol{n}!$, is defined by

$$n! = \begin{cases} 1 & \text{if } n = 0 \\ 1 \times 2 \times \cdots \times n & \text{if } n > 0 \end{cases}$$

Write a function that, given an integer $n \geq 0$, computes n factorial.

Object-Centered Design

Behavior. To describe how the function should behave, we might begin by looking at how to solve the problem by hand. We would probably begin with 1, multiply it by 2, multiply that product by 3, and so on, until we multiply it by n. For example, to find 5!, we might do the following computation:

$$\begin{array}{r} 1 \\ \times 2 \\ \hline 2 \\ \times 3 \\ \hline 6 \\ \times 4 \\ \hline 24 \\ \times 5 \\ \hline 120 \end{array}$$

If we want our function to imitate this approach, we need to identify the various objects in the solution and the roles they play. It should be clear that we are keeping a running product and incrementing a counter:

9. This section provides only an introduction to repetition structures. This material is used only in the *Case Study* sections of this chapter and the next and in a few examples and exercises in Section 5.4 so that it is possible to defer its study until Chapter 7 if one prefers to study all repetition structures together.

$$
\begin{array}{rl}
1 & \leftarrow \text{initial running product} \\
\times 2 & \leftarrow \text{initial count} \\ \hline
2 & \leftarrow \text{new running product} \\
\times 3 & \leftarrow \text{new count} \\ \hline
6 & \leftarrow \text{new running product} \\
\times 4 & \leftarrow \text{new count} \\ \hline
24 & \leftarrow \text{new running product} \\
\times 5 & \leftarrow \text{new count} \\ \hline
120 & \leftarrow \text{new running product}
\end{array}
$$

Our list of objects can thus be summarized as follows:

	Software Objects			
Problem Objects	**Type**	**Kind**	**Movement**	**Name**
nonnegative integer	`int`	variable	received	*n*
the running product	`int`	variable	returned	*product*
the counter	`int`	variable	none (local)	*count*

We can specify the problem as follows:

Receive: n, an integer

Precondition: $n \geq 0$

Return: $product = n!$, an integer

From this information, we can write a stub for the function:

```
int factorial(int n)
{
}
```

To fill in the body of this stub, we must consider the operations required in the computation.

Operations. Analysis of the operations performed in the preceding approach gives the following list:

i. Check the precondition ($n \geq 0$)
ii. Declare and initialize two integer variables (*product* and *count*)
iii. Multiply two integers (*product* and *count*) and assign the result to an integer (*product*)
iv. Increment an integer variable (*count*)
v. Repeat Operations iii and iv so long as *count* is less than or equal to *n*

In Chapter 3, we saw how the `assert` mechanism can be used for the first operation,

```
assert(n >= 0);
```

or we could use an if statement:

```
if (n < 0)
{
  cout << "n must be nonnegative -- returning 0" << endl;
  return 0;
}
```

The second operation is also familiar:

```
int product = 1;
int count = 2;
```

We have also seen how to perform Operation iii,

```
product *= count;
```

and Operation iv:

```
count++;
```

The difficulty lies with the last operation. How can statements be executed more than once? Here we will use a C++ `for` **loop** to repeatedly execute a statement once for each number in a given range.

Algorithm. The idea of the `for` loop can be captured in pseudocode as shown in the following algorithm for our problem:

Algorithm for Factorial Computation

1. Initialize *product* to 1.
2. Repeat the following for each value of *count* in the range 2 to *n*:
   Multiply *product* by *count*.
3. Return *product*.

Coding. The C++ function in Figure 4.8 implements this algorithm.

Fig. 4.8 Function `factorial()`. (Part 1 of 2)

```
/* factorial computes the factorial of a nonnegative integer.
 *
 * Receive:      n, an integer
 * Precondition: n is nonnegative
 * Return:       n!
 ***************************************************************/

#include <cassert>             // assert()
using namespace std;
```

Fig. 4.8 Function `factorial()`. (Part 2 of 2)

```
int factorial(int n)
{
   assert(n >= 0);
   int product = 1;
   for (int count = 2; count <= n; count++)
      product *= count;

   return product;
}
```

Testing. To test this function, we can write a simple driver program like that in Figure 4.9 to display the values returned by the function for some easy-to-check inputs. Note in the sample runs that both valid and invalid input values are used. The results indicate that `factorial()` computes correct values for valid inputs (at least those we tried), and the `assert()` mechanism prevents output of values for negative inputs. Once it has been fully tested, `factorial()` could be moved to a library as described in Section 4.6 for convenient reuse by programs that need this mathematical function.

Fig. 4.9 Driver for `factorial()`. (Part 1 of 2)

```
/* factDriver.cpp is a driver program to test the factorial function
 *
 ***************************************************************/

#include <iostream>
using namespace std;

int factorial(int n);

int main()
{
   cout << "To compute n!, enter n: ";
   int theNumber;
   cin >> theNumber;
   cout << theNumber << "! = "
        << factorial(theNumber) << endl;
}

/*** Insert the #include directive and the definition of
     factorial() from Figure 4.8 here. ***/
```

Fig. 4.9 Driver for `factorial()`. (Part 2 of 2)

Sample runs:

```
To compute n!, enter n: 1
1! = 1

To compute n!, enter n: 2
2! = 2

To compute n!, enter n: 5
5! = 120

To compute n!, enter n: -1
factorial9.cpp:22: failed assertion 'n >= 0'
-1! = Abort
```

REPEATED EXECUTION: THE `for` STATEMENT

If we once again think of executing a program as being analogous to driving on a roadway, then a repeated execution of a portion of the program is analogous to driving onto a race track, circling it for a certain number of laps, and then leaving the track to resume traveling on the roadway:

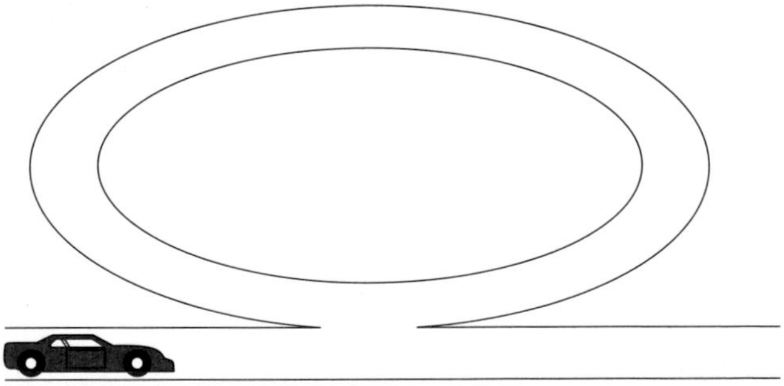

Notice that there are three parts to this repetition mechanism (also called a **loop**):

1. *Initialization* ("entering the track")
2. *Repeated execution* ("circling the track")
3. *Termination* ("leaving the track")

One of the statements provided in C++ for executing a statement more than once is the `for` **statement** like that shown in Figure 4.8:

```
for (int count = 2; count <= n; count++)
   product *= count;
```

(Other forms of the `for` statement as well as other repetition statements will be studied in Chapter 7.) It executes a statement *repeatedly*, once for each number in the range 2 through `n`. More precisely, when it is executed, this `for` statement behaves as shown in the flow graph

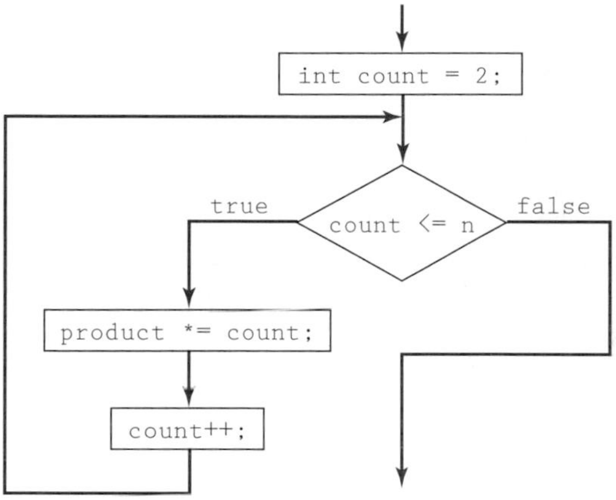

or as a box diagram:

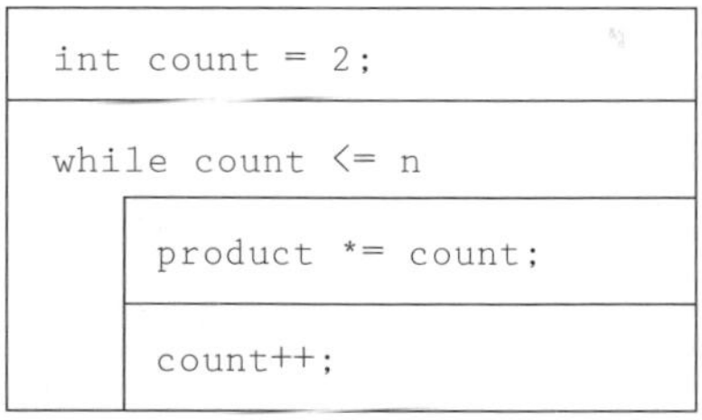

When execution reaches the loop, the variable `count` is created and initialized to 2. The value of `count` is then tested against `n`. If `count` exceeds `n`, repetition ceases and execution continues with the `return` statement that follows the `for` statement in Figure 4.8. However, if `count` is less than or equal to `n`, then the `*=` statement controlled by the loop is executed, so `product` is multiplied by `count`. The value of `count` is then incremented by the expression `count++`, after which execution returns to the top of the loop where the boolean expression `count <= n` is re-evaluated and the cycle starts again. This cyclic behavior continues so long as the boolean expression evaluates to `true`.

Another way to understand the execution of such a loop is with a **trace table,** which traces the execution of the loop's statements, one at a time. The following is a trace table for the execution of `factorial(5)`:

Time	Statement Executed	product	count	Comment
0	`int count = 2;`	1	2	loop initialization
1	`count <= n`	1	2	`true`, loop executes

Time	Statement Executed	product	count	Comment
2	`product *= count;`	2	2	`product` updated
3	`count++;`	2	3	`count` incremented
4	`count <= n`	2	3	`true`, loop executes
5	`product *= count;`	6	3	`product` updated
6	`count++;`	6	4	`count` incremented
7	`count <= n`	6	4	`true`, loop executes
8	`product *= count;`	24	4	`product` updated
9	`count++;`	24	5	`count` incremented
10	`count <= n`	24	5	`true`, loop executes
11	`product *= count;`	120	5	`product` updated
12	`count++;`	120	6	`count` incremented
13	`count <= n`	120	6	`false`, repetition ceases

The `for` statement has the following general form:

`for` Statement

Form:

```
for (init_expression; boolean_expression; step_expression)
    statement
```

where

`for` is a keyword;

`init_expression`, *`boolean_expression`*, and *`step_expression`* are C++ expressions;

`statement` is a C++ statement (simple or compound).

Purpose: When execution reaches a `for` statement, the following actions occur:

1. *`init_expression`* is evaluated.
2. *`boolean_expression`* is evaluated.
3. If *`boolean_expression`* is true, then
    a. *`statement`* is executed,
    b. *`step_expression`* is evaluated,
    c. control returns to Step 2.

Otherwise
    execution continues with the statement following the `for` statement.

Note that like the `if` statement, a `for` loop controls access to a *`statement`*, called the **loop body**, which can be either a single statement, as in

```
for (int count = 2; count <= n; count++)
   product *= count;
```

or a block of statements:

```
cout << "How many values? ";
int numValues;
cin >> numValues;
for (int count = 1; count <= numValues; count++)
{
   cin >> newValue;
   sum += newValue;
   sumOfSquares += newValue * newValue;
}
```

Note also that allowing the *`step_expression`* to be an arbitrary expression makes the C++ `for` loop quite flexible. For example, to count downwards from 10 to 1, we could write

```
for (int value = 10; value >= 1; value--)
   cout << value << ' ';
```

which will display

```
10 9 8 7 6 5 4 3 2 1
```

Similarly, to count from 0 to 2 by 0.5, we could write

```
for (double counter = 0.0; counter <= 2.0; counter += 0.5)
   cout << counter << ' ';
```

which will produce output like the following:

```
0 0.5 1 1.5 2
```

Finally, note that when the `for` statement is being used to count by ones, the prefix and the postfix forms of the increment (or decrement) operator can be used interchangeably. That is, to count from 1 to 10, we can write either

```
for (int count = 1; count <= 10; count++)
   statement
```

or

```
for (int count = 1; count <= 10; ++count)
   statement
```

The two are interchangeable, because both expressions add 1 to the value of `count`, which is the value being used to control the loop.

PROCESSING SEVERAL INPUT VALUES

The driver program in Figure 4.9 for computing factorials suffers from one major drawback: It processes only one value of `n`. To compute factorials for other values, the program must be re-executed, which involves retyping its name, reclicking on its icon, or whatever is necessary for a particular system.

A more user-friendly program would permit the user to process any number of values before it terminated. One way to do this is to have the user specify in advance how many values are to be processed and then *wrap* the body of the program in a `for` loop that counts from 1 to that number:

```
// ...
int main()
{
   cout << "This program computes n! for n >= 0.\n"
           "How many factorials do you wish to compute? ";
   int numValues;
   cin >> numValues;
   for (int count = 1; count <= numValues; count++)
   {
      cout << "\nEnter n: ";
      int n;
      cin >> n;
      cout << n << "! = " << factorial(n) << endl;
   }
}
// ...
```

A sample run might appear as follows:

```
This program computes n! for n >= 0.
How many factorials do you wish to compute? 3

Enter n: 5
5! = 120

Enter n: 2
2! = 2

Enter n: 1
1! = 1
```

By enclosing the critical portion of a driver program within a loop, we can process several input data values without having to re-execute the program.

One problem with this approach is that it requires knowing how many input values there will be. When the set of input values is very large, counting the values may be inconvenient or even impractical. A common alternative that does not require this is to use a **while loop**, which we only introduce briefly here. This repetition structure, along with other kinds of loops, is studied in detail in Chapter 7.

REPEATED EXECUTION: THE `while` STATEMENT

While loops are implemented in C++ using a `while` **statement** of the following form:

The `while` Statement

Form:

```
while (loop_condition)
    statement
```

where

`while` is a C++ keyword;

`loop_condition` is a boolean expression;

`statement` is a simple or compound statement.

Behavior: When execution reaches a `while` statement:

1. *`loop_condition`* is evaluated.
2. If *`loop_condition`* is true:
   a. The specified *`statement`*, called the *body* of the loop, is executed.
   b. Control returns to step 1.

   Otherwise
   execution continues with the statement following the `while` statement.

Figure 4.10 illustrates how a while loop can be used to repeatedly input integers whose factorials are to be calculated, stopping when the user enters a negative value.

Fig. 4.10 Computing several factorials. (Part 1 of 2)

```
/* factorials.cpp is a driver program to test the factorial
 * function.  It computes any number of factorials.
 *
 ************************************************************/

#include <iostream>              // cin, cout, <<, >>
using namespace std;

int factorial(int n);
```

Fig. 4.10 Computing several factorials. (Part 2 of 2)

```
int main()
{
   int aNumber;
   cout << "To compute n!, enter n (a negative number to quit): ";
   cin >> aNumber;
   while (aNumber >= 0)
   {
      cout << theNumber << "! = "
           << factorial(aNumber) << "\n\n";
      cout << "Enter next value of n (negative to quit): ";
      cin >> aNumber;
   }
}

/*** Insert the #include directive and the definition of
     factorial() from Figure 4.8 here. ***/
```

Sample run:

```
To compute n!, enter n (a negative number to quit): 1
1! = 1

Enter next value of n (negative to quit): 2
2! = 2

Enter next value of n (negative to quit): 5
5! = 120

Enter next value of n (negative to quit): 6
6! = 720

Enter next value of n (negative to quit): -1
```

Quick Quiz 4.4

For Questions 1–8, describe the output produced.

1.
```
for (int i = 1; i <= 5; i++)
   cout << "Hello\n";
```

2.
```
for (int i = 1; i < 4; i++)
   cout << "Hello";
```

3.
```
for (int i = 1; i <= 5; i += 2)
    cout << "Hello\n";
```

4.
```
for (int i = 1; i < 7; i++)
    cout << i << ' ' << i + 1 << endl;
```

5.
```
for (int i = 6; i > 0; i--)
    cout << endl << i*i << endl;
```

6.
```
for (int i = 6; i <= 6; i++)
    cout << "Hello\n";
```

7.
```
for (int i = 6; i <= 5; i++)
    cout << "Hello\n";
```

8.
```
for (int i = 1; i <= 10; i++)
{
    cout << i << endl;
    i++;
}
```

9. How many lines of output are produced by the following?

```
for (int i = 1; i <= 50; i += 2)
{
   cout << i << "  ";
   if (i % 5 == 0)
      cout << endl;
}
```

Exercises 4.4

For Exercises 1–6, describe the output produced.

1.
```
for (int i = 0; i <= 3; i++)
    cout << i << " squared = " << i*i << endl;
```

2.
```
for (int i = 5; i > 0; i--)
    cout << i << " squared = " << i*i << endl;
```

3.
```
int k = 5;
for (int i = k; i <= 5; i++)
{
    cout << i + k << endl;
    k = 1;
}
```

4.
```
int s = 5;
for (int i = s; i < 5; i++)
    cout << i + s << endl;
cout << "***\n";
```

5.
```
int s = 1;
while (s <= 16)
{
   cout << 2*s << endl;
   s *= 2;
}
```

6.
```
int s = 20;
while (s/2 < 10)
{
   cout << 2*s << endl;
   s /= 2;
}
```

For Exercises 7 and 8, write functions that will do what is required. To test these functions, you should write driver programs as instructed in Programming Problems 21 and 22 at the end of this chapter.

7. For a positive integer n, use a `for` loop to find the sum $1 + 2 \ldots + n$ and return this sum.
8. For two integers m and n with $m \leq n$, use a `for` loop to find the sum $m + m + 1 + \cdots + n$ and return this sum.

For Exercises 9–14, write a loop to do what is asked for.

9. Display the squares of the first 100 positive integers in increasing order.
10. Display the cubes of the first 50 positive integers in decreasing order.
11. Display the square roots of the first 25 odd positive integers.
12. Display a list of points (x, y) on the graph of $y = x^3 - 3x + 1$ for x ranging from -2 to 2 in steps of 0.1.
13. Display the value of x, starting at 10.0, and decrease x by 0.5 as long as x is positive.
14. Calculate and display the squares of consecutive positive integers until the difference between a square and the preceding one is greater than 50.

Part of the Picture
Computability Theory

At the beginning of this chapter, we were limited to designing functions that applied operations to objects in a sequential fashion. The statements presented in Sections 4.3 and 4.4 now allow us to design functions that apply operations *selectively* or *repetitively*.

Selection and repetition enable us to build functions that are more powerful than those limited to sequential execution. There are functions that use sequence and selection for which there is no equivalent function that uses only sequential execution. Similarly, there are functions that use sequence, selection, and repetition for which there is no equivalent function that uses only sequence and selective execution.

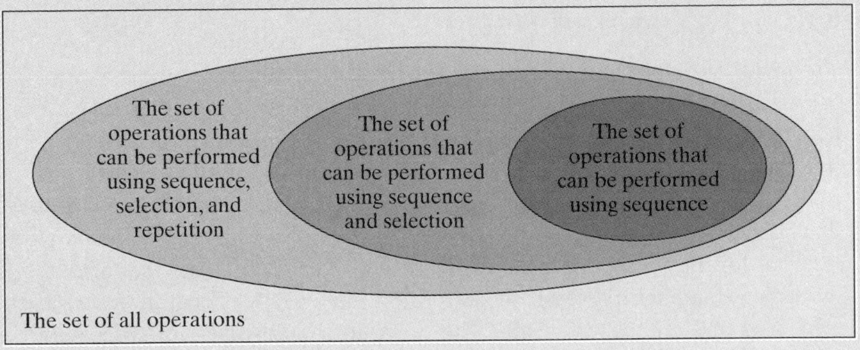

Fig. 4.11 Venn Diagram of operations.

Stated differently, *the set of all operations that can be built using only sequential execution is a proper subset of the set of all operations that can be built using sequence and selection. And the set of all operations that can be built using only sequential and selective execution is a proper subset of the set of all operations that can be built using sequence, selection, and repetition.* The **Venn Diagram** in Figure 4.11 pictures the relationship between these three categories of functions. Selection statements allow us to design and implement operations that are more powerful than those we can build using only sequence; and adding repetition statements allows us to design and implement operations that are more powerful than those that can be built using only sequence and selection.

This is a result from *computability theory*, a branch of computer science that investigates (from a theoretical viewpoint) interesting questions such as the following:

- What can (or cannot) be computed?
- How can functions be classified, and what relationships exist among those classes?
- What is the most efficient algorithm for solving a particular problem?

Rather than ask questions about programs written in an existing language or that run on a particular hardware platform, both of which become obsolete all too soon, theoreticians represent programs *abstractly*, using mathematical models (e.g., *the set of all functions that use only sequence*). The advantage of this is that when a theoretician discovers something that is true about the model, then that result is true for all programs represented by that model, regardless of the language in which those programs are written and regardless of the hardware on which those programs execute! This **language and hardware independence** gives theoretical work a sense of *timelessness*: Although programming languages and hardware platforms come and go, theoretical results endure.

4.5 Case Study: An Eight-Function Calculator

PROBLEM

Write an eight-function calculator program that allows the user to perform addition, subtraction, multiplication, division, exponentiation, base-ten logarithm, factorial, and quit operations.

Object-Centered Design

Behavior. The program will display on the screen a menu of the eight operations, telling the user to enter +, -, *, /, ^ (for exponentiation), `l` (for logarithm), `!` (for factorial), or `q` (for quit) to specify the operation to be performed. The program will read the operation from the keyboard. If the user enters `q`, execution will terminate. Otherwise, the program will display on the screen a prompt for the first operand, which it will then read from the keyboard. If the operation requires two operands, the program will display on the screen a prompt for the second operand, which it will then read from the keyboard. The program will then compute the result of performing the specified operation using the operand(s) provided and output this result. The program should repeat this behavior until the user specifies the `q` operation.

Starting from this statement of the program's behavior, you should try to complete the solution to the problem by first identifying the problem's objects and operations and organizing them into an algorithm. Then, following the examples of this chapter, see if you can translate your algorithm into code. If you have difficulty, see the book's Web site for a detailed description of the object and operation lists, algorithms, and C++ code that implements the algorithms.

4.6 An Introduction to Libraries

In the preceding sections, we have seen how functions enable us to extend the collection of operations provided in C++. If a problem requires some new operation, we can define a function to perform that operation and then call it, just as if C++ did provide it.

Although this is a significant improvement over using only expressions, it does not by itself make it easy for us to reuse our work. For example, to use the function `factorial()` in a different program, we have to copy its prototype and its definition from the program in Figure 4.9 and insert them at the appropriate places in the new program. We might use the *copy-and-paste* capabilities of a text editor or word processor to do this. If we needed the function `fahrToCelsius()` from Figure 4.2 in a new program, we might use this same *copy-and-paste* method or we might simply make a copy of the program in Figure 4.2, delete everything between the prototype and definition of `fahrToCelsius()`, and then write the new program between this prototype and definition.

Although these approaches may be acceptable in languages not designed for reusability, C++ provides a better approach by supporting **libraries**, which are files containing items that can be shared by different programs and by other libraries. C++ inherited the idea of libraries from its parent language C, which defined a number of standard libraries, some of which we have described in earlier chapters.

Libraries are one feature that make C a powerful language, because they make it possible to share commonly used functions between different programs. For example, we noted in Chapter 2 that the standard C library `cstdlib` provides the function `exit()` that can be used to terminate execution of a program at any point in the program. When executed, the call

```
exit(1);
```

will terminate a program and make its return value 1. (Recall from Chapter 1 that a C++ main program normally returns the value 0.) To use `exit()`, we need only include the library's header file in the program:

```
#include <cstdlib>
```

The C++ libraries provide a variety of different functions, several of which are described in Appendix D.[10] In this section, we give a brief description of how such libraries are constructed.

CONSTRUCTING A LIBRARY

If we examine the libraries of functions provided in the various C++ implementations, we see that the functions in each library are *related* in some way. For example, the `iostream` library provides functions for performing input and output, and the `cmath` library provides functions that are commonly needed in mathematical computations. It would be silly (and confusing) to put the `sqrt()` function in the `iostream` library or to put one of the input functions in the `cmath` library.

The first step in constructing a library, therefore, is to identify its *organizing principle*; that is, what kind of functions it will contain. For example, if we intend to store the temperature-conversion function `fahrToCelsius()` in a library, we might decide that the library will contain items that are in some way related to heat and temperature, just as the `iostream` library contains functions that are related to input and output streams. We will call this library `Heat`.

Once we have an organizing principle for the library, we must identify the particular items that we want it to provide. By careful planning and trying to anticipate what items related to heat might be reused, we hope to save time in the future—libraries involve long-term rather than short-term planning.

The organizing principle helps us decide what items to include in our library. For example, if our `Heat` library is to contain our `fahrToCelsius()` function, then it should also include the inverse operation for Celsius-to-Fahrenheit conversions. Functions to convert a temperature in each scale to Kelvin and back are other appropriate additions.

It is important to note that we are not limited to storing functions in a library. For example, we might also store important heat-related constants in our library, such as the heat of fusion of water (79.71 calories/gram) and the heat of vaporization of water (539.55 calories/gram). The important thing is to identify useful items that are related by our library's organizing principle and put them into the library so that a user can retrieve and use these items (and thus avoid "reinventing the wheel").

Once the items that the library is to contain have been selected, we are ready to begin building it. A library is a collection of the following files:

- *A **header file** that contains the declarations and prototypes of the items in the library.* It is inserted into a program (or another library) using a `#include` directive. It serves as an *interface* between the library and a program that uses the library and is thus sometimes called the library's **interface file**.

10. The header files that C++ inherits from C have been renamed in standard C++ by prepending `c` to their names and dropping the `.h` extension. For example, the C header files `stdlib.h`, `math.h`, and `ctype.h` are now named `cstdlib`, `cmath`, and `cctype`, respectively. If your compiler is not fully ISO/ANSI-C++ compliant, you may have to use the original names.

- *An **implementation file** that contains the definitions of items not defined in the header file*. It must be separately compiled and then linked to a program needing to access its contents (as described later in this section).
- *A **documentation file** that contains documentation for the items in the library.*[11]

Building the Header File. A header file contains declarations of all items stored in the library. For functions stored in the library, it contains the *prototypes* of the functions, but usually *not their definitions*. Thus, just as `iostream` (or `iostream.h` in older versions of C++) is a file containing declarations of items needed to perform stream input and output, *Heat.h* will be a header file containing declarations of items needed for processing heat-related values. It might begin as shown in Figure 4.12.

Fig. 4.12 Header file for library `Heat`.

```
/* Heat.h provides an interface for a library of
 * heat-related constants and functions.
 *
 * Created by: Jane Roe, August, 2001, at Dooflingy Industries.
 * Modification History: Kelvin functions added January 2002 -- JR.
 ******************************************************************/

const double HEAT_OF_FUSION = 79.71;            // calories per gram

const double HEAT_OF_VAPORIZATION = 539.55;     // calories per gram

double fahrToCelsius(double tempFahr);          // degrees Celsius

double celsiusToFahr(double tempCels);          // degrees Fahrenheit

double fahrToKelvin(double tempFahr);           // degrees Kelvin

double kelvinToFahr(double tempKelv);           // degrees Fahrenheit

double celsiusToKelvin(double tempCels);        // degrees Kelvin

double kelvinToCelsius(double tempKelv);        // degrees Celsius
```

If a program includes this header file (using a `#include` directive) before its main function, the compiler will insert these statements into the program at that point. Since these statements are declarations of the library's constants and prototypes of the library's functions, these items can be used at any point thereafter in the program.

11. An alternative approach is to document each object and function in the header file. However, this tends to clutter the header file and reduce its overall readability. For this reason, we will put this documentation in a separate file.

It is not necessary to compile the header file separately. It gets compiled because it is *inserted* into a program; that is, when the program that names it in an `#include` directive is compiled, the contents of the header file also get compiled.

Building the Implementation File. As noted earlier, the *definitions* of a library's functions are usually stored in the implementation file of the library.[12] The implementation file is so named because it implements (i.e., defines) the functions that are declared in the header file. Part of the implementation file *Heat.cpp*[13] for our library `Heat` is given in Figure 4.13.

Fig. 4.13 Implementation file for library `Heat`.

```
/* Heat.cpp provides the function implementations for Heat,
 * a library of heat-related constants and functions.
 *
 * Created by: Jane Roe, August 2001, at Dooflingy Industries.
 * Modification History: Kelvin functions added January 2002 -- JR.
 ******************************************************************/

#include "Heat.h"

//----------------------------------------

double fahrToCelsius(double tempFahr)
{
   return (tempFahr - 32.0) / 1.8;
}

//----------------------------------------

double celsiusToFahr(double tempCels)
{
   return tempCels * 1.8 + 32.0;
}

// . . . Definitions of other functions omitted to save space . . .
```

It is important to note that, unlike the header file, a library's implementation file must be compiled. This is the reason that this implementation file contains the line

```
#include "Heat.h"
```

12. Functions that are sufficiently simple (e.g., whose bodies consist of 5 or fewer operations) can be defined in the header file, provided the definition is preceded by the `inline` modifier.

13. Although the name of a library's header file usually has a `.h` extension, the extension for an implementation file is the same as that of a source file (e.g., `.cpp`) since (like a source file) it must be compiled.

in addition to the definitions of the various temperature-related functions. When the library's implementation file is compiled, the compiler will insert and process the function prototypes from the header file and then process their definitions in the library's implementation file. Because the compiler processes both the prototypes and the definitions of the functions, it can check that they are *consistent;* if it detects any inconsistencies, the compiler can display an error message, alerting you to the problem.

It is also important to note the following:

- Items defined in the implementation file that are declared in the header file can be accessed in any program that (i) uses the `#include` directive to insert the header file and (ii) links to the implementation file.
- Items defined in the implementation file that are *not* declared in the header file *cannot* be accessed outside of the implementation file, even by a program that inserts the header file.

Stated simply, items declared in the header file can be thought of as **public** information, whereas items declared in the implementation file are **private** within the library.

Building the Documentation File. The documentation file is a copy of the header file, but it is annotated with documentation that describes each object and provides the specification for each function prototype. Figure 4.14 shows part of this documentation file for library `Heat`. We have named it *Heat.doc,* but *Heat.txt* would also be appropriate.

Fig. 4.14 Documentation file for library `Heat`. (Part 1 of 2)

```
/* Heat.doc provides the documentation for Heat,
 * a library of heat-related constants and functions.
 *
 * Created by: Jane Roe, August 2001, at Dooflingy Industries.
 * Modification History: Kelvin functions added January 2002 -- JR.
 ******************************************************************/

// the amount of heat needed to change water from liquid to solid
const double HEAT_OF_FUSION = 79.71;           // calories per gram

// the amount of heat needed to change water from liquid to gas
const double HEAT_OF_VAPORIZATION = 539.55;    // calories per gram

/* fahrToCelsius converts a temperature from Fahrenheit to Celsius.
 *
 * Receive:  A Fahrenheit temperature
 * Return:   The equivalent Celsius temperature
 */
double fahrToCelsius(double tempFahr);        // degrees Celsius
```

Fig. 4.14 Documentation file for library `Heat`. (Part 2 of 2)

```
/* celsiusToFahr converts a temperature from Celsius to Fahrenheit.
 *
 * Receive:  A Celsius temperature
 * Return:   The equivalent Fahrenheit temperature
 */
double celsiusToFahr(double tempCels);      // degrees Fahrenheit

// ... Other functions omitted to save space ...
```

Such a documentation file serves a secondary purpose: As an annotated copy of the header file, it serves as a *backup* for the header file.

USING A LIBRARY IN A PROGRAM

Once the library `Heat` has been constructed, it can be used in a program like that in Figure 4.15 for solving a temperature-conversion problem.

Fig. 4.15 Converting a temperature—version 3. (Part 1 of 2)

```
/* f2c.cpp converts a temperature from Fahrenheit to Celsius,
 * using function fahrToCelsius() that is stored in library Heat.
 *
 * Input:   tempFahrenheit
 * Output:  tempCelsius
 *******************************************************************/

#include <iostream>    // cin, cout, <<, >>
using namespace std;
#include "Heat.h"      // our library's header file

int main()
{
   cout << "This program converts a temperature\n"
           "from Fahrenheit to Celsius.\n";

   cout << "\nEnter a Fahrenheit temperature: ";
   double tempFahrenheit;
   cin >> tempFahrenheit;

   double tempCelsius = fahrToCelsius(tempFahrenheit);
```

Fig. 4.15 Converting a temperature—version 3. (Part 2 of 2)

```
   cout << tempFahrenheit << " degrees Fahrenheit is equivalent to "
        << tempCelsius << " degrees Celsius\n";
}
```

Execution of this program is identical to that in Figure 4.2. In this program, however, the prototype of `fahrToCelsius()` before the main function has been replaced by the line

```
#include "Heat.h"
```

and the definition of `fahrToCelsius()` is no longer present. The prototype and the definition of `fahrToCelsius()` are not given in this file, because the prototype is in the header file of library `Heat` and the definition is in the library's implementation file.

It is important to note and understand the difference between the notation

```
#include "Heat.h"
```

used to include the `Heat` library's header file and the different notation

```
#include <iostream>
```

used to include the `iostream` library's header file. If the name of a library's header file is surrounded by *angle brackets* (< and >), the C++ compiler will search for that file in one or more special system `include` directories. The exact location of these directories is implementation dependent.[14] By contrast, if the name of a library's header file is enclosed in *double quotes*, the C++ compiler will search for that file in the directory that contains the source file being compiled.

C++ also permits the programmer to store a library in a different directory (e.g., a library directory) and then instruct the compiler to search that directory when looking for files named by `#include` directives. The details of how to do this vary from one system to another.[15]

TRANSLATING A LIBRARY

Translation of a program consists of two separate steps:

1. **compilation,** in which a source program is translated to an equivalent machine-language program, called an *object program*, which is stored in an *object file*,[16]
2. **linking,** in which any calls to functions that are defined within a library are linked to their definitions, creating an *executable program*, which is stored in an *executable file*.

---

14. See your instructor or your C++ documentation for their location on your system.
15. In *Metrowerks CodeWarrior*, this is done by adding the directory to the list in the *Access Paths* dialogue box, found under the *Edit→PPC Std C++ Console Settings* menu choice. (Select *Target→Access Paths*.) In GNU C++, this is done using the `-I Path` switch, where `Path` is the path to the new directory.
16. Many IDEs like *Metrowerks CodeWarrior* and *Visual C++* require a programmer to create a project, in which the object files are stored. Unix object files end in the extension `.o`; DOS object files end in the extension `.OBJ`.

Since a programmer-defined library must also be compiled (if it isn't already), translation of a program that uses a library may require three separate actions:

1. Separate compilation of the program's source file, creating an object file.
2. Separate compilation of the library's implementation file, creating a different object file (unless the library's implementation file has already been compiled).
3. Linking the function calls in the program's object file to the function definitions in the library's object file, creating an executable program.

It makes no difference whether the source program or the library's implementation file is compiled first, but *both source and library implementation files must be compiled before linking can be performed.* The following diagram illustrates this process:

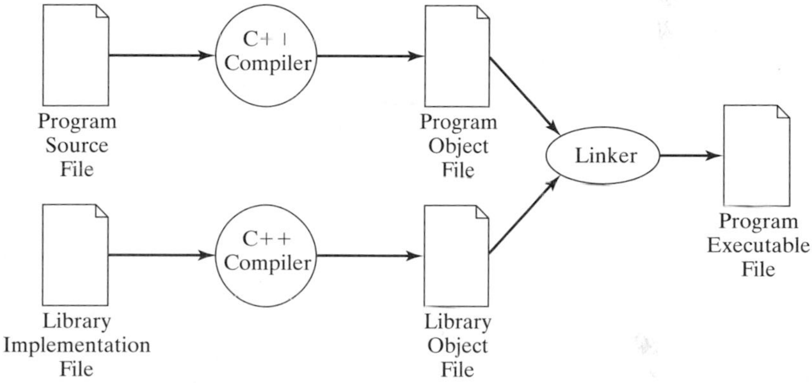

While the mechanics of translation differ from one system to another, there are two basic approaches: translation from the *command-line* and translation using a *project file*. In a command-line environment such as Unix, Linux, or MS-DOS, the user interacts with the computer by typing commands. Compiling and linking the source code in the files *f2c.cpp* and *Heat.cpp* thus requires several commands. For example, if we are using the GNU C++ compiler (g++) on a Unix system, we begin by entering the command to separately compile the source file `f2c.cpp`,

```
g++ -c f2c.cpp
```

which creates the object file `f2c.o`. Next, we do the same for the library's implementation file,

```
g++ -c Heat.cpp
```

which creates a second object file `Heat.o`. Finally, we link these two object files together,

```
g++ f2c.o Heat.o -o f2c
```

which produces a binary executable file named `f2c` that can be executed simply by typing its name:

```
f2c
```

In an integrated development environment such as *Metrowerks CodeWarrior* or *Visual C++*, a multifile translation is coordinated by creating a special file called a *project*.[17] By selecting a menu choice (such as `Project→Add Files`), a dialogue box appears through which one can add source files such as *f2c.cpp* and *Heat.cpp* (but *not* header files like *Heat.h*) to the project. Once this has been done, translation and execution can be accomplished using the `Run` menu choice (usually `Project→Run`, or `Compile→Run`), which automatically compiles each file in the project, links the resulting object files into a binary executable, and then runs that executable.

Although the extra step of compiling a library separately from the source program may seem like an inconvenience, it has two significant benefits:

1. The compilation time for the source program is significantly reduced.
2. Any errors that occur are (most likely) confined to the source program.

These long-term advantages far outweigh the short-term inconvenience.

To illustrate this, suppose that we have written a library containing a large number of functions that a friend wishes to use in a program she is writing. Because C++ allows us to link together separately-compiled files, translation of her program requires

1. compilation of her source program and
2. linking her resulting object file to our library's object file.

By contrast, if it were necessary to recompile the library's implementation file each time she translated her program, the translation would probably take much longer. Moreover, since our library is compiled separately (and, we hope, is error free), any errors generated during compilation must lie in her source file. *Separate compilation and linking eliminate needless recompilation of a library, and allow errors to be isolated within a file.*

Object-Centered Design

INCORPORATING FUNCTIONS AND LIBRARIES

Until now, we have designed software solutions to problems using object-centered design (OCD), which we described as follows:

Behavior: State how you want the program to behave as precisely as possible.

Objects: Identify the objects in the problem description and categorize them.

Operations: Identify the operations that are needed to solve the problem.

Algorithm: Arrange the operations on the objects in an order that solves that problem.

Now that we have seen how to build functions and store them in libraries, we need to integrate these new capabilities into OCD. Since a function can be thought of as a way to

---

17. In place of a *project*, many command-line environments provide a `make` utility that uses a special file called a `Makefile` to coordinate the multifile translation. Discussion of the `make` utility is beyond the scope of this text—for an introduction, see our lab manual; or for a complete discussion, see *Mastering Make* by Tondo, Nathanson, and Yount (Prentice Hall, 1994).

extend C++ by adding an operation not predefined in the language, we will expand OCD as follows:

Behavior: State how you want the program to behave as precisely as possible.

Objects: Identify the objects in the problem description, and categorize them.

Operations: Identify the operations that are needed to solve the problem.
If an operation is not predefined, then:

a. Write a function to implement that operation.
b. If that function seems likely to be reused in the future, store it in a library.

Algorithm: Arrange the operations on the objects in an order that solves that problem.

Thus, any time a problem requires an operation that is not provided in C++, we will write a function to implement that operation. Functions that are likely to be reused in the future should be stored in a library instead of in the file containing the main function.

SUMMARY

Libraries are fundamental to the object-oriented approach to programming, because they provide the following benefits:

Functions in a Library Are Reusable. A library *extends the language* by making additional items—functions, constants, and so on—available to any program (or other library). There is no need for a programmer to "reinvent the wheel" each time these items are needed.

Libraries Hide Implementation Details. To use the items in a library, the programmer needs to know only the information in the header file; the details in the implementation file are of no concern. The header and documentation files must be provided to users, but the source code in the implementation file need not be made available—only its compiled object file, so that it can be linked to their programs. The details in the implementation file can thus remain "hidden" in the machine code of the object file provided to the user. This **information hiding** makes it possible to use the library without being concerned about these details. For example, one can use the square root function `sqrt()` from the `cmath` library without worrying about the details of how the operation is performed.

Libraries Make Programs Easier to Maintain. Information hiding is one of the most important benefits of using libraries, because it makes programs using the libraries *easier to maintain.* If programmers were permitted to access the contents of the implementation file, they might be tempted to use the implementation details in their programs. However, if the implementation file were subsequently changed (e.g., perhaps a faster square-root function is devised and substituted for the old one), then such programs might no longer work correctly. Maintaining such programs requires that they be modified to remove the

describe another way to build such a library where the conversion functions are stored in a `Temperature` class. Figure 4.16 shows how we could use such a Fahrenheit-to-Celsius conversion function of this kind.

Fig. 4.16 Temperature conversion using a `Temperature` class method.

```
/* f2c.cpp computes the Celsius equivalent of a Fahrenheit temperature,
 * using a class method.
 * ...
 ********************************************************************/

#include <iostream>
using namespace std;
#include "Temperature.h"

int main()
{
   cout << "To convert Fahrenheit to Celsius,\n"
        << " enter a Fahrenheit temperature: ";
   double fahrTemp;
   cin >> fahrTemp;

   double celsTemp = Temperature::fahrToCels(fahrTemp);

   cout << "The equivalent temperature is " << celsTemp << endl;
}
```

The new feature in this program is its use of the *class method* `fahrToCels()`. To use such a method, we must send a message to the *class*, not to an *object*. The C++ notation for invoking a class method is

```
ClassName::method_name(argument_list)
```

where `::` is the C++ **scope operator**. The statement

```
double celsTemp = Temperature::fahrToCels(fahrTemp);
```

in the preceding program effectively tells the compiler, "*Invoke the function named* `fahrToCels()` *found in class* `Temperature`, *pass it the value* `fahrTemp`, *and store the result in variable* `celsTemp`."

To build `fahrToCels()`, we can "wrap" a `Temperature` class around a prototype of function `fahrToCels()` and then (because it is fairly simple) define `fahrToCels()` in *Temperature.h* below the class declaration. Figure 4.17 gives the details.

Fig. 4.17 Temperature conversion using a `Temperature` class method.

```
/* Temperature.h provides a Temperature class that (so far)
 *   provides class methods for temperature conversions.
 * ...
 *****************************************************************/

#include <cassert>     // assert()
using namespace std;

const double MIN_FAHRENHEIT = -459.67,
             MIN_CELSIUS    = -273.15,
             MIN_KELVIN     = 0;

class Temperature
{
public:
  static double fahrToCels(double tempFahr);
  static double fahrToKelv(double tempFahr);
  static double celsToFahr(double tempCels);
  static double celsToKelv(double tempCels);
  static double kelvToFahr(double tempKelv);
  static double kelvToCels(double tempKelv);
  // ... other Temperature class method prototypes ...
};

inline double Temperature::fahrToCels(double tempFahr)
{
   assert(tempFahr >= MIN_FAHRENHEIT)
   return (tempFahr - 32.0) / 1.8;
}

inline double Temperature::celsToFahr(double tempCels)
{
   assert(tempCels >= MIN_CELSIUS);
   return tempCels * 1.8 + 32.0;
}

// ... Definitions of other Temperature class methods ...
```

Figure 4.17 introduces several new features of C++:

- Just as we can wrap variable declarations within a class, we can wrap function declarations (i.e., their prototypes) within a class.
- If we declare a function inside a class using the `static` modifier, then that function is a **class method** that specifies one of the messages that can be sent to the class (using the scope operator `::`). The **keyword** `static` informs the compiler that what follows is the prototype of a class method:

```
class Temperature
{
      // ...
      static double fahrToCels(double tempFahr);
 };
```

- A "normal" function declared inside a class (i.e., without using the `static` modifier) is an **instance method** that specifies one of the messages that can be sent to an object whose type is that class. We will examine instance methods in the *OBJECTive Thinking* section of the next chapter.
- In the *definition* of a method (outside the class), its name must be qualified using the name of its class and the scope operator or a linking error will occur.

```
class Temperature
{
     // ...
     static double fahrToCels(double tempFahr);
};

inline double Temperature::fahrToCels(double tempFahr)
{
    // ...
}
```

As we observed in Footnote 12, simple operations can be defined in the header file. In this case, they should be defined using the `inline` modifier. If this is not done, a *linking error* will result in some versions of C++. More complicated operations should be defined in a separate implementation file, and the `inline` modifier should be omitted. (See Figure 4.13.)

EXAMPLE CLASS METHODS: `Sphere` OPERATIONS

In Section 1.4, we saw how a `Sphere` object could be used to simplify sphere-related problems, such as computing the weight of the world's largest ball of twine or computing the average density of our planet. These programs solved the problem by building a `Sphere` object (e.g., `aSphere`) and sending it instance messages (e.g., `aSphere.getWeight()`). Figure 4.18 presents a slightly more complex solution to the weight-of-a-sphere problem that uses a `Sphere` class, but does not create any `Sphere` objects. Instead, it uses a `Sphere` class method named `computeWeight()`.

Fig. 4.18 Weight of a sphere using a `Sphere` class method.

```
/* sphereWeight.cpp computes the weight of a sphere,
 * given its radius and density, using a class method.
 * ...
 *****************************************************************/

#include <iostream>
using namespace std;
#include "Sphere.h"

int main()
{
   cout << "To compute the weight of a sphere,\n"
        << " enter its radius and density: ";
   double radius, density;
   cin >> radius >> density;

   double weight = Sphere::computeWeight(radius, density);

   cout << "The sphere's weight is " << weight << endl;
}
```

In order for a `Sphere` class to respond to the `computeWeight()` message, we must declare a method named `computeWeight()` in the public section of the class using the `static` modifier. Since `computeWeight()` is a fairly simple calculation, we define it in *Sphere.h*, below the class declaration, using the `inline` keyword. Figure 4.19 gives the details.

Fig. 4.19 A `Sphere` class providing class methods. (Part 1 of 2)

```
/* Sphere.h provides a Sphere class that (so far)
 * provides class methods for several basic operations.
 * ...
 *****************************************************************/

#include <cmath>        // pow()
using namespace std;

const double PI = 3.14159;
```

Fig. 4.19 A `Sphere` class providing class methods. (Part 2 of 2)

```
class Sphere
{
 public:
   Sphere();
   // ... other Sphere instance method prototypes ...

   static double computeWeight(double radius, double density);
   static double computeDensity(double radius, double weight);
   static double computeRadius(double density, double weight);
   // ... other Sphere class method prototypes ...

 private:
   // ... attribute variable declarations omitted ...
};

inline double Sphere::computeWeight(double radius, double density)
{
   if (radius > 0 && density > 0)
      return density * 4.0 * PI * pow(radius, 3) / 3.0;
   else
      return 0.0;
}

// ... other Sphere class methods left as exercises ...
```

Note again that we must give the qualified name (i.e., `Sphere::computeWeight()`) when defining a method outside of the class. Otherwise, a **linking error** will result when we try to send the corresponding message to our class:

```
Link Error   : undefined 'computeWeight(double,double)'
Referenced from 'main' in sphereWeight.cpp
```

The *compilation* phase succeeds, because our class contains a prototype for the method.[18] But the *linking* phase fails because without the `Sphere::` before the name of the method, the compiler treats the definition as that of a normal function named `computeWeight()`—as opposed to a method from our `Sphere` class named `computeWeight()`—and the linker cannot find a method definition that corresponds to our message.

18. Recall that the compiler uses prototypes/declarations to check that function/method calls are correct. Because a function/method may be compiled separately, the compiler does not check function/method calls against definitions. The *linker* checks that a function/method definition exists for each function/method called.

CLASS METHODS AND VARIABLES

NOTE

NOTE

As these examples illustrate, a class method defines a message that can be sent to a class to perform some operation. Generally speaking, if a class-related operation does not need to reference any of the instance variables in a class, then it should probably be implemented as a class method. (Operations that must access instance variables must be implemented as instance methods.) *Class methods are not permitted to access instance variables.*

Within a class, declaring a method as `static` specifies that the method is a **class method**. Similarly, preceding a variable declaration by `static` within a class specifies that the variable is a **class variable**. Whereas each instance of a class has its own distinct copies of all instance variables, class variables are *shared* by all instances of the class. *Class methods may access class variables; instance methods may access both class variables and instance variables.* We will learn more about class variables in Section 8.7 and instance methods in our next *OBJECTive Thinking* section.

Quick Quiz 4.7

1. The two basic categories of methods are ________ methods and ________ methods.
2. With respect to sending messages, what distinguishes the two kinds of methods in Question 1?
3. Write a statement to invoke a class method named `m()` in a class named `C`, sending it the argument `a`.
4. The modifier ________ must be used in the declaration of a class method.
5. (True or false) Methods declared in a class are usually defined outside the class.
6. The ________ operator, denoted by ________, is used to attach the name of a class to the name of a method being defined.
7. Class variables are declared using the modifier ________.
8. (True or false) Class variables are shared by all instances of a class.
9. (True or false) Class methods may access both class variables and instance variables.
10. (True or false) Instance methods may access both class variables and instance variables.

Exercises 4.7

In these exercises, you are to write methods for the classes in this section. You should test each method with a driver program similar to those in the text. (See the programming problems for this section.)

For Exercises 1–4, add definitions of the class methods to the class `Temperature`. (See Figure 4.17.)

1. `fahrToKelv()`
2. `celsToKelv()`
3. `kelvToFahr()`
4. `kelvToCels()`

For Exercises 5 and 6, add definitions of the class methods to the class `Sphere`. (See Figure 4.19.)

5. `computeDensity()`
6. `computeRadius()`
7. For class `Temperature`, add a prototype and a definition of a method that receives a wind speed in miles per hour and a temperature and returns the wind chill for that wind speed and temperature. (See the introduction to Figure 4.4 for the formula for wind chill.)
8. Proceed as in Exercise 7, but replace wind speed with relative humidity and return the heat index. (See Exercise 18 in Section 4.2.)
9. For the time class in Exercise 2 of Section 3.8, write a declaration and a definition of a class method that receives a time and returns the total number of minutes (an integer) that have elapsed since midnight for that time. For example, for 10:30:45 AM, the method should return the value 630.
10. Proceed as in Exercise 9, but return the number of seconds that have elapsed since midnight.

CHAPTER SUMMARY

Key Terms & Notes

`#include` directive
abstraction
argument
`automatic` object
block
boolean expression
box diagram
call to a function
class method
class variable
compilation
compound statement
condition
declaration
documentation file
driver program
executable file
executable program
flow diagram
`for` statement
function
function body
function declaration
function definition
function heading
function member
function prototype
function stub
header file
`if` statement
implementation file
indefinite loop
information hiding
instance method
instance variables
interface file
library
linking
local object
loop
loop body
method
movement
nested `if` statements
object file
object program
parameter
postcondition

precondition	separate compilation
private	sequential execution
public	specification
receive	subprogram
repetition	termination (or exit) condition
`return` statement	trace table
return value	Venn Diagram
scope operator (: :)	`void` keyword
selection	`while` statement

- A function provides a way to encapsulate code so that it can be reused.
- Like variables and constants, a function must be declared before it can be used. The declaration of a function is also called a prototype and has the form

```
returnType functionName(parameter_declaration_list);
```

- The general form of a function definition is:

```
function heading
function body
```

where the heading has the general form

```
returnType functionName(parameter_declaration_list)
```

and the body is a sequence of statements enclosed in curly braces ({ and }):

```
{
  statements
}
```

- When a function is called, the arguments are associated with the parameters from left to right—first argument with the first parameter, the second argument with the next parameter, and so on, until the matching is complete. There should be the same number of arguments as parameters and each argument's type must be compatible with the type of the corresponding parameter.
- Execution transfers from a function back to the caller when a `return` statement is encountered or the end of the function is reached.
- No `return` statement is required for functions whose return type is `void`.
- Like programs, functions should be rigorously tested to ensure correctness. This involves writing driver programs that call the functions with specific values and display the values they return.
- A function's documentation should include a comment that describes its specification.
- A *specification* for a function should include descriptions of values the function receives—parameters and their types; values input to the function; what it returns; values it outputs; preconditions; and postconditions.

- Local variables, constants, and parameters exist only while a function is executing and thus can be accessed only within the function. This means that other functions may reuse the name of a local for some other purpose without causing a conflict.
- Some problems require control mechanisms that are more powerful than sequential execution, namely, selection and repetition.
- *Sequential execution* refers to execution of a sequence of statements in the order in which they appear, so that each statement is executed exactly once.
- *Selective execution* refers to selecting and executing exactly one of a collection of alternative actions.
- The `if` statement is the most common selection structure for selecting between two alternatives.
- A *block* (or *compound statement*) groups a sequence of statements into a single statement by enclosing them in curly braces ({ and }).
- When one of the alternatives in an `if` statement contains another `if` statement, the second `if` statement is said to be *nested* in the first. In this case, an `else` clause is matched with the nearest preceding unmatched `if`.
- There are three parts to a repetition mechanism (also called a loop): *initialization*, *repeated execution*, and *termination*.
- A `for` loop is one of the repetition structures provided in C++.
- A `while` loop can be used to implement an input loop.
- A library is a collection of the following files:
  - *Header file*: A header file contains declarations and prototypes of the library's items, is also called the *interface file* because it acts as an interface between the library and client programs, and is inserted into a program (or another library) using a directive of the form `#include "Library.h"`.
  - *Implementation file*: An implementation file contains definitions of items not defined in the header file. It must be separately compiled and then linked to a client program. Items defined here and declared in the header file can be accessed in any program that `#include`s the header file and links to this implementation file. Items defined here, but not declared in the header file cannot be accessed outside of this implementation file, even by a program that `#include`s the header file.
  - *Documentation file*: A documentation file contains documentation for the library's items.
- Methods fall into one of two basic categories:
  - *class method*: defines a message that can be sent to a *class*. Their declarations inside a class are modified by the keyword `static`. Calls to them have the form

    ```
    ClassName::method_name(argument_list)
    ```

    where `::` is the C++ *scope operator*
  - *instance method*: defines a message that can be sent to an *object* (i.e., an instance of a class). Calls to them have the form

    ```
    object_name.method_name(argument_list)
    ```

  For either kind, in their definitions (outside the class), their names must be qualified using the name of the class and the scope operator or a linking error will occur.

Programming Pointers

Program Style and Design

1. *Functions should be documented in the same way as programs.* The documentation should include the following:
   - *a statement of what it does;*
   - *its specification, which consists of those of the following that apply:*
     - *what it receives—i.e., its parameters;*
     - *what is input to the function;*
     - *preconditions—restrictions or limitations on the parameters' values in order for the function to work properly;*
     - *what it returns;*
     - *what it outputs;*
     - *postconditions—effects produced by the function.*

   In this text, to avoid cluttering the header and implementation files, we place the documentation for functions stored in a library in a separate documentation file.
2. *Functions are separate program components, and the white space in a program should reflect this.* In this text, we
   - *insert appropriate documentation before each function defined in the main function's file, to separate it from other program components;*
   - *indent the declarations and statements within each function.*
3. *All guidelines for programming style apply to functions.*
4. *Once a problem has been analyzed to identify the problem's objects and the operations needed to solve it, an algorithm should be constructed that specifies the order in which the operations are applied to the objects.*
5. *Operations that are not predefined (or are nontrivial) in C++ should be encoded as functions, separate from the main function.*
6. A *function that encodes an operation should be designed in the same manner as the main function.*
7. *A function that returns no values should have its return type declared as* `void`.
8. *A function that receives no values should have no parameters within the parentheses of the function heading.*
9. *If a problem requires the selection of one or more operations, use a selection statement like the* `if` *statement.*
10. *If a problem requires the repetition of one or more operations, and the number of repetitions can be computed in advance, use a repetition statement like the* `for` *statement.*
11. *If a problem involves a set of data values whose size is not known in advance, a repetition statement like the* `while` *statement can be used to read and process the values.*
12. *If a function is sufficiently general that it might someday prove useful in solving a different problem, a library should be constructed to store that function, rather than declaring and defining it in the program's source file.*
13. *A library's files should be documented in much the same way as programs.* For each library, provide a special documentation file that describes clearly, precisely, and completely the contents of the library and how to use items in it, any special algorithms it implements, and other useful information such as the author, a modification history, and so on. This documentation

file should be kept in the same place as the other files of a library, so that users can refer to that file in order to understand and use the items stored in the library.

14. *When the header file of a less commonly used library is inserted in a program (using* `#include`*), a comment should be used to explain its purpose.* For example, simply writing

```
#include <cstdlib>
```

tells the reader nothing about why the library is needed in this program. A simple comment

```
#include <cstdlib>     // exit()
```

tells the reader what role the library is playing in solving the particular problem.

15. *Libraries provide the following benefits:*
    - *A library extends the language, since its contents can be made available to any program or to another library.*
    - *The items in a library's interface can be used without being concerned about the details of their implementation.*
    - *Programs and libraries can be compiled separately. Changing the implementation file of a library requires recompilation of only that implementation file.*
    - *Libraries provide another level of modularity in software design; related functions and other objects can be grouped together in independent libraries.*

WATCH OUT

Potential Pitfalls

1. *When a function is called, the list of arguments is matched against the list of parameters from left to right, with the leftmost argument associated with the leftmost parameter, the next argument associated with the next parameter, and so on. The number of arguments must be the same as the number of parameters (for exceptions see the description of default arguments on the text's Web site), and the type of each argument must be compatible with the type of the corresponding parameter.* For example, consider the function with the heading

```
int f(int number1, int number2)
```

The statements

```
y = f(x);
```

and

```
y = f(2, "Joe");
```

are incorrect. In the first case, the number of arguments (1) does not agree with the number of parameters (2). In the second case, the string `"Joe"` can not be passed to the integer parameter `number2`.

2. *Identifiers defined within a function (e.g., parameters, local variables, and local constants) are defined only during the execution of that function; they are undefined both before and after its execution.* Any attempt to use such identifiers outside the function (without redeclaring them) is an error. For example, in the function

```
void f(int x, float y)
{
   int a, b;
   //...
}
```

neither the local variables a and b nor the parameters x and y can be accessed outside of function f().

3. *If a function changes the value of its parameter, the value of the corresponding argument is not altered*[19]. A parameter is a completely separate variable into which the argument value is copied. Any change to the parameter changes the copy, not the corresponding argument. For example, if a function f() is defined as

```
int f(int x)
{
   x *= 5;
}
```

and then called by

```
//...
int y = 1,
    z;
   .
   .
   .
z = f(y);
//...
```

the value of y is still 1 following the call to function f(). Even if the calling function uses an argument with the same name as the corresponding parameter,

```
int x = 1;
z = f(x);
```

the value of x will still be 1 after the function call.

4. *A function must be declared before it is called.* For example, if the function f() is to call the function g(), then a prototype of g() must precede its call in f():

```
int g(...);  // prototype of function g
   .
   .
   .
int f(...)    // definition of function f
{
   //...
   int x = g(...); // call to function g
   //...
}
```

5. *Each { must have a matching }*. To make it easier to find matching braces, we align each { with its corresponding }.

6. *One of the most common C++ errors is using an assignment operator (=) when an equality operator (==) is intended. Each equality comparison in a boolean expression should be double-checked to make certain that the equality operator is being used and not the assignment operator.* It is easy to forget that in C++ = is the assignment operator and, consequently, to incorrectly encode an instruction of the form

19. Except as noted in Footnote 7.

If *variable* is equal to *value*, then

statement

as

```
if (variable = value)
   statement
```

perhaps because = is used in many programming languages to check equality. However, instead of testing whether `variable` is equal to `value`, the condition in this `if` statement assigns `value` to `variable`. If `value` happens to be zero, then the result of the assignment is zero, which C++ interprets as false, and so the *statement* will not be executed, regardless of the value of `variable`. If `value` is nonzero, then the result of the assignment is nonzero, which C++ interprets as true, and so `statement` will be executed. For example, execution of the following incorrect function for finding the reciprocal of a real number,

```
double recip(double x)
{
   if (x = 0)
   {
      cout << "\n***Error:  Cannot divide by zero!\n";
      return 0.0;
   }
   else
      return 1.0 / x;
}
```

will always produce a division-by-zero error, regardless of the value of parameter `x`, because

- `x` is not compared to zero, but is assigned the value zero, which changes the value of `x` to 0 and produces the value 0 as its result;
- the value 0 (produced by the assignment operator) is treated as false by the `if` statement, and thus the statement

  ```
  return 1.0 / x;
  ```

  is selected; and
- the expression `1.0 / x` is evaluated (and since `x` was set to 0, a division-by-zero error occurs).

7. *In a nested if statement, each* `else` *clause is matched with the nearest preceding unmatched* `if`. For example, consider the following statements, which are given without indentation:

```
if (x > 0)
if (y > 0)
z = x + y;
else
z = x + abs(y);
w = x * y * z;
```

With which `if` is the `else` associated? According to the rule just stated, these statements are executed as

```
if (x > 0)
   if (y > 0)
      z = x + y;
```

```
    else
        z = x + abs(y);
w = x * y * z;
```

where the `else` clause matches the `if` clause containing the condition `y > 0`. Use indentation and alignment to show such associations.

8. *When using repetition, care must be taken to avoid infinite looping.* In a `for` statement, be sure that the boolean expression controlling repetition eventually becomes true. For example, executing the code fragment

```
for (double num = 0.0; num != 1.0; num += 0.3)
    cout << num << endl;
```

results in an infinite loop

```
0.0
0.3
0.6
0.9
1.2
 .
 .
 .
```

because the boolean expression controlling the loop is always false. Rewriting the loop as

```
for (double num = 0.0; num <= 1.0; num += 0.3)
    cout << num << endl;
```

corrects the problem.

9. *In a `for` loop, neither the control variable nor any variable involved in the loop condition should be modified within the body of the `for` loop, since it is intended to run through a specified range of consecutive values.* Strange or undesirable results may be produced otherwise. To illustrate, the statement

```
for (int i = 1; i <= 4; i++)
{
    cout << i << endl;
    i++;
}
```

produces the output

```
1
3
```

The statement

```
for (int i = 1; i <= 4; i++)
{
    cout << i << endl;
    i--;
}
```

results in an infinite loop, displaying the output

```
1
1
1
1
.
.
.
```

10. *If a function needs things from a library, the header file of that library must be inserted (using `#include`) before the definition of that function.* For example, if a function attempts to perform input using the `istream` data object `cin` and

```
#include <iostream>
using namespace std;
```

does not precede the function's definition, then an error message such as the following is produced:

```
cin:  Unknown identifier
```

11. *The implementation file of a library should always insert the header file of that library (using `#include`) so that the compiler can verify that each function's prototype is consistent with its definition.* Failure to follow this rule is a common source of **linking errors**.
12. *A function that is defined in the implementation file of a library but not declared in that library's header file cannot be called outside the library (but it can be called inside the library).* For example, if a library's implementation file contains the two function definitions

```
int f(...)
{
 //...
}

int g(...)
{
 //...
}
```

and the library's header file declares `g()` but does not declare `f()`, then

`g()` can be called by a program in which `#include` is used to insert the library's header file, but `f()` cannot be called,

`f()` can call `g()` because there is a declaration of `g()` before the definition of `f()` in the header file, and `g()` can call `f()` because the definition of `f()` precedes that of `g()`.

13. *To use a class method, one must send a message to the* class, *not to an* object*:*

```
ClassName::method_name(argument_list)
```

14. *The declaration of a class method must begin with the* `static` *modifier; otherwise, the method is an instance method. The qualified name of the method—*`ClassName::methodName()`*—must be used when defining it outside the class or a* **linking error** *will result.*
15. *Class methods are not permitted to access instance variables.*

Programming Problems

Section 4.2

1. Write a driver program to test the temperature-conversion function `celsiusToFahr()` of Exercise 1.
2. Write a driver program to test the monetary-conversion functions `US_to_Canadian()` and `Canadian_to_US()` of Exercises 2 and 3.
3. Write a driver program to test the function `range()` of Exercise 4.
4. Write a driver program to test the function `wages()` of Exercise 5.
5. Write a driver program to test the circle-processing functions of Exercises 6 and 7.
6. Write a driver program to test the rectangle-processing functions of Exercises 8 and 9.
7. Write a driver program to test the triangle-processing functions of Exercises 10 and 11.
8. Write a driver program to test the culture-of-bacteria function of Exercise 12.
9. Write a driver program to test the time-conversion functions of Exercises 13–16.
10. Write a driver program to test the phone-number function of Exercise 17.
11. Write a driver program to test the heat-index function of Exercise 18.
12. Write a driver program to test the stick-number functions of Exercise 19.
13. Complete Problem 12 by writing and testing the additional functions needed to display all digits.

Section 4.3

14. Write a driver program to test the distance-calculation function of Exercise 11.
15. Write a driver program to test the quadratic-equation function of Exercise 12. Execute the program with the following values for A, B, and C: 1, –5, 6; 1, –2, 1; 1, 0, 4; 1, 1, 1; 2, 1, –3.
16. Modify the quadratic-equation function of Exercise 12 so that it returns 0 if the quadratic equation has no real roots (discriminant is negative), 1 if it has a repeated real root (discriminant is 0), and 2 if it has two distinct real roots (discriminant is positive). Test the function with a driver program using the values in Problem 15 for A, B, and C.
17. Construct a driver program to test the pollution-index function in Exercise 13 and execute it with the following data: 20, 45, 75, 35, 60.
18. Construct a driver program to test the wind-chill function in Exercise 14 and execute it with the following data: –80, 10, 0, –70, –10, –5, 10, –20, –40.
19. Write a program that reads an employee's number, hours worked, and hourly rate; calls a function to calculate his or her wages; and then displays the employee information, including wages. All hours over 40 are paid at 1.5 times the regular hourly rate. Execute the program with the following values for employee number, hours worked, and hourly rate: 123, 38, 7.50; 175, 39.5, 7.85; 223, 40, 9.25; 375, 44.5, 8.35.
20. Write a wage-calculation program like the one in Problem 19, but with the following modification: If an employee's number is greater than or equal to 1000, the program should read an annual salary and calculate the employee's weekly pay as this salary divided by 52. If the employee's number is less than 1000, wages are calculated on an hourly basis, as described in Problem 19. Execute the program with the data in Problem 19 and the following data: 1217, 25500; 1343, 31775.

Section 4.4

21. Write a driver program to test the summation function of Exercise 7.
22. Write a driver program to test the summation function of Exercise 8.

23. The sequence of *Fibonacci numbers* begins with the integers 1, 1, 2, 3, 5, 8, 13, 21, . . . where each number after the first two is the sum of the two preceding numbers. Write a program that reads a positive integer n and uses a `for` loop to generate and display the first n Fibonacci numbers.

24. Ratios of consecutive Fibonacci numbers 1/1, 1/2, 2/3, 3/5, . . . approach the *golden ratio* $(\sqrt{5}-1)/2$. Modify the program in Problem 23 so that it also displays the decimal values of the ratios of consecutive Fibonacci numbers.

25. A certain product is to sell for `unitPrice` dollars. Write a program that reads values for `unitPrice` and `totalNumber` and then produces a table showing the total price of from 1 through `totalNumber` units. The table should have a format like the following:

```
Number of Units    Total Price
===============    ===========
              1        $ 1.50
              2        $ 3.00
              3        $ 4.50
              4        $ 6.00
              5        $ 7.50
```

26. Suppose that at a given time, genotypes AA, AB, and BB appear in the proportions x, y, and z, respectively, where $x = 0.25$, $y = 0.5$, and $z = 0.25$. If individuals of type AA cannot reproduce, the probability that one parent will donate gene A to an offspring is

$$p = \frac{1}{2}\left(\frac{y}{y+z}\right)$$

since $y/(y+z)$ is the probability that the parent is of type AB and $\frac{1}{2}$ is the probability that such a parent will donate gene A. Then the proportions x', y', and z' of AA, AB, and BB, respectively, in each succeeding generation are given by

$$x' = p^2, \qquad y' = 2p(1-p), \qquad z' = (1-p)^2$$

and the new probability is given by

$$p' = \frac{1}{2}\left(\frac{y'}{y'+z'}\right)$$

Write a program to calculate and display the generation number and the proportions of AA, AB, and BB under appropriate headings for 30 generations. (Note that the proportions of AA and AB should approach 0, since gene A will gradually disappear.)

27. Write a program that uses an input loop to read data values as shown in the following table, calculates the miles per gallon in each case, and displays the values with appropriate labels:

Miles Traveled	Gallons of Gasoline Used
231	14.8
248	15.1
302	12.8
147	9.25

Miles Traveled	Gallons of Gasoline Used
88	7
265	13.3

28. Write a program that uses an input loop to read several values representing miles, converts miles to kilometers (1 mile = 1.60935 kilometers), and displays all values with appropriate labels.

29. Write a program to read a set of numbers, count them, and calculate and display the mean, variance, and standard deviation of the set of numbers. The *mean* and *variance* of numbers x_1, $x_2, \ldots, x_n$ can be calculated using the formulas

$$\text{mean} = \frac{1}{n}\sum_{i=1}^{n} x_i, \qquad \text{variance} = \frac{1}{n}\sum_{i=1}^{n} x_i^2 - \frac{1}{n^2}\left(\sum_{i=1}^{n} x_i\right)^2$$

The *standard deviation* is the square root of the variance.

Section 4.6

30. Construct a library `Exchange` that contains the monetary-conversion functions from Exercises 2 and 3 in Section 4.2. Write a driver program to test your library.

31. Construct a library `Geometry` that contains the functions from Exercises 6–11 in Section 4.2. Write a driver program to test your library.

32. Write a program to read one of the codes `C` for circle, `R` for rectangle, or `T` for triangle, and the radius of the circle, the sides of the rectangle, or the sides of the triangle, respectively. Using the functions in the library `Geometry` of Problem 31, the program should then calculate and display with appropriate labels the perimeter and the area of that geometric figure.

33. Construct a library `Time` that contains the time-conversion functions from Exercises 13–16 in Section 4.2. Write a driver program to test your library.

34. Write a library containing functions to compute the surface area and volume of a sphere. For a sphere of radius r, these values can be calculated using

$$\text{Surface Area} = 4\pi r^2$$

$$\text{Volume} = \frac{4\pi r^3}{3}$$

Write a driver program to test your library.

35. Write a library `Cylinder` containing functions to compute the total surface area, lateral surface area, and volume of a right-circular cylinder. For a cylinder of radius r and height h, these can be calculated using

$$\text{Total Surface Area} = 2\pi r(r + h)$$

$$\text{Lateral Surface Area} = 2\pi rh$$

$$\text{Volume} = \pi r^2 h$$

Write a driver program to test your library.

36. Construct a library `Measures` containing functions that will allow a user to freely convert within the following categories of measurement:

Length: inches, feet, yards, miles
Weight: ounces, pounds, tons
Volume: teaspoons, tablespoons, cups, quarts, gallons

Section 4.7*

37. Write a driver program to test the class method `fahrToKelv()` of Exercise 1.
38. Write a driver program to test the class method `celsToKelv()` of Exercise 2.
39. Write a driver program to test the class method `kelvToFahr()` of Exercise 3.
40. Write a driver program to test the class method `kelvToCels()` of Exercise 4.
41. Write a driver program to test the class method `computeDensity()` of Exercise 5.
42. Write a driver program to test the class method `computeRadius()` of Exercise 6.
43. Write a driver program to test the wind-chill class method of Exercise 7.
44. Write a driver program to test the heat-index class method of Exercise 8.
45. Write a driver program to test the elapsed-minutes class method of Exercise 9.
46. Write a driver program to test the elapsed-seconds class method of Exercise 10.

CHAPTER 5
Using Classes

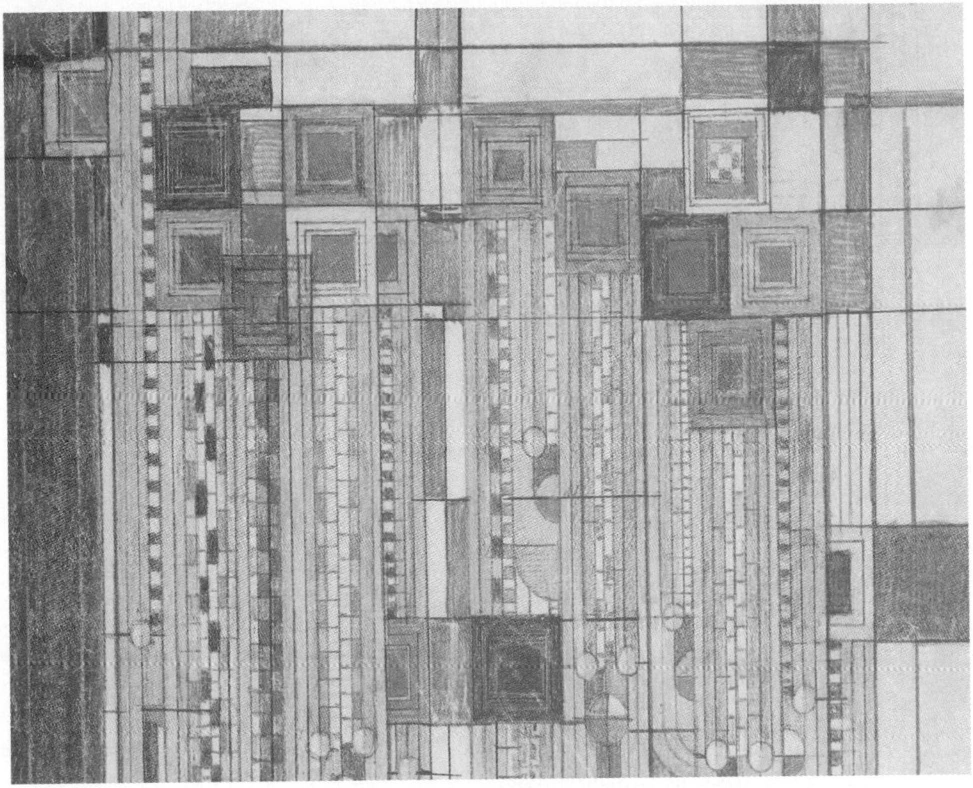

The old order changeth, yielding place to the new.

-Alfred, Lord Tennyson

Buying a new tire costs less than reinventing the wheel.

-V. Orehck III (fictitious)

The moving finger writes; and having writ
Moves on: not all your piety nor wit
Shall lure it back to cancel half a line,
Nor all your tears wash out a word of it.

-The Rubaiyat

Chapter Contents

Chapter Objectives

- Study another example of software development using OCD.
- Introduce enough of the basic features of classes so that one knows what they are and how to use them.
- Study the input (`istream`) and output (`ostream`) classes.
- Study the `string` class.
- (Optional) Look at how a (user-defined) random integer class can be used in simulations.
- (Optional) Take a first look at how to develop instance methods.

The word *class* is often used to describe a group or category of objects that have a set of attributes in common. For example, the high school football teams in one state are described as

- *class A*, if they have fewer than 100 students in three grades;
- *class AA*, if they have between 101 and 500 students in three grades;
- *class AAA*, if they have between 501 and 1000 students in three grades;
- *class AAAA*, if they have 1000 or more students in three grades.

The U.S. Navy describes ships as belonging to certain *classes;* for example, *Skipjack class, Thresher class*, and *Sturgeon class* have been used to characterize different kinds of submarines. Economists describe families as *lower class, middle class,* or *upper class,* based on their annual income. Used in this way, the word *class* is a synonym for the word *type*, since it provides a name for a group of related objects.

In Chapter 2 we studied some of the types provided in C++, including `int`, `long`, `unsigned`, `double`, `char`, and `bool`. These are called **fundamental types**, because they can be used to model basic objects like numbers and characters. However, consider modeling the name of a person. Since a name consists of several characters and the fundamental type `char` can only store single characters, the `char` type is inadequate to model a name.

For situations like this where the fundamental types are inadequate, C++ allows a programmer to create a new type for modeling a problem's object by building a **class**. A class can thus be thought of as an *extension* to C++; by building a class and storing it in a library, a programmer can add new types to C++ that other programmers can use.

In this chapter, we examine three types that have been added to C++ using the class mechanism: the `istream` class for modeling a computer's keyboard, the `ostream` class for modeling a computer's screen, and the `string` class for modeling arbitrary sequences of characters. None of these types existed in the original C++ language; all of them have been added to the language by creating the corresponding classes. The optional *OBJECTive Thinking* section takes a first look at how instance methods can be added to a class to define messages that can be sent to objects whose type is that class. The *Part of the Picture* section shows how simulations can be performed using a random number generator.

5.1 Introductory Example: "The Farmer in the Dell"

PROBLEM

"The Farmer in the Dell" is a children's song that many people have sung at one time or another:

The farmer in the dell
The farmer in the dell
Hi-ho, the derry-o
The farmer in the dell

The farmer takes a wife
The farmer takes a wife
Hi-ho, the derry-o
The farmer takes a wife

The wife takes a child
The wife takes a child
Hi-ho, the derry-o
The wife takes a child

The child takes a nurse
. . .

The nurse takes a cow
. . .

The cow takes a dog
. . .

The dog takes a cat
. . .

The cat takes a rat
. . .

The rat takes the cheese
. . .

The cheese stands alone
The cheese stands alone
Hi-ho, the derry-o
The cheese stands alone

We want to write a program that prints the lyrics of this song.

Object-Centered Design

Preliminary Analysis. One obvious solution is a "brute force" solution, in which the program consists of a large main function containing a single output statement that displays the lyrics on the screen:

```
int main()
{
   cout << "The farmer in the dell\nThe farmer in the dell\n"
           "Hi-ho, the derry-o\nThe farmer in the dell\n\n"
           "The farmer takes a wife\nThe farmer takes a wife\n"
           "Hi-ho, the derry-o\nThe farmer takes a wife\n\n"
           "The wife takes a child\nThe wife takes a child\n"
           "Hi-ho, the derry-o\nThe wife takes a child\n\n"

           // etc., etc., etc.
}
```

However, writing such a program is tiresome and boring, because we are typing almost exactly the same thing over and over again. *Anytime a plan requires repeating the same work over and over, there is something wrong with the plan!*

If we examine the structure of the song and identify what is common to the verses, we see that each verse has the following form:

The *restOfLine*
The *restOfLine*
Hi-ho, the derry-o
The *restOfLine*

In the first verse, *restOfLine* is "farmer in the dell"; in the second verse, it is "farmer takes a wife"; and so on, until in the tenth verse, *restOfLine* is "cheese stands alone". This suggests that the song can be viewed as a sequence of verses, rather than as a single monolithic song. More precisely, what we might do is write a function to display on the screen a single verse of the song, with a `string` parameter to store *restOfLine* and then call that function 10 times, passing it different lines.

Behavior. Our program should display on the screen the lyrics of a verse of "The Farmer in the Dell" using "farmer in the dell", followed by a verse using "farmer takes a wife", followed by a verse using "wife takes a child", and so on.

Objects. In this approach, our objects are as follows:

	Software Objects		
Problem Objects	Type	Kind	Name
screen	`ostream`	varying	`cout`
lyrics of a Farmer-in-the-Dell verse	`string`	constant	none
"farmer in the dell"	`string`	constant	none
"farmer takes a wife"	`string`	constant	none
"wife takes a child"	`string`	constant	none
"child takes a nurse"	`string`	constant	none
"nurse takes a cow"	`string`	constant	none
"cow takes a dog"	`string`	constant	none
"dog takes a cat"	`string`	constant	none
"cat takes a rat"	`string`	constant	none
"rat takes the cheese"	`string`	constant	none
"cheese stands alone"	`string`	constant	none

Operations. There are these operations to perform:

i. Display a string on the screen
ii. Construct a verse of the song using:
   a. "farmer in the dell"
   b. "farmer takes a wife"
   c. "wife takes a child"
   d. "child takes a nurse"
   e. "nurse takes a cow"
   f. "cow takes a dog"
   g. "dog takes a cat"
   h. "cat takes a rat"
   i. "rat takes the cheese"
   j. "cheese stands alone"

Since the operation "Construct a verse of the song using ______" is not predefined in C++, we will design a function to perform this operation.

Algorithm. Once we have such a function `verse()`, we simply call it 10 times, once for each of the preceding phrases: Thus, we can solve our problem with the following algorithm, which eliminates the redundant coding that afflicts the brute force approach:

Algorithm for Displaying the Lyrics of *The Farmer in the Dell*

Call `verse()` with each of the 10 arguments listed.

Function's Behavior. Our function must receive from its caller a phrase to complete the first, second, and last lines of a verse. It should construct a verse of "The Farmer in the Dell" using that phrase and return that verse to the calling function.

Function's Objects. Our behavioral description contains these objects:

	Software Objects			
Problem Objects	**Type**	**Kind**	**Movement**	**Name**
screen	`ostream`	varying	none	`cout`
a phrase	`string`	varying	received (in)	*restOfLine*
a verse of "The Farmer in the Dell"	`string`	constant	returned (out)	*aVerse*

From these objects, we can specify the problem our function solves as follows:

Receive: *restOfLine*, a `string` object

Return: a verse of "The Farmer in the Dell" using *restOfLine*.

Function's Operations. To construct a function having the specified behavior, we need the following operations:

i. Build *aVerse*, a `string` consisting of the lyrics to a verse of "The Farmer in the Dell," containing *restOfLine* in the first, second, and last lines
ii. Return *aVerse* to the caller

Algorithm for Function. After our analysis of the structure of a verse, we arrive at the following sequence of steps to solve the problem:

Algorithm for Function `verse()`

1. Build *aVerse* = "\nThe" + *restOfLine* + "\n"
   "The" + *restOfLine* + "\n"
   "Hi-ho, the derry-o\n"
   "The" + *restOfLine* + "\n".
2. Return *aVerse*.

The listed values are all strings, and the C++ `string` class provides the + operator to perform the necessary operation of *concatenating* (i.e., joining) two strings into a single string. Each operation in this algorithm is thus predefined, and we can continue to the coding phase.

Coding. Now that we have an algorithm for the program and for the function, we can proceed to code the program. Figure 5.1 presents the solution. Compared with the brute force approach, it is surely more *space efficient* (i.e., it is shorter) and exhibits good design style, because its structure reflects the structure of the song.

Fig. 5.1 "The Farmer in the Dell". (Part 1 of 3)

```
/* dellFarmer.cpp displays the lyrics for "The Farmer in the Dell"
 * using a function verse().
 *
 * Input:  none
 * Output: lyrics for the "The Farmer in the Dell"
 *******************************************************************/

#include <iostream>                  // cin, cout, >>, <<
#include <string>                    // string
using namespace std;

string verse(string restOfLine);

int main()
{
   cout << verse("farmer in the dell")
        << verse("farmer takes a wife")
        << verse("wife takes a child")
        << verse("child takes a nurse")
        << verse("nurse takes a cow")
        << verse("cow takes a dog")
        << verse("dog takes a cat")
        << verse("cat takes a rat")
        << verse("rat takes the cheese")
        << verse("cheese stands alone") << endl;
}

/* verse() builds one verse of "The Farmer in the Dell".
 *
 * Receive: restOfLine, a string.
 * Return:  a verse with restOfLine inserted appropriately.
 *************************************************************/

string verse(string restOfLine)
{
   const string aVerse =
                         "\nThe " + restOfLine + "\n" +
                         "The " + restOfLine +  "\n" +
                         "Hi-ho, the derry-o\n" +
                         "The " + restOfLine + "\n";
   return aVerse;
}
```

Fig. 5.1 "The Farmer in the Dell". (Part 2 of 3)

Sample run:

```
The farmer in the dell
The farmer in the dell
Hi-ho, the derry-o
The farmer in the dell

The farmer takes a wife
The farmer takes a wife
Hi-ho, the derry-o
The farmer takes a wife

The wife takes a child
The wife takes a child
Hi-ho, the derry-o
The wife takes a child

The child takes a nurse
The child takes a nurse
Hi-ho, the derry-o
The child takes a nurse

The nurse takes a cow
The nurse takes a cow
Hi-ho, the derry-o
The nurse takes a cow

The cow takes a dog
The cow takes a dog
Hi-ho, the derry-o
The cow takes a dog

The dog takes a cat
The dog takes a cat
Hi-ho, the derry-o
The dog takes a cat

The cat takes a rat
The cat takes a rat
Hi-ho, the derry-o
The cat takes a rat
```

Fig. 5.1 "The Farmer in the Dell". (Part 3 of 3)

```
The rat takes the cheese
The rat takes the cheese
Hi-ho, the derry-o
The rat takes the cheese

The cheese stands alone
The cheese stands alone
Hi-ho, the derry-o
The cheese stands alone
```

5.2 Introduction to Classes

In Chapter 2, we saw that a programmer can model items in a computation by declaring variables and constants whose types are the predefined fundamental C++ types—`int`, `double`, `bool`, `char`, and their variations. For example, we used

```
const double HOURLY_WAGE = 6.75;
double hours;
```

to declare `HOURLY_WAGE` and `hours` to model the hourly wage and hours worked by student employees. In Chapter 4, we saw that a programmer can effectively create new operations for a computation by declaring and defining functions, such as the temperature-conversion function whose prototype was

```
double fahrToCelsius(double tempFahr);
```

These C++ features are adequate for many programming tasks in which the items being modeled are sufficiently simple.

The problem, however, is that most objects in the real world are not simple. For example, suppose that we want to represent cars. If we begin by thinking of the different characteristics of a car, we can quickly compile a sizeable list:

1. name (Acura Integra, Chevrolet Impala, Pontiac GrandAm, Volkswagen Beetle, . . .)
2. number of doors
3. number of cylinders
4. engine size

.
.
.

Suppose, for simplicity, that we use only these four characteristics. One way to proceed would be to declare a separate variable for each of these characteristics:

```
string carName;
int carDoors;
int carCylinders;
int carEngineSize;
```

This approach is on the right track, but it has some serious deficiencies. To see why, consider a function to display the information about a car via `cout`:

```
void printCarInfo(string itsName, int itsDoors,
                  int itsCylinders, int itsEngineSize)
{
   cout << itsName << endl
        << "Doors: " << itsDoors << endl
        << "Cylinders: " << itsCylinders << endl
        << "Engine Size: " << itsEngineSize << endl;
}
```

Given such a function and the variables defined earlier, we can call it as follows:

```
printCarInfo(carName, carDoors, carCylinders, carEngineSize);
```

A function to input information about a car would be similar (with one major difference that we will see in Chapter 8) and would be called in virtually the same way:

```
readCarInfo(carName, carDoors, carCylinders, carEngineSize);
```

The problems with this approach should be clear: Every function we define for a "car operation" must have a separate parameter for each attribute needed by that operation. Similarly, each function call must pass the correct argument to each of those parameters. Obviously, the more complex the object, the more information must be passed and the more cumbersome this approach becomes. Just imagine how inelegant a program would be if it had 50 function calls, each having 100 or more arguments!

The basic difficulty with this approach is that there is *one* kind of object (a car) that we want to model, and yet we must pass *more than one* piece of information to the operations. To solve this problem, C++ provides the **class**. When programmers create a class, they create a *new type*, with space for the characteristics of objects of that type. For example, the type `string` used in Figure 5.1 is actually a class that was created by some programmer.

In the discussion that follows, we will describe the major features of classes, leaving most of the details for a later chapter (and the optional *OBJECTive Thinking* sections in each chapter). By the end of this section, you should know what a class is and how to use one.

DATA ENCAPSULATION

Classes provide a way to encapsulate the characteristics of an object within a single "wrapper." For example, to create a class named `Car` with the characteristics described previously, we could use

```
class Car
{
 public:
   string itsName;
   int itsDoors;
   int itsCylinders;
   int itsEngineSize;
   // ... declarations of identifiers for other attributes
};
```

The identifiers `itsName`, `itsDoors`, `itsCylinders`, and `itsEngineSize` are called the **instance variables** (or **data members** or **attribute variables**) of the class.[1]

The name of the class, `Car`, is treated by C++ as *the name of a new type* and can therefore be used to declare objects:

```
Car dadsCar,
    momsCar;
```

Such declarations create distinct `Car` objects, each of which can store its own characteristics:

dadsCar		momsCar	
Yugo	itsName	Porsche 911	itsName
2	itsDoors	2	itsDoors
4	itsCylinders	8	itsCylinders
120	itsEngineSize	454	itsEngineSize

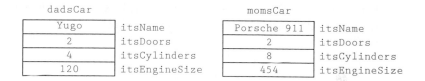

(We will see how to initialize the data members of a class object in Chapter 11—see also the *OBJECTive Thinking* section in Chapter 3.)

This encapsulation is important, because a single object like `dadsCar` now contains all of its own information. This solves our earlier problem, because it allows us to pass a complicated object to a function by using just one argument (and declaring just one parameter); for example,

```
void printCarInfo(Car theCar)
{
   cout << theCar.itsName << endl
        << "Doors: " << theCar.itsDoors << endl
        << "Cylinders: " << theCar.itsCylinders << endl
        << "Engine Size: " << theCar.itsEngineSize << endl;
   // ... and possibly more ...
}
```

Any *public* member of a class object can be accessed using **dot notation**. The expression

```
theCar.itsDoors
```

will access the `itsDoors` member of the `Car` object associated with parameter `theCar`.

If we call this function with

```
printCarInfo(dadsCar);
```

the values of the data members of `dadsCar` will be displayed:

```
Yugo
Doors: 2
Cylinders: 4
Engine Size: 120
```

1. The keyword `public:` is used in this class declaration because the members of a class will be private otherwise, which means they cannot be accessed from outside. An alternative is to use a C-style **struct** in which the members are public by default; simply replace the word `class` with `struct`, and remove the keyword `public:`.

If we call the same function with a different argument,

```
printCarInfo(momsCar);
```

the values of `momsCar`'s data members will be displayed:

```
Porsche 911
Doors: 2
Cylinders: 8
Engine Size: 454
```

For a complicated object, the class thus provides a convenient way to package the data items needed to describe that object in one container. This is what is meant by **data encapsulation**.

ENCAPSULATING OPERATIONS

There is more to classes than data encapsulation. Besides making it possible to package the data characteristics of an object, classes can also store functions that make up the *operations* or *messages* that we can send to such objects. For example, to declare an input message `read()` and an output message `print()` for our `Car` class, we could write

```
class Car
{
 public:
   void read();
   void print();
   // ... function prototypes for other operations
 private:
   string itsName;
   int itsDoors;
   int itsCylinders;
   int itsEngineSize;
   // ... declarations of other instance variables
};
```

The members `read()` and `print()` are called **instance methods** or **function members**. Each instance method performs its particular operation using the data members of the class. For example, the `print()` function could be defined by

```
void Car::print()
{
   cout << itsName << '\n'
        << "Doors: " << itsDoors << '\n'
        << "Cylinders: " << itsCylinders << '\n'
        << "Engine Size: " << itsEngineSize << endl;
   // ... and possibly more ...
}
```

The unusual `Car::` notation indicates that `print()` is a member of the `Car` class, which permits it to directly access the (private) instance variables.

Usually, we would provide a rich set of instance methods as operations on the objects we are modeling. When this is done, the instance variables are designated `private` as shown in class `Car` to prevent users of the class from performing unauthorized operations. However, since this is only an introduction to classes, we will keep our example simple and use only the two function members `read()` and `print()`.

When class objects are declared, as in

```
Car dadsCar,
    momsCar;
```

each has its own instance variables. When we send a message to an object, it responds to that message by executing the corresponding method, which accesses its instance variables. For example, to display the information stored in `dadsCar`, we can send it the `print()` message

```
dadsCar.print();
```

To display the information stored in `momsCar`, we would send it the `print()` message

```
momsCar.print();
```

Similarly, the statement

```
momsCar.read();
```

sends `momsCar` the `read()` message, which fills the instance variables in `momsCar` with values extracted from `cin`; and

```
dadsCar.read();
```

sends `dadsCar` the `read()` message to fill its instance variables with input values. An instance method is thus what gets executed when we send an object a message.

Classes also make it possible to redefine C++ operators. For example, the `string` class redefines the + function so that when it is given two strings, it *concatenates* (joins) those strings. The declaration

```
string name = "Popeye" + " the " + "Sailor";
```

thus initializes the object `name` with the `string` value `"Popeye the Sailor"`. We can also overload operators for classes we build. For example, we could overload the input and output operators for our `Car` class, which would enable us to write statements like

```
cout << "Enter dad's car:\n";
cin >> dadsCar;
cout << "Dad's car is " << dadsCar << endl;
```

Redefining a function with a new definition is called **overloading** that function, a topic discussed in Chapter 8.

Once a class has been built, it is usually stored in a library, with its declaration stored in the library's header file and the definitions of its nontrivial function members in an implementation file. To use the class, a program must include the library's header file.

NOTE

This brief introduction to classes should indicate their importance in C++. Classes are the single biggest difference between C++ and its parent language C. (In fact, prior to 1983, the C++ language was called "C with Classes.") An important part of learning to program in C++ is learning how to use the standard classes that are part of the language, to avoid reinventing the wheel. In the sections that follow, we will examine three of these classes: `ostream`, `istream`, and `string`.

SUMMARY

C++ provides the class mechanism for building types to represent complicated objects. This mechanism allows us to create a single structure that encapsulates (i) *instance variables* or *data members* defining the characteristics of the object and (ii) *instance methods* or *function members* defining the operations on the object. Class members that are designated `public` within the class can be accessed using *dot notation.*

✔ Quick Quiz 5.2

1. Packaging data items needed to describe an object in one container is known as data ________.
2. Classes have two kinds of members: ________ members and ________ members.
3. Redefining a function with a new definition is called ________ that function.
4. Public members of a class can be accessed using ________ notation.

Questions 5–7 assume the following declarations:

```
class Date
{
 public:
   void display();
 private:
   string month;
   int day;
   int year;
};

Date birth;
```

5. List the instance variables of `Date`.
6. List the instance methods of `Date`.
7. Write a statement to call the `display()` method in `birth`.

5.3 The `istream` and `ostream` Classes

When C++ was first developed in 1980, it did not have its own I/O system, but instead relied upon the I/O system of its parent language C.[2] Jerry Schwarz, one of the early users

2. The C standard I/O system provided in `cstdio` is fully usable in C++, but its use is discouraged because its design and use reflect the procedural approach of C and not the object-oriented approach of C++.

of C++, decided to see just how powerful these new things called classes really were and used them to develop a better I/O system. After much work, feedback from users, and revision, the resulting set of classes is today's `iostream` library. Two of these classes are the `istream` class and the `ostream` class, which we examine in this section.[3]

THE `istream` CLASS

One problem in designing a general–purpose model for input is that where the input comes from depends on how users are interacting with the program. Regardless of whether they are using a computer terminal on a mainframe, a workstation, or a microcomputer, the input to the program must come from that terminal's keyboard. What complicates the problem is that the program to which the input is being sent may reside on the same computer or it may be running on an entirely different computer across a network.

The challenge in creating a modern I/O system is to provide a single system that hides this complexity from the programmer—to create an *abstraction* for input that programmers can use without having to concern themselves with the messy details of how data actually gets from the keyboard to the program. What model can capture the basic idea of *every* input system, regardless of the low-level details?

Streams. Building on an idea from C and Unix, Bjarne Stroustrup, the designer of C++, developed such an abstraction, which he called a **stream**. Stroustrup envisioned a stream of characters flowing from the keyboard to a program, like a stream of water flowing from one place to another. Schwarz used this idea to create the `istream` class—a class representing a flow of characters from an arbitrary input device to an executing program:

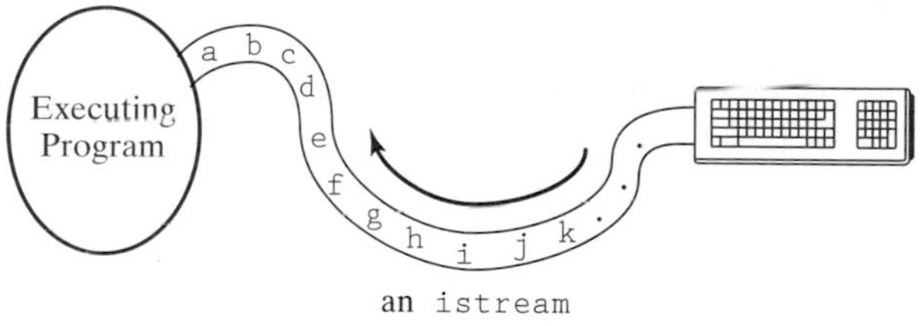

He then defined an `istream` object in the `iostream` library, so that any C++ program that included the library's header file would automatically have an input stream flowing from the keyboard to the program. This object is named `cin`:

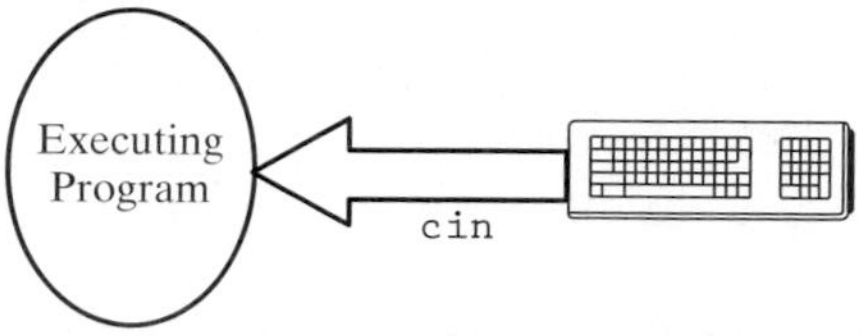

3. `istream` and `ostream` are really specializations of class templates `basic_istream` and `basic_ostream` to type char, which are derived from the `basic_ios` class that handles the low-level details of formatting, buffers, and so on. Using `wchar_t` instead of `char` produces wide-character streams `wistream` and `wostream`. (See Chapter 9 for more details.)

The >> Operator. Schwarz also defined the input operator >> so that when it is applied to an `istream` object and a variable,

```
istream_object >> variable
```

the operator tries to extract a sequence of characters corresponding to a value of the type of *`variable`* from *`istream_object`*. If there are no characters, it *blocks execution* from proceeding until characters are entered.

To illustrate, suppose that `cin` is initially empty, and the following statements are executed:

```
int age;
cin >> age;
```

When the >> operator attempts to read an integer value for `age`, it finds that `cin` is empty and so blocks execution. If the user enters `18`, the characters `1` and `8` are entered into the `istream` named `cin`,

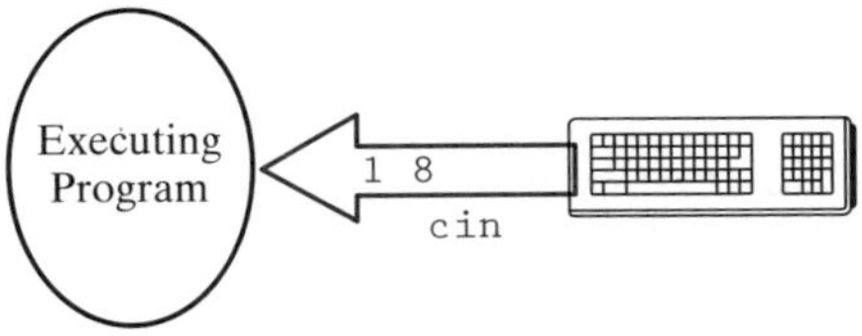

and since `cin` is now no longer empty, the >> operator resumes its execution. It reads the characters `1` and `8` from the `istream`, converts them to the integer value 18, and stores this value into its right operand `age`.

Because the behavior of the >> operator is to extract values from an `istream`, it is often called the *extraction operator*.

Status Methods. In our discussion of the >> operator, we assumed that the user entered appropriate values. Suppose, however, in the preceding example that `18` was mistyped as `q8`. The stream `cin` will then contain the characters `q` and `8`:

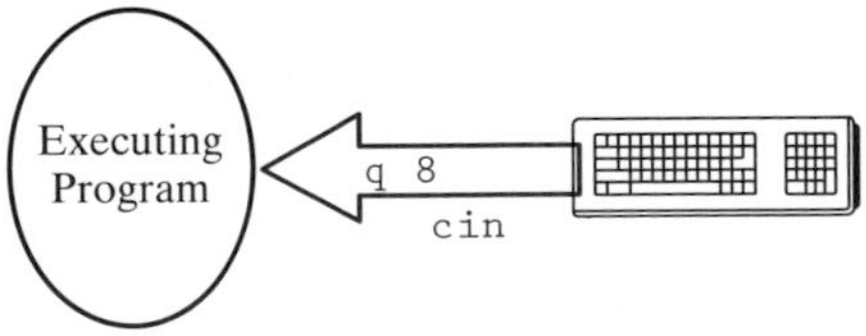

What happens when the >> operator tries to extract an integer and encounters the character `q`?

One of the attributes of an `istream` is its **state** or condition. If all is well with the stream, its state is said to be *good*. If something has gone wrong with the stream, its state is *bad*. If the last operation on the stream did not succeed, its state is *fail*. The `istream` class essentially maintains a boolean variable called a **flag** for each of these states, with the *good* flag initialized to true and the *bad* and *fail* flags initialized to false.

In our scenario, if the >> operator encounters the letter `q` while trying to read an integer, it will set the stream's *good* flag to false, its *bad* flag to true, and its *fail* flag to true. In general, if either the *bad* or *fail* flag is true, then the *good* flag is false. In most circumstances, if the *bad* flag is true, then the *fail* flag is also true, and vice versa.

For each of these flags, the `istream` class provides a boolean method having the same name as its flag, that reports on the value of that flag.[4]

Message	Returns True if and only if
`cin.good()`	all is well in the `istream`
`cin.bad()`	something is wrong with the `istream`
`cin.fail()`	the last operation could not be completed

We can use the `good()` message to check that an input step has succeeded:

```
assert( cin.good() );
```

Alternatively, we could use one of the other status messages; for example,

```
assert( !cin.fail() );
```

Combined with the `assert()` mechanism, these status methods provide a simple way to guard against data-entry errors.

The `clear( )` Method. Once the *good* flag of an `istream` has been set to false, no subsequent input operations can be performed on that stream until its state is cleared. This is accomplished by sending the stream a `clear()` message,

```
cin.clear();
```

which resets the good flag to true and the other flags to false. As we shall see in Chapter 7, this `clear()` message is useful in writing fool-proof loops for reading data values.

The `ignore( )` Method. The `clear()` method resets the status flags, but it does not actually remove the offending input from the `istream`. For this, the `istream` class provides the `ignore()` method. As its name implies, it can be used to ignore one or more characters in the stream. The message

```
cin.ignore();
```

will skip the next character in `cin`.

More generally, the `ignore()` message can be sent with arguments,

```
cin.ignore(num_chars_to_skip, stop_char);
```

where *`num_chars_to_skip`* is an integer expression and *`stop_char`* is a character. This form of `ignore()` will skip *`num_chars_to_skip`* characters in `cin`, unless

4. There is a fourth *end-of-file* state that occurs when the last input operation encountered an end-of-file mark before finding any data. This state can be checked by sending an `istream` the `eof()` message.

stop_char is encountered. The default value of *num_chars_to_skip* is 1 and the default value of *stop_char* is the end-of-file mark.[5] For example, the message

```
cin.ignore(1024, ' ');
```

might be used to skip all characters up to the next blank (assuming it is within the next 1024 characters), and

```
cin.ignore(1024, '\n');
```

to skip all characters remaining on a given line of input (assuming that the end of the line is within 1024 characters). Combined with `clear()`, `ignore()` is useful for detecting bad input characters and removing them from the input stream:

```
cin >> variable;
if (cin.fail())      // e.g., invalid input character
{
  cin.ignore(1024, '\n\);
  cin.clear();
}
```

White space. One of the nice features of the >> operator is that, by default, it *skips leading* **white space**—blanks, tabs, and returns. To illustrate, consider the statements

```
double height, weight;
cout << "Enter your height (inches) and weight (pounds): ";
cin >> height >> weight;
```

and suppose that the user enters 70.5 and 180. Then `cin` contains the following characters where ␣ represents a blank and ↵ represents the return character:

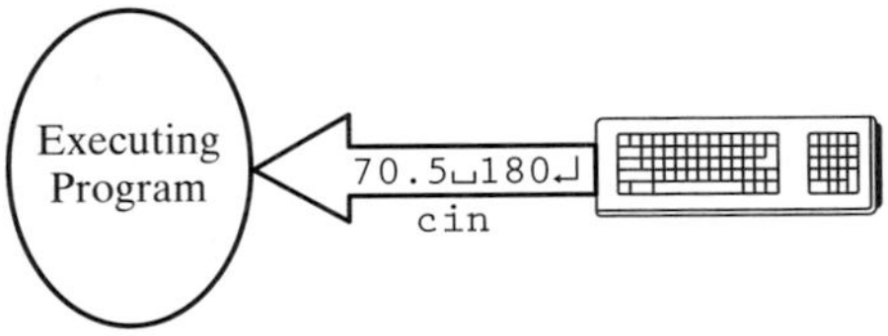

When the input statement

```
cin >> height >> weight;
```

is executed, the first (leftmost) >> reads 70.5 and stores it in `height`, leaving the blank (␣) unread:

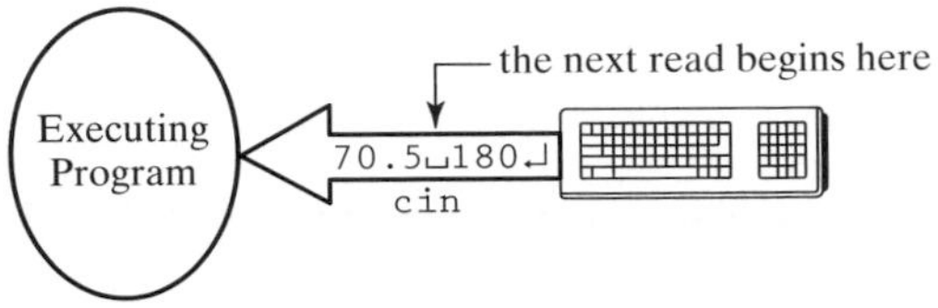

5. Different operating systems use different control characters as an end-of-file mark. On Unix systems and the Macintosh, `Control-d` can be entered as this mark, while DOS-based systems use `Control-z` followed by `Enter`.

The second >> begins reading where the previous one left off, but since the first character is a blank, it skips this character:

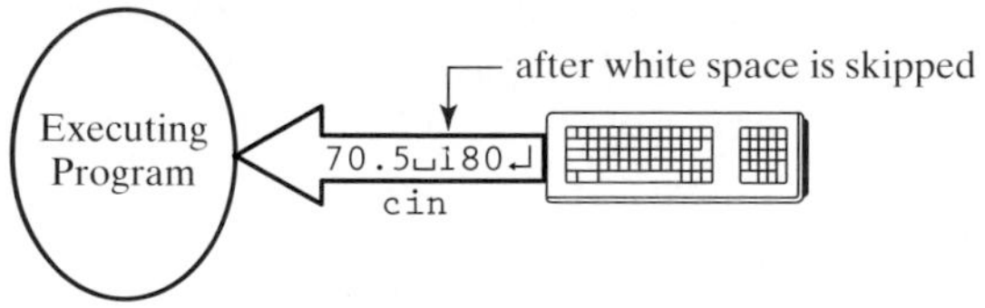

It then reads 180 and stores it in `weight`:

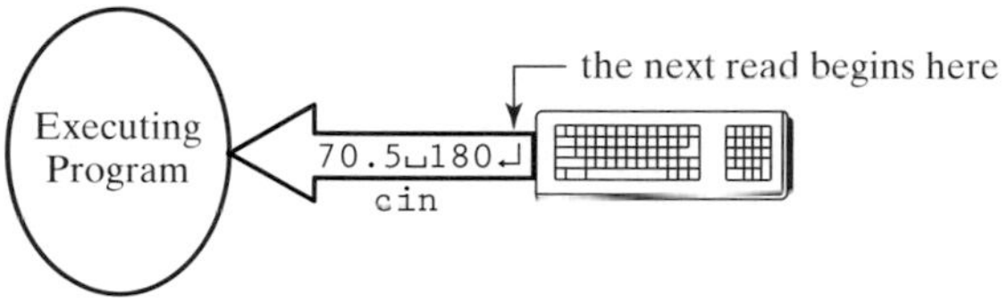

The return character is left unread in the stream. Since a return character is a white-space character, it will be skipped by any subsequent calls to the >> operator.

Note that white space is skipped even when reading a single character, as in

```
char ch;
cin >> ch;
```

>> will read the first non-white-space character from `cin` into `ch`. Any leading white-space characters in `cin` will be skipped.

Suppose, however, that we want to read all characters, including white-space characters; for example, a word-processing program may need to count the lines of input by reading each input character and incrementing a counter each time that character is a return character. One way to read white-space characters is to use an **input manipulator** —an identifier that changes some property of the `istream` when it is used in an input statement. If we use the `noskipws` **manipulator** in an input statement,

```
cin >> ... >> noskipws ...
```

then in all subsequent input, white-space characters will not be skipped. The `skipws` **manipulator** can be used to reactivate white-space skipping.[6]

Alternatively, the `istream` class provides a method named `get()` that reads a single character without skipping white space. More precisely, the message

```
cin.get(ch);
```

where `ch` is of type `char`, will read the next character from `cin` into `ch`, regardless of whether it is a white-space character.

---

6. As noted before, some older C++ compilers may not support the use of manipulators in this way. It may be necessary to include the `iomanip` library and use `resetiosflags(ios::skipws)` in the input statement to turn off white-space skipping and `setiosflags(ios::skipws)` to turn it back on.

THE `ostream` CLASS

Just as the idea of a stream of characters abstractly describes the nature of input, it also describes the nature of output. This level of abstraction is needed because of the different destinations to which the output might be sent. If a text-only computer terminal is being used, then the output from the program must be sent to that terminal's screen. By contrast, if a computer running a windowing system (e.g., X-windows, Macintosh, or Windows 2000) is being used, then the output must be sent to the appropriate window on that machine. Complicating things even more is the fact that a program may be running *locally* (i.e., on the local computer) or *remotely* (i.e., on a different machine across a network).

The abstract notion of a stream can be used to hide these low-level details from the programmer, and so the `iostream` library provides the `ostream` class to represent the "flow" of characters from an executing program to an arbitrary output device:

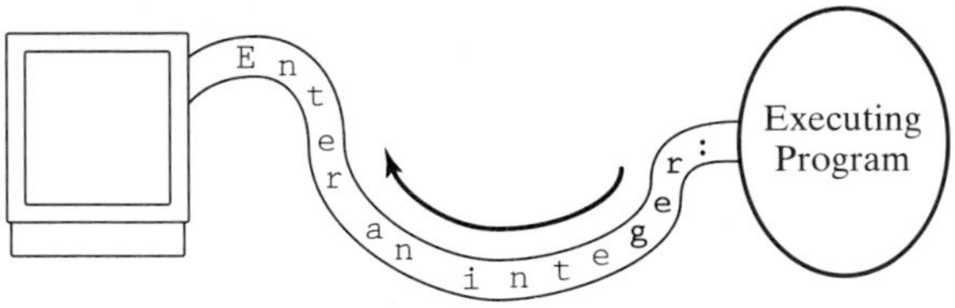

an `ostream`

Any C++ program that includes the `iostream` library will automatically have the following output streams from the program to whatever device the user is using for output—a window, a terminal, etc.:

`cout`: the standard buffered output stream for displaying normal output

`cerr and clog`: standard output streams for displaying error or diagnostic messages (`clog` is buffered; `cerr` is not)

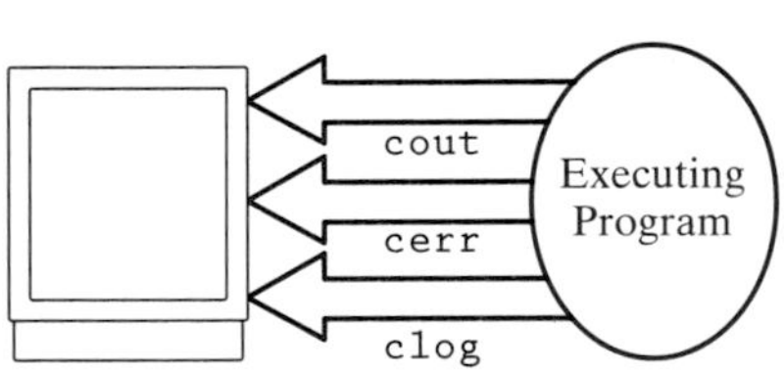

The `assert()` mechanism typically writes its diagnostic messages to `cerr`.

The << Operator. Schwarz also defined the << operator so that when it is applied to an `ostream` object and an expression

```
ostream_object << expression
```

it will evaluate the expression, convert its value into the corresponding sequence of characters, and insert those characters into the `ostream` object. Thus, if the constant `PI` is defined by

```
const double PI = 3.1416;
```

then, in the output statement

```
cout << PI;
```

the << function converts the double value 3.1416 into the corresponding characters 3, ., 1, 4, 1, and 6 and inserts each character into cout:

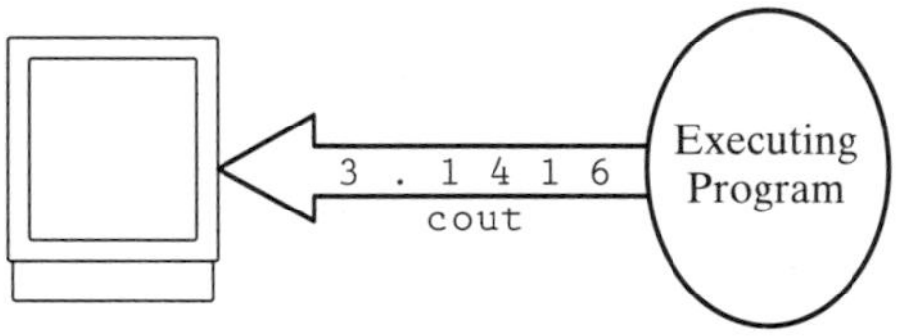

Unlike cerr, which is unbuffered, characters actually remain in cout or clog, without appearing on the screen, until the ostream is *flushed*, which, as its name suggests, empties the stream onto the screen. This can sometimes cause confusion. For example, suppose that we insert output statements in a function to trace calls to the function:

```
double f(double x, double y)
{
   cout << "Entering f";
      .
      .
      .
   cout << "Exiting f";
   return z;
}
```

The output "Entering f" may not appear on our screen when we expect it to, because the ostream is not being flushed.

One common way to flush an ostream is to use an **output manipulator**—an identifier that affects the ostream itself when it is used in an output statement, rather than simply generating a value to appear on the screen. The manipulator most often used to flush an output stream is the endl **manipulator:**

```
double f(double x, double y)
{
   cout << "Entering f" << endl;
      .
      .
      .
   cout << "Exiting f" << endl;
   return z;
}
```

This manipulator inserts a newline character ('\n') into the ostream and then flushes it, thus ending a line of output.[7]

---

7. If one prefers to let the operating system schedule when an output stream should be flushed— for example, because there is a large volume of output—then '\n' should be used to advance to a new line of output rather than endl.

A less commonly used alternative is the `flush` **manipulator,** which simply flushes the `ostream` without inserting anything:

```
double f(double x, double y)
{
   cout << "Entering f" << flush;
     .
     .
     .
   cout << "Exiting f" << flush;
   return z;
}
```

Of course, without insertion of a newline character, the output will appear on the same line,

```
Entering fExiting f
```

which is the reason `endl` is usually used instead.

The `ostream cout` *is also flushed automatically whenever the* `istream cin` *is used.* Thus, when the statements

```
cout << "Enter radius: ";
double radius;
cin >> radius;
```

are executed, the call to the `<<` operator inserts the prompt `"Enter radius: "` into the `ostream`,

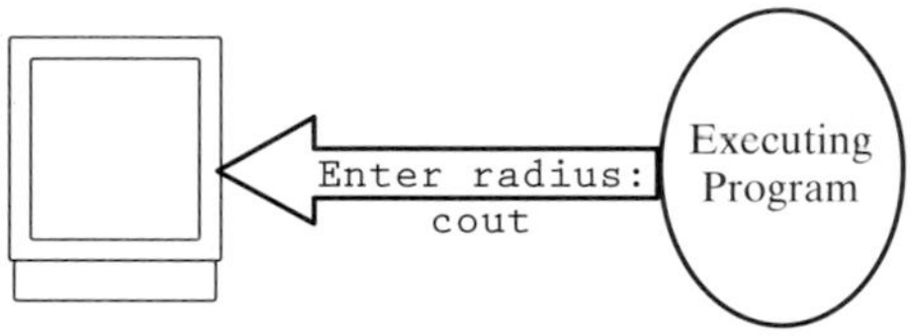

but it is actually the later sending of the `>>` message to `cin` that moves the prompt `"Enter radius: "` out of the `ostream` and onto your screen or window:

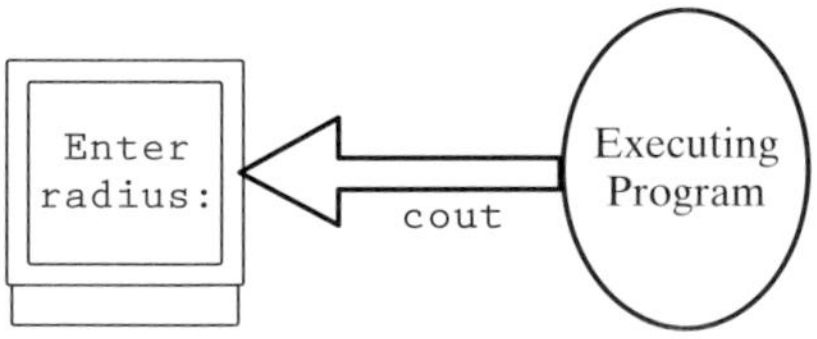

FORMAT CONTROL

The form in which a value is displayed or is entered is called its *format*, and **format manipulators** can be used to specify various format features. For example, in the statement

```
cout << "\nThe total revenue for these installations is $"
     << fixed << showpoint
     << revenue << endl;
```

`fixed` is a format manipulator that ensures that subsequent real values will be displayed in fixed-point notation instead of in scientific notation, and `showpoint` is a format manipulator that ensures that the decimal point will be displayed. The following is a complete list of the format manipulators provided by the `iostream` class. They and other manipulators are described in more detail in Chapter 9.[8]

Format Manipulator	Description
`fixed`	Use fixed-point notation for real values.
`scientific`	Use scientific notation for real values.
`showpoint`	Show decimal point and trailing zeros for whole real numbers.
`noshowpoint`	Hide decimal point and trailing zeros for whole real numbers.
`dec`	Use base-10 notation for integer input or output.
`hex`	Use base-16 (hexadecimal) notation for integer input or output.
`oct`	Use base-8 (octal) notation for integer input or output.
`showbase`	Display integer values indicating their base (e.g., `0x` for hex).
`noshowbase`	Display integer values without indicating their base.
`showpos`	Display + sign for positive values.
`noshowpos`	Do not display + sign for positive values.
`boolalpha`	Read or display `bool` values as `true or false`.
`noboolalpha`	Do not read or display `bool` values as `true` or `false`.
`uppercase`	In scientific, use E; in hexadecimal, use symbols A–F.
`nouppercase`	In scientific, use e; in hexadecimal, use symbols a–f.
`flush`	Write contents of stream to screen (or file).
`endl`	Insert newline character into output stream and flush the stream.
`left`	Left justify displayed values; pad with fill character on the right.
`right`	Right justify displayed values: pad with fill character on the left.
`internal`	Pad with fill character between sign or base and value.
`skipws`	Skip white space on input.
`noskipws`	Do not skip white space on input.

As we have seen, manipulators affect the stream into which they are inserted. For example, if we were to write

```
int i = 17;
cout << showbase
     << oct << i << endl
     << dec << i << endl
     << hex << i << endl;
```

---

8. As we noted before, some older C++ compilers may not support the use of format manipulators in this way. For example, it may be necessary to include the `iomanip` library, use `setiosflags(ios::fixed | ios::showpoint)` in the output statement, and use `resetiosflags(`*`ios::flagname`*`)` to reset the `ostream` to its default value. See Chapter 9 for more details.

then the result would be

```
021
17
0x11
```

because $21_8 = 17_{10} = 11_{16}$.

Some format manipulators require arguments, and to use them, the `iomanip` library must be included. There are many programs in which we want to specify the number of decimal places, or **precision**, to use in displaying real values. For this, `iomanip` provides the `setprecision(n)` manipulator, which sets the number of decimal places of precision in subsequent reals to *n*. We might use it, for example, to display monetary values rounded to two decimal places:

```
cout << "\nThe total equipment cost is $"
     << fixed << showpoint
     << setprecision(2)
     << equipmentCost << endl;
```

WATCH OUT

Another kind of format has to do with the space or *field* in which a data value is displayed. The width of an output field is 0 by default and automatically grows to accommodate the value being displayed. This is convenient, because it is what the programmer usually wants. However, there are some situations where we would like to have a field wider than the data value. The `setw(n)` manipulator can be used to set the width of the *next* field to *n*. However, every insertion automatically resets the field width to zero, and so `setw()` *must be used immediately prior to the insertion of each value whose field width is to be nonzero.*

To illustrate the use of `setw()`, suppose that we are creating a budget report and want the decimal points in our monetary values to be aligned. If we use

```
cout << showpoint << fixed
     << setprecision(2)
     << "Expenditures:  $" << expenditures << endl
     << "Receipts:      $" << receipts << endl
     << "-----------------------" << endl
     << "Profit:        $" << profit << endl;
```

then the output appears as follows:

```
Expenditures:     $1013.51
Receipts:         $998.49
------------------------
Profit:           $15.02
```

This would look better if the decimal points were aligned, and one way to do this is to use the `setw()` manipulator to increase the size of the field for the monetary values, and the `right` manipulator to right justify the values in these fields:

```
cout << showpoint << fixed
     << setprecision(2) << right
     << "Expenditures:  $" << setw(7) << expenditures << endl
```

```
     << "Receipts:       $" << setw(7) << receipts << endl
     << "------------------------" << endl
     << "Profit:         $" << setw(7) << profit << endl;
```

which generates the output

```
Expenditures:   $1013.51
Receipts:       $ 998.49
------------------------
Profit:         $  15.02
```

When a value is smaller in width than its field, the character used to fill the empty part of a field is called the **fill character**. It is a *space* by default, but it can be changed to another character *ch* by using the `setfill(ch)` manipulator. For example, if we changed the preceding output statement to

```
cout << showpoint << fixed
     << setprecision(2) << right
     << setfill('*')
     << "Expenditures:   $" << setw(7) << expenditures << endl
     << "Receipts:       $" << setw(7) << receipts << endl
     << "------------------------" << endl
     << "Profit:         $" << setw(7) << profit << endl;
```

the resulting output will be

```
Expenditures:   $1013.51
Receipts:       $*998.49
------------------------
Profit:         $**15.02
```

Quick Quiz 5.3

1. Who designed the C++ language?
2. Who developed the classes that constitute the `iostream` library?
3. What are two of the main classes in the `iostream` library?
4. A(n) __________ is an abstraction that models how input gets from the keyboard to a program, or from a program to the screen.
5. __________ is a class for inputting characters from an arbitrary input device to an executing program.
6. __________ is an `istream` object defined in the `iostream` library, which is a stream from the keyboard to a program.
7. Three states of an `istream` are __________, __________, and __________.
8. The statement `assert(cin.______);` will stop program execution if there is a data-entry error.
9. The method __________ in the `istream` class is used to reset the states of an input stream.
10. The method __________ in the `istream` class is used to skip characters in an input stream.
11. (True or false) By default, `>>` skips white space in an input stream.
12. (True or false) The method `get()` skips white space in an input stream.

13. _________ is a class for outputting characters from an executing program to an arbitrary output device.
14. _________ and _________ are `ostream` objects defined in the `iostream` library, which are streams from a program to an output device.
15. Two manipulators that can be used to flush an output stream are _________ and _________.
16. (True or false) When the statement

```
cout << setw(10) << 1.234 << 5.678 << endl;
```

is executed, the real numbers 1.234 and 5.678 will be displayed in 10-space fields.

17. (True or false) When the statement

```
cout << setprecision(1) << 1.234 << 5.678 << endl;
```

is executed, the real numbers 1.2 and 5.7 will be displayed.

Exercises 5.3

For Exercises 1–11, assume that `i1`, `i2`, and `i3` are `int` variables; `r1`, `r2`, and `r3` are `double` variables; and `c1`, `c2`, and `c3` are `char` variables. Tell what value, if any, will be assigned to each of these variables, or explain why an error occurs, when the input statements are executed with the given input data.

1.
```
cin >> i1 >> i2 >> i3
    >> r1 >> r2 >> r3;
```
Input:
```
1     2   3
4 5.5 6.6
```

2.
```
cin >> i1 >> i2 >> i3;
cin >> r1 >> r2 >> r3;
```
Input:
```
1
2
3
4
5
6
```

3.
```
cin >> i1 >> r1;
cin >> i2 >> r2;
cin >> i3 >> r3;
```
Input:
```
1 2.2
3 4.4
5 6.6
```

4.
```
cin >> i1 >> i2 >> i3
    >> r1 >> r2 >> r3;
```
Input:
```
1 2.2
3 4.4
5 6.6
```

5.
```
cin >> i1 >> c1 >> r1
    >> i2 >> c2 >> r2
    >> i3 >> c3 >> r3;
```
Input:
```
1 2.2
3 4.4
5 6.6
```

6.
```
cin >> noskipws
    >> i1 >> c1 >> r1
    >> c2 >> i2 >> skipws
    >> r2 >> i3 >> r3;
```
Input:
```
1 2.2
3 4.4
5 6.6
```

7.
```
cin >> i1 >> c1 >> i2
    >> c2 >> i3 >> c3;
```
Input: `1A 2B 3C`

8. `cin >> i1 >> i2 >> i3;` Input: `012 345 678`
9. `cin >> dec >> i1 >> i2 >> i3;` Input: `012 345 678`
10. `cin >> oct >> i1 >> i2 >> i3;` Input: `012 345 678`
11. `cin >> hex >> i1 >> i2 >> i3;` Input: `12 3A BC`

For Exercises 12–20, assume that alpha and beta are real variables with values –2567.392 and 0.0004, respectively, and that num1 and num2 are integer variables with values 12 and 436, respectively. Show precisely the output that each of the sets of statements produces, or explain why an error occurs.

12. `cout << num2 << num2 + 1 << num2 + 2;`

13. `cout << num2 << setw(4) << num2 + 1 << num2 + 2;`

14. `cout << num1 << num1 + 1 << num1 + 2;`

15. `cout << oct << num1 << num1 + 1 << num1 + 2;`

16. `cout << showbase << oct << num1 << num1 + 1 << num1 + 2;`

17. `cout << hex << num1 << num1 + 1 << num1 + 2;`

18. `cout << showbase << hex << num1 << num1 + 1 << num1 + 2;`

19.
```
cout << fixed << showpoint << right
     << setw(9) << setprecision(3) << alpha << endl
     << setw(10) << setprecision(5) << beta << endl
     << setw(7) << setprecision(4) << beta << endl;
```

20.
```
cout << scientific << showpoint << left
     << setprecision(1) << setw(10) << alpha << endl
     << setw(5) << beta << endl
     << "Tolerance:"
     << setw(12) << setprecision(3) << beta << endl;
```

For Exercises 21 and 22, assume that i and j are integer variables with values 15 and 8, respectively; that ch is a character variable whose value is 'c'; and that x and y are real variables with values 2559.50 and 8.015, respectively. Show precisely the output produced, or explain why an error occurs.

21.
```
cout << setw(j) << setprecision(2)
     << fixed << showpoint << right
     << "New balance =" << x << ' ' << setw(i % 10) << ch
     << setw(j) << setprecision(j-6) << y << endl;
```

22.
```
cout << i =" << setw(i) << i
     << fixed << showpoint << right
     << "j = << setw(j) << setprecision(j) << j << endl
     << setw(j) << i << ' '
     << setw(i) << j << endl;
```

For Exercises 23–26, assume that n1 and n2 are integer variables with values 987 and –6789, respectively; that r1 and r2 are real variables with values 12.3456 and –0.00246, respectively; and that ch is a character variable with the value 'T'. For each, write an output statement that uses these variables and format manipulators to produce the given output. (The underlining dashes are shown here only to help you determine the spacing.)

23.
```
   12.3  T   987
----------------
-6789TTT-0.00246
----------------
```

24.
```
 12.35  -0.0025
-----------------
 12.345600T***987
-----------------
```

25.
```
Values: 12.34560 and -0.00246
-----------------------------
```

26.
```
Observations:  12.3 and -0.0
-----------------------------
Locations:       987 and  6789
-----------------------------
```

5.4 Computing with `string` Objects

The word *compute* usually suggests arithmetic computations performed on numeric data; thus computers are sometimes thought to be mere "number crunchers"—devices whose only purpose is to process numeric information—and in the early days of computing, this was largely true.

However, to facilitate communication between a human and a running program, computer scientists soon devised a code by which alphabetic characters could be represented and manipulated. Since words consist of sequences or **strings** of characters, the problem of storing and processing strings of characters followed naturally. In this section, we examine C++'s solution to the problem, the standard `string` class. It is declared in the header file `string` (*not* `string.h`, which is a C library), which must be included to use the class.

DECLARING `string` OBJECTS

Since `string` is the name of a class and the name of a class is a type, `string` objects can be declared and initialized in the same manner as other objects we have studied.[9] For example, the declaration

```
string name;
```

creates a `string` object named `name` and initializes it to an **empty string**, which contains no characters. A literal for the empty string can be written as two consecutive double quotes ("").

A declaration of a `string` object can also initialize that object by providing a `string` expression for its initial value. For example, the declarations

```
string play = "Hamlet",
       author = "W. Shakespeare",
       mainCharacter = play;
```

create three `string` objects `play`, `author`, and `mainCharacter` and initialize `play` to contain 6 characters,

play	H	a	m	l	e	t

9. The class `string` is really a specialization of the class template `basic_string` to type `char`. (Class templates are described in Section 10.6.) Also, a recent feature added to C++ is the ability to read input from a `string` or write output to a `string`. This is made possible by means of **string streams** defined in the `<sstream>` library (see Chapter 9).

`author` to contain 14 characters,

author	W	.		S	h	a	k	e	s	p	e	a	r	e

and `mainCharacter` to contain a copy of the string in `play`:

mainCharacter	H	a	m	l	e	t

These `string` objects are *variables*, and they can be assigned new values as in

```
play = "The Tempest";
mainCharacter = "Prospero";
```

and these two objects will be modified:

play	T	h	e		T	e	m	p	e	s	t

mainCharacter	P	r	o	s	p	e	r	o

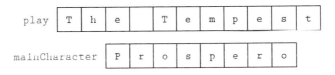

Constant `string` objects are defined by preceding a normal string declaration with the keyword `const`; for example,

```
const string PASSWORD = "Romeo-Romeo";
```

As with other constants, the `string` value of such objects cannot subsequently be changed.

STRING I/O

String input and output are quite similar to input and output for other types of objects, because the `string` class has overloaded the << operator to perform `string` output and the >> operator to perform `string` input.

Output. The output operator << can be used to display `string` literals and expressions. For example, the statements

```
string name = "John Doe";
cout << "My name is " << name << ".\n";
```

will display

```
My name is John Doe.
```

Input Using >>. The input operator >> can be used to input values for `string` variables. For example, consider the following statements:

```
cout << "Enter your name: ";
string name;
```

```
cin >> name;
cout << "Welcome, " << name << "!\n";
```

If these statements are executed and the user enters `Al`,

```
Enter your name: Al
Welcome, Al!
```

we see that the string `Al` is assigned to `name`. If, however, the user enters `Al E. Cat` instead, execution will proceed as follows:

```
Enter your name: Al E. Cat
Welcome, Al!
```

The string `Al` is assigned to `name` as before, but what happened to the `E. Cat`?

When the input operator `>>` is applied to a string object, it gets the next "word" from the input stream, that is, the next sequence of characters that contains no **white-space** characters (spaces, tabs, and newlines). More precisely, `>>` *removes leading white-space characters from an* `istream` *until a non-white-space character is encountered, and then continues extracting characters and transferring them into a* `string` *object until a white-space character is encountered, which is left in the* `istream`. In the preceding example, the unread characters `E. Cat` (including the space before the `E`) remain in the `istream` and will be read by subsequent input statements, which is probably not what was intended.

For this reason, it is a good idea to *always prompt the user as precisely as possible when reading* `string` *values using* `>>`; for example,

```
cout << "Enter your first name (e.g., Jane): ";
string firstName;
cin >> firstName;
```

or

```
cout << "\nEnter your full name (e.g., John Quincy Doe): ";
string firstName,
       middleName,
       lastName;
cin >> firstName >> middleName >> lastName;
```

Input Using `getline()`. Sometimes we want to read an entire line of text into a `string` variable. This can be done using the function `getline()` provided in the `string` library. For example, if we rewrite the earlier code segment as

```
cout << "Enter your name: ";
string name;
getline (cin, name);
cout << "Welcome, " << name << "!\n";
```

and the user enters `Al`, execution will proceed as before:

```
Enter your name: Al
Welcome, Al!
```

However, if the user instead enters `Al E. Cat`, execution will produce

```
Enter your name: Al E. Cat
Welcome, Al E. Cat!
```

because the `getline()` function reads *the entire line*. More precisely, *the* `getline()` *function extracts characters from an* `istream` *and transfers them into a* `string` *variable until a newline character is encountered, which is removed from the* `istream`, *but is not stored in the* `string` *variable.*

WATCH OUT

Thus, to read an *entire line* of input, the `getline()` function should be used. To read a *word* of input, the input operator `>>` should be used. *Caution must be exercised, however, when using both* `>>` *and* `getline()`. For example, a newline character that terminates input of characters via `>>` is left in the `istream`, and a subsequent attempt to read a string using `getline()` would terminate as soon as this newline is encountered with the result that no characters are read.

OTHER STRING OPERATIONS

The `string` class provides several other operations. We will discuss the more commonly used operations here; others are described in Appendix D.

The Subscript Operation. Variables that can only store a single value at a time are called **scalar variables**. In contrast, a `string` object can be viewed as a *container* for storing a sequence of values. Each *element* of a `string` object is like a scalar `char` variable in that it can store a single character and can have the character operations performed on it.

When a `string` object is created, the compiler automatically associates an integer called an **index** with each character in the string. For example, suppose that `name` is declared by

```
string name = "John Doe";
```

When this declaration is encountered, a container is automatically built for the object `name`, with each element of `name` being numbered, starting from zero, and the characters `J`, `o`, `h`, `n`, a blank, `D`, `o`, and `e` are stored in these elements:

name	J	o	h	n		D	o	e
	0	1	2	3	4	5	6	7

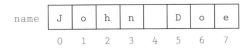

The **subscript operator** `[]` uses the index of an element to access the character stored in that element. An expression of the form

`string_object[index]`

accesses the element at the specified *`index`* of *`string_object`*. To illustrate, consider the following assignment statements:

```
name[1] = 'a';
name[2] = name[3];
name[3] = 'e';
name[5] = 'R';
```

The first assignment changes the element at index 1 of `name` to 'a'. The second assignment copies the element 'n' at index 3 to the element at index 2. The third assignment changes the element at index 3 to 'e'. The final assignment changes the element at index 5 to 'R'. The result is that `name` is changed as follows:

name	J	a	n	e		R	o	e
	0	1	2	3	4	5	6	7

To process all of the characters in a string individually, a `for` loop as described in Section 4.4 can be used in conjunction with the subscript operator. For example, to display the characters of `name` in reverse order,

```
eoR enaJ
```

we could use the `for` loop

```
for (int i = 7; i >= 0; i--)
   cout << name[i];
```

On the first pass through the loop, `i` is 7, and so the last element's value is displayed; on the next pass, `i` is 6, and so the next-to-last element's value is displayed; and so on.

This example assumes that the index of the last element is 7 and will no longer work correctly if a larger or smaller `string` value is assigned to `name`. To avoid this difficulty, we need to be able to find the *size* of a string.

The `size()` Method. To determine the **size** of a given `string` object, we can send it the `size()` message, which returns the number of characters in that string. For example, the message

```
name.size()
```

will return the value 8.

Note that because indices start at zero, *the index of the last character in a string is always* `size() - 1`. This means that the earlier `for` loop for displaying the reverse of `name` could be better written

```
for (int i = name.size() - 1; i >= 0; i--)
   cout << name[i];
```

If `name` is `"Jane Roe"`, then `name.size()` is 8, so 7 is the index of the final character. If `name` is `"William Shakespeare"`, then `name.size()` is 19, so 18 is the index of the final character. By using `name.size() - 1` as the index of the final character, this loop will always correctly begin with the last character in `name`, regardless of the string stored in it.

The `empty()` Method. As we noted earlier, a string containing no characters is called the empty string. To test whether a string is empty, we can send it the `empty()` message. This method returns the boolean value `true` if the `string` object to which it is sent is empty and `false` otherwise. For example, if we declare

```
string oneString,
       anotherString = "Hi There";
```

then the expression

```
oneString.empty()
```

returns `true`, while the expression

```
anotherString.empty()
```

returns `false`.

Assignment. The assignment operator can be used to assign values to variable `string` objects. The size of the `string` object will be the number of characters in the `string` value being assigned. For example,

```
string quote = "To be is to do - Aristotle.";
```

will initialize `quote` with the indicated string so that `quote.size()` will be 27. If we later assign

```
quote = "To do is to be - Sartre.";
```

then this new string replaces the string in `quote`, and `quote.size()` changes to 24. Similarly, a later assignment

```
quote = "Doobee-Doobee-Doo - Sinatra.";
```

will change `quote`'s value as indicated and `quote.size()` to 28.

In each of these examples, the value assigned has been a `string` literal, but a string object can also be assigned to another string object. For example, the declarations

```
string today = "Monday",
       yesterday;
```

initialize `today` to contain the string `"Monday"` and `yesterday` to an empty string:

today	M	o	n	d	a	y
	0	1	2	3	4	5

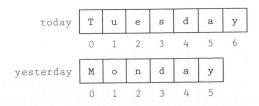

If we subsequently write

```
yesterday = today;
today = "Tuesday";
```

then `yesterday` is assigned the value `"Monday"` and the value of `today` is changed to `"Tuesday"`:

today	T	u	e	s	d	a	y
	0	1	2	3	4	5	6

yesterday	M	o	n	d	a	y
	0	1	2	3	4	5

The Relational Operators. The relational operators have all been overloaded in class `string` and can be used to compare `string` objects. For each operation, the elements of the string operands are compared element by element until a mismatch occurs or the end of one (or both) of the strings is reached.

To illustrate, consider the declarations

```
string hisName = "James",
       herName = "Jan";
```

The objects produced are

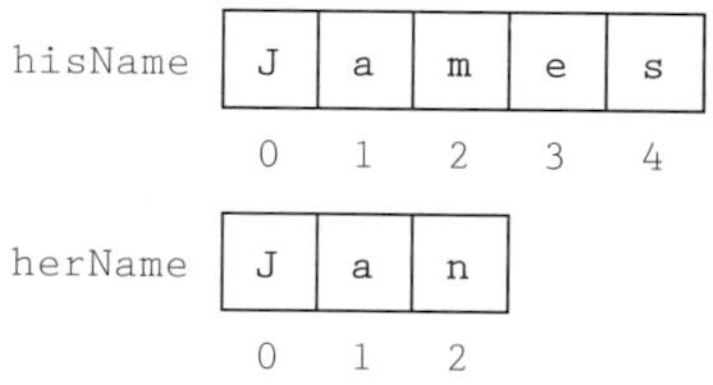

If these two objects are compared with the boolean expression

```
hisName < herName
```

the < function begins by comparing the characters at index 0:

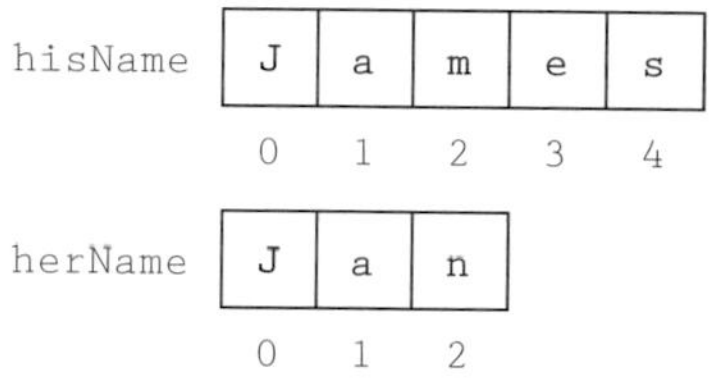

Since these characters are the same, the function compares the next two characters,

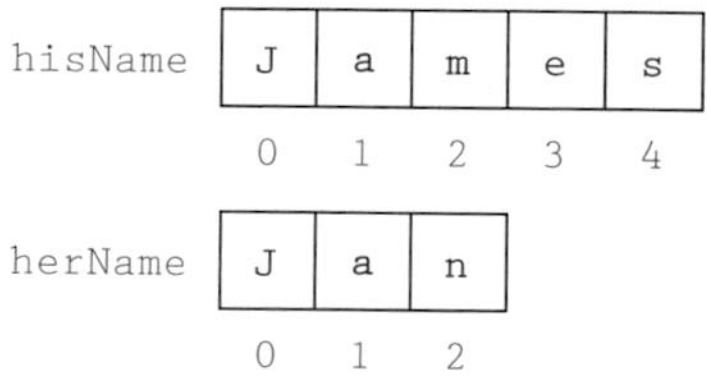

and, because they are also the same, it proceeds to the next two characters:

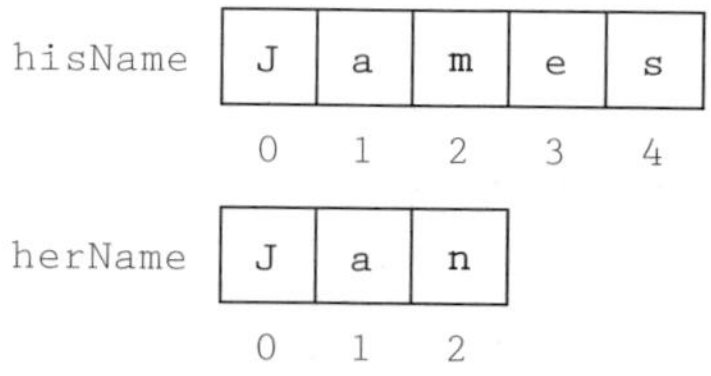

Here, the first mismatch occurs. Since the character code for `'m'` is less than the character code for `'n'` (see Appendix A), the < function returns `true`, indicating that `"James"`

is less than "Jan". If the end of one of the strings is reached without a mismatch, then the shorter string is considered to be less than the longer one. For example,

```
herName < "Jane"
```

returns true. If the ends of both strings are reached without a mismatch, the strings are of course, equal.

Expressions involving the other relational operators such as

```
hisName == herName

hisName != herName

hisName > herName

hisName <= herName

hisName >= herName
```

use this same character-by-character comparison. For the given values of hisName and herName, they will return false, true, false, true, and false, respectively.

Concatenation. Another useful string operation is **concatenation**—combining two strings into a single string. For example, the concatenation of the string "list" and the string "en" produces the string "listen". Ordering is important in concatenation—if we concatenate the string "en" and the string "list", the string "enlist" is produced. The concatenation operation can be thought of as forming a string whose value is the second string appended to the first string.

The plus symbol (+) has been overloaded in class string so that when its two operands are string objects or character string literals, concatenation is performed. For example, given the declarations

```
string state = "Michigan",
       greatLake;
```

the statement

```
greatLake = "Lake " + state;
```

will concatenate the string literal "Lake " and the string stored in state and assign the resulting string to greatLake:

greatLake	L	a	k	e		M	i	c	h	i	g	a	n
	0	1	2	3	4	5	6	7	8	9	10	11	12

Concatenation thus builds a larger string out of two smaller string values. The concatenation operator returns the string object it produces, so that multiple concatenations can be chained together, as in

```
string firstName = "Popeye",
       middleName = "the",
       lastName = "Sailor",
       fullName = firstName + " " + middleName + " " + lastName;
```

which initializes `fullName` to be a `string` object containing

```
Popeye the Sailor
```

To append `man` to this string, we could write

```
fullName = fullName + "man";
```

but the += shortcut

```
fullName += "man";
```

is preferable. In either case, `"man"` is appended to the `string` in `name` so that the value in `fullName` is `"Popeye the Sailorman"`.

The `substr()` Method. The subscript operation provides access to a particular character in a string, but it is sometimes useful to access a substring of characters. To illustrate, suppose that the following string objects have been declared:

```
string fullName = "John Quincy Doe",
       firstName,
       middleName,
       lastName;
```

fullName	J	o	h	n		Q	u	i	n	c	y		D	o	e
	0	1	2	3	4	5	6	7	8	9	10	11	12	13	14

Also, suppose we want to access the first, middle, or last name within `fullName`. The `substr()` message makes this easy. The assignments

```
firstName = fullName.substr(0, 4);
middleName = fullName.substr(5, 6);
lastName = fullName.substr(12, 3);
```

set the value of `firstName` to `"John"`, the value of `middleName` to `"Quincy"`, and the value of `lastName` to `"Doe"`, leaving `fullName` unchanged.

The general form to send a `string` object the `substr()` message is

`string_object``.substr(`*`first, num_chars`*`)`

where *`first`* is the index in *`string_object`* of the first character to be selected and *`num_chars`* is the size of the substring to be selected. It returns a `string` value consisting of the *`num_chars`* characters beginning at position *`first`* in *`string_object`*.

Note the differences between this *substring* method and the *subscript* operation:

Subscript Operation	Substring Method
Invoked using square brackets: `[]`	Invoked using `substr` and parentheses: `substr()`
Takes one argument: an index	Takes two arguments: an index and a size
Returns a `char` value	Returns a `string` value

WATCH OUT

Another difference is that the subscript operation does not check that the index it receives is within the bounds of the string; hence, logic errors can occur and go undetected if one tries to access a position past the end of the string, as in

```
string name = "Sam";
char initial = name[4];          // ERROR, but no notification
```

When these statements are executed, `initial` will be assigned whatever "garbage" character happens to be two characters past the end of `"Sam"`.

By contrast, the `substring()` member function checks the validity of its index. If one tries to access a substring that begins past the end of the string,

```
string name1 = "Sam",
name2 = name1.substr(4, 2);   // ERROR: fatal
                              // with notification
```

an **out-of-bounds exception** will occur and execution of the program terminated. If the size passed to `substr()` is larger than the number of characters remaining in the string,

```
string name1 = "Sam",
       name2 = name1.substr(1, 5);   // ERROR: no notification
```

the size argument (5) will be ignored and all of the characters from the specified starting position (1) to the end of the string will be selected.

The `replace()` Method. We have seen that the `substr()` message does not modify the `string` object to which it is sent. However, it is sometimes necessary to modify some portion of a `string`, leaving the rest of it unaltered. To accomplish this, we can send a `string` object the `replace()` message. To illustrate, consider again the declaration:

```
string fullName = "John Quincy Doe";
```

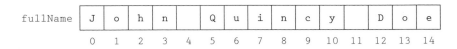

fullName	J	o	h	n		Q	u	i	n	c	y		D	o	e
	0	1	2	3	4	5	6	7	8	9	10	11	12	13	14

Execution of the statement

```
fullName.replace(0, 4, "Jane");
```

replaces the first four characters in `fullName` with `"Jane"`:

fullName	J	a	n	e		Q	u	i	n	c	y		D	o	e
	0	1	2	3	4	5	6	7	8	9	10	11	12	13	14

Individual characters can also be replaced with the `replace()` function. For example, the statement

```
fullName.replace(12, 1, "R");
```

will replace the single character at index 12 with R, changing the last name to "Roe":

fullName	J	a	n	e		Q	u	i	n	c	y		R	o	e
	0	1	2	3	4	5	6	7	8	9	10	11	12	13	14

In the preceding examples, the length of fullName did not change, because the replacement string and the substring being replaced had the same length. In general, however, they may have different lengths. For example, execution of the statement

```
fullName.replace(5, 6, "Eyre");
```

replaces the six-character substring "Quincy" with the four-character string "Eyre". As a result, the size of fullName decreases from 15 to 13:

fullName	J	a	n	e		E	y	r	e		R	o	e
	0	1	2	3	4	5	6	7	8	9	10	11	12

The general form to send a string object the replace() message is

string_object.replace(*first*, *num_chars*, *replacement*);

where *first* is the index of the first character to be replaced, *num_chars* is the number of characters to be replaced, and *replacement* is a string object, string literal, or character. It modifies *string_object* by replacing the substring *string_object*.substr(*first*, *num_chars*) with *replacement*; the size of *string_object* increases or decreases as necessary. Bounds checking is performed to ensure that *first* is a valid index of *string_object*.

The erase() Method. Another useful string operation is removal of a substring. To accomplish this, we can send a *string* object the erase() message. For example, consider the declaration

```
string commonName = "John Quincy Doe";
```

which initializes the string object commonName as

commonName	J	o	h	n		Q	u	i	n	c	y		D	o	e
	0	1	2	3	4	5	6	7	8	9	10	11	12	13	14

Execution of the statement

```
commonName.erase(5, 7);
```

removes the seven characters starting at position 5 from commonName,

commonName	J	o	h	n		D	o	e
	0	1	2	3	4	5	6	7

and the size of commonName decreases to 8.

The general form to send a `string` object the `erase()` message is

```
string_object.erase();
```

or

```
string_object.erase(first, num_chars);
```

where *`first`* is the index of the first character to be removed and *`num_chars`* is the number of characters to be removed. The first version makes *`string_object`* the empty string, removing all of its characters. The second version modifies *`string_object`* by removing the substring *`string_object`*`.substr(`*`first,num_chars`*`)`. The length of *`string_object`* decreases by *`num_chars`*. Bounds checking is performed to ensure that *`first`* is a valid index of *`string_object`*.

The `insert()` Method. The inverse of the removal operation for a `string` object is the insertion of a substring into a string. To accomplish this, we can send a `string` object the `insert()` message. For example, consider the declaration

```
string signature = "Jane Doe";
```

which initializes `signature` to `"Jane Doe"`:

signature	J	a	n	e		D	o	e
	0	1	2	3	4	5	6	7

Execution of the statement

```
signature.insert(5, "E. ");
```

inserts the string `"E. "` into `signature` beginning at position 5, giving

signature	J	a	n	e		E	.		D	o	e
	0	1	2	3	4	5	6	7	8	9	10

The size of `signature` increases to 11.

The general form to send a `string` object the `insert()` message is

```
string_object.insert(position, new_string);
```

where *`position`* is the index at which insertion is to begin, and *`new_string`* is a `string` object, `string` literal, or a character. It modifies *`string_object`* by inserting the *`new_string`* with its first character at *`position`*. The size of *`string_object`* increases by *`new_string`*`.size()`. Bounds checking is performed to ensure that *`position`* is a valid index of *`string_object`*.

The `find()` and `rfind()` Methods. Another common string operation is finding the location of a given string within another string, an operation known as **pattern matching.**

The `string` class provides two methods for this purpose: `find()` and `rfind()`. For example, given the declaration

```
string quote = "If it walks like a duck, "
               "and quacks like a duck,\n"
               "then it just may be a duck - Reuther";
```

the `find()` message in the statement

```
int position = quote.find("duck", 0);
```

will search `quote` for the substring `"duck"`, beginning the search at index 0. In this case, the value 19 will be returned since the first occurrence of the substring `"duck"` within object `quote` is at index 19. The positions of later occurrences of the same substring `"duck"` can be found by starting the search one past the last `position`. For example, if `position` is 19, the statement

```
position = quote.find("duck", position + 1);
```

will search for `"duck"` again, but starting from the character at index 20. In this case, the value returned will be 43, which is assigned to `position`. A subsequent execution of this statement

```
position = quote.find("duck", position + 1);
```

will begin the search at position 44 and return the value 71. If we try again,

```
position = quote.find("duck", position + 1);
```

the search will fail, and the value returned will be `npos`, a special **class constant** (–1 on many systems) defined within the `string` class. As shown later, to access a class constant, the name of the class and the scope operator (`::`) must be attached to it—`string::npos`.

The `find()` and `replace` messages can be sent to a `string` object in a loop to find and replace all occurrences of a string in that object. For example, we might use a while loop (described in Section 4.4) as in the following statements that replace all occurrences of `"a duck"` in `quote` with `"an aardvark"`:

```
int position = quote.find ("a duck", 0);
while (position != string::npos)
{
   quote.replace (position, 6, "an aardvark");
   position = quote.find ("a duck", position + 1);
}
```

The general form to send a `string` object the `find()` message is

`string_object``.find(`*`pattern`*`, `*`position`*`)`

where *`pattern`* is a `string` object or `string` literal, and *`position`* is the index at which the search is to commence. It returns the index at which the substring *`pattern`* begins within *`string_object`*. If *`pattern`* is not found (i.e., if the search *fails*), `string::npos` is returned. Bounds checking is performed to ensure that *`position`* is a valid index of *`string_object`*.

In general, it is good programming practice to check the return values of operations that can easily fail (such as pattern matching) to ensure that they are successful before continuing. For example, suppose that we search `quote` for some string:

```
int location = quote.find(some_string, 0);
```

WATCH OUT

If *`some_string`* is a value that does not occur within `quote`, `find()` will return the value `string::npos` and a subsequent access to `quote` using `location` may generate a fatal out-of-bounds exception. It would be better to check the value of `location` with an `if` statement, for example (as described in Section 4.3):

```
int location = quote.find(some_string, 0);
if (location == string::npos)
   cerr << some_string << " does not occur within \'quote\'";
else
{
   // ... process using valid location value
}
```

The method `find()` searches in a forward direction, by incrementing the index being examined. To search in a backward direction, the `string` class provides the method `rfind()`. It is used in a manner similar to the `find()` method, except that the search should begin at the index of the last character instead of the first character. For example, the statement

```
int rPosition = quote.rfind("duck", quote.size() - 1);
```

will search `quote` for the substring `"duck"` in a backward direction, starting at its last character. For the value of `quote` given earlier, the value 71 will be returned, since the last occurrence of the substring `"duck"` within object `quote` is at index 71. Earlier occurrences can be found by starting at `rPosition - 1`, one position before that located in the previous search.

Other Search Methods. The `find()` and `rfind()` methods are used to search a string for a substring. To search a `string` object for the first occurrence of any of a set of characters, the `string` class provides the `find_first_of()` method, which searches a string in a forward direction for the first occurrence of any of a given list of characters. To illustrate, consider the declaration

```
string quote = "I wouldn't want to belong to any club\n"
               "that would accept me as a member "
               "- Groucho Marx.";
```

To find the index of the first vowel in `quote`, we can use

```
position = quote.find_first_of ("aeiouAEIOU", 0);
```

and the following statements to find all vowels:

```
position = quote.find_first_of ("aeiouAEIOU", 0);
while (position != string::pos)
{
   cout << position << ' ';
   position = quote.find_first_of ("aeiouAEIOU", position + 1);
}
```

Execution of these statements produces

```
0 3 4 12 17 20 22 27 29 35 40 44 45 49 52 57 59 62 65 68 75 76 79 82
```

The general form to send a `string` object the `find_first_of()` message is

string_object`.find_first_of(`*pattern*`,` *position*`)`

where *pattern* is a `string` object, `string` literal, or character and *position* is the index at which the search is to begin. It returns the index ≥ *position* of the first occurrence of any character in *pattern* within *string_object*. If no character in *pattern* is found, the predefined constant `npos` is returned. Bounds checking is carried out to ensure that *position* is a valid index of *string_object*.

The `string` class also provides other character-searching methods, including the following:

- *string_object*`.find_last_of(`*pattern*`,` *position*`)`
  returns the index ≤ *position* of the *last* occurrence of any of the characters in *pattern*.
- *string_object*`.find_first_not_of(`*pattern*`,` *position*`)`
  returns the index ≥ *position* of the *first* occurrence of a character *not* in *pattern*.
- *string_object*`.find_last_not_of(`*pattern*`,` *position*`)`
  returns the index ≤ *position* of the *last* occurrence of a character *not* in *pattern*.

These complementary operations simplify some kinds of searches. For example, to find the consonants in `quote` with the `find_first_of()` function, *pattern* would have to list all 21 consonants in both uppercase and lowercase:

```
"bcdfghjklmnpqrstvwxyzBCDFGHJKLMNPQRSTVWXYZ"
```

It is much simpler to use the `find_first_not_of()` function and the string of vowel characters for *pattern*:

```
firstConsonantIndex = quote.find_first_not_of("AEIOUaeiou", 0);
```

✔ Quick Quiz 5.4

1. A string that contains no characters is called a(n) ________ string.
2. Write a declaration that initializes a `string` variable `label` to an empty string.
3. Write a declaration that initializes a `string` constant `UNITS` to “meters”.
4. If the input for the statement `cin >> s1 >> s2;`, where `s1` and `s2` are `string` variables, is

```
ABC
    DEF GHI
```

then `s1` will be assigned the value ________ and `s2` the value ________.

Questions 5–22 assume the following declarations:

```
string s1 = "shell",
       s2 = "seashore",
       s3 = "She sells seashells by the seashore.",
       s4;
```

For Questions 5–19 find the value of the expression, and for 20–22 give the new value of the variable (`s1`, `s2`, or `s3`).

5. `s1[2]`
6. `s2.size()`
7. `s4.size()`
8. `s3.empty()`
9. `s4.empty()`
10. `s1 > s2`
11. `s1 < s3`
12. `s2 + s1`
13. `s1.substr(0,3)`
14. `s3.find("sea", 0)`
15. `s3.rfind("sea", 35)`
16. `s3.find_first_of("abc",0)`
17. `s3.find_last_of("abc",35)`
18. `s3.find_first_not_of("abc",0)`
19. `s3.find_last_not_of("abc",35)`
20. `s1.replace(0, 2, 'b');`
21. `s2.insert(3, "1 on the ");`
22. `s3.erase(9, 13);`

Exercises 5.4

Exercises 1–26 assume the following declarations:

```
string s1,
       s2 = "row, row, row your boat",
       s3 = "row",
       s4 = "boat.";
```

For Exercises 1–21, find the value of the expression or explain why an error occurs.

1. `s2[3]`
2. `s1.size() + s4.size()`
3. `s3 < s4`
4. `s3 <= s2`
5. `s3 + s4`
6. `"fl" + s4.substr(1,3) + " a " + s4`
7. `s2.substr(1,3)`
8. `s3.substr(1,3)`
9. `s2.find("ow", 1)`
10. `s2.find("ow", 2)`
11. `s2.find("ow", 12)`
12. `s2.rfind("ow", 12)`

Fig. 5.2 Dice-roll simulation. (Part 3 of 3)

```
                                    // display the result
     cout << "The relative frequency of " << numberOfSpots
          << " was " << double(occurrences) / double(numberOfRolls)
          << "\n\n";

     cout << "Enter number of spots to count (2-12, 0 to stop): ";
     cin >> numberOfSpots;
   }                                 // end input loop
}
```

Sample run:

```
This program simulates a given number of dice rolls,
counting the number of times a given roll occurs.

How many times are the dice to be rolled? 10000

Enter number of spots to count (2-12, 0 to stop): 2
The relative frequency of 2 was 0.0281

Enter number of spots to count (2-12, 0 to stop): 6
The relative frequency of 6 was 0.1365

Enter number of spots to count (2-12, 0 to stop): 7
The relative frequency of 7 was 0.1691

Enter number of spots to count (2-12, 0 to stop):  8
The relative frequency of 8 was 0.141

Enter number of spots to count (2-12, 0 to stop): 11
The relative frequency of 11 was 0.0543

Enter number of spots to count (2-12, 0 to stop): 0
```

NORMAL DISTRIBUTIONS

Most random number generators generate random numbers having a **uniform distribution**, but they can also be used to generate random numbers having other distributions. The **normal distribution** is especially important because it models many physical processes. For example, the heights and weights of people, the lifetime of light bulbs, the tensile strength of steel produced by a machine, and, in general, the variations in parts produced in almost any manufacturing process have normal distributions. The normal distribution has the familiar bell-shaped curve,

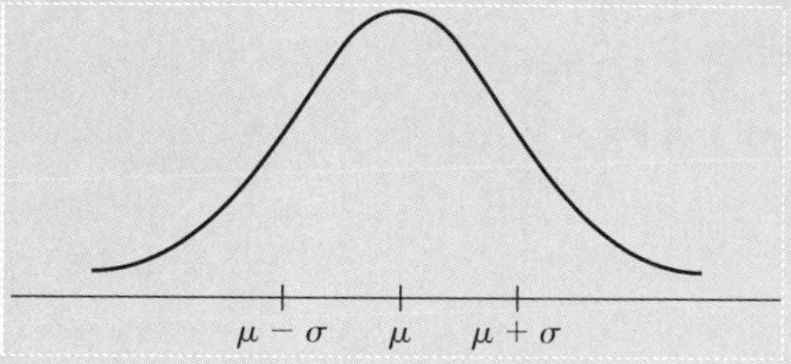

where μ is the mean of the distribution, σ is the standard deviation, and approximately two thirds of the area under the curve lies between $\mu - \sigma$ and $\mu + \sigma$.

A normal distribution having $\mu = 0$ and $\sigma = 1$ is called a **standard normal distribution,** and random numbers having approximately this distribution can be generated quite easily from a uniform distribution with the following algorithm:

Algorithm for the Standard Normal Distribution

1. Set *sum* equal to 0.
2. Do the following 12 times:
   a. Generate a random number *x* from a uniform distribution.
   b. Add *x* to *sum*.
3. Calculate $z = sum - 6$.

The numbers *z* generated by this algorithm have an approximate standard normal distribution. To generate random numbers *y* having a normal distribution with mean μ and standard deviation σ, we simply add the following step to the algorithm:

4. Calculate $y = \mu + \sigma * z$.

Implementing this algorithm as a program is left as an exercise.

* Optional arguments `lower_bound` and `upper_bound` can be used with the `generate()` method to alter the range in the random number to be generated.

5.6* OBJECTive Thinking: Instance Methods

In earlier *OBJECTive Thinking* sections, we have seen how to build a class containing instance variables and how to initialize those variables using a constructor. We have also seen how to build a class containing class methods, which define messages that can be sent to a class. In this section, we take a first look at **instance methods**, which define messages that can be sent to an *object* (i.e., an *instance of a class*).

There are several different kinds of instance methods, including the following:

- an **accessor** is an instance method that retrieves the value of an instance variable;
- a **mutator** is an instance method that modifies the value of an instance variable;
- a **converter** is an instance method that returns a different representation (usually a different type) of the object to which it is sent; and

- a **utility** is an instance method that other methods use to avoid redundant coding.

In this section, we will see how to write accessor methods.

ACCESSORS FOR CLASS Name

In Section 3.8, we built the Name class to represent a person's name, including instance variables and constructors:

```
#include <string>        // the string class
using namespace std;
class Name
{
 public:
   Name();
   Name(string first, string middle, string last);
   // ... other Name-operation declarations go here
 private:
   string myFirstName,
          myMiddleName,
          myLastName;
};

inline Name::Name()
{
   myFirstName = myMiddleName = myLastName = "";
}

inline Name::Name(string first, string middle, string last)
{
   myFirstName = first;
   myMiddleName = middle;
   myLastName = last;
}
```

As we saw, such a class allows us to declare Name variables:

```
#include "Name.h"
int main()
{
   Name hisName("John", "Paul", "Jones"),
        herName("Mary", "Anne", "Smith");
}
```

It would obviously be useful if we could send Name objects messages to retrieve their various components, such as the first name, the middle name, the last name, the initials, and so on. We can accomplish this by defining an accessor method for each particular message we wish to be able to send. Figure 5.3 shows the prototypes and definitions of four accessor methods: getFirstName(), getLastName(), getMiddleInitial(), and getSignature().

Fig. 5.3 Some name accessor methods. (Part 1 of 2)

```
/* Name.h presents accessor methods for class Name.
 * ...
 */

#include <iostream>      // ostream class
#include <string>        // the string class
#include <cassert>       // assert()
using namespace std;

class Name
{
 public:
   Name();
   Name(string first, string middle, string last);

   string getFirstName() const;
   string getLastName() const;
   char   getMiddleInitial() const;
   string getSignature() const;

   void   print(ostream& out) const;

 // ... other Name-operation declarations go here

 private:
   string myFirstName,
   myMiddleName,
   myLastName;
};

// ... constructor definitions omitted ...

inline string Name::getFirstName() const
{
   return myFirstName;
}

inline string Name::getLastName() const
{
   return myLastName;
}
```

Fig. 5.3 Some name accessor methods. (Part 2 of 2)

```
inline char Name::getMiddleInitial() const
{
   assert(myMiddleName.size() > 0);
   return myMiddleName[0];
}

inline string Name::getSignature() const
{
   return getFirstName() + ' '
          + getMiddleInitial() + ". "
          + getLastName();
}

inline void Name::print(ostream& out) const
{
   out << getFirstName() + ' '
          + getMiddleName() + ' '
          + getLastName();
}
```

Because an output method like `print()` retrieves and displays the values of the instance variables, it can be thought of as a kind of accessor method, and so we have included it here.

As we have seen before, for such relatively simple functions, we can define them using the `inline` modifier in the header file below the class declaration. However, the code in Figure 5.3 introduces some new features that deserve further explanation:

- We saw in Section 4.7 that the prototype of a class method must be preceded by the keyword `static`. By contrast, no special keyword is needed for the prototype of an instance method. A "normal" function prototype that appears within a class declaration thus declares an instance method.
- As with a class method, an instance method must be defined using its qualified name, consisting of the name of the class, the scope operator (`::`), and the name of the method.
- Each of these instance methods is an *accessor*, which means it accesses and returns some *attribute* of a class. A common name for an accessor is get*X*(), where *X* is the name of the attribute being accessed.
- The heading of an accessor method is usually followed by the keyword `const`. This keyword tells the compiler that such a method may not modify any of the instance variables, and any attempt to do so should produce an error. In general, any instance method that does not modify instance variables should be declared and defined as a `const` method.

- From the definitions of `getFirstName()`, `getLastName()`, and `getMiddleInitial()`, we see that an instance method can directly access the instance variables.
- In the definition of `getSignature()`, we see that an instance method can invoke other instance methods. When executed, this is the conceptual equivalent of an object sending itself messages. While most accessor methods simply return the value of their corresponding instance variable, some attributes (e.g., a middle initial or a signature) may not be stored, because they can be easily computed.
- In order for an output method like `print()` to work with an arbitrary `ostream` (i.e., `cout`, `cerr`, `clog`, ...), we must pass the particular `ostream` to which we want to print as an argument to the method. This implies that the method must have an `ostream` parameter. However a 'normal' parameter is a *copy* of its argument, and we do not want our method to make such a copy.[10] To "turn off" the copy mechanism and have our parameter refer directly to the actual `ostream` argument being passed, we can declare a parameter whose type is `ostream&`. Such a parameter is called a **reference parameter**, and they are discussed in detail in Chapter 8.

Given such a class stored in *Name.h*, a programmer can now send `Name` objects these messages in order to access these attributes, as shown in the following program.

Fig. 5.4 Driver for class `Name`. (Part 1 of 2)

```
/* nameDriver.cpp tests class Name.
 * ... documentation omitted to save space ...
 ******************************************************************/

#include <iostream>                // cin, cout, >>, <<
#include "Name.h"                  // Name
using namespace std;

int main()
{
   Name hisName("John", "Paul", "Jones"),
        herName("Mary", "Anne", "Smith");

    cout << hisName.getSignature() << "\n\n";

    herName.print(cout);
}
```

10. The results of inserting characters into a copy of `cout`, `cerr`, or `clog` are unpredictable. Such copying would also waste a great deal of time.

Fig. 5.4 Driver for class `Name`. (Part 2 of 2)

Sample run:

```
John P. Jones

Mary Anne Smith
```

Note that to print `herName` to `cout`, we must pass `cout` as an argument with the `print()` message.

The general form of an instance method definition is

```
[inline] type ClassName::method_name ( param_dec_list ) [const]
   Block
```

where the brackets around `inline` and `const` indicate that these keywords are optional, *`type`* is the method's return-type, *`ClassName`* is the name of the class of which it is a method, and *`param_dec_list`* is a list of parameters for the method. If simple enough to define in the header file, its definition should be preceded by `inline`. If the method does not modify any instance variables, its header should be followed by `const` in both its declaration and its definition.

ACCESSORS FOR CLASS `Student`

In Section 3.8, we also saw how to build a `Student` class that included instance variables for a student's name, id number, hourly wage, and hours worked, as well as constructors to initialize them:

```
#include "Name.h"
class Student
{
 public:
   Student();
   Student(string first, string middle, string last,
           int id);
   Student(string first, string middle, string last,
           int id, double wage, double hours);
   // ... other Student-operation declarations go here
 private:
   Name   myName;
   int    myIdNumber;
   double myHourlyWage,
          myHoursWorked;
};

inline Student::Student()
{
   myIdNumber = 0;
```

```
   myHourlyWage = 0.0;
   myHoursWorked = 0.0;
}

inline Student::Student(string first, string middle, string
                        last, int id)
{
   myName = Name(first, middle, last);
   myIdNumber = id;
   myHourlyWage = 0.0;
   myHoursWorked = 0.0;
}

inline Student::Student(string first, string middle, string
                        last, int id, double wage, double
                        hours)
{
   myName = Name(first, middle, last);
   myIdNumber = id;
   myHourlyWage = wage;
   myHoursWorked = hours;
}
```

We can create accessor methods for each of these attributes as shown in Figure 5.5.

Fig. 5.5 Student accessor methods. (Part 1 of 2)

```
/* Student.h defines Student accessor methods.
 * ... documentation omitted to save space ...
 *****************************************************************/

#include <iostream>        // ostream class
#include <string>          // string class
#include "Name.h"          // Name class
using namespace std;

class Student
{
 public:
    // ... constructors omitted -- see above & Section 3.8

    Name getName() const;
    int  getIdNumber() const;
    double getHourlyWage() const;
    double getHoursWorked() const;

    void print(ostream& out) const;
```

Fig. 5.5 Student accessor methods. (Part 2 of 2)

```
    // ... other operations omitted ...

 private:
    Name   myName;
    int    myIdNumber;
    double myHourlyWage;
    double myHoursWorked;
};

// ... constructor definitions omitted -- see above & Section 3.8

inline Name Student::getName() const
{
   return myName;
}

inline int Student::getIdNumber() const
{
   return myIdNumber;
}

inline double Student::getHourlyWage() const
{
   return myHourlyWage;
}

inline void Student::print(ostream& out) const
{
   myName.print(out);
   out << ' ' << getIdNumber()
       << ' ' << getHourlyWage()
       << ' ' << getHoursWorked();
}

// ... other method definitions omitted ...
```

Given such a class and methods in *Student.h*, a programmer can now send a `Student` object messages to retrieve its attributes, as shown in Figure 5.6:

Fig. 5.6 A driver for class `Student`.

```
/* studentDriver.cpp tests class Student.
 * ... documentation omitted to save space ...
 *****************************************************************/

#include <iostream>                // cin, cout, >>, <<
using namespace std;
#include "Student.h"               // Student

int main()
{
   Student oneStudent("Alex", "Bob", "Colt", 1234, 7.25, 15.0),
           anotherStudent("Debra", "Ellen", "Fazio", 9876);

   oneStudent.print(cout);
   cout << '\n';
   anotherStudent.getName().print(cout);
   cout << ' ' << herName.getIdNumber() << endl;
}
```

Sample run:

```
Alex Bob Colt 1234 7.25 15
Debra Ellen Fazio 9876
```

From this program, we see that, where appropriate, we can chain messages together. The statement

```
anotherStudent.getName().print(cout);
```

begins by sending the object `anotherStudent` the `getName()` message,

```
anotherStudent.getName().print(cout);
```

which returns a `Name` object containing that student's name. We then send that `Name` object the `print()` message:

```
anotherStudent.getName().print(cout);
```

Since the `print()` message is being sent to a `Name` object, this invokes the method `Name::print()`, whose definition is in *Name.h.* (See Figure 5.3.)

This concludes our introduction to instance methods and accessor methods. In our next *OBJECTive Thinking* section (see Section 6.6), we will examine instance methods called *mutators* and see how they differ from accessors.

Quick Quiz 5.6

1. Instance methods define messages that are sent to ________ .
2. A(n) ________ is an instance method that retrieves some attribute of a class.
3. A(n) ________ is an instance method that modifies the value of an instance variable.
4. A(n) ________ is an instance method that returns a different representation of an object.
5. A(n) ________ is an instance method that other methods to avoid redundant coding.
6. (True or false) The prototype of an instance method must be preceded by the keyword `static`.
7. The keyword ________ can be appended to the heading of a method's declaration and definition to prevent it from modifying any instance variables.

Exercises 5.6

The following exercises ask you to add various accessor methods to the classes considered in this section. You should test these with driver programs like those asked for in Programming Problems 29–35 at the end of the chapter.

For Exercises 1–4, write prototypes and definitions for the required methods.

1. A `getFirstAndLastName()` accessor method for class `Name` that returns a string of the form *Firstname Lastname*
2. A `getLastFirstMiddleInitial()` accessor method for class `Name` that returns a string of the form *Lastname, Firstname M.* (where *M* is the middle initial)
3. `getRadius()`, `getDensity()`, and `getWeight()` accessor methods for class `Sphere` in Section 4.7
4. A `print()` accessor method for class `Sphere` in Section 4.7

For Exercises 5–8, extend the given classes by adding accessor methods for all of the instance variables and a `print()` accessor method.

5. The class `Temperature` in Section 4.7
6. The time class in Exercise 2 of Section 2.3 (See also Exercises 2 and 7 in Section 3.8 and Exercises 9 and 10 in Section 4.7.)
7. The date class in Exercise 3 of Section 2.3 (See also Exercises 3 and 8 in Section 3.8.)
8. The phone-number class in Exercise 4 of Section 2.3 (See also Exercises 4 and 9 in Section 3.8.)

CHAPTER SUMMARY

Key Terms & Notes

<< operator
>> operator
accessor method
attribute variable
bad state
Bjarne Stroustrup
class
class constant
concatenation
converter method

- data encapsulation
- data member
- deterministic
- dot notation
- empty string
- encapsulation
- `endl` manipulator
- extraction operator
- fail state
- fill character
- flag
- `flush` manipulator
- format manipulator
- function member
- fundamental type
- good state
- `get()`
- index
- input manipulator
- insertion operator
- instance method
- instance variable
- `istream`
- mutator method
- normal distribution
- `npos`
- `ostream`
- out-of-bounds exception
- output manipulator
- overloading
- pattern matching
- precision
- pseudorandom number
- random number generator
- randomness
- reference parameter
- scalar variable
- `setfill()`
- simulation
- standard normal distribution
- state
- stream
- `string`
- `string::npos`
- string stream
- struct
- subscript operator (`[]`)
- uniform distribution
- utility method
- white space

- Classes provide a way to encapsulate the characteristics of an object.
- Encapsulation with a class is important because it makes it possible for a single object to contain all of its own information, which in turn makes it possible to pass a complicated object to a function by using just one argument.
- Public members of a class object can be accessed using dot notation.
- Instance variables are designated private to prevent users of the class from performing unauthorized operations on them.
- Instance methods get executed when messages are sent to objects.
- The state of an `istream`—good, bad, fail—can be checked by sending a message—`good()`, `bad()`, `fail()`—to the `istream` object (e.g., `cin`). The `clear()` message can be used to reset states and the `ignore()` message to skip characters in the stream.
- The input operator `>>` skips leading white space (space, tab, or newline). The `noskipws` and `skipws` manipulators can be used to turn this feature off or on. The `get()` method provides a useful alternative for reading any character, whether white space or not.
- The `endl` manipulator inserts a newline character (`'\n'`) into an `ostream` to end a line of output and then flushes it. The `ostream cout` is flushed automatically whenever the `istream cin` is used.

- The format of output is controlled by inserting format manipulators into output lists. Except for `setw()`, which affects only the next output value, these manipulators control the format of all subsequent output in the program unless changed by some other manipulator.
- When the input operator `>>` is applied to a `string` object, it extracts characters from an `istream` and transfers them into a `string` object until a white-space character is encountered.
- The `getline()` function stops extracting and transferring characters when a newline character is encountered. In can thus be used to read an entire line of input. To read characters only up to the next white-space character, the input operator `>>` should be used.
- The characters in a `string` object are indexed, beginning with 0. An expression of the form *`string_object[index]`* accesses the element at the specified *`index`* of *`string_object`*. The index of the last character is always *`string_object`*`.size() - 1`.
- Random number generators are used in simulations to model processes that involve randomness.
- *Class methods* define messages sent to a class; *instance methods* define messages sent to an object (i.e., an instance of a class).
- Prototypes of class methods are preceded by the keyword `static`; prototypes of instance methods are not.
- Like class methods, definitions of instance methods must use qualified names of the form *`ClassName`*`::`*`methodName`*, and if they are simple, they are inlined by prepending the keyword `inline` and placed below the class declaration in the class' header file.
- Important kinds of instance methods are
  - *accessors*: retrieve values of instance variables;
  - *mutators*: modify values of instance variables;
  - *converters*: produce a different representation of an object;
  - *utilities*: used by other methods to simplify coding.
- Headings of accessor methods are usually followed by the keyword `const`, which prevents a method from modifying the class' instance variables.

Programming Pointers

Program Style and Design

1. *If any of the objects needed to solve a problem have been identified, but cannot be defined using the fundamental types, examine the predefined classes of C++ to see if any of them is appropriate for representing such objects.* Don't be afraid to discuss your problem with experienced programmers who may know of classes that will make the problem easier to solve.
2. *If any of the operations needed to solve a problem involve a class object, study the available documentation for that class to see if any of its methods perform that operation* . In the worst case, this may involve looking at the header file for that class and experimenting with the methods.
3. *If you find yourself doing the same work repeatedly, look for what you are doing wrong. A primary tenet of object-centered programming is "Don't reinvent the wheel!"* Ifyoufindyourself writing redundant code, isolate the code in a function and call the function wherever it is needed.

WATCH OUT

Potential Pitfalls

1. *When values for variables are read using* `>>`*, leading white-space characters are skipped and characters are read and removed from the* `istream` *until white-space or some other character that cannot belong to a value of that type is encountered; this character that terminates input is left in the stream.* The characters that were read are then converted to a value of the type of the variable for which a value is being read. For example, if `intVal` is an `int` variable and `cin` contains

   ```
   1234.56
   ```

   the statement `cin >> intVal;` will read the characters `1`, `2`, `3`, and `4` and assign the integer 1234 to `intVal`. The remaining characters will stay in the `istream cin` for the next input operation:

   ```
   .56
   ```

2. *In the preceding Programming Pitfall, if no character in an* `istream` *is found that can belong to a value of the required type, the input operation is said to fail, and the value of the variable remains unchanged* . For example, if the statement `cin >> intVal;` is executed again, no characters will be read and removed because the period (`.`) cannot be a part of an `int` value, the value of `intVal` remains unchanged, and `cin` is unchanged. The result is that an infinite loop can easily result. Including a statement like

   ```
   if (cin.fail()) exit(1);
   ```

   after the input statement can be used to detect this condition and terminate repetition.
3. *The first character in a string object has index 0.* This zero-based indexing is a legacy from C, the parent language of C++, that simplifies the mapping of a subscript access `string_object[index]` to an actual memory address.
4. *Be careful when using both* `>>` *and* `getline()` *for input.* A newline character that terminates input of characters via `>>` will be left in the `istream` and a subsequent attempt to read a string using `getline()` will not read any characters because it terminates as soon as this newline is encountered.
5. *The* `string` subscript operation *uses square brackets containing an index,*

   ```
   stringVariable[index]
   ```

   whereas the `string` substring operation *uses parentheses containing an index and a size:*

   ```
   string_object.substr(index, num_chars)
   ```

6. *Run-time bounds checking is performed on most* `string` *functions that use an index* . Th bounds checking causes an out-of-bounds exception if the index is negative or greater than the size of the string, which terminates the program and displays a diagnostic.
7. *Run-time bounds checking is not performed on the subscript operation.* Special care must be taken when accessing the characters of a string with the subscript operator, to ensure that all accesses fall within the boundaries of the string.
8. *To fill a* `string` *object with a word from an* `istream`*, use the input operator* `>>`*:*

   ```
   cin >> someString;
   ```

   To fill a `string` *object with a line from an* `istream`*, use the* `getline()` *function:*

   ```
   getline(cin, someString);
   ```

Programming Problems

Section 5.1

1. Write a program to display the lyrics of "Happy Birthday to You."
2. Write a program to display the lyrics of "Old MacDonald had a Farm."
3. Write a program to display the lyrics of "This Old Man."
4. Write a program to display the lyrics of "She'll be Comin' 'Round the Mountain."
5. Write a program to display the lyrics of "When the Saints Go Marchin' In."
6. Write a program to display the lyrics of "The Hokey Pokey."

Sections 5.2–5.5

7. Write a driver program to test the name-conversion function of Exercise 28.
8. Write a driver program to test the name-conversion function of Exercise 29.
9. Write a program to print personalized contest letters like those frequently received in the mail. They might have a format like that of the following sample. The user should enter the three strings in the first three lines, and the program then prints the letter with the underlined locations filled in.

```
Mr. John Q. Doe
123 SomeStreet
AnyTown, AnyState 12345

Dear Mr. Doe:
How would you like to see a brand new Cadillac parked in front of 123
SomeStreet in AnyTown, AnyState? Impossible, you say? No, it isn't,
Mr. Doe. Simply keep the enclosed raffle ticket and validate it by
sending a $100.00 tax-deductible political contribution and 10 labels
from Shyster & Sons chewing tobacco. Not only will you become eligi-
ble for the drawing to be conducted on February 29 by the independent
firm of G. Y. P. Shyster, but you will also be helping to reelect Sam
Shyster.   That's all there is to it, John. You may be a winner!!!
```

Note: Programming Problems 10–28 require use of the selection or repetition statements introduced in Chapter 4.

10. Write a driver program to test the name-of-a-month function of Exercise 30.
11. Write a driver program to test the number-of-a-month function of Exercise 31.
12. Write a driver program to test the case-conversion functions of Exercise 32.
13. Write a driver program to test the function `replace_all()` of Exercise 33.
14. Write a driver program to test the palindrome-checker function of Exercise 34.
15. There are 3 teaspoons in a tablespoon, 4 tablespoons in a quarter of a cup, 2 cups in a pint, and 2 pints in a quart. Write a program to convert units in cooking. The program should call for the input of the amount, the units, and the new units desired.
16. Write a function to count occurrences of a string in another string. Then write a driver program to input a string and then input several lines of text, using the function to count occurrences of the string in the lines of text.
17. Write a program to input a string and then input several lines of text, determine whether the first string occurs in each line, and if so, print asterisks (`*`) under each occurrence.

18. Reverend Zeller developed a formula for computing the day of the week on which a given date fell or will fall. Suppose that we let a, b, c, and d be integers defined as follows:

    a = the number of a month of the year, with March = 1, April = 2, and so on, with January and February being counted as months 11 and 12 of the preceding year

    b = the day of the month

    c = the year of the century

    d = the century

    For example, July 31, 1929 gives $a = 5$, $b = 31$, $c = 29$, $d = 19$; January 3, 1988 gives $a = 11$, $b = 3$, $c = 87$, $d = 19$. Now calculate the following integer quantities:

    w = the integer quotient $(13a - 1)/5$

    x = the integer quotient $c/4$

    y = the integer quotient $d/4$

    $z = w + x + y + b + c - 2d$

    $r = z$ reduced modulo 7; that is, r is the remainder of z divided by 7: $r = 0$ represents Sunday; $r = 1$ represents Monday, and so on

    Write a function `day_of_the_Week()` that receives the name of a month, the day of the month, and a year and returns the name of the day of the week on which that date fell or will fall. Write a program that inputs several strings representing dates, calls the function `day_of_the_Week()`, and displays the day returned by the function.

    a. Verify that December 12, 1960 fell on a Monday, and that January 1, 1991 fell on a Tuesday.
    b. On what day of the week did January 25, 1963 fall?
    c. On what day of the week did June 2, 1964 fall?
    d. On what day of the week did July 4, 1776 fall?
    e. On what day of the week were you born?

19. The game of Hangman is played by two persons. One person selects a word and the other tries to guess the word by guessing individual letters. Design and implement a program to play Hangman.

20. Write a function that accepts two character strings and determines whether one is an anagram of the other; that is, whether one character string is a permutation of the characters in the other string. For example, "dear" is an anagram of "read," as is "dare." Write a driver program to test your function.

Part of the Picture: Simulation

21. A coin is tossed repeatedly, and a payoff of 2^n dollars is made, where n is the number of the toss on which the first head appears. For example, TTH pays $8, TH pays $4, and H pays $2 (T-tails, H-heads). Write a program to simulate playing the game several times and to print the average payoff for these games.

22. Suppose that a gambler places a wager of $5 on the following game: A pair of dice is tossed, and if the result is odd, the gambler loses his wager. If the result is even, a card is drawn from a standard deck of 52 playing cards. If the card drawn is an ace, 3, 5, 7, or 9, the gambler wins the value of the card (with aces counting as 1, Jacks as 11, Queens as 12, and Kings as 13); otherwise, he loses. What will be the average winnings for this game? Write a program to simulate the game.

23. Johann VanDerDoe, centerfielder for the Klavin Klodhoppers, has the following lifetime hitting percentages:

Out	63.4%
Walk	10.3%
Single	19.0%
Double	4.9%
Triple	1.1%
Home run	1.3%

Write a program to simulate a large number of times at bat, for example, 1000, for Johann, counting the number of outs, walks, singles, and so on, and calculating his

$$\text{batting average} = \frac{\text{number of hits}}{\text{number of times at bat} - \text{number of walks}}$$

24. The classic *drunkard's walk problem* is as follows: Over an 8-block line, the home of an intoxicated chap is at block n, $1 < n < 8$, and a pub is at block 1. Our poor friend starts at block n and wanders at random, one block at a time, either toward or away from home. At any intersection, he moves toward the pub with a certain probability, say 2/3, and toward home with a certain probability, say 1/3. Having gotten either home or to the pub, he remains there. Write a program to simulate 500 trips in which he starts at block 2, another 500 in which he starts at block 3, and so forth up to block 7. For each starting point, calculate and print the percentage of time he ends up at home and the average number of blocks he walked on each trip.

25. A slab of material is used to shield a nuclear reactor, and a particle entering the shield follows a random path by moving forward, backward, left, or right with equal likelihood, in jumps of one unit. A change of direction is interpreted as a collision with an atom in this shield. Suppose that after 10 such collisions, the particle's energy is dissipated and that it dies within the shield, provided that it has not already passed back inside the reactor or outside through the shield. Write a program to simulate particles entering this shield and to determine what percentage of them reaches the outside.

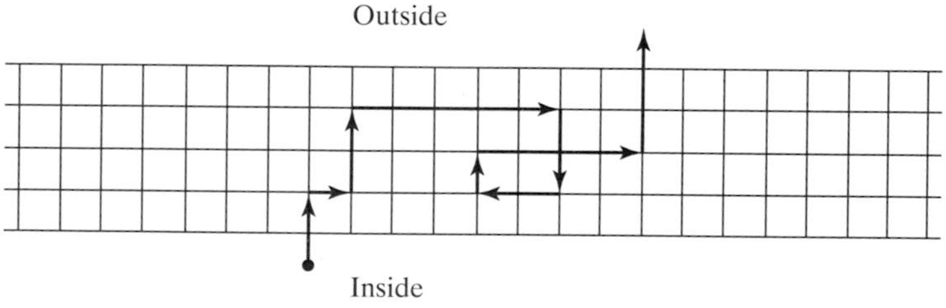

26. Consider a quarter circle inscribed in a square whose sides have length 1:

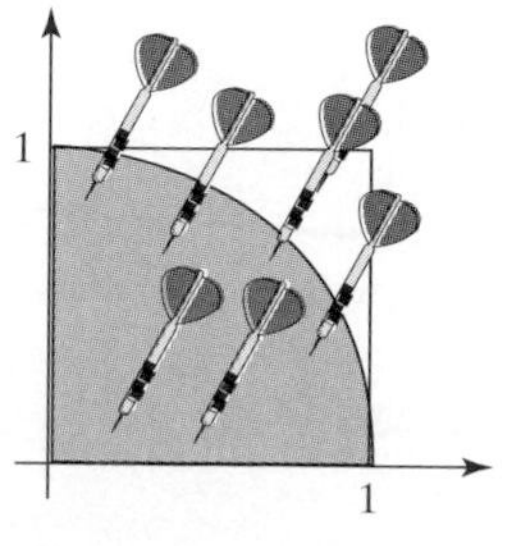

Imagine throwing q darts at this square and counting the total number p that hit within the quarter circle. For a large number of throws, we would expect

$$\frac{p}{q} \sim \frac{area\ of\ quarter\ circle}{area\ of\ square} = \frac{\pi}{4}.$$

Write a program to approximate π using this method. To simulate throwing the darts, generate two random numbers X and Y and consider point (X,Y) as being where the dart hits.

27. The famous *Buffon Needle problem* is as follows: A board is ruled with equidistant parallel lines, and a needle of length equal to the distance between these lines is dropped at random on the board. Write a program to simulate this experiment and estimate the probability p that the needle crosses one of these lines. Display the values of p and $2/p$. (The value of $2/p$ should be approximately equal to a well-known constant. What constant is it?)
28. The tensile strength of a certain metal component has an approximate normal distribution with a mean of 10,000 pounds per square inch and a standard deviation of 100 pounds per square inch. Specifications require that all components have a tensile strength greater than 9800; all others must be scrapped. Write a program that uses the algorithm described in this section to generate 1000 normally distributed random numbers representing the tensile strength of these components, and determine how many must be rejected.

Section 5.6

29. Write a driver program to test the class `Name` as modified in Exercise 1.
30. Write a driver program to test the class `Name` as modified in Exercise 2.
31. Write a driver program to test the class `Sphere` as modified in Exercises 3 and 4.
32. Write a driver program to test the class `Temperature` as modified in Exercise 5.
33. Write a driver program to test the time class as modified in Exercise 6.
34. Write a driver program to test the date class as modified in Exercise 7.
35. Write a driver program to test the phone-number class as modified in Exercise 8.

CHAPTER 6

Selection

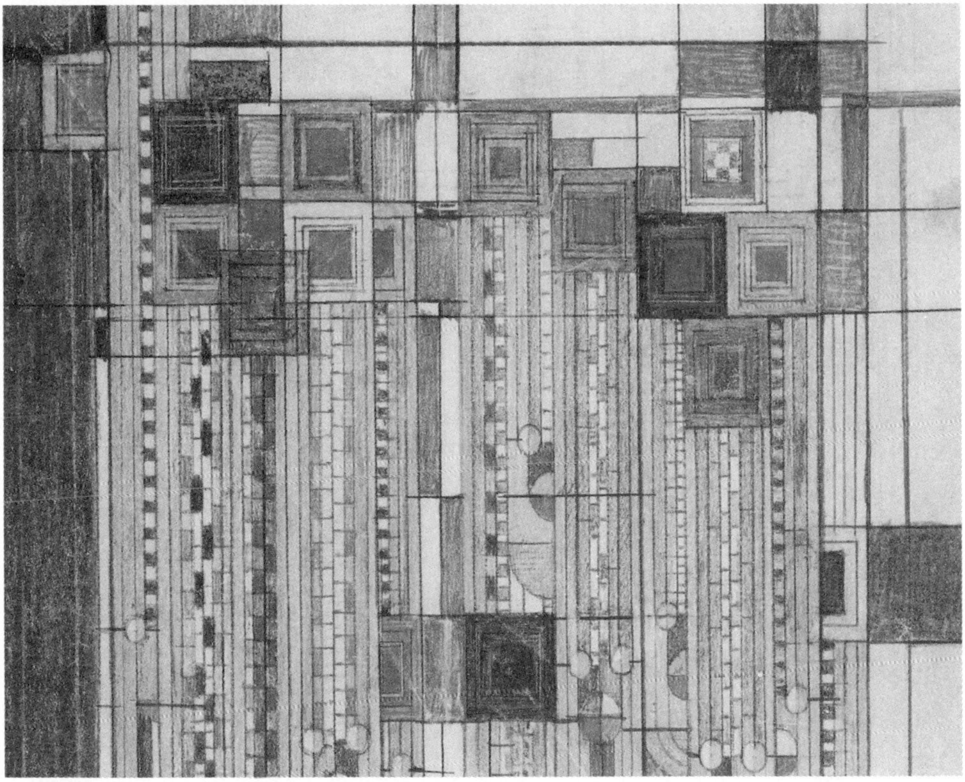

When you get to the fork in the road, take it.

-Yogi Berra

If you don't know where you're going, you'll wind up somewhere else.

-Yogi Berra

We are all special cases.

-Albert Camus

"Would you tell me, please, which way I ought to go from here?"
"That depends a great deal on where you want to get to," said the Cat.

-Lewis Carroll

If you believe you can, you probably can. If you believe you won't, you most assuredly won't. Belief is the ignition switch that gets you off the launching pad."

-Denis Waitley

Chapter Contents

Chapter Objectives

- Expand on the introduction to selection structures in Chapter 4.
- Examine the `if` statement in detail.
- Study the `switch` statement and how it can be used to implement certain multialternative selections.
- Introduce conditional expressions.
- (Optional) See how boolean expressions can be used to model logical circuits.
- (Optional) Study the architecture of typical computer systems.
- (Optional) Take a first look at mutator methods in classes.

In Chapter 4, we saw that functions play an important role in programming in C++ and that the logical flow of execution through them is governed by three basic control mechanisms: **sequence**, **selection**, and **repetition**. We also looked at some examples of functions that used an `if` statement to perform selective execution and the `for` and `while` statements to perform repetitive execution. Our introductions to these statements were quite brief, however, and so we will take a closer look at them in this chapter and the next. This chapter describes the `if` statement in detail and introduces the `switch` statement that sometimes provides a more efficient way to perform selection. The special *Part of the Picture* sections describe the role of boolean expressions in logical circuit design and offer a close look at computer architecture. The optional *OBJECTive Thinking* section introduces mutator methods that use selection structures to check the validity of values being assigned to a class' instance variables.

6.1 Introductory Example: School Mascots

PROBLEM

The Big 10 Conference of the NCAA consists of the following universities, whose mascots are as shown:

University	Common Name	Mascot
University of Illinois	Illinois	Fighting Illini
University of Indiana	Indiana	Hoosiers
University of Iowa	Iowa	Hawkeyes
University of Michigan	Michigan	Wolverines
Michigan State University	Michigan State	Spartans
University of Minnesota	Minnesota	Golden Gophers
Northwestern University	Northwestern	Wildcats
Ohio State University	Ohio State	Buckeyes
Pennsylvania State University	Penn State	Nittany Lions
Purdue University	Purdue	Boilermakers
University of Wisconsin	Wisconsin	Badgers

Our problem is to develop a function `mascot()` that, given the name of a Big 10 university, returns its mascot.[1]

Object-Centered Design

Behavior. Our function should receive from its caller the name of a Big 10 university. It should return the university's mascot.

Objects. From this behavior description, we identify two objects in the problem:

	Software Objects			
Problem Objects	Type	Kind	Movement	Name
the name of a Big 10 university	`string`	varying	received	*university*
its mascot	`string`	varying	returned	none

The problem can be specified in terms of these objects as follows:

Receive: *university*, a `string`

Precondition: *university* is the common name of a Big 10 university,

---

1. We have restricted our universities to the Big 10 conference to keep the problem manageable in size. Extending the function to include additional universities is straightforward and is left as an exercise.

Return: the mascot of that university, a `string`

Given this specification, we can build the following stub for our function:

```
string mascot(string university)
{
}
```

Operations. From the problem description, we can identify 11 operations:

i. Compare *university* to "Michigan State University"; if true, return "Spartans"
ii. Compare *university* to "Northwestern University"; if true, return "Wildcats"
iii. Compare *university* to "Ohio State University"; if true, return "Buckeyes"

.
.
.

xi. Compare *university* to "University of Wisconsin"; if true, return "Badgers"

Because the `string` class defines the equality operator (==) to compare two `string` values, a series of `if` statements can be used to perform these operations.

Algorithm. These operations can be organized into the following algorithm. To save the user from having to enter "University" or "University of", we will use the common name for each school.

Algorithm for Big 10 University Mascot Computation

1. If *university* is "Illinois"
   return "Fighting Illini".
2. Otherwise, if *university* is "Indiana"
   return "Hoosiers".
3. Otherwise, if *university* is "Iowa"
   return "Hawkeyes".
4. Otherwise, if *university* is "Michigan State"
   return "Spartans".
5. Otherwise, if *university* is "Minnesota"
   return "Golden Gophers".
6. Otherwise, if *university* is "Northwestern"
   return "Wildcats".
7. Otherwise, if *university* is "Ohio State"
   return "Buckeyes".
8. Otherwise, if *university* is "Penn State"
   return "Nittany Lions".
9. Otherwise, if *university* is "Purdue"
   return "Boilermakers".
10. Otherwise, if *university* is "Michigan"
    return "Wolverines".

11. Otherwise, if *university* is "Wisconsin"
    return "Badgers".
12. Otherwise
    a. Display an error message.
    b. Return on empty string as a default value.

Coding. Given this algorithm, completing our function is straightforward, as shown in Figure 6.1.

Fig. 6.1 The `mascot()` function. (Part 1 of 2)

```
/* mascot() returns the mascot for a Big 10 university.
 *
 * Receive:      university, a string
 * Precondition: university is a Big 10 university
 * Return:       the (string) mascot of university
 **********************************************************/

string mascot(string university)
{
   if (university == "Illinois")
      return "Fighting Illini";
   else if (university == "Indiana")
      return "Hoosiers";
   else if (university == "Iowa")
      return "Hawkeyes";
   else if (university == "Michigan")
      return "Wolverines";
   else if (university == "Michigan State")
      return "Spartans";
   else if (university == "Minnesota")
      return "Golden Gophers";
   else if (university == "Northwestern")
      return "Wildcats";
   else if (university == "Ohio State")
      return "Buckeyes";
   else if (university == "Penn State")
      return "Nittany Lions";
   else if (university == "Purdue")
      return "Boilermakers";
   else if (university == "Wisconsin")
      return "Badgers";
```

Fig. 6.1 The `mascot()` function. (Part 2 of 2)

```
   else
   {
      cerr << "mascot: " << university
           << " is not known by this program!";
      return "";
   }
}
```

Testing. To test this function, we write a simple driver program like that in Figure 6.2. Note that it uses `getline()` to read the name of a university because some names consist of more than one word (e.g., Michigan State, Penn State). If we used the input operator >>, only the first word of such names would be read, as described in Section 5.4.

Fig. 6.2 Driver for the `mascot()` function. (Part 1 of 2)

```
/* mascotDriver.cpp is a driver program for the mascot() function.
 *
 * Input:  names of Big 10 schools
 * Output: prompts, mascots of schools
 ***************************************************************/

#include <iostream>                // cin, cout, <<, >>
#include <string>                  // string, ==, getline()
using namespace std;

string mascot(string university);

int main()
{
   string school;

   cout << "\nEnter a Big 10 school (Q to quit): ";
   getline(cin, school);
   while (school != "Q" && school != "q")
   {
      cout << mascot(school) << endl;
      cout << "\nEnter a Big 10 school (Q to quit): ";
      getline(cin, school);
   }
}
```

Fig. 6.2 Driver for the `mascot()` function. (Part 2 of 2)

```
/*** Insert definition of mascot() from Figure 6.1 here ***/
```

Sample run:

```
Enter a Big 10 school (Q to quit): Michigan
Wolverines

Enter a Big 10 school (Q to quit): Ohio State
Buckeyes

Enter a Big 10 school (Q to quit): Missouri
Mascot: Missouri is not known by this program!

Enter a Big 10 school (Q to quit): Minnesota
Golden Gophers

Enter a Big 10 school (Q to quit): Q
```

The sample run indicates that the function is working correctly.

6.2 Selection: The `if` Statement

In Section 4.3, we introduced the `if` statement and saw that there are three different forms:[2]

the **single-branch** or **simple** `if` form:

```
if (boolean_expression)
   statement
```

the **dual-branch** or `if-else` form:

```
if (boolean_expression)
   statement1
else
   statement2
```

the **multibranch** or `if-else-if` form:

```
if (boolean_expression1)
   statement1
else if (boolean_expression2)
   statement2
```

2. This section extends the introduction to the `if` statement in Section 4.3. Thus, if this section was omitted earlier, it should be covered now.

```
...
else if (boolean_expression_n)
   statement_n
else
   statement_n+1
```

The boolean expressions in these `if` statements are sometimes called **conditions**.

Although these may look like three distinct statements, C++ really has only one `if` statement with two different forms:

The `if` Statement (General Form)

Forms:

```
if (boolean_expression)
   statement_1
```

or

```
if (boolean_expression)
   statement_1
else
   statement_2
```

where

`if` and `else` are keywords; and

statement$_1$ and *statement*$_2$ are C++ statements (either simple or compound).

Purpose: If the *boolean_expression* is true, then *statement*$_1$ is executed and *statement*$_2$ is bypassed, if present. If the *boolean_expression* is false, then *statement*$_1$ is bypassed and *statement*$_2$ is executed, if present. In either case, execution continues with the next statement in the program.

UNDERSTANDING THE MULTIBRANCH `if`

While it may look like a different statement, the multibranch or `if-else-if` form is really an `if` statement of the second form where *statement*$_2$ is another `if` statement, and this `if` statement also is of the second form with *statement*$_2$ another `if` statement, and so on. That is, a multibranch form is simply a series of **nested** `if` statements written as one.

To illustrate this, if we were to write a five-branch `if-else-if` and we were to start each new `if` statement on a new line with each `else` aligned with its corresponding `if`, our code would appear as follows:

```
if (boolean_expression_1)
   statement_1
```

```
else
   if (boolean_expression_2)
      statement_2
   else
      if (boolean_expression_3)
         statement_3
      else
         if (boolean_expression_4)
            statement_4
         else
            statement_5
```

However, the free-form nature of C++ allows us to begin each nested `if` on the same line as the preceding `else` and align the `else-if` combinations:

```
if (boolean_expression_1)
   statement_1
else if (boolean_expression_2)
   statement_2
else if (boolean_expression_3)
   statement_3
else if (boolean_expression_4)
   statement_4
else
   statement_5
```

This latter style reflects more clearly the multibranch nature and is therefore more readable. It is important, however, to understand that each `else` is really a continuation of the preceding `if`:

```
if (boolean_expression_1)
    statement_1
else if (boolean_expression_2)
    statement_2
else if (boolean_expression_3)
    statement_3
else if (boolean_expression_4)
    statement_4
else
    statement_5
```

WATCH OUT

PITFALL: THE DANGLING-ELSE PROBLEM

We have just seen that the multibranch form of the `if` statement is actually an `if-else` form

```
if (boolean_expression)
   statement_1
else
   statement_2
```

in which $statement_2$ is another `if` statement. However, suppose that $statement_1$ is another `if` statement; for example,

```
if (x > 0)
   if (y > 0)
      z = sqrt(x) + sqrt(y);
```

When such nested `if` statements are followed by an `else`, it is not evident with which `if` the `else` corresponds. Does the `else` match the outer `if`?

```
if (x > 0)
    if (y > 0)
        z = sqrt(x) + sqrt(y);
else
    cerr << "\n*** Unable to compute z!" << endl;
```

Or does it match the inner `if`?

```
if (x > 0)
if (y > 0)
    z = sqrt(x) + sqrt(y);
else
    cerr << "\n*** Unable to compute z!" << endl;
```

This ambiguity is known as the **dangling-else problem**, and C++ resolves it by stipulating that;

NOTE

In a nested `if` *statement, an* `else` *is matched with the nearest preceding unmatched* `if`.

Thus, for the preceding `if` statement, the second matching is used; that is, the `else` is associated with the inner `if` (whose condition is `y > 0`). Consequently, the output statement is executed only in the case that `x` is positive and `y` is nonpositive. If we wish to associate this `else` with the outer `if`, we can force the association by enclosing the inner `if` in curly braces as follows:

```
if (x > 0)
{
   if (y > 0)
      z = sqrt(x) + sqrt(y);
}
else
   cerr < "*** Unable to compute z!" << endl;
```

Putting the inner `if` inside a **block** makes it a complete statement, so that the `else` must associate with the outer `if`. Thus, the output statement is executed whenever `x` is nonpositive.

WATCH OUT

PITFALL: CONFUSING = AND ==

We describe now what is probably *the most common error in constructing boolean expressions*, and, as a consequence, in `if` statements. We begin by examining two features of C++ that are relevant to this problem.

1. *True and false in C++*. To maintain compatibility with its parent language C, in any boolean context, C++ interprets the value 0 as equivalent to the boolean value `false` and any nonzero value as equivalent to the boolean value `true`.[3] Thus, the statement

   ```
   if (0)
      cout << "T\n";
   else
      cout << "F\n";
   ```

   will always display `F` because the condition controlling the selection is zero, which C++ treats as false. Similarly, the statement

   ```
   if (23)
      cout << "T\n";
   else
      cout << "F\n";
   ```

   will always display `T` because the condition controlling the selection is nonzero, which is interpreted as true in C++.

2. *Assignments are expressions*. We saw in Chapter 3 that in C++, assignment (=) is an operator that returns the value being assigned as its result. For example, the assignment expression

   ```
   x = 23
   ```

   does two things: It assigns `x` the value 23 and it produces the value 23 as its result. Similarly, the assignment

   ```
   x = 0
   ```

   both assigns `x` the value 0 and produces the value 0 as its result.

By themselves, neither of these C++ features is particularly troublesome, but when coupled with the similarity of the assignment and equality operators, they make it easy to write `if` statements that contain logical errors. To illustrate, suppose that a programmer encodes the instruction

If `x` *is equal to zero, then*
   Display the character string "Zero"
Otherwise
   Display the character string "Nonzero"

---

3. C has no `bool` type. In its place, C uses the zero/nonzero mechanism described here.

as

```
if (x = 0)
   cout << "Zero\n";
else
   cout << "Nonzero\n";
```

Because the assignment operator

```
x = 0
```

is used instead of an equality comparison

```
x == 0
```

and the value returned by the assignment operator is the value that was assigned, this statement is equivalent to

```
if (0)
   cout << "Zero\n";
else
   cout << "Nonzero\n";
```

Because 0 is treated as false, the statement to output `Nonzero` will *always* be selected, regardless of the value of `x`.

Similarly, if a programmer writes

```
cout << MENU;              // display menu of choices: A, B, C
cin >> choice;
if (choice = 'A')
   statement1              // do something when choice is A
else if (choice = 'B')
   statement2              // do something else when choice is B
else if (choice = 'C')
   statement3              // do something else when choice is C
else
   cout << choice << " must be A, B, or C.\n";
```

then the statement associated with choice `A` will *always* be selected, regardless of the value entered by the user. The reason is that instead of the first condition testing whether `choice` is equal to `A`,

```
choice == 'A'
```

it assigns `choice` the numeric code of `A` (65 in ASCII):

```
choice = 'A'
```

The result produced by the assignment operator is the value assigned (65), and so this `if-else-if` form is equivalent to

```
cout << MENU;         // display menu of choices: A, B, C
cin >> choice;
if (65)
   statement1              // do something when choice is A
```

```
else if (choice = 'B')
   statement2                // do something else when choice is B
else if (choice = 'C')
   statement3                // do something else when choice is C
else
   cout << choice << " must be A, B, or C.\n";
```

Because nonzero values are treated as true, the value 65 is treated as true, so `statement1` will be executed, and `statement2`, `statement3`, and the output statement will be bypassed, regardless of the value of `choice`.

This kind of error is one of the most frequent errors in constructing boolean expressions. Unfortunately, these errors can be fiendishly difficult to find, because the equality operator (==) and the assignment operator (=) are similar in appearance. *Any time an algorithm calls for an equality comparison, the code that implements the algorithm should be carefully checked to ensure that an assignment operator has not been inadvertently used instead of the equality operator*

Exercises 6.2

1. Describe the output produced by the following poorly indented program segment:

```
int number = 4;
double alpha = -1.0;
if (number > 0)
   if (alpha > 0)
      cout << "first\n";
else
   cout << "second\n";
   cout << "third\n";
```

Exercises 2 and 3 refer to the following `if` statement, where `honors`, `awards`, and `goodStudent` are of type `bool`:

```
if (honors)
   if (awards)
      goodStudent = true;
   else
      goodStudent = false;
else if (!honors)
   goodStudent = false;
```

2. Write a simpler `if` statement that is equivalent to this one.
3. Write a single assignment statement that is equivalent to this `if` statement.
4. What output (if any) will be produced by the statement

```
int x = 0,
    y;
if ((x = 15) > y)
   cout << "Yes\n";
else
   cout << "No\n";
```

if y has the value (a) 10? (b) 20?

For Exercises 5–9, you are asked to write functions. To test these functions, you should write driver programs as instructed in Programming Problems 1–5 at the end of this chapter.

5. In a certain region, pesticide can be sprayed from an airplane only if the temperature is at least 70°, the relative humidity is between 15 and 35 percent, and the wind speed is at most 10 miles per hour. Write a boolean-valued function `okToSpray()` that receives three numbers representing temperature, relative humidity, and wind speed and returns true if the conditions allow spraying and false otherwise.
6. A certain credit company will approve a loan application if the applicant's income is at least \$25,000 or the applicant's assets are at least \$100,000; in addition, the applicant's total liabilities must be less than \$50,000. Write a boolean-valued function `creditApproved()` that receives three numbers representing income, assets, and liabilities and returns true if the criteria for loan approval are satisfied and false otherwise.
7. Write a function that returns true if the value of an `int` parameter `year` is the number of a leap year and return false otherwise. (A leap year is a multiple of 4; and if it is a multiple of 100, it must also be a multiple of 400.)
8. Write a function that returns the number of days in a given `int` parameter `month` (1, 2, . . . , 12) of a given parameter `year`. Use Exercise 7 to determine the number of days if the value of `month` is 2.
9. Proceed as in Exercise 8, but assume that `month` is a `string` variable whose value is the name of a month.

6.3 Selection: The `switch` Statement

An `if` statement can be used to implement a multialternative selection statement in which exactly one of several alternative actions is selected and performed. In the `if-else-if` form described in the preceding section, a selection is made by evaluating one or more boolean expressions. Because selection conditions can usually be formulated as boolean expressions, an `if-else-if` form can be used to implement virtually any multialternative selection.

In this section, we describe another multialternative selection statement called the `switch` statement. Although it is not as general as the `if` statement, it is more efficient for implementing certain forms of selection. As usual, we begin with an example that illustrates the use of the statement.

EXAMPLE: TEMPERATURE CONVERSIONS

In the early sections of Chapter 4, we considered the problem of converting temperatures from the Fahrenheit scale to the Celsius scale. In Section 4.2, we constructed a function to do this conversion, and in Section 4.6, we showed how a library `Heat` could be created to store various functions for converting temperatures between the Fahrenheit, Celsius, and Kelvin scales.

Now that we know about selective execution, we can consider a more general version of the problem—writing a program that allows the user to choose which conversion to be performed: Fahrenheit to Celsius (or vice versa), Fahrenheit to Kelvin (or vice versa), or Celsius to Kelvin (or vice versa).

Problem. Write a program that allows the user to perform arbitrary temperature conversions.

Object-Centered Design

Behavior. Our program should display on the screen a menu of the six possible conversion options and then read the desired conversion from the keyboard. Next, it should display on the screen a prompt for a temperature, which it should read from the keyboard. The program should then display the result of converting the input temperature, as determined by the specified conversion.

Objects. From our behavioral description, we have the following objects in this problem: [4]

	Software Objects		
Problem Objects	**Type**	**Kind**	**Name**
menu	`string`	constant	*MENU*
conversion	`char`	varying	*conversion*
temperature	`double`	varying	*temperature*
result	`double`	varying	*result*

We can thus specify the problem as follows:

Input: *temperature* (a `double`) and *conversion* (a `char`)

Precondition: *conversion* is in the range A–F (or a–f) . . .

Output: *MENU*, prompts for input, and the result of converting the temperature

Operations. Our behavioral description leads to the following list of operations:

i. Display prompts and *MENU* (strings) on the screen
ii. Read *temperature* (a `double`) from the keyboard
iii. Read *conversion* (a `char`) from the keyboard
iv. Select the conversion function corresponding to conversion and apply it to *temperature*

All of these are provided in C++. For Operation iv, we must compare *conversion* to each of the valid menu choices and, based upon that comparison, select an appropriate conversion function.

4. Since almost every problem will use the screen, keyboard, and prompt objects, we will omit them from our lists of objects and simply assume that they are needed. This will save space and will also allow us to focus our attention on user-defined objects.

Algorithm. The following algorithm applies this strategy:

Algorithm to Convert Arbitrary Temperatures

1. Display *MENU* via `cout`.
2. Read *conversion* from `cin`.
3. Display a prompt for a temperature via `cout`.
4. Read *temperature* from `cin`.
5. If *conversion* is 'A' or 'a'
   Convert *temperature* from Fahrenheit to Celsius and store in *result*.
   Otherwise, if *conversion* is 'B' or 'b'
   Convert *temperature* from Celsius to Fahrenheit and store in *result*.
   Otherwise, if *conversion* is 'C' or 'c'
   Convert *temperature* from Celsius to Kelvin and store in *result*.
   Otherwise, if *conversion* is 'D' or 'd'
   Convert *temperature* from Kelvin to Celsius and store in *result*.
   Otherwise, if *conversion* is 'E' or 'e'
   Convert *temperature* from Fahrenheit to Kelvin and store in *result*.
   Otherwise, if *conversion* is 'F' or 'f'
   Convert *temperature* from Kelvin to Fahrenheit and store in *result*.
   Otherwise
   Display an error message.

Coding and Testing. We could implement the algorithm using an `if-else-if` construct:

```
if (conversion == 'A' || conversion == 'a')
   result = fahrToCelsius(temperature)
else if (conversion == 'B' || conversion == 'b')
   result = celsiusToFahr(temperature);
      .
      .
      .
else
{
   cerr << "\n*** Invalid conversion: " << conversion << endl;
   result = 0.0;
}
```

The C++ `switch` statement, however, provides a more convenient way to do this, as shown in the program in Figure 6.3.[5]

---

5. This program uses the conversion functions from the library `Heat` from Section 4.6. If this section was omitted, simply replace the directive `#include "Heat.h"` with the prototypes of the conversion functions and append the definitions of these functions after the main program.

Fig. 6.3 Arbitrary temperature conversions. (Part 1 of 2)

```
/* convertTemp.cpp converts temperatures from one scale to another.
 *
 * Input:  menu choices, temperatures
 * Output: menu, temperatures on other scale
 ******************************************************************/

#include <iostream>      // cin, cout, <<, >>
#include <string>        // string
using namespace std;
#include "Heat.h"        // fahrToCelsius(), celsiusToFahr(), ...

int main()
{
   const string MENU = "To convert arbitrary temperatures, enter:\n"
                       "   A - to convert Fahrenheit to Celsius;\n"
                       "   B - to convert Celsius to Fahrenheit;\n"
                       "   C   to convert Celsius to Kelvin;\n"
                       "   D - to convert Kelvin to Celsius;\n"
                       "   E - to convert Fahrenheit to Kelvin; or\n"
                       "   F - to convert Kelvin to Fahreneht.\n"
                       " --> ";
   cout << MENU;
   char conversion;
   cin >> conversion;

   cout << "\nEnter the temperature to be converted: ";
   double temperature;
   cin >> temperature;

   double result;
   switch (conversion)
   {
      case 'A': case 'a':
                     result = fahrToCelsius(temperature);
                     break;
      case 'B': case 'b':
                     result = celsiusToFahr(temperature);
                     break;
      case 'C': case 'c':
                     result = celsiusToKelvin(temperature);
                     break;
```

Fig. 6.3 Arbitrary temperature conversions. (Part 2 of 2)

```
      case 'D': case 'd':
                      result = kelvinToCelsius(temperature);
                      break;
      case 'E': case 'e':
                      result = fahrToKelvin(temperature);
                      break;
      case 'F': case 'f':
                      result = kelvinToFahr(temperature);
                      break;
      default:
                      cerr << "\n*** Invalid conversion: "
                           << conversion << endl;
                      result = 0.0;
   }

   cout << "The converted temperature is " << result << endl;
}
```

Sample run:

```
To convert arbitrary temperatures, enter:
   A - to convert Fahrenheit to Celsius;
   B - to convert Celsius to Fahrenheit;
   C - to convert Celsius to Kelvin;
   D - to convert Kelvin to Celsius;
   E - to convert Fahrenheit to Kelvin; or
   F - to convert Kelvin to Fahreneht.
--> B
Enter the temperature to be converted: 100
The converted temperature is 212
```

Note the convenience of the `switch` statement: By allowing us to specify the cases for a given alternative, we can test the value of `conversion` quite conveniently, regardless of whether it is uppercase or lowercase:

```
switch (conversion)
{
   case 'A': case 'a':
      result = FahrToCelsius(temperature);
      break;
         .
         .
         .
}
```

The equivalent `if-else-if` version seems clumsy by comparison, and many people find it to be more work and less readable. In addition, using a `switch` statement to select from among several alternatives is typically *more time efficient* than using an `if` statement, as discussed at the end of this section.

FORM OF THE `switch` STATEMENT

The C++ `switch` statement has the following general form:

The `switch` Statement

Form:

```
switch (expression)
{
   case_list1 :
                  statement_list1;
   case_list2 :
                  statement_list2;
          .
          .
          .
   case_listn :
                  statement_listn
   default :
                  statement_listn+1
}
```

where

`switch` and `default` are keywords;

`expression` is an integer (or integer-compatible) expression;

each *`case_list`* $_i$ is a sequence of cases of the form

`case constant_value :`

the `default` clause is optional; and

each *`statement_list`* $_i$ is a sequence of statements.

Purpose: When the `switch` statement is executed, *`expression`* is evaluated. If the value of *`expression`* is in *`case_list`* $_i$, then execution begins in *`statement_list`* $_i$ and continues until one of the following is reached:

a `break` statement

a `return` statement

the end of the `switch` statement

If the value of *expression* is not in any $case\_list_i$, then $statement\_list_{n+1}$ in the default clause is executed. If the default clause is omitted and the value of *expression* is not in any $case\_list_i$, then execution "falls through" the `switch` statement.

Note that *expression* must be an integer-compatible expression (in particular, it may not evaluate to a real or a `string` value).

THE `break` STATEMENT

As illustrated in the program in Figure 6.3, each of the statement lists in a `switch` statement usually ends with a `break` **statement** of the form

```
break;
```

When it is executed, this statement transfers control to the first statement following the `switch` statement. As we will see in the next chapter, the `break` statement can also be used to terminate repetition of a loop. In both situations, `break` has the same behavior: Execution jumps to the first statement following the `switch` statement or loop in which it appears.

DROP-THROUGH BEHAVIOR

An important feature to remember when using the `switch` statement is its *drop-through behavior*. To illustrate it, suppose we had written the `switch` statement in Figure 6.3 without the `break` statements:

```
switch (conversion)
{
   case 'A': case 'a':
                          result = fahrToCelsius(temperature);
   case 'B': case 'b':
                          result = celsiusToFahr(temperature);
   case 'C': case 'c':
                          result = celsiusToKelvin(temperature);
   case 'D': case 'd':
                          result = kelvinToCelsius(temperature);
   case 'E': case 'e':
                          result = fahrToKelvin(temperature);
   case 'F': case 'f':
                          result = kelvinToFahr(temperature);
   default:
                          cerr << "\n*** Invalid conversion: "
                               << conversion << endl;
                          result = 0.0;
}
cout << "The converted temperature is " << result << endl;
```

The output produced when this modified version is run may be rather unexpected. Here is one example:

```
To convert arbitrary temperatures, enter:
A - to convert Fahrenheit to Celsius;
```

```
B - to convert Celsius to Fahrenheit;
C - to convert Celsius to Kelvin;
D - to convert Kelvin to Celsius;
E - to convert Fahrenheit to Kelvin; or
F - to convert Kelvin to Fahreneht.
--> B

Enter the temperature to be converted: 100
*** Invalid conversion: B
The converted temperature is 0
```

As in the sample run in Figure 6.3, the value of `conversion` is `B`, so control is transferred to the statement:

```
result = celsiusToFahr(temperature);
```

However, there is no `break` following this statement to transfer control past the other statements, and so execution drops through to the statement in the next case, which resets `result`:

```
result = celsiusToKelvin(temperature);
```

Again, there is no `break` statement, so execution drops through to the statement in the next case, which resets `result` again:

```
result = kelvinToCelsius(temperature);
```

This drop-through behavior continues until a `break`, a `return`, or the end of the `switch` statement is reached. Because there are no `break` or `return` statements here, execution proceeds through the next two cases and reaches the `default` case, which displays

```
*** Invalid conversion: B
```

and sets result to zero. The output statement following the `switch` then displays

```
The converted temperature is 0
```

WATCH OUT

To avoid this behavior, we must remember to end each statement list in a `switch` statement with a `break` (or `return` statement), except for the final statement list, where it is not necessary.

The program in Figure 6.3 uses the `switch` statement in a `main` function, but it is perhaps more commonly used to control selection in functions other than `main`. In this case, the function is probably using the `switch` to select its return value, and so a `return` statement can be used instead of a `break` statement. The following example illustrates this.

EXAMPLE: CONVERTING NUMERIC CODES TO NAMES

Problem. Suppose that a university uses numeric codes to store certain information about a student: 1 for freshman, 2 for sophomore, 3 for junior, 4 for senior, and 5 for graduate. When information about a freshman named Jane Doe is displayed, output of the form

```
Doe, Jane D. (Freshman)
```

is more descriptive than

```
Doe, Jane D.     (1)
```

Write a function that, given the numeric code of a year for some student, returns the name of the year corresponding to that code (e.g., 1 → `Freshman`, 2 → `Sophomore`, and so on).

Object-Centered Design

Behavior. Our function should receive a year code and should return the corresponding year name.

Objects. From our behavioral description, we have two objects in the problem:

Problem Objects	Software Objects			
	Type	Kind	Movement	Name
a year code	`int`	varying	received	*yearCode*
the name of the year	`string`	varying	returned	none

We can thus specify the problem as

Receive: *yearCode*, an integer

Precondition: *yearCode* is in the range 1–5 . . .

Return: character string corresponding to that year code ("Freshman", "Sophomore", . . .)

From this specification, we can build the following stub for our function:

```
string yearName(int yearCode)
{
}
```

Operations. From the behavioral description, we have only one operation:

Return the name of the year corresponding to *yearCode*.

Here, the key word is *corresponding*. Because we must return the name of the year corresponding to *yearCode*, we must compare *yearCode* to each of the possible year codes and then select an appropriate `return` statement.

Algorithm. The following algorithm applies this strategy.

Algorithm to Convert a Year Code

If *yearCode* is 1
  Return "Freshman".
Otherwise, if *yearCode* is 2
  Return "Sophomore".
Otherwise, if *yearCode* is 3
  Return "Junior".

Otherwise, if *yearCode* is 4
    Return "Senior".
Otherwise, if *yearCode* is 5
    Return "Graduate".
Otherwise
    Display an error message.
    Return the empty string.

Although we clearly could implement this algorithm using an `if` statement, the function in Figure 6.4 solves this problem using a `switch` statement. Note that no `break` statements are required in the cases of this `switch`. The function uses the `switch` to select a `return` statement, and a `return` statement causes execution of the function to terminate.

Fig. 6.4 Year-code conversion.

```
/* yearName() returns the name of a year, given a year code.
 *
 * Receive: an int year code (1-5)
 * Return:  the appropriate (string) year name
 *          (Freshman, Sophomore, Junior, Senior, Graduate)
 *****************************************************************/

string yearName(int yearCode)
{
   switch (yearCode)
   {
      case 1:
               return "Freshman";
      case 2:
               return "Sophomore";
      case 3:
               return "Junior";
      case 4:
               return "Senior";
      case 5:
               return "Graduate";
      default:
               cerr << "yearName: code error: " << yearCode << endl;
               return "";
   }
}
```

Testing. To test our function, we can write a simple driver program like that in Figure 6.5. The sample runs indicate that the function is behaving correctly for some valid values and an invalid value.

Fig. 6.5 Driver to test `yearName()`.

```
/* yearDriver.cpp is a driver program to test function YearName().
 *
 * Input:  none
 * Output: names of years (Freshman, Sophomore, ... )
 ***************************************************************/

#include <iostream>                    // cout, <<
#include <string>                      // string
using namespace std;

string yearName(int yearCode);

int main()
{
   int number;
   cout << "Enter the number of a class year: ";
   cin >> number;
   cout << yearName(number) << endl;
}

/*** Insert the definition of yearName() from Figure 6.4 here ***/
```

Sample runs:

```
Enter the number of a class year: 1
Freshman

Enter the number of a class year: 3
Junior

Enter the number of a class year: 6
YearName: code error: 6
```

CASES WITH NO ACTION

Occasionally, no action is required for certain values of the expression in a `switch` statement. In such situations, the statement lists associated with these values should consist of a single `break` or `return` statement, so that no action is taken. For example, a program to count aces and face cards might use a `switch` statement like the following:

```
char card;
int aces = faceCards = 0;
```

```
    .
    .
    .
switch (card)
{
   case 'A' :
                                       aces++;
                                       break;
   case 'J': case 'Q': case 'K':
                                       faceCards++;
                                       break;
   case '2': case '3': case '4': // these 'cards' are
   case '5': case '6': case '7': //  not being counted
   case '8': case '9': case '0':
                                       break;
   default:
                                       cout << "*** Illegal card: "
                                            << card << endl;
}
```

Note that white space is ignored in the case lists and statement lists. Where these items are positioned is largely a matter of personal style, but the goal should be to write readable `switch` statements in which there is a clear association between each case list and its corresponding statement list.

It is important to remember that *the expression and the constants in the case lists must be integer compatible (*e.g., `int`, `char`, *and so on).* In particular, they may not be real or string expressions. For example, we cannot write the preceding `switch` statement as

```
string card;
int aces = faceCards = 0;
    .
    .
    .
switch (card)
{
   case "ACE":                    aces++;        // STRINGS
                                  break;         // ARE
   case "JACK": case "QUEEN":                    // NOT
   case "KING":                   faceCards++;   // ALLOWED
                                  break;
    .
    .
    .
}
```

because the expression controlling a `switch` statement must be integer-compatible, which precludes `string` and real expressions.

CHOOSING THE PROPER SELECTION STATEMENT

Now that we have two different ways to perform multialternative selection, it is important to understand when an `if-else-if` should be used and when a `switch` statement is appropriate. If a selection step in an algorithm is written in the form

If *expression* is equal to $constant_1$
    $statement\_list_1$
Otherwise, if *expression* is equal to $constant_2$
    $statement\_list_2$

.
.
.

Otherwise, if *expression* is equal to $constant_n$
    $statement\_list_n$
Otherwise
    $statement\_list_{n+1}$

and if *expression* is integer compatible, then this selection step is most effectively coded as a `switch` statement:

```
switch (expression)
{
   case constant1:
                     statement_list1
                     break;
   case constant2:
                     statement_list2
                      break;
     .
     .
     .
   case constantn:
                     statement_listn
                     break;
   default:
                     statement_listn+1
}
```

The reason is that in the `if-else-if` form, execution of $statement\_list_1$ requires the evaluation of one boolean expression, execution of $statement\_list_2$ requires the evaluation of two boolean expressions, . . . , and execution of $statement\_list_n$ (or $statement\_list_{n+1}$) requires the evaluation of n boolean expressions. Because it takes time to evaluate each expression, there is a performance penalty associated with statements that occur later in an `if-else-if` construct.

For example, we already saw that it would be *correct* to code the temperature-conversion algorithm at the beginning of this section using an `if-else-if` as follows:

```
if (conversion == 'A' || conversion == 'a')
   result = fahrToCelsius(temperature);
else if (conversion == 'B' || conversion == 'b')
   result = celsiusToFahr(temperature);
else if (conversion == 'C' || conversion == 'c')
   result = celsiusToKelvin(temperature);
```

```
else if (conversion == 'D' || conversion == 'd')
   result = kelvinToCelsius(temperature);
else if (conversion == 'E' || conversion == 'e')
   result = fahrToKelvin(temperature);
else if (conversion == 'F' || conversion == 'f')
   result = kelvinToFahr(temperature);
else
{
   cerr << "\n*** Invalid conversion: " << conversion << endl;
   result = 0.0;
}
```

But this requires that 12 boolean expressions be evaluated for a Kelvin-to-Fahrenheit conversion, whereas only one is evaluated for a Fahrenheit-to-Celsius conversion.

By contrast, a `switch` statement is usually implemented so that each statement list requires approximately one comparison,[6] regardless of whether it is first or last. A `switch` statement is thus to be preferred over the `if-else-if` when

1. the equality (==) comparison is being performed;
2. the same expression (e.g., `conversion`) is being compared in each condition; and
3. the value to which this expression is being compared is `int` compatible.

6.4 Example: Computing Letter Grades

PROBLEM

In many courses, students submit homework, take tests, and take a final exam. In comput ing a final grade, the average scores for these components are calculated, multiplied by a weighting factor, and then added to give a final weighted average. A program is needed that, given averages for homework, tests, and a final exam score, will compute a student's letter grade, assuming that homework constitutes 20 percent, tests 50 percent, and the final exam 30 percent of the final grade.

Object-Centered Design

Behavior. Our program should display on the screen a prompt for the homework average, test average, and the final-exam score. It should then read these quantities from the keyboard and compute the final weighted average. From the weighted average, it should compute the corresponding letter grade and display this grade.

Objects. From the statement of the problem and our behavioral description, we can identify the following objects in the problem:

---

6. The mechanism by which this is accomplished is beyond the scope of this text. The interested reader should see, for example, *Compiler: Principles, Techniques and Tools* by Aho, Sethi, and Ullman (Reading, Mass.: Addison–Wesley, 1986).

Problem Objects	Software Objects		
	Type	Kind	Name
homework average	`double`	varying	*homeworkAverage*
test average	`double`	varying	*testAverage*
final-exam score	`double`	varying	*examScore*
final weighted average	`double`	varying	*finalAverage*
homework weight	`double`	constant	*HOMEWORK_WEIGHT*
test weight	`double`	constant	*TEST_WEIGHT*
final-exam weight	`double`	constant	*EXAM_WEIGHT*
letter grade	`char`	constant	*grade*

The problem can then be specified as follows:

Input: *homeworkAverage*, *testAverage*, and *examScore*, three real values

Output: The letter grade earned

Operations. From our behavioral description, we can identify the following operations:

i. Display a prompt (a character string) on the screen
ii. Read three (real) quantities from the keyboard
iii. Compute a weighted average using the three inputs and three weights
iv. Compute the letter grade corresponding to a weighted average
v. Display that (`char`) letter grade

Operations i, ii, and v are predefined, and iii is a simple formula:

finalAverage = *HOMEWORK_WEIGHT* * *homeworkAverage* +
TEST_WEIGHT * *testAverage* +
EXAM_WEIGHT * *examScore*

Operation iv is more complicated, so we will write a function to perform it.

Algorithm. Once we have a function to perform operation iv, we can solve our problem using the following algorithm:

Grade-Computation Algorithm

1. Prompt for the homework average, test average, and exam score.
2. Enter *homeworkAverage, testAverage, and examScore.*
3. Calculate *finalAverage* = *HOMEWORK_WEIGHT* * *homeworkAverage* +
   TEST_WEIGHT * *testAverage* +
   EXAM_WEIGHT * *examScore.*
4. Calculate and display the letter grade corresponding to *finalAverage.*

Function's Problem. Calculate the letter grade corresponding to a weighted average.

Function's Behavior. The function should receive from its caller a weighted average, which is a real value. It should return the letter grade corresponding to that weighted average.

Function's Objects. From our behavioral description, we can identify the following objects for this problem:

Problem Objects	Software Objects			
	Type	Kind	Movement	Name
the weighted average	`double`	varying	received (in)	*weightedAverage*
the corresponding letter grade	`char`	constant	returned (out)	none

We can thus specify the behavior of our function as

Receive: *weightedAverage*, a `double`

Return: the (`char`) letter grade corresponding to *weightedAverage*

and from this specification, we can build a stub for the function:

```
char letterGrade(double weightedAverage)
{
}
```

Function's Operations. The key to our problem is recognizing that it requires selective execution. The function must return a letter grade for a given value of *weightedAverage*, as given by the following table:

weightedAverage	Return
$weightedAverage \geq 90$	A
$80 \leq weightedAverage < 90$	B
$70 \leq weightedAverage < 80$	C
$60 \leq weightedAverage < 70$	D
$weightedAverage < 60$	F

Function's Coding. We could perform this operation using an `if` statement, as described in Section 6.2, but a `switch` statement is more efficient. There are, however, two problems to be resolved. First, the parameter `weightedAverage` will be of type `double` (i.e., a real) and the expression in a `switch` statement cannot be a real. This problem can be solved by converting `weightedAverage` to an `int` value,

```
int(weightedAverage)
```

which truncates the decimal portion of `weightedAverage`.

The second problem is that when `weightedAverage` has been converted from a real to an integer, there are still 10 or more values in each case list. For example, the values for a 'B' are

80, 81, 82, 83, 84, 85, 86, 87, 88, 89

This means that a case list like

```
case 80: case 81: case 82: case 83: case 84:
case 85: case 86: case 87: case 88: case 89:
```

would be required for each grade to be displayed. However, if we divide each of these values by 10, the same quotient (8) results. Thus, assuming that the weighted average does not exceed 100, we can use the expression

```
int(weightedAverage) / 10
```

in a `switch` statement that will have manageable case lists. The function in Figure 6.6 uses this approach.

Fig. 6.6 Grade computation.

```
/* letterGrade() computes the grade for a given weightedAverage.
 *
 * Receive:      a (double) weighted average
 * Precondition: 0 <= weightedAverage <= 100
 * Return:        the appropriate (char) letter grade (A, B, C, D, or F)
 *****************************************************************/

char letterGrade(double weightedAverage)
{
   switch ( int(weightedAverage) / 10 )
   {
      case 10:                 // int(100)/10 -> 10
      case 9:                  // int(90-99)/10 -> 9
              return 'A';
      case 8:                  // int(80-89)/10 -> 8
              return 'B';
      case 7:                  // int(70-79)/10 -> 7
              return 'C';
      case 6:                  // int(60-69)/10 -> 6
              return 'D';
      default:                 // not so good!
              return 'F';
   }
}
```

Coding and Testing. We can now code the algorithm for the original problem, as shown in Figure 6.7.

Fig. 6.7 The letter-grade program. (Part 1 of 2)

```
/* grader.cpp computes a final course average using the homework
 * average, the average on tests, and a final-exam score and
 * assigns a letter grade.
 *
 * Input:  three real values representing a student's homework
 *            average, average on tests, and a final-exam score
 * Output: the final average and the letter grade
 ******************************************************************/

#include <iostream>                    // cin, cout, >>, <<
using namespace std;

char letterGrade(double weightedAverage);

int main()
{
   const double HOMEWORK_WEIGHT = 0.2, // weights for homework,
                TEST_WEIGHT = 0.5,     //   tests,
                EXAM_WEIGHT = 0.3;     //   and the exam.

   cout << "This program computes a final course grade using the\n"
           "homework average, test average, and a final exam "
           "score.\n";

   cout << "\nEnter the homework average, test average, "
           "and exam score:\n";

   double homeworkAverage,       // the average of the homework scores
          testAverage,           // the average of the test scores
          examScore;             // the final-exam score

   cin >> homeworkAverage >> testAverage >> examScore;

   double finalAverage = HOMEWORK_WEIGHT * homeworkAverage +
                         TEST_WEIGHT * testAverage +
                         EXAM_WEIGHT * examScore;

   char grade = letterGrade(finalAverage);    // the letter grade received
```

Fig. 6.7 The letter-grade program. (Part 2 of 2)

```
   cout << "Final Average = " << finalAverage
        << ", Grade = " << grade << "\n\n";
}

/*** Insert definition of letterGrade() from Figure 6.6 here ***/
```

Sample runs:

```
This program computes a final course grade using the
homework average, test average, and a final-exam score.

Enter the homework average, test average, and exam score:
100 100 100
Final Average = 100, Grade = A

. . .
Enter the homework average, test average, and exam score:
30 40 50
Final Average = 41, Grade = F

. . .
Enter the homework average, test average, and exam score:
56.2 62.7 66.5
Final Average = 62.54, Grade = D

. . .
Enter the homework average, test average, and exam score:
87.5 91.3 80
Final Average = 87.15, Grade = B
```

✔ Quick Quiz 6.4

For the following questions, assume that `number` is an `int` variable, `code` is a `char` variable, and `x` is a `double` variable.

1. If `number` has the value 99, tell what output is produced by the following `switch` statement, or indicate why an error occurs:

```
switch(number)
{
   case 99:
               cout << number + 99 << endl;
               break;
```

```
    case -1:
                cout << number - 1 << endl;
                break;
    default:
                cout << "default\n";
}
```

2. Proceed as in Question 1, but suppose that the `break` statements are omitted.
3. Proceed as in Question 1, but suppose that `number` has the value 50.
4. Proceed as in Question 2, but suppose that `number` has the value 50.
5. Proceed as in Question 1, but suppose that `number` has the value –1.
6. Proceed as in Question 2, but suppose that `number` has the value –1.
7. If the value of `code` is the letter `B`, tell what output is produced by the following `switch` statement, or indicate why an error occurs:

```
switch (code)
{
    case 'A': case 'B':
                            cout << 123 << endl;
                            break;
    case 'P': case 'R': case 'X':
                            cout << 456 << endl;
                            break;
}
```

8. Proceed as in Question 7, but suppose that the value of `code` is the letter `X`.
9. Proceed as in Question 7, but suppose that the value of `code` is the letter `M`.
10. If the value of `x` is 2.0, tell what output is produced by the following `switch` statement, or indicate why an error occurs:

```
switch (x)
{
    case 1.0:
                cout << x + 1.0 << endl;
                break;
    case 2.0:
                cout << x + 2.0 << endl;
                break;
}
```

Exercises 6.4

1. Write a `switch` statement that increases `balance` by adding `amount` to it if the value of the character variable `transCode` is `'D'`; decrease `balance` by subtracting `amount` from it if `transCode` is `'W'`; display the value of `balance` if `transCode` is `'P'`; and display an illegal-transaction message otherwise.
2. Write a `switch` statement that, for two given integers `a` and `b`, and a given character `operation`, computes and displays `a + b`, `a - b`, `a * b`, or `a / b` according to whether `operation` is `'+'`, `'-'`, `'*'`, or `'/'` and displays an illegal-operator message if it is not one of these.

For Exercises 3–6, write functions that use `switch` statements to compute what is required. To test these functions, you should write driver programs as instructed in Programming Problems 9–12 at the end of this chapter.

3. Given a number representing a TV channel, return the call letters of the station that corresponds to that number, or some message indicating that the channel is not used. Use the following channel numbers and call letters (or use those that are available in your locale):

   2: WCBS
   4: WNBC
   5: WNEW
   7: WABC
   9: WOR
   11: WPIX
   13: WNET

4. Given a distance less than 1000, return a shipping cost as determined by the following table:

Distance	Cost
0 through 99	5.00
At least 100 but less than 300	8.00
At least 500 but less than 600	10.00
At least 600 but less than 1000	12.00

5. Given the number of a month, return the name of a month (or an error message indicating an illegal month number).
6. Proceed as in 5, but return the number of days in a month. (See Exercise 7 of Section 6.2 regarding the determination of leap years.)

6.5 Selection: Conditional Expressions

The selection statements (`if` and `switch`) we have considered thus far are similar to statements provided by other languages. However, C++ has inherited a third selection mechanism from its parent language C, an expression that produces either of two values, based on the value of a boolean expression (also called a *condition*).

To illustrate it, consider a simplified form of the letter-grade computation problem from the preceding section, in which we wish to determine whether a student is passing or failing, based on an average of homework average, test average, and final exam score. If `average` is this average, the output statement

```
cout << "You are "
     << ( (average > PASS_FAIL_LINE) ? "passing." : "failing." );
```

will display

```
You are passing.
```

if the condition `average > PASS_FAIL_LINE` is true, but it will display

```
You are failing.
```

if the condition `average > PASS_FAIL_LINE` is false.

Because the value produced by such expressions depends on the value of their condition, they are called **conditional expressions**[7] and have the following general form:

The Conditional Expression

Form:

condition ? $expression_1$: $expression_2$

where

condition is a boolean expression; and

$expression_1$ and $expression_2$ are type-compatible expressions.

Behavior: *condition* is evaluated.

If the value of *condition* is true (i.e., nonzero),

then the value of $expression_1$ is returned as the result.

If the value of *condition* is false (i.e., zero),

then the value of $expression_2$ is returned as the result.

Note that in a conditional expression, only one of $expression_1$ and $expression_2$ is evaluated. Thus, an assignment such as

```
reciprocal = ( (x == 0) ? 0 : 1 / x);
```

is safe because if the value of `x` is zero, the expression `1 / x` will not be evaluated, and so no division-by-zero error results. A conditional expression can thus sometimes be used in place of an `if` statement to guard a potentially unsafe operation. When it is used as a subexpression in another expression, the conditional expression should be enclosed in parentheses, because its precedence is lower than most of the other operators. (See Appendix C.)

This mechanism has many different uses, because it can be used anywhere that an expression can appear. In fact, the conditional expression can be used in place of most `if-else` statements. To illustrate, suppose that we wanted to write a function `largerOf()` to find the maximum of two `int` values. Although we could do this with an `if` statement,

```
int largerOf(int value1, int value2)
{
   if (value1 > value2)
      return value1;
```

7. A conditional expression has the form `C ? A : B` and is actually a *ternary* (three-operand) operation, in which `C`, `A`, and `B` are the three operands, and `? :` is the operator.

```
    else
        return value2;
}
```

a conditional expression provides a simpler alternative:

```
int largerOf(int value1, int value2)
{
    return ( (value1 > value2) ? value1 : value2);
}
```

Using such a function, we can write

```
max = largerOf(x, y);
```

and `max` will be assigned the larger of the two values `x` and `y`.

As a final example, suppose that `numCourses` is an `int` variable containing the number of courses a student is taking in the current semester. Then the output statement

```
cout << "\nYou are taking " << numCourses << " course"
     << ( (numCourses == 1) ? "" : "s" )
     << " this semester.\n";
```

will display the *singular* message

```
You are taking 1 course this semester.
```

if `numCourses` is equal to 1 and will display a *plural* message if `numCourses` has a value other than 1:

```
You are taking 3 courses this semester.
```

Exercises 6.5

1. Describe the operation that the following function performs:

```
int doSomething1(int value)
{
    return ( (value >= 0) ? value : -value );
}
```

2. Describe the operation that the following function performs:

```
char doSomething2(char ch)
{
    return ( ( ('A' <= ch) && (ch <= 'Z') ) ? ch+32 : ch );
}
```

3. Write conditional expressions that can replace the blanks in the output statement

```
cout << ____ << month << '/'
     << ____ << day << '/'
     << ____ << year % 100<< endl;
```

so that the output produced will be as follows:

month	day	year	**Output**
12	25	1999	12/25/99
10	1	1980	10/01/80
7	4	1976	07/04/76
2	2	2002	02/02/02

4. Write a conditional expression that can replace the blank in the output statement

```
cout << ____ << number << endl;
```

so that the output produced will be as follows:

number	**Output**
123	123
23	023
3	003

5. Write a function `smallerOf()` that returns the smaller of two given integer values.
6. Using nested conditional expressions, write a function:
   a. `largestOf()` that, given three `int` values, returns the largest of the three;
   b. `smallestOf()` that, given three `int` values, returns the smallest of the three.
7. The mathematician Carl Friedrich Gauss discovered that the sum of the integers from 1 through n is given by the form

$$\frac{n(n+1)}{2}$$

Using a conditional expression, construct a function `sum()` that returns the value according to Gauss's formula if the value of its parameter is positive and zero otherwise.

Part of the Picture
Boolean Logic and Digital Design

The *Part of the Picture: Introduction to Computer Organization* section in Chapter 0 and the *Part of the Picture: Computer Architecture* introduced in the next section of this chapter describe one of a computer's components, the CPU (central processing unit). The arithmetic operations performed by the CPU must be carried out using special electrical circuits called **logic circuits** that are used to implement boolean (or digital) logic in hardware. In this section, we investigate the design of such circuits, which is one small part of the broader area of computer architecture.

EARLY WORK

The foundations of circuit design were laid in the early 1900s by the English mathematician George Boole, after whom the C++ `bool` type is named. Boole formalized several axioms of logic, resulting in an algebra for writing logical expressions, which have since come to be known as boolean expressions.

In C++ syntax, some of the basic axioms of boolean logic are as follows:*

	The Relational Laws		
1a.	`!(X == Y) ≡ (X != Y)`	1b.	`!(X != Y) ≡ (X == Y)`
2a.	`!(X < Y) ≡ (X >= Y)`	2b.	`!(X >= Y) ≡ (X < Y)`
3a.	`!(X > Y) ≡ (X <= Y)`	3b.	`!(X <= Y) ≡ (X > Y)`
	The Boolean Laws		
4a.	`X || false ≡ X`	4b.	`X && false ≡ false`
5a.	`X || true ≡ true`	5b.	`X && true ≡ X`
	Idempotent Laws		
6a.	`X || X ≡ X`	6b.	`X && X ≡ X`
	Involution Law		
7a.	`!(!X) ≡ X`		
	Laws of Complementarity		
8a.	`X || (!X) ≡ true`	8b.	`X && (!X) ≡ false`
	Commutative Laws		
9a.	`X || Y ≡ Y || X`	9b.	`X && Y ≡ Y && X`
	Associative Laws		
10a.	`(X || Y) || Z ≡ X || (Y || Z)`	10b.	`(X && Y) && Z ≡ X && (Y && Z)`
	Distributive Laws		
11a.	`X && (Y || Z) ≡ (X && Y) || (X && Z)`	11b.	`X || (Y && Z) ≡ (X || Y) && (X || Z)`
	Simplification Theorems		
12a.	`(X && Y) || (X && !Y) ≡ X`	12b.	`(X || Y) && (X || !Y) ≡ X`
13a.	`X || (X && Y) ≡ X`	13b.	`X && (X || Y) ≡ X`
14a.	`(X || !Y) && Y ≡ X && Y`	14b.	`(X && !Y) || Y ≡ X || Y`
	DeMorgan's Laws		
15a.	`!(X && Y) ≡ !X || !Y`	15b.	`!(X || Y) ≡ !X && !Y`

It is especially useful for programmers to know DeMorgan's Laws because they can simplify complicated boolean expressions. As a simple illustration, suppose that `done` and `error` are `bool` objects, and consider the following `if` statement:

```
if (!done && !error)
// ... do something...
```

DeMorgan's law tells us that the boolean expression involving two negated values,

```
!done && !error
```

can be simplified to

```
!(done || error)
```

The original expression contained two NOT operations and one AND operation, but the simplified expression contains only one NOT operation and one OR operation—one less operation. Applying DeMorgan's law repeatedly to a boolean expression of the form

$$!b_1 \ \&\& \ !b_2 \ \&\& \ \ldots \ \&\& \ !b_n$$

containing n NOTs and $n - 1$ ANDs, gives the simpler expression

$$!(b_1 \ || \ b_2 \ || \ \ldots \ || \ b_n)$$

containing only one NOT and $n - 1$ ORs. The complexity of the expression is thus reduced by $n - 1$ NOT operations, which can result in a significant increase in performance.

DIGITAL CIRCUITS

With the invention of the digital computer in the late 1930s, the work of Boole moved from obscurity to prominence. The axioms and theorems of his boolean algebra became extremely important as mathematicians, engineers, and physicists sought to build the arithmetic and logic circuitry of the early computers. These circuits utilize three basic electronic components: the **AND gate,** the **OR gate,** and the **NOT gate** or **inverter,** whose symbols are as follows:

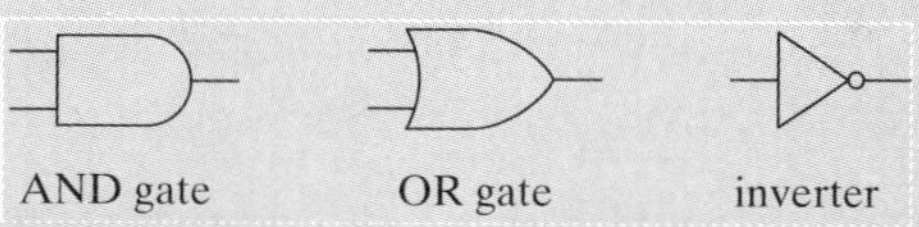

The inputs to these gates are electrical voltages, where a voltage that exceeds a certain threshold value is interpreted as 1 (i.e., true), and a voltage below that threshold is interpreted as 0 (i.e., false). In the case of an AND gate, a 1 is produced only when there are 1s on both input lines. An OR gate produces a 1 only when there is a 1 on at least one of the input lines. The output of a NOT gate is the opposite of its input. Because these three components behave in the same fashion as the AND, OR, and NOT operators from boolean algebra, a circuit can be constructed to represent any boolean expression, and boolean expressions can be used to design circuits!

CIRCUIT DESIGN: A BINARY HALF-ADDER

To illustrate, consider the problem of adding two binary digits `digit1` and `digit2`. The truth table below summarizes the behavior of the addition operation, which produces two results—a `sum` bit and a `carry` bit:

digit1	digit2	carry	sum
0	0	0	0
0	1	0	1
1	0	0	1
1	1	1	0

There are two important things to note:

1. The `carry` output is 1 (true) only when `digit1` and `digit2` are both 1 (true).
2. The `sum` output is 1 (true) only when `digit1` is 0 (false) and `digit2` is 1 (true), or when `digit1` is 1 (true) and `digit2` is 0 (false).

It is easy to see that we can represent these outputs by the following pair of boolean expressions:

```
bool carry = digit1 && digit2,
     sum = (!digit1 && digit2) || (digit1 && !digit2);
```

The expression for `sum` has the form `(!A && B) || (A && !B)` and can be simplified by applying the axioms from boolean logic as follows:

```
(!A && B) || (A && !B)
        ⇓                          (Apply 9a to switch two operands of ||)
(A && !B) || (!A && B)
        ⇓                          (Apply 11b with X = (A && !B), Y =
                                   !A, Z = B)
((A && !B) || !A) && ((A && !B) || B)
        ⇓                          (Apply 14b to second expression with X = A
                                   and Y = B)
((A && !B) || !A) && (A || B)
        ⇓                          (Apply 9a to switch two operands of first &&)
((!B && A) || !A) && (A || B)
        ⇓                          (Apply 14b to first expression with X = !B and
                                   Y = !A)
(!B || !A) && (A || B)
        ⇓                          (Apply 15a to first || expression with X = B
                                   and Y = A)
!(B && A) && (A || B)
        ⇓                          (Apply 9a to switch two operands of first &&)
!(A && B) && (A || B)
        ⇓                          (Apply 9a to switch two operands of second &&)
(A || B) && !(A && B)
```

This means that the boolean expression for `sum` can be rewritten as

```
sum = (digit1 || digit2) && !(digit1 && digit2);
```

which has one less NOT operation than the original expression.

This may seem like a lot of work for not much improvement. On the contrary, this simplification means that a circuit for this expression will require one less inverter than a circuit for the original expression and will therefore be less expensive to manufacture. If half-adders are mass-produced, then this circuit may be manufactured millions of times with a savings that is millions of times the cost of an inverter!

Using the boolean expressions

```
bool carry = digit1 && digit2,
sum = (digit1 || digit2) && !(digit1 && digit2);
```

for `sum` and `carry`, we can design the following circuit, called a **binary half-adder**, that adds two binary digits:

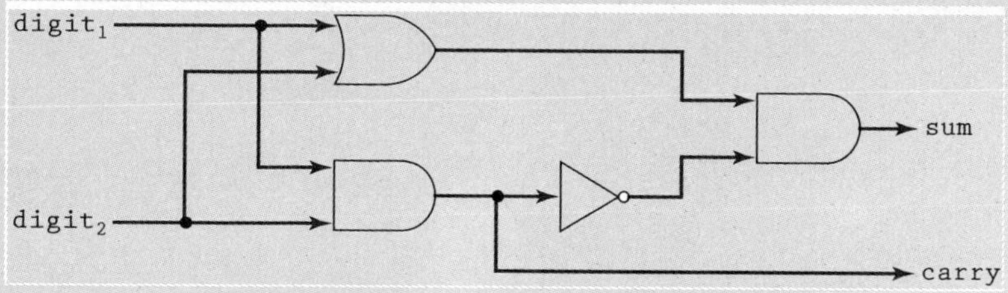

It accepts two inputs, `digit1` and `digit2`, and produces two outputs, `sum` and `carry`.

Once a boolean expression is found to represent a circuit, it is easy to write a simple program to check its behavior. For example, the program in Figure 6.8 simulates the action of a binary half-adder. It reads binary digits (0 or 1) for `digit1` and `digit2`. The values of the two boolean expressions representing the sum and carry outputs are then assigned to the variables `sum` and `carry`, respectively, and are displayed.

Fig. 6.8 A binary half-adder. (Part 1 of 2)

```
/* halfadder.cpp calculates the outputs from boolean expressions
 * that represent the logical circuit for a binary half-adder.
 *
 *  Input (keyboard): two binary digits
 *  Output (screen):  two binary values representing the sum and carry
 *                    that result when the input values are added
 ***********************************************************************/

#include <iostream>                        // cout, cin, <<, >>
using namespace std;

int main()
{
   cout << "Enter two binary inputs: ";
   short digit1, digit2;                   // the two binary inputs
   cin >> digit1 >> digit2;
                                           // the two circuit outputs
   bool sum   = (digit1 || digit2) && !(digit1 && digit2),
        carry = (digit1 && digit2);

   cout << "Carry = " << carry << " Sum = " << sum << "\n\n";
}
```

Fig. 6.8 A binary half-adder. (Part 2 of 2)

Sample runs:

```
Enter two binary inputs: 0 0
Carry = 0 Sum = 0

Enter two binary inputs: 0 1
Carry = 0 Sum = 1

Enter two binary inputs: 1 0
Carry = 0 Sum = 1

Enter two binary inputs: 1 1
Carry = 1 Sum = 0
```

A binary *full-adder* for adding two binary digits and a carry bit and an *adder* for numbers having more than one binary digit are described in the Programming Problems at the end of the chapter.

* In the statements of these laws, the symbol ≡ denotes *is equivalent to*. A statement of the form $p \equiv q$ means that p and q always have the same truth values (true or false).

Part of the Picture
Computer Architecture
by William Stallings

At a top level, a computer consists of processor, memory, and I/O components, with one or more modules of each type. These components are interconnected in some fashion to achieve the main function of the computer, which is to execute programs. Thus, there are four main structural elements:

- **Processor:** Controls the operation of the computer and performs its data processing functions. When there is only one processor, it is often referred to as the *central processing unit* (*CPU*).
- **Main Memory:** Stores data and programs. This memory is typically volatile; it is also referred to as *real memory or primary memory.*
- **I/O Modules:** Move data between the computer and its external environment. The external environment consists of a variety of external devices, including secondary memory devices, communications equipment, and printers.
- **System Interconnection:** Some structure and mechanisms that provide for communication among processors, main memory, and I/O modules.

So begins Professor Stalling's comprehensive and detailed description of the components of a computer. Unfortunately, space restrictions prevent us from including all of this *Part of the Picture* section here, but it is available on the text's Web site.

6.6* OBJECTive Thinking: Mutator Methods

In the *OBJECTive Thinking* section of the last chapter, we saw how to define accessor methods, which are probably the simplest category of instance methods—messages that can be sent to an object. We also saw how to build a simple output method to write an object's attributes to an `ostream`. In this section, we will examine the complementary operations:

- **mutator methods** that let a programmer change the value of an instance variable; and
- **input methods** that let a user define an object using values read from an `istream`.

Mutators are so-named because they change (or mutate) the attributes of an object to which they are sent. As such, a mutator usually receives one or more arguments that specify the new value(s) for the object's attributes. Similarly, an input method defines a message that when sent to an object will set that object's instance variables to values read from an `istream`.

Thus, mutators and input methods both change an object's attributes. The main difference between them is where they get their values: Mutators change attributes to values received via parameters, while input methods change attributes to values read from an `istream`.

Special **validation code** is a necessity in mutators and input methods to ensure that the values passed as arguments or read from the stream are valid attribute values. This code usually takes the form of `if` statements (or `asserts`) that check these incoming values.

NAME MUTATORS AND INPUT METHODS

We have seen previously how to define a `Name` class that provides instance variables, con structors, and accessors. The highlighted code in Figure 6.9 shows how to define mutators and an input method for this class.

Fig. 6.9 Class `Name` mutator and input methods. (Part 1 of 2)

```
/* Name.h presents accessor methods for class Name.
 * ...
 */

#include <iostream>      // ostream class
#include <string>        // the string class
#include <cassert>       // assert()
using namespace std;

class Name
{
 public:
   Name();                                    // constructors
   Name(string first, string middle, string last);
```

Fig. 6.9 Class `Name` mutator and input methods. (Part 2 of 2)

```
   string getFirstName() const;              // accessors
   string getLastName() const;
   char   getMiddleInitial() const;
   string getSignature() const;

   void setFirstName(string newFirstName);   // mutators
   // setMiddleName() left as an exercise
   void setLastName(string newLastName);

   void print(ostream& out) const;           // I/O methods
   void read(istream& in);

 // ... other Name-operation declarations go here

 private:
   string myFirstName,
          myMiddleName,
          myLastName;
};

// ... constructor, accessor definitions omitted ...

inline void Name::setFirstName(string newFirstName)
{
   myFirstName = newFirstName;
}

// setMiddleName() left as an exercise

inline void Name::setLastName(string newLastName)
{
   myLastName = newLastName;
}

inline void Name::read(istream& in)
{
   in >> myFirstName >> myMiddleName >> myLastName;
}
```

If we compare the prototypes and definitions of these methods with those of their corresponding accessor and output methods from Section 5.6, we see several basic differences:

- An accessor retrieves the value of an attribute; a mutator is used to change an attribute's value.
- The names of accessors and mutators are usually chosen to reflect their differences:
  - An accessor's name is usually `getX()`, where *X* is the name of the attribute being retrieved.
  - A mutator's name is usually `setX()`, where *X* is the name of the attribute being changed.
- Because they do not change the values of instance variables, accessors are declared and defined as `const` methods by placing the keyword `const` at the end of their heading. By contrast, mutators change the values of instance variables and thus cannot be `const` methods.
- Because they do not change the values of instance variables—they simply read and display such values—output methods are declared as `const` methods. By contrast, input methods change values of instance variables and thus cannot be `const` methods.

Given these methods in class `Name`, a programmer can now send a `Name` object mutator and input messages, as shown in Figure 6.10.

Fig. 6.10 Driver for class `Name`. (Part 1 of 2)

```
/* nameDriver.cpp tests class Name.
 * ... documentation omitted to save space ...
 *************************************************************************/

#include <iostream>                // cin, cout, >>, <<
#include "Name.h"                  // Name
using namespace std;

int main()
{
   cout << "Enter a full name (first, middle, last): ";
   Name aName;
   aName.read(cin);
   aName.print(cout);
   cout << endl;
   aName.setFirstName("Yertle");
   aName.setLastName("Turtle");
   aName.print(cout);
}
```

Fig. 6.10 Driver for class `Name`. (Part 2 of 2)

Sample run:

```
Enter a full name (first, middle, last): Popeye the Sailorman
Popeye the Sailorman
Yertle the Turtle
```

Note that we have not used any validation code in the `Name` mutator and input methods. This is because there are no well-defined rules for what constitutes a valid name. (For example, "Moon Unit Zappa" is a perfectly valid, albeit unusual, name.) Our next example will illustrate validation code.

SPHERE MUTATORS AND INPUT METHODS

We have seen previously how to define a `Sphere` class that provides instance variables and constructors; and the definitions of accessor methods were left as exercises in Section 5.6. We now examine one way that `Sphere` mutator methods might be defined.

Defining mutators for our `Sphere` class is a bit tricky, because the values of the three sphere attributes (*radius*, *density*, and *weight*) are all related by the formula

$$weight = density \times 4\pi\frac{r^3}{3}$$

or an equivalent variation. This means that a mutator cannot arbitrarily change the three attributes; the relationship between the three given by this formula must remain true.[8] If a sphere's *radius* and *density* are changed, then the *weight* must also change according to this formula. If only the *radius* is changed (so the *density* remains fixed), then the *weight* still must change according to this formula. Similarly, changing only the *weight* and leaving the *radius* fixed forces the *density* to change.

Here we will consider only the mutators and input methods in which two of the three attributes are provided; as we have seen, the value of the third attribute is then determined by the preceding formula. Prototypes for these methods are highlighted in Figure 6.11. Mutators and output methods in which only one attribute is provided and another remains fixed are left to the exercises.

Fig. 6.11 A `Sphere` class providing class methods. (Part 1 of 2)

```
/* Sphere.h provides a Sphere class
 * that illustrates mutator methods.
 * ...
 ********************************************************************/
```

8. A relationship between a class' attributes that must always remain true is called a **class invariant**. We will consider class invariants in more detail later.

Fig. 6.11 A `Sphere` class providing class methods. (Part 2 of 2)

```
#include <iostream>   // istream
#include <cmath>      // pow()
using namespace std;

const double PI = 3.14159;

class Sphere
{
 public:
   Sphere();

   double getWeight() const;
   // ... other Sphere accessors omitted...

   void setRadiusAndDensity(double radius, double density);
   void setRadiusAndWeight(double radius, double weight);
   void setDensityAndWeight(double density, double weight);

   void print(ostream& out) const;
   void readRadiusAndDensity(istream& in);
   void readRadiusAndWeight(istream& in);
   void readDensityAndWeight(istream& in);

   // ... other Sphere operations omitted...

 private:
   double myRadius, myWeight, myDensity;
};

// ... "simple" Sphere method definitions...
```

Since a sphere whose radius, density, or weight is nonpositive is meaningless, each of these methods has a precondition. For example, the precondition for `setRadiusAndDensity(newRadius, newDensity)` is

```
newRadius > 0 && newDensity > 0
```

Each method must verify that its precondition is true before modifying any attribute variables. Doing so is the role of a method's validation code.

Up to now, we have been using a threshold of three to five operations for methods to be considered "simple" enough to define them in a class' header file. When we design an algorithm for the current methods, we find that the number of operations in each method definition is well above this threshold. As a result, we will put the definitions of these methods in the separately compiled implementation file *Sphere.cpp*. Figure 6.12 shows the definitions of two of these methods, `setRadiusAndDensity()` and `readRadiusAndDensity()`.

Fig. 6.12 Definitions of nontrivial `Sphere` methods in `Sphere.cpp`. (Part 1 of 2)

```
/* Sphere.cpp defines the nontrivial methods of class Sphere.
 * ... other documentation omitted
 ******************************************************************/

#include "Sphere.h"       // our Sphere class

void Sphere::setRadiusAndDensity(double radius, double density)
{
   if (radius > 0 && density > 0)      // validate arguments
   {                                   // update attributes
      myWeight = density * 4.0 * PI * pow(radius, 3) / 3.0;
      myRadius = radius;
      myDensity = density;
   }
   else                                // precondition failed
   {
      cerr << "setRadiusAndDensity(r, d): invalid arguments "
           << " r = " << radius << ", d = " << density;
      myRadius = myDensity = myWeight = 0.0;
   }
}

// ... other Sphere mutators left as exercises ...

void Sphere::readRadiusAndDensity(istream& in)
{
   double newRadius, newDensity;
   in >> newRadius >> newDensity;        // read inputs from in

   if (newRadius > 0 && newDensity > 0) // validate inputs
   {                                    // update attributes
      myWeight = newDensity * 4.0 * PI * pow(newRadius, 3) / 3.0;
      myRadius = newRadius;
      myDensity = newDensity;
   }
```

Fig. 6.12 Definitions of nontrivial `Sphere` methods in `Sphere.cpp`. (Part 2 of 2)

```
   else                                     // precondition failed
   {
      cerr << "readRadiusAndDensity(in): invalid input values "
           << " r = " << newRadius << ", d = " << newDensity;
      myRadius = myDensity = myWeight = 0.0;
   }
}
```

Note that the basic structure of the two methods is very similar: Each gets some values, validates them, and then updates the instance variables, displaying a warning message if necessary. Their main difference is in where they get the values they use to modify the instance variables. This similarity of structure between mutators and input methods is not uncommon.

Given these definitions, a programmer can now write a client program that uses the `Sphere` class like that shown in Figure 6.13.

Fig. 6.13 Driver for class `Sphere`.

```
/* sphereDriver.cpp tests class Sphere.
 * ... documentation omitted to save space ...
 **************************************************************/

#include <iostream>                   // cin, cout, >>, <<
#include "Sphere.h"                   // Sphere
using namespace std;

int main()
{
   cout << "Enter a sphere's radius and density: ";
   Sphere aSphere;
   aSphere.readRadiusAndDensity(cin);

   cout << "The sphere's weight is "
        << aSphere.getWeight() << endl;
}
```

Sample run:

```
Enter a sphere's radius and density: 6.5 14.6
The sphere's weight is 16795
```

Once the attributes, constructors, accessors, mutators, and I/O methods of a class have been defined, that class is ready to use in many applications. In later *OBJECTive Thinking* sections, we will examine utility and converter methods, which add more functionality to a class to make it more convenient to use.

✔ Quick Quiz 6.6

1. A(n) ________ method changes values of instance variables with values sent to it as arguments.
2. A(n) ________ method changes values of instance variables with values from an `istream`.
3. ________ code is necessary in mutators and input methods to ensure that values passed as arguments or read from an `istream` are valid.
4. (True or false) An accessor method should be declared to be a `const` method, but a mutator should not.
5. (True or false) An input method should be declared to be a `const` method, but an output method should not.

Exercises 6.6

The following exercises ask you to add various mutator and output methods to the classes considered in this section. You should test these with driver programs like those asked for in Programming Problems 22–28 at the end of the chapter.

1. Declare and define the mutator `setMiddleName()` for the `Name` class.
2. Write a definition of the `setRadiusAndWeight()` mutator for the `Sphere` class.
3. Proceed as in Exercise 2, but for the `setDensityAndWeight()` mutator.
4. Write a definition of the `readRadiusAndWeight()` input method for the `Sphere` class.
5. Proceed as in Exercise 4, but for the `readDensityAndWeight()` input method.
6. Write declarations and definitions of the following mutator methods for the `Sphere` class:
   (a) `setRadiusWithDensityFixed()` (b) `setRadiusWithWeightFixed()`
7. Write declarations and definitions of the following mutator methods for the `Sphere` class:
   (a) `setDensityWithRadiusFixed()` (b) `setDensityWithWeightFixed()`
8. Write declarations and definitions of the following mutator methods for the `Sphere` class:
   (a) `setWeightWithRadiusFixed()` (b) `setWeightWithDensityFixed()`

For Exercises 9–13, Design and code appropriate mutators and input methods for the specified class.

9. The class `Student` in Section 5.6.
10. The class `Temperature` described in Section 4.7 (See also Exercise 5 of Section 5.6.)
11. The time class in Exercise 2 of Section 2.3 (See also Exercises 2 and 7 in Section 3.8, Exercises 9 and 10 in Section 4.7, and Exercise 6 of Section 5.6.)
12. The date class in Exercise 3 of Section 2.3 (See also Exercises 3 and 8 in Section 3.8 and Exercise 7 of Section 5.6.)
13. The phone-number class in Exercise 4 of Section 2.3 (See also Exercises 4 and 9 in Section 3.8 and Exercise 8 of Section 5.6.)

CHAPTER SUMMARY

Key Terms & Notes

AND gate
binary half-adder
block
`break` statement
central processing unit (CPU)
class invariant
condition
conditional expression
continuous behavior
dangling-else problem
drop-through behavior
dual-branch or `if-else` form
input method
inverter
logic circuit
logic gate
multialternative selection
multibranch if or if-`else-if` form
mutator method
nested OR gate
NOT gate
repetition
selection
sequence
single-branch or simple `if` form
`switch` statement
ternary operation
validation code

- The multibranch `if` is a series of nested if statements written as one.
- In a nested `if`, each `else` is matched with the nearest preceding unmatched `if`.
- Be sure to use the == operator for equality comparisons, and not = (assignment). Any time an algorithm calls for an equality comparison, the code that implements the algorithm should be carefully checked to ensure that = (assignment) has not been inadvertently used instead of the == (equality operator).
- To prevent drop-through behavior in a `switch` statement, remember to end the statement list in each case with a `break` or `return` statement (except for the final statement list, where it is not needed).
- Remember that the type of the expression of a `switch` and the constants in its case lists must be integer compatible. Note that they may not be real or string expressions.
- In deciding which statement to use to implement a selection, use a `switch` if all of the following hold, and an `if` otherwise:
  1. An equality (==) comparison is being performed.
  2. The same expression is being compared in each condition.
  3. The expression being compared is integer compatible.
- Conditional expressions can be used in place of many `if-else` statements and sometimes provide a simpler alternative.
- Mutators and input methods both change an object's attributes; mutators change them to values received via parameters, while input methods change them to values read from an `istream`. Both must check these values to ensure that they are valid attribute values.
- Because they do not change the values of instance variables, accessors and output methods are declared and defined as const methods by placing the keyword `const` at the end of their

headings; mutators and input methods may not be const methods because they do change the values of instance variables.

- Before modifying instance variables, mutators and input methods must verify that any necessary preconditions are true.

Programming Pointers

Program Style and Design

In this text, we use the following conventions for formatting the selection statements considered in this chapter.

1. *For an* `if` *statement,* `if (boolean_expression)` *is on one line, with its statement indented on the next line. If there is an* `else` *clause,* `else` *is on a separate line, aligned with* `if`*, and its statement* is *indented on the next line. If the statements are compound, the curly braces are aligned with the* `if` *and* `else` *and the statements inside the block are indented.*

```
if (boolean_expression)
   statement_1
else
   statement_2

if (boolean_expression)
{
   statement_1
      .
      .
      .
   statement_k
}
else
{
   statement_k+1
      .
      .
      .
   statement_n
}
```

An exception is made when the `if-else-if` *form is used to implement a multialternative selection structure. In this case the format used is*

```
if (boolean_expression_1)
   statement_1
else if (boolean_expression_2)
   statement_2
      .
      .
      .
else if (boolean_expression_n)
   statement_n
else
   statement_n+1
```

When the statements are compound, the curly braces are aligned with the first `if` *and all subsequent* `else`*s and the statements inside the blocks are indented.*

2. *For a* `switch` *statement,* `switch (expression)` *is on one line, with its curly braces aligned and on separate lines; each case list is indented within the curly braces, and each statement list and* `break` *or* `return` *statement is indented past its particular case list.*

```
switch (expression)
{
   case_list1:
               statement_list1
               break;           //or return
   case_list2:
               statement_list2
               break;           //or return
     .
     .
     .
   case_listn:
               statement_listn
               break;           // or returnn
   default:
               statement_listn+1
}
```

Alternatively, each `statement_list` $_i$ may be positioned on the same line as `case_list` $_i$.

3. *Program defensively by using the* `if` *statement to test for illegal values.* This provides an alternative to the `assert()` mechanism that does not terminate the program on a failed precondition. For an example, see the first `if` statement in the function `printLetter-Grade()` in the next programming pointer.
4. *Multialternative selection constructs can be implemented more efficiently with an* `if-else-if` *construct than with a sequence of separate* `if` *statements.* For example, consider the function

```
void printLetterGrade(int score)
{
   if (score < 0 || score > 100)
      cout << score << " is not a valid score.\n";
   if (score >= 90) && (score <= 100))
      cout << "A\n";
   if ((score >= 80) && (score < 90))
      cout << "B\n";
   if ((score >= 70) && (score < 80))
      cout << "C\n";
   if ((score >= 60) && (score < 70))
      cout << "D\n";
   if (score < 60)
      cout << "F\n";
}
```

Here, all the `if` statements are executed for each score processed and five of the boolean expressions are compound expressions, so that a total of 16 operations are performed, regardless of the score being processed. By contrast, for the function

```
void printLetterGrade(int score)
{
   if (score < 0 || score > 100)
      cout << score << " is not a valid score \n";
```

```
   else if (score >= 90)
      cout << "A\n";
   else if (score >= 80)
      cout << "B\n";
   else if (score >= 70)
      cout << "C\n";
   else if (score >= 60)
      cout << "D\n";
   else
      cout << "F\n";
}
```

most of the boolean expressions are simple, and not all of them are evaluated for each score, so that only three to seven operations are performed, depending on the score being processed.

5. *Multialternative selection statements of the form*

```
if (variable == constant_1)
   statement_1
else if (variable == constant_2)
   statement_2
      .
      .
      .
else if (variable == constant_n)
   statement_n
else
   statement_n+1
```

where `variable` and each `constant`$_i$ are `int` compatible, are usually implemented more efficiently using a `switch` statement like that in the preceding Programming Pointer 2, with `expression` replaced by `variable` and `case_list`$_i$ by `case constant`$_i$. For example, we might implement `printLetterGrade()` even more efficiently as follows:

```
void printLetterGrade(int score)
{
   switch (score / 10)
   {
      case 10: case 9:
                          cout << "A\n"; break;
      case 8:
                          cout << "B\n"; break;
      case 7:
                          cout << "C\n"; break;
      case 6:
                          cout << "D\n"; break;
      case 5: case 4:
      case 3: case 2:
      case 1: case 0:
                          cout << "F\n"; break;
      default:
                          cout << score
                               << " is not a valid score.\n";
   }
}
```

This version of `printLetterGrade()` will perform the same number of operations regardless of the value of `score`.

A second advantage of the `switch` statement is that a problem solution implemented with a `switch` is often more readable than an equivalent solution implemented using an `if` statement. For example, consider the problem of classifying the value of a `char` variable `ch` as an arithmetic operator (`+`, `-`, `*`, `/`, `%`), a relational operator (`<`, `>`), an assignment operator (=), or a punctuation symbol (semicolon or comma). Using a `switch` statement, we might write

```
switch (ch)
{
   case '+': case '-':
   case '*': case '/':
   case '%':
                     cout << "Arithmetic operator\n";
                     break;
   case '<': case '>':
                     cout << "Relational operator\n";
                     break;
   case '=':
                     cout << "Assignment operator\n";
                     break;
   case ';': case ',':
                     cout << "Punctuation\n";
                     break;
   default:
                     cout << "identification of "
                          << ch << " is not supported.\n";
}
```

which is more readable than an equivalent implementation using an `if` statement:

```
if ((ch == '+') || (ch == '-')  || (ch == '*')
 || (ch == '/') || (ch == '%'))
   cout << "Arithmetic operator\n";
else if ((ch == '<') || (ch == '>'))
   cout << "Relational operator\n";
else if (ch == '=')
   cout << "Assignment operator\n";
else if ((ch == ';') || (ch == ','))
   cout << "Punctuation\n";
else
   cout << "identification of " << ch
        << " is not supported.\n";
```

The potential error of inadvertently substituting the assignment operator (=) for one of the several equality operators (==) in this `if` statement is also avoided by the `switch` statement.

WATCH OUT

Potential Pitfalls

1. *One of the most common errors in an `if` statement is using an assignment operator (=) when an equality operator (==) is intended.* See Potential Pitfall 6 at the end of Chapter 4.
2. *When real quantities that are algebraically equal are compared with ==, the result may be a false boolean expression, because most real numbers are not stored exactly.* For example, even though the two real expressions `x * (1/x)` and `1.0` are algebraically equal, the boolean expression `x * (1/x) == 1.0` may be false for some real numbers `x`.

3. *In a nested `if` statement, each `else` clause is matched with the nearest preceding unmatched `if`.* Indentation and alignment of each `else` with its corresponding `if` should be used to make these associations clear. See Potential Pitfall 7 at the end of Chapter 4.
4. *Each `switch` statement and block must contain matching curly braces.* A missing `}` can be very difficult to locate. In certain situations, the compiler may not find that a `{` is unmatched until it reaches the end of the file. In such cases, an error message such as

```
Error...: Compound statement missing } in function ...
```

will be generated.
5. *The selector in a `switch` statement must be integer compatible.* In particular, the values of the selector in case lists
   - may *not* be real constants, such as 1.5, – 2.3, 3.414159 or 2.998E8, and
   - may *not* be string constants such as `"JACK"`, `"QUEEN"`, or `"KING"`.
6. *A `switch` statement has drop-through behavior. Execution of the statement list in a particular case will continue on into subsequent cases until a `break`, a `return`, or the end of the `switch` statement is reached.* To avoid this behavior, you must remember to end each statement list in a `switch` statement with a `break` or `return` statement (except for the final statement list, where it is not necessary).

Programming Problems

Section 6.2

1. Write a driver program to test the function `okToSpray()` of Exercise 5.
2. Write a driver program to test the function `creditApproved()` of Exercise 6.
3. Write a driver program to test the leap-year function of Exercise 7.
4. Write a driver program to test the days-in-a-month function of Exercise 8.
5. Write a driver program to test the days-in-a-month function of Exercise 9.
6. Suppose that charges by a gas company are based on consumption according to the following table:

Gas Used	Rate
First 70 cubic meters	$5.00 minimum cost
Next 100 cubic meters	5.0¢ per cubic meter
Next 230 cubic meters	2.5¢ per cubic meter
Above 400 cubic meters	1.5¢ per cubic meter

Write a function that computes the charges for a given amount of gas usage. Use this function in a program in which the meter reading for the previous month and the current meter reading are entered, each a four-digit number and each representing cubic meters, and that then calculates and displays the amount of the bill. (*Note:* Because of rollover, the current reading may be less than the previous one; for example, the previous reading may be 9897, and the current one may be 0103. Execute the program with the following meter readings: 3450, 3495; 8810, 8900; 9950, 0190; 1275, 1982; 9872, 0444.)

7. Write a program that reads values for the coefficients A, B, C, D, E, and F of the equations

$$Ax + By = C$$
$$Dx + Ey = F$$

of two straight lines, and then determine whether the lines are parallel (their slopes are equal) or the lines intersect. If they intersect, determine whether the lines are perpendicular (the product of their slopes is equal to – 1).

8. Write a program that reads the coordinates of three points and then determines whether they are collinear.

Section 6.4

9. Write a driver program to test the TV-channel function of Exercise 3.
10. Write a driver program to test the distance-cost function of Exercise 4.
11. Write a driver program to test the month-name function of Exercise 5.
12. Write a driver program to test the days-in-month function of Exercise 6.
13. Locating avenues' addresses in mid-Manhattan is not easy; for example, the nearest cross street to 866 Third Avenue is 53rd Street, whereas the nearest cross street to 866 Second Avenue is 46th Street. To locate approximately the nearest numbered cross street for a given avenue address, the following algorithm can be used:

    Cancel the last digit of the address, divide by 2, and add or subtract the number given in the following abbreviated table:

1st Ave.	Add 3
2nd Ave.	Add 3
3rd Ave.	Add 10
4th Ave.	Add 8
5th Ave. up to 200	Add 13
5th Ave. up to 400	Add 16
6th Ave. (Ave. of the Americas)	Subtract 12
7th Ave.	Add 12
8th Ave.	Add 10
10th Ave.	Add 14

    Write a function that uses a `switch` statement to determine the number of the nearest cross street for a given address and avenue number according to the preceding algorithm. Then write a program to test your function.

14. A wholesale office supply company discounts the price of each of its products depending on the number of units bought and the price per unit. The discount increases as the numbers of units bought or the unit price increases. These discounts are given in the following table:

Number Bought	0–10.00	Unit Price (dollars) 10.01–100.00	100.01–
1–9	0%	2%	5%
10–19	5%	7%	9%
20–49	9%	15%	21%
50–99	14%	23%	32%
100–	21%	32%	43%

Write a function that calculates the percentage discount for a specified number of units and unit price. Use this function in a program that reads the number of units bought and the unit price and then calculates and prints the total full cost, the total amount of the discount, and the total discounted cost.

15. An airline vice president in charge of operations needs to determine whether the current estimates of flight times are accurate. Because there is a larger possibility of variations due to weather and air traffic in the longer flights, he allows a larger error in the time estimates for them. He compares an actual flight time with the estimated flight time and considers the estimate to be too large, acceptable, or too small, depending on the following table of acceptable error margins:

Estimated Flight Time in Minutes	Acceptable Error Margin in Minutes
0–29	1
30–59	2
60–89	3
90–119	4
120–179	6
180–239	8
240–359	13
360 or more	17

For example, if an estimated flight time is 106 minutes, the acceptable error margin is 4 minutes. Thus, the estimated flight time is too large if the actual flight time is less than 102 minutes, or the estimated flight time is too small if the actual flight time is greater than 110 minutes; otherwise, the estimate is acceptable. Write a function that uses a `switch` statement to determine the acceptable error for a given estimated flight time, according to this table. Use your function in a program that reads an estimated flight time and an actual flight time and then determines whether the estimated time is too large, acceptable, or too small. If the estimated flight time is too large or too small, the program should also print the amount of the overestimate or underestimate.

16. Write a function `convertLength()` that receives a real value and two strings `inUnits` and `outUnits`, then converts the value given in `inUnits` to the equivalent metric value in `outUnits` and displays this value. The function should carry out the following conversions:

`inUnits`	`outUnits`	
`I`	`c`	(inches to centimeters; 1 in. = 2.54001 cm)
`F`	`c`	(feet to centimeters; 1 ft = 30.4801 cm)
`F`	`m`	(feet to meters; 1 ft = 0.304801 m)
`Y`	`m`	(yards to meters; 1 yd = 0.914402 m)
`M`	`k`	(miles to kilometers; 1 mi = 1.60935 km)

Also, write a driver program to test your function. What happens if you enter units other than those listed?

17. Proceed as in Problem 16, but write a function `convertWeight()` that carries out the following conversions:

inUnits	outUnits	
`O`	`g`	(ounces to grams; 1 oz = 28.349527 g)
`P`	`k`	(pounds to kilograms; 1 lb = 0.453592 kg)

18. Proceed as in Problem 16, but write a function `convertVolume()` that carries out the following conversions:

inUnits	outUnits	
`P`	`l`	(pints to liters; 1 pt = 0.473167 L)
`Q`	`l`	(quarts to liters; 1 qt = 0.94633 L)
`G`	`l`	(gallons to liters; 1 gal = 3.78541 L)

19. Write a menu-driven program to test the three functions `convertLength()`, `convertWeight()`, and `convertVolume()` of Problems 16–18. It should allow the user to select one of three options according to whether lengths, weights, or volumes are to be converted; read the value to be converted and the units; and then call the appropriate function to carry out the conversion.

Part of the Picture: Boolean Logic and Digital Design

20. A *binary full-adder* has three inputs: the two bits `a` and `b` being added, and a "carry-in" bit `cIn` (representing the carry bit that results from adding the bits to the right of `a` and `b` in two binary numbers). It can be constructed from two binary half-adders and an OR gate:

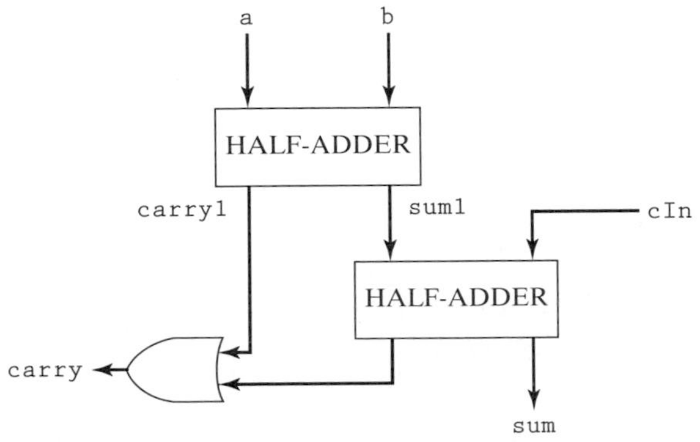

a. Write boolean expressions for

i. `sum1` and `carry1` in terms of `a` and `b`

ii. `sum` and `carry` in terms of `cIn`, `sum1`, and `carry1`

b. Write a program to implement this binary full-adder, and use it to verify the results shown in the following table:

a	b	cIn	sum	carry
0	0	0	0	0
0	0	1	1	0
0	1	0	1	0
0	1	1	0	1
1	0	0	1	0
1	0	1	0	1
1	1	0	0	1
1	1	1	1	1

21. An adder to calculate binary sums of two-bit numbers

```
       a2 a1
     + b2 b1
     -------
 cOut s2 s1
```

where `s1` and `s2` are the sum bits and `cOut` is the carry-out bit, can be constructed from a binary half-adder and a binary full-adder:

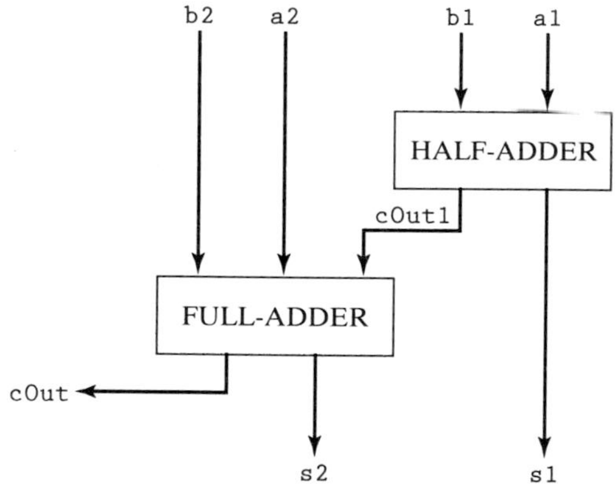

a. Write logical expressions for

i. `s1` and `cOut1` in terms of `a1` and `b1`

ii. `s2` and `cOut` in terms of `a2`, `b2`, and `cOut1`

b. Write a program to implement this adder and use it to demonstrate that 00 + 00 = 000, 01 + 00 = 001, 01 + 01 = 010, 10 + 01 = 011, 10 + 10 = 100, 11 + 10 = 101, and 11 + 11 = 110.

Section 6.6

22. Write a driver program to test the class `Name` as modified in Exercise 1.

23. Write a driver program to test the class `Sphere` as modified in Exercises 2–8.
24. Write a driver program to test the class `Student` as modified in Exercise 9.
25. Write a driver program to test the class `Temperature` as modified in Exercise 10.
26. Write a driver program to test the time class as modified in Exercise 11.
27. Write a driver program to test the date class as modified in Exercise 12.
28. Write a driver program to test the phone-number class as modified in Exercise 13.
29. Use the `Name` class as modified in Exercise 1 and the date class as modified in Exercise 12 in a program that reads the current date and then reads a person's name and date of birth and displays that person's name, birthdate, and how old she will be on her birthday this year.

Note: The next two problems require the use of the repetition statements introduced in Section 4.4.

30. Use the `Sphere` class as modified in Exercises 2–8 in a program that models the inflation of a spherical balloon. It should read a sphere's initial radius, density, and weight, and an increment factor, and then generate a table showing how the weight changes as the radius increases. Use a `for` loop that increases the sphere's radius by the increment factor on each repetition.
31. Use the time class as modified in Exercise 11 in a program that simulates a digital clock. It should read a start time and then display consecutive times in one-second intervals for a specified number of seconds.

CHAPTER 7

Repetition

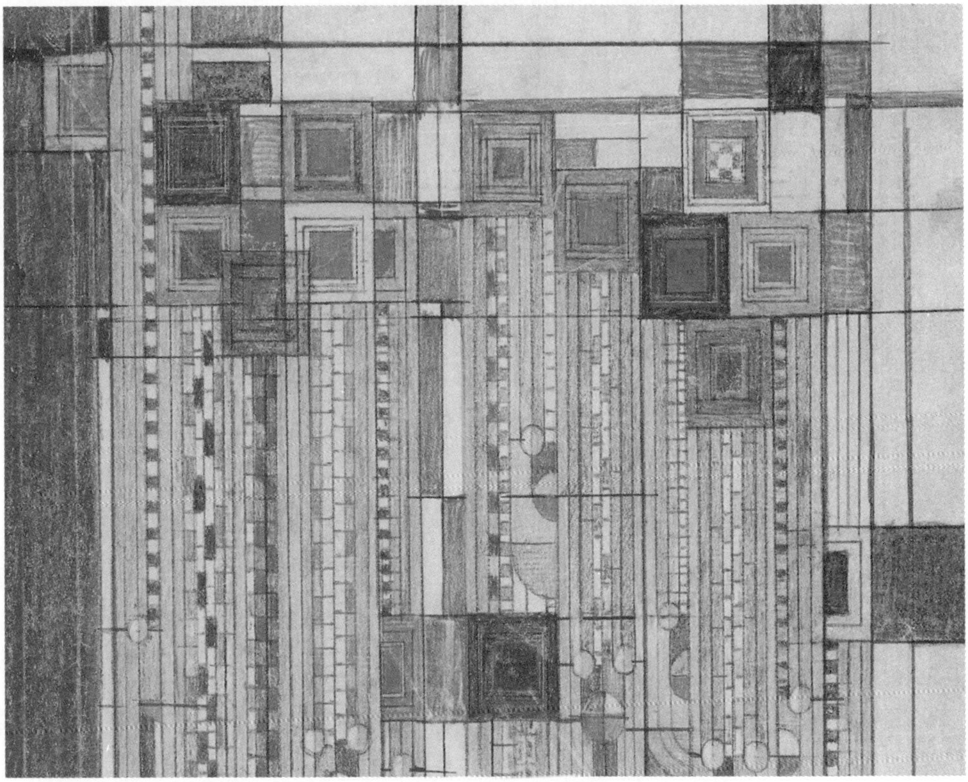

Progress might be a circle, rather than a straight line.

-Eberhard Zeidler

But what has been said once can always be repeated.

-Zeno of Elea

Its déjà vu all over again.

-Yogi Berra

A rose is a rose is a rose.

-Gertrude Stein

Chapter Contents

Chapter Objectives

- Expand on the introduction to repetition structures in Chapter 4.
- Examine for loops and C++'s `for` statement in detail.
- Study while and do loops and the corresponding C++ `while` and `do` statements.
- Look at various kinds of input loops: counting, sentinel controlled, and query controlled.
- Consider some aids to choosing the right kind of loop to use in a problem.
- (Optional) Take a first look at the important area of computer science known as algorithm analysis.
- (Optional) Introduce the important object-oriented concept of code reusability via inheritance.

As we saw in Chapter 4, the three control behaviors used in writing functions are **sequence, selection,** and **repetition.** In Chapter 6, we examined selection in detail, and in this chapter we take a closer look at the third control structure, repetition.

7.1 Introductory Example: The Punishment of Gauss

Although sequence and selection are powerful control mechanisms, they are by themselves not powerful enough to solve all computing problems. In this section, we consider a problem that can be solved using the most familiar C++ repetition statement: the `for` loop.

THE SUMMATION PROBLEM

Our problem begins with an incident in the life of Carl Friedrich Gauss, one of the greatest mathematicians of all time. When Gauss was young, he attended a school in Brunswick, Germany. One day when the students were being particularly mischievous, the teacher asked them to sum the integers from 1 to 100, expecting that this would keep them busy for awhile. However, Gauss produced the correct answer (5050) almost immediately, using a particularly clever approach described in the *Part of the Picture* section later in this chapter.

Although calculating the sum of the integers from 1 to 100 is not a particularly important computation, a generalization of this problem has many applications. The problem is to construct a function that, given a positive integer n, calculates and returns the sum of the integers from 1 to n:

$$1 + 2 + \cdots + n$$

Thus, Gauss and his classmates were asked to compute a particular *instance* of the summation problem with $n = 100$.

Object-Centered Design

Behavior. The function should receive the value n from its caller. It should compute the sum $1 + \cdots + n$ and return this value to its caller.

Objects. Obviously, the value n is required if we are to compute the sum of the integers from 1 to n. We can thus list the following objects for this problem:

	Software Objects			
Problem Objects	Type	Kind	Movement	Name
The limit value, n	integer	varying	received	n
$1 + 2 + \ldots + n$	integer	varying	returned	none

This allows us to specify the problem as follows: Write a function `sum()` that will

Receive: an integer value n

Return: $1 + 2 + \cdots + n$

This specification lets us build a stub for this function:

```
int sum(int n)
{
}
```

Operations. Because most of us do not have Gauss' ability, we will solve this problem using the approach probably used by his classmates (and intended by his teacher). We simply begin adding consecutive integers, keeping a running total as we proceed:

```
  0   ← running total
 +1   ← count
 ---
  1   ← running total
 +2   ← count
 ---
  3   ← running total
 +3   ← count
 ---
  6   ← running total
 +4   ← count
 ---
 10   ← running total
 +5   ← count
 ---
 15   ← running total
  .
  .
  .
```

This procedure consists of the following steps:

1. Initialize a *running total* to 0.
2. Initialize *count* to 1.
3. Loop through the following steps:
   a. Add *count* to the *running total.*
   b. Add 1 to *count.*

The steps in the loop must be repeated as long as the value of *count* is less than or equal to *n*. Thus, if *n* has the value 100, the loop must be repeated so long as the value of *count* is less than or equal to 100:

```
   .
   .
   .
 4950   ← running total
+ 100   ← count
 ----
 5050   ← running total
```

It is apparent that this procedure uses two previously unmentioned quantities—the *running total* and the *count*—and that when the procedure is finished, the value of the *running total* is the sum of the integers from 1 to *n* and is therefore the value to be returned by the function. We can thus amend our list of objects in this problem as follows:

	Software Objects			
Problem Objects	**Type**	**Kind**	**Movement**	**Name**
The limit value, *n*	int	varying	received	*n*
1 + 2 + ... + *n*	int	varying	returned	*runningTotal*
A counter	int	varying	none	*count*

Operations. The preceding description of how the problem can be solved suggests that the following operations are needed:

i. Receive an integer (*n*)
ii. Initialize an integer (*runningTotal* to 0, *count* to 1)
iii. Add two integers (*count* and *runningTotal*) and store the result
iv. Repeat the preceding step for each value of *count* in the range 1 through *n*
v. Return an integer (*runningTotal*)

All of these can be implemented using predefined C++ operations and functions. In particular, the repetition in (iv) can be implemented using a `for` loop.

Algorithm. We organize these operations in the following algorithm:

Algorithm for the Summation Problem

1. Initialize *runningTotal* to 0.
2. For each value of *count* in the range 1 through *n*:
   Add *count* to *runningTotal*.
3. Return *runningTotal*.

Coding and Testing. Note that the two data objects *runningTotal* and *count* are not received by the function, but they are required to solve the problem. It is important to remember that such objects should be declared as *local variables within the definition of the function*. By contrast, *n* must be *received* from the caller, and so it is declared as a *parameter* of the function. Figure 7.1 gives a definition of `sum()`. In the next section, we will consider in more detail the `for` statement used to implement the loop in `sum()`.

Fig. 7.1 Function `sum()`—`for` loop version. (Part 1 of 2)

```
/* sum(n) computes the sum of the integers from 1 to n.
 *
 * Receive:       n, an integer
 * Precondition:  n > 0
 * Return:        the sum 1 + 2 + ... + n
 ************************************************************/

int sum (int n)
{
   assert(n > 0);

   int runningTotal = 0;
```

Fig. 7.1 Function `sum()–for` loop version. (Part 2 of 2)

```
   for (int count = 1; count <= n; count++)
      runningTotal += count;

   return runningTotal;
}
```

The program in Figure 7.2 uses this function to solve specific summation problems. The prototype of `sum()` is placed before `main()`, and its definition follows `main()`. Alternatively, `sum()` could be stored in a library (e.g., `MyMath`) so that other programs needing to compute sums can use it. In this case, we would store the definition of `sum()` in the implementation file and the prototype of `sum()` in the header file, and use a directive such as `#include "MyMath.h"` (instead of including the prototype of `sum()` and its definition in the source program).

Fig. 7.2 Driver program for function `sum()`. (Part 1 of 2)

```
/* summation.cpp is a driver program to test function sum().
 *
 *   Input:   an integer n
 *   Output:  the sum of the integers from 1 through n
 ****************************************************************/

#include <iostream>             // cout, cin, <<, >>
#include <cassert>              // assert
using namespace std;

int sum(int n);                  // prototype for sum()

int main()
{
  cout << "This program computes the sum of the integers from "
          "1 through n.\n";

  cout << "Enter a value for n: ";
  int n;
  cin >> n;

  cout << "--> 1 + ... + " << n << " = " << sum(n) << endl;
}

/*** Insert the definition of function sum()
     from Figure 7.1 here. ***/
```

Fig. 7.2 Driver program for function `sum()`. (Part 2 of 2)

Sample runs:

```
This program computes the sum of the integers from 1 through n.
Enter a value for n: 5
--> 1 + ... + 5 = 15

This program computes the sum of the integers from 1 through n.
Enter a value for n: 100
--> 1 + ... + 100 = 5050
```

7.2 Repetition: The `for` Loop

Counting loops, or **counter-controlled loops**, are loops in which a set of statements is executed once for each value in a specified range:

for each value of a *counter_variable* in a specified range:
    statement

For example, our solution to the summation problem uses a counting loop to execute the statement

```
runningTotal += count;
```

once for each value of `count` in the range 1 through *n*.

Because counting loops are used so often, nearly all programming languages provide a special statement to implement them. In C++, this is the `for` **statement** or `for` **loop.** The four components of a counting `for` loop were introduced in Section 4.4:[1]

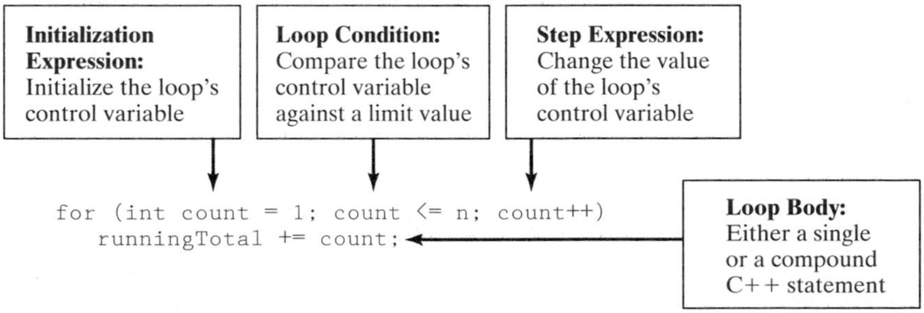

As noted in Chapter 4, a **trace table** is a good tool to trace the action of a loop (especially in debugging). For example, in the first sample run of Figure 7.1 where the value 5 is entered for `n`, the loop counts through the values 1 through 5, so that the body of the

1. This section extends the introduction to the `for` statement in Section 4.4. Thus, if this section was omitted earlier, it is recommended that it be covered now.

`for` loop is executed five times. The following table shows the value of the various variables and loop condition as the function `sum()` executes:

`count`	`n`	`count <= n`	**Action**	`runningTotal`
1	5	true	Execute loop body	1
2	5	true	Execute loop body	3
3	5	true	Execute loop body	6
4	5	true	Execute loop body	10
5	5	true	Execute loop body	15
6	5	false	Terminate repetition	15

A similar trace table for the second sample run where `n` has the value 100 would show that the loop counts through the values 1 through 100, so that the loop body is executed 100 times.

There are two forms of the `for` statement that are commonly used to implement counting loops: an ascending form, in which the loop control variable is incremented,

```
for (int control_variable = initial_value;
         control_variable <= limit_value;
         increment_expression)
   statement
```

and a descending form, in which the loop control variable is decremented:

```
for (int control_variable = initial_value;
         control_variable >= limit_value;
         decrement_expression)
   statement
```

The first form counts through an *ascending range*, and the second counts through a *descending range*.

To illustrate the first form, consider the following `for` statement:

```
for (int number = 1; number <= 10; number++)
   cout << number << '\t' << number * number << endl;
```

Here, `number` is the control variable, the initial value is `1`, the limit value is `10`, and the increment expression is `number++`. This `for` loop will execute the statement

```
cout << number << '\t' << number * number << endl;
```

once for each value of `number` in the ascending range 1 through 10. On the first pass through the loop, `number` will have the value 1; on the second pass it will have the value 2; and so on until the final pass when `number` will have the value 10. Thus, the output produced will be

```
1       1
2       4
3       9
4       16
```

```
5        25
6        36
7        49
8        64
9        81
10       100
```

By using an appropriate increment expression, a `for` statement can be used to step through a range of values in increments of size other than 1. For example, the `for` statement

```
for (int number = 0; number <= 100; number += 20)
   cout << number << '\t' << number * number << endl;
```

uses the expression

```
number += 20
```

to count upwards in increments of 20, producing the output

```
0        0
20       400
40       1600
60       3600
80       6400
100      10000
```

The second form of a `for` loop performs a decrement operation following each execution of the loop body. For example, the following loop

```
for (int number = 10; number >= 6; number--)
   cout << number << '\t' << number * number << endl;
```

will count downward from 10 to 6, producing the output:

```
10       100
9        81
8        64
7        49
6        36
```

Note that whereas the ascending form continues the repetition as long as the control variable is less than or equal to the limit value, the descending form is counting downwards, and so must continue the repetition as long as the control variable is *greater than or equal to* the limit value.

The loop condition in the preceding examples of `for` loops have all used <= or >= to test if the value of the control variable has reached its limit value. In some problems, however, it may be more natural to use < instead of <= or > instead of >=. For example, in a loop that counts through the (integer) number of degrees in a circle, it seems more intuitive to write

```
for (int degrees = 0; degrees < 360; degrees++)
   . . .
```

than to use `degrees <= 359` for the loop condition.

In fact, in some problems, we may not even know the limiting value of the control variable. For example, to calculate and print all sums of consecutive integers, 1, 1 + 2, 1 + 2 + 3, . . ., until this sum exceeds 1000, we could use the following `for` loop:

```
int sum = 0;
for (int count = 1; sum <= 1000; count++)
{
   sum += count;
   cout << sum << endl;
}
```

NESTED `for` LOOPS

The statement that appears within a `for` statement may itself be a `for` statement; that is, one `for` loop may be *nested within* another `for` loop. When this happens, the two loops behave something like the hands of a clock:

```
for (int hours = 1; hours <= 12; hours++)
   for (int minutes = 0; minutes < 60; minutes++)
      cout << hours << ':'
           << setw(2) << setfill('0') << minutes << endl;
```

The *inner* 'minutes' loop executes sixty times for each execution of the *outer* 'hours' loop:

```
1:00
1:01
1:02
  .
  .
  .
1:59
2:00
2:01
2:02
  .
  .
  .
2:59
3:00
  .
  .
  .
```

The inner loop thus acts like a clock's minutes hand, and the outer loop acts like the clock's hours hand.

To see how nested loops can be useful, consider the problem of printing a multiplication table by calculating and displaying products of the form `x * y` for each `x` in the range 1 through `lastX` and each `y` in the range 1 through `lastY` (where `lastX` and `lastY` are arbitrary integers). Such a multiplication table can be easily generated using nested `for` statements, as shown in Figure 7.3.

Fig. 7.3 Printing a multiplication table. (Part 1 of 2)

```
/* multTable.cpp calculates and displays a multiplication table.
 *
 * Input:   lastX and lastY, the largest numbers to be multiplied
 * Output:  a list of products: 1*1 ... lastX * lastY
 ****************************************************************/

#include <iostream>            // cout, cin, <<, >>, right
#include <iomanip>             // setw()
using namespace std;

int main()
{
   cout << "This program constructs a multiplication table\n"
           "for the values 1*1 through lastX*lastY.\n";

   int lastX,          // the largest numbers being multiplied
       lastY,
       product;        // the product of the two numbers

   cout << "\nEnter two integer limit values (lastX and lastY): ";
   cin >> lastX >> lastY;

   for (int x = 1; x <= lastX; x++)
      for (int y = 1; y <= lastY; y++)
      {
         product = x * y;
         cout << right
              << setw(2) << x << " * "
              << setw(2) << y << " = "
              << setw(3) << product << endl;
      }
}
```

Sample run:

```
This program constructs a multiplication table
for the values 1*1 through lastX*lastY.
```

Fig. 7.3 Printing a multiplication table. (Part 2 of 2)

```
Enter two integer limit values (lastX and lastY): 3 4
 1 *  1 =   1
 1 *  2 =   2
 1 *  3 =   3
 1 *  4 =   4
 2 *  1 =   2
 2 *  2 =   4
 2 *  3 =   6
 2 *  4 =   8
 3 *  1 =   3
 3 *  2 =   6
 3 *  3 =   9
 3 *  4 =  12
```

In the sample run, `lastX` is given the value 3 and `lastY` the value 4. When control reaches the outer loop, its control variable `x` is assigned its initial value 1. The statement it controls (the inner loop) is then executed, which counts through the values 1 through 4 for `y` and thus calculates and displays the first four products: 1 * 1, 1 * 2, 1 * 3, and 1 * 4. Control then passes from the inner loop to the increment expression of the outer loop, where the value of `x` is incremented to 2. The statement it controls (the inner loop) is then executed again. It again counts through the values 1 through 4 for `y`, but since the value of `x` is now 2, this pass calculates and displays the next four products: 2 * 1, 2 * 2, 2 * 3, and 2 * 4. The control variable `x` is then incremented to 3, so that when the inner loop is executed again, the last four products, 3 * 1, 3 * 2, 3 * 3, and 3 * 4, are produced. `x` is then incremented (to 4), making the loop condition `x <= lastX` false, so that repetition stops. The compound statement

```
{
   product = x * y;
   cout << setw(2) << x << " * "
        << setw(2) << y << " = "
        << setw(3) << product << endl;
}
```

is executed a total of 12 times, because the inner loop is executed 4 times for each of the 3 executions of the outer loop.

WATCH OUT

Words of Warning

A `for` loop must be constructed carefully to ensure that its initialization expression, loop condition, and increment expression will eventually cause the loop condition to become false. In particular:

> *If the body of a counting loop alters the values of any variables involved in the loop condition, then the number of repetitions may be changed.*

It is generally considered poor programming practice to alter the value of any variables in the loop condition within the body of a counting loop, because this can produce unexpected results. For example, execution of

```
int limit = 1;
for (int i = 0; i <= limit; i++)
{
   cout << i << endl;
   limit++;
}
```

produces an infinite sequence of integers[2]

```
0
1
2
3
.
.
.
```

because on each pass through the loop, the expression `limit++` increments `limit` by 1 before `i++` increments `i`. As a result, the loop condition `i <= limit` is always true.

Similarly, the loop

```
for (int i = 0; i <= limit; i++)
{
   cout << i << '\n';
   i--;
}
```

will output infinitely many zeros,

```
0
0
0
.
.
.
```

because the expression `i--` in the body of the loop decrements `i` by 1 before the step expression `i++` increments it by 1. As a result, `i` is always 0 when the loop condition is tested.

THE FOREVER LOOP

The primary use of `for` loops is to implement counting loops where the number of repetitions is known (or can be computed) in advance. For example, in computing the sum of

---

2. In some environments, execution will terminate when `i` is `MAXINT` and `limit` is `MAXINT + 1 = MININT`.

the integers from 1 to `n`, we know that the loop's body must be executed exactly `n` times. However, there are many problems in which the number of repetitions cannot be determined in advance. For these situations, most modern programming languages provide a general loop statement that provides for *indefinite repetition*. This loop is often implemented by a statement that is different from the statements used for other loops.[3]

C++, however, does not provide a separate statement for indefinite loops, but instead allows the programmer to construct such a loop from other loops. One way this can be done is by removing the initialization expression, the loop condition, and the step expression from a `for` loop, as illustrated in the following general form:[4]

The Forever Loop

Form:

```
for ( ; ; )              // forever loop
   statement
```

where

`for` is a C++ keyword and

`statement` is a simple or a compound statement (but is usually compound).

Behavior: The specified statement is executed infinitely many times, unless it contains a `break` or `return` statement (usually an `if-break` or `if-return` combination).

If a `break` statement is encountered, execution of the loop will terminate and will continue with the statement following the loop.

If a `return` statement is encountered, the loop and the function containing it are terminated and control returns to the calling function.

Because such a loop contains no loop condition specifying the condition under which repetition terminates, it is an **indefinite loop** that executes the statements in its body without stopping.[5] We will call such a loop a **forever loop.**

To illustrate, consider the following forever loop:

```
for ( ; ; )                       // forever loop
   cout << "Help ! I'm caught in a loop!\n";
```

---

3. *Ada* and *Turing* have the `loop` statement, *Modula-2* and *Modula-3* the `LOOP` statement, and *Fortran 90* the `DO` loop.
4. Alternatively, we can achieve the same effect with either of these forms:

   `while (true)` *`statement`* or `do` *`statement`* `while (true);`
5. This will still be an indefinite loop if the initialization expression and the step expression are retained. Sometimes it is convenient to use one or both of them.

This statement will produce the output

```
Help ! I'm caught in a loop!
Help ! I'm caught in a loop!
Help ! I'm caught in a loop!
Help ! I'm caught in a loop!
       .
       .
       .
```

an unlimited number of times, unless the user *interrupts* execution (usually by pressing the `Control` and `C` keys).

To avoid this infinite looping behavior, the body of a forever loop is usually a compound statement, containing

1. those statements that must be repeatedly executed in order to solve the problem and
2. a statement that will *terminate* execution of the loop when some condition is satisfied.

The terminating statement is usually an `if-break` **combination**—an `if` statement containing a `break` statement,

```
if (condition) break;
```

where *`condition`* is a boolean expression. Execution of a `break` statement within a loop terminates execution of the loop and transfers control to the statement following the loop.

Note that unlike other loops (counting loops and the loops considered in the next sections), repetition continues as long as the condition in the `if-break` combination is *false*—it terminates when the condition becomes true. To distinguish this condition from the loop conditions of the other loops, we will call it a **termination condition** instead of a *loop condition*.

Most forever loops, therefore, have the form

```
for (;;)                                    // loop:
{
   statement_list1
   if (termination_condition) break;
   statement_list2
}                                           // end loop
```

where either *`statement_list`*$_1$ or *`statement_list`*$_2$ can be empty.

To illustrate forever loops, here is a useful utility function called `getMenuChoice()` that receives a menu and the characters that denote the first and last choices on the menu. (A precondition of this function is that the menu choices are a closed range such as A–D.) It repeatedly displays the menu and reads the user's choice until that choice is in the range of valid choices:

```
char getMenuChoice(string MENU,
                   char firstChoice, char lastChoice)
{
   char choice;                           // what the user enters
```

```
      for (;;)                                // loop:
      {
         cout << MENU;                        //    statement_list1
         cin >> choice;
                                              // if break combination
         if ((choice >= firstChoice) && (choice <= lastChoice))
            break;
                                              //    statement_list2
         cerr << "\nI'm sorry, but " << choice
              << " is not a valid menu choice.\n";
      }                                       // end loop

      return choice;
   }
```

The effect here is to "trap" the user inside the forever loop until a valid menu choice is entered. For each invalid menu choice, the termination condition is false, so the `break` statement is bypassed and the output statement displays an error message. Control then returns to the beginning of the loop for the next repetition and gives the user another chance. When a valid choice is entered, the termination condition becomes true, so the `break` statement is executed and transfers control to the `return` statement following the loop.

A statement related to `break` that is sometimes useful for modifying (but not terminating) execution of a loop is a **`continue` statement**. When it is executed, control transfers to the enclosing loop, the current iteration is terminated, and a new one begins. If there is no enclosing loop, a compile-time error results. The `continue` statement is useful when one wants to skip to the bottom part of a loop if a certain condition is true:

```
   for (...)
   {
      ...
      if (condition) continue;
      //— Skip from here to end of loop body if
      //— condition is true and begin a new iteration
   }
```

Returning from a Loop. In functions like `getMenuChoice()` where the statement following a forever loop is a `return` statement, it is slightly more efficient to replace the `break` statement with a `return` statement:

```
   char getMenuChoice(string MENU,
                      char firstChoice, char lastChoice)
   {
      char choice;                            // what the user enters
      for (;;)                                // loop:
      {
         cout << MENU;                        //    statement_list1
         cin >> choice;
```

```
                                       // if break combination
      if ((choice >= firstChoice) && (choice <= lastChoice))
         return choice;
                                       //    statement_list2
      cerr << "\nI'm sorry, but " << choice
           << " is not a valid menu choice.\n";
   }                                   // end loop
}
```

As before, if the user enters an invalid choice, an error message is displayed and the body of the loop is repeated. However, when the user enters a valid choice, the termination condition is true, and so the `return` statement is selected. Since execution of a `return` statement causes the function to terminate, it also terminates the loop in the function.

7.3 Repetition: The `while` Loop

A loop of the form

loop
    if (termination_condition) exit the loop.
    other statements
end loop

in which the termination test occurs before the loop statements are executed is called a **pretest** or **test-at-the-top** loop. Such loops can be implemented in C++ using a forever loop:

```
for (;;)                              // loop:
{
   if (termination_condition) break;
   statement_list2
}                                     // end loop
```

However, C++ provides another statement with a simpler syntax for these pretest loops—the `while` **statement** or `while` **loop** that we introduced briefly in Section 4.4. We will use a `while` loop to solve the following problem.

EXAMPLE: FOLLOW THE BOUNCING BALL

Suppose that when a ball is dropped, it bounces from the pavement to a height one-half of its previous height. We want to write a program that will simulate the behavior of the ball when it is dropped from a given height. It should display the number of each bounce and the height of that bounce, repeating this until the height of the ball is very small (e.g., less than 1 millimeter).

Object-Centered Design

Behavior. The program should first obtain the initial height. It should then display 1 and the height of the first rebound, display 2 and the height of the second rebound, and so on, until the height of the rebound is less than some very small number.

Objects. Given this description of the problem, we can identify the following data objects:

	Software Objects		
Problem Objects	**Type**	**Kind**	**Name**
The current height	real	varying	*height*
The bounce number	integer	varying	*bounce*
A very small number	real	constant	*SMALL_NUMBER*

This list allows us to specify the problem as follows:

Input: The initial *height* of a ball

Output: For each rebound of the ball:
the number of the rebound and
the height of that rebound,
assuming that the height of each rebound is one-half the previous height

Operations. The operations that must be performed on these objects are as follows:

i. Input a real value (the original *height*)
ii. Initialize *bounce* to zero
iii. Divide the *height* by 2 (to compute the rebound height)
iv. Increment *bounce*
v. Display the current *bounce* number and *height*
vi. Repeat operations iii–v as long as *height* ≥ *SMALL_NUMBER*

Algorithm. Each of these operations is available through the operators and statements of C++. However, for the loop in (vi) we must ask where the termination condition should be placed. It should be clear that if *height* is initially less than *SMALL_NUMBER*, then none of the operations in (iii–v) should be performed. This suggests that we use a pretest loop as in the following algorithm:

Algorithm for Bouncing Ball Problem

1. Initialize *bounce* to 0.
2. Prompt for and read a value for *height*.

3. Display original *height* value with appropriate label.
4. Loop:
   a. If *height* < *SMALL_NUMBER*, terminate the repetition.
   b. Replace *height* with *height* divided by 2.
   c. Add 1 to *bounce*.
   d. Display *bounce* and *height*.
5. End loop.

Coding. We could code this algorithm using a pretest form of a forever loop, but as we noted earlier, the C++ `while` loop has a simpler syntax. The program in Figure 7.4 implements this algorithm, using a `while` loop to implement the loop in Step 4.[6]

Fig. 7.4 The bouncing ball. (Part 1 of 2)

```
/* bouncingBall.cpp calculates and displays the rebound heights
 * of a dropped ball.
 *
 * Input:  a real height from which a ball is dropped.
 * Output: for each rebound of the ball from the pavement below:
 *            the number of the rebound and
 *            the height of that rebound
 *         assuming that the height of each rebound
 *         is one-half the previous height
 ****************************************************************/

#include <iostream>                    // <<, >>, cout, cin
using namespace std;

int main()
{
  const double SMALL_NUMBER = 1.0e-3;     // 1 millimeter

  cout << "This program computes the number and height\n"
       << "of the rebounds of a dropped ball.\n";
```

6. A `for` loop could also be used:

```
for (int bounce = 0; height >= SMALL_NUMBER; bounce++)
{
   height /= 2;
   cout << "Rebound # " << bounce << ": "
        << height << " meters" << endl;
}
```

Fig. 7.4 The bouncing ball. (Part 2 of 2)

```
   cout << "\nEnter the starting height (in meters): ";
   double height;
   cin >> height;

   cout << "\nStarting height: " << height << " meters\n";

   int bounce = 0;
   while (height >= SMALL_NUMBER)
   {
      height /= 2.0;
      bounce++;
      cout << "Rebound # " << bounce << ": "
           << height << " meters" << endl;
   }
}
```

Sample run:

```
This program computes the number and height
of the rebounds of a dropped ball.

Enter the starting height (in meters): 15

Starting height: 15 meters
Rebound # 1: 7.5 meters
Rebound # 2: 3.75 meters
Rebound # 3: 1.875 meters
Rebound # 4: 0.9375 meters
Rebound # 5: 0.46875 meters
Rebound # 6: 0.234375 meters
Rebound # 7: 0.117188 meters
Rebound # 8: 0.0585938 meters
Rebound # 9: 0.0292969 meters
Rebound # 10: 0.0146484 meters
Rebound # 11: 0.00732422 meters
Rebound # 12: 0.00366211 meters
Rebound # 13: 0.00183105 meters
Rebound # 14: 0.000915527 meters
```

THE `while` STATEMENT

While loops are implemented in C++ using a `while` **statement** of the following form;

The `while` Statement

Form:

```
while (loop_condition)
   statement
```

where

`while` is a C++ keyword;

`loop_condition` is a boolean expression; and

`statement` is a simple or compound statement.

Behavior: When execution reaches a `while` statement:

1. *`loop_condition`* is evaluated.
2. If *`loop_condition`* is true:
   a. The specified *`statement`*, called the **body** of the loop, is executed.
   b. Control returns to Step 1.

   Otherwise

   Control is transferred to the statement following the `while` statement.

Like a `for` loop, a `while` loop has a loop condition that controls repetition. The placement of this loop condition before the body of the loop is significant because it means that a while loop is a pretest loop, so that when it is executed, this condition is evaluated before the body of the loop is executed. This can be pictured as follows:

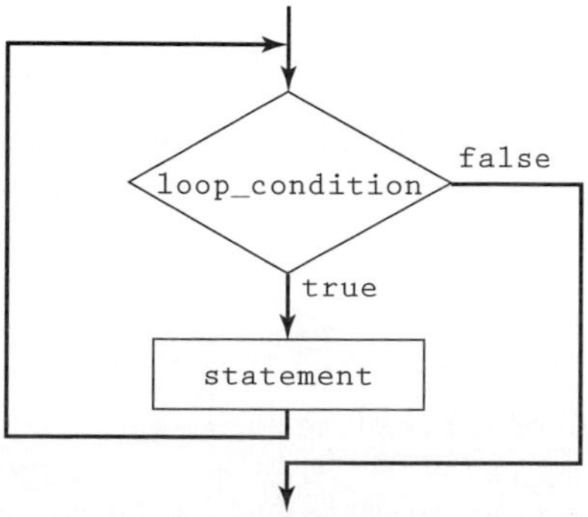

As this diagram indicates, execution of the specified statement is repeated as long as the loop condition remains true and terminates when it becomes false. For example, the following table provides a partial trace of the repetitions of the `while` loop in Figure 7.4, showing the values of the relevant data objects:

`height`	`bounce`	`height >= SMALL_NUMBER`	Action
15.0	0	true	Execute loop body
7.5	1	true	Execute loop body
3.75	2	true	Execute loop body
1.875	3	true	Execute loop body
⋮	⋮	⋮	⋮
0.00183105	13	true	Execute loop body
0.000915527	14	false	Terminate repetition

The preceding diagram indicates that the loop condition is evaluated before the loop body is executed; thus, if this condition is initially false, the body of the loop will not be executed. Stated differently, the body of a pretest loop will be executed *zero or more times*, and so these loops are said to exhibit **zero-trip behavior**. Thus, in the program in Figure 7.4, if the value entered for `height` is less than `SMALL_NUMBER`, the statements in the `while` loop will not be executed, because the condition `height >= SMALL_NUMBER` that controls the repetition will be false the first time it is evaluated. As we shall see, it is this zero-trip behavior that distinguishes the `while` loop from other noncounting C++ loops. It is important to keep this characteristic in mind when designing a solution to a problem, because it influences the decision of which loop to use.

LOOP CONDITIONS VS. TERMINATION CONDITIONS

A forever loop continues the repetition when its condition is false and terminates the repetition when that condition is true. A `while` loop behaves in the opposite manner, continuing the repetition as long as its condition is true and terminating the repetition when its condition is false. Stated differently, the condition controlling a `while` loop must always be the *negation* of the condition controlling an equivalent forever loop:

```
for (;;)                              while (!condition)
{                                     {
   if (condition) break;                 statements
   statements                         }
}
```

To illustrate, the `while` loop in the bouncing-ball program in Figure 7.4 continues the repetition so long as `height` is greater than or equal to `SMALL_NUMBER`:

```
while (height >= SMALL_NUMBER)
{
   height /= 2.0;
   bounce++;
   cout << "Rebound # " << bounce << ": "
        << height << " meters" << endl;
}
```

The equivalent forever loop version would control the repetition by terminating when `height` is less than `SMALL_NUMBER`:

```
for (;;)
{
   if (height < SMALL_NUMBER) break;
   height /= 2.0;
   bounce++;
   cout << "Rebound # " << bounce << ": "
        << height << " meters" << endl;
}
```

WATCH OUT

Words of Warning

As with other loops, it is important to ensure that the body of a `while` loop will eventually cause its loop condition to become false, since otherwise an *infinite loop* will result. To illustrate, consider the while loop:

```
counter = 1;
while (counter < 100)
{
   cout << counter << endl;
   counter--;
}
```

Here, `counter` is initially less than 100, and since `counter--` decrements `counter` by 1, the value of `counter` will always be less than 100.[7] Thus, the condition `counter < 100` will always be true, resulting in an infinite loop, producing the output

```
 1
 0
-1
-2
-3
 .
 .
 .
```

7. In some environments, repetition will terminate when `counter` becomes `MININT` because the next value of `counter` will then be `MAXINT`.

```
    i++;
    j--;
}
cout << i << j << k << endl;
```

9.
```
i = 0;
j = 10;
for (;;)
{
    k = 2 * i + j;
    if (k > 20) break;
    cout << i << j << k << endl;
    if (i + j < 10) break;
    i++;
    j--;
}
cout << i << j << k << endl;
```

10.
```
i = 5;
for (;;)
{
    cout << i;
    i -= 2;
    if (i < 1) break;
    j = 0;
    for (;;)
    {
        j++;
        cout << j;
        if (j >= i)  break;
    }
    cout << "###\n";
}
cout << "***\n";
```

11.
```
k = 5;
i = 32;
while (i > 0)
{
    cout << "base-2 log of " << i << " = " << k << endl;
    i /= 2;
    k--;
}
```

12.
```
i = 1;
while (i*i < 10)
{
    j = i;
    while (j*j < 100)
    {
      cout << i + j << endl;
      j *= 2;
    }
    i++;
}
cout << "\n*****\n";
```

13.
```
i = 1;
do
{
    k = i * i * i - 3 * i + 1;
    cout << i << k << endl;
    i++;
}
while (k <= 2);
```

14.
```
i = 0;
do
{
    j = i * i * i;
    cout << i;
    do
    {
      k = i + 2 * j;
      cout << j << k;
      j += 2;
    }
    while (k <= 10);
    cout << endl;
    i++;
}
while (j <= 5);
```

Each of the loops in the following program segment is intended to find the smallest value of `number` for which the product $1 \times 2 \times \cdots \times$ `number` is greater than `limit`. For each of Exercises 15–17, make three trace tables, one for each loop, that display the values of `number` and `product` for the given value of `limit`. Assume that `number`, `product`, and `limit` have been declared to be of type `int`.

```
/* A. Using a while loop */
  number = 0;
  product = 1;
  while (product <= limit)
  {
    number++;
    product *= number;
  }
/* B. Using a do loop */
  number = 0;
  product = 1;
  do
  {
    number++;
    product *= number;
  }
  while (product <= limit);
/* C. Using a test-in-the middle loop */
  number = 0;
  product = 1;
  for (;;)
  {
    number++;
    if (product > limit) break;
    product *= number;
  }
```

15. `limit` = 20
16. `limit` = 1
17. `limit` = 0

For Exercises 18–22, write a loop to do what is required.

18. Display the value of x and decrease x by 0.5 as long as x is positive.
19. Display the squares of the first 50 positive even integers in increasing order.
20. Display the square roots of the real numbers 1.0, 1.25, 1.5, 1.75, 2.0, . . . , 5.0.
21. The sequence of *Fibonacci numbers* begins with the integers 1, 1, 2, 3, 5, 8, 13, 21, . . . where each number after the first two is the sum of the two preceding numbers. Display the Fibonacci numbers less than 500.
22. Repeatedly prompt for and read a real number until the user enters a positive number.

For Exercises 23–27, write functions that will do what is required. To test these functions, you should write driver programs as instructed in Programming Problems 1–5 at the end of this chapter.

23. Given a real number x and a nonnegative integer n, use a loop to calculate x^n, and return this value.
24. Proceed as in Exercise 23, but allow n to be negative. (x^{-n} is defined to be $1/x^n$, provided $x \neq 0$.)
25. Given a positive integer n, return the sum of the proper divisors of n, that is, the sum of the divisors that are less than n. For example, for $n = 10$, the function should return $1 + 2 + 5 = 8$.

26. Given an integer n, return true if n is prime and false otherwise. (A *prime number* is an integer $n > 1$ whose only divisors are 1 and n.)
27. Given a positive integer n, return the least nonnegative integer k for which $2^k \geq n$.

7.5 Input Loops

One important use of loops is to input a collection of values into a program. Because the number of data values may not be known before repetition begins, we need some method to signal that the end of the data has been reached. In this section, we look at three different approaches: *sentinels, counting*, and *queries*. To illustrate how these three techniques are used, we will use each of them in solving the problem of calculating the average of a set of failure times.

RUNNING EXAMPLE: MEAN TIME TO FAILURE

One important statistic that is used in measuring the reliability of a component in a circuit is the *mean time to failure*, which can be used to predict the circuit's lifetime. This is especially important in situations in which repair is difficult or even impossible, such as a computer circuit in a satellite. Suppose that an engineering laboratory has been awarded a contract by NASA to evaluate the reliability of a particular component for a future space probe to Mars. As part of this evaluation, an engineer at this laboratory has tested several of these circuits and recorded the time at which each failed. She now wishes to develop a program to process this data and determine the mean time to failure.

Object-Centered Design

Behavior. The program should display on the screen prompts for input and read a series of component failure times from the keyboard. It should count these failure times and compute their sum and the average failure time. The program should then display this average.

Objects. In addition to the usual screen, keyboard, and prompts, we can identify the following objects in this problem:

Problem Objects	Software Objects		
	Type	Kind	Name
failure time	`double`	varying	*failureTime*
sum of the failure times	`double`	varying	*failureTimeSum*
number of components	`int`	varying	*numComponents*
average of the failure times	`double`	varying	*meanFailureTime*

Operations. To solve this problem, we need the following operations:

i. Initialize an integer (*numComponents*)
ii. Display a string (prompt) and input a real (*failureTime*)

iii. Add a real (*failureTime*) to a real (*failureTimeSum*)
iv. Increment an integer (*numComponents*)
v. Repeat Operations ii–iv once for each component
vi. Divide a real (*failureTimeSum*) by an integer (*numComponents*) and store the result in a real (*meanFailureTime*)
vii. Perform Operation vi only if *numComponents* ≠ 0

Algorithm. We can organize these operations into the following algorithm:

Algorithm to Calculate Mean Time to Failure

1. Initialize *numComponents* to 0 and *failureTimeSum* to 0.0.
2. Loop:
   a. Prompt for and read a *failureTime*.
   b. Add *failureTime* to *failureTimeSum*.
   c. Increment *numComponents* by 1.
   End loop.
3. If *numComponents* ≠ 0
   a. Calculate *meanFailureTime* = *failureTimeSum* / *numComponents*.
   b. Display *meanFailureTime* and *numComponents*.
   Otherwise
   Display a "No Data" message.

The question we must answer is this: Which of the loops provided in C++ should we use to implement the loop in Step 2?

INPUT LOOPS: THE SENTINEL APPROACH

The first approach is the **sentinel approach** introduced in Section 4.4. It uses a special value called an **end-of-data flag** or **sentinel** to mark the end of the data values to be processed.

Forever Loops and Sentinels. The program in Figure 7.7 uses a forever loop to implement the sentinel approach.

Fig. 7.7 The sentinel approach in a forever loop. (Part 1 of 3)

```
/* failureTime.cpp uses a forever loop and a sentinel to process a
 * collection of failure times and find the mean time to failure.
 *
 *  Input:        a collection of component failure times
 *  Precondition: failure times >= 0
 *  Output:       prompts and the average of the failure times
*************************************************************/
```

Fig. 7.7 The sentinel approach in a forever loop. (Part 2 of 3)

```
#include <iostream>                  // <<, >>, cout, cin
using namespace std;

int main()
{
   cout << "Computing Component Mean Time to Failure\n\n";

   int    numComponents = 0;
   double failureTime,
          failureTimeSum = 0.0;

   for (;;)                 // or while (true)
   {
      cout << "Enter a failure time (-1 to quit): ";
      cin >> failureTime;

      if (failureTime < 0) break;

      failureTimeSum += failureTime;
      numComponents++;
   }

   if (numComponents != 0)
      cout << "\nThe mean failure time of the "
           << numComponents << " components is "
           << failureTimeSum / numComponents << endl;
   else
      cerr << "\nNo failure times to process!\n";
}
```

Sample run:

```
Computing Component Mean Time to Failure

Enter a failure time (-1 to quit): 2.3
Enter a failure time (-1 to quit): 2.4
Enter a failure time (-1 to quit): 2.5
Enter a failure time (-1 to quit): 2.6
```

Fig. 7.7 The sentinel approach in a forever loop. (Part 3 of 3)

```
Enter a failure time (-1 to quit): 2.7
Enter a failure time (-1 to quit): -1

The mean failure time of the 5 components is 2.5
```

As the comment at the beginning of the forever loop indicates, a `while` statement could also be used to implement the input loop:

```
while(true)
{
   cout << "Enter a failure time (-1 to quit): ";
   cin >> failureTime;

   if (failureTime < 0) break;

   failureTimeSum += failureTime;
   numComponents++;
}
```

And as we noted earlier, a `do` statement could also be used, but this is not as common. The choice of which statement to use to implement an input loop is largely a matter of programmer preference. In this text, we will use the forever-loop version.

If we examine this and earlier examples for similarities, we see the following pattern:

Pattern for Sentinel Input Loop (Indefinite Loop Version)

```
for (;;)          // or while(true)
{
   Display a prompt (for a data value).
   Read theValue to be processed.
   If (theValue is the sentinel) terminate the repetition.
   Process theValue.
}
```

This pattern provides a succinct and intuitive way to input any data set for which a sentinel value exists.

While Loops and Sentinels. Before indefinite loops and statements to exit from loops became common features of programming languages, the `while` loop as described in Section 7.3 was the only loop available to implement the sentinel approach. It is still used by some programmers, and so we should understand how it works. We gave some examples of its usage in Section 4.4, but we will review it here. The basic pattern is as follows:

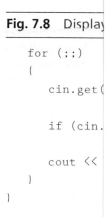

Pattern for Sentinel Input Loop (while Loop Version)

Display a prompt for a data value.
Read *theValue* to be processed.
while (*theValue* is not the sentinel)
{
    Process *theValue*.
    Display a prompt for a data value.
    Read *theValue* to be processed.
}

For example, a `while` loop version of the sentinel loop used in the mean-time-to-failure program in Figure 7.7 would be written as follows:

```
cout << "Enter a failure time (-1 to quit): ";
cin >> failureTime;
while (failureTime >= 0)
{
   failureTimeSum += failureTime;
   numComponents++;

   cout << "Enter a failure time (-1 to quit): ";
   cin >> failureTime;
}
```

Note the two input steps, one before the loop and one at the bottom of the loop. Obviously, the input step inside the loop is needed to read new data values. But one is also needed before the loop, because the `while` loop is a pretest loop and tests its condition before the body of the loop is executed. For this condition to compare an input value with the sentinel, a value must be input before the beginning of the loop.

In the past, when the `while` loop was the only noncounting loop provided in a language, a programmer had no choice but to do this extra coding when designing a sentinel loop, but the addition of indefinite loops and loop-exit statements in modern languages makes it possible to avoid this redundant code. Although the duplicate code is not a major violation of OOP's "don't-reinvent-the-wheel" tenet, it does require redundant coding, violating the spirit of object-oriented programming. We will therefore use the forever loop version of the sentinel approach in this text.

A Problem with Sentinels. To use the sentinel approach, there must be some value that is not a valid data value to use as a sentinel. For the mean-time-to-failure problem, all failure times are nonnegative numbers, and so any negative value can serve as the sentinel.

The second drawback is one that we discussed in Section 5.3: Once any `istream` status flag other than *good* is set, no subsequent input actions have any effect until the status flags are cleared. In some versions of C++ it is possible to read values *after* the eof mark has been read by calling the `istream` function member `clear()` to reset the status flags. The simple program in Figure 7.9 illustrates how this is done. It reads two lists of numbers and computes the sum of the numbers in the first list and the product of the numbers in the second list. The end of each list is indicated by using the eof mark as a sentinel. As illustrated, this technique works in gnu C++; but it may not work in some other versions of C++.

Fig. 7.9 Processing two lists. (Part 1 of 2)

```
/* processLists.cpp processes two lists, summing the values in one,
 * and finding the product of the values in the other.
 *
 * Input:   two sequences of numbers
 * Output:  the sum of the numbers in the first sequence,
 *          the product of the numbers in the second sequence.
 *****************************************************************/

#include <iostream>          // <<, cout, cin, get, eof(), clear()
using namespace std;

int main()
{
   cout << "This program reads two lists, summing the first\n"
           "and finding the product of the numbers in the second.\n\n"
           "Enter the list to be summed (end list with eof):\n";

   double number,
          sum = 0;

   for (;;)                                     // read 1st list
   {
      cin >> number;
      if (cin.eof()) break;
      sum += number;
   }

                                                //eof flag is set,
   cin.clear();                                 // so clear it
   // This may not work in some versions of C++
   cout << "\nEnter the list to be multiplied (end list with eof):\n";

   double product = 1;
```

Fig. 7.9 Processing two lists. (Part 2 of 2)

```
   for (;;)                                          // read 2nd list
   {
      cin >> number;
      if (cin.eof()) break;
      product *= number;
   }

   cout << "\nThe sum of the first list is " << sum << "\nand "
        << "the product of the second list is " << product << endl;
}
```

Sample run (Unix System with gnu C++):

```
This program reads two lists, summing the first
and finding the product of the numbers in the second.

Enter the list to be summed (end list with eof):
1 2 3 4 5 6
^D
Enter the list to be multiplied (end list with eof):
10 9 8 7
^D
The sum of the first list is 21
and the product of the second list is 5040
```

INPUT LOOPS: THE COUNTING APPROACH

Another way to process a set of input values is to first input the number of values in the data set and then use a counting loop to read and process that many values. Figure 7.10 is a modification of the mean-time-to-failure program in Figure 7.7 that uses this approach.

Fig. 7.10 The counting approach. (Part 1 of 2)

```
/* failureTime.cpp uses a counting loop to process a collection
 * of failure times and find the mean time to failure.
 *
 *  Input:  the number of component failure times and
 *          the collection of failure times
 *  Output: prompts and the average of the failure times
 *****************************************************************/
```

Fig. 7.10 The counting approach. (Part 2 of 2)

```
#include <iostream>                          // <<, >>, cout, cin
using namespace std;

int main()
{
   cout << "Computing Component Mean Time to Failure\n\n";

   int numComponents;
   double failureTime,
          failureTimeSum = 0.0;

   cout << "How many failure times will be entered? ";
   cin >> numComponents;

   for (int count = 1; count <= numComponents; count++)
   {
      cout << "Enter failure time #" << count << ": ";
      cin >> failureTime;

      failureTimeSum += failureTime;
   }

   if (numComponents > 0)
      cout << "\nThe mean failure time of the "
           << numComponents << " components is "
           << failureTimeSum / numComponents << endl;
   else
      cerr << "\nNo failure times to process!\n";
}
```

Sample run:

```
Computing Component Mean Time to Failure

How many failure times will be entered? 5
Enter failure time #1: 2.3
Enter failure time #2: 2.4
Enter failure time #3: 2.5
Enter failure time #4: 2.6
Enter failure time #5: 2.7

The mean failure time of the 5 components is 2.5
```

Conceptually, this approach is quite simple. We ask the user how many values are to be entered and then use a `for` loop to read and process that many values. The general pattern is as follows:

Pattern for Counting Input Loop

Display a prompt for the number of values to be processed.

Read *numberOfValues* to be processed.

```
for (int var = 1; var <= numberOfValues; var++)
{
    Display a prompt for a data value.
    Read theValue to be processed.
    Process theValue.
}
```

One disadvantage of this approach is its lack of flexibility. The number of data values entered must be exactly the number specified at the beginning of execution. If a user discovers during the input of the data values that there will be more (or fewer) values than were specified, there is no way out, except to abort the program and reexecute it. A related disadvantage is that the counting loop requires that we know in advance how many values will be entered. This may be difficult to determine for large data sets. The program is much more user friendly if the computer, rather than the user, does the counting.

INPUT LOOPS: THE QUERY APPROACH

Each of the preceding kinds of input loops has its disadvantages. The sentinel approach can only be used in problems where there is a suitable value to use as the sentinel. The eof mark is platform dependent. The counting loop approach requires knowing in advance the number of values to be entered.

The final approach we consider is to **query the user** at the end of each repetition to determine whether there is more data to process. Although not without its disadvantages, this approach is the most broadly applicable.

The program in Figure 7.11 is a modification of the mean-time-to-failure programs in Figures 7.7 and 7.10 that uses this query approach. It asks the query

```
Do you have more data to enter (y or n)?
```

and then reads the user's response from the keyboard. Repetition continues until the user answers `y` or `Y`, and the loop condition

```
response == 'y' || response == 'Y'
```

then terminates the repetition.

Fig. 7.11 The query approach. (Part 1 of 2)

```
/* failureTime.cpp uses a query-controlled loop to process a
 * collection of failure times and find the mean time to failure.
 *
 *  Input:    a collection of component failure times and
 *            user's response to "more data?" query
 *  Output:   prompts and the average of the failure times.
 ****************************************************************/

#include <iostream>                      // <<, >>, cout, cin
using namespace std;

int main()
{
   cout << "Computing Component Mean Time to Failure\n";

   int numComponents = 0;
   double failureTime,
          failureTimeSum = 0.0;

   char response;
   do
   {
      cout << "\nEnter a failure time: ";
      cin >> failureTime;

      failureTimeSum += failureTime;
      numComponents++;

      cout << "Do you have more data to enter (y or n)? ";
      cin >> response;
   }
   while (response == 'y' || response == 'Y');

   cout << "\nThe mean failure time of the "
        << numComponents << " components is "
        << failureTimeSum / numComponents << endl;
}
```

Sample run:

```
Computing Component Mean Time to Failure
```

Fig. 7.11 The query approach. (Part 2 of 2)

```
Enter a failure time: 2.3
Do you have more data to enter (y or n)? y

Enter a failure time: 2.4
Do you have more data to enter (y or n)? y

Enter a failure time: 2.5
Do you have more data to enter (y or n)? y

Enter a failure time: 2.6
Do you have more data to enter (y or n)? y

Enter a failure time: 2.7
Do you have more data to enter (y or n)? n

The mean failure time of the 5 components is 2.5
```

In problems where it is reasonable to assume that there is at least one data value to be entered and processed, the query and the corresponding loop condition are placed at the bottom of the loop, making it a posttest loop.[9] This suggests the following *pattern* for a query-controlled input loop:

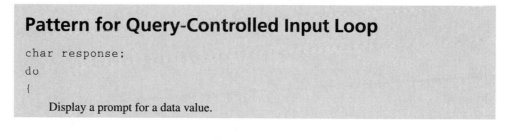

Pattern for Query-Controlled Input Loop

```
char response;
do
{
   Display a prompt for a data value.
```

9. In problems where there might be no values to enter and process, a forever loop can be used:

```
for (;;)
{
   cout << "\nDo you wish to continue (y or n)? "
   char response;
   cin >> response;
   if (response == 'n' || response == 'N') break;
   cout << "\nEnter a value: ";
   double value;
   cin >> value;
   // process value
}
```

```
      Input theValue to be processed.
      Process theValue.
      Display a query that asks if there is more data.
      Input the user's response (y or n).
   }
   while ((response != 'n') && (response != 'N'));
```

Query Functions. The code to perform a query tends to clutter a loop, and this may obscure the program's structure. One way to avoid this is to use a **query function** like the following to perform the query, read the user's response, and return true or false based on the response:

```
bool moreValues()
{
   char answer;
   cout << "Do you have more values to enter (y or n)? ";
   cin >> answer;
   return (answer == 'y') || (answer == 'Y');
}
```

Since it returns a boolean value, a call to such a query function can be used as a loop condition. For example, we could modify the mean-time-to-failure program of Figure 7.11 to use the query function `moreData()` to control the input loop:

```
int main()
{
        .
        .
        .
   do
   {
      cout << "\nEnter a failure time: ";
      cin >> failureTime;
      failureTimeSum += failureTime;
      numComponents++;
   }
   while ( moreValues() );
        .
        .
        .
}
```

Each time execution reaches the loop condition, the function `moreValues()` is called. It queries the user, reads the response, and returns true if the response was either `y` or `Y` and returns false otherwise. If `moreValues()` returns true, the body of the `do` loop is repeated, but if it returns false, repetition is terminated.

This version of a query-controlled loop is easier to read than the earlier version in Figure 7.11 because the statements that perform the querying (including the declaration of a character variable to hold the response) are now hidden in the function `moreValues()`.

Another advantage of this approach is that a query function can be stored in a library (e.g., `Queries`), from which it can be accessed by any program requiring a query-controlled loop. Since the particular query

```
Do you have more values to enter (y or n)?
```

may be less appropriate for a different program, such a library might contain a variety of query functions, such as:

`moreValues()`:	asks if there are more values
`done()`:	asks if the user is done
`notDone()`:	asks if the user wants to continue

A program that uses the `#include` directive to insert the library's header file can use whichever query function is most appropriate.

The general pattern of a loop controlled by a query function is as follows:

Pattern for Input Loop Controlled by a Query Function

```
bool queryFunction();    // or #include "QueryLibrary"
   .
   .
   .
do
{
    Display a prompt for a data value.
    Input theValue to be processed.
    Process theValue.
}
while ( queryFunction() );
```

The Disadvantage of the Query Approach. The sentinel and counting approaches require one interaction by the user to enter each data value, but the query approach requires two—one for the data value and one for the response to the query. This doubling of user effort may make the query approach too cumbersome for large data sets. (If the data values come in groups, however, the query approach may be less cumbersome and more appropriate.)

7.6 Choosing the Right Loop

With so many different kinds of loops, it can be difficult for a programmer to decide which is best for a particular problem. One simple guideline is the following:

The choice of a loop should be determined by the nature of the problem.

This means that choosing a loop is part of the design phase of program development. It should be done only after the algorithm has been developed in some detail, because the algorithm will provide clues as to which loop to use.

DECISION #1: USE A COUNTING LOOP OR A GENERAL LOOP?

The first question to ask is,

Does the algorithm require counting through some fixed range of values?

If the answer is yes, then a counting loop is needed, and a `for` loop is the appropriate choice. However, if solving the problem does not involve repeating the execution of statements a fixed number of times, then one of the more general loops—`while`, `do`, or forever—is a better choice.

DECISION #2: WHICH GENERAL LOOP?

If one of the general loops should be used, then the next question is, Which one? One way to proceed is to begin with a *generic loop* of the form

Loop
    body-of-the-loop
End loop.

in the algorithm. Then continue to develop the algorithm, adding any necessary initialization statements before the loop together with the statements that make up the body of the loop:

initialization statements
Loop
    $statement_1$
    .
    .
    .
    $statement_n$
End loop.

Finally, formulate an appropriate termination condition and determine where it should be placed in the loop. This will determine which kind of loop to use:

If the termination condition appears

- at the beginning of the loop, the loop is a pretest loop—choose a `while` loop;

- at the bottom of the loop, the loop is a posttest loop—choose a `do` loop;
- within the list of statements, the loop is a test-in-the-middle loop—choose a forever loop with an `if-break` (or `if-return`) combination.

To illustrate, consider again the problem of designing an algorithm for the bouncing-ball problem of Section 7.3. Using a generic loop, we write a first version of the algorithm as follows:

1. Initialize *bounce* to 0.
2. Enter a value for *height*.
3. Display original *height* value with appropriate label.
4. Loop:
   Replace *height* with *height* divided by 2.
   Add 1 to *bounce*.
   Display *bounce* and *height*.
5. End loop.

Because repetition is to stop when *height* is less than some *SMALL_NUMBER*, the condition

height < *SMALL_NUMBER*

can be used as a termination condition for the loop. However, the user could have entered zero or a negative value for *height*, in which case the body of the loop should not be executed. Thus, we should evaluate this condition immediately upon entering the loop:

1. Initialize *bounce* to 0.
2. Enter a value for *height*.
3. Display original *height* value with appropriate label.
4. Loop:
   a. If *height* < *SMALL_NUMBER*, terminate the repetition.
   b. Replace *height* with *height* divided by 2.
   c. Add 1 to *bounce*.
   d. Display *bounce* and *height*.
   End loop.

This is a pretest loop, and we should therefore use a `while` loop to implement it.

By contrast, if we reconsider the sentinel approach to reading a collection of values, we begin by constructing the generic loop

Loop:
  Display a prompt for input.
  Input *theValue*.
  Process *theValue*.
End loop.

Since we are using the sentinel approach, an appropriate termination condition is

theValue is the sentinel

Before this termination condition can be evaluated, *theValue* must have been read, which means that the termination condition must appear after the input statement. Also, a sentinel value must not be processed, which means that the termination condition should be placed before the processing statements:

Loop:
  a. Display a prompt for input.
  b. Input *theValue*.
  c. If *theValue* is the sentinel, terminate repetition.
  d. Process *theValue*.
End loop.

This is a test-in-the-middle loop, and we can use a forever loop to implement it.

Quick Quiz 7.6

1. Name the three kinds of input loops.
2. A special value used to signal the end of data is called a(n) ______ or ______.
3. (True or false) A disadvantage of using a `while` loop instead of a forever loop for sentinel-based input is that duplicate input steps are required.
4. The eof flag is set when a special character called the ______ mark is read.
5. The method ______ from class `istream` is used to check the eof flag.
6. (True or false) One advantage of using the eof mark is that it is platform independent.
7. (True or false) The counting method of input is one of the most flexible methods.
8. A ______ is a question asked of the user to determine whether there are more data values.

7.7 Case Study: Calculating Depreciation

PROBLEM

Depreciation is a decrease in the value over time of some asset due to wear and tear, decay, declining price, and so on. For example, suppose that a company purchases a new computer system for $200,000 that will serve its needs for five years. After that time, called the *useful life* of the computer, it can be sold at an estimated price of $50,000, which is the computer's salvage value. Thus, the value of the computing equipment will have depreciated $150,000 over the five-year period. The calculation of the value lost in each of several years is an important accounting problem, and there are several ways of calculating this quantity. We want to write functions that use some of these methods to calculate depreciation for each year of an item's useful life and display tables that show these annual depreciations.

Object-Centered Design

Behavior. Each function should receive from its caller the amount to be depreciated and the number of years in an item's useful life. The function should then output to the screen a depreciation table that displays the depreciation for each year.

Objects. The objects in this problem are straightforward:

Problem Objects	Software Objects			
	Type	Kind	Movement	Name
The amount to be depreciated	real	varying	received	*amount*
The item's useful life (in years)	integer	varying	received	*numYears*
The annual depreciation	real	varying	—	*depreciation*

Each function will have the same specification:

Receive: *amount* and *numYears*

Output: a depreciation table

There are several different methods of calculating depreciation. One standard method is the **straight-line method**, in which the amount to be depreciated is divided evenly over the specified number of years. For example, straight-line depreciation of $150,000 over a five-year period gives an annual depreciation of $150,000 / 5 = $30,000:

Year	Depreciation
1	$30,000
2	$30,000
3	$30,000
4	$30,000
5	$30,000

With this method, the value of an asset decreases a fixed amount each year.

Another common method of calculating depreciation is called the **sum-of-the-years'-digits method**. To illustrate it, consider again depreciating $150,000 over a five-year period. We first calculate the "sum of the years' digits," 1 + 2 + 3 + 4 + 5 = 15. In the first year, 5/15 of $150,000 ($50,000) is depreciated; in the second year, 4/15 of $150,000 ($40,000) is depreciated; and so on, giving the following depreciation table:

Year	Depreciation
1	$50,000
2	$40,000
3	$30,000
4	$20,000
5	$10,000

See if you can write two depreciation functions, one to display a depreciation table using the straight-line method and another to display a depreciation table using the sum-of-the-years'-digits method. Each will make use of a counting loop to output the table. Then write a menu-driven program that lets the user select from four options: (a) Enter information about a new item. (b) Use straight-line depreciation. (c) Use sum-of-the-years'-digits depreciation. (d) Quit the program. Use a do loop to force the user to select one of these options.

Compare your solution with the one given on the book's Web site. You might also look at this solution if you have difficulty with any of these functions or with the program. It is a complete solution that uses OCD to develop the functions and the program and contains code for them. A sample run of the program also is shown.

Part of the Picture
Introduction to Algorithm Analysis

In the incident described in Section 7.1, the student Gauss responded almost immediately when he was given the problem of summing the integers from 1 through 100. The simplicity and efficiency of his algorithm compared to the repetitive algorithm we used is an indication of his genius. We will describe his algorithm here and use it to introduce the area of computer science known as *algorithm analysis* .

To compute the sum of the integers from 1 through 100, Gauss perhaps observed that writing the sum forward,

$$sum = 1 + 2 + 3 + \ldots + 98 + 99 + 100$$

and then backward,

$$sum = 100 + 99 + 98 + \ldots + 3 + 2 + 1$$

and then adding corresponding terms in these two equations gives

$$\begin{aligned} 2 \times sum &= 101 + 101 + \cdots + 101 + 101 \\ &= 100 \times 101 \end{aligned}$$

Thus the sum is equal to

$$sum = \frac{100 \times 101}{2} = 5050$$

Applying his algorithm to the more general summation problem, we begin with the sum

$$sum = 1 + 2 + 3 + \ldots + (n - 2) + (n - 1) + n$$

reverse it,

$$sum = n + (n - 1) + (n - 2) + \cdots + 3 + 2 + 1$$

and then add these two equations to get

$$\begin{aligned} 2 \times sum &= (n + 1) + (n + 1) + \cdots + (n + 1) + (n + 1) \\ &= n \times (n + 1) \end{aligned}$$

Dividing by 2 gives

$$sum = \frac{n \times (n + 1)}{2}$$

This formula implies that function `sum()` can be written without using a loop at all, as shown in Figure 7.12.

Fig. 7.12 Function `sum()`—no-loop version.

```
/* sum(n) computes the sum of the integers from 1 to n
 * using Gauss's formula.
 *
 * Receive:      n, an integer
 * Precondition: n > 0
 * Return:       the sum 1 + 2 + ... + n
 ***********************************************************/

int sum(int n)
{
   return n * (n + 1) / 2;
}
```

This solution is better than one that uses a loop, because it solves the same problem in less time. To see why, suppose that we want to compute the sum of the integers from 1 through 1000. A version of `sum()` that uses a loop (such as that in Figure 7.1) must repeat the body of the loop 1000 times. That means it must perform

1,000 additions of `count` to `runningTotal`,
1,000 assignments of that result to `runningTotal`,
1,000 increments of `count`, and
1,000 comparisons of `count` to `n`,

for a total of 4,000 operations. For an arbitrary value of `n`, each of these operations would be performed `n` times for a total of 4`n` operations. We say that the number of operations performed by the loop version of `Sum()` **grows linearly** with the value of its parameter `n`.

By contrast, the final version of `sum()` always does

1 addition,
1 multiplication, and
1 division,

for a total of 3 operations, *regardless of the value of* `n`. Thus, the time taken by the last version of `sum()` is **constant**, no matter what the value of its parameter `n`.

This is our first look at an important area of computer science called **analysis of algorithms**. We have seen two algorithms that solve the summation problem. To determine which of them is "better," we analyze the number of operations each requires to solve the problem. The algorithm using Gauss's formula solves the problem in constant time, while the algorithm using a loop solves the problem in time proportional to `n`, and consequently, Gauss's algorithm is to be preferred.

7.8* OBJECTive Thinking: Code Reuse through Inheritance

Repetition statements, like those we have studied in this chapter, provide a kind of code reuse—the statements in the body of the loop can be reused several times within the same program:

```
for (int i = 1; i <= n; i++)
   // ... repeat something n times
```

NOTE

Functions provide a similar kind of code reuse by allowing a programmer to reuse the same code (the body of the function) wherever the function is called in a program. Function libraries provide a third kind of code reuse, by allowing a programmer to reuse the same functions in different programs. Class libraries provide a fourth kind of code reuse, by allowing a programmer to reuse the same objects in different programs. In this *OBJECTive Thinking* section, we will see a fifth kind of code reuse: an **inheritance mechanism** whereby one class whose attributes include all those of another class can reuse the attributes of that other class. *It is this inheritance mechanism that distinguishes object-oriented languages and design from non-object-oriented approaches*

INHERITANCE

We begin with a simple example to illustrate the benefit of inheritance. In the preceding and earlier *OBJECTive Thinking* sections (See Section 6.6) we have built a `Name` class that represents three-part names—first name, middle name, and last name. Some people, however, have *titles* as part of their names; for example, *Doctor*, *Judge*, *Reverend*, *Father*, and *Senator*. In this section, we consider how to represent such names.

One option would be to design a new class, containing four string instance variables—one to represent the person's title and the remaining three to represent their first, middle, and last names—plus constructors to initialize them and accessors, mutators, and I/O methods to manipulate them. The problem is that much of the code in this new class will be identical to or very similar to the code we have already written for our `Name` class. As soon as we recognize that this approach leads to redundant coding, it should make us stop and think, because *anytime we find ourselves writing redundant code, there is usually a better approach*.

NOTE

The "better approach" in this case is to recognize that our new class is a specialized kind of `Name`—a `Name` with a title in front of it. This is the key: *When a new class is a specialization of an existing class, we can use the C++ inheritance mechanism to derive the new class from the existing class*. To illustrate, we can write

```
#include "Name.h"     // the Name class

class TitledName : public Name
{
   // attributes and operations of TitledName
};
```

and our new class `TitledName` will inherit all of the attributes and operations of class `Name`.

All that leaves for us to do in class `TitledName` is add the attributes and operations that deal with the title part of a titled name—all of the attributes and operations that deal with the name part are inherited. Figure 7.13 shows the details.

Fig. 7.13 `TitledName`, a class derived from `Name`. (Part 1 of 2)

```
/* TitledName.h illustrates the use of inheritance in C++.
 * ... other documentation omitted ...
 **************************************************************/

#include "Name.h"                  // our Name class

class TitledName : public Name    // a TitledName is a Name
{
 public:
   TitledName();
   TitledName(string title, string fName, string mName, string lName);

   string getTitle() const;
   void setTitle(string newName);

   void read(istream& in);
   void print(ostream& out) const;
   // ... other methods omitted ...

 private:
   string myTitle;
};


inline TitledName::TitledName()
 : Name()                         // use parent constructor
{                                 //  to initialize inherited vars
   myTitle = "";
}

inline TitledName::TitledName(string title, string fName,
                              string mName, string lName)
 : Name(fName, mName, lName)      // use parent constructor
{                                 //  to initialize inherited vars
   myTitle = title;
}
```

Fig. 7.13 `TitledName`, a class derived from `Name`. (Part 2 of 2)

```
inline string TitledName::getTitle() const
{
   return myTitle;
}

inline void TitledName::setTitle(string newTitle)
{
   myTitle = newTitle;
}

inline void TitledName::read(istream& in)
{
   in >> myTitle;          // read the title -- it's first
   Name::read(in);         // read the name using parent method
}

inline void TitledName::print(ostream& out) const
{
   out << myTitle;         // print the title -- it's first
   Name::print(out);       // print the name using parent method
}
```

Given this code, a `TitledName` object will automatically have the instance variables `myFirstName`, `myMiddleName`, and `myLastName` from class `Name`, without our having to redefine them in class `TitledName`. We can also send it any of the messages declared in class `Name`. We can thus send a `TitledName` object a message like `getFirstName()`, `setLastName()`, or `getMiddleInitial()`, because the `TitledName` object inherits them from class `Name`.

In object-oriented terminology, `Name` is called a **parent class** or **superclass**, and `TitledName` is called a **child class** or **subclass**. The relationship between a child class and its parent is often depicted graphically, as follows:

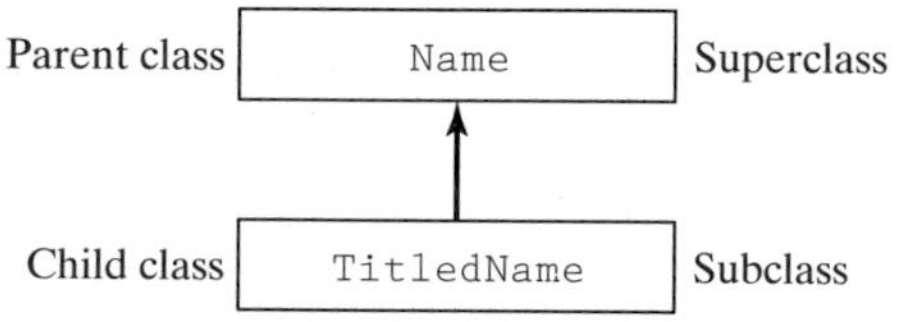

The arrow in such diagrams denotes the **is-a relationship**: A `TitledName` *is a* specialized kind of `Name` and inherits all of its attributes. Anytime we can describe the relationship between two objects using this *is-a* relation, classes for those objects can be built using inheritance.

Given this class, a programmer can now declare `TitledName` objects and send them messages from either class `Name` or class `TitledName`, as shown in Figure 7.14:

Fig. 7.14 A `TitledName` driver program.

```
// titledNameDriver.cpp

#include "TitledName.h"       // class TitledName

int main()
{
  cout << "\nEnter a titled name: ";
  TitledName aTitledName;
  aTitledName.read(cin);                             // overridden

  cout << aTitledName.getLastName() << ", "          // inherited
       << aTitledName.getTitle() << ' '              // not inherited
       << aTitledName.getFirstName() << ' '          // inherited
       << aTitledName.getMiddleInitial() << ". "     // inherited
       << endl;
}
```

Sample Run:

```
Enter a titled name: President George Walker Bush
Bush, President George W.
```

We will now look at several parts of the code in Figure 7.13 that require additional explanation.

Constructors and Initialization. In our `Name` class, the instance variables are all private, even to a subclass like `TitledName`. Because of this, our `TitledName` class constructors and methods cannot access them directly, but must instead do so using the constructors and methods provided by class `Name`.

To initialize the inherited members, our constructors use a special feature of C++ called an **initialization list** that lies between a constructor's heading and body:

```
Classname::ClassName( parameterDeclarations )
  : InitializationList
Body
```

The most common form of the initialization list is simply a call to the constructor of a parent class,

```
ParentClassname( initial_values )
```

where *initial_values* is a list of values to be passed to *ParentClassname*'s constructor. For example, our `TitledName` default-value constructor uses this mechanism to invoke the default-value constructor of class `Name`:[10]

```
inline TitledName::TitledName()
 : Name()
{
   myTitle = "";
}
```

Given this constructor, the object declaration

```
TitledName aTitledName;
```

will cause all four of the string instance variables within it to be initialized to default (empty string) values.

Similarly, our `TitledName` explicit-value constructor uses an initialization list to invoke the `Name` explicit-value constructor:

```
inline TitledName::TitledName(string title, string fName,
                              string mName, string lName)
 : Name(fName, mName, lName)
{
   myTitle = title;
}
```

Since this constructor passes some of its parameters—`fName`, `mName`, and `lName`—on to the explicit-value constructor of its parent class, the object declaration

```
TitledName presidentOfUS("President", "George",
                         "Walker", "Bush");
```

will use the two explicit-value constructors in concert to initialize the object's instance variables:

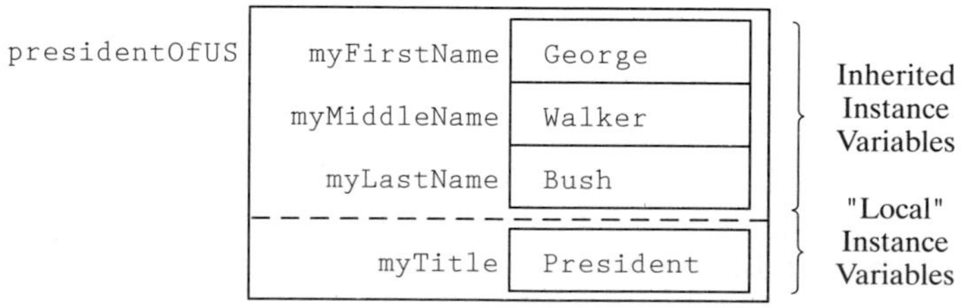

10. Instance variables may also be initialized in the initialization list. To illustrate, we could have written

```
inline TitledName::TitledName()
 : Name(), myTitle("")
{}
```

to initialize `myTitle`, instead of the definition given in Figure 7.13.

Accessor and Mutator Methods. The `TitledName` class inherits all of the accessor and mutator methods of its parent class `Name`. Since the operations these methods provide are independent of the title that goes with a name, we can use them just as they are. All that leaves for us to write are the accessor and mutator methods for the instance variable `myTitle`. Doing so is straightforward, as shown in Figure 7.13.

I/O Methods. The input/output methods `read()` and `print()` of class `TitledName` must read and display the *title* part of a `TitledName` object in addition to the first, middle, and last names, which means that we must redefine them in class `TitledName`. In object-oriented terminology, these definitions are said to **override** the definitions of `print()` and `read()` that the `TitledName` class inherits from class `Name`.

Except for reading or displaying the title part of a name, however, the rest of what these methods must do is exactly the same as the corresponding methods in class `Name`. When this is the case, the `Name` methods can be reused in the definitions of the `TitledName` methods by attaching the qualifier `Name::` to their names:

```
inline void TitledName::print(ostream& out) const
{
   out << myTitle;
   Name::print(out);
}

inline void TitledName::read(istream& in)
{
   in >> myTitle;
   Name::read(in);
}
```

In general, a child class method can invoke a particular method from its parent class using the notation:

```
ParentClass::ParentClassMethod( arguments )
```

When a `print()` or `read()` message is sent to a `TitledName` object, the methods defined in class `TitledName` are the ones that will be executed rather than the methods inherited from class `Name`. Thus, in the program in Figure 7.14, the expression

```
aTitledName.getLastName()
```

invokes the inherited method `getLastName()` because `TitledName` does not override `getLastName()`; but the expression

```
aTitledName.read(cin)
```

uses the `read()` method of class `TitledName`, overriding the inherited method from class `Name`.

WATCH OUT

In the definitions of `print()` and `read()`, the expressions `Name::print(out)` and `Name::read(in)` invoke the `print()` and `read()` methods from the parent class `Name`. The `Name::` notation must not be omitted, or the `print()` method will call *itself* over and over again. Such a mistake is called an **infinite recursion** and behaves similarly to an infinite loop.

A General Principle. There is one simple principle that governs the writing of constructors and methods of a child class:

> *The constructors and methods of a class should only access directly instance variables that are defined within the same class. Inherited instance variables should be accessed through inherited constructors or methods.*

Note how our constructors and I/O methods follow this principle:

- Each of the `TitledName` constructors directly initializes the new instance variable `myTitle`. The inherited instance variables are initialized using the corresponding `Name` constructor.
- The `print()` method directly accesses instance variable `myTitle`. It leaves the responsibility of displaying the inherited instance variables to the method `Name::print()`.
- The `read()` method directly accesses instance variable `myTitle`. It leaves the responsibility of filling the inherited instance variables with input values to the method `Name::read()`.

INHERITANCE AND OBJECT-ORIENTED DESIGN

In the "real world," objects do not exist in a vacuum. Instead, they are often related in some way, and much of science deals with the classification of real-world objects according to these relationships. For example, protons, neutrons, and electrons are all *subatomic particles*. Hydrogen, helium, and lithium are all *elements*. Pencils, pens, and stylii are all *writing instruments*. Chijuajuas, mastiffs, and collies are all *dogs*. Whales, pigs, dogs, and people are all *mammals*. Mums, roses, and tulips are all *flowers*. Mammals and flowers are both *living things*.

We might depict these relationships graphically as follows:

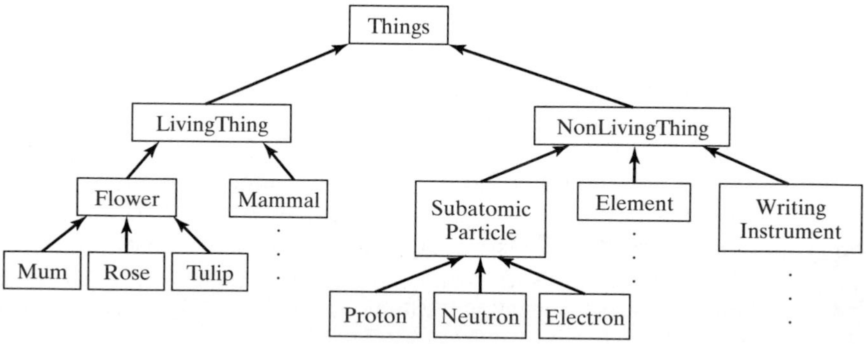

Since each arrow in our diagram represents the *is-a* relationship, we can create an efficient software representation of these relationships using the inheritance mechanism. To represent this hierarchy, we could write

```
class Thing
{
   // attributes and operations common to all things
};

class LivingThing : public Thing
{
   // attributes and operations common to all living things
};

class NonLivingThing : public Thing
{
   // attributes and operations common to all nonliving things
};

class Flower : public LivingThing
{
   // attributes and operations common to all flowers
};

class Mammal : public LivingThing
{
   // attributes and operations common to all mammals
};

class SubatomicParticle : public NonLivingThing
{
   // attributes and operations common to all subatomic particles
};

class Element : public NonLivingThing
{
   // attributes and operations common to all elements
};

class WritingUtensil : public NonLivingThing
{
   // attributes and operations common to all writing utensils
};
```

and so on. Inheritance can thus be used to create **class hierarchies** in which every subclass is related to its superclass by the *is-a* relationship.

One advantage of this approach is that by storing all attributes and operations common to a particular class of objects in that class, redundant coding can be essentially eliminated because all subclasses will automatically inherit the common code from their superclass. Another advantage is that when one class in the hierarchy is modified—for example, via maintenance or a software upgrade—all of its subclasses automatically inherit the changes. Similarly, if we fix an error in some method of a class, all subclasses automatically inherit the fix.

Object-Oriented Design

Object-oriented design (OOD) is the process of designing software that consists of class hierarchies in order to take advantage of inheritance. In fact, the steps involved in OOD are a natural extension to those of object-centered design (OCD):

1. Identify the objects in your problem.
   a. If an object cannot be directly represented with an existing type, build a class to represent such objects.
   b. Where appropriate, *use inheritance to consolidate common attributes and operations within superclasses, and derive each class from the appropriate superclasses.*
2. Identify the operations in your problem.
   a. If an operation is not predefined, write a function to perform that operation.
   b. Where appropriate, *identify a class that should be responsible for providing that operation, and define the operation as a method of that class.*
3. Organize the objects and operations identified in Steps 1 and 2 into an algorithm that solves your problem.

When is it appropriate to use inheritance to relate two classes? Once again, there is a simple guiding principle:

> *It is appropriate for a class B to be derived from another class A, if and only if every message that can be sent to an object of type A can appropriately be sent to any object of type B.*

Thus, it was appropriate to derive our `TitledName` class from class `Name` because every message that can be sent to a `Name` object is also appropriate for a `TitledName` object. By contrast, if we wished to create a `PetsName` class to represent names of animal pets, it would not be appropriate to derive `PetsName` from `Name`, because some `Name` messages would be inappropriate to send to a `PetsName` object—for example, most pets have no middle names.

This was our first look at OOD. We hope it has given you new food for thought regarding software design. We will revisit OOD in a future *OBJECTive Thinking* section. (See Section 12.5.)

Quick Quiz 7.8

1. ________ is what distinguishes object-oriented languages and design from non-object-oriented ones.
2. ________ makes it possible to derive one class from another class and reuse the attributes of that class.

   For Questions 3–8, assume that class `A` is derived from class `B`; `B` contains methods named `m1()` and `m2()`; `A` contains a method named `m1()`, but not one named `m2()`; and that `obj` is an `A` object.
3. A is called a(n) ________ class of `B`.

4. B is called a(n) ________ class of A.
5. The relationship between A objects and B objects is known as the ________ relationship.
6. The declaration of A would begin `class A :` ________ B.
7. The version of `m1()` in A is said to ________ the version of `m1()` in B.
8. Which version of `m1()` would be invoked by the expression `obj.m1()`, A's or B's or neither?
9. (True or false) The expression `obj.m2()` will invoke the method `m2()` from B.
10. How could the definition of `m1()` for class A invoke the method `m1()` from class B?
11. In OOD, class ________ are designed in order to take advantage of inheritance.

Exercises 7.8

For Exercises 1–4, draw a diagram that pictures an appropriate class hierarchy to model the given objects.

1. Circle, triangle, square, rectangle, polygon, geometric figure, hexagon
2. Bulldog, Chihuahua, Collie, Miniature Collie, horse, cat, reptile, dog, snake, lizard, canine, mammal, animal
3. Driver's license, chauffeur's license, hunting license, pet license, duck-hunting license, fishing license, deer-hunting license, dog license, marriage license, license
4. Bank account, savings account, loan, checking account, student loan, free checking account, money-market savings account, home equity loan, graduate-school student loan

For Exercises 5–8, add at least 4 more classes to the hierarchies of Exercises 1–4.

5. The hierarchy in Exercise 1
6. The hierarchy in Exercise 2
7. The hierarchy in Exercise 3
8. The hierarchy in Exercise 4

For Exercises 9–11, proceed as in Exercises 5–8, but make a class hierarchy with at least 12 classes with the given class at the top and that contains at least 3 levels.

9. Motorized vehicles
10. Computer equipment
11. Shoes
12. Write declarations for:
    a. A class *License* with a person's name, age, and id number as attributes; a constructor method that initializes the instance variables; and an output method.
    b. A subclass *HuntingLicense* with the name of the prey as a new attribute; a constructor method that initializes the instance variables; an accessor for this new attribute; and an output method that overrides that in the *License* class.
13. Write a declaration for a subclass *DeerHuntingLicense* of the *HuntingLicense* class in Exercise 12 with a new attribute that indicates whether hunting does is permitted, a constructor method that initializes the instance variables, an accessor and a mutator for this new attribute, and an output method that overrides that in the *HuntingLicense* class.

14. Write declarations for:
    a. A class *BankAccount* with a customer's name, account number, and account balance as attributes; a constructor method that initializes the instance variables; and a method that displays the account number and the current balance.
    b. A subclass *CheckingAccount* with service charge as a new attribute; a constructor method that initializes the instance variables; a deposit method; and a withdrawal method.
    c. A subclass *Loan* with interest rate as a new attribute; a constructor method; a make-payment method; and an add-interest method.
15. Write a declaration for a subclass *StudentLoan* that is a subclass of the *Loan* class in Exercise 14 with the loan term (number of years to pay it off) and monthly payment as new attributes; a constructor method that initializes the instance variables; and a method that returns the number of payments remaining.

CHAPTER SUMMARY

Key Terms & Notes

analysis of algorithms
`break` statement
child class
class hierarchy
`continue` statement
counting (or counter-controlled) loop
counting input loop
do loop
`do` statement
end-of-data flag
end-of-file mark
`for` loop
`for` statement
forever loop
grows linearly
`if-break` combination
indefinite loop
infinite recursion
inheritance
initialization list
inner loop
is-a relationship
labeled statement
nested loops
object-oriented design (OOD)
one-trip behavior
outer loop
override
parent class
platform dependent
posttest loop
pretest loop
query-controlled input loop
query function
query the user
repetition
selection
sentinel
sentinel approach
sequence
subclass
superclass
termination condition
test-at-the-bottom loop
trace table
`while` loop
`while` statement
zero-trip behavior

- A trace table is a good tool to trace the action of a loop (especially in debugging).

- By using an appropriate increment expression, a `for` statement can be used to step through a range of values with any increment.
- It is (usually) unwise to change the value of any variables in the loop condition within the body of a counting loop, because this can produce unexpected results; in particular, the number of repetitions may change.
- An indefinite loop can be implemented in C++ with a `for` statement with no loop condition, `for(;;){ ... }`; or a `while` statement of the form `while(true){ ... }` can be used.
- A forever loop continues repetition when its termination condition is false and terminates repetition when that condition is true.
- A `break` statement can be used to terminate execution of an enclosing loop or `switch` statement. It terminates the innermost enclosing loop or `switch`.
- In some cases, a `return` statement is a useful alternative to `break` for terminating execution of a function and returning to the calling function.
- A `continue` statement is useful for skipping the rest of the current iteration and beginning a new one.
- A *while* loop is a *pretest* (or test-at-the-top) loop. It continues repetition so long as its condition is true and terminates repetition when that condition is false. A while loop has *zero-trip behavior*.
- A *do* loop is a *posttest* (or test-at-the-bottom) loop. Because its loop body will always be executed at least once before the loop condition is tested, it is said to have *one-trip behavior*.
- Three common kinds of input loops are
  - *counting* loops in which the number of input items is known in advance;
  - *sentinel-controlled* loops in which an end-of-data flag (or sentinel) signals the end of data, and
  - *query-controlled* loops in which the user is asked whether there is more data
- The following guidelines may help with deciding which kind of loop to use:
  1. If the algorithm requires counting through some fixed range of values, use a counting loop.
  2. If a general loop is required, use a generic indefinite loop to formulate the algorithm. Then determine where the termination condition should go. If at the beginning, use a while loop; if at the end, use a do loop; if somewhere else, use a forever loop with an `if-break` or `if-return`.
- Anytime you find yourself writing redundant code, you should realize that there is probably a better approach.
- The inheritance mechanism is what distinguishes object-oriented languages and design from non-object-oriented approaches.
- A declaration of a child class has the form

```
class ChildClassName : public ParentClassName
{ . . . }
```

- A child class method can invoke a method from its parent class using the notation

```
ParentClassName::ParentClassMethod(arguments)
```

- The constructors and methods of a class should only access directly instance variables that are defined within the same class. Inherited instance variables should be accessed through inherited constructors or methods.
- Object-oriented design (OOD) is the process of designing software that consists of class hierarchies in order to take advantage of inheritance.
- When one class in a hierarchy is corrected or modified in any way—for example, via maintenance or a software upgrade—all of its subclasses automatically inherit the changes.

Programming Pointers

Program Style and Design

1. *The statement in a* `for`, `while`, `do`, *and forever loop is indented. If the statement is compound, the curly braces are aligned with the* `for`, `while`, *or* `do`, *and the statements inside the block are indented. In a* `do` *loop,* `do` *is aligned with its corresponding* `while`:

```
for (...)
   statement
```

```
for (...)
{
   statement_1
      .
      .
      .
   statement_n
}
```

```
while(loop_condition)
   statement
```

```
while(loop_condition)
{
   statement_1
      .
      .
      .
   statement_n
}
```

```
do
   statement
while (loop_condition);
```

```
do
{
   statement_1
      .
      .
      .
   statement_n
}
while (loop_condition);
```

2. *Sequence, selection, and repetition are the only control structures needed to compute anything that can be computed.*
3. *Repetition structures can be implemented in C++ using the* `for`, `while`, *and* `do` *statements, and it is important to select the one that best implements the repetition structure required in a given problem* Some guidelines for choosing the appropriate loop are as follows:
   - *The* `for` *loop is most appropriate for performing repetition when the number of repetitions can be determined before the loop is entered .*

- *The* `while` *loop is most appropriate for performing repetition when zero-trip behavior is desired.* Since the loop condition appears at the top of the loop, the body of the loop will not be entered inadvertently if the loop condition is false initially.
- *The* `do` *loop is most appropriate for performing repetition when one-trip behavior is desired.* Since the loop condition appears at the bottom of the loop, the body of the loop will be executed at least once before repetition is terminated.
- *The forever loop can be used to perform repetition when neither zero-trip nor one-trip behavior is desired.* An `if-break` or an `if-return` combination is usually used to terminate repetition.

Potential Pitfalls

1. *Care must be taken to avoid infinite looping* .

   - The loop condition of a `for` loop must eventually become *false;* the body of a `while` loop or a `do` loop must contain statements that eventually cause its loop condition to become *false*. For example, the code fragment

     ```
     x = 0.0;
     do
     {
        cout << x << endl;
        x += 0.3;
     }
     while (x != 1.0);
     ```

     produces an infinite loop:

     ```
     0.0
     0.3
     0.6
     0.9
     1.2
     1.5
     1.8
     .
     .
     .
     ```

     Since the value of `x` is never equal to 1.0, repetition is not terminated.

   - The body of a forever loop should always contain an `if-break` or `if-return` combination, and statements that ensure that the termination condition of the loop will eventually become true.

2. *In a* `while` *loop, the loop condition that controls repetition is evaluated before execution of the body of the loop. In a* `do` *loop, the loop condition that controls repetition is evaluated after execution of the body of the loop.* Thus, the body of a `while` loop will not be executed if the loop condition is false initially, but the statements in a `do` loop are always executed at least once.
3. *The* `for`, `while`, `do`, *and forever loops control a single statement* For example, the following poorly indented segment

```
for (int i = 1; i <= 10; i++)
   j = i*i;
   cout << j << endl;
```

will display only a single value,

```
100
```

since the output statement is outside the body of the loop. Likewise, the segment

```
int count = 1;
while (count <= 10)
   cout << count << '\t' << count*count << endl;
   count++;
```

will produce an infinite loop,

```
1     1
1     1
1     1
   .
   .
   .
```

because the statement that increments `count` is outside the body of the loop.

4. *In a* `do` *loop, the closing* `while (`*`loop_condition`*`)` *must be followed by a semicolon, or a syntax error will result.*
5. *In a* `for` *loop, neither the control variable nor any variable involved in the loop condition should be modified within the body of the loop, since it is intended to run through a specified range of values* Strange and undesirable results may be produced otherwise. To illustrate, the statement

```
for (int i = 1; i <= 4; i++)
{
   cout << i << endl;
   i++;
}
```

produces the output

```
1
3
```

The statement

```
for (int i = 1; i <= 4; i++)
{
   cout << i << endl;
   i--;
}
```

results in an infinite loop, displaying the output

```
1
1
1
```

```
1
.
.
.
```

6. *Each use of the equality operator in a loop condition should be double checked to make certain that the assignment operator is not being used* Using = instead of == is one of the easiest errors to make. This error is illustrated by the following code fragment:

```
do
{
   // ... do some processing ...

   cout << "Do you wish to continue (y or n)? ";
   cin >> answer;
}
while (answer = 'y');
```

This loop will be executed infinitely many times, regardless of what the user enters, because

1. the loop condition is an *assignment* that sets `answer` to `y` (it is not a *comparison*);
2. the assignment operator (=) produces the value that was assigned as its result;
3. this assignment thus produces the value 121 (the ASCII value of character `y`); and
4. C++ treats any nonzero value as true.

Similarly, the forever loop

```
for
{
   cout << "\nPlease enter an integer value (0 to quit): ";
   cin >> value;

   if (value = 0) break;

   // ... do something with value ...
}
```

is an infinite loop, because the termination condition in its `if-break` combination is an assignment, not a comparison. Because the result of that assignment is zero, and C++ uses zero to represent the value false, this termination condition will always be false, and so the `break` statement will never be executed.

7. *Invoking a parent-class method from within a child-class method overriding it without using a qualifier of the form* `ParentClass::` *will result in infinite recursion.*

Programming Problems

Section 7.4

1. Write a driver program to test the power function of Exercise 23.
2. Write a driver program to test the power function of Exercise 24.
3. Write a driver program to test the sum-of-divisors function of Exercise 25.
4. Write a driver program to test the prime-checker function of Exercise 26.
5. Write a driver program to test the power-of-two function of Exercise 27.

6. Write a program that displays the following multiplication table:

	1	2	3	4	5	6	7	8	9
1	1								
2	2	4							
3	3	6	9						
4	4	8	12	16					
5	5	10	15	20	25				
6	6	12	18	24	30	36			
7	7	14	21	28	35	42	49		
8	8	16	24	32	40	45	56	64	
9	9	18	27	36	45	54	63	72	81

7. A positive integer is said to be a *deficient, perfect*, or *abundant* number if the sum of its proper divisors is less than, equal to, or greater than the number, respectively. For example, 8 is deficient because its proper divisors are 1, 2, and 4, and $1 + 2 + 4 < 8$; 6 is perfect, because $1 + 2 + 3 = 6$; 12 is abundant, because $1 + 2 + 3 + 4 + 6 > 12$. Write a program that classifies n as being deficient, perfect, or abundant for $n = 20$ to 30, then for $n = 490$ to 500, and finally for $n = 8120$ to 8130. It should use the function from Exercise 25 to find the sum of the proper divisors. *Extra:* Find the smallest odd abundant number. *Warning:* An attempt to find an odd perfect number will probably fail, because none has ever been found although it has not been proven that such numbers do not exist.

8. The Rinky Dooflingy Company currently sells 200 dooflingies per month at a profit of $300 per dooflingy. The company now spends $2000 per month on advertising and has fixed operating costs of $1000 per month that do not depend on the volume of sales. If the company doubles the amount spent on advertising, sales will increase by 20 percent. Write a program that displays under appropriate headings the amount spent on advertising, the number of sales made, and the net profit. Begin with the company's current status, and successively double the amount spent on advertising until the net profit "goes over the hump," that is, begins to decline. The output should include the amounts up through the first time that the net profit begins to decline.

9. The *divide-and-average* algorithm for approximating the square root of any positive number a is as follows: Take any initial approximation x that is positive, and then find a new approximation by calculating the average of x and a / x, that is, $(x + a / x) / 2$. Repeat this procedure with x replaced by this new approximation, stopping when x and a / x differ in absolute value by some specified error allowance, such as 0.00001. Write a program that reads values for x, a, and the small error allowance and then uses this divide-and-average algorithm to find the approximate square root of x. Have the program display each of the successive approximations. Execute the program with $a = 3$ and error allowance = 0.00001, and use the following initial approximations: 1, 10, 0.01, and 100. Also execute the program with $a = 4$, error allowance = 0.00001, and initial approximations 1 and 2.

10. Write a program that accepts a positive integer and gives its prime factorization; that is, expresses the integer as a product of primes or indicates that it is a prime. (See Exercise 26 for the definition of a prime number.)

Sections 7.5–7.6

11. Write a program to read a set of numbers, count them, and find and print the largest and smallest numbers in the list and their positions in the list.

12. Write a program that reads an exchange rate for converting English currency to U.S. currency and then reads several values in English currency and converts each amount to the equivalent U.S. currency. Display all amounts with appropriate labels. Use sentinel-controlled or end-of-file-controlled loops for the input.

13. Proceed as in the Problem 12, but convert several values from U.S. currency to English currency.

14. One method for finding the *base-b representation* of a positive integer given in base-10 notation is to divide the integer repeatedly by *b* until a quotient of zero results. The successive remainders are the digits from right to left of the base-*b* representation. For example, the binary representation of 26 is 11010_2, as the following computation shows:

$$
\begin{array}{r}
0 \text{ R } 1 \\
2\overline{)1} \text{ R } 1 \\
2\overline{)3} \text{ R } 0 \\
2\overline{)6} \text{ R } 1 \\
2\overline{)13} \text{ R } 0 \\
2\overline{)26} \phantom{\text{ R } 0}
\end{array}
$$

Write a program to accept various integers and bases and display the digits of the base-*b* representation (in reverse order) for each integer. You may assume that each base is in the range 2 through 10.

15. Proceed as in Problem 14, but convert integers from base 10 to hexadecimal (base 16). Use a `switch` statement to display the symbols A, B, C, D, E, and F for 10, 11, 12, 13, 14, and 15, respectively.

16. Write a program that reads the amount of a loan, the annual interest rate, and a monthly payment and then displays the payment number, the interest for that month, the balance remaining after that payment, and the total interest paid to date in a table with appropriate headings. (The monthly interest is $r / 12$ percent of the unpaid balance after the payment is subtracted, where r is the annual interest rate.) Use a function to display these tables. Design the program so it can process several different loan amounts, interest rates, and monthly payments, including at least the following triples of values: $100, 18 percent, $10 and $500, 12 percent, $25. (*Note:* In general, the last payment will not be the same as the monthly payment; the program should show the exact amount of the last payment due.)

17. Proceed as in Problem 16, but with the following modifications: During program execution, have the user enter a payment amount and a day of the month on which this payment was made. The monthly interest is to be calculated on the *average daily balance* for that month. (Assume, for simplicity, that the billing date is the first of the month.) For example, if the balance on June 1 is $500 and a payment of $20 is received on June 12, the interest will be computed on (500 * 11 + 480 * 19) / 30 dollars, which represents the average daily balance for that month.

18. Suppose that on January 1, April 1, July 1, and October 1 of each year, some fixed *amount* is invested and earns interest at some annual interest rate r compounded quarterly (that is, $r / 4$ percent is added at the end of each quarter). Write a program that reads a number of years and that calculates and displays a table showing the year, the yearly dividend (total interest earned for that year), and the total savings accumulated through that year. Design the program to process several different inputs and to call a function to display the table for each input.

19. *A possible modification/addition to your program:* Instead of investing *amount* dollars each quarter, invest *amount* / 3 dollars on the first of each month. Then in each quarter, the first payment earns interest for three months ($r / 4$ percent), the second for two months ($r / 6$ percent), and the third for one month ($r / 12$ percent).

Section 7.8

20. Modify Programming Problem 29 of Chapter 6 for displaying people's age on their birthday this year so that it uses the `TitledName` class instead of the `Name` class.
21. Write a program to test the license classes and subclasses in Exercises 12 and 13.
22. Write a program to test the bank account classes and subclasses in Exercises 14 and 15.

CHAPTER 8

Functions in Depth

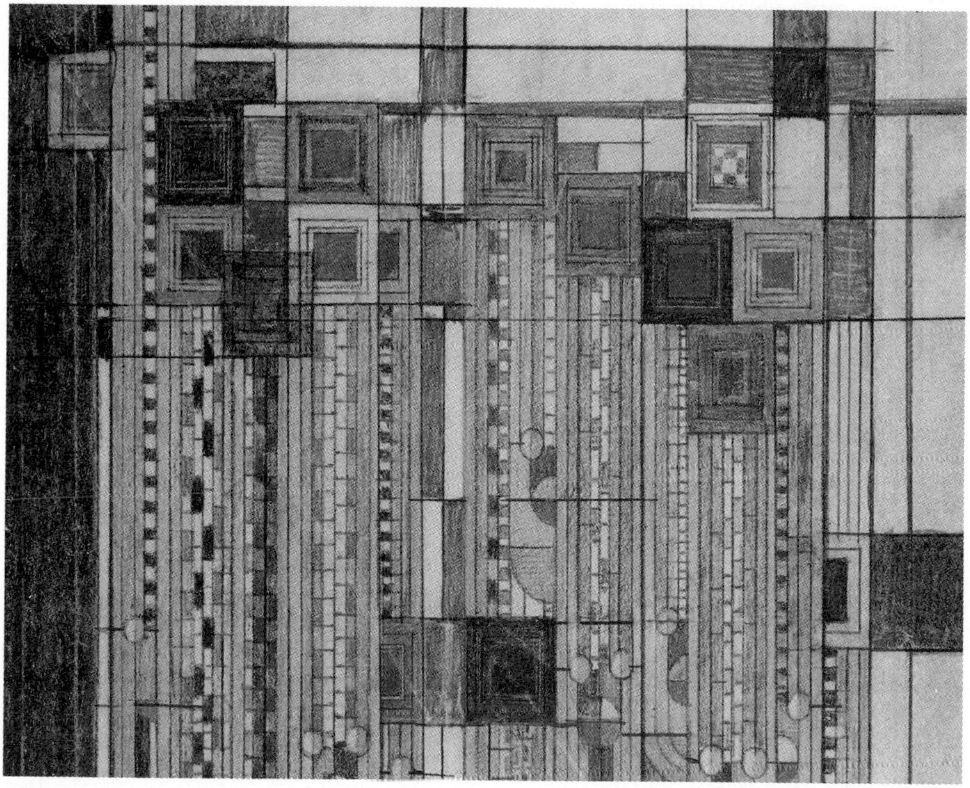

On two occasions I have been asked [by members of Parliament], 'Pray, Mr. Babbage, if you put into the machine wrong figures, will the right answers come out?' I am not able rightly to apprehend the kind of confusion of ideas that could provoke such a question.

-Charles Babbage

Fudd's law states: "What goes in must come out." Aside from being patently untrue, Fudd's law neglects to mention that what comes out need not bear any resemblance to what went in.

-V. Orehck III (fictitious)

So, Naturalists observe, a flea

Hath smaller fleas that on him prey;

And these have smaller fleas to bite 'em
and so proceed ad infinitum.

-Jonathan Swift

Before one can understand recursion, one must understand recursion.

-V. Orehck III (fictitious)

Chapter Contents

Chapter Objectives

- Expand on the introduction to functions in Chapter 4.
- Take a detailed look at parameter passing—reference parameters in particular.
- See what the advantages of inlining are and when it should be used.
- Study C++'s scope rules, function overloading, and templates.
- (Optional) Introduce recursion by describing it and illustrating it with two examples.
- (Optional) Take a first look at numerical computing.
- (Optional) Expand on earlier discussions of class and instance variables and examine scope rules for classes.

We have seen that designing a solution to a problem involves identifying the *objects* needed to solve the problem as well as the *operations* that must be applied to those objects. Thus far the problems we have examined have required operations that were either provided by C++ or were such that functions could easily be constructed to perform them. Functions are thus one mechanism to implement operations not provided in C++.

In this chapter, we study C++ functions in greater detail. We begin by introducing *reference parameters*, a new mechanism for passing values to and from functions. We then look at inlining, scope, overloading, templates, and recursion. The *Part of the Picture* section introduces the area of computer science that studies numerical methods and some of their applications, and the optional *OBJECTive Thinking* section examines scope rules for classes and the special role of destructor methods.

8.1 Introductory Example: One-Step Integer Division

PROBLEM

We saw in Chapter 3 that C++ provides separate operators for calculating the quotient and the remainder that result when one integer is divided by another integer:

> `op1 / op2` produces the *quotient* of the division of `op1` by `op2` and
>
> `op1 % op2` produces the *remainder* of the division of `op1` by `op2`.

Thus, the expression `5 / 3` produces `1`, the quotient of the division, and `5 % 3` produces the remainder `2`. Suppose that we want to perform both of these operations in a single step. Can we write a C++ function that, given two integer operands, returns both the quotient and the remainder?

Object-Centered Design

Behavior. Our function should receive two integer operands. It should compute and return the quotient and the remainder that result when the first integer is divided by the second, provided that the second operand is not zero.

Objects. Four problem objects can be identified from our behavioral description:

	Software Objects			
Problem Objects	**Type**	**Kind**	**Movement**	**Name**
the first operand	`int`	varying	received (in)	*op1*
the second operand	`int`	varying	received (in)	*op2*
the quotient of their division	`int`	varying	returned (out)	*quotient*
the remainder of their division	`int`	varying	returned (out)	*remainder*

Note that two numbers (*quotient* and *remainder*) are to be returned by the function. Technically, a C++ function cannot *return* two values because execution of a `return` statement immediately terminates execution of the function. Thus it will not work to write

```
int divideInts(int op1, int op2)
{
   return op1 / op2;
   return op1 % op2;   // Execution won't get here!
}
```

because the second `return` statement will never be reached, since execution of the function will terminate when the first `return` statement is reached. Moreover, a function's `return` statement has the form

```
return expression;
```

and so only a single value can be returned to the caller using the `return` statement.[1]

Since we cannot return multiple values, we might try to communicate back to the caller through some additional parameters. For example, we might try writing

```
int divideInts(int op1, int op2, int quotient, int remainder)
{
   quotient = op1 / op2;
   remainder = op1 % op2;
}
```

and then call the function as follows:

```
int quot = 0,
    rem = 0;
divideInts(4, 3, quot, rem);
```

This is a good idea, but unfortunately, it will not work because C++ parameters are by default *copies* of their corresponding arguments. That is, the parameter `quotient` contains a copy of its argument `quot`, and the parameter `remainder` contains a copy of its argument `rem`. When it executes, `divideInts()` modifies these copies, leaving the arguments `quot` and `rem` unchanged.

What we need is a way to "turn off" this mechanism that causes parameters to be copies of their arguments. For this purpose, C++ provides **reference parameters** that, instead of being copies of their parameters, refer all accesses directly back to their arguments. Since we will use this mechanism, we should amend our object list as follows:

	Software Objects			
Problem Objects	**Type**	**Kind**	**Movement**	**Name**
the first operand	`int`	varying	received (in)	*op1*
the second operand	`int`	varying	received (in)	*op2*
the quotient of their division	`int`	varying	sent back (out)	*quotient*
the remainder of their division	`int`	varying	sent back (out)	*remainder*

1. The `return` statement can also be used without an expression; in this case, execution of the function terminates but no value is returned—the function is a `void` **function**.

This gives the following specification:

Receive: *op1*, an integer, and
op2, an integer

Precondition: $op2 \neq 0$

Send back: *quotient*, an integer, and
remainder, an integer

The stub for a function satisfying this specification is as follows:

```
void divideInts(int op1, int op2,
                int& quotient, int& remainder)
{
}
```

An ampersand (`&`) in a parameter declaration specifies that the parameter is a reference parameter. Ordinary parameters (like `op1` and `op2`) are copies of their arguments, and so only move values *into* a function; reference parameters (like `quotient` and `remainder`) refer back to their arguments, and so move values both *into and out of* a function.

Operations. From our behavioral description, we have the following operations:

i. Check that an integer (*op2*) is nonzero
ii. Compute the *quotient* from the division of two integers
iii. Compute the *remainder* from the division of two integers

Algorithm. These steps comprise an algorithm for our problem:

Algorithm for One-Step Integer Division

1. Check that *op2* is nonzero. If it is, terminate execution.
2. Compute *quotient* = *op1* / *op2*.
3. Compute *remainder* = *op1* % *op2*.

Coding. Figure 8.1 shows the complete definition of the function. Note that because values are communicated back to the caller via reference parameters, `void` is used to indicate that the function returns no value (via a `return` statement).

Fig. 8.1 One-step integer division. (Part 1 of 2)

```
/* divideInts performs integer division in 1 step.
 *
 * Receive:      op1 and op2, two integers
 * Precondition: op2 is nonzero
 * Send back:    quotient and remainder, two integers
 * Uses:         assert()
 ****************************************************************/
```

Fig. 8.1 One-step integer division. (Part 2 of 2)

```
void divideInts(int op1, int op2, int& quotient, int& remainder)
{
   assert (op2 != 0);
   quotient = op1 / op2;
   remainder = op1 % op2;
}
```

Testing. Figure 8.2 presents a simple driver program that tests this function by displaying a table of division results obtained by repeatedly calling `divideInts()`.

Fig. 8.2 Driver program for `divideInts()`. (Part 1 of 2)

```
/* intDivision.cpp displays a table of integer division results.
 *
 * Output: A table of the quotients and remainders produced by
 *         the divisions i/j with i and j running from 1 to 4
 ******************************************************************/

#include <iostream>                    // <<, cout, endl
#include <cassert>                     // assert()
using namespace std;

void divideInts(int op1, int op2, int& quotient, int& remainder);

int main()
{
   cout << "                         Division Table\n\n";

   int quot,                           // variables to hold the values
       rem;                            //  sent back from divideInts()

   for (int j = 1; j <= 4; j++)
   {
      for (int i = 1; i <= 4; i++)
      {
         divideInts(i, j, quot, rem);
         cout << i << " divided by " << j
              << " gives a quotient of " << quot
              << " and a remainder of " << rem << endl;
      }
      cout << endl;
   }
}
```

Fig. 8.2 Driver program for `divideInts()`. (Part 2 of 2)

```
/*** Insert definition of divideInts() from Figure 8.1 here. ***/
```

Sample run:

```
                Division Table

1 divided by 1 gives a quotient of 1 and a remainder of 0
2 divided by 1 gives a quotient of 2 and a remainder of 0
3 divided by 1 gives a quotient of 3 and a remainder of 0
4 divided by 1 gives a quotient of 4 and a remainder of 0

1 divided by 2 gives a quotient of 0 and a remainder of 1
2 divided by 2 gives a quotient of 1 and a remainder of 0
3 divided by 2 gives a quotient of 1 and a remainder of 1
4 divided by 2 gives a quotient of 2 and a remainder of 0

1 divided by 3 gives a quotient of 0 and a remainder of 1
2 divided by 3 gives a quotient of 0 and a remainder of 2
3 divided by 3 gives a quotient of 1 and a remainder of 0
4 divided by 3 gives a quotient of 1 and a remainder of 1

1 divided by 4 gives a quotient of 0 and a remainder of 1
2 divided by 4 gives a quotient of 0 and a remainder of 2
3 divided by 4 gives a quotient of 0 and a remainder of 3
4 divided by 4 gives a quotient of 1 and a remainder of 0
```

Note that the driver program displays (among other things) the values of the arguments `quot` and `rem`. It should be evident from the sample run that each time function `divideInts()` assigns values to its parameters `quotient` and `remainder`, the values of the corresponding arguments `quot` and `rem` are changed in the driver. Each call to function `divideInts()` thus moves two values back to its caller; by changing the values of its two reference parameters, it simultaneously changes the values of their corresponding arguments.

Once tested, `divideInts()` can be stored in a library (e.g., `MyMath`) for reuse by other programs. Such programs need only include the library's header file and then link in the object file produced by compiling its implementation file.

8.2 Parameters in Depth

The rule that governs the relationship between an argument (the value supplied when a function is called) and its corresponding parameter (the variable in the function's heading for storing the argument) is called a **parameter-passing mechanism**. In this section, we examine the various mechanisms available in C++ for passing parameters.

VALUE PARAMETERS

The simplest parameter-passing mechanism is the one that occurs by default. It is named **call-by-value**, and parameters whose values are passed using this mechanism are called **value parameters**. The rule governing them is as follows:

Value Parameter

Form:

```
type parameter_name
```

Description: A value parameter is a *distinct variable* containing a *copy* of its argument. Therefore, any modification of a value parameter within the body of a function *has no effect on the value* of its corresponding argument.

All of the parameters that we have seen in earlier chapters have been value parameters. For example, in the temperature-conversion function in Figure 4.2,

```
double fahrToCelsius(double tempFahr)
{
   return (tempFahr - 32.0) / 1.8;
}
```

the variable `tempFahr` is a value parameter. If `theHighTemp` is a `double` variable whose value is 92.0 and we call

```
celsTemp = fahrToCelsius(theHighTemp);
```

then a memory location is allocated for parameter `tempFahr` and the value of `the-HighTemp` (92.0) is *copied* into it. The function then is executed using this value.

Similarly, in the `mascot()` function in Figure 6.1,

```
string mascot(string university)
{
   if (university == "Illinois")
      return "Fighting Illini";
   else if (university == "Indiana")
      return "Hoosiers";
            .
            .
            .
}
```

the parameter `university` is a value parameter. If `school` is a `string` variable whose value is `"Michigan State"`, then when this function is called,

```
cout << mascot(school) << endl;
```

a memory location is allocated for parameter `university` and the value of `school` is copied into it. The function is then executed using this value.

NOTE

Because a value parameter is a distinct variable containing a copy of its argument, *any changes a function makes to a value parameter have no effect on the corresponding argument*. Thus, we could have written the factorial function from Figure 4.8 as follows:

```
int factorial(int n)
{
   assert(n >= 0);

   int product = 1;

   while (n > 1)
   {
      product *= n;
      n--;
   }

   return product;
}
```

Because parameter `n` is a distinct variable containing a copy of whatever argument is passed, function `factorial()` can freely change the value of `n` without changing the value of the corresponding argument in the caller.

REFERENCE PARAMETERS

If we examine the function `divideInts()` in Figure 8.1,

```
void divideInts(int op1, int op2,
                int& quotient, int& remainder)
{
   quotient = op1 / op2;
   remainder = op1 % op2;
}
```

we see that the parameters `op1` and `op2` are value parameters. However, the parameters `quotient` and `remainder` have an ampersand (`&`) between their type and their name. When used this way in a parameter declaration, the ampersand indicates that values should be passed to the parameter using the **call-by-reference** mechanism. Such parameters are thus called **reference parameters**. The rule governing them is as follows:

Reference Parameter

Form:

```
type& parameter_name
```

Description: Reference parameters are *aliases* of (alternate names for) their corresponding arguments.

Therefore, any change to the value of a reference parameter within the body of a function *changes the value* of its corresponding argument.

To illustrate, suppose that `i` is 5 and `j` is 3 in the function call

```
divideInts(i, j, quot, rem);
```

The value parameters `op1` and `op2` are distinct variables into which the arguments `i` and `j` are copied:

By contrast, `quotient` and `remainder` are reference parameters, and so they become aliases, or alternative names, for their arguments `quot` and `rem`:

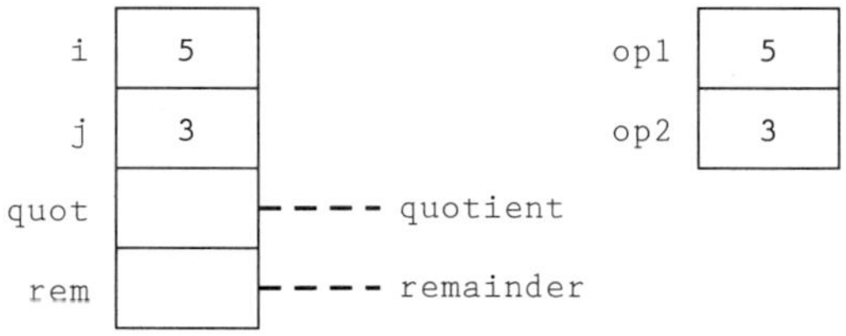

This means that when function `divideInts()` assigns a value to its reference parameter `quotient`, the value of the corresponding argument `quot` is changed,

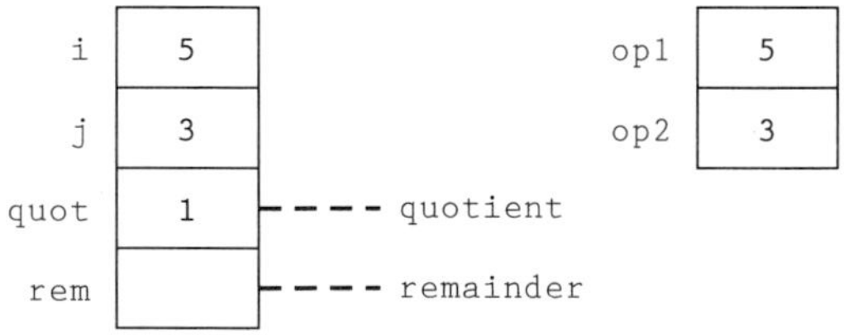

and when `divideInts()` assigns a value to its reference parameter `remainder`, the value of the corresponding argument `rem` is changed:

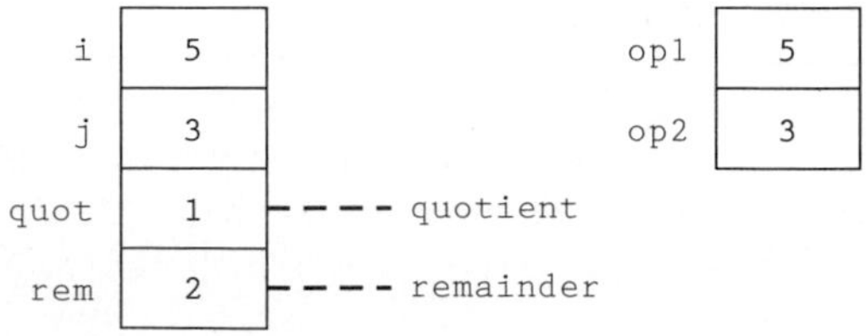

Thus, to design a function like `divideInts()` that sends back more than one value to its caller, we can proceed as follows:

1. Define a reference parameter for each value to be communicated back to the caller:

```
void divideInts(int op1, int op2,
                int& quotient, int& remainder)
```

2. Assign to the reference parameters the values that must be communicated back:

```
quotient = op1 / op2;
remainder = op1 % op2;
```

3. Call the function with a *variable* argument for each reference parameter:

```
divideInts(i, j, quot, rem);
```

When the function terminates, the values of the argument variables will be changed to the values the function assigned to its reference parameters.

WATCH OUT

Common Errors. Because reference parameters can change the values of the corresponding arguments, these arguments must be objects whose values can be changed, that is, they must be variables. The argument corresponding to a value parameter can be a constant or literal, but *the argument corresponding to a reference parameter must be a* ***variable***. For example, the function call

```
divideInts(40, 3, 4, 5);
```

causes a compilation error because `4` and `5` are not variables. By contrast, if `quot` and `rem` are the `int` variables defined earlier, then the call

```
divideInts(40, 3, quot, rem);
```

is valid. Following the call, the value of `quot` will be 13 and the value of `rem` will be 1.

The type of an argument corresponding to a reference parameter must match the type of that parameter. Thus, if `doubleQuot` and `doubleRem` are `double` variables and we call `divideInts()` with them as arguments,

```
divideInts(40, 3, doubleQuot, doubleRem);
```

a compilation error will result because their types do not match the types of their corresponding parameters.

`const` REFERENCE PARAMETERS

From the preceding discussion, it may seem that when an object's movement is *out of* (and perhaps also *into*) a function, it should be passed using the *call-by-reference* mechanism, and when movement is *only into* a function, it should be passed using the *call-by-value* mechanism. However, there is an alternative to the call-by-value mechanism that is sometimes preferred.

A Problem with Value Parameters. As we have seen, a call-by-reference parameter is an alias of its argument, but a call-by-value parameter is a distinct variable into which the argument's value is copied. When the type of a value parameter is one of the fundamental types (e.g., `int`, `char`, `double`, . . .), the time needed to do this copying is usually negligible, but it might not be when the argument being passed is a *class object* (e.g., `string`, `ostream`, or `istream`).

To illustrate, recall that the `mascot()` function in Figure 6.1 had a value parameter whose type was `string`:

```
string mascot(string university)
{
   if (university == "Illinois")
      return "Fighting Illini";
   else if (university == "Indiana")
      return "Hoosiers";
            .
            .
            .
}
```

Suppose that `mascot()` is called with `school` as an argument,

```
cout << mascot(school) << endl;
```

where `school` is a `string` variable whose value is `"Penn State"`. Before `mascot()` can begin execution, two actions must occur:

1. Sufficient space must be allocated for the parameter `university` to hold its argument:

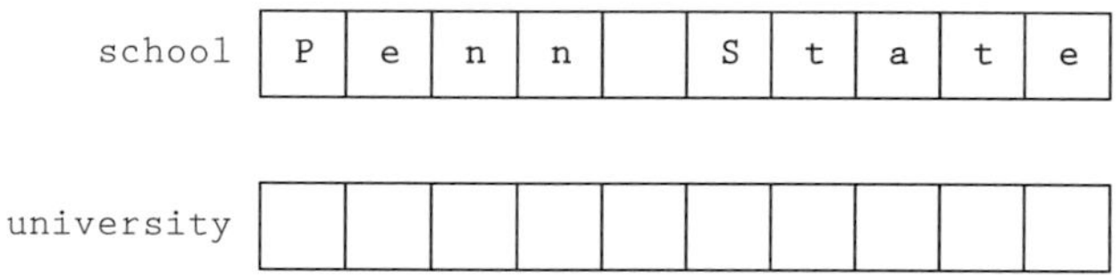

2. The argument must be copied into this space:

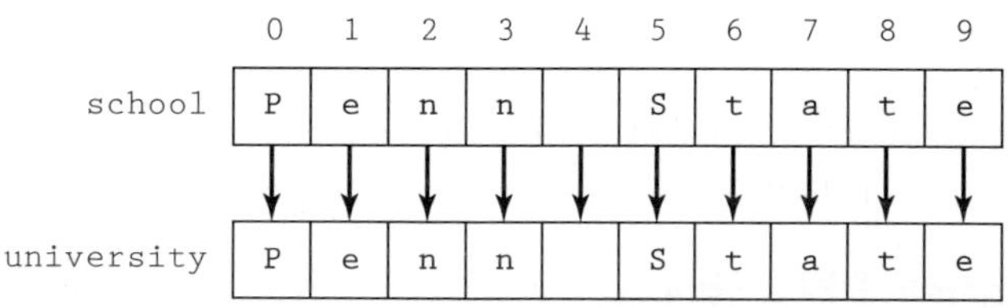

In this example, ten characters must be copied into the parameter's space, and the longer the argument, the greater the number of characters that must be copied. Such copying takes time, increasing the overall execution time of the function. In general, *if a parameter whose type is a class is a value parameter, then the corresponding class argument must be copied, which can be time inefficient.*

NOTE

Reference Parameters. Call-by-reference does not suffer this time inefficiency because a reference parameter is an alias for its argument—no copying is required. To avoid the time-consuming copying of values required by call-by-value, many programmers in languages other than C++ always pass large arguments such as classes by reference, regardless of whether their movement is out of or into the function. To illustrate, suppose that we make `university` a reference parameter in the function `mascot()`:

```
string mascot(string& university)
{
      .
      .
      .
}
```

Then, in a call like

```
cout << mascot(school) << endl;
```

the parameter `university` simply becomes an alias for its argument `school`:

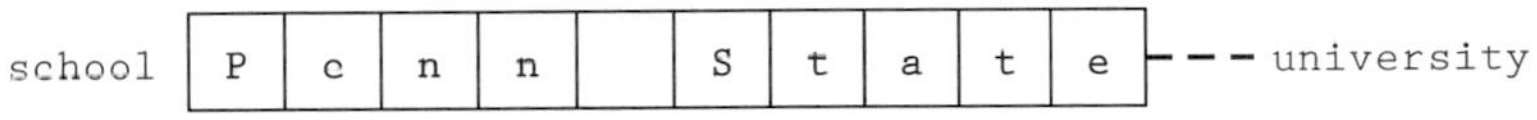

No copying occurs, avoiding the time inefficiency of the call-by-value mechanism.

There is a danger with this approach, however. Suppose that the definition of function `mascot()` contains the common error of using assignment (=) instead of comparison (==) in the `if` statement:

```
string mascot(string& university)
{
   if (university = "Illinois")
      return "Fighting Illini";
            .
            .
            .
}
```

As explained in Section 6.2, `university` will be assigned the string `"Illinois"`. The result of this assignment is this string, and since it is nonzero, it will be treated as `true` in this context, causing `"Fighting Illini"` to be returned regardless of the original value of `university`. This is obviously an error. But a much more serious and much less obvious error occurs when this function is called as in

```
cout << mascot(school) << endl;
```

where `school` has the value `"Penn State"`. Since `university` is a reference parameter, it is an alias for its argument `school`, and so the change in the value of `university` also changes the value of `school` from `"Penn State"` to `"Illinois"`, which compounds the error!

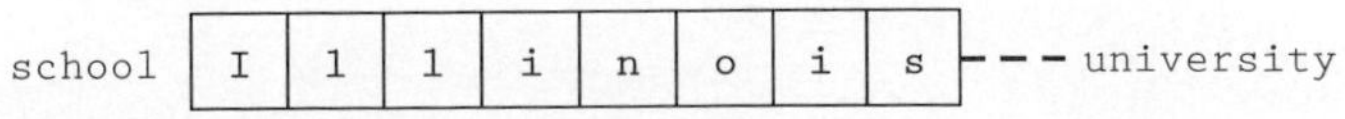

WATCH OUT

This is the danger with reference parameters: *If a function mistakenly changes the value of a reference parameter, the value of the corresponding argument is also changed, and the compiler cannot detect such mistakes.* Because of such unintended or unexpected changes, one should look carefully at the prototype of each function that is used to see if it has reference parameters.

It follows that for safety reasons, one should not use reference parameters in functions simply to avoid the inefficiency of the call-by-value mechanism (unless they are declared to be const as shown next). Also, when a function needs to pass back only one value, a `return` statement should be used and not a reference parameter. Safety is increased and, in addition, such functions (unlike void functions) can be called from within an expression.

`const` **Reference Parameters.** C++ provides a third method for passing parameters called the `const` **reference mechanism** that, for values whose movement is *in only,* avoids both the time inefficiency of the call-by-value mechanism and the potential for error of the call-by-reference mechanism. To illustrate, the parameter `university` in `mascot` can be defined as a `const` reference parameter as follows:

```
string mascot(const string& university)
{
   if (university == "Illinois")
      return "Fighting Illini";
          .
          .
          .
}
```

The effect of the `const` reference mechanism is twofold:

1. Like the reference mechanism, a `const` reference parameter is an *alias* of its corresponding argument, and so no time is wasted copying the argument:

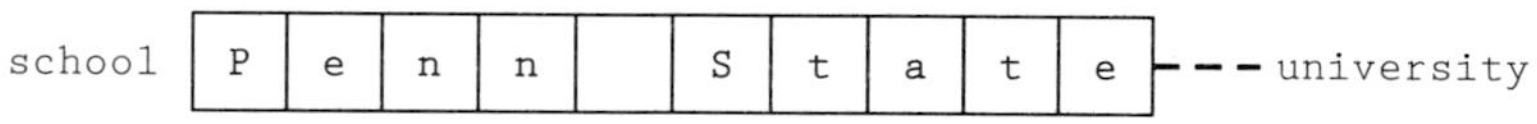

2. Unlike the reference mechanism, a `const` reference parameter is a **read-only** variable, which means that if the function tries to change the value of the parameter, the compiler will generate an error message, alerting the programmer to the mistake:

```
string mascot(const string& university)
{
   if (university = "Illinois")
                              // COMPILATION ERROR (Good!)
      return "Fighting Illini";
          .
          .
          .
}
```

NOTE

For these reasons, *the* `const` *reference mechanism is the preferred way to define parameters whose types are classes (or other large objects) and whose movement is in but not out of a function or method.*

USING PARAMETERS

Learning to use the three different kinds of parameters correctly is not difficult, but it does require us to expand the way we think about constructing functions. To define a function's parameters, a programmer must know precisely the *movement* of the function's objects: What values are received by the function (*in* values) and what values are returned to the caller (*out* values). Jumping in and writing a function without having a clear specification of the problem that includes a description of how values move into and out of the function often leads to wasted work.

Once the movement of a function's objects is known, the following guidelines can be used to decide what kind of parameters are needed:

P1. If a value is only received by a function from its caller and its type is a fundamental type, define a *value parameter* to receive that object. This is also the case if the function needs to make a copy of a received object so that this copy can be changed.

P2. If a value is only received by a function from its caller and its type is a class (or it is some other large object), define a `const` *reference parameter* to receive that value.

P3. If only one value must be communicated back to its caller, then have the *function return* that value as its result via a `return` statement.

P4. If more than one value must be communicated back to its caller, use *reference parameters* for those values to change argument variables in the caller.

The examples in the next section illustrate how these rules can be applied.

8.3 Examples of Parameter Usage

There are many problems that require passing more than one value back to the function's caller. In this section we consider three such problems: decomposing a name, designing a coin dispenser, and swapping the values of two variables. To save space, we will abbreviate the derivations of their solutions.

PROBLEM 1: DECOMPOSING A NAME

A person's full name has three parts: a first name, a middle name, and a last name. Our first problem is to write a function that, given a person's full name, passes back his or her first name, middle name, and last name.

Behavior. The function must receive from its caller a full name. It must decompose this full name into a first name, a middle name, and a last name, and send all of these back to the caller.

Objects. From the behavior, we can identify the following objects:

Problem Objects	Software Objects			
	Type	Kind	Movement	Name
full name	`string`	varying	received (in)	*fullName*
the first name	`string`	varying	send back (out)	*firstName*
the middle name	`string`	varying	send back (out)	*middleName*
the last name	`string`	varying	send back (out)	*lastName*

This gives the following specification for the function:

Receive: *fullName*, a `string` value

Precondition: *fullName* contains a *firstName, a middleName,* and a *lastName*, separated by spaces

Send Back: *firstName, middleName, lastName*

Because *fullName* is a class object that is received from its caller, we define it as a `const` reference parameter, according to Rule P2 in the preceding section. Because *firstName, middleName* and *lastName* are communicated back to the caller, we define these objects as reference parameters, according to Rule P4. This gives the following stub for our function:

```
void decomposeName(const string& fullName, string& firstName,
                   string& middleName, string& lastName)
{
}
```

Operations. In order to decompose *fullName* into its three components, we must perform the following operations:

i. Extract and assign the first name in *fullName* to *firstName*
ii. Extract and assign the second name in *fullName* to *middleName*
iii. Extract and assign the third name in *fullName* to *lastName*

One way to accomplish this[2] is to use the `string` method `substr()` to do the extraction, but it requires the index at which to begin and the number of characters to be extracted. To see how to find these, we will work through an example.

Suppose that `fullName` is `"John Quincy Doe"`:

`fullName`	J	o	h	n		Q	u	i	n	c	y		D	o	e
	0	1	2	3	4	5	6	7	8	9	10	11	12	13	14

2. See Section 9.4 for a simpler approach using the `sstream` library.

For the first name, the index at which to begin is zero; the index for the middle name is one past the first blank (5); and for the last name, the index is one past the second blank (12). We thus need to find the index values of the first and second blanks, and for this we can use the `string` function member `find()`.

The number of characters to be extracted for the first name is equal to the index of the first blank (4). For the second name it is equal to the index of the second blank (11) minus the index of the first blank (4) minus one (= 6). The number of characters to be extracted for the last name is equal to the size of the `fullName` (15) minus the index of the second blank (11) minus one (= 3). Note that, for simplicity, we are assuming that only one blank separates the first, middle, and last names.

Algorithm. We can organize these observations into the following algorithm:

Algorithm for Name Decomposition

1. Use `find()` to find the index of the first blank in *fullName*.
2. Use `substr()` to extract *firstName*.
3. Use `find()` to find the index of the second blank in *fullName*.
4. Use `substr()` to extract *middleName*.
5. Use `size()` and the result of 3 to find the number of characters in *lastName*.
6. Use `substr()` to extract *lastName*.

Coding. Given this algorithm, we can define our function as shown in Figure 8.3, which also contains a driver program to test it. Note that because a search can fail, it is always a good idea to check the value returned by `find()`, either with an `assert()` (as in `decomposeName()`) or with an `if` statement.

Fig. 8.3 Name decomposition. (Part 1 of 2)

```
/* decomposeNameDriver.cpp tests function decomposeName().
 *
 * Input:  a person's full name
 * Output: the person's first name, middle name, and last name
 ***************************************************************/

#include <iostream>                  // cout, cin, <<, >>
#include <string>                    // string, getline
using namespace std;

void decomposeName(const string& fullName, string& firstName,
                   string& middleName, string& lastName);

int main()
{
   cout << "Enter a full name: ";
   string fullName;
   getline(cin, fullName);
```

Fig. 8.3 Name decomposition. (Part 2 of 2)

```
   string fName, mName, lName;
   decomposeName(fullName, fName, mName, lName);

   cout << fName << endl
        << mName << endl
        << lName << endl;
}

/* decomposeName breaks down a full name into its 3 parts.
 *
 * Receive:      fullName, a string
 * Precondition: fullName contains 3 names separated by blanks
 * Send back:    the 3 parts: firstName, middleName and lastName
 *************************************************************/

#include <cassert>         // assert()
using namespace std;

void decomposeName(const string& fullName, string& firstName,
                   string& middleName, string& lastName)
{
   int firstBlankIndex = fullName.find(' ', 0);
   assert(firstBlankIndex != string::npos);
   firstName = fullName.substr(0, firstBlankIndex);

   int secondBlankIndex = fullName.find(' ', firstBlankIndex + 1);
   assert(secondBlankIndex != string::npos);
   middleName = fullName.substr(firstBlankIndex + 1,
                            secondBlankIndex - firstBlankIndex - 1);

   int fullNameSize = fullName.size();

   lastName = fullName.substr(secondBlankIndex + 1,
                            fullNameSize - secondBlankIndex - 1);
}
```

Sample run:

```
Enter a full name: John Quincy Doe
John
Quincy
Doe
```

PROBLEM 2: DESIGNING A COIN DISPENSER

An automated cash register has two inputs: the amount of a purchase and the amount given as payment. It computes the number of dollars, quarters, dimes, nickels, and pennies to be given in change. The cashier returns the dollars to the customer, but the coins are returned by an automatic coin dispenser. Our problem is to write a function that models this dispenser.

Behavior. Our function must receive the amount of a purchase and the amount given as payment. It must compute and send back the number of dollars to be returned by the cashier and the number of coins of each denomination to be returned by the coin dispenser.

Objects. Identifying the objects in this problem is relatively easy:

Problem Objects	Software Objects			
	Type	Kind	Movement	Name
the amount of the purchase	`double`	varying	received (in)	*purchaseAmount*
the amount of the payment	`double`	varying	received (in)	*payment*
how many dollars in change	`int`	varying	sent back (out)	*dollars*
how many quarters in change	`int`	varying	sent back (out)	*quarters*
how many dimes in change	`int`	varying	sent back (out)	*dimes*
how many nickels in change	`int`	varying	sent back (out)	*nickels*
how many pennies in change	`int`	varying	sent back (out)	*pennies*

We can then specify the function as follows:

Receive: *purchaseAmount*, the (real) amount of the purchase
payment, the (real) amount of the payment

Precondition: *payment* >= *purchaseAmount*

Send back: *dollars*, the (integer) number of dollars in change
quarters, the (integer) number of quarters in change
dimes, the (integer) number of dimes in change
nickels, the (integer) number of nickels in change
pennies, the (integer) number of pennies in change

Using Rule P1, we define *purchaseAmount* and *payment* as value parameters, and using Rule P4, we define *dollars*, *quarters*, *dimes*, *nickels*, and *pennies* as reference parameters. We can then construct the following stub for the function `makeChange()`:

```
void makeChange(double purchaseAmount,   // amount of purchase
                double payment,          // amount of payment
                int& dollars,            // dollars of change
                int& quarters,           // quarters of change
```

```
                   int& dimes,               // dimes of change
                   int& nickels,             // nickels of change
                   int& pennies)             // pennies of change
{
}
```

Operations. To determine the sequence of operations needed to make change, we will work through a specific example. Suppose that the amount of a purchase is $8.49 and we pay with a $10.00 bill. We clearly must begin by subtracting the purchase amount from the payment to get the total amount of change ($1.51). This is a real value, but our return values are integers. So we must at some point convert this real value to an integer value. One approach would be to store the total amount of change (1.51) as a real value and perform a separate conversion as each return value is computed. However, this requires doing the same thing six times — an indication that there is probably a better way. Also, real values are not stored exactly (e.g., 1.51 might be stored as 1.50999...), and thus it is better to convert the real amount of change (1.51) into an integer value (151) at the outset, ensuring that no significant digits are lost. This can be done by multiplying the real amount of change by 100, adding 0.5, and then truncating the fractional part of the result. The following examples illustrate this computation:

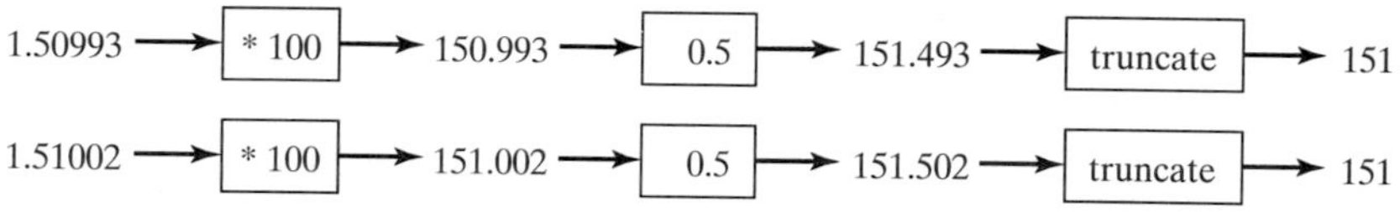

The result of this computation is the change in cents, and we will store this value in a local (variable) object *change*.

Algorithm. We can now construct the following algorithm to solve the problem:

Algorithm to Make Change

1. Compute *change* as the difference between *payment* and *purchaseAmount*, in cents.
2. If *change* is positive, then
   a. Compute *dollars* in *change* and remove *dollars* from *change*.
   b. Compute *quarters* in *change* and remove *quarters* from *change*.
   c. Compute *dimes* in *change* and remove *dimes* from *change*.
   d. Compute *nickels* in *change* and remove nickels *from change*.
   e. Compute *pennies* in *change*.

   Otherwise

   Set each of *dollars*, *quarters*, *dimes*, *nickels*, and *pennies* to zero.

Once *change* has been computed as the amount of change in cents, the number of dollars of change can be computed using integer division, dividing the value of *change* by 100:

```
dollars = change / 100;  // for change = 151, dollars equals 1
```

The remaining change is the remainder that results from this division:

```
change %= 100;              // for change = 151, change becomes 51
```

The number of quarters remaining in *change* can then be computed in a similar manner by dividing *change* by 25,

```
quarters = change / 25;
```

The remainder of this division is then the amount of change remaining to be dispensed as dimes, nickels, and pennies:

```
change %= 25;
```

Similar calculations are used to determine the number of dimes, nickels, and pennies.

Coding. The complete function is given in Figure 8.4.

Fig. 8.4 Computing change. (Part 1 of 2)

```
/* makeChange() computes the dollars, quarters, dimes, nickels, and
 * pennies in change given the amount of a purchase and the amount paid.
 *
 * Receive:      purchaseAmount, the (real) amount of the purchase,
 *               payment, the (real) amount of the payment
 * Precondition: purchaseAmount <= payment
 * Send back:    dollars, the (integer) number of dollars,
 *               quarters, the (integer) number of quarters,
 *               dimes, the (integer) number of dimes,
 *               nickels, the (integer) number of nickels, and
 *               pennies, the (integer) number of pennies in change
 ***************************************************************/

void makeChange(double purchaseAmount, // amount of purchase
                double payment,        // amount of payment
                int& dollars,          // dollars of change
                int& quarters,         // quarters of change
                int& dimes,            // dimes of change
                int& nickels,          // nickels of change
                int& pennies)          // pennies of change
{
  int change = int(100.0 * (payment - purchaseAmount) + 0.5);
```

Fig. 8.4 Computing change. (Part 2 of 2)

```
   if (change > 0)
   {
      dollars = change / 100;         // 100 pennies per dollar
      change %= 100;                  // compute remaining change

      quarters = change / 25;         // 25 pennies per quarter
      change %= 25;                   // compute remaining change

      dimes = change / 10;            // 10 pennies per dime
      change %= 10;                   // compute remaining change

      nickels = change / 5;           // 5 pennies per nickel
      pennies = change % 5;           // pennies are all that's left
   }
   else
   {
      cerr << "*** Purchase amount: " << purchaseAmount
           << " exceeds payment: " << payment << endl;
      dollars = quarters = dimes = nickels = pennies = 0;
   }
}
```

It should be noted that we could write this function more succinctly using the `divideInts()` function from Section 8.1. We simply change the `if` statement in the function to

```
if (change > 0)
{
   divideInts(change, 100, dollars, change);
   divideInts(change, 25, quarters, change);
   divideInts(change, 10, dimes, change);
   divideInts(change, 5, nickels, pennies);
}
else
{
   cerr << "*** Purchase amount: " << purchaseAmount
        << " exceeds payment: " << payment << endl;
   dollars = quarters = dimes = nickels = pennies = 0;
}
```

We can test our function by writing a driver program that reads two amounts `itemCost` and `amountPaid`, calls `makeChange()` to calculate the change that must be given, and then displays the amounts sent back by `makeChange()`. Figure 8.5 presents a driver program that uses a sentinel-controlled loop to process several amounts.

Fig. 8.5 Driver program for `makeChange()`. (Part 1 of 2)

```
/* makeChangeDriver.cpp tests function makeChange().
 *
 * Input:  the cost of an item and the amount paid
 * Output: the change in terms of numbers of dollars, quarters,
 *         dimes, nickels, and pennies
 *****************************************************************/

#include <iostream>                    // cout, cin, <<, >>
#include <string>                      // string
using namespace std;

void makeChange(double purchaseAmount, double payment,
                int& dollars, int& quarters, int& dimes,
                int& nickels, int& pennies);

int main()
{
   cout << "This program tests a change-making function...\n\n";

   double itemCost,              // a purchase
          amountPaid;            // what was paid

   int numDollars,               // variables for
       numQuarters,              //  the values
       numDimes,                 //  to be output
       numNickels,
       numPennies;

   for (;;)
   {
      cout << "Enter item cost (negative to quit) and amount paid: ";
      cin >> itemCost;

      if (itemCost < 0) break;

      cin >> amountPaid;

      makeChange(itemCost, amountPaid, numDollars,
                 numQuarters, numDimes, numNickels, numPennies);
```

Fig. 8.5 Driver program for `makeChange()`. (Part 2 of 2)

```
      cout << "The change from this purchase is:\n"
           << numDollars << " dollars,\n"
           << numQuarters << " quarters,\n"
           << numDimes << " dimes,\n"
           << numNickels << " nickels, and\n"
           << numPennies << " pennies\n\n";
   }
}

/*** Insert definition of makeChange() from Figure 8.4 here. ***/
```

Sample run:

```
This program tests a change-making function...

Enter item cost (negative to quit) and amount paid: 1.01 2.00
The change from this purchase is:
0 dollars,
3 quarters,
2 dimes,
0 nickels, and
4 pennies

Enter item cost (negative to quit) and amount paid: 1.34 5.00
The change from this purchase is:
3 dollars,
2 quarters,
1 dimes,
1 nickels, and
1 pennies

Enter item cost (negative to quit) and amount paid: 9.99 10.00
The change from this purchase is:
0 dollars,
0 quarters,
0 dimes,
0 nickels, and
1 pennies

Enter item cost (negative to quit) and amount paid: -1
```

PROBLEM 3: INTERCHANGING THE VALUES OF TWO VARIABLES

There are certain problems in which it is necessary to interchange the values of two variables. For example, one approach to reverse the characters in a `string` is to interchange its first and last characters, interchange its second and next-to-last characters, and so on.

Because this "swapping" operation is useful in many problems, it is worthwhile to construct a function to perform it and store the function in a library. Given such a function, we can call

```
swap(ch1, ch2);
```

to exchange the values of character variables `ch1` and `ch2` or call

```
swap(aString[i], aString[j]);
```

to exchange the values of the characters at indices `i` and `j` within `aString`.

Behavior. Describing the function's behavior is straightforward: It must receive values of two variables, swap them, and send the interchanged values back.

Objects. If we assume for this example that two character variables are to have their values interchanged, then we can list the data objects needed to perform this operation as follows:

	Software Objects			
Problem Objects	**Type**	**Kind**	**Movement**	**Name**
the first variable	`char`	varying	received (in) and sent back (out)	*first*
the second variable	`char`	varying	received (in) and sent back (out)	*second*

Note the unusual movement of this function: Because the value of *first* must be changed to the value of *second*, *first* must be sent back and *second* must be received. Because the value of *second* must be changed to the value of *first*, *first* must be received and *second* passed back. Thus both have *in–out* movement, and we can specify the function as follows:

Receive: *first*, a (`char`) variable
second, a (`char`) variable

Sent back: *first*, containing the value of *second*
second, containing the value of *first*

Since this specification indicates that two values are to be sent back, Rule P4 can be applied with *first* and *second* as reference parameters because they are sent back as well as received. This allows us to construct the following stub for the function `swap()`:

```
void swap(char& first, char& second)
{
}
```

Operations. Since we are only interchanging values of two variables, the only operation needed will be assignment.

Algorithm. To perform the swap operation, we cannot simply assign the value of *second* to *first* (or vice versa), because the value of *first* will be overwritten and lost. Instead, the correct approach is to define an auxiliary variable to use in the interchange:

Algorithm to Interchange Two Values

1. Copy *first* to *temporary.*
2. Copy *second* to *first.*
3. Copy *temporary* to *second.*

Coding. The function `swap()` in Figure 8.6 implements this algorithm:

Fig. 8.6 Interchanging the values of two variables.

```
/* swap exchanges the values of two variables.
 *
 * Receive:   first, a (char) variable
 *            second, a (char) variable
 * Send back: first, containing the value of second
 *            second, containing the value of first
 *******************************************************/

void swap(char& first, char& second)
{
   char temporary = first;
   first = second;
   second = temporary;
}
```

Given such a function, other functions can use it to exchange the values of two character variables. For example, the following function receives a string and returns that string reversed:

```
string reverse(const string& originalString)
{
   string resultString = originalString;
   int begin = 0,
       end = resultString.size() - 1;

   while (begin < end)
   {
      swap(resultString[begin], resultString[end]);
      begin++;
      end--;
   }
```

```
    return resultString;
}
```

Quick Quiz 8.3

1. The parameter-passing mechanism that occurs by default is call-by-__________.
2. A __________ parameter contains a copy of the corresponding argument.
3. If a __________ parameter is changed in the body of the function, then the value of the corresponding argument is not changed.
4. If a __________ parameter is changed in the body of the function, then the value of the corresponding argument is also changed.
5. Placing a(n) ________ between a parameter's type and its name indicates that the parameter is a reference parameter.

Questions 6–11 assume the following function definition

```
void f(int x, int & y, int & z)
{
   z = y = x * x + 1;
}
```

and the following declarations in the calling function:

```
int a = 0, b = 1, c = 2, d = 3;
const int E  = 4;
```

6. (True or false) After `d = f(a, b, c);` is executed, `d` will have the value 1.
7. (True or false) After `f(a, b, c);` is executed, `b` and `c` will both have the value 1.
8. (True or false) After `f(c, d, E);` is executed, `d` will have the value 5.
9. (True or false) After `f(c+1, c-1, d);` is executed, `d` will have the value 10.
10. (True or false) The function call `f(c, d, E);` makes `z` a `const` reference parameter.
11. Rewrite the definition of `f()` so that `x` is a `const` reference parameter.
12. Given the function definition

    ```
    void change(int number, string & a, string & b, string & c)
    {
       const string BAT = "bat";
       if (number < 3)
       {
          a = BAT;
          b = BAT;
       }
       else
          c = BAT;
    }
    ```

    what output will the following program segment produce?

    ```
       string str1 = "cat", str2 = "dog", str3 = "elk";
       change(2, str1, str2, str3);
       cout << "String = " << str1 << str2 < str3 << endl;
    ```

Exercises 8.3

Exercises 1–11 assume the following program skeleton:

```
#include <cmath>
using namespace std;

void calculate(double a, double & b,
               int m, int & k, int & n, char & c);

int main()
{
   const double PI = 3.14159;
   const int TWO = 2;
   const char INITIAL = 'N';

   int month, day, year, p, q;
   double hours, rate, amount, u, v;
   char code, dept;
}
```

Determine whether the given statement can be used to call the function `calculate()`. If it cannot be used, explain why.

1. `calculate(u, v, TWO, p, q, code);`
2. `calculate(PI, u, TWO, p, v, dept);`
3. `calculate(hours, PI, TWO, day, year, dept);`
4. `calculate(13, hours, PI, 13, year, dept);`
5. `calculate(PI * hours, PI, TWO, day, year, dept);`
6. `calculate(PI, PI * hours, TWO, day, year, dept);`
7. ```
   while (u > 0)
      calculate(u, v, TWO, p, q, code);
   ```
8. `calculate(0, hours, (p + 1) / 2, day, year, code)`
9. `calculate(sqrt(amount), rate, 7, p, q, INITIAL);`
10. ```
    while (amount > 0)
       calculate(TWO, amount, day, p + q, day, dept);
    ```
11. `cout << calculate(u, v, TWO, p, q, code);`

The following exercises ask you to write functions to compute various quantities. To test these functions, you should write driver programs as instructed in Programming Problems 1–3 at the end of this chapter.

12. Write a function that receives a weight in pounds and ounces and returns the corresponding weight in grams (1 oz = 28.349527 g).
13. Write a function that receives a weight in grams and returns the corresponding weight in pounds and ounces.
14. Write a function that receives a measurement in yards, feet, and inches and returns the corresponding measurement in centimeters (1 in. = 2.54001 cm).

15. Write a function that receives a measurement in centimeters and returns the corresponding measurement in yards, feet, and inches.
16. Write a function that receives a time in the usual representation of hours and minutes and a character value that indicates whether this is A.M. ('A') or P.M. ('P') and returns the corresponding military time.
17. Write a function that receives a time in military format and returns the corresponding time in the usual representation in hours, minutes, and A.M. / P.M. For example, a time of 0100 should be returned as 1 hour, 0 minutes, and 'A' to indicate A.M.; and a time of 1545 should be returned as 3 hours, 45 minutes, and 'P' to indicate P.M.

8.4 Inline Functions

We have seen that when one function `f()` calls another function `g()`, execution is transferred from `f()` to `g()`. When `g()` terminates, a second transfer of control is necessary to return execution back to `f()`. Each of these transfers takes time—a great deal of time in fact, compared to the speed at which a computer normally operates. *Each function call significantly increases the amount of time required for a program to execute.*

In many situations, the *overhead* associated with function calls is acceptable, but there are other problems in which time is so important that this overhead cannot be tolerated. For these problems, C++ provides *inlining* of functions.[3]

One of the details we omitted (for simplicity) in the description of function definitions in Section 4.2 is that a definition can be preceded by a function specifier, which provides the compiler with special instructions about the function:

```
function_specifier return_type
                     function_name(parameter_declaration_list)
{
   statement_list
}
```

One such specifier is the `inline` **specifier**, which instructs the compiler to use the C++ inline mechanism to avoid the overhead of normal function calls.

To illustrate, suppose that we want to inline the temperature-conversion function `fahrToCelsius()` in Figure 4.2. We can do so by preceding its prototype and its definition with the `inline` specifier:

```
inline  double fahrToCelsius(double tempFahr);
                .
                .
                .
inline  double fahrToCelsius(double tempFahr)
{
   return (tempFahr - 32.0) / 1.8;
}
```

3. The inline specifier effectively provides a fourth parameter passing mechanism that is known as *call-by-name*, or *macro-substitution*. For a discussion of this mechanism, see, for example, *Compilers: Principles, Techniques and Tools,* by Aho, Sethi, and Ullman (Reading, Mass.: Addison–Wesley, 1986).

When the function prototype and definition occur in the same file as in Figure 4.2, both must be labeled as `inline`. Otherwise, there will be a mismatch between the function's prototype and its definition, and a compiler error results.

The `inline` specifier suggests to the C++ compiler that it *replace each call to this function with the body of the function, with the arguments for that function call substituted for the functions parameters.*[4] For example, the compiler is being asked to effectively replace the function call in the statement

```
tempCelsius = fahrToCelsius(tempFahrenheit);
```

with the body of the function, but with the argument `tempFahrenheit` substituted for the parameter `tempFahr`:

```
tempCelsius = (tempFahrenheit - 32.0) / 1.8;
```

The effect of the `inline` specifier is to ask the compiler to take additional *compile time* to perform this substitution *for each call* to the function. This saves *run time*, because the elimination of each function call means that no transfers of execution need to be performed, eliminating the overhead incurred by those function calls.

INLINE FUNCTIONS AND LIBRARIES

NOTE

The normal procedure for a function stored in a library is to put its prototype in the library's header file and its definition in the implementation file. This separation is not allowed, however, if we want to inline a function. *An* `inline` *library function must be defined in the header file.*

To illustrate, suppose that a library `MyMath` contains, among other mathematical functions, the function `sum()` from Figure 7.12, with the prototype of `sum()` in `MyMath.h` and its definition in `MyMath.cpp`. To designate `sum()` as an inline function, we would remove its definition from the implementation file and replace its prototype in the header file with this definition, preceding it with the `inline` specifier, as shown in Figure 8.7.

Fig. 8.7 Inline library functions. (Part 1 of 2)

```
/* This header file provides an interface for library MyMath.
 * It contains prototypes and inline definitions of non-predefined
 * math functions.
 * ... remaining opening documentation omitted ...
 ***************************************************************/

int factorial(int n);
```

4. This *suggestion* may be ignored by the compiler if it judges that the function definition is too complicated to be inlined efficiently.

Fig. 8.7 Inline library functions. (Part 2 of 2)

```
inline int sum(int n)
{
   return n * (n + 1) / 2;
}

// ... other function prototypes and/or inline definitions
```

These steps are necessary because the only part of the library that the compiler sees when it compiles a program is the header file, which is inserted when it processes the `#include` directive. If the *compiler* (and not the *linker*) is to replace calls to a function with the function's definition, a function's entire definition must be visible to the compiler, which means that it must be moved from the implementation file to the header file.

TO INLINE OR NOT TO INLINE: A SPACE–TIME TRADE-OFF

Because inlined functions eliminate the overhead of function calls and make programs run faster, it may be tempting to make all functions inline. There is, however, a *space–time tradeoff*: a program that uses inlined functions may indeed run *faster* than its non-inlined equivalent, but it may also be much *larger* and thus require more memory.

To see why this happens, we must realize that, unlike the simple examples we have been using, functions written for real-world software projects typically (1) contain many statements, and (2) may be called at many different places in a program. When such a function is inlined, *each substitution of the function's body for its call replaces a single statement (the call) with many statements (the body)*, which increases the overall size of the program.

More generally, suppose that we are working on a software project and write a function `f()` that is called at N different places in our program. Let S_{prog} denote the size of the program (including the definition and calls of `f()`) and S_{fun} denote the size of function `f()`. If `f()` is not implemented as an inline function, the total space needed for the program is simply

$$S_{prog}$$

but if it is inlined, the program's total space will be approximately

$$S_{prog} + N \times S_{fun}$$

Thus, if the size of function `f()` is more than a few operations and `f()` is called many times, then substituting the body of `f()` at each call will significantly increase the overall size of the program, a phenomenon known as **code bloat**.

To avoid code bloat, we recommend that `inline` *be used with restraint:* If a function uses just a few operations (such as the `fahrToCelsius()` and `sum()` functions), then designate it as `inline` to eliminate the overhead associated with calling the function. But if a function uses many operations (e.g., more than 5 or 6), do not use `inline`.[5]

Quick Quiz 8.4

1. (True or false) Function calls increase the execution time of a program.
2. The _________ specifier provides a way to avoid the overhead of function calls.
3. Describe what inlining a function suggests to the compiler.
4. For the function definition

```
inline int f(int n)
{ return n * (n + 1) / 2; }
```

   how will the compiler modify the statement `cout << f(number);` ?
5. If a library function is inlined, then the function must be defined in the ________ file of the library.
6. (True or false) Programs that use `inline` functions will usually run faster.
7. (True or false) Programs that use `inline` functions will usually require less memory.

8.5 Scope, Overloading, and Templates

As we have seen, identifiers are used to name the objects and functions in a program. For example, the library `MyMath` in Figure 8.7 might contain two summation functions, one to calculate sums of the form $1 + 2 + ... + n$ and another to calculate sums of the form $m + (m{+}1) + (m{+}2) + ... + (n{-}1) + n$. Although we might use different names for the functions, this is not necessary. We can name them both `sum()`:

```
inline int sum(int n)
{
   return n * (n + 1) / 2;
}

inline int sum(int m, int n)
{
   assert(m < n);
   return (n - m + 1) * (n + m) / 2;
}
```

These definitions indicate the following:

1. The same identifier can be used in different functions without conflict (e.g., parameter `n`).
2. Two functions can have the same name.

However, if we try to use the same identifier to define two different objects in the same function as in

5. There are situations where the use of `inline` will increase the size of a program without producing any gain in its execution speed. See, for example, *Effective C++*, by Scott Meyers (Reading, Mass.: Addison–Wesley, 1992).

```
void f()
{
   int value;
   ...
   char value;       // ERROR!
   ...
}
```

a compilation error results.

These examples raise an important question:

What rules govern the use of and/or access to an identifier?

As we shall see, some rules govern access to identifiers in general, and other rules govern access to identifiers that are names of functions. In this section, we describe these rules.

SCOPE: IDENTIFIER ACCESSIBILITY

The **scope** of an identifier is that portion of a program where that identifier is the name of a constant, variable, or function that can be accessed. For example, consider again the definitions of the two summation functions. The identifier n is used in both definitions, but it has two distinct scopes. In the first function, n is the name of the first parameter, and any uses of n in the body of that function refer to that parameter:

```
int sum (int n)
{
   return n * (n + 1) / 2;
}

int sum(int m, int n)
{
   return (n - m + 1) * (n + m) / 2;
}
```

This is sometimes described by saying that *the body of the first function lies within the scope of its parameter* n.

In the second function, the identifier n is the name of the second parameter, and so any use of n in that function refers to that object:

```
int sum(int n)
{
   return n * (n + 1) / 2;
}

int sum(int m, int n)
{
   return (n - m + 1) * (n + m) / 2;
}
```

The body of the second function lies within the scope of its parameter n (and within the scope of its parameter m as well).

WATCH OUT

Any attempt to access an identifier outside its scope produces a compilation error
For example, if we changed the definition of the first function to

```
int sum(int n)
{
   m = 1;
   return (n - m + 1) * (n + m) / 2;
}
```

then an error message like

```
Identifier 'm' is undeclared
```

would be generated when the function is compiled, because there is no identifier `m` whose scope reaches the body of that function. Understanding scope is important for understanding certain compilation errors.

Stated simply, the scope of an identifier depends on *where the identifier is declared.* The scopes of the identifiers we have seen thus far have been determined by four simple rules:[6]

S1. If an identifier is declared within a block,
then its scope runs from its declaration to the end of the block.

S2. If an identifier is a parameter of a function,
then its scope is the body of the function.

S3. If an identifier is declared in the initialization expression of a `for` loop,
then its scope runs from its declaration to the end of the loop.

S4. If an identifier is a declared outside all blocks and is not a parameter,
then its scope runs from its declaration to the end of the file.

Note that an identifier's scope always begins at some point following its declaration. This observation can be summarized in the single rule:

> *An identifier must be declared before it can be used.*

A Quick Example. To illustrate how the compiler uses these rules, suppose that we were to rewrite the `getMenuChoice()` function from Section 7.2 as follows:

```
char getMenuChoice(const string& MENU,
                   char firstChoice, char lastChoice)
{
   for (;;)
   {
      cout << MENU;
      char choice;
      cin >> choice;
```

6. Scope Rule S3 was a late addition to the C++ standard; thus, some versions of C++ that are not fully ANSI-compliant may not implement it. Also, there are other rules that govern the scope of identifiers declared in namespaces (later in this section) and classes (see Chapter 11).

```
      if (choice >= firstChoice && choice <= lastChoice)
         break;

      cerr << "\nI'm sorry, but " << choice
           << " is not a valid menu choice.\n";
   }
   return choice;                   // ERROR!
}
```

When this function is compiled, the `return` statement generates an error message like

```
Identifier 'choice' is undeclared
```

(Before continuing, use the scope rules to try to find the cause of the error.)

The problem is that by Rule S1, the scope of `choice` only runs through the last statement of the block that is the body of the loop. Since the `return` statement appears after the block, it lies outside the scope of `choice`, and so the compiler generates an error when it attempts to access `choice`. The problem can be avoided by moving the declaration of `choice` to the outermost block of the function, thus ensuring that all statements that refer to `choice` lie within its scope:

```
char getMenuChoice(const string& MENU,
                   char firstChoice, char lastChoice)
{
   char choice;

   for (;;)
   {
      cout << MENU;
      cin >> choice;

      if (choice >= firstChoice && choice <= lastChoice)
         break;

      cerr <<"\nI'm sorry, but " << choice
           << " is not a valid menu choice.\n";
   }
   return choice;                   // OK!
}
```

Objects Declared Outside All Blocks. Although we have not put any declarations of variables or constants outside *all* blocks, we have done so with prototypes of functions. For example, in Figure 8.3, the prototype of the function `decomposeName()` precedes the main function, so that the identifier `decomposeName` is declared outside all blocks. By Scope Rule S4, its scope thus extends from its declaration to the end of the file:

```
#include <iostream>
#include <string>
using namespace std;

void decomposeName(const string& fullName, string& firstName,
                   string& middleName, string& lastName);
```

```
int main()
{
   cout << "Enter a full name: ";
   string fullName;
   getline(cin, fullName);

   string fName, mName, lName;
   decomposeName(fullName, fName, mName, lName);

   cout << fName << endl
        << mName << endl
        << lName << endl;
}
   .
   .
   .
```

This is the reason why a function prototype *must* precede calls to a function. Since a prototype is a declaration of the function, it begins the scope of the function. Calls to the function thus lie within its scope.

Identifiers that are declared in a library's header file, such as `cin`, `cout`, `cerr`, and `clog` in `iostream` and the class `string` in the header file `string`, are also governed by Rule S4. When the compiler processes a `#include` directive outside all blocks as in

```
#include <iostream>
using namespace std;

int main()
{
   ...
}
```

then all objects in that file are inserted outside all blocks and thus fall under Rule S4. The scope of such declarations thus extends from their declarations (i.e., from the `#include` directive) to the end of the file. Thus, if we were to write

```
#include <iostream>
using namespace std;

int main()
{
   ...
}

void g()
{
   ...
}
```

then both `main()` and `g()` lie within the scope of `cin`, `cout`, `cerr`, and `clog`. By contrast, if we write

```
int main()
{
   ...
}

#include <iostream>
using namespace std;

void g()
{
   ...
}
```

then any attempt to access `cin`, `cout`, `cerr`, or `clog` in `main()` will result in a compilation error, because `main()` does not lie within their scope.

Scopes of `for`-Loop Control Variables. Rule S3 that governs the scope of an identifier declared in the initialization expression of a `for` loop deserves special attention, because it is easy to make mistakes when using several `for` loops if this rule is not well understood. To illustrate, suppose that a programmer writes a program containing two `for` loops as follows:

```
int main()
{
   ...
   for (int i = 1; i <= someLimit; i++)
      // ... do something with i
   ...
   for (i = 1; i <= someLimit; i++)            // ERROR!
      // ... do something with i again
   ...
}
```

When the program is compiled, an error message like

```
Identifier 'i' is undeclared
```

is generated by the first line of the second for loop. The reason for this is that by Rule S3, the scope of `i` begins at its declaration and ends at the end of the first `for` loop:

```
int main()
{
   ...
   for (int i = 1; i <= someLimits; i++)
      // ... do something with i
   ...

   for (i = 1; i <= someLimit; i++)            // ERROR!
      // ... do something with i gain
   ...
}
```

As a result, the second loop lies outside the scope of `i`, so that when an attempt is made there to reuse `i`, it is no longer available, and the compiler generates an error.

Such an error can be corrected in several ways. One way is to redeclare `i` in the second loop, so that a new scope for `i` is present in that loop:

```
int main()
{
   ...
   for (int i = 1; i <= someLimit; i++)
      // ... do something with i
   ...
   for (int i = 1; i <= someLimit; i++)              // Ok!
      // ... do something with i again
...
}
```

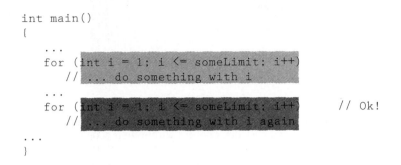

Another solution is to move the declaration of `i` *before* the first loop, so that it is governed by Rule S1 instead of Rule S3, and both loops fall within its scope:

```
int main()
{
   ...
   int i;
   for (i = 1; i <= someLimit; i++)
      // ... do something with i
   ...
   for (i = 1; i <= someLimit; i++)              // Ok!
      // ... do something with i again
   ...
}
```

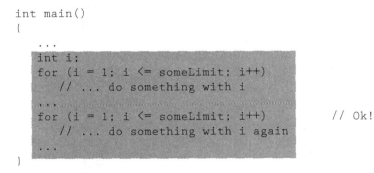

Name Conflicts. Our discussion of scope would not be complete without mentioning the following rule:

> *Within the scope of an identifier, no redeclaration of that identifier that results in an ambiguity for the compiler is permitted.*

As a simple illustration, suppose that we write

```
int main()
{
   int value = 1;

   double value = 2.0;           // ERROR!

   cout << value << endl;
}
```

The redeclaration of `value` creates an *ambiguity* for the compiler, because in the output statement, it is unclear which `value` is to be displayed. From the standpoint of the compiler, `value` is declared as the name of an `int` object, starting the scope of the identifier `value`. When the compiler encounters a second declaration of the same name that it cannot distinguish from the first declaration, a **name conflict** arises,

```
int main()
{
   int value = 1;

   double value = 2.0;          // ERROR!

   cout << value << endl;
}
```

and so the compiler generates an error. By contrast, there is no name conflict in the following, because the scopes of the two versions of `value` do not overlap:

```
int main()
{
   ...
   if (x > 0)
   {
      int value = 1;
      cout << value << endl;
   }
   else
   {
      double value = 2.0;
      cout << value << endl;
   }
}
```

The compiler will eliminate ambiguity between names whenever it can. To illustrate, consider the following example:

```
int main()
{
   int value = 1;
   {
      double value = 2.3;
      cout << value << endl;
   }
   cout << value << endl;
}
```

The effect here is that the outer (`int`) version of `value` will be hidden from the statements within the scope of the nested version of `value`. Because `value` is redeclared in its own *nested block*, the compiler will assume that accesses within the scope of the nested

Note that the return type of a function is not a part of its signature. Thus, two functions with different return types but with identical signatures cannot have the same name.

Names should be overloaded only when it is appropriate. Otherwise, the code you write may be very difficult to read and understand. Different functions that perform the same operation (e.g., summation, finding the minimum operation, finding the maximum) on different data types are prime candidates for overloading. But giving operations that have nothing to do with each other the same name simply because the language allows you to do so is an abuse of the overloading mechanism and is deplorable programming style.

It should be evident that overloading has been used since Chapter 1. For example, the operators +, -, *, and / are all overloaded so that they can be applied to any of the numeric types. In the expression

```
2.0 / 5.0
```

the C++ compiler uses the real division operation (which produces the value 0.4), but in the integer expression

```
2 / 5
```

it uses the integer division operation (which produces the value 0). Many of the other operators, including <<, >>, =, +=, -=, *=, /=, <, >, ==, <=, >=, and != , have also been overloaded with multiple definitions. For an expression of the form

$operand_1$ $operator$ $operand_2$

the compiler simply matches the types of $operand_1$ and $operand_2$ against the signatures of the available definitions of *operator* to determine which definition to apply.

FUNCTION TEMPLATES

In Section 8.3, we considered a function to interchange the values of two character variables:

```
void swap(char& first, char& second)
{
   char temporary = first;
   first = second;
   second = temporary;
}
```

This function works well so long as the values we wish to exchange are two `char` values. But the swap operation is needed in many different problems such as sorting a list of strings, interchanging the smaller and larger of two integers, and interchanging two rows in a table of `doubles`. The preceding function, however, can be used only to exchange the values of two `char` objects and not `string` values, `int` values, `double` values, and so on.

One solution would be to create a library of overloaded `swap()` functions, one for each type of value we may ever want to interchange:

```
/* This swap library provides a collection of functions
 * for interchanging the values of two variables.
 * ...
 ***********************************************************/
```

```
inline void swap(bool& first, bool& second)
{
   bool temporary = first;
   first = second;
   second = temporary;
}

inline void swap(char& first, char& second)
{
   char temporary = first;
   first = second;
   second = temporary;
}

inline void swap(short& first, short& second)
{
   short temporary = first;
   first = second;
   second = temporary;
}

inline void swap(int& first, int& second)
{
   int temporary = first;
   first = second;
   second = temporary;
}

inline void swap(long& first, long& second)
{
   long temporary = first;
   first = second;
   second = temporary;
}

inline void swap(float& first, float& second)
{
   float temporary = first;
   first = second;
   second = temporary;
}

inline void swap(double& first, double& second)
{
   double temporary = first;
   first = second;
   second = temporary;
}

inline void swap(long double& first, long double& second)
{
   long temporary = first;
```

```
   first = second;
   second = temporary;
}
```

Given such a library, we could interchange two values of any of the fundamental types simply by using the `#include` directive to insert this file and then calling a `swap()` function:

```
...
#include "swap.h"

int main()
{
   int i1 = 11,
       i2 = 22;
   double d1 = 11.1,
          d2 = 22.2;

   swap(i1, i2);
   cout << i1 << ' ' << i2 << endl;

   swap(d1, d2);
   cout << d1 << ' ' << d2 << endl;
}
```

The compiler will select the appropriate version of `swap()` by matching the types of the arguments in the function call with the signatures of the functions in the library.

Suppose, however, that we find that we need to exchange the values of two class (e.g., `string`) objects. We could add yet another definition to `swap.h`,

```
inline void swap(string& first, string& second)
{
   string temporary = first;
   first = second;
   second = temporary;
}
```

However, each definition of `swap()` is doing exactly the same thing (on a different type of data). This should raise red flags for us, because we have said before that *anytime we find ourselves repeating the same work, there is probably a better way.*

Parameters for Types. Here, the better way is to recognize that the only differences in any of these definitions are the three places where a type is specified. It would be nice if we could define the function and leave these types "blank," to be filled in later,

```
inline void swap( ________& first,  ________& second)
{
   ________ temporary = first;
   first = second;
   second = temporary;
}
```

and somehow *pass the type* to the function when we called it. Then we could replace all of these definitions with one.

This is effectively what C++ allows us to do, as shown in Figure 8.8.

Fig. 8.8 The `swap()` template.

```
/* swap.h provides a template that generates functions
 * for interchanging the values of two variables.
 * ...
 **************************************************************/

template<typename Item>
inline void swap(Item& first, Item& second)
{
   Item temporary = first;
   first = second;
   second = temporary;
}
```

Rather than specify that the function is to exchange two values of a particular type such as `char`, `int`, and so on, this definition uses the identifier `Item` as a place-holder for the type of the value to be exchanged. More precisely, the line

```
template<typename Item>
```

informs the compiler of two things:

1. This definition is a **template**: *a pattern from which the compiler can create a function.*
2. The identifier `Item` is the name of a **type parameter** for this definition that will be given a value when the function is called.[7]

The rest of the definition simply specifies the behavior of the function, using the type parameter `Item` in place of any specific type.

Using this version of the `swap` library, we can now write

```
#include "swap.h"
#include <iostream>
#include <string>
using namespace std;
```

7. C++ allows either of the keywords `typename` or `class` to be used to specify the "type" of a type parameter. Because the keyword `class` is used in other places in C++, we will use `typename` in this text to avoid confusion. When you see `class` used in template declarations in other examples of code (especially in older code), just remember that, in this case, the word *class* is being used as a synonym for *type*.

```
int main()
{
   int i1 = 11,
       i2 = 22;
   swap(i1, i2);
   cout << i1 << ' ' << i2 << endl;

   double d1 = 33.3,
          d2 = 44.4;
   swap(d1, d2);
   cout << d1 << ' ' << d2 << endl;

   string s1 = "Hi",
          s2 = "Ho";
   swap(s1, s2);
   cout << s1 << ' ' << s2 << endl;
}
```

When the compiler encounters the first call to `swap()`,

```
swap(i1, i2);
```

in which the two arguments `i1` and `i2` are of type `int`, it uses the pattern given by our template to generate a new definition of `swap()` in which the type parameter `Item` is replaced by `int`:

```
inline void swap(int& first, int& second)
{
   int temporary = first;
   first = second;
   second = temporary;
}
```

When it reaches the second call,

```
swap(d1, d2);
```

where the two arguments `d1` and `d2` are of type `double`, the compiler will use the same pattern to generate a second definition of `swap()` in which the type parameter `Item` is replaced by `double`:

```
inline void swap(double& first, double& second)
{
   double temporary = first;
   first = second;
   second = temporary;
}
```

When the compiler reaches the final call,

```
swap(s1, s2);
```

in which the two arguments `s1` and `s2` are of type `string`, it will use the same pattern to generate a third definition of `swap()` in which the type parameter `Item` is replaced by `string`:

```
inline void swap(string& first, string& second)
{
   string temporary = first;
   first = second;
   second = temporary;
}
```

We are spared from all of the redundant coding of the earlier approach because the compiler is providing multiple versions of the swap operation as they are needed.

Templates vs. Overloading. If there are several versions of the same operation to be encoded as functions, it may not be clear whether one should write several functions that overload the same name or write one function template. The following guideline helps with making this decision:

> If each version of the operation behaves in exactly the same way,
> regardless of the type of data being used,
> then define a **function template** to perform the operation.
>
> Otherwise, define a separate function for each operation,
> and use **overloading** to give them the same name.

Thus, because each version of `swap()` uses the three-way swap and behaves in exactly the same manner regardless of the type of values being interchanged, a function template is appropriate.

By contrast, the two summation functions we considered earlier use different formulas and thus behave differently. These operations are therefore best performed by two separate functions that overload the name `sum()`.

The reasoning behind this guideline should be clear. When the compiler creates a function definition from a template, it blindly replaces each occurrence of the type parameter with the type of the arguments. As a result, each definition created from a template must behave in exactly the same way, except for the type of data being operated upon. Overloading has no such restriction and so can be used for a wider variety of operations.

✔ Quick Quiz 8.5

1. The part of a program where an identifier refers to a particular object or function is called the ________ of that identifier.
2. (True or false) A compilation error results if an identifier is accessed within its scope.
3. The scope of an identifier declared within a block runs from its declaration to the ________.
4. The scope of a parameter is the ________.

5. What will the following statements produce?

```
for (int i = 0; i < 3; i++)
   cout << i << endl;
cout << "i is now " << i << endl;
```

6. A function's __________ is a list of the types of its parameters.
7. Two functions are said to be overloaded if they have the same __________.
8. A function's name can be overloaded provided no two definitions of the function have the same __________.
9. A __________ is a pattern from which a function can be constructed.
10. Templates may have __________ parameters, but ordinary functions may not.
11. Given the template definition

```
template<typename something>
void print(something x)
{ cout << "****" << x << "***\n"; }
```

describe what the compiler will do when it encounters the statements

```
int number = 123;
print(number);
```

8.6* A Brief Introduction to Recursion

All the examples of function calls considered thus far have involved one function `f()` calling a different function `g()` (with the calling function `f()` often being the main function). However, a function `f()` may also *call itself*, a phenomenon known as **recursion**, and in this section, we show how **recursion**, is implemented in C++. Many examples of recursion could be given, but we will consider only two of the classic ones: calculating factorials and the Towers of Hanoi problem. Others are given in the exercises and in Chapter 15 where we revisit recursion.

EXAMPLE 1: THE FACTORIAL PROBLEM REVISITED

To illustrate the basic idea of recursion, we reconsider the problem of calculating the factorial function.

Objects. The objects and specification of this problem were given in Section 4.4. The specification

Receive: *n*, an integer.

Return: $n! = 1 \times 2 \times \cdots \times n$

gives rise to the following stub for the function:

```
int factorial(int n)
{
}
```

Operations. Although the first definition of the factorial $n!$ of an integer n that one usually learns (and the one we used in Section 4.4) is

$$n! = \begin{cases} 1 & \text{if } n \text{ is } 0 \\ 1 \times 2 \times \ldots n & \text{if } n > 0 \end{cases}$$

it would be foolish to use it to calculate a sequence of consecutive factorials; that is, to multiply together the numbers from 1 through n each time:

$$0! = 1$$
$$1! = 1$$
$$2! = 1 \times 2 = 2$$
$$3! = 1 \times 2 \times 3 = 6$$
$$4! = 1 \times 2 \times 3 \times 4 = 24$$
$$5! = 1 \times 2 \times 3 \times 4 \times 5 = 120$$

A great deal of the effort would be redundant, because it is clear that once a factorial has been calculated, it can be used to calculate the next factorial. For example, given the value 4!, the value 5! can be computed simply by multiplying the value of 4! by 5:

$$5! = 5 \times 4! = 5 \times 24 = 120$$

This value of 5! can in turn be used to calculate 6!,

$$6! = 6 \times 5! = 6 \times 120 = 720$$

and so on. Indeed, to calculate $n!$ for any positive integer n, we need only know the value of 0! and the fundamental relation between one factorial and the next:

$$n! = n \times (n-1)!$$

In general, a function is said to be **defined recursively** if its definition consists of two parts:

1. An **anchor or base case**, in which the value of the function is specified for one or more values of the parameter(s),
2. An **inductive** or **recursive step**, in which the function's value for the current value of the parameter(s) is defined in terms of previously defined function values and/or parameter values

For the factorial function, we have

$0! = 1$	(the anchor or base case)
For $n > 0$, $n! = n \times (n-1)!$	(the inductive or recursive step)

The first statement specifies a particular value of the function, and the second statement defines its value for n in terms of its value for $n - 1$.

Algorithm. This approach to calculating factorials leads to the following recursive definition of $n!$:

$$n! = \begin{cases} 1 & \text{if } n \text{ is } 0 \\ n \times (n-1)! & \text{if } n > 0 \end{cases}$$

This definition can be used as an algorithm[8] for completing the stub of `factorial()`. To see how it works, consider using it to calculate 5!. We must first calculate 4! because 5! is defined as the product of 5 and 4!. But to calculate 4!, we must calculate 3!, because 4! is defined as $4 \times 3!$. And to calculate 3!, we must apply the inductive step of the definition again, $3! = 3 \times 2!$, then again to find 2!, which is defined as $2! = 2 \times 1!$, and once again to find $1! = 1 \times 0!$. Now we have finally reached the anchor case:

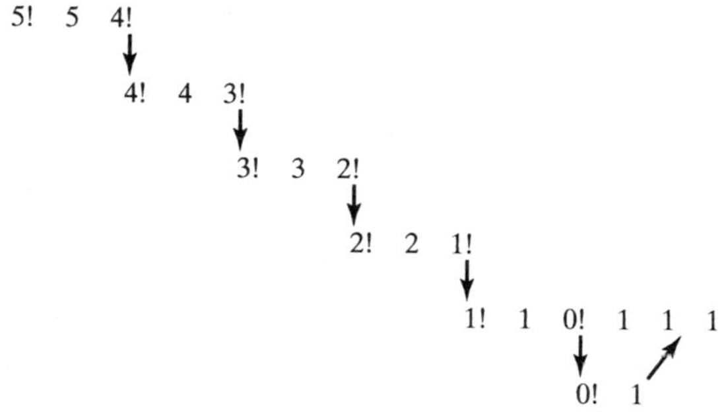

Since the value of 0! is given, we can now backtrack to find the value of 1!, then backtrack again to find the value of 2!,

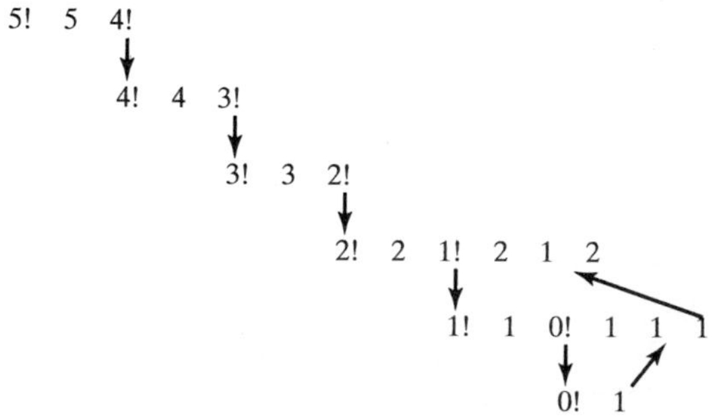

and so on, until we eventually obtain the value 120 for 5!:

---

8. Note that a recursive definition with a slightly different anchor case can be constructed by observing that 0! and 1! are both 1. Although this alternative definition leads to a slightly more efficient implementation of `factorial()`, we will use the simpler definition in this introduction to recursion.

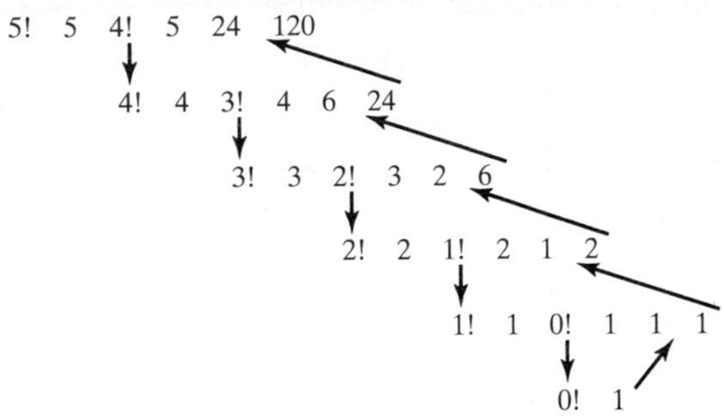

As this example demonstrates, a recursive definition may require considerable bookkeeping to record information at the various levels of the recursion, because this information is used *after* the anchor case is reached to *backtrack* from one level to the preceding one. Fortunately, most modern high-level languages (including C++) support recursion by automatically performing all of the necessary bookkeeping and backtracking.

Coding. Figure 8.9 shows a definition of `factorial()` that implements this algorithm:

Fig. 8.9 Computing `n!` recursively.

```
/* factorial computes n! recursively.
 *
 * Receive:      n, an integer
 * Precondition: n is nonnegative
 * Return:       n!
 ******************************************/

int factorial(int n)
{
   assert(n >= 0);
   if (n == 0)
      return 1;                      // anchor case
   else
     return n * factorial(n-1);      // inductive step
}
```

When this function is called with an argument greater than zero, the inductive step

```
else
   return n * factorial(n-1);
```

causes the function to call itself repeatedly, each time with a smaller parameter, until the anchor case

```
if (n == 0)
   return 1;
```

is reached.

To illustrate, consider the statement

```
int fact = factorial(4);
```

that calls the function `factorial()` to calculate 4!. Since the value of `n` (4) is not 0, the inductive step executes

```
return n * factorial(n-1);
```

which calls `factorial(3)`. Before control is transferred to `factorial(3)`, the current value (4) of the parameter `n` is saved so that the value of `n` can be restored when control returns. This might be pictured as follows:

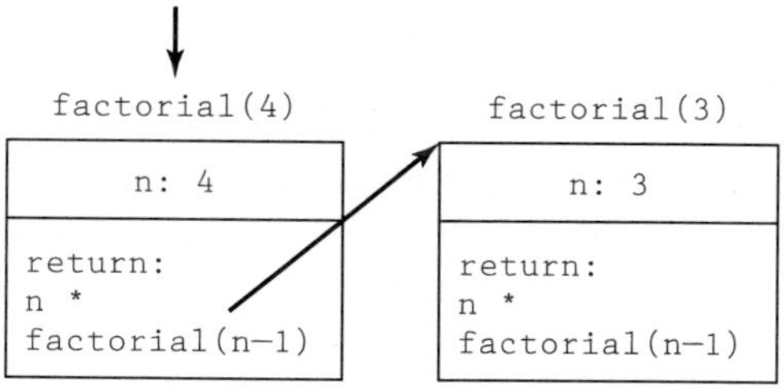

Since the value of `n` (3) in this function call is not 0, the inductive step in this second call to `factorial()` generates another call `factorial(n-1)` passing it the argument 2. Once again, the value of `n` (3) is saved so that it can be restored later:

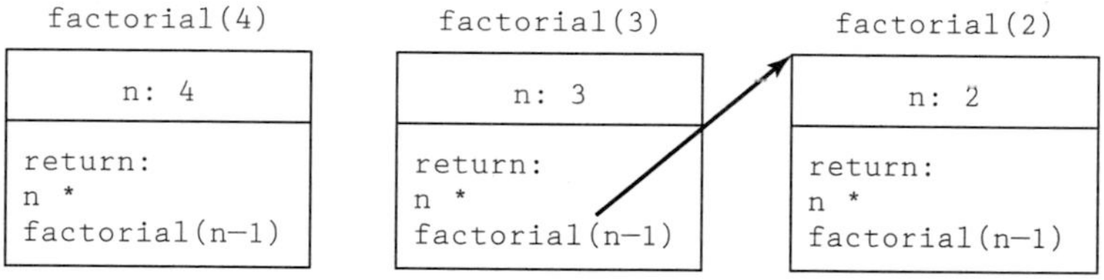

Since the value of `n` (2) in this function call is not 0, the inductive step in this third call to `factorial()` generates another call `factorial(n-1)` passing it the argument 1. Once again, the value of `n` (2) is saved so that it can be restored later. The call `factorial(1)` in turn generates another call, `factorial(0)`:

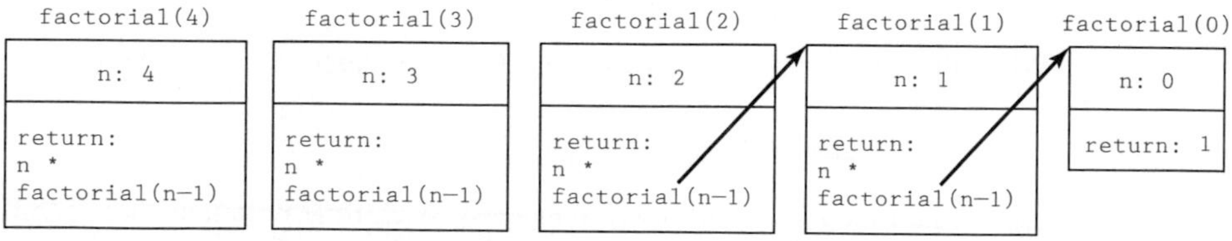

Because the anchor condition

```
if (n == 0)
   return 1;
```

is now satisfied in this last function call, no additional recursive calls are generated. Instead, the value 1 is returned as the value for `factorial(0)`:

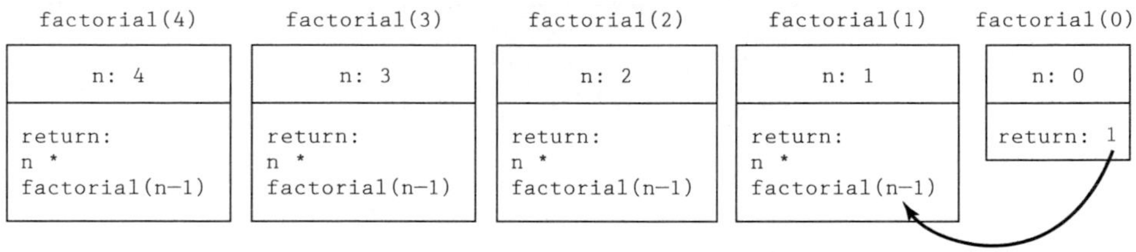

Now that `factorial(0)` has completed its computation, execution resumes in `factorial(1)` where this returned value can now be used to complete the evaluation of

```
n * factorial(n - 1) =  1 * factorial(0) = 1 * 1  = 1
```

giving 1 as the return value for `factorial(1)`:

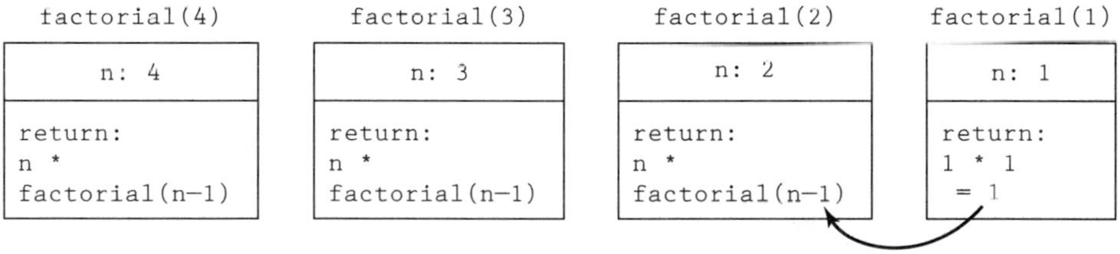

Once `factorial(1)` has completed its computation, execution resumes in `factorial(2)` where the return value of `factorial(1)` can now be used to complete the evaluation of

```
n * factorial(n - 1) =  2 * factorial(1) = 2 * 1  = 2
```

giving 2 as the return value for `factorial(2)`:

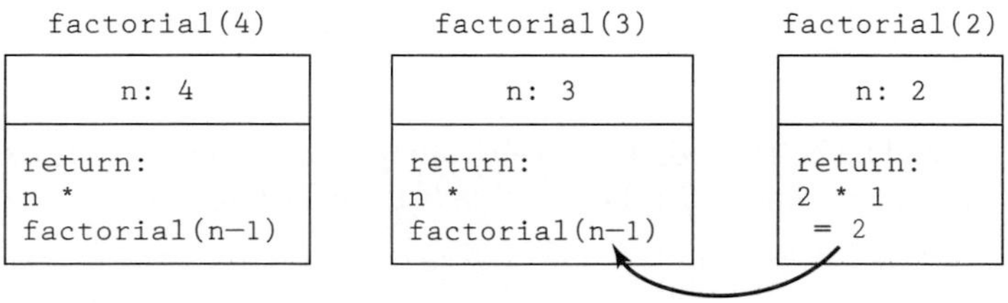

Since `factorial(2)` has completed its computation, execution resumes in `factorial(3)` where the return value of `factorial(2)` is used to complete the evaluation of

```
n * factorial(n - 1) =  3 * factorial(2) = 3 * 2  = 6
```

giving 6 as the return value for `factorial(3)`:

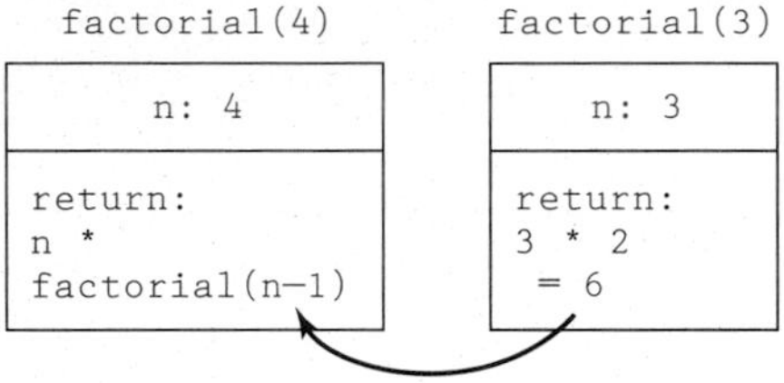

This completes the function call to `factorial(3)`, and so execution resumes in the call to `factorial(4)`, which computes and returns the value

```
n * factorial(n - 1) = 4 * factorial(3) = 4 * 6 = 24
```

giving 24 as the return value for `factorial(4)`:

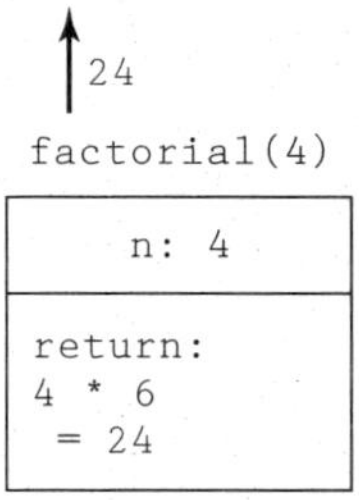

Note that in the definition `factorial()`, we used an `assert()` to test that the parameter `n` is not negative. To see the reason for this, consider what would happen if we had not tested this precondition and the function were called with a negative integer, as in

```
int fact = factorial(-1);
```

Since –1 is not equal to 0, the inductive step

```
else
   return n * factorial(n-1);
```

would be performed, recursively calling `factorial(-2)`. Execution of this call would begin, and since – 2 is not equal to 0, the inductive step

```
else
   return n * factorial(n-1);
```

would be performed, recursively calling `factorial(-3)`. This behavior would continue until memory was exhausted, at which point the program would terminate abnormally, possibly producing an error message like

```
Stack overruns Heap.
```

Such behavior is described as **infinite recursion** and is obviously undesirable. To avoid it, we programmed defensively by including the parameter-validity check.

EXAMPLE 2: TOWERS OF HANOI

The **Towers of Hanoi** problem is to solve the puzzle shown in the following figure, in which one must move the disks from the left peg to the right peg according to the following rules:

1. When a disk is moved, it must be placed on one of the three pegs.
2. Only one disk may be moved at a time, and it must be the top disk on one of the pegs.
3. A larger disk may never be placed on top of a smaller one.

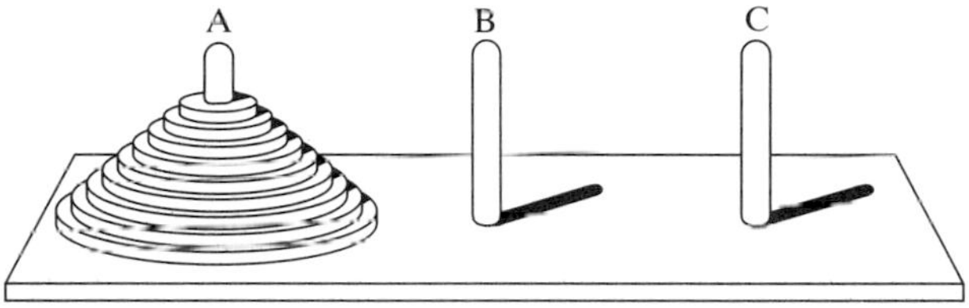

The following *game tree* shows the various configurations that are possible in the problem with two disks; the highlighted path in the tree shows a solution to the two-disk problem:

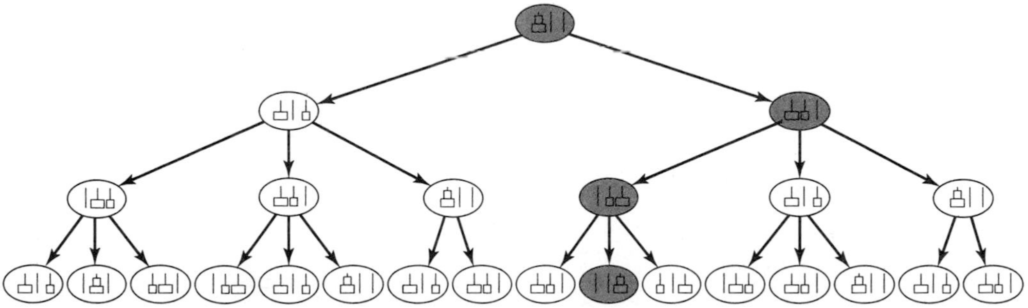

Legend has it that the priests in the Temple of Bramah were given a puzzle consisting of a golden platform with three diamond needles on which were placed sixty-four golden disks. The priests were to move one disk per day, following the preceding rules, and when they had successfully finished moving the disks to another needle, time would end. (*Question:* If the priests moved one disk per day and began their work in year 0, when would time end?)

Novices usually find the puzzle easy to solve for a small number of disks, but they have more difficulty as the number of disks grows to seven, eight, and beyond. To a computer scientist, however, the Towers of Hanoi puzzle is easy: We begin by identifying a base case, for which the problem is trivial to solve:

If there is one disk, then move it from Peg A to Peg C.

The puzzle is thus easily solved for one disk. We then seek an inductive solution for $n > 1$ disks, in which we assume that a solution exists for $n - 1$ disks:

1. *Move the topmost n – 1 disks from Peg A to Peg B, using Peg C for temporary storage.*
2. *Move the final disk remaining on Peg A to Peg C.*
3. *Move the n – 1 disks from Peg B to Peg C, using Peg A for temporary storage.*

This scheme is implemented by the recursive function `move()` in Figure 8.10, which solves the Towers of Hanoi puzzle for n disks:

Fig. 8.10 Solving the Towers of Hanoi problem recursively.

```
/* move is a recursive function to solve the Hanoi Towers puzzle.
 *
 *  Receive:
 *    n, the number of disks to be moved;
 *    source, the needle the disks are to be moved from;
 *    destination, the needle the disks are to be moved to; and
 *    spare, the needle that can be used to store disks temporarily.
 *******************************************************************/

void move(int n, char source, char destination, char spare)
{
   if (n <= 1)                                  // anchor
      cout << "Move the top disk from " << source << " to "
           << destination << endl;
   else
   {                                            // inductive case
      move(n-1, source, spare, destination);
      move(1, source, destination, spare);
      move(n-1, spare, destination, source);
   }
}
```

Figure 8.11 presents a driver program that uses `move()` to solve the Hanoi Towers problem and an execution in which the problem is solved for 4 disks.

Fig. 8.11 Towers of Hanoi driver program. (Part 1 of 2)

```
/* hanoitowers.cpp solves the Towers of Hanoi puzzle recursively.
 *
 * Input:  numDisks, the number of disks to be moved
 * Output: a sequence of moves that solve the puzzle
 ****************************************************************/

#include <iostream>
using namespace std;

void move(int n, char source, char destination, char spare);

int main()
{
   const char PEG1 = 'A',                // the three pegs
              PEG2 = 'B',
              PEG3 = 'C';

   cout << "This program solves the Hanoi Towers puzzle.\n\n";

   cout << "Enter the number of disks: ";
   int numDisks;                         // the number of disks to be moved
   cin >> numDisks;
   cout << endl;

   move(numDisks, PEG1, PEG2, PEG3);     // the solution
}

/*** Insert definition of move() from Figure 8.10 here. ***/
```

Sample run:

```
This program solves the Hanoi Towers puzzle.

Enter the number of disks: 4

Move the top disk from A to B
Move the top disk from A to C
Move the top disk from B to C
Move the top disk from A to B
Move the top disk from C to A
```

Fig. 8.11 Towers of Hanoi driver program. (Part 2 of 2)

```
Move the top disk from C to B
Move the top disk from A to B
Move the top disk from A to C
Move the top disk from B to C
Move the top disk from B to A
Move the top disk from C to A
Move the top disk from B to C
Move the top disk from A to B
Move the top disk from A to C
Move the top disk from B to C
```

✔ Quick Quiz 8.6

1. _______ is the phenomenon of a function calling itself.
2. Name and describe the two parts of a recursive definition of a function.
3. (True or false) A nonrecursive function for computing some value may execute more rapidly than a recursive function that computes the same value.
4. For the following recursive function, find `f(5)`:

```
int f(int n)
{
    if (n == 0)
        return 0;
    else
        return n + f(n - 1);
}
```

5. For the function in Question 4, find `f(0)`.
6. For the function in Question 4, suppose that + is changed to * in the inductive step. Find `f(5)`.
7. For the function in Question 4, what happens with the function call `f(-1)`?

Exercises 8.6

Exercises 1–12 assume the following function `f`:

```
void f(int num)
{
    if ((1 <= num) && (num <= 8))
    {
        f(num - 1);
        cout << num;
    }
```

```
    else
        cout << endl;
}
```

For Exercises 1–3, tell what output is produced by the function call.

1. `f(3);`
2. `f(7);`
3. `f(10);`

4–6. Tell what output is produced by the function calls in Exercises 1–3 if `num - 1` is replaced by `num + 1` in the function definition.

7–9. Tell what output is produced by the function calls in Exercises 1–3 if the `cout << num;` statement and the recursive call to `f()` are interchanged.

10–12. Tell what output is produced by the function calls in Exercises 1–3 if a copy of the statement `cout << num;` is inserted before the recursive call to `f()`.

13. Given the following function `f()`, use the method illustrated in this section to trace the sequence of function calls and returns in evaluating `f(1, 5)`:

```
int f(int num1, int num2)
{
    if (num1 > num2)
        return 0;
    else if (num2 == num1 + 1)
        return 1;
    else
        return f(num1 + 1, num2 - 1) + 2;
}
```

14. Proceed as in Exercise 13, but for `f(8, 3)`.

Exercises 15–17 assume the following function `g()`:

```
void g(int num1, int num2)
{
    if (num2 <= 0)
        cout << endl;
    else
    {
        g(num1 - 1, num2 - 1);
        cout << num1;
        g(num1 + 1, num2 - 1);
    }
}
```

15. What output is produced by the function call `g(14, 4)`? (*Hint:* First try `g(14, 2)`, then `g(14, 3)`).

16. How many letters are output by the call `g(14, 10)`?

17. If the `cout << num1;` statement is moved before the first recursive call to `g()`, what output will be produced by `g(14, 4)`?

For Exercises 18–22, determine what is calculated by the given recursive function.

18.
```
void f(unsigned n)
{
   if (n == 0)
      return 0;
   else
      return n * f(n - 1);
}
```

19.
```
double f(double x, unsigned n)
{
   if (n == 0)
      return 0;
   else
      return x + f(x, n - 1);
}
```

20.
```
unsigned f(unsigned n)
{
   if (n < 2)
      return 0;
   else
      return 1 + f(n / 2);
}
```

21.
```
unsigned f(unsigned n)
{
   if (n == 0)
      return 0;
   else
      return f(n / 10) + n % 10;
}
```

The following exercises ask you to write functions to compute various quantities. To test these functions, you should write driver programs as instructed in Programming Problems 8–11 at the end of this chapter.

22. Write a recursive power function that calculates x^n, where x is a real value and n is a nonnegative integer.

23. Write a recursive function that returns the number of digits in a nonnegative integer.

24. Write a recursive function `printReverse()` that displays an integer's digits in reverse order.

25. Modify the recursive power function in Exercise 22 so that it also works for negative exponents. One approach is to modify the recursive definition of x^n so that for negative values of n, division is used instead of multiplication and n is incremented rather than decremented:

$$x^n = \begin{cases} 1 & \text{if } n \text{ is zero} \\ x^{n-1} * x & \text{if } n \text{ is greater than } 0 \\ x^{n+1}/x & \text{otherwise} \end{cases}$$

26. For the function `move()` in Figure 8.10, trace the execution of the function call `move(4, 'A', 'B', 'C');` far enough to produce the first five moves. Does your answer agree with the program output in Figure 8.11?
27. Proceed as in Exercise 26, but for the call `move(5, 'A', 'B' , 'C')`.

Part of the Picture

Numerical Methods

Mathematical models are used to solve problems in a wide variety of areas including science, engineering, business, and the social sciences. Many of these models consist of ordinary algebraic equations, differential equations, systems of equations, and so on, and the solution of the problem is obtained by finding solutions for these equations. Methods for solving such equations that can be implemented in a computer program are called **numerical methods,** and the development and analysis of such numerical methods is an important area of study in computer science.

Some of the major types of problems in which numerical methods are routinely used include the following:

1. *Curve fitting.* In many applications, the solution of a problem requires analyzing data consisting of pairs of values to determine whether the items in these pairs are related. For example, a sociologist might wish to determine whether there is a linear relationship between educational level and income level.
2. *Solving equations*. Such problems deal with finding the value of a variable that satisfies a given equation.
3. *Integration*. The solution of many problems such as finding the area under a curve, determining total revenue generated by sales of an item, calculating probabilities of certain events, and calculating work done by a force require the evaluation of an integral. Often these integrals can only be evaluated using numerical techniques.
4. *Differential equations*. Differential equations are equations that involve one or more derivatives of unknown functions. Such equations play an important role in many applications, and several effective and efficient numerical methods for solving these equations have been developed.
5. *Solving linear systems*. Linear systems consist of several equations, each of which has several unknowns. A solution of such a system is a collection of values for these unknowns that satisfies all of the equations simultaneously.

Here we introduce a simple, but practical, introduction to one of these areas: integration.

APPROXIMATING AREAS OF REGIONS

One important problem in calculus is finding the area of a region bounded below by the x-axis, above by the graph of a function $y = f(x)$, on the left by a vertical line $x = a$, and on the right by a vertical line $x = b$:

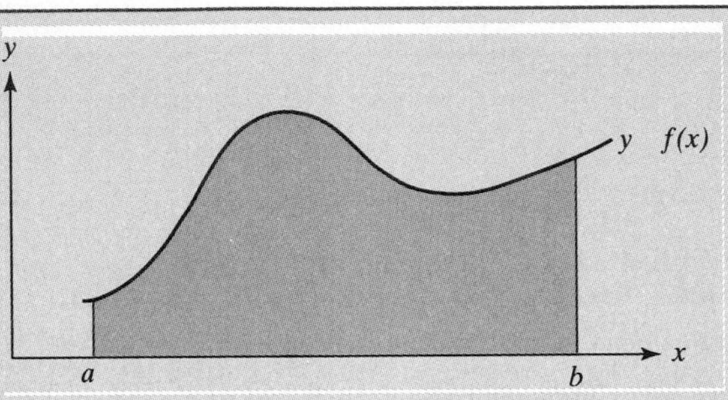

More generally, the problem is to approximate the integral $\int_a^b f(x)dx$.

A commonly used method for approximating this area is to divide the region into strips and approximate the area of each strip with the area of some geometric figure for which an area formula is known. One such method that uses trapezoids is described on the Web site for this text. This description derives the trapezoidal formula and implements this with a function `trapezoidalArea()`. One of the Programming Problems describes Simpson's method that uses parabolas instead of trapezoids.

There are many problems where it is necessary to compute the area under a curve (or the more general problem of calculating an integral). One such problem is the following.

PROBLEM: ROAD CONSTRUCTION

A construction company has contracted to build a highway for the state highway commission. Several sections of this highway must pass through hills from which large amounts of dirt must be excavated to provide a flat and level roadbed.

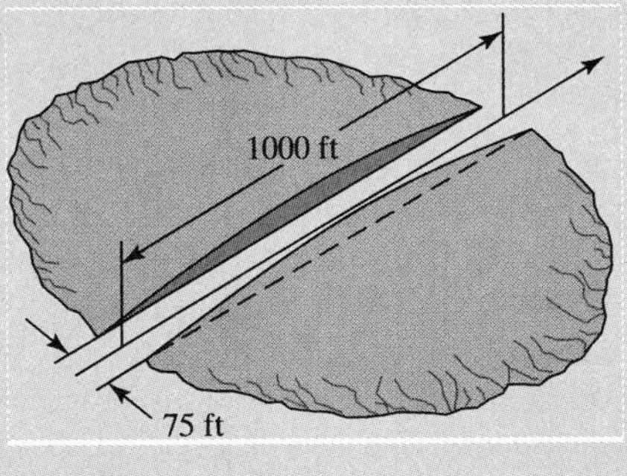

To estimate the construction costs, the company needs to know the volume of dirt that must be excavated from the hill.

Object-Centered Design

To estimate the volume of dirt to be removed, we can assume that the height of the hill does not vary from one side of the road to the other. The volume can then be calculated as

(Volume = cross-sectional area of the hill) × (width of the road)

The cross-sectional area of the hill can be computed using the trapezoidal method.

The rest of the OCD development of a solution to this problem is included on the book's Web site. A program along with a sample run is also included.

8.7* OBJECTive Thinking: Class Variables, Instance Variables, and Scope

In our previous *OBJECTive Thinking* sections, we have seen various aspects of building class types, including how to build classes, how to write constructors that let us initialize instance variables, how to use constructors to define objects, and how to build methods by which we can send messages to such objects. In Figure 4.7, we also saw how to build *class methods*—messages that were sent to *classes* rather than to objects—by prepending the keyword `static` to a method's prototype.

In this section, we will see that in addition to providing a mechanism for class methods, C++ also provides a means of declaring and initializing *class variables*. Once we have seen this mechanism, we will discuss how scope rules apply to C++ classes.

CLASS VARIABLES

Suppose that a programmer is using our `Sphere` class from earlier *OBJECTive Thinking* sections in some 3-D graphics program. It is possible that this program might need to keep track of the number of `Sphere` objects that have been created. The traditional way to do this is for the programmer to declare a counter variable and then increment it each time a `Sphere` is constructed:

```
int sphereCount = 0;
    .
    .
    .
Sphere aSphere;
sphereCount++;
```

This approach works, but it requires the user of our class to do the bookkeeping.

An alternative approach is for our `Sphere` class itself to keep track of how many instances of itself have been created. The basic idea is to add a counter variable to the class, add an accessor method for that variable, and then (since the `Sphere` constructor is invoked each time a `Sphere` object is created) increment that counter in the `Sphere` constructor:

```
class Sphere
{
 public:
   Sphere();
   int getNumberOfSpheres();
   // ... other method prototypes ...
```

```
 private:
   double myRadius, myDensity, myWeight;
   int numberOfSpheres;  // WILL BE MODIFIED LATER
   // ... other variable declarations ...
};

inline Sphere::Sphere()
{
   myRadius = myDensity = myWeight = 0.0;
   numberOfSpheres++;
}

inline int Sphere::getNumberOfSpheres()
{
   return numberOfSpheres;
}

// ... other method definitions ...
```

Unfortunately, declaring `numberOfSpheres` as an instance variable will not work for this purpose, because its value will be initialized to zero each time a a new `Sphere` object is created. What we want is for `numberOfSpheres` to be initialized only *once*, when the program begins running, and to be incremented each time we build a new `Sphere`.

For situations like this, C++ provides **class variables**. Unlike instance variables, whose storage is associated with an *object*, the storage of a class variable is associated with the *class*. We can thus solve our problem by

- declaring `numberOfSpheres` as a class variable instead of as an instance variable;
- initializing `numberOfSpheres` to zero exactly once;
- incrementing `numberOfSpheres` in the constructor; and
- declaring `getNumberOfSpheres()` as a class method instead of as an instance method.

Each of these is straightforward, as illustrated in Figure 8.12.

Fig. 8.12 Class variable declaration, initialization, and access. (Part 1 of 2)

```
/* Sphere.h illustrates the use of a class variable.
 * ...
 **********************************************************/

class Sphere
{
 public:
   Sphere();
   // ... other methods omitted ...
   static int getNumberOfSpheres();
```

Fig. 8.12 Class variable declaration, initialization, and access. (Part 2 of 2)

```
 private:
   double myRadius, myDensity, myWeight;
   static int numberOfSpheres;
};

int Sphere::numberOfSpheres = 0;

inline Sphere::Sphere()
{
   myRadius = myDensity = myWeight = 0.0;
   numberOfSpheres++;
}

inline int Sphere::getNumberOfSpheres()
{
   return numberOfSpheres;
}
```

There are several things to note in this example:

- Just as a class method is declared by prepending `static` to its prototype, a class variable is declared by prepending `static` to its declaration:

```
static int numberOfSpheres;
```

- A class variable is initialized by a special class variable initialization statement that is executed exactly once, just before the main method begins execution. This statement specifies the type of the variable, the class of which it is a member, the scope operator, the name of the variable, the assignment operator, and the initial value:

```
int Sphere::numberOfSpheres = 0;
```

- A constructor (or an instance method) can access and modify the value of a class variable:

```
inline Sphere::Sphere()
{
   myRadius = myDensity = myWeight = 0.0;
   numberOfSpheres++;
}
```

- Accessors for class variables are usually class methods. Constructors and instance methods can access both class variables and instance variables, but a class method is only permitted to access class variables:

```
inline int Sphere::getNumberOfSpheres()
{
   return numberOfSpheres;
}
```

By incrementing our class variable each time the constructor executes, we are able to keep count of how many `Sphere` objects a program has created. Figure 8.13 presents a driver program that illustrates this.

Fig. 8.13 Testing class variables and methods. (Part 1 of 2)

```
/* sphereDriver.cpp tests our Sphere class variable & method.
 * ...
 ************************************************************/

#include <iostream>
using namespace std;
#include "Sphere.h"

int main()
{
  for (;;)
  {
    cout << "\nEnter a positive value (0 to quit): ";
    int aValue;
    cin >> aValue;
    if (aValue < 1) break;
    Sphere aSphere;
    cout << "Total number of spheres: "
         << Sphere::getNumberOfSpheres() << endl;
  }
}
```

Sample Run:

```
Enter a positive value (0 to quit): 1
Total number of spheres: 1

Enter a positive value (0 to quit): 1
Total number of spheres: 2

Enter a positive value (0 to quit): 1
Total number of spheres: 3
```

Fig. 8.13 Testing class variables and methods. (Part 2 of 2)

```
Enter a positive value (0 to quit): 1
Total number of spheres: 4

Enter a positive value (0 to quit): 0
```

Each time we declare a `Sphere` object, the `Sphere` constructor increments `numberOfSpheres`. In general, class variables like `numberOfSpheres` are useful in any situation where a class needs to keep track of some activity of its objects.

DESTRUCTORS

In the program in Figure 8.13, there is only one `Sphere` object in existence at any one time. Suppose, however, that many `Sphere` objects may exist (i.e., consume memory) at any given time and we need to know how many there are.

The preceding approach increments our class variable each time a `Sphere` is created. But to count the number of `Sphere` objects *in existence* (as opposed to the number that have been created), we must decrement class variable `numberOfSpheres` each time a `Sphere` ceases to exist—whenever control moves outside of the scope of that `Sphere`. To illustrate, consider the loop in Figure 8.13:

```
for (;;)
{
   . . .
   Sphere aSphere;
   . . .
}
```

Each time control moves through the loop, the object `aSphere` comes into existence, and each time control leaves the loop body to begin the next repetition, `aSphere` ceases to exist.

To keep a count of the number of `Sphere` objects in existence, we need to be able to decrement `numberOfSpheres` each time a `Sphere` ceases to exist. To do this, we need an operation for class `Sphere` that is the opposite of a constructor—one that is automatically executed whenever an object ceases to exist. Such an operation is called a **destructor**.

Just as the name of a constructor is always the same as the name of a class, *the name of a destructor is always the ~ (tilde) character followed by the name of the class.* Figure 8.14 illustrates how a destructor can be declared and defined.

Fig. 8.14 Destructor declaration and definition. (Part 1 of 2)

```
/* Sphere.h illustrates a class destructor.
 * ...
 ****************************************************************/
```

Fig. 8.14 Destructor declaration and definition. (Part 2 of 2)

```
class Sphere
{
 public:
   Sphere();
   ~Sphere();
   // ... other methods omitted ...
   static int getNumberOfSpheres();

 private:
   double myRadius, myDensity, myWeight;
   static int numberOfSpheres;
};

int Sphere::numberOfSpheres = 0;

inline Sphere::Sphere()
{
   myRadius = myDensity = myWeight = 0.0;
   numberOfSpheres++;
}

inline Sphere::~Sphere()
{
   numberOfSpheres--;
}

inline int getNumberOfSpheres()
{
   return numberOfSpheres;
}
```

NOTE *The C++ compiler automatically invokes a destructor at the end of the scope of any instance of the class (i.e., an object), just as it automatically invokes the constructor at the declaration of any instance of the class.* Compare the code and execution of Figure 8.15 with that of Figure 8.13 to see the difference this makes.

Fig. 8.15 Testing destructor execution. (Part 1 of 2)

```
/* sphereDriver.cpp tests our Sphere class variable & method.
 * ...
 **************************************************************/
```

Fig. 8.15 Testing destructor execution. (Part 2 of 2)

```
#include <iostream>
using namespace std;
#include "Sphere.h"          // now contains a destructor

int main()
{
  for (;;)
  {
    cout << "\nEnter a positive value (0 to quit): ";
    int aValue;
    cin >> aValue;
    if (aValue < 1) break;
    Sphere s0; // construct a Sphere object
    cout << "Inside the loop, total number of spheres is: "
         << Sphere::getNumberOfSpheres() << endl;
  } // Sphere destructor gets called here for s0 each repetition

  cout << "\nOutside the loop, total number of spheres is: "
       << Sphere::getNumberOfSpheres() << endl;
  Sphere s1, s2, s3; // construct 3 Sphere objects
  cout << "At the end, total number of spheres is: "
       << Sphere::getNumberOfSpheres() << endl;
} // Sphere destructor gets called here for s1, s2, and s3
```

Sample Run:

```
Enter a positive value (0 to quit): 9
Inside the loop, total number of spheres is: 1

Enter a positive value (0 to quit): 9
Inside the loop, total number of spheres is: 1

Enter a positive value (0 to quit): 9
Inside the loop, total number of spheres is: 1

Enter a positive value (0 to quit): 0

Outside the loop, total number of spheres is: 0
At the end, total number of spheres is: 3
```

You should make certain that you understand why the programs in Figure 8.13 and Figure 8.15 produce the output they do.

What have we learned?

- Preceding an attribute variable's declaration with `static` makes it a class variable. Attribute variable declarations without the `static` specifier are instance variables.
- Instead of being initialized in a constructor, class variables are initialized by a special initialization statement outside of the class. Such statements are executed once, just before a program's main function begins execution.
- Just as a constructor can perform any desired action when an object is created, a destructor is an operation that can perform any desired action when an object is destroyed.
- The name of a destructor is always ~ followed by the name of the class. A destructor may not have parameters and, therefore, may not be overloaded with multiple definitions.

CLASS SCOPE

In Section 8.5, we saw that there are several rules of scope that govern the accessibility of identifiers in a program. With a bit of thought, it should be evident that the attribute variables of a class do not follow these rules. To illustrate, we revisit the `Sphere` class:

```
class Sphere
{
 public:
   Sphere();
   ~Sphere();

   static int getNumberOfSpheres();
 private:
   double myRadius, myDensity, myWeight;
   int numberOfSpheres;
};

int Sphere::numberOfSpheres = 0;

inline Sphere::Sphere()
{
  myRadius = myDensity = myWeight = 0.0;
  numberOfSpheres++;
}

inline Sphere::~Sphere()
{
  numberOfSpheres--;
}
```

```
inline int Sphere::getNumberOfSpheres()
{
  return numberOfSpheres;
}
```

If the `Sphere` attribute variables `myRadius`, `myDensity`, `myWeight`, and `numberOfSpheres` were governed by the "normal" C++ scope rules, then using Rule S1, their scopes would begin at their declarations and would end at the end of the block containing them—that is, at the end of class `Sphere`. However, we have seen that the definition of an instance method can access the attribute variables, even if that method definition resides in a different file (e.g., `Sphere.cpp`)! Clearly, the scope of an attribute variable is not the same as the scope of a normal variable.

To govern the identifiers declared in a class, we add a fifth scope rule to those we defined in Section 8.5:

S5.a If an identifier is declared anywhere within a class,
then its scope begins at the beginning of its class and ends at the end of its class, but extends into every constructor, destructor, and method[9] of the class.

From a slightly different perspective, the methods of a class may be considered to be a part of their class—that is why, in their definitions, their names must be preceded by the name of the class and the scope operator. From this perspective, it makes sense that methods be able to access any identifier declared within their class.

To govern the difference between public and private identifiers, we add a final rule:

S5.b If an identifier is declared in a public section of a class:

- If it is an instance variable or method, it may be accessed outside of the class using the name of the instance and dot notation.
- Otherwise (e.g., it is a class variable or method), it may be accessed outside of the class using the name of the class and the scope operator.

The C++ scope rules may seem complex and difficult. However, if you master them and keep them in mind as you program, you (i) will make far fewer programming errors and (ii) will find it easier to correct those that you do make. Practice makes perfect!

✔ Quick Quiz 8.7

1. Storage of a class variable is associated with the ________ rather than an object, which is the case for instance variables.
2. The declaration of a class variable must begin with the keyword ________.
3. (True or false) A class constructor is used to initialize a class variable.

9. As noted earlier, class variables can be accessed by both instance and class methods; instance variables, however, can only be accessed by instance methods.

4. (True or false) Constructors and instance methods can access both instance variables and class variables.
5. (True or false) Class methods can access both instance variables and class variables.

For Questions 6–9, assume that `C` is a class.

6. `C`'s ________ is invoked whenever an instance of `C` is declared.
7. `C`'s ________ is invoked whenever an instance of that class is destroyed.
8. The name of `C`'s constructor is ________.
9. The name of `C`'s destructor is ________.

CHAPTER SUMMARY

Key Terms & Notes

alias
anchor
argument
base case
call-by-reference
call-by-value
class scope
class variable
code bloat
`const` reference parameter
destructor
hole in the scope
inductive step
`inline` specifier
namespace
numerical mehod
overload
parameter
parameter-passing mechanism
recursion
recursive definition of a function
recursive step
reference parameter
scope
signature
template
type parameter
`using` directive
value parameter

- By default, parameters are value parameters; their values are *copies* of the corresponding arguments. Thus, changing the value of a value parameter has no effect on the value of the corresponding argument.
- Reference parameters are aliases for their corresponding arguments; they refer to the same memory locations. Thus, changing the value of a reference parameter also changes the value of the corresponding argument. This argument must be a variable.
- A parameter is specified to be a reference parameter by inserting an ampersand (`&`) between its type and its name in the function heading.
- An alternative to a value parameter that does not require copying the value of the corresponding argument is a `const` reference parameter. Such a parameter is preferred when its type is a class (or it is some other large object) and the movement is into, but not out of the function.

- A `const` reference parameter is specified by inserting the keyword `const` before the parameter's type and an ampersand (`&`) after its type.
- Use a `return` statement to send back a single value from a function; use reference parameters to send back multiple values.
- A simple function can be inlined to avoid the overhead of calling that function and thereby reduce execution time. Prepend the keyword `inline` to the function heading to do this.
- Inlined functions cannot be split with prototypes in a header (`.h`) file and definitions in an implementation (`.cpp`) file.
- Use restraint with inlining functions, since code bloat may result otherwise.
- The scope of an identifier is the portion of a program where the object or function that it names can be accessed.
- The basic scope rules for an identifier are as follows:
  - *Declared in a block*: from declaration to end of block
  - *Parameter*: body of the function
  - *In initialization of for loop*: from declaration to end of loop body
  - *Declared outside all blocks* : from declaration to end of file
  - *Declared in a class* : the entire class including every method of the class; if declared in the public section, it can be accessed outside the class using the name of an instance and dot notation for instance variables and methods or using the class name and the scope operator for class variables and methods.
- A `using` clause makes names in a namespace available without qualification.
- The signature of a function is the list of its parameter types. A function may overload another function—that is, have the same name—provided they have different signatures.
- Preceding the prototype and the definition of a function with a template clause of the form

  ```
  template<typename  T>
  ```

  converts the function into a function template, which is a type-independent pattern for a function. When the function is called, the compiler will use the types of the arguments to determine what type to substitute for `T` and generate a type-specific function.
- A recursive function must have an anchor that will eventually be executed and cause a return from the function. It must also have an inductive step that specifies the current action of the function in terms of previously defined actions.
- Unlike instance variables, whose storage is associated with an object, the storage of a class variable is associated with the class. All instances of that class share this same variable rather than have their own copies of it.
- A class variable is declared by prepending the keyword `static` to its declaration. It is initialized by a special class variable initialization statement of the form

  ```
  type ClassName::variableName = initial_value;
  ```

  that is executed exactly once, just before the main method begins execution.
- Constructors and instance methods can access both instance and class variables; class methods can access only class variables.

- A class constructor is invoked whenever an instance of that class is declared. A class destructor is called whenever the lifetime of an instance of that class is over.
- The name of a class destructor has the form `~ClassName()`.

Programming Pointers

Program Style and Design

1. *Functions should be documented in the same way that programs are.* The documentation should include specifications and descriptions of
   - the *purpose* of the function;
   - any items that must be *received by* the function from its caller;
   - any items that must be *input* to the function;
   - any items that are *returned or sent back by* the function to its caller;
   - any items that are *output* by the function.
2. *Follow the same stylistic standards for functions that are used for main programs*.
3. *Declare variable objects as close as possible to their first use.* This practice increases the readability of a program by keeping the use of an object and its declaration close together. It also aids with debugging because it delays the scope of an identifier as late as possible, which minimizes the number of variables to keep track of at any given point in the program.

   The primary exception is that *variables should not be casually declared within loops*, because such variables must be constructed anew on every repetition of the loop, and this slows execution.
4. *Parameters should be declared as determined by the* ***specification*** *of a function: If the specification for a function stipulates that*
   - *the function* **receives and does not return** *a nonclass value, then define a value parameter to hold that value;*
   - *the function* **receives and does not return** *a class value, then define a* `const` **reference** *parameter to hold that value*;
   - *the function* **returns a single value**, *then use a* `return` *statement in the function*;
   - *the function* **returns** *(and perhaps also receives) more than one value, then define a* **reference** *parameter to hold each of these values*.
5. *All variables that are used within a function should be defined within that function, either as parameters (if named in the specification) or as local variables (if required by the algorithm, but not named in the specification)*. Following this guideline keeps functions self-contained and increases their generality and hence their reusability.
6. *Only simple functions should be specified as being inline functions*. Substitution of an inline function's body for each of its calls can increase a program's size considerably if the function is nontrivial or it is called at several places in the program.
7. *Recursive functions should be clearly marked as such*. For clarity and readability, the anchor case and inductive steps of a recursive function should be marked with comments.

Potential Pitfalls

1. *When a function is called, the number of arguments should be the same as the number of parameters in the function heading.* [10] For example, consider the function prototype

```
int maximum(int number1, int number2);
```

If `i`, `j`, and `k` are integer variables, the function call

```
larger1 = maximum(i, j, k);
```

will generate an error, because the number of arguments does not match the number of parameters.

2. *The type of an argument corresponding to a value parameter should be compatible with the type of that parameter.* For example, for the function `maximum()` in Potential Pitfall 1, the statement

```
larger2 = maximum(someValue, 3.75);
```

is incorrect, because a real value such as `3.75` should not be passed to the integer parameter `number2`, since a loss of precision will occur.

3. *An argument that corresponds to a reference parameter must be a variable whose type matches the type of that parameter; it may not be a constant or an expression.* For example, the function with prototype

```
void findTaxes(double income,
               double & netIncome, double & tax);
```

cannot be called by the statement

```
findTaxes(salary, 3525.67, incomeTax);
```

because the constant `3525.67` cannot be associated with the reference parameter `netIncome`.

4. *Changing the value of a reference parameter changes the value of the corresponding argument.* Check carefully the prototype of each function that is used to see if it has any reference parameters; changes in their values may lead to unexpected or unintended changes in the values of arguments.

5. *A function's parameters (and non-static local variables) are allocated memory only during execution of that function; there is no memory associated with them either before or after execution of that function.* Any attempt to use these parameters outside the function will thus generate an error.

6. *An identifier must be declared before it can be used.* For example, if the function `findTaxes()` calls the function `calculate()`, then a prototype (or definition) of `calculate()` must precede the definition of `findTaxes()`.

---

10. An exception is when one or more parameters at the end of the parameter list have *default arguments* (see the text's Web site for more details); for example,

```
void f(int x, int y = 0, double z = 3.5);
```

As the following examples show, this function may be called with 1, 2, or 3 arguments:

`f(1, 2, 4.9);`	Within `f`, x will have the value 1, y the value 2, and z the value 4.9.
`f(1, 2);`	Within `f`, x will have the value 1, y the value 2, and z the value 3.5.
`f(1);`	Within `f`, x will have the value 1, y the value 0, and z the value 3.5.

```
void calculate(parameter_list);
   . . .
void findTaxes();
{
   . . .
   calculate(argument_list);
   . . .
}
```

Programming Problems

Section 8.3

1. Write a driver program to test the weight-conversion functions of Exercises 12 and 13.
2. Write a driver program to test the length-conversion function of Exercises 14 and 15.
3. Write a driver program to test the time-conversion function of Exercises 16 and 17.
4. With **polar coordinates** (r, θ) of a point P, the first polar coordinate r is the distance from the origin to P, and the second polar coordinate θ is the angle from the positive x-axis to the ray joining the origin with P.

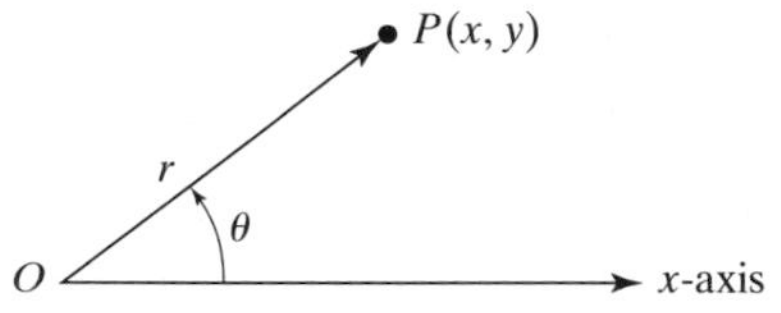

The formulas that relate polar coordinates of a point to its **rectangular coordinates** (x, y) are

$$x = r\cos\theta$$

$$y = r\sin\theta$$

Write a function `convert()` that converts polar coordinates to rectangular coordinates. Use it in a program that reads the polar coordinates for several points and calls `convert()`, which calculates and returns the rectangular coordinates for each point. The program should display both pairs of coordinates.

5. Write a function `calculateTaxes()` that calculates and returns the amount of city income tax and the amount of federal income tax to be withheld from an employee's pay for one pay period. Assume that city income tax withheld is computed by taking 1.15 percent of gross pay on the first $40,000 earned per year and that federal income tax withheld is computed by taking the gross pay less $50 for each dependent claimed and multiplying by 20 percent.

   Use this function in a program that for each of several employees reads the employee's number, number of dependents, hourly pay rate, city income tax withheld to date, federal income tax withheld to date, and hours worked for this period and then calls function `calculateTaxes()` to find the amount of taxes to be withheld. The program should then display the employee number, gross pay and net pay for this pay period, the amount of city income tax and the amount of federal income tax withheld for this pay period, and the total amounts withheld through this pay period.

6. The **greatest common divisor** of two integers a and b, GCD(a, b), not both of which are zero, is the largest positive integer that divides both a and b. The **Euclidean algorithm** for finding

this greatest common divisor of a and b is as follows: Divide a by b to obtain the integer quotient q and remainder r, so that $a = bq + r$. (If $b = 0$, GCD(a, b) = a.) Then GCD(a, b) = GCD(b, r). Replace a with b and b with r, and repeat this procedure. Since the remainders are decreasing, eventually a remainder of 0 will result. The last nonzero remainder is GCD(a, b). For example,

$$\begin{aligned} 1260 &= 198 \times 6 + 72 & \text{GCD}(1260, 198) &= \text{GCD}(198, 72) \\ 198 &= 72 \times 2 + 54 & &= \text{GCD}(72, 54) \\ 72 &= 54 \times 1 + 18 & &= \text{GCD}(54, 18) \\ 54 &= 18 \times 3 + 0 & &= 18 \end{aligned}$$

(*Note:* If either a or b is negative, replace it with its absolute value.) The **least common multiple** of a and b, LCM(a, b), is the smallest nonnegative integer that is a multiple of both a and b, and can be calculated using

$$\text{LCM}(a, b) = \frac{|a \times b|}{\text{GCD}(a, b)}$$

Write a program that reads two integers and then calls a function that calculates and passes back the greatest common divisor and the least common multiple of the integers. The program should then display the two integers together with their greatest common divisor and their least common multiple.

7. The graph of a person's emotional cycle $y = f(x)$ is a sine curve having an amplitude of 1 and a period of 28 days. On a given day, the person's emotional index is $f(age)$, where *age* is his or her age in days. Similarly, the physical and intellectual cycles are sine curves having an amplitude of 1 and periods of 23 and 33 days, respectively. Write a function that receives a person's age and returns his or her physical, intellectual, and emotional indices for the current day. Write another function to compute a person's biorhythm index, which is the sum of the physical, intellectual, and emotional cycles. Write a driver program to test your functions.

Section 8.6*

8. Write a driver program to test the power function of Exercise 22.
9. Write a driver program to test the digit-counting function of Exercise 23.
10. Write a driver program to test the reverse-printing function of Exercise 24.
11. Write a driver program to test the modified power function of Exercise 25.
12. Write a test driver for one of the functions in Exercises 18–21. Add output statements to the function to trace its actions as it executes. For example, the trace displayed for `f(21)` for the function `f` in Exercise 20 should have a form like

```
f(21) = 1 + f(10)
   f(10) = 1 + f(5)
      f(5) = 1 + f(2)
         f(2) = 1 + f(1)
            f(1) returns 0
         f(2) returns 1
      f(5) returns 2
   f(10) returns 3
f(21) returns 4
```

where the indentation level reflects the depth of the recursion. (*Hint:* This can be accomplished by declaring a variable `level` outside all blocks, initially zero, that is incremented when the function is entered and decremented just before exiting the function.)

13. Write a recursive function that prints a nonnegative integer with commas in the correct locations. For example, it should print 20131 as 20,131. Write a driver program to test your function.
14. The Euclidean algorithm for finding the greatest common divisor of two integers (not both zero) is described in Problem 6. Write a recursive function that calculates the greatest common divisor of two integers using the Euclidean algorithm. Write a driver program to test your function.
15. The sequence of *Fibonacci numbers*, 1, 1, 2, 3, 5, 8, 13, 21, . . . , (see Programming Problem 23 in Chapter 4) can be defined recursively by

$$f_1 = f_2 = 1 \qquad \text{(anchor)}$$

$$\text{For } n \geq 3,\ f_i = f_{i-1} + f_{i-2} \qquad \text{(inductive step)}$$

A recursive function seems like a natural way to calculate these numbers. Write such a function and then write a driver program to test your function. (*Note:* You will probably find that this function is very inefficient. See if you can figure out why by tracing some function calls as was done in the text.)

16. Consider a network of streets laid out in a rectangular grid, for example,

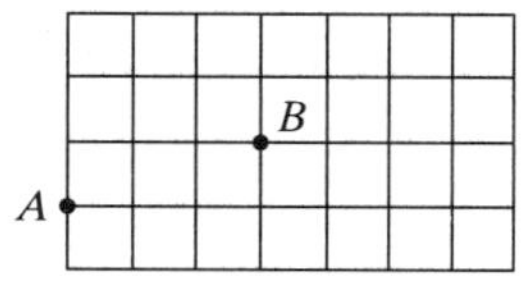

In a *northeast path* from one point in the grid to another, one may walk only to the north (up) and to the east (right). For example, there are four northeast paths from A to B in the preceding grid:

Write a recursive function to count the number of northeast paths from one point to another in a rectangular grid. Write a driver program to test your function.

CHAPTER 9
Files and Streams

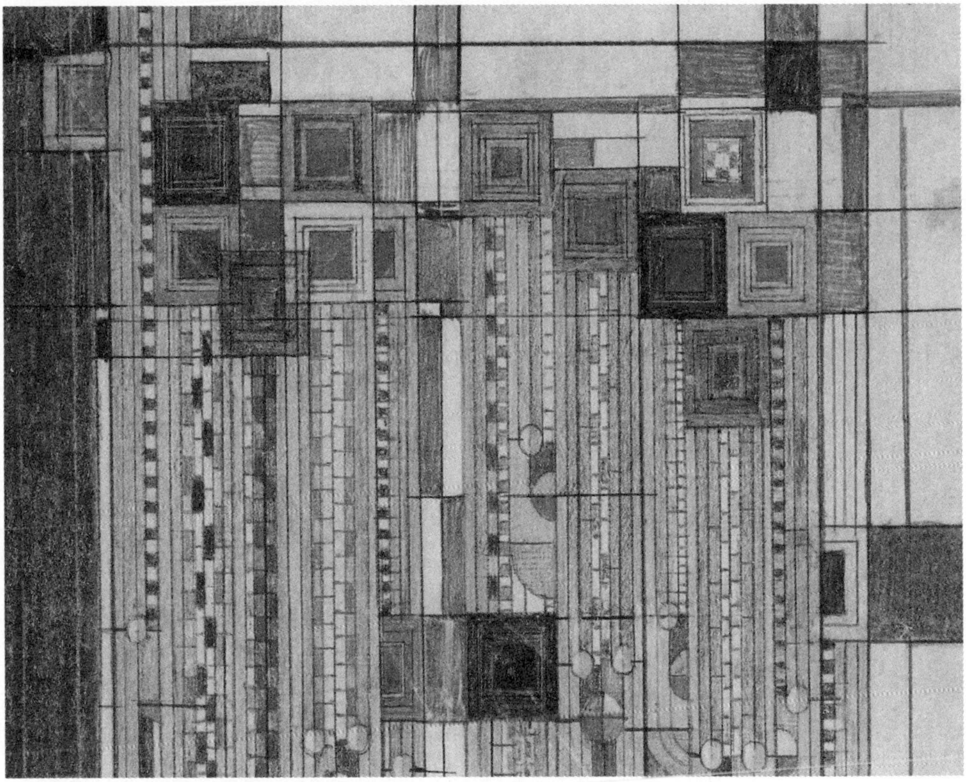

I can only assume that a "Do Not File" document is filed in a "Do Not File" file.

-Senator Frank Church

The goal is information at your fingertips.

-Bill Gates

The next best thing to knowing something is knowing where to find it.

-Samuel Johnson

. . . it became increasingly apparent to me that, over the years, Federal agencies have amassed vast amounts of information about virtually every American citizen. This fact, coupled with technological advances in data collection and dissemination, raised the possibility that information about individuals conceivably could be used for other than legitimate purposes and without the prior knowledge or consent of the individuals involved.

-President Gerald R. Ford

The rights of the people to be secure in their persons, houses, papers, and effects against unreasonable searches and seizures, shall not be violated. . . .

-Fourth Amendment of the U. S. Constitution

Chapter Contents

Chapter Objectives

- Use OCD to solve a problem involving files.
- Study C++'s support for input and output with files.
- Examine how C++ uses interactive and file streams to carry out I/O.
- See how to open and close file streams and how to use them for file I/O.
- Look at string streams and how they can be used for I/O.
- (Optional) Learn about the role files play in database-management systems.
- (Optional) Show how I/O operations using streams can be defined for classes.
- (Optional) Study how class converters can use string streams.

Many computer users have had the unfortunate experience of having their word processor (or text editor) unexpectedly fail while they were editing a document. This is especially annoying because all of the information entered since the last save operation is lost. This happens because a word processor is an executable program, and the information being edited (documents, programs, input data, etc.) is stored in the section of main memory allocated to the word processor. When the word processing program terminates, this memory is deallocated and its contents are lost.

To minimize this problem, many word processors and text editors provide an **autosave** feature that saves the information being edited in some *stable* location (such as secondary memory) so that information is not lost, even if a power outage should occur. Examples of secondary memory include hard disks, floppy disks, compact disks, and magnetic tapes.

Information that is saved in secondary memory must be stored in such a way that

1. it can be retrieved in the future and
2. it is kept separate from all other documents, programs, and so on that are saved.

To achieve these goals, secondary memory is organized into distinct containers called **files**, in which information can be stored. When a document must be edited, the word processor *loads* it from secondary memory to main memory by *reading* from the file in which it is stored. The operation of saving information to secondary memory involves *writing* the information to a file.

Files can be classified by the kind of data stored in them. Those that contain textual characters (such as the source code for a program, numbers entered with a text editor, etc.) are called **text files**. By contrast, files whose contents are not characters represented using ASCII or some other standard coding scheme for text (such as the binary code for a compiled program or the control codes for a word processor) are called **binary files**. In this chapter, we will discuss input and output using text files.

In addition to providing a stable place to store *programs* indefinitely, files can also be used to store data. If a large set of data values is to be processed, then those values can be stored in a file, and a program can be written to read these values from the file and process them. This capability is especially useful in testing and debugging a program because the data does not have to be reentered each time the program is executed. In this chapter, we will examine the file-processing features of C++.

9.1 Introductory Example: Weather Data Analysis

Until now our programs have been *interactive*, meaning that the user entered data directly from the keyboard in response to prompts or queries displayed on the screen. There are many problems, however, in which the sheer volume of data to be processed makes it impractical to enter it from the keyboard. For such problems, the data can be stored in a file, and the program designed to read data values from that file. In this section, we look at one such problem.

PROBLEM: PROCESSING METEOROLOGICAL DATA

A meteorologist must record and process large amounts of weather-related data. One part of the data consists of thousands of atmospheric pressure readings that were recorded every 15 minutes for the past year. This data has been stored in a file named `pressure.dat`, and the minimum, the maximum, and the average of these readings must be computed. A program is needed to read this data, calculate these statistics, and write the results to an output file.

Object-Centered Design

Behavior. For maximum flexibility, our program should display on the screen a prompt for the name of the input file containing the pressure readings to be processed and then read this filename from the keyboard. It should then read an arbitrary number of values from that file, compute the minimum, maximum, and average of those values. The program should display on the screen a prompt for the name of the output file, which is entered from the keyboard. It must then write the minimum, maximum, and average to that output file.

Objects. In addition to the objects identified in the preceding behavior, the program must maintain a count of how many values have been read and their sum, because these values are needed to compute the average of a collection of values. This gives the following list of objects needed to solve the problem:

	Software Objects		
Problem Objects	**Type**	**Kind**	**Name**
The name of the file in which the pressure readings are stored	`string`	varying	*inputFileName*
A pressure reading	`double`	varying	*reading*
The number of readings	`int`	varying	*count*
The minimum reading	`double`	varying	*minimum*
The maximum reading	`double`	varying	*maximum*
The sum of the readings	`double`	varying	*sum*
The average reading	`double`	varying	none (*sum* /*count*)
The name of the file to which the results are to be written	`string`	varying	*outputFileName*

From this list, we can specify the problem as follows:

Input(keyboard):	*inputFileName*, a string naming an input file
Input(*inputFileName*):	sequence of pressure readings
Input(keyboard):	*outputFileName*, a string naming an output file
Output(*outputFileName*):	the minimum, maximum, and average of the input values

Operations. From our behavioral description, the following operations are needed:

i. Prompt for and read a string (*inputFileName* and *outputFileName*) from the keyboard
ii. Initialize *count, sum, maximum*, and *minimum* to specific values
iii. Read a real value (*reading*) stored in a file
iv. Increment an integer variable (*count*) by 1
v. Add a real value (*reading*) to a real value (*sum*)
vi. Update *minimum* with *reading*, if necessary
vii. Update *maximum* with *reading*, if necessary
viii. Repeat Operations iii–vii until the end of the file is reached
ix. Write real values (*minimum, maximum, sum/count*) to an output file

All of these operations can be performed by C++ operations, functions, and statements that we have studied, except those that involve files (iii, viii, and ix). These (and other) file-processing operations are the topics of study in this chapter.

As we shall see, there are three additional administrative operations required to read from or write to a file.

- In order for a program to read from a file, C++ requires that a special object called an `ifstream` be **opened** to connect that file with the program.
- In order for a program to write to a file, a special object called an `ofstream` must be **opened** to connect the program and that file.
- When a program is done using a file, the `ifstream` or `ofstream` to that file should be **closed**.

This adds two more objects to our list of objects,

Problem Objects	Software Objects		
	Type	Kind	Name
Stream from program to input file	`ifstream`	varying	*inStream*
Stream from program to output file	`ofstream`	varying	*outStream*

and two more operations to our list of operations:

x. *Open* a stream to a file
xi. *Close* a stream to a file

Algorithm. The preceding operations can be organized into the following algorithm:

Algorithm for Processing Meteorological Data

1. Prompt for and read the name of the input file into *inputFileName*.
2. Open an `ifstream` named *inStream* to the file whose name is in *inputFileName*. (If this fails, display an error message and terminate the algorithm.)
3. Initialize *count* to 0; *sum* to 0.0; *maximum* to the smallest possible (real) value; and *minimum* to the largest possible (real) value.

4. Loop:
   a. Read a (real) value for *reading* from *inStream.*
   b. If the end-of-file mark was read, exit the loop.
   c. Increment *count.*
   d. Add *reading* to *sum.*
   e. If *reading* is less than *minimum*
      Set *minimum* to *reading.*
   f. If *reading* is greater than *maximum*
      Set *maximum* to *reading.*

   End loop.
5. Close *inStream.*
6. Prompt for and read the name of the output file into *outputFileName.*
7. Open an `ofstream` named *outStream* to the file whose name is in *outputFileName.* (If this fails, display an error message and terminate the algorithm.)
8. Write *count* to *outStream.*
9. If *count* is greater than zero
   Write *minimum, maximum,* and *sum/count* to *outStream.*
10. Close *outStream.*

Coding. Once one is familiar with the file-processing capabilities of C++, encoding the preceding algorithm in a program like that in Figure 9.1 is straightforward. The file-processing features used in this program will be described in the following sections.

Fig. 9.1 Reading a file of meteorological data. (Part 1 of 3)

```
/* meteorology.cpp reads meteorological data stored in a file;
 * computes the minimum, maximum, and average of the readings;
 * and writes these statistics to an output file.
 *
 *  Input(keyboard): names of the input and output files
 *  Input(file):     a sequence of meteorological readings
 *  Output(file):    the number of readings, the minimum reading,
 *                   the maximum reading, and the average reading
 ******************************************************************/

#include <iostream>                  // cin, cout
#include <fstream>                   // ifstream, ofstream
#include <string>                    // string, getline()
#include <cassert>                   // assert()
#include <cfloat>                    // DBL_MIN and DBL_MAX
using namespace std;

int main()
{
   cout << "This program computes the number, maximum, minimum, and\n"
           "average of an input list of numbers in one file,\n"
           "and places its results in another file.\n\n";
```

Fig. 9.1 Reading a file of meteorological data. (Part 2 of 3)

```
// ----------- Input Section ----------------------------------

cout << "Enter the name of the input file: ";
string inputFileName;
getline(cin, inputFileName);                 // get name of input file
                                             // open an input stream
ifstream inStream;                           //  to the input file,
inStream.open(inputFileName.data());         //  establish connection,
assert( inStream.is_open() );                //  and check for success

int count = 0;                               // number of values
double reading,                              // value being processed
       maximum = DBL_MIN,                    // largest seen so far
       minimum = DBL_MAX,                    // smallest seen so far
       sum = 0.0;                            // running total

for (;;)                                     // loop:
{
   inStream >> reading;                      //  read a value

   if ( inStream.eof() ) break;              //  if eof, quit

   count++;                                  //  update: count,
   sum += reading;                           //          sum,
   if (reading < minimum)
      minimum = reading;                     //          minimum,
   if (reading > maximum)
      maximum = reading;                     //          maximum
}                                            // end loop

inStream.close();                            // close the connection

// ------------ Output Section --------------------------------

cout << "Enter the name of the output file: ";
string outputFileName;
getline(cin, outputFileName);
                                             // open an output stream
ofstream outStream(outputFileName.data());//  to the output file,
                                             //  establish connection,
assert( outStream.is_open() );               //  and check for success
                                             // write results to file
outStream << "\n--> There were " << count << " values";
```

Fig. 9.1 Reading a file of meteorological data. (Part 3 of 3)

```
   if (count > 0)
      outStream << "\n\tranging from " << minimum
                << " to " << maximum
                << "\n\tand their average is " << sum / count
                << endl;

   outStream.close();                           // close the stream

   cout << "Processing complete.\n";
}
```

By allowing the user to enter the name of the input file to be processed, the program provides a convenient way to process the data values in *any* input file, which simplifies testing its correctness. Note that we use the `string` library function `getline()` to read the name of the file. This permits the user to enter multiword file names, as allowed by some operating systems. If we had used the input operator (>>), then only single-word names could be entered.

Testing. To test the correctness of the program, we construct several **test files** in which we place a small set of data values that will be used to check whether the program is performing correctly. For example, we might place an ascending sequence of numbers

```
11
12
13
14
15
```

in one file `test1.dat`, a descending sequence

```
99 98 97 96 95 94 93 92 91
```

in another file `test2.dat`, two sets of numbers separated by a blank line

```
4 5 6
1 2 3

9 8
7
```

in yet another file `test3.dat`, and so on. We thus create test files that *exercise* the program, looking for conditions under which it fails. Figure 9.2 shows sample runs of the program using the first two files. Once the program has been thoroughly tested, we can execute it using the original data file (`pressure.dat`) and have confidence in the results it produces.

Fig. 9.2 Testing the program in Figure 8.1.

Sample run #1:

```
This program computes the number, maximum, minimum, and
average of an input list of numbers in one file
and places its results in another file.

Enter the name of the input file: test1.dat
Please enter the name of the output file: test1.out
Processing complete.
```

Listing of `test1.out`:

```
--> There were 5 values
    ranging from 11 to 15
    and their average is 13.
```

Sample run #2:

```
This program computes the number, maximum, minimum, and
average of an input list of numbers in one file
and places its results in another file.

Enter the name of the input file: test2.dat
Please enter the name of the output file: test2.out
Processing complete.
```

Listing of `test2.out`:

```
--> There were 9 values
    ranging from 91 to 99
    and their average is 95.
```

Note that in these sample runs of the program, the only things output to the screen are the opening message, the prompts for the names of the input and output files, and a termination message. The rest of the output is written to the output file specified by the user. The only things input from the keyboard are the two filenames. All other input data is read from the input file.

9.2 `ifstream` and `ofstream` Objects

In this section, we examine the types and operations provided by the `fstream` library for performing file I/O.

DECLARING fstream OBJECTS

Recall that with interactive I/O, the iostream library automatically establishes the following connections (among others) between programs executing in main memory and I/O devices:

1. An istream object named cin connects the program and the keyboard.
2. An ostream object named cout connects the program and the screen.[1]

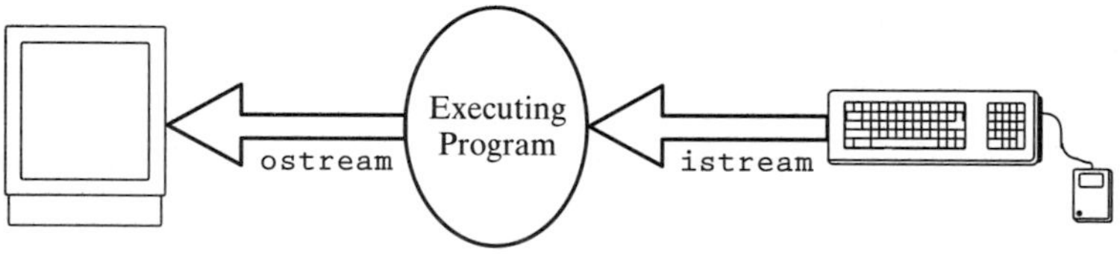

These streams are constructed automatically for interactive programs, but if a program is to perform input from or output to a text file, it must construct streams for this purpose. This operation is called opening the streams. **Opening a stream** creates a connection between a program (in main memory) and a text file (stored on some secondary memory device such as a disk drive).

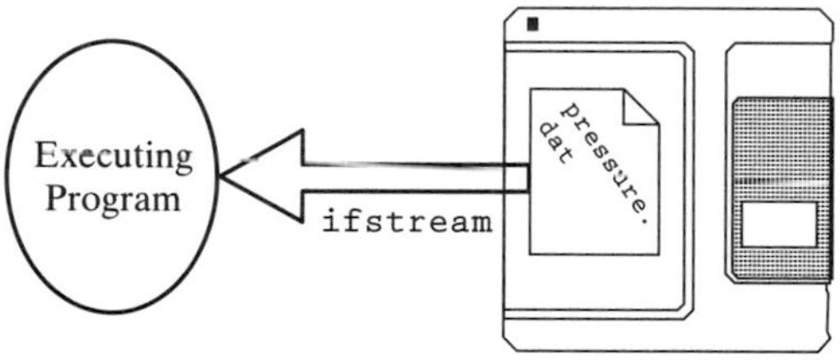

As illustrated in the program in Figure 9.1, a program that is to read from a file must open an ifstream to that file, and a program that is to write to a file must open an ofstream to that file. An fstream object can be used both for input from and output to a file. These classes are declared in the fstream library, so that any program wishing to use these classes must contain the #include <fstream> directive.[2]

Declaring a File Stream. Before a program can read values from a text file, it must construct an ifstream object to act as a connection from the file to the program. This can be done with a declaration of the form

```
ifstream input_stream_name;
```

---

1. The ostream objects cerr and clog are also established as connections between the program and the screen.
2. As noted before, older C++ compilers may require <fstream.h> in place of <fstream> and removal of the using namespace std; line.

Similarly, a program that writes values to a text file must first construct an `ofstream` object to act as a connection from the program to the file. This can be accomplished with

```
ofstream output_stream_name;
```

For example, the program in Figure 9.1 uses the declaration

```
ifstream inStream;
```

to construct an `ifstream` object named `inStream`. Using `fstream` instead of `ifstream` or `ofstream` constructs an `fstream` object that can be used both for input from and output to a file.

THE BASIC `fstream` OPERATIONS

It is important to understand that the classes `ifstream`, `ofstream`, and `fstream` are *derived from* the classes `istream`, `ostream`, and `iostream`, respectively, which means that these classes have been constructed as *extensions* of the `istream`, `ostream`, and `iostream` classes. As a result, all of the operations on `istream`, `ostream`, and `iostream` objects can also be performed on `ifstream`, `ofstream`, and `fstream` objects, respectively, along with several new operations that are limited to file streams. (In the terminology of Section 7.8, `ifstream`, `ofstream`, and `fstream` are *subclasses* of `istream`, `ostream`, and `iostream`, respectively, and *inherit* their operations.) Some of the most commonly used operations are as follows:

`open()`	a message that establishes a connection between a program and a file
`is_open()`	a boolean message that returns true if a file was opened successfully and returns false otherwise
`>>`	an operator that inputs a value from a file that has been opened for input
`getline()`	a function that reads a line of text from a file into a `string` object
`<<`	an operator that outputs a value to a file that has been opened for output
`eof()`	a boolean message that returns true if the last input operation read the end-of-file mark and returns false otherwise
`close()`	a message that terminates a connection between a program and a file

We now examine each of these operations in more detail.

The `open()` Message. The declarations

```
ifstream inStream;
ofstream outStream;
```

declare the objects `inStream` and `outStream` as uninitialized `fstreams`—as *potential* connections between a program and files. These potential connections become *actual* connections by sending them the `open()` message. In the program in Figure 9.1, the statement

```
inStream.open( inputFileName.data() );
```

initializes the `ifstream` object `inStream` by establishing it as a connection between the program and the file whose name is stored in the `string` object `inputFileName`. So if `inputFileName` contains the string `"pressure.dat"`, then the program is connected to the file `pressure.dat`:

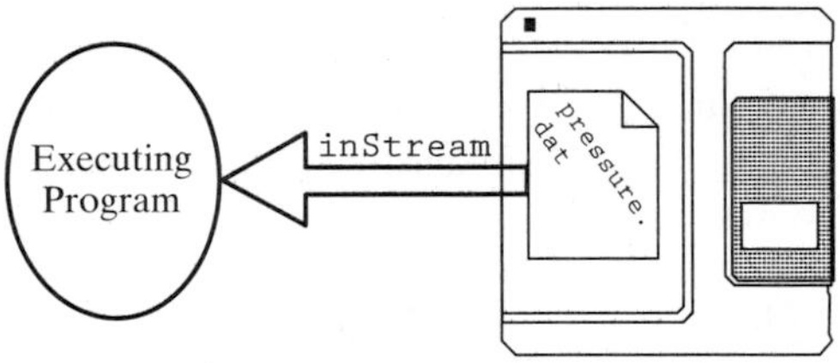

For a file name stored in a `string` object, the message `data()` or `c_str()` must be used to extract the string of characters stored in that `string` object. (`c_str()` appends a terminating null character—see Section 10.2—whereas `data()` does not.)

To illustrate, consider a small version of the file `pressure.dat`:

```
11.1 22.2 33.3 44.4
55.5 66.6 77.7
88.8 99.9
```

It is important to realize that a **text file** like this is simply a *sequence of characters*. Such files are created by the operating system, which automatically places a special **end-of-file mark** at the end of the file. If we use the symbol ƀ to represent a blank, the symbol ↲ to represent a newline, and the symbol ◊ to represent the end-of-file mark, then after the statement

```
inStream.open( inputFileName.data() );
```

has been executed, `inStream` may be visualized as

```
↓
11.1ƀ22.2ƀ33.3ƀ44.4↲55.5ƀ66.6ƀ77.7↲88.8ƀ99.9↲◊
                 inStream
```

where the down-arrow (↓) indicates the **read position**, denoting the next character to be read.

The `open()` message can also be used to open `ofstream` objects as connections to output files. For example, given the declaration

```
ofstream outStream;
```

the statement

```
outStream.open("NewFile.out");
```

creates a new file named `NewFile.out` containing only the end-of-file mark and then establishes `outStream` as a connection between the program and the file:

`outStream`

In this diagram, the down-arrow (↓) represents the **write position**—the position at which the next output value will be placed in the stream.

A (simplified) general form of the `open()` message is as follows:

The `open()` Message

Form:

`fstream_name.open(file_name);`

where

`fstream_name` is the name of the file stream being initialized;

`file_name` is the (character string) name of a data file.

Action: The object *`fstream_name`* is initialized as a connection between the executing program and the file named *`file_name`*.

WATCH OUT

By default, opening an `ofstream` to a file is *destructive*. That is, if a file named `NewFile.out` exists and the statement

```
outStream.open("NewFile.out");
```

is executed, any old contents of `NewFile.out` will be destroyed.

For situations where this destruction is undesirable, the `open()` message can be sent with a second **mode argument**, which can be any of the following:

Mode	Description
`ios::in`	The default mode for `ifstream` objects. Open a file for input, nondestructively, with the read position at the file's beginning.
`ios::trunc`	Open a file, and delete any contents it contains (i.e., *truncate* it).
`ios::out`	The default mode for `ofstream` objects. Open a file for output, using `ios::trunc`.
`ios::app`	Open a file for output, but nondestructively, with the write position at the file's end (i.e., for *appending*).
`ios::ate`	Open an existing file with the read position (`ifstream` objects) or write position (`ofstream` objects) at the end of the file.
`ios::binary`	Open a file in binary mode.

To illustrate, to open an `ofstream` to a file named `ExistingFile.out` and add data at the end of the file, we can use `ios::app` as a second argument, as follows:

```
outStream.open("ExistingFile.out", ios::app);
```

This second argument makes the `open()` message *nondestructive* so that the old contents of `ExistingFile.out` are preserved, and any additional values written to the file will be *appended* to it. The file modes can also be combined using the bitwise-or (|) operator. For example,

```
fstream inoutStream;
inoutStream.open("TwoWayFile", ios::in | ios::out);
```

opens the file `TwoWayFile` for both input and output.

Initialization at Declaration. An alternative to declaring an `fstream` and then sending it the `open()` message is to initialize it *when it is declared.* Just as a variable can be initialized in its declaration,

```
int sum = 0;
```

C++ also allows a file stream to be initialized when it is declared. For example, instead of using

```
ofstream outStream;
outStream.open( outputFileName.data() );
```

to declare the second (output) `fstream` and then sending it the `open()` message, the program in Figure 9.1 used[3]

```
ofstream outStream( outputFileName.data() );
```

This statement both declares `outStream` as an `ofstream` and opens it as a connection to the file whose name is stored in `outputFileName`.

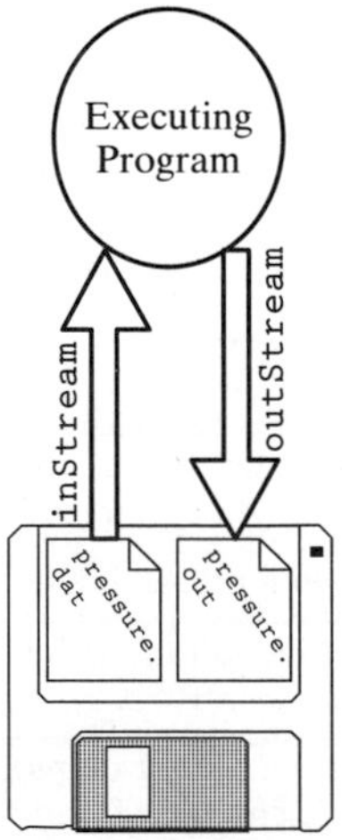

3. Like the examples in the *OBJECTive Thinking* section of Chapter 3, this declaration is using an explicit-value constructor of a class—`ofStream`—to do this initialization.

The general form of an initializing declaration of a file stream is as follows:

fstream Initializing Declaration

Forms:

```
ifstream fstream_name(file_name, mode);
ofstream fstream_name(file_name, mode);
fstream fstream_name(file_name, mode);
```

where

fstream_name is the name of the file stream being initialized;

file_name is the (character string) name of a data file; and

mode is the optional mode argument described earlier.

Action: The object *fstream_name* is initialized as a connection between the executing program and the file named *file_name*.

The trade-offs in the two initialization mechanisms are the following:

- Using the `open()` message is perhaps more readable than using the initializing declaration since it explicitly states the operation being performed. It also makes repeated attempts to open a stream possible as shown in the function in Figure 9.3. Moreover, an open operation is common in programming languages.
- Initializing a file stream object is an easily forgotten detail since we do not need to initialize `cin` or `cout` before we use them. Initializing such objects at their declaration is thus perhaps less error prone because it eliminates having to remember to use the `open()` operation.

The two mechanisms are functionally equivalent, however, and the choice is largely a matter of programming style.

WATCH OUT

Programming Defensively—the `is_open()` Message. There are a number of errors that can occur in opening a stream to a file. To illustrate, consider the following attempt to initialize an `ifstream` to an input file:

```
ifstream inStream(file_name);
```

If the file *file_name* does not exist or cannot be found, then the open operation fails. Obviously, if this happens, any subsequent attempts to read from that file will also fail. Consequently,

the success or failure of a call to open a file should always be ***tested*** *before proceeding with any additional operations on the file.*

This testing is easily done using the boolean message `is_open()` whose form is as follows.[4]

The `is_open()` Message

Use:

```
fstream_name.is_open();
```

where

`fstream_name` is the name of a file stream that serves as a connection to some file.

Action: `is_open()` returns:

`true` if *`fstream_name`* was successfully opened;

`false` if the open operation failed.

In the program in Figure 9.1, we used the `assert()` mechanism to check for successful opens:

```
assert( inStream.is_open() );
```

and

```
assert( outStream.is_open() );
```

This provides a succinct way to test each file stream and terminate the program if it failed to open. A more user-friendly approach is used in the following function.

An `interactiveOpen()` Function. Quite often when a stream is opened to a file, the user must be queried for the name of the file, which must be stored in a string and then used to open the file. The details of carrying out these steps tend to clutter the code and can be hidden by encapsulating them in a function. Figure 9.3 gives a pair of such functions that overload the name `interactiveOpen()` to allow both `ifstream` and `ofstream` objects to be conveniently opened. They might be stored in a library—for example, in a `Query` library that also contains the interactive query functions from Section 7.5—to simplify the task of opening a stream to a file.

These two functions allow the user repeated chances to enter a file name—perhaps to correct a typo—and are consistent with the practice of many programmers to try to *recover from errors whenever possible and exit gracefully when it isn't.*

---

4. Some compilers that are not fully ISO/ANSI-C++ compliant may not provide the `is_open()` function. In this case, the success or failure of the open operation can be tested using the `good()` or `fail()` messages; for example, `assert(inStream.good());` or `assert(!inStream.fail());`.

Fig. 9.3 interactiveOpen().

```
#include <iostream>                         // cin, cout, >>, <<
#include <fstream>                          // ifstream, ofstream
#include <string>                           // string, getline()
using namespace std;

// --- Open an ifstream interactively --------------------

void interactiveOpen(ifstream & theIFStream)
{
   char response;
   do
   {
      cout << "Enter the name of the input file: ";
      string inputFileName;
      getline(cin, inputFileName);

      theIFStream.open(inputFileName.data());

      if (theIFStream.is_open()) break;
      cerr << "\n***InteractiveOpen(): unable to open "
           << inputFileName << "\nTry again (Y or N)? ";
      cin >> response;
   }
   while (response != 'N' && response != 'n');
}

// --- Open an ofstream interactively --------------------

void interactiveOpen(ofstream & theOFStream)
{
   char response;
   do
   {
      cout << "Enter the name of the output file: ";
      string outputFileName;
      getline(cin, outputFileName);

      theOFStream.open(outputFileName.data());

      if (theOFStream.is_open()) break;
```

Fig. 9.3 `interactiveOpen()`. (Continued)

```
      cerr << "\n***InteractiveOpen(): unable to open "
           << outputFileName << "\nTry again (Y or N)? ";
      cin >> response;
    }
    while (response != 'N' && response != 'n');
}
```

The Input Operator. One of the most elegant features of C++ is its *consistency*—its use of the same operators to perform tasks that are functionally similar. The task of performing input from a file is an example of this consistency, because input from an `ifstream` is performed in the same manner as input from an `istream`. That is, once an `ifstream` has been established as a connection to some file, the same input operator (`>>`) we have used to input data from the keyboard using an `istream` (i.e., `cin`) can now be used to input data from a file via the `ifstream` to that file. Thus, in the program in Figure 9.1, the statement

```
inStream >> reading;
```

gets the next value from the file connected to the program through the `ifstream` object `inStream` and stores it in the variable `reading`. For example, given `inStream` as described earlier,

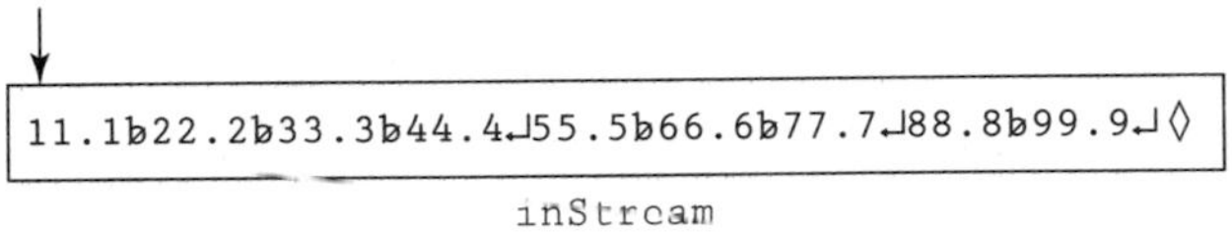

execution of this input statement reads the characters `'1'`, `'1'`, `'.'`, `'1'` and then stops upon encountering the blank. The characters are then converted to the real value `11.1`, which is stored in variable `reading`:

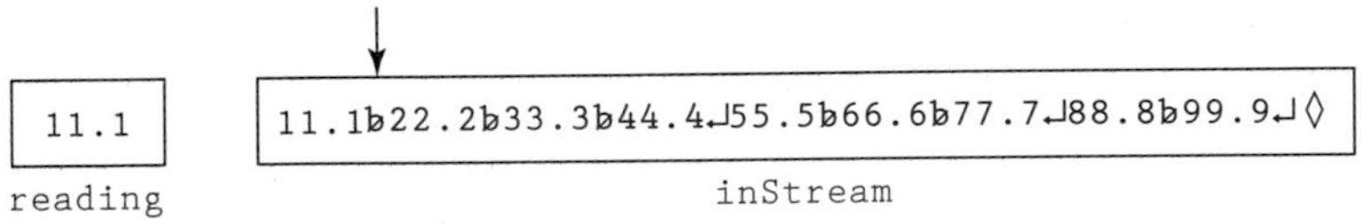

In the next repetition of the loop, execution of the statement

```
inStream >> reading;
```

skips the blank, reads the characters `'2'`, `'2'`, `'.'`, `'2'`, and then stops upon encountering the next blank. The characters are converted to the real value `22.2`, which is stored in variable `reading`.

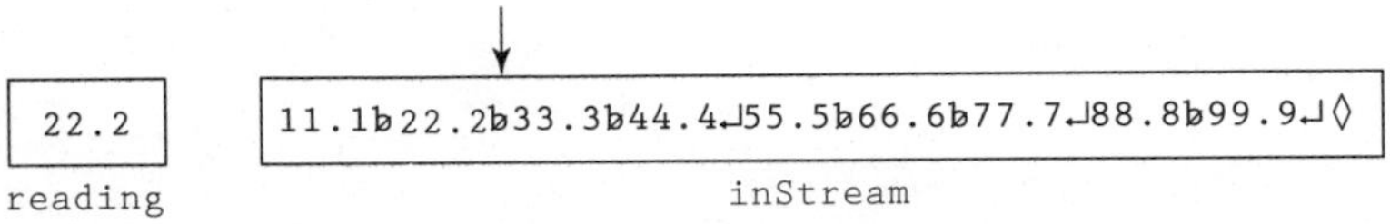

In subsequent repetitions of the loop, the value `33.3` is read in exactly the same way,

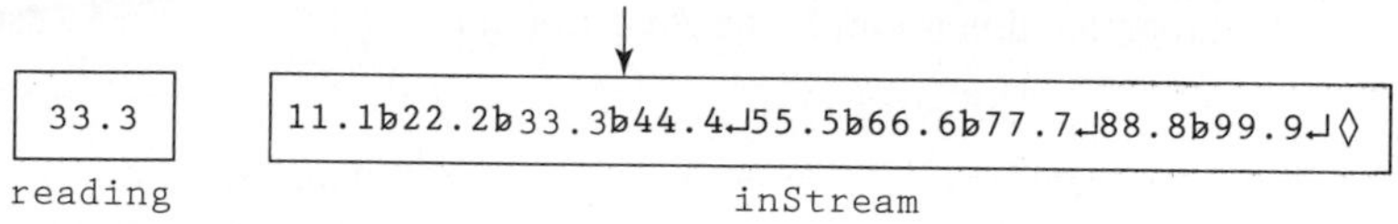

as is the value `44.4`, except that reading stops at the newline character instead of at a blank:

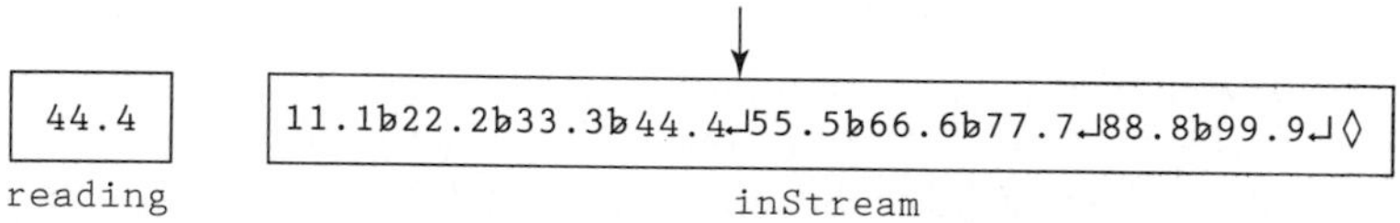

(Recall that any *white-space* character—blank, tab, or newline—serves to delimit numbers.) Subsequent repetitions of the loop read the remaining values in the same way until only the `99.9` remains unread:

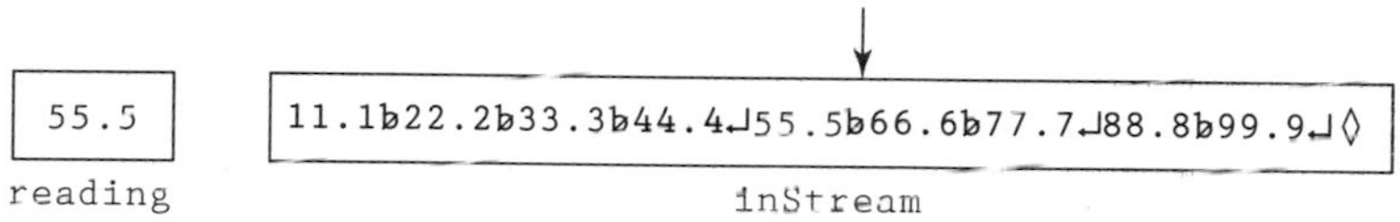

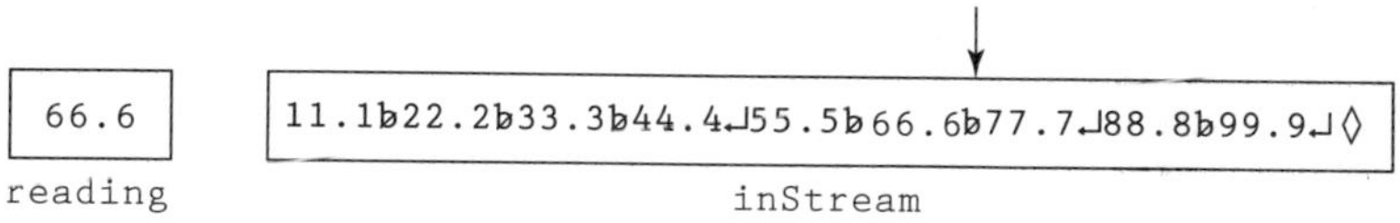

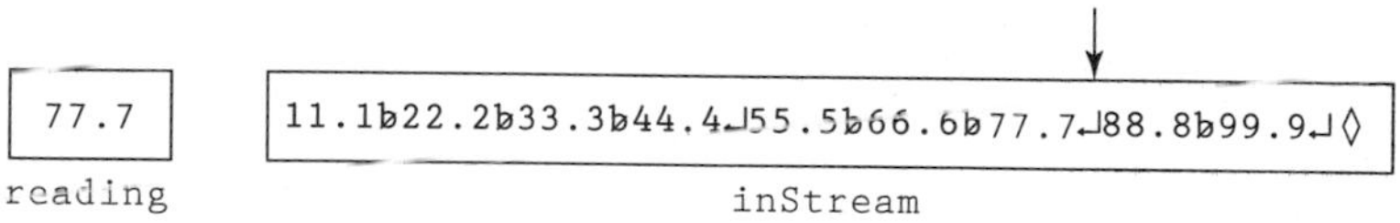

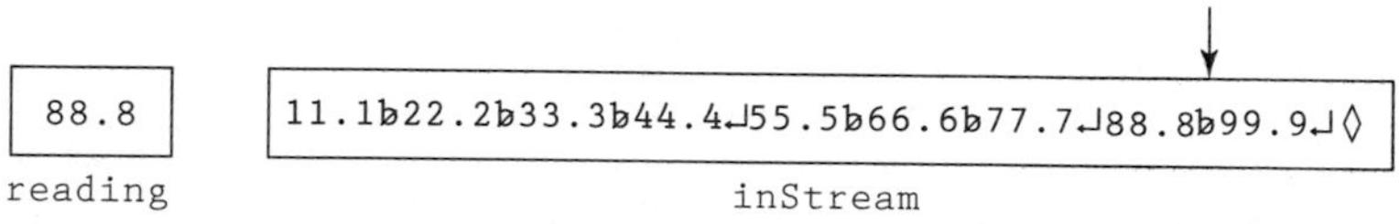

The next repetition skips the blank, reads the four characters `'9'`, `'9'`, `'.'`, `'9'`, and stops when the newline is encountered:

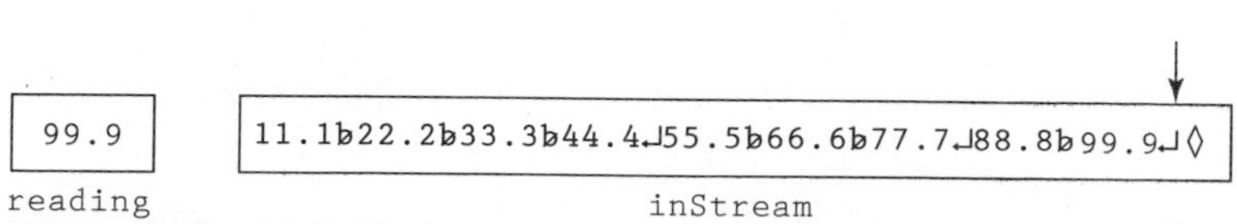

On the final trip through the loop, the input statement attempts to read a value, but finds no data before the end-of-file mark. This causes the member function `eof()` to return the value `true`, which terminates the loop. (See the discussion of `eof()` later in this section.)

Note that this is similar to what would happen if we were to use the statement

```
cin >> reading;
```

to get the next `double` value from the keyboard and store it in `reading`. The only difference is that the input operator would extract values from the `istream` named `cin` instead of from the `ifstream` named `inStream`.

Input is consistent in the `iostream` library because the same operator (>>) is used to input a `double` value from an `istream` object such as `cin` and to input a `double` value from an `ifstream` object such as `inStream`. The only difference in these operations is the type of their first operand. As we saw in Section 7.5, when the same operator (such as >>) can be applied to operands of different types, that operator is said to be **overloaded**. Just as we overloaded the function `swap()` by defining its behavior for a variety of types, the designer(s) of the `fstream` library overloaded the >> operator so that it can be applied to `ifstream` objects as well as `istream` objects.

The `getline()` Function. As we saw in Chapter 5, the `string` library provides a utility function named `getline()` that, given an `istream` object and a `string` object, fills the `string` object with a line of input from the `istream`. Since an `ifstream` is a specialized kind of `istream`, we can also use `getline()` for input from an `ifstream`.

This function is most commonly used in files that are organized into lines. For example, if `nameStream` is an `ifstream` to a file containing a list of names,

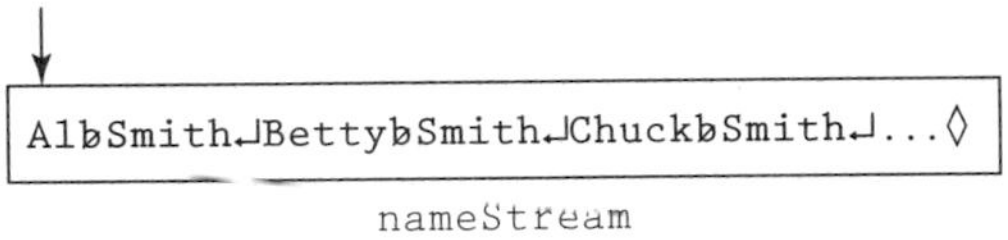

we can either use the input operator >>

```
inStream >> firstName >> lastName;
```

to read the individual name components into `string` objects `firstName` and `lastName`,

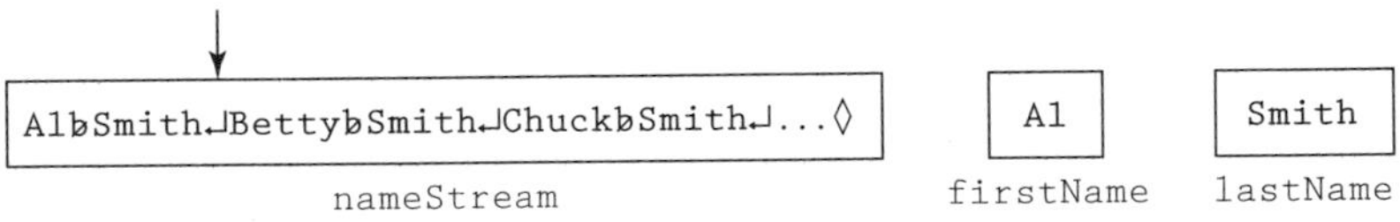

or we can use the `getline()` function

```
getline(inStream, name);
```

and read the entire first line into a `string` object `name`:

We can thus describe the `getline()` function as follows:

The `getline()` Function

Use:

```
getline(stream_object, string_object);
```

where

stream_object is an `istream` or `ifstream` connected to a file; and

string_object is a variable `string` object.

Action: Reads characters from *stream_object*, storing them in *string_object*, until a newline character is read (but is not stored in *string_object*).

Note the difference in how the input operator and the `getline()` function treat the newline character: `>>` leaves it unread in the stream (and will skip it as leading white space on the next read), whereas `getline()` reads it, but does not add it to the end of the `string` object.

WATCH OUT

This difference between `>>` and `getline()` can cause difficulty if calls to them are carelessly intermixed. To illustrate, suppose that `empStream` is an `ifstream` connected to a file containing employee numbers and employee names, each on a separate line:

```
101
Al Smith
102
Betty Smith
...
```

Then `empStream` can be visualized as follows:

```
↓
101↵Al␢Smith↵102↵Betty␢Smith↵...◊
```

empStream

Now, consider the following input loop:

```
int empNumber;
string empName;
```

```
for (;;)
{
   empStream >> empNumber;
   getline (empStream, empName);

   if (empStream.eof()) break;

   // Process empNumber and empName
}
```

The problem here is that when the input operation has read the employee number,

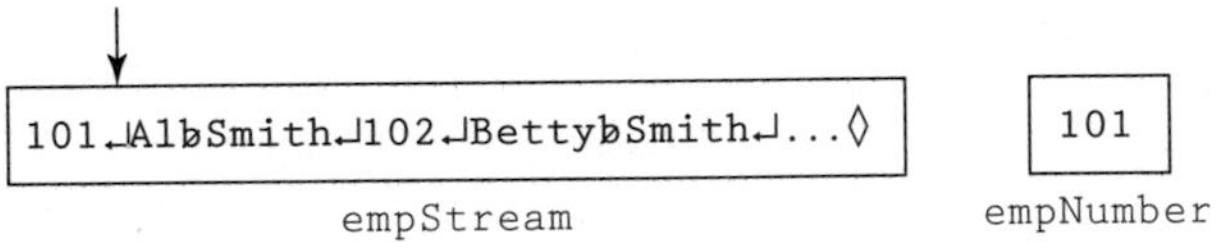

it leaves the newline unread in the stream. Since the character at the read position is a newline and `getline()` stops when it reads a newline, it will stop immediately, leaving `empName` empty:

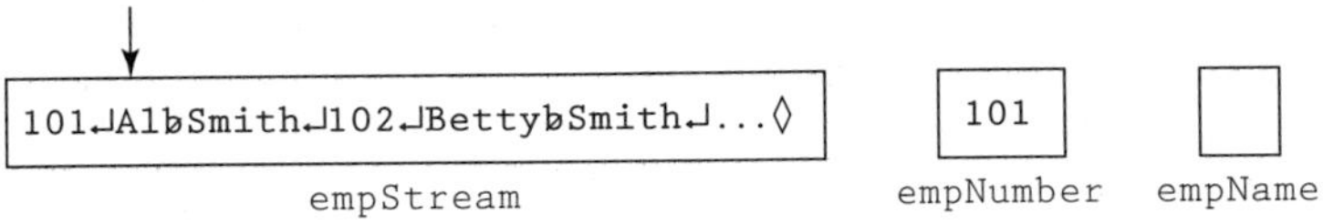

`empNumber` and `empName` will then not be processed in the way we expect, which is clearly a problem. Even worse, when control returns to the top of the loop and the input statement tries to extract a value for `empNumber`, the read position is at the `"A"` in `"Al Smith"`:

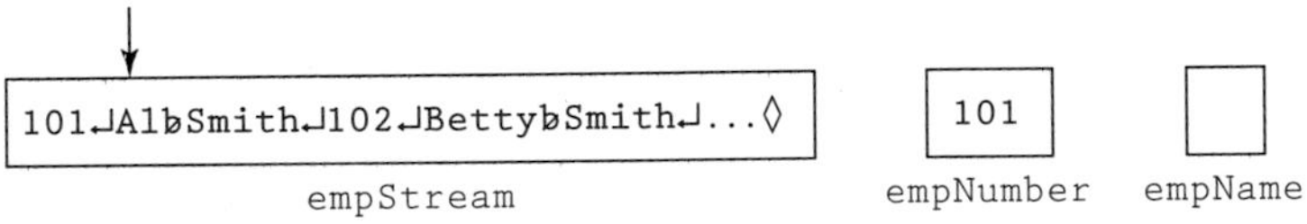

Since `"A"` is not an integer, this will set the *fail* and/or *bad* status bits of `empStream`, but not the *eof* bit. Once a bit other than *good* is set, no subsequent input operations will succeed, and so no progress is made towards the end-of-file mark. This, combined with `eof()` being false, means that execution is stuck in an infinite loop!

The solution to the problem is to follow the input operation with a call to the stream function member `get()` to explicitly consume the newline character following each extraction of a value for `empNumber`:

```
int empNumber;
string name;
char theNewLine;
```

```
for (;;)
{
   empStream >> empNumber;      // this leaves unread newline at
   empStream.get(theNewLine); //  the read position; get() it
   getline(empStream, name);  //  so getline() won't trip on it

   if (empStream.eof()) break;

   // Process empNumber and name
}
```

Now, when our input loop executes, `101` is read into `empNumber`,

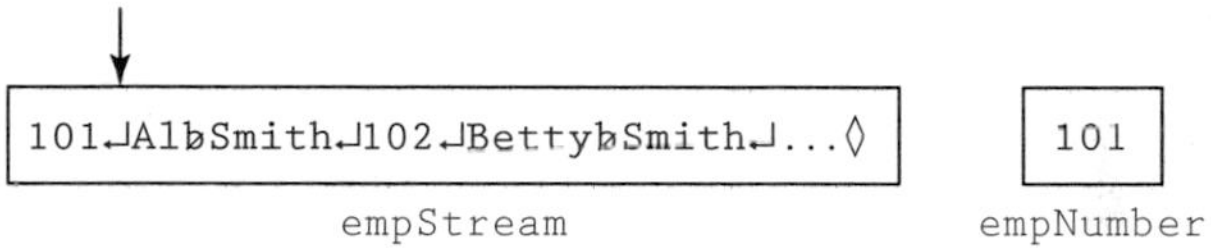

after which the call to `get()` moves the read position past the newline,

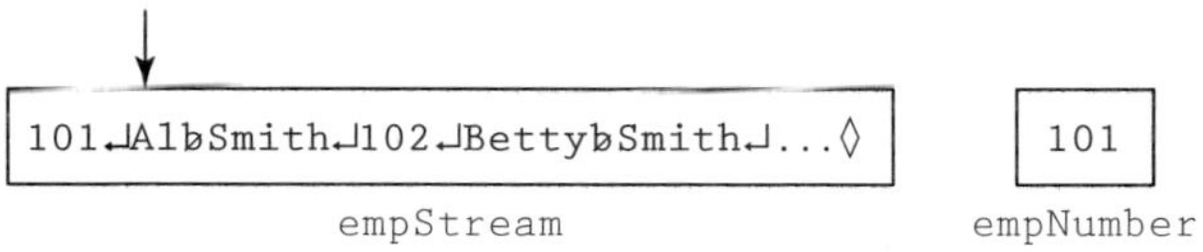

and the call to `getline()` correctly reads `"Al Smith"` into `empName`:

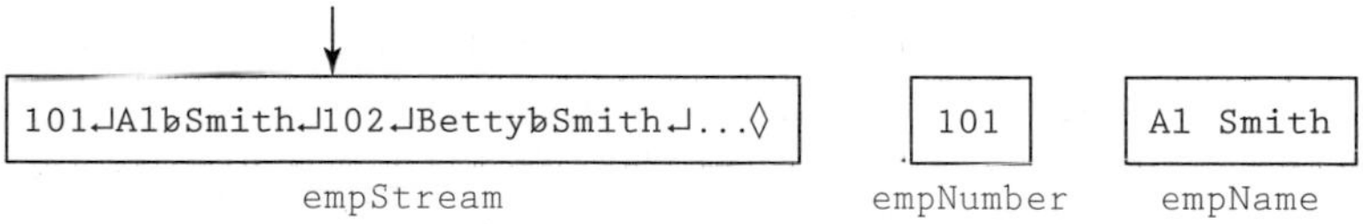

Both values are now available to be processed, and the stream is left in the correct state for the next repetition.

The `eof()` Message. We saw in Section 7.5 that the end-of-file mark can be used as a sentinel value to control an input loop as follows:

```
for (;;)
{
   cin >> inputValue;

   if ( cin.eof() ) break;

   // ... process inputValue
}
```

Such a loop will continue to execute until the user enters an end-of-file mark as a sentinel to indicate that no more data is to be entered.

In the program in Figure 9.1, the main processing loop has a similar form:

```
for (;;)
{
   inStream >> reading;

   if ( inStream.eof() ) break;

   // ...process reading
}
```

Here, the message

```
inStream.eof()
```

behaves exactly like

```
cin.eof()
```

except that the user need not enter an end-of-file mark to make the function return `true`, because the file from which we are reading already contains such a mark:

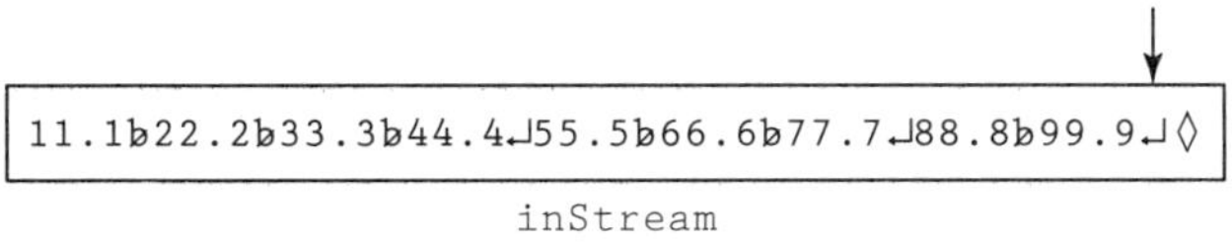

`inStream.eof()` returns `true` following execution of the statement

```
inStream >> reading;
```

provided there is no data between the read position and the end-of-file mark. The variable `reading` retains the value it had on the last pass through the loop.

The `eof()` Message

Use:

`fstream_name``.eof()`

where

`fstream_name` is the name of a stream that serves as a connection to some file.

Action: `eof()` returns:

`true`, if the last input operation on *`fstream_name`* failed because the end-of-file mark was encountered; in this case, input variables retain the last value successfully read;

`false`, otherwise.

Again, we see a pleasing consistency in the I/O libraries because `eof()` is a message that can be sent to both `ifstream` objects and `istream` objects. This is an example of the usefulness of the C++ *inheritance* mechanism (see Section 7.8)—`eof()` is actually a method of the class `ios`, from which other I/O-stream classes are derived. These other classes (`istream` and `ifstream`) inherit `eof()` from the base class `ios` (which all of them hold in common) and thus avoid redundant redefinitions of their own `eof()` functions.

The Output Operator. Just as the input operator is overloaded to perform consistently with both `istream` and `ifstream` objects, the output operator (`<<`) is overloaded to behave consistently with both `ostream` and `ofstream` objects. For example, as we saw in Figure 9.1, we can declare

```
ofstream outStream( outputFileName.data() );
```

to open an output connection between a program and a file whose name is stored in the `string` object `outputFileName`. The `ofstream` object `outStream` is initially empty, containing only the end-of-file mark:

outStream

The program in Figure 9.1 contains statements to write results to an output file via `outStream`:

```
outStream << "\n--> There were a total of " << count <<
             " values.";

if (count > 0)
   outStream << "\n\tranging from " << minimum
             << " to " << maximum
             << "\n\tand their average is " << sum / count
             << endl;
```

Execution of the first statement inserts the appropriate characters into `outStream`,

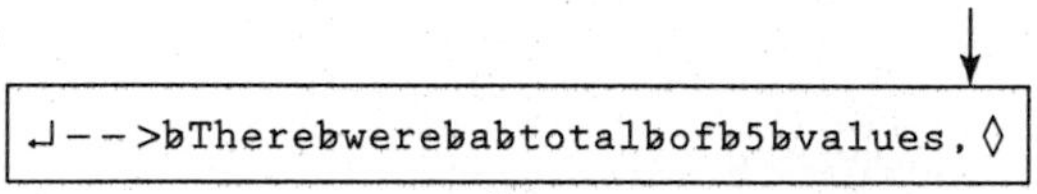

outStream

and execution of the output statement within the `if` statement inserts the remaining characters:

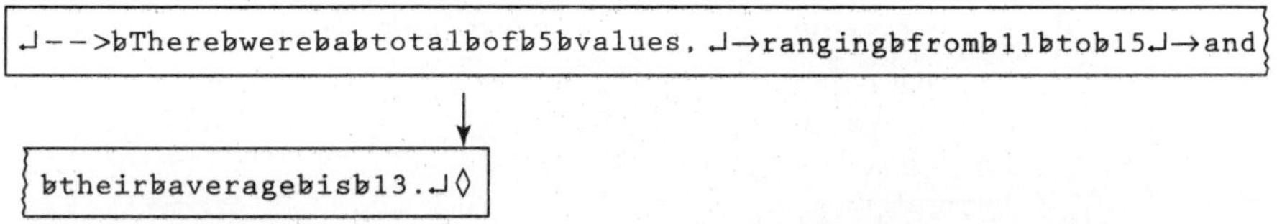

outStream

Here we have used the right-arrow symbol (→) to represent a tab character.

Execution of the program simply displays the introductory message on the screen, prompts for the names of the input and output files, and then displays a `Processing complete` message; all other output has been sent to the output file via `outStream` instead of to the screen via `cout`.

The `close()` Message. We have seen that the initialization of a file stream establishes that object as a connection between a program and a file. A file stream is disconnected when execution leaves the scope of the `fstream` just as a local variable's value is lost when execution leaves the scope of that variable. In particular, a file stream declared within a function will be disconnected when execution leaves that function (if not before).

A file stream can be disconnected explicitly by sending it the `close()` message. In the program in Figure 9.1, the statements

```
inStream.close();
```

and

```
outStream.close();
```

sever the connection between the program and the input file and the output file, respectively. We can describe the `close()` operation as follows:

The `close()` Message

Use:

`fstream_name``.close();`

where

`fstream_name` is the name of a stream that serves as a connection to some output file.

Action: The executing program and the file are disconnected, and *`fstream_name`* becomes undefined.

In the program in Figure 9.1, the effect of the statement

```
outStream.close();
```

is to write the contents of the `ofstream` named `outStream`

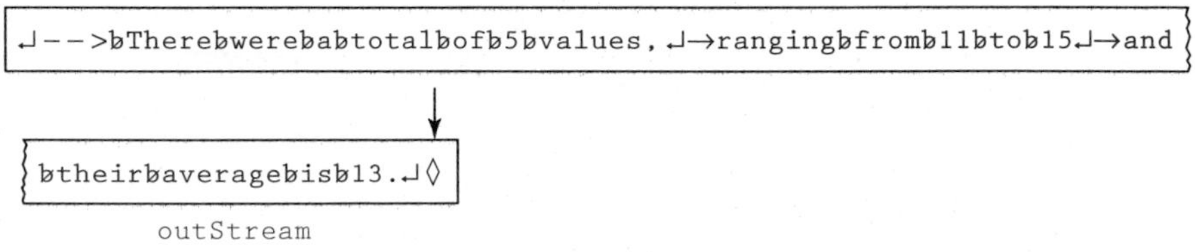

to the output file (e.g., test1.out), which we might visualize as

```
-->There were a total of 5 values,
   ranging from 11 to 15
   and their average is 13.
```

The close() message must be used whenever it is necessary to disconnect a file stream before reaching the end of its scope. For example, if we write values to a file and then want to open that file and read from it, the output stream to that file must be disconnected first. But even though a file stream is closed automatically when execution reaches the end of its scope, it is nevertheless considered good programming practice to use close() to disconnect every file stream when it is no longer needed.

One situation where this is important is in programs that use many different files, because many operating systems place a limit on the number of files a program may have open simultaneously.[5] This means that if a program tries to open more files than allowed, the operating system will terminate the program abnormally. This problem can be avoided by always using the close() message to sever the connection between a program and a file when the program is done using it. This keeps the number of open files associated with the program from growing beyond the limit allowed by the operating system.

FILE STREAMS AS PARAMETERS

NOTE

File streams, like any other types of objects, may be used as arguments to user-defined functions. In this case, however, *the parameters corresponding to file stream arguments must be reference parameters*, because, as we have seen,

- reading from an ifstream alters the read position in that ifstream;
- writing to an ofstream alters the write position in that ofstream.

The file stream parameter must be defined as a reference parameter so that these changes to the stream in the function are propagated back to the caller of the function.

SUMMARY

The following points summarize some of the important points regarding file I/O in C++:

- A text file is simply a container for characters stored on a secondary memory device.
- A file cannot be accessed directly from a program, but must be accessed indirectly through a file stream—an abstract conduit between the program and the file through which the program can perform input from or output to the file.
- Either the initialization-at-declaration mechanism or the open() message can be used to connect a file stream to a file.
- If an ifstream is opened to a file, then the file stream is initialized with the contents of that file and the read position at the first character in the file stream.

5. For example, the original Unix systems allowed a program to have a maximum of 15 files open simultaneously.

- If an `ofstream` is opened to a file, then the stream is initialized as empty (containing only the end-of-file mark) with the write position at the end-of-file mark. Any previous contents of the file are destroyed.
- If an `ofstream` is opened to a file using the mode `ios::app`, then the file must exist and the stream is initialized with the contents of that file with the write position at the end of the file.
- The input operator (>>) can be used to extract the first value following the read position in an `ifstream`. The read position is advanced to the first character past the input value. Any initial white-space characters are skipped. Numeric values are delimited by nonnumeric characters.
- The `string` library `getline()` function can be used to extract the line of input beginning at the read position in an `ifstream` and store the extracted characters in a `string` variable. The function stops storing characters as soon as it reaches a newline character, and it leaves the read position at the first character beyond that newline. Care must be taken when intermixing calls to `getline()` and calls to the input operator.
- The output operator (<<) can be used to insert a value into an `ofstream` at the write position. The write position is advanced to the point immediately following the value.
- The `close()` message should be used to disconnect a stream from a file when that file is no longer needed.

✔ Quick Quiz 9.2

1. The `iostream` library establishes a(n) _____ object named _____ that connects a program and the keyboard.
2. The `iostream` library establishes a(n) _____ object named _____ that connects a program and the screen.
3. In order for a program to read data from a file, a(n) _____ object must connect the program to that file.
4. In order for a program to write output to a file, a(n) _____ object must connect the program to that file.
5. The types of streams needed to connect a program and a file are declared in the _____ library.
6. (True or false) Almost none of the operations on `iostreams` can be performed on file streams.
7. Write a statement to declare a file stream named `inputStream` that will be used for input from a file and another statement that uses the `open()` function to connect this stream to a file named `EmployeeInfo`.
8. Repeat Question 7, but use the initialization-at-declaration mechanism.
9. Repeat Question 7, but for a file stream named `outputStream` that will be used for output to a file named `EmployeeReport`.
10. Repeat Question 9, but use the initialization-at-declaration mechanism.
11. Modify your answers to Questions 7 and 8 so that the user inputs the name of the file into a `string` variable `inputFileName`.

12. (True or false) The declaration `ifstream inStream("Info");` will destroy the contents of the file named `Info`.
13. (True or false) The declaration `ofstream outStream("Info");` will destroy the contents of the file named `Info`.
14. Write a statement that will stop program execution if an attempt to open the `ifstream` `inputStream` fails.
15. Write a statement that will extract an entire line from the `ifstream` in Question 14.
16. Write a statement that will display the message `"End of file"` for the `ifstream` in Question 14 when the end-of-file mark is reached.
17. Write a statement to disconnect the `ifstream` in Question 14.

Exercises 9.2

1. Using both the (a) `open()` function and (b) the initialization-at-declaration mechanism, write statements to declare and open a file stream named `inputStream` as a connection to an input file named `InData`.
2. Proceed as in Exercise 1, but open an `fstream` named `outputStream` as a connection to an output file named `OutData`.
3. Proceed as in Exercise 1, but declare a `string` variable `inputFileName`, and read the name of the input file into it.
4. Proceed as in Exercise 2, but declare a `string` variable `outputFileName`, and read the name of the output file into it.

For Exercises 5–7, assume that `num1`, `num2`, `num3`, and `num4` are integer variables and that *`inStream`* is an `ifstream` connected to a file containing the following data:

```
1  -2 3↵
4 -5 6↵
7       -8     9↵
```

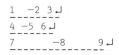

Tell what values will be assigned to these variables when the statements are executed.

5. `inStream >> num1 >> num2 >> num3 >> num4;`
6.
```
inStream >> num1 >> num2;
inStream >> num3;
inStream >> num4;
```
7.
```
inStream >> num1 >> num2;
inStream >> num3 >> num4;
```

For Exercises 8–12, assume that `inStream` has been opened as a connection to an input file that contains the data

```
123  45.6↵
X78 -909.8 7↵
-65 $  432.10↵
```

If LINE_LENGTH has been defined by

```
const int LINE_LENGTH = 8;
```

we can move the read position to the beginning of the first line with the statement

```
friendStream.seekg(0 * LINE_LENGTH, ios::beg);
```

to the beginning of the second line with

```
friendStream.seekg(1 * LINE_LENGTH, ios::beg);
```

and in general, to the beginning of the `i`th line with the statement

```
friendStream.seekg((i-1) * LINE_LENGTH, ios::beg);
```

Thus, the statement

```
friendStream.seekg(2*LINE_LENGTH, ios::beg);
```

will move the read position 16 bytes from the beginning of the file:

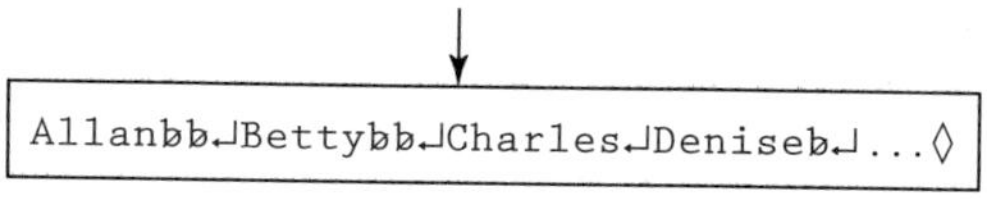

friendStream

Similarly, the statement

```
friendStream.seekg(LINE_LENGTH, ios::cur);
```

can be used to move the read position from the beginning of one line to the beginning of the next line:

friendStream

The function `seekg()` thus allows us to adjust the read position in any way that is useful in solving a particular problem.

It should be apparent that seeking with a negative offset from the base `ios::beg` or seeking with a positive offset from the base `ios::end` is not desirable. Such operations will set the stream status *fail* bit, disabling all subsequent operations on the stream until the status bits are reset using the `clear()` message.

`tellg()`. It is sometimes convenient to think of a stream as a *list* of characters, in which each position has its own number or *index*, similar to a `string` object:

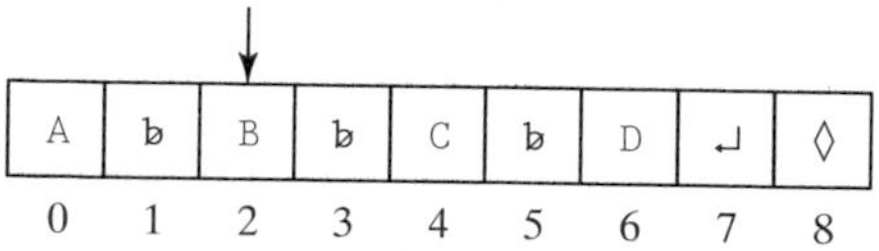

inStream

The `tellg()` method can be used to find the index of the read position. For example, the statements

```
inStream.seekg(0, ios::end);
long lastPosition = inStream.tellg();
```

will (1) move the read position to the end-of-file mark,

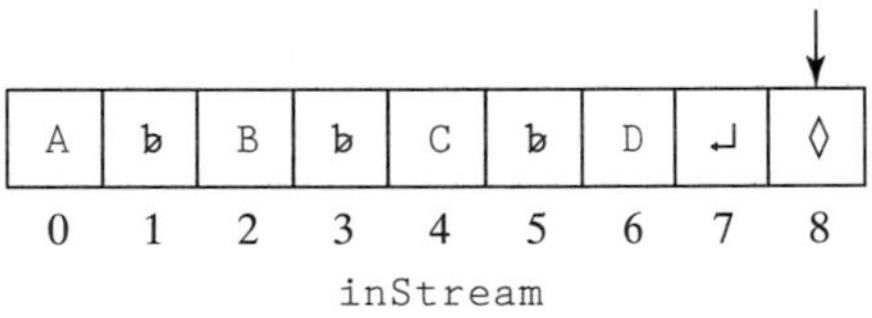

and (2) store the index of the end-of-file mark (i.e., 8) in `lastPosition`. Note that because the index of the first character is always zero, the index of the end-of-file mark is always the number of characters in the file (not counting the end-of-file mark). A text-processing program could use this fact to determine how many characters are in a file, rather than counting them one at a time.

Knowing the index of the last character allows us to find the middle of a file. For example, the statements

```
inStream.seekg(0, ios::end);

long lastPosition = inStream.tellg(),
     middlePosition = (lastPosition + 1) / 2;

inStream.seekg(middlePosition, ios::beg);
```

can be used to move the read position to the middle character in `inStream`:

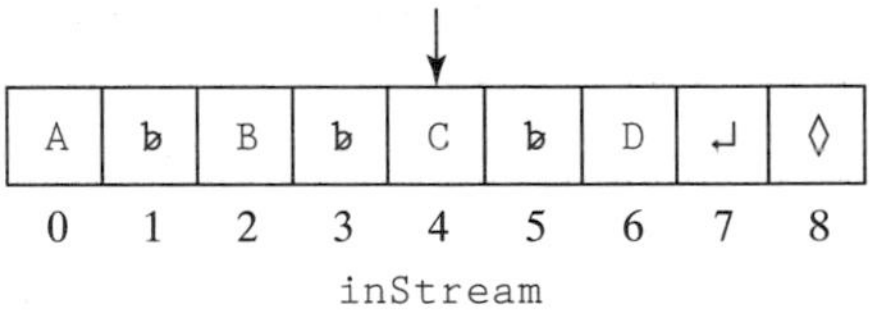

It should be evident that like `seekg()`, `tellg()` is most useful for files that are organized into lines or records of fixed lengths. To illustrate, suppose that in the earlier example using the file `Friends`, the read position has moved away from the beginning of a line,

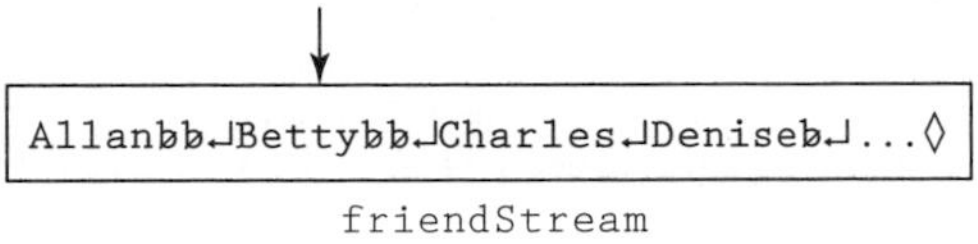

and we want to advance it to the next line. Because `friendStream.tellg()` returns the index of the current read position (11), the statement

```
long offBy = friendStream.tellg() % LINE_LENGTH;
                                   // how far past beginning of line
```

can be used to compute the number of characters (`offBy` = 3) that the read position is past the beginning of the current line; and the following statement can then be used to move the read position forward to the beginning of the next line:

```
friendStream.seekg(LINE_LENGTH - offBy, ios::cur);
                                   // go to beginning of next line
```

`seekp()` and `tellp()`. The methods `seekg()` and `tellg()` can only be used with input streams, because they only manipulate the read position within a stream. The write position within an `ostream` or `ofstream` can be manipulated by using the functions `seekp()` and `tellp()`.[8] These messages behave in the same manner as `seekg()` and `tellg()`, respectively, but must be sent to output streams.

THE `peek()` AND `putback()` MESSAGES

Two other methods allow the programmer to do some useful, if unconventional, operations on an input stream. These methods are named `peek()` and `putback()`, and their names describe the operations they perform.

`peek()`. The `peek()` message allows the programmer to *look ahead* in an input stream. This operation is similar to the `get()` message, in that both return the next character in the stream, but `get()` advances the read position and `peek()` does not.

To illustrate, consider a problem that the C++ compiler has when reading a C++ program from a stream. One of the tasks of a compiler is **lexical analysis**, which breaks the source program down into a sequence of indivisible symbols, called **tokens**. This task is accomplished by a special object called the **lexical analyzer**, which the compiler contacts whenever it needs the next token. For each identifier, each keyword, each operator, and each punctuation mark, the compiler has a distinct token. For example, the compiler might refer to the + operator as `PLUS_TOKEN`, the ++ operator as `INCREMENT_TOKEN`, and the += operator as `PLUS_EQUALS_TOKEN`.

One problem for the compiler is to distinguish the three tokens that begin with the + character. Suppose, for example, that the compiler's input stream is named `inStream` and appears as follows:

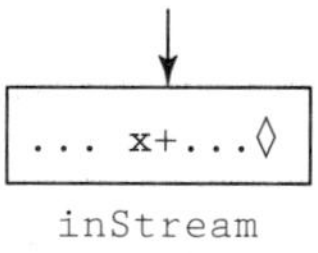

Suppose further that the compiler asks its lexical analyzer for the next token, which executes the statement:

```
inStream.get(ch);
```

8. The `'p'` in `seekp()` and `tellp()` refers to the fact that one *puts* values into the stream being manipulated (i.e., that it is an output stream).

Clearly, this will retrieve the value `'+'` and advance the read position:

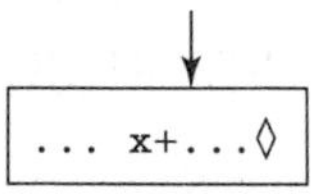

inStream

In order to determine which operation the programmer specified, the lexical analyzer needs more information: If the next character is an equal sign (=), then the operator is +=; if the next character is another +, the operator is the increment operator ++; and if the next character is a white-space character, a letter, a digit, a single quote, or a double quote, then the operator is simply the plus operator +. The `peek()` function makes it possible to look ahead at the next character without actually moving the read position:[9]

```
nextCh = inStream.peek();                  // look ahead at next char

if (nextCh == '=')                         // if it's an =
{
   inStream.get(nextCh);                   //    get the char
   return PLUS_EQUALS_TOKEN;               //    and return +=
}
else if (nextCh == '+')                    // else if it's another +
{
   inStream.get(nextCh);                   //    get the char
   return INCREMENT_TOKEN;                 //    and return ++
}
else if (isspace(nextCh)                   // else if it's whitespace
         || isalnum(nextCh)                //   a letter or a digit,
         || nextCh == '\''                 //   a single quote, or
         || nextCh == '"')                 //   a double quote,
   return PLUS_TOKEN;                      //    just return +
else                                       // else
   // ... generate error message           //    illegal token
```

Thus, if

```
inStream.peek()
```

returns the character `y`, then the lexical analyzer can infer that `inStream` contains

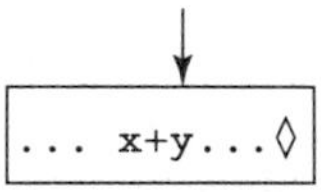

inStream

indicating that the plus operator + was specified, and not ++ or +=. The `y` is left in the stream where it can be subsequently processed in the normal fashion the next time the compiler asks the lexical analyzer for a token.

---

9. Recall from Chapter 3 that the `cctype` library function `isalnum(`*ch*`)` returns true if and only if its argument *ch* is an alphanumeric character. Similarly, `isspace(`*ch*`)` returns true if and only if its argument *ch* is a white-space character.

`putback()`. An alternative approach is provided by the `putback()` message, whose effect is to cause its character argument to be put back into the input stream, so that the next call to `get()` will input that character.

As an example, consider again the compiler problem, where the lexical analyzer has used `get()` to retrieve the character + from `inStream`:

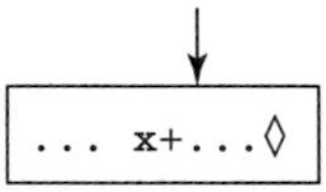

inStream

An alternative to using `peek()` would be to use `get()` to retrieve the next character,

```
inStream.get(nextCh);
```

and then use `putback()` to return it to `inStream`, if necessary:

```
if (nextCh == '=')                    // if it's an =
   return PLUS_EQUALS_TOKEN;          //   just return +=
else if (nextCh == '+')               // else if it's another +
   return INCREMENT_TOKEN;            //   just return ++
else if (isspace(nextCh)              // else if it's white space
         || isalnum(nextCh)           //  a letter or a digit,
         || nextCh == '\''            //  a single quote, or
         || nextCh == '"')            //  a double quote
{
   inStream.putback(nextCh);          // put it back for now
   return PLUS_TOKEN;                 //   and return +
}
else                                  // else
   // ...generate error message       //   illegal token
```

Thus, if the value of `nextCh` were `y`, the `putback()` function would return that character to the stream so that the next time the compiler asks the lexical analyzer for a token, its call to `get()` will retrieve that character.

THE `setstate()` MESSAGE

The `clear()` message can be used to reset the status bits of a stream. In addition to clearing the stream-status bits, it is sometimes useful to be able to set them. This can be done using the stream method `setstate()`.

To illustrate, suppose that we have a problem involving the seven colors red, orange, yellow, green, blue, indigo, and violet and we want to write a `readColor()` function to input a color, similar to the `getline()` function provided by the `string` library. Our function will read a word from a stream into a `string` variable, which it then passes back to the caller via a reference parameter.

But what do we do if the user enters an invalid value, a word that is not one of the seven colors? If we wish to handle this situation in a way that is consistent with the `iostream` library, then our function should set the *fail* status bit in the stream from which we attempted to read. Figure 9.6 shows how the stream function member `setstate()` can be used to do this.

Fig. 9.6 Setting stream-status flags.

```
void readColor(istream & theStream, string & theColor)
{
  string theWord;
  theStream >> theWord;

  if (theWord == "red" || theWord == "orange" ||
      theWord == "yellow" || theWord == "green" ||
      theWord == "blue" || theWord == "indigo" ||
      theWord == "violet")
      theColor = theWord;
  else
  {
     theStream.seekg(-theWord.size(), ios::cur); // unread the word
     theStream.setstate(ios::failbit);           // indicate failure
  }
}
```

By setting the *fail* status bit in the stream, this function leaves the handling of the error up to its caller. For example, a programmer wishing to treat this as a fatal error can write

```
string aColor;
readColor(cin, aColor);
assert( cin.good() );
```

and if the user enters any word other than a valid color value, the call to `assert()` will terminate the program. By contrast, a programmer who wishes to treat this occurrence as a nonfatal error and have the user try again, can write

```
string aColor;
for (;;)
{
   readColor(cin, aColor);
   if ( cin.good() ) break;
   cout << "Try again: ";
   cin.clear();
   cin.ignore(80, '\n');
}
```

and the user will be given more chances to enter a valid value. Such flexibility is a hallmark of good design, because it leaves the decision of how to handle the problem up to users of the function, allowing them to choose the approach they prefer.

The `setstate()` message can be used to set the status bits in a stream, which are referred to by the following names:

Status Bit	Description
`ios::badbit`	The *bad* bit: 1 if an unrecoverable error occurred, 0 otherwise.
`ios::failbit`	The *fail* bit: 1 if a recoverable error occurred, 0 otherwise.
`ios::eofbit`	The *eof* bit: 1 if the end-of-file mark was read, 0 otherwise.

In practice, `setstate()` is rarely passed `ios::eofbit`, since that is set by the input operations.

The Formatting Manipulators. As we saw in Chapter 5, the `iostream` library and its companion library `iomanip` provide manipulators for controlling the format of `ostream` and `ofstream` objects. Manipulators can be divided into two categories: those without arguments and those that require arguments.

Manipulators without Arguments. The manipulators that do not require arguments are available in the `iostream` library. Some of these manipulators are given in the following table:

Manipulator	Description
`boolalpha`	Use strings `true` and `false` for I/O of boolean values
`noboolalpha`	Use integers `1` and `0` for I/O of boolean values
`scientific`	Use floating-point (scientific) notation
`fixed`	Use fixed-point notation
`showpoint`	Show decimal point and trailing zeros for whole real numbers
`noshowpoint`	Hide decimal point and trailing zeros for whole real numbers
`showpos`	Display positive values with a + sign
`noshowpos`	Display positive values without a + sign
`dec`	Display integer values in base 10
`oct`	Display integer values in base 8
`hex`	Display integer values in base 16
`showbase`	Display integer values indicating their base (e.g., `0x` for hex).
`noshowbase`	Display integer values without indicating their base
`uppercase`	In hexadecimal, use symbols A–F; in scientific, use E
`nouppercase`	In hexadecimal, use symbols a–f; in scientific, use e
`skipws`	Skip white space on input
`noskipws`	Don't skip white space on input
`flush`	Write contents of stream to screen (or file)

Manipulator	Description
`endl`	Insert newline character and flush the stream
`left`	Left justify displayed values, pad with fill character on right
`right`	Right justify displayed values (except strings), pad with fill character on left
`internal`	Pad with fill character between sign or base and value

As we saw in Chapter 5, manipulators are inserted into the stream. But instead of appending values to the stream (except for `endl`), they affect the format of values that are subsequently inserted into the stream. For example, if we were to write

```
int i = 17;

cout << showbase
     << oct << i << endl
     << dec << i << endl
     << hex << i << endl;
```

then the following values would be displayed

```
021
17
0x11
```

because $21_8 = 17_{10} = 11_{16}$.

Manipulators Requiring Arguments. To use the manipulators that require arguments, the file `<iomanip>` must be included. The following table gives some of these manipulators:

Manipulator	Description
`setprecision(`*`num`*`)`	Set the number of decimal digits to be displayed to *`num`*
`setw(`*`num`*`)`	Display *the next value* in a field whose width is *`num`*
`setfill(`*`ch`*`)`	Set the fill character to *`ch`* (blank is the default)

When a real number is inserted into a stream, the number of digits that are displayed to the right of the decimal point is called the **precision** of the number. As we have seen before, this characteristic can be controlled with the `setprecision()` manipulator.

We have also seen that when a number is inserted into a stream, it is first placed into a **field**, which is then inserted into the stream. The size of this field is controlled by the `setw()` manipulator. If the size of the field is less than the size of the value being displayed, the field is automatically expanded to the same size as the value. If the size of the field exceeds the size of the value being displayed, then the empty positions in the field are filled with the **fill character** (by default, a blank), whose value is set by the `setfill()` manipulator.

Here is a simple code fragment that illustrates the use of these manipulators:

```
cout << fixed << showpoint              // show decimal pt, sign
     << setprecision(2)                 // 2 decimal places
     << setfill('*') << left            // pad with *, left justify
     << setw(6) << 1.0/3.0 << endl      // print value
     << setfill('$') << right           // pad with $, rt justify
     << setw(6) << 1.0/3.0 << endl;     // print value
```

When executed, this statement produces the following output:

```
0.33**
$$0.33
```

Note that unlike `setprecision()`, `setw()` affects only the next value inserted into the stream, so `setw()` must precede *each* insertion of a value whose field width we wish to specify.

To display a column of figures with their decimal points aligned, the `right` manipulator can be used with `setprecision()` and `setw()`. For example, to display a table of square roots to seven decimal places, we could write this code segment:

```
cout << fixed << showpoint << right
     << setprecision(7) << setfill('.');

for (int i = 1; i <= 10; i++)
   cout << setw(2) << i << setw(12) << sqrt(i) << endl;
```

Executing these statements produces the output

```
 1....1.0000000
 2....1.4142136
 3....1.7320508
 4....2.0000000
 5....2.2360680
 6....2.4494897
 7....2.6457513
 8....2.8284271
 9....3.0000000
10....3.1622777
```

STRING STREAMS

C++ also permits us to read input from a `string` or to write output to a `string`. This is made possible by means of **string streams** defined in the `<sstream>` library:[10]

`istringstream`	For input from a string
`ostreamstream`	For output to a string
`stringstream`	For input from and output to a string

---

10. The corresponding types for wide characters (of type `wchar_t`) are `wistringstream`, `wostringstream`, and `wstringstream`.

The message `str()` can be used to convert a string stream to a `string`, and vice versa:

`strstream.str(s);`	Set string stream `strstream` to a copy of `string s`
`str(strstream)`	Returns a `string` that is a copy of the string in `strstream`

The program in Figure 9.7 illustrates the use of string streams. It constructs an `istringstream` from the string `date`, uses the input operator `>>` to read the individual words and integers, and displays them. It then outputs strings and integers to the `ostringstream ostr`, uses `str()` to extract the string from `ostr`, and displays it. (See Section 9.5 for more examples of the usefulness of string streams.)

Fig. 9.7 String streams. (Part 1 of 2)

```
/* stringStreamDemo.cpp illustrates the use of string streams.
 *   Input (istringstream istr):  word1, word2, month, day, comma, year
 *   Output (istringstream ostr): these words separated by ***
 *   Output (ostream cout):       the string stored in ostr
 ************************************************************************/

#include <iostream>
#include <iomanip>
#include <sstream>
using namespace std;

int main()
{
   string date = "Independence Day: July 4, 1776";
   istringstream istr(date);
   string word1, word2, month;
   int day, year, one = 1;
   char comma;

   istr >> word1 >> word2 >> month >> day >> comma >> year;
   cout << "Contents of string stream istr:\n"
        << word1 << "***" << word2 << "***" << month << "***"
        << day << "***" << comma << "***" << year << endl;

   ostringstream ostr;
   ostr << "New Year's "<< word2 << "January"
        << setw(2) << one << ", "<< year + 226;
   cout << ostr.str() << endl;
}
```

Fig. 9.7 String streams. (Part 2 of 2)

Sample run:

```
Contents of string stream istr:
Independence***Day:***July***4***,***1776
New Year's Day: January 1, 2002
```

Quick Quiz 9.4

1. (True or false) Sequential access refers to being able to access an item in a file directly by specifying its sequential position in the file.
2. (True or false) Direct access refers to being able to access an item in a file directly by specifying its offset from the beginning of the file.
3. Another name for direct access is ________ access.
4. The ________ function can be used to find the location of the read position in an `istream`, and the ________ function can be used to move to that position.
5. Write a statement that moves the read position in the `ifstream inputStream` to the third character from the beginning of the stream.
6. Proceed as in Question 5, but move the read position to the third character past the current position.
7. Proceed as in Question 5, but move the read position to the last character in the stream.
8. Write statements to display the next character in the file stream of Question 5, and remove it from the `fstream`.
9. Write statements to display the next character in the file stream of Question 5 without removing it from the file stream. Do this in two different ways.
10. ________ can be used to control the format of `ofstream` objects.

Part of the Picture
Database Systems
by Keith Vander Linden, Calvin College

One of our local supermarket chains keeps detailed records of its products, sales, customers, and supplies. They can tell you the current price of any item in any of their stores, who supplied it, and how long it's been on the shelf. They can tell you how many people bought tortilla chips at the rock-bottom sale price last weekend and whether they also bought salsa and bean dip to go with them. Not surprisingly, this level of record keeping produces a staggering volume of information, commonly called **data**. Why do they go to all this trouble? The answer—they have to make business decisions, and these decisions are based on data. The more accurate and detailed the data, the better the decisions can be. Was the rock-bottom sale price for the chips too high, or too low? Did they make an overall profit? How many units of chips should they buy next time? The data can help answer these questions and thus are critical to business in a competitive market.

This use of data is not unique to the grocery business. Banks keep records of our accounts and our transactions, universities and colleges keep records of our tuition costs and our performance, airlines keep records on which planes are flying where and who has paid to ride on them. As in the case of the supermarket, these data sets can become very large and must be maintained for long periods of time. Furthermore, they must be conveniently accessible to many people. It is useful, therefore, to store and maintain them on computers. The data sets themselves, when stored on a computer, are commonly called **databases,** and the programs designed to maintain them are called **database–management systems.**

The current chapter has discussed files, and it is not hard to see that their ability to store large amounts of data in a persistent manner is important for database systems. Section 9.1 gave an example of how files can be used to maintain a small meteorological database. As we work with that database, however, a problem arises: The database will change, as all realistic databases do. We may, for example, want to add temperature readings to the pressure readings already contained there. Adding this information to the file is easy enough, but we must also modify the code by adding an additional variable to store the temperature and an extra input command to read the value, and we must know the order in which the pressure and temperature readings are stored in the file. Another complication would arise if we wanted to add information on the particular instruments used to collect the readings. This would probably require a separate file of information for each of the instruments, new code to read and process this file, and some additional code allowing us to record which readings were taken with which instruments.

What started as a fairly simple problem, with a small driver program and a single data file, has become much more complex. In addition, this complexity is likely to increase as the database grows and as more and more people want to access it. Database systems are designed to address these problems. Although varied, they tend to provide a number of common facilities:

- *High-level views of the data* —Databases allow programmers to view the data at a higher level, ignoring some of the details of the location and format of the files.
- *Access routines*—A high-level view of the data wouldn't be of much use if the programmer couldn't retrieve and manipulate the data. Database systems, therefore, provide what is called a **query language**, which provides a set of operations that a programmer can use when accessing and manipulating a database.
- *Support for large databases*—Databases tend to be large, frequently too large to fit into a computer's main memory. For example, the supermarket database mentioned earlier maintains approximately one *terabyte* of data, that's 10^{12} bytes or 1,000 gigabytes. Database systems are designed to manipulate large databases such as this without reading them into memory all at once.
- *Security*—It is frequently important to restrict access to sensitive or proprietary data in a database. Most database systems provide this capability.
- *Data sharing* —The data stored in a database is often of interest to many different people. Several people may, therefore, want to retrieve or modify the data at the same time. Database systems typically provide a check-in/check-out protocol for the data, much like the protocol for checking out books at a public library. This ensures that only one person can manipulate the data at a time.

THE RELATIONAL MODEL

Different models may be used to design a database system, each of which attempts to provide the features just mentioned. One particular model, called the **relational model**, has become an industry standard. In this model, the database is viewed as a set of tables with one row for each entry. For instance, the data from a simple employee database would be viewed as follows:

Name	IDNumber	Pay Rate	Department
John	45678	7.50	Accounting
Mark	56789	8.75	Accounting
Paul	67891	9.35	Marketing
Matt	78912	10.50	Accounting
Gabe	89123	6.35	Marketing
Joel	91234	10.50	Development
Naomi	98765	7.15	Development
Jamie	12345	9.15	Development
April	23456	8.75	Accounting
Jodi	34567	10.50	Service

In this set of data, called a **table**, the top row specifies the contents of each column of data. In this case we have the employee's name, ID number, pay rate, and department. The table has one row, called a **record**, for each employee, and each record has one entry for each column, called a **field**. We will call this table the `Employee` table. Note that there is no mention here of the files that contain the data or in what format the data is represented. The database system takes care of these details, so the programmer doesn't have to.

One popular query language for the relational model is called **SQL** (for "Structured Query Language"). SQL provides commands to add data for tables, retrieve data from tables, and modify data in tables. For example, consider the following command:

```
SELECT *
FROM Employee
WHERE Rate = 10.5;
```

This command will retrieve, or *select*, all the records (specified by the `"*"`) from the `Employee` table that have a pay rate of $10.50. The resulting records are as follows:

Name	IDNumber	Pay Rate	Department
Matthew	78912	10.50	Accounting
Joel	91234	10.50	Development
Jodi	34567	10.50	Service

Note that the result is itself a table. This elegant feature allows the output of one SQL command to be used as the input to another.

To gain a better understanding of the relationship between file manipulation and database management, Professor Vander Linden has built a simple relational database system with a scaled-down implementation of the select command. See the book's Web site for this example. It includes program code as well as exercises for you to work with the example.

FURTHER READING

The field of database systems is active, both in research and in applications. If you are interested in reading additional material, consider going to the following sources:

- Ullman and Widom's text, *A First Course in Database Systems* , Prentice Hall, 1997—This is a good, current overview of the field of database systems. It covers the relational model and also deals with newer object-oriented approaches to database modeling.
- E. F. Codd's original paper, "A Relational Model of Data for Large Shared Data Banks," *Communications of the ACM* , 1970, 13(6), pages 377–387—This is a classic paper on the relational database model.
- For information on some current database systems, try visiting the Oracle or Sybase corporation Web sites: `www.oracle.com; www.sybase.com.`

9.5* OBJECTive Thinking: Objects and Streams

In previous *OBJECTive Thinking* sections, we have seen how to build classes that provide instance variables, constructors, accessors, mutators, and I/O methods. In this section, we examine two different ways that streams can be used in conjunction with objects:

- reading an object's attributes from a file, and
- converting an object to a string representation.

Both of these operations use streams, but in somewhat different ways.

OBJECTS AND FILE I/O

In the *OBJECTive Thinking* section of Chapter 6, we defined `read()` methods for classes `Name` and `Student` that fill an object with values read from an `istream`. The `read()` methods we defined there can also be used to read from an `ifstream` because:

1. Our `read()` methods extract their values from an `istream` passed as an argument.
2. An `ifstream` is a specialized kind of `istream` (i.e., `ifstream` is derived from `istream`).
3. An instance of a derived class can be passed as an argument to a parameter whose type is its parent class.

This means, for example, that because we can read a value for a `Name` object from the keyboard by sending it a `read()` message with `cin` as an argument,

```
aName.read(cin);
```

we can also send it a `read()` message with an open `ifstream` as an argument,

```
ifstream fin("nameFile.txt");
aName.read(fin);
```

and our `read()` method will then extract its values from `nameFile.txt` instead of from the keyboard.

Similarly, in the *OBJECTive Thinking* section of Chapter 5 we saw how to define a `print()` method that displays an object's attributes by inserting them into an `ostream`. The `print()` methods we defined there can also be used to write to an `ofstream` because:

1. Our `print()` methods insert their values into an `ostream` they are passed as an argument.
2. An `ofstream` is a specialized kind of `ostream` (i.e., `ofstream` is derived from `ostream`).
3. An instance of a derived class can be passed as an argument to a parameter of its parent class.

This means, for example, that because we could write a value for a `Student` object to the screen by sending it the `print()` message with `cout` or `cerr` as an argument,

```
aStudent.print(cout);
```

we can also send it a `print()` message with an open `ofstream` as an argument,

```
ofstream fout("studentFile.txt");
aStudent.print(fout);
```

and our `print()` method will then write its values to `studentFile.txt`, instead of to the screen.

To illustrate, suppose that the file `nameFile.txt` contains the following entries:

```
John Jacob Jingle-Heimer-Schmidt
Little Bo Peep
Little Jackie Horner
Yertle the Turtle
```

Then we can write a program like that in Figure 9.8 to read and display the contents of this file.

Fig. 9.8 Filling an object with data from a file. (Part 1 of 2)

```
// nameDriver.cpp

#include <iostream>    // cout
#include <fstream>     // ifstream
#include "Name.h"
using namespace std;

int main()
{
   ifstream fin("nameFile.txt");
   Name aName;
```

Fig. 9.8 Filling an object with data from a file. (Part 2 of 2)

```
   for (;;)
   {
      aName.read(fin);

      if ( fin.eof() ) break;

      aName.print(cout);
   }

   fin.close();
}
```

Sample run:

```
John Jacob Jingle-Heimer-Schmidt
Little Bo Peep
Little Jackie Horner
Yertle the Turtle
```

CONVERTER METHODS

Streams can also be used to simplify the design of **converter methods**. As its name implies, a converter is an operation that, given an object of one type, produces an equivalent representation of that object in a different type. Classes commonly provide converters to convert between an object and its string representation.

There are two kinds of converters:

- **Accessor converters** are methods that return a representation of an object as a different type.
- **Constructor converters** are constructors (similar to explicit-value constructors) that, given a value of some different type, initialize a new object's attributes using that value.

Because most data items can be represented by one or more characters, and because strings provide a convenient way to convey sequences of characters, it is common for a class to provide conversions to and from strings. To illustrate this, we will build these converters for our `Name` class.

`Name`-to-string and string-to-`Name` Converters. The `Name` class we introduced in Section 2.3 contains three string instance variables: one for the *first name*, one for the *middle name*, and one for the *last name*. Because these three attributes are all stored as strings, it is easy to build a `Name`-to-string converter accessor using the concatenation operator. The string-to-`Name` converter constructor requires a bit more work, but is still fairly easy, thanks to the string-stream library. Figure 9.9 gives the prototypes and definitions.

Fig. 9.9 `Name` converter operations.

```
/* Name.h provides the Name class.
 * ... other documentation omitted ...
 ****************************************************************/

#include <string>              // class string
#include <sstream>             // istringstream, ostringstream
using namespace std;

class Name
{
 public:
   // ... other constructors omitted ...
   Name(string fullName);       // convert string to Name

   string asString() const;     // convert Name to string
   // ... other methods omitted ...

 private:
   string myFirstName, myMiddleName, myLastName;
};

// Definitions of converters
inline Name::Name(string fullName)
{
   istringstream ssin(fullName);
   ssin >> myFirstName >> myMiddleName >> myLastName;
}

inline string Name::asString() const
{
   return myFirstName + ' ' + myMiddleName + ' ' + myLastName;
}
```

As we mentioned earlier, defining the `Name`-to-string accessor converter `asString()` is quite easy. Since each instance variable is a string, this method simply returns the result of concatenating these three strings (with separating spaces).

Defining a constructor to convert a string into a `Name` is not much more work, thanks to the `istringstream` class from the `sstream` library. (See Section 9.4.) As we saw, an `istringstream` is an object that lets us read values from a string using the extraction (`>>`) operator in the same manner as from an `istream`. All we need to do is pass the string in question to the `istringstream` constructor and then extract the values from the resulting `istringstream`.

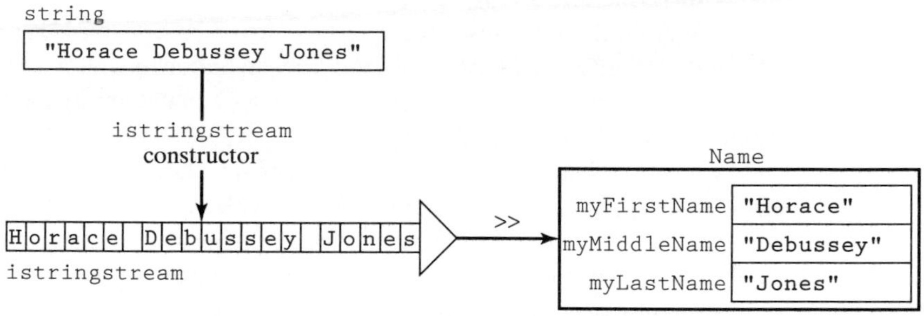

Once we have these operations defined, a programmer can use them to convert between Name values and string values, as shown in Figure 9.10.

Fig. 9.10 Driver to test Name converter operations.

```
/* nameDriver.cpp tests the Name class converter operations.
 * ... other documentation omitted ...
 *******************************************************************/

#include <string>              // class string
#include <iostream>            // cin, cout, ...
using namespace std;
#include "Name.h"

int main()
{
  string fullNameString = "Horace Debussey Jones";
  Name aName(fullNameString);             // convert string to Name

  string nameString = aName.asString(); // convert Name to string

  aName.print(cout);                      // output Name
  cout << "\n" << nameString << endl;     // output string
}
```

Sample Execution:

```
Horace Debussey Jones
Horace Debussey Jones
```

Our asString() converter method was easy to define because all of the attributes to be converted to strings were themselves strings. In our next example, we will see how to convert an object to a string when its instance variables are not strings.

Sphere-to-string and string-to-Sphere Converters. The Sphere class we introduced in Section 2.3 contains three double instance variables: myRadius, myDensity, and myWeight. Since the string concatenation operator (+) is not defined for double values, we cannot define an asString() converter method for class Sphere the same way we did for class Name.

However, in addition to the istringstream class that can be used to extract values from a string, the sstream library also provides an ostringstream class we can use to insert values into a string. That is, we can define an asString() method for class Sphere by building an ostringstream object, inserting our three double attributes and separating spaces into it using the insertion operator (<<), and then sending the ostringstream object the str() message to retrieve the string it contains. Figure 9.11 provides the details.

Fig. 9.11 Sphere converter operations. (Part 1 of 2)

```
/* Sphere.h provides the Sphere class.
 * ... other documentation omitted ...
 ****************************************************************/

#include <string>              // class string
#include <sstream>             //istringstream, ostringstream
using namespace std;

class Sphere
{
 public:
   // ... other constructors omitted ...
   Sphere(string sphereAttributes);  // convert string to Name

   string asString() const;          // convert Sphere to string
   // ... other methods omitted ...

 private:
   double myRadius, myDensity, myWeight;
};

inline Sphere::Sphere(string sphereAttributes)
{
   istringstream ssin(sphereAttributes);
   ssin >> myRadius >> myDensity >> myWeight;
}
```

Fig. 9.11 Sphere converter operations. (Part 2 of 2)

```
inline string Sphere::asString() const
{
   ostringstream ssout;
   ssout << myRadius << ' ' << myDensity << ' ' << myWeight;
   return ssout.str();
}
```

Similar to our approach in class `Name`, the string-to-`Sphere` constructor converter builds an `istringstream` named `ssin`, passing it the string to be processed. It then extracts `double` values from it using the extraction operator (>>). Our `Sphere`-to-string accessor converter builds an empty `ostringstream` named `ssout`, inserts `double` values into it using the insertion operator (<<), sends the `ostringstream` object the `str()` message to retrieve its string, and returns that string to the caller.

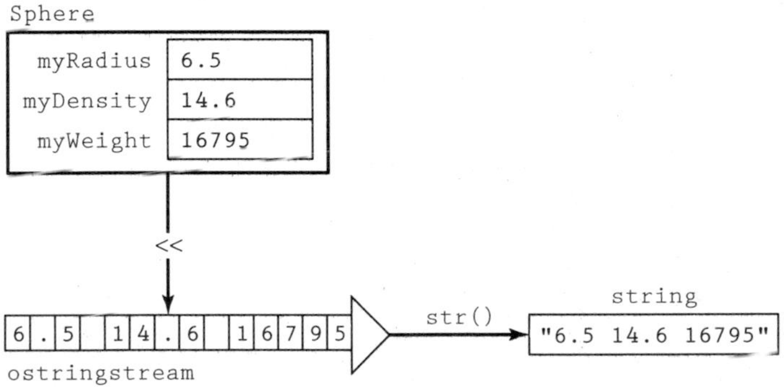

The converters we have been considering are thus useful for storing objects to and retrieving objects from a file. An object-to-string converter can store the representation of an object in a file, and the string-to-object converter can read this string representation of a object from a file and convert it into an object representation. Figure 9.12 illustrates this for `Sphere` objects.

Fig. 9.12 Driver to test `Sphere` converter operations. (Part 1 of 2)

```
/* sphereDriver.cpp tests the Sphere class converter operations.
 * ... other documentation omitted ...
 **************************************************************/

#include <string>             // class string
#include <iostream>           // cin, cout, ...
#include <fstream>            // ifstream, ofstream
#include "Sphere.h"
using namespace std;
```

Fig. 9.12 Driver to test `Sphere` converter operations. (Part 2 of 2)

```
int main()
{
  cout << "\nTo compute the weight of a sphere,\n"
       << " enter its radius and density: ";
  Sphere aSphere;
  aSphere.readRadiusAndDensity(cin);
                                       // store aSphere in a file
  ofstream fout("Sphere.txt");
  fout << "Sphere\n" << aSphere.asString() << endl;
  fout.close();
                                       // now, read info back
  ifstream fin("Sphere.txt");
  string classString, attributeString;
  getline(fin, classString);
  getline(fin, attributeString);
  fin.close();
                                       // rebuild object
  if (classString == "Sphere")
  {
     Sphere sameSphere(attributeString);
     sameSphere.print(cout);
     cout << endl;
  }
  else
  {
     cerr << "Unexpected class: " << classString << endl;
     exit(1);
  }
}
```

Sample Execution:

```
To compute the weight of a sphere,
 enter its radius and density: 6.5 14.6
Sphere, radius: 6.5, density: 14.6, weight: 16795
```

Contents of file `Sphere.txt`:

```
Sphere
6.5 14.6 16795
```

Converters thus provide an alternative approach to file I/O that may be more convenient if the `read()` and `print()` methods are tailored for interactive I/O.

Note that by storing the name of the class in a file along with the attribute string, we can store objects of *different* types in the same file. To read such objects back from the file, a program can use a loop containing an `if-else-if` statement to construct the appropriate objects:

```
for (;;)
{
   getline(fin, classString);
   getline(fin, attributeString);

   if ( fin.eof() ) break;

   if (classString == "Sphere")
   {
      Sphere aSphere(attributeString);
      // ... do whatever with aSphere
   }
   else if (classString == "Box")
   {
      Box aBox(attributeString);
      // ... do whatever with aBox
   }
   .
   .
   .
   else
   {
      cerr << "Unknown class: " << classString << endl;
      exit(1);
   }
}
```

Using string streams. We can send the `str()` message to either an `istringstream` or an `ostringstream` to extract the string it contains—that is, `str()` is an accessor converter method! The `>>` operator should only be applied to an `istringstream`, and the `<<` operator should only be applied to an `ostringstream`.

In situations where it is necessary to both insert and extract values, the `sstream` library provides the `stringstream` class. As with the other classes, the `str()` message can be used to extract the string from a `stringstream`. But, in addition, the `>>` operator can be used to extract individual values from it, *and* the `<<` operator can be used to insert values into it.

All three of these classes (`istringstream`, `ostringstream`, `stringstream`) provide a default constructor that initializes the string stream to be empty and an explicit-value constructor that initializes the string stream to a string passed as an argument. In Figure 9.11, the `ostringstream` in our accessor converter is initialized using the default constructor and the `istringstream` in our constructor converter is initialized using the explicit-value constructor.

The following table summarizes the behaviors of the three `sstream` classes:

	`str()`	`<<`	`>>`
`istringstream`	yes	no	yes
`ostringstream`	yes	yes	no
`stringstream`	yes	yes	yes

Exercises 9.5

1. Write converter methods for the phone-number class in Exercise 4 of Section 2.3. (See also Exercises 4 and 9 of Section 3.8 and Exercise 8 of Section 5.6.)
2. Write converter methods for the time class in Exercise 2 of Section 2.3. (See also Exercises 2 and 7 of Section 3.8, Exercises 9 and 10 of Section 4.7, and Exercise 6 of Section 5.6.)
3. Write converter methods for the date class in Exercise 3 of Section 2.3. (See also Exercises 3 and 8 of Section 3.8 and Exercise 7 of Section 5.6.)
4. Write converter methods for the class `Student` of Section 5.6.

CHAPTER SUMMARY

Key Terms & Notes

accessor converters
binary file
`close()` function
closing a stream
converter method
data
data base
`data()`
direct access
end-of-file mark
end-of-line mark
`eof()` function
field
file
fill character
format manipulators
`fstream` library
`getline()` function
`ifstream`
input operator (`>>`)
`is_open()` function
`istringstream`
manipulator
mode argument
`ofstream`
`open()` function
opening a stream
`ostringstream`
output operator(`<<`)
overload
precision
random access
read position
sequential access
`sstream` library
stream
`stringstream`
test file
text file
virus
write position

- Text files are simply sequences of characters, some of which may be special characters that mark the end of a line or the end of the file.
- Before input from / output to a file can be performed, a file stream must first be connected to that file; this is called *opening* that stream. Either the initialization-at-declaration mechanism or the `open()` message can be used to open a file stream. If the file's name is stored in a string object, the `data()` or `c_str()` method must be used to extract the character string from the string object.
- Each attempt to open a file should always be tested to see if it succeeded—for example, with the `is_open()` function—before proceeding with other operations on the file.
- `ifstream` objects are used for file input; `ofstream` objects are used for file output.
- Because the file stream classes `ifstream`, `ofstream`, and `fstream` are derived from the `istream`, `ostream`, and `iostream` classes, respectively, all of the operations from these latter classes can also be performed on the corresponding file stream objects.
- By default, opening an `ifstream` to a file initializes the file stream with the contents of that file with the read position at the first character in the stream. Opening an `ofstream` initializes the file stream as empty (containing only the end-of-file mark) with the write position at the end-of-file mark. Any previous contents of the file are destroyed. If the mode `ios::app` is used, then the file must exist and the stream is initialized with the contents of that file with the write position at the end of the file.
- Applying the input operator (`>>`) to an `ifstream` will extract the first value following the read position in the stream, skipping initial white-space characters, and advance the read position to the first character past the input value. Numeric values are delimited by nonnumeric characters.
- The `getline()` function can be used to extract the line of input beginning at the read position in an `ifstream` and store the characters in a string variable, leaving the read position at the first character beyond the first newline character encountered. Care must be taken when intermixing calls to `getline()` and the input operator because `>>` leaves the newline character in the file.
- The output operator (`<<`) can be used to insert a value into an `ofstream` at the write position, advancing it to the point immediately following the value.
- It is considered good programming practice to disconnect a file stream from a file using the `close()` message when that file is no longer needed.
- Parameters corresponding to file stream arguments must be reference parameters so that changes to the stream are passed back to the calling function.
- Streams are useful in writing converter methods that, given an object of one type, produce an equivalent representation of that object in a different type.

Programming Pointers

Program Style and Design

1. *If a program is to read data from a file, an* `ifstream` *must be declared and initialized as a connection between the program and the file. If it is to write data to a file, an* `ofstream` *must be declared and initialized as a connection between the program and the file*. The three basic steps for file-processing programs are as follows:

- **a.** Declare and open an `ifstream` object for each input file and an `ofstream` object for each output file to establish connections between the program and the files.
- **b.** Perform the desired processing with the file via the file streams.
- **c.** Close each file stream, severing the connection with the file.

2. *A forever loop controlled by the* `ifstream` *function member* `eof()` *can be used to read data from a file via an* `ifstream`:

```
ifstream theStream("SomeFile");

for (;;)
{
   // read a value from theStream
   if (theStream.eof()) break;
   // process the value
}
```

Some programmers prefer the `while` loop version:

```
// read a value from theStream
while (!theStream.eof())
{
   // process the value
   // read a value from theStream
}
```

Potential Pitfalls

1. *Before a file stream can be used, it must be opened as a connection to a particular file*. There are two ways to do this. The simplest way is to initialize the stream with the name of the file in the stream's declaration:

```
ofstream outStream("OutputFile.TXT");
```

Alternatively, the stream can be declared and opened separately, using the `open()` function member:

```
ofstream outStream;
outStream.open("OutputFile.TXT");
```

2. *When opening a stream to a file, the name of the file must be given as a character string.* For example, to open an `ifstream` named `inStream` to a file named `Text`, we can write

```
ifstream inStream("Text");
```

because `"Text"` is a character string literal. However, if the name of the file is stored in a string variable named `fileName`, then the function member `data()` or `c_str()` must be used to extract the character string stored in `fileName`:

```
ifstream inStream(filename.data());
```

3. *The operations performed on a file stream must be consistent with the mode by which it was initialized*. Applying the input operator to an `ofstream` or applying the output operator to an `ifstream` will generate a compilation error.
4. *When inputting values, the extraction operator (>>) skips over any leading white-space characters (blanks, tabs, and newlines); the member functions* `get()` *and* `getline()` *do not.* For example, if the user enters

```
A↵
B↵
C↵
```

then the `istream` named `cin` can be visualized as follows:

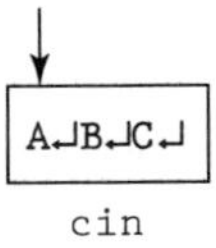

Now, if the statements

```
cin >> letter1;
cin >> letter2;
cin >> letter3;
```

are executed, then `'A'` is read and stored in `letter1`,

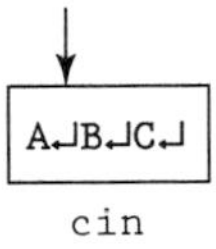

the newline (as white space) is skipped and the value `'B'` is read and stored in `letter2`,

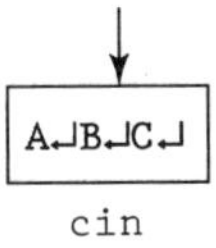

and the newline (as white space) is skipped and the value `'C'` is read and stored in `letter3`,

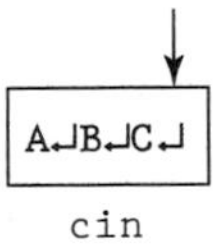

leaving the final newline unread. By contrast, if the statements

```
cin.get(letter1);
cin.get(letter2);
cin.get(letter3);
```

are executed, then the value `'A'` is read and stored in `letter1` as before,

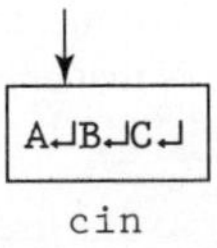

but the newline value `'\n'` is read and stored in `letter2`

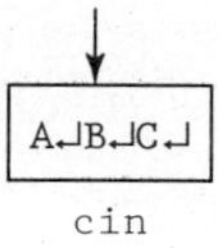

and the value `'B'` is read and stored in `letter3`,

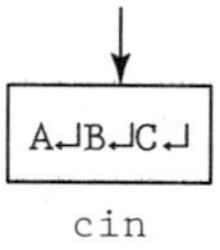

leaving the second newline, `'C'`, and third newline unread.

5. *Care must be taken when mixing calls to* `>>` *and* `getline()`. If a call to `>>` precedes a call to `getline()` and the values being read are separated by a newline character, then an additional call to `get()` should be inserted between `>>` and `getline()` to consume the newline character. Otherwise, `getline()` will stop reading immediately when it encounters that newline, and the `string` variable for which a value is being read will retain its previous value.
6. *When values are read using* `>>`, *leading white space is skipped and then characters are read and removed from the stream until a white-space, end-of-file, or some other character that cannot belong to a value of that type is encountered; this character that terminates input is left in the stream*. The characters that were read are then converted to a value of the type of the variable for which a value is being read. For example, if `intVal` is an `int` variable and `cin` contains

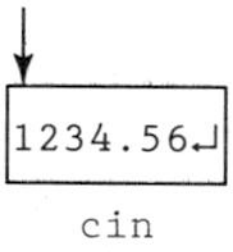

the statement `cin >> intVal;` will read the characters `1`, `2`, `3`, and `4` and assign the integer 1234 to `intVal`. The remaining characters will stay in `cin` for the next input operation:

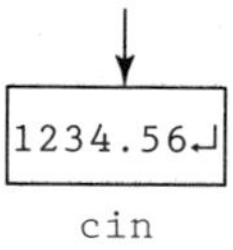

7. *In the preceding Potential Pitfall, if no character in a stream is found—including the end-of-file mark—that can belong to a value of the required type, the input operation is said to fail, and the value of the variable remains unchanged.* For example, if the statement `cin >> intVal;` is executed again, no characters will be read and removed because the period `(.)` cannot be a part of an `int` value, the value of `intVal` remains unchanged, and the `istream` is unchanged. The result is that an infinite loop can easily result. Including a statement like

```
if (cin.fail()) break;
```

after the input statement can be used to detect this condition and terminate repetition.

8. *A file stream should always be closed using the member* `close()` *once use of that stream has been completed.*
9. *Parameters to hold file stream arguments must be* **reference parameters** *because an input or output operation changes the stream's read or write position, respectively.*
10. *Once the eof, bad, or fail state bits have been set in a stream, no subsequent operations can be performed on that stream until those bits have been cleared (using the* `clear()` *member)— but see Potential Pitfall 7.*

Programming Problems

Sections 9.1–9.3

1. Write a program to concatenate two files; that is, to append one file to the end of the other.
2. Write a program that reads a text file and counts the vowels in the file.
3. Write a program that reads a text file and counts the occurrences in the file of a specified string entered during execution of the program.
4. Write a program that reads a text file and counts the characters in each line. The program should display the line number and the length of the shortest and longest lines in the file, as well as the average number of characters per line.
5. Write a program to copy one text file into another text file in which the lines are numbered 1, 2, 3, . . . with a number at the left of each line.
6. Write a program that reads a text file and writes it to another text file, but with leading blanks and blank lines removed. Run this program using as input files the last two C++ programs you have written, and comment on whether you think indenting C++ programs makes them more readable.
7. Write a file-pagination program that reads a text file and prints it in blocks of 20 lines. If after printing a block of lines, there still are lines in the file, the program should allow the user to indicate whether more output is desired; if so, the next block should be printed; otherwise, execution of the program should terminate.
8. People from three different income levels, A, B, and C, rated each of two different products with a number 0 through 10. Construct a file in which each line contains the income level and product rankings for one respondent. Then write a program that reads this information and calculates the following:

   a. for each income bracket, the average rating for product 1;
   b. the number of persons in income bracket B who rated both products with a score of 5 or higher;
   c. the average rating for product 2 by persons who rated product 1 lower than 3.

   Label all output, and design the program so that it automatically counts the respondents.
9. Write a program to search the file `Users` (see descriptions following this problem set) to find and display the resources used to date for specified users whose identification numbers are entered during execution of the program.
10. Write a program to search the file `Inventory` (see descriptions following this problem set) to find an item with a specified item number. If a match is found, display the item number and the number currently in stock; otherwise, display a message indicating that it was not found.
11. At the end of each month, a report is produced that shows the status of each user's account in `Users` (see descriptions following this problem set). Write a program to accept the current date and produce a report of the form

```
                    USER ACCOUNTS--mm/dd/yy
                      RESOURCE                RESOURCES
USER-ID                 LIMIT                    USED
-----------------------------------------------------
10101                   $750                    $381
10102                   $650                    $599***
  .                       .                       .
  .                       .                       .
  .                       .                       .
```

where mm/dd/yy is the current data and the three asterisks (***) indicate that the user has already used 90 percent or more of the resources available to him or her.

12. Write a program that reads a text file, counting the nonblank characters, the nonblank lines, the words, and the sentences and then calculates the average number of characters per word and the average number of words per sentence. You may assume the following: The file contains only letters, blanks, commas, periods, semicolons, and colons; a word is any sequence of letters that begins a line or is preceded by one or more blanks and that is terminated by a blank, comma, semicolon, colon, period, or the end of a line; and a sentence is terminated by a period.

13. (Project) Write a menu-driven program that uses the files `Student` and `Student-Update` (see descriptions following this problem set) and allows (some of) the following options. For each option, write a separate function so that options and corresponding functions can be easily added or removed.

    1. Locate a student's permanent record when given his or her student number, and print it in a nicer format than that in which it is stored.
    2. This option is the same as Option 1, but locate the record when given the student's name.
    3. Print a list of all student names and numbers in a given class (1, 2, 3, 4, 5).
    4. This is the same as Option 3 but for a given major.
    5. This option is the same as Option 3, but for a given range of cumulative GPAs.
    6. Find the average cumulative GPAs for (a) all females, (b) all males, (c) all students with a specified major, and (d) all students.
    7. Produce updated grade reports with the following format (where xx is the current year):

```
                GRADE REPORT -- SEMESTER 2   5/29/xx

                      DISPATCH UNIVERSITY

10103           James L. Johnson

                      GRADE              CREDITS
                      =====              =======
ENGL 176                C                   4
EDUC 268                B                   4
EDUC 330                B+                  3
P E 281                 C                   3
ENGR 317                D                   4

Cumulative Credits:    28
Current GPA:         1.61
Cumulative GPA:      2.64
```

Here, letter grades are assigned according to the following scheme: A = 4.0, A– = 3.7, B+ = 3.3, B = 3.0, B– = 2.7, C+ = 2.3, C = 2.0, C– = 1.7, D+ = 1.3, D = 1.0, D– = 0.7, and F = 0.0. (See Programming Problem 3 in Chapter 2 for details on the calculation of GPAs.)

8. This is the same as Option 7, but instead of producing grade reports, it produces a new file containing the updated total credits and new cumulative GPAs.
9. Produce an updated file when a student (a) drops or (b) adds a course.
10. Produce an updated file when a student (a) transfers into or (b) withdraws from the university.

Section 9.4

14. Suppose that each line of a file contains a student's last name and exam scores. Write a program that reads and counts the scores, then calculates the mean score and reads through the file again to calculate the variance and standard deviation. Display how many numbers there are and their mean, variance, and standard deviation with appropriate labels. If $\bar{x}$ denotes the mean of the numbers $x_1, \ldots, x_n$, the *variance* is the average of the squares of the deviations of the numbers from the mean:

$$variance = \frac{1}{n}\sum_{i=1}^{n}(x_i - \bar{x})^2$$

and the *standard deviation* is the square root of the variance.

15. Letter grades are sometimes assigned to numeric scores by using the grading scheme commonly called *grading on the curve.* In this scheme, a letter grade is assigned to a numeric score, according to the following table:

x = Numeric Score	Letter Grade
$x < m - \frac{3}{2}\sigma$	F
$m - \frac{3}{2}\sigma \le x < m - \frac{1}{2}\sigma$	D
$m - \frac{1}{2}\sigma \le x < m + \frac{1}{2}\sigma$	C
$m + \frac{1}{2}\sigma \le x < m + \frac{3}{2}\sigma$	B
$m + \frac{3}{2}\sigma \le x$	A

Here, m is the mean score and σ is the standard deviation. Extend the program of Problem 14 to read the student information in the file, calculate the mean and standard deviation of the scores, and produce another file containing each student's name, exam score, and the letter grade corresponding to that score.

16. Information about computer terminals in a computer network is maintained in a file. The terminals are numbered 1 through 100, and information about the nth terminal is stored in the nth line of the file. This information consists of a terminal type (string), the building in which it is located (string), the transmission rate (integer), an access code (character), and the date of last service (month, day, year). Write a program to read terminal numbers from the keyboard and directly access the line in the file for each terminal by moving the read position directly to that line. The program should retrieve and display the information about that terminal.

17. Extend the program of Problem 16 to accept a date of service along with each terminal number, and in addition to displaying terminal information on the screen, produce a new updated file containing the terminal number and date of service for each terminal processed during execution.
18. Extend the program of Problem 17 to close the input file and output file, reopen them for input, and then produce a new file containing the information of the original file, but with the dates of service updated with the information from the update file.

Section 9.5*

19. Modify the program in Figure 9.8 so that the output is to a file instead of to the screen.
20. Using the converter methods in Exercise 4 for the class `Student`, write a program that builds a file of students whose values are entered interactively.
21. Using the converter methods in Exercise 4 for the class `Student`, write a program that searches a file of students for a particular student whose name is entered interactively and displays that student's information.

DESCRIPTIONS OF DATA FILES

The following describe the contents of data files used in exercises in the text. Listings of them are available on the book's Web site.

`Inventory:`

Item number: an integer
Number currently in stock: an integer (in the range 0 through 999)
Unit price: a real value
Minimum inventory level: an integer (in the range 0 through 999)
Item name: a character string

File is sorted so that item numbers are in increasing order.

`Student:`

This is a file of student records organized as follows: They are arranged so that student numbers are in increasing order.

Student number: an integer
Student's name: two character strings (last, first) and a character (middle initial)
Hometown: two character strings of the form city, state
Phone number: a character string
Gender: a character (M or F)
Year: a one-digit integer (1, 2, 3, 4, or 5 for special)
Major: a character string
Total credits earned to date: an integer
Cumulative GPA: a real value

`StudentUpdate:`

This is a file of student grade records organized as follows. They are sorted so that student numbers are in increasing order. There is one update record for each student in the file `Student`.

Student number: an integer (same as those used in the file `Students`)

For each of five courses:

Course name: a seven-character string (e.g., CPSC185)

Letter grade: a two-character string (e.g., A–, B+, C ␢, where the last string is a C followed by a blank)

Course credit: an integer

`Users:`

This is a file of computer system records organized as follows. They are arranged so that identification numbers are in increasing order.

Identification number: an integer

User's name: two strings of the form last name, first name

Password: a string

Resource limit (in dollars): an integer with up to four digits

Resources used to date: a real value

`LeastSquaresFile:`

This is a text file in which each line contains a pair of real numbers representing the x-coordinate and the y-coordinate of a point.

CHAPTER 10

Arrays, `vector<T>`s, and STL

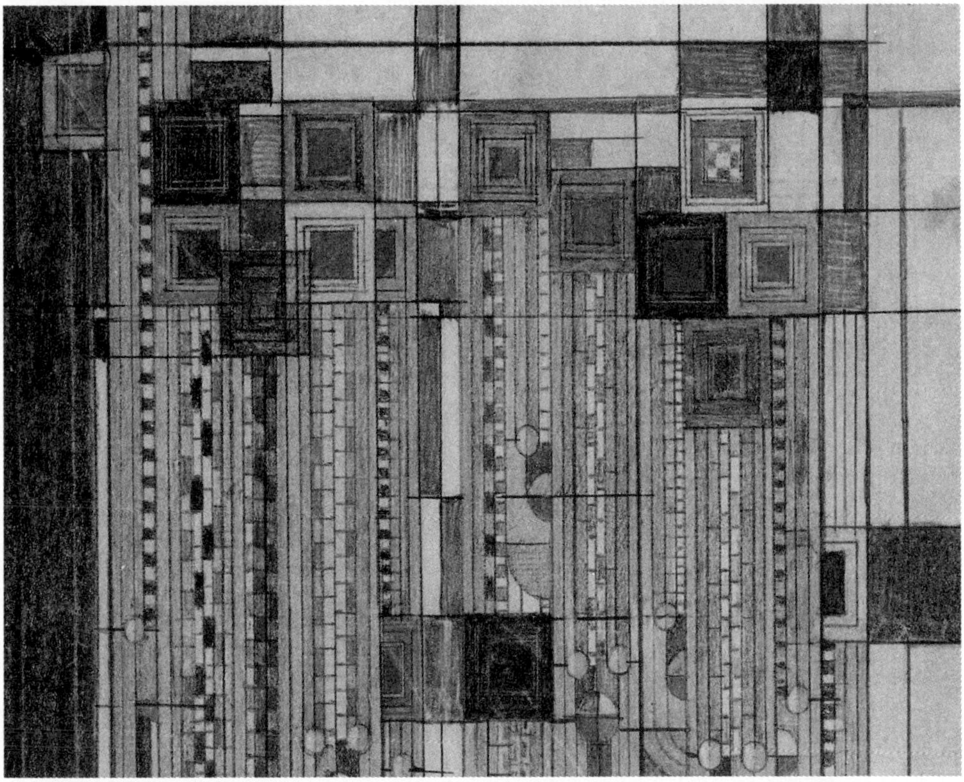

With silver bells, and cockle shells,

And pretty maids all in a row.

-Mother Goose

I've got a little list, I've got a little list.

-Gilbert and Sullivan, The Mikado

Get your ducks in a row and then cook their goose. (Pause). Gooses. (Pause). Geese. (Pause). Whatever they're called, cook'em!

-V. Orehck III (fictitious)

Chapter Contents

Chapter Objectives

- Use OCD to solve a list-processing problem using an array.
- Investigate one-dimensional arrays as implemented in C++.
- Study the important problems of sorting and searching lists.
- Study in some detail the `vector<T>` class template.
- Take a quick peek at the Standard Template Library (STL).
- (Optional) Indicate STL's role in component-based programming.
- (Optional) Illustrate how a class can store a sequence of values.

In this chapter, we combine two ideas that may, at first glance, seem unrelated. The first is the idea of *processing sequences* of values. For example, in Section 9.1 we considered the problem of finding the minimum, maximum, and mean of a sequence of atmospheric pressure readings. The second idea is that of *indexed* (or *subscripted*) *variables*. In Chapter 5, we presented the `string` class that makes it possible to store a collection of characters in a single object. A `string` object `aString` is an indexed object, which means that `aString[i]` can be used to access the character of `aString` whose index is `i`.

As we will see in this chapter, these two ideas can be combined to give a powerful mechanism for solving problems that involve processing sequences of noncharacter data (such as atmospheric-pressure readings). This processing can often be done most efficiently if the entire sequence can be stored in some indexed object `valueSequence` so that the value stored in any location `i` can be accessed directly by using the expression `valueSequence[i]`.

An **array** is such a variable. It is more general than a `string` object, because it is not limited to storing `char` values. An array can be declared to store values of any type: `char`, `int`, and `double` values, as well as class objects such as `string`. In short, an array can be defined to store values of any type that has been declared prior to the declaration of the array.

In the first two sections of this chapter, we introduce **C-style arrays** that C++ inherits from its parent language C. For these arrays, the programmer must specify the size of the array in its declaration, and once the program is compiled, this size cannot be changed without changing the array declaration and recompiling the program. Consequently, such arrays are called **fixed-size arrays**. In later sections, we will introduce `vector<T>`, a C++ standard class template that eliminates many of the limitations of C-style arrays. The optional *OBJECTive Thinking* section demonstrates how classes can store sequences of values.

10.1 Introductory Example: Quality Control

We begin with a problem that can be solved using C-style arrays.

PROBLEM: MEAN TIME TO FAILURE

An electronics company uses a robot to manufacture circuit boards that have five different components. A quality-control engineer monitors the robot by checking each circuit board and recording in a file the number of defective components on that board:

```
0  0  1  0  0  0  2  0  4  0  0  0  1  0  0  0  0  2
0  0  0  0  1  0  0  3  0  0  0  0  0  0  2  0  0  0
3  0  0  0  0  0  0  0  0  1  0  0  0  0  0  0  0  2
0  0  0  0  1  0  0  0  0  0  1  0  0  0  0  0  1  0
```

To analyze the overall performance of the robot, a program that generates a **frequency distribution** is needed. The frequency distribution should show the number of boards in which there were no defective components, one defective component, two defective components, three defective components, four defective components, and five defective components:

```
58 had 0 failed components (80.6%)
7 had 1 failed components (9.7%)
4 had 2 failed components (5.6%)
2 had 3 failed components (2.8%)
1 had 4 failed components (1.4%)
0 had 5 failed components (0%)
```

Such an analysis may help a company decide whether to upgrade its equipment. Weighing the cost of a new robot (that presumably makes fewer mistakes) against the cost of repairing or discarding 19.4 percent of the circuit boards helps in making an informed decision.

Object-Centered Design

Behavior. The program should display on the screen a prompt for the name of the input file, read this name from the keyboard, and then open a stream to that file. It should then use an input loop to read the data values from the file stream, counting the occurrences of each 0, 1, 2, 3, 4, and 5. It should then display the number and percentages of occurrences of each 0, 1, 2, 3, 4, and 5.

Objects. The objects in this problem are as follows:

	Software Objects		
Problem Objects	**Type**	**Kind**	**Name**
The name of the input file	`string`	varying	*inputFileName*
A stream to the input file	`ifstream`	varying	*inStream*
The number of circuit boards	`int`	varying	*numCircuitBoards*
Each data value	`int`	varying	*numFailures*
The number of 0s	`int`	varying	*count*[0]
The number of 1s	`int`	varying	*count*[1]
The number of 2s	`int`	varying	*count*[2]
The number of 3s	`int`	varying	*count*[3]
The number of 4s	`int`	varying	*count*[4]
The number of 5s	`int`	varying	*count*[5]

Operations. The operations needed to solve the problem are:

i. Display a string on the screen
ii. Read a string from the keyboard
iii. Open a stream to a file whose name is stored in a string
iv. Read data values from the stream, counting occurrences of 0, 1, 2, 3, 4, and 5
v. Display the number and percentage of occurrences of 0, 1, 2, 3, 4, and 5

Each of these operations is either predefined in C++ or is easily implemented using only a few statements.

Algorithm. The program must read from the data file and count the number of occurrences of each number in the file. One approach would be to declare six different counter variables,

```
int count0 = 0, count1 = 0, count2 = 0,
    count3 = 0, count4 = 0, count5 = 0;
```

and then use a `switch` statement to select the appropriate counter to be incremented:

```
inStream >> score;
if (inStream.eof()) break;
```

```
switch (score)
{
   case 0: count0++;
           break;
   case 1: count1++;
           break;
   case 2: count2++;
           break;
   case 3: count3++;
           break;
   case 4: count4++;
           break;
   case 5: count5++;
           break;
}
```

However, such a solution is clumsy, because it requires that we declare and manage six different counters. Moreover, it is *not scalable*: if the company creates a new product with 10 components or 100 components, then the program must be modified extensively.

A **C-style array** provides a better solution. We define a single array object with space for six different integer values:

```
const int SIZE = 6;
int count[SIZE] = {0};
```

This definition creates an indexed variable named `count` that can store six integers. Each of these integers has a different index in the range 0 to 5. That is, the first integer in `count` has index 0, the second integer in `count` has index 1, . . . , and the last integer in `count` has the index 5. The definition also initializes each of these integers to 0. We can visualize such an object as follows:

count	0	0	0	0	0	0
	[0]	[1]	[2]	[3]	[4]	[5]

Because `count` has index values ranging from 0 to 5 and these values coincide with the number of components on the circuit board, we can use this one array to count the occurrences of each of the values 0 through 5. We can write statements like

```
inStream >> numFailures;
if (inStream.eof()) break;
count[numFailures]++;
```

to add 1 to the integer in `count` whose index is `numFailures`. For example, if `numFailures` is 2, then execution of

```
count[numFailures]++;
```

will increment the integer in `count` whose index is 2:

	[0]	[1]	[2]	[3]	[4]	[5]
count	0	0	1	0	0	0

The following algorithm for solving the quality-control problem uses this approach.

Algorithm for Quality Control Analysis

1. Prompt for and read the name of the input file into *inputFileName*.
2. Open an `ifstream` named *inStream* to the file whose name is in *inputFileName*. (If this fails, display an error message and terminate the algorithm.)
3. Initialize *numCircuitBoards* to 0.
4. Initialize each integer in the array *count* to 0.
5. Loop:
   a. Read an integer *numFailures* from *inStream*.
   b. If the end-of-file mark was read, exit the loop.
   c. Increment the element of *count* indexed by *numFailures*.
   d. Increment *numCircuitBoards*.

   End loop.
6. Close *inStream*.
7. For each *index* in the range 0 through 5
   Display *index* and *count*[*index*] with appropriate labels.

Coding. The program in Figure 10.1 implements this algorithm. It uses the function `interactiveOpen()` from Figure 9.3 to open the file containing the failure data.

Fig. 10.1 Quality-control failure frequency distribution. (Part 1 of 3)

```
/* qualityControl.cpp shows a distribution of component failure
 * rates that are stored in an input file.
 *
 *  Input(file):    a sequence of failure rates
 *  Output(screen): the number and percentage of occurrences
 *                      of each failure rate
 ***************************************************************/

#include <iostream>                  // cout, <<, fixed, showpoint
#include <fstream>                   // ifstream, >>, eof(), close()
#include <iomanip>                   // setprecision()
#include <string>                    // string, getline()
```

Fig. 10.1 Quality-control failure frequency distribution. (Part 2 of 3)

```
#include "Query.h"                  // interactiveOpen() Fig. 9.3
using namespace std;

const int CAPACITY = 6;             // # of array elements

int main()
{
   cout << "Quality Control: "
           "Component Failure Frequency Distribution.\n\n";

   ifstream inStream;
   interactiveOpen(inStream);
   int count[CAPACITY] = {0},               // array of counters
       numFailures,                         // input variable
       numCircuitBoards = 0;                // # of input values

   for (;;)                                 // loop:
   {
      inStream >> numFailures;              //   read input value
      if (inStream.eof()) break;            //   if done, stop reading
      count[numFailures]++;                 //   increment its counter
      numCircuitBoards++;                   //   one more input value
   }                                        // end loop
   inStream.close();                        // close the stream

   cout << "\nOut of " << numCircuitBoards << " circuit boards:\n"
        << setprecision(1) << fixed << showpoint;

   for (int i = 0; i < CAPACITY; i++)       // output counters
      cout << count[i] << " had " << i
           << " failed components ("       // and percentages
           << double(count[i]) / numCircuitBoards * 100
           << "%)" << endl;
}
```

Sample run:

```
Quality Control: Component Failure Frequency Distribution.

Enter the name of the input file: failureData.txt
```

Fig. 10.1 Quality-control failure frequency distribution. (Part 3 of 3)

```
Out of 71 circuit boards:
57 had 0 failed components (80.3%)
7 had 1 failed components (9.9%)
4 had 2 failed components (5.6%)
2 had 3 failed components (2.8%)
1 had 4 failed components (1.4%)
0 had 5 failed components (0.0%)
```

10.2 C-Style Arrays

The program in Figure 10.1 uses the definitions

```
const int CAPACITY = 6;            // # of array elements
    .
    .
    .
int count[CAPACITY] = {0};         // array of counters
    .
    .
    .
```

to construct `count` as an array of six integers, with each integer being initialized to 0. The first part of the definition

```
int count[CAPACITY]= {0};       // array of counters
```

instructs the compiler to reserve a block of memory large enough to hold six integer values and associates the name `count` with this block. Since `count` has room for six integers, its **capacity** is said to be 6. The integer-sized spaces in `count` are called **elements** and are indexed from 0 through 5:

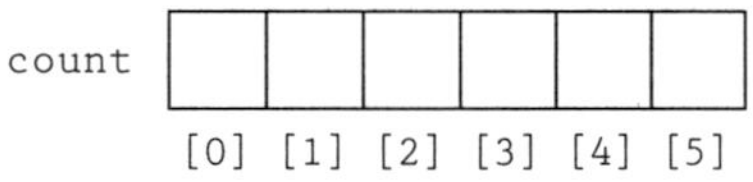

NOTE

Unlike some languages, *C++ arrays are **zero-based**; that is, the index of the first element of any C++ array is always zero.*

The second part of the definition,

```
int count[CAPACITY] = {0};    // array of counters
```

initializes the first element of `count` to 0, and as described later, the remaining elements are initialized to zero by default:

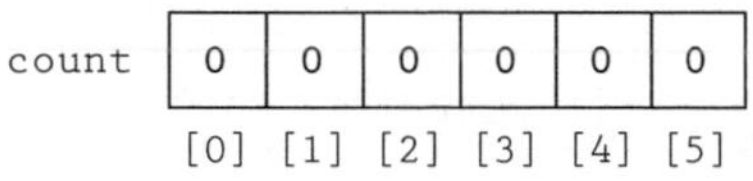

Whereas the capacity of an array is the number of values that it can store, its **size** is *the number of values it actually contains*. Both the capacity and the size of `count` are `6`.

In this example, `count` is an array of integers, but the elements of an array may be of any type. For example, the declarations

```
const int NUM_ELEMENTS = 4;
char charArray[NUM_ELEMENTS];       // array of 4 char elements
long intArray[NUM_ELEMENTS];        // array of 4 long elements
string stringArray[NUM_ELEMENTS]; // array of 4 string elements
```

construct three arrays, each having four elements (i.e., having *capacity* `4`), but each containing no values (i.e., each having *size* `0`). `charArray` has space for four characters (stored in four bytes):

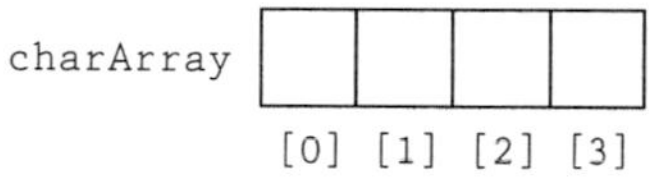

`intArray` has space for four long integers (stored in 16 bytes):

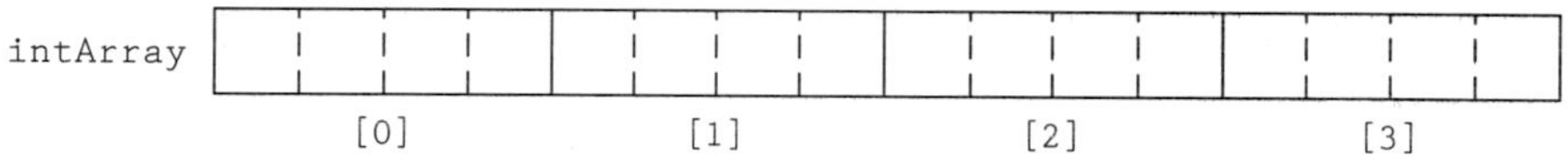

`stringArray` has space for four `string` objects, for which the storage requirements vary according to the lengths of the `string` values being stored.

These declarations are examples of the following (simplified) general form of an array declaration:

Array Declaration (simplified)

Form:

```
type array_name[CAPACITY];
```

where

`type` is any defined type (predefined or programmer-defined);

`array_name` is the name of the array object being defined; and

`CAPACITY` is the number of values the object can contain.

Purpose: Instructs the compiler to reserve sufficient storage to hold `CAPACITY` objects of type *type*, and associates the name `array_name` with that storage.

To understand the implications of an array declaration, it is useful to contrast a `char` array and a `string` object:

```
const int CAPACITY = 16;
char charArray[CAPACITY];
string aString;
```

The capacity of `charArray` is fixed at 16 bytes and cannot change during program execution. By contrast, the object `aString` is a container with a varying capacity (initially of capacity zero); it will automatically grow as needed, according to the number of characters stored in it.

It is important to remember this property of C-style arrays: Unlike a `string` object, *the capacity of a C-style array is fixed when the program is compiled.* If we try to enter the capacity at run time as in

```
cout << "Enter the number of components: ";
int arrayCapacity;
cin >> arrayCapacity;
int count[arrayCapacity];              // ERROR!
```

a compilation error will result. The reason is that the memory for a C-style array is allocated by the compiler, and so the capacity of the array must be available when its definition is compiled.[1]

Define Capacity with a Constant, Not a Literal. It is good programming practice to use integer constants to specify the capacity of arrays as in

```
const int CAPACITY = 5;
double count[CAPACITY];
   .
   .
   .
for (int i = 0; i < CAPACITY; i++)
   cout << count[i];
```

rather than using integer literals:

```
int count[5];
   .
   .
   .
for (int i = 0; i < 5; i++)
   cout << count[i];
```

This makes the program more flexible. It is often necessary to adjust the capacity of an array several times before the final version of a program is completed or to modify the capacity after the program has been in use for some time. If literals are used,

---

1. For run-time-allocated arrays as described in Section 14.2, the capacity can be specified during execution.

making these modifications requires finding and changing each literal throughout the entire program:

```
double count[100];
     .
     .
     .
for (int i = 0; i < 100; i++)
   cout << count[i];
```

But if a named constant (such as `CAPACITY`) is used throughout the program, then modifying the capacity of the array requires only a single modification—change the declaration of the named constant:

```
const int CAPACITY = 100;
double count[CAPACITY];
     .
     .
     .
for (int i = 0; i < CAPACITY; i++)
   cout << count[i];
```

When the program is recompiled, the compiler will update all uses of `CAPACITY` with the new value, saving time and ensuring consistent capacities in all array accesses.

ARRAY INITIALIZATION

As we have noted, simple array declarations of the form

```
type array_name[capacity];
```

specify no initialization for the array. Because no initial values are supplied, such arrays will usually contain whatever "garbage" values remain from prior use of the memory block allocated to the array.

Because an array can store different values, it cannot be initialized with a single value:

```
int intArray[CAPACITY] = 0;      // ERROR!
```

Instead, an **array literal** can be used; this is a sequence of initializing values listed between curly braces, `{` and `}`, and separated by commas; for example,

```
const int CAPACITY = 10;

int intArray[CAPACITY] = {9,8,7,6,5,4,3,2,1,0};
```

The first value in the list is stored in the first array element, the second value in the second element, and so on, resulting in an object that can be pictured as follows:

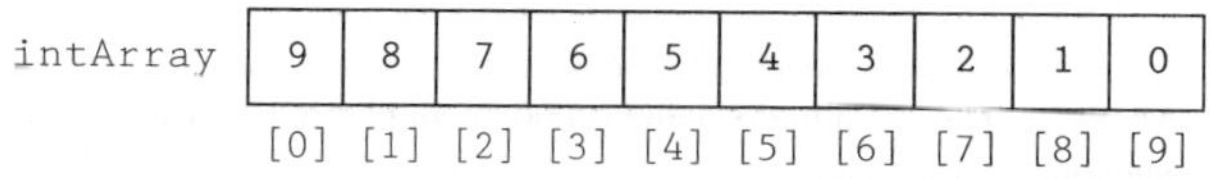

The `for` loop that generates the program's output also uses the subscript operator:

```
for (int i = 0; i < CAPACITY; i++)         // output counters
   cout << count[i] << " had " << i
        << " failed components ("          // and percentages
        << double(count[i]) / numCircuitBoards * 100
        << "%)" << endl;
```

In the first pass through the loop, `i` is `0`, so `count[i]` accesses the value `58`, producing the output

```
58 had 0 failed components (80.6%)
```

In the second pass, `i` is `1`, so `count[i]` accesses the value `7`, producing the output

```
7 had 1 failed components (9.7%)
```

The remaining lines of output are generated in a similar way.

It is worth noting that any operation that is defined for a given type can be applied to an array element of that type. For example, any operation that can be applied to the type `double` can be applied to an element of a `double` array named `realArray`, as in

```
#include <cmath>                      // sqrt()
      .
      .
      .
for (int i = 0; i < CAPACITY; i++)
   cout << sqrt(realArray[i]);  // sqrt() takes a double argument
```

Similarly, any operation that is defined for the type `char` can be applied to any of the elements of a `char` array. This is illustrated in the following statements that convert all lowercase characters in the `char` array `name` to uppercase:

```
#include <cctype>                            // islower(), toupper()
      .
      .
      .
for (int i = 0; name[i] != '\0'; i++) // Each of these char
   if (islower(name[i]))                //   functions takes
      name[i] = toupper(name[i]);       //   a char argument
```

PROCESSING ARRAYS WITH `for` LOOPS

A `for` loop is useful for implementing many array operations, because its loop-control variable can be used to count through the index values of the array. The indices of an array declared by

```
someType someArray[CAPACITY];
```

range from `0` through `CAPACITY - 1`. Thus, each element of an array can be accessed in turn by using the subscript operation with the loop-control variable in the body of a `for` loop that counts from 0 to `CAPACITY - 1`:

```
for (int i = 0; i < CAPACITY; i++)
   // ... do something with someArray[i]
```

We have seen, for example, that the program in Figure 10.1 uses a `for` loop to display the elements of the array `count` in order:

```
for (int i = 0; i < CAPACITY; i++)
   cout << count[i] << " had " << i        // output counters
        << " failed components ("          // and percentages
        << double(count[i]) / numCircuitBoards * 100
        << "%)" << endl;
```

Similarly, if `dubArray` is an array of real numbers and we wish to sum the first `numValues` values stored in it, we can write

```
double sum = 0.0;

for (int i = 0; i < numValues; i++)
   sum += dubArray[i];
```

In mathematical formulas, notation like v_i has historically been used to denote the *i*th element in a subscripted variable *v*. Because of this convention, single-letter identifiers like `i`, `j`, and `k` are commonly used as names for array indices. This is one of the few cases where single-letter identifiers are acceptable as names of objects.

ARRAYS AS PARAMETERS

Functions can be written that accept arrays via parameters and then operate on the arrays by operating on individual array elements. For example, we could encapsulate the preceding statements for adding the elements of a `double` array in the following function:

```
/* arraySum() computes the sum of the first itsSize
 *   double values stored in an array.
 *
 * Receive: theArray, an array of double values
 *          itsSize, an integer
 * Return:  the sum of the values
 ***************************************************************/

double arraySum(const double theArray[], int itsSize)
{
   double sum = 0.0;              // sum of the array elements

   for (int i = 0; i < itsSize; i++)
      sum += theArray[i];

   return sum;
}
```

As this example illustrates, placing a pair of brackets (`[]`) after the name of a parameter indicates that the parameter is an array and that it is not necessary to specify the capacity of the array. In this case, *there is no restriction on the capacity of the array that is passed to the function*.

WATCH OUT

It is also important to remember that *arrays are automatically passed by reference.* That is, simply specifying that a parameter is an array makes it a reference parameter, without using the usual ampersand (`&`) notation. If the function modifies the array, then the corresponding argument will also be modified. If this is undesirable, it can be prevented by declaring the array as a `const` parameter, as we did with `theArray` in the function `arraySum()`.

THE `typedef` MECHANISM

C++ has inherited another mechanism from its parent language C that can be used to *increase the readability of a program and to make some types easier to use.* This is the `typedef` **declaration**, the simplest form of which is

```
typedef ExistingTypeName NewTypeName ;
```

This declaration makes the name *`NewTypeName`* a *synonym* for *`ExistingTypeName`*, which is some existing type.

For example, suppose that we put

```
typedef double Item_Type;
  . . .
Item_Type someFunction( ... Item_Type param, ... );
  . . .
```

in some library. The `typedef` declaration makes the word `Item_Type` a synonym for `double`, and it may be used any place that the word `double` is used. If sometime later we change this declaration to possible

```
typedef float Item_Type;
```

NOTE

then all occurrences of the type `Item_Type`, including all those in any program that `#includes` this library, will automatically become synonyms for `float`. *Being able to change all occurrences of a type identifier simply by changing it in one declaration is one of the important advantages of the* `typedef` *mechanism.*

A different form of `typedef` declaration used for arrays

```
typedef element_type NewTypeName [CAPACITY];
```

associates the name *`NewTypeName`* with arrays whose capacity is *`CAPACITY`* (which may be omitted) and whose elements are of type *`element_type`*. For example, the declarations

```
const int CAPACITY = 6;                // # of array elements
typedef int IntegerArray[CAPACITY];    // an array type
```

associate the name `IntegerArray` with arrays whose elements are integers and whose capacity is 6. This new type identifier can then be used to declare the types of variables, constants, and the return types of functions. For example, if we inserted the preceding `typedef` declaration of `IntegerArray` after the definition of `CAPACITY` in the program in Figure 10.1, we could then use `IntegerArray` to declare the array `count`:

```
IntegerArray count = {0};
```

Such `typedef`s are usually placed outside all blocks (typically after the `#include` directives) so that they have global scope and can be used to declare objects in all the functions that follow. The following code segment illustrates:

```
   .
   .
   .
typedef double DoubleArray[100];
double arraySum(DoubleArray theArray, int itsSize);

int main ()
{
   . . .
   DoubleArray tempReadings;   // array of temperature readings
   int numReadings;            // number of readings
   .
   .
   .
   // calculate the mean temperature
   double meanTemp =
            arraySum(tempReadings, numReadings) / numReadings;
   .
   .
   .
}

/* Function arraySum . . .
         . . .           */
double arraySum(DoubleArray theArray, int itsSize)
{
   // . . . definition of arraySum given earlier
}
```

Here the type identifier `DoubleArray` is used to declare the array `tempReadings` in the main program and to specify the type of the parameter `dubArray` in the prototype and in the definition of the function `arraySum()`. This makes these declarations easier to read than if we had used the array declarations everywhere (and this is especially true for multidimensional arrays as described in Chapter 13).

OUT-OF-RANGE ERRORS

WATCH OUT

It is important to note that *no checking is done to ensure that indices stay within the range determined by an array's declaration* and that strange results may be obtained when an index is allowed to get out of bounds. This is illustrated by the program in Figure 10.2.

Fig. 10.2 Why array indices must stay in bounds. (Part 1 of 3)

```
/* outOfRange.cpp demonstrates aberrant behavior
 * resulting from out-of-range errors.
 ************************************************/
```

Fig. 10.2 Why array indices must stay in bounds. (Part 2 of 3)

```
#include <iostream>                // cout, <<
using namespace std;

const int CAPACITY = 4;
typedef int IntArray[CAPACITY];

void printArray(char name, IntArray x, int numElements);

int main()
{

   IntArray a = {0, 1, 2, 3},
            b = {4, 5, 6, 7},
            c = {8, 9, 10, 11};
   int below = -3,
       above = 6;

   printArray('a', a, 4);
   printArray('b', b, 4);
   printArray('c', c, 4);

   b[below] = -999;
   b[above] = 999;

   cout << endl;
   printArray('a', a, 4);
   printArray('b', b, 4);
   printArray('c', c, 4);
}

#include <iomanip>                 // setw()

/* printArray() displays an int array.
 *
 * Receives:  name, a character, and x, an int array
 * Output:    name of array, and 4 values stored in it
 *************************************************/
void printArray(char name, IntArray x, int numElements)
{
   cout << name << " = ";
   for (int i = 0; i < numElements; i++)
      cout << setw(5) << x[i];
   cout << endl;
}
```

Fig. 10.2 Why array indices must stay in bounds. (Part 3 of 3)

Sample run:

```
a =      0      1    2    3
b =      4      5    6    7
c =      8      9   10   11

a =      0   -999    2    3
b =      4      5    6    7
c =      8      9  999   11
```

We see that even though there are no statements of the form a[i] = *value*; or c[i] = *value*; to change values stored in a and c, the second element of a was changed to -999 and the third element of c was changed to 999.[3]

This happens because the memory location being accessed is typically determined by simply counting forward or backward from the **base address** of the array—the address of the first element in the array. Thus, the illegal array references b[-3] and b[6] accessed the memory locations associated with a[1] and c[2]

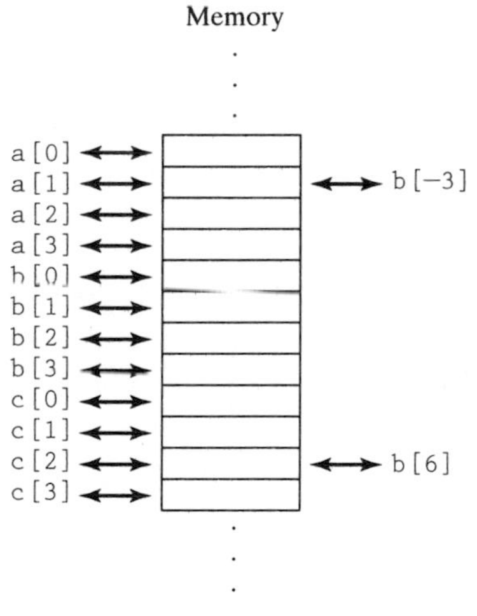

3. The output on your system may not agree exactly with that shown in the sample run. For example, some systems allocate memory from higher addresses to lower, and the output in this case will probably appear as follows:

```
a =      0     1    2    3
b =      4     5    6    7
c =      8     9   10   11

a =      0     1  999    3
b =      4     5    6    7
c =      8  -999   10   11
```

Thus, modifying b[-3] and b[6] changed a[1] and c[2], respectively. This change is obviously undesirable! An array reference such as b[500] that is very much out of range will likely cause the program to "crash." As this example demonstrates, it is important to check that the index is not out of range.

PREDEFINED ARRAY OPERATIONS

The C++ string class provides a rich set of predefined operations on string objects. This raises the question: *What predefined operations are there for arrays?*

C++ has inherited from C the **C standard library**, which provides a variety of functions for processing character arrays. These functions are divided among several different libraries, including <cstring>, <cstdlib>, and <cstdio>.[4] Also, the iostream operators have been overloaded to operate on char arrays, allowing us to write

```
char name[CAPACITY];
   .
   .
   .
cin >> name;
```

to fill a character array name with characters from the keyboard. Similarly, we can simply write

```
cout << name;
```

to display the contents of a character array name.

However, there are virtually *no* similar operations or libraries of standard predefined functions for operating on numeric (or other) arrays. For example, there is no operation or function to input or output a numeric array. We must implement all such operations ourselves.

One of the reasons for this disparity is that functions typically use loops to process arrays. As we saw earlier, these loops begin processing with the value at index 0 and terminate after processing the final value in the array. A character-array-processing function "knows" that it has processed the final value in a character array when it reaches the NUL character that marks the end of the string:

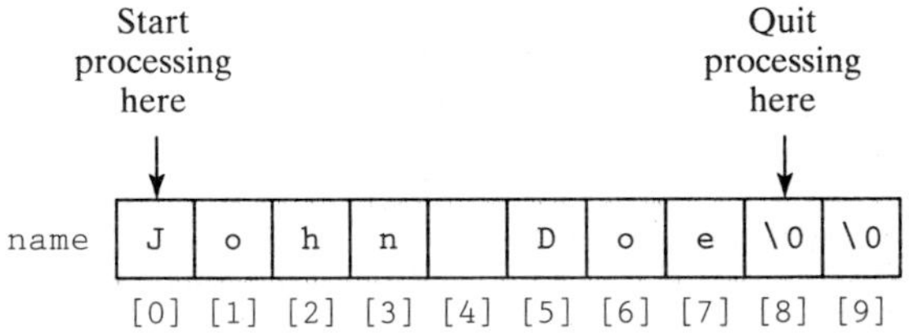

Even though the capacity and size of name differ, a function can still determine when to quit processing.

4. The string class eliminates the need for most of these functions in C++. They are described in Appendix D.

However, there is no numeric equivalent of the NUL character that can be used to mark the end of a sequence of numbers. For example, if we want to process the integers in the following `intArray`,

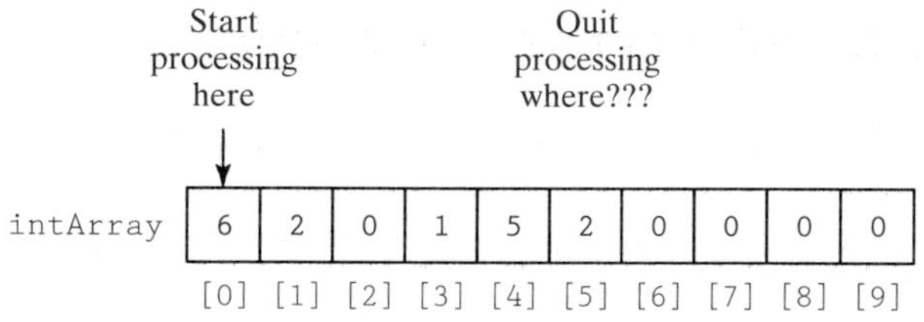

we have no way of knowing how many data values to process, because we do not know which of the zeros are values stored in the array and which are default zeros used to fill the array.

A NON-OOP APPROACH

Because there is no end-of-sequence value comparable to the NUL character, a function that processes an array of numbers must use some alternative mechanism to determine when the final number has been processed. One solution is to pass both the array and its size to the function and then use this size in the computation, as in the `arraySum()` function:

```
double arraySum(DoubleArray theArray, int itsSize)
{
   double sum = 0.0;            // sum of the array elements

   for (int i = 0; i < itsSize; i++)
      sum += theArray[i];

   return sum;
}
```

Unfortunately, this means that passing a sequence of values to `arraySum()` requires two arguments instead of one, which is *not consistent with the aims of object-oriented programming*. That is, if we wish to treat a sequence of values as a single object (which is the reason for storing the values in an array), then it should only be necessary to pass that one object to the function.

There are, therefore, two significant problems with C-style arrays:

1. The capacity of a C-style array cannot change during program execution.
2. One of the principles of the object-oriented programming is that *an object should be self-contained*, which means that it should carry within itself all of the information necessary to describe and operate on it. Operations on C-style arrays, however, need at least two pieces of information: the array and some way to identify its final value (e.g., its size). In particular, C-style arrays carry neither their size nor capacity within them, and so *C-style arrays are not self-contained objects*.

We will look briefly at two containers provided in C++ that solve these problems.

AN OOP APPROACH: valarray<T> AND vector<T>

We have seen that the C++ class mechanism allows different data members to be stored within a single object. This provides a solution to the second problem—by storing an array, its capacity, and its size within a class structure, a single class object can encapsulate all three pieces of information. This is the approach used in the C++ containers valarray<T> and vector<T>.[5] They also provide solutions to the first problem because their capacities can change.

One important use of arrays is in vector processing and other numeric computation in science and engineering. In mathematics, the term *vector* refers to a sequence (one-dimensional array) of real values on which various arithmetic operations are performed; for example, +, –, scalar multiplication, and dot product. Because much numeric work relies on the use of such vectors, highly efficient libraries are essential in many fields. For this reason, C++ provides the standard library <valarray>, which is designed to carry out vector operations very efficiently.

A valarray<T> is basically a class that contains a C-style array whose elements are of type T, which is a numeric type, and that has several built-in operations that are important in numeric computations. The following are two declarations of valarrays:

```
valarray<double> v0;
valarray<int> v1(100);
```

The first creates v0 as an empty valarray of doubles, and the second creates v1 as a valarray containing 100 int values, initially 0. Both of these valarrays can be resized later, if necessary.

A vector<T> is similar to a valarray<T> in that it contains a C-style array whose elements are of type T and it has several built-in operations. The fundamental difference, however, is that the type T need not be numeric—it can be *any* type—and the operations are more general-purpose operations.

Because valarrays are limited to numeric problems whereas vectors can be used in a much wider range of problems, we will focus on vectors in this chapter. More information about valarrays is available on the book's Web site and in the sequel[6] to this text. We will consider vectors in more detail in Section 10.5.

Quick Quiz 10.2

Questions 1–16 assume the following definitions:

```
double a[5],
       b[5] = {0},
       c[5] = {1},
       d[5] = {0,0,0,0,0},
       e[5] = {1,2,3,4,5};
```

---

5. Each of these containers is actually a *class template*. See Section 10.6 for more information about templates.
6. *C++: An Introduction to Data Structures* by Larry Nyhoff (Upper Saddle River, NJ: Prentice Hall, Inc., 1999). A second edition is scheduled to appear in 2003.

```
char f[5] = {'a', 'b'},
     g[8] = "abcde";
typedef int alpha[5];
alpha beta;
```

1. (True or false) a is an array indexed 0, 1, 2, 3, 4, 5.
2. (True or false) All elements of a are initialized to 0.
3. (True or false) All elements of b are initialized to 0.
4. (True or false) All elements of c are initialized to 1.
5. (True or false) The definition of d could be shortened to `double d[5] = {0};`.
6. (True or false) The definition of b could be shortened to `double b[5] = 0;`.
7. (True or false) `e[3] == 3`.
8. The capacity of a is __________.
9. (True or false) `f[2]` is the NUL character.
10. (True or false) The definition of f could also be written `char f[5] = "ab";`.
11. (True or false) `g[5]` contains an end-of-string mark.
12. (True or false) `alpha` is an array indexed 0, 1, 2, 3, 4.
13. (True or false) `beta` is an array indexed 0, 1, 2, 3, 4.
14. The address of `a[0]` is called the __________ address of a.
15. (True or false) The output produced by `cout << e << endl;` will be `12345`.
16. (True or false) The output produced by `cout << f << endl;` will be `ab`.
17. (True or false) C-style arrays are self-contained.
18. Arrays are passed as __________ parameters.

For Questions 19–22, assume the declarations

```
int number[5] = {1};
typedef double Dubber[5];
Dubber xValue;
```

Tell what values will be assigned to the array elements.

19.
```
for (int i = 0; i <= 4; i++)
    xValue[i] = double(i) / 2.0;
```

20.
```
for (int i = 0; i < 5; i++)
    if (i % 2 == 0)
        number[i] = 2 * i;
    else
        number[i] = 2 * i + 1;
```

21.
```
for (int i = 1; i < 5; i++)
    number[i] = 2 * number[i - 1];
```

22.
```
for (int i = 3; i >= 0; i--)
    number[i] = 2 * number[i + 1];
```

Exercises 10.2

For Exercises 1–8, assume that the following declarations have been made:

```
const int LITTLE = 6,
          MEDIUM = 10,
          BIG = 128;
int i, j, n = 10,
    temp,
    number[MEDIUM] = {99, 33, 44, 88, 22, 11, 55, 111, 66, 77};
char ch,
     letterCount[BIG];
typedef double LittleDouble[LITTLE];
LittleDouble value;
```

Tell what value (if any) will be assigned to each array element, or explain why an error occurs:

1.
```
for (i = 0; i < MEDIUM; i++)
   number[i] = i / 2;
```
2.
```
for (i = 0; i < LITTLE; i++)
   number[i] = i * i;
for (i = LITTLE; i < MEDIUM; i++)
   number[i] = number[i - 5];
```
3.
```
for (i = 0; i < 3; i++)
   value[i] = 0;
for (i = 3; i < LITTLE; i++)
   value[i] = 1;
```
4.
```
for (i = 1; i < LITTLE; i += 2)
{
   value[i - 1] = double(i) / 2.0;
   value[i] = 10.0 * value[i - 1];
}
```
5.
```
i = 0;
while (i != 10 )
{
   if (i % 3 == 0)
      number[i] = 0;
   else
      number[i] = i;
   i++;
}
```
6.
```
number[1] = 1;
i = 2;
do
{
   number[i] = 2 * number[i - 1];
```

```
      i++;
   }
   while (i < MEDIUM);
```
7.
```
   for (ch = 'A'; ch <= 'F'; ch++)
      if (ch == 'A')
         letterCount[ch] = 1;
      else
         letterCount[ch] = letterCount[ch - 1] + 1;
```
8.
```
   for (i = 0; i < n - 1; i++)
      for (j = 0; j < n - i - 1; j++)
         if (number[j] > number[j + 1])
         {
            temp  = number[j];
            number[j] = number[j + 1];
            number[j + 1] = temp;
         }
```

For Exercises 9–15, write definitions of the given arrays in two ways: (a) without using `typedef` and (b) using `typedef`.

9. An array with capacity 10 in which each element is an integer.
10. An array whose indices are integers from 0 through 10 and in which each element is a real value.
11. An array with capacity 10 in which each element is an integer, all of which are initially 0.
12. An array that can store five `strings`.
13. An array that can store five characters and is initialized with the vowels a, e, i, o, and u.
14. An array that can store 100 values, each of which is either `true` or `false`.

For Exercises 15–18, write definitions and statements to construct the given array.

15. An array whose indices are the integers from 0 through 99 and in which the value stored in each element is the same as the index.
16. An array whose indices are the integers from 0 through 99 and in which the values stored in the elements are the indices in reverse order.
17. An array of capacity 50 in which the value stored in an element is true if the corresponding index is even and false otherwise.
18. An array whose indices are the decimal ASCII values (0–127), such that the value stored in an element is `true` if the index is that of a vowel and `false` otherwise.

Exercises 19–25 ask you to write functions to do various things. Also, include any `typedef` declarations that are needed. To test these functions, you should write driver programs as instructed in Programming Problems 1–5 at the end of this chapter.

19. Return the smallest value stored in an array of integers.
20. Return the largest value stored in an array of integers.
21. Return the range of values stored in an array of integers; that is, the difference between the largest value and the smallest value.
22. Return `true` if the values stored in an array are in ascending order and `false` otherwise.

LINEAR INSERTION SORT

Linear insertion sort is based on the idea of repeatedly inserting a new element into a list of already sorted elements so that the resulting list is still sorted. The following sequence of diagrams demonstrates this method for the list 67, 33, 21, 84, 49, 50, 75. The sorted sublist produced at each stage is highlighted.

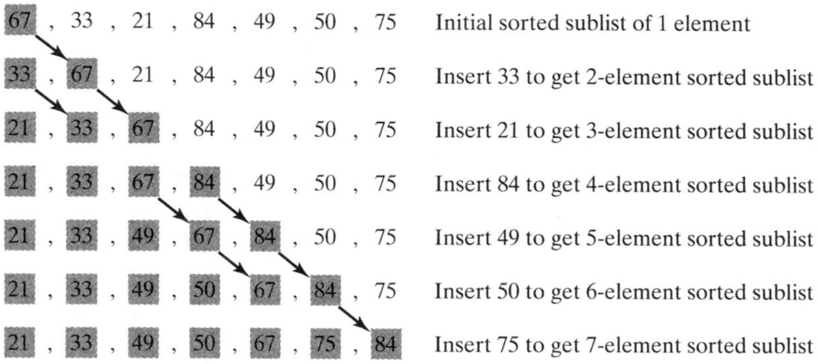
67 , 33 , 21 , 84 , 49 , 50 , 75 Initial sorted sublist of 1 element
33 , 67 , 21 , 84 , 49 , 50 , 75 Insert 33 to get 2-element sorted sublist
21 , 33 , 67 , 84 , 49 , 50 , 75 Insert 21 to get 3-element sorted sublist
21 , 33 , 67 , 84 , 49 , 50 , 75 Insert 84 to get 4-element sorted sublist
21 , 33 , 49 , 67 , 84 , 50 , 75 Insert 49 to get 5-element sorted sublist
21 , 33 , 49 , 50 , 67 , 84 , 75 Insert 50 to get 6-element sorted sublist
21 , 33 , 49 , 50 , 67 , 75 , 84 Insert 75 to get 7-element sorted sublist

The following algorithm describes this procedure for lists stored in arrays. At the *i*th stage, $x[i]$ is inserted into its proper place among the already sorted $x[0], ..., x[i-1]$. We do this by comparing $x[i]$ with each of these elements, starting from the right end, and shifting them to the right as necessary.

Linear Insertion Sort Algorithm

For $i = 1$ to $n - 1$ do the following:
// Insert $x[i]$ into its proper position among $x[0], ..., x[i-1]$.
a. Set *nextElement* equal to $x[i]$.
b. Set j equal to i.
c. While $j > 0$ and *nextElement* $< x[j-1]$ do the following:
// Shift element to the right to open a spot.
i. Set $x[j]$ equal to $x[j-1]$.
ii. Decrement j by 1.
// Now drop *nextElement* into the open spot.
d. Set $x[j]$ equal to *nextElement*.

As the foregoing diagram indicates, fewer elements in the already sorted sublist have to be moved for a larger value being inserted than for a smaller one. In particular, if the list is already sorted, no elements have to move! Thus, unlike simple selection sort, linear insertion sort takes advantage of any partial ordering of the elements that already exists.

*QUICKSORT

The **quicksort** method of sorting is one of the fastest methods of sorting and is most often implemented by a recursive algorithm. The basic idea of quicksort is to choose some element called a **pivot** and then to perform a sequence of exchanges so that all elements that are less than this pivot are to its left and all elements that are greater than the pivot are to its right. This correctly positions the pivot and divides the (sub)list into two smaller sublists, each of which may then be sorted independently in the *same* way. This **divide-and-conquer** strategy leads naturally to a recursive sorting algorithm.

To illustrate this splitting of a list into two sublists, consider the following list of integers:

75, 70, 65, 84, 98, 78, 100, 93, 55, 61, 81, 68

If we select the first number as the pivot, we must rearrange the list so that 70, 65, 55, 61, and 68 are placed before 75, and 84, 98, 78, 100, 93, and 81 are placed after it. To carry out this rearrangement, we search from the right end of the list for an element less than 75 and from the left end for an item greater than 75:

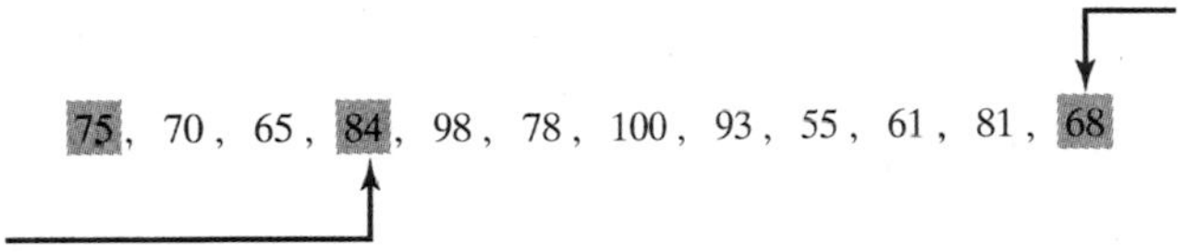

This locates the two numbers 68 and 84, which we now interchange to obtain

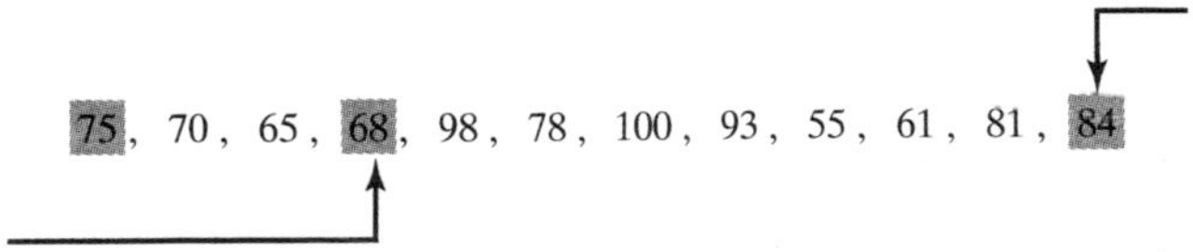

We then resume the search from the right for a number less than 75 and from the left for a number greater than 75:

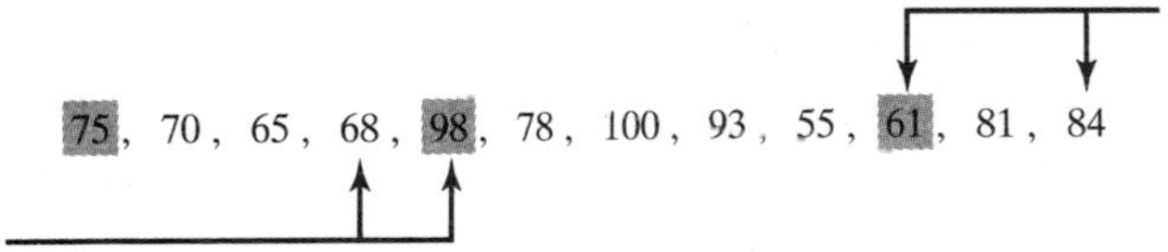

This locates the numbers 61 and 98, which are then interchanged:

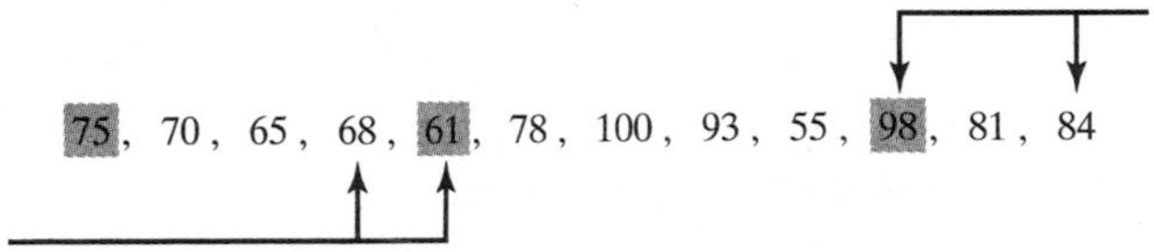

A continuation of the searches locates 78 and 55:

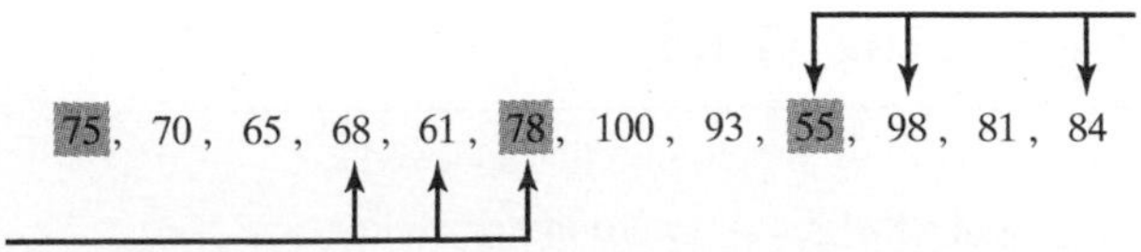

Interchanging these gives

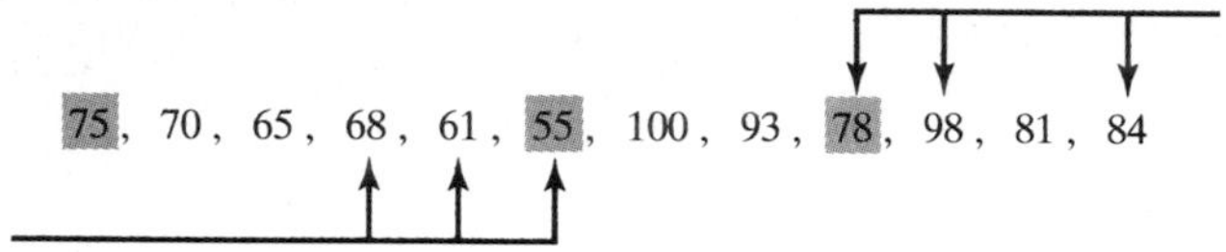

Now, when we resume our search from the right, we locate the element 55 that was found on the previous search from the left:

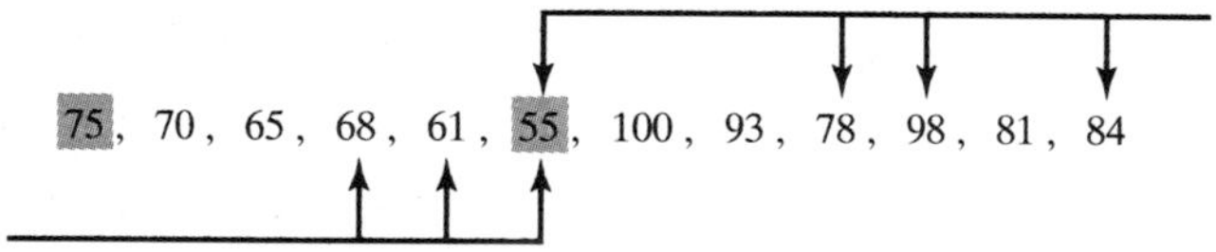

The "pointers" for the left and right searches have thus met, and this signals the end of the two searches. We now interchange 55 and the pivot 75:

55, 70, 65, 68, 61, 75, 100, 93, 78, 98, 81, 84

Note that all elements to the left of 75 are less than 75 and that all those to its right are greater than 75. Thus, the pivot 75 has been properly positioned.

The left sublist

55, 70, 65, 68, 61

and the right sublist

100, 93, 78, 98, 81, 84

can now be sorted *independently, using any sorting scheme desired.* Quicksort uses the same scheme we have just illustrated for the entire list; that is, these sublists must themselves be split by choosing and correctly positioning one pivot element (the first) in each of them.

A recursive method to sort a list is then easy to write, and we leave it as an exercise. The anchor case occurs when the list being examined is empty or contains a single element; in this case, the list is in order, and nothing needs to be done. The inductive case occurs when the list contains two or more elements, in which case the list can be sorted by

1. splitting the list into two sublists;
2. recursively sorting the left sublist; and
3. recursively sorting the right sublist.

✔ Quick Quiz 10.3

1. Describe how simple selection sort works.
2. Describe how linear insertion sort works.

3. (True or false) Linear insertion sort performs well for small lists.
4. Describe how quicksort uses a divide-and-conquer sorting strategy.
5. The item properly positioned at each call to quicksort is called a(n) ________.

Exercises 10.3

For each of the arrays x in Exercises 1–4, show x after each of the first four passes of simple selection sort.

1.

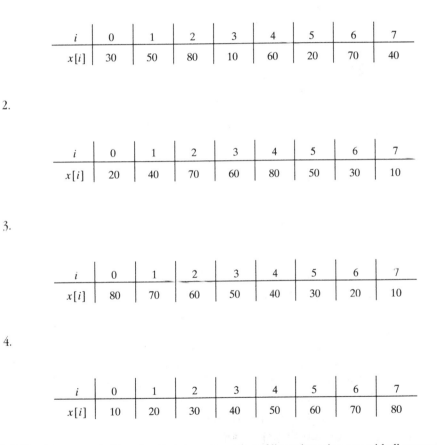

i	0	1	2	3	4	5	6	7
$x[i]$	30	50	80	10	60	20	70	40

2.

i	0	1	2	3	4	5	6	7
$x[i]$	20	40	70	60	80	50	30	10

3.

i	0	1	2	3	4	5	6	7
$x[i]$	80	70	60	50	40	30	20	10

4.

i	0	1	2	3	4	5	6	7
$x[i]$	10	20	30	40	50	60	70	80

5–8. For the arrays x in Exercises 1–4, trace the action of linear insertion sort with diagrams like that in the text.

9. One variation of simple selection sort for a list stored in an array $x[0], \ldots, x[n-1]$ is to locate both the smallest and the largest elements while scanning the list and to position them at the beginning and the end of the list, respectively. On the next scan, this process is repeated for the sublist $x[1], \ldots, x[n-2]$, and so on. Write an algorithm to implement this double-ended selection sort.

10–13. For the arrays *x* in Exercises 1–4, show *x* after each pass of the double-ended selection sort described in Exercise 9.

14. For the following array *x*, give a sequence of diagrams like those in the text that trace the action of quicksort as it splits the list by properly positioning the pivot 45:

i	0	1	2	3	4	5	6	7	8	9
x[*i*]	45	20	50	30	80	10	60	70	40	90

10.4 Searching

Another important problem is **searching** a collection of data for a specified item and retrieving some information associated with that item. For example, one searches a telephone directory for a specific name in order to retrieve the phone number listed with that name. We consider two kinds of searches, linear search and binary search.

LINEAR SEARCH

A **linear search** searches consecutive elements in the list, beginning with the first element and continuing until either the desired item is found or the end of the list is reached. To illustrate, suppose that we have the following array x of values,

x	[0]	[1]	[2]	[3]	[4]	[5]	[6]
	33	55	11	77	66	22	44

and that we search the list for 66. Using linear search, we start at the beginning and compare each value in the sequence against 66. After five comparisons, we successfully locate the desired element. If we were searching for 60 instead of 66, then after seven comparisons—the number of values in the container—and not finding it, we could conclude that 60 is not present. In general, linear search requires *n* comparisons to determine that a sequence with *n* elements does not contain a specific value.

The following algorithm uses this method for searching a list of *n* elements stored in an array, *x*[0], *x*[1], ..., *x*[*n* – 1], for *itemSought*. It returns the location of *itemSought* if the search is successful, or the value *n* otherwise.

Linear Search Algorithm

1. Initialize *location* to 0 and *found* to false.
2. While *location* < *n* and not *found*, do the following:
   If *itemSought* is equal to *x*[*location*], then
      Set *found* to true.
   Otherwise
      Increment *location* by 1.

BINARY SEARCH

If a list has been sorted, we can use a different method called **binary search**. To illustrate it, suppose that the preceding array x has been sorted,

x	[0]	[1]	[2]	[3]	[4]	[5]	[6]
	11	22	33	44	55	66	77

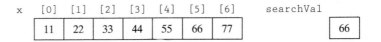

and we search the list for 66. We begin by examining the middle element in the sequence (44 in this case):

x	[0]	[1]	[2]	[3]	[4]	[5]	[6]	searchVal
	11	22	33	44	55	66	77	66

Since 66 (the value we are seeking) is greater than 44, we ignore the middle value and all values to its left and repeat the process by comparing 66 with the middle value in the remainder of the list (66 in this case),

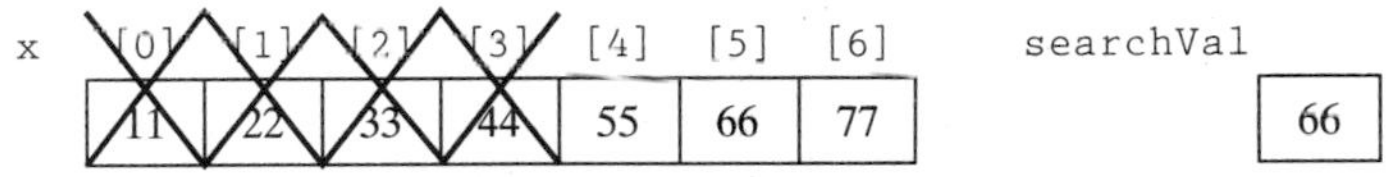

and we successfully locate the desired element. Note that in contrast to the five comparisons required by linear search to locate this value, binary search required only two comparisons.

If we had been searching for 60 instead of 66, then in the preceding step, since 60 is less than 66, we would ignore the middle value and all values to its right and repeat the process by comparing 60 to the middle value in the remainder of the list (55 in this case):

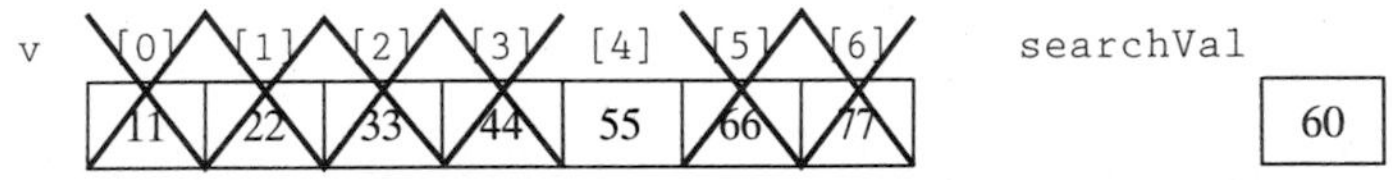

Since there is just one value remaining and it is not equal to the value we are seeking (60), we conclude that 60 is not present. Determining this required just three comparisons, in contrast to the seven comparisons required by linear search.

In general, linear search may require n comparisons to locate a particular item, but binary search will require at most $\log_2 n$ comparisons. For example, for a list of 1024 ($= 2^{10}$) items, binary search will locate an item using at most 10 comparisons, whereas linear search may require 1024 comparisons.

The following algorithm uses binary search to search a list of n elements stored in an array, $x[0], x[1], ..., x[n-1]$, that has been ordered so the elements are in ascending order. If *itemSought* is found, its location in the array is returned; otherwise, the value n is returned.

Binary Search Algorithm

1. Initialize *first* to 0 and *last* to $n - 1$. These values represent the positions of the first and last items of the list or sublist being searched.
2. Initialize *found* to false.
3. While $first \le last$ and not *found*, do the following:
   a. Find the middle position in the sublist by setting *middle* equal to the integer quotient (*first* + *last*) / 2.
   b. Compare *itemSought* with *x*[*middle*]. There are three possibilities:
      i. *itemSought* < *x*[*middle*]: *itemSought* is in the first half of the sublist; set *last* equal to *middle* – 1.
      ii. *itemSought* > *x*[*middle*]: *itemSought* is in the second half of the sublist; set *first* equal to *middle* + 1.
      iii. *itemSought* = *x*[*middle*]: *itemSought* has been found; set *location* equal to *middle* and *found* to true.
4. If *found*, return *middle*; otherwise, return *n*.

10.5 Example: Processing Employee Information

PROBLEM

The Rinky Dooflingy Corporation keeps track of employee seniority and salaries in a file `employeeData.txt`, in which the first line in the file describes the employee with the most seniority, the second line describes the employee with next highest seniority, and so on. Each line contains an employee's name in last-name, first-name order, followed by his or her weekly salary:

```
Somebody, Jane      950.00
Yahyah, Noah        845.00
Newman, Alfred      735.00
    .
    .
    .
```

The problem is that the company paymaster uses this file to write the paychecks in order of seniority, but the company mailboxes are in alphabetical order. As a result, putting the paychecks into the mail boxes takes an inordinate amount of time. A program is needed to read the information in `employeeData.txt` and create a second file in which the employees are listed in alphabetical order.

Object-Centered Design

Behavior. The program should open a stream to the file named `employeeData.txt`. It should then read a sequence of employee records from the stream, and close it. After this, it should sort this sequence so that the last names are in alphabetical order. Next, it should open a stream to a file named `payrollData.txt`, write the sorted sequence of employee records to the file stream, and then close the stream.

Objects. From the statement of the problem and our behavioral description, we have the following objects:

Problem Objects	Software Objects		
	Type	Kind	Name
the stream to the input file	`ifstream`	varying	*inStream*
name of the input file	`string`	constant	`"employeeData.txt"`
a line of employee info	`string`	varying	*empLine*
a sequence of employee records	`vector<string>`	varying	*empVector*
the stream to the output file	`ofstream`	varying	*outStream*
name of the output file	`string`	constant	`"payrollData.txt"`

We could use an array to store the sequence of employee records. However, as we observed in Section 10.2, this would require setting some *fixed* capacity for it, but we do not know at the outset how many employee records there are in the file. As we shall see, the C++ `vector<T>` class template provides a convenient way to store an arbitrarily long sequence of values of type `T`. Thus, we will use a `vector<string>` object to store the sequence of lines of text from the input file.

Operations. From the behavioral description, we find the following operations:

i. Open a stream to an input file
ii. Read a sequence of employee records from a file stream
iii. Close a file stream
iv. Sort a sequence of employee records
v. Open a stream to an output file
vi. Write a sequence of employee records to a file stream

Each of these operations is either predefined in C++ or is easily implemented with a few simple statements. In particular, we need not code one of the methods from Section 10.3 for the sorting operation because C++ provides a `sort()` function template that works on a wide variety of objects, including `vector<T>` objects. Our task is further simplified by the format of the input file: Because an employee's last name is the first item on each line, we can simply read the file a line at a time and then sort these lines.

Algorithm. Our algorithm is thus as follows:

Algorithm for Sorting Problem

1. Open an `ifstream` named *inStream* to "employeeData.txt".
   (If this fails, display an error message and terminate the algorithm.)
2. Loop:
   a. Read a line from *inStream* into *empLine*.

   b. If the eof mark was read, terminate repetition.
   c. Append *empLine* to *empVector.*

  End loop.
3. Close *inStream.*
4. Sort the lines in *empVector.*
5. Open an `ofstream` named *outStream* to "payrollData.txt".
   (If this fails, display an error message, and terminate the algorithm.)
6. For each index *i* of *empVector*:
   Write *empVector*[*i*] to *outStream.*
7. Close *outStream.*

Note that because we do not know how many employee records are in `employee-Data.txt`, we must use an indefinite loop in Step 2. Once this step is finished, the number of employees is known, and so we can use a `for` loop in Step 6.

Coding. The program in Figure 10.3 is a complete implementation of this algorithm in C++. It uses two new features of C++: the `vector<T>` class template and the `sort()` algorithm template, each of which is a standard component of C++.

Fig. 10.3 Sorting a file of employee records. (Part 1 of 3)

```
/* empRecords.cpp sorts a sequence of employee records from a file
 * so they are arranged with the last names in alphabetical order.
 *
 * Input (file):    employee records
 * Output (screen): user messages
 * Output (file):   sorted employee records
 *****************************************************************/

#include <iostream>                       // cout, <<, >>
#include <fstream>                        // ifstream, ofstream
#include <string>                         // string
#include <cassert>                        // assert()
#include <vector>                         // vector<T>
#include <algorithm>                      // sort()
using namespace std;

int main()
{
   cout << "This program sorts the data in a file"
        << " named 'employeeData.txt'.\n";

   ifstream inStream("employeeData.txt");     // input stream
   assert(inStream.is_open());
```

Fig. 10.3 Sorting a file of employee records. (Part 2 of 3)

```
   vector<string> empVector;                    // sequence-holder

   string empLine;                              // input variable

   for (;;)                                     // loop:
   {
      getline(inStream, empLine);               //   read a name
      if (inStream.eof()) break;                //   quit if eof
      empVector.push_back(empLine);             //   append name
   }                                            // end loop

   inStream.close();                            // close stream

   sort(empVector.begin(), empVector.end());    // sort vector

   ofstream outStream("payrollData.txt");       // output stream
   assert(outStream.is_open());

   for (int i = 0; i < empVector.size(); i++)   // display
      outStream << empVector[i] << endl;        // vector

   outStream.close();

   cout << "\nProcessing complete. See 'payrollData.txt'.\n";
}
```

Listing of input file `employeeData.txt`**:**

```
Somebody, Jane     950.00
Yahyah, Noah       845.00
Newman, Alfred     735.00
Bigfoot, Ben       425.00
Valyou, Mary       300.00
Smith, Nancy       195.00
Juan, John         175.00
Doe, John          150.00
Buck, John         150.00
Deere, John        150.00
```

Fig. 10.3 Sorting a file of employee records. (Part 3 of 3)

Sample run:

```
This program sorts the data in a file named 'employeeData.txt'.

Processing complete.
```

Listing of output file `payrollData.txt`:

```
Bigfoot, Ben        425.00
Buck, John          150.00
Deere, John         150.00
Doe, John           150.00
Juan, John          175.00
Newman, Alfred      735.00
Smith, Nancy        195.00
Somebody, Jane      950.00
Valyou, Mary        300.00
Yahyah, Noah        845.00
```

In the next section, we examine the `vector<T>` class template in depth.

10.6 The `vector<T>` Class Template

A QUICK REVIEW OF FUNCTION TEMPLATES

In Section 8.5, we introduced **function templates**, which are patterns for functions from which the compiler can create actual function definitions. A template typically has a **type parameter** that is used as a place holder for a type that will be supplied when the function is called. For example, we considered the following function template:

```
template <typename Item>
void swap(Item& first, Item& second)
{
   Item temporary = first;
   first = second;
   second = temporary;
}
```

When `swap()` is called with

```
swap(int1, int2);
```

the compiler creates an instance of `swap()` in which the type-parameter `Item` is replaced by `int`—the type of the variables whose values are being exchanged. But when `swap()` is called with

```
swap(char1, char2);
```

the compiler creates an instance of `swap()` in which `Item` is replaced by `char`. Function templates thus allow a programmer to create **generic functions**—functions that are *type independent.*

CLASS TEMPLATES

In addition to function templates, C++ also allows **class templates**, which are type-independent patterns from which actual classes can be defined. These are useful for building **generic container classes**—objects that store other objects. In the early 1990s, Alex Stepanov and Meng Lee of Hewlett Packard Laboratories extended C++ with an entire library of class and function templates, which has come to be known as the **Standard Template Library (STL)** and is one of the standard C++ libraries.

One of the simplest containers in STL is the `vector<T>` class template, which can be thought of as a type-independent pattern for a self-contained array class whose capacity can change. A simplified form of its declaration is

```
template <typename T>
class vector
{
  // details of vector omitted...
};
```

where `T` is a parameter for the type of values to be stored in the container. To illustrate its use, consider the following definitions:

```
vector<double> realVector;
vector<string> stringVector;
```

When it processes the first definition, the compiler will create a definition of class `vector` in which each occurrence of `T` is replaced by `double` and will use this class to construct an object named `realVector`. When it processes the second definition, the compiler will create a second definition of class `vector` in which each occurrence of `T` is replaced by `string` and will use this class to construct an object named `stringVector`.[7]

Because a class template is a parameterized pattern from which a class can be built and not an actual class itself, its name includes its `<T>` parameter, as in `vector<T>`, to distinguish it from an actual class, which is not parameterized.

DEFINING vector<T> OBJECTS

The definition

```
vector<string> empVector;
```

---

7. Since class names must be unique, whenever the compiler builds an actual class from a class template, it gives the new class a unique name formed by combining the name of the class and its parameterized type(s), a process known as **name mangling**. For example, `vector<double>` and `vector<string>` might be mangled to `vector_d` and `vector_s`, respectively.

in the program of Figure 10.3 creates an **empty** vector<string>, meaning a vector that can store string values and whose size and capacity are both zero. As the program demonstrates, having a capacity of zero is not a problem, because a vector<T> object can increase its capacity as necessary during program execution.

Preallocating a vector<T> Object. Sometimes it is useful to *preallocate* the capacity of a vector<T>. (See the discussion of push_back() later.) This can be done by passing the desired initial capacity as an argument to the object being constructed. For example, if we write

```
vector<string> empVector(10);
```

then empVector will be constructed as a vector of string values whose capacity is 10. Its size will also be 10 since these string values will be initialized (by default) to strings of length 0 that contain no characters:

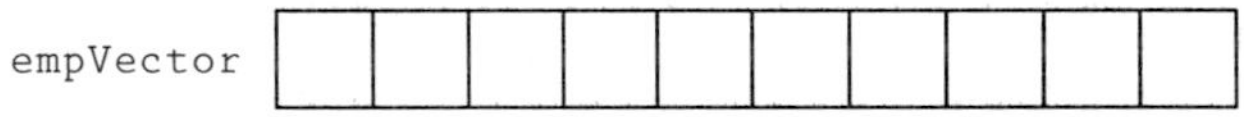

Unlike a C-style array whose capacity must be known at compile time, the space for a vector<T> object is allocated during program execution. This allows us to write code like the following that provides *interactive control* over the capacity of a vector<T>:

```
int numberOfEmployees
cin >> numberOfEmployees;
vector<string> empVector(numberOfEmployees);
```

Whatever value the user enters for numberOfEmployees will be the initial capacity (and size) of empVector.

Preallocating and Initializing a vector<T> Object. A third form of a vector<T> definition can be used both to preallocate the capacity of a vector<T> object and to initialize each element to a specified value. For example, the definition

```
vector<double> realVector(10, 0);
```

will construct realVector as a vector of double values, with capacity 10, and containing 10 zeros (making its size also 10):

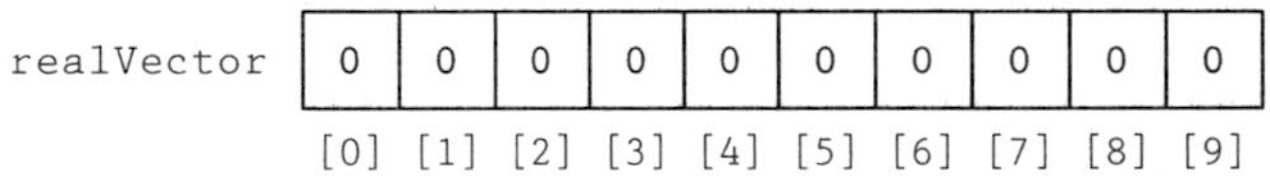

Similarly, the definition

```
vector<string> names(4, "Jane Doe");
```

will construct names as a vector of four string values, each initialized to "Jane Doe":

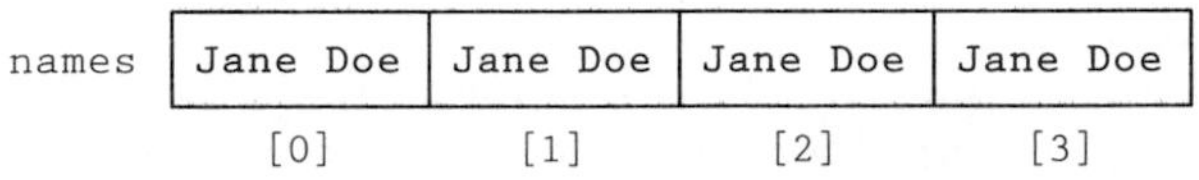

The three forms of vector<T> definitions can be summarized as follows:

vector<T> Definition

Forms:

```
vector<element_type> object_name;
vector<element_type> object_name(initial_capacity);
vector<element_type> object_name(initial_capacity,
                                 initial_value );
```

where

element_type is any known type;

object_name is the name of the vector object being defined;

initial_capacity is an integer expression; and

initial_value is an object of type *element_type*.

Purpose: Define a varying-capacity object capable of storing values of type *element_type*.

Form 1 constructs *object_name* with capacity and size 0.

Forms 2 and 3 both construct *object_name* with capacity *initial_capacity* and with size *initial_capacity*. Form 2 initializes the elements to default values of type *element_type*. Form 3 initializes each element to *initial_value*.

vector<T> FUNCTION MEMBERS

C++ provides a rich set of operations for vector<T>. As we shall see, these operations allow a vector<T> to be treated much like an array or valarray, but without some of the limitations of C-style arrays and valarrays. The following table lists some of these operations:

Operation	Description
vector<*Type*> *v*; vector<*Type*> *v*(*n*); vector<*Type*> *v*(*n*, *initVal*);	Construct *v* as a vector<*type*> of capacity 0 Construct *v* as a vector<*type*> of capacity *n*, size *n*, and each element initialized to a default *type* value Construct *v* as a vector<*type*> of capacity *n*, size *n*, and each element initialized to *initVal*
v.capacity() *v*.size() *v*.empty()	Return the number of values *v* can store Return the number of values *v* currently contains Return true if and only if *v* contains no values (i.e., *v*'s size is 0)

Operation	Description
`v.reserve(n);`	Grow *v* so that its capacity is *n* (does not affect *v*'s size)
`v.push_back(value);` `v.pop_back();`	Append *value* at *v*'s end Erase *v*'s last element
`v.front()` `v.back()`	Return a reference to *v*'s first element Return a reference to *v*'s last element

The Constructors. The first group of operations provide the three main ways to construct a `vector<T>`. We have already described these in some detail.

Checking Size and Capacity. The second group of operations show how much more self-contained `vector<T>` objects are than C-style arrays:

- `v.size()` returns the number of values in *v*. As with C-style arrays and `valarray`s, *the index of the first value of a* `vector<T>` *is always 0*; but unlike arrays and `valarray`s, which provide no way to identify the final values stored in them, *the index of the last value stored in a* `vector<T>` *object v is always* `v.size() - 1`.
- `v.empty()` is a faster alternative to the boolean expression `v.size() == 0`.
- `v.capacity()` returns the current capacity of *v*.
- `v.reserve()` can be used to increase the capacity of *v*, but this is more often done implicitly using `v.push_back()`.

To illustrate the use of these methods, suppose that we write

```
vector<int> intVector;
cout << intVector.capacity() << ' '
     << intVector.size() << endl;
```

The output produced will be

```
0 0
```

because `intVector` is an empty container. But if we change the declaration of `intVector` to

```
vector<int> intVector(3);
```

the values

```
3 3
```

will be displayed, because `intVector` has space for three values and contains three undefined `int` values. The same output will be produced if we use the declaration

```
vector<int> intVector(3, 0);
```

because `intVector` has space for three values and contains three values, each of which is 0:

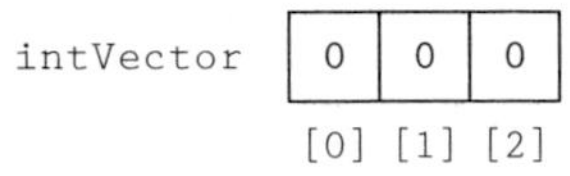

Appending and Removing Values. The third group of operations shows how values can be appended to or removed from a `vector<T>`. A statement of the form

```
v.push_back(value);
```

appends *value* to the end of *v* and increases its size by 1. If necessary, the capacity of *v* is increased to accommodate the new value.

To illustrate, execution of the statements

```
vector<int> intVector;
cout << intVector.capacity() << ' '
     << intVector.size() << endl;
for (int i = 0; i <= 64; i++)
{
   intVector.push_back(i);
   cout << intVector.capacity() << ' '
        << intVector.size() << endl;
}
```

on one machine produced

```
0 0
1 1
2 2
4 3
4 4
8 5
8 6
8 7
8 8
16 9
 .
 .
 .
16 16
32 17
32 18
 .
 .
 .
32 32
64 33
 .
 .
 .
64 64
```

We see that the capacity of `intVector` increased to 1 when the first value was added to it and then doubled each time more space was needed. When the declaration of `intVector` was changed to

```
vector<int> intVector(3, 0);
```

execution of the statements produced

```
3 3
6 4
6 5
6 6
12 7
12 8
 .
 .
 .
12 12
24 13
 .
 .
 .
24 24
48 25
 .
 .
 .
48 48
96 49
 .
 .
 .
96 68
```

Here, we see that the capacity is initially 3, as expected, but when a fourth value is appended to the full intVector, its capacity doubles from 3 to 6. Similarly, when the capacity of intVector is 6 and we add a seventh value, its capacity doubles again (to 12).

This behavior is a compromise between allocating many small blocks of memory (which wastes time) and allocating only a few large blocks of memory (which wastes space). It can be produced by declaring the vector<T> as nonempty or by using the function member reserve() to set the initial capacity of an empty vector<T>. The reserve() method can also be used to override the doubling feature of a vector<T>'s capacity.

The method *v*.pop_back() can be used to remove the last value in *v*. This will decrease the size of *v* by 1, but it does not change its capacity.

Accessing the First and Last Values. The front() and back() messages can be used to access the first and last values in a vector<T>. More precisely, if realVector is the vector

	[0]	[1]	[2]
realVector	4.3	7.2	5.9

then front() and back() can be used to retrieve the first and last values, as in

```
cout << realVector.front() << ' '
     << realVector.back() << endl;
```

which will display

```
4.3 5.9
```

These methods can also be used to change the first and last values, as in

```
realVector.front() = 1.1;
realVector.back() = 9.0;
```

which will modify `realVector` as follows:

realVector	1.1	7.2	9.0
	[0]	[1]	[2]

vector<T> OPERATORS

There are four basic **operators** defined in `vector<T>`:

Operator	Description
v[i]	Access the element of *v* whose index is i
v1 = *v2*	Assign a copy of *v2* to *v1*
v1 == *v2*	Return true if and only if *v1* has the same values as *v2*, in the same order
v1 < *v2*	Return true if and only if *v1* is lexicographically less than *v2*

The Subscript Operator. The first operator is the familiar subscript operator that provides convenient access to the element with a given index. As we have noted, the index of the first element of a `vector<T>` is always 0, and the expression *vectorName*`.size() - 1` is always the index of the final value in *vectorName*. This allows all of the values stored in a `vector<T>` to be processed using a `for` loop and the subscript operator, as we saw in the program in Figure 10.3:

```
for (int i = 0; i < empVector.size(); i++)     // display
   outStream << empVector[i] << endl;          // vector
```

The `vector<T>` subscript operation is thus similar to that of `string` objects and C-style arrays.

When Not to Use Subscript. There is one important difference between `vector<T>`s and C-style arrays and `valarray`s. To illustrate this difference, suppose that we wrote the following function to read values into a `vector<T>`:

```
template <typename T>
void read(istream& in, vector<T>& theVector)
```

```
{
   int count = 0;
   for (;;)
   {
      in >> theVector[count]; // LOGIC ERROR:
      if (in.eof()) break;    //  size & capacity not updated!
      count++;
   }
}
```

WATCH OUT

This does not work correctly because *if the subscript operator is used to append values to a* vector<T>, *neither its size nor its capacity is modified. The* push_back() *method should always be used to append values to a* vector<T>, because it updates the vector's size (and if necessary, its capacity).[8] Figure 10.4 shows one way to write a correct, generic vector<T> input function that uses the end-of-file mark as a sentinel value:

Fig. 10.4 vector<T> input from an istream.

```
/* read() fills a vector<T> with input from a stream.
 *
 * Receives:     type parameter T,
 *               an istream and a vector<T>
 * Input:        a sequence of T values
 * Precondition: operator >> is defined for type T
 * Passes back:  the modified istream and the modified vector<T>
****************************************************************/

template <typename T>
void read(istream& in, vector<T>& theVector)
{
   T inputValue;

   for (;;)
   {
      in >> inputValue;
      if ( in.eof() ) break;
      theVector.push_back(inputValue);
   }
}
```

8. The push_back() method also correctly updates the iterator returned by the end() function member, while the subscript operator does not. STL algorithms will thus not work properly if subscript is used to append values to a vector<T>.

Given this function template, the statements

```
vector<double> realVector;
read(cin, realVector);
```

will cause the compiler to create a definition of `read()` in which each occurrence of `T` has been replaced by `double`, and the call to `read()` will be linked to this definition. If, in the same program, we write

```
vector<string> stringVector;
read(cin, stringVector);
```

then the compiler will create a second definition of `read()` in which each occurrence of `T` is replaced by `string`, and this second call to `read()` will be linked to this definition.

Because an `ifstream` is a specialized form of `istream`, this same function template can be used to fill a `vector<T>` from a file by passing an open `ifstream` to that file as an argument to `read()`:

```
ifstream fin("data.txt");
read(fin, realVector);
```

When to Use Subscript. Once a `vector<T>` contains values, *then and only then* should the subscript operator be used to access (or change) those values. For example, Figure 10.5 presents a generic output function that uses a `for` loop and the subscript operator to display the values in a `vector<T>`.

Fig. 10.5 `vector<T>` output.

```
/* print() writes a vector<T> to a stream.
 *
 * Receives:       type parameter T
 *                 an ostream and a vector<T>
 * Output:         each T value stored in theVector to ostream out
 * Precondition:   operator << is defined for type T
 * Passes back:    the modified ostream
*****************************************************************/

template <typename T>
void print(ostream& out, const vector<T>& theVector)
{
   for (int i = 0; i < theVector.size(); i++)
      out << theVector[i] << ' ';
}
```

Given this function template and the statements

```
vector<double> realVector(5, 1.1);
print(cout, realVector);
```

the compiler will generate a definition of `print()` in which each occurrence of `T` is replaced by `double`. When executed, it will produce the output

```
1.1 1.1 1.1 1.1 1.1
```

Because an `ofstream` is a specialized form of `ostream`, this same function template can be used to write a `vector<T>` to a file by passing an open `ofstream` to that file as an argument to `print()`:

```
ofstream fout("data.txt");
print(fout, realVector);
```

Because these functions are useful in many problems, they should probably be stored in a library (e.g., `myVector.h`) so that any program can easily reuse them.

The Assignment Operator. The assignment operator (=) is straightforward, behaving exactly as one would expect. For example, the definitions

```
vector<int> v1;
vector<int> v2(5, 1);
```

create `v1`, an empty `vector<int>`, and `v2`, a nonempty `vector<int>`:

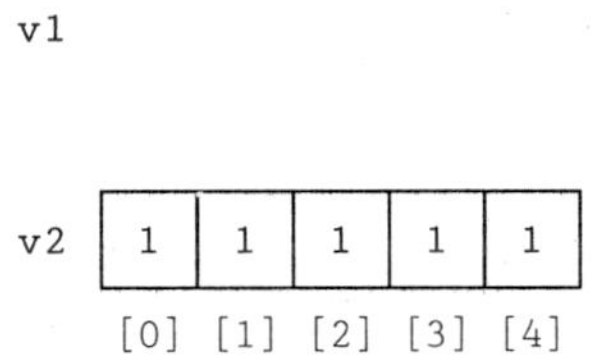

A subsequent assignment statement

```
v1 = v2;
```

changes `v1` to a copy of `v2`:

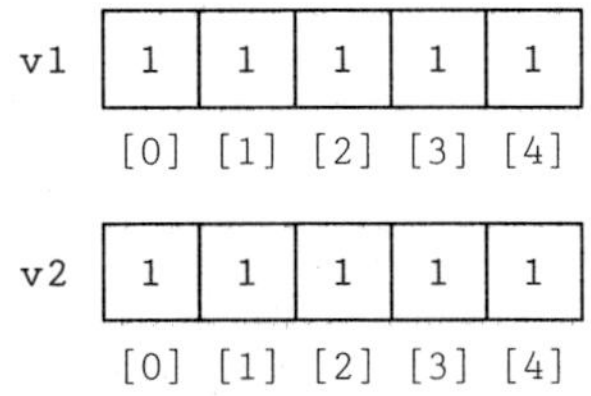

The Equality Operator. The equality operator (==) is also straightforward. It compares its operand's element by element and returns true if and only if they are identical; that is, their sizes match and their values match. For example, the definitions

```
vector<int> v1(4, 1);
vector<int> v2(5, 1);
```

produce two similar but not identical vector<int> objects:

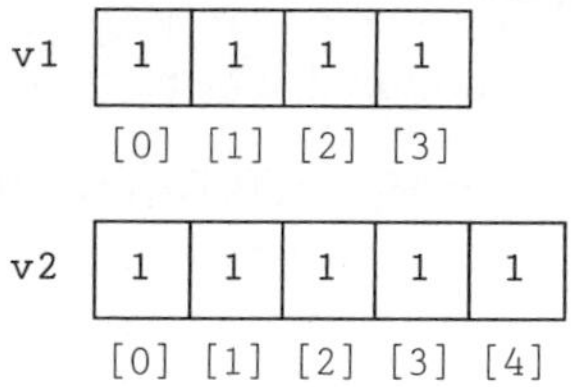

When these are compared using the equality operator,

```
if (v1 == v2)
// ... do something appropriate
```

the expression produces the value false, because v1 and v2 are not identical.

The Less-Than Operator. The less-than operator (<) is also defined for vector<T> objects. It behaves much like the string less-than operation, performing an element-by-element comparison until a mismatch (if any) occurs. If the mismatched element in the left operand is less than the corresponding element in the right operand, the operation returns true; otherwise, it returns false. If all the elements of both vector<T> objects are compared and no mismatch is found, the operation returns false.

To illustrate, suppose that the two vector<int> objects v1 and v2 have the following values:

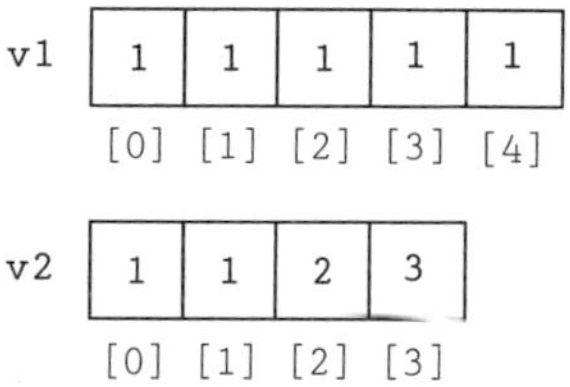

When these are compared using the less-than operator,

```
if (v1 < v2)
// ... do something appropriate
```

the values at index 0 are compared first. Because they are equal, the function moves on and examines the values at index 1. Once again, the values are equal, so it moves on and examines the values at index 2. Now, the value (1) at index 2 in v1 is less than the value (2) at index 2 in v2, the < operation returns true.

If the values of v1 and v2 are

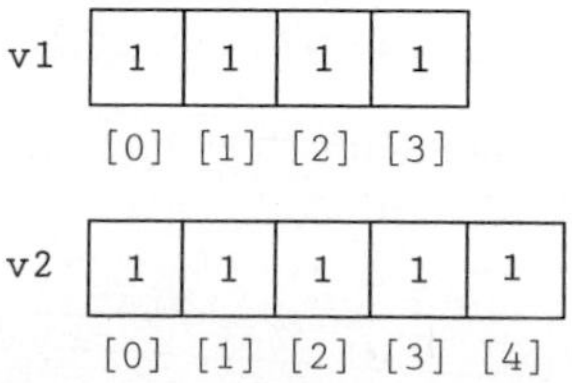

the values at index 0 are compared. Because they match, the values at index 1 are compared. This continues through the values at index 2, and the function moves on and examines the values at index 3. Because we have reached the end of `v1` but not the end of `v2` and no mismatch has occurred, the operation returns `true`.

`vector<T>` Function Members Involving Iterators. As we have seen, the elements of a `vector<T>` can be accessed using an index and the subscript operator. However, some of the `vector<T>` operations (and those for other STL containers described in the next section) require a different method of access using objects called **iterators**. Basically, an **iterator** is a class object that can "point at" an element of a container by storing its memory address and has built-in operations that can access the value stored there and move from one element to another.

Each STL container provides its own group of iterator types and (at least) two methods that return iterators:

- `begin()`: Returns an iterator positioned at the first element in the container
- `end()`: Returns an iterator positioned immediately after the last value in the container

The following table gives the `vector<T>` versions of these methods and other important operations that use iterators:

Method	Description
`v.begin()` `v.end()`	Return an iterator positioned at *v*'s first value Return an iterator positioned immediately after *v*'s last value
`v.rbegin()` `v.rend()`	Return a reverse iterator positioned at *v*'s last value Return a reverse iterator positioned one element before *v*'s first value
`v.insert(pos, value);` `v.insert(pos, n, value);`	Insert *value* into *v* at iterator position *pos* Insert *n* copies of *value* into *v* at iterator position *pos*
`v.erase(pos);` `v.erase(pos1, pos2);`	Erase the value in *v* at iterator position *pos* Erase the values in *v* from iterator positions *pos1* to *pos2*

For `vector<T>`, an iterator declaration has the form

```
vector<T>::iterator iter = initial-value;
```

where the initialization is optional. Three of the important operators on such iterators are:

`iter++`	Moves `iter` forward to the next element of a vector
`iter--`	Moves `iter` backward to the preceding element of a vector
`*iter`	Accesses the value at the position pointed to by `iter`

The following statements show how iterators can be used in a loop to output a `vector<double> v`:

```
for (vector<double>::iterator iter = v.begin();
                               iter != v.end(); iter++)
```

```
    cout << *iter << "  ";
cout << endl;
```

More details about the use of iterators in `vector<T>` can be found on the book's Web site.

DECISION: USE A `vector<T>` OR A C-STYLE ARRAY?

We have now seen two different ways to store a sequence of values of the same type: the C-style array and the C++ `vector<T>` class template. (We will not consider `valarrays` here because they can be used only for numeric values.) This raises the question:

> *When should a C-style array be used, and when should a C++* `vector<T>` *be used?*

Whereas the C-style array is a legacy of programming in the early 1970s, the C++ `vector<T>` was designed in the early 1990s and thus incorporates over 20 years of additional programming wisdom. This design of `vector<T>` (along with the other class templates in STL) gives it some definite advantages over C-style arrays, making it the preferred choice in many situations:

- The capacity of a `vector<T>` can change during execution; the capacity of a C-style array is fixed at compile time (except as noted below) and cannot be changed without recompiling the program.
- A `vector<T>` is a self-contained object; the C-style array is not. If the same operation can be implemented with either container, the array version will require more parameters.
- A `vector<T>` is a class template, and its function members (augmented with the STL algorithms) provide ready-to-use implementations of many common operations. The C-style array requires that we reinvent the wheel for most operations, and `valarray` operations are limited to numeric applications.

But there are times when the strengths of an array outweigh the convenience of using a `vector<T>`:

- If one does not need all the operations provided for `vector<T>`s, but those for arrays are adequate or nearly so, then a "lean and mean" array that doesn't have all the overhead of `vector<T>` or a class containing an array with a few new operations will perform more efficiently.
- The automatic increases in a `vector<T>`'s capacity can result in considerable waste of memory. For example, if we need to store 1050 elements and start with an empty `vector<T>`, repeated capacity increases will produce a `vector<T>` with 2048 elements, almost twice as many as are needed. Also, each increase in the capacity requires copying the elements from the old container into the new; this can be very time consuming if the elements are large objects.
- In addition to the arrays we have considered in this chapter, C and C++ also provide run-time allocated arrays. (See Section 14.2.) These arrays have all

the features we have described, but also have the additional property that their capacities can be specified during execution.

ARRAY AND vector<T> LIMITATIONS

One weakness that arrays, valarrays, and the vector<T>s all have in common is that inserting and deleting elements at positions other than at the end can be quite time consuming, especially for large sequences. For example, consider the following ordered sequence of ten integers:

23, 25, 34, 48, 61, 79, 82, 89, 91, 99

If these values are stored in an array, valarray<int>, or vector<int> and we wish to insert the value 56 into its proper position, then the fifth through the tenth values must be shifted one position to the right to make room for the new value:

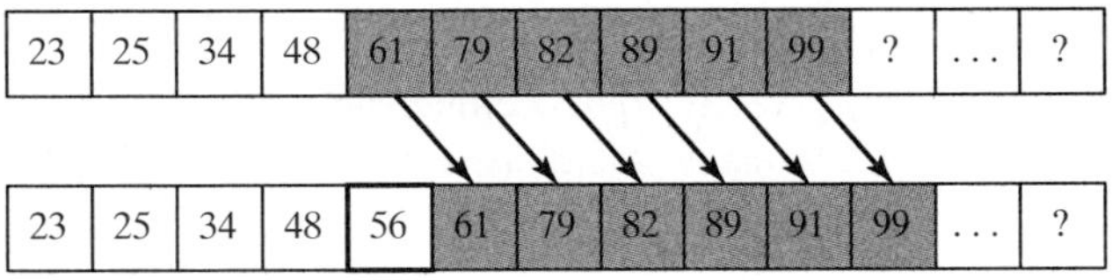

Erasing a value from the sequence also requires moving values; for example, to remove the second number, we must shift the third through the eleventh values one position to their left to "close the gap":

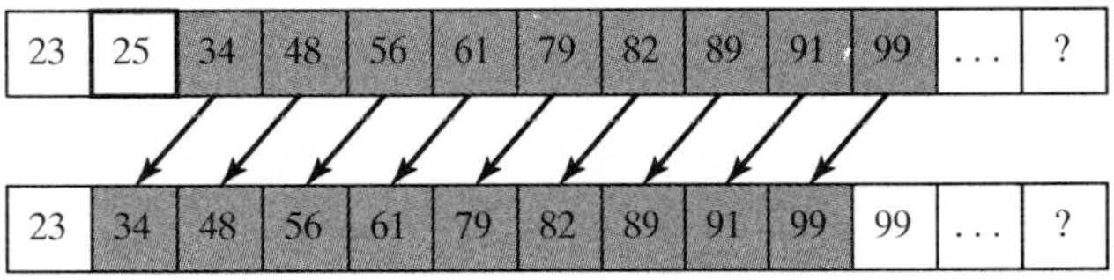

If insertions and erasures are restricted to the ends of the sequence, then array and vector<T> implementations that do not require moving elements are possible. Two important special cases are stacks and queues. A **stack** is a sequence in which values may be inserted **(pushed)** and removed **(popped)** at only one end, called the **top** of the stack.[9] If elements may be inserted only at one end (the **back**) and removed only at the other (the **front**), the sequence is called a **queue**. STL provides standardized *adaptor* class templates for building such objects out of other containers. (See Chapter 15 for more information on stacks and queues.)

In summary, arrays and vector<T> objects work well for storing sequences in which insertions and deletions are infrequent or are restricted to the end of the list. **Dynamic** sequences whose sizes may vary greatly during processing and those in which items are frequently inserted or deleted anywhere in the sequence are better stored in *linked lists*, which are described in Chapter 14.

---

9. This is the source of the names for vector<T>'s push_back() and pop_back() methods.

✔ Quick Quiz 10.6

Questions 1–15 assume that the following statements have been executed:

```
vector<int> a, b(5), c(5, 1), d(5, 0);
d.push_back(77);
d.push_back(88);
```

1. The type of values stored in a is __________.
2. The capacity of a is __________, and its size is __________.
3. The capacity of b is __________, and its size is __________.
4. The capacity of c is __________, and its size is __________.
5. The capacity of d is __________, and its size is __________.
6. What output is produced by
```
cout << c.front() << ' ' << c.back() << endl;
```
7. What output is produced by
```
cout << d.front() << ' ' << d.back() << endl;
```
8. (True or false) `a.empty()`.
9. (True or false) `c < d`.
10. (True or false) `c[1] == 1`.
11. What output is produced by
```
for (int i = 0; i < c.size(); i++)
   cout << c[i] << ' ';
```
12. What output is produced by
```
d.pop_back();
for (int i = 0; i < d.size(); i++)
   cout << d[i] << ' ';
```
13. `d.begin()` returns an iterator positioned at __________ in d.
14. `d.end()` returns an iterator positioned at __________.
15. (True or false) `vector<T>` objects are self-contained.

For Questions 16–19, assume only the declarations

```
vector<double> xValue(5, 0);
vector<int> number(5, 1);
```

Describe the contents of the `vector<T>` after the statements are executed.

16.
```
for (int i = 0; i <= 4; i++)
   xValue.push_back(double(i) / 2.0)
```
17.
```
for (int i = 0; i < 5; i++)
   if (i % 2 == 0)
      number.push_back(2 * i);
   else
      number.push_back(2 * i + 1);
```
18.
```
for (int i = 1; i < 5; i++)
   number.push_back(2 * number[i - 1]);
```

19.
```
for (int i = 1; i <= 3; i++)
    number.pop_back();
for (int i = 1; i <= 3; i++)
    number.push_back(2);
```
20. When, where, and by whom was the Standard Template Library (STL) developed?
21. A(n) __________ is a sequence in which values may be inserted and removed at only one end.
22. A(n) __________ is a sequence in which values may be inserted only at one end and removed only at the other end.

Exercises 10.6

For Exercises 1–12, assume that the following declarations have been made

```
vector<int> number,
            v(10, 20),
            w(10);
int num;
```

and that for exercises that involve input, the following values are entered:

```
99 33 44 88 22 11 55 66 77 -1
```

Describe the contents of the given vector<T> after the statements are executed.

1.
```
for (int i = 0; i < 10; i++)
    number.push_back(i / 2);
```
2.
```
for (int i = 0; i < 6; i++)
    w.push_back(i / 2);
```
3.
```
for (;;)
{
    cin >> num;
    if (num < 0) break;
    number.push_back(num);
}
```
4.
```
for (int i = 0; i <= 5; i++)
    number.push_back(i);
for (int i = 0; i < 2; i++)
    number.pop_back();
for (int i = 0; i <= 5; i++)
    number.push_back(i);
```

For Exercises 5–10, assume that the loop in Exercise 3 has been executed.

5.
```
for (int i = 0; i < number.size() - 1; i += 2)
    number[i] = number[i + 1];
```

6.
```
number.pop_back();
    number.push_back(number.front());
```
7.
```
int temp = number.front();
number.front() = number.back();
number.back() = temp;
```
8.
```
sort(number.begin(), number.end());
```
9.
```
for (int i = 0; i < number.size(); i++)
    w.pushback(number[i] + v[i]);
```
10.
```
while (v < number)
{
    v.erase(v.begin());
    number.erase(number.begin());
}
```

For Exercises 11–15, write a definition for a `vector<T>` having the given properties.

11. Can store `long int` values.
12. Capacity 10 and each element is a `long int`.
13. Capacity 10 and each element is a `long int`, all of which are initially 0.
14. Capacity 5, size 5, and each element contains a string, initially `"xxx"`.
15. Capacity 100 and each element is either `true` or `false`.

For Exercises 16–18, write definitions and statements to construct a `vector<T>` with the required properties.

16. Stores the sequence of integers from 0 through 99.
17. Stores the sequence of integers from 0 through 99 in reverse order.
18. Has capacity 50 and the value stored in an element is true if the corresponding index is even and is false otherwise.

Exercises 19–25 ask you to write functions to do various things. To test these functions, you should write driver programs as instructed in Programming Problems 21–23 at the end of this chapter.

19. Returns `true` if the values stored in a `vector<double>` are in ascending order and `false` otherwise.
20. Finds the range of values stored in a `vector<double>`, that is, the difference between the largest value and the smallest value.

Exercises 21–25 deal with operations on *n-dimensional vectors*, which are sequences of n real numbers and which are studied and used in many areas of mathematics and science. They can obviously be modeled in C++ by `vector<double>`s of capacity n. In the description of each operation, A and B are assumed to be n-dimensional vectors:

$$A = (a_1, a_2, \ldots, a_n)$$

$$B = (b_1, b_2, \ldots, b_n)$$

21. Compute and return the sum of two n-dimensional vectors:

$$A + B = (a_1 + b_1, a_2 + b_2, \ldots, a_n + b_n)$$

22. Compute and return the difference of two n-dimensional vectors:

$$A - B = (a_1 - b_1, a_2 - b_2, \ldots, a_n - b_n)$$

23. Compute and return the product of a scalar (real number) and an n-dimensional vector:

$$cA = (ca_1, ca_2, \ldots, ca_n)$$

24. Compute and return the magnitude of an n-dimensional vector:

$$|A| = \sqrt{a_1^2 + a_2^2 + \ldots + a_n^2}$$

25. Compute and return the inner (or dot) product of two n-dimensional vectors (which is a scalar):

$$A \cdot B = a_1 \times b_1 + a_2 \times b_2 + \cdots + a_n \times b_n = \sum_{i=1}^{n} (a_i \times b_i)$$

10.7 An Overview of the Standard Template Library

In addition to the built-in operations on `vector<T>` objects that we have described, there are several other operations that can be performed on `vector<T>`s (and other containers). However, to understand them, we need to know more about the C++ Standard Template Library (STL).

THE ORGANIZATION OF STL

As we noted earlier, the Standard Template Library is a library of C++ class and function templates developed by Alex Stepanov and Meng Lee of Hewlett Packard Laboratories in the early 1990s. When the C++ standard was finalized, this library was included as one of the standard C++ libraries.

STL has several different kinds of components, including the following:

1. **Containers:** A group of class templates that provide standardized, generic, off-the-shelf structures for storing data. These containers are

   `vector`
   `list`
   `deque`
   `stack`
   `queue`
   `priority_queue`
   `map` and `multimap`
   `set` and `multiset`

2. **Iterators:** A generic means of accessing, finding the successor of, and finding the predecessor of a container element
3. **Algorithms:** A group of function templates that provide standardized, generic, off-the-shelf functions for performing many of the most common operations on container objects.

In order for the algorithms in STL to be truly generic, they must be able to operate on any container. To make this possible, each container provides iterators for the algorithms to use. Iterators thus provide the interface that is needed for STL algorithms to operate on STL containers.

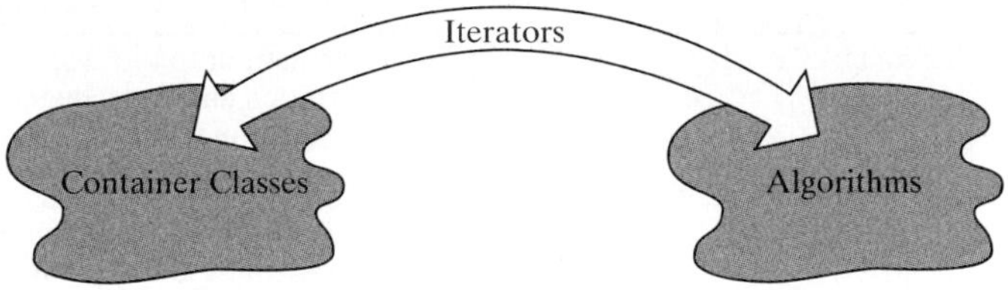

The program in Figure 10.3 gives an illustration of this when it calls

```
sort(empVector.begin(), empVector.end());
```

The `sort()` function is a generic STL algorithm that requires two iterators: one to the first element in the sequence and one to just past the end of the sequence. As we have seen, `empVector.begin()` returns an iterator that points to the first element of `empVector`, and `empVector.end()` returns an iterator that points just beyond its last element. More information about iterators is given on the book's Web site.

STL ALGORITHMS

Like `sort()`, most of the algorithms in the Standard Template Library are function templates designed to operate on *a sequence of elements*, rather than on a specific container. The STL way of designating a sequence for an algorithm is by using two iterators:[10]

- An iterator positioned at the first element in the sequence
- An iterator positioned *after* the last element in the sequence

In the discussion that follows, we will refer to these two iterators as *begin* and *end*, respectively.

STL provides over 80 algorithm templates. An in-depth examination of these algorithms is beyond the scope of this text and is left for the sequel. (See Footnote 6.) The table that follows provides a brief introduction to what is available. *All of these algorithms are in the* `<algorithm>` *library except for* `accumulate()`, *which was moved to the* `<numeric>` *library in the final C++ standard.*

Algorithm	Description
`accumulate(`*`begin`*`, `*`end`*`, `*`init`*`)`	Return the sum of the values in the sequence; *`init`* is the initial value for the sum (e.g., 0 for integers, 0.0 for reals)
`binary_search(`*`begin`*`, `*`end`*`, `*`value`*`)`	Return `true` if *`value`* is in the sorted sequence; if not present, return `false`
`find(`*`begin`*`, `*`end`*`, `*`value`*`)`	Return an iterator to *`value`* in the unsorted sequence; if not present, return *`end`*
`count(`*`begin`*`, `*`end`*`, `*`value`*`)`	Return how many times *`value`* occurs in the sequence
`fill(`*`begin`*`, `*`end`*`, `*`value`*`);`	Assign *`value`* to every element in the sequence

10. If an entire container were passed to an algorithm, then the algorithm would affect the entire container. Passing iterators to the beginning and end of the sequence allows an algorithm to act on a subset of the container's elements.

Algorithm	Description
`for_each(begin, end, f);`	Apply function *f* to every element in the sequence
`lower_bound(begin, end, value);` `upper_bound(begin, end, value);`	Return an iterator to the *first* position at which *value* can be inserted and the sequence remain sorted Return an iterator to the *last* position at which *value* can be inserted and the sequence remain sorted
`max_element(begin, end)` `min_element(begin, end)`	Return an iterator to the maximum sequence value Return an iterator to the minimum sequence value
`next_permutation(begin, end);` `prev_permutation(begin, end);`	Shuffle the sequence to its next permutation, and return `true` (If there is none, return `false`) Shuffle the sequence to its previous permutation, and return `true` (If there is none, return `false`)
`random_shuffle(begin, end);`	Shuffle the values in the sequence randomly
`replace(begin, end, old, new);`	In the sequence, replace each value *old* with *new*
`reverse(begin, end);`	Reverse the order of the values in the sequence
`sort(begin, end);`	Sort the sequence into ascending order
`unique(begin, end);`	In the sequence, replace any consecutive occurrences of the same value with one instance of that value

Familiarity with the standard algorithms in C++ can save considerable time and effort and allow us to write functions that are more streamlined and efficient. The function in Figure 10.6 and the example following it illustrate this. The function finds the mean of the values in a `vector<double>`, using the `accumulate()` algorithm from the `<numeric>` library. This eliminates the need to write a `for` loop to sum the values in the vector and also eliminates the need to define a variable to store that sum.

Fig. 10.6 Finding the mean of a `vector<double>`.

```
/* mean() finds the mean value in a vector<double>.
 *
 * Receive:      vec, a vector<double>
 * Precondition: vec is not empty
 * Return:       the mean of the values in vec
 * Note: Must #include <numeric> to use accumulate()
 ****************************************************************/

double mean(const vector<double>& vec)
{
   if ( vec.empty() )
   {
      cerr << "\n***mean(vector): vector is empty!\n" << endl;
      return 0.0;
   }
   else
      return accumulate(vec.begin(), vec.end(), 0.0) / vec.size();
}
```

Now suppose that the following `vector<double>` named `scores` contains a sequence of ten scores given by judges in some competition:

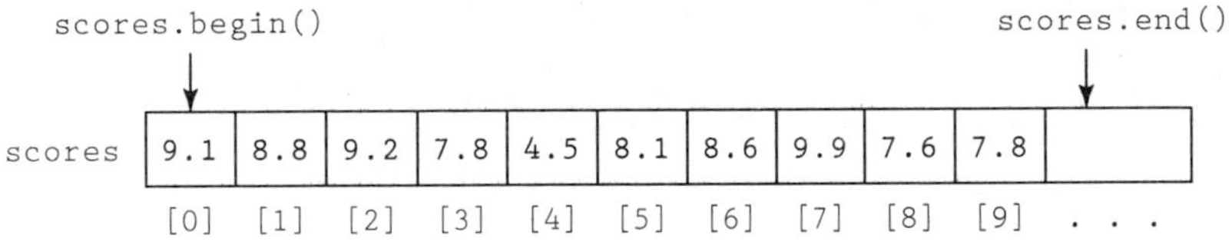

To reduce the effect of bias, the high score (9.9) and the low score (4.5) are to be thrown out, and the mean of the remaining scores computed.

Eliminating the low score can be done in one step using STL's `min_element()` algorithm to position an iterator at 4.5 and then pass this iterator to the `vector<T>` function member `erase()`,

```
scores.erase( min_element( scores.begin(), scores.end() ) );
```

The maximum score can be erased using the same approach with the `max_element()` algorithm:

```
scores.erase( max_element( scores.begin(), scores.end() ) );
```

The result is that the 4.5 and 9.9 are erased from `scores`, the remaining values are shifted to the left to fill their spaces, and `scores.size()` and `scores.end()` are appropriately updated:

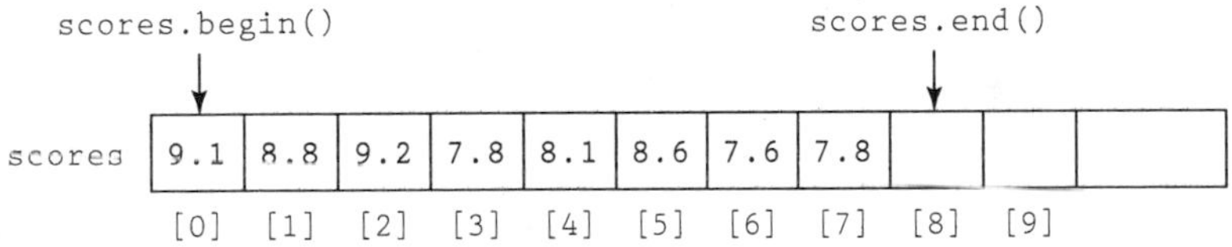

The resulting vector can then be passed to the function `mean()` in Figure 10.6 to compute the average score.

10.8 Case Study: Processing Test Scores

PROBLEM

Professor von Neuperson has a file containing the class roster for each class she teaches. To help with processing the grades for her classes, she would like a program that will allow her to enter a test score for each student in the file; calculate the mean of the scores, excluding the lowest and the highest score; and then display each person's name and score and the difference between that score and the mean. For example, if the mean score is 75, the program should display something like

```
... 82 (+7)
```

for a score of 82, and

```
. . . 69 (-6)
```

for a score of 69.

Object-Centered Design

Behavior. The program should display on the screen a prompt for the name of the class roster file and read its name from the keyboard. It should then read a sequence of names from the input file. The program should then read a sequence of test scores from the keyboard, prompting for them using the sequence of names. It should eliminate the outliers of this sequence—the high and low scores—and then compute the mean of the sequence of test scores. Finally, the program should display this mean value and then display the sequences of names and test scores, along with the difference of each test score from the mean.

Objects. Although most of the objects in our behavioral description are familiar, two of them require special attention: the sequence of names and the sequence of scores. Each of these sequences can be stored in a vector<T> for an appropriate type T.

Problem Objects	Software Objects		
	Type	Kind	Name
name of the class roster file	string	varying	*inputFileName*
the sequence of names	vector<string>	varying	*names*
the sequence of scores	vector<double>	varying	*scores*
the outliers of the sequence	double, double	varying	none
the mean score	double	varying	*meanScore*
the difference of a score and the mean score	double	varying	none

Operations. The operations specified in our behavioral description are as follows:

i. Read a string from the keyboard
ii. Open a stream to an input file
iii. Read a sequence of string values from the file stream into a vector<string>
iv. Read a sequence of double values from the keyboard into a vector<double>, using a sequence of string values stored in a vector<string> as prompts
v. Eliminate the outliers of a sequence of double values
vi. Compute the mean of a sequence of double values stored in a vector<double>

vii. Display a `double`

viii. Display the sequence of `string` values stored in a `vector<string>`, a corresponding sequence of `double` values stored in a `vector<double>`, and the difference of two `double` values

Operations i, ii, and viii are predefined, and a straightforward modification of the `read()` function of Figure 10.4 can be used for Operation iii. In the last section, we saw that Operation v can be done with two statements, and the `mean()` function from Figure 10.6 provides Operation vi. We will need a function `promptAndRead()` to perform Operation iv and another function `printResults()` for Operation viii.

See if you can write these two functions. Be sure to test them with driver programs. After you're confident of their correctness, write a program that solves the original problem, using the two functions you wrote and those mentioned earlier. When you finish (or if you have difficulty), you might look at the solution on the book's Web site. A complete solution is given there including the design, coding, and testing of the two functions `promptAndRead()` and `printResults()` and of the program for the original problem.

Part of the Picture

Component Programming

Before the Industrial Revolution, a *smith* was an important part of nearly every community. His job was to manufacture whatever metal components the members of the community might need. For example, if a horse lost a shoe, the owner of the horse would pay the smith to make a new horseshoe that was the correct size. In the absence of factories to mass-produce horseshoes and other common items in standard sizes, each new shoe had to be made from scratch.

This all changed with the Industrial Revolution. Once entrepreneurs identified markets for standard items such as horseshoes and built factories to produce them, these items could be mass produced much less expensively than if they were made by hand.

A second result of the Industrial Revolution was the advent of interchangeable components. No two horseshoes made by a smith were exactly alike; each was simply close enough to the correct size to do the job. By contrast, mass-produced items were virtually identical and were thus interchangeable. This made possible the assembly lines that make consumer products such as automobiles out of standardized components—pistons, axles, wheels, and so on. If a car's axle broke, no smith was needed to laboriously manufacture a new one. Instead, a replacement that was virtually identical could be ordered from the manufacturer.

COMPUTER HARDWARE

The same revolution occurred in computer hardware during the 1970s. The processors in early computers were built by hand and cost thousands or millions of dollars, but the invention of the microprocessor in the early 1970s made it possible to mass-produce the processor in a chip, some of which cost less than $100.

With the mass production of computer components has come interchangeability. When one memory or processor chip wears out, it can be unplugged from its circuit board and replaced by another chip that is functionally identical, even if the replacement is made by a different manufacturer. By using inexpensive, functionally identical components that connect in a standardized way, the cost of manufacturing and repairing computing systems has decreased dramatically since 1970.

COMPUTER SOFTWARE

The same revolution has begun in computing software. Historically, programmers have worked like the preindustrial smith, manually building from scratch the objects and operations needed to solve particular problems.

A step forward occurred in 1988 with the standardization of the C language and its many function libraries. Once the functions in these libraries were standardized, they became like software components that could be "plugged in" as needed, reducing programming effort and cost. However, such libraries only provided standardized operations, not objects.

With the publication of the ISO/ANSI standard for C++ in 1997and its embrace of the Standard Template Library, standardized objects such as istream, ostream, string, vector<T>, list<T>, set<T>, map<T>, and so on have become a reality. Because such objects have a well-defined set of operations that can be applied to them, they can be "plugged in" to programs as needed, an approach called **component programming**. By eliminating the need to build such objects from scratch, component programming increases programmer productivity, which reduces the cost of software.

To use such objects effectively, a programmer must be familiar with the operations they provide. For example, in the phone-number problem from Section 5.5, it was necessary to check whether each character in a string was a digit. If a programmer simply knew that C++ had a string class, without investigating the operations it provides, he or she might be tempted to write code like the following to perform this checking:

```
for (int i = 0; i < aString.size(); i++)
   if (aString[i] != '0' && aString[i] != '1' &&
       aString[i] != '2' && aString[i] != '3' &&
       aString[i] != '4' && aString[i] != '5' &&
       aString[i] != '6' && aString[i] != '7' &&
       aString[i] != '8' && aString[i] != '9')
      phoneError("A phone number can have only digits");
```

This approach is the programming equivalent of manually beating a horseshoe out of a bar of metal. It is far more costly in terms of time and effort than using the standardized operation:

```
if (aString.find_first_not_of("0123456789", 0) != string::npos)
   phoneError("A phone number can have only digits");
```

In the same fashion, a programmer needing to locate an item named value within a sequence might begin correctly by storing the sequence in a vector<T>, but then unnecessarily write a function to search the vector<T> for the value,

```
template <typename T>
int search(const vector<T>& theVec, const T& searchVal)
{
   for (int i = 0; i < theVec.size(); i++)
      if (theVec[i] == searchVal)
         return i;

   return -1;
}
   .
   .
   .
int index = search(vec, value);
```

and then call this function in some statement like

```
if ( search(itemVec, itemSought) != -1 ) // item found
   . . .
```

The STL find() algorithm provides an efficient, standardized way to solve this problem,

```
if ( find(itemVec.begin(), itemVec.end(), itemsought)
        != itemVec.end() )                 // item found
   . . .
```

and requires far less work. STL thus provides both standardized objects and algorithms.

Of course, practice is required to become familiar with the standardized components and their capabilities. Much of learning to program is becoming familiar with what standard objects are available and what operations can be performed on them. We hope that our introduction to STL objects and algorithms will whet your appetite to explore them further.

10.9* OBJECTive Thinking: Objects and Sequences

In this chapter, we have seen three mechanisms for storing sequences of values: C-style arrays, valarray<T>s, and vector<T>s. Any of these can be used in conjunction with classes to store sequences within a class. In this section, we build a Dataset class to illustrate how a class can use a vector<T> to store a sequence of values.

OVERVIEW OF A Dataset CLASS

A **dataset** is a sequence of measurements that describe some phenomenon, usually recorded over some regular interval—hourly, daily, weekly, monthly, yearly, and so on. Hourly temperature readings, daily sales figures, monthly pollution levels, and annual rainfall measurements are some examples.

A class to represent a dataset must, therefore, store a *sequence*, usually of numbers. Since a dataset might contain any number of values, arrays and valarrays are not the best choices for storage; thus, we will use an instance variable of type vector<double> to store this sequence. Often a dataset also has a *title* that labels the data in the sequence. We can store such a title in an instance variable of type string.

Some of the useful operations on datasets are the following:

- an explicit-value constructor to initialize our instance variables using values read from a file (since datasets are often stored in files)
- an accessor method to retrieve the *title* attribute
- an accessor method to retrieve the *sequence* attribute
- an accessor method to retrieve the *i*th data value in the sequence
- an output method to display the dataset
- methods to compute various statistics on the dataset, including:
  - minimum value
  - maximum value

- mean (average) value
- median value
- standard deviation

The declaration in Figure 10.7 implements the preceding rudimentary outline for our dataset class. In the remainder of this section, we will give definitions of the operations that are highlighted in color; the others are left as exercises.

Fig. 10.7 A `Dataset` Class declaration. (Part 1 of 2)

```
/* Dataset.h provides a class to represent datasets.
 * ...
 ****************************************************************/

#include <iostream>                       // ostream
#include <fstream>                        // ifstream
#include <vector>                         // vector
#include <string>                         // string
#include <cassert>                        // assert()
using namespace std;

class Dataset
{
  public:
    // constructor
    Dataset(const string& fileName);

    // accessors
    string         getTitle()          const;
    vector<double> getValues()         const;
    double         getValue(int index) const;

    // output
    void           print(ostream& out) const;

    // statistics
    double         getMin()            const;
    double         getMax()            const;
    double         getMean()           const;
    double         getMedian()         const;
    double         getStandardDev()    const;

    // ... other operations omitted ...
```

Fig. 10.7 A `Dataset` Class declaration. (Part 2 of 2)

```
 private:
    string          myTitle;
    vector<double> myValues;
};
```

A DATASET CONSTRUCTOR

To initialize the attribute variables with data from a file, we first must open an `ifstream` to that file and then check that it has opened successfully. Then to initialize `myTitle`, we will first `peek()` at the first character in the file to see if it is alphabetic. If it is, we will read the rest of that line into `myTitle`; but if it is not, we will set `myTitle` to a default value. To initialize `myValues`, we will need to use an input loop like that in Figure 10.4 and then close the `ifstream` from which we are reading.

The only tricky part of this operation is determining whether the first line of the file is the title. We peek at the first character, and if it is an alphabetic character, we assume that the first line is the title of the dataset; otherwise, we set `myTitle` to a default title. This approach works correctly, so long as the title of the dataset begins with an alphabetic character.

Figure 10.8 gives a definition of an explicit-value constructor that behaves in this manner. Since it is nontrivial, we place this definitions in a separately compiled implementation file `Dataset.cpp`.

Fig. 10.8 A `Dataset` constructor. (Part 1 of 2)

```
/* Dataset.cpp defines nontrivial Dataset operations.
 * ...
 *************************************************************/

#include "Dataset.h"
#include <cctype>                          // isalpha()
#include <numeric>                         // accumulate()
#include <algorithm>                       // sort()
using namespace std;

Dataset::Dataset(const string& fileName)
{
  ifstream fin( fileName.data() );  // open stream
  assert( fin.is_open() );          // validate

  char ch = fin.peek();             // check for title
```

Fig. 10.8 A Dataset constructor. (Part 2 of 2)

```
   if ( isalpha(ch) )                  // if present
      getline(fin, myTitle);           //    initialize myTitle
   else
      myTitle = "Untitled data set"; //    set default title

   double aValue;
   for (;;)                            // initialize myValues
   {
      fin >> aValue;                   //    read a value
      if ( fin.eof() ) break;          //    if successful
      myValues.push_back(aValue);      //      append it to myValues
   }
   fin.close();                        // close the stream
}
```

THE getTitle() AND getValue() ACCESSORS

As is often the case, the accessor methods are almost trivial; getTitle() simply returns the value of myTitle; and getValue(*i*) checks its preconditions and then retrieves the value at index *i* within myValues. Because they are so simple, we inline these functions as shown in Figure 10.9.

Fig. 10.9 Definitions of some Dataset accessors.

```
/* Dataset.h provides a class to represent datasets.
 * ...
 ****************************************************************/

// ... #includes and other Dataset operations omitted
 ...
// ... end of class declaration

inline string Dataset::getTitle() const
{
   return myTitle;
}

inline double Dataset::getValue(int index) const
{
   assert(0 <= index && index < myValues.size());
   return myValues[index];
}
```

THE getMean() METHOD

In Figure 10.6, we saw how to compute the mean of a sequence of values stored in a vector<T>. Our getMean() method uses essentially the same approach. Because this is somewhat more complex than the accessors in Figure 10.9, we define it in the implementation file Dataset.cpp, as shown in Figure 10.10.

Fig. 10.10 Computing the mean of a Dataset.

```
/* Dataset.cpp defines nontrivial Dataset operations.
 * ...
 ******************************************************************/

// ... #includes and other Dataset operations omitted

double Dataset::getMean() const
{
   assert( !myValues.empty() );
   double sum = accumulate(myValues.begin(), myValues.end(), 0.0);
   return sum / myValues.size();
}
```

THE getMedian() METHOD

The mean of a dataset is the average value in a dataset. The median is a value *m* such that one-half of the values in the dataset are less than or equal to *m* and one-half of them are greater than or equal to *m*. In some cases, the median provides a better indicator of the "middle value" of a dataset than does the mean.

One way to compute the median is to sort the dataset. For an odd number of values, the middle value of the sorted dataset is the median; for an even number of values, the average of the two middle values can be taken as the median. Figure 10.11 gives a definition of getMedian() that uses this approach. As before, this is a nontrivial operation, and so we define it (along with the "helper" function even()) in the implementation file Dataset.cpp.

Fig. 10.11 Computing the median of a Dataset.

```
/* Dataset.cpp defines nontrivial Dataset operations.
 * ...
 ******************************************************************/

// ... #includes and other Dataset operations omitted
```

Fig. 10.11 Computing the median of a `Dataset`.

```
inline bool even(int i)
{
   return i % 2 == 0;
}

double Dataset::getMedian() const
{
   vector<double> copy = myValues;
   sort( copy.begin(), copy.end() );

   int mid = copy.size() / 2,      // integer division
       mid1 = mid - 1;

   if ( even( copy.size() ) )
       return (copy[mid] + copy[mid1]) / 2;
   else
       return copy[mid];
}
```

Note that a *copy* of `myValues` is sorted so that the order of the values in `myValues` is not changed. This is important because the values in `myValues` usually are measurements recorded over time so their order is significant, and a method like `getMedian()` should not alter that order.

TESTING CLASS `Dataset`

Once we have these methods defined, we have a class that provides a significant level of functionality. To test its correctness, we might create some files containing datasets for which it is easy to verify the results produced by the operations in the `Dataset` class. For example, we might place the following entries in the file `data1.txt`,

```
Rainfall Readings
1
2
2
1
1
2
```

and a different, but still easy-to-verify, dataset in `data2.txt`:

```
Temperature Readings
40
30
30
```

Figure 10.12 presents a program that uses the `Dataset` class to compute the mean and median of a dataset stored in a file.

Fig. 10.12 Testing class `Dataset`.

```
// meanAndMedian.cpp

#include "Dataset.h"          // Dataset
#include <iostream>           // cin, cout
using namespace std;

int main()
{
   cout << "\nEnter the name of the data file: ";
   string fileName;
   getline(cin, fileName);
   Dataset dSet(fileName);

   cout << "Dataset: "                        << dSet.getTitle()
        << "\n The mean value is: "           << dSet.getMean()
        << ",\n and the median value is: "    << dSet.getMedian()
        << endl;
}
```

Sample Runs:

```
Enter the name of the data file: data1.txt
Dataset: Rainfall Readings
 the mean value is: 1.5,
 and the median value is: 1.5

Enter the name of the data file: data2.txt
Dataset: Temperature Readings
 the mean value is: 33.3333,
 and the median value is: 30
```

Note how simple this program is. It (and other programs that use our `Dataset` class) can be easy to write because of the functionality provided by the `Dataset` class. Our program need only build an instance of the class, send it the appropriate messages, and output the required information.

NOTE

This is an important goal of object-oriented programming: *Build powerful classes that provide the functionality to solve a wide variety of problems so that programs using those classes are straightforward and easy to write*

Exercises 10.9

The following exercises ask you to add various methods to the DataSet class described in this section. You should also test them with short driver programs like that in Figure 10.12 as Programming Problems 38–45 at the end of this chapter ask you to do.

1. Define the getValues() accessor method whose prototype is given in Figure 10.7.
2. Define the print() output method whose prototype is given in Figure 10.7.
3. Define the getMin() and getMax() accessor methods whose prototypes are given in Figure 10.7.
4. Define the getStandardDev() method whose prototype is given in Figure 10.7.
5. Add a default-value constructor to class Dataset to initialize the instance variables appropriately for an empty dataset.
6. Add a read() mutator to class Dataset that, given the name of a file containing a data set (title and values), sets myTitle to the title and myValues to the values.
7. Add a setTitle() mutator to class Dataset that, given a string, changes myTitle to that string.
8. Add a setValues() mutator to class Dataset that, given a vector<double>, changes myValues to that vector<double>.
9. Add an addValues() mutator to class Dataset that, given a Dataset, appends the values in that Dataset to myValues.

CHAPTER SUMMARY

Key Terms & Notes

algorithm
array
array capacity
array components
array declaration
array elements
array literal
array size or length
base address
binary search
C standard library
capacity
class template
component programming
container
C-style array
dataset
divide-and-conquer
dynamic
element
end-of-string mark
frequency distribution
function template
generic container class
generic function
index
indexed variable
iterator
length attribute
linear insertion sort
linear search
name mangling
null (NUL) character
pivot
queue
quicksort

searching
simple selection sort
size
sorting
stack
Standard Template Library (STL)
subscript operation
subscripted variable
type parameter
`typedef` declaration
`valarray`
`vector<T>`
zero-based

- A simple form of an array declaration is `type name[CAPACITY];`, where `type` is the type of elements in the array, `CAPACITY` is the number of elements the array can store, and `name` is the name of the array. The values in the array `name` will be undefined and will likely contain "garbage" values.
- In an array declaration, it is good programming practice to use an integer constant rather than an integer literal to specify the capacity of the array.
- An array can be initialized with an array literal, `type name[CAPACITY] = {list};`, where `list` is a list of values of type `type` that will be stored in `name[0]`, `name[1]`, ... If there are fewer than `CAPACITY` values in `list`, the remaining components of `name` will be filled with zeros.
- For an array declaration of the form `type name[] = {list};`, the capacity of `name` will be the number of values in `list`.
- C++ arrays are zero-based; that is, the index of the first element is zero.
- For the standard C-string-processing functions to work correctly with a `char` array, the capacity of the array should always be at least one more than the size of the largest string to be stored in the array so there is room for the null character that is used as an end-of-string mark.
- The value at index `i` in an array named `name` can be accessed using the subscript operator in an expression of the form `name[i]`.
- A `for` loop whose loop-control variable is an array index is useful for implementing array operations, because it can vary this index in an indexed variable.
- Arrays may be passed to functions via parameters and may also be returned by functions.
- Arrays are automatically passed as reference parameters.
- Two significant limitations on C-style arrays are:
  - Their capacity cannot change during program execution.
  - They are not self-contained, which violates the spirit of OOP.
- `valarrays` are designed to carry out vector operations very efficiently. Also, unlike C-style arrays, they have several built-in operations.
- Simple selection sort repeatedly selects one element of a list— for example, the smallest—and correctly positions it.
- Linear insertion sort inserts list elements into an already-sorted sublist.
- Quicksort uses a divide-and-conquer approach to sort a list recursively and is one of the fastest sorting methods for large lists.
- Linear search can be used with any list. Binary search is faster than linear search, but can only be used with ordered lists.

- The `vector<T>` class template is an array-based container whose capacity can increase to accommodate new elements.
- The index of the first value of a `vector<T>` object *v* is always 0; the index of the last value is `v.size() - 1`. The subscript operator `[]` can be used to access any of the elements in this range.
- The subscript operator should not be used to append values to a `vector<T>` because it will not update the size of the `vector<T>` or cause the capacity to increase if the `vector<T>` is full. The `push_back()` method should always be used instead.
- An important goal of object-oriented programming is to build powerful classes that provide the functionality to solve a wide variety of problems so that programs using those classes are straightforward and easy to write.

Programming Pointers

Program Style and Design

1. *C-style arrays, valarrays, and* `vector<T>`*s can be used to store sequences of values* since the elements of an array, `valarray`, or `vector<T>` all have the same type.
2. *If a problem involves a sequence of unknown or varying length, or requires the use of an operation that is predefined for a* `vector<T>`*, store the sequence in a* `vector<T>` *instead of in a C-style array or a valarray.* The `vector<T>` class template provides a standardized, variable-capacity, self-contained object for storing sequences of values, and STL provides many predefined `vector<T>` operations.
3. *Do not reinvent the wheel.* When a problem requires an operation on a `vector<T>`, thoroughly review the `vector<T>` function members and STL algorithms to see if the operation is already defined or if there are other operations that make yours easier to implement.
4. *When using C-style arrays, always define their capacity using a constant, not a literal.* Such a constant can be used to control `for` loops, passed to functions, and so on, which simplifies program maintenance if the array must be resized.

Potential Pitfalls

1. *In C++, the subscript operator is a pair of square brackets, not a pair of parentheses.* An attempt to access element `i` of an array `a` by using `a(i)` will be interpreted by the C++ compiler as a call to a function named `a`, passing it the argument `i`. A compile-time error will result unless such a function exists, in which case a logical error will result.
2. *The first element of a C++ array,* `valarray`*, or* `vector<T>` *has the index value 0—not 1, as in many programming languages.* Forgetting this can produce some puzzling results. To illustrate, suppose that a programmer attempts to fill and output a `char` array named `anArray` as follows:

```
//...
for (int i = 1, i < CAPACITY; i++)   // read in elem-by-elem
   cin.get(anArray[i]);
//...
cout << anArray;                     // display A
```

If the user enters

```
WXYZ
```

no output will be produced. The reason for this is that the contents of `anArray` are

anArray	\0	W	X	Y	Z	\0	\0	\0	. . .
	[0]	[1]	[2]	[3]	[4]	[5]	[6]	[7]	. . .

because all the array elements were initialized to the NUL character. Because the first element of the array contains the NUL character (which is used to terminate character strings), all predefined operations will treat that array as though it contains the empty string.

3. *A character string literal is invisibly terminated with the NUL character* `'\0'`, *and a character array must leave room for this character.* Most of the standard operations for processing character arrays use the NUL character as an end-of-string marker. If a program mistakenly constructs a character array containing no terminating character or somehow overwrites the terminating character of a string with some nonnull value, the results are unpredictable, but can easily produce a run-time error.
4. *No checking is performed to ensure that array,* `valarray`, *or* `vector<T>` *indices stay within the range of valid indices.* As the program in Figure 10.2 demonstrates, out-of-range indices can produce obscure errors whose source can be very difficult to find.
5. *Array arguments are automatically passed by reference; thus, if a function changes an array parameter, the corresponding array argument will also be changed.* If a function has an array parameter through which a value is being passed back to its caller, it is a mistake to declare the array as a reference parameter. If a function has an array parameter that is being received, but not returned, that parameter should be declared as a `const` parameter.
6. *Always append new values to a* `vector<T>` *using its* `push_back()` *function member.* The size, capacity, and iterators of a `vector<T>` are all correctly updated by `push_back()`. None of these are updated by the subscript operator, however, so it should never be used to append values to (or insert values beyond the size of) a `vector<T>`.
7. *When nesting STL templates (or using the STL* `stack`, `queue`, *or* `priority_queue` *adaptors), leave a space between the two* `>` *symbols.* A common mistake is to forget this and write

```
vector<vector<int>> myGrid;
```

to define `myGrid` as a vector of vectors. The compiler will read the `>>` as the output operator, and since this makes no sense in this context, a compilation error will result. The proper approach is to leave a space:

```
vector< vector<int> > myGrid;
```

Programming Problems

Section 10.2

1. Write a driver program to test the min and max functions of Exercises 19 and 20.
2. Write a driver program to test the range function of Exercise 21.
3. Write a driver program to test the ascending-order function of Exercise 22.
4. Write a driver program to test the insert function of Exercise 23.
5. Write a driver program to test the remove function of Exercise 24.
6. The Rinky Dooflingy Company records the number of cases of dooflingies produced each day over a four-week period. Write a program that reads these production numbers and stores them

in an array. The program should then accept from the user a week number and a day number and should display the production level for that day. Assume that each week consists of five workdays.

7. The Rinky Dooflingy Company maintains two warehouses, one in Chicago and one in Detroit, each of which stocks at most 25 different items. Write a program that first reads the product numbers of items stored in the Chicago warehouse and stores them in an array `Chicago`, and then repeats this for the items stored in the Detroit warehouse, storing these product numbers in an array `Detroit`. The program should then find and display the *intersection* of these two lists of numbers; that is, the collection of product numbers common to both sequences. The lists should not be assumed to have the same number of elements.

8. Repeat Problem 7, but find and display the *union* of the two lists, that is, the collection of product numbers that are elements of at least one of the sequences of numbers.

9. Suppose that a row of closed mailboxes are numbered 1 through 150 and that, beginning with mailbox 2, we open the doors of all the even-numbered mailboxes. Next, beginning with mailbox 3, we go to every third mail box, opening its door if it is closed and closing it if it is open. We repeat this procedure with every fourth mailbox, then every fifth mailbox, and so on. Using an array to model the mailboxes, write a program to determine which mailboxes will be closed when this procedure is completed.

10. If $\bar{x}$ denotes the mean of a sequence of numbers $x_1, x_2, \ldots, x_n$, the *variance* is the average of the squares of the deviations of the numbers from the mean,

$$variance = \frac{1}{n}\sum_{i=1}^{n}(x_i - \bar{x})^2$$

and the *standard deviation* is the square root of the variance. Write functions to calculate the mean, variance, and standard deviation of the values stored in an array and a driver program to test your functions.

11. Write a program that reads a list of real numbers representing numeric scores, stores them in an array, calls the functions from Problem 10 to calculate their mean and standard deviation, and then calls another function to display the letter grade corresponding to each numeric score as determined using the grading-on-the-curve method described in Problem 15 at the end of Chapter 9.

12. A prime number is an integer greater than 1 whose only positive divisors are 1 and the integer itself. The Greek mathematician Eratosthenes developed an algorithm, known as the *Sieve of Eratosthenes*, for finding all prime numbers less than or equal to a given number n; that is, all primes in the range 2 through n. Consider the list of numbers from 2 through n. Two is the first prime number, but the multiples of 2 (4, 6, 8, . . .) are not, and so they are crossed out in the list. The first number after 2 that was not crossed out is 3, the next prime. We then cross out from the list all higher multiples of 3 (6, 9, 12, . . .). The next number not crossed out is 5, the next prime, and so we cross out all higher multiples of 5 (10, 15, 20, . . .). We repeat this procedure until we reach the first number in the list that has not been crossed out and whose square is greater than n. All the numbers that remain in the list are the primes from 2 through n. Write a program that uses this sieve method and an array to find all the prime numbers from 2 through n. Run it for $n = 50$ and for $n = 500$.

Section 10.3

13. Write and test a method for simple selection sort.

14. Write and test a method for linear insertion sort.

15. Write and test a method for quicksort.

16. Write and test a method for double-ended selection sort described in Exercise 9.

17. The investment company of Pickum & Loozem has been recording the trading price of a particular stock over a 15-day period. Write a program that reads these prices and sorts them into increasing order, using one of the sort methods in Problems 13–16. The program should display the trading range (i.e., the lowest and the highest prices recorded) and also the median price. (See the discussion preceding Figure 10.11.)

Section 10.4

18. Write and test a method for linear search.

19. Write and test a method for binary search.

20. The Rinky Dooflingy Company manufactures different kinds of dooflingies, each identified by a product number. Write a program that reads product numbers and prices and stores these values in two arrays, `number` and `price`; `number[0]` and `price[0]` are the product number and unit price for the first item, `number[1]` and `price[1]` are the product number and unit price for the second item, and so on. The program should then allow the user to select one of the following options:

    (a) Retrieve and display the price of a product whose number is entered by the user. (Use the linear search procedure developed in Problem 17 to determine the index of the specified item in the array number.)

    (b) Print a table displaying the product number and the price of each item.

Section 10.6

21. Write a driver program to test the ascending-order function of Exercise 19.

22. Write a driver program to test the range function of Exercise 20.

23. Write a menu-driven calculator program that allows a user to repeatedly select and perform one of the operations on n-dimensional vectors in Exercises 21–25.

24. Proceed as in Problem 6 for retrieving production levels, but use a `vector<T>` to store the production numbers.

25. Proceed as in Problem 7 for finding the intersection of two lists, but use a `vector<T>` to store the lists.

26. Proceed as in Problem 8 for finding the union of two lists, but use a `vector<T>` to store the lists.

27. Proceed as in Problem 9, but use a `vector<T>` to model the mailboxes.

28. Proceed as in Problem 10 for calculating the mean, variance, and standard deviation of a sequence of scores, but use a `vector<T>` to store the scores.

29. Proceed as in Problem 11 for grading on the curve, but use `vector<T>`s instead of arrays.

30. Proceed as in Problem 12 for finding prime numbers using the Sieve Method of Eratosthenes, but use a `vector<T>` instead of an array.

31. Proceed as in Problem 16 for finding the range of stock prices, but store the prices in a `vector<T>` and use STL's `sort` algorithm to sort the prices.

32. Proceed as in Problem 19 for processing product numbers and prices, but use `vector<T>`s instead of arrays.

33. Write a function to perform addition of large integers, for which there is no limit on the number of digits. (*Suggestion:* Treat each number as a sequence, each of whose elements is a block of digits of the number. For example, the integer 179,534,672,198 might be stored with

block[0] = 198, block[1] = 672, block[2] = 534, and block[3] = 179. Then add the integers (lists) element by element, carrying from one element to the next when necessary.) Write a driver program to test your function.

34. Proceed as in Problem 32, but for subtraction of large integers.
35. Proceed as in Problem 32, but for multiplication of large integers.
36. Proceed as in Problem 32, but for division of large integers.
37. Write a big-integer calculator program that allows the user to enter two large integers and the operation to be performed and that calls the appropriate function from Problems 32–35 to carry out the designated operation.

Section 10.9

38. Write a driver program to test the Dataset class with the getValues() accessor method of Exercise 1 added.
39. Write a driver program to test the Dataset class with the print() output of Exercise 2 added.
40. Write a driver program to test the Dataset class with the getMin() and getMax() accessor methods of Exercise 3 added.
41. Write a driver program to test the Dataset class with the getStandardDev() method of Exercise 4 added.
42. Write a driver program to test the Dataset class with the default-value constructor of Exercise 5 added.
43. Write a driver program to test the Dataset class with the read() mutator of Exercise 6 added.
44. Write a driver program to test the Dataset class with the setTitle() and setValues() mutators of Exercises 7 and 8 added.
45. Write a driver program to test the Dataset class with the addValues() mutator of Exercise 9 added.

CHAPTER 11

Building Classes

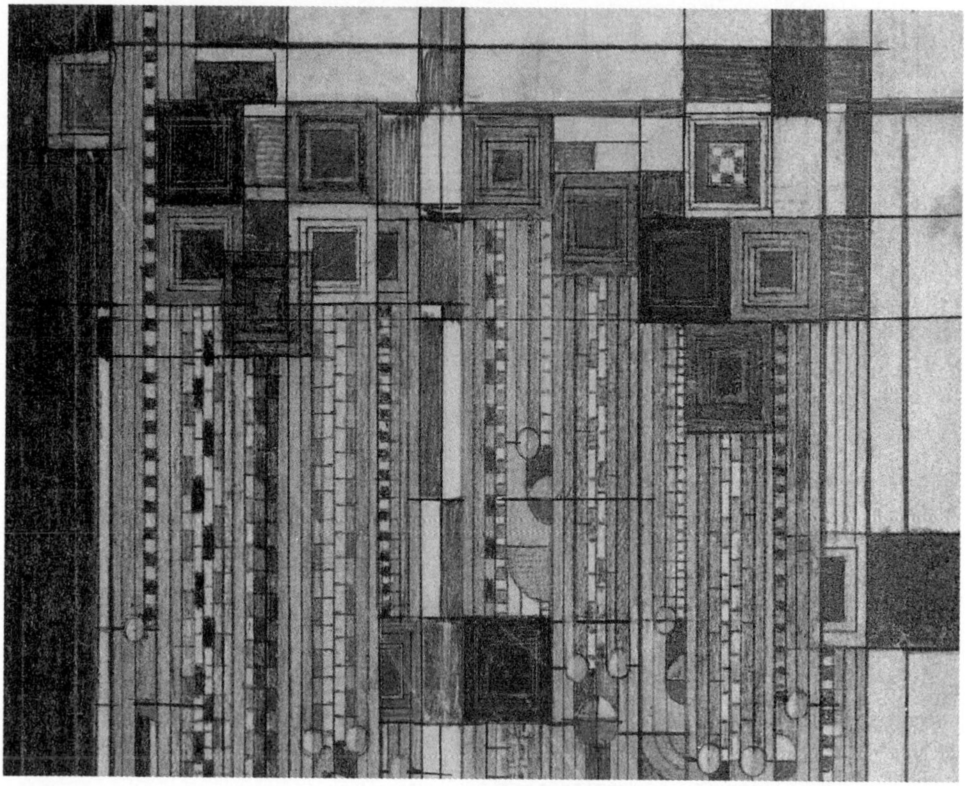

The old order changeth, yielding place to new.

-Alfred, Lord Tennyson

. . . All manner of things—everything that begins with an M . . . such as mousetraps, and the moon, and memory, and muchness—you know you say things are "much of a muchness."

-The Dormouse in Lewis Carroll's
-Alice's Adventures in Wonderland

I'd never join a club that would accept someone like me as a member.

-Groucho Marx

If this stuff were easy, everyone and their parents would be doing it.

-V. Orehck III (fictitious)

Chapter Contents

Chapter Objectives

- See an example of how OCD is applied in a problem where there are no predefined types for some of the objects.
- Learn how classes are designed and built.
- Study the ideas of encapsulation and information hiding that underlie class design.
- See how to implement attributes as instance variables.
- Describe the roles of
  - → class constructors,
  - → accessor methods,
  - → mutator methods,
  - → converter methods, and
  - → utility methods.
- Illustrate the preceding features by building a complete class to model temperatures.
- See how operators can be overloaded.
- See how input and output operators can be overloaded.
- (Optional) Give an overview of artificial intelligence and some of the topics of study in this area of computer science.

We have seen that designing a C++ program involves identifying the objects in a problem and then using types to create software representations of those objects. Once these objects are created, programming consists of applying to those objects the operations needed to solve the problem.

We have also seen that when there is no predefined type that suffices to model an object, the C++ class can be used to create a new type to represent the object. Classes thus provide a way to extend the C++ language, allowing it to represent an ever-increasing number of objects.

Until now, we have for the most part *used* classes that someone else built. In this chapter, we learn how to *build* them ourselves and study the ideas of encapsulation and information hiding that underlie class design. If you have been reading the optional *OBJECTive Thinking* sections of the preceding chapters, this chapter will review and reinforce the content of those earlier sections. If you have not been reading them, you may wish to go back and do so after studying the material in this chapter to review and reinforce the concepts we present here.

The *OBJECTive Thinking* section in this chapter deals with *operator overloading* and *friend functions*, which are important topics. For this reason, we have not marked this section as optional, since we recommend that it be covered.

11.1 Introductory Example: Modeling Temperatures

As usual, we begin with a problem.

PROBLEM: TEMPERATURE CONVERSION

Write a program that, given a temperature in Fahrenheit, Celsius, or Kelvin, will display the equivalent temperature in each of the scales.

PRELIMINARY ANALYSIS

In Chapter 4, we saw that a Fahrenheit temperature could be modeled using a `double` variable,

```
double tempFahrenheit = 0.0;     // Brrrrr!
```

because such an object has only a single attribute—its number of degrees. However, the problem here is to model a temperature having two attributes—its *number* of *degrees* and its *scale* (Fahrenheit, Celsius, or Kelvin). Of course, we could model this using two variables:

```
char myScale = 'F';
double myDegrees = 0.0;
```

But this requires two data items (`myScale` and `myDegrees`) to model a single object (a temperature). To apply some function `g()` to a temperature, we would have to pass it each of the data items used in our model,

```
g(myScale, myDegrees);
```

instead of being able to pass a single object:

```
g(theTemperature);
```

Similarly, displaying a temperature would require an output statement like

```
cout << myDegrees << myScale;
```

instead of simply

```
cout << theTemperature;
```

This approach is not too inconvenient for objects that can be described with two attributes, but it quickly becomes unmanageable as the complexity of the object being modeled increases. Just think how many data items would be needed to represent a tax form like that shown in Figure 11.1.

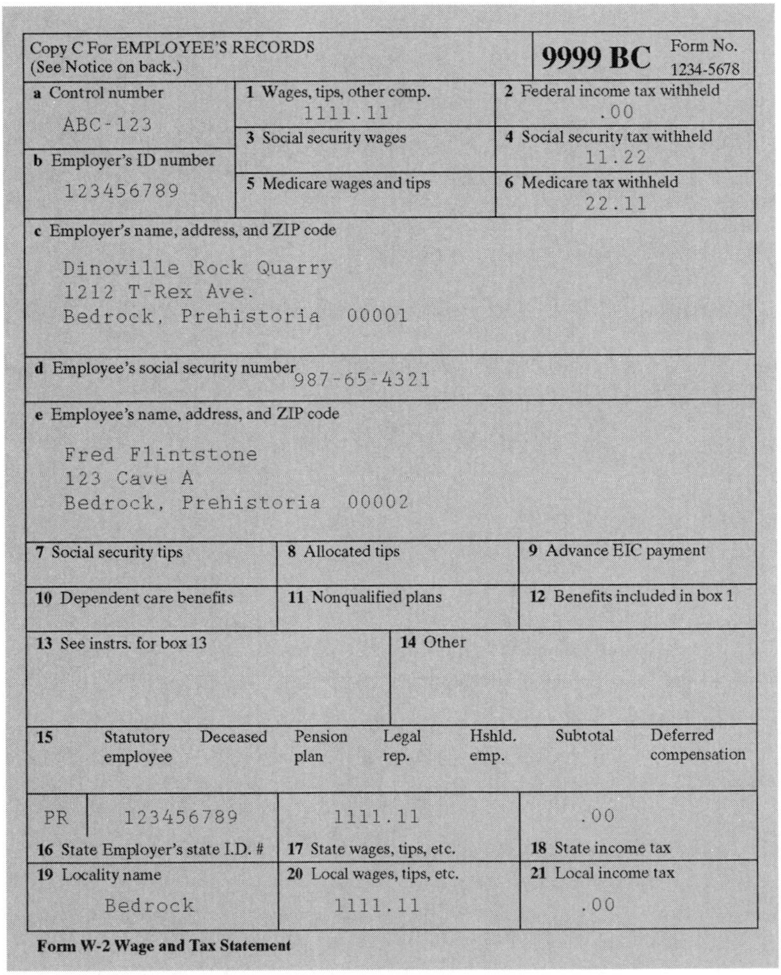

Copy C For EMPLOYEE'S RECORDS
(See Notice on back.)
9999 BC Form No. 1234-5678
a Control number ABC-123
1 Wages, tips, other comp. 1111.11
2 Federal income tax withheld .00
3 Social security wages
4 Social security tax withheld 11.22
b Employer's ID number 123456789
5 Medicare wages and tips
6 Medicare tax withheld 22.11
c Employer's name, address, and ZIP code
Dinoville Rock Quarry
1212 T-Rex Ave.
Bedrock, Prehistoria 00001
d Employee's social security number 987-65-4321
e Employee's name, address, and ZIP code
Fred Flintstone
123 Cave A
Bedrock, Prehistoria 00002
7 Social security tips
8 Allocated tips
9 Advance EIC payment
10 Dependent care benefits
11 Nonqualified plans
12 Benefits included in box 1
13 See instrs. for box 13
14 Other
15 Statutory employee Deceased Pension plan Legal rep. Hshld. emp. Subtotal Deferred compensation
PR 123456789
16 State Employer's state I.D. #
1111.11
17 State wages, tips, etc.
.00
18 State income tax
19 Locality name Bedrock
20 Local wages, tips, etc. 1111.11
21 Local income tax .00
Form W-2 Wage and Tax Statement

Fig. 11.1 An income tax form.

EXTENDING OBJECT-CENTERED DESIGN

In Chapter 4, we extended object-centered design to situations where some *operation* needed to solve a problem is not predefined:

1. Identify the behavior required to solve the problem.
2. Identify the objects.
3. Identify the operations.

   For each operation that is not predefined:
   - **a.** **Define a function to perform that operation.**
   - **b.** **If that operation is reusable, store it in a library.**
4. Organize the objects and operations into an algorithm.
5. Encode the algorithm in C++.
6. Test and maintain the program.

In the temperature problem, however, we have a situation that is not covered by these rules: The object (a `Temperature`) has a *type* that is not predefined. In Chapter 5, we suggested that when an object has multiple attributes, making it impossible to represent it with predefined types, a C++ class can be used to create a new type that has those attributes. Thus, we need to extend object-centered design again to cover this new situation:

1. Identify the behavior required to solve the problem.
2. Identify the objects.

   For each object that cannot be directly represented with the existing types:
   - **a.** **Design and build a class to represent such objects.**
   - **b.** **Store it in a class library.**
3. Identify the operations.

   For each operation that is not predefined:

   If the operation is an operation on a class object from Step 2a

   Design and build a class method to perform that operation.

   Otherwise
   - **a.** Design and build a function to perform that operation.
   - **b.** If the operation is reusable, store it in a library.
4. Organize the objects and operations into an algorithm.
5. Encode the algorithm in C++.
6. Test and maintain the program.

For the temperature problem, therefore, we should create a `Temperature` class containing both the scale and degrees of an arbitrary temperature and function members to perform temperature conversions. Given such a class, solving the problem is straightforward.

Object-Centered Design

Behavior. Our program should display on the screen a prompt for a temperature (degrees and scale) and should then read a temperature from the keyboard. It should then display the Fahrenheit, Celsius, and Kelvin equivalents of that temperature.

Objects. We can identify the following objects in our problem:

	Software Objects		
Problem Objects	**Type**	**Kind**	**Name**
A temperature	`Temperature`	varying	*theTemperature*
Its Fahrenheit equivalent	`Temperature`	varying	none
Its Celsius equivalent	`Temperature`	varying	none
Its Kelvin equivalent	`Temperature`	varying	none

Operations. The operations needed to solve this problem are as follows:

i. Display a string on the screen
ii. Read a *Temperature* from an `istream`
iii. Determine the Fahrenheit equivalent of a *Temperature*
iv. Determine the Celsius equivalent of a *Temperature*
v. Determine the Kelvin equivalent of a *Temperature*
vi. Display a *Temperature* to an `ostream`

Here, only Operation i is predefined. The `Temperature` class will have function members that perform Operations ii–vi.

Algorithm. Assuming the availability of a `Temperature` class that provides Operations ii–vi, we can organize the preceding operations into the following algorithm:

Algorithm for Temperature Conversion

1. Via `cout`, display a prompt for a temperature.
2. From `cin`, read a temperature into *theTemperature*.
3. Via `cout`, display
   a. the Fahrenheit equivalent of *theTemperature*,
   b. the Celsius equivalent of *theTemperature*,
   c. the Kelvin equivalent of *theTemperaure*.

Coding. Given a `Temperature` class (stored in a header file `Temperature.h`) that provides the required operations, we can encode this algorithm in C++ as shown in Figure 11.2.

Fig. 11.2 A temperature-conversion program. (Part 1 of 2)

```
/* tempConversion.cpp displays a temperature in Fahrenheit,
 * Celsius, and Kelvin, using class Temperature.
 *
 *  Input:  an arbitrary Temperature
 *  Output: its Fahrenheit, Celsius and Kelvin equivalents
 *****************************************************************/

#include <iostream>                         // >>, <<, cin, cout
using namespace std;
#include "Temperature.h"                    // Temperature

int main()
{
   cout << "This program shows the Fahrenheit, Celsius, and\n"
           "Kelvin equivalents of a temperature.\n\n";

   char response;
   Temperature theTemperature;               // construction

   do
   {
      cout << "Enter a temperature (e.g., 98.6 F): ";

      theTemperature.read(cin);              // input

      cout << "--> ";                        // output
      theTemperature.inFahrenheit().print(cout);
      cout << " == ";
      theTemperature.inCelsius().print(cout);
      cout << " == ";
      theTemperature.inKelvin().print(cout);
      cout << endl;
```

Fig. 11.2 A temperature-conversion program. (Part 2 of 2)

```
      cout << "\nDo you have more temperatures to convert? ";
      cin >> response;
   }
   while (response == 'Y' || response == 'y');
}
```

Sample run:

```
This program shows the Fahrenheit, Celsius, and
Kelvin equivalents of a temperature.

Enter a temperature (e.g., 98.6 F): 212 F
--> 212 F == 100 C == 373.15 K

Do you have more temperatures to convert? Y
Enter a temperature (e.g., 98.6 F): 0 C
--> 32 F == 0 C == 273.15 K

Do you have more temperatures to convert? Y
Enter a temperature (e.g., 98.6 F): 100 K
--> -279.67 F == -173.15 C == 100 K

Do you have more temperatures to convert? N
```

We will design and build the `Temperature` class in the following sections, and use it to illustrate the principles of class design.

11.2 Designing a Class

As with programs, creating a class consists of two phases:

1. the design phase in which we plan the class;
2. the implementation phase in which we encode this design in C++.

This section explores the first phase. Sections 11.3 and 11.4 will examine the implementation phase.

CLASS DESIGN

Designing a class consists of identifying two things:

- its **behavior:** the *operations* that can be applied to a class object;
- its **attributes:** the *data* that must be stored to characterize a class object.

The behavior is usually identified first, because it is often not obvious what the attributes of the class should be, and identifying the class behavior can sometimes clarify them. Also, if the behaviors are identified first, before any of the attribute details are fixed, they will be independent of any particular details of how the attributes are implemented. This *independence from implementation details* is very important in good class design.

THE EXTERNAL AND INTERNAL PERSPECTIVES

Up to now, our approach to programming has mostly been that of an observer looking from outside the program into its details. Since we reside outside the program, this is a natural way to begin, and as long as we are merely *using* predefined classes, this **external perspective** is adequate.

One of the basic ideas in class design is **object autonomy**, embodied in **the I-can-do-it-myself principle**, which means that an object should carry within itself the ability to perform its operations. That is, rather than viewing a class operation as manipulation of an object by a program, object autonomy views a class operation as an object taking an action. To incorporate the I-can-do-it-myself principle into the design of a class, we must shift our perspective from that of an external observer to that of the object being designed. More precisely, we want to think through our design as though *we are the object*. The resulting approach describes an object in first person terminology, and is called the **internal perspective**.

As a simple illustration of the difference, rather than referring to the `Temperature` data members as *its* degrees and *its* scale (which imply we are outside, looking in), we will refer to them as *my* degrees and *my* scale (indicating that we are the object, looking out). This approach leads to a natural implementation of the I-can-do-it-myself principle, resulting in an autonomous object.

In the sections that follow, we will use *both* perspectives. When working in a program and using a class, we will use the external perspective. When working inside a class or building its function members, we will use the internal perspective.

`Temperature` BEHAVIOR

From an internal perspective, a `Temperature` object must provide the following operations if the program in Figure 11.2 is to work:

i. Define myself *implicitly* by initializing my degrees and scale with default values
ii. Read a temperature from an `istream` and store it in my data members
iii. Compute the Fahrenheit temperature equivalent to me
iv. Compute the Celsius temperature equivalent to me
v. Compute the Kelvin temperature equivalent to me
vi. Display my degrees and scale using an `ostream`

Although these operations suffice to solve the problem at hand, designing a reusable class involves identifying other operations that a user of the class is likely to need. To that end, we might extend our list with the following operations:

vii. Define myself *explicitly* by initializing my degrees and scale with specified values
viii. Identify my number of degrees
ix. Identify my scale
x. Compute my temperature raised by a given number of degrees
xi. Compute my temperature lowered by a given number of degrees
xii. Compare myself to another `Temperature` object using any of the six relational operators (==, `!=`, <, >, <=, >=)
xiii. Assign another `Temperature` value to me using the assignment operator (=)

This is not an exhaustive list, but it is a good start and will serve to introduce the details of class implementation. Other operations can be added later.

The last operation, assignment, is already provided. For any class we define, the C++ compiler creates a *default assignment operation*, so that a statement like

```
temp2 = temp1;
```

can be used to copy the data members of `temp1` into `temp2`. We must implement the other operations ourselves as methods or functions, as described in Section 11.4.

`Temperature` ATTRIBUTES

To identify a class' attributes, it is a good idea to go through the list of behaviors and identify what information each of them requires. If the same information is required by several different operations, then such information is probably one of the object's attributes.

For example, if we examine the first twelve operations in our list, Operations i and vi–xi indicate that, from an internal perspective, a `Temperature` object has the following attributes:

1. my degrees and
2. my scale.

In fact, these are the only attributes needed for class `Temperature`. For other classes, a complete set of attributes may not be evident at the outset. In this case, others can be added later, when the implementation of an operation requires an attribute not on the list.

11.3 Implementing Class Attributes

Once we have a design for a class, we can use it as a blueprint for implementing the class. Since we want the class to be reusable, it is declared in a library header file (e.g., `Temperature.h`) and the nontrivial operations are usually defined in a separately compiled implementation file (e.g., `Temperature.cpp`). As suggested in Chapter 4, the documentation for the class and its function members are commonly put in a separate documentation file (e.g., `Temperature.doc`).

Given a class design that includes its attributes, the first task is to define objects to represent those attributes. For our `Temperature` class, we can represent the number of degrees with a real object, and the scale with a character object. Thus, in `Temperature.h`, we write

```
/* Temperature.h is the header file for class Temperature.
 * ...
 ******************************************************************/

double myDegrees;
char   myScale;        // 'F', 'C', or 'K'
```

These will become the **data members** or **instance variables** of our `Temperature` class. We will begin the names of instance variables with the prefix `my` to indicate that these are attributes of the class and to reflect our internal perspective. And as with all identifiers, the name of a data member should be *self-documenting*, describing the attribute being stored.

IMPLEMENTATION DECISIONS

We could have used `string` to define `myScale` if we wanted to store the entire name of the scale, but we chose `char` instead because temperatures are usually written using a single character for the scale (e.g., 98.6 F, 100 C, 273 K). The best choice in some situations may not be clear, but a decision must be made before we can proceed. Such implementation decisions can always be revised later if they prove unwise.

ENCAPSULATION

Once we have defined objects for the instance variables of our class, we can actually create the class by wrapping a **class declaration** around these objects (again, in `Temperature.h`):

```
class Temperature
{
 public:
```

```
                                       // to be filled in later
   private:
     double myDegrees;
     char   myScale;
  };
```

WATCH OUT

Don't forget the semicolon after the closing curly brace. Like all declarations, a class declaration must be terminated by a semicolon.

This declaration creates a new type named `Temperature`. If we use this type to declare objects as in

```
#include "Temperature.h"
   .
   .
   .
Temperature temp1,
            temp2;
```

then `temp1` and `temp2` are two distinct `Temperature` objects, each containing two instance variables: a `double` named `myDegrees` and a `char` named `myScale`. We might picture these objects as follows:

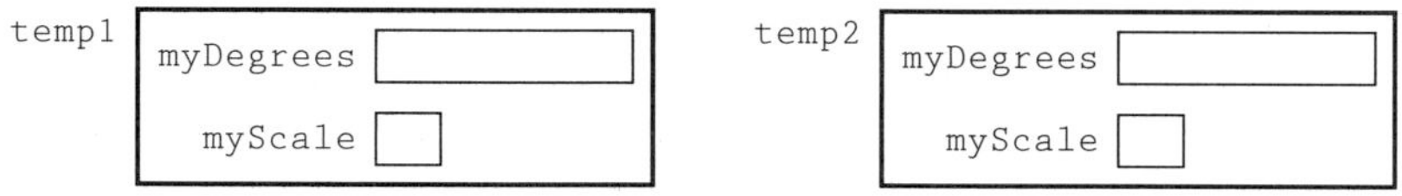

Wrapping the instance variables in a class declaration and then using the class as a type to declare an object makes it possible for an object to store values of different types. In the vocabulary of programming languages, we say that class `Temperature` **encapsulates** the `double` instance variable `myDegrees` and the `char` instance variable `myScale`. Encapsulation allows a single object to store values of different types.

INFORMATION HIDING

We have defined `myScale` as a `char`, but we might decide in the future to define it as a `string` so it could store the name of a temperature scale instead of only its first letter. The possibility that the instance variables of a class may be revised is the reason for preceding their declarations with the keyword `private`. If we omit the `private` specifier, a program can directly access the instance variable `myScale` as in

```
if (temp1.myScale == 'F')
   // do something with Fahrenheit temp1
```

However, if we were to later change the type of `myScale`, this revision would *break* that program, making it necessary to rewrite some of it as well. In some situations, the required revisions may be so extensive that software is not ready on time or is more expensive than was predicted, the obvious result of which is a loss of sales or productivity.

The root of the problem is allowing a programmer to access the instance variables of the class. By making them *private*, we prevent such direct access. If, for example, `myScale` is private and a program tries to access it as before, then an error message such as

```
Member 'myScale' of class 'Temperature' is private
```

will be generated.

This aspect of class design is called **information hiding**. By preventing a program from directly accessing the instance variables of a class, we hide that information, thus removing the temptation to access those variables directly.

It is good programming style to hide all instance variables of a class by making them ***private.***

Once we have the instance variables encapsulated and hidden, we are almost ready to begin implementing the class operations.

CLASS INVARIANTS

Before defining class operations, we should identify any restrictions there may be on the values of the instance variables of our class. For example, we might stipulate that the only valid values for the instance variable `myScale` will be the characters `F`, `C`, or `K`. For the instance variable `myDegrees`, we know of no bound on how high a temperature can go, but we will use absolute zero (0 K, which is equivalent to –273.15° C and –459.67° F) for a lower bound. If we identify and specify such restrictions at the outset, then we can implement the various class operations in a way that ensures that they are observed.

To document such limitations concisely, we usually define a condition (i.e., a boolean expression) that describes the restrictions. We have already said that the value of `myScale` must be one of the characters `F`, `C`, or `K`. From this, we can express the restrictions on the instance variables with the following boolean expression:

```
   myScale == 'F' && myDegrees >= -459.67
|| myScale == 'C' && myDegrees >= -273.15
|| myScale == 'K' && myDegrees >= 0.0
```

Once we have a description of these restrictions, we then want to make certain that nothing we write violates that condition—we want it to be `true`, both before and after each call to a class operation. Because this condition will be true throughout the class, it is called a **class invariant**. When such an invariant can be defined, it is good practice to record it in both the class documentation file and in the header file near the instance variable(s) it governs.

CONDITIONAL COMPILATION AND A CLASS "WRAPPER"

Whenever a program stored in a file is compiled, it is first examined by a special program called the **preprocessor**. The preprocessor scans through the file doing some preliminary analysis before the file is passed on to the compiler itself. For example, the preprocessor strips all comments from the program so that the compiler need not spend time finding them, only to ignore them. Another task of the preprocessor is to process all **preprocessor directives**, which are lines that begin with a # character such as

```
#include FileName
```

When it encounters this directive, the preprocessor finds the file named *`FileName`* and inserts it at that point in the program.

WATCH OUT

For large projects consisting of many library files, it is customary for each file to include whatever class declarations it needs. This means that the same class could be declared in several different places in a project, and this results in an error because C++ does not permit a class to be declared more than once.

However, no error results if the header file `<iostream>` is included more than once. Why? Because the contents of `<iostream>` are wrapped in directives that basically tell the preprocessor, "*If this is the first time you have seen this class, go ahead and process the declaration. If you have seen it before, skip the declaration.*"

Thus, before we proceed to implement the class operations, we need to surround the class `Temperature` with directives that tell the preprocessor to do the same for class `Temperature`:

```
#ifndef TEMPERATURE
#define TEMPERATURE

class Temperature
{
 public:
                          // to be filled in later

 private:                 //             Class invariant:
   double myDegrees;  //      myScale == 'F' && myDegrees >= -459.67
   char   myScale;    //   || myScale == 'C' && myDegrees >= -273.15
                          //   || myScale == 'K' && myDegrees >=  0.0
};

#endif
```

These are called **conditional-compilation directives** because of what they do. The directive

```
#ifndef TEMPERATURE
```

instructs the preprocessor, "*If* `TEMPERATURE` *is not defined, then continue processing as usual. Otherwise, skip everything between here and the first* `#endif` *directive you encounter.*"[1] Because `TEMPERATURE` is undefined the first time the preprocessor examines the file, it proceeds on to the next line. Here it encounters the directive

```
#define TEMPERATURE
```

which defines the identifier `TEMPERATURE`. The preprocessor then continues and processes the class declaration and passes it on to the compiler.

If the preprocessor should encounter `Temperature.h` a second time, the first thing it sees is the directive

```
#ifndef TEMPERATURE
```

---

1. The compiler will also stop skipping text if it encounters a `#else` or `#elif` directive, which behave like the `else` or the `else if` in an `if` statement.

This time, however, `TEMPERATURE` is defined, and so the preprocessor skips everything between that point and the `#endif` directive.

The result is that *the class declaration is only processed once, regardless of how many different files include* `Temperature.h`. Every class should be wrapped in these directives to prevent redeclaration errors if the header file is included more than once in a project. Customarily, the identifier used with the `#ifndef` and `#define` directives (`TEMPERATURE` in this case) is the name of the class in all uppercase letters.

11.4 Implementing Class Operations

Once the attributes of a class are defined, encapsulated, hidden, and wrapped, we are ready to begin implementing the class operations. This is done by writing **methods**, which are also known as **function members**. We will begin our study of how they are defined by looking at a simple example: an output method that displays a `Temperature` via an `ostream` (Operation vi in our list). It is a good practice to define such output operations early, because displaying the instance variables of a class object can help us test the correctness of the remaining operations.

`Temperature` OUTPUT

From an external perspective, the purpose of an output method `print()` is to allow a programmer to display the values that make up a class object. In our case, a programmer should be able to write

```
temp1.print(cout);
```

to display the degrees and scale in a `Temperature` object `temp1` to `cout`, and write

```
temp2.print(cerr);
```

to display the degrees and scale of `temp2` to `cerr`.

As an autonomous object, a `Temperature` should be able to display itself. From the internal perspective, a call to `print()` can thus be viewed as a **message** the program is sending to *you* (a `Temperature` object), with `cout` as an argument—like someone else telling you

"Hey you! Print yourself using `cout`."

The definition of `print()` must therefore provide the instructions that I (a `Temperature` object) apply to my instance variables to perform the operation.

Applying object-centered design from the internal perspective gives the following specification for the operation's behavior:

Receive: *out*, the `ostream` to which information is to be written

Output: `myDegrees` followed by a space and then `myScale`

Send back: *out*, with `myDegrees`, a space, and `myScale` inserted into it

It is important that the specification of a method be phrased from the internal perspective, because we want our operations to reflect the I-can-do-it-myself approach: As a `Temperature` object, when I receive a `print(`*`out`*`)` message, I insert the values stored in `myDegrees` and `myScale` into *`out`*.

Figure 11.3 shows a definition of this operation. Because of its simplicity, we define it using the `inline` specifier, in the header file `Temperature.h`, following the class declaration (but before the `#endif` preprocessor directive).

Fig. 11.3 Displaying a `Temperature`.

```
// ... Class declaration goes here ...

// ------- Output method -----------------------------

inline void Temperature::print(ostream& out) const
{
   out << myDegrees << ' ' << myScale;
}
```

From an external perspective, sending this message to a `Temperature` object will display the instance variables `myDegrees` and `myScale` of that object, so the statement

```
temp1.print(cout);
```

will display the data members of `temp1` via `cout`, while

```
temp2.print(cerr);
```

will display the data members of `temp2` via `cerr`. In Section 1.6, we will see how to overload the output operator (`<<`) to display a `Temperature` value in the usual manner.

Note that as a `Temperature` method, `print()` must be invoked using **dot notation.** Put differently, `print()` must be sent as a message to a `Temperature` object. If we attempt to call `print()` without using dot notation,

```
print(cout);            // ERROR!
```

the compiler will generate an error, because we have not specified a `Temperature` object to receive the message.

In this first look at the definition of a method, we introduced a number of new features, and we will now look at each of these in more detail.

Full Method Names. The first new feature is the name of the method:

```
inline void Temperature::print(ostream& out) const
```

In the definition of a method, *preceding the name of the method by the name of a class and the* **scope operator (::)** *tells the compiler the class to which the method belongs.* The resulting name is called the **fully-qualified name** of the method (or **full name** for short).

WATCH OUT

It is important to use the full name in the definition of methods, because *methods can access the private members of their class, but normal functions cannot.* If the full name is not used in a method's definition, as in

```
inline void print(ostream& out) const    // Not a method
{
   out << myDegrees << ' ' << myScale;    // ERROR!
}
```

the compiler views this as a normal (nonmember) function, and errors like

```
Identifier 'myDegrees' is not defined
Identifier 'myScale' is not defined
```

will be generated, since the private data members of a class are invisible to a nonmember function.

Full names are also important because they permit methods of different classes to have the same name and signature. For example, we might declare classes X, Y, and Z, each having its own print() method. By using the full name to define each print() method, the compiler can distinguish one method definition from another:

```
void X::print(ostream& out)
{
      // send instance variables of X to out...
}
void Y::print(ostream& out)
{
      // send instance variables of Y to out...
}
void Z::print(ostream& out)
{
      // send instance variables of Z to out...
}
```

Constant Methods. The next new feature in print() is the keyword const at the end of the method heading:

```
inline void Temperature::print(ostream & out) const
```

This informs the compiler that print() is a **constant method** of class Temperature, which means that it may not change any of the instance variables. Any attempt to modify an instance variable in this method will be caught by the compiler as an error. *All methods that do not alter the instance variables of the class should be declared as* const *methods.*

NOTE

Before a method's definition will compile correctly, a prototype of that method must be stored inside the class declaration. If the method is to be visible outside of the class, this prototype must be stored in the public section of the class. Also, since the print() prototype refers to the type ostream, we must include the iostream header file:

```
#include <iostream>                          // ostream, ...
using namespace std;

class Temperature
{
 public:
   void print(ostream& out) const;

 private:              //         Class invariant:
   double myDegrees;  //     myScale == 'F' && myDegrees >= -459.67
   char   myScale;    //  || myScale == 'C' && myDegrees >= -273.15
                      //  || myScale == 'K' && myDegrees >= 0.0
};
```

Note that for a constant method, the `const` specifier must also be used in its prototype. Also note that it is not necessary to specify `inline` or the full name of the method within the class itself. Keeping these prototypes simple reduces clutter within the class declaration and thus increases readability. For the same reason, the methods of a class should be documented in a separate file. To complete our method `print()`, therefore, we add documentation for it to the library's documentation file (`Temperature.doc`).

Of course, before the `print()` method is of any use, the instance variables `myDegrees` and `myScale` must contain values. We therefore turn our attention to two operations that can be used to initialize these instance variables.

The Default-Value Constructor

As we have seen, a `Temperature` definition

```
Temperature temp1,
            temp2;
```

defines `temp1` and `temp2` as objects that might be pictured as follows:

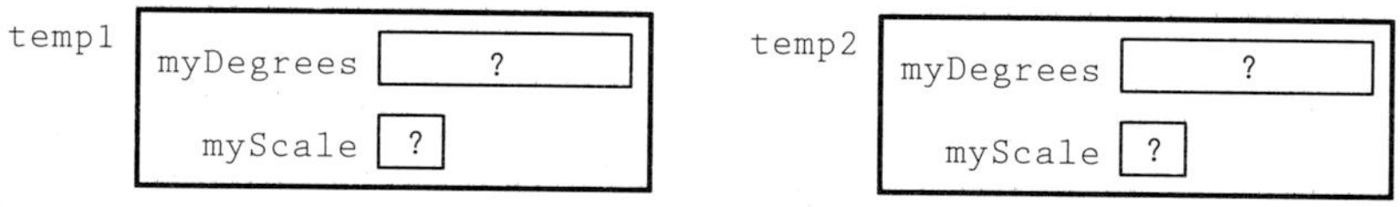

The question marks indicate that the instance variables in these objects are undefined—their values are indeterminate. Some versions of C++ may initialize `myDegrees` to 0 and `myScale` to the null character `'\0'`. In other versions, their initial values may be whatever "garbage values" correspond to the strings of bits in the memory locations allocated to them; for example, one version initialized `myDegrees` to –9.3E61 and `myScale` to a nonexistent character whose numeric code was –52. Since garbage values like these do not represent valid temperatures, we would certainly prefer that the preceding definitions define `temp1` and `temp2` with some default initial value of our choosing (e.g., 0 degrees Celsius) and that satisfies the class invariant:

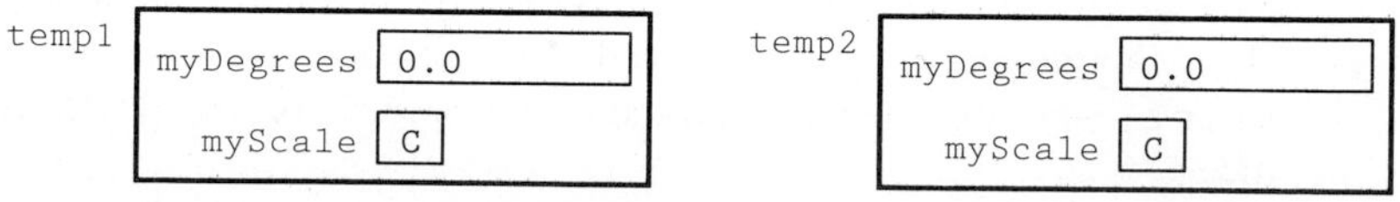

Constructors. C++ allows such initialization behavior to be performed by a class operation. More precisely, to initialize the instance variables of a class, C++ allows us to define special operations called **constructors.** *The name of a constructor is always the same as the name of the class.*

To be autonomous, a `Temperature` object should be able to initialize itself. Applying the I-can-do-it-myself principle, a constructor defines the sequence of actions that I (a `Temperature` object) take to initialize my instance variables when I am defined. Applying object-centered design from this internal perspective gives the following specification for the behavior of this **default-value constructor**:

Postcondition: `myDegrees == 0.0 && myScale == 'C'`

We specify the behavior of a constructor using a **postcondition**, a boolean expression that must be `true` when the operation terminates. A postcondition is needed to specify the behavior, because a constructor (unlike a function) cannot return anything to its caller.

Figure 11.4 shows the definition of a default-value constructor for class `Temperature`. Because of the simplicity of this operation, we define it as `inline` and place its definition in `Temperature.h`, after the declaration of class `Temperature`.

Fig. 11.4 The `Temperature` default-value constructor.

```
// ------- Default-value constructor ------------ ------------

inline Temperature::Temperature()
{
   myDegrees = 0.0;
   myScale = 'C';
}
```

Here again, we see some new features. The first is that there is no return type between `inline` and the method's full name because constructors have no return type, not even `void`. As an initialization operation, a constructor never returns anything to its caller. Its sole purpose is to initialize the instance variables of a class.

Next comes the full name of the operation, in which the first `Temperature` is the name of the class of which the operation is a member, `::` is the scope operator, and then follows the name of the operation:

```
inline Temperature::Temperature()
```

Since the name of a constructor is always the same as the name of its class, the name of the operation is also `Temperature`.

Note that there is no `const` at the end of the constructor's heading. A constructor is not a constant operation because it modifies the instance variables of the class (by initializing them).

We must also store a prototype of this operation in the public section of the class declaration:

```
class Temperature
{
 public:
   Temperature();
   void print(ostream & out) const;

 private:               //            Class invariant:
   double myDegrees; //     myScale == 'F' && myDegrees >= -459.67
   char   myScale;   // || myScale == 'C' && myDegrees >= -273.15
                     // || myScale == 'K' && myDegrees >= 0.0
};
```

As before, we omit the `inline` and use the normal name of the operation instead of its full name. We also add its documentation to `Temperature.doc.`

Given this much, a programmer can now write a short program to test the class declaration and method definitions:

```
#include <iostream>
using namespace std;
#include "Temperature.h"

int main()
{
   Temperature temp1;        // the compiler sends temp1 the
                             //  'initialize yourself' message
   temp1.print(cout);
}
```

When this program is executed, it will display the values

```
0 C
```

This output is produced because whenever the C++ compiler processes the definition of a class object, it searches the class for a constructor it can use to initialize that object. If it finds such a constructor, it invokes that operation to initialize the object.[2] *The constructor is automatically called by the compiler whenever a class object is defined.* For this reason, ***always provide one or more constructors when building a class.***

NOTE

EXPLICIT-VALUE CONSTRUCTORS

The constructor we just defined only allows us to initialize a `Temperature` object to the value 0 degrees Celsius. It would be more useful to allow initializations to arbitrary temperatures. This can be accomplished by overloading the constructor with a second definition that receives the initial values via its parameters. These initial values will be specified in an object's declaration.

---

2. In the case of an `inline` constructor, it actually inserts statements to perform the initialization specified by the body of the constructor:

```
temp1.myDegrees = 0.0;
temp1.myScale = 'C';
```

(Note that such access to the instance variables in statements like these does not violate their privacy; the private section is still protected from direct access by a programmer.)

Unlike the default-value constructor, this operation receives its initialization values from the caller, and so our constructor must supply parameters to hold those values. Since there is the possibility of the caller passing initial values that would produce an invalid temperature value, the method must check them to ensure that the class invariant holds.

From the internal perspective, object-centered design gives us the following specification for the operation's behavior—for user convenience, we are allowing the scale to be in either upper or lower case:

Receive: *initialDegrees*, a `double`
initialScale, a `char`

Precondition: *initialScale* is one of {'f', 'c', 'k', 'F', 'C', 'K'} and *initialDegrees* is valid for *initialScale*

Postcondition: `myDegrees` == *initialDegrees* && `myScale` == *initialScale* in uppercase

Checking Temperature Validity. A similar check will be needed for our input method to verify that the values entered by the user comprise a valid temperature. To avoid redundant coding, we will define a utility method named `isValid()` that, given a `char` and a `double`, returns `true` if and only if they comprise a valid temperature. We can specify its behavior as follows:

Receive: *degrees*, a `double`
scale, a `char`

Return: *true* if *degrees* and *scale* comprise a *valid* temperature and *false* otherwise

Using the restrictions imposed in the class invariant, we have the following algorithm for this method:

Algorithm for Checking Temperature Validity

1. Receive *degrees*, *scale* from caller.
2. If *scale* is 'c' or 'C'
   return the result of comparing *degrees* >= –273.15.
   Else if *scale* is 'f' or 'F'
   return the result of comparing *degrees* >= –459.67.
   Else if *scale* is 'k' or 'K'
   return the result of comparing *degrees* >= 0.0.
   Else
   return false.

Since this algorithm is nontrivial to implement, it should not be defined as an `inline` method. Instead, this method should be defined in the class implementation file (`Temperature.cpp`). Figure 11.5 presents one possible definition.

Fig. 11.5 Checking `Temperature` validity.

```
/* Temperature.cpp defines nontrivial Temperature operations.
 *  ...
 ******************************************************************/

#include "Temperature.h"                    // class Temperature

// ------- Utility method ----------------------------------

bool Temperature::isValid(double degrees, char scale)
{
   switch (scale)
   {
      case 'F': case 'f':                   // Fahrenheit
         return degrees >= MIN_FAHRENHEIT;
      case 'C': case 'c':                   // Celsius
         return degrees >= MIN_CELSIUS;
      case 'K': case 'k':                   // Kelvin
         return degrees >= MIN_KELVIN;
      default:                              // otherwise, invalid
         return false;
   }
}
```

Note that we use three constants `MIN_FAHRENHEIT`, `MIN_CELSIUS`, and `MIN_KELVIN` for our comparisons, rather than the "magic" numbers –459.67, –273.15, and 0.0. Since these constants seem likely to be generally useful, we define them in the class header file `Temperature.h`.

We must also provide a prototype of this method in our class. We could write

```
class Temperature
{
 public:
   // ... other prototypes
   bool isValid(double degrees, char scale) const;

 private:                 //           Class invariant:
   double myDegrees; //     myScale == 'F' && myDegrees >= -459.67
   char   myScale;   // || myScale == 'C' && myDegrees >= -273.15
                     // || myScale == 'K' && myDegrees >= 0.0
};
```

However, such a prototype would make this an *instance method*—a message that must be sent to an *object*. That is, a function would have to invoke this method by writing something like

```
Temperature temp1;
if ( temp1.isValid(someDouble, someChar) )
   // ... do something
```

NOTE

This is unwise, because method `isValid()` does not access any of the instance variables of our class; instead, it gets all of the information it uses via its parameters. When a method does not access the instance variables of a class, it is inefficient to implement that method as an instance method, because instance methods must be sent to an object. Instead, it is preferable to define it as a **class method**, by preceding its prototype with the `static` **modifier**:

```
class Temperature
{
 public:
   // ... other prototypes
   static bool isValid(double degrees, char scale);

 private:              //             Class invariant:
   double myDegrees;   //     myScale == 'F' && myDegrees >= -459.67
   char   myScale;     //  || myScale == 'C' && myDegrees >= -273.15
                       //  || myScale == 'K' && myDegrees >= 0.0
};
```

Class methods are messages that can be sent to a ***class*** *using the scope operator*, instead of to an object using the dot operator. A function can thus use this method as follows:

```
if ( Temperature::isValid(someDouble, someChar) )
   // ... do something
```

As we shall see shortly, a method of the same class can invoke `isValid()` directly, without the inconvenience of specifying the class and the scope operator.

The Explicit-Value Constructor. Once we have an `isValid()` method like that shown in Figure 11.5, we can resume work on our explicit-value constructor. Figure 11.6 presents a definition of this operation. Because of its complexity, it should *not* be designated `inline`. Instead, its definition should be stored in the class implementation file (`Temperature.cpp`) so that it can be compiled separately. Note that the full name of this constructor is exactly the same as the full name of the default-value constructor in Figure 11.4. Like any function, a constructor can be overloaded with multiple definitions, so long as the signature (i.e., list of parameter types) of each definition is distinct.

Fig. 11.6 The `Temperature` explicit-value constructor. (Part 1 of 2)

```
/* Temperature.cpp defines the nontrivial Temperature operations.
 *  ...
 *******************************************************************/
```

Fig. 11.6 The `Temperature` explicit-value constructor. (Part 2 of 2)

```
#include "Temperature.h"                // class Temperature
#include <cctype>                       // islower(), toupper()
#include <cstdlib>                      // exit()
using namespace std;

// ------- Explicit-value constructor ------------------------

Temperature::Temperature(double initialDegrees, char initialScale)
{
  if ( isValid(initialDegrees, initialScale) )
  {
    if (islower(initialScale))              // if scale is lowercase
      initialScale = toupper(initialScale); // convert it to uppercase

    myDegrees = initialDegrees;             //  proceed with
    myScale = initialScale;                 //  initialization
  }                                         // otherwise, error msg
  else
  {
    cerr << "\n*** Temperature constructor received invalid params "
         << initialDegrees << ' ' << initialScale << endl;
    exit(1);
  }
}
```

To use this operation, we must place its prototype in the public portion of class `Temperature`:

```
class Temperature
{
 public:
   Temperature();
   Temperature(double initialDegrees, char initialScale);
   static bool isValid(double degrees, char scale);
   void print(ostream & out) const;

 private:               //           Class invariant:
   double myDegrees;    //    myScale == 'F' && myDegrees >= -459.67
   char   myScale;      // || myScale == 'C' && myDegrees >= -273.15
                        // || myScale == 'K' && myDegrees >= 0.0
};
```

We also add its documentation to `Temperature.doc`.

Given this prototype, a programmer can now write

```
#include <iostream>
#include "Temperature.h"
using namespace std;

int main()
{
   Temperature temp1(98.6, 'F'),
               temp2;

   temp1.print(cout); cout << endl;
   temp2.print(cout); cout << endl;
}
```

When this program is compiled and linked to the `Temperature` object file, the values

```
98.6 F
0 C
```

will be displayed when the program is executed. In the definitions

```
Temperature temp1(98.6, 'F'),
            temp2;
```

the object `temp1` is constructed using the explicit-value constructor, and `temp2` is constructed using the default-value constructor. These objects are thus initialized as follows:

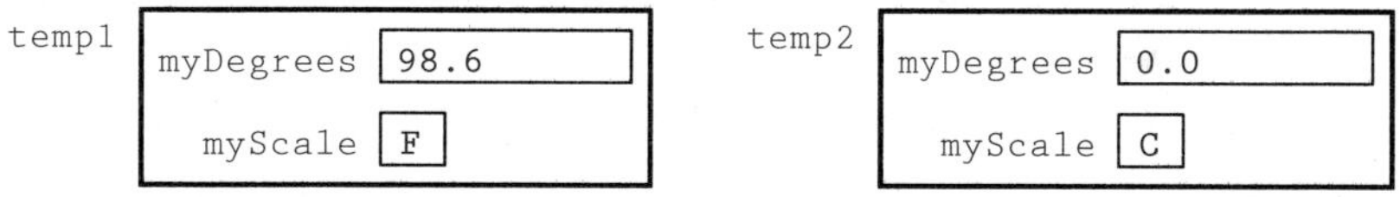

Class Object Initialization. The syntax of the explicit-value constructor deserves comment. As noted earlier, when the C++ compiler processes the definition of a class object, it searches the class for a constructor it can use to initialize the object. When it sees a "normal" class object definition (without arguments) like

```
Temperature temp2;
```

the compiler searches the class for a constructor that has no parameters. Finding one, it uses that constructor to perform the initialization.

When the compiler sees a class object definition for which arguments are specified,

```
Temperature temp1(98.6, 'F');
```

it searches the class for a constructor whose signature matches the types of the arguments. When it finds such a constructor, the compiler inserts a call to that constructor to perform the initialization.

This syntax should not seem completely unfamiliar. In Chapter 9, we saw that an `ifstream` object can be initialized with the name of a file; for example,

```
ifstream inStream("weather.dat");
```

Such a statement is using an `ifstream` explicit-value constructor to open the stream to the file whose name it is passed as an argument.

According to the C++ standard, any object can be initialized in this way. Instead of writing

```
double sum = 0.0;
char middleInitial = 'C';
```

we could write

```
double sum(0.0);
char middleInitial('C');
```

The C++ standard actually suggests that the latter approach is the *preferred* way to initialize an object. The syntax using = is simply provided as a convenient shorthand to this approach.

Now that we have constructors that allow `Temperature` objects to be initialized, we proceed to build the two simplest methods of class `Temperature`.

ACCESSOR METHODS

An **accessor method** is a method that allows some attribute of the class to be read, but not modified. From an external perspective, a programmer should be able to send the message

```
temp1.getDegrees()
```

to access the number of degrees in a `Temperature` object `temp1` and send the message

```
temp1.getScale()
```

to access the scale of `temp1`.

An autonomous `Temperature` object will know how many degrees it has. From an internal perspective, when I (a `Temperature`) receive the `getDegrees()` message, I should return the number of degrees I have. We thus have this simple specification for the behavior of `getDegrees()`:

Return: `myDegrees`

The specification of the behavior of `getScale()` is similar:

Return: `myScale`

Figure 11.7 shows the definitions of these methods. Because of the simplicity of these methods, we define them as `inline` methods and store their definitions in the class header file `Temperature.h`. Because these methods read, but do not modify the instance variables, they are designated as `const` methods.

Fig. 11.7 `Temperature` accessor methods. (Part 1 of 2)

```
// ------- Degrees extractor ------------------------------------

inline double Temperature::getDegrees() const
{
   return myDegrees;
}
```

Fig. 11.7 `Temperature` accessor methods. (Part 2 of 2)

```
// ------- Scale extractor ---------------------------------------

inline char Temperature::getScale() const
{
   return myScale;
}
```

As with all methods, prototypes must be stored in the class declaration:

```
class Temperature
{
 public:
   Temperature();
   Temperature(double initialDegrees, char initialScale);

   double getDegrees() const;
   char getScale() const;

   void print(ostream & out) const;

   static bool isValid(double degrees, char scale);

 private:               //           Class invariant:
   double myDegrees;  //     myScale == 'F' && myDegrees >= -459.67
   char   myScale;    //  || myScale == 'C' && myDegrees >= -273.15
                      //  || myScale == 'K' && myDegrees >= 0.0
};
```

NOTE

It is our practice to group method prototypes within a class declaration according to purpose, with blank lines separating each group. For example, constructors, accessors, and I/O methods all have distinct purposes, so we group their prototypes accordingly.

From an external perspective, when the `getDegrees()` message is sent to a `Temperature` object, it will return the value stored in the `myDegrees` instance variable of that object. To illustrate, given the declarations

```
Temperature temp1(98.6, 'F'),
            temp2;
```

the expression

```
temp1.getDegrees()
```

will access the value of the `myDegrees` data member of `temp1` (i.e., 98.6), while the expression

```
temp2.getDegrees()
```

will access the value of the myDegrees data member of temp2 (i.e., 0.0). The getScale() method behaves in a similar manner using the myScale instance variable.

Temperature INPUT

Next, we provide a method to read a Temperature value from an istream. A statement such as

```
temp2.read(cin);
```

should read a number and a character from cin and store them in temp2.myDegrees and temp2.myScale, respectively.

From an internal perspective, the definition of read() contains the instructions that I (as an autonomous Temperature object) must follow to input a temperature. From this perspective, object-centered design gives the following specification:

Receive:	*in*, an istream containing a double and a char
Input:	*inDegrees*, the double value, and *inScale*, the char value
Precondition:	*inScale* is one of {'f', 'c', 'k', 'F', 'C', 'K'} and *inDegrees* is valid for *inScale*
Send back:	*in*, with *inDegrees* and *inScale* extracted from it
Postcondition:	myDegrees == *inDegrees* && myScale == *inScale*

For user convenience, we accept the scale in either upper- or lowercase, and convert lowercase entries to uppercase. To guard against invalid input values, we must check that the degrees and scale entered satisfy the precondition before modifying the data members. If they do not, we will set the fail bit in the istream and leave further corrective action up to the caller.

Due to the complexity of this method, we do not define it as inline, and so this definition should be stored in Temperature.cpp, for separate compilation. Since this method modifies the Temperature instance variables, it is *not* defined as a const method. Figure 11.8 presents an implementation of this method. Note that as in the explicit-value constructor, we use the isValid() class method to check the method's precondition.

Fig. 11.8 Temperature input. (Part 1 of 2)

```
// ------- Temperature Input -----------------------------------

void Temperature::read(istream& in)
{
  double inDegrees;                   // temporary variables to
  char inScale;                       //   store the input values
```

Fig. 11.8 `Temperature` input. (Part 2 of 2)

```
  in >> inDegrees >> inScale;           // read values from in

  if ( isValid(inDegrees, inScale) ) // if they're valid
  {
    if ( islower(inScale) )             //   if scale is lower case
      inScale = toupper(inScale);       //     convert it to upper case

    myScale = inScale;                  //   assign input values
    myDegrees = inDegrees;              //    to instance variables
  }
  else                                  // otherwise
    in.setstate(ios::failbit);          //   set fail bit in stream
}                                       //    and return
```

As a function member, a prototype of this method must be added to the class declaration:

```
class Temperature
{
 public:
   Temperature();
   Temperature(double initialDegrees, char initialScale);

   double getDegrees() const;
   char getScale() const;

   void print(ostream& out) const;
   void read(istream& in);

   static bool isValid(double degrees, char scale);

 private:              //          Class invariant:
   double myDegrees; //    myScale == 'F' && myDegrees >= -459.67
   char   myScale;   // || myScale == 'C' && myDegrees >= -273.15
                     // || myScale == 'K' && myDegrees >= 0.0
};
```

We finish by adding the documentation for this method to the library documentation file.

Given this method, a programmer can now use `read()` to input temperatures from an `istream` or from an `ifstream`. For example, to build an input loop, we could use any temperature with an invalid scale as a sentinel value:

```
Temperature temp1;

for (;;)
{
```

```
      cout << "Enter a temperature, as in 98.6 F (0 A to quit): ";
      temp1.read(cin);

      if (cin.fail()) break;

      // ... process the temperature in temp1 ...
   }
```

Once this fragment is compiled and linked to the `Temperature` object file, a series of temperature values can be read from the keyboard and processed. In Section 11.6, we will see how to overload the input operator (>>) to read `Temperature` values in the usual manner.

CONVERSION METHODS

Next, we examine the methods that produce equivalent temperatures in different scales. We begin with the `inFahrenheit()` method.

From an internal perspective, I (an autonomous `Temperature` object) should be able to compute the Fahrenheit `Temperature` equivalent to myself. Object-centered design produces the following specification for this behavior:

Return: The Fahrenheit temperature equivalent of myself

Since the particular formula used to compute the return value depends on the current value of `myScale`, a selection statement is needed to select the appropriate formula. The resulting method is sufficiently complex that it is not defined as `inline`. Since the method accesses, but does not modify any of the data members, it is defined as a constant method. Figure 11.9 presents an implementation of this method.

Fig. 11.9 The `inFahrenheit()` method.

```
// ------- Fahrenheit conversion method ----------------

Temperature Temperature::inFahrenheit() const
{
   switch (myScale)
   {
      case 'F':
         return Temperature(myDegrees, 'F');
      case 'C':
         return Temperature(myDegrees * 1.8 + 32.0, 'F');
      case 'K':
         return Temperature((myDegrees - 273.15) * 1.8 + 32.0, 'F');
   }
}
```

Note how this method constructs the `Temperature` value to be returned. It calls the explicit-value `Temperature` constructor to build the appropriate value in each case of the `switch` statement. For example, in the first case, the expression

```
Temperature(myDegrees, 'F')
```

passes the arguments `myDegrees` and `'F'` to the `Temperature` explicit-value constructor, which constructs a `Temperature` object from these values and returns it to `inFahrenheit()`. The method `inFahrenheit()` then uses this `Temperature` object as its return value for this case. Note also that because the class invariant ensures the validity of `myDegrees` and `myScale`, we need not check for other cases.

As always, we must place a prototype of this method in the class declaration:

```
class Temperature
{
 public:
   Temperature();
   Temperature(double initialDegrees, char initialScale);

   double getDegrees() const;
   char getScale() const;

   Temperature inFahrenheit() const;

   void read(istream & in);
   void print(ostream & out) const;

   static bool isValid(double degrees, char scale);

 private:                 //            Class invariant:
   double myDegrees;  //     myScale == 'F' && myDegrees >= -459.67
   char   myScale;    //  || myScale == 'C' && myDegrees >= -273.15
                      //  || myScale == 'K' && myDegrees >= 0.0
};
```

The methods `inCelsius()` and `inKelvin()` are similar and are left as exercises.

Given these methods, our `Temperature` class provides the minimal functionality necessary for the program in Figure 11.2 to run as indicated:

```
int main()
{
   // ...
   Temperature theTemperature;
   theTemperature.read(cin);

   cout << "\n-->";
   theTemperature.inFahrenheit().print(cout); cout << " == ";
   theTemperature.inCelsius().print(cout);    cout << " == ";
   theTemperature.inKelvin().print(cout);     cout << endl;
   // ...
}
```

Note the **chaining** of messages in the statement

```
theTemperature.inFahrenheit().print(cout);
```

The chained messages are processed from left to right. First, the `inFahrenheit()` message is sent to `theTemperature`, which returns a (temporary) `Temperature` object. The `print()` message is then sent to this (temporary) `Temperature` object, which displays itself.

This method of outputting `Temperature` values works correctly, but it is far less elegant than if we could use the input and output operators (>> and <<) on `Temperature` objects:

```
Temperature theTemperature;
cin >> theTemperature;

cout << "\n-->";
     << theTemperature.inFahrenheit() << " == "
     << theTemperature.inCelsius() << " == "
     << theTemperature.inKelvin() << endl;
```

To accomplish this, we must overload these operators with new definitions that specify how to output a `Temperature`. Doing so does not require much code, but some subtle issues must be addressed. We introduce operator overloading next, but defer the overloading of the I/O operators to the *OBJECTive Thinking* section at the end of this chapter.

OVERLOADING OPERATORS

Each of the preceding operations has been implemented as a "normal" method, in that its name was an identifier. For some operations (addition, subtraction, relational comparisons, and I/O), it is often more convenient to define an *operator* to perform them. Just as normal functions and methods can be overloaded, C++ allows operators to be overloaded for classes. Such **operator overloading** is the topic we examine next.

The Relational Operators. As we noted earlier, it would be useful if we could compare two `Temperature` objects using relational operators. This would allow a computerized thermometer to be programmed with statements like

```
if (yourTemperature > Temperature(98.6, 'F'))
   cout << "You have a fever!\n";
```

or a computer-controlled thermostat to be programmed with statements like

```
while (houseTemperature < Temperature(20, 'C'))
   runFurnace();
```

To permit such operations, we must overload the relational operators for class `Temperature`. We will do this for two of them, the less-than operator (<) and the equality operator (==). The others are similar and are left as exercises.

To compare two temperatures using <, we need to overload the < operator. To do this, we can define a `Temperature` method with the name `operator<`. Similarly, to overload the == operator, we define a method with the name `operator==`. In general, *we can overload an arbitrary operator whose symbol is Δ by defining a method with the name* **operatorΔ**, provided it has a signature distinct from that of any existing definition of `operatorΔ`.

If `operator<()` is defined as a `Temperature` method, an expression like

```
houseTemperature < Temperature(20, 'C')
```

is treated by the C++ compiler as the message

```
houseTemperature.operator<( Temperature(20, 'C') )
```

Intuitively, such a call is sending the less-than message to `houseTemperature`, along with a `Temperature` argument (20 degrees Celsius in this case). From the internal perspective, I (an autonomous `Temperature`) should return `true` if and only if I am less than that `Temperature` argument.

Using object-centered design, we can specify the behavior of `operator<` as follows:

Receive: *rightOperand*, a `Temperature` value

Return: `true` if and only if I am less than *rightOperand*

Note that an expression like

```
Temperature(0, 'C') < Temperature(32, 'F')
```

should return `false`, since these two temperatures are in fact equal! The implementation of `operator<` is thus complicated by the possibility that `myScale` and *rightOperand*.`myScale` are not the same. Figure 11.10 shows one way that this method can be implemented:

Fig. 11.10 Overloading operator <. (Part 1 of 2)

```
// ------- less-than ---------------------------------------

bool Temperature::operator<(const Temperature& rightOperand) const
{
   Temperature localTemp;          // the equivalent of rightOperand,
                                   //  but in my scale
   switch (myScale)
   {
      case 'C': localTemp = rightOperand.inCelsius();
                break;
```

Fig. 11.10 Overloading operator <. (Part 2 of 2)

```
      case 'F': localTemp = rightOperand.inFahrenheit();
                break;
      case 'K': localTemp = rightOperand.inKelvin();
                break;
   }
   return myDegrees < localTemp.getDegrees();
}
```

This implementation of the method resolves the problem of mismatched scales by using a local `Temperature` object `localTemp`, which it sets to the equivalent of `rightOperand` in the same scale as the `Temperature` object receiving the message. Once we have two temperatures in the same scale, we can simply compare their `myDegrees` members using the less-than operation.[3]

The equality (==) operator can be overloaded using a similar approach, as shown in Figure 11.11:

Fig. 11.11 Overloading operator ==.

```
// ------- equality ------------------------------------------

bool Temperature::operator==(const Temperature& rightOperand) const
{
   Temperature localTemp;          // the equivalent of rightOperand,
                                   //  but in my scale
   switch (myScale)
   {
      case 'C': localTemp = rightOperand.inCelsius();
                break;
      case 'F': localTemp = rightOperand.inFahrenheit();
                break;
      case 'K': localTemp = rightOperand.inKelvin();
                break;
   }

   return myDegrees == localTemp.getDegrees();
}
```

3. A class method can directly access the private data members in class objects it receives as parameters. For readability, we use an object's accessor method, rather than directly accessing its data members.

Both of these methods are sufficiently complicated that they should not be defined as `inline`,[4] but should instead be stored in `Temperature.cpp` where they can be separately compiled.

Prototypes for these operations must be placed in the class declaration as shown in Figure 11.12. Documentation for these methods is placed in `Temperature.doc`. The remaining relational operators can be overloaded in a similar fashion and are left as exercises.

SUMMARY: THE `Temperature` CLASS

Figure 11.12 presents a final version of the `Temperature` class declaration. The complete files `Temperature.h` and `Temperature.cpp` can be found on the book's Web site. Other operations (+ and -) that might be added are described in the exercises.

Fig. 11.12 The `Temperature` class declaration. (Part 1 of 2)

```
/* Temperature.h declares class Temperature.
 * ...
 ***************************************************************/

#ifndef TEMPERATURE
#define TEMPERATURE

#include <iostream>                        // istream, ostream
using namespace std;

const double MIN_FAHRENHEIT = -459.67;
const double MIN_CELSIUS    = -273.15;
const double MIN_KELVIN     = 0.0;

class Temperature
{
 public:                                   // The class interface
   Temperature();
   Temperature(double initialDegrees, char initialScale);
```

4. An alternative version can eliminate the redundant code by isolating it in a private auxiliary method named `compare()` that, given a `Temperature` *rightOperand*, returns a negative value if I am less than *rightOperand*, 0 if we are equal, and a positive value if I am greater than *rightOperand*. Each relational operator can then be defined in one statement using `compare()`:

```
inline bool Temperature::operator<(const Temperature& rightOperand)
{
   return compare(rightOperand) < 0;
}
```

Fig. 11.12 The `Temperature` class declaration. (Part 2 of 2)

```
  double getDegrees() const;
  char getScale() const;

  Temperature inFahrenheit() const;
  Temperature inCelsius() const;
  Temperature inKelvin() const;

  bool operator<  (const Temperature& rightOperand) const;
  bool operator== (const Temperature& rightOperand) const;
  // ... other relational operators omitted ...

  void print(ostream& out) const;
  void read(istream& in);

  static bool isValid(double degrees, char scale);

 private:                //            Class invariant:
  double myDegrees;  //      myScale == 'F' && myDegrees >= -459.67
  char   myScale;    //   || myScale == 'C' && myDegrees >= -273.15
                     //   || myScale == 'K' && myDegrees >= 0.0
};

// ... Definitions of inline operations go here ...

#endif
```

Class Structure. As Figure 11.12 illustrates, every class has two parts:

- the **public** portion of the class, consisting of those components (data or operations) that are accessible outside the class; and
- the **private** portion of the class, consisting of those components (data or operations) that can only be accessed inside the class.

As mentioned earlier, class operations are usually declared in the public section and **attribute variables** (instance variables or class variables) in the private portion of the class. This makes the attribute variables inaccessible to programs using the class, preventing programmers from writing programs that depend upon those particular details.

The Class Interface. The benefit of keeping attribute variables private is that it forces programs to interact with a class object through its public operations. The set of public operations can thus be thought of as an **interface** between the class and programs that use it. Since the interface provides the sole means of operating on class objects, it is important that it be well designed—a good interface must provide all of the functionality needed to operate on a class object. *Designing a good interface thus requires much time and thought and should not be hurried.*

One reason for designing the interface carefully is that a class interface must be stable. If it changes frequently, then programs that use the class must be revised often to accommodate the changes. Programmers will eventually tire of revising their programs and stop using the class. A stable interface is only possible if it is carefully designed from the outset.

If an interface is stable, then any program that uses the class solely through the interface will not break even if the private portion of the class (its attribute variables) is modified extensively. Such extensive modifications are common in maintaining or upgrading many real-world systems. Attribute variables of a class may be replaced by others that more efficiently represent the object being modeled. If the interface is stable, the time required to upgrade such a system is only the time to modify the attribute variables and instance method definitions; a program that uses the class and its methods requires no modifications. This in turn simplifies program maintenance, which saves time and money.

The public section of a class need not come first, but we will usually place it there so that it is easy to find. Since it provides the class interface, most readers are more interested in it than in the private (inaccessible) details.

Although most classes will have this simple two-part structure, C++ does allow classes to have multiple public and private sections. Thus, the general structure of a class is as follows:

Class Declaration Statement

Form:

```
class ClassName
{
    PublicPart_1
    PrivatePart_1
    PublicPart_2
    PrivatePart_2
        .
        .
        .
    PublicPart_n
    PrivatePart_n
};
```

where

ClassName is an identifier naming the class;

each $PublicPart_i$ consists of the keyword `public:` and a list of declarations of members (or friends) of the class; and each *PrivatePart$_i$* consists of the keyword `private:` and a list of declarations of members (or friends) of the class.

Purpose: Define a new data type *ClassName*, which is a class consisting of the specified private and public parts. Each component (data or function) declared in a private part is accessible only within the class. Each component (data or function) declared in a public part is accessible outside the class.

✔ Quick Quiz 11.4

1. For an object that cannot be directly represented with existing types, we design and build a(n) ________ to represent it and store it in a(n) ________.
2. The behavior of a class object is the collection of ________ that can be applied to the object.
3. The attributes of a class object consist of the ________ that must be stored to characterize the object.
4. (True or false) The attributes of a class are usually identified before the behavior.
5. Object autonomy is embodied in the ________ principle.
6. ________ allows a single object to store values of different types.
7. What is the purpose of hiding instance variables in a class?
8. Instance variables are hidden by declaring them to be ________.
9. Before a program is compiled, it is first examined by the ________.
10. All lines that begin with a(n) ________ character are preprocessor directives.
11. Directives of the form

    ```
    #ifndef name
    #define name
        .
        .
        .
    #endif
    ```

    are called ________ directives.
12. Class operations are implemented using ________.
13. (True or false) Specifications of methods should usually be formulated from an external perspective.
14. In the definition of a method, the name of the method is preceded by the ________ and the ________ operator.
15. A method that does not alter the instance variables of the class should be declared as a(n) ________ method by attaching the keyword ________ at the end of its heading.
16. A constructor in a class `Employee` will be named ________.
17. Name and describe two kinds of constructors.
18. The ________ (public or private) portion of a class acts as an interface between the class and programs that use it.
19. Write a declaration for a class `Employee` that has two instance variables, `myID` of type `int`, and `myName` of type `string`, an output method, and an input method.

Exercises 11.4

For Exercises 1 and 2, add methods to class `Temperature` to implement the specified operation. You should write a driver program to test these methods as Programming Problems 1–2 at the end of the chapter ask you to do.

1. Add methods to class `Temperature` that convert a `Temperature` value to (a) Celsius; (b) Kelvin.
2. Overload `operator+` for class `Temperature` so that expressions like `temp + 3.6` can be used to increase a `Temperature` value by a `double` amount.
3. Overload `operator-` for class `Temperature` so that expressions like `temp - 3.6` can be used to decrease a `Temperature` value by a `double` amount.

For Exercises 4–9, define the private portion of a class to model the given item.

4. Cards in a deck of playing cards.
5. Time measured in hours, minutes, and seconds.
6. A telephone number as area code, local exchange, and number.
7. Position of a checker on a board.
8. A point (x, y) in a Cartesian coordinate system.
9. A point (r, θ) in a polar coordinate system.

For Exercises 10–15, completely implement a class for the specified objects, supplying a complete set of operations for the class. You should write a driver program to test your class as Programming Problems 3–8 at the end of the chapter ask you to do.

10. Exercise 4
11. Exercise 5
12. Exercise 6
13. Exercise 7
14. Exercise 8
15. Exercise 9

For Exercises 16–18, develop a class for the given information and then write operations appropriate for an object of that type. You should write a driver program to test your class as Programming Problems 9–11 at the end of the chapter ask you to do.

16. Information about a person: name, birthday, age, gender, social security number, height, weight, hair color, eye color, and marital status.
17. Statistics about a baseball player: name, age, birthdate, and position (pitcher, catcher, infielder, outfielder).
18. Weather statistics: date; city and state, province, or country; time of day; temperature; barometric pressure; weather conditions (clear skies, partly cloudy, cloudy, stormy).

For Exercises 19–21, write appropriate class declarations to describe the information in the specified file. See the end of Chapter 9 for descriptions of these files.

19. `Student`

20. `Inventory`
21. `Users`

11.5 Case Study: Retrieving Student Information

Once we are able to create classes, we can represent complex objects in software. In this section, the problem is to build an information retrieval system that a university registrar might use to maintain student records.

PROBLEM: INFORMATION RETRIEVAL

The registrar at IO University has a data file named `students.txt` that contains student records:

```
111223333 Bill Board
Freshman    16.0  3.15

666554444 Jose Canusee
Sophomore   16.0  3.25

777889999 Ben Dover
Junior      16.0  2.5

333221111 Stan Dupp
Senior      8.0  3.75

444556666 Ellie Kat
Senior      16.0  3.125

999887777 Isabelle Ringing
Junior      16.0  3.8
      .
      .
      .
```

Each pair of lines in this file has the form

studentNumber firstName lastName
studentYear credits gradePointAverage

where

studentNumber is a nine-digit (integer) student ID number;
firstName, lastName, and *studentYear* are character strings;
credits is the (real) number of credits this student carried this semester; and
gradePointAverage is the (real) grade-point average of this student this semester.

The registrar at IOU needs a program that will let her enter student numbers and that will retrieve and display the information for those students.

Object-Centered Design

Behavior. The program should read a sequence of students from the input file `students.txt`. It should then repeatedly prompt for and read a student ID number from the keyboard, search the sequence of students for the position of the student with that student ID number, and if found, display the information for that student.

Objects. An abbreviated list of the objects in this problem is as follows:

	Software Objects		
Problem Objects	**Type**	**Kind**	**Name**
A sequence of students	`vector<Student>`	varying	*studentVec*
Name of the input file	`string`	constant	*INPUT_FILE*
A student ID number	`long`	varying	*studentID*
The position of the student	`vector<T>::iterator`	varying	position
A student	`Student`	varying	none

As we saw in Chapter 10, we can use a `vector<T>` to store a sequence of objects of type `T`. However, we need to store a sequence of students. Since there is no predefined type that allows us to represent a student object, we will need to build a `Student` class for this.

Operations. The operations needed to solve this problem are as follows:

i. Read a sequence of students from the input file
ii. Display a prompt
iii. Read a long integer from the keyboard
iv. Search a sequence of students for one with a particular ID number
v. Display a student
vi. Repeat Steps ii–v an arbitrary number of times

We can accomplish Step iv using the Standard Template Library's `find()` algorithm. However, `find()` requires that the relational operators < and == be defined for objects being compared, so we add these operations to our list:

vii. Compare two `Student` objects using <
viii. Compare two `Student` objects using ==

Algorithm. Given a `Student` class that provides the appropriate operations, we can organize these operations into the following algorithm:

Algorithm for Student Information Retrieval

1. Read a sequence of students from *INPUT_FILE* into *studentVec*.
2. Repeatedly do the following:

    a. Prompt for and read *studentID*.

b. Search *studentVec* for the student with *studentID*, returning its *position*.
c. If the search was successful
   Display the student at *position*.
   Otherwise
   Display an error message.

Before we can code this algorithm, we must build a `Student` class. From an internal perspective, the behaviors required of a `Student` include the following:

- Initialize myself with default values
- Initialize myself with explicitly supplied values
- Read my attributes from an `istream` and store them in me
- Display my attributes using an `ostream`
- Compare myself and another `Student` using the < and == relational operators

These are the minimal operations needed to solve the problem. To make the class truly reusable, we should add (at least) the following operations:

- Access any of my attributes
- Compare myself and another `Student` using the != , >, <=, and >= operators

The `Student` attributes required to solve this problem include the attributes stored in the input file:

my id number, my first name, my last name, my year, my credits, and *my GPA*.

See if you can build the class `Student` to have the attributes and operations just described. To help you get started, Figure 11.13 presents the class declaration containing prototypes for the operations and instance variables for the attributes. Its contents should be placed in a file named *Student.h*, which would also contain inlined definitions of all of the operations, except for the two constructors and the I/O operations, which should be placed in *Student.cpp*. You should also prepare a documentation file for this class. When you have finished (or if you have difficulty) you can compare your definitions of the operations with those given on the text's Web site.

Fig. 11.13 The header file for class `Student`. (Part 1 of 2)

```
/* Student.h declares class Student.
 * ... Add your documentation here
 *******************************************************/

#ifndef STUDENT                              // compile-once
#define STUDENT                              //  wrapper

#include <iostream>                          // istream, ostream
#include <string>                            // string
using namespace std;
```

Fig. 11.13 The header file for class `Student`. (Part 2 of 2)

```
class Student
{
 public:                                        // The Interface
                                                //  constructors
   Student();
   Student(long idNumber, const string & firstName,
            const string & lastName, const string & year,
            double credits, double gpa);
                                                //  accessors
   long   getID() const;
   string getFirstName() const;
   // ... Add getLastName(), getYear(), getCredits(), and getGPA()
                                                //  relational ops
   bool operator== (const Student& rightOperand) const;
   bool operator!= (const Student& rightOperand) const;
   // ... Add operators <, >, <=, and >=.
   // ...  See the exercises at the end of this section for
   // ...  information about these operators.
                                                //  I/O
   void read(istream& in);
   void print(ostream& out) const;

 private:                                       // Implementation Details
                                                // Examples:
  long   myIDNumber;                            //   123456789
  string myFirstName,                           //   Jane
         myLastName,                            //   Doe
         myYear;                                //   Senior
  double myCredits,                             //   15.0
         myGPA;                                 //   3.75
};

// ** Put definitions of all accessors and relational operators here.
// ...
// ** Definitions of the constructors and the I/O methods are more
// ** complicated and should be put in Student.cpp.

#endif
```

Coding. Given class `Student` and the Standard Template Library, our algorithm for the original problem is relatively easy to implement. The basic idea is to define a `vector<Student>` object named `studentVec` to store the sequence of `Student` values from the input file:

```
vector<Student> studentVec;
```

The effect of this is to create a vector of student objects that we can visualize as follows:

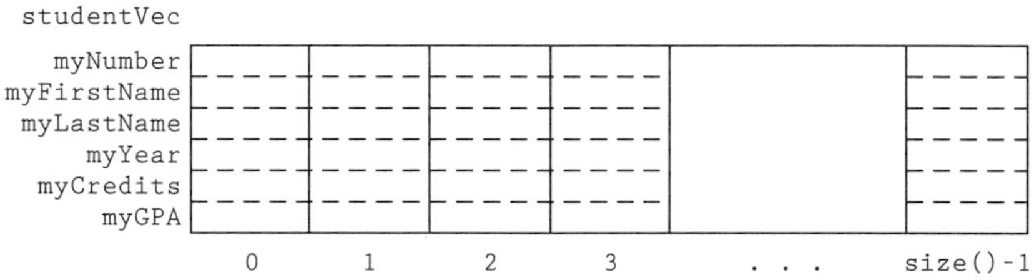

We can then apply any of the `vector<T>` operations described in Chapter 10 and the STL algorithms such as `sort()` or `find()` to `studentVec`.

Figure 11.14 gives part of a program that implements our algorithm using this approach. Add the items described in the comments, and execute your program with the file `students.txt` shown. Also shown in Figure 11.14 is a sample run of the program. Compare your program's output with that shown and your solution with that given on the book's Web site.

Fig. 11.14 Student information retrieval. (Part 1 of 3)

```
/* registrar.cpp retrieves a student's data from a file
 *  using their id #.
 * Input (file):     a sequence of Students
 * Input (keyboard): one or more student numbers
 * Output:           that student's data
 *************************************************************/

// ... #includes go here ...

void fill(vector<Student>& sVec, const string& fileName);
int main()
{
  const string INPUT_FILE = "students.txt";

  cout << "This program provides an information retrieval system\n"
          "  by reading a series of student records from "
       << '\'' << INPUT_FILE << '\''
       << "\n  and then allowing retrieval of any student's data.\n";
```

Fig. 11.14 Student information retrieval. (Part 2 of 3)

```
  // 1. Declare studentVec and use fill() to read Students into it

  // 2. Loop:
  //       a. Prompt for and read an integer studentID
  //       b. Search studentVec for Student with that studentID
  //       c. If such a Student object was found
  //             Display the Student object
  //          Otherwise
  //             Display a "not found" message
}

// ... Definition of fill() goes here
```

Listing of input file `students.txt`:

```
111223333 Bill Board
Freshman  16.0 3.15

666554444 Jose CanuSee
Sophomore 16.0 3.25

777889999 Ben Dover
Junior    16.0  2.5

333221111 Stan Dupp
Senior    8.0 3.75

444556666 Ellie Kat
Senior    16.0 3.125

999887777 Isabelle Ringing
Junior    16.0  3.8
```

Sample run:

```
This program provides an information retrieval system
  by reading a series of student records from 'students.dat'
  and then allowing retrieval of any student's data.
```

Fig. 11.14 Student information retrieval. (Part 3 of 3)

```
Enter the ID # of a student (eof to quit): 333221111

 333221111 Stan Dupp
      Senior 16.0000  3.7500

Enter the ID # of a student (eof to quit): 123456789
There is no student with ID # 123456789.

Enter the ID # of a student (eof to quit): 999887777

 999887777 Ringing, Isabelle
      Junior  8.0000  3.8000

Enter the ID # of a student (eof to quit): ^D
```

Taking the time to implement an object as a class is an *investment for the future*—if the registrar subsequently asks us to write a program to create a list of all students who will be graduating with honors, our `Student` class makes this easy:

```
// ...open inStream and outStream...

cout << "Seniors whose GPA is 3.5 or greater:\n";
for (;;)
{
   aStudent.read(inStream);

   if ( inStream.eof() ) break;

   if (aStudent.getYear() == "Senior"
       && aStudent.getGPA() >= 3.5)
   {
      aStudent.print(outStream);
      outStream << endl;
   }
}

// ... close inStream and outStream ...
```

By planning for the future when we design a class, we save ourselves and others a great deal of time and effort.

Note that thus far, the I/O for these classes is a bit clumsy. Code like

```
cout << '\n';
aStudent.print(cout);
cout << endl;
```

is far less elegant than would be the case if the output operator were overloaded:

```
cout << '\n' << aStudent << endl;
```

See the *OBJECTive Thinking* section that follows to see how to overload the input and output operators.

11.6 OBJECTive Thinking: Operator Overloading and Friends

We have already seen that methods like `read()` and `print()` provide a way to define I/O operations for classes like `Temperature` and `Student`. However, these methods do not coordinate well with the normal `iostream` I/O operators. For example, in the program in Figure 11.2, we had to perform I/O of a `Temperature` object using `read()` and `print()` as follows:

```
. . .
char response;
Temperature theTemperature;

do
{
   cout << "\nEnter a temperature (e.g., 98.6 F): ";
   theTemperature.read(cin);

   cout << "-->";
   theTemperature.inFahrenheit().print(cout);
   cout << " = ";
   theTemperature.inCelsius().print(cout);
   cout << " = ";
   theTemperature.inKelvin().print(cout);
   cout << endl;

   cout << "Do you have more temperatures to convert? ";
   cin >> response;
}
while (response == 'Y' || response == 'y');
```

Performing I/O of `Student` objects in the preceding section is equally inelegant, using the `read()` and `print()` methods of class `Student`. It would be preferable if we could instead extract/insert class values from/into streams using the customary stream input and output operators (>> and <<). We will now overload `operator<<` using our `print()` method and overload `operator>>` using `read()`. Doing so does not require much code, but to do so correctly requires that some subtle issues be addressed.

The first issue is that unlike `operator<` and `operator==`, we cannot define `operator<<` as a method of a class. To see why, recall that if an operator whose symbol is Δ is defined as a method of a class, and `object` is an object of that class, then the expression

```
object Δ operand
```

is treated by the compiler as

```
object.operatorΔ(operand)
```

If this observation is applied to the output expression

```
cout << someTemperature
```

then it should be evident that `operator<<` must be defined as a method of class `ostream`, not class `Temperature`. This would require that we add a new prototype for `operator<<` to the declaration of `ostream`, but on most platforms, users are not permitted to modify the header files that come with the system (nor would this be wise).

Fortunately, C++ provides a way around this problem. If the operator whose symbol is Δ is defined as a normal function—one that acts upon its operands via parameters—and not as a method, then the expression

```
object Δ operand
```

is treated by the compiler as the function call

```
operatorΔ(object, operand)
```

More precisely, if we wish to use

```
cout << someTemperature;
```

then we need to define a nonmember function `operator<<` that the compiler can call as

```
operator<<(cout, someTemperature);
```

We can thus define `operator<<` as a normal function, using an external perspective. Using object-centered design gives the following specification of the function's behavior:

Receive:	*out*, the `ostream` to which values are being written *theTemp*, the `Temperature` object whose value is being written
Output:	*theTemp*`.myDegrees` and *theTemp*`.myScale`
Send back:	*out*, containing the inserted values
Return:	*out*, for use by a subsequent output operation

Figure 11.15 presents the implementation of `operator<<`. Because most of the required functionality is already available via the `print()` method of class `Temperature`, our function merely sends its parameter `theTemp` the `print()` message and then returns its `ostream` parameter. The resulting function is simple enough to define as `inline`, and so we store it in the class header file `Temperature.h`. Because it is a normal function (i.e., not a method), no prototype is placed within the class declaration.

Fig. 11.15 Overloading operator << for class temperature.

```
// ------- Temperature ostream output -------------------------

inline ostream& operator<<(ostream& out, const Temperature& theTemp)
{
   theTemp.print(out);   // tell theTemp to print itself
   return out;
}
```

The output operator for the class `Student` of the preceding section is almost identical,[5] as shown in Figure 11.16:

Fig. 11.16 Overloading operator << for class student.

```
// ------- Student ostream output ---------------------------

inline ostream& operator<<(ostream& out, const Student& aStudent)
{
   aStudent.print(out);   // tell aStudent to print itself
   return out;
}
```

These functions are deceptively simple. They seemingly just receive an `ostream` and a class operand and send the `print()` message to their class operand with the `ostream` operand as an argument. Because `print()` inserts values into its `ostream` operand `out`, `out` is defined as a reference parameter.

However, the functions also return `out` and the return type of each function is `ostream&`, something we have not seen before. These are the two most subtle parts of the function, and we will deal with them separately. What we say below applies both to `Temperature` objects and `Student` objects; however, to keep the presentation concise, we will discuss only the function for `Temperature` objects.

The << operator returns `out` so that output operations can be chained. That is, when we insert two `Temperature` objects `temp1` and `temp2` into `cout`,

```
cout << temp1 << temp2;
```

5. In fact, the only difference between the two functions is the type of their second parameter. As indicated in Section 8.5, a template may be used in such situations to avoid the redundant coding:

```
template<typename T>
inline ostream& operator<<(ostream& out, const T& anObject)
{
   anObject.print(out);
   return out;
}
```

A similar approach can be used for the input operator described later in this section.

there are two different calls to `operator<<`, and these are executed from left to right. To distinguish them, suppose that we number the output operators as follows:

$\texttt{cout <<}_1\ \texttt{temp1 <<}_2\ \texttt{temp2;}$

In executing these functions from left to right, the compiler treats them as nested function calls, with `<<`$_1$ being performed first, as the "inner" call:

$\texttt{operator<<}_2\texttt{(operator<<1(cout, temp1), temp2);}$

The return-value from `<<`$_1$ is thus used as the left argument to `<<`$_2$:

$\texttt{operator<<}_2\texttt{(operator<<}_1\texttt{'s return\_value, temp2);}$

The subtle point is that since the left operand of `operator<<` is the `ostream` into which values are inserted, `<<`$_2$ will try to insert `temp2` into whatever value `<<`$_1$ returns.

From this, it should be apparent that `<<`$_1$ must return an `ostream` for use by `<<`$_2$. Moreover, the `ostream` that `<<`$_1$ returns should be the same `ostream` into which `<<`$_1$ inserted its value, and so it should return its parameter `out`, rather than a particular `ostream` such as `cout`. If `operator<<` were to explicitly return `cout`,

```
inline ostream& operator<<(ostream& out,
                           const Temperature& theTemp)
{
   theTemp.print(out);
   return cout;            // LOGIC ERROR!
}
```

then a code fragment like

```
ifstream dataStream("datafile");
// ...
dataStream << temp1 << temp2;
```

would correctly insert `temp1` into the `ifstream` named `dataStream`, but would incorrectly insert `temp2` into `cout`. To avoid this, `operator<<` must return its parameter `out`, which, as an alias for the stream into which values are being inserted, returns the appropriate stream.

The other subtle point has to do with the return type of `operator<<`. Why did we define its return type as `ostream&`? The reason is that when a C++ function returns a value in the usual fashion, it actually returns a *copy* of the value to the caller of the function.[6] That is, if we had defined the function to simply return an `ostream`,

```
inline ostream operator<<(ostream& out,
                          const Temperature& theTemp)
{
   theTemp.print(out);
   return out;
}
```

---

6. The caller maintains this copy, called a *temporary*, as long as it is needed and then discards it.

then the `return` statement would create a copy of parameter `out`, which, as a reference parameter, would create a copy of its argument. That means that in an output expression like

```
cout << temp1 << temp2;
```

`temp1` would be inserted into `cout`, but `temp2` would be inserted into a copy of `cout`, the result of which is unpredictable.

To avoid such copying, C++ allows a function to be defined with a **reference return type**. The effect is to "turn off" the copying mechanism and return the actual object. Thus, when we write

```
inline ostream& operator<<(ostream& out,
                           const Temperature& theTemp)
{
   theTemp.print(out);
   return out;
}
```

we are telling the compiler, "Don't return a copy of `out`, but instead return the actual `ostream` for which it is an alias."[7]

Figure 11.17 presents a definition of the input operator for class `Temperature`, which is similar.

Fig. 11.17 Overloading operator >> for class temperature.

```
// ------- istream input for a Temperature -------------------

inline istream& operator>>(istream& in, Temperature& theTemp)
{
   theTemp.read(in);
   return in;
}
```

Note that since the output operator does not modify the `Temperature` being displayed, it was declared to be a constant reference parameter. The input operator, however, does modify its `Temperature` parameter, so it is declared as a reference parameter. A similar function[8] can be defined for our `Student` class, as shown in Figure 11.18.

7. The reference return type cannot be used to circumvent the scope rules—if you try to use a reference return type to return an object defined within the function (i.e., a local), the compiler will generate an error message.
8. As described earlier in Footnote 5, a single template can be defined and stored in a header file (e.g., *ClassIO.h*) which can then be included (via `#include`) by any class that defines `print()`, and `read()`, but wishes to use the I/O operators.

Fig. 11.18 Overloading operator >> for class student.

```
// ------- istream input for a Student -----------------------

inline istream& operator>>(istream& in, Student& aStudent)
{
   aStudent.read(in);
   return in;
}
```

Given these I/O operations for `Temperature` objects, we can rewrite the temperature-conversion program of Figure 11.2 as shown in Figure 11.19. A similar rewrite of the student information retrieval program of the preceding section is left as an exercise.

Fig. 11.19 A temperature-conversion program using << and >>. (Part 1 of 2)

```
/* tempConversion.cpp displays a temperature in Fahrenheit,
 * Celsius, and Kelvin, using class Temperature.
 *
 *  Input:  an arbitrary Temperature
 *  Output: its Fahrenheit, Celsius and Kelvin equivalents
 ***************************************************************/

#include <iostream>                          // >>, <<, cin, cout
using namespace std;
#include "Temperature.h"                     // Temperature

int main()
{
   cout << "This program shows the Fahrenheit, Celsius, and\n"
           "Kelvin equivalents of a temperature.\n\n";

   char response;
   Temperature theTemperature;               // construction

   do
   {
      cout << "Enter a temperature (e.g., 98.6 F): ";

      cin >> theTemperature;                 // input
```

Fig. 11.19 A temperature-conversion program using << and >>. (Part 2 of 2)

```
      cout << "--> "                          // output
           << theTemperature.inFahrenheit()
           << " == "
           << theTemperature.inCelsius()
           << " == "
           << theTemperature.inKelvin()
           << endl;

      cout << "\nDo you have more temperatures to convert? ";
      cin >> response;
   }
   while (response == 'Y' || response == 'y');
}
```

This completes our implementation of the various `Temperature` operations.

FRIEND FUNCTIONS

Although most operations on a class object can be defined as methods, there are some occasions when this is not possible. For example, we just saw that the `iostream` insertion operator (`<<`) could not be defined as a `Temperature` method because its left operand is an `ostream`, not a `Temperature`:

```
cout << "The temperature is " << temp1 << endl;
```

Our solution was to define a "normal" function for `operator<<` that used the `Temperature print()` method to perform its task:

```
inline ostream& operator<<(ostream& out,
                           const Temperature& theTemp)
{
   theTemp.print(out);
   return out;
}
```

Now, suppose that we want to define `operator<<` without calling `print()`—for example, suppose that our `Temperature` class had no `print()` method. If `operator<<` attempts to access the instance variables of its parameter `theTemp` directly,

```
inline ostream & operator<<(ostream& out,
                            const Temperature& theTemp)
{
   out << theTemp.myDegrees << ' ' // ERROR!
      << theTemp.myScale;          // ERROR!
   return out;
}
```

the compiler will generate error messages like

```
Member 'myDegrees' is private in class 'Temperature'
Member 'myScale' is private in class 'Temperature'
```

The compiler is enforcing the information-hiding mechanism by not allowing the function to access the private instance variables of our class.

But suppose that the only reasonable way to define some operation requires that a function be able to access the private instance variables of a class. In such rare situations, C++ allows a class to grant this special access privilege to the function by specifying that it is a **friend**.

To illustrate, suppose that we delete the `print()` method from class `Temperature`. Then we *can* define `operator<<` as

```
inline ostream & operator<<(ostream& out,
                             const Temperature& theTemp)
{
   out << theTemp.myDegrees << ' '
       << theTemp.myScale;
   return out;
}
```

provided we place a prototype of `operator<<` within the class, preceded by the keyword `friend`:

```
class Temperature
{
 public:                                    // The class interface
         .
         .
         .
   friend ostream& operator<<(ostream& out,
                               const Temperature& theTemp);
         .
         .
         .
 private:                                   // The hidden details
   double myDegrees;
   char myScale;
};
```

The same definition that previously produced compilation errors will now compile correctly, because by naming the function as a `friend`, the class is granting this function access to its private section. Note that this does not allow a programmer to circumvent the information-hiding mechanism, because only a person able to alter the class declaration can insert a `friend` prototype.

Note also that `operator<<` is not designated as a `const` function. This is because it is not a method and `const` *can only be applied to methods.*

We can also replace the `read()` method with a `friend` version of `operator>>`:

```
class Temperature
{
 public:                              // The class interface
          .
          .
          .

   friend ostream& operator<<(ostream& out,
                              const Temperature& theTemp);
   friend istream& operator>>(istream& in,
                              Temperature& theTemp);

          .
          .
          .

 private:                             // The hidden details
   double myDegrees;
   char myScale;
};
```

We can then define `operator>>` as a normal function that directly accesses the instance variables of its parameter `theTemp`. Because of the relative complexity of this definition, it should not be designated as `inline` and should be stored in `Temperature.cpp` for separate compilation:

```
istream& operator>>(istream& in, Temperature& theTemp)
{
   double inDegrees;                  // temporary variables to
   char inScale;                      // store the input values
   in >> inDegrees >> inScale;        // read the values
                                      // if they're valid:
   if ( Temperature::isValid(inDegrees, inScale) )
   {
      if (islower(inScale))           // if scale is LC
         inScale = toupper(inScale);  //  convert to UC

     theTemp.myScale = inScale;       // assign input values
     theTemp.myDegrees = inDegrees;   //  to data members
   }

   else                               // otherwise
     in.setstate(ios::failbit);       // set fail bit, without
   }                                  // changing attributes

   return in;
}
```

Use of `friend`. The `friend` mechanism is rarely needed to define class operations. As we saw with class `Temperature`, most operations on a class object can be defined as methods, so the `friend` mechanism is not needed for them.

NOTE

When the left operand of an operation is of a type different from the class being built, then a method cannot be used and a normal function must be defined. But even in such infrequent cases, a public intermediary function (like `print()` or `read()`) can be defined which that function can call. The only circumstances where the `friend` mechanism is an absolute necessity are when the left operand of the operation is of some type different from the class being built and the operation must directly access the instance variables of the class.

Because it embodies the external approach to defining class operations (in which a function manipulates an object from outside) instead of the *I-can-do-it-myself* principle of the object-oriented approach, we will use the `friend` mechanism only in those rare circumstances where it is a necessity.

Exercises 11.6

1. Overload the input and output operators for the phone-number class in Exercise 4 of Section 2.3. (See also Exercises 4 and 9 in Section 3.8 and Exercise 8 of Section 5.6.)
2. Overload the input and output operators for the time class in Exercise 2 of Section 2.3. (See also Exercises 2 and 7 in Section 3.8, Exercises 9 and 10 in Section 4.7, and Exercise 6 of Section 5.6.)
3. Overload the input and output operators for the date class in Exercise 3 of Section 2.3. (See also Exercises 3 and 8 in Section 3.8 and Exercise 7 of Section 5.6.)

Part of the Picture
Artificial Intelligence
by Keith Vander Linden

Just over an hour into the sixth game of their chess match, Garry Kasparov, the reigning world champion, conceded defeat to Deep Blue, a chess-playing computer developed by IBM corporation. Kasparov lost the match, held in May of 1997, 3.5 games to 2.5 games. It marked the first time a computer program had defeated a world chess champion in anything approaching tournament conditions.

Although this result came as a surprise to many, it has been clear for some time that a computer would eventually beat a world champion player. Since their introduction to tournament play in the late 1960s, chess programs have made steady progress, defeating a chess master in 1983, a grandmaster in 1988, and now the world champion. This is by no means the end of the story, however. There are reservations concerning the validity of this most recent match: It was not really a tournament setting with multiple players, Kasparov was not allowed to study Deep Blue's previous matches, and he was under considerable pressure to hold off a perceived "attack on humanity" by computer programs. Nevertheless, another milestone has been passed.

The construction of game-playing programs such as Deep Blue is part of a subfield of computer science known as **artificial intelligence**, or **AI**. Roughly speaking, AI is an attempt to program computers to perform intelligent tasks. Giving a precise definition of AI is difficult, however, and most AI textbooks spend a laborious opening chapter attempting to characterize the field. This difficulty comes about for two reasons: (1) because intelligent behavior is complex and hard to define and (2) because the styles of programming used to implement this behavior are diverse.

Read the rest of Professor Vander Linden's introduction to the area of artificial intelligence on the book's Web site. It describes several of the topics studied in AI and some of the programming techniques and concludes with a description and code for a simple dice game called Not-One.

CHAPTER SUMMARY

Key Terms & Notes

accessor method
artificial intelligence
attribute
attribute variable
behavior
chaining
class
class declaration
class invariant
class method
conditional-compilation directive
constant method
constructor
data member
default-value constructor
dot notation
encapsulate
explicit-value constructor
external perspective
friend function
fully-qualified name
function member
I-can-do-it-myself principle
information hiding
instance variable
interface
internal perspective
message
method
object autonomy
object-centered design
operator overloading
postcondition
preprocessor
preprocessor directive
private
public
reference return type
scope operator
`static` modifier

- Independence from implementation details is very important in good class design.
- When working in a program and using a class, use an *external* perspective of an observer/user of the class. When working inside a class or building its function members, use an *internal* perspective of the object being designed.
- Like all declarations, a class declaration must be terminated by a semicolon.
- Two basic principles of class design are as follows:

  encapsulation , which allows a single object to store values of different types and is accomplished by wrapping a class declaration around them;

  information hiding , which prevents direct access to attribute variables by making them private in the class declaration.

- When there are restrictions on the values of a class' instance variables, a *class invariant* that specifies these restrictions should be formulated and checked whenever the instance variables are modified.
- Every class should be wrapped in conditional-compilation directives to prevent redeclaration errors if the header file is included more than once in a project.
- Methods that do not alter the instance variables of the class should be declared as `const` methods.
- Constructors are used to initialize the instance variables of a class. The name of a constructor is always the same as the name of the class.
- Methods that get all of the information they use via parameters and do not access any instance variables should normally be defined as *class* methods rather than instance methods.
- Class methods are messages that can be sent to a class using the scope operator (`::`); instance methods are messages that can be sent to an object using the dot operator (`.`).
- An operator Δ can be overloaded by defining a function with the name `operatorΔ`, provided it has a signature distinct from that of any existing definition of `operatorΔ`.
- Designing a good class interface—which consists of its public operations—requires much time and thought and should not be hurried. If it changes frequently, then programs that use the class must be revised often. If it is stable, then programs that use the class solely through the interface will not break even if the private portion of the class (its attribute variables) is modified.
- By naming a function as a friend, a class can grant this function access to its private section.

Programming Pointers

Program Style and Design

1. *When an object in a program cannot be represented directly using predefined types, define a class to represent such objects.* The class is the central mechanism for defining new types in C++. Remember, the language was originally called "C with classes."
2. *Use classes to define new types whose values consist of multiple attributes of arbitrary types.*

   One purpose of a class is to permit different data types to be encapsulated in a single object. For example, to model an address, we might declare

```
class Address
{
 public:
      // ... Interface omitted ...
 private:
   int    myHouseNumber;
   string myStreet;
   string myCity;
   string myState;
   int    myZipCode;
};
```

3. *Use indentation to reflect the structure of your class, since this increases its readability.*
4. *Use descriptive identifiers for the instance variables that reinforce the I-can-do-it-myself principle.* For example, begin each name with the prefix `my`.
5. *Place the class interface first in the class declaration so that it is easy to find.* Then users of your class can find the class interface without wading through all of its private details.
6. *Keep all instance variables of a class private, and provide accessor methods to retrieve the values of those members.* One purpose of a class is to hide implementation details from programs that use an object. Providing a carefully designed set of interface methods and preventing programs from accessing the instance variables except through this interface simplifies program maintenance.
7. *If a method does not modify the instance variables of a class, then it should be declared and defined as a constant method by placing the keyword* `const` *at the end of its heading*. Doing so lets the compiler help you find logic errors if such methods inadvertently change the value of a instance variable (or call a function that might do so).
8. *Put inlined definitions of simple methods after the class declaration in the header file for that class.* C++ does allow simple methods to be defined inside the class declaration, but doing so clutters the declaration, reducing its readability, so this practice should be avoided.
9. *Define more complicated methods in a separately compiled implementation file.* If a definition is stored in the header file, it will be recompiled every time a program that includes that definition is compiled, which wastes time. Storing a definition in a separately compiled implementation file eliminates this extra work.
10. *Only overload an operator to perform an operation that is consistent with its symbol.* For example, the standard `string` class overloads + to perform concatenation, which is the equivalent of adding two `string` values. Avoid being cute and abusing the overloading mechanism by giving operators counter-intuitive definitions since this reduces the readability of the code.

Potential Pitfalls

1. *Members of a class that are declared following the keyword* `private:` *are not accessible outside of the class*. Private members of a class can only be accessed by methods and friend functions.
2. *In definitions of the methods of a class, the method's name must be qualified with the name of the class and the scope operator (* `::` *).* For example, given a class declaration

```
class Point
{
 public:
   void print(ostream & out) const;
  private:
   double myX,
          myY;
};
```

the `print()` function for this class could be defined as

```
inline void Point::print(ostream & out)
{
   out << '(' << myX << ',' << myY << ')';
}
```

3. *The name of the constructor is the same as the name of the class, and the constructor has no return type.* For example, given a class declaration

```
class Point
{
 public:
   Point(double xVal, double yVal);
   // ...
 private:
   double myX,
          myY;
};
```

the constructor for this class could be defined as

```
Point::Point(double xVal, double yVal)
{
 myX = xVal;
 myY = yVal;
}
```

4. *Errors that result from inadvertent modification of the values of instance variables in a class can be difficult to find. To avoid such errors, methods that access instance variables, but do not modify them should be constant methods.* This is accomplished by placing the keyword `const` after the closing parentheses that follows their parameter lists. For example, given a class declaration

```
class Point
{
 public:
   double getX() const;
   // ...
 private:
   double myX,
          myY;
};
```

the accessor function `getX()` could be defined as

```
inline double Point::getX() const
{
   return myX;
}
```

5. *It is good practice to surround a class declaration with conditional compilation preprocessor directives.*

```
#ifndef CLASSNAME
#define CLASSNAME

ClassDeclaration

#endif
```

to avoid errors when multiple files insert that declaration using the `#include` *directive.* To see why, suppose that the class `Point` described previously has been declared, and we use it to create two new classes, `Line` and `Rectangle`:

```
#include "Point.h"

class Line
{
 public:
   // ...
 private:
   double mySlope;
   Point myYIntercept;
};
```

```
#include "Point.h"

class Rectangle
{
 public:
   //...
 private:
   Point myUpperLeft,
         myLowerRight;
};
```

Now if a graphing program should use the `#include` directive to insert both `Line.h` and `Rectangle.h`, then `Point` is declared twice, generating an error. By surrounding the declaration of `Point` as follows,

```
#ifndef POINT
#define POINT

class Point
{
   // ...
};

#endif
```

the code declaring class `Point` will be processed in whichever header file is processed first, but skipped in the header file that is processed second, eliminating the error.

6. *A friend function must be named as such by the class of which it is a friend.* This is accomplished by preceding its declaration with the keyword `friend` in the class declaration. However, the friend mechanism should only be used in situations where a method cannot be used and direct access to the instance variables of a class object is required.

Programming Problems

Section 11.4

1. Write a driver program to test the temperature converter methods of Exercise 1.
2. Write a driver program to test the methods `operator+()` and `operator-()` of Exercises 2 and 3.
3. Write a driver program to test the playing-cards class of Exercise 9.
4. Write a driver program to test the time class of Exercise 10.
5. Write a driver program to test the phone-number class of Exercise 11.
6. Write a driver program to test the checker-board class of Exercise 12.
7. Write a driver program to test the Cartesian-coordinate class of Exercise 13.
8. Write a driver program to test the polar-coordinate class of Exercise 14.
9. Write a driver program to test the personal-information class of Exercise 15.

10. Write a driver program to test the baseball-player class of Exercise 16.
11. Write a driver program to test the weather-statistics class of Exercise 17.
12. The *point–slope equation* of a line having slope m and passing through point P with coordinates (x_1, y_1) is $y - y_1 = m(x - x_1)$.
    - **(a)** Write a class for a `CartesianPoint`, described by its x- and y- coordinates, with all appropriate operations on such objects.
    - **(b)** Write a `LineSegment` class, described by two `CartesianPoint` endpoints. In addition to the usual operations, this class should provide operations to compute
        - **(i)** the midpoint of the line segment joining two points and
        - **(ii)** the equation of the perpendicular bisector of this line segment.
    - **(c)** Write a class for a `Line`, described by its slope and a point on the line, with operations that
        - **(i)** find the point–slope equation of the line and
        - **(ii)** find the slope–intercept equation of the line.
    - **(d)** Write a program to read the point and slope information for two lines and to determine whether they intersect or are parallel. If they intersect, find the point of intersection and also determine whether they are perpendicular.
13. Write a program that accepts a time of day in military format and finds the corresponding standard representation in hours, minutes, and A.M./P.M., or accepts the time in the usual format and finds the corresponding military representation. For example, the input 0100 should produce 1:00 A.M. as output, and the input 3:45 P.M. should give 1545. Use a class to store the time and provide extraction or conversion functions to display the time in either format.
14. A *rational number* is of the form a/b, where a and b are integers with $b \neq 0$. Write a program to do rational number arithmetic, representing each rational number as a class that has instance variables for the numerator and the denominator. The program should read and display all rational numbers in the format a/b, or simply a if the denominator is 1. The following examples illustrate the menu of commands that the user should be allowed to enter:

Input	Output	Comments
3/8 + 1/6	13/24	$a/b + c/d = (ad + bc)/bd$ reduced to lowest terms
3/8 – 1/6	5/24	$a/b - c/d = (ad - bc)/bd$ reduced to lowest terms
3/8 * 1/6	1/16	$a/b * c/d = ac/bd$ reduced to lowest terms
3/8 / 1/6	9/4	$a/b\, /\, c/d = ad/bc$ reduced to lowest terms
3/8 I	8/3	Invert a/b
8/3 M	2 + 2/3	Write a/b as a mixed fraction
6/8 R	3/4	Reduce a/b to lowest terms
6/8 G	2	Greatest common divisor of numerator and denominator
1/6 L 3/8	24	Lowest common denominator of a/b and c/d
1/6 < 3/8	true	$a/b < c/d$?
1/6 <= 3/8	true	$a/b \le c/d$?
1/6 > 3/8	false	$a/b > c/d$?
1/6 >= 3/8	false	$a/b \ge c/d$?

Input	Output	Comments
3/8 = 9/24	true	$a/b = c/d$?
2/3 X + 2 = 4/5	X = –9/5	Solution of linear equation $(a/b)X + c/d = e/f$

15. A *complex number* has the form $a + bi$ where a and b are real values and $i^2 = -1$. The standard C++ library includes a class `complex` for processing complex numbers. Examine the structure of this class to find the operations it provides and what data members it uses.
16. Using the `complex` type, write a program to find the roots (real or complex) of a quadratic equation. (See Programming Problem 3 of Chapter 3.)

Section 11.6

17. Write a driver program to test the input and output operators for the phone-number class in Exercise 1.
18. Write a driver program to test the input and output operators for the time class in Exercise 2.
19. Write a driver program to test the input and output operators for the date class in Exercise 3.

CHAPTER 12

Classes and Enumerations

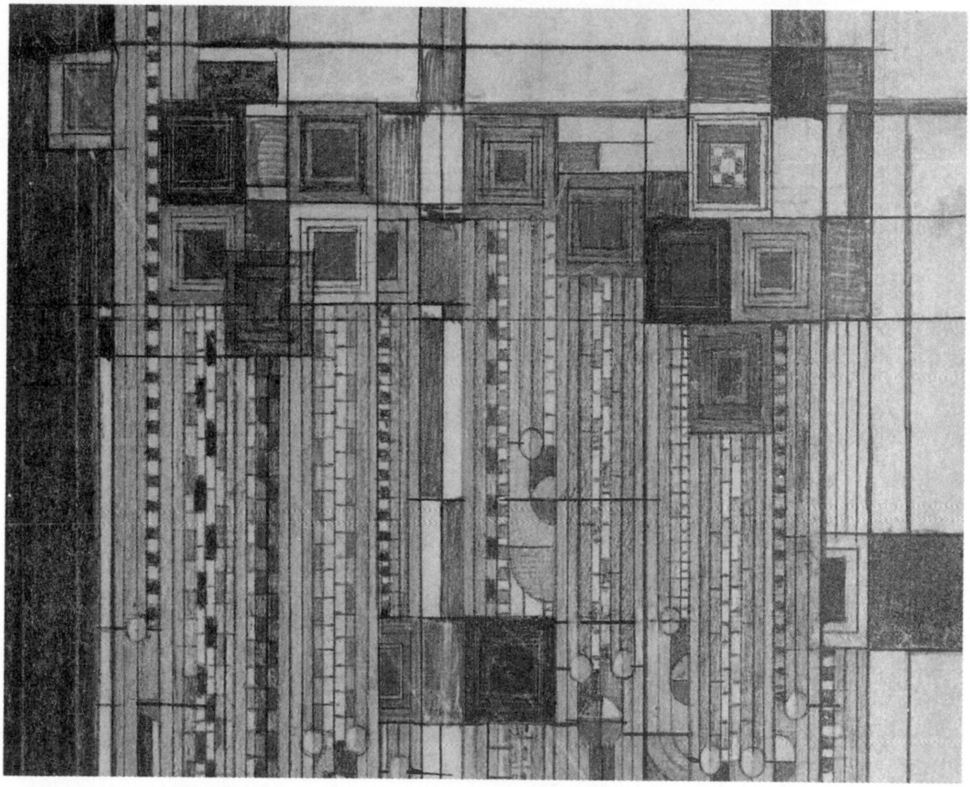

God created the integers; all the rest is the work of man.

-Leopold Kronecker

Roses are 0, violets are 3 ???

-(orig.)

This guy Roy G. Biv—now he was one COLORFUL character . . .

-V. Orehck III (fictitious)

Chapter Contents

Chapter Objectives

- See an example of how enumerations are used in a problem involving objects whose attributes cannot be modeled in a natural and efficient way using only the fundamental types.
- Learn how to declare and use C-style enumerations.
- See how C-style enumerations can be replaced by object-oriented enumerations.
- Look at an application that shows how enumerations can be used to model real-world objects.
- (Optional) Introduce the essential object-oriented properties of inheritance and polymorphism.

The *fundamental types* provided in C++ make it possible to represent objects whose values are integers, reals, characters, and so on. The C++ *class types* make it possible to represent complex objects having multiple attributes, and in the objects we have examined thus far, these attributes have been represented using the fundamental types. Some real-world objects, however, may have attributes that cannot be modeled in a natural and efficient way using only the fundamental types, for example,

- a person's gender: *female* or *male;*
- an automobile's manufacturer: *Buick, Chevrolet, Chrysler, Ferrari, Ford, Mercedes Benz, Honda, Saab, Toyota, Volkswagen*, . . . (to name just a few);
- a craftsman's expertise: *apprentice, journeyman, master;*
- athletic shoes designed for specific sports: *running shoes, tennis shoes, cross trainers, volleyball shoes, basketball shoes*, . . . (another long list).

Each of these attributes could be represented using the `string` type, but this can result in very inefficient programs. To see why, suppose that an object has an attribute named `hue`, whose value is one of the seven colors: *RED, ORANGE, YELLOW, GREEN, BLUE, INDIGO*, and *VIOLET*. One approach is to use a `string` object to represent these colors:

```
string hue;  // "RED", "ORANGE", ..., "VIOLET"
```

The object `hue` can then be assigned a character `string` color value, can be compared using the `string` relational operators, and so on. The problem is that using a `string` can be very time inefficient, since a seemingly simple assignment such as

```
hue = "ORANGE";
```

may actually require six assignments—one for each character being assigned. Comparisons can be time consuming for the same reason. The boolean expression in the `if` statement

```
if (hue == "VIOLET")
   doSomethingWith(hue);
```

may require six comparisons, one for each character in `VIOLET`.

An alternative approach is to represent such attributes using the `int` type, but this is clumsy and results in programs that are hard to read. For example, if we represent `hue` as an integer,

```
int hue;    // 1 - RED, 2 - ORANGE, ..., 7 - VIOLET
```

we avoid the inefficiency of the `string` type, because the assignment

```
hue = 2;
```

requires just one integer assignment. Similarly, a comparison

```
if (hue == 4)
   doSomethingWith(hue);
```

involves only one integer comparison.

The difficulty with this approach is remembering which integer is associated with which color. Is *RED* represented by zero or one? What is the fourth color? The programmer is forced to remember this object-to-integer mapping and use it consistently. This is annoying, because maintaining such a mapping is a mechanical process and could just as well be done by the computer. It would be much more convenient to simply write

```
hue = ORANGE;
```

or

```
if (hue == RED)
   doSomethingWith(hue);
```

There is an alternative that makes it possible to use statements like these—define a bunch of constants, one for each color:

```
const int RED = 1;
const int ORANGE = 2;
```

```
        .
        .
        .
```

The assignment and `if` statements given earlier,

```
hue = ORANGE;
   ...
if (hue == RED)
   doSomethingWith(hue);
```

can then be used. But the problem of remembering which integer is associated with which color still remains.

Fortunately, C++ provides a mechanism that avoids these problems, allowing the programmer to construct objects whose values are names of real-world entities like colors, genders, days, and so on. In this chapter, we will first examine this mechanism, called an *enumeration*, as a feature that C++ inherits from C and then we will see how these enumerations can be transformed into object-oriented enumerations.

12.1 Introductory Example: Wavelengths of Colors

As usual, we begin with an example to introduce this chapter's topic.

PROBLEM

Botanist Dawn N. Baum studies conifers and how their needles absorb light. To help with her research, she has hired us to write a program that, given one of the colors red, orange, yellow, green, blue, indigo, or violet, will display the wavelength of light associated with that color.

Object-Centered Design

Behavior. The program should display on the screen a prompt for a color and then read the color from the keyboard. It should then compute and display on the screen the wavelength of light associated with that color.

Objects. In addition to the usual screen, keyboard, and prompt objects, this problem involves the following objects:

	Software Objects		
Problem Objects	**Type**	**Kind**	**Name**
A color	`Color`	varying	*theColor*
The associated wavelength	`double`	varying	*wavelength*

As we saw in the introduction to this chapter, using the type `string` to represent *theColor* would not be very efficient. We will instead create a new type named `Color` that avoids these inefficiencies.

Operations. Solving this problem involves the following operations:

i. Output a `string` via an `ostream`
ii. Read a `Color` value via an `istream`
iii. Compute the (`double`) wavelength associated with a given `Color` value
iv. Display a `double` via an `ostream`

Of these operations, i and iv are predefined, but we will need to write functions to perform Operations ii and iii.

Algorithm. Given functions to perform each of these operations, we can organize them into the following algorithm:

Algorithm for Color Wavelengths

1. Via `cout`, display a prompt for a color.
2. From `cin`, read a color into *theColor.*
3. Compute *wavelength,* the wavelength associated with *theColor.*
4. Via `cout`, display *wavelength.*

Coding. The program in Figure 12.1 implements the preceding algorithm. It uses the type `Color` defined in *Color.h.* In the next section, we will see how to build this type `Color` in a way that is both efficient and readable.

Fig. 12.1 A `Color`–wavelength program. (Part 1 of 2)

```
/* wavelength.cpp computes the wavelength of light for a given Color.
 *
 * Input:        theColor, a Color value
 * Precondition: theColor is one of RED, ORANGE, YELLOW,
 *                  GREEN, BLUE, INDIGO, VIOLET
 * Output:       the wavelength of light corresponding to theColor
 ************************************************************/

#include <iostream>                     // cin, cout
using namespace std;
#include "Color.h"                      // Color

int main()
{
   cout << "To compute the wavelength corresponding to a given color,\n"
        << "enter a color (e.g., RED): ";
   Color theColor;
   cin >> theColor;
   double lambda = wavelength(theColor);
   cout << "\nThe corresponding wavelength is " << lambda << endl;
}
```

Fig. 12.1 A `Color`–wavelength program. (Part 2 of 2)

Sample run:

```
To compute the wavelength corresponding to a given color,
enter a color (e.g., RED): BLUE

The corresponding wavelength is 4.7e-07
```

12.2 C-Style Enumerations

The declaration

```
enum Color {RED, ORANGE, YELLOW, GREEN, BLUE, INDIGO, VIOLET};
```

creates a new type named `Color` whose values are the seven colors listed between the curly braces. Because the valid values are explicitly listed or *enumerated* in the declaration, this kind of type is called an **enumeration**.

ENUMERATION DECLARATIONS

The declaration of an enumeration must

1. provide a name for the enumeration, which becomes the name of a new type, and
2. explicitly list all of the values (called **enumerators**) of this new type.

In this example, `Color` is the name of the enumeration, and its enumerators are the identifiers

```
RED, ORANGE, YELLOW, GREEN, BLUE, INDIGO, VIOLET
```

When the compiler encounters such a declaration, it performs an object-to-integer mapping, associating the integer 0 with the first identifier in this list, the integer 1 with the second, and so on. Thus, for the preceding declaration, the compiler makes the following associations:

RED	ORANGE	YELLOW	GREEN	BLUE	INDIGO	VIOLET
↕	↕	↕	↕	↕	↕	↕
0	1	2	3	4	5	6

As another example,

```
enum Gender {FEMALE, MALE};
```

declares a new type `Gender` whose values are the identifiers `FEMALE` and `MALE`; the compiler will associate the integer 0 with `FEMALE` and the integer 1 with `MALE`. Similarly, the declaration

```
enum HandTool {HAMMER, PLIERS, SAW, SCREWDRIVER};
```

constructs a new type `HandTool` whose values are `HAMMER`, `PLIERS`, `SAW`, and `SCREWDRIVER` and associates the integers 0, 1, 2, and 3 with these identifiers, respectively. By contrast, neither of the declarations

```
enum Zipcodes {12531, 14405, 21724, 30081};    // ERROR!
enum LetterGrades {A, A-, B+, B, B-, C+, C,     // ERROR!
                   C-, D+, D, D-, "FAIL" };
```

is a valid enumeration, because each contains items that are not valid identifiers.

C++ also allows the programmer to specify explicitly the values given to the enumerators. For example, the declaration

```
enum NumberBase {BINARY = 2,
                 OCTAL = 8,
                 DECIMAL = 10,
                 HEX = 16, HEXADECIMAL = 16};
```

associates the identifiers `BINARY`, `OCTAL`, `DECIMAL`, `HEX`, and `HEXADECIMAL` with the values 2, 8, 10, 16, and 16, respectively. Similarly, if we wished to have the values 1, 2, . . . , 7 associated with the seven colors given earlier (instead of 0 through 6), we could use the declaration

```
enum Color {RED = 1, ORANGE = 2, YELLOW = 3, GREEN = 4,
            BLUE = 5, INDIGO = 6, VIOLET = 7};
```

or more compactly,

```
enum Color {RED = 1, ORANGE, YELLOW, GREEN, BLUE, INDIGO, VIOLET};
```

because the integer associated with an enumerator is, by default, one more than the integer associated with the preceding enumerator. The `iostream` library uses an enumeration declaration something like

```
enum Flag {GOOD_BIT = 1, BAD_BIT, FAIL_BIT = 4, EOF_BIT = 8};
```

which associates `1` with `GOOD_BIT`, `2` with `BAD_BIT`, `4` with `FAIL_BIT`, and `8` with `EOF_BIT`.[1]

These examples illustrate the flexibility of C++—the integers associated with the names need not be distinct, nor must they be given in ascending order, although it is good programming style to do so.

The general form of an enumeration declaration is as follows:

Enumeration Declaration Statement

Form:

```
enum TypeName { List };
```

---

1. Because each enumerator is a power of 2, each has a 1 at a different position in its binary representation. Such enumerators are called **bit masks** and make it possible to efficiently store a boolean value such as an `iostream` status attribute using only a single bit of memory.

where

`TypeName` is an identifier naming a new type;

`List` is a list of the values for the new type, separated by commas, each of which is a valid

IDENTIFIER

or an initialization expression of the form

IDENTIFIER = *integer_constant*

Purpose: Define a new data type whose values are the identifiers in `List`. Each identifier is associated with an integer as follows:

If an item in `List` has the form *IDENTIFIER* = *integer_constant*, then *integer_constant* is associated with *IDENTIFIER*;

otherwise if it is the first item in the list,

0 is associated with the *IDENTIFIER*;

otherwise,

1 + (the integer associated with the preceding identifier) is associated with the *IDENTIFIER*.

Because the compiler essentially treats an enumeration as a series of constant integer declarations, we will use the same uppercase naming convention for enumerators that we use for constant objects.

DEFINING ENUMERATION OBJECTS

To illustrate how enumerations are used, consider the following expansion of enumeration `Color`:

```
enum Color {COLOR_UNDERFLOW = -1,       // too-low indicator
            RED, ORANGE, YELLOW, GREEN, // 0-3
            BLUE, INDIGO, VIOLET,       // 4-6
            COLOR_OVERFLOW,             // too-high indicator
            NUMBER_OF_COLORS = 7};
```

Here, we added the identifiers `COLOR_UNDERFLOW` and `COLOR_OVERFLOW` as values to indicate out-of-range errors. As we will see later, these values can be used to keep from "falling off the ends of the list." We also added the identifier `NUMBER_OF_COLORS`, whose value is the number of values in the list, because this count is often useful.

If it is worthwhile to define a new type, it is usually worth taking the time to store that type in a library so that it can be easily reused. We thus store this declaration of type `Color` in a header file *Color.h* so that programs like that in Figure 12.1 can use it simply by including this header file.

Given this type, we can declare a `Color` object named `theColor` as in Figure 12.1. Enumeration objects can also be initialized when they are declared:

```
Color theColor = YELLOW;
```

USING ENUMERATIONS

In addition to defining enumeration objects, an enumeration can be used as the index of an array. For example, suppose that we define `colorArray` as follows:

```
double colorArray[NUMBER_OF_COLORS] = {0.0};
```

This definition builds the object `colorArray` as a fixed-size array with index values 0 through 6. Because the C++ compiler treats the identifiers `RED` through `VIOLET` as the integer values 0 through 6, we can visualize `colorArray` as follows:

colorArray	0.0	0.0	0.0	0.0	0.0	0.0	0.0
	[RED]	[ORANGE]	[YELLOW]	[GREEN]	[BLUE]	[INDIGO]	[VIOLET]

The `Color` enumerators can then be used with the subscript operator to access the array elements.

In the same way, an extra enumerator like `NUMBER_OF_COLORS` can be used to provide a `vector<T>` with an initial size:

```
vector<double> colorVector(NUMBER_OF_COLORS, 0.0);
```

This defines `colorVector` as a varying-sized object, initially with seven elements:

colorVector	0.0	0.0	0.0	0.0	0.0	0.0	0.0
	[RED]	[ORANGE]	[YELLOW]	[GREEN]	[BLUE]	[INDIGO]	[VIOLET]

C-STYLE ENUMERATION OPERATIONS

Many enumeration operations are predefined. For example, an enumeration object can be assigned a value, used as a parameter, compared using the relational operators, and so on. But other operations must be defined by the creator or user of the enumeration. For example, the program in Figure 12.1 requires computing the wavelength corresponding to a `Color` value. Since there is no predefined operation to do this, one must be provided. The function in Figure 12.2 shows one way to do this. Because this `Color` operation is nontrivial, its definition should be stored in the library's implementation file *Color.cpp* and its prototype in the header file *Color.h*.

Fig. 12.2 Computing `Color` wavelength. (Part 1 of 2)

```
// ------ Wavelength of a Color --------------------------------

double wavelength(Color aColor)
{
   switch(aColor)
   {
      case RED:
                     return 6.5E-7;
```

Fig. 12.2 Computing `Color` wavelength. (Part 2 of 2)

```
      case ORANGE:
                     return 6.0E-7;
      case YELLOW:
                     return 5.8E-7;
      case GREEN:
                     return 5.2E-7;
      case BLUE:
                     return 4.7E-7;
      case INDIGO:
                     return 4.4E-7;
      case VIOLET:
                     return 4.1E-7;
      default:
                     cerr << "\n*** wavelength: invalid color "
                             "received!\n";
                     return 0.0;
   }
}
```

A program like that in Figure 12.1 can call this function,

```
double lambda = wavelength(theColor);
```

and the argument `theColor` will be passed to the function via parameter `aColor`. The function's `switch` statement will then select and return the appropriate wavelength.

The program in Figure 12.1 also requires that we be able to read a `Color` value from the keyboard using `operator>>`, which is not predefined. As shown in Section 11.6, overloading the input function is a bit complicated; therefore, we will derive it in more detail.

Function Behavior. The function `operator>>()` should receive `istream` and `Color` parameters from its caller. Because an `istream` is a stream of characters, this function should read a sequence of characters from the `istream` into a `string` object. For user convenience, we will allow these characters to be either upper- or lowercase and design the function to convert the characters in this string to uppercase, if necessary. Based upon the value of that string, the function must assign the corresponding `Color` enumerator to the `Color` parameter. If the string does not correspond to any valid `Color` enumerator, the *fail* bit should be set in the `istream`. Finally, the function should return its `istream` parameter (so that input operations can be chained).

Function Objects. The objects in this problem are as follows:

	Software Objects			
Problem Objects	**Type**	**Kind**	**Movement**	**Name**
An `istream`	`istream`	varying	received (in), sent back (out), and returned	`in`
A `Color`	`Color`	varying	received (in) and sent back (out)	*aColor*
A `string`	`string`	varying	none	*colorString*

The specification of the operation is thus:

Receive: *in*, an `istream`
aColor, a `Color` object

Precondition: *in* contains a string corresponding to a `Color` value

Input: a string from *in*

Send back: *in* with the string removed
aColor, containing the `Color` corresponding to the string read from *in*

Return: *in* (for chaining)

From this, we can write the following stub for the function:

```
istream& operator>>(istream& in, Color& aColor)
{
   // ... to be filled in shortly ...
   return in;
}
```

Function Operations. The operations in this problem are as follows:

i. Receive arguments from the caller
ii. Read a `string` from an `istream`
iii. Convert the characters in a `string` to uppercase, if necessary
iv. Assign to the `Color` parameter `aColor` the enumerator corresponding to the `string` (or set the *fail* bit in the `istream` if there is no such `Color` enumerator)

Function Algorithm. We can organize these operations into the following algorithm:

Algorithm for color input

0. Receive *in* and *aColor* from the caller.
1. From *in*, read a string into *colorString*.
2. For each index *i* in *colorString*:
   If *colorString*[*i*] is lowercase, convert it to uppercase.
3. If *colorString* == "RED"
   Assign enumerator RED to *aColor*.

Else if *colorString* == "ORANGE"
  Assign enumerator ORANGE to *aColor.*
Else if *colorString* == "YELLOW"
  Assign enumerator YELLOW to *aColor.*
Else if *colorString* == "GREEN"
  Assign enumerator GREEN to *aColor.*
Else if *colorString* == "BLUE"
  Assign enumerator BLUE to *aColor.*
Else if *colorString* == "INDIGO"
  Assign enumerator INDIGO to *aColor.*
Else if *colorString* == "VIOLET"
  Assign enumerator VIOLET to *aColor.*
Else
  Set the *fail* bit in stream *in.*

4. Return *in.*

Function Coding. Given this algorithm, we can fill in the function's stub as shown in Figure 12.3. Because this is a nontrivial function, we store its definition in the `Color` library's implementation file, *Color.cpp*, and place its prototype in *Color.h.*

Note that we must perform selection using the `string` object `colorString`. Because the selector in a `switch` statement cannot be based on a string value, we must use a multibranch `if` statement to perform the selection.

Fig. 12.3 `Color` input. (Part 1 of 2)

```
// ------ Color Input ----------------------------------------
#include <string>                // string
#include <cctype>                // islower(), toupper()
using namespace std;

istream& operator>>(istream& in, Color& aColor)
{
   string colorString;
   in >> colorString;

   for (int i = 0; i < colorString.size(); i++)
      if (islower(colorString[i]))
         colorString[i] = toupper(colorString[i]);
   if (colorString == "RED")
      aColor = RED;
   else if (colorString == "ORANGE")
      aColor = ORANGE;
   else if (colorString == "YELLOW")
      aColor = YELLOW;
   else if (colorString == "GREEN")
      aColor = GREEN;
```

Fig. 12.3 `Color` input. (Part 2 of 2)

```
   else if (colorString == "BLUE")
      aColor = BLUE;
   else if (colorString == "INDIGO")
      aColor = INDIGO;
   else if (colorString == "VIOLET")
      aColor = VIOLET;
   else
      in.setstate(ios::failbit);

   return in;
}
```

Given this function, the program in Figure 12.1 can now contain the statements

```
Color theColor
cin >> theColor;
```

and since `theColor` is of type `Color`, the compiler will search for a version of `operator>>` whose signature is `(istream&, Color&)`. Finding its prototype in *Color.h*, the compiler will allow the call to proceed. The linker will then search for a definition with this signature. Upon finding it in *Color.cpp*, the linker will bind the function call to this definition.

OTHER ENUMERATION OPERATIONS

Because we are building a `Color` library, it makes sense to provide additional `Color` operations that might be useful.

Output. As we saw in Figure 12.3, all I/O is performed at the character level, and the input function basically reads `string` values and maps them to `Color` values. The output function `operator<<` must therefore perform the opposite `Color`-to-`string` mapping and write the resulting `string` to an `ostream`. Figure 12.4 gives a definition of this function that, because of its complexity, should be defined in *Color.cpp*.

Fig. 12.4 `Color` output. (Part 1 of 2)

```
// ------ Color Output -------------------------------------------

ostream& operator<<(ostream& out, Color aColor)
{
   switch(aColor)
   {
      case RED:
                     out << "RED";
                     break;
```

Fig. 12.4 `Color` output. (Part 2 of 2)

```
      case ORANGE:
                  out << "ORANGE";
                  break;
      case YELLOW:
                  out << "YELLOW";
                  break;
      case GREEN:
                  out << "GREEN";
                  break;
      case BLUE:
                  out << "BLUE";
                  break;
      case INDIGO:
                  out << "INDIGO";
                  break;
      case VIOLET:
                  out << "VIOLET";
                  break;
      default:
                  cerr << "\n*** operator<<: invalid color "
                          "received!\n";
   }
   return out;
}
```

As described earlier, the compiler treats an enumeration as a special kind of integer. This has two implications for this function:

1. If a function receives but does not pass back an enumeration value, the value should be passed using the call-by-value mechanism. That is, since an enumeration is not a class, an enumeration value should not be passed using the `const` reference mechanism.
2. Because we are using an enumeration (as opposed to a `string`), we can use a `switch` statement to perform the selection.

Once the function is defined and its prototype stored in *Color.h*, a programmer can write

```
cout << "Color me " << theColor << endl;
```

and if the value of `theColor` is `BLUE`, then

```
Color me BLUE
```

will be displayed.

Successor. A *successor function* is a function that, given a value *v*, returns the value that follows *v* in the list of enumerators. For example, given `RED`, a successor function will return `ORANGE`; given `ORANGE`, it will return `YELLOW`; and so on; given `VIOLET`, however, it will return `COLOR_OVERFLOW`, one of our "illegal" `Color` enumerators.

Figure 12.5 presents a function `next()` that provides this operation for our `Color` enumeration. As usual, the complexity of this function implies that it be stored in *Color.cpp*.

Fig. 12.5 `Color` successor.

```
// ------ Color Successor ---------------------------------------

Color next(Color aColor)
{
   switch (aColor)
   {
      case RED:
                     return ORANGE;
      case ORANGE:
                     return YELLOW;
      case YELLOW:
                     return GREEN;
      case GREEN:
                     return BLUE;
      case BLUE:
                     return INDIGO;
      case INDIGO:
                     return VIOLET;
      case VIOLET:
                     return COLOR_OVERFLOW;
      default:
                     cerr << "\n*** next(): invalid color received!\n";
                     return COLOR_OVERFLOW;
   }
}
```

This function shows why the enumerators `COLOR_UNDERFLOW` and `COLOR_OVERFLOW` were added. By providing these extra "invalid" values at each end of the enumerator list, we provide an error value for the function to return when there is no valid return value.

We can use this function to drive a `for` loop that iterates through the `Color` values:

```
for (Color aColor = RED; aColor <= VIOLET;
                         aColor = next(aColor))
   cout << aColor << ' ';
```

On each repetition, the call to `next()` returns the successor to `aColor`, and so this statement produces

```
RED ORANGE YELLOW GREEN BLUE INDIGO VIOLET
```

For the final repetition (when `aColor` is `VIOLET`), the call to `next()` returns `COLOR_OVERFLOW`. Because the compiler treats `VIOLET` as 6 and `COLOR_OVERFLOW` as 7, the condition

```
aColor <= VIOLET
```

is evaluated as

```
COLOR_OVERFLOW <= VIOLET     // 7 <= 6?
```

which is `false`, terminating the repetition.

Predecessor. Whereas a successor function returns the next value in a sequence, a predecessor function returns the previous value in the sequence. A predecessor function is similar to the successor function and is left as an exercise.

LIBRARIES AND TYPES

As we saw with classes, the true purpose of a library is as follows:

The purpose of a library is to store

1. a type declaration and
2. the operations on objects of that type.

That is, a library is intended to be a container for a type, including the collection of functions that form the basic operations on that type. In the case of type `Color`, we would define a library named *Color*. In its interface file *Color.h*, we would store the declarations of `Color` and the various `Color` operations, as shown in Figure 12.6:

Fig. 12.6 The `Color` interface file. (Part 1 of 2)

```
/* Color.h contains the interface for enumeration Color.
 * ...
 ************************************************************/

#include <iostream>                      // istream, ostream
using namespace std;

// --- The type
enum Color {COLOR_UNDERFLOW = -1,         // too-low error
            RED, ORANGE, YELLOW, GREEN,   // 0-3
            BLUE, INDIGO, VIOLET,         // 4-6
            COLOR_OVERFLOW,               // too-high error
            NUMBER_OF_COLORS= 7};
```

Fig. 12.6 The `Color` interface file. (Part 2 of 2)

```
// --- Its interface
istream& operator>>(istream& in, Color& aColor);
ostream& operator<<(ostream& out, Color aColor);
Color next(Color aColor);
Color previous(Color aColor);
double frequency(Color aColor);
double wavelength(Color aColor);
// ... additional Color operations ...
```

The corresponding definitions of the `Color` operations would then be stored in the library's implementation file *Color.cpp* and documentation in its documentation file *Color.doc*.

Given this library, a program can now use the type `Color` and its operations simply by including the library's header file (*Color.h*) as in Figure 12.1. After the program is compiled, the resulting object file must be linked with the definitions in the implementation object file.

Quick Quiz 12.2

1. The compiler treats an enumerator as a special kind of ________.
2. (True or false) `enum T {1, 2, 3, 4};` is a valid enumeration declaration.
3. (True or false) `enum T {FORTY, FIFTY, SIXTY};` is a valid enumeration declaration.
4. (True or false) `enum T {FORTY-ONE, FIFTY-ONE, SIXTY-ONE};` is a valid enumeration declaration.

Questions 5–14 use the following declarations:

```
enum English {ZERO, ONE, TWO, THREE, FOUR};
enum German {EIN = 1, ZWEI, DREI, VIER};
enum PigLatin {EROZAY, EETHRAY = 3, IVEFAY = 5, IXSAY};
enum Nonsense {FEE, FI = 6, FO, FUM, FOO = 3, BAR};
```

5. What value is associated with `THREE`?
6. What value is associated with `DREI`?
7. What value is associated with `IXSAY`?
8. What value is associated with `FEE`?
9. What value is associated with `FUM`?
10. What value is associated with `BAR`?
11. What type is defined by the last declaration?
12. In the last declaration, `FUM` is called a(n) ________.
13. (True or false) `EETHRAY < IVEFAY`.
14. (True or false) `FOO > BAR`.
15. (True or false) An enumeration parameter should not be declared using the `const` reference mechanism.

16. (True or false) Enumerations may be used as array indices.
17. Write an enumeration declaration for the names of the days of the week.
18. What is the main purpose of a library?

Exercises 12.2

1. Write an enumeration `MonthAbbrev`, whose values are abbreviations of the months of the year and consist of the first three letters of the months' names.

Exercises 2–7 assume the enumerated type `MonthAbbrev` of Exercise 1. For each, find the value of the given expression.

2. `JAN < AUG`
3. `SEP <= SEP`
4. `SEP + 1`
5. `APR - 1`
6. `AUG + 2`
7. `AUG - 2`

Exercises 8–13 ask you to develop a library for the enumerated type `MonthAbbrev` of Exercise 1. To test this library, you should write driver programs as instructed in Programming Problem 1 at the end of this chapter.

8. Construct a header file for the type `MonthAbbrev` that defines it together with (at least) I/O operations and a successor operation.
9. Construct an implementation file for the header file of Exercise 8.
10. Write a documentation file to complete the library for the type `MonthAbbrev` of Exercises 8 and 9.
11. Write a function whose parameter is the number of a month and whose value is the corresponding value of type `MonthAbbrev`. Add this function—its prototype, definition, and documentation—to the appropriate files in the library for the type `MonthAbbrev` of Exercises 8–10.
12. Write a function whose parameters are a nonnegative integer `n` and a month abbreviation `abbrev` and that finds the "`n`th successor" of `abbrev`. The 0th successor of `abbrev` is `abbrev` itself; for `n` > 0, the `n`th successor of `abbrev` is the `n`th month following `abbrev`. For example, the fourth successor of `AUG` is `DEC`, and the sixth successor of `AUG` is `FEB`. Add this function—its prototype, definition, and documentation—to the appropriate files in the library for the type `MonthAbbrev` of Exercises 8–10.
13. Proceed as in Exercise 12, but define the function recursively.

Exercises 14–16 ask you to develop a library for an enumerated type `Day` for the names of the days of the week. To test this library, you should write driver programs as instructed in Programming Problem 2 at the end of this chapter.

14. Construct a header file for type `Day`. It should at least have I/O operations and a successor operation.
15. Construct an implementation file for the type `Day` of Exercise 14.
16. Write a documentation file to complete the library for the type `Day` of Exercises 14 and 15.

12.3 Object-Oriented Enumerations

Because C-style enumerations are not classes, they suffer from two drawbacks:

1. The operations on a C-style enumeration cannot be defined as methods, and so C-style enumerations are not consistent with the I-can-do-it-myself principle.
2. Because there is no class invariant, operations on a C-style enumeration cannot assume that valid values will be passed to an enumeration parameter.

Both of these deficiencies can be overcome by replacing a C-style enumeration with a class.

DECLARING ENUMERATION CLASSES

As we saw in Chapter 11, building a class consists of carefully designing the class and then using that design as a blueprint to implement the class.

Class Design. Recall that the first step in designing a class is to list the operations it should provide. Applying the internal perspective to the design of a `Color` class, we might list the following:

- Initialize myself to a default color value
- Initialize myself to an explicitly supplied color value
- Return my wavelength
- Return my frequency
- Display my value on a given `ostream`
- Read a color value from a given `istream` into me
- Compare myself with another `Color` using any of the relational operators
- Increment myself to the color value that follows mine
- Decrement myself to the color value that precedes mine

Again, this is not an exhaustive list, but it will be adequate to illustrate the use of enumerations with classes.

Class Implementation. Once we have identified what operations the class is to provide, we are ready to begin implementing its data members. From our list of operations, it should be evident that the class needs to store a color value. To represent a color value, we begin by declaring an enumeration named `ColorValue`, in the class header file *Color.h*:

```
enum ColorValue {COLOR_UNDERFLOW = -1,
                 RED, ORANGE, YELLOW, GREEN,
                 BLUE, INDIGO, VIOLET,
                 COLOR_OVERFLOW,
                 NUMBER_OF_COLORS = 7};
```

We can then declare a variable that can store a `ColorValue`:

```
ColorValue myColorValue;
```

This will be the only instance variable of the class and so we wrap it, but not the declaration of ColorValue, within a declaration of class Color:

```
enum ColorValue {COLOR_UNDERFLOW = -1,
                 RED, ORANGE, YELLOW, GREEN,
                 BLUE, INDIGO, VIOLET,
                 COLOR_OVERFLOW,
                 NUMBER_OF_COLORS = 7};
class Color
{
 public:
   // ... to be filled in later ...
 private:
   ColorValue myColorValue;
};
```

We thus have *two* types: ColorValue, which is the name of an enumeration of color values, and Color, which is the name of a class that contains an instance variable of type ColorValue. However, no operations will be defined for type ColorValue; its sole purpose is to support the declaration of the instance variable myColorValue. Instead, all operations will be defined as methods (or friends) of class Color. By declaring ColorValue outside of class Color, the various ColorValue enumerators (RED, ORANGE, . . .) can be used as is, both by the class and by any program that uses this class.[2]

To finish our class declaration, we wrap it and the declaration of ColorValue inside preprocessor directives that prevent it from being compiled more than once:

```
#ifndef COLOR
#define COLOR

enum ColorValue {COLOR_UNDERFLOW = -1,
                 RED, ORANGE, YELLOW, GREEN,
                 BLUE, INDIGO, VIOLET,
                 COLOR_OVERFLOW,
                 NUMBER_OF_COLORS = 7};
class Color
{
 public:
   // ... to be filled in later ...
 private:
   ColorValue myColorValue;
};

#endif
```

Given this much, a definition

```
Color hue;
```

2. If ColorValue were declared publicly within class Color, then any use of an enumerator outside of the class would have to be qualified with the name of the class and the scope operator (e.g., Color::RED, Color::ORANGE, etc.).

will define hue as a Color object that we might visualize as follows:

Of course, to provide hue with an initial value, we need to supply a Color constructor, so we proceed to the implementation of the Color operations.

DEFINING COLOR OPERATIONS

The Class Invariant. The value of the class' instance variable myColorValue must be one of the ColorValue enumerators that names a color. Thus, an invariant for the class Color is

```
myColorValue == RED || myColorValue == ORANGE ||
myColorValue == YELLOW || myColorValue == GREEN ||
myColorValue == BLUE || myColorValue == INDIGO ||
myColorValue == VIOLET
```

Our implementations of the class constructors and other operations that can modify this instance variable must ensure that this invariant is never violated. Other operations that use the instance variable can then be assured that its value satisfies this condition.

The Default-Value Constructor. As a default color value, we might choose any of the colors. Here we will use the first valid color value RED. Applying object-centered design from the internal perspective gives the following specification of the behavior of the default-value constructor:

Postcondition: myColorValue == RED

Figure 12.7 gives a Color constructor that guarantees this postcondition. Because this method is so simple, we define it as inline in *Color.h* (between the declaration of the class Color and the #endif directive). We store its prototype in the public section of class Color, as shown in Figure 12.14.

Fig. 12.7 The Color default-value constructor.

```
// ------ Default-Value Constructor ----------------------------

inline Color::Color()
{
   myColorValue = RED;
}
```

A programmer can now write

```
Color hue;
```

and `hue` will be auto-initialized to the color `RED`:

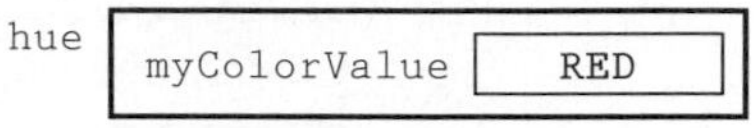

The Explicit-Value Constructor. If we want to initialize a `Color` object with some value other than `RED`, we must, of course, supply a second constructor. Applying object-centered design from an internal perspective gives the following specification of its behavior:

Receive: *initialColorValue*, a `ColorValue`

Precondition: *initialColorValue* is one of `RED, . . . , VIOLET`

Postcondition: `myColorValue` == *initialColorValue*

Figure 12.8 presents a `Color` constructor that ensures that the precondition and postcondition are satisfied and thus guarantees that the class invariant remains true. As before, we define this explicit-value constructor as `inline` in *Color.h*, between the declaration of the class `Color` and the `#endif` directive.

Fig. 12.8 The `Color` explicit-value constructor.

```
// ------ Explicit-Value Constructor ---------------------------

#include <cassert>                              // assert()
using namespace std;

inline Color::Color(ColorValue initialColorValue)
{
   assert(RED <= initialColorValue && initialColorValue <= VIOLET);
   myColorValue = initialColorValue;
}
```

The declaration

```
Color hue(BLUE);
```

will construct `hue` and initialize it with the color value `BLUE`:

`Color` **Wavelength.** Next on our list of operations is a function to "return my wavelength." We can specify its behavior as follows:

Return: the (`double`) wavelength corresponding to `myColorValue`

The method in Figure 12.9 satisfies this specification. Because this operation should not alter any of the class instance variables, it is defined as a `const` method. Note that it also need not include a default case in the `switch` statement because of the class invariant. Because of the relative complexity of this function, we put its prototype in the public section of class `Color` (see Figure 12.14) and its definition in a separately compiled implementation file *Color.cpp*.

Fig. 12.9 `Color` wavelength.

```
/* Color.cpp provides the implementation of class Color operations
 * ...
 *****************************************************************/

#include "Color.h"                          // class Color

// ---     wavelength ----------------------------------------
double Color::wavelength() const
{
   switch (myColorValue)
   {
      case RED:
                    return 6.5E-7;
      case ORANGE:
                    return 6.0E-7;
      case YELLOW:
                    return 5.8E-7;
      case GREEN:
                    return 5.2E-7;
      case BLUE:
                    return 4.7E-7;
      case INDIGO:
                    return 4.4E-7;
      case VIOLET:
                    return 4.1E-7;
   }
}
```

A programmer can now write

```
cout << hue.wavelength() << endl;
```

and the appropriate wavelength for the color in `hue` will be displayed. A method to compute the frequency of a `Color` is straightforward and is left as an exercise.

`Color` I/O. As explained in Section 11.6, the extraction operator (`>>`) should not be defined as a method of a class other than `istream`. We will therefore use the same approach used there: Define a public `read()` method, and then overload `operator>>` as a "normal" function that uses `read()`. The behavior of this `read()` method can be specified as follows:

Receive: *in*, an `istream`

Input: *colorString*, a character string

Precondition: *colorString* is one of "RED", "ORANGE", . . . , "VIOLET"

Postcondition: `myColorValue` contains the `ColorValue` corresponding to *colorString*

Send back: *in* with the character string literal removed

Figure 12.10 gives a definition of `read()` that satisfies this specification. Because the method can modify `myColorValue`, it must ensure that the class invariant remains true. And because it is relatively complicated, it is defined in *Color.cpp*. The prototype of this method must, of course, be stored in the public section of class `Color`, as shown in Figure 12.14.

Fig. 12.10 `Color` input (function member). (Part 1 of 2)

```
#include <string>                               // string
#include <cctype>                               // islower(), toupper()
using namespace std;

// ------- Input Method ----------------------------------
void Color::read(istream& in)
{
   string colorString;                                 // read string
   in >> colorString;

   for (int i = 0; i < colorString.size(); i++)    // convert case
      if (islower(colorString[i]))                 // if needed
         colorString[i] = toupper(colorString[i]);
   if (colorString == "RED")                       // map to ColorValue
      myColorValue = RED;
   else if (colorString == "ORANGE")
      myColorValue = ORANGE;
   else if (colorString == "YELLOW")
      myColorValue = YELLOW;
   else if (colorString == "GREEN")
      myColorValue = GREEN;
   else if (colorString == "BLUE")
      myColorValue = BLUE;
   else if (colorString == "INDIGO")
      myColorValue = INDIGO;
```

Fig. 12.10 `Color` input (function member). (Part 2 of 2)

```
   else if (colorString == "VIOLET")
      myColorValue = VIOLET;
   else
   {
      cerr << "\n*** read(): invalid color-value received!\n";
      in.setstate(ios::failbit);
   }
}
```

A programmer can now write

```
hue.read(cin);
```

to read a color value for `hue`.

Of course, it would be more convenient if we could use the operator `>>` to read a `Color`. Because this operation must be defined as a nonmember function, its specification is as follows:

Receive: *in*, an `istream`
theColor, a `Color`

Input: a character string

Precondition: the input string is one of "RED", "ORANGE", . . . , "VIOLET"

Send back: *in*, with the character string literal removed
theColor, containing the `ColorValue` corresponding to the input string

Return: *in*, for chaining of input operations

Although this specification is somewhat complicated, the definition of the function is quite simple, thanks to the `read()` method. We can therefore inline `operator>>` in *Color.h*, as shown in Figure 12.11. Because `operator>>` is not a method of class `Color`, no prototype is placed in the declaration of the class.[3]

Fig. 12.11 `Color` input (NonMember function).

```
// ------- Function Input -----------------------------------
inline istream& operator>>(istream& in, Color& theColor)
{
   theColor.read(in);
   return in;
}
```

---

3. If `operator>>` were to directly assign a `ColorValue` to the private member `theColor.myColorValue`, instead of using the public `theColor.read()` method to do so indirectly, then it would be necessary for class `Color` to contain a prototype of `operator>>` naming it as a `friend`.

Given this definition, a statement like

```
cin >> hue;
```

can be used to read a color value from the keyboard into `hue`.

A `Color` output operation can be provided using a similar approach and is left as an exercise.

Relational Operators. Unlike `operator<<` and `operator>>`, the relational operators ==, !=, <, >, <=, and >= can be overloaded as methods of class `Color`. However, if we implement these operations using *methods*, then a boolean expression like

```
someColor == RED
```

will be valid, but an expression

```
RED == someColor
```

will not be valid, because such an expression sends `RED` (a `ColorValue` object) the == message with a `Color` argument, and there is no definition of `operator==` with such a signature. Put differently, the equality operation will not be symmetric if we define `operator==` as a `Color` method.

This problem can be circumvented by defining `operator==` as a "normal" function. Its behavior can be specified as

Receive: *left*, a `Color`, and *right*, another `Color`

Return: `true` if and only if *left*.`myColorValue` == *right*.`myColorValue`

The other relational operators have similar specifications. For example,

Receive: *left*, a `Color`, and *right*, another `Color`

Return: `true` if and only if *left*.`myColorValue` < *right*.`myColorValue`

is a specification for the less-than operation.

Figure 12.12 presents definitions of `operator==`, `operator<`, and `operator<=` satisfying these specifications. Because they are relatively simple, we define them as `inline` in *Color.h*.

Fig. 12.12 `Color` relational operators. (Part 1 of 2)

```
// ------- Equality ---------------------------------------
inline bool operator==(const Color& left, const Color& right)
{
   return left.myColorValue == right.myColorValue;
}

// ------- Less-than --------------------------------------
inline bool operator<(const Color& left, const Color& right)
{
   return left.myColorValue < right.myColorValue;
}
```

Fig. 12.12 `Color` relational operators. (Part 2 of 2)

```
// ------- Less-than-or-equal ---------------------------------
inline bool operator<=(const Color& left, const Color& right)
{
   return left.myColorValue <= right.myColorValue;
}

// ... remaining relational operators omitted
```

If we try to compile these functions, an error message is generated because they are functions (not methods) trying to access the private `myColorValue` data members of their operands. Either the class must provide a public accessor method to access `myColorValue`, or it must specify that these functions are friend functions, as shown in Figure 12.14. Once this is done, a programmer can compare two `Color` objects in statements like

```
if (hue1 == hue2)
   // ... do whatever is appropriate for equal colors
```

or

```
if (hue1 < hue2)
   // ... do whatever is appropriate
```

Although it is less obvious, we can also compare a `Color` and a `ColorValue`:

```
if (hue == VIOLET)
   // ... do something appropriate
```

or

```
if (ORANGE < hue)
   // ... do something appropriate
```

Even though there are no definitions of `operator==` or `operator<` with the signature `(Color, ColorValue)` or `(ColorValue, Color)`, such comparisons still work. When the compiler encounters the comparison

```
hue == VIOLET
```

it searches for a definition of `operator==` whose signature is `(Color, ColorValue)`. Because there is none, it uses the explicit-value constructor to build a `Color` out of a `ColorValue` and then uses the definition of `operator==` whose signature is `(Color, Color)`. The compiler thus uses the explicit-value constructor to build `VIOLET` into a `Color`, which it then passes to the definition of `operator==` whose signature is `(Color, Color)`.

Fig. 12.15 An O-O `Color`–wavelength program. (Part 2 of 2)

```
#include <iostream>                          // cin, cout
using namespace std;
#include "Color.h"                           // Color

int main()
{
   cout << "\nTo compute the wavelength of a given "
        << "color,\nenter a color (e.g., RED): ";
   Color theColor;
   cin >> theColor;

   double lambda = theColor.wavelength();

   cout << "\nThe corresponding wavelength is " << lambda << endl;
}
```

The behavior of this program is identical to that of Figure 12.1, but the `Color` used by this program is a class, not a C-style enumeration, and is thus more consistent with the I-can-do-it-myself principle. That is, the program in Figure 12.1 uses the external approach by applying `wavelength()` as a function to a `Color`, but the program in Figure 12.15 uses the internal approach by sending a `wavelength()` message to a `Color` object, which then responds to that message.

This completes our introduction to enumerations in classes. By planning for the future and providing useful functions like ++ and -- (even though they are not needed to solve the problem at hand), we produce a first class data type that is useful in other problems. For example, this extra functionality makes it quite easy to display a table of colors and their wavelengths:

```
for (Color hue = RED; hue <= VIOLET; hue++)
   cout << hue << ' ----- ' << hue.wavelength() << endl;
```

Also, as the `Color` example of this section and the `Rock` class in the next illustrate, enumeration-based classes, together with functions that provide useful operations on them, allow objects from the real world to be represented using their real-world names, both by *programmers* as they write programs and by *users* as they execute programs.

✔ Quick Quiz 12.3

1. What are two of the main drawbacks of C-style enumerations?
2. (True or false) If a class is used to provide operations on an enumeration, it is customary to place the enumeration declaration outside of the class declaration.
3. Why is it important that class operations do not violate the class invariants?
4. The compiler may use a(n) _______ constructor in a class `C` to perform automatic conversion of a type to type `C`.
5. For prefix ++, the signature of `operator++` is _______; and for postfix ++, the signature of `operator++` is _______.

Exercises 12.3

1. Redesign the type `MonthAbbrev` described in Exercises 1–12 of Section 12.2 so that it is a class instead of an enumeration type.
2. Redesign the type `Day` described in Exercises 14–16 of Section 12.2 so that it is a class instead of an enumeration type.
3. Design a `Date` class to model dates consisting of a month name (given by an enumeration), a day number, and a year number. Operations should at least include input and output.
4. Design a class for doing simple arithmetic with names of numbers (given by an enumeration); for example, zero, one, two, . . . , nine, ten. Operations should at least include input, output, and some of the relational operators.
5. Design a `PlayingCard` class to model playing cards (using enumerations for suits and card values). Operations should at least include input and output. Also formulate appropriate class invariants.

12.4 Case Study: Geological Classification

Objects are often organized into groups that share similar characteristics. To illustrate, consider the following:

- A doctor might be described as an internist, a pediatrician, a surgeon, a gynecologist, a family practitioner, or some other specialty, according to his or her area of training.
- Members of the animal kingdom are organized into groups (called phyla) according to whether they have vertebrae, the relative positions of their nervous and digestive systems, and their outer covering.
- The elements are organized into groups according to the number of electrons in the outermost shell of one of their atoms.

These are just a few of the many situations in which we **classify** objects. By classifying objects into groups according to their characteristics, objects that are in some way similar become related by their group membership.

The library developed in this section illustrates how enumerations can be used to create software simulations of classifications from the real world. The problem we will consider is a simplified rock-classification problem.

In geology, rocks are classified according to the nature of their origin. More precisely, a given rock is described as

- *igneous*, if it is volcanic in origin (i.e., formed as the result of solidifying magma);
- *metamorphic*, if the rock was formed under conditions of high temperature and pressure; and
- *sedimentary*, if the rock was formed from the laying down of deposits of sediment.

Igneous rocks include basalt, granite, and obsidian. Metamorphic rocks include marble, quartzite, and slate. Sedimentary rocks include dolomite, limestone, sandstone, and shale.

Knowing the different categories of rocks can make outdoor activities (such as backpacking and canoeing) more interesting. For example, if one is hiking through a valley whose walls contain layers of sandstone, then one can conclude that the walls of the valley were probably once under water and may contain fossils of water creatures. By contrast, a valley whose walls consist of granite means that there was once a volcano in the vicinity, and finding it can make for an interesting diversion in the hike.

It is relatively easy to write a program that, given the name of a rock, describes some of its characteristics. Figure 12.16 gives an example of such a program.

Fig. 12.16 A rock-classification program. (Part 1 of 2)

```
/* geology.cpp allows a user to retrieve information about rocks.
 *
 * Receive: the name of a rock
 * Output:  the known information about that rock
 ****************************************************************/

#include <iostream>                          // cin, cout
using namespace std;
#include "Rock.h"                            // class Rock

int main()
{
   cout << "This program provides information about "
           "specific rocks.\n";

   Rock aRock;                               // input variable
   char response;                            // query response

   do
   {
      cout << "\nEnter the name of a rock: ";
      cin >> aRock;

      if ( cin.good() )
         cout << endl << aRock
              << " is classified as a(n) " << aRock.kind()
              << " rock, and\n its texture is " << aRock.texture()
              << endl;
      else
      {
         cerr << "That kind of rock is not supported." << endl;
         cin.clear();
      }
```

Fig. 12.16 A rock-classification program. (Part 2 of 2)

```
      cout << "\nEnter 'c' to continue, anything else to quit: ";
      cin >> response;
   }
   while (response == 'c');
}
```

Sample run:

```
This program provides information about specific rocks.

Enter the name of a rock: sandstone

Sandstone is classified as a(n) SEDIMENTARY rock, and
 its texture is COARSE.

Enter 'c' to continue, anything else to quit: c

Enter the name of a rock: obsidian

Obsidian is classified as a(n) IGNEOUS rock, and
 its texture is FINE.

Enter 'c' to continue, anything else to quit: q
```

The interesting thing about the preceding program is that it allows the user to communicate in real-world terms (the names of rocks), rather than through some artificial mechanism (such as a numeric representation of rocks). This is accomplished by using the techniques of the last section to create the type `Rock` as a class that uses an enumeration `RockName` whose values are the names of common rocks.

Because the class `Rock` might be useful in other geological programs, it should be stored in a library to facilitate its reuse. Figure 12.17 contains part of a header file for such a library. If you follow the `Color` example of the preceding section, you should have no difficulty completing it. After you finish, compare your file with that given on the book's Web site.

Fig. 12.17 Class `Rock` header file. (Part 1 of 2)

```
/* Rock.h provides the declaration of class Rock.
 *
 * Class Invariant:
 *    The value of myRockName is one of the following:
 *       BASALT, DOLOMITE, GRANITE, LIMESTONE, MARBLE,
 *       OBSIDIAN, QUARTZITE, SANDSTONE, SHALE, SLATE
 ******************************************************************/
```

Fig. 12.17 Class `Rock` header file. (Part 2 of 2)

```
#ifndef ROCK
#define ROCK

#include <iostream>                          // istream, ostream
using namespace std;
#include "RockKind.h"                        // class RockKind
#include "RockTexture.h"                     // class RockTexture

// Add a declaration of an enumeration RockName here; see the
// opening documentation for the rock names to use.

class Rock
{
 public:                                          // constructors:
   Rock();                                        //  default value
   Rock(RockName initialRock);                    //  explicit value

   void read(istream & in);                       // input
   void print(ostream & out) const;               // output

   RockKind kind() const;                         // igneous, ...
   RockTexture texture() const;                   // coarse, ...

   // Add prototypes for both forms of ++ and -- as well as for
   // the six relational operators:  <, >, ==, <=, >=, !=

 private:
   RockName myRockName;
};

// ---- Put definitions of the constructors,
// ---- the operators <<, >>,
// ---- and the relational operators here.

#endif
```

Note that this class depends upon the classes `RockKind` and `RockTexture`, each of which has its own header file. Since there are three real-world kinds of rocks, a `RockKind` class can be created with an enumeration of its own, whose values are the various kinds of rocks as shown in Figure 12.18. Again, you should have no difficulty completing it. One version of this file is included on the book's Web site. A class `RockTexture` can be created using a similar `RockTextureName` enumeration and is left as an exercise.

Fig. 12.18 Class `RockKind` header file.

```
/* RockKind.h declares class RockKind.
 *
 *    The value of myRockKindName is one of the following:
 *       IGNEOUS, METAMORPHIC, SEDIMENTARY,
 ***************************************************************/

#ifndef ROCK_KIND
#define ROCK_KIND

enum RockKindName {KIND_UNDERFLOW = -1,
                   IGNEOUS, METAMORPHIC, SEDIMENTARY,
                   NUMBER_OF_KINDS,
                   KIND_OVERFLOW = NUMBER_OF_KINDS};

#include <iostream>                    // istream, ostream
using namespace std;

class RockKind
{
 public:                               // constructors:
   RockKind();                         //  default value
   RockKind(RockKindName initialRock); //  explicit value

   // --- Add prototypes for print(), read(), ++ and -- (both forms),
   // --- and the six relational operators here.

 private:
   RockKindName myRockKindName;
};

// ---- Put definitions of the constructors,
// ---- the operators <<, >>,
// ---- and the relational operators here.

#endif
```

The implementation file *RockKind.cpp* for class `RockKind` will contain the definitions of the nontrivial `RockKind` function members: `read()`, `print()`, `operator++`, and `operator--`. You should be able to write these definitions by imitating those for the corresponding operations in the `Color` class of the preceding section. (If you have difficulty, see the book's Web site.) An implementation file for class `RockTexture` is similar and is left as an exercise.

The implementation file *Rock.cpp* will have definitions of these same operations `read()`, `print()`, `operator++`, and `operator--`, but for the `Rock` class. It will also contain definitions of the methods `kind()` and `texture()`. To help you with these definitions, here is one for `kind()`:

```
/* Rock.cpp defines the nontrivial members of class Rock.
*************************************************************
*/

#include "Rock.h"
   .
   .
   .

RockKind Rock::kind() const
{
   switch (myRockName)                    // if the rock is...
   {
      case BASALT: case GRANITE:          //  any of these, then
      case OBSIDIAN:                      //    it's igneous
         return RockKind(IGNEOUS);
      case MARBLE: case QUARTZITE:        //  any of these, then
      case SLATE:                         //    it's metamorphic
         return RockKind(METAMORPHIC);
      case DOLOMITE: case LIMESTONE:      //  any of these, then
      case SANDSTONE: case SHALE:         //    it's sedimentary
         return RockKind(SEDIMENTARY);
   }
   .
   .
   .
```

After you finish these three files, you will have developed a collection of classes that solve a real-world problem. Obviously, the problem has been simplified considerably, but the final solution does illustrate quite realistically how enumeration classes can be used to model real-world objects.

Part of the Picture

The C++ Type Hierarchy

At this point, we have examined many of the types available in C++. Figure 12.19 presents a diagram in which these types are organized into a **type hierarchy** that shows their relationships to one another. This hierarchy provides a map of the richness of the C++ language that shows where we have been and where we have not yet explored. The sequel to this text explores the types not examined in this text.*

* *C++: An Introduction to Data Structures* by Larry Nyhoff (Upper Saddle River, NJ: Prentice Hall, Inc. 1999). A second edition is scheduled to appear in 2003.

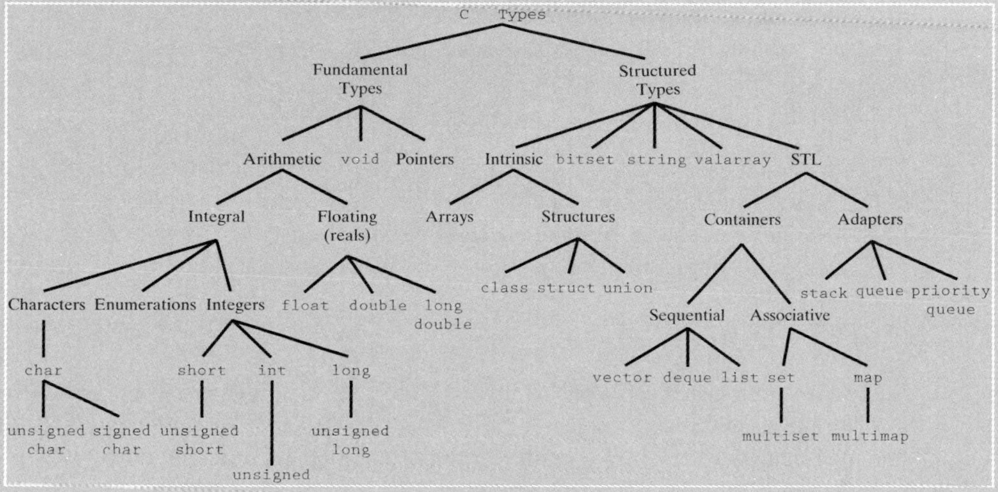

Fig. 12.19 The C++ type hierarchy.

12.5* OBJECTive Thinking: Inheritance and Polymorphism

Enumerations provide one means of representing real-world values in software. However, it is noteworthy that "pure" object-oriented programming languages like Smalltalk and Java do not provide an enumeration mechanism. One reason is that a similar effect can be achieved using the inheritance mechanism that was introduced in Section 7.8. The main idea is to use a class to represent the basic type (e.g., `Color`) and then build a subclass for each different value of that type (e.g., `Red`, `Orange`, ..., `Violet`).

To illustrate, observe that we can represent the colors by building a class hierarchy like that shown in the following diagram:

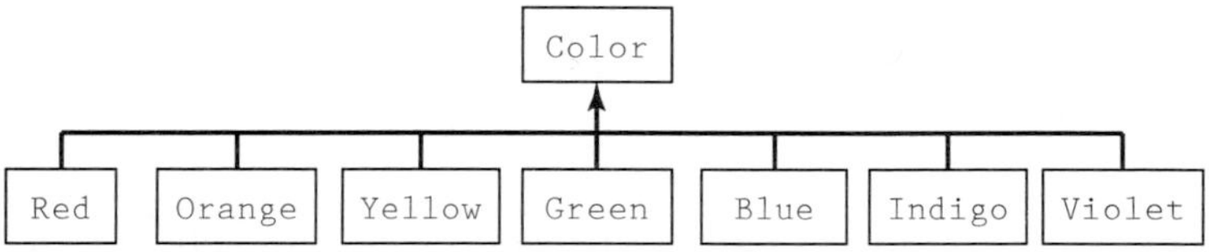

The parent class `Color` will consolidate the attributes that each of its child classes has in common. For example, each color has a *name* attribute. Since this attribute is common to all colors, we can store it as a string in the parent class `Color`, from where each child class can inherit it. The parent class can also define methods that are common to each child class, and thus avoid redundant coding.

Given such a hierarchy, a programmer can use an expression like:

```
new Red()
```

or

```
new Violet()
```

to create a Red or Violet object. The space for such objects is allocated when the expression executes (i.e., at *run-time*), rather than at *compile time* like objects declared in the usual fashion.

HANDLES

While we could declare Red, Orange, ..., or Violet variables, the preferred approach is to declare a single variable that can refer to a Red, Orange, ..., or Violet object. Such a variable is called a **handle**, because we will use it to access objects of any of the child classes in our hierarchy. To illustrate, we can declare a handle for this hierarchy by writing

```
Color* colorHandle;
```

Such a declaration creates a variable named colorHandle that is capable of referring to a Red object, an Orange object, ..., or a Violet object.[6] The type Color* tells the compiler that colorHandle may refer to a Color object or to any object whose class is a subclass of Color. Thus, we can write

```
colorHandle = new Red();
```

and colorHandle will refer to a newly allocated Red object:[7]

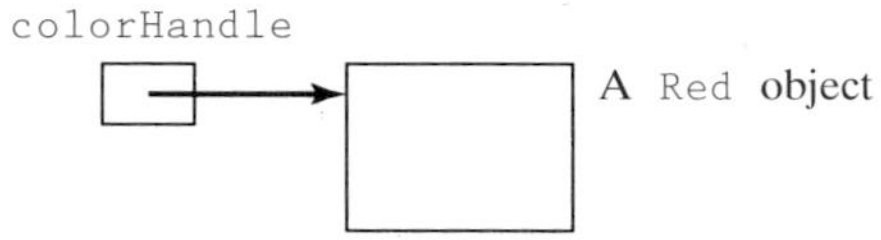

Or we can write

```
colorHandle = new Violet();
```

and colorHandle will refer to a newly allocated Violet object:

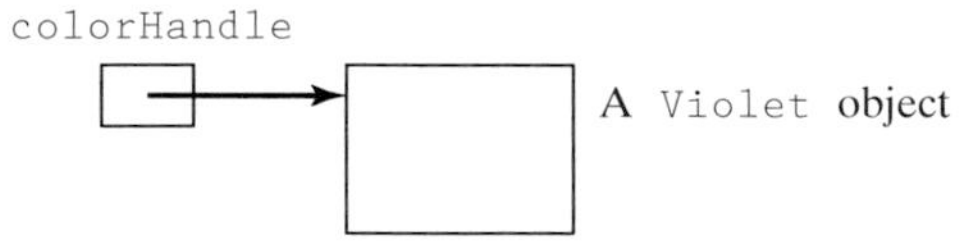

The same handle can be used to "grab" any Color object; and since Red, Orange, ..., Violet are subclasses of Color, this same handle can be used to "grab" Red, Orange, ..., Violet objects as well. Because a handle "points at" an object, they are also called **pointer variables**.

To send a message to an object through its handle, C++ uses a special **arrow operator** -> instead of dot notation. To illustrate, we can send the wavelength() message to the object referred to by colorHandle using the expression:

```
colorHandle->wavelength()
```

---

6. The phrase "capable of referring to" is another way of saying "can store the address of."
7. The expression new *ClassName* constructs a new instance of class *ClassName* and returns its address.

Such an expression relays the `wavelength()` message to the object to which `colorHandle` refers. If that object's class defines or inherits a method for that message, then that method executes.[8] So it is up to us as designers to ensure that

NOTE

If we wish to send to send a message to an object via a handle, then every object to which that handle might refer must define (or inherit) a method for that message.

To illustrate, Figure 12.20 presents a version of our program that displays a table of colors, wavelengths, and frequencies:

Fig. 12.20 An O-O color table. (Part 1 of 2)

```
/* colorTable.cpp displays a table of colors, wavelengths & frequencies.
 * ...
 *******************************************************************/

#include <iostream>                         // cin, cout
#include <iomanip>                          // setw()
using namespace std;
#include "Color.h"                          // Color hierarchy

int main()
{
   cout << "\nColor       Wavelength       Frequency\n"
        << "=======================================\n";

   Color* colorHandle = new Red();
   Color* saveHandle = 0;
   while (colorHandle != 0)
   {
      cout << left << setw(10) << colorHandle
           << right << setw(10) << colorHandle->wavelength()
           << setw(20) << colorHandle->frequency() << endl;
      saveHandle = colorHandle;
      colorHandle = colorHandle->next();
      delete saveHandle;
   }
}
```

8. If the object's class does not define or inherit a method for that message, a run-time error results.

Fig. 12.20 An O-O color table. (Part 2 of 2)

Sample Run:

```
Color          Wavelength          Frequency
=========================================
Red               6.5e-07          4.61231e+14
Orange              6e-07          4.99667e+14
Yellow            5.8e-07          5.16897e+14
Green             5.2e-07          5.76538e+14
Blue              4.7e-07          6.37872e+14
Indigo            4.4e-07          6.81364e+14
Violet            4.1e-07          7.3122e +14
```

As this program indicates, 0 may be used to initialize a handle that has no value; a handle with value 0 is said to be a **null handle**. It may also be used with the equality operator to determine whether a handle refers to an object, as shown in the condition controlling the while loop. 0 may also be a return value: When a `Violet` object receives the `next()` message, it returns 0.

As mentioned earlier, the `new` operator allocates space for an instance of its argument and returns the address of that space. With the ability to allocate space comes the responsibility to deallocate it. The last three lines of the `for` loop accomplish this. The statement

```
saveHandle = colorHandle;
```

makes `saveHandle` refer to the same object as `colorHandle`:

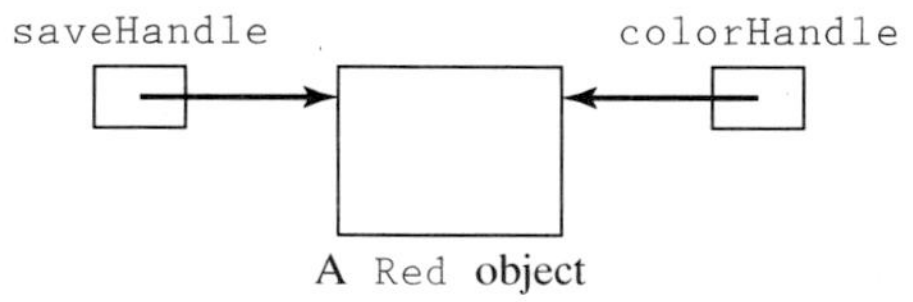

This statement is necessary to avoid losing a handle on the object to which `colorHandle` refers. When the statement

```
colorHandle = colorHandle->next();
```

is executed, the handle `colorHandle` then refers to the object returned by `next()`:

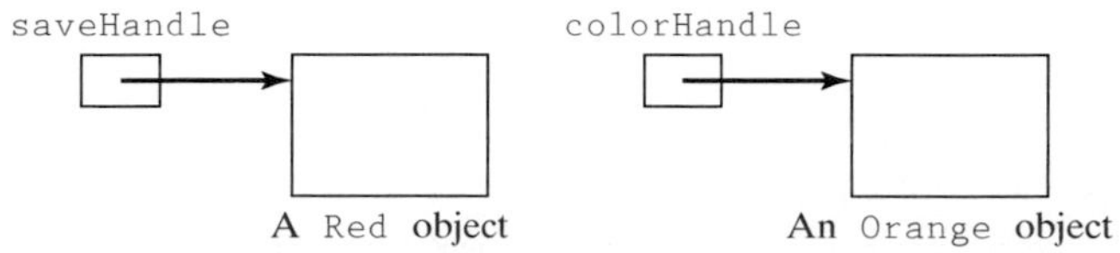

Execution of the statement

```
delete saveHandle;
```

then reclaims the space occupied by the object to which `saveHandle` refers:

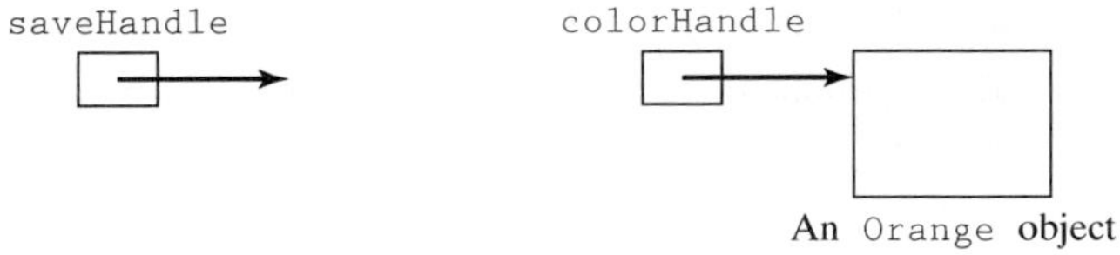

If a program does not "clean up" after itself in this manner, then it is said to *leak memory.* **Memory leaks** are the result of neglecting to use `delete` to reclaim space that has been allocated using `new`. As such, they reflect sloppy programming and, in a large program, can lead to seemingly random crashes that occur when free memory has been exhausted.

In order for this code to work as described, we have to define the eight classes shown in our hierarchy and distribute the following operations among them:

- A constructor for each class
- An accessor method for a `Color`'s *name* attribute
- The output operator for a `Color` handle
- The `wavelength()` method for a `Color`
- The `frequency()` method for a `Color`
- The `next()` method, to get the successor of a `Color`

In addition, we might add the following operations to make the classes more generally useful:

- Methods to convert string values to `Color` objects and vice versa
- The input operator for a `Color` handle
- The six relational operators, so that `Color` objects can be compared
- The `previous()` method, to get the predecessor of a `Color`

Defining all 16 of these operations for each class would be a huge amount of work. Fortunately, we can identify those operations that are common to each of our `Color` subclasses and define them in class `Color`. Each subclass can then inherit this common functionality from a single definition instead of having to define the same (redundant) functionality over and over. The general rules of thumb are as follows:

1. If a method elicits the same behavior for each subclass object, then define that method in the parent class.
2. If a method elicits a different behavior for each subclass object, then define that method in each subclass.[9]

---

9. If a method elicits different behaviors in some subclasses and the same behavior in others, an intermediate class can be derived from the parent class to store the method common to the latter subclasses, which can then be derived from the intermediate class.

With a bit of study (and experience), we can identify the following methods as having the same behavior in all subclasses of `Color`:

- the accessor for the *name* attribute
- the input operator
- the output operator
- methods to convert string values to `Color` objects and vice versa
- the six relational operators
- the `frequency()` method

This leaves only a constructor, the `next()` and `previous()` methods, and the `wavelength()` method for each subclass to provide. To illustrate, Figure 12.21 presents a part of the header file *Colors.h*, showing the class declarations it contains:

Fig. 12.21 A `Color` class hierarchy. (Part 1 of 2)

```
/* Colors.h provides a Color hierarchy.
 * ...
 *****************************************************************/

#ifndef COLORS
#define COLORS

#include <iostream>                        // cin, cout
#include <string>
using namespace std;
class Color
{
 public:
   Color(const string& colorName);

   string asString() const;
   static Color* fromString(const string& name);

   virtual double wavelength() const = 0;
   double frequency() const;

   virtual Color* next()        const = 0;
   // previous() left as an exercise

   friend bool operator==(const Color& left, const Color& right);
   friend bool operator!=(const Color& left, const Color& right);
```

Fig. 12.21 A `Color` class hierarchy. (Part 2 of 2)

```
   friend bool operator<=(const Color& left, const Color& right);
   friend bool operator>=(const Color& left, const Color& right);
   friend bool operator< (const Color& left, const Color& right);
   friend bool operator> (const Color& left, const Color& right);

 private:
   string myName;
};

class Red : public Color
{
 public:
   Red();
   virtual double wavelength() const;
   virtual Color* next() const;
   // previous() left as an exercise
};
class Orange : public Color
{
 public:
   Orange();
   virtual double wavelength() const;
   virtual Color* next() const;
   // previous() left as an exercise
};
// ... Classes Yellow, Green, Blue, & Indigo omitted ...

class Violet : public Color
{
 public:
   Violet();
   virtual double wavelength() const;
   virtual Color* next() const;
   // previous() left as an exercise
};
//... inline function definitions for Color and subclasses go here

#endif
```

2. *Use uppercase letters for enumerators.* Enumerators are similar to constant objects, so we use the same stylistic conventions.
3. *Pad enumerations with underflow/overflow values at the ends of the identifier list.* This provides "illegal" values that functions can return in error situations or that can be used as sentinel values.
4. *Use enumeration classes instead of C-style enumerations so that*
   a. *objects of that type are self-contained and*
   b. *class invariants can be enforced.*

   Doing so results in a class of objects that reflects the I-can-do-it-myself principle.
5. *For enumeration classes, define the relational operators as nonmember functions to preserve the symmetric property of the relation.* For example, if an expression of the form `e == c` is valid, then the expression `c == e` should also be valid. With enumeration classes, this is somewhat tricky because `e` and `c` may not have the same type. If `e` is an enumeration object and `c` is an enumeration class object, then one way to resolve this is for the enumeration class to (1) name the relational operators as `friend` functions that compare two enumeration class objects and (2) supply an explicit-value constructor to perform automatic type conversion. This allows the compiler to transparently construct `e` into an enumeration class object, allowing it to be compared to `c`.
6. *Declare every class in its own header file.* By doing so, a program that wants to use a class can include its header file without having to include classes that are not being used.

WATCH OUT

Potential Pitfalls

1. *Values listed in an enumeration must be legal identifiers and may not be overloaded.* For example, the declaration

```
enum PassengerType {FIRST-CLASS, COACH, STANDBY}; // ERROR!
```

   is not allowed because `FIRST-CLASS` is not a legal identifier. The declarations

```
enum Weekday {MONDAY, TUESDAY, WEDNESDAY, THURSDAY, FRIDAY};
enum VacationDay {FRIDAY, SATURDAY, SUNDAY}; // ERROR!
```

   are not allowed because the same identifier (`FRIDAY`) may not be used in two declarations.
2. *Values of an enumerated data type cannot be input or output unless the I/O operators are overloaded.* Otherwise, such values must be input as and will be displayed as the corresponding integers.

Programming Problems

Section 12.2

1. Write a driver program to test the library for the enumerated type `MonthAbbrev` of Exercises 1–12.
2. Write a driver program to test the library for the enumerated type `Day` of Exercises 14–16.

Sections 12.3

3. Write a driver program to test the enumeration class `MonthAbbrev` of Exercise 1.
4. Use the type `MonthAbbrev` of Exercise 1 in a program that prompts for and reads the rainfall for each month and then calculates and displays the average monthly rainfall for the year.

5. Add a method to class `MonthAbbrev` of Exercise 1 whose parameter is a year in the range from 1538 through 2004 and that returns the number of days in the month. Remember that February has 28 days, except in a leap year, when it has 29. A leap year is one in which the year number is divisible by four except for centesimal years (those ending in 00); these centesimal years are not leap years unless the year number is divisible by 400. Thus 1996 and 2000 were leap years, but 1995 and 1900 were not. Test the new method with a driver program.
6. Use the method of Problem 5 in a program that reads two dates (month and a day) in the same year and then calculates and displays the number of days between these two dates.
7. Write a driver program to test the enumeration class `Day` of Exercise 2.
8. Use the type `Day` of Exercise 2 in a program that first reads an employee's name and hourly pay rate, and then for each weekday (Monday through Friday) prompts for and reads the number of hours worked by that employee. Display the total hours worked and the pay for each employee. (Assume that hours over 40 are paid at the overtime rate of 1.5 times the regular hourly rate.)
9. Use the type `Day` of Exercise 2 in a program that first reads a customer's account number and current balance, and then for each weekday (Monday through Friday) prompts for and reads a series of transactions by that customer of the form D (deposit) or W (withdrawal), followed by an amount, and updates the balance with this amount. Display the new balance after all transactions for the week have been processed.
10. Write a driver program to test the enumeration class `Date` of Exercise 3.
11. Modify the program in Problem 6 so that it uses the type `Date` of Exercise 3 and determines the number of days between any two dates.
12. Use the type `Date` of Exercise 3 to develop a class `Event` to model events scheduled for specified dates. Use this class in a program that reads several events and stores these in a `vector` (or array) of `Events`. After all the events have been entered, the program should display a schedule of events in chronological order.
13. Write a driver program to test the name-of-number enumeration class of Exercise 4.
14. Add some simple arithmetic operations to the name-of-number enumeration class of Exercise 4. Use the modified class in a program that models a simple calculator in which the user "speaks" the names of the numbers.
15. Write a driver program to test the enumeration class `PlayingCard` of Exercise 5.
16. Use the type `PlayingCard` of Exercise 5 in a program that deals random hands of cards, making certain that none of them have been dealt already. (For more of a challenge, design the program to play a simple card game such as Go Fish!).
17. (*Project*) Design a class `PeriodicTable` to model the periodic table of elements, using an enumeration whose values are the element abbreviations (e.g., `H`, `He`, `Li`, . . .). Construct I/O operations for it, and add functions that return: the atomic number of the element, the atomic weight of the element, the number of protons (and/or neutrons) in the nucleus of the element, the period of the element, the group of the element, and any other useful operations that represent standard information that can be extracted from the periodic table. Then write a menu-driven program that allows a user to obtain the information about any element whose symbol they input.
18. (*Project*) Design an enumeration class `Sword` in which the enumerators are `SHORT`, `BROAD`, `LONG`, and `TWOHANDED`, and which has the following operations: I/O; a function `reach()` that returns the length of a `Sword` object (e.g., 18 inches, 24 inches, 36 inches, and 48 inches, respectively); and a function `speed()` that returns the time required to swing a `Sword` object as a value proportional to its length. Write a program that allows its user to pick the weapons of two duelists and then provides a blow-by-blow account of a simulated duel.

19. (*Group Project*) Have one group member proceed as in Problem 18, but have a second group member build another library that defines the type `Armor` with enumerators `NONE`, `LEATHER`, `CHAIN`, and `PLATE` with the following operations: I/O; a `protection()` method that returns the degree to which the `Armor` object protects its wearer (e.g., 0.0, 0.50, 0.75, and 0.95, respectively); a `weight()` method that returns the degree to which a wearer of the `Armor` object is slowed in swinging a weapon (e.g., 0, 2, 4, 8). Write the duel-simulation program in such a way that the user can choose both the duelists' weapons and armor and that both are considered in the simulation.

Section 12.5

20. Write a program equivalent to that in Figure 12.1, but that uses the `Color` class hierarchy.
21. (*Project*) The city of Drib has a brand new aviary that houses a few of each of the following birds:

    - gray geese that eat bugs and walk about calling "Honk!"
    - brown ostriches that eat grass and walk about calling "Neek-neek!"
    - brown screech owls that eat mice and fly about calling "Screeeeeeeeeeeeech!"
    - white snow owls that eat mice and fly about calling "Hoo!" from 1 to 4 times
    - parrots that eat fruit and fly about calling "Squawk!" (most are green.)
    - parrots that eat fruit and fly about calling "Polly wanna cracker!", "Pieces of eight!", "You're a pretty boy!", and "I wonder if this thing can talk." Most of these are red.

    Build a `Bird` class hierarchy to model this aviary. Some obvious attributes are color, call, food, and movement. The parent class `Bird` could have different subclasses for walking and flying birds. Goose and ostrich classes would be subclasses of the walking-bird class and parrot and owl subclasses of the flying bird class. Write a program to test you class hierarchy.
22. (*Group Project*) Design the `Rock` hierarchy and implement the `Rock` class described in this section. Have different members of the group build the various subclasses. The group together should then build a program to generate a `Rock`-classification table equivalent to that in Figure 12.20.

CHAPTER 13

Multidimensional Arrays and Vectors

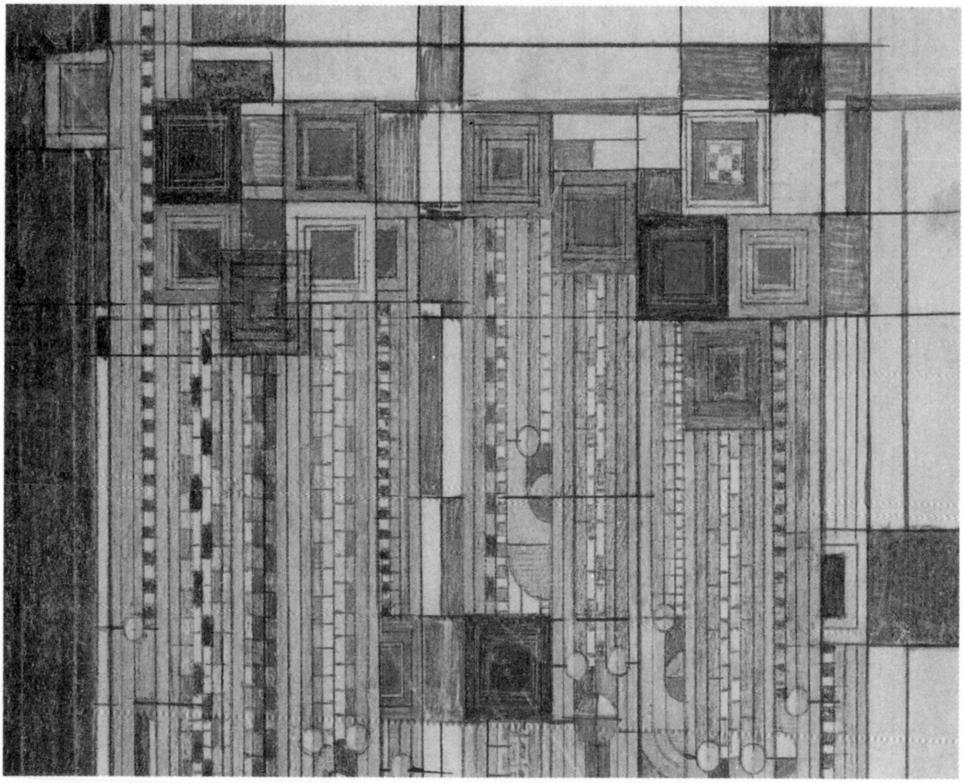

We are columns left alone
of a temple once complete.

-Christopher Cranch

A teacher who can arouse a feeling for one single good action,
for one single good poem,
accomplishes more than he who fills our memory with row on row
of natural objects, classified with name and form.

-Johann Wolfgang Von Goethe

Would someone please wake the person in row 3, seat 6?

-V. Orehck III (during a lecture on matrices)

Chapter Contents

Chapter Objectives

- Use OCD to solve a problem involving a mileage chart, using a two-dimensional array to store the chart.
- Learn how to declare and use C-style multidimensional arrays.
- See how C-style multidimensional arrays can be replaced by multi-dimensional `vector<T>`s.
- Build a `vector<T>`-based library for processing matrices.
- (Optional) Introduce some of the key ideas and techniques in computer graphics.
- (Optional) Review the basic object-oriented property of inheritance, illustrating it with a `Matrix` class derived from vectors of vectors.

In Chapter 10, we introduced C-style arrays and `vector<T>` class templates and used them to store sequences of values. Each of the containers considered in that chapter had *one dimension:* its *length*, which is the number of values in the sequence.

C++ also allows arrays and vectors of more than one dimension. As we shall see, a *two-dimensional* array or vector can be used to store a data set whose values are arranged in *rows and columns*. Similarly, a *three-dimensional* array or vector is an appropriate storage structure when the data can be arranged in *rows, columns,* and *ranks*. When there are several characteristics associated with the data, still higher dimensions may be useful, with each dimension corresponding to one of these characteristics. In this chapter, we show how to use such multidimensional arrays in C++ programs.

13.1 Introductory Example: Mileage between Cities

PROBLEM

The German transportation tycoon Otto Bonn is expanding his trucking business into Florida, with shipping centers in Daytona Beach, Gainesville, Jacksonville, Miami, Tallahassee, and Tampa. He has hired us as software consultants to create a computerized mileage chart for his truck drivers. Given any two of these cities, our program must display the approximate mileage between them.

PRELIMINARY ANALYSIS

From a road atlas, we can find the following mileages between Florida cities:

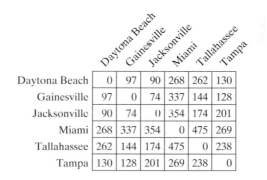

	Daytona Beach	Gainesville	Jacksonville	Miami	Tallahassee	Tampa
Daytona Beach	0	97	90	268	262	130
Gainesville	97	0	74	337	144	128
Jacksonville	90	74	0	354	174	201
Miami	268	337	354	0	475	269
Tallahassee	262	144	174	475	0	238
Tampa	130	128	201	269	238	0

The basic idea is to create a software representation of such a chart and then use it to look up the distance between any two of the cities.

Object-Centered Design

Behavior. For simplicity, our program will begin by displaying on the screen a numbered menu of the cities. It should then read the numbers of two cities from the keyboard. Next, it should look up the mileage between those cities in a software mileage chart. Finally, it should display that mileage.

Objects. From the behavior, we identify the following objects in this problem:

	Software Objects		
Problem Objects	**Type**	**Kind**	**Name**
A menu of cities	`string`	constant	*CITY_MENU*
The number of a city	`int`	varying	*city1*
The number of another city	`int`	varying	*city2*
A mileage chart	`int[][]`	constant	*MILEAGE_CHART*
The mileage	`int`	varying	*mileage*

As we shall see, the type `int[][]` refers to a two-dimensional array of integers, which provides a convenient way to represent the mileage chart.

Operations. Our behavioral description gives the following set of operations:

i. Define a two-dimensional array with initial values
ii. Display a string on the screen
iii. Read two integers from the keyboard
iv. Look up an entry in the two-dimensional array
v. Output an integer

Algorithm. These operations are easily organized into the following algorithm:

Algorithm for City Mileages

1. Define *MILEAGE_CHART*, a two-dimensional array of city mileages, and *CITY_MENU*, a menu of the supported cities.
2. Via `cout`, display *CITY_MENU*.
3. From `cin`, read two integers into *city1* and *city2*.
4. Compute *mileage*, by looking up *MILEAGE_CHART*[*city1*][*city2*].
5. Via `cout`, display *mileage*.

Coding. The preceding algorithm is easily encoded in C++, as shown in Figure 13.1.

Fig. 13.1 A mileage calculator. (Part 1 of 2)

```
/* findMileage.cpp computes the mileage between two cities.
 *
 * Input:        city1 and city2, two integers representing cities
 * Precondition: for n cities, city1 and city2 are in the range 0..n-1
 * Output:       the mileage between city1 and city2
 ******************************************************************/

#include <iostream>                         // cin, cout, <<, >>
#include <string>                           // string
using namespace std;

int main()
{
   const int NUMBER_OF_CITIES = 6;
   const int MILEAGE_CHART[NUMBER_OF_CITIES][NUMBER_OF_CITIES]
     = { {  0,  97,  90, 268, 262, 130 },    // Daytona Beach
         { 97,   0,  74, 337, 144, 128 },    // Gainesville
         { 90,  74,   0, 354, 174, 201 },    // Jacksonville
```

Fig. 13.1 A mileage calculator. (Part 2 of 2)

```
        { 268, 337, 354,   0, 475, 269 },      // Miami
        { 262, 144, 174, 475,   0, 238 },      // Tallahassee
        { 130, 128, 201, 269, 238,   0 } };    // Tampa

   const string CITY_MENU
      = "To determine the mileage between two cities,\n"
        "please enter the numbers of 2 cities from this menu:\n\n"
        "     0 for Daytona Beach,    1 for Gainesville\n"
        "     2 for Jacksonville,     3 for Miami\n"
        "     4 for Tallahassee,      5 for Tampa\n\n"
        "--> ";

   cout << CITY_MENU;
   int city1, city2;
   cin >> city1 >> city2;

   int mileage = MILEAGE_CHART[city1][city2];

   cout << "\nThe mileage between those 2 cities is "
        << mileage << " miles.\n";
}
```

Sample run:

```
To determine the mileage between two cities,
please enter the numbers of 2 cities from this menu:

     0 for Daytona Beach,    1 for Gainesville
     2 for Jacksonville,     3 for Miami
     4 for Tallahassee,      5 for Tampa

--> 2 5

The mileage between those 2 cities is 201 miles.
```

13.2 C-Style Multidimensional Arrays

There are many problems in which the data being processed can be naturally organized as a *table*. The mileage problem in the preceding section is such a problem since mileage charts are commonly given in tabular form. For these problems, two-dimensional arrays provide a way to build a software model of a table.

DEFINING A TWO-DIMENSIONAL ARRAY

The program in Figure 13.1 illustrates how a two-dimensional array can be defined and initialized. The statements

```
const int NUMBER_OF_CITIES = 6;
const int MILEAGE_CHART[NUMBER_OF_CITIES][NUMBER_OF_CITIES]
  = { {   0,  97,  90, 268, 262, 130 },    // Daytona Beach
      {  97,   0,  74, 337, 144, 128 },    // Gainesville
      {  90,  74,   0, 354, 174, 201 },    // Jacksonville
      { 268, 337, 354,   0, 475, 269 },    // Miami
      { 262, 144, 174, 475,   0, 238 },    // Tallahassee
      { 130, 128, 201, 269, 238,   0 } };  // Tampa
```

define the object `MILEAGE_CHART` as a constant two-dimensional array of integers, consisting of six rows and six columns, which we might visualize as follows:

	[0]	[1]	[2]	[3]	[4]	[5]
[0]	0	97	90	268	262	130
[1]	97	0	74	337	144	128
[2]	90	74	0	354	174	201
[3]	268	337	354	0	475	269
[4]	262	144	174	475	0	238
[5]	130	128	201	269	238	0

As with one-dimensional arrays, each dimension of a two-dimensional array is indexed starting with zero, so the six rows are indexed from zero to five as are the six columns. As we shall see, these row and column indices are used to uniquely identify each element in the array.

This example shows how a two-dimensional array object can be initialized by listing the initial values in curly braces. Although not required, the values for each row are often enclosed in their own pair of curly braces to make the declaration more readable by delimiting the values of each row.

Two-dimensional arrays like `MILEAGE_CHART` that have the same number of rows as columns are called *square* arrays. But nonsquare arrays are needed for some problems. For example, consider the monitor screen of a computer being used in a command-line (text-only) mode. Typically, such a screen can display 24 lines, with 80 characters on each line. The standard way to describe the screen is in terms of horizontal rows and vertical columns, with the rows numbered from 0 through 23 and the columns numbered from 0 through 79. The position at row 0 and column 0 is usually in the upper left corner of the screen, giving the screen the following layout:

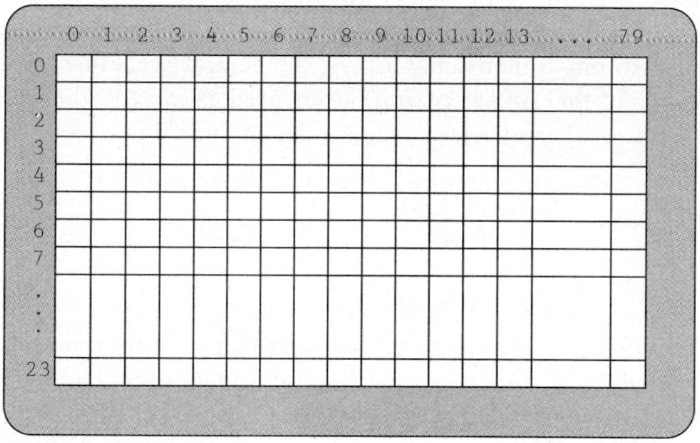

Such a screen can be modeled in software using a two-dimensional array of characters, declared as follows:

```
const int ROWS = 24,
          COLUMNS = 80;
char screen[ROWS][COLUMNS];
```

Note that this definition creates `screen` as a two dimensional array *variable* object, whereas `MILEAGE_CHART` in Figure 13.1 is a two-dimensional array *constant* object.

The `typedef` mechanism introduced in Chapter 10 to define an identifier as a synonym for a one-dimensional array type can also be used for multidimensional arrays. For example, to declare the identifier `MileageTable` as a synonym for an array of double values representing mileages, we would write

```
const int NUMBER_OF_CITIES = 6;
typedef double MileageArray[NUM_CITIES][NUM_CITIES];
```

We can then use this new type to define the two-dimensional array `MileageArray` object:

```
const MileageArray  MILEAGE_CHART
  = { {   0,  97,  90, 268, 262, 130 },     // Daytona Beach
      {  97,   0,  74, 337, 144, 128 },     // Gainesville
      {  90,  74,   0, 354, 174, 201 },     // Jacksonville
      { 268, 337, 354,   0, 475, 269 },     // Miami
      { 262, 144, 174, 475,   0, 238 },     // Tallahassee
      { 130, 128, 201, 269, 238,   0 } };   // Tampa
```

Similarly, we might define the type `MonitorScreen` by

```
const int ROWS = 24,
          COLUMNS = 80;
typedef char MonitorScreen[ROWS][COLUMNS];
```

and then use this new type to declare the variable `screen` by

```
MonitorScreen screen;
```

PREDEFINED TWO-DIMENSIONAL ARRAY OPERATIONS

As with one-dimensional arrays, the central predefined operation for two-dimensional arrays is the **subscript operation** used to access the elements of an array. A one-dimensional array uses a single subscript operator to access an element:

```
double aOneDimensionalArray[10];
      .
      .
      .
aOneDimensionalArray[0] = 2.5;
```

Objects like `MILEAGE_CHART` and `screen` are two-dimensional objects and require two subscript operators, one for each dimension. The element in row 0, column 0 of `MILEAGE_CHART` can be accessed using

```
MILEAGE_CHART[0][0]
```

The element of `MILEAGE_CHART` in the second column of the first row can be accessed using

```
MILEAGE_CHART[0][1]
```

the first element of the third using

```
MILEAGE_CHART[2][0]
```

and the element at row 4, column 3 using

```
MILEAGE_CHART[4][3]
```

and so on. In general, the notation

```
MILEAGE_CHART[r][c]
```

can be used to access the value at row `r` and column `c`. The program in Figure 13.1 looked up the mileage between `city1` and `city2`,

```
int mileage = MILEAGE_CHART[city1][city2];
```

by accessing the element at row `city1` and column `city2`.

Because `MILEAGE_CHART` is a constant object, we are only permitted to read (i.e., look up) its values. If we try to change one of `MILEAGE_CHART`'s elements as in

```
cin >> MILEAGE_CHART[r][c];
```

the compiler will generate an error because we may not alter the value of a constant object.

By contrast, the object `screen` described earlier is a *variable* object, so values can be assigned to it. For example, the statement

```
screen[0][0] = 'X';
```

assigns the character `'X'` to the element in row `0` and column `0`.

DEFINING TWO-DIMENSIONAL ARRAY OPERATIONS

For operations other than subscript on a two-dimensional array, we must write functions to perform them. Operations on one-dimensional arrays typically use a `for` loop to count through the index values:

```
for (int i = 0; i < howManyValues; i++)
   // ... do something with oneDimensionalArray[i]
```

Operations that access the values stored in a two-dimensional array use two nested `for` loops: an outer loop counting through the rows and an inner loop counting through the columns:

```
for (int r = 0; r < howManyRows; r++)
   for (int c = 0; c < howManyColumns; c++)
      // ... do something with twoDimensionalArray[r][c]
```

For example, to fill the object `screen` with blanks, we can use a function like the following:

```
void clearScreen(MonitorScreen theScreen,
                 int numRows, int numColumns)
{
   for (int row = 0; row < numRows; row++)
      for (int col = 0; col < numColumns; col++)
         theScreen[row][col] = ' ';
}
```

To display `screen` via `cout`, we could use

```
void display(MonitorScreen theScreen,
             int numRows, int numColumns)
{
   for (int row = 0; row < numRows; row++)
   {
      for (int col = 0; col < numColumns; col++)
         cout << theScreen[row][col];
      cout << endl;
   }
}
```

Each pass through the inner loop displays all the characters in one row of `theScreen` and then moves to a new line before displaying the characters in the next row.

Primitive graphics functions can also be designed using this technique. For example, here is a function that can be used to draw a box of arbitrary size at an arbitrary position on a `MonitorScreen`:

```
void drawBox(MonitorScreen theScreen,        // 2-D array
             int numRows, int numColumns,    // its size
             int topRow, int leftCol,        // upper left corner
             int bottomRow, int rightCol,    // bottom right   "
             char drawChar)                  // outline character

{
   assert(0 <= topRow && topRow < numRows);
   assert(0 <= leftCol && leftCol < numColumns);
   assert(0 <= bottomRow && bottomRow < numRows);
   assert(0 <= rightCol && rightCol < numColumns);
```

```
      // draw top & bottom edges
      for (int col = leftCol; col <= rightCol; col++)
         theScreen[topRow][col] =
            theScreen[bottomRow][col] = drawChar;

      // draw left & right edges
      for (int row = topRow; row <= bottomRow; row++)
         theScreen[row][leftCol] =
            theScreen[row][rightCol] = drawChar;
   }
```

Other functions can use primitive graphics functions like `drawBox()` to draw more complex patterns on `screen`. For example, the following function can be used to fill `screen` with nested boxes:

```
   void drawNestedBoxes(MonitorScreen theScreen,
                        int numRows, int numColumns,
                        char drawChar)
   {
      for (int offset = 0; offset < numRows/2; offset += 2)
         drawBox(theScreen, numRows, numColumns, offset, offset,
                 numRows - offset - 1, numColumns - offset - 1,
                 drawChar);
   }
```

Given the object named `screen` defined previously, the following sequence of function calls can be used to initialize, draw on, and display `screen`:

```
   clearScreen(screen, ROWS, COLUMNS);
   drawNestedBoxes(screen, ROWS, COLUMNS, 'X');
   display(screen, ROWS, COLUMNS);
```

When executed, the output from function `display()` appears as follows:

```
XXXXXXXXXXXXXXXXXXXXXXXXXXXXXXXXXXXXXXXXXXXXXXXXXXXXXXXXXXXXXXXXXXXXXXXXXXXXXXXX
X                                                                              X
X XXXXXXXXXXXXXXXXXXXXXXXXXXXXXXXXXXXXXXXXXXXXXXXXXXXXXXXXXXXXXXXXXXXXXXXXXXXX X
X X                                                                          X X
X X XXXXXXXXXXXXXXXXXXXXXXXXXXXXXXXXXXXXXXXXXXXXXXXXXXXXXXXXXXXXXXXXXXXXXXXX X X
X X X X                                                                    X X X
X X X X XXXXXXXXXXXXXXXXXXXXXXXXXXXXXXXXXXXXXXXXXXXXXXXXXXXXXXXXXXXXXXXXXX X X X
X X X X X                                                              X X X X
X X X X X XXXXXXXXXXXXXXXXXXXXXXXXXXXXXXXXXXXXXXXXXXXXXXXXXXXXXXXXXXXXXX X X X X
X X X X X X                                                        X X X X X
X X X X X X XXXXXXXXXXXXXXXXXXXXXXXXXXXXXXXXXXXXXXXXXXXXXXXXXXXXXXXX X X X X X
X X X X X X X                                                    X X X X X X
X X X X X X X                                                    X X X X X X
X X X X X X XXXXXXXXXXXXXXXXXXXXXXXXXXXXXXXXXXXXXXXXXXXXXXXXXXXXXXXX X X X X X
X X X X X                                                          X X X X X
X X X X XXXXXXXXXXXXXXXXXXXXXXXXXXXXXXXXXXXXXXXXXXXXXXXXXXXXXXXXXXXXXXXX X X X X
X X X X                                                                X X X X
X X X XXXXXXXXXXXXXXXXXXXXXXXXXXXXXXXXXXXXXXXXXXXXXXXXXXXXXXXXXXXXXXXXXXXX X X X
X X X                                                                      X X X
X X XXXXXXXXXXXXXXXXXXXXXXXXXXXXXXXXXXXXXXXXXXXXXXXXXXXXXXXXXXXXXXXXXXXXXXXX X X
X X                                                                          X X
X XXXXXXXXXXXXXXXXXXXXXXXXXXXXXXXXXXXXXXXXXXXXXXXXXXXXXXXXXXXXXXXXXXXXXXXXXXXX X
X                                                                              X
XXXXXXXXXXXXXXXXXXXXXXXXXXXXXXXXXXXXXXXXXXXXXXXXXXXXXXXXXXXXXXXXXXXXXXXXXXXXXXXX
```

Using Enumerations. As a second application of two-dimensional arrays, suppose that four times a day, water temperatures are recorded at each of three discharge outlets of the cooling system of a nuclear power plant. These temperature readings can be arranged in a table having four rows and three columns:

	Location		
Time	Outlet1	Outlet2	Outlet3
12 A.M.	65.5	68.7	62.0
6 A.M.	68.8	68.9	64.5
12 P.M.	70.4	69.4	66.3
6 P.M.	68.5	69.1	65.8

In this table, the three temperature readings at 12 A.M. are in the first row, the three temperatures at 6 A.M. are in the second row, and so on. We might model such a table by first declaring an enumeration for the row indices,

```
enum Row {ROW_UNDERFLOW = -1, MIDNIGHT, SIX_AM, NOON, SIX_PM,
          NUM_TIMES, ROW_OVERFLOW = 4};
```

and another enumeration for the indices of the columns,

```
enum Column {COLUMN_UNDERFLOW = -1, OUTLET1, OUTLET2, OUTLET3,
             NUM_OUTLETS, COLUMN_OVERFLOW = 3};
```

Recall that the C++ compiler treats `MIDNIGHT`, `SIX_AM`, `NOON`, `SIX_PM`, and `NUM_TIMES` as equivalent to 0, 1, 2, 3, and 4, respectively; and `OUTLET1`, `OUTLET2`, `OUTLET3`, and `NUM_OUTLETS` as equivalent to 0, 1, 2, and 3, respectively. This means that the declaration

```
double temperatureGrid[NUM_TIMES][NUM_OUTLETS];
```

defines `temperatureGrid` as a two-dimensional array, consisting of four rows and three columns. The C++ compiler thus reserves 12 memory locations for this object and associates `temperatureGrid` with these memory locations. We can visualize this as follows:

temperatureGrid:	[OUTLET1]	[OUTLET2]	[OUTLET3]
[MIDNIGHT]			
[SIX_AM]			
[NOON]			
[SIX_PM]			

The notation

```
temperatureGrid[NOON][OUTLET2]
```

thus refers to the element in row `NOON` and column `OUTLET2` of `temperatureGrid`. In general, the notation

```
temperatureGrid[r][c]
```

refers to the entry in row `r` and column `c`, that is, to the temperature recorded at time `r`, location `c`.

As before, the `typedef` mechanism can be used to declare the name `TableOfTemperatures` as a type denoting a two-dimensional array of real values,

```
typedef double TableOfTemperatures[NUM_TIMES][NUM_OUTLETS];
```

and this type can then be used to declare `temperatureGrid` to be an object whose type is `TableOfTemperatures`:

```
TableOfTemperatures temperatureGrid;
```

DECLARING THREE-DIMENSIONAL ARRAYS

To illustrate the use of an array with more than two dimensions, suppose that the temperatures in the last example are recorded for one week, so that seven such tables are collected:

Saturday

Time	Location Outlet1	Outlet2	Outlet3
12 A.M.	66.5	69.4	68.4
6 A.M.	68.4	71.2	69.3
12 P.M.	70.1	71.9	70.2
6 P.M.	69.5	70.0	69.4

⋰

Monday

Time	Location Outlet1	Outlet2	Outlet3
12 A.M.	63.7	66.2	64.3
6 A.M.	64.0	66.8	64.9
			66.3
			65.8

Sunday

Time	Location Outlet1	Outlet2	Outlet3
12 A.M.	65.5	68.7	62.0
6 A.M.	68.8	68.9	64.5
12 P.M.	70.4	69.4	66.3
6 P.M.	68.5	69.1	65.8

The collection of these tables can be modeled with a **three-dimensional array** object, declared by

```
enum DayName {DAY_UNDERFLOW = -1, SUNDAY, MONDAY, TUESDAY,
              WEDNESDAY, THURSDAY, FRIDAY, SATURDAY,
              NUM_DAYS, DAY_OVERFLOW = 7};

enum Row {ROW_UNDERFLOW = -1, MIDNIGHT, SIX_AM, NOON, SIX_PM,
          NUM_TIMES, ROW_OVERFLOW = 4};

enum Column {COLUMN_UNDERFLOW = -1, OUTLET1, OUTLET2, OUTLET3,
             NUM_OUTLETS, COLUMN_OVERFLOW = 3};

typedef double
   ThreeDimTemperatureArray[NUM_DAYS][NUM_TIMES][NUM_OUTLETS];

ThreeDimTemperatureArray temperature;
```

The object `temperature` can then be used to store these 84 temperature readings.

OPERATIONS ON THREE-DIMENSIONAL ARRAYS

Subscript. A single subscript operator is needed to access an element in a one-dimensional array and two subscript operators are needed to access an element in a two-dimensional array, so it seems reasonable that three subscript operators are needed to access an element in a three-dimensional array. For example,

```
temperature[MONDAY][MIDNIGHT][OUTLET3]
```

refers to the temperature recorded on Monday at 12 A.M. at the third outlet; that is, the value 64.3 in the second table, first row, and third column. In general,

```
temperature[d][t][o]
```

is the temperature recorded on day `d` at time `t` for outlet `o`.

Other Operations. Other operations on three-dimensional arrays can be encoded as functions. Typically, these use three nested `for` loops to run through the elements of the array. For example, if a file contains a week's 84 temperature readings, the following function can be used to read the values from that file into `temperature`:

```
void read(ifstream & in, ThreeDimTemperatureArray temperature,
          int numDays, int numTimes, int numOutlets)
{
   for (int d = 0; d < numDays; d++)
      for (int t = 0; t < numTimes; t++)
         for (int o = 0; o < numOutlets; o++)
            in >> temperature[d][t][o];

}
```

Functions can be defined to perform any operation we need on a three-dimensional array.

HIGHER-DIMENSIONAL ARRAYS

In some problems, arrays with even more dimensions may be useful. For example, suppose that a retailer maintains an inventory of jeans. She carries several different brands of jeans and for each brand she stocks a variety of styles, waist sizes, and inseam lengths. A four-dimensional array can be used to record the inventory, with each element of the array being the number of jeans of a particular brand, style, waist size, and inseam length currently in stock. The first index represents the brand; thus, it might be of type

```
enum BrandType {LEVI, WRANGLER, GAP, LEE, EDDIE_BAUER,
               NUM_BRANDS};
```

(We will omit the *underflow* and *overflow* enumerators in this example, to save space.) The second index represents styles and is of type

```
enum StyleType {FLAIR, BOOT_LEG, CARGO, CARPENTER,
               RELAXED_FIT, ORIGINAL_FIT, NUM_STYLES};
```

The third and fourth indices represent waist size and inseam length, respectively. For waist sizes ranging from 28 through 48 and inseam lengths ranging from 26 through 36, we might declare enumerations as follows:

```
enum WaistType {W28, W29, W30, W31, W32, W33, W34, W35, W36,
                W37, W38, W39, W40, W41, W42, W43, W44, W45,
                W46, W47, W48, NUM_WAIST_SIZES};
enum InseamType {I26, I27, I28, I29, I30, I31, I32, I33, I34,
                 I35, I36, NUM_INSEAM_SIZES};
```

A program to maintain the inventory can then declare the type

```
typedef int
   JeansArray[NUM_BRANDS][NUM_STYLES]
             [NUM_WAIST_SIZES][NUM_INSEAM_SIZES];
```

and then use this type to define a four-dimensional array `jeans` having indices of the types just described:

```
JeansArray jeans;
```

The value of the expression

```
jeans[LEVI][BOOT_LEG][W32][I31]
```

is the number of Levi's boot-leg 32×31 jeans that are in stock. The statement

```
jeans[brand][style][waist][inseam]--;
```

can be used to record the sale (i.e., decrement the inventory) of one pair of jeans of a specified `brand`, `style`, `waist` size, and `inseam` length.

As these examples illustrate, n-dimensional arrays can be defined and subscript operators can be used to access the array elements. C++ places no limit on the number of dimensions of an array, but the number of values in each dimension must be specified. The general form of an array declaration is as follows:

Array Declaration

Form:

ElementType arrayName[DIM_1][DIM_2] . . . [DIM_n];

where

ElementType is any known type;

arrayName is the name of the array being defined; and

each DIM_i must be a nonnegative integer (constant) value.

Purpose: Defines an n-dimensional object whose elements are of type *ElementType*, in which $DIM_1, DIM_2, \ldots, DIM_n$ are the number of elements in each dimension.

Array of Arrays Declarations. One way to view a multidimensional array is as an **array of arrays**; that is, an array whose elements are other arrays. For example, consider the nuclear power plant's temperature grid described earlier:

```
double temperatureGrid[NUM_TIMES][NUM_OUTLETS];
```

Since `NUM_TIMES` is 4, this table can be thought of as a one-dimensional array, whose four elements are its rows:

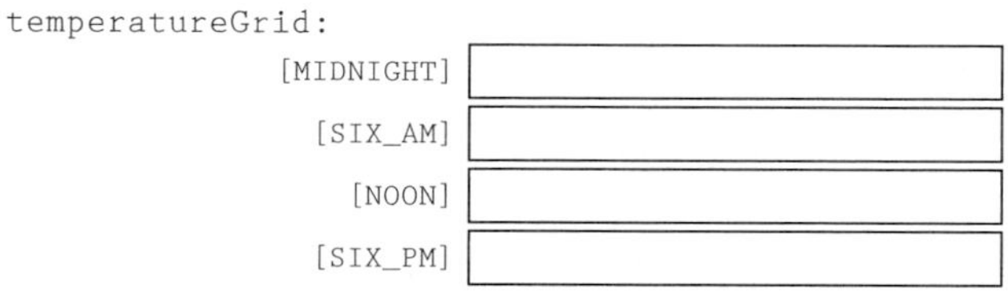

Of course, each row in `temperatureGrid` is itself a one-dimensional array of three real values:

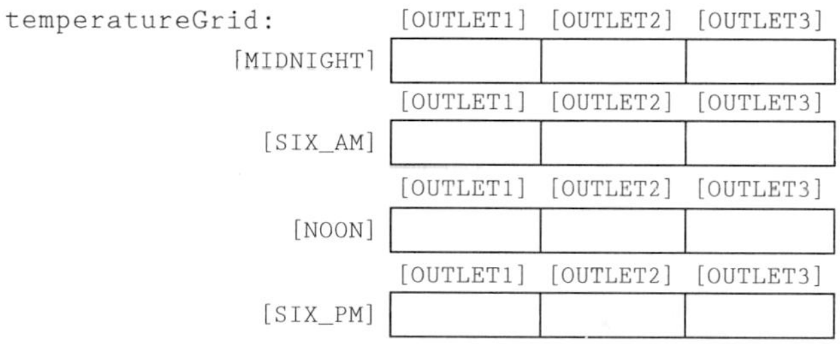

A table can thus be viewed as a one-dimensional array whose components are also one-dimensional arrays.

C++ allows array declarations to be given in a form that reflects this perspective. If we first declare the type identifier `TemperatureList` as a synonym for an array of outlet readings,

```
enum Column {COLUMN_UNDERFLOW = -1, OUTLET1, OUTLET2, OUTLET3,
             NUM_OUTLETS, COLUMN_OVERFLOW = 3};
typedef double TemperatureList[NUM_OUTLETS];
```

the objects of type `TemperatureList` are one-dimensional arrays of `double` values. We can then use this new type to declare a second type `TemperatureTable` as an array whose elements are `TemperatureList` objects:

```
enum Row {ROW_UNDERFLOW = -1, MIDNIGHT, SIX_AM, NOON, SIX_PM,
          NUM_TIMES, ROW_OVERFLOW = 4};
typedef TemperatureList TemperatureTable[NUM_TIMES];
```

This declares the name `TemperatureTable` as a new type, whose objects are two-dimensional arrays of double values. The resulting type can then be used to define a two-dimensional array object `temperatureGrid`, as before:

```
TemperatureTable temperatureGrid;
```

Regardless of which approach is used, the notation

```
temperatureGrid[SIX_AM]
```

refers to the second row of temperatures in the table,

	[OUTLET1]	[OUTLET2]	[OUTLET3]
[SIX_AM]			

and the notation

```
temperatureGrid[SIX_AM][OUTLET2]
```

to the second entry in this row.

This idea can be extended to higher-dimensional arrays. For example, the three-dimensional array of temperature tables considered earlier can also be thought of as an array of arrays. In particular, since one temperature table was recorded for each day, the entire three-dimensional array can be viewed as an array of temperature tables, meaning a one-dimensional array whose components are two-dimensional arrays. If we adopt this point of view, we might declare the three-dimensional array `temperature` by adding the declarations

```
enum DayName {DAY_UNDERFLOW = -1, SUNDAY, MONDAY, TUESDAY,
              WEDNESDAY, THURSDAY, FRIDAY, SATURDAY,
              NUM_DAYS, DAY_OVERFLOW = 7};
typedef TemperatureTable ThreeDimTemperatureArray[NUM_DAYS];
ThreeDimTemperatureArray temperature;
```

to the preceding declarations. This may make it clearer that the notation

```
temperature[MONDAY]
```

refers to the entire temperature table that was recorded on Monday; that is, `temperature[MONDAY]` is the two-dimensional array corresponding to the following temperature table:

	Location		
Time	Outlet1	Outlet2	Outlet3
12 A.M.	63.7	66.2	64.3
6 A.M.	64.0	66.8	64.9
12 P.M.	72.7	69.9	66.3
6 P.M.	66.6	68.0	65.8

As in the previous example, each row in a temperature table can be viewed as a one-dimensional array of temperatures, and each table can therefore be viewed as a one-dimensional array of the temperature arrays. The doubly indexed expression

```
temperature[MONDAY][MIDNIGHT]
```

refers to the first row in the temperature table for `Monday`,

63.7	66.2	64.3

and the triply indexed expression

```
temperature[MONDAY][MIDNIGHT][OUTLET3]
```

accesses the third temperature in this row:

```
64.3
```

DRAWBACKS OF C-STYLE ARRAYS

The drawbacks of C-style arrays can be summarized in one sentence:

C-style arrays are not self-contained objects.

When we define a function to implement an array operation, we must pass not only the array, but also the bound on each of its dimensions. To illustrate, the function `read()` to read values from a file into a `ThreeDimTemperatureArray` must receive not only the `ifstream` to the file and the `ThreeDimTemperatureArray`, but also the number of days, number of times, and number of outlets:

```
void read(ifstream & in, ThreeDimTemperatureArray temperature,
          int numDays, int numTimes, int numOutlets)
{
   for (int day = 0; day < numDays; day++)
      for (int time = 0; time < numTimes; time++)
         for (int outlet = 0; outlet < numOutlets; outlet++)
            in >> temperature[day][time][outlet];
}
```

The reason is that an array is not a class and thus does not have instance variables in which these attributes can be stored.

One solution is to imitate what we did with C-style enumerations in the preceding chapter: Build array classes. For example, we might build a class for two-dimensional arrays of `doubles` like the following:

```
const int MAX_ROWS = 20;
const int MAX_COLUMNS = 20;
typedef double ElementType;
/* or for a class template: template <typename ElementType> */

class TwoDimArray
{
 public:
   /* Basic operations such as input and output methods.
      Also, since the subscript operator [] is defined for
      C-style arrays but not for TwoDimArray objects, we
      need to overload the operator[] function. */

 private:
   ElementType myArray[MAX_ROWS][MAX_COLUMNS];
   int myRows;      // number of rows and
   int myColumns;   // columns of data I currently store
   // . . . other instance variables as needed . . .
};
```

For three-dimensional arrays, we could define a similar `ThreeDimArray` class and so on for higher dimensions.

This is an acceptable way to transform C-style arrays into C++ array classes, especially when one prefers or needs "lean and mean" array objects that do not have a lot of overhead from infrequently used operations or if one needs special array operations.[1] The disadvantage, however, is that one must implement all of the operations.

In the next section, we will explore an alternative approach: higher-dimensional `vector<T>`s.

✔ Quick Quiz 13.2

1. A(n) ________ array is useful for storing data arranged in rows and columns.
2. A(n) ________ array is useful for storing data arranged in rows, columns, and ranks.
3. Arrays with the same number of rows as columns are said to be ________ arrays.

Questions 4–14 refer to the following two-dimensional array:

mat:

	[0]	[1]	[2]	[3]
[0]	11	22	0	43
[1]	1	−1	0	999
[2]	−5	39	15	82
[3]	1	2	3	4
[4]	44	33	22	11

Find the value of each expression in Questions 4–9.

4. `mat[2][3]`
5. `mat[4][1]`
6. `mat[1][1]`
7. `mat[0][0] + mat[0][1]`
8. `mat[0][0] + mat[1][0]`
9. `mat[3]`

Find the value of x in each of Questions 10–14:

10.
```
int x = 0;
for (int i = 0; i <= 4; i++)
   x += mat[i][1];
```
11.
```
int x = 0;
for (int j = 0; j < 4; j++)
   x += mat[1][j];
```
12.
```
int x = 0;
for (int k = 0; k <= 3; k++)
   x += mat[k][k];
```
13.
```
int x = 0;
for (int i = 0; i < 5; i++)
   for (int j = 0; j < 4; j++)
      x += mat[i][j];
```

1. It is even better if one uses run-time allocated arrays as described in Section 14.2.

14.
```
int x = 0;
for (int j = 0; j < 4; j++)
   for (int i = 0; i < 5; i++)
      x += mat[i][j];
```
15. The main drawback of C-style arrays is that they are not ________ objects.

Exercises 13.2

Exercises 1–6 assume that the following declarations have been made:

```
enum Color {RED, YELLOW, BLUE, GREEN, WHITE, BLACK, NUM_COLORS};
typedef bool BitArray[2][2][2][2];
typedef int Shirt[NUM_COLORS][10][20];
typedef Shirt ShirtStock[5];
```

How many elements can be stored in an array of each type?

1. `int[50][100]`
2. `char[26][26]`
3. `bool[2][2][2]`
4. `BitArray`
5. `Shirt`
6. `ShirtStock`

Exercises 7–10 assume that the following declarations have been made:

```
typedef int Array3x3[3][3];
Array3X3 mat;
```

Tell what value (if any) is assigned to each array element, or explain why an error occurs.

7.
```
for (int i = 0; i < 3; i++)
   for (int j = 0; j < 3; j++)
      mat[i][j] = i + j;
```
8.
```
for (int i = 0; i < 3; i++)
   for (int j = 2; j >= 0; j--)
      if (i == j)
         mat[i][j] = 0;
      else
         mat[i][j] = 1;
```
9.
```
for (int i = 0; i < 3; i++)
   for (int j = 0; j < 3; j++)
      if (i < j)
         mat[i][j] = -1
      else if (i == j)
         mat[i][j] = 0;
      else
         mat[i][j] = 1;
```

10.
```
for (int i = 0; i < 3; i++)
{
   for (int j = 0; j < i; j++)
      mat[i][j] = 0;
   for (j = i; j < 3; j++)
      mat[i][j] = 2;
}
```

Exercises 11–14 assume that the following declarations have been made:

```
char logo[2][10] = {"Computers", "and More!"};
```

Tell what output will be produced or explain why an error occurs.

11.
```
for (int i = 0; i < 2; i++)
{
   for (int j = 0; j < 9; j++)
      cout << logo[i][j];
   cout << endl;
}
```

12.
```
for (int j = 0; j < 9; j++)
{
   for (int i = 0; i < 2; i++)
      cout << logo[i][j];
   cout << endl;
}
```

13.
```
for (int i = 0; i < 2; i++)
{
   for (int j = 0; j < 9; j++)
      cout << logo[j][i];
   cout << endl;
}
```

14.
```
for (int i = 0; i < 2; i++)
{
   for (int j = 8; j >= 0; j--)
      cout << logo[i][j];
   cout << endl;
}
```

15. Write a function that, given a `TemperatureTable` (as declared in this section), will calculate and return the average temperature at each of the three locations.
16. Construct two enumerations: `AutoModel`, whose values are ten different automobile models, and `EmployeeName`, whose values are the names of eight employees of an auto dealership. Using these types, overload the I/O operators with definitions to perform input and output of sales tables. The output operator should display the sales table with the rows labeled with the automobile models and the columns labeled with the employee's names.

17. Like one-dimensional arrays, multidimensional arrays are stored in a block of consecutive memory locations, and address translation formulas are used to determine the location in memory of each array element. To illustrate, consider a 3×4 array `a` of integers, and assume that an integer can be stored in one memory word. If `a` is allocated memory in a row-wise manner and b is its base address, then the first row of `a`, `a[0][0]`, `a[0][1]`, `a[0][2]`, `a[0][3]`, is stored in words b, $b + 1$, $b + 2$, $b + 3$; the second row in words $b + 4$ through $b + 7$; and the third row in words $b + 8$ through $b + 11$.

Address	*Memory*	*Array Element*
	⋮	
b		a[0][0]
$b + 1$		a[0][1]
$b + 2$		a[0][2]
$b + 3$		a[0][3]
$b + 4$		a[1][0]
$b + 5$		a[1][1]
$b + 6$		a[1][2]
$b + 7$		a[1][3]
$b + 8$		a[2][0]
$b + 9$		a[2][1]
$b + 10$		a[2][2]
$b + 11$		a[2][3]
	⋮	

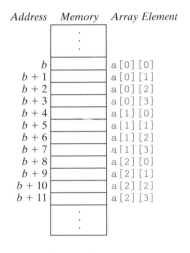

In general, `a[i][j]` is stored in word $b + 4i + j$.

a. Give a similar diagram and formula if `a` is a 3×3 array of integer values.

b. Give a similar diagram and formula if `a` is a 3×4 array of `double` values, where `double` values require two words for storage.

13.3 Multidimensional vector<T> Objects

In the preceding section, we noted some of the drawbacks associated with C-style arrays and indicated how we could get around them by "wrapping" an array inside a class. This is in fact the approach used in `vector<T>` (except that it uses run-time allocated arrays as described in Section 14.2). In this section, we will explore how we can use `vector<T>`s to create self-contained higher-dimensional objects. Using the operations already provided in `vector<T>` and applying the STL algorithms to `vector<T>` objects will save us work.[2] Applying them to higher dimensional objects requires some care, however, since this is not as straightforward as using them with one-dimensional objects.

Among the methods provided by `vector<T>` are three constructors whose prototypes (in simplified form) are as follows:

```
vector();
vector(int n);
vector(int n, T initialValue);
```

2. There are several `vector<T>` operations that are not used, however, which means that this approach will have more overhead than array classes we might build in the manner described at the end of the preceding section.

The first constructs an empty vector<T> object; the second constructs a vector<T> object with capacity n and fills it with a default value of type T; and the third constructs a vector<T> object with capacity n and fills it with the specified initialValue. For example, the declarations

```
vector<double> aVector;

const int INITIAL_CAPACITY = 10;
vector<double> bVector(INITIAL_CAPACITY);

vector<double> cVector(INITIAL_CAPACITY, 1.0);
```

construct aVector as a vector of doubles, initially empty; bVector as a vector of 10 (undefined) doubles; and cVector as a vector of 10 doubles, all initialized to 1.0:

aVector										
bVector	?	?	?	?	?	?	?	?	?	?
cVector	1.0	1.0	1.0	1.0	1.0	1.0	1.0	1.0	1.0	1.0

It is the last two types of constructor that make it possible to build multidimensional vector<T> objects.

TWO-DIMENSIONAL vector<T> OBJECTS

A Two-Step Approach. Suppose that we want to build a two-dimensional object named table consisting of three rows and four columns. We might begin by defining a one-dimensional vector<T> object named initialRow whose capacity is the desired number of columns (4) and filling it with some initial value:

```
const int COLUMNS = 4;
vector<double> initialRow(COLUMNS, 0.0);
```

This builds a one-dimensional vector named initialRow, whose size and capacity are each 4:

	[0]	[1]	[2]	[3]
initialRow:	0.0	0.0	0.0	0.0

In the same way that a two-dimensional C-style array can be viewed as an array of arrays, a **vector of vectors** is a two-dimensional object. We can thus define the two-dimensional object table as a vector of vectors, using the desired number of rows (3) as its capacity, and with the object initialRow as its initial value:

```
const int ROWS = 3;
vector< vector<double> > table(ROWS, initialRow);
```

WATCH OUT

Note the space separating `double>` and `>`. *It is important to remember the space between the angle brackets (> >), because if we write*

```
vector<vector<double>> table(ROWS, initialRow);   // ERROR!
```

the compiler will mistake >> for the input (or right-shift) operator, which will result in a compilation error.

Because each element of `table` is a `vector<initialRow>`, and `initialRow` is a `vector<double>`, the compiler will use `initialRow` to initialize each element of `table`. The result is that `table` is constructed as a 3 × 4 vector of vectors, in which each of the three rows is a copy of `initialRow`:

table:	[0]	[1]	[2]	[3]
[0]	0.0	0.0	0.0	0.0
[1]	0.0	0.0	0.0	0.0
[2]	0.0	0.0	0.0	0.0

A single-subscript expression such as

```
table[0]
```

refers to the first row of `table`,

table:	[0]	[1]	[2]	[3]
[0]	0.0	0.0	0.0	0.0

and a double-subscript expression such as

```
table[0][2]
```

refers to an element within the specified row of `table`:

table:	[0]	[1]	[2]	[3]
[0]	0.0	0.0	0.0	0.0

In general, the expression

```
table[r][c]
```

can be used to access the value stored in column `c` of row `r`.

A One-Step Approach. We can define the same vector of vectors in one step by using a more concise (although somewhat less readable) form that avoids the need to define the object `initialRow`:

```
const int ROWS = 3;
const int COLUMNS = 4;
vector< vector<double> >
                    table(ROWS, vector<double>(COLUMNS, 0.0));
```

This uses the `vector<T>` constructor twice: an "outer" call,

```
vector< vector<double> >
                table( ROWS, vector<double>(COLUMNS, 0.0));
```

and nested within it, an "inner" explicit call to the same constructor:

```
vector< vector<double> >
                table(ROWS, vector<double>(COLUMNS, 0.0));
```

This inner constructor builds a nameless `vector<double>` object containing four zeros (like `initialRow` in the two-step approach). This nameless vector of `double` values is then passed as the initial value to the outer call to the constructor, which uses it to initialize each of its three vector elements. The result is the same 3×4 vector of vectors of `double` values as before:

table:	[0]	[1]	[2]	[3]
[0]	0.0	0.0	0.0	0.0
[1]	0.0	0.0	0.0	0.0
[2]	0.0	0.0	0.0	0.0

The `typedef` mechanism can be used to improve the readability of this one-step approach:

```
typedef vector<double> TableRow;
typedef vector<TableRow> Table;
```

The first `typedef` declares the name `TableRow` as a type that is a synonym for a one-dimensional vector of `double`s. The second `typedef` then declares the name `Table` as a synonym for a two-dimensional vector of `TableRow` values; that is, a vector of vectors of `double`s. For reusability, we might put these declarations in a header file *Table.h* as shown in Figure 13.2.

Fig. 13.2 A header file for type `Table`.

```
/* Table.h contains the declarations for type Table.
 * ...
 *******************************************************/

#include <vector>
using namespace std;

typedef vector<double> TableRow;
typedef vector<TableRow> Table;

// ... prototypes of Table operations
```

A program that includes *Table.h* can then use

```
Table aTable;
```

to define an object `aTable` as an empty two-dimensional `Table`. To define a nonempty `Table`, we can use

```
const int ROWS = 3,
          COLUMNS = 4;
Table theTable(ROWS, TableRow(COLUMNS, 0.0));
```

The result is a definition that is more readable than that given earlier and that eliminates the error described there caused by forgetting a space between two > symbols.

TWO-DIMENSIONAL vector<T> OPERATIONS

We have already seen that double-subscript expressions of the form `theTable[r][c]` can be used to access the element at row `r` and column `c` in `theTable`. In addition to the subscript operator, other `vector<T>` messages can be sent to two-dimensional vectors. We will look briefly at two of these methods.

The `size( )` Method. If `theTable` is the 3 × 4 two-dimensional vector described earlier, then the expression

```
theTable.size()
```

returns 3, the number of rows in `theTable`. The expression

```
theTable[r].size()
```

can be used to find the number of columns in row `r`, because `theTable[r]` is the vector of `double` values in `theTable` whose index is `r`, and applying `size()` to that vector returns the number of values in it. If `theTable` is **rectangular** so that each row has same number of elements, we can apply `size()` to any row to get the number of columns in `theTable`. If `theTable` is a **jagged table**—different rows have different sizes—`size()` must be applied to each row separately.

The `push_back()` Method. Suppose that we need to add a new (fourth) row to `theTable`. This can be done by using the `vector<T>` method `push_back()`:

```
theTable.push_back( TableRow(COLUMNS, 0.0) );
```

Since `TableRow` has been declared as a synonym for `vector<double>`, the expression

```
TableRow(COLUMNS, 0.0)
```

is a call to the `vector<T>` constructor to build a nameless vector of zeros. The `push_back()` message then appends this vector to the existing rows in `theTable`:

theTable:	[0]	[1]	[2]	[3]
[0]	0.0	0.0	0.0	0.0
[1]	0.0	0.0	0.0	0.0
[2]	0.0	0.0	0.0	0.0
[3]	0.0	0.0	0.0	0.0

To add a fifth column to `theTable`, we can use `push_back()` to append a `double` value to each row of `theTable`, because each row in `theTable` is itself a vector of `double` values:

```
for (int row = 0; row < theTable.size(); row++)
   theTable[row].push_back(0.0);
```

theTable:	[0]	[1]	[2]	[3]	[4]
[0]	0.0	0.0	0.0	0.0	0.0
[1]	0.0	0.0	0.0	0.0	0.0
[2]	0.0	0.0	0.0	0.0	0.0
[3]	0.0	0.0	0.0	0.0	0.0

We can also use `push_back()` to build nonrectangular tables. To illustrate, consider the following statements:

```
Table aTable;

for (int cols = 1; cols <= 3; cols++)
   aTable.push_back( TableRows(cols, 0.0) );
```

Initially, `aTable` is constructed as an empty vector. The first pass through the `for` loop constructs a nameless vector containing one zero and appends it to `aTable`:

aTable:	[0]
[0]	0.0

The second pass through the `for` loop constructs and appends another nameless vector containing two zeros:

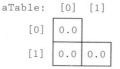

aTable:	[0]	[1]
[0]	0.0	
[1]	0.0	0.0

The third pass through the `for` loop constructs and appends a third nameless vector of three zeros:

aTable:	[0]	[1]	[2]
[0]	0.0		
[1]	0.0	0.0	
[2]	0.0	0.0	0.0

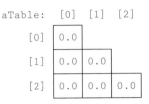

Two-dimensional vectors thus need not be square, nor even rectangular—they can also be jagged.

DEFINING TWO-DIMENSIONAL `vector<T>` FUNCTIONS

The subscript and other `vector<T>` operations can be used as "building blocks" for operations that are not predefined for two-dimensional vectors. The following examples illustrate this.

Two-Dimensional `vector` Output. The function in Figure 13.3 displays a two-dimensional vector via an `ostream`. Note how it uses the `size()` method and subscript operations. For reusability, we define this function in a separately compiled implementation file *Table.cpp* and place a prototype in *Table.h* (see Figure 13.2).

Fig. 13.3 A `Table` output operation.

```
/* Table.cpp defines various Table operations.
 * ...
 ****************************************************/

#include "Table.h"

void print(ostream& out, const Table& aTable)
{
   for (int row = 0; row < aTable.size(); row++)
   {
      for (int col = 0; col < aTable[row].size(); col++)
         out << aTable[row][col] << '\t';
      out << endl;
   }
}
```

For the `Table` object `theTable` defined previously,

```
print(cout, theTable);
```

will display `theTable` as follows:

```
0    0    0    0
0    0    0    0
0    0    0    0
```

Note that because `size()` is applied separately to each row in the inner `for` loop, this function can be used to display jagged tables in addition to square and rectangular tables.

Two-Dimensional `vector` Input. The data for a table is often stored in a file, and an operation to fill a two-dimensional vector from a file is thus a useful operation. There are several ways to implement such an operation. The approach used by the function `fill()` in Figure 13.4 resembles the way C-style arrays are input. The number of rows and number of columns in the table are read from the first line of the file, and these values are used to preallocate a local two-dimensional vector of the appropriate dimensions, which is then filled with values from the file. Again, for reusability, we would store this function in *Table.cpp* and put a prototype in *Table.h* .

Fig. 13.4 A `Table` input operation.

```
#include <fstream>        // ifstream
#include <cassert>        // assert()
using namespace std;

void fill(const string& fileName, Table& aTable)
{
   ifstream in(fileName.data());               // open stream to file
   assert(in.is_open());                       // verify

   int rows,                                   // variables
       cols;                                   //   for dimensions
   in >> rows >> cols;                         // read dimensions

   Table locTable(rows, TableRow(cols));       // construct a local
                                               //   rows x cols table
   for (int r = 0; r < rows; r++)              // for each row
      for (int c = 0; c < cols; c++)           //   input cols values
         in >> locTable[r][c];                 //     into row
                                               // assign locTable to aTable
   aTable = locTable;                          //   so it has correct
                                               //     dimensions
   in.close();                                 // close stream
}
```

This function constructs a local `Table locTable` that has the correct number of rows and columns. A pair of nested `for` loops is then used to fill this table with values from the file. Assigning this table to the reference parameter aTable destroys the corresponding Table argument and constructs a new one whose capacity will match exactly the dimensions of the table stored in the file when fill() terminates.

An alternative approach is to leave the number of rows and columns unspecified, read values from the file, use push_back() to append the values to a vector that stores a row of the table, and, at the end of the row, use push_back() again to append that vector to the vector of vectors. The function load() in Figure 13.5 uses this approach.

Fig. 13.5 A Table input operation.

```
void load(const string& fileName, Table& aTable)
{
   ifstream in(fileName.data());          // open stream to file
   assert(in.is_open());                  // verify

   Table locTable;                        // an empty local table
   double aValue;                         // input variable
   char separator;                        // to test for '\n'

   for (;;)                               // loop:
   {
      TableRow aRow;                      //  start with an empty row
      for (;;)                            //  loop:
      {
         separator = in.peek();           //    peek at the next char
         if (separator == '\n') break;    //    if at end of row, exit
         in >> aValue;                    //    read a value
         if (in.eof()) return;            //    if eof, quit
         aRow.push_back(aValue);          //    append value to row
      }                                   //   end loop
      in.get(separator);                  //   consume the newline
      locTable.push_back(aRow);           //   append row to table
   }                                      // end loop

   aTable = locTable;                     // assign locTable to aTable
   in.close();                            // close stream
}
```

The advantage of this approach is its generality. The input file need not contain the table's dimensions, only the table data. Also, because each row corresponds to one line from the input file, load() can be used to read square, rectangular, or jagged tables, and it requires no information in the input file other than the table's data. Its disadvantage is that a significant portion of the vector's memory may be wasted, because when push_back() expands the capacity of a vector, memory is allocated in large blocks.

Quick Quiz 13.3

1. (True or false) A vector of vectors is a two-dimensional object.
2. (True or false) The declaration

```
vector<vector<int>> intTable(3, vector<int>(4, 0));
```

will cause a compile-time error.

Questions 3–8 assume the following declarations:

```
typedef vector<double> TableRow;
typedef vector<TableRow> Table;
Table qqTab(5, TableRow(4, 0.0));
```

3. `qqTab` will have ________ rows and ________ columns.
4. Write an expression to change the element in the second row and third column of `qqTab` to 1.1.
5. What is the value of `qqTab.size()`?
6. What is the value of `qqTab[0].size()`?
7. Write a statement to append the value 99.9 at the end of the second row of `qqTab`.
8. Write statements to append a row containing 4 zeros at the bottom of `qqTab`.

Exercises 13.3

For each of the following exercises, write a function for type `Table` to do what is required.

1. A function `setElem()` that, for a given row `r`, column `c`, and `double` value `element`, sets the value in row `r`, column `c` to `element`.
2. A function `rowSum()` that sums the values in a given row of a `Table`.
3. A function `columnSum()` that sums the values in a given column of a `Table`.
4. A function `rowAverage()` that, given a row number, computes the average of the values in that row.
5. A function `rowStdDeviation()` that, given a row number, computes the standard deviation of the values in that row. (See Programming Problem 10 at the end of Chapter 10.)
6. A function `columnAverage()` that, given a column number, computes the average of the values in that column.
7. A function `columnStdDeviation()` that, given a column number, computes the standard deviation of the values in that column. (See Programming Problem 10 at the end of Chapter 10.)

13.4 Case Study: `vector<T>`-Based Matrices

A two-dimensional numeric array having m rows and n columns is called an $m \times n$ **matrix**. There are many important applications of matrices because there are many problems that can be solved most easily using matrices and matrix operations. Thus, a `Matrix` class would be very useful and the task at hand is to build such a class.

To begin, we must know what matrix operations to include. Here we will confine our attention to addition, subtraction, multiplication, and transpose. The **sum** of two matrices that have the same number of rows and the same number of columns is defined as follows: If A_{ij} and B_{ij} are the entries in the ith row and jth column of $m \times n$ matrices A and B, respectively, then $A_{ij} + B_{ij}$ is the entry in the ith row and jth column of the sum, which will also be an $m \times n$ matrix. For example,

$$\begin{bmatrix} 1 & 0 & 2 \\ -1 & 3 & 5 \end{bmatrix} + \begin{bmatrix} 4 & 2 & 1 \\ 7 & 0 & 3 \end{bmatrix} = \begin{bmatrix} 5 & 2 & 3 \\ 6 & 3 & 8 \end{bmatrix}$$

The **difference** of two such matrices is obtained simply by replacing + by –; for example,

$$\begin{bmatrix} 1 & 0 & 2 \\ -1 & 3 & 5 \end{bmatrix} - \begin{bmatrix} 4 & 2 & 1 \\ 7 & 0 & 3 \end{bmatrix} = \begin{bmatrix} -3 & -2 & 1 \\ -8 & 3 & 2 \end{bmatrix}$$

The **product** of two matrices is more difficult to calculate. For $A * B$ to be defined, the number of columns in A must match the number the number of rows in B. So suppose that A is an $m \times n$ matrix and B is an $n \times p$ matrix. The product C of A and B is an $m \times p$ matrix with the entry C_{ij}, which appears in the ith row and the jth column, given by

$$\begin{aligned} C_{ij} &= \text{the sum of the products of the entries in row } i \text{ of } A \\ &\quad\ \text{with the entries in column } j \text{ of } B \\ &= A_{i1} \times B_{1j} + A_{i2} \times B_{2j} + \cdots + A_{in} \times B_{nj} \end{aligned}$$

To illustrate, suppose that A is the 2×3 matrix

$$\begin{bmatrix} 1 & 0 & 2 \\ 3 & 0 & 4 \end{bmatrix}$$

and that B is the 3×4 matrix

$$\begin{bmatrix} 4 & 2 & 5 & 3 \\ 6 & 4 & 1 & 8 \\ 9 & 0 & 0 & 2 \end{bmatrix}$$

Because the number of columns (3) in A equals the number of rows in B, the product matrix is defined. The entry in the first row and first column is obtained by multiplying the first row of A with the first column of B, element by element, and adding these products:

$$\begin{bmatrix} \boxed{1 \ \ 0 \ \ 2} \\ 3 \ \ 0 \ \ 4 \end{bmatrix} \begin{bmatrix} \boxed{4} & 2 & 5 & 3 \\ \boxed{6} & 4 & 1 & 8 \\ \boxed{9} & 0 & 0 & 2 \end{bmatrix}$$

$$1*4 + 0*6 + 2*9 = 22$$

Similarly, the entry in the first row and second column is

$$\begin{bmatrix} \boxed{1 \ 0 \ 2} \\ 3 \ 0 \ 4 \end{bmatrix} \begin{bmatrix} 4 & \boxed{2} & 5 & 3 \\ 6 & \boxed{4} & 1 & 8 \\ 9 & \boxed{0} & 0 & 2 \end{bmatrix}$$

$$1*2 + 0*4 + 2*0 = 2$$

The complete product matrix is the 2×4 matrix given by

$$\begin{bmatrix} 22 & 2 & 5 & 7 \\ 48 & 6 & 15 & 17 \end{bmatrix}$$

BUILDING A `Matrix` CLASS: THE EXTERNAL APPROACH

If we imitate the `Table` class in the preceding section, then building a `Matrix` class is quite easy, because a matrix can be thought of as a vector of vectors of numbers. We can simply use a `typedef` statement to declare the name `Matrix` as an alias for `vector< vector<double> >`. To make this declaration reusable, we would place it in a `Matrix` library header *Matrix.h*:

```
/* Matrix.h provides the type Matrix and its
 * operation prototypes.
 ********************************************/

#include <vector>
using namespace std;
#include "Table.h"                    // Table prototypes

typedef vector<double> MatrixRow;
typedef vector< MatrixRow > Matrix;

// ... Matrix operation prototypes go here
```

A program that includes this header file can now define an empty `Matrix` object as follows:

```
Matrix aMatrix;
```

A nonempty `Matrix` can be defined using the same approach as in the preceding section:

```
const int ROWS = 3,
          COLS = 4;
Matrix theMatrix(ROWS, MatrixRow(COLS, 0.0));
```

This definition builds `theMatrix` as a 3×4 matrix and sets each of its elements to zero.

theMatrix:	[0]	[1]	[2]	[3]
[0]	0.0	0.0	0.0	0.0
[1]	0.0	0.0	0.0	0.0
[2]	0.0	0.0	0.0	0.0

Matrix OPERATIONS

Because the identifier Matrix is a synonym for vector< vector<double> >, any operation defined for vector< vector<double> > can be applied to a Matrix object. For example, the double-subscript operation can be used to access a particular element of a Matrix; that is, theMatrix[r][c] is the entry of theMatrix in row r and column c. Similarly, the size() function can be used to determine the number of rows in a Matrix.

In addition, because Matrix is a synonym for vector< vector<double> > and Table is also a synonym for vector< vector<double> >, the operations defined for Table (e.g., fill() from Figure 13.4) can also be applied to Matrix objects. Including the directive #include "Table.h" in *Matrix.h* adds the prototypes of these operations.

Operations that are specific to matrices such as addition, subtraction, and multiplication must be defined as functions. See if you can overload the functions operator+, operator-, and operator* for Matrix objects. Put prototypes for them in *Matrix.h* and their definitions in the implementation file *Matrix.cpp*. Be sure to write a driver program to test them. When you finish (or you have difficulty), see the versions on the text's Web site.

APPLICATION: SOLVING LINEAR SYSTEMS

A linear system is a set of linear equations, each of which involves several unknowns; for example,

$$
\begin{aligned}
5x_1 - x_2 - 2x_3 &= 11 \\
-x_1 + 5x_2 - 2x_3 &= 0 \\
-2x_1 - 2x_2 + 7x_3 &= 0
\end{aligned}
$$

is a linear system of three equations involving the three unknowns x_1, x_2, and x_3. A solution of such a system is a collection of values for these unknowns that satisfies all of the equations simultaneously.

This linear system can also be written as a single matrix equation

$$A*x = b$$

where A is the 3×3 **coefficient matrix**, b is the 3×1 **constant vector**, and x is the 3×1 **vector of unknowns**:

$$
A = \begin{bmatrix} 5 & -1 & -2 \\ -1 & 5 & -2 \\ -2 & -2 & 7 \end{bmatrix}, \quad x = \begin{bmatrix} x_1 \\ x_2 \\ x_3 \end{bmatrix}, \quad b = \begin{bmatrix} 11 \\ 0 \\ 0 \end{bmatrix}
$$

One method for solving a linear system is called **Gaussian elimination**. It is described on the text's Web site.

Quick Quiz 13.4

1. A two-dimensional numeric array having *m* rows and *n* columns is called a(n) ________.

Questions 2–6 assume the following matrices:

$$A = \begin{bmatrix} 1 & 0 & 2 \\ 3 & 0 & 4 \end{bmatrix}, B = \begin{bmatrix} 1 & 0 \\ 2 & -1 \\ 1 & 3 \end{bmatrix}, C = \begin{bmatrix} 3 & 2 \\ 1 & 0 \\ -1 & -2 \end{bmatrix}$$

2. $A * B$ will be a(n) _______ × _______ matrix.
3. Calculate $A * B$.
4. Calculate $B * A$, or explain why it is not defined.
5. Calculate $B * C$, or explain why it is not defined.
6. Calculate $C * B$, or explain why it is not defined.
7. Calculate $B + C$, or explain why it is not defined.
8. Calculate $B - C$, or explain why it is not defined.

Part of the Picture
Computer Graphics

Computer graphics is the area of computing that studies how information can be modeled and manipulated using pictures on a computer screen. To provide graphics capabilities, a computer screen is usually organized as a two-dimensional array (e.g., 480 × 640) of picture elements, called **pixels**. Primitive graphics operations include the ability to set a particular pixel to a given color (black or white on a monochrome screen). From these primitive operations, higher-level graphics operations can be implemented to draw lines, boxes, circles, text, and so on. From these operations, classes can be built to represent graphical user interface (GUI) objects, including *Window, Pane, Button, ScrollBar, CheckBox*, and so on.

Functions that perform graphics operations are typically stored in *graphics libraries* so they are easy to access. However, in order for such functions to be as efficient as possible, they are often written as low-level (e.g., assembly language) functions. Because of this, graphics functions cannot usually be ported between different hardware platforms or operating systems. Implementations of C++ for different platforms have historically had different graphics libraries:

- The *Xlib* and *Xt* libraries provide low-level and high-level graphics (respectively) C functions for the *X-window system*. X is the graphical environment on most Unix systems.
- *The Microsoft Foundation Classes* (MFC) is a C++ library providing graphics objects and operations for *MS Windows*. Visual C++ GUIs are generally built using MFC.
- *PowerPlant classes* is a C++ library for the MacOS available from Metrowerks CodeWarrior. CodeWarrior also runs on MS Windows and includes support for MFC, making it a good environment for developing applications for both MacOS and MS-Windows.
- *The CMUgraphics library* is a simple graphical library developed at Carnegie–Mellon University (see http://www.cs.cmu.edu/~mjs/apcs.html) as a teaching resource. This library is available for both MacOS and MS-Windows systems, providing (some) code portability across personal computers.
- *Qt* is an object-oriented C++ graphical environment from Trolltech (see http://www.trolltech.com/). With implementations for MacOS X, Unix, and Windows, Qt is the first C++ graphical library providing code portability across all three major platforms.

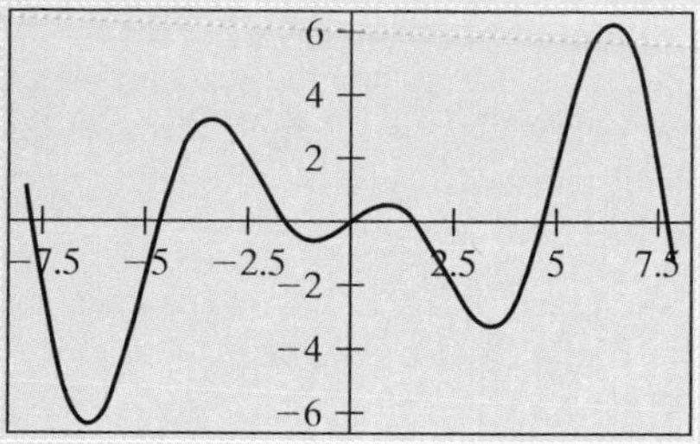

Fig. 13.6 Plot of $y = x * \cos(x)$ produced by Mathematica.

To illustrate the use of a graphics library, we have implemented a class named `CartesianSystem`, whose source code can be found on the text's Web site. This class is built as an extension of the *window* class provided in the CMUgraphics library. Graphics operations (e.g., `drawAxes()`, `drawLine()`, `drawFunction()`, and so on) are provided as methods of class `CartesianSystem`.

EXAMPLE: FUNCTION GRAPHING

Function Graphing. The number and quality of software packages that can be used to generate high-resolution graphs of functions are increasing rapidly. For example, Figure 13.6 shows the graph of $y = x * \cos(x)$ for $-8 \leq x \leq 8$ produced by the powerful software package Mathematica™.

The window containing the plot shown in Figure 13.6 is similar to the two-dimensional character array `screen` presented in Section 13.1 in that it is simply a two-dimensional array of points (pixels). The following enlarged view of the portion of the graphics window near the origin shows clearly the grid structure of this part of the window:

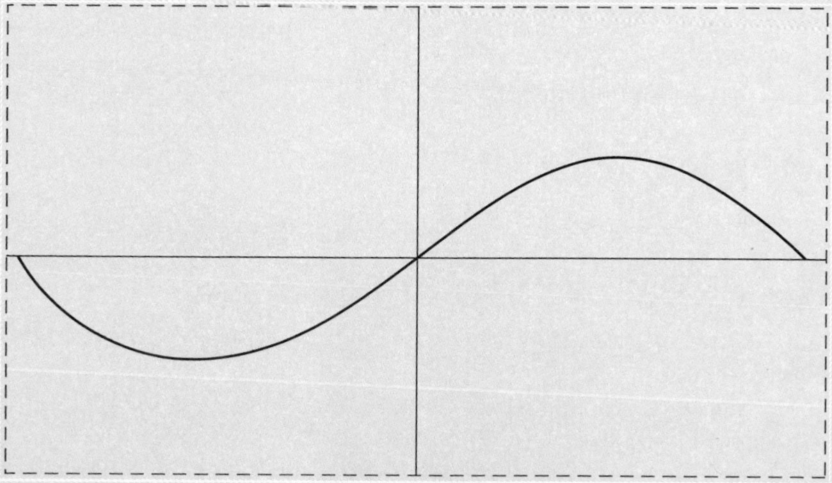

The class `CartesianSystem` contains a method `drawFunction()` for plotting a graph of a function. To draw the graph of a given function *f(x)*, it uses a loop to iterate through the *x* values. For each such *x* value, the *y* value nearest the actual function value $y = f(x)$ is determined, and the point (x, y) is mapped into the appropriate pixel in the window. This pixel is then set to a color different from the background by using a primitive graphics command.

The program in Figure 13.7 uses the `drawFunction()` method of class `CartesianSystem` to plot the functions $f(x) = x$, and $f(x) = x * cos(x)$. It also illustrates the use of several other `CartesianSystem` methods.

Fig. 13.7 Plotting a function. (Part 1 of 2)

```
/* functionPlotter.cpp demonstrates use of class CartesianSystem.
 *
 * Note:  We plot two functions f(x) and g(x).
 */

#include "CartesianSystem.h"
#include <cmath>                             // sin(), cos(), ...
using namespace std;
                                             // functions to be plotted
double f(double x);
double g(double x);

int main()
{
   cout << "This program graphs two functions\n"
        << " (currently y = x*cos(x) and y = x)."
        << "\n\nEnter the first and last X values: ";
   double xFirst, xLast;
   cin >> xFirst >> xLast;
   cout << "\nEnter the first and last Y values: ";
   double yFirst, yLast;
   cin >> yFirst >> yLast;

   CartesianSystem grid(xFirst, yFirst, xLast, yLast);

   grid.setPenWidth(3);
   grid.drawFunction(g, BLUE);
   grid.drawFunction(f, RED);
}

double f(double x) { return x * cos(x); }
double g(double x) { return x; }
```

Fig. 13.7 Plotting a function. (Part 2 of 2)

Sample run:

```
This program graphs two functions...
 (currently y = x*cos(x) and y = x.)

Please enter the minimum and maximum x values: -8 8

Please enter the minimum and maximum y values: -7 7
```

The sample run produced the output in Figure 13.8 (but see the text's Web site for color images).*

Figure 13.10 presents a second example, in which we use the `CartesianSystem` default constructor, and show how to draw circles and rectangles. We also use the blocking `waitForMouseClick()` and `clear()` methods to separate a series of drawings. The result is a "slide-show" effect.

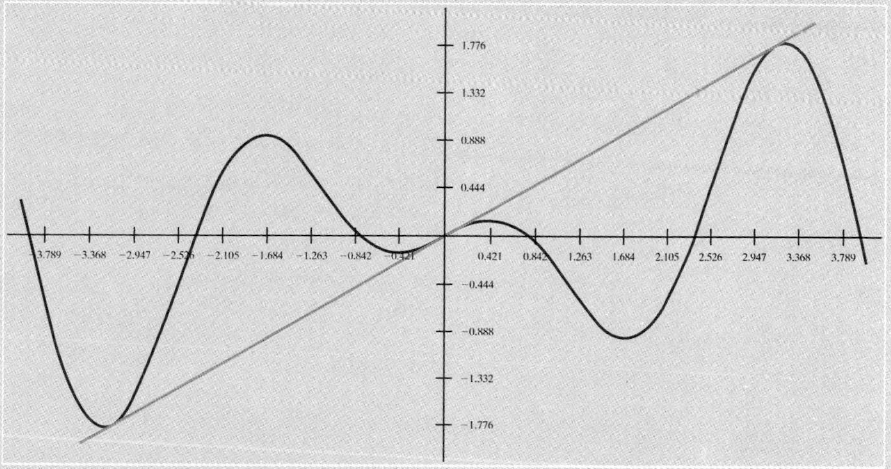

Fig. 13.8 Output of function plotter.

Fig. 13.9 A function "slide show."

```
/* functionSlideShow.cpp demonstrates the use of
 *  various CartesianSystem methods.
 * ...
 */

#include "CartesianSystem.h"
#include <cmath>                          // sin(), cos()
using namespace std;
                                          // functions to be plotted
double f(double x);
double g(double x);

int main()
{
   CartesianSystem grid;

   grid.setPenWidth(3);
   grid.drawRectangle(-1, -1, 1, 1, PURPLE, FRAME);
   grid.drawCircle(0, 0, 1, GREEN, FRAME);
   grid.drawFunction(g, BLUE);
   grid.drawFunction(f, RED);

   grid.waitForMouseClick();
   grid.clear(YELLOW);
   grid.setPenWidth(3);
   grid.drawFunction(g, DKGREEN);
   grid.drawFunction(f, BLUE);

   grid.waitForMouseClick();
   grid.clear(BLACK);
   grid.drawAxis(YELLOW, 3);
   grid.drawFunction(g, AQUA);
   grid.drawFunction(f, RED);
}

double f(double x) { return x * cos(x); }
double g(double x) { return x; }
```

Because this program performs no explicit textual I/O, the only output is the graphical output of the program as shown in Figure 13.10. Again, see the text's Web site for color images.

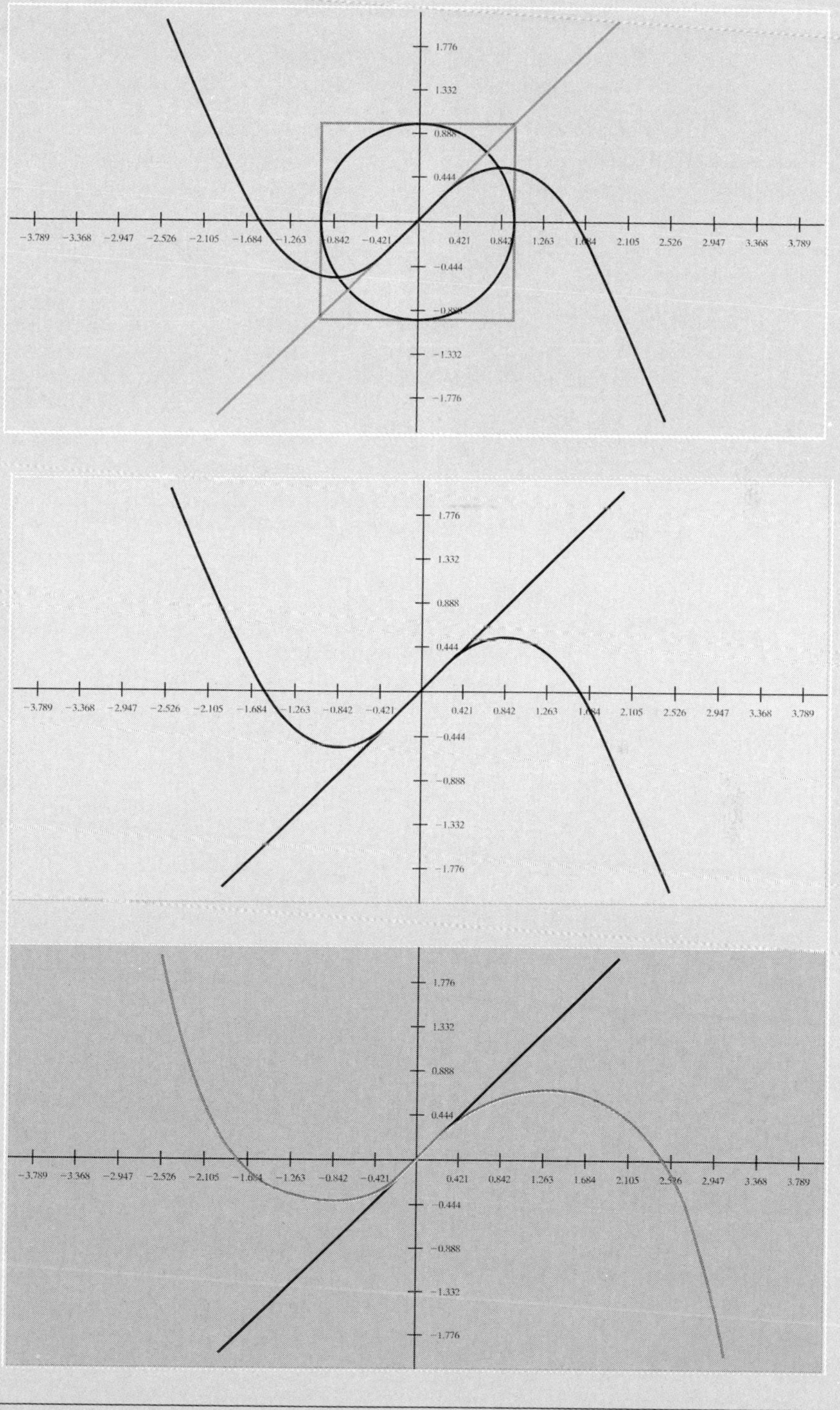

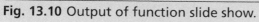

Fig. 13.10 Output of function slide show.

GUI WINDOWS APPLICATION PROGRAMMING

In a *command-line environment, programs are text oriented,* in that they communicate with their users primarily by writing text to the screen; and a user communicates with the program by typing text at the keyboard.

By contrast, when a program (called a *GUI application*) is written to take advantage of the capabilities of a **graphical user interface (GUI)** environment like MacOS or MS-Windows, the program must coordinate the construction and destruction of screen graphics objects such as windows, menus, and dialogue boxes. In addition to user activity at the keyboard, it must also respond to the user clicking the mouse buttons, and the same user action may require different responses, depending on where the mouse is pointing. GUI applications thus entail considerably more complexity than text-oriented programs.

Figure 13.12 illustrates this with a simple application that uses the CMUgraphics library and our `CartesianSystem` class. It simply constructs a `CartesianSystem` object named `grid` and then enters a loop that waits for mouse-clicks and displays the grid and pixel coordinates of each mouse-click at the click-point.

Fig. 13.11 Using mouse-clicks. (Part 1 of 2)

```
/* mouseExample.cpp is a simple example using mouse-clicks.
 * ...
 */

#include "CartesianSystem.h"
#include <sstream>
using namespace std;

void plotPoint(double x, double y,
               int column, int row, CartesianSystem& cs);

int main()
{
   CartesianSystem grid;

   cout << "\nClick the mouse 5 times in different places on the grid.\n";
   double x, y; int row, column;
   for (int i = 0; i < 5; i++)
   {
      grid.waitForMouseClick(x, y, column, row);
      plotPoint(x, y, column, row, grid);
   }
}
```

Fig. 13.11 Using mouse-clicks. (Part 2 of 2)

```
void plotPoint(double x, double y,     // CartesianSystem coords,
               int column, int row,    // window (pixel) coords.
               CartesianSystem& cs)    // where to plot
{
   ostringstream sout;                          // 1. build stringstream
   sout << setprecision(DEFAULT_PRECISION) //    containing the
        << '(' << x << ',' << y << ") : [" //    info we want to
        << column << ',' << row << ']';    //    display
   cs.drawString(x, y, sout.str());             // 2. display it
}
```

When executed, this program displays a `CartesianSystem` window and then waits for the user to take an action:

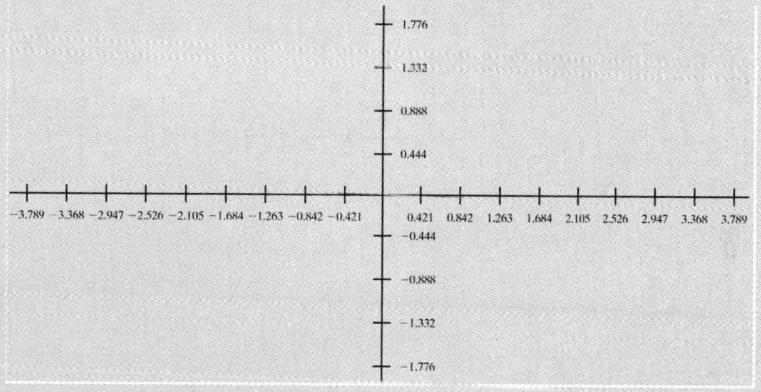

If the left mouse button is clicked within the window, the coordinates to which the mouse is pointing are displayed at that position, as illustrated in the next screen shot:

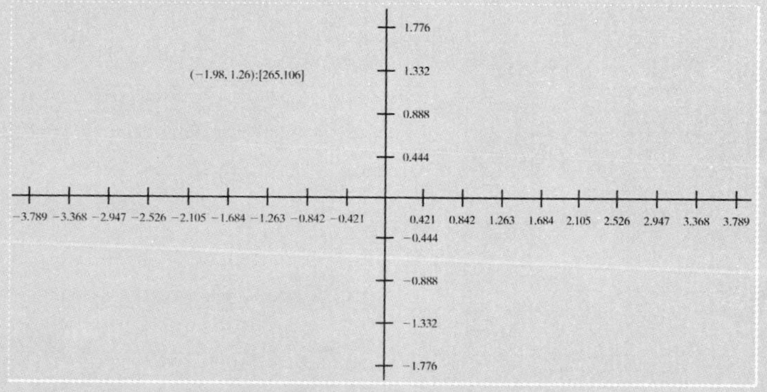

The program handles and displays five mouse-clicks. Note that for each mouse-click, our `plotPoint()` function displays its `CartesianSystem` coordinates in parentheses, and the window (pixel) coordinates in square brackets:

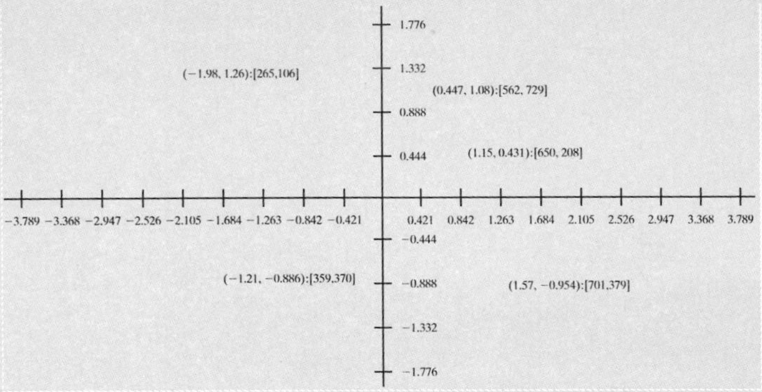

The drawing methods in *CartesianSystem.h* draw in the `CartesianSystem`'s frame of reference. To draw in the window's (pixel) frame of reference, the corresponding methods from the CMUgraphics header file *Graphics.h* can be used:

`CartesianSystem` **methods**	`window` **methods (Graphics.h)**
`drawPixel(x, y, color)`	`DrawPixel(column, row)`
`drawLine(x0, y0, x1, y1, color)`	`DrawLine(c0, r0, c1, r1)`
`drawRectangle(x0, y0, x1, y1, color, style, width, height)`	`DrawRectangle(c0, r0, c1, r1, style, width, height)`
`drawCircle(x, y, radius, color, style)`	`DrawCircle(col, row, style)`
`drawEllipse(x0, y0, x1, y1, color, style)`	`DrawEllipse(c0, r0, c1, r1, style)`
`drawArc(x, y, radius, startDegrees, arcDegrees, color, style)`	`DrawArc(col, row, radius, startDegrees, arcDegrees, style)`
`drawString(x, y, string, color)`	`DrawString(col, row, apString)`
`drawNumber(x, y, double, color)`	*none*
none	`DrawInteger(col, row, int)`
`drawFunction(function, color)`	*none*
`drawAxis(color, penSize)`	*none*
`waitForMouseClick()`	*none*
`waitForMouseClick(x, y, col, row)`	`WaitMouseClick(col, row)`
`getMousePosition(x, y, col, row)`	`GetMouseCoord(col, row)`
`getKeyPress(ch)`	`GetKeyPress(ch)`

CartesianSystem methods	window methods (Graphics.h)
setPenWidth(width)	SetPen(width)
setFont(size, style, family)	SetFont(size, style, family)
none	SetBrush(color)
getWidthInPixels()	GetWidth()
getHeightInPixels()	GetHeight()
minX()	*none*
maxX()	*none*
minY()	*none*
maxY()	*none*
deltaX()	*none*
deltaY()	*none*
xToColumn(x)	*none*
yToRow(y)	*none*
columnToX(col)	*none*
distanceToPixels(distance)	*none*

Because our CartesianSystem class is derived from the CMUgraphics window class, it inherits all of the window methods. Thus, we may send a CartesianSystem object the drawLine() message to draw a line in the CartesianSystem frame of reference, or we can send it the DrawLine() message to draw a line in the window's (pixel) frame of reference. We refer the interested reader to the files *CartesianSystem.doc* and *Graphics.h* for more information.

* Using CodeWarrior on MacOS, the programs in Figures 13.8 and 13.9 compile correctly, but generate numerous *linker warnings*, apparently because of redundant definitions in the CMUgraphics library and CodeWarrior's libraries. It is not a good practice to ignore warnings, but in this case the programs run correctly despite them.

13.5* OBJECTive Thinking: The Matrix Class Revisited

In Section 13.4, we built a Matrix library, using typedef to declare the name Matrix as a type and then defined "normal" functions to act as operations on a Matrix. This approach does not reflect the I-can-do-it-myself philosophy of the internal approach of object-centered design; operations like fill() and print() are functions that manipulate their Matrix parameter, rather than messages being sent to a Matrix object.

To build a Matrix that reflects the I-can-do-it-myself approach, we must somehow declare the name Matrix as the name of a class and then define operations like fill() and print() as methods of that class. We can do this using the C++ inheritance mechanism.

Using Inheritance. The *OBJECTive Thinking* section of Chapter 7 described how the C++ inheritance mechanism lets a class inherit the methods and variables of another class. We can use this inheritance mechanism to build a `Matrix` class that inherits the data and methods of a vector of vectors of `double` values and then add our specialized `Matrix` operations to the new class. Figure 13.12 shows the C++ syntax for this.

Fig. 13.12 Deriving `Matrix` from a two-dimensional vector.

```
/* Matrix.h derives class Matrix from a two-dimensional vector
 * of doubles.
 * . . .
 ****************************************************************/

#include <vector>
using namespace std;

typedef vector<double> OneDimVector;
typedef vector<OneDimVector> TwoDimVector;

class Matrix : public TwoDimVector
{
 public:
   Matrix(unsigned rows, unsigned columns);
   unsigned rows() const;
   unsigned columns() const;
   void print(ostream& out) const;
   void read(istream& in);
   Matrix operator*(const Matrix& Mat1) const;
   // ... additional operations omitted ...

 private:
   unsigned myRows,
            myColumns;
};

// ... definitions of simple Matrix operations go here as inline...
```

Recall that the first line of the class declaration

```
class Matrix : public TwoDimVector
```

declares that the class `Matrix` (a *child class*, or *derived class*, or *subclass*) is derived from the class `TwoDimVector` (the *parent class*, or *base class*, or *superclass*). This means that every `Matrix` object *is a* `TwoDimVector` object. This means, for example, that even though there is no prototype for an `empty()` method in class `Matrix`, the vector message `empty()` can be sent to a `Matrix` object because `Matrix` inherits it from `TwoDimVector`:

```
Matrix aMatrix;
   . . .
if ( aMatrix.empty() ) // ... aMatrix is empty
```

Similarly, `push_back()` can be used with `Matrix` objects as in

```
const int COLUMNS = 10;
aMatrix.push_back(OneDimVector(COLUMNS, 0.0));
```

to append a row of ten zeros to `aMatrix`, because `Matrix` inherits the `push_back()` method from `TwoDimVector`. And once a `Matrix` has been given a set of values, the subscript operator can be used to access those values

```
aMatrix[r][c]
```

because `Matrix` also inherits this vector operation. Inheritance thus saves us a great deal of work in building the `Matrix` class.

Constructor. As shown in Section 7.8, a child class constructor can call a parent class constructor to initialize the data members the child inherits from the parent by using the **member initialization list** mechanism of the form

```
Child::Child(ChildConstructorParameterList)
   : Parent(ParentConstructorArgumentList)
{ StatementList }
```

Figure 13.13 shows the definition of the constructor for class `Matrix` that uses this approach. Because of its simplicity, we inline it in the header file `Matrix.h`, following the declaration of class `Matrix`.

Fig. 13.13 The `Matrix` m × n constructor.

```
inline Matrix::Matrix(unsigned rows, unsigned columns)
: TwoDimVector( rows, OneDimVector(columns) )
{
   myRows = rows;
   myColumns = columns;
}
```

Note that the constructor is simple enough to be inlined. This is frequently the case when using a member initialization list, because most of the work is done by the parent class constructor.

To illustrate what happens with this constructor, consider the following declaration of a `Matrix` object:

```
Matrix theMatrix(3, 4);
```

When it is encountered, the `Matrix` constructor first calls the `TwoDimVector` constructor, sending it the desired number of rows (3) and columns (4). That constructor is executed and allocates space for a 3 × 4 two-dimensional vector that will store the element of `theMatrix` (and it initializes `TwoDimVector` instance variables as necessary). When it finishes, the statements in the body of the `Matrix` constructor are executed and initialize the new `Matrix` instance variables `myRows` and `myColumns`:

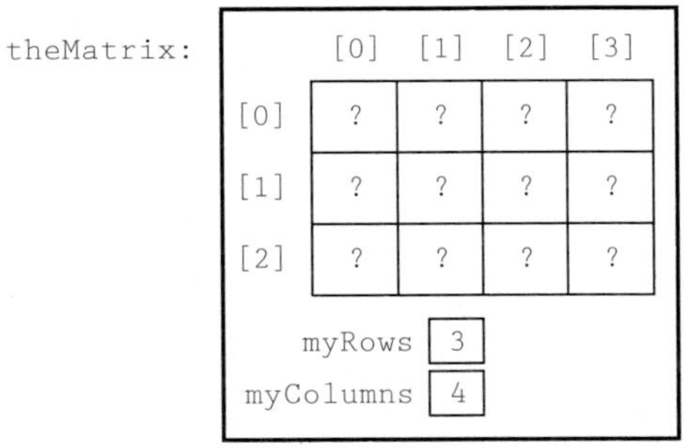

Similarly, we can write

```
cout << "Enter the number of rows and columns in the matrix: ";
int numRows, numColumns;
cin >> numRows >> numColumns;
Matrix aMatrix(numRows, numColumns);
```

and `aMatrix` will be constructed with `numRows` rows and `numColumns` columns.

The `rows()` and `columns()` Methods. In addition to the `Matrix` constructors, we must define its specialized operations. We begin with accessors that return the dimensions of the matrix, that is, the number of rows and columns—that is, the values stored in `myRows` and `myColumns`, as shown in Figure 13.14. Like nearly all accessors, they are simple enough to inline in *Matrix.h*.

Fig. 13.14 `rows()` and `columns()` of a `Matrix`.

```
// Number of rows in a Matrix
inline unsigned Matrix::rows() const
{
   return myRows;
}

// Number of columns in a Matrix
inline unsigned Matrix::columns() const
{
   return myColumns;
}
```

Given these functions, a programmer can now send the messages `aMatrix.rows()` and `aMatrix.columns()` to determine the number of rows and the number of columns in `aMatrix`.

The Output Operation. Because an output function is helpful in debugging other operations, we will define it next. Our approach will be that described in Chapter 11:

1. Define an output method `print()`, and then
2. overload `operator<<()` as an external function that invokes `print()`.

A specification for the `print()` method (from an internal perspective) is as follows:

Receive: *out*, an `ostream`

Output: My values, each row on a separate line

Send back: *out*, containing the output values

Figure 13.15 shows a definition of `print()` that satisfies this specification. Because of its complexity, we put this definition in the implementation file *Matrix.cpp*.

Fig. 13.15 The `Matrix print()` method.

```
void Matrix::print(ostream& out) const
{
   for (int i = 0; i < myRows; i++)
   {
      for (int j = 0; j < myColumns; j++)
         out << (*this)[i][j] << '\t';
      out << endl;
   }
}
```

NOTE

This method uses a special feature that C++ provides to allow objects to refer to themselves. *Every class object contains a predefined local variable named* `this` *whose value is the address of the object so that the value of the dereferenced variable* `*this` *is the object itself.*[3] Thus, in `print()`, `*this` will refer to the `Matrix` object to which the `print()` message was sent, and since class `Matrix` inherits the vector subscript operator, `[]` can be applied to `*this`.[4]

3. As we will see in the next chapter, `this` is a *pointer variable*, and *dereferencing* it with the operator `*` produces the value stored in the memory location to which it points.
4. An alternative way to define `print()` that does not use `this` is to use iterators (see Section 10.6). We leave this as an exercise for those who have studied iterators.

Given the `print()` method, it is easy to overload `operator<<()` as shown in Figure 13.16. Because of its simplicity, we put this inlined definition in *Matrix.h* following the class declaration. This function makes it possible to write statements such as

```
cout << aMatrix;
```

to display the value of a `Matrix`.

Fig. 13.16 Output Operator `<<` for `Matrix`.

```
inline ostream& operator<<(ostream& out, const Matrix& theMatrix)
{
   theMatrix.print(out);
   return out;
}
```

The Input Operation. In a similar way, we can define an input operation for the class `Matrix`. We first define a `read()` method to input the entries of a `Matrix` from an istream and then overload `operator>>()` to invoke `read()`. Figure 13.17 shows the definition of `read()`. It is defined in *Matrix.cpp* and prototyped inside the class. The inlined definition of `operator>>()` in Figure 13.18 would be placed in *Matrix.h* following the class declaration.

Fig. 13.17 The `Matrix read()` operation.

```
void Matrix::read(istream& in)
{
   for (int i = 0; i < myRows; i++)
      for (int j = 0; j < myColumns; j++)
         in >> (*this)[i][j];
}
```

Fig. 13.18 Input operator `>>` for `Matrix`.

```
inline istream& operator>>(istream& in, Matrix& theMatrix)
{
   theMatrix.read(in);
   return in;
}
```

Other Matrix Operations. In Section 13.4, we described the addition, subtraction, and multiplication operations on matrices. These surely are operations that should be added to our `Matrix` class. We leave implementations of these operations by methods as exercises.

Exercises 13.5

1. Add a constructor to the class `Matrix` that, upon receiving a vector of `double` values, builds a `Matrix` object containing one row containing the elements of that vector.
2. Add a constructor to the class `Matrix` that, upon receiving a vector of `double` values, builds a `Matrix` object containing one column containing the elements of that vector.
3. Add the + operation to the class `Matrix`. (See Section 13.4 for a definition of matrix addition.)
4. Add the `-` operation to the class `Matrix`. (See Section 13.4 for a definition of matrix subtraction.)
5. Add the `*` operation to the class `Matrix`. (See Section 13.4 for a definition of matrix multiplication.)
6. Add a method to class `Matrix` to find the transpose of a matrix, which is defined as follows: If A is an $m \times n$ matrix and A_{ij} is the entry in the ith row and jth column of A, then the **transpose** of A is an $n \times m$ matrix T in which $T_{ji} = A_{ij}$, for all indices i and j. For example, if A is the 2×3 matrix

$$\begin{bmatrix} 1 & 0 & 2 \\ -1 & 3 & 5 \end{bmatrix}$$

the transpose of A is the 3×2 matrix

$$\begin{bmatrix} 1 & -1 \\ 0 & 3 \\ 2 & 5 \end{bmatrix}$$

CHAPTER SUMMARY

Key Terms & Notes

array of arrays
column
graphical user interface (GUI)
inheritance
jagged tables (arrays)
$m \times n$ matrix
matrix addition
matrix multiplication
matrix subtraction
member initialization list
multidimensional array
multidimensional vector
rank
rectangular array
row
square array
subscript operator
`this`
three-dimensional array
two-dimensional array
`typedef` mechanism
vector of vectors

- Two-dimensional arrays or vectors are useful for storing a data set whose values are arranged in rows and columns. Three-dimensional arrays or vectors are useful when the data set values are arranged in rows, columns, and ranks.
- As with one-dimensional arrays, each dimension of a multidimensional array is indexed starting with zero.

- A two-dimensional array can be viewed as a one-dimensional array whose components are also one-dimensional arrays. A three-dimensional can be viewed as a one-dimensional array whose components are two-dimensional arrays. In general, an n-dimensional can be viewed as a one-dimensional array whose components are $(n - 1)$-dimensional arrays.
- The main drawback of C-style arrays is that they are not self-contained objects. In a function to implement an array operation, we must pass not only the array, but also the bound on each of its dimensions. One solution is to wrap an array in a class that contains operations for it.
- Multidimensional vectors are constructed as vectors of vectors and are self-contained objects, having all the built-in operations of `vector<T>`s.
- Inheritance saves a great deal of work by allowing operations in a parent class to be applied to a child class object without redefining those operations.
- A child class constructor can use the member initialization list mechanism to invoke a constructor of its parent class.
- Every class object contains a predefined local variable named `this` whose value is the address of the object so that the value of the dereferenced variable `*this` is the object itself.

Programming Pointers

Many of the programming pointers given for one-dimensional arrays at the end of Chapter 10 also apply to multidimensional arrays, and the reader should refer to those for an expanded discussion.

Program Style and Design

1. *Like one-dimensional arrays, multidimensional array objects should be stored within a class, so that*
   - *the number of elements in each dimension and*
   - *the operations on the object*

   can be encapsulated within a single package. This makes it easier to reuse the work that was invested in building that object and its operations.
2. *Use of a multidimensional array or vector is appropriate when a table of data values, a list of tables, and so on must be stored in main memory for processing.* Using a multidimensional array or vector when it is not necessary, however, can tie up a large block of memory locations. The amount of memory required to store a multidimensional array/vector may be quite large, even though each index is restricted to a small range of values. For example, the three-dimensional array `threeD` declared by

   ```
   typedef int ThreeDimArray[20][20][20];
   ThreeDimArray threeD;
   ```

   requires $20 \times 20 \times 20 = 8000$ memory locations.
3. *If a function must receive a class object that contains an array or vector member, then the parameter to hold that object should be declared as a reference parameter.* It is especially important that class objects be passed as constant reference parameters rather than as value parameters, because the time and memory required to copy class objects as value parameters can greatly slow the execution of a function.
4. *Do not reinvent the wheel.* When a problem requires an operation on a multidimensional vector, review the `vector<T>` function members and STL algorithms to see if the operation is already defined or if there are other operations that make yours easier to implement.

WATCH OUT

Potential Pitfalls

1. *In C++, multiple indices are each enclosed in brackets ([and]) and attached to the array/vector object.* In some languages, a single pair of brackets (or parentheses) is used to enclose a list of indices. However, attempting to access the value in row `i` and column `j` of a two-dimensional array `A` in C++ by using `A[i, j]` will cause a compile-time error.
2. *The first element of a C++ array or vector has the index value 0, not 1 as in many programming languages.*
3. *In subscript operations, no checking is performed to ensure that array or vector indices stay within the range of valid indices.*
4. *Assignment of one array to another is not permitted. The assignment operator may be used with vectors, however.*
5. *Arrays and vectors cannot be input/output simply by including the array name in an input/output list.*
6. *Array arguments are automatically passed by reference.*
7. *When using vectors of vectors, leave a space between the two > symbols.* A common mistake is to forget this and to define a vector of vectors with a statement like

   ```
   vector<vector<int>> myGrid;
   ```

   The compiler will read the >> as the output (or right-shift) operator, and since this makes no sense in this context, a compilation error will result. The correct approach is to leave a space:

   ```
   vector< vector<int> > myGrid;
   ```

8. *When processing the elements of a multidimensional array/vector using nested loops, the loops must be arranged so that the indices vary in the appropriate order.* To illustrate, suppose that the two-dimensional array `table` is declared by

   ```
   typedef int Array3x4[3][4];
   Array3x4 table;
   ```

   and the following data values are to be read into the array:

   ```
   11  22  27  35  39  40  48  51  57  66  67  92
   ```

   If these values are to be read and assigned in a row-wise manner so that the value is the matrix

   ```
   11  22  27  35
   39  40  48  51
   57  66  67  92
   ```

   then the following nested `for` loops are appropriate:

   ```
   for (int row = 0; row < 3; row++)
      for (int col = 0; col < 4; col++)
         cin >> table[row][col];
   ```

   If the order of these loops is reversed,

   ```
   for (int col = 0; col < 4; col++)
      for (int row = 0; row < 3; row++)
         cin >> table[row][col];
   ```

   then `table` will be loaded column-by-column, instead of row-by-row,

   ```
   11  35  48  66
   22  39  51  67
   27  40  57  92
   ```

   and operations applied to `table` will produce incorrect results.

Programming Problems

Sections 13.1–13.3

1. Write a program to calculate and display the first ten rows of Pascal's triangle. The first part of the triangle has the form

```
        1
      1   1
    1   2   1
  1   3   3   1
1   4   6   4   1
```

in which each row begins and ends with 1, and each of the other entries in a row is the sum of the two entries just above it. If this form for the output seems too challenging, you might display the triangle as

```
1
1  1
1  2  1
1  3  3  1
1  4  6  4  1
```

2. A demographic study of the metropolitan area around Dogpatch divided it into three regions (urban, suburban, and exurban,) and published the following table showing the annual migration from one region to another (the numbers represent percentages):

	Urban	Suburban	Exurban
Urban	1.1	0.3	0.7
Suburban	0.1	1.2	0.3
Exurban	0.2	0.6	1.3

For example, 0.3 percent of the urbanites (0.003 times the current population) move to the suburbs each year. The diagonal entries represent internal growth rates. Using a two-dimensional array with an enumerated type for the indices to store this table, write a program to determine the population of each region after 10, 20, 30, 40, and 50 years. Assume that the current populations of the urban, suburban, and exurban regions are 2.1, 1.4, and 0.9 million, respectively.

3. The famous mathematician G. H. Hardy once mentioned to the brilliant young Indian mathematician Ramanujan that he had just ridden in a taxi whose number he considered to be very dull. Ramanujan promptly replied that, on the contrary, the number was very interesting because it was the smallest positive integer that could be written as the sum of two cubes (that is, written in the form $x^3 + y^3$, with x and y integers) in two different ways. Write a program to find the number of Hardy's taxi.

4. A certain professor has a file containing a table of student grades, where the first line of the file contains the number of students and the number of scores in the table; each row of the table represents the exam scores of a given student and each column represents the scores on a given exam. The maximum possible score on each exam was 100 points. Write a program that, given the name of such a file, generates a report summarizing the overall percentage for each student and the average score on each exam.

5. The group CAN (Citizens Against Noise) has collected some data on the noise level (measured in decibels) produced at seven different speeds by six different models of cars. This data is summarized in the following table:

	Speed (MPH)						
Car	**20**	**30**	**40**	**50**	**60**	**70**	**80**
0	88	90	94	102	111	122	134
1	75	77	80	86	94	103	113
2	80	83	85	94	100	111	121
3	68	71	76	85	96	110	125
4	77	84	91	98	105	112	119
5	81	85	90	96	102	109	120

Write a program that will display this table in easy-to-read format and that will calculate and display the average noise level for each car model, the average noise level at each speed, and the overall average noise level.

6. Suppose that a certain automobile dealership sells ten different models of automobiles and employs eight salespersons. A record of sales for each month can be represented by a table in which each row contains the number of sales of each model by a given salesperson and each column contains the number of sales by each salesperson of a given model. For example, suppose that the sales table for a certain month is as follows:

```
0 0 2 0 5 6 3 0
5 1 9 0 0 2 3 2
0 0 0 1 0 0 0 0
1 1 1 0 2 2 2 1
5 3 2 0 0 2 5 5
2 2 1 0 1 1 0 0
3 2 5 0 1 2 0 4
3 0 7 1 3 5 2 4
0 2 6 1 0 5 2 1
4 0 2 0 3 2 1 0
```

Write a program to produce a monthly sales report, displaying the monthly sales table in the form:

```
                          Salesperson
  Model :    1    2    3    4    5    6    7    8:   Totals
-----------------------------------------------------------
    1   :    0    0    2    0    5    6    3    0  :    16
    2   :    5    1    9    0    0    2    3    2  :    22
    3   :    0    0    0    1    0    0    0    0  :     1
    4   :    1    1    1    0    2    2    2    1  :    10
    5   :    5    3    2    0    0    2    5    5  :    22
    6   :    2    2    1    0    1    1    0    0  :     7
    7   :    3    2    5    0    1    2    0    4  :    17
    8   :    3    0    7    1    3    5    2    4  :    25
    9   :    0    2    6    1    0    5    2    1  :    17
   10   :    4    0    2    0    3    2    1    0  :    12
-----------------------------------------------------------
 Totals :   23   11   35    3   15   27   18   17
```

As indicated, the report should also display the total number of automobiles sold by each salesperson and the total number of each model sold by all salespersons.

7. Suppose that the prices for the ten automobile models in Problem 6 are as follows:

Model #	Model Price
0	$17,450
1	$19,995
2	$26,500
3	$25,999
4	$10,400
5	$18,885
6	$11,700
7	$14,440
8	$17,900
9	$19,550

Write a program to read this list of prices and the sales table given in Problem 6 and calculate the total dollar sales for each salesperson and the total dollar sales for all salespersons.

8. A certain company has a product line that includes five items that sell for $100, $75, $120, $150, and $35. There are four salespersons working for this company, and the following table gives the sales report for a typical week:

Salesperson Number	Item Number				
	1	2	3	4	5
1	10	4	5	6	7
2	7	0	12	1	3
3	4	9	5	0	8
4	3	2	1	5	6

Write a program to do the following:

(a) Compute the total dollar sales for each salesperson.
(b) Compute the total commission for each salesperson if the commission rate is 10 percent.
(c) Find the total income for each salesperson for the week if each salesperson receives a fixed salary of $500 per week in addition to commission payments.

9. A certain company manufactures four electronic devices using five different components that cost $10.95, $6.30, $14.75, $11.25, and $5.00, respectively. The number of components used in each device is given in the following table:

Device Number	Component				
	1	2	3	4	5
1	10	4	5	6	7
2	7	0	12	1	3
3	4	9	5	0	8
4	3	2	1	5	6

Write a program to calculate:

(a) The total cost of each device
(b) The total cost of producing each device if the estimated labor cost for each device is 10 percent of the cost in Part (a)

10. A number of students from several different engineering sections performed the same experiment to determine the tensile strength of sheets made from two different alloys. Each of these strength measurements is a real number in the range 0 through 10. Write a program to read several lines of data, each consisting of a section number and the tensile strength of the two types of sheets recorded by a student in that section, and store these values in a two-dimensional array. Then calculate:

(a) For each section, the average of the tensile strengths for each type of alloy
(b) The number of persons in a given section who recorded strength measures of 5 or higher
(c) The average of the tensile strengths recorded for alloy 2 by students who recorded a tensile strength lower than 3 for alloy 1

11. A *magic square* is an $n \times n$ table in which each of the integers 1, 2, 3, . . . , n^2 appears exactly once and all column sums, row sums, and diagonal sums are equal. For example, the following is a 5×5 magic square in which all the rows, columns, and diagonals add up to 65:

17	24	1	8	15
23	5	7	14	16
4	6	13	20	22
10	12	19	21	3
11	18	25	2	9

The following is a procedure for constructing an $n \times n$ magic square for any odd integer n. Place 1 in the middle of the top row. Then after integer k has been placed, move up one row and one column to the right to place the next integer $k + 1$, unless one of the following occurs:

(a) If a move takes you above the top row in the jth column, move to the bottom of the jth column and place the integer $k + 1$ there.

(b) If a move takes you outside to the right of the square in the ith row, place $k + 1$ in the ith row at the left side.

(c) If a move takes you to an already filled square or if you move out of the square at the upper right-hand corner, place $k + 1$ immediately below k.

Write a program to construct an $n \times n$ magic square for any odd value of n.

12. Consider a square grid, with some cells empty and others containing an asterisk. Define two asterisks to be *contiguous* if they are adjacent to each other in the same row or in the same column. Now suppose that we define a *blob* as follows:

(a) A blob contains at least one asterisk.

(b) If an asterisk is in a blob, then so is any asterisk that is contiguous to it.

(c) If a blob has more than two asterisks, then each asterisk in it is contiguous to at least one other asterisk in the blob.

For example, there are four blobs in the partial grid

*			*	*			*		*	*
							*		*	*

seven blobs in

*		*		*				*	*	*
					*				*	
*				*						

and only one in

		*	*	*		*	*	*		
				*		*		*		
				*	*	*				

Write a program that uses a recursive function to count the number of blobs in a square grid. Input to the program should consist of the locations of the asterisks in the grid, and the program should display the grid and the blob count.

13. The game of *Life*, invented by the mathematician John H. Conway, is intended to model life in a society of organisms. Consider a rectangular array of cells, each of which may contain an organism. If the array is assumed to extend indefinitely in both directions, each cell will have eight neighbors, the eight cells surrounding it. Births and deaths occur according to the following rules:

(a) An organism is born in an empty cell that has exactly three neighbors.

(b) An organism will die from isolation if it has fewer than two neighbors.

(c) An organism will die from overcrowding if it has more than three neighbors.

The following display shows the first five generations of a particular configuration of organisms:

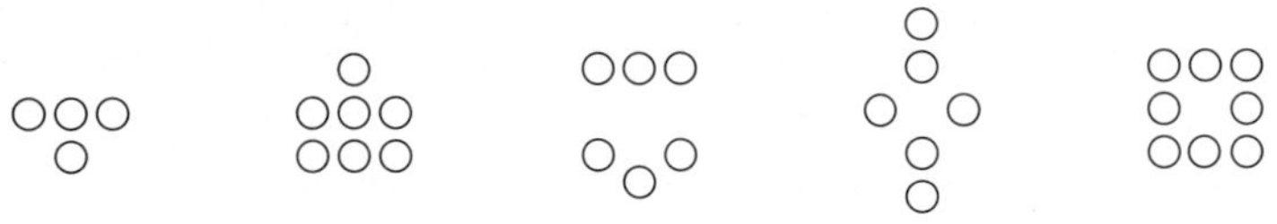

Write a program to play the game of *Life* and investigate the patterns produced by various initial configurations. Some configurations die off rather quickly; others repeat after a certain number of generations; others change shape and size and may move across the array; and still others may produce "gliders" that detach themselves from the society and sail off into space.

14. The game of Nim is played by two players. There are usually three piles of objects, and on his or her turn, each player is allowed to take any number (at least one) of objects from one pile. The player taking the last object loses. Write a program that allows the user to play Nim against the computer. You might have the computer play a perfect game, or you might design the program to "teach" the computer. One way for the computer to "learn" is to assign a value to every possible move, based on experience gained from playing games. The value of each possible move is stored in some array; initially, each value is 0. The value of each move in a winning sequence of moves is increased by 1, and those in a losing sequence are decreased by 1. At each stage, the computer selects the best possible move (that having the highest value).
15. Write a program that allows the user to play tic-tac-toe against the computer.

Part of the Picture: Computer Graphics

16. Each "slide" in the output produced by Figure 13.10 displays the same function. Modify the program in Figure 13.10 so that it will display a different function on each slide (and adding more slides).
17. Add a method to class `CartesianSystem` to plot graphs of parametric equations of the form

$$x = x(t), \quad y = y(t), \quad a \le t \le b$$

18. A *scatter plot* of a set of data pairs (x, y) of real numbers is obtained simply by plotting these points. Add a method to class `CartesianSystem` to produce a scatter plot of a set of data pairs read from a file. Execute your program using `LeastSquaresFile` (see the description at the end of Chapter 9).
19. We noted that the ideas in this section can be modified to carry out *visual image processing* and *enhancement*. Make a file that represents light intensities of an image in digitized form; say, with intensities from 0 through 9. Write a program that reads these intensities from the file and then reconstructs and displays them using a different character for each intensity. This image might then be enhanced to sharpen the contrast. For example, gray areas might be removed by replacing all intensities in the range 0 through some value by 0 (light) and intensities greater than this value by 9 (dark). Design your program to accept a threshold value that distinguishes light from dark and then enhances the image in the manner described.
20. An alternative method for enhancing an image (see Problem 19) is to accept three successive images of the same object and, if two or more of the intensities agree, to use that value; otherwise, the average of the three values is used. Modify the program of Problem 19 to use this technique for enhancement.

Sections 13.4 & 13.5

21. Write a driver program to test the `Matrix` constructor in Exercise 1 of Section 13.5.
22. Write a driver program to test the `Matrix` constructor in Exercise 2 of Section 13.5.
23. Write a driver program to test the `Matrix` addition operator in Exercise 3 of Section 13.5.
24. Write a driver program to test the `Matrix` subtraction operator in Exercise 4 of Section 13.5.
25. Write a driver program to test the `Matrix` multiplication operator in Exercise 5 of Section 13.5.
26. Write a driver program to test the `Matrix` transpose function in Exercise 6 of Section 13.5.
27. A company produces three different products. They are processed through four different departments, A, B, C, and D, and the following table gives the number of hours that each department spends on each product:

Product	A	B	C	D
1	20	10	15	13
2	18	11	11	10
3	28	0	16	17

The cost per hour of operation in each of the departments is as follows:

Department	A	B	C	D
Cost per hour	\$140	\$295	\$225	\$95

Write a program that uses matrix multiplication to find the total cost of each of the products.

28. The vector-matrix equation

$$\begin{bmatrix} N \\ E \\ D \end{bmatrix} = \begin{bmatrix} \cos\alpha & -\sin\alpha & 0 \\ \sin\alpha & \cos\alpha & 0 \\ 0 & 0 & 1 \end{bmatrix} \begin{bmatrix} \cos\beta & 0 & \sin\beta \\ 0 & 0 & 0 \\ -\sin\beta & 0 & \cos\beta \end{bmatrix} \begin{bmatrix} 1 & 0 & 0 \\ 0 & \cos\gamma & -\sin\gamma \\ 0 & \sin\gamma & \cos\gamma \end{bmatrix} \begin{bmatrix} I \\ J \\ K \end{bmatrix}$$

is used to transform local coordinates (I, J, K) for a space vehicle to inertial coordinates (N, E, D). Write a program that reads values for α, β, and γ and a set of local coordinates (I, J, K) and then uses matrix multiplication to determine the corresponding inertial coordinates.

29. A *Markov chain* is a system that moves through a discrete set of states in such a way that when the system is in state i, there is probability P_{ij} that it will next move to state j. These probabilities are given by a transition matrix P, whose (i, j) entry is P_{ij}. It is easy to show that the (i, j) entry of P^n then gives the probability of starting in state i and ending in state j after n steps.

    To illustrate, suppose that there are two urns A and B containing a given number of balls. At each instant, a ball is chosen at random and is transferred to the other urn. This is a Markov chain if we take as a state the number of balls in urn A and let P_{ij} be the probability that a ball is transferred from A to B if there are i balls in urn A. For example, for four balls, the transition matrix P is given by

$$\begin{bmatrix} 0 & 1 & 0 & 0 & 0 \\ 1/4 & 0 & 3/4 & 0 & 0 \\ 0 & 1/2 & 0 & 1/2 & 0 \\ 0 & 0 & 3/4 & 0 & 1/4 \\ 0 & 0 & 0 & 1 & 0 \end{bmatrix}$$

Write a program that reads a transition matrix P for such a Markov chain and calculates and displays the value of n and P^n for several values of n.

30. A *directed graph*, or *digraph*, consists of a set of vertices and a set of directed arcs joining certain of these vertices. For example, the following diagram pictures a directed graph having five vertices numbered 1, 2, 3, 4, and 5, and seven directed arcs joining vertices 1 to 2, 1 to 4, 1 to 5, 3 to 1, 3 to itself, 4 to 3, and 5 to 1:

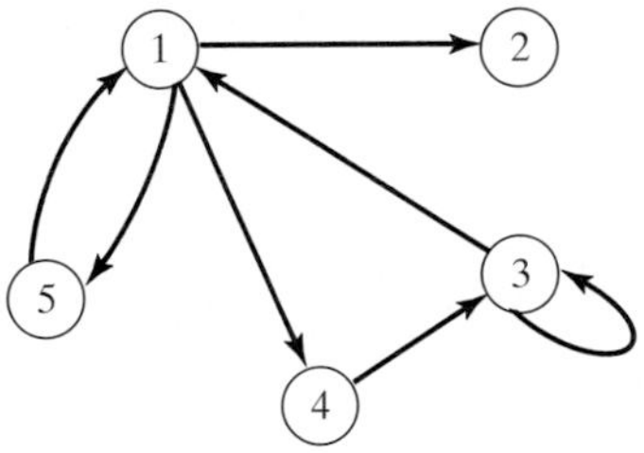

A directed graph having n vertices can be represented by its *adjacency matrix*, which is an $n \times n$ matrix, with the entry in the ith row and jth column 1 if vertex i is joined to vertex j, and 0 otherwise. The adjacency matrix for this graph is

$$\begin{bmatrix} 0 & 1 & 0 & 1 & 1 \\ 0 & 0 & 0 & 0 & 0 \\ 1 & 0 & 1 & 0 & 0 \\ 0 & 0 & 1 & 0 & 0 \\ 1 & 0 & 0 & 0 & 0 \end{bmatrix}$$

If A is the adjacency matrix for a directed graph, the entry in the ith row and jth column of A^k gives the number of ways that vertex j can be reached from the vertex i by following k edges. Write a program to read the number of vertices in a directed graph and a collection of ordered pairs of vertices representing directed arcs, construct the adjacency matrix, and then find the number of ways that each vertex can be reached from every other vertex by following k edges for some value of k.

CHAPTER 14

Pointers, Run-Time Allocation, and Linked Lists

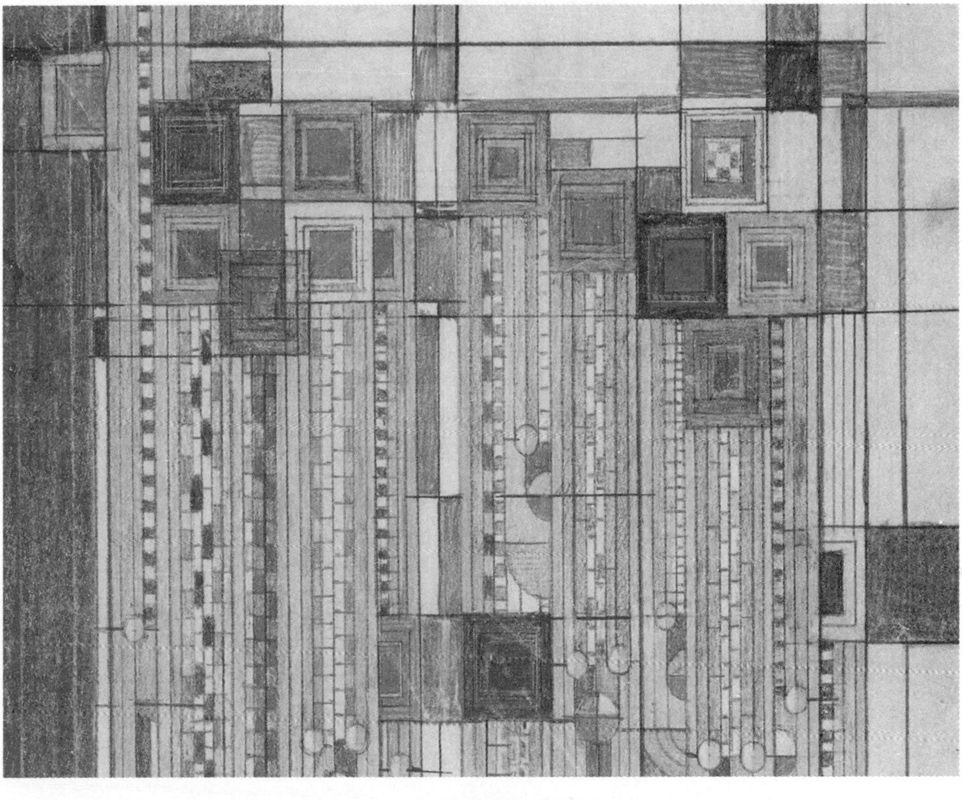

[Pointers] are like jumps, leaping wildly from one part of a data structure to another. Their introduction into high-level languages has been a step backward from which we may never recover.

-C. A. R. Hoare

He's making a list, and checking it twice, gonna' find out who's naughty or nice . . .

-Christmas Carol: "Santa Claus Is Coming to Town"

. . . is the sort of person who keeps a list of all of his lists.

-V. Orehck III (fictitious)

Chapter Contents

Chapter Objectives

- Study pointers and the operations provided for them in C++.
- See how memory is allocated and deallocated during run time.
- Study linked lists and see how they solve the problems with insertion and deletion for arrays and `vector<T>`s.
- See how to build a `LinkedList` class.
- Look at STL's `list<T>` class template, its operations, and how it is implemented as a doubly-linked list.
- Look at how command-line arguments can be implemented in C++.
- (Optional) Take another brief look at algorithm efficiency and how it is measured.
- (Optional) Study how handles and polymorphism are powerful tools in building class hierarchies.

In Chapters 10 and 13, we saw two different data structures that C++ provides for storing sequences of values: arrays and `vector<T>`s. One significant difference between these two kinds of objects is the way in which they are defined. For the kind of arrays we considered, their capacities *must* be specified at *compile time* as in the following declaration of `anArray`:

```
const int CAPACITY = 50;
int anArray[CAPACITY];
```

While a `vector<T>` object can be defined in a similar way,

```
const int CAPACITY = 50;
vector<int> aVector(CAPACITY);
```

its capacity can also be specified at *run time*:

```
cout << "Enter the number of values to be stored: ";
int capacity;
cin  >> capacity;
vector<int> aVector(capacity);
```

This is a basic difference between the two kinds of objects: The array's storage is determined (and is fixed) when the program is compiled, but the storage of a `vector<T>` object is determined (and can change) while the program executes. The `string` class is similar to `vector<T>` in that a `string` object's storage automatically adjusts to the number of characters being stored.

To build arrays whose capacities can be specified at run time and other structures whose storage can grow (and shrink) during execution, C++ provides a way to request and return memory during program execution. To understand this feature and how to use it, we must first study *pointers* and *indirection*.

14.1 Introduction to Pointer Variables

As usual, we begin with a program. The purpose of the program in Figure 14.1 is only to introduce the basics of pointers and indirection. It is not intended to show how pointers are typically used in programs.[1]

Fig. 14.1 Using indirection. (Part 1 of 2)

```
/* indirection.cpp illustrates indirection and pointer variables.
 *
 * Output: addresses of memory locations and the integers
 *         stored there
 *****************************************************************/

#include <iostream>
using namespace std;

int main()
{
   int i = 11,
       j = 22,
       k = 33;

   int* iPtr = &i;
   int* jPtr = &j;
   int* kPtr = &k;
```

1. For some versions of C++, it may be necessary to use `(void*)`*`pointerVariable`* in an output statement for addresses to display correctly.

Fig. 14.1 Using indirection. (Part 2 of 2)

```
   cout << "\nAt address " << iPtr
        << ", the value " << *iPtr << " is stored.\n"
        << "\nAt address " << jPtr
        << ", the value " << *jPtr << " is stored.\n"
        << "\nAt address " << kPtr
        << ", the value " << *kPtr << " is stored.\n";
}
```

Sample run:

```
At address 0x0053AD78, the value 11 is stored.

At address 0x0053AD7C, the value 22 is stored.

At address 0x0053AD80, the value 33 is stored.
```

DECLARING AND INITIALIZING POINTERS

We begin with the second set of declarations in the program in Figure 14.1:

```
int* iPtr = &i;
int* jPtr = &j;
int* kPtr = &k;
```

There are two new items in these statements:

1. An asterisk (`*`) following the type name in a declaration of the form

   ```
   Type* variableName;
   ```

   declares that *`variableName`* can store *the address of* a memory location where a value of the specified *`Type`* is stored.[2] Such variables are often called **pointer variables**, or simply **pointers**. Thus, the declarations

   ```
   int* iPtr;
   int* jPtr;
   int* kPtr;
   ```

   declare that `iPtr`, `jPtr`, and `kPtr` are pointer variables, each of which can store the address of a memory location where an `int` is stored. The type of each of these variables is `int*`.

---

2. The asterisk need not be attached to the type identifier; for example, this declaration could also be written `Type * variableName;` or `Type *variableName;`.

2. The ampersand operator (`&`) can be used as a unary prefix operator on a variable name,

    ```
    &variable_name
    ```

    and *returns the address* with which `variableName` is associated, and so `&` is called the **address-of operator**. Thus, the expressions `&i`, `&j`, and `&k` return the addresses (or references[3]) associated with variables `i`, `j`, and `k`, respectively.

Combining these two pieces of information, we see that the declarations

```
int* iPtr = &i;
int* jPtr = &j;
int* kPtr = &k;
```

declare `iPtr`, `jPtr`, and `kPtr` as pointer variables, each of which can store the address of a memory location containing an `int`, and they initialize `iPtr` to the address of variable `i`, `jPtr` to the address of variable `j`, and `kPtr` to the address of variable `k`. In the sample run in Figure 14.1, the address associated with variable `i` is the hexadecimal value `0x0053AD78`, the address of `j` is `0x0053AD7C`, and the address of `k` is `0x0053AD80`. We can visualize the layout of the program's data in memory as follows:[4]

0x0053AD78	11	i
0x0053AD7C	22	j
0x0053AD80	33	k
	0x0053AD78	iPtr
	0x0053AD7C	jPtr
	0x0053AD80	kPtr

WATCH OUT

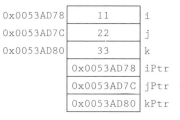

It is important to remember that

> *in a declaration, an asterisk operator * must precede each identifier that is to serve as a pointer.*

Thus,

```
double* ptr1,
      * ptr2;
```

is a correct declaration of `ptr1` and `ptr2` as pointers to `double`s. Had we written

```
double* ptr1,
        ptr2;
```

---

3. The word *reference* is used as a synonym for *address*. In fact, this is the origin of the phrase *reference parameter*—the value of a reference parameter is actually the address of its argument, rather than a copy of the argument.
4. Note that (using hexadecimal arithmetic)
    0x0053AD7C – 0x0053AD78 = 4
    and
    0x0053AD80 – 0x0053AD7C = 4
    which indicates that the size of an `int` on this particular machine is 4 bytes (32 bits).

however, only `ptr1` would be a pointer variable; `ptr2` would be an ordinary `double` variable. To avoid making this mistake, we will normally use a separate declaration for each pointer variable:

```
double* ptr1;
double* ptr2;
```

Using `typedef` for Readability. An alternative notation that does not require the repeated use of the asterisk in pointer declarations is to use `typedef` to rename a pointer type. For example, we could first declare

```
typedef int* IntPointer;
```

in Figure 14.1 and then use `IntPointer` to declare the pointers:

```
IntPointer iPtr = &i,
           jPtr = &j,
           kPtr = &k;
```

Such declarations improve the readability of pointer declarations, especially when pointer parameters are being declared.

BASIC POINTER OPERATIONS

C++ supports a variety of operations on pointers, including initialization, dereferencing, I/O, assignments, comparisons, and arithmetic. We examine each of these in turn.

Initialization. When a pointer variable is initialized to an address, as in

```
int* iPtr = &i;
```

that address must be the address of an object whose type is the same as the type to which the pointer points. The pointer is said to be **bound** to that type. For example, the declarations

```
double doubleVar;
int* iPtr = &doubleVar;        // ERROR
```

will cause a compiler error, because an integer pointer may only store addresses of integer objects.

One important exception is that 0 can be assigned to any pointer variable. The value that results is called the **null pointer value** for that type and 0 is often called the **null address**. Thus, the declarations

```
char* cPtr = 0;
int* iPtr = 0;
double* dPtr = 0;
```

are all valid initializations using the null address.

The null address can also be used in a boolean expression to indicate whether a pointer is pointing to anything:

```
if (dPtr == 0)
   // dPtr is not currently pointing to anything
```

```
else
   // dPtr is pointing to a memory location
```

As we shall see, such comparisons are especially important when pointers are used to store the addresses of blocks of memory allocated during execution.

Indirection and Dereferencing. Pointer variables not only store addresses, but also provide access to the values stored at those addresses. An expression of the form

```
*pointerVariable
```

can be used to access the value at the address stored in `pointerVariable`. It can be thought of as going to the reference (address) stored in `pointerVariable` and accessing the value stored at that address. To illustrate, in the sample run of Figure 14.1, the value of the expression

```
iPtr
```

is `0x0053AD78`, and the value of the expression

```
*iPtr
```

is 11, because 11 is the value stored at address `0x0053AD78`:

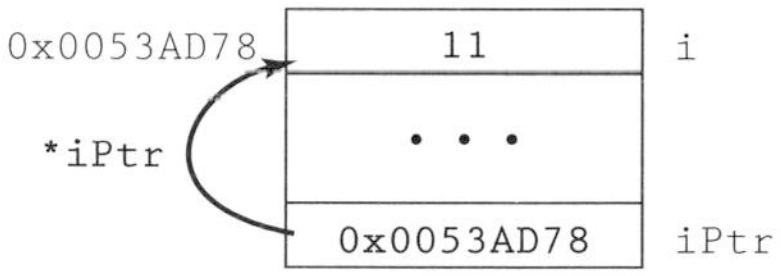

For the same reason, the values of the expressions `*jPtr` and `*kPtr` are 22 and 33, respectively. Thus, the value of variable `i` can be accessed via the expression `*iPtr`, the value of `j` via `*jPtr`, and the value of `k` via `*kPtr`. In general, the value of a variable `v` can be *accessed indirectly* by applying the `*` operator to a pointer variable `vPtr` whose value is the address of `v`. For this reason, the `*` operator is called the **indirection operator**. Since *reference* is another term for *address* and applying the indirection operator to a pointer variable accesses the value at the address stored in that pointer variable, applying the indirection operator to a pointer variable is called **dereferencing** that pointer variable.

We have already used this indirect access technique in earlier chapters. For example, we saw in Section 13.5 that each class object contains a pointer variable `this` whose value is the address of the object that contains it and that dereferencing `this` provides a way to (indirectly) access that object. We might picture this as follows:

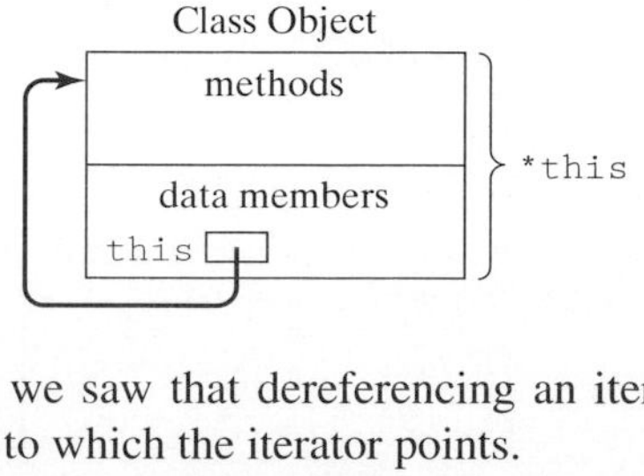

Similarly, in Section 10.6, we saw that dereferencing an iterator provides access to the value stored at the position to which the iterator points.

The indirection operator can be applied more than once to produce additional levels of indirection. For example, the declarations

```
typedef int* IntPointer;      // or without using typedef:
IntPointer * ptr;             //      int** ptr;
```

declare `ptr` to be a pointer to a memory location that contains a pointer to another memory location where an `int` can be stored.

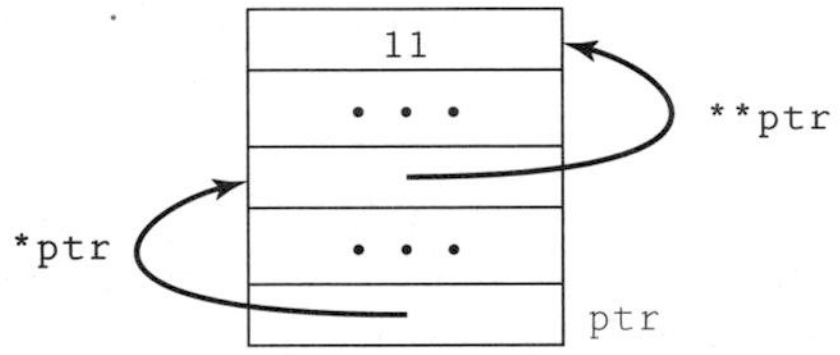

The indirection operator can be used on either side of an assignment statement. If the statement

```
i = *jPtr;
```

were added to the program in Figure 14.1, the value of `i` would be changed from 11 to 22, because dereferencing `jPtr` produces the value 22 stored at address `0x0053AD7C` and this value would be assigned to `i`. The statement

```
*iPtr = j;
```

would produce the same result. `*iPtr` refers to the memory location with address `0x0053AD78`, and the assignment operator copies the value of `j` (22) into this memory location. Since this address is associated with the variable `i`, the effect is to change the value of `i`.

As we noted earlier, the purpose of the program in Figure 14.1 was to introduce the basics of pointers and indirection. Pointers are not often used to store addresses that are associated with names. Instead, as we shall see, pointers are used to store and retrieve values in memory locations with which *no name* has been associated.

Pointers to Class Objects. Although the program in Figure 14.1 does not do so, we can also declare pointers to class objects and use them to store the addresses of objects. For example, in Chapter 11 we built a `Temperature` class that we used to define `Temperature` objects such as

```
Temperature temp1(98.6, 'F');
```

Given such an object, we could declare a pointer to a `Temperature` and use it to store the address of that object,

```
Temperature* tempPtr = &temp1;
```

which can be pictured as follows:

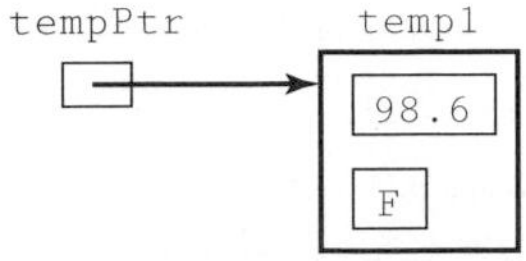

The members of `temp1` can be accessed (indirectly) via `tempPtr`. For example, `temp1` has a `getScale()` method that returns the value (`'F'`) of its `myScale` instance variable. The `getScale()` message can be sent to `temp1` via `tempPtr`, and this can be done in two ways. One way is combine the indirection operator with the dot operator and write

```
(*tempPtr).getScale()
```

In this expression, the pointer `tempPtr` is first dereferenced to access the object to which it points (i.e., `temp1`), and the dot operator is then used to send that object the `getScale()` message.

This notation is rather cumbersome, because it involves two operators and the indirection operation *must be parenthesized* since it has lower priority than the dot operator. Thus, C++ provides a more convenient notation that accomplishes the same thing in one operation:

```
tempPtr->getScale()
```

Here `->` is the **class pointer selector operator** whose left operand is a *pointer* to a class object and whose right operand is a *member* of the class object. This operator provides a convenient way to access that object's members, and the "arrow" notation clearly indicates that the member is being accessed through a pointer.

I/O. In the program in Figure 14.1, we displayed the addresses associated with `i`, `j`, and `k` by displaying the values of `iPtr`, `jPtr`, and `kPtr`, which stored these addresses.[5] In a similar manner, to find the addresses associated with `iPtr`, `jPtr`, and `kPtr`, we could write

```
cout << "\n iPtr is stored at address " << &iPtr
     << ",\n jPtr is stored at address " << &jPtr
     << ", and\n kPtr is stored at address " << &kPtr
     << endl;
```

The address-of operator allows us to determine the exact memory address at which an object is stored, whereas pointer variables allow us to store these addresses.

WATCH OUT

Just as the value of a pointer can be output using `<<`, an address could be input and stored in a pointer variable using `>>`. However, this is rarely done, because we usually are not interested in the address of the memory location storing a value, only in the value itself. In fact, it is dangerous to input address values because an attempt to access a memory address outside the space allocated to an executing program will result in a fatal run-time error.

Assignment. Although the program in Figure 14.1 does not illustrate it, pointer variables can be assigned the values of other pointer variables that are *bound to the same type*. For example, if we were to add the statement

```
jPtr = iPtr;
```

---

5. See Footnote 1 about the use of `void*`.

to the program, then the value of `iPtr` would be copied to `jPtr` so that both have the same memory address as their value; that is, both point to the same memory location, as the following diagrams illustrate:

Before the assignment:

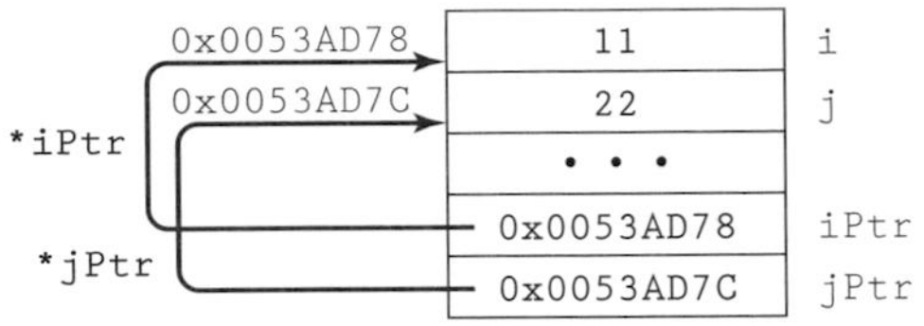

After the assignment `jPtr = iPtr;`:

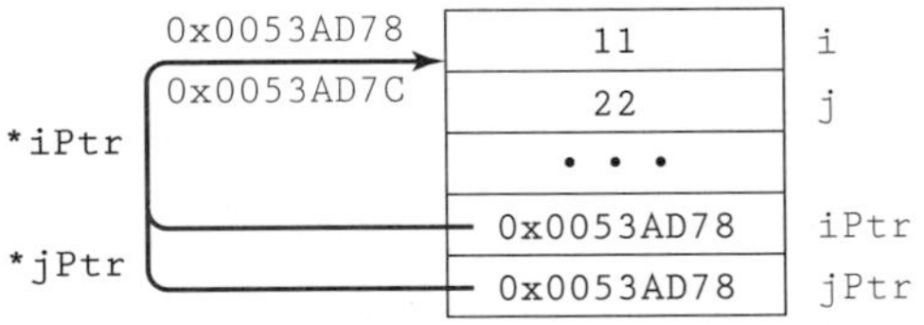

After the assignment statement is executed, `jPtr` no longer points to `j`, but now points to `i`. Thus, applying the indirection operator to `jPtr` will access the memory location associated with `i`. For example, an output statement

```
cout << *jPtr;
```

will display the value 11 instead of 22, and the statement

```
*jPtr = 44;
```

will change the value at address `0x0053AD78` (i.e., the value of `i`) from 11 to 44:

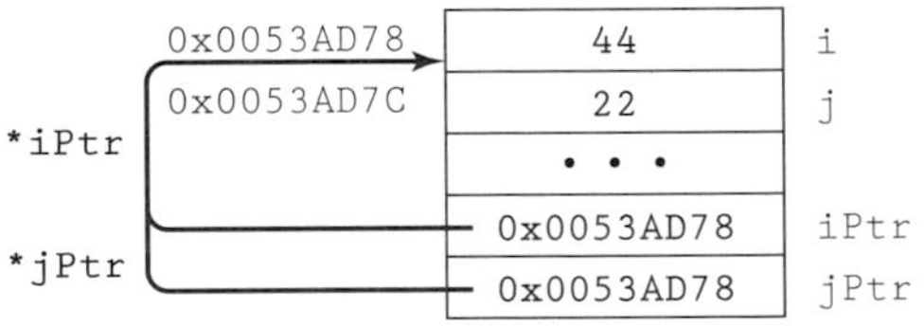

WATCH OUT

We have included this example to show that pointers are a very powerful (and dangerous) feature of programming languages. Statements that change the value of a variable in a statement in which that variable is not named are generally considered to be poor programming practice, because they make programs difficult to debug by hiding such changes. In the preceding example, the expressions `*iPtr` and `*jPtr` are alternate names for variable `i` and are sometimes called **aliases** for `i`. A function that changes a variable's value through an alias for that variable is said to exhibit the **aliasing problem**.

Comparison. The relational operators can be used to compare two pointers that are *bound to the same type*. The most common operation is to use == and != to determine if two pointer variables both point to the same memory location. For example, the boolean expression

```
iPtr == jPtr
```

is valid and returns true if and only if the address in `iPtr` is the same as the address in `jPtr`. However, if pointers `nPtr` and `dPtr` are declared by

```
int* nPtr;
double* dPtr;
```

the comparison

```
nPtr == dPtr    // ERROR!
```

will result in a compilation error, because `nPtr` and `dPtr` are bound to different types.

The *null address may be compared with any pointer variable.* For example, the conditions

`nPtr != 0`   and   `dPtr == 0`

are both valid boolean expressions.

Pointer Arithmetic. To explain arithmetic operations on pointers, it is helpful to make use of a C++ operator that we have not used up to now. This is the `sizeof` **operator**, which may be applied to any type *T* or to any expression and returns

- the number of bytes required to store a value of type *T*, or
- the number of bytes required to store the value of the expression.

The `sizeof` operator can thus be applied to either types or expressions:

```
sizeof(type-specifier)
sizeof expression
```

Note that in the first case, the type specifier must be enclosed within parentheses.

To illustrate, the expression

```
sizeof(char)
```

evaluates to 1, because `char` values are allocated one byte. Similarly, if `longVar` is of type `long int`, the expression

```
sizeof longVar
```

will evaluate to 4, because `long int` objects are stored in four bytes.

Understanding the `sizeof` operator makes it easier to understand pointer arithmetic. We consider the increment and decrement operations first because they are probably the most commonly used arithmetic operations on pointer variables. For a pointer variable `ptr` declared by

```
Type* ptr;
```

the increment statement

```
ptr++;
```

adds the value `sizeof(`*`Type`*`)` to the address in `ptr`. Similarly, a decrement statement

```
ptr--;
```

subtracts the value `sizeof(`*`Type`*`)` from the address in `ptr`. If *`intExpr`* is an integer expression, a statement of the form

```
ptr += intExp;
```

adds the value *`intExp`* `* sizeof(`*`Type`*`)` to `ptr`, and

```
ptr -= intExp;
```

subtracts the value *`intExp`* `* sizeof(`*`Type`*`)` from `ptr`.

To illustrate how these operations are used, suppose that `ptr` is a pointer whose value is the address of the first element of an array of `double` elements:

```
double dArray[10];             // array of 10 doubles
double* ptr = &(dArray[0]); // pointer to first elem of dArray
```

The last declaration could also be written

```
double* ptr = dArray;          // pointer to first elem of dArray
```

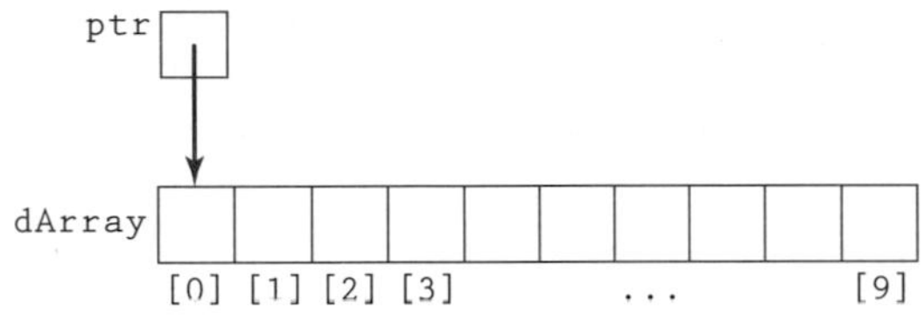

Now consider the following loop:

```
for (int i = 0; i < 10; i++)
{
   *ptr = 0;
   ptr++;
}
```

On the first pass through the loop, `ptr` is dereferenced and the value 0 is assigned to the memory location at that address. `ptr` is then incremented, which adds `sizeof(double)` to its value, effectively making `ptr` point to the second element of the array:

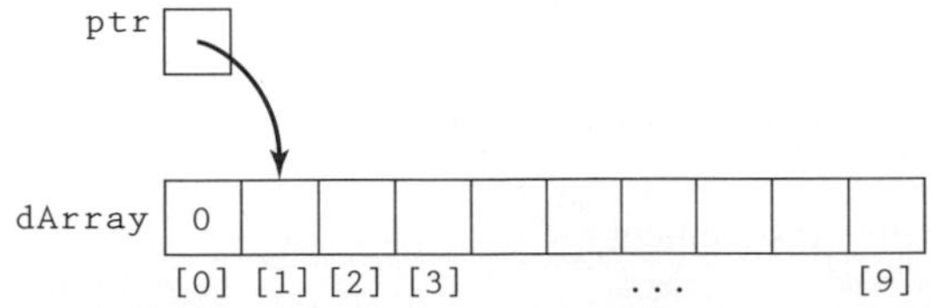

The next pass again dereferences `ptr`, sets that memory location to zero, and increments `ptr`:

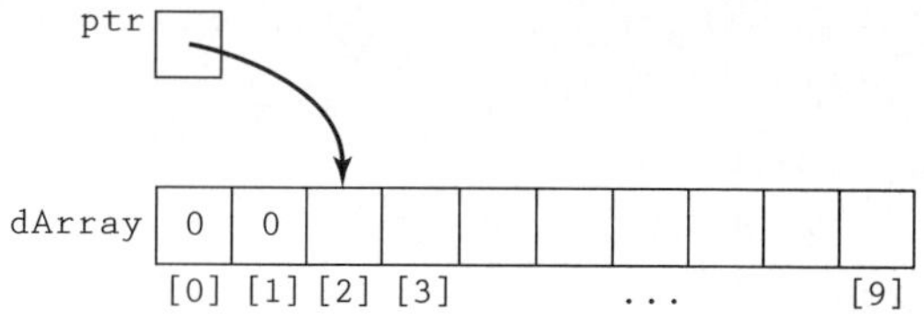

This continues with each subsequent iteration. On the final pass, the last element of the array is set to zero. Then after `ptr` is incremented, it points to the first address past the end of the array:

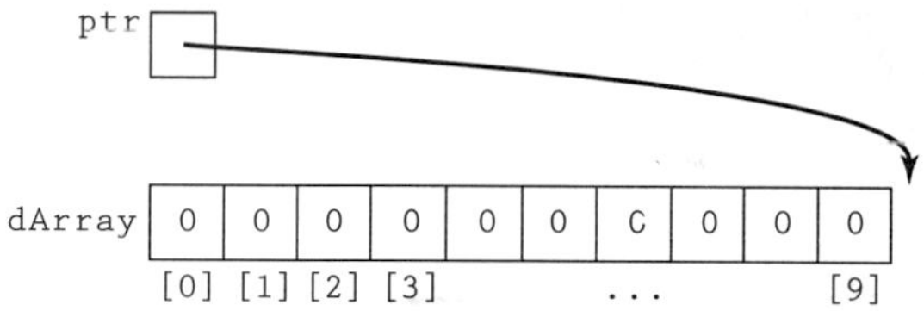

A pointer can thus be used to move through consecutive blocks of memory, accessing them in whatever way a particular problem requires.

From these examples, it should be apparent that pointers are the basis for **iterators**, which, as we saw in Section 10.7, are provided by Standard Template Library containers for accessing the values they store. Iterators are in fact implemented using pointers and behave in much the same way, with ++ being used to move the iterator to the next value in the container, `--` to move the iterator to the previous value in the container, and `*` to dereference the iterator and access the value to which it "points."

Pointers as Arguments and Parameters. Pointers may also be passed as arguments to functions. The parameters corresponding to such arguments may be either value or reference parameters, but the pointer argument and the corresponding parameter must be bound to the same type. The return type of a function may also be a pointer.

Quick Quiz 14.1

1. A pointer variable stores a(n) ________.
2. ________ is the address-of operator.
3. ________ is the dereferencing operator.
4. ________ is the indirection operator.
5. ________ is the class pointer selector operator.

Questions 6–18 assume the declarations

```
double * x,
       y = 1.1;
```

and that `double` values are stored in eight bytes of memory. Answer each of Questions 6–12 with (a) address or (b) `double` value:

6. The value of `x` will be a(n) ________.
7. The value of `y` will be a(n) ________.
8. The value of `&y` will be a(n) ________.
9. The value of `&x` will be a(n) ________.
10. The value of `*x` will be a(n) ________.
11. The value of `(*x) * y` will be a(n) ________.
12. The word "reference" is a synonym for a(n) ________.
13. In the assignment `x = 0;`, `0` is called the ________ address.
14. The output produced by the statements `x = &y; cout << *x;` is ________.
15. The output produced by the statements `x = &y; *x = 3.3; cout << y;` is ________.
16. (True or false) `sizeof(double) == sizeof y`.
17. (True or false) `sizeof(double) == sizeof(*x)`.
18. If the output produced by `cout << x;` is `0x12a30`, the value of `x+4` is ________.

Exercises 14.1

Exercises 1–9 assume the following declarations:

```
int i1 = 11,
    i2 = 22;
double d1 = 3.45,
       d2 = 6.78;
class Point
{
 public:
   double x() { return xCoord; }
   double y() { return yCoord; }
 private:
   double xCoord, yCoord;
};
```

1. Write declarations for variables `p1` and `p2` whose values will be addresses of memory locations in which a `double` can be stored.
2. Write a statement to assign the address of `d1` to the variable `p1` in Exercise 1, or explain why this is not possible.
3. Write a statement to assign the address of `i2` to the variable `p2` in Exercise 1, or explain why this is not possible.
4. Write declarations for a variable `q` whose value will be a memory location in which a `Point` object can be stored.
5. Write declarations that initialize variables `ptr1` and `ptr2` with the addresses of `i1` and `i2`, respectively.
6. Write a statement that will make variables `p1` and `p2` of Exercise 1 point to the same memory location.

7. Write a statement that will copy the value stored in the memory location pointed to by `ptr2` into the memory location pointed to by `ptr1`, for `ptr1` and `ptr2` as in Exercise 5.
8. Write a statement to output the *x*-coordinate and the *y*-coordinate of the point in the memory location pointed to by the variable `q` of Exercise 4.
9. Write statements that use the variables `p1` and `p2` of Exercise 2, but *not* the variables `d1` and `d2` to interchange the values of `d1` and `d2`.

For Exercises 10–16, use the `sizeof` operator to find how many bytes your C++ compiler allocates for the given data type:

10. `int`
11. `float`
12. `double`
13. `short int`
14. A `string` whose value is `"Bye!"`
15. A `string` whose value is `"Auf Wiedersehen!"`
16. Pointers to the types in Exercises 10–15.
17. Using the address-of operator, find the starting addresses your C++ compiler associates with the constant `SIZE` and each of the variables in the following declarations:

```
const int SIZE = 10;
char charArray[SIZE];
int intArray[SIZE];
double doubleArray[SIZE];
char charVar;
```

18. Use the `sizeof` operator to find the number of bytes allocated by your C++ compiler to `SIZE` and each of the variables in Exercise 17.
19. Using `typedef`, declare a type `CharPointer` that is a synonym for pointers to type `char`.

Exercises 20–22 assume an array declaration like the following:

```
double anArray[10];
```

20. Use the address-of operator to find the address of the first element of `anArray`.
21. Find the value associated with the name `anArray`.
22. What can you conclude from the results of Exercises 20 and 21?

14.2 Run-Time Allocation Using `new` and `delete`

In the first part of Chapter 10, we saw that the definition of a C-style array

```
const int CAPACITY = 10;
double arrayName[CAPACITY];
```

causes the compiler to allocate a block of memory large enough to hold ten `double` values and associate the starting address of that block with the name *`arrayName`*. Such fixed-size arrays have two drawbacks:

- If the size of the array exceeds the number of values to be stored in it, then memory is wasted by the unused elements.

- If the size of the array is smaller than the number of values to be stored in it, then the problem of array overflow may occur.

At the root of these problems is the fact that the capacity of a C-style array is fixed when the program is *compiled*. In our example, the size of the block of memory allocated for `arrayName` cannot be changed, except by editing the declaration of `CAPACITY` and then recompiling the program.

What is needed are arrays whose capacities are specified during execution. Such *run-time arrays* can be constructed using the mechanism C++ provides for run-time memory allocation. At its simplest, such a mechanism requires two operations:

1. Acquire additional memory locations as they are needed
2. Release memory locations when they are no longer needed

C++ provides the predefined operations `new` and `delete` to perform these two operations of memory allocation and deallocation during program execution.

THE `new` OPERATION

The `new` operation is used to request additional memory from the operating system during program execution. The general form of such a request is as follows:

The `new` Operation

Form:

```
new Type
```

Purpose: Issue a run-time request for a block of memory that is large enough to hold a value of the specified *Type*. If the request can be granted, `new` returns the address of the block of memory; otherwise, it returns the null address.

Since the `new` operation returns an address and addresses can be stored in pointer variables, this operation is almost always used in conjunction with a pointer. For example, when the statements

```
int* intPtr;
intPtr = new int;
```

are executed, the expression `new int` issues a request to the operating system for a memory block large enough to store an `int` value (that is, for `sizeof(int)` bytes of memory). If the operating system is able to grant the request, `intPtr` will be assigned the address of this memory block. Otherwise, if all available memory has been exhausted, `intPtr` will be assigned the null address 0. Because of this possibility, the value returned by `new` should always be tested before it is used:

```
assert(intPtr != 0);
```

or

```
if (intPtr == 0)
{
   cerr << "\n*** No more memory!\n";
   exit(1);
}
```

If `intPtr` is assigned a nonzero value, the newly allocated memory location is an **anonymous variable**; that is, it is an allocated memory location that has no name associated with it. For example, suppose `new` returns the address `0x020`:

Because there is no name associated with this newly allocated memory, it *cannot be accessed directly* in the same way other variables are accessed. However, its address is stored in `intPtr`, so this anonymous variable can be *accessed indirectly* by dereferencing `intPtr`:

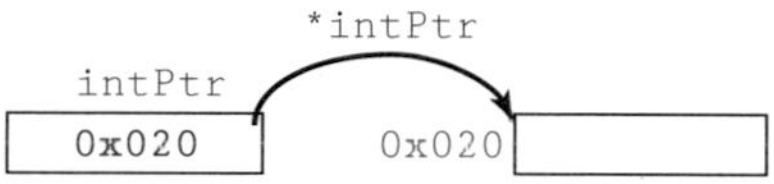

Statements such as the following can be used to operate on this anonymous variable:

```
cin >> *intPtr;        // store input value in the new integer

if (*intPtr < 100)     // apply relational ops to new integer
   (*intPtr)++;        // apply arithmetic ops to new integer
else
   *intPtr = 100;      // assign values to the new integer
```

In short, anything that can be done with an "ordinary" integer variable can be done with this anonymous integer variable by accessing it indirectly via `intPtr`.

Allocating Arrays with `new`. In practice, `new` is rarely used to allocate space for scalar values like integers. Instead, it is used to allocate space for either arrays or anonymous class objects. To illustrate the former, consider an integer array object `anArray` declared by

```
int anArray[10];
```

The value associated with the name `anArray` is the **base address** of the array, that is, the address of the first element of the array.[6] The type of object `anArray` is `int[10]`.

---

6. This is one reason that the assignment operator cannot be used to copy a "normal" array—the statement

```
alpha = beta;
```

would attempt to copy the starting address of `beta` into `alpha`, as opposed to copying the elements of `beta`.

A type such as `int[10]` can be used with `new` to allocate the memory for an array at run time. For example, the statements

```
int * arrayPtr;
arrayPtr = new int[10];
```

allocate space for an array of ten integers. Until the second statement is executed, `arrayPtr` is simply a pointer variable whose value is undefined. After it is executed (assuming that sufficient memory is available), `arrayPtr` contains the base address of the *newly allocated* array. If that address is `0x032`, we might picture the situation as follows:

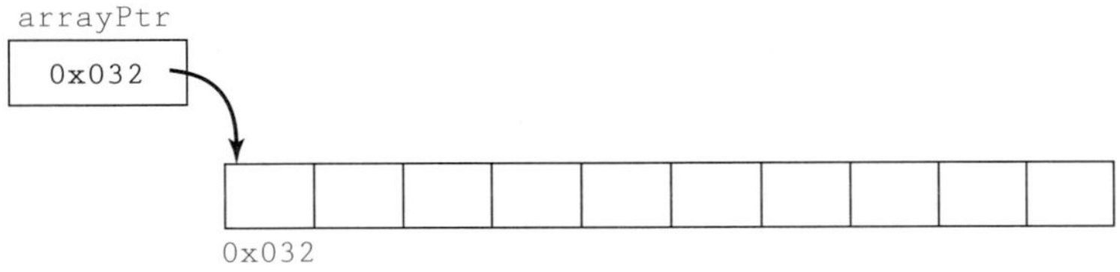

But we have seen previously that the value associated with the name of a compile-time allocated array is its base address. This means that

> *if the base address of a run-time allocated array is stored in a pointer variable, then the elements of that array can be accessed via the pointer in exactly the same way that the elements of a compile-time allocated array are accessed via its name, by using the subscript operator* (`[]`).

That is, the first element of the new array can be accessed using the notation `arrayPtr[0]`, the second element using `arrayPtr[1]`, the third element using `arrayPtr[2]`, and so on:

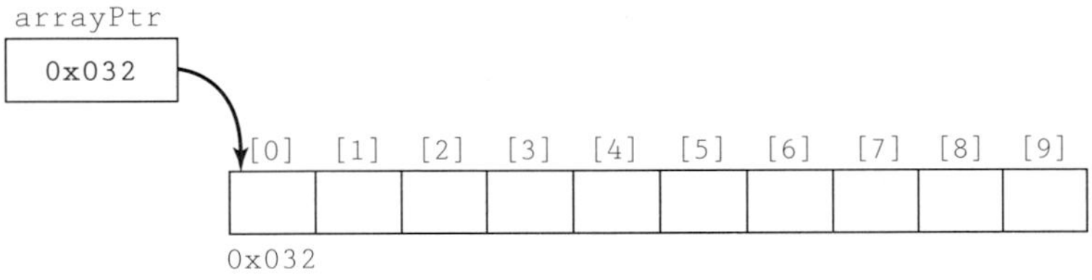

The value of the pointer variable `arrayPtr` is the base address of the array, and for a given index `i`, the subscript operator

```
arrayPtr[i]
```

simply accesses the memory location `arrayPtr + i`.

The advantage of run-time allocation is that it is not necessary to know the capacity of the array at compile time. For example, we can write

```
cout << "How many entries? ";        // find out how big the
cin >> numEntries;                   //   array should be
```

```
double *dPtr =                          // allocate an array
       new double[numEntries];          //   with that capacity
assert(dPtr != 0)                       // check for success

cout << "Enter your values.\n";         // fill it with values
for (int i = 0; i < numEntries; i++)
   cin >> dPtr[i];
...
```

Unlike arrays whose memory is allocated at compile time, arrays whose memory is allocated at run time can be tailored to the exact size of the list to be stored in them. The wasted memory problem is solved because the array will not be too large. The overflow problem is solved because the array will not be too small.

This is precisely the approach used by the `vector<T>` class template, whose structure might be something like the following:

```
template<typename T>
class vector
{
 public:
   vector();
   vector(int n);
   ...
 private:
   T * tPtr;
   int myCap;    // my capacity
   ...
};
```

Note the instance variable that is a pointer to a value of type `T`. The default-value `vector<T>` constructor simply initializes this pointer to the null address to signify an empty vector:

```
template<typename T>
vector<T>::vector()
{
   tPtr = 0;
   myCap = 0;
   ...
}
```

But the explicit-value `vector<T>` constructor uses `new` to dynamically allocate an array of `n` elements, each of which is of type `T`:

```
template<class T>
vector<T>::vector(int n)
{
   tPtr = new T[n];
   if (tptr != 0)
     ...
```

```
        myCap = n;
        . . .
    }
```

The definition of a vector object

```
vector<int> intVector(10);
```

uses this second constructor to build intVector as follows:

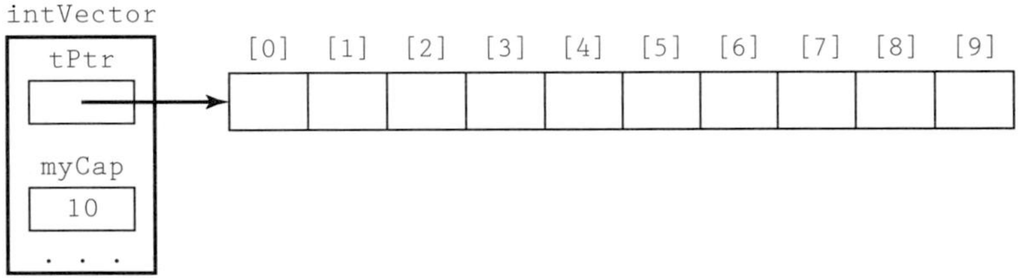

The other vector<T> operations simply access the elements of this anonymous array via the tPtr instance variable.

As we noted in Section 13.2, when one prefers or needs "lean and mean" array objects that do not have the overhead of infrequently used vector<T> operations or if one needs special array operations, we can wrap an array in a class and add operations to make it self-contained. We also noted that the best way to do this is to use an array that is allocated at run time. To do this, we can proceed as just described for vector<T>, using a pointer instance variable to store the base address of the array and having the array class' constructor use new to allocate memory for the array. Other operations that will be needed are described in what follows for vector<T>, but they are easily adaptable to array classes.

In summary, the new operator can be used to allocate anonymous array variables at run time, and the capacities of these arrays can be tailored to the number of values being stored in the arrays. By storing the base address of an array in a pointer variable, most things that can be done with a compile-time allocated array can be done with the run-time allocated array via the pointer.[7]

The Copy Constructor. There are situations in which a copy of an object needs to be constructed. For example, when an argument is passed to a function via a value parameter, the compiler must construct the parameter as a copy of the argument. Similarly, when a function returns a local object, the function terminates, ending the lifetime of that object, so the compiler builds an (anonymous) copy of the object called a *temporary* to transmit the return value back to the caller.

To make copies of a class object, the compiler supplies a **default copy constructor**, which simply copies the members of the object byte by byte. This default copy constructor works fine, except when the object being copied contains an instance variable that is a

---

7. While doing so is a bit simplistic, some programmers like to think of the name of a compile-time allocated array as a *constant pointer*, because like a pointer, the evaluation of such a name produces the array's base address, and like a constant, C++ does not allow that value to be altered.

pointer. To see why, suppose that the compiler uses it to make a copy of the following object named `intVector`:

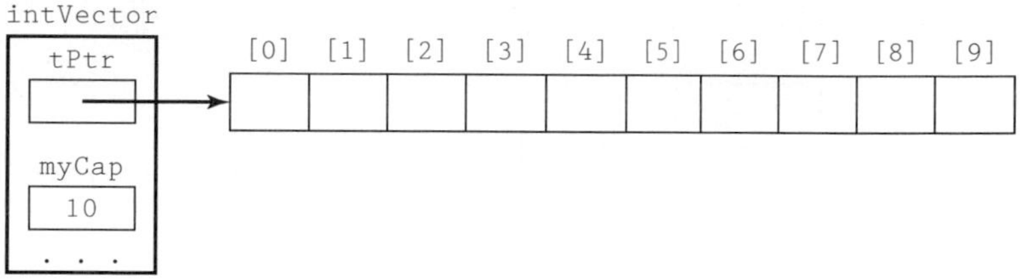

When the default copy constructor copies the instance variables of `intVector`, it blindly copies them. Although it correctly copies `myCap` and it copies `tPtr`, it does not copy the run-time allocated array, because that array is not an instance variable of `intVector`. The result can be pictured as follows:

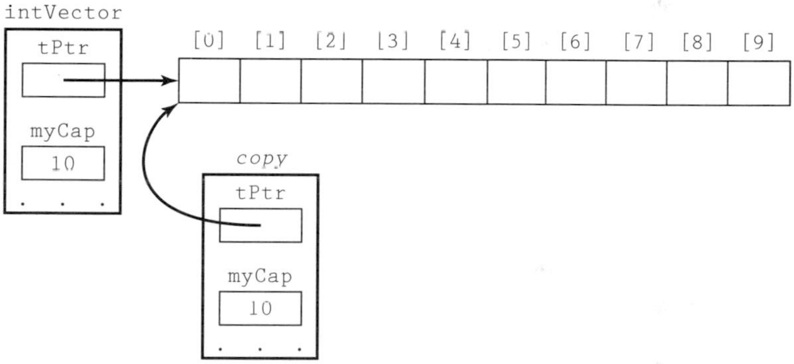

WATCH OUT

That is, when a class contains an instance variable that is a pointer, *the default copy constructor does not make a distinct copy of the object pointed to by the pointer.* This can be a problem. For example, if *`copy`* is a value parameter in a function and the function modifies the array pointed to by *`copy`*'s instance variable `tPtr`, these modifications will simultaneously change the array of `intVector`. This should not happen with a value parameter!

This kind of copying is known as a **shallow copy**. What is needed is a **deep copy** operation that makes a *distinct* copy of a class object containing a pointer instance variable. To accomplish this, C++ allows a class to define its own copy constructor. For example, a copy constructor for `vector<T>` might look something like the following:

```
template<class T>
vector<T>::vector(const vector<T>& original)
{
   myCap = original.capacity();       // copy capacity info.
   tPtr = new T[myCap];               // get a distinct array
   for (int i = 0; i < myCap; i++)    // copy original's array
      tPtr[i] = original[i];          //  into our new one
   ...
}
```

Unlike the default copy constructor, this one will allocate a distinct anonymous array, store its address in the pointer instance variable, and then copy the values from the original object's array into this new array. The result will be a completely distinct copy:

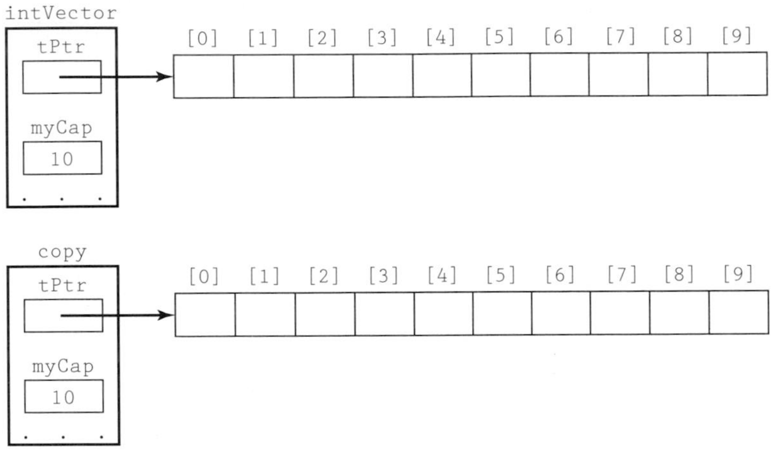

The general form of a copy constructor for an arbitrary class is as follows:

Class Copy Constructor

Form:

```
ClassName(const ClassName & original)
```

where

`ClassName` is the name of the class containing this function; and

`original` is a reference to the object being copied.

Purpose: This function is used by the compiler to construct a copy of the argument corresponding to *`original`*. The compiler calls this function whenever such a copy is needed, including the following:

- An object of type *`ClassName`* is passed as a value parameter
- The return value of a function is of type *`ClassName`*
- An object of type *`ClassName`* is initialized when it is declared
- The evaluation of an expression produces an intermediate (or temporary) value of type *`ClassName`*

Note that the parameter of a copy constructor *must* be a reference parameter (and should be a `const` reference parameter, as well) because if it is defined as a value parameter, then a call to the operation will cause the following:

1. Passing `original` as a value parameter means that a copy of `original` must be made.
2. To make a copy of `original` as a value parameter, the copy constructor is called again (with `original` as its argument).
3. To pass `original` as a value parameter to that copy constructor, a copy of `original` is needed.
4. To make a copy of `original`, the copy constructor is called again (with `original` as its argument).

.
.
.

An infinite recursion results! Defining `original` as a reference parameter avoids this infinite recursion because the reference (address) of `original` is passed, instead of a copy of `original`.

THE `delete` OPERATION

When execution of a program begins, the program has available to it a "pool" of unallocated memory locations, called the **free store** or **heap**. The effect of the `new` operation is to request the operating system to

1. remove a block of memory from the free store,
2. allocate that block to the executing program.

The executing program can use this block if it stores its address (the value produced by the `new` operation) in a pointer variable.

The size of the free store is limited, and each execution of `new` causes the pool of available memory to shrink. If a call to `new` requests more memory than is available in the free store, then the operating system is unable to fill the request and `new` returns the null address 0.

Memory that is no longer needed can be returned to the free store by using the **`delete` operation**. Just as `new` is a request by the executing program for memory from the free store, the `delete` operation is a request to return memory to the free store. Such memory can then be reallocated to the program by a subsequent `new` operation. The `new` and `delete` operations are thus complementary:

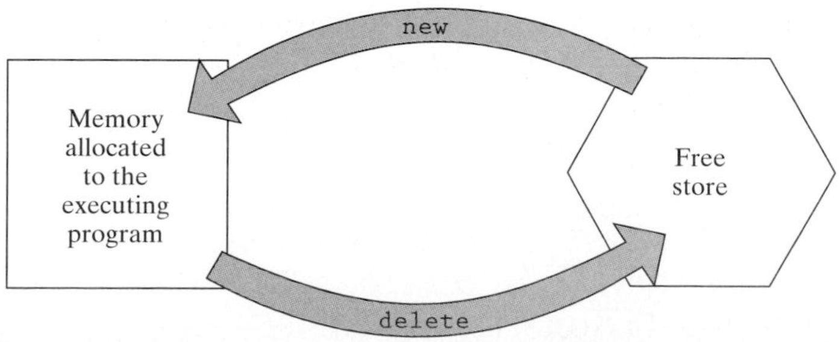

The general form of the `delete` operation is as follows:

The `delete` Operation

Form:

```
delete pointerVariable
```

or

```
delete [] arrayPointerVariable
```

Purpose: The first form frees the run-time allocated object whose address is stored in *pointerVariable*. The second form frees the run-time allocated array object whose address is stored in *arrayPointerVariable*.

For example, if `intPtr` has been allocated memory from the free store with

```
int* intPtr = new int;
```

then the statement

```
delete intPtr;
```

will release the memory location pointed to by `intPtr`, making it available for allocation at a later time. Following the operation, the value of `intPtr` will be undefined, and so the result of any attempt to dereference it,

```
*intPtr
```

is unpredictable, possibly producing a run-time error.

Similarly, if `dPtr` is a pointer to the first element of an array allocated at run time, as in

```
cin >> numValues;
double *dPtr = new double[numValues];
```

then that array's memory can be returned to the free store with

```
delete [] dPtr;
```

Memory Leaks. It is important for programs that allocate memory using `new` to deallocate that memory using `delete`. To see why, consider the following innocent-looking code:

```
do
{
   int * intPtr = new int[10];
   assert(intPtr != 0);

   // ... use the array via intPtr to solve a problem
```

```
        cout << "\Do another (y or n)? ";
        cin >> answer;
    }
    while (answer != 'n');
```

The first time the loop executes, an array of 10 integers will be allocated:

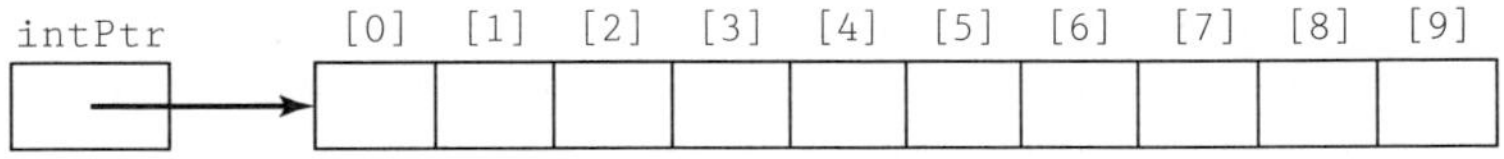

The second time the loop executes, a second array will be allocated and its address stored in `intPtr`. However, `delete` was not used to return the first array to the free store, and so it is still allocated to the program:

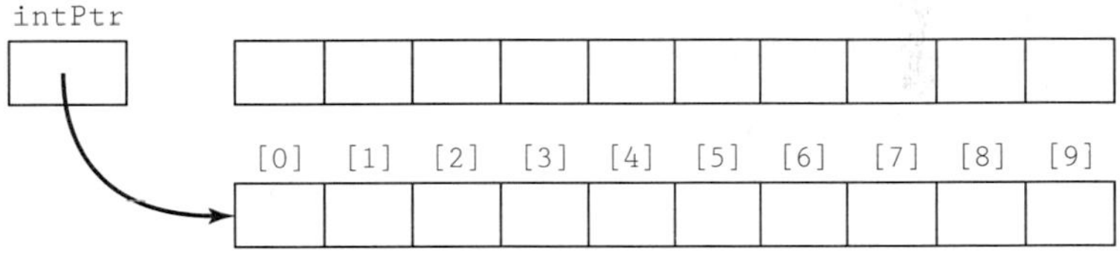

Since `intPtr` was the only means of accessing the first anonymous array and we overwrote its address in `intPtr`, that array is now "lost" or "marooned" memory—it can neither be accessed by the program, nor returned to the free store.

The third time the loop executes, a third array is allocated and its address stored in `intPtr`, marooning the second anonymous array:

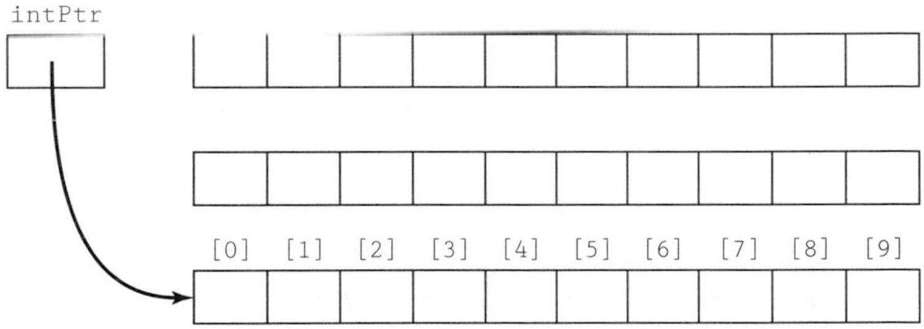

With each repetition of the loop, ten more memory locations will be lost. If the loop executes enough times, the assertion (`intPtr != 0`) will fail and terminate the program. Because such code loses memory over time, this situation is called a **memory leak**.

To avoid memory leaks, the memory to which a pointer points should always be deallocated before the pointer is assigned a new address:

```
    do
    {
        int * intPtr = new int[10];
        assert(intPtr != 0);
```

```
      // ... use the array via intPtr to solve a problem

      delete [] intPtr;

      cout << "\Do another (y or n)? ";
      cin >> answer;
   }
   while (answer != 'n');
```

This will ensure that the memory pointed to by a pointer is released to the free store and thus avoid a memory leak.

Destructors. We saw earlier that the `vector<T>` constructor could use `new` to request an anonymous array at run time. Since the pointer by which this array is accessed is a private instance variable, how is this anonymous array deallocated? Stated differently, how does `vector<T>` avoid a memory leak?

In addition to *constructor* operations that are used to define objects of the class, C++ also allows a class to define a special **destructor** operation to do any necessary "clean-up" activities at the end of a class object's lifetime. These activities include using `delete` to release memory allocated at run time. For example, the `vector<T>` destructor might be written as follows:

```
template<class T>
vector<T>::~vector()
{
   delete [] tPtr;   // deallocate array
   tPtr = 0;         // reset pointer to null
   myCap = 0;        // update capacity
   // ...
}
```

The compiler will automatically invoke this destructor at the end of a `vector<T>` object's lifetime, so that the object can "clean up after itself." This illustrates the primary role of a destructor, which is to reclaim any storage that was allocated to the object at run time.

The name of a destructor is always the name of the class preceded by the tilde (~) character:

The Class Destructor

Form:

```
~ClassName()
```

Purpose: The compiler calls this function to destroy objects of type *`ClassName`* whenever such objects should no longer exist:

- At the end of the main function for *`ClassName`* objects that are declared within `main()` as static or global objects

- At the end of each block in which a nonstatic `ClassName` object is declared
- At the end of each function containing a `ClassName` parameter
- When a `ClassName` object allocated at run time is destroyed using `delete`
- When an object containing a `ClassName` instance variable is destroyed
- When an object whose type is derived from type `ClassName` is destroyed (see Sections 7.8 and 13.5)
- When a compiler-generated `ClassName` copy (made by the copy constructor) is no longer needed

Note that like a constructor, a destructor has no return type. However, unlike a constructor, a destructor cannot have parameters, and thus can have only a single definition.

By providing a destructor for any class that uses run-time allocated memory, a class object will automatically release that memory at the end of its lifetime, avoiding a memory leak. This makes class objects self-contained, which is another characteristic of good design.

The Assignment Operator. In addition to a default copy constructor, the C++ compiler also provides for each class a default definition for the assignment operator (=) that, like the default copy constructor, simply does a byte-by-byte copy of the object being assigned. As with the copy constructor, this works fine unless the class has a pointer instance variable.

The problem is similar to the copy constructor problem: If `v1` and `v2` are two vector objects defined by

```
vector<int> v1(10), v2;
```

and we subsequently assign `v1` to `v2`,

```
v2 = v1;
```

the default assignment operator will simply copy the instance variables of `v1` into those of `v2`. This works fine for `myCap`, but not for the instance variable `tPtr`:

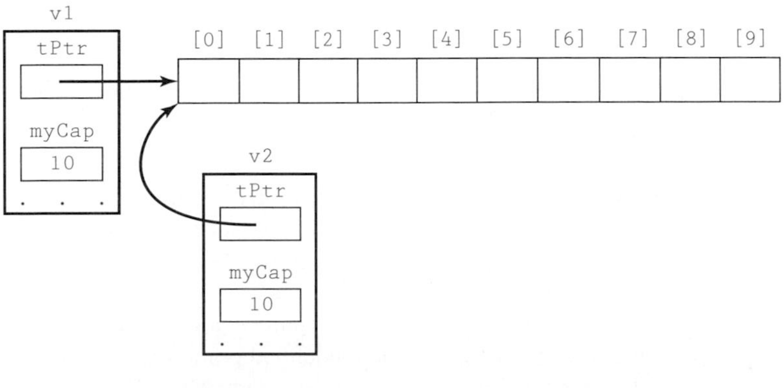

That is, the default assignment operator does not make a *distinct* copy of a class object that contains a pointer instance variable. This means that the class designer must overload the assignment operator, which *must* be defined as a method. For example, we might overload the assignment operator for class `vector<T>` by writing something like the following:

```
template<class T>
vector<T>& vector<T>::operator=(const vector<T>& original)
{
   if (this != &original)                    // check for v = v
   {
      if (myCap != original.capacity())     // if necessary
      {                                      //   deallocate
         delete [] tPtr;                     //   old array
         tPtr = new T[original.capacity()];//  get a new one
      }
      myCap = original.size();               //  copy capacity
      for (int i = 0; i < myCap; i++)        //  copy original's
         tPtr[i] = original[i];              //  array into our
                                             //    new one
      // copy any other instance variables...
   }
   return *this;                   // return ourself for
}                                  // chaining: v1 = v2 = v3
```

The behavior is similar to that of the copy constructor, with two main differences. One is that whereas the copy constructor simply builds a *new* object, the assignment message may be sent to an *existing* object. If that object already has a run-time allocated array whose capacity is different from that of `original`, then that array should be replaced with one whose capacity is the same as that of `original`. To do this, the old array must be deallocated with `delete`, to avoid a memory leak. However, we only want to do all of this if `original` is distinct from this object (the receiver of this message), and so we must guard these steps with an `if` statement and the condition `(this != &original)`.

The second difference is that the copy constructor returns no value and thus has no return type, but the assignment operation should return the object on the left-hand side of the assignment to support chained assignments. That is, an assignment like

```
v3 = v2 = v1;
```

must first assign `v1` to `v2`, and then assign `v2` to `v3`. Since such a call will be processed as

```
v3.operator=(v2.operator=(v1));
```

the expression `v2.operator=(v1)` must return `v2`. From an internal perspective, when an object receives the `operator=` message, it must return *itself*. Two different actions must be taken in order for this to occur correctly:

1. As we saw in Chapter 13, C++ allows a class method to refer to the receiver of a message by means of the predefined pointer `this`, whose value is the address of the object to which the message is sent. The statement

   ```
   return *this;
   ```

thus dereferences the pointer named `this`, effectively returning the object to which the `operator=` message was sent.

2. Normally, a `return` statement in a function,

```
return object;
```

first uses the copy constructor to build a copy of *`object`* and then returns this copy. This extra copying can be avoided by *declaring the function's return-type as a reference:*

```
ReturnType& FunctionName( Parameters );
```

This tells the compiler to return the actual *`object`* named by the `return` statement, rather than a copy of it.[8]

Given such a method, the preceding vector assignment

```
v2 = v1;
```

will replace the previous contents of `v2` with a distinct copy of `v1`:

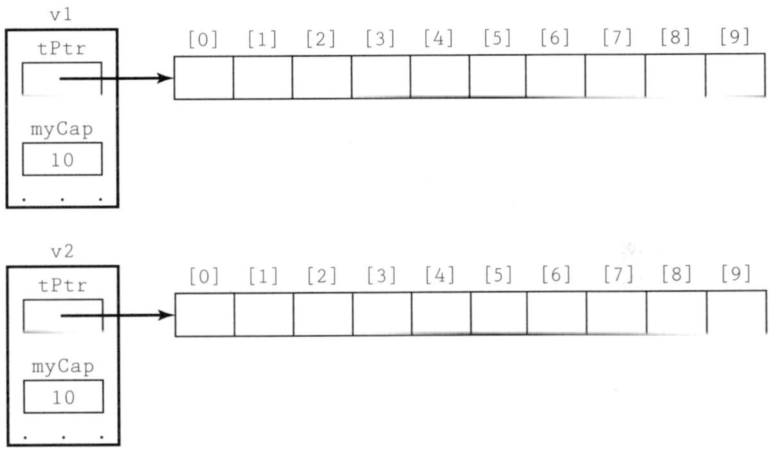

The general form of the assignment operation can be described as follows:

Assignment Operation

Form:

```
ClassName& ClassName::operator=
                    (const ClassName& original)
```

8. It follows that the object being returned cannot be a local variable or a value parameter if the return type of the function is a reference, since its lifetime ends when the function terminates. The reference return type can thus be used to return reference parameters (e.g., see the definitions of `operator<<` and `operator>>` in previous chapters) or the object receiving the message (e.g., `*this`).

```
{
   // ... if not self assignment,
   // ... make a copy of original

   return *this;
}
```

where

ClassName is the name of the class containing this function; and

original is a reference to the object being assigned.

Purpose: For classes that have pointer instance variables, overload `operator=` to make the object receiving this message a distinct copy of *original*. `operator=` *must* be defined as a method of the class.

SUMMARY

The following is a general rule of thumb to remember when designing a class:

If a class allocates memory at run time using `new`, then it should provide

- a *copy constructor* that the compiler can use to make distinct copies;
- an *assignment operator* that a programmer can use to make distinct copies;
- a *destructor* that releases the run-time allocated memory to the free store.

Remembering this rule will help you to build classes whose objects are self-contained, that are free of memory leaks, and that behave in the way a user expects.

✔ Quick Quiz 14.2

1. (Run or compile) Memory for a C-style array is allocated at ________ time; memory for a `vector<T>` object is allocated at ________ time.
2. The ________ operation is used to request memory during program execution. If not enough memory is available, it returns ________; otherwise, it returns the ________ of a block of memory. The newly allocated memory location is a(n) ________ variable.
3. The ________ operation is used to release memory during program execution.
4. The base address of a run-time allocated array is stored in a ________.
5. Given the declarations

   ```
   int a[] = {44, 22, 66, 11, 77, 33};
   int* p = a;
   ```

   what is the value of `p[2]`?
6. Write a prototype for the copy constructor of a class named `C`.
7. Write a prototype for the destructor of a class named `C`.

8. (True or false) The parameter of a copy constructor should always be a value parameter to ensure that a distinct copy is made.
9. (True or false) The assignment operator for a class must be a method.
10. When the compiler makes a copy of a class object by using the default copy constructor, it simply copies the object's members ________ by ________.
11. When is it essential that a class have its own copy constructor and why?
12. The problem of run-time memory getting marooned is called a(n) ________.
13. When an object's lifetime is over, the compiler calls the object's ________.
14. When is it essential that a class have its own destructor and why?
15. When is it essential that a class have its own assignment operator and why?

Exercises 14.2

For Exercises 1–10, write C++ statements to do what is asked.

1. Declare a `char` pointer variable named `charPtr`.
2. Allocate an anonymous `char` variable, storing its address in `charPtr`.
3. Input a character value and store it in the anonymous variable of Exercise 2.
4. Display the value of the anonymous variable of Exercise 2.
5. Convert the case of the value of the anonymous variable of Exercise 2 using character-processing functions such as `isupper()` and `tolower()` from `cctype`.
6. Declare a `double` pointer variable named `doublePtr`.
7. Allow the user to enter *n*, the number of values to be processed; then allocate an anonymous array of *n* `double` values, storing its address in `doublePtr`.
8. Fill the anonymous array of Exercise 7 with *n* input values, entered from the keyboard.
9. Compute and display the average of the values in the anonymous array of Exercise 7.
10. Deallocate the storage of the anonymous array of Exercise 7.
11. Find the base address of the anonymous array allocated in Exercise 7 and draw a memory map showing the addresses of its first few elements.
12. Describe the output produced by the following statements:

```
int * foo, * goo;

foo = new int;
*foo = 1;
cout << (*foo) << endl;
goo = new int;
*goo = 3;
cout << (*foo) << (*goo) << endl;
*foo = *goo + 3;
cout << (*foo) << (*goo) << endl;
foo = goo;
*goo = 5;
cout << (*foo) << (*goo) << endl;
*foo = 7;
cout << (*foo) << (*goo) << endl;
```

```
goo = foo;
*foo = 9;
cout << (*foo) << (*goo) << endl;
```

14.3 Introduction to Linked Lists

Although arrays and vector<T>s are easy to use to store sequences of values, they do have limitations. One limitation is that values can be efficiently added to the sequence or removed from it only at its *back*. If a problem requires that values be inserted or removed anywhere else, much shifting of elements may be required.

To illustrate, consider the following array (or vector<T>) and suppose that we want to add 99 at the front of the list. To make room for this new value, all of the elements of the array must be shifted one position to the right. This is very inefficient for large arrays and large elements, because they must all be copied from one location to another.

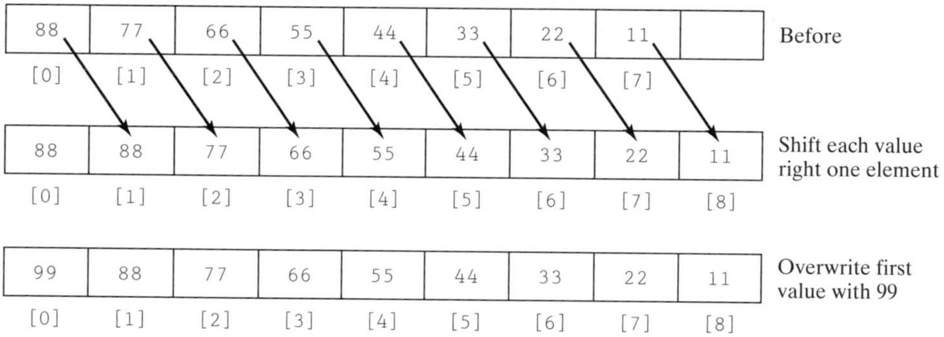

The same problem occurs when any element other than the one at the end of the sequence must be removed. All of the elements that follow it must be shifted one position to the left to close the gap. The following diagram illustrates this when the first element is removed:

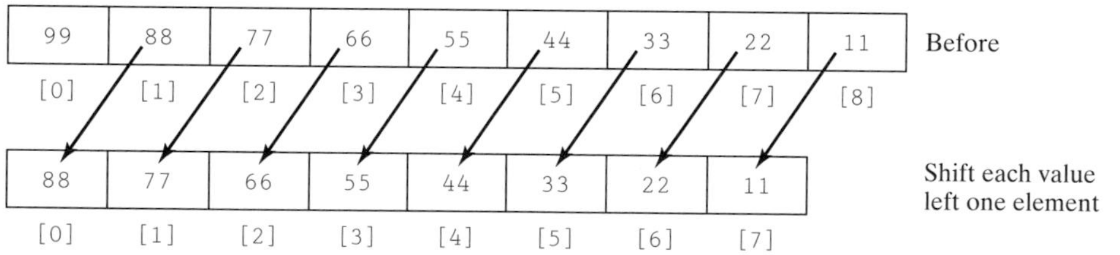

For problems where many such within-the-sequence insertions and deletions are required, a *linked list* should be used. It allows values to be inserted or removed anywhere in a sequence without any of this copying.

WHAT ARE THEY?

A **linked list** is a series of **nodes** linked together by pointers. In addition to space for the data being stored, each node has a pointer to the node containing the next value in the list.

A pointer to the node storing the first list element must also be maintained. This will be the null value, if the list is empty.

To illustrate, a linked list storing the integers storing 9, 17, 22, 26, 34 might be pictured as follows:

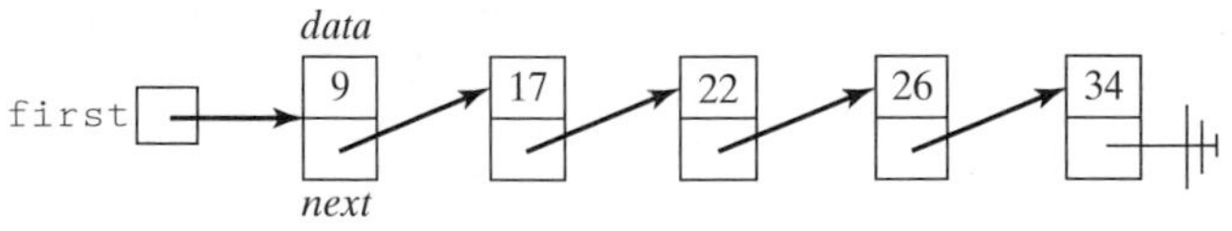

In this diagram, arrows represent links, and `first` points to the first node in the list. The *data* part of each node stores one of the elements of the list, and each arrow from a *next* part represents a pointer. The symbol in the last node (a version of the ground symbol used in electrical engineering) represents a null link and indicates that this list element has no successor.

Insert Operation. To see how linked lists make it possible to avoid the data-shifting problem of arrays and `vector<T>`s, suppose that we wish to insert 20 after 17 in the preceding linked list and that `predptr` points to the node containing 17. We first obtain a new node (via the `new` operator) temporarily pointed to by `newptr` and store 20 in its data part:

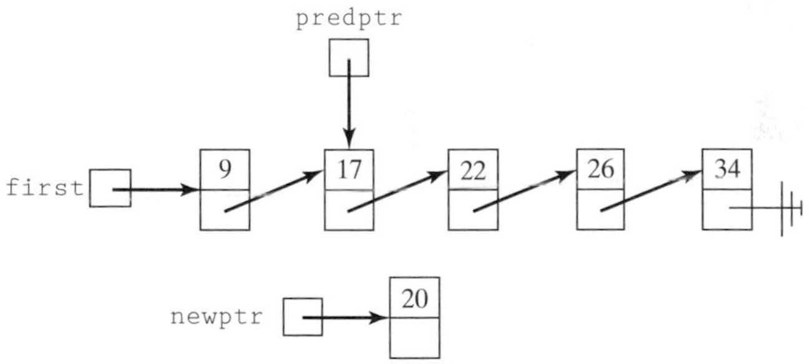

We insert it into the list by first setting its next part equal to the link in the node pointed to by `predptr` so that it points to its successor:

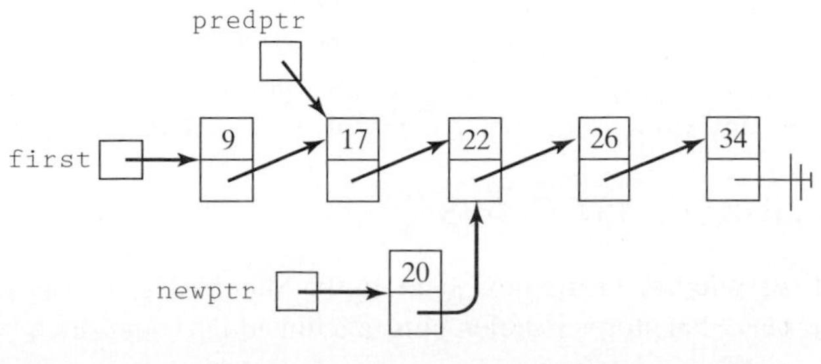

Now reset the link in the predecessor node to point to this new node:

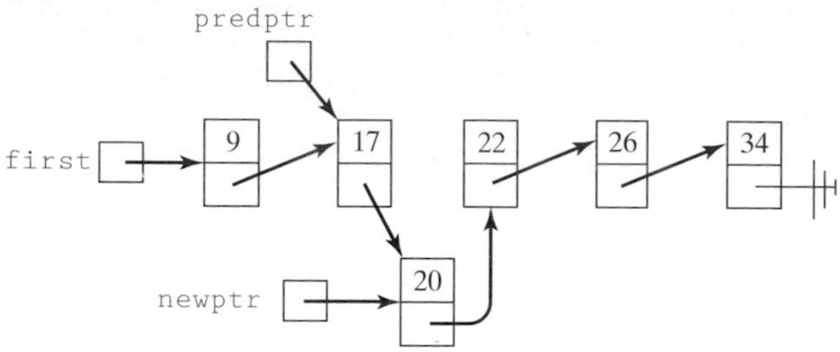

This same procedure also works for inserting a value at the end of the list. Check this for yourself by following the steps to append 55 to the list.

Inserting at the beginning of list, however, requires a modification of the last two steps, because there is no predecessor to which we can attach the node:

- Set the next part of the new node equal to `first`, which makes it point to the first node in the list.
- Then change `first` to point to the new node.

Work through this procedure yourself to insert 5 at the beginning of the list.

Note that only three instructions are needed to insert a value at any point in the list. *No shifting of list elements is required!*

Delete Operation. Deleting elements from a linked list can also be done very efficiently, as the following diagram demonstrates:

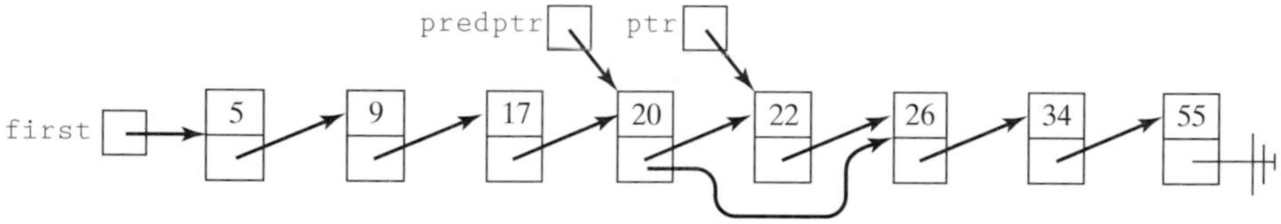

Here `ptr` points to the node to be deleted and `predptr` to its predecessor. We need only perform a bypass operation by setting the link in the predecessor to point to `ptr`'s successor. To avoid a memory leak, the deleted node should be returned to the free store (via `delete`).

Once again, this same procedure also works at the end of the list. Convince yourself of this by deleting 55. Also, a modification is needed when deleting the first node because there is no predecessor. It consists of simply resetting `first` to point to the second node in the list and then returning this node to the storage pool of available nodes. Check this for yourself by seeing how 5 would be deleted from the above list.

Like insertion, this is a very efficient operation—only two instructions are needed to delete any value in the list. *No shifting of list elements is required!*

A LINKED LIST CLASS

As we will see in the next section, the Standard Template Library has a `list<T>` class template that stores list elements in a linked list (but which have a more complex structure than we have been considering). Like most of the other STL containers, `list<T>` provides many list operations, because it is intended for use in a wide variety of list processing problems. As we have noted before, there are times when one doesn't need or want all of the operations, and a "lean and mean" linked-list class that contains the basic list operations would be more suitable. We will now indicate how such a class might be designed and implemented.

Nodes. Before we can build a linked list class, we must first consider how to implement the nodes that make up a linked list. Since each node has two different parts—a data part and a next part—it is natural to have a `Node` class with two instance variables, `data` and `next`. The instance variable `data` will be of a type that is appropriate for storing a list element, and the `next` member will be a pointer to the node that stores the successor of this element:

```
class Node
{
 public:
   . . .
   DataType data;
   Node * next;
};
```

Note that this definition of a `Node` is a *recursive (or self-referential) definition* because it uses the name `Node` in its definition: The `next` member is defined as a pointer to a `Node`.

You might wonder why we have made the instance variables of `Node` public. This is because the declaration of class `Node` will be placed inside another class `LinkedList`. Making the instance variables of `Node` public makes them accessible to all of the methods and friend functions of `Linked List`.[9] However, the `Node` class will be inside the private section of the class `LinkedList`, so these instance variables will not be accessible outside the class:

```
#ifndef LINKEDLIST
#define LINKEDLIST

template <typename DataType>
class LinkedList
{
 private:
   /*** Node class ***/
   class Node
   {
    public:
     // Node's operations
        . . .
```

9. Instead of a class, we could use a *struct*, whose members are public by default. However, it is common practice to use structs for C-style structs that contain no function members and classes when there are. See also Footnote 10.

```
      // Node's instance variables
       DataType data;
       Node * next;
    };
    typedef Node* NodePointer;

 public:
  // LinkedList's methods
    . . .
 private:
  // LinkedList's instance variables
   . . .
};
. . .
#endif
```

Only one instance variable for the `LinkedList` class is needed: a pointer to the first node. However, several operations are easier to implement if we add another instance variable to keep a count of the list elements. Thus we would put the following declarations in the class:

```
// LinkedList's instance variables
  NodePointer first;     // points to first node
  int mySize;            // number of nodes
```

A typical `LinkedList<int>` object `intList` might then be pictured as follows:

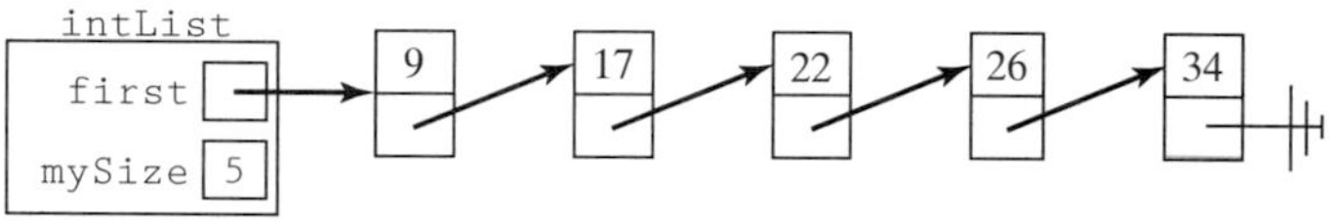

As we will see in the next section where we look at STL's version of a linked-list class, there are many different operations on linked lists. Here we will describe only some of the basic ones. To save space, we will leave most of the details of implementing these with methods and functions as exercises.

Constructor. The constructor creates an empty list. It need only make `first` a null pointer and initialize `mySize` to 0:

```
//--- Constructor
template <typename DataType>
inline LinkedList::LinkedList()
{
   first = 0;
   mySize = 0;
}
```

List Traversals. Several list operations such as sorting and searching requiring **traversing** the list; that is, starting with the first node, process the data part of a node in the required manner, and then move to the next, repeating this as long as necessary. The following statements show the basic technique for traversing the entire list:

```
ptr = first;        // ptr is of type NodePointer
while (ptr != 0)
{
   /* Appropriate statements to process
      ptr->data are inserted here */
   ptr = ptr->next;
}
```

Replacing the comment inside the loop with an output statement would produce an output operation for `LinkedList`.

Insert and Delete. The descriptions we gave earlier for the insert and delete operations lend themselves easily to algorithms and then to definitions of methods for these operations. Recall that they both require having a pointer positioned at the node that precedes the point of insertion or deletion. Positioning this pointer is done with an appropriate version of list traversal.

Assuming that `predptr` has been positioned, we can insert a node with code like the following. It assumes that the class `Node` has an explicit-value constructor that creates a node containing a specified data value and sets its `next` pointer to 0:

```
newptr = new Node(dataVal);    // newptr of type NodePointer
if (predptr != 0)              // Not inserting at front
{
   newptr->next = predptr->next;
   predptr->next = newptr;
{
else                           // Inserting at front
{
   newptr->next = first;
   first = newptr;             // reset first
}
```

And we can delete the specified node with code like the following:

```
if (predptr != 0)              // Not deleting first node
{
   ptr = predptr->next;
   predptr->next = ptr->next;  // bypass
{
else                           // Deleting first node
{
   ptr = first;
   first = ptr->next;          // reset first
}
delete ptr;                    // return node to free store
```

Destructor. We would need to add a destructor to `LinkedList` for the same reason as for run-time arrays. If we don't provide one, the default destructor used by the compiler for a linked list will cause memory leaks. The compiler deallocates memory for the instance variables `first` and `mySize`, but the nodes in the linked list will be marooned:

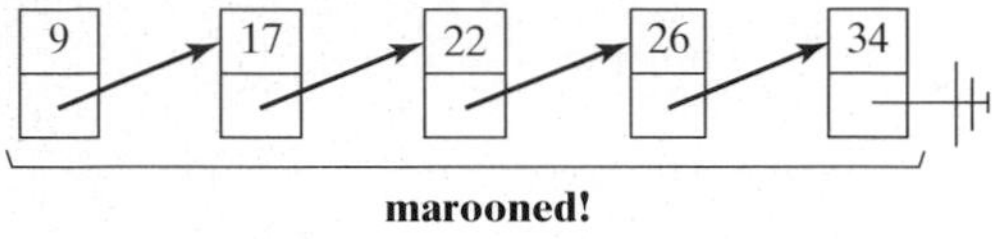

There are several ways to implement a destructor, but perhaps the most natural one is to do a traversal, deleting each node as we go.

Copy Constructor and Assignment. A copy constructor also is needed for the same reasons as for run-time arrays. If we don't provide one, the default copy constructor (which just does byte-by-byte copying) used by the compiler for a linked list like `intList` will produce

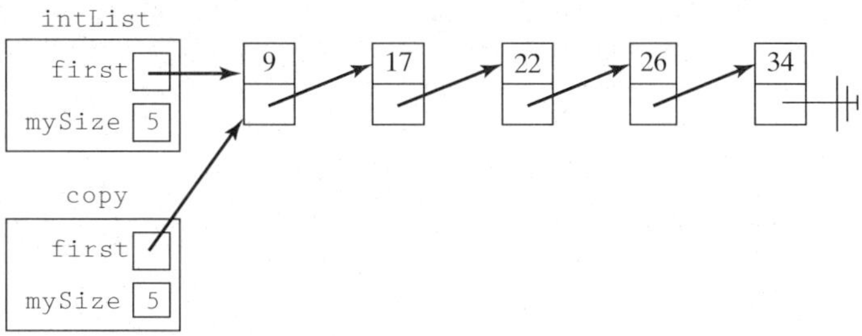

For the same reason, an assignment operator must be provided. Both of these are list traversals where we copy each list element into a new node and link the nodes together. We leave the details as exercises.

✔ Quick Quiz 14.3

1. (True or false) Values can be inserted at the end of a `vector<T>` more efficiently than at its front.
2. In a linked list, values are stored in ________ that are linked together by ________ .
3. The two parts of a node are a(n) _______ part and a(n) _______ part.
4. If a node has no successor, its link is set to a special _______ value.
5. One of the strengths of arrays is that an item can be inserted at any point without moving any array elements. (True or false).
6. One of the strengths of a linked list is that an item can be deleted at any point without moving any list elements. (True or false).

Exercises 14.3

In the following exercises you may assume that operations as described in the text can be used to obtain a new node from the storage pool and to return nodes to the storage pool, and that there is a special null value.

Exercises 1–7 assume that `p1`, `p2`, and `p3` are pointers to `Node`s and that the following statements have been executed:

```
p1 = new Node;
p2 = new Node;
p3 = new Node;
```

Tell what will be displayed by each of the code segments, or explain why an error occurs.

1.
```
p1->data = 123;
p2->data = 456;
p1->next = p2;
p2->next = 0;
cout << p1->data << "  " << p1->next->data << endl;
```

2.
```
p1->data = 12;
p2->data = 34;
p1 = p2;
cout << p1->data << "  " << p2->data << endl;
```

3.
```
p1->data = 12;
p2->data = 34;
*p1 = *p2;
cout << p1->data << "  " << p2->data << endl;
```

4.
```
p1->data = 123;
p2->data = 456;
p1->next = p2;
p2->next = 0;
cout << p2->data << "  " << p2->next->data << endl;
```

5.
```
p1->data = 12;
p2->data = 34;
p3->data = 34;
p1->next = p2;
p2->next = p3;
p3->next = 0;
cout << p1->data << "  " << p1->next->data << endl;
cout << p2->data << "  " << p2->next->data << endl;
cout << p1->next->next->data << endl;
cout << p3->data << endl;
```

6.
```
p1->data = 111;
p2->data = 222;
p1->next = p2;
p2->next = p1;
cout << p1->data << "  " << p2->data << endl;
cout << p1->next->data << endl;
cout << p1->next->next->data << endl;
```

7.
```
p1->data = 12;
p2->data = 34;
p1 = p2;
p2->next = p1;
cout << p1->data << "  " << p2->data << endl;
cout << p1->next->data << "  " << p2->next->data << endl;
```

Exercises 8–17 ask you to add operations to the `LinkedList` class begun in this section. You should test each one with a driver program as Programming Problems 1–9 ask you to do.

8. Add a `print()` method.
9. Overload the output operator (`<<`).
10. Add a `search()` method that searches the linked list for a given item and returns a pointer to the node where the item is found or a null pointer if the search is unsuccessful.
11. Add an `insert()` method that has two parameters: the item to be inserted and an integer parameter that specifies the position (counting from 0) where it is to be inserted.
12. Write a version of the `insert()` method in Exercise 11 whose parameters are the item to be inserted and a pointer to the predecessor of the item to be inserted (null if there is none).
13. Add a `delete()` method that has an integer parameter that specifies the position (counting from 0) of the list element to be deleted.
14. Write a version of the `delete()` method in Exercise 13 that has as a parameter a pointer to the predecessor of the item to be deleted (null if there is none).
15. Write code for a version of a list traversal that determines the average of a linked list of real numbers.
16. Write a boolean-valued `LinkedList` method that determines whether the data items in the list are arranged in ascending order.
17. Write a `LinkedList` method to reverse the list. Do not copy the list elements; rather, reset links and pointers so that `first` points to the last node and all links between nodes are reversed.

14.4 The STL `list<T>` Class Template

In our description of the C++ Standard Template Library in Section 10.7, we saw that it provides a variety of other storage containers besides `vector<T>` and that one of these containers is named `list<T>`. Now that we have seen anonymous variables and how C++ pointers provide indirect access to them and have studied simple linked lists, we are ready to examine the `list<T>` class template and its implementation.

Organization of `list<T>` Objects. To see how `list<T>` stores a sequence of values, suppose that `aList` is defined by

```
list<int> aList;
```

and consider the following sequence of insert operations:

```
aList.push_back(77);
aList.push_back(66);
aList.push_front(88);
```

A simplified picture of the resulting object aList is

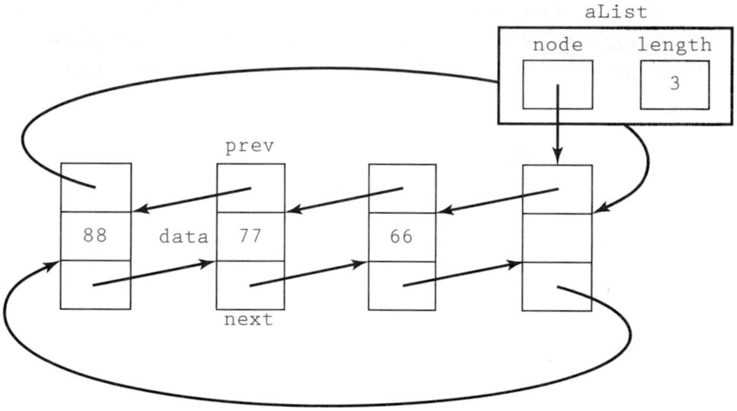

The values 88, 77, and 66 are stored in a variation of the linked lists studied in the preceding section called a **circular doubly-linked list with a head node**. It is doubly linked because each node has two pointers, prev to its predecessor and next to its successor. It is circular because the next pointer in the last node is not null, but rather points to the "empty" (rightmost) node, which is the head node; and similarly, the prev pointer in the first node points to the head node instead of being null. Note that the instance variable node (which we called first in LinkedList in the preceding section) points to this head node rather than to the first node that stores a data value.

The list<T> class template declares the type list_node as a protected struct,[10] as follows:

```
template<typename T>
class list
{
   // ... previous part of list class  ...
protected:
   struct list_node
   {
      list_node* prev;      // pointer to the node containing
                            //   the previous value
      T data;               // the value being stored in
                            //   this node
      list_node* next;      // pointer to the node containing
                            //   the next value
   };
   // ... remainder of list class ...
};
```

10. A **struct** is exactly the same as a class, except that all of its members are by default public, whereas those of a class are by default private. By declaring a list_node as a *struct* within class list, the list operations can directly access the list_node instance variables. By declaring list_node *protected* within class list, casual users of class list are prevented from accessing it or its instance variables, while classes derived from list are permitted to do so.

SOME list<T> OPERATIONS

In the remainder of this section, we examine a collection of the most useful `list<T>` operations. For some of these, we look at how they are implemented. More details about these are given on the text's Web site, where a complete table of the `list<T>` operations is given.

The `list<T>` Default-Value Constructor. Perhaps the most basic `list<T>` operation is the default-value constructor. When a programmer writes

```
list<int> aList;
```

the default-value constructor builds an empty linked list `aList`, for which a (simplified) picture is

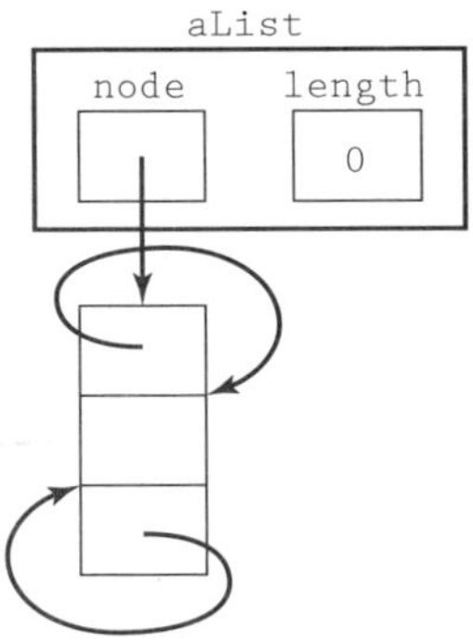

As shown in the diagram, the default class constructor allocates an empty node, which is the head node, and stores the address of this node in its instance variable `node`. In the STL `list<T>` class template, this head node plays a central role: Its `next` member always points to the node containing the *first* value in the sequence (or to the head node, if the list is empty); and its `prev` member always points to the node containing the *last* value in the sequence (or to the head node, if the list is empty). The main advantages of this organization are that there is always at least one node in the list (i.e., the head node) and every node has a predecessor and a successor. These properties simplify several of the list operations. In particular, the insert and delete operations we considered in the preceding section do not have to consider two cases of whether there is a predecessor or not.

The `size()` and `empty()` Methods. Two of the simplest `list<T>` operations are `size()` and `empty()`. The `size()` method is a simple accessor for the `length` instance variable; it returns the number of values currently stored in the list. The `empty()` method is nearly as simple, returning `true` if there are no values in the list (`length` == 0) and `false` otherwise.

The `begin()` and `end()` Iterator Methods. As with `vector<T>`, the `list<T>` class template provides two methods, `begin()` and `end()`, that return iterators to the front and past the end of the list, respectively. The `begin()` method returns a pointer to the first node, by returning the address stored in the `next` member of the head node. By contrast, the `end()` function returns a pointer pointing beyond the last node containing a data value by returning the address of the head node:

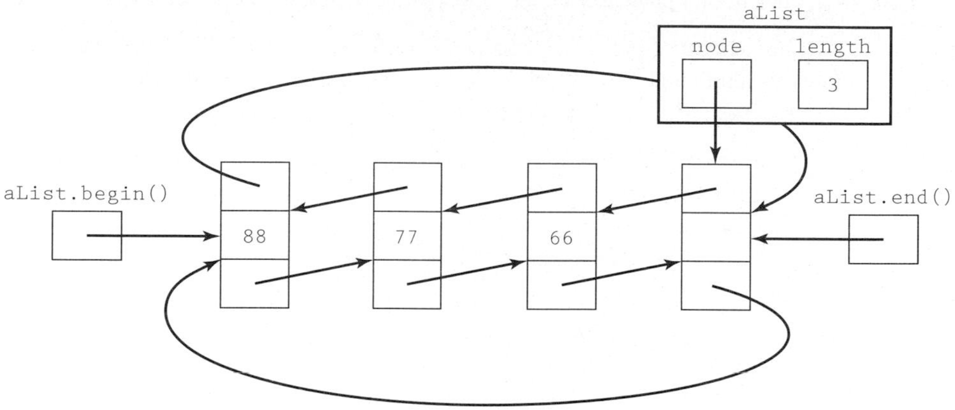

Iterators and Pointers. From our discussion of iterators in Chapter 10 and our discussion of pointers in this chapter, it should be evident that an iterator is an *abstraction* of a pointer, hiding some of its details and eliminating some of its hazards.

To illustrate, the `list<T>` class template contains a declaration of a class `list<T>::iterator` that contains its own pointer instance variable named `node`:

```
template<class T>
class list
{
 // ... previous list members omitted ...

 public:
   class iterator        // ... some simplification here ...
   {
    protected:
      list_node* node; // ... and here ...

      // ... other iterator members omitted...
   };

   // ... other list members omitted ...
};
```

The `iterator` class overloads `operator*` so that it returns the value (`node->data`) stored in the node pointed to by the iterator's `node` member. It also overloads `operator++` to "increment" the iterator to the next node in the list (`node = node->next`) and overloads `operator--` similarly to "decrement" the iterator to the previous node in the list (`node = node->prev`).

The `front()` and `back()` Members. Like `vector<T>`, `list<T>` provides methods to access the first and last values in the sequence. These are implemented by dereferencing the iterators returned by the `begin()` and `end()` operations. Since the `list<T>::iterator` class overloads `operator*` to return the data value stored in a node, the expression `*begin()` can be used to access the first value in the sequence, and the expression `*(--end())` can be used to access the last value in the sequence. Note that `*` has higher precedence than `--`, so the parentheses are necessary in this last expression.

The `insert()`, `push_front()`, and `push_back()` Methods. The `list<T>` class template provides several operations to insert a new data value, including:

- *aList*`.push_back(`*newValue*`);` which appends *newValue* to *aList*
- *aList*`.push_front(`*newValue*`);` which prepends *newValue* to *aList*
- *aList*`.insert(`*anIterator, newValue*`);` which inserts *newValue* into *aList* ahead of the value pointed to by *anIterator*

Of these three, `insert()` is the most general; `push_back()` and `push_front()` simply invoke `insert()`, passing *aList*`.begin()` and *aList*`.end()` to *anIterator*, respectively.

The insert operation is carried out in much the same way that we described for singly-linked lists in the preceding section. The only differences are that there are four links to set instead of two and we don't have to consider special cases for the ends of the list:

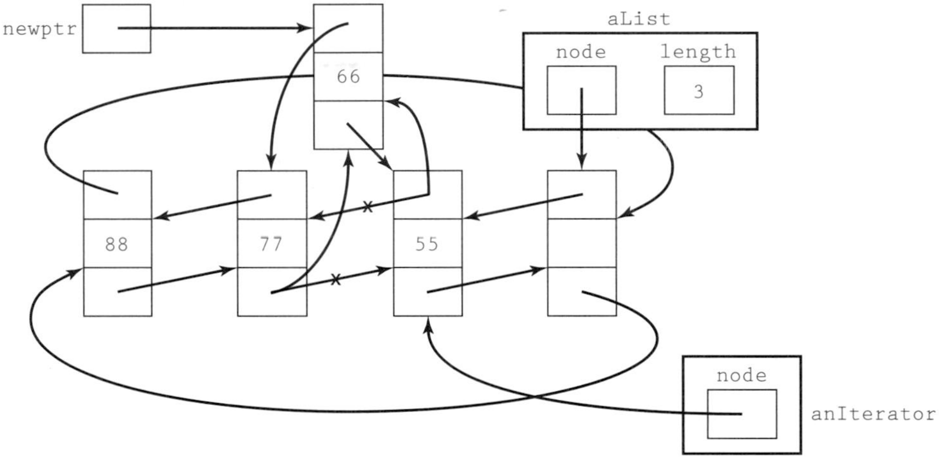

The `pop_back()`, `pop_front()`, `erase()`, and `remove()` Methods. There also are several different operations provided by `list<T>` to remove a value from a sequence:

- *aList*`.pop_back();` removes the last value from *aList*
- *aList*`.pop_front();` removes the first value from *aList*
- *aList*`.erase(`*anIterator*`);` removes the value pointed to by *anIterator* from *aList*
- *aList*`.remove(`*aValue*`);` removes all occurrences of *aValue* from *aList*

The `pop_back()`, `pop_front()`, and `remove()` operations are implemented using the `erase()` function. This function removes a node in much the same way that we described for singly linked lists in the preceding section. One difference is that there are two links that need to be changed—one for a forward bypass and one for the backward bypass. Also, there are no special cases for deleting one of the end nodes.

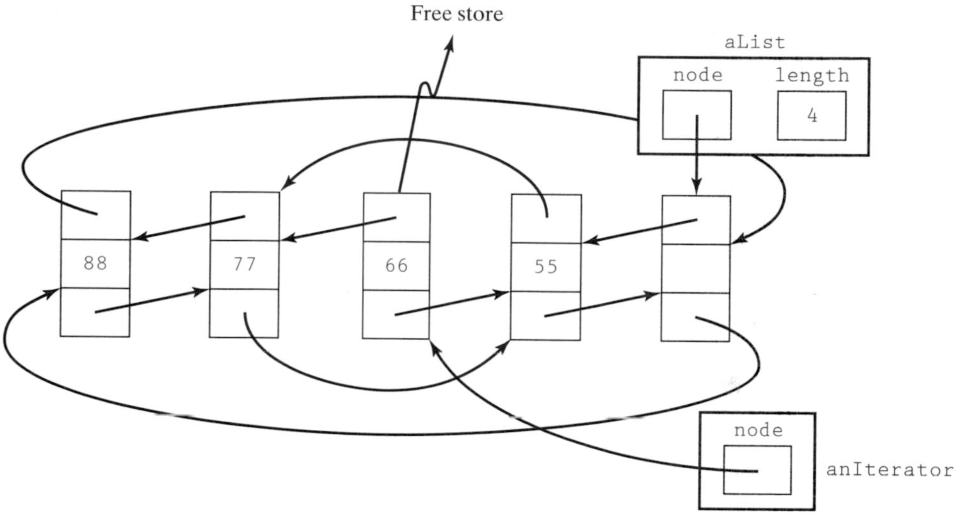

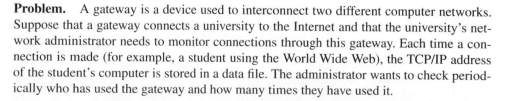

AN APPLICATION: INTERNET ADDRESSES

The TCP (Transmission Control Protocol) and IP (Internet Protocol) communication protocols specify the rules computers use in exchanging messages on the Internet. TCP/IP addresses are used to uniquely identify computers in the Internet; for example, `www.ksc.nasa.gov` is the address of a site at the NASA Kennedy Space Center. Such an address is made up of four fields that represent specific parts of the Internet,

host.subdomain.subdomain.rootdomain

which the computer will translate into a unique TCP/IP numeric address. This address is a 32-bit value, but it is usually represented in a dotted-decimal notation by separating the 32 bits into four 8-bit fields, expressing each field as a decimal integer, and separating the fields with a period; for example, at the time of this writing, `198.119.202.36` was the TCP/IP numeric address for the site at the NASA Kennedy Space Center. (A *Part of the Picture* detailing the TCP/IP Communications Architecture written by William Stallings is available on the text's Web site.)

Problem. A gateway is a device used to interconnect two different computer networks. Suppose that a gateway connects a university to the Internet and that the university's network administrator needs to monitor connections through this gateway. Each time a connection is made (for example, a student using the World Wide Web), the TCP/IP address of the student's computer is stored in a data file. The administrator wants to check periodically who has used the gateway and how many times they have used it.

Solution. The TCP/IP addresses will be read from the file and stored in a linked list of nodes, each of which will store an address and the number of times that address appeared in the data file. As each address is read, we check if it is already in the list. If it is, we increment its count by 1; otherwise, we simply insert it at the end of the list. After all the addresses in the file have been read, the distinct addresses and their counts are displayed.

The program in Figure 14.2 uses this approach to solve the problem. The addresses are stored in a `list<AddressCounter>` object named `addrCntList`, where `AddressCounter` is a small class containing two instance variables (`address` and `count`), input and output methods, and a `tally()` method to increment the `count` instance variable. Also, `operator==()` is overloaded so that STL's `find()` algorithm can be used to search the list.

Fig. 14.2 Internet addresses. (Part 1 of 3)

```
/* internet.cpp reads TCP/IP addresses from a file and produces a
 *  list of distinct addresses and a count of how many times each
 *  appeared in the file. The addresses and counts are stored in a
 *  linked list.
 *
 * Input (keyboard): name of file containing addresses
 * Input (file):     addresses
 * Output:           a list of distinct addresses and their counts
 *****************************************************************/

#include <cassert>                    // assert
#include <string>                     // string
#include <iostream>                   // cin, cout, >>, <<
#include <iomanip>                    // setw()
#include <fstream>                    // ifstream, is_open()
#include <list>                       // list<T>
#include <algorithm>                  // find
using namespace std;

//-------------- Begin class AddressItem ------------------------
class AddressCounter
{
 public:
   void read(istream & in) { in >> address; count = 1; }

   void print(ostream & out) const
   { out << setw(15) << left << address
         << "\t occurs " << count << " times\n"; }

   void tally() { count++; }
```

Fig. 14.2 Internet addresses. (Part 2 of 3)

```
   friend bool operator==(const AddressCounter& addr1,
                          const AddressCounter& addr2);

 private:
   string address;
   int count;
};

inline bool operator==(const AddressCounter& addr1,
                       const AddressCounter& addr2)
{ return addr1.address == addr2.address; }

//----------------- End class AddressCounter -------------------

typedef list<AddressCounter> TCP_IP_List;

int main()
{
   string fileName;                        // file of TCP/IP addresses
   TCP_IP_List addrCntList;                // list of addresses

   ifstream inStream;                      // open file of addresses
   cout << "Enter name of file containing TCP/IP addresses: ";
   cin >> fileName;
   inStream.open(fileName.data());
   assert(inStream.is_open());

   AddressCounter item;                    // one address & its count
   for (;;)                                // input loop:
   {
      item.read(inStream);                 //   read an address
      if (inStream.eof()) break;           //   if eof, quit

      TCP_IP_List::iterator it =           //   is item in list?
        find(addrCntList.begin(), addrCntList.end(), item);
      if (it != addrCntList.end())         //   if so:
        (*it).tally();                     //    ++ its count
      else                                 // otherwise
        addrCntList.push_back(item);       // add it to the list
   }                                       // end loop
```

Fig. 14.2 Internet addresses. (Part 3 of 3)

```
   cout << "\nAddresses and Counts:\n\n";  // output the list
   for (TCP_IP_List::iterator it = addrCntList.begin();
                              it != addrCntList.end(); it++)
      (*it).print(cout);
}
```

Listing of file *ipAddresses.dat* used in sample run:

```
128.159.4.20
123.111.222.333
100.1.4.31
34.56.78.90
120.120.120.120
128.159.4.20
123.111.222.333
123.111.222.333
77.66.55.44
100.1.4.31
123.111.222.333
128.159.4.20
```

Sample run:

```
Enter name of file containing TCP/IP addresses: ipAddresses.dat

Addresses and Counts:

128.159.4.20      occurs 2 times
123.111.222.333   occurs 3 times
100.1.4.31        occurs 1 times
34.56.78.90       occurs 0 times
120.120.120.120   occurs 0 times
77.66.55.44       occurs 0 times
```

14.5 Pointers and Command-Line Arguments

As we know by now, every C++ program has a function whose name is `main`. The main function differs from other programmer-defined functions in a number of ways. One of the differences is that arguments are passed to the main function, using an array of pointers. How this is done is the topic of this section.

The main function cannot be called directly. Instead, we can think of it as being *called* when a program is *executed*. In **command-line environments** such as the Unix operating system, the Command Prompt of Windows 2000, and the DOS prompt in earlier versions of the Windows operating system, a program is executed by entering its name following the operating system prompt. For example, on a Unix system, the operating system prompt is often the **$** symbol, so to invoke the text editor `emacs` on a computer running Unix, we might enter the command

```
$ emacs
```

and the program will begin executing. In any command-line environment, entering the name of a C++ program on the command line can be thought of as issuing a call to the main function of that program.

To edit a C++ source file in the Unix environment, we can enter a command of the form

```
$ emacs SourceFileName
```

When invoked in this way, the program (`emacs`) begins execution, searches for the file named *`SourceFileName`*, and (assuming that it is found) opens it for editing. In this example, the file that we wish to edit (*`SourceFileName`*) is an example of a **command-line argument**. Just as entering the name of the program (`emacs`) is like calling the main function of a program, entering the name of the program followed by *`SourceFileName`* is like calling the main function of a program and passing it *`SourceFileName`* as an argument.

Command-line arguments are used with many of the system commands in command-line environments such as Unix. For example, the command `mkdir projects` is used in Unix to create a new subdirectory named `projects`. Similarly, the command `cd projects` will change location in the directory structure to the subdirectory `projects`. In each case, a program is being executed (one named `mkdir` and the other named `cd`), and the name `projects` is passed to that program as an argument. In this section, we examine the mechanism by which a main function can receive and process command-line arguments. The techniques discussed can be used in any C++ command-line environment.

PARAMETERS OF THE MAIN FUNCTION

The general form of the main function is

```
int main(parameterList)
{
   statementList
}
```

In all of our programs up to this point, the *`parameterList`* has been empty, but this need not be the case. A main function can be declared with a parameter list consisting of two predefined parameters:

- `argc` (the `arg`ument `c`ount), an integer; and
- `argv` (the `arg`ument `v`ector), an array of pointers to characters.

As a legacy from C, the standard way to declare these parameters in a main function is[11]

```
int main (int argc, char* argv[])
{
   // ... body of the main function ...
}
```

When a C++ program with the parameters `argc` and `argv` declared in the parameter list of its main function is executed from the command line, two things occur automatically:

1. If `n` character strings were entered on the command line, the value of `argc` is set to `n`.
2. The value of `argv[0]` is the address of the first character string of the command line.

   The value of `argv[1]` is the address of the second character string of the command line.

   .
   .
   .

   The value of `argv[n-1]` is the address of the `n`th character string of the command line.

To illustrate, consider the simple C++ program in Figure 14.3.

Fig. 14.3 Introducing `argc` and `argv`.

```
/* commandLine.cpp demonstrates the use of parameters argc and argv.
 *
 * Output: The value of argc, followed by each string in argv.
 ****************************************************************/

#include <iostream>
using namespace std;

int main(int argc, char* argv[])
{
   cout << "\nThere are " << argc
        << " strings on the command line:\n";

   for (int i = 0; i < argc; i++)
      cout << '\t' << "argv[" << i << "] contains: "
           << argv[i] << endl;
}
```

11. C has no classes and thus has no `string` class. Instead, C permits character strings to be stored in character arrays (`char []`), and passed to functions via character pointer (`char *`) parameters, with the value of a character string literal being the address of its first character. Hence, there is a close relationship between character strings, arrays, and pointers in C.

In this program the parameter list of the main function contains declarations of `argc` and `argv`. If the compiled version of this program is stored in a file named `commandLine`, then `commandLine` can be executed by entering the command

```
$ commandLine
```

which produces the output:

```
There are 1 strings on the command line:
   argv[0] contains: commandLine
```

Thus, within `commandline`, `argc` has the value `1`, and `argv[0]` refers to the character string `commandLine`. If we execute `commandline` by entering the command

```
$ commandLine I want an argument
```

then the output will be

```
There are 5 strings on the command line:
   argv[0] contains: commandLine
   argv[1] contains: I
   argv[2] contains: want
   argv[3] contains: an
   argv[4] contains: argument
```

From these examples, it should be evident that the values of `argc` and `argv` depend on what the user enters on the command line when invoking the program. If the user enters the name of the program followed by *`i`* arguments, then the value of `argc` will be *`i`* `+ 1`, the number of character strings entered on the command line; `argv[0]` will refer to the name of the program; and `argv[1]` through *`argv[i]`* will refer to the *`i`* arguments that were entered.

EXAMPLE: A SQUARE ROOT CALCULATOR

As a simple illustration of the use of `argv` and `argc`, consider the problem of designing a square root calculator that allows the user to enter the value(s) to be processed on the command line and that then calculates and displays the square roots of each value. For example, if the command

```
$ sroot 4 9 16 25
```

is entered, the values 2, 3, 4, and 5 are to be displayed.

Since the program must process command-line arguments, it *receives* the arguments through the parameters of the main function (i.e., `argc` and `argv`). Here are some possibilities of what the user might enter:

```
$ sroot        // error — no data to process (argc is 1)
$ sroot A      // error — non-numeric data (argc is 2, argv[1] is "A")
$ sroot -1     // error — negative data (argc is 2, argv[1] is "-1")
$ sroot 9      // one value (argc is 2, argv[1] is "9")
$ sroot 4 9    // two values (argc is 3, argv[1] is "4", argv[2] is "9")
```

From the first example, we see that valid input requires `argc` > 1. Also, each `argv[i]` refers to a character string, and we must take the square root of a value of type `double`. This means that the character string stored in `argv[i]` must be converted to the corresponding `double` value. Fortunately, C++ provides the `strtod()` function in `cstdlib` that performs this operation.[12] That function can also be used to make our program more foolproof by checking its return value—`strtod()` returns 0 if it is unable to convert the string to a numeric value, which is the case in the second and third examples. Once we have converted the character string to the corresponding `double` value, all that remains is to find its square root, which is easy, using the `sqrt()` function declared in `cmath`. We then simply display the value and its square root.

We can thus construct the following algorithm, which checks that at least one command-line argument has been given and if so, uses a loop to process each argument.

Algorithm for `sroot`.

1. If *argc* is less than 2, display an "incorrect usage" error message and quit.
2. For each integer *i* in the range 1 through *argc* – 1:
   a. Get *inValue*, the `double` equivalent to argument *i*.
   b. If *inValue* > 0
      Display *inValue* and its square root.
   Else
      Display an "invalid data" error message.

Encoding this algorithm in C++ is straightforward, as shown in Figure 14.4.

Fig. 14.4 Encoding `sroot`. (Part 1 of 3)

```
/* sroot.cpp displays the square roots of a sequence of values,
 *     specified by the user on the command line.
 *
 *   Receive: One or more numeric (double) values
 *   Output:  The square roots of the input values
 *****************************************************************/

#include <iostream>                  // cin, cout, <<, >>
#include <cmath>                     // sqrt()
#include <cstdlib>                   // strtod()
using namespace std;
```

12. More accurately, the `strtod()` function is a legacy from C, the parent language of C++. An `istringstream` can also be used to perform the conversion.

Fig. 14.4 Encoding `sroot`. (Part 2 of 3)

```
int main(int argc, char* argv[])
{
   if (argc < 2)
   {
      cout << "\n*** Usage: sroot List-of-Positive-Numbers \n\n";
      return 1;
   }

   double inValue;                    // double equivalent of an argument

   for (int i = 1; i < argc; i++)
   {
      inValue = strtod(argv[i], 0);
      if (inValue >= 0)
         cout <<"\n--> The square root of " << inValue
              << " is " << sqrt(inValue) << endl;
      else
         cout << "\n*** " << argv[i] << " is not a valid data item;"
              << "\n*** must be numeric and positive.\n"
              << endl;
   }
}
```

Sample runs:

```
$ sroot

*** Usage: sroot List-of-Positive-Numbers

$ sroot 4

--> The square root of 4 is 2

$ sroot 4 ABC 7 9

--> The square root of 4 is 2

*** ABC is not a valid data item;
*** must be numeric and positive.
```

Fig. 14.4 Encoding `sroot`. (Part 3 of 3)

```
--> The square root of 7 is 2.64575

--> The square root of 9 is 3
```

COMMAND-LINE ARGUMENTS: FILES AND SWITCHES

To remove an object file `prog.o` created by compiling a C++ program on a Unix system, we might enter the command

```
$ rm prog.o
```

Here, the file to be removed, `prog.o`, is the argument to the command. It should be clear that the `rm` command can retrieve the name of this file using `argc` and `argv`.

To remove all such object files from the current directory, one can use the command

```
$ rm *.o
```

Because Unix shells treat the asterisk (`*`) as a **wild card** that matches any character string, the arguments to the `rm` command become all files of the form *`FileName`*`.o`. The `rm` command then removes all such files from the file system.

Using wild cards can be risky, because it is easy to remove files inadvertently. To reduce this risk, an alternative form of the `rm` command can be used:

```
$ rm -i *.o
```

Instead of blindly removing all files that end with `.o`, the command-line argument `-i` causes the `rm` command to (`i`nteractively) prompt the user for the removal of each file. For example, execution of this command might proceed as follows:

```
delete mystats.o? y
delete change.o? n
delete minmax.o? y
delete sroot.o? y
```

It should be clear that the `rm` command can use `argc` and `argv` to check for the presence of the `-i` argument and behave interactively if it is present, but noninteractively if it is absent.

Command-line arguments like `-i` that alter the behavior of a program are called **switches** and are common in command-line operating systems such as Unix.

In summary, most command-line arguments fall into one of three categories:

1. *values* that the program processes;
2. *files* that the program reads from or writes to (see Chapter 9);
3. *switches* that in some way alter the behavior of the program.

The main function parameters `argc` and `argv` provide a mechanism whereby a program can retrieve such arguments.

Part of the Picture
Algorithm Efficiency

When we study the **time efficiency** of algorithms in computer science, we do not concern ourselves with real (wall-clock) time, because that varies with the language in which the algorithm is encoded, the quality of the code, the quality of the compiler, the speed of the computer on which the code is executed, and various other factors. Instead, we study the number of *steps* an algorithm takes as a function of the size of the problem it solves. For example, the following method for the summation problem uses a for loop that iterates n times:

```
long summation(long n)
{
   long result = 0;
   for (int count = 1; count <= n; count++)
      result += count;
   return result;
}
```

Because its for loop executes n times, we say that this version requires **linear time**, or **time proportional to** n, written **O(*n*),** to compute the sum of the first *n* positive integers. By contrast, here is another version that computes $1 + 2 + \ldots + n$ using the formula credited to Carl Friedrich Gauss, one of the greatest mathematicians of all time:

```
long summation(long n)
{
   return n * (n + 1) / 2;
}
```

As noted in the *Part of the Picture* section of Chapter 7, because this second version computes the sum in 3 steps (1 addition, 1 multiplication, and 1 division) regardless of the value of n, we say that it does so in **constant time**, or **time proportional to 1**, expressed as **O(1).** Since it solves the same problem more quickly, this second method is *more time efficient* than the first.

Time efficiency is a major consideration in deciding between a vector<T> and a list<T> to store a sequence to solve a given problem, because different containers have different time efficiencies for the same operation. For example, appending a value to the end of either kind of container takes negligible time. This means that if a problem involves the manipulation of a sequence, but appending (or removing from the end) is the only sequence operation needed to solve the problem, then it makes no difference whether you store the sequence in a vector<T> or a list<T>. The push_back() method of each requires O(1) time.

By contrast, it is far more time consuming to access the middle value in a list<T> than in a vector<T> or array. For arrays and vector<T>s, the operation *v[i]* can access the value at index *i* in *constant* (i.e., O(1)) time, because the element at index *i* is (*i* × the size of one element) past the beginning of the array or vector, which allows the element's address to be computed in constant time. For a list<T>, there is no subscript operation, so finding the value at index *i* requires a list traversal, beginning at the head node and following *i* successive links to reach the appropriate node. If every index *i* is equally likely to be accessed, we will on average have to follow *n/2* links, making this a *linear* (i.e., O(*n*)) time operation. This implies that if a problem involves the manipulation of a sequence and involves a large number of accesses to values other than the first or last value in the sequence, then an array or a vector<T> should be chosen to store the sequence, because those accesses will be much faster using a list<T>.

Fig. 14.5 The `Bird` parent class. (Part 2 of 2)

```
inline string Bird::getKind() const { return myKind; }

#endif
```

As described in Section 12.5, the `= 0` at the end of the `virtual` methods makes `Bird` an **abstract class**, which means that no instances of class `Bird` can be created. This is as it should be, because in our design, only instances of subclasses like `Chicken`, `Duck`, and so on know how to respond to the `getCall()` message.

We next build the `FlyingBird` subclass of `Bird`. It defines the `getMovement()` method, as shown in Figure 14.6. However, because it does not define `getCall()`, which was declared pure `virtual` in class `Bird`, the compiler automatically classifies class `FlyingBird` as an abstract class too, and any attempt to create an instance of it will produce an error.

Fig. 14.6 The `FlyingBird` intermediate class.

```
/* FlyingBird.h declares class FlyingBird, a subclass of Bird. */

#ifndef FLYING_BIRD
#define FLYING_BIRD

#include "Bird.h"

class FlyingBird : public Bird
{
 public:
   FlyingBird(const string& kind);

   virtual string getMovement() const;
};

inline FlyingBird::FlyingBird(const string& kind) : Bird(kind) {}

inline string FlyingBird::getMovement() const { return "flew"; }

#endif
```

Note that the `FlyingBird` constructor has a parameter for the *kind* attribute, which it passes along to the `Bird` constructor. With no attribute variables, there remains nothing else for the constructor to do. Note also that `FlyingBird` does not store the *movement* attribute in an instance variable: It simply provides a definition of `getMovement()` that returns the appropriate string literal. (We use the *movement*'s past tense for the purposes of our simulation.)

The declaration of class WalkingBird is similar to that of FlyingBird, as shown in Figure 14.7.

Fig. 14.7 The WalkingBird intermediate class.

```
/* WalkingBird.h declares class WalkingBird, a subclass of Bird. */

#ifndef WALKING_BIRD
#define WALKING_BIRD

#include "Bird.h"

class WalkingBird : public Bird
{
 public:
   WalkingBird(const string& kind);

   virtual string getMovement() const;
};

inline WalkingBird::WalkingBird(const string& kind) : Bird(kind) {}

inline string WalkingBird::getMovement() const { return "walked"; }

#endif
```

We next move down our hierarchy to the Hawk class, which is one of the simplest of the bottom-level classes, as shown in Figure 14.8:

Fig. 14.8 The Hawk "bottom-level" class. (Part 1 of 2)

```
/* Hawk.h declares class Hawk, a subclass of FlyingBird. */

#ifndef HAWK
#define HAWK

#include "FlyingBird.h"

class Hawk : public FlyingBird
{
 public:
   Hawk();

   virtual string getCall() const;
};
```

Fig. 14.8 The `Hawk` "bottom-level" class. (Part 2 of 2)

```
inline Hawk::Hawk() : FlyingBird("hawk") {}

inline string Hawk::getCall() const { return "kir-reeeee"; }

#endif
```

The `Hawk` constructor simply passes its kind along to its superclass (`FlyingBird`) constructor (which in turn passes it along to the `Bird` constructor). Since the `Hawk` class "knows" its call, it provides the definition for the `getCall()` method. Because `Hawk` defines `getCall()` and inherits a definition of `getMovement()`, all of the pure virtual methods have definitions, so the compiler can create instances of class `Hawk`.

Most of the other bottom-level class declarations are similar. Figure 14.9 shows a declaration of one of them—the class `Chicken`.

Fig. 14.9 The `Chicken` "bottom-level" class.

```
/* Chicken.h declares class Chicken, a subclass of WalkingBird. */

#ifndef CHICKEN
#define CHICKEN

#include "WalkingBird.h"

class Chicken : public WalkingBird
{
 public:
   Chicken();

   virtual string getCall() const;
};

inline Chicken::Chicken() : WalkingBird("chicken") {}

inline string Chicken::getCall() const { return "cluck-cluck"; }

#endif
```

The only bottom-level class that differs slightly from the others is the `Duck` class, because a `Duck` may either fly or waddle. As a result, the `Duck` class overrides the definition of `getMovement()` inherited from class `FlyingBird` with a new definition that selects randomly the inherited "flew" movement or the "waddled" movement. To elicit this random behavior, we use the RandomInt class from Chapter 5, as shown in Figure 14.10. The remaining bottom-level classes are similar and are left as exercises.

Fig. 14.10 The Duck "bottom-level" class.

```
/* Duck.h declares class Duck, a subclass of FlyingBird. */

#ifndef DUCK
#define DUCK

#include "FlyingBird.h"

class Duck : public FlyingBird
{
 public:
   Duck();

   virtual string getCall() const;
};

inline Duck::Duck() : FlyingBird("duck") {}

inline string Duck::getCall() const { return "quack-quack"; }

inline string Duck::getMovement() const
{
   RandomInt coin(0, 1);
   return (coin == 0) ? FlyingBird::getMovement() : string("waddled");
}

#endif
```

Once we have our class hierarchy implemented, we are ready to write the program to simulate the aviary. The basic idea is to do the following:

1. Define a vector of seven Bird* handles.
2. Using new, initialize each element of the vector to a dynamically allocated instance of a different bottom-level class.
3. Loop:
   a. Generate a random integer within the range of vector indices.
   b. Use that integer to index into the vector.
   c. Display the result of sending that vector element the getKind(), getMovement(), and getCall() messages.

   End loop.

4. Use `delete` to deallocate the bottom-level class instances.

The implementation of this algorithm can be seen in Figure 14.11.

Fig. 14.11 The aviary simulation. (Part 1 of 2)

```
/* aviary.cpp simulates sitting in an aviary. */

#include "Chicken.h"
#include "Duck.h"
#include "GreenParrot.h"
#include "Hawk.h"
#include "Jabberwock.h"
#include "Peacock.h"
#include "RedParrot.h"
#include "RandomInt.h"
#include <iostream>
#include <vector>
using namespace std;

int main()
{
   const int NUMBER_OF_BIRDS = 7;

   vector<Bird*> birdVec(NUMBER_OF_BIRDS);

   birdVec[0] = new Chicken();
   birdVec[1] = new Duck()
   birdVec[2] = new GreenParrot();
   birdVec[3] = new Hawk();
   birdVec[4] = new Jabberwock();
   birdVec[5] = new Peacock();
   birdVec[6] = new RedParrot();

   cout << "\nWelcome to the Bird Aviary!\n"
        << "\nTo remain in the aviary, keep pressing 'Enter';\n"
        << " enter any other character to leave:\n\n";
   int i;
   Bird* aBird;
   char response;
   RandomInt d7(0, NUMBER_OF_BIRDS-1);
```

Fig. 14.11 The aviary simulation. (Part 2 of 2)

```
   for (;;)
   {
      cin.get(response);

      if (response != '\n') break;

      i = d7.generate();
      aBird = birdVec[i];
      cout << "A " << aBird->getKind()
           << " just " << aBird->getMovement()
           << " by, calling \"" << aBird->getCall()
           << "\"...\n" << endl;
   }

   for (i = 0; i < NUMBER_OF_BIRDS; i++)
      delete birdVec[i];

   cout << "\nGood-bye, and come again!" << endl;
}
```

It is worth noting that we defined the handle aBird solely for readability. We could have instead omitted aBird, and then written the output statement as

```
cout << "A " << birdVec[i]->getKind()
     << " just " << birdVec[i]->getMovement()
     << " by, calling \"" << birdVec[i]->getCall()
     << "\"...\n" << endl;
```

This works because birdVec is a vector of Bird* handles that we might picture as follows:

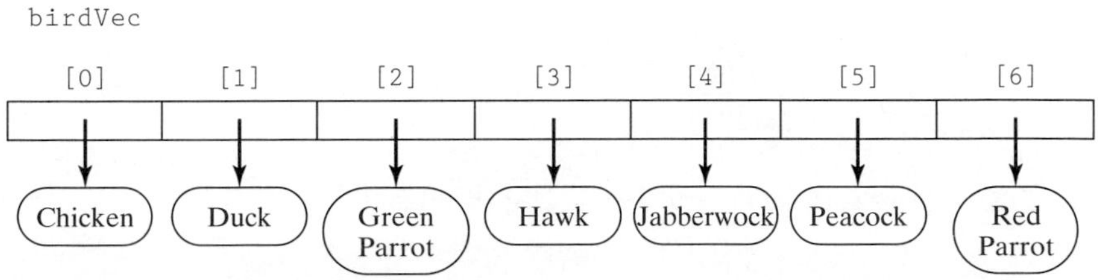

If the randomly generated integer in variable i is 3, then the statement

```
aBird = birdVec[i];
```

simply makes `aBird` and `birdVec[3]` both handles for the same object,

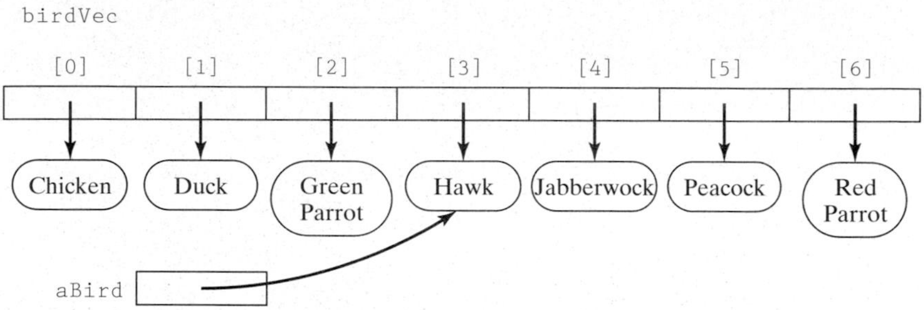

so we can send messages to that object by using either `birdVec[i]` or `aBird` as its handle.

Figure 14.12 shows a sample run of the program, using the symbol ↵ to represent the ENTER or RETURN character. Note that the duck randomly flies by or waddles by, as specified by the `Duck::getMovement()` method.

Fig. 14.12 An aviary sample run. (Part 1 of 2)

Sample Run:

```
Welcome to the Bird Aviary!

To remain in the aviary, keep pressing 'Enter';
 enter any other character to leave:

↵
A jabberwock just whiffled by, calling "burble-burble"...

↵
A hawk just flew by, calling "kir-reeeee"...

↵
A red parrot just flew by, calling "squawwwwwwwwwk"...

↵
A duck just waddled by, calling "quack-quack"...

↵
A chicken just walked by, calling "cluck-cluck"...
↵
```

Fig. 14.12 An aviary sample run. (Part 2 of 2)

```
A duck just flew by, calling "quack-quack"...

q↵

Goodbye, and come again!
```

Pointers and run-time allocation thus provide two benefits: (i) They allow a programmer to define *containers* whose sizes can grow (and possibly shrink) during program execution. (ii) They allow a programmer to define *handles* by which polymorphic messages can be sent to objects.

With the Standard Template Library providing a broad assortment of containers that can be used in an "off-the-shelf" manner, it might seem as though beginning programmers no longer need to master programming with pointers. This is not the case, however, because of the need to use pointers as handles to objects and because the situation sometimes arises where a container is needed that STL does not provide. We will see an example of such a situation at the beginning of the next chapter.

Exercises 14.6

1. Write declarations for the following:
   a) A class *License* with a person's name, age, and id number as attributes; a constructor method that initializes the instance variables; and an output method.
   b) A subclass *HuntingLicense* with the name of the prey as a new attribute; a constructor method that initializes the instance variables; an accessor for this new attribute; and an output method that overrides that in the *License* class.
2. Write a declaration for a subclass *DeerHuntingLicense* of the *HuntingLicense* class in Exercise 2 with a new attribute that indicates whether hunting does is permitted, a constructor method that initializes the instance variables, an accessor and a mutator for this new attribute, and an output method that overrides that in the *HuntingLicense* class.
3. Write declarations for the following:
   a) A class *BankAccount* with a customer's name, account number, and account balance as attributes; a constructor method that initializes the instance variables; and a method that displays the account number and the current balance.
   b) A subclass *CheckingAccount* with service charge as a new attribute; a constructor method that initializes the instance variables; a deposit method; and a withdrawal method.
   c) A subclass *Loan* with interest rate as a new attribute; a constructor method; a make-payment method; and an add-interest method.
4. Write a declaration for a subclass *StudentLoan* that is a subclass of the *Loan* class in Exercise 3 with the loan term (number of years to pay it off) and monthly payment as new attributes; a constructor method that initializes the instance variables; and a method that returns the number of payments remaining.

CHAPTER SUMMARY

Key Terms & Notes

abstract class
address-of operator (&)
alias
aliasing problem
anonymous variable
assignment operator
asterisk operator (*)
base address
bound
circular doubly-linked list with a head node
circular linked list
class pointer selector operator (->)
command-line argument
command-line environment
compile-time allocation
constant time
copy constructor
deep copy
default copy constructor
`delete` operation
dereference
destructor
dotted-decimal notation
doubly-linked list
free store
gateway
handle
head node
heap
indirection operator
Internet Protocol (IP)
IP address
iterator
linear time
linked list
memory leak
`new` operation
node
null address
null pointer value
O(1)
O(n)
pointer
pointer variable
polymorphism
pure virtual method
reference
run-time allocation
shallow copy
singly-linked list
`sizeof` operator
struct
TCP/IP
time efficiency
Transmission Control Protocol (TCP)
traversing
virtual method
wild card

- In a declaration, an asterisk operator * must precede each identifier that is to serve as a pointer.
- 0 can be assigned to any pointer variable; 0 is called the *null pointer* value for that type and is also often called the *null address*.
- An address assigned to a pointer variable must be the address of an object whose type is the same as the type to which the pointer is bound in its declaration.
- The term *reference* is another term for *address*, so applying the indirection operator (*) to a pointer variable is called *dereferencing* that pointer.

- The value of a pointer variable `ptr` is simply the address stored within `ptr`; the expression `*ptr` uses the address stored in the pointer to access (indirectly) the contents of the memory location at that address.
- Pointers can be assigned the values of other pointers that are *bound to the same type*. The null address may be assigned to any pointer.
- The relational operators == and != can be used to compare two pointers that are *bound to the same type*. The null address may be compared with any pointer.
- An expression of the form `new` *`Type`* issues a run-time request for a block of memory large enough to store an object of the specified *`Type`*. If the request can be granted, `new` returns the address of the block of memory; otherwise, it returns the null address (0).
- An anonymous variable can be accessed indirectly by dereferencing a pointer to it.
- Unlike arrays whose memory is allocated at compile time, arrays whose memory is allocated at run time can be tailored to the size of the sequence to be stored in them.
- If `ptr` points to the base address of an array, then `ptr[i]` can be used to access the element at location `i` and is equivalent to writing `*(ptr + i)`.
- If a class has no copy constructor, the compiler supplies a default version that simply copies the members of an object byte by byte. This works fine except when the object being copied contains an instance variable that is a pointer; it makes a copy of the address stored in the pointer, but not a copy of the object to which it points.
- The parameter of a copy constructor must be a reference parameter (and should be a `const` reference parameter) to avoid infinite recursive calls to the copy constructor itself to make a copy of the (value) parameter.
- For objects that use run-time allocated memory, a class destructor should be provided to reclaim this memory.
- If a class has no assignment operator, the compiler supplies a default version that simply copies the members of an object byte by byte. This has the same problem as the default copy constructor for objects with instance variables that are pointers.
- If a class allocates memory at run time using `new`, then it should provide
  - a copy constructor that the compiler can use to make distinct copies;
  - an assignment operator that a programmer can use to make distinct copies;
  - a destructor that releases the run-time allocated memory to the free store, thus avoiding memory leaks.
- Singly-linked lists consist of a series of nodes, each of which has a data part and a pointer to the next node. A node in a doubly-linked list also has a pointer to the preceding node.
- Items can be inserted in and removed from linked lists more efficiently than for arrays and vectors.
- Values can be passed to the `main()` function in a program via the `argc` (argument count) and `argv` (argument vector) parameters.
- No instances of an abstract class can be created.
- Two important uses of pointers and run-time allocation are to define
  - containers that can grow (and possibly shrink) during program execution;
  - handles by which polymorphic messages can be sent to objects.

Programming Pointers

Program Style and Design

Pointers permit the implementation of flexible data structures like vector<T> and list<T> from the Standard Template Library. When using such objects, we must select the data structure that best fits the problem to be solved. More precisely, if one is storing a sequence of values and the problem requires access to arbitrary values within the sequence, then a vector<T> is an appropriate container for storing the sequence. However, if one is storing a sequence and the problem requires many insertions and deletions anywhere except at the end of the sequence, then a list<T> provides an efficient means of storing and manipulating such a sequence.

The pointers used to implement list<T> and vector<T> have memory addresses as values. Consequently, the manner in which pointer variables are used is quite different from that in which other kinds of variables are processed, and this can cause special difficulties for both beginning and experienced programmers. Pointers are used to store the addresses of objects whose memory is allocated at run time. Consequently, operations on such objects that

- create the object require that its memory be explicitly allocated using new;
- destroy the object require that its memory be explicitly deallocated using delete;
- modify the size of the object require that its old memory be deallocated and then new memory of the correct size be reallocated.

When designing classes that have pointer instance variables, *always* define a **copy constructor**, the **assignment operator**, and a **destructor**.

WATCH OUT

Potential Pitfalls

The operations used to process pointers are quite different from those used to process objects whose memory is allocated at compile time. Some of the main features to remember when using pointer variables and run-time allocation in C++ programs are as follows:

1. *Use the* typedef *mechanism and descriptive identifiers to declare pointer types.* This increases the readability of programs, which reduces the likelihood of errors and makes errors easier to find when they do occur.
2. *Each pointer variable is bound to a fixed type; a pointer is the address of a memory location in which only a value of that type can be stored.* For example, if pPtr and qPtr are pointer variables declared by

```
int* pPtr;
double* qPtr;
```

then pPtr is bound to the type int and qPtr to the type double. Memory locations pointed to by pPtr can store only int values, whereas those to which qPtr points can store only double values.

3. *Care must be used when operating on pointers because they have memory addresses as values.*
   - *A pointer* `ptr` *can be assigned a value in the following ways:*

     `ptr = &obj;` (where `obj` is an object of the type to which `ptr` points)

     `ptr = 0;` (the null address)

     `ptr = anotherPtr;` (where `anotherPtr` is a pointer bound to the same type as `ptr`)

     `ptr = new Type;` (where *Type* is the type to which `ptr` points)

   - *Arithmetic operations on pointers are restricted.* For example, pointer values (memory addresses) cannot be added, subtracted, multiplied, or divided. However, an integer value `i` can be added to or subtracted from the value of a pointer variable, which changes the address in the pointer by `i * sizeof(Type)`, where *Type* is the type to which the pointer is bound.
   - *Relational operators can be used to compare pointers, but the two pointers must be bound to the same type, or one or both may be the null address.*
   - *Pointers may be used as parameters, but corresponding parameters and arguments must be bound to the same type.* A function may also return a pointer as its return value, but the type to which that pointer is bound must be the same as the type to which the function is declared to point.
4. *Do not confuse memory locations with the contents of memory locations.* If `ptr` is a pointer, its value is the address of a memory location; `*ptr` refers to the contents of that location. Both `ptr++` and `(*ptr)++` are valid (if `ptr` is bound to a type for which ++ is defined), but the first increments the address in `ptr`, while the second increments the contents of the memory location at that address.
5. *The null address ≠ undefined.* A pointer becomes defined when it is assigned the address of a memory location or the null address. Assigning a pointer the null address is analogous to initializing a numeric variable to zero.
6. *If the value of a pointer* `ptr` *is undefined or the null address, then an attempt to dereference* `ptr` *is an error.* Doing so may produce cryptic run-time error messages.
7. *When memory is allocated at run time with the* `new` *operation, the value returned by* `new` *should be tested before proceeding, to ensure that the operation was successful.* The `assert()` mechanism provides a convenient way to do this. For example, if `ptr` is a pointer in which we are storing the address of a newly allocated block of memory,

   ```
   ptr = new SomeType;
   ```

   then the assertion

   ```
   assert(ptr != 0);
   ```

   can be used to verify that the `new` operation returned a valid (non-null) address.
8. *Memory locations that were once associated with a pointer variable and that are no longer needed should be returned to the free store by using the delete function.* Special care is required so that memory locations are not rendered inaccessible. For example, if `pPtr` and `qPtr` are pointer variables bound to the same type, the assignment statement

   ```
   pPtr = qPtr ;
   ```

   causes `pPtr` to point to the same memory location as that pointed to by `qPtr`. If the program should execute

   ```
   delete qPtr;
   ```

then the memory previously pointed to by `qPtr` is deallocated, leaving an invalid address in `pPtr`, so that any attempt to dereference `pPtr` (i.e., `*pPtr`) will usually generate a run-time error. This difficulty occurs so frequently, it has a special name—the **dangling pointer problem.**

9. *Never rely upon the default copy constructor or assignment operator for a class containing a pointer instance variable.* When a class contains a pointer instance variable, these default operations will not make distinct copies of an object. The **aliasing problem** can result, since changes to a copy of an object can inadvertently change the original object, producing a difficult-to-find logical error.

Programming Problems

Sections 14.3 & 14.4

1. Write a driver program to test the `print()` method of Exercise 8.
2. Write a driver program to test the output operator of Exercise 9.
3. Write a driver program to test the `search()` method of Exercise 10.
4. Write a driver program to test the `insert()` methods of Exercises 11 and 12.
5. Write a driver program to test the `delete()` methods of Exercises 13 and 14.
6. Complete the `LinkedList` class template by adding to the methods in Problems 1–5. Basic operations should include a constructor, a destructor, a copy constructor, assignment, and the basic list operations: empty, output, insert, delete, and search.
7. Write a driver program to test the average method of Exercise 15.
8. Write a driver program to test the ascending-order method of Exercise 16.
9. Write a driver program to test the list-reversal method of Exercise 17.
10. Design and implement a class `BigInt` whose values are large integers with perhaps hundreds of digits. Overload the addition operator to add two large integers. Treat each number as a list, each of whose elements is a block of digits of the number. Add the intcgers (lists) element by element, carrying from one element to the next when necessary.
11. Proceed as in Problem 10, but add a subtraction operator. Write a two-function `BigInt` calculator program to test your class.
12. Extend class `BigInt` from Problem 11 by overloading the multiplication operator.
13. Extend class `BigInt` from Problem 12 by overloading the division operator (more challenging).
14. A limited number of tickets for the Hoops championship basketball game go on sale tomorrow, and ticket orders are to be filled in the order in which they are received. Write a program that a box-office cashier can use to enter the names and addresses of the persons ordering tickets together with the number of tickets requested and stores this information in a list. The program should then produce a sequence of mailing labels (names, addresses, and number of tickets) for orders that can be filled. Check that no one receives more than four tickets and that multiple requests from the same person are disallowed.
15. A *polynomial of degree n* has the form

$$a_0 + a_1x + a_2x^2 + \ldots + a_nx^n$$

where $a_0, a_1, \ldots, a_n$ are numeric constants called the *coefficients* of the polynomial and $a_n \neq 0$. For example,

$$1 + 3x - 7x^3 + 5x^4$$

is a polynomial of degree 4 with integer coefficients 1, 3, 0, –7, and 5. Design and implement a `Polynomial` class that can represent any such polynomial. Store only the nonzero coefficients and the corresponding exponents in a list. Provide input and output operators, displaying polynomials in the usual mathematical format with x^n written as $x \uparrow n$ or x ^ n. Use your class in a program that reads a polynomial and then reads values for x and evaluates the polynomial for each value.

16. Extend the class `Polynomial` in Problem 15 to add two polynomials.

17. Extend the class `Polynomial` in Problems 15 and 16 to multiply two polynomials.

18. In an ordered list, all operations that modify the list are designed to ensure that its elements remain in ascending order. Build an `OrderedList` class template derived from class `list<T>` that exhibits this characteristic.

19. Write a "quiz-tutor" program, perhaps on a topic from one of the early chapters or some other topic about which you are knowledgeable. The program should read a question and its answer from a file, display the question, and accept an answer from the user. If the answer is correct, the program should go on to the next question. If it is not correct, store the question in a list. When the file of questions is exhausted, the questions that were missed should be displayed again (in their original order). Keep a count of the correct answers and display the final count. Also, display the correct answer when necessary in the second round of questioning.

20. Suppose that jobs entering a computer system are assigned a job number and a priority from 0 through 9. The numbers of jobs awaiting execution by the system are kept in a *priority queue*. A job entered into this queue is placed ahead of all jobs of lower priority, but after all those of equal or higher priority. Write a program to read one of the letters `R` (remove), `A` (add), or `L` (list). For `R`, read a job number and remove it from the priority queue; for `A`, read a job number and priority, and then add it to the priority queue in the manner just described; and for `L`, list all the job numbers in the queue.

21. Write a program to read the records from the file `Student` (see the file descriptions at the end of Chapter 9), and construct five linked lists of records containing a student's name, number, and cumulative GPA, one list for each class. Store these records in a `vector` of `list<T>s`. After the lists have been constructed, sort each list, and then print each of them with appropriate headings. *Note:* If `aList` is a `list<T>` object, then `alist.sort();` will sort `aList` provided `<` is defined for type `T` objects. In this exercise, you must overload `operator<()` to define what it means for one student record to be less than another.

22. The number of elements in a list may grow so large that finding a value in the list cannot be done efficiently. One way to improve performance is to maintain several smaller linked lists. Write a program to read several lines of uppercase text and to produce a text concordance, which is a list of all distinct words in the text. Store distinct words beginning with `A` in one linked list, those beginning with `B` in another, and so on. After all the text lines have been read, sort each list (see Problem 21), and then print a list of all these words in alphabetical order.

23. Modify the program of Problem 22 so that the concordance also includes the frequency with which each word occurs in the text.

24. In addition to the words in a section of text, a concordance usually stores the numbers of selected pages on which there is a significant use of the word. Modify the program of Problem 22 so that the numbers of all lines in which a word appears are stored along with the word itself. The program should display each word together with its associated line numbers in ascending order.

Section 14.5

25. Write a program `binary` so that the command

    `binary` *DecimalValue*

    will calculate and display the binary representation of *DecimalValue*.

26. The *median* of a list of *n* numbers is a value such that *n*/2 of the values are greater than that value, and *n*/2 of the values are less than that value. The usual procedure to find the median is to sort the list and then pick the middle number as the median if the list has an odd number of elements, or the average of the two middle numbers if the number of elements is even. Write a program to find the median of a list, so that the command

    ```
    median FileName
    ```

    will calculate and display the median of the values in file *`FileName`*, but the command

    ```
    median
    ```

    will calculate and display the median of a list of numbers entered from the keyboard.

27. Write a program so that the following command will make a copy of *`File1`* with the name *`File2`*:

    ```
    copy File1 File2
    ```

28. Write a program so that the following command will display the specified file on the screen, one page (23 lines) at a time, waiting between pages until the user presses some key:

    ```
    page File
    ```

Section 14.6

29. Write a program to test the license classes and subclasses in Exercises 1 and 2.

30. Add subclasses for the following kinds of licenses to the license class hierarchy of Problem 29, and extend the program to test them: chauffeur's license, pet license, duck-hunting license, fishing license, deer-hunting license, dog license, and marriage license.

31. Write a program to test the bank-account classes and subclasses in Exercises 3 and 4.

32. Add subclasses for the following kinds of accounts to the bank-account class hierarchy of Problem 31 and extend the program to test them: savings account, student loan, free checking account, money-market savings account, home equity loan, and graduate-school student loan.

33. A company has two payroll categories: managers and programmers are paid a monthly salary, while secretaries and consultants are paid on an hourly basis. Design and test a class hierarchy to represent the company's employees who are managers or programmers. Then write a program to generate the monthly paychecks for these employees.

34. Add a `Secretary` class to the employee hierarchy of Problem 33. Use a program like the payroll generator to test your class.

35. Add a `Consultant` class to the employee hierarchy of Problem 33. Use a program like the payroll generator to test your class.

36. Add a class to the employee hierarchy of Problem 33 for a new category of employees who are paid on a contract basis. Each such employee is paid a specified amount for a certain task performed. For example, reviewers check documentation, advertising materials, and so on and are paid a specified amount for each document.

37. Add a class to the employee hierarchy of Problem 33 for reviewers as described in Problem 36.

38. Following the example of the bird hierarchy in this section, redesign the rock class from Section 12.4 as a class hierarchy with a rock class at the top, subclasses for igneous, metamorphic,

and sedimentary rocks and bottom-level classes for basalt, granite, obsidian, marble, quartzite, slate, dolomite, limestone, sandstone, and shale.

39. Find information about the following rocks and add appropriate classes to the rock hierarchy of Problem 38 to model them: (a) pea; (b) soapstone; (c) pumice.
40. Design, build, and test a class hierarchy to represent geometric figures including circles, triangles, squares, rectangles, polygons, and hexagons.
41. Design, build, and test a class hierarchy to represent animals including bulldogs, Chihuahuas, Collies, Miniature Collies, horses, cats, reptiles, dogs, snakes, lizards, canines, and mammals.

CHAPTER 15

Data Structures

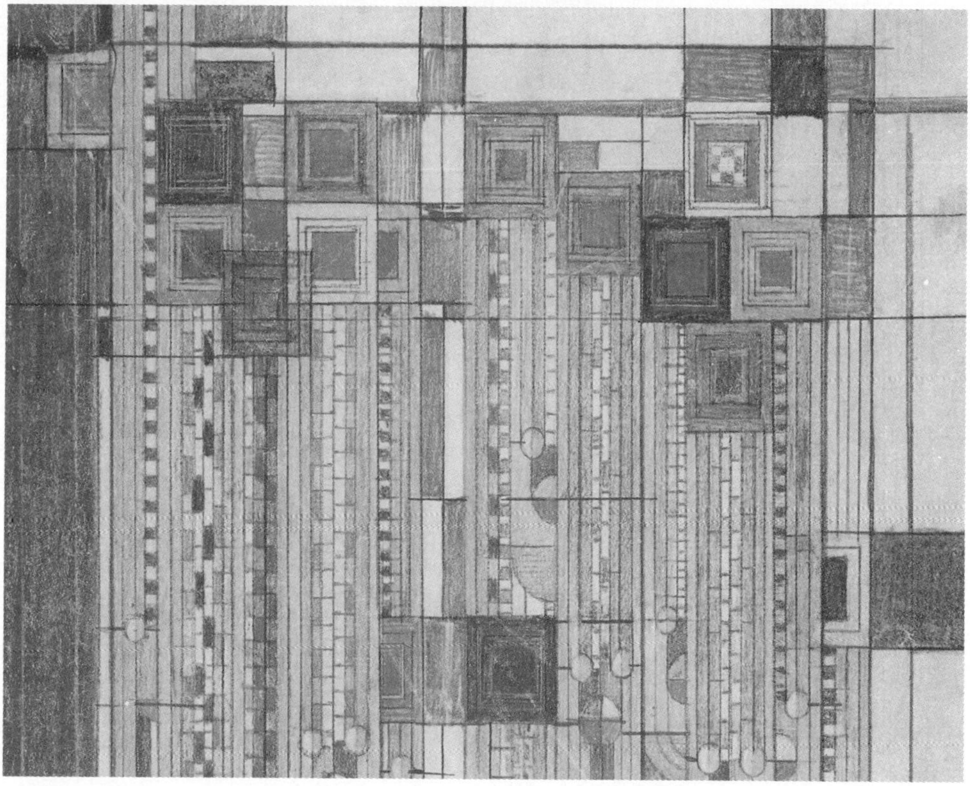

I've got a little list, I've got a little list.

-Gilbert and Sullivan, The Mikado

I think that I shall never see,
A poem lovely as a tree.

-Joyce Kilmer

Woodman, spare that tree!

-George Pope Morris

Chapter Contents

Chapter Objectives

- Examine some of the containers/data structures provided in C++ for storing collections of data.
- Study the important data structures stack and queue.
- Take another look at recursion and what stacks have to do with it.
- Learn about two-dimensional linked structures—binary trees.
- (Optional) Take a peek at expert systems in AI.

In previous chapters, we have seen that C++ provides several mechanisms for storing collections of values. These include

- C-style array (has a fixed capacity);
- `vector<T>` (can grow and is best used when insertions or deletions occur only at the end of the sequence);
- Linked lists (can grow or shrink; insertions and deletions may occur anywhere).

In this chapter, we examine some of the other structures that C++ provides for storing collections of data, which are known as **containers** or **data structures**.

15.1 Introductory Example: The Binary Representation of Integers—Stacks

In this section, we study a problem that can be conveniently solved using a specialized structure called the **stack**. We will begin with the problem, then examine the stack and how it can be used to solve the problem.

PROBLEM: DISPLAYING A NUMBER'S BINARY REPRESENTATION

Data values are stored in computer memory using a binary representation. In particular, positive integers are commonly stored using the base-two representation described in the *Part of the Picture: Data Representation* section of Chapter 2. This means that the base-ten representation of an integer that appears in a program or in a data file must be converted to a base-two representation. One algorithm for carrying out this conversion uses repeated division by 2, with the successive remainders giving the binary digits in the base-two representation from right to left. For example, the following computation shows that the base-two representation of 26 is 11010:

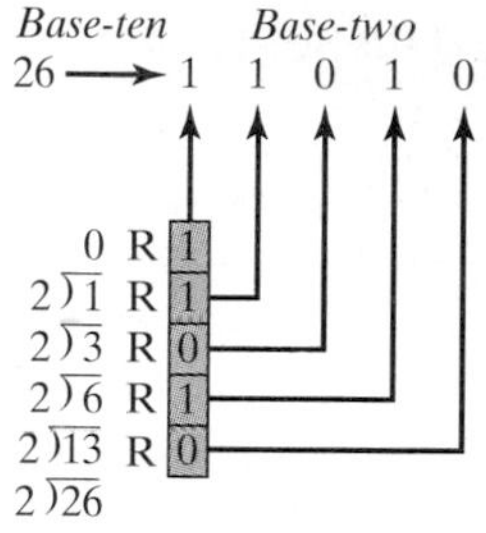

We can generalize this approach to determine the base-*b* representation for any value of *b* between 2 and 36 inclusive, simply by dividing by *b* instead of 2 and using the symbols a, b,..., z as base-*b* digits (in addition to 0–9) when $b > 10$. For example, the base-eight representation of 95 is 137_8 and the base-sixteen representation of 95 is $5f_{16}$, which we can compute as follows:

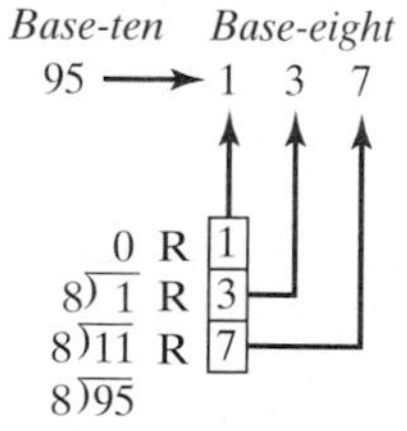

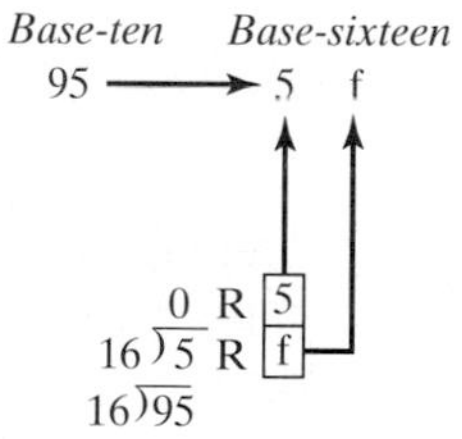

(The base-sixteen digits for ten, eleven, twelve, thirteen, fourteen, and fifteen are a, b, c, d, e, and f, respectively.) Our problem is to write a method that will output the base-*b* representation of a given base-ten number.

One of the difficulties in this problem is that the order in which remainders are generated is the opposite of the order in which they must be output. For example, in determining the binary representation of 26, the *first* remainder,

$$26 \% 2 = 0$$

is the *last* binary digit that we must display. Similarly, the *second* remainder we compute,

$$13 \% 2 = 1$$

produces the *next-to-the-last* binary digit that we must display. This pattern continues until we generate the final remainder,

$$1 \% 2 = 1$$

which produces the first binary digit that we must display.

THE STACK CONTAINER

The preceding diagrams suggest one approach to solving this problem. What is needed is a special kind of list to store the remainders—a container where the delete operation always removes the value that was most recently inserted to the list. The values in such a list must, therefore, be maintained in **Last-In-First-Out (LIFO)** order; that is, the last item inserted is the first item to be removed. Such a list is called a **stack** (or a **push-down stack**) because it functions in the same manner as a spring-loaded stack of plates or trays used in a cafeteria:

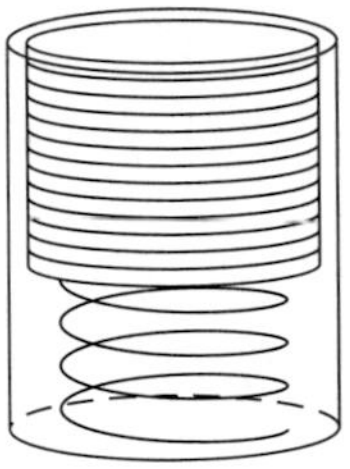

Plates are added to the stack by *pushing* them onto the top of the stack. When a plate is removed from the top of the stack, the spring causes the next plate to *pop* up. For this reason, the operations to insert a value into and delete a value from a stack are commonly called **push** and **pop**, respectively.[1] The most recently added value is called the **top** value. If the stack contains no plates, then it is described as **empty**. These properties of a stack in a cafeteria illustrate the four standard stack operations:

1. *empty*(): returns true if there are no values in the stack and false otherwise
2. *top*( ): returns a copy of the value at the top of the stack
3. *push*(*v*): adds a value *v* at the top of the stack

1. This is the source of the `push_back()` and `pop_back()` method names in `vector<T>` and `list<T>`.

4. *pop*( ): removes the value at the top of the stack

A stack can be used to solve the base-conversion problem. To display the base-*b* representation of an integer in the usual left-to-right sequence, we must "stack up" the remainders generated during the repeated division by *b* by pushing them onto a stack. When the division process terminates, we can retrieve the remainders from this stack in the required "last-in-first-out" order by popping them from the stack.

If we have a stack class available, we can use the following algorithm to convert from base-10 to base-*b* and display the result:

Base-Conversion Algorithm

/* This algorithm displays the representation of a base-10 number in any *base* from 2 through 36.

Receive: *number*, an int;
base, the base to which we want to convert *number*

Precondition: *number* > 0 and 2 ≤ *base* ≤ 36

Return: the base-*base* representation of *number*, as a `string`

*/

1. Create an empty stack to hold the remainders.
2. While *number* ≠ 0, do the following:
   a. Calculate the *remainder* that results when *number* is divided by *base*.
   b. Push *remainder* onto the stack of remainders.
   c. Replace *number* by the integer quotient of *number* divided by *base*.
3. Declare *result* as an empty `string`.
4. While the stack of remainders is not empty, do the following:
   a. Remove the *remainder* from the top of the stack of remainders.
   b. Convert *remainder* to its base-*base* equivalent.
   c. Concatenate the base-*base* equivalent of *remainder* to *result*.
5. Return *result*.

The diagram in Figure 15.1 traces this algorithm for the integer 26 and base 2. Figure 15.2 presents a program containing a `convertDecimal()` function that implements this algorithm.

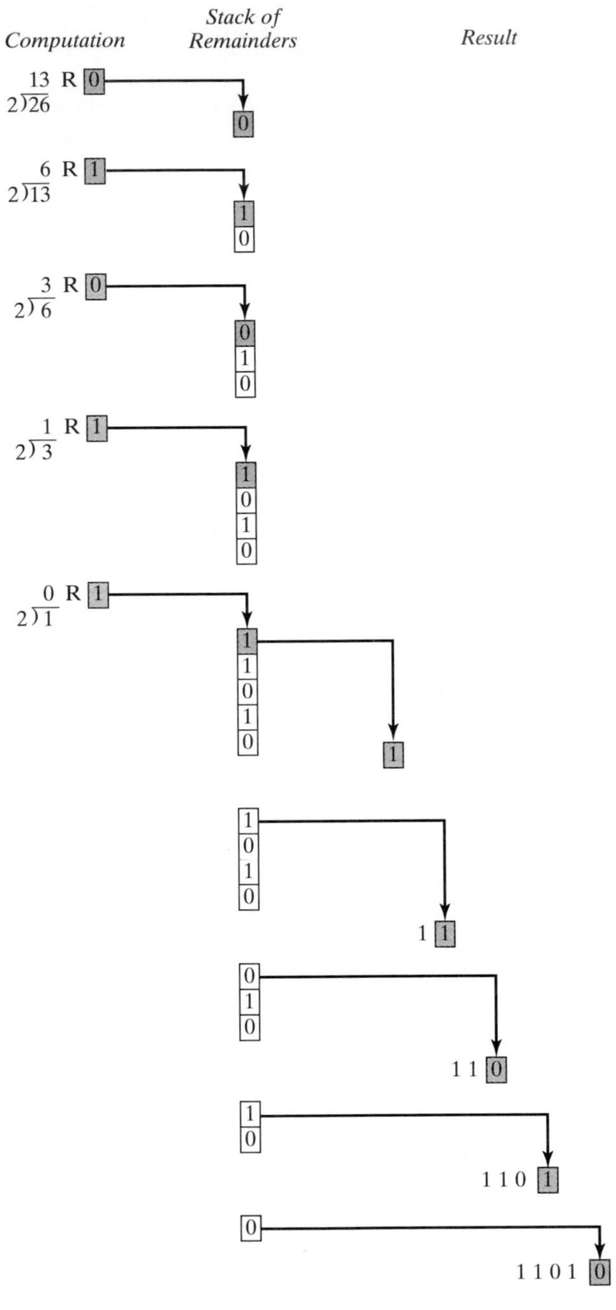

Fig. 15.1 Using a stack in base-two conversion.

Fig. 15.2 Converting decimal integers. (Part 1 of 3)

```
/* decimalConverter.cpp converts an int value to
 *   its representation in a different base.
 * Input:  number, a positive decimal integer
 *         base, the base to which it is to be converted
 * Output: the base representation of number
 */

#include <iostream>        // cin, cout, cerr, ...
#include <stack>           // stack<T>
using namespace std;

string convertDecimal(int number, int base);

int main()
{
   cout << "To convert a decimal integer to a different base,\n"
        << " enter a positive integer: ";
   int number;
   cin >> number;
   cout << " then enter the base to which it is to be converted: ";
   int base;
   cin >> base;

   cout << '\n' << convertDecimal(number, base)
        << " is the base-" << base
        << " representation of " << number << endl;
}

char baseDigit(int value);

/* convertDecimal() converts a decimal value to its base representation
 * Receive:      number, an int; and
 *               base, an int
 * Precondition: number is positive &&
 *               2 <= base && base <= 35
 * Return:       a string giving the base-base representation of number
 */
string convertDecimal(int number, int base)
{
   stack<int> intStack;
   int remainder;
```

Fig. 15.2 Converting decimal integers. (Part 2 of 3)

```
   do
   {
      remainder = number % base;
      intStack.push(remainder);
      number /= base;
    }
    while (number != 0);

   string resultString = "";
   char digitChar;
   while ( !intStack.empty() )
   {
      remainder = intStack.top();
      intStack.pop();
      digitChar = baseDigit(remainder);
      resultString += digitChar;
   }

   return resultString;
}

/* Table look-up routine for mapping 0-35 to 0-z
 * Receive:          value, an int.
 * Precondition:     0 <= value && value <= 35
 * Return:           the 0-z representation of value
 */

char baseDigit (int value)
{
   const int VALUES_SUPPORTED = 36;
   const char resultArray[VALUES_SUPPORTED] =
     { '0', '1', '2', '3', '4', '5', '6', '7', '8', '9',
       'a', 'b', 'c', 'd', 'e', 'f', 'g', 'h', 'i', 'j',
       'k', 'l', 'm', 'n', 'o', 'p', 'q', 'r', 's', 't',
       'u', 'v', 'w', 'x', 'y', 'z'};

   char result = '*';
   if (0 <= value && value < VALUES_SUPPORTED)
      result = resultArray[value];
   else
```

Fig. 15.2 Converting decimal integers. (Part 3 of 3)

```
      cerr << "\n** baseDigit(value): "
           << value << " outside of range 0.."
           << VALUES_SUPPORTED-1 << endl;

   return result;
}
```

Sample runs:

```
To convert a decimal integer to a different base,
 enter a positive integer: 32
 then enter the base to which it is to be converted: 2

100000 is the base-2 representation of 32

To convert a decimal integer to a different base,
 enter a positive integer: 32
 then enter the base to which it is to be converted: 8

40 is the base-8 representation of 32

To convert a decimal integer to a different base,
 enter a positive integer: 32
 then enter the base to which it is to be converted: 16

20 is the base-16 representation of 32


To convert a decimal integer to a different base,
 enter a positive integer: 255
 then enter the base to which it is to be converted: 16
ff is the base-16 representation of 255
```

The `convertDecimal()` function in this program relies heavily upon the C++ Standard Template Library's `stack<T>` container. We will now take a look at this container.

THE `stack<T>` ADAPTER

In the Standard Template Library, an **adapter** is a component that acts as a "wrapper" around another component, giving it a new interface. As we indicated previously, a stack is a specialized kind of container for storing sequences, and we have already seen that

STL provides containers such as `vector<T>` and `list<T>` for storing sequences. The designers of STL recognized that they could reuse the work they had invested in building these sequential containers if they built `stack<T>` as an adapter of one of them—`vector<T>`, `list<T>`, or `deque<T>` (described in Section 15.2).

To illustrate, the declaration of `intStack` in Figure 15.2,

```
stack<int> intStack;
```

uses the default constructor in `stack<T>` to create `intStack` and uses STL's default `stack<T>` implementation as an adapter of a `deque<T>`.[2] But if we want a `stack<T>` to be built using one of the other two containers, we can specify this in the declaration. For example,

```
stack<int, list<int> > intListStack;
```

declares `intListStack` as a `stack<T>` that is built using the `list<T>` template; and the declaration

```
stack<int, vector<int> > intVectorStack;
```

declares `intVectorStack` as a `stack<T>` that is built using the `vector<T>` template.

Each of these constructors builds a stack, but the underlying implementations are different. The object `intListStack` will be implemented using STL's *linked list* (and thus use memory fairly efficiently, but provide slightly slower versions of `push()` and `pop()`):

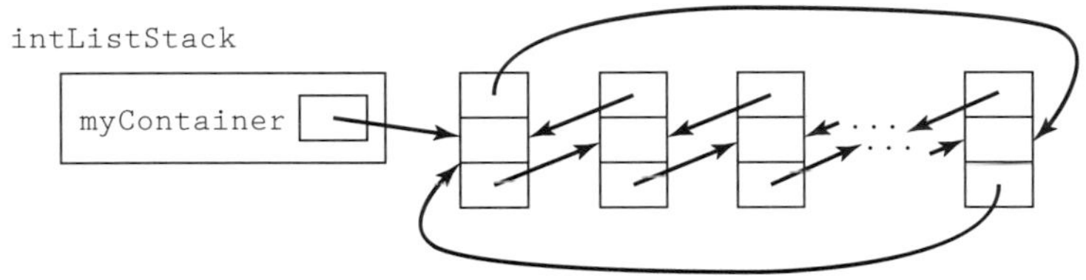

The object `intVectorStack` will be implemented using STL's *vector* (and thus on average probably provide the fastest versions of `push()` and `pop()`, while possibly using more memory than necessary):

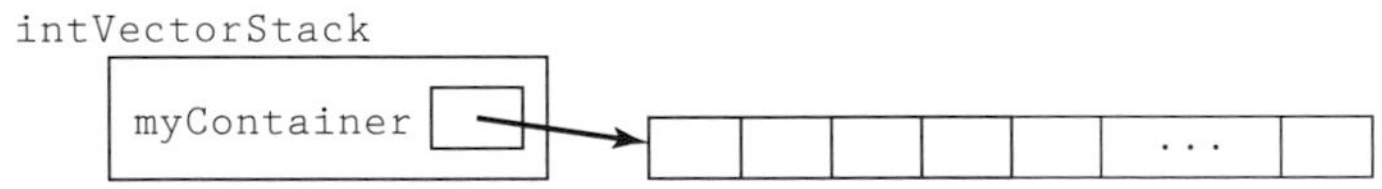

And the object `intStack` will be implemented using STL's default implementation as an adapter of `deque<T>`, which we will describe in more detail in the next section. Which of these to use depends on the problem:

- If speed is the primary concern and one has no memory constraints, using STL's default `stack<T>` implementation or as an adapter of the `vector<T>` template is probably the best choice.

---

2. The default `stack<T>` constructor builds the stack using the `deque<T>` template so this declaration could also be written `stack<T, deque<T> >`.

- If conserving memory is more important than blazing speed, using stack<T> to provide an alternative interface to the list<T> template is probably the best choice.

THE stack<T> METHODS

The program in Figure 15.2 illustrates several of the messages that can be sent to a stack<T>, regardless of its underlying implementation details. These messages include:[3]

- void push(T *aValue*)—place *aValue* on the top of the stack
- void pop()—remove the top value of the stack
- T top()—retrieve (but do not remove) the T value that is on top of the stack
- bool empty()—return true if and only if the stack contains no values

Thus, in the program in Figure 15.2, we "stacked up" the remainders by writing (within a loop)

```
intStack.push(remainder);
```

Likewise, to remove the remainders in LIFO order, we wrote (within a loop)

```
remainder = intStack.top();
intStack.pop();
```

And to control the repetition of these statements, we wrote

```
while ( !intStack.empty() )
{
   // ...
}
```

Because the list<T>, vector<T>, and deque<T> containers have many of the same operations, these stack<T> operations are relatively easy to implement. For example, because they all provide the push_back() method, the push() method for a stack is easy to implement:

```
template<typename T, typename Container>
inline void stack<T, Container>::push(T aValue)
{
   myContainer.push_back(aValue);
}
```

Here, myContainer is an instance variable in which the values are actually stored.

The other methods are equally easy to implement. Just as push() is basically a renaming of the internal container's push_back(), the pop(), top(), empty(), and size() operations are essentially renamings of the internal container's pop_back(), back(), empty(), and size() operations, respectively. The

---

3. STL also defines a size() method that returns the number of values in the stack, and the == and < operators for stack<T>. Stacks s1 and s2 will be compared element by element from bottom to top to determine if they are the same (s1 == s2 will be true) or whether the first element where they differ is less than the corresponding element in the other stack (s1 < s2 will be true).

stack<T> component thus provides a simpler interface to the container it wraps, which is the hallmark of an adapter.

Quick Quiz 15.1

1. Convert 1234 to a base-two number.
2. Convert 1234 to a base-eight number.
3. Convert 1234 to a base-sixteen number.
4. The last element added to a stack is the _______ one removed. This behavior is known as maintaining the list in _______ order.
5. What are the four standard stack operations?
6. A container that "wraps" another container, giving it a new interface, is called a(n) _______.

Questions 7–9 assume the declaration `stack<int> s;`. List the elements from bottom to top that s will contain after the code segment is executed, or indicate why an error occurs.

7.
```
s.push(123);
s.push(456);
s.pop();
s.push(789);
s.pop();
```
8.
```
s.push(111);
int i = s.top();
s.push(222);
s.pop();
s.push(i);
```
9.
```
for (int i = 0; i < 5; i++)
    s.push(2*i);
s.pop();
s.pop();
```

Exercises 15.1

1. Convert 2748 to a base-two number.
2. Convert 2748 to a base-eight number.
3. Convert 2748 to a base-sixteen number.

Exercises 4–7 assume the declaration `stack<int> s;`. List the elements from bottom to top that s will contain after the code segment is executed, or indicate why an error occurs.

4.
```
s.push(10);
s.push(22);
s.push(37);
s.pop();
s.pop();
```

5.
```
s.push(10);
s.push(9);
s.push(8);
while (!s.empty())
    s.pop();
s.push(7);
```
6.
```
for (int i = 0; i <= 5; i++)
    s.push(10*i);
```
7.
```
s.push(11);
s.push(s.top());
s.pop();
```

15.2 Queues, Deques, and Priority Queues

In the preceding section, we examined the stack—a special kind of container in which values are always inserted and removed from the same end. In this section, we examine some other special-purpose containers. We begin with queues and look later at deques and priority queues.

APPLICATIONS OF QUEUES

A **queue** is a container in which values are always added at one end, called the **rear** or **tail**, and removed from the opposite end, called the **front** or **head**. Queues abound in everyday life, because they provide a fair way to schedule things that are waiting for some kind of service. For example,

- a line of persons waiting to check out at a supermarket,
- a line of vehicles at a toll booth,
- a line of planes waiting to take off at an airport, and
- a line of persons waiting to purchase a ticket for a film

are all queues. Arriving customers, vehicles, planes, and the like enter the line at the rear and are removed from the line and served when they reach the front of the line, so that the first person to enter the queue is the first person served.

Because the first thing to enter the queue has been waiting the longest, it seems *fair* that it should be the first one served. (People get irritated when others "jump ahead" of them in a line, because this *fairness principle* is violated.) Stated differently, whereas a stack exhibits last-in-first-out (LIFO) behavior; a queue exhibits **first-in-first-out (FIFO)** behavior.

In addition to lines of people, vehicles, and planes waiting for service, queues are also commonly used to model waiting lines that arise in the operation of computer systems. These queues are formed whenever more than one process requires a particular resource such as a printer, a disk drive, the central processing unit, and so on. As processes request a particular resource, they are placed in a queue to wait for service by that resource.

As one example, several personal computers may be sharing the same printer, and a **spool**[4] **queue** is used to schedule output requests in a first-come-first-served manner. If a print job is requested and the printer is free, it is immediately assigned to this job. While this output is being printed, other jobs may need the printer, and so they are placed in a spool queue to await their turns. When the output from the current job terminates, the printer is released from that job and is assigned to the first job in the spool queue.

Another important use of queues in computing systems is **input/output buffering**. I/O buffering is important because a single disk operation (e.g., read from or write to a file) can take thousands (or millions) of times as long as a single CPU operation. Consequently, if the processing of a program must be suspended while the disk is accessed, program execution is slowed dramatically. One common solution to this problem uses sections of main memory known as **buffers** and transfers data between the program and these buffers rather than directly between the program and the disk.

C++ `ifstream` and `ofstream` objects automatically buffer file I/O. In the declaration

```
ifStream fin("inputFile.txt");
```

`inputFile.txt` is opened, and some of its data is transferred from the disk to an input buffer in main memory while the central processing unit (CPU) is processing the next statement(s). When the program attempts to read from `fin`,

```
fin >> aValue;
```

the next value stored in this buffer is retrieved. While this value is being processed, additional data values can be transferred from the disk file to the buffer. Clearly, the buffer must be organized as a first-in-first-out structure, that is, as a queue. A queue-empty condition indicates that the input buffer is empty, and program execution is suspended while the operating system attempts to load more data into the buffer or signals the end of file.

THE `queue<T>` ADAPTER

Like STL's `stack<T>` container, `queue<T>` is an adapter for which the default container that is wrapped is a `deque<T>`, described later in this section. The declaration

```
queue<string> stringQueue;
```

thus defines `stringQueue` as a queue in which strings can be stored in a `deque<T>`. The container that is given a new interface may also be a `list<T>`. Thus, the declaration

```
queue<string, list<string> > stringListQueue;
```

---

4. "Spool" is an acronym for **S**imultaneous **P**eripheral **O**peration **O**n-**L**ine.

defines stringListQueue as a queue in which the strings are stored in a list<string>. However, queue<T> cannot wrap a vector<T>, for reasons we will see shortly.

The methods provided for queue<T> are similar to those for stack<T>:[5]

- bool empty()—return true if and only if there are no values in the queue
- void push(T *aValue*)—append *aValue* to the end of the queue
- void pop()—remove the value at the front of the queue
- T front()—retrieve (but do not remove) the T value at the front of the queue
- T back()—retrieve (but do not remove) the T value at the back of the queue

Implementations of most of these queue<T> methods are similar to those we saw for stack<T> and are essentially just renamings of the container being adapted. Here, for example, is a definition of the push() method:

```
template<typename T, typename Container>
inline void queue<T, Container>::push(T aValue)
{
   myContainer.push_back(aValue);
}
```

Note that as with a stack<T>, when we send the push() message to a queue<T>, the value we are pushing gets appended to the back of the queue's container using the push_back() method. However, when we send the pop() message to a queue<T>, the value is removed from the *front* of the container:

```
template<typename T, typename Container>
inline void queue<T, Container>::pop()
{
   myContainer.pop_front();
}
```

This is the reason that a queue<T> cannot adapt a vector<T>. As we saw in Section 10.6, inserting or deleting at the front of an array or vector requires extensive copying that is very inefficient. To discourage programmers from writing inefficient code, vector<T> does not provide pop_front() or push_front() methods. Since we cannot send the pop_front() message to a vector<T>, we cannot use a vector<T> as the underlying container for a queue<T>.

Fortunately, this is not much of a hardship. The reason is that the default implementations of both stack<T> and queue<T> use a container called a *deque*, which we discuss next.

THE deque<T> CONTAINER

The word **deque** stands for *double-ended queue*. It is a good container to choose for any problem that requires the storage of a sequence of values and manipulation of the values at either end of that sequence.

---

5. size(), ==, and < are also provided in queue<T>.

The Standard Template Library's `deque<T>` is a container that (among many others) supports these operations:

- `void push_back(T aValue)`—insert *aValue* at the end of the deque
- `void pop_back()`—remove the value at the back of the deque
- `void push_front(T aValue)`—insert *aValue* at the front of the deque
- `void pop_front()`—remove the value at the front of the deque
- `T front()`—retrieve (but do not remove) the `T` value at the front of the deque
- `T back()`—retrieve (but do not remove) the `T` value at the back of the deque
- `bool empty()`—return true if and only if there are no values in the deque
- `int size()`—return the number of values in the deque

From this list, a `deque<T>` might seem to resemble a `list<T>`; however, the subscript operator (and indeed almost all other `vector<T>` operations) can be used with a `deque<T>`. So what are the differences between `deque<T>`, `vector<T>`, and `list<T>`? The following table summarizes the major differences:

	`vector<T>`	`list<T>`	`deque<T>`
`push_back()`	O(1)	O(1)	O(1)
`push_front()`	*none*	O(1)	O(1)
`pop_back()`	O(1)	O(1)	O(1)
`pop_front()`	*none*	O(1)	O(1)
`operator[]`	O(1)	*none*	O(1)
`insert()`	O(n)	O(1)	O(n)
`erase()`	O(n)	O(1)	O(n)

Thus, a `deque<T>` is a container that, for the most part, mirrors the behavior of a `vector<T>`, except that where adding and removing an element at the front of a `vector<T>` would require O(n) time, the internal structure of a `deque<T>` permits these operations to be performed in O(1) time. An explanation of this structure is left for the sequel to this text.[6]

It is because of this efficient implementation of these ends-of-the-sequence operations that `deque<T>` is used as the default container for the `stack<T>` and `queue<T>` adapters.

THE `priority_queue<T>` CONTAINER

While queues are usually associated with fairness, there is a special kind of queue in which the order of the values in the queue is determined by some principle that need not be first-in-first-out. Such a queue is known as a **priority queue** because the ordering of its elements depends on their priorities or values relative to one another. For example, a

6. *C++: An Introduction to Data Structures* by Larry Nyhoff (Upper Saddle River, NJ: Prentice Hall, Inc. 1999). A second edition is scheduled to appear in 2003.

multitasking operating system often uses a priority queue to decide which task or process to run next, with tasks that must meet real-time requirements (e.g., video or audio streaming) receiving the highest priority, tasks owned by the operating system receiving the next highest priority, tasks owned by a user receiving the next highest priority, and so on.

The Standard Template Library provides a `priority_queue<T>` container for such situations (defined in the *queue* header file). By default, a `priority_queue<T>` organizes its values so that the "highest" value is at its front, followed by the "next-highest" value, and so on, with the "lowest" value at its back.

The program in Figure 15.3 illustrates the difference between a `queue<T>` and a `priority_queue<T>`:

Fig. 15.3 Comparing the `queue<T>` and `priority_queue<T>` containers. (Part 1 of 2)

```
// priorityQueueTest.cpp

#include <iostream>          // cin, cout, cerr, ...
#include <queue>             // queue<T>, priority_queue<T>
using namespace std;

int main()
{
   string name = "JoeSmith";
   priority_queue<char> pQ;
   queue<char> q;

   for (int i = 0; i < 5; i++)
   {
      q.push(name[i]);     // insert into normal queue
      pQ.push(name[i]);    // insert into priority queue
   }

   while ( !q.empty() )           // output normal queue values
   {
      cout << q.front();
      q.pop();
   }
   cout << endl;

   while ( !pQ.empty() )           // output priority queue values
   {
      cout << pQ.top();
      pQ.pop();
   }
   cout << endl;
}
```

Fig. 15.3 Comparing the queue<T> and priority_queue<T> containers. (Part 2 of 2)

Sample run:

```
JoeSmith
tomiheSJ
```

When we output the values in q, they come in FIFO order—the order in which they were inserted—as we would expect. However, when we output the values in pQ, they come in *priority order*, according to their ASCII values. Thus, 't' is at the front of pQ because of all of the letters we inserted, it has the highest ASCII value (116). Likewise 'J' is at the back of pQ, because it has the lowest ASCII value (75) in this particular sequence.

Note that the priority_queue<T> container does not provide a front() method. Instead, it provides a top() method, to reflect that the value being retrieved has the highest priority of any of its items.

To avoid inefficiency, the priority_queue<T> container uses advanced techniques that guarantee that its push() and pop() routines take at most $O(\log_2(n))$ time.[7] This is much faster than $O(n)$, and it ensures that push() and pop() require a minimal amount of time.

Like stack<T> and queue<T>, STL's priority_queue<T> is an adapter. Because of its special internal structure, it can be used with a vector<T> or a deque<T> as its internal container, but not a list<T>. The default container is a vector<T>.

A priority queue is thus a useful container for any situation in which we wish to treat a sequence's values in some prioritized order. Because it effectively sorts its values, operator< and operator== must be defined for any object we place in a priority_queue<T>.

Quick Quiz 15.2

1. Explain how a queue differs from a stack.
2. The last element added to a queue is the (first or last) _______ one removed.
3. A stack exhibits LIFO behavior; a queue exhibits _______ behavior.
4. A(n) _______ queue is used to schedule output requests.
5. Queues are used to organize sections of main memory called _______ used to hold input/output data being transferred between a program and disk.
6. A(n) _____ is a double-ended queue.

Questions 7–9 assume only the declaration queue<int> q;. List the elements from front to back that q will contain after the code segment is executed, or indicate why an error occurs.

7.
```
q.push(123);
q.push(456);
```

7. A priority_queue<T> usually relies on an internal organization known as a **heap**, whose structure is beyond the scope of this text, but is described in the sequel (see Footnote 6).

```
q.pop();
q.push(789);
q.pop();
q.push(111);
int i = q.front();
```

8.
```
q.push(222);
q.pop();
q.push(i);
```

9.
```
for (int i = 0; i < 5; i++)
    q.push(2*i);
q.pop();
q.pop();
```

Exercises 15.2

Exercises 1–3 assume the declaration `queue<int> q;`. List the elements from front to back that `q` will contain after the code segment is executed, or indicate why an error occurs.

1.
```
for (int k = 1; k <= 5; k++)
    q.push(10*k);
```

2.
```
q.push(11);
q.push(22);
q.push(q.front());
q.pop();
q.push(33);
q.push(q.back());
q.pop();
q.push(44);
```

3.
```
q.push(10);
q.push(9);
q.pop();
q.pop();
q.pop();
q.push(8);
```

Exercises 4–6 assume the declaration `deque<int> q;`. List the elements from front to back that `q` will contain after the code segment is executed, or indicate why an error occurs.

4.
```
q.push_front(11);
q.push_front(22);
q.push_back(33);
q.pop_front();
q.push_back(44);
q.push_front(55);
```

```
    q.pop_back();
    q.push_back(66);
```
5.
```
for (int k = 1; k <= 5; k++)
   if (k % 2 == 0)
      q.push_front(10*k);
   else
      q.push_back(10*k);
```
6.
```
q.push_back(10);
q.push_back(9);
q.pop_front();
q.pop_front();
q.pop_back();
q.push_front(8);
```

For Exercises 7–10, tell what output will be produced by the program in Figure 15.3 for the given input.

7. `stack`
8. `computer`
9. `Recursion`
10. `STLisgreat`

15.3 Recursion Revisited

In Section 8.6, we saw that C++ permits a function definition to call itself, a technique called *recursion*. Now that we know about stacks, we are able to see how recursion works. We begin with an example.

EXAMPLE: RECURSIVE EXPONENTIATION

In Section 8.6, we looked at how the factorial function can be computed recursively. Another classic example of a function that can be calculated recursively is the power function that calculates x^n, where x is a real value and n is a nonnegative integer. The first definition of x^n that one learns is usually an iterative (nonrecursive) one,

$$x^n = \underbrace{x \times x \times \cdots \times x}_{n x\text{'s}}$$

and later one learns that x^0 is defined to be 1. (For convenience, we assume here that x^0 is 1 also when x is 0, although in this case, it is usually left undefined.)

A specification of the function is straightforward,

Receive: x, a real value;
n, an integer

Return: x^n, a real value

and suggests the following function stub:

```
double power(double x, int n)
{
}
```

To solve a problem recursively, we must identify the anchor and inductive cases. The anchor step is clear: $x^0 = 1$. For the inductive case, we look at an example:

$$5.0^4 = 5.0 \times 5.0 \times 5.0 \times 5.0 = (5.0 \times 5.0 \times 5.0) \times 5.0 = 5.0^3 \times 5.0$$

In general,

$$x^n = x^{n-1} \times x$$

Combining our anchor and inductive steps provides the following recursive definition of x^n:

$$x^n = \begin{cases} 1 & \text{if } n \text{ is zero} \quad \text{(the anchor case)} \\ x^{n-1} \times x & \text{if } n \text{ is greater than } 0 \quad \text{(the inductive case)} \end{cases}$$

As Figure 15.4 shows, writing a recursive C++ function from this definition is straightforward.

Fig. 15.4 Performing exponentiation recursively.

```
/* power() recursively computes x raised to the power n.
 * Receive:   x, a real value, and
 *            n, an integer
 * Return:    x raised to the power n
 ***************************************************************/

double power(double x, int n)
{
   if (n == 0)
      return 1.0;                         //anchor case
   else if (n > 0)
      return power (x, n - 1) * x;        //inductive step (n > 0)
   else                                   // invalid parameter n
   {
      cerr << "*** power(x,n): n is negative.\n";
      return -1.0;
   }
}
```

When it processes a function definition (recursive or not), the C++ compiler creates a special structure called an **activation record**. This record contains space for that function's parameters, local variables, return value, caller, and other information that can vary from call to call. During execution, each program has a special data structure called its **run-time stack**, which is a stack of these activation records. Whenever a function is called, an activation record is pushed onto the run-time stack; and whenever a function terminates, the run-time stack is popped, and control returns to the function whose activation record is uncovered. The effect, therefore, is that the top of the run-time stack is always an activation record for whatever function is currently executing.

To illustrate, consider what happens when the function call `power(3.0, 4)` occurs. An activation record for `power()` is pushed onto the run-time stack, in which `x` is 3.0 and `n` is 4:

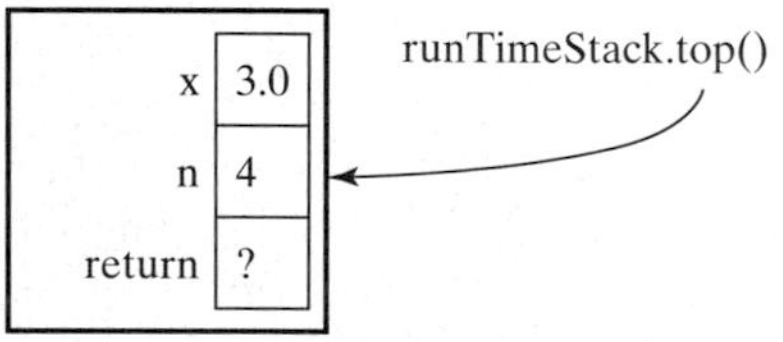

The function begins executing, and since `n` is 4, the expression `power(3.0, 3) * 3` must be evaluated to get the return value; and this expression has a new invocation of `power()`. This causes a new activation record to be pushed onto the run-time stack:

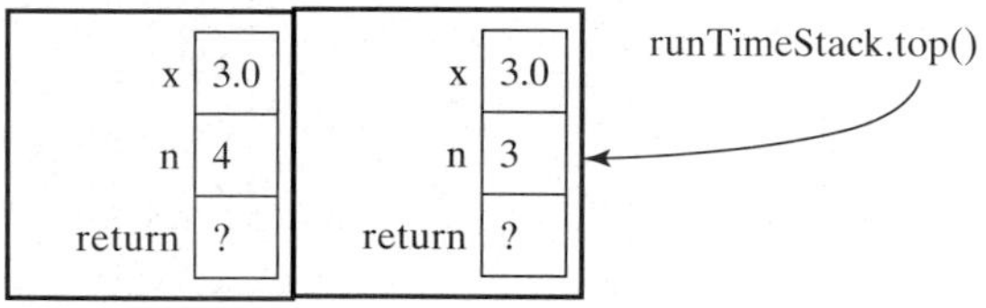

This new function begins executing, and since `n` is 3, the function encounters the expression `power(3.0, 2) * 3.0`, which involves a new invocation of `power()`. This causes a new activation record to be pushed onto the run-time stack:

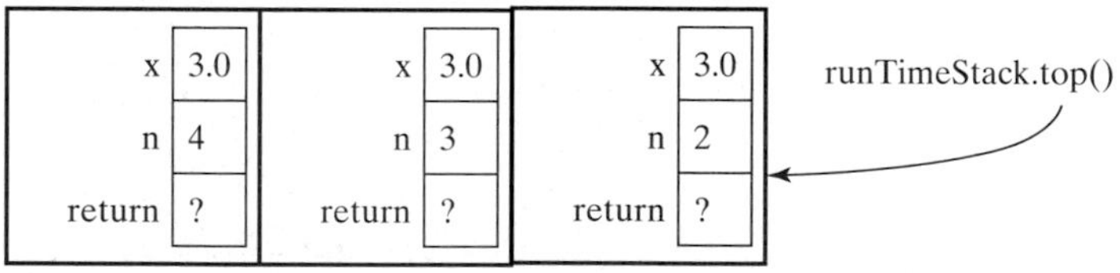

This new function begins executing, and since `n` is 2, the function encounters the expression `power(3.0, 1) * 3.0`, which produces another new invocation of `power()`. This causes a new activation record to be pushed onto the run-time stack:

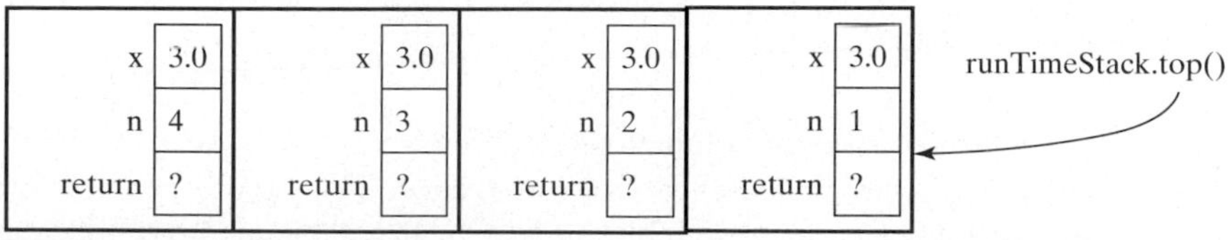

This new function begins executing, and since `n` is 1, the function encounters the expression `power(3.0, 0) * 3.0`, which causes another new invocation of `power()`. A new activation record is pushed onto the run-time stack:

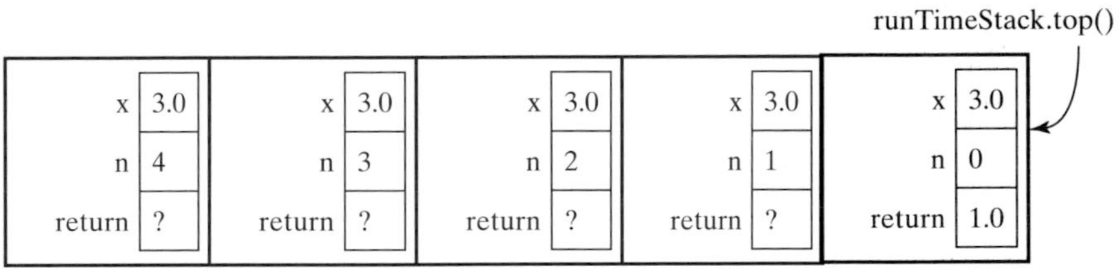

This new function begins executing, and since `n` is 0, the anchor case has been reached, stopping the recursion, and the function returns the value 1. The sequence of recursive calls from an initial call to the anchor case is sometimes referred to as the *winding phase* of the recursion, because it's like winding the spring of a wind-up clock until it's fully wound.

Once the anchor case has been reached, the backtracking behavior begins that actually performs the computation. The run-time stack is popped, and control then returns to the function whose activation record is now on top (i.e., `power(3.0, 1)`), in the middle of the expression `power(3.0, 0) * 3.0`, which now evaluates to `1.0 * 3.0`:

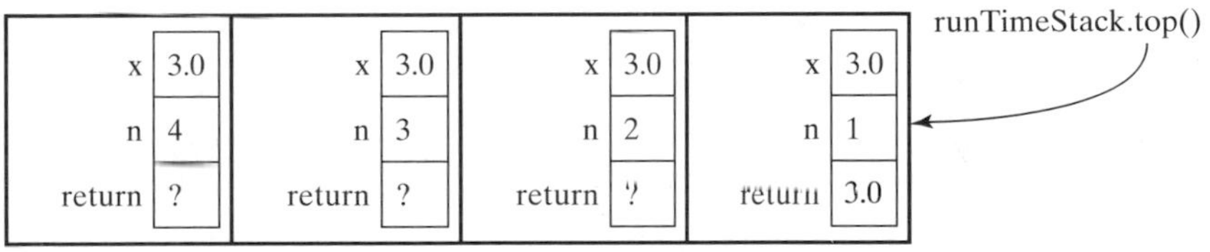

Since that is the end of that function, the run-time stack is then popped, and control returns to the function whose activation record is exposed (i.e., `power(3.0, 2)`), in the middle of the expression `power(3.0, 1) * 3.0`, which now evaluates to `3.0 * 3.0`:

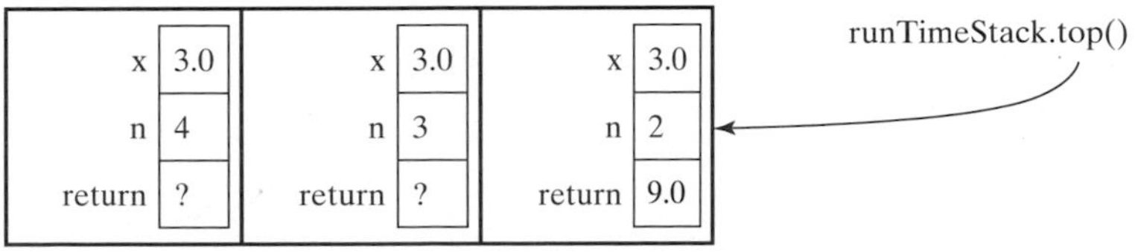

That is the end of that function, so the run-time stack is popped, and control then returns to the function whose activation records is now on top (i.e., `power(3.0, 3)`), in the middle of the expression `power(3.0, 2) * 3.0`, which now evaluates to `9 * 3.0`:

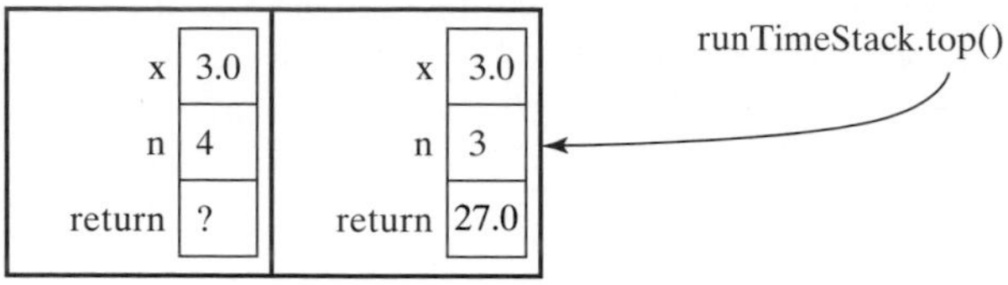

That is the end of that function, so the run-time stack is popped, and control returns to the function whose activation record is uncovered (i.e., `power(3.0, 4)`), in the middle of the expression `power(3.0, 3) * 3.0`, which now evaluates to `27 * 3.0`:

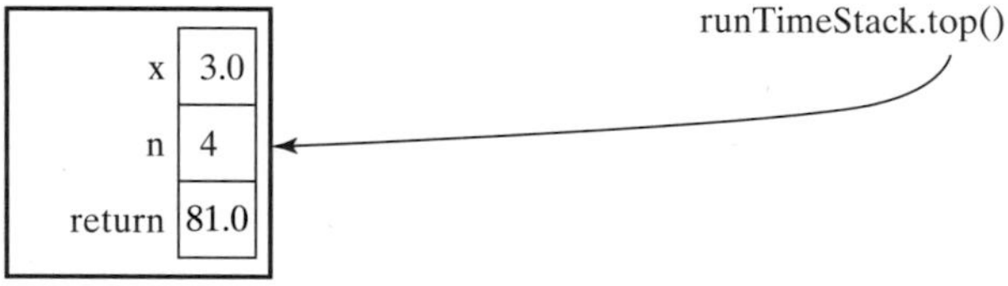

The result (`81.0`) is the return value of the call `power(3.0, 4)`.

This phase in which values are returned from the anchor case back through each of the previous calls is sometimes referred to as the *unwinding phase* of the recursion, because like a wind-up clock performing its task as its spring unwinds, a recursive function performs its task by unwinding the recursive calls stacked up in its winding phase.

The run-time stack thus plays a pivotal role in managing recursion. During the winding phase of a recursive call, activation records are pushed onto the run-time stack until the anchor case is reached. During the unwinding phase, activation records are popped from the run-time stack, until control returns to the original caller.

EXAMPLE: DRY BONES!

"Dry Bones" is a song known as a *spiritual*—a song whose lyrics referred to a story from the Bible that carried themes of hope and freedom;

```
Ezekiel cried, "Dem dry bones!"
Ezekiel cried, "Dem dry bones!"
Ezekiel cried, "Dem dry bones!"
Oh, hear the word of the Lord.
The foot bone connected to the leg bone,
The leg bone connected to the knee bone,
The knee bone connected to the thigh bone,
The thigh bone connected to the back bone,
The back bone connected to the neck bone,
The neck bone connected to the head bone,
Oh, hear the word of the Lord!
Dem bones, dem bones, gonna walk aroun'
Dem bones, dem bones, gonna walk aroun'
Dem bones, dem bones, gonna walk aroun'
```

```
Oh, hear the word of the Lord.
The head bone connected to the neck bone,
The neck bone connected to the back bone,
The back bone connected to the thigh bone,
The thigh bone connected to the knee bone,
The knee bone connected to the leg bone,
The leg bone connected to the foot bone,
Oh, hear the word of the Lord!
Dem bones, dem bones, gonna walk aroun'
Dem bones, dem bones, gonna walk aroun'
Dem bones, dem bones, gonna walk aroun'
Oh, hear the word of the Lord.
```

It is based on a powerful vision by the Old Testament prophet Ezekiel in which a valley of dry bones becomes reconnected as he prophesies. It uses the imagery of scattered bones being reconnected to encode the same message of hope conveyed in this vision. (See Ezekiel 37.)

The structure of the song is interesting, because it can be partitioned into the following steps, which together comprise an algorithm for printing the song:

a. Print the `"Ezekiel cried"` variation of the chorus.
b. Print the *bone lyrics* from foot to head.
c. Print the `"Dem bones"` variation of the chorus.
d. Print the *bone lyrics* from head to foot.
e. Print the `"Dem bones"` variation of the chorus.

Because of the reversal in Steps b and d, the actions performed in Steps b–d can be described using recursion with Step c as an anchor case.

An expanded version of this example on the text's Web site contains more about the history and purpose of spirituals. It also explains how to develop a recursive algorithm for displaying the song and how to implement it in code.

Like the Towers of Hanoi example in Section 8.6, this example demonstrates that recursion is not limited to functions such as `power()` that return numerical values. Instead, recursion can be applied to solve any of the wide variety of problems whose solutions are inherently recursive. In the next section, we see how recursion can actually simplify the operations on certain kind of containers.

15.4 An Introduction to Trees

In the preceding chapter, we saw how a linked list can be implemented by linking together structures called *nodes*. We also saw that the main advantage of linked lists over arrays/vectors is that values can be inserted at any point in a linked list without having to move values to make room for the new value; and items can be deleted without having to move values to close the gaps. The primary weakness of linked lists is that the elements cannot be accessed directly (except those at the ends of the list). This limits the kinds of algorithms that can be applied to linked lists; those that work well for arrays and vectors may not perform well for linked lists.

To demonstrate the problem, we consider the algorithms for searching lists considered in Section 10.4. One of these is **linear search** in which one searches consecutive elements in the list, beginning with the first element and continuing until either the desired item is found or the end of the list is reached. For example, consider the following vector `v` of values:

v	[0]	[1]	[2]	[3]	[4]	[5]	[6]
	11	22	33	44	55	66	77

To use linear search to find out whether the value 60 is present, we start at the beginning and compare each value in the sequence against 60. After seven comparisons—the number of values in the container—we determine that 60 is not present. In general, linear search requires O(n) time to determine that a sequence with n elements does not contain a specific value.[8]

The other search algorithm we studied was **binary search**, which requires that the sequence be sorted. We begin by examining the middle element in the sequence (44 in this case):

v	[0]	[1]	[2]	[3]	[4]	[5]	[6]	searchVal
	11	22	33	44	55	66	77	60

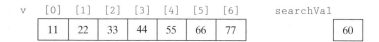

Since 60 (the value we are seeking) is greater than 44, we ignore the middle value and all values to its left and repeat the process by comparing 60 to the middle value in the remainder of the list (66 in this case):

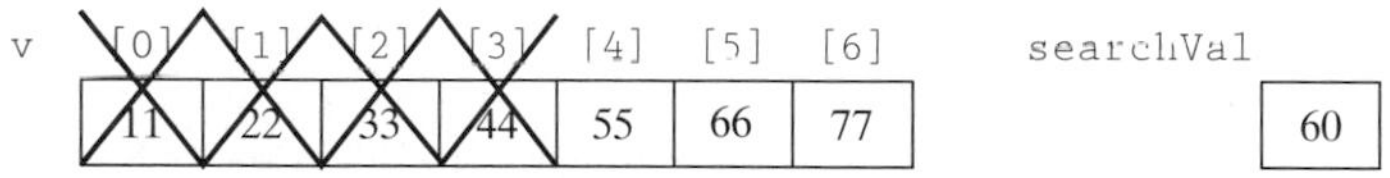

Since 60 is less than 66, we ignore the middle value and all values to its right and repeat the process by comparing 60 to the middle value in the remainder of the list (55 in this case):

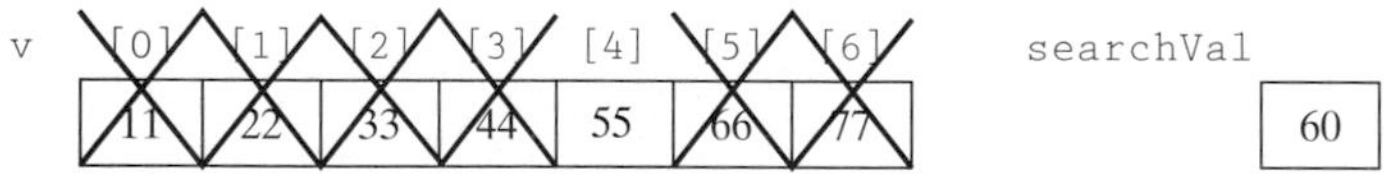

Since there is just one value remaining and it is not equal to the value we are seeking (60), we conclude that 60 is not present. Determining this required just three comparisons, and in general, the binary search algorithm can determine whether any value is in a sorted container with n elements in O($\log_2 n$) time.

In addition to assuming that the sequence is sorted, the binary search algorithm depends on the ability to directly access any value in the container, since any of them may

8. If our linear search algorithm assumes that the sequence is sorted, then it may be able to stop a bit earlier; on average, however, the number of comparisons will still be proportional to the length of the sequence or O(n).

be the middle element in a sublist to be searched. Because of this, binary search works no better than linear search for a linked list because the values in such a container cannot be accessed directly. To access the middle element of a linked list, as required by binary search, we must go through all the nodes that precede it.

This raises an interesting question: Is it possible to link the nodes together in some other way so that its elements can be searched more quickly than is possible in a linearly-linked structure? To see what would be needed to make it possible to search a list in a binary-search-like manner, consider the ordered list of integers again:

11, 22, 33, 44, 55, 66, 77

The first step in a binary search requires examining the middle element in the list. Direct access to this element is possible if we maintain a link to the node storing it:

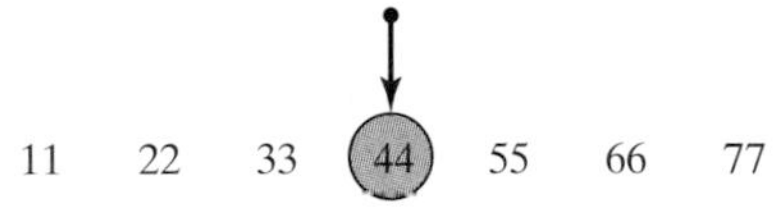

For the next step, one of the two sublists, the left half or the right half, must be searched and both must therefore be accessible from this node. This is possible if we maintain two links, one to each of these sublists. Since these sublists are searched in the same manner, these links should refer to nodes containing the middle elements in these sublists:

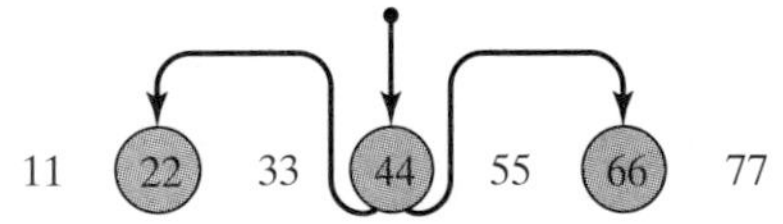

By the same reasoning, in the next step, links from each of these "second-level" nodes are needed to access the middle elements in their sublists:

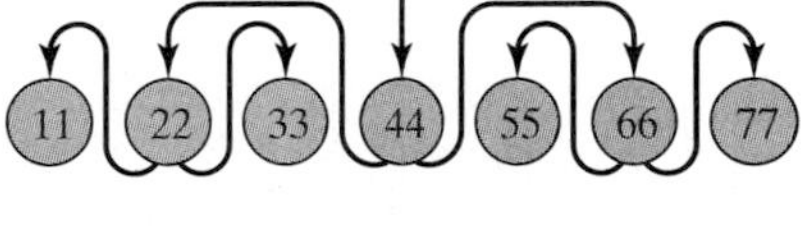

The resulting structure is usually drawn so that it has a treelike shape:

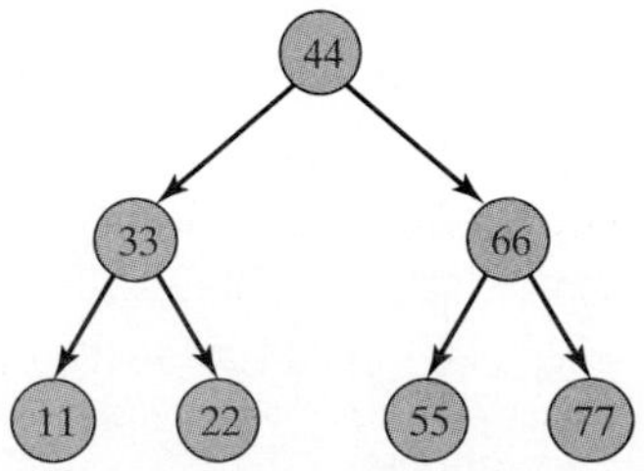

This structure is called a *binary search tree* and is a special kind of *binary tree*, which is a special instance of a more general structure called a *tree*.

TREE TERMINOLOGY AND EXAMPLES

A **tree** consists of a finite collection of **nodes** linked together in such a way that if the tree is not empty, then one of the nodes, called the **root**, has no incoming links, but every other node in the tree can be reached from the root by following a unique sequence of consecutive links.

Trees derive their names from the treelike diagrams that are used to picture them. For example, the following shows a tree having nine vertices in which the node labeled 1 is the root. As this diagram indicates, trees are usually drawn upside down, with the root at the top and the **leaves**—that is, nodes with no outgoing links—at the bottom. Nodes that are directly accessible from a given node (by using only one link) are called the **children** of that node, and a node is said to be the **parent** of its children. For example, in the following tree, node 3 is the parent of nodes 5, 6, and 7, and these nodes are the children of node 3 and are called **siblings**.

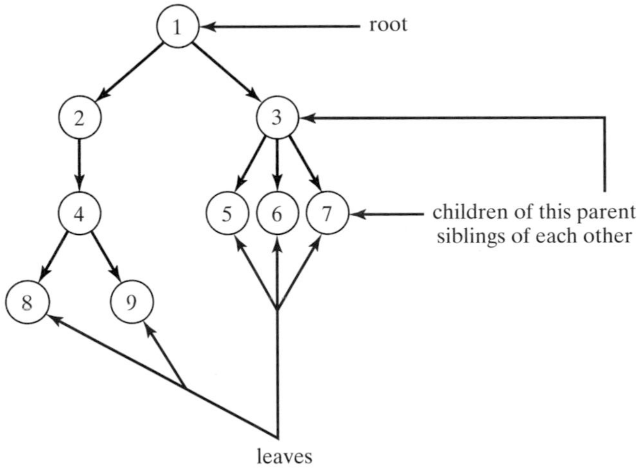

Applications of trees are many and varied. For example, a **genealogical tree** such as the following is a convenient way to picture a person's descendants:

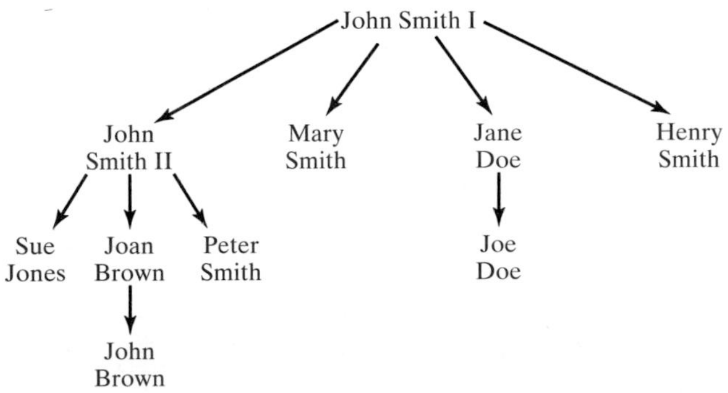

Game trees like that for the Towers of Hanoi problem in Section 8.6 are used to analyze games and puzzles. **Parse trees** are used to check a program's syntax. For example, the following is a parse tree for the expression 2 * (3 + 4):

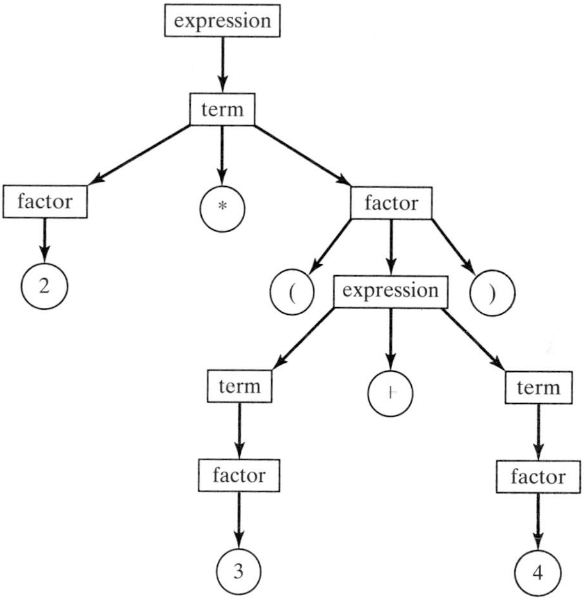

EXAMPLES OF BINARY TREES

Binary trees are trees in which each node has at most two children. Such trees are especially useful in modeling processes in which some experiment or test with two possible outcomes (for example, off or on, 0 or 1, false or true, down or up, yes or no) is performed repeatedly. For example, the following binary tree might be used to represent the possible outcomes of flipping a coin three times:

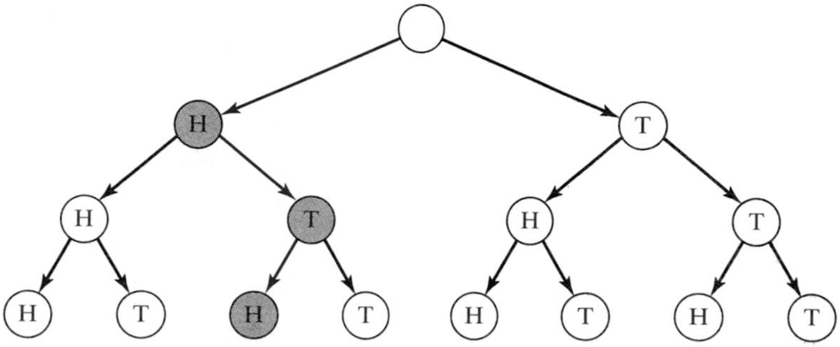

Each path from the root to one of the leaf nodes corresponds to a particular outcome, such as HTH (a head followed by a tail followed by another head), as highlighted in the diagram.

Similarly, a binary tree can be used in coding problems such as in encoding and decoding messages transmitted in Morse code, a scheme in which characters are represented as sequences of dots and dashes, as shown in the following table:

A	·–	M	––	Y	–·––
B	–···	N	–·	Z	––··
C	–·–·	O	–––	1	·––––
D	–··	P	·––·	2	··–––
E	·	Q	––·–	3	···––
F	··–·	R	·–·	4	····–
G	––·	S	···	5	·····
H	····	T	–	6	–····
I	··	U	··–	7	––···
J	·–––	V	···–	8	–––··
K	–·–	W	·––	9	––––·
L	·–··	X	–··–	0	–––––

In this case, the nodes in a binary tree are used to represent the characters, and each link from a node to its children is labeled with a dot or a dash, according to whether it leads to a left child or to a right child, respectively. Thus, part of the tree for Morse code is

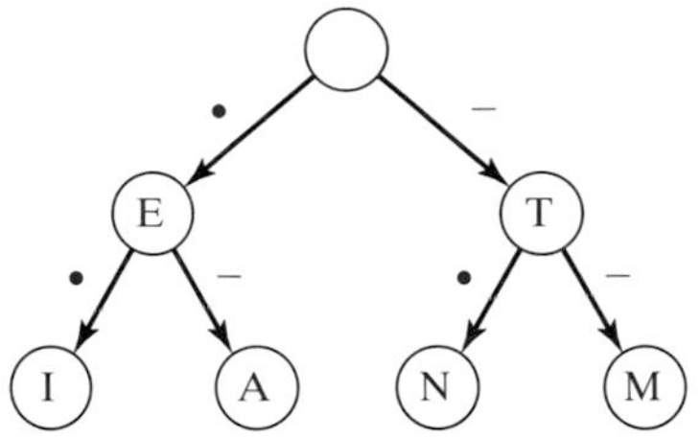

The sequence of dots and dashes labeling a path from the root to a particular node corresponds to the Morse code for that character; for example, `. .` is the code for I, and `- .` is the code for N.

Decision-making processes can be modeled as a series of "yes-or-no" questions, and a binary tree can thus be used to model that process. Each non-leaf node is used to store a question, and if an affirmative answer to a question leads to another question, then the two nodes are connected with a link labeled "yes". Similarly, if a negative answer to a question leads to another question, then the two nodes are connected with a link labeled "no". Since there are only two choices for each question, the resulting structure is a binary tree with decisions at its leaf nodes. The problem of making a single choice from among many choices is solved simply by descending through the tree until a leaf node (i.e., a decision) is reached.

For problems in some areas, solutions can be obtained by designing decision trees that mimic the choices experts would make in solving these problems. For example, programs to help a person prepare their income tax returns have some of the expertise of a tax accountant encoded within them. Similarly, programs that lead a person through the steps of writing a will have some of the expertise of an estate lawyer encoded within them. Programs that control a robot that welds automobile components on an assembly line are based on the knowledge of an expert welder. In general, programs that exhibit expertise in some area through the use of a knowledge base are called **expert systems**, and the study of such systems is one of the branches of artificial intelligence. A simple example of an expert system is given in the *Part of the Picture* section later in this chapter.

IMPLEMENTING BINARY TREES

A binary tree can be represented by a multiply-linked structure in which each node has two links, one connecting the node to its left child and the other connecting it to its right child. Such nodes can be represented by a public class named `Node` that has three instance variables:

```
template <typename DataType>
. . .
class Node
{
 public:
 //... Constructors and methods go here
   DataType myValue;
   Node*    myLeft;
   Node*    myRight;
};
```

The two pointers `myLeft` and `myRight` point to the left and right children, respectively, or are null if the node does not have a left or right child:

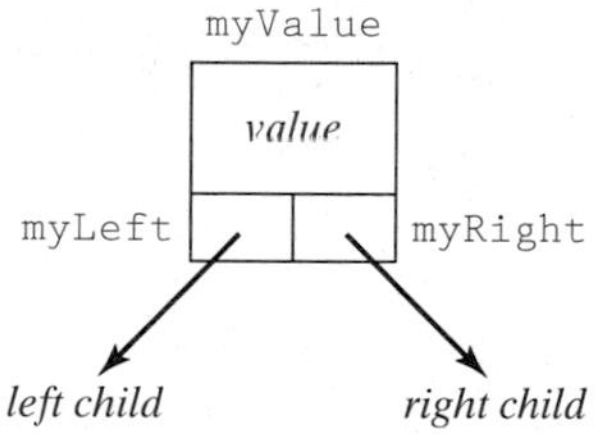

A leaf node is thus characterized by `myLeft` and `myRight` both being null:

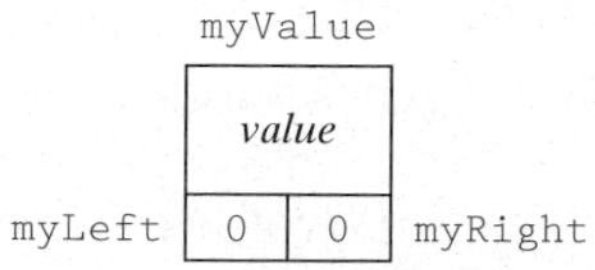

We can hide our `Node` structure within the private section of a `BinaryTree` class template declaration, to prevent programmers from accessing its details directly:

```
template <typename DataType>
class BinaryTree
{
 public:
   // ... constructors and methods go here

 private:
   class Node
   {
    public:
      // ... Node constructors and methods
      DataType myValue;
      Node*    myLeft;
      Node*    myRight;
   };

   // ... BinaryTree instance variables go here
};
```

One of the instance variables in a `BinaryTree` class would be a pointer `myRoot` to the node that is the root of the tree; and for convenience, we might also add an instance variable `mySize` that keeps track of the number of nodes in the tree:

```
template <typename DataType>
class BinaryTree
{
 public:
   // ... constructors and methods go here
 private:
   // ... declaration of class Node goes here
   // BinaryTree instance variables
   Node* myRoot;
   int   mySize;
};
```

Given such a class, the binary tree

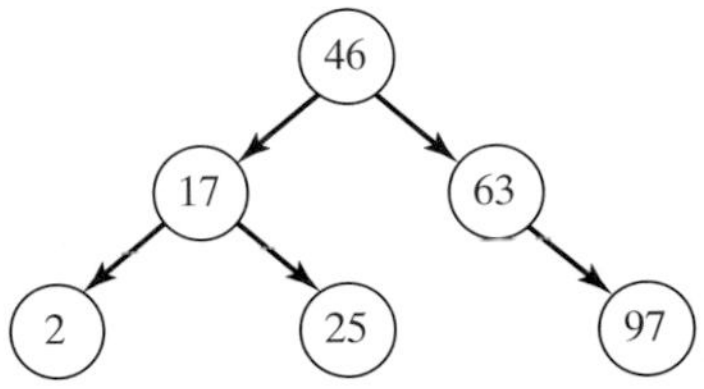

can be represented as the following linked structure:

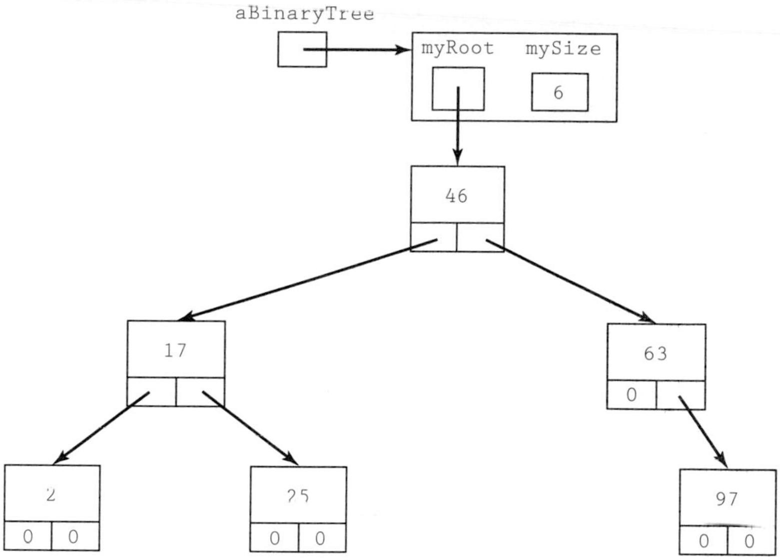

BINARY SEARCH TREES

In the preceding binary tree, the value in each node is greater than all values in its **left subtree** (if there are any) and less than all values in its **right subtree** (if there are any). A binary tree having this property is called a **binary search tree (BST)** because, as we noted at the beginning of this section, it can be searched using an algorithm much like the binary search algorithm for lists:

Search Algorithm for a BST

1. Initialize a pointer *currentNode* to the node containing the root and *found* to false.
2. While *currentNode* is not null and *found* is false, do the following:
   If the *item* being sought is:
      Less than the value referred to by *currentNode->myValue*
         Set *currentNode* = *currentNode->myLeft*;
      Greater than the value referred to by *currentNode->myValue*
         Set *currentNode* = *currentNode->myRight;*
      Else
         Set *found* to true.

To illustrate, suppose that we wish to search the preceding BST for 25. We begin at the root, and since 25 is less than the value 46 in this root, we know that the desired value is located to the left of the root; that is, it must be in the left subtree, whose root is 17:

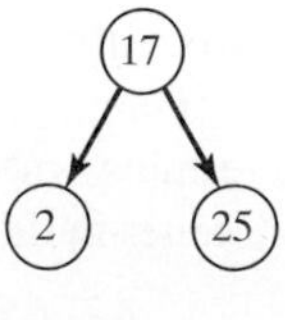

Now we continue the search by comparing 25 with the value in the root of this subtree. Since 25 > 17, we know that the right subtree should be searched:

Examining the value in the root of this one-node subtree locates the value 25.

Similarly, to search for the value 55, after comparing 55 with the value in the root, we are led to search its right subtree:

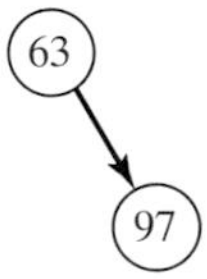

Now, because 55 < 63, if the desired value is in the tree, it will be in the left subtree. However, since this left subtree is empty, we conclude that the value 55 is not in the tree.

Figure 15.5 presents an implementation of the BST search algorithm.

Fig. 15.5 `BST search()` method.

```
template <typename DataType>
bool BST<DataType>::search(const DataType& item) const
{
   Node* currentNode = root;       // search pointer
   bool found = false;             // indicates if item already in BST
   while (currentNode != 0 && !found)
   {
      if (item < currentNode->myValue)              // descend left
         currentNode = currentNode->myLeft;
      else if (item > currentNode->myValue)         // descend right
         currentNode = currentNode->myRight;
      else                                          // item found
         found = true;
   }
  return found;
}
```

Because each pass through the while loop effectively eliminates one subtree (i.e., approximately half of the remaining nodes) from consideration, this method will, except for "lop-sided" BSTs, determine whether `item` is in the BST in $O(\log_2 n)$ comparisons, where n is the number of values in the BST.

TREE TRAVERSALS

Another important operation is **traversal**, that is, moving through a binary tree, visiting each node exactly once. And suppose for now that the order in which the nodes are visited is not relevant. What is important is that we visit each node, not missing any, and that the information in each node is processed exactly once.

One simple recursive scheme is to traverse the binary tree as follows:

1. Visit the root and process its contents.
2. Traverse the left subtree.
3. Traverse the right subtree.

To illustrate this algorithm, let us consider the following binary tree:

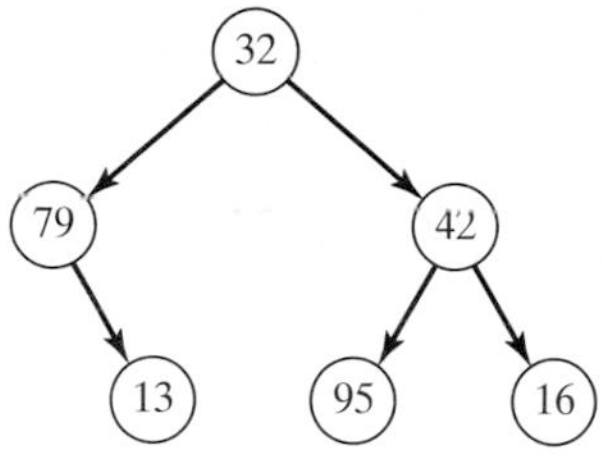

If we simply display a node's contents when we visit it, we begin by displaying the value 32 in the root of the binary tree. Next we must traverse the left subtree; after this traversal is finished, we then must traverse the right subtree; and when this traversal is completed, we will have traversed the entire binary tree.

(I)

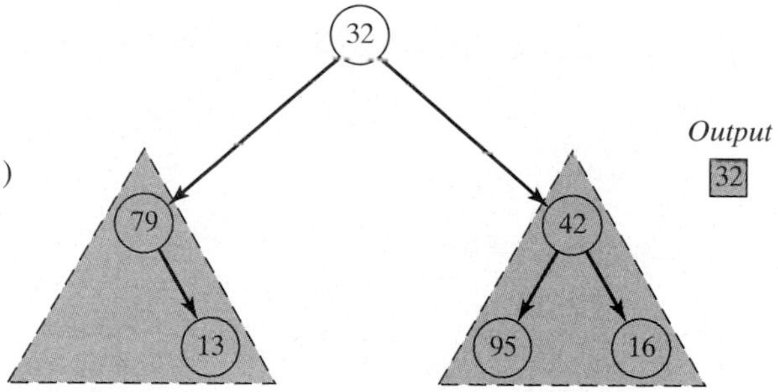

Thus the problem has been reduced to the traversal of two smaller binary trees. We consider the left subtree and visit its root. Next we must traverse its left subtree and then its right subtree.

(II)

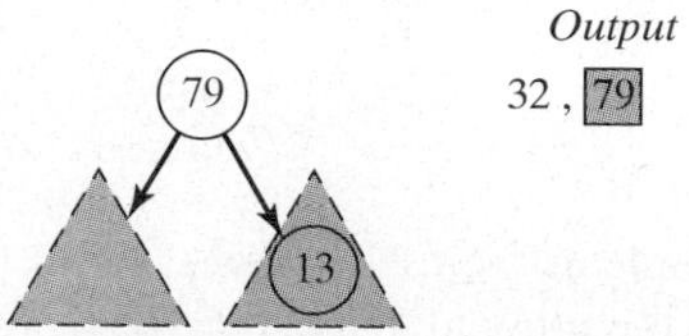

The left subtree is empty, and we need do nothing. So we turn to traversing the right subtree. We visit its root and then must traverse its left subtree followed by its right subtree:

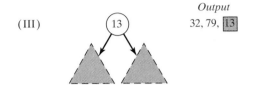

(III)

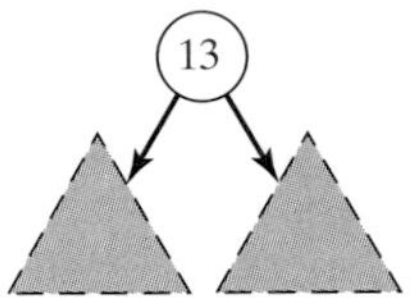

Output

32, 79, **13**

As both subtrees are empty, no action is required to traverse them. Consequently, traversal of the binary tree in diagram III is complete, and since this was the right subtree of the tree in diagram II, traversal of this tree is also complete.

This means that we have finished traversing the left subtree of the root in the original binary tree in diagram I, and we finally are ready to begin traversing the right subtree. This traversal proceeds in a similar manner. We first visit its root, displaying the value 42 stored in it; then traverse its left subtree: and then its right subtree:

(IV)

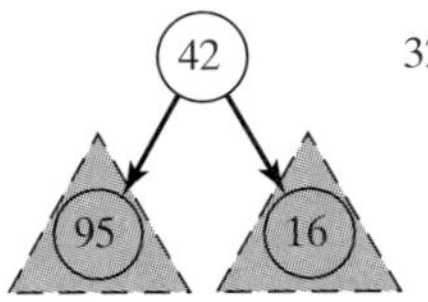

Output

32, 79, 13, **42**

The left subtree consists of a single node with empty left and right subtrees and is traversed as described earlier for a one-node binary tree:

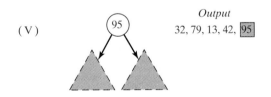

(V)

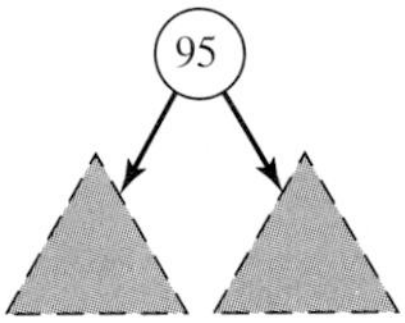

Output

32, 79, 13, 42, **95**

The right subtree is traversed in the same way:

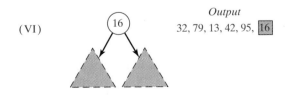

(VI)

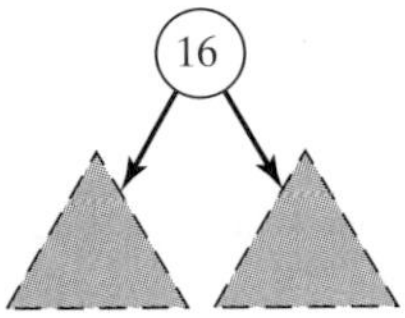

Output

32, 79, 13, 42, 95, **16**

This completes the traversal of the binary tree in diagram IV and thus completes the traversal of the original tree in diagram I.

As this example demonstrates, traversing a binary tree recursively requires three basic steps, which we shall denote N, L, and R:

N: Visit a node.
L: Traverse the left subtree of a node.
R: Traverse the right subtree of a node.

We performed these steps in the order listed here, but in fact, there are six different orders in which they can be carried out: LNR, NLR, LRN, NRL, RNL, and RLN. For example, the ordering LNR corresponds to the following recursive traversal algorithm:

```
If the binary tree is empty then            // anchor
   Do nothing.
Else do the following:                      // inductive step
   L: Traverse the left subtree.
   N: Visit the root.
   R: Traverse the right subtree.
```

For the preceding binary tree, this LNR traversal visits the nodes in the order 79, 13, 32, 95, 42, 16.

The first three orders, in which the left subtree is traversed before the right, are the most important of the six traversals and are commonly called by other names:

LNR ↔ Inorder
NLR ↔ Preorder
LRN ↔ Postorder

To see why these names are appropriate, consider the following **expression tree**, a binary tree used to represent the arithmetic expression

$$A - B*C + D$$

by representing each operand as a child of a parent node representing the corresponding operator:

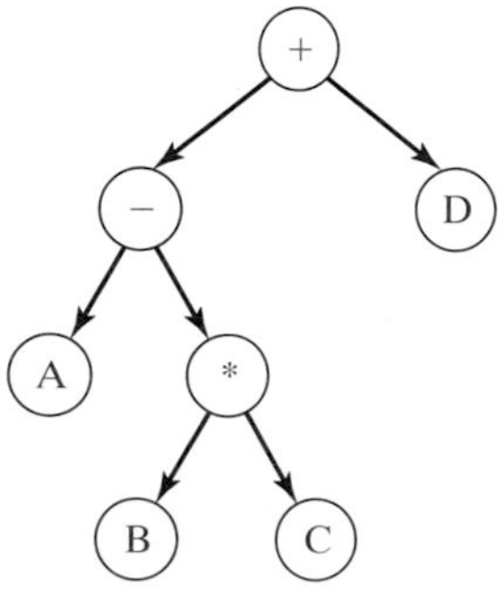

An **inorder** traversal of this expression tree produces the **infix** expression

$$A - B*C + D$$

A **preorder** traversal gives the **prefix** expression, in which an operator precedes its operands:

$$+-A*BCD$$

And a **postorder** traversal yields the **postfix** expression—also called **Reverse Polish Notation** (RPN)—in which an operator follows its operands:

$$ABC* - D +$$

NOTE

It should be noted that an *inorder traversal visits the nodes in a BST in ascending order.* The reason is that in a binary search tree, for each node, all of the values in the left subtree are smaller than the value in this node, which is less than all values in its right subtree. Because an inorder traversal is an LNR traversal, it follows that it must visit the nodes in ascending order.

Figure 15.6 presents a use of inorder traversal in displaying the values in a BST. We use a two-method approach: a nonrecursive `BST` method (since our `BST` is not recursively defined) that uses a recursive `Node` method (since a `Node` is recursively defined).

Fig. 15.6 `BST` and `Node print()` methods.

```
template <typename DataType>
void BST<DataType>::print(ostream& out) const
{
   if (myRoot != 0)             // if I am not empty
      myRoot->print(out);       //    invoke recursive Node print()
}

template <typename DataType>
void BST<DataType>::Node::print(ostream& out) const
{
  if (myLeft != 0)            // if my left subtree is not empty
     myLeft->print(out);      //    display its values first

  out << myData << ' ';       // display my value

  if (myRight != 0)           // if my right subtree is not empty
     myRight->print(out);     //    display its values last
}
```

The `Node::print()` method implements the inorder traversal algorithm by recursively displaying everything in its left subtree, then displaying its own value, and finally recursively displaying everything in its right subtree.

CONSTRUCTING BSTS

A binary search tree can be built by repeatedly inserting elements into a BST that is initially empty (`myRoot` is null). The method used to determine where an element is to be inserted is similar to that used to search the tree. In fact, we need only modify `search()` to maintain a pointer to the parent of the node currently being examined as we descend the tree, looking for a place to insert the item. Figure 15.7 shows a method that uses this approach.

Fig. 15.7 BST `insert()` method.

```
template <typename DataType>
void BST<DataType>::Insert(const DataType & item)
{
   Node* currentNode = root,       // search pointer
         parentNode = 0;           // pointer to parent of current node
   bool found = false;             // indicates if item already in BST

   while (currentNode != 0 && !found)
   {
      parentNode = currentNode;
      if (item < currentNode->myValue)               // descend left
         currentNode = currentNode->myLeft;
      else if (item > currentNode->myValue)          // descend right
         currentNode = currentNode->myRight;
      else                                           // item found
         found = true;
   }
   if (found)
      cerr << "Item already in the tree\n";
   else
   {
      currentNode = new Node(item);       // construct node ctg item
      if (parentNode == 0)                // empty tree
         root = currentNode;
      else if (item < parentNode->data)   // insert to parent's left
         parentNode->myLeft = currentNode;
      else                                // insert to parent's right
         parentNode->myRight = currentNode;
   }
}
```

To illustrate, the following sequence of diagrams indicates how 35 would be inserted into the binary search tree given earlier:

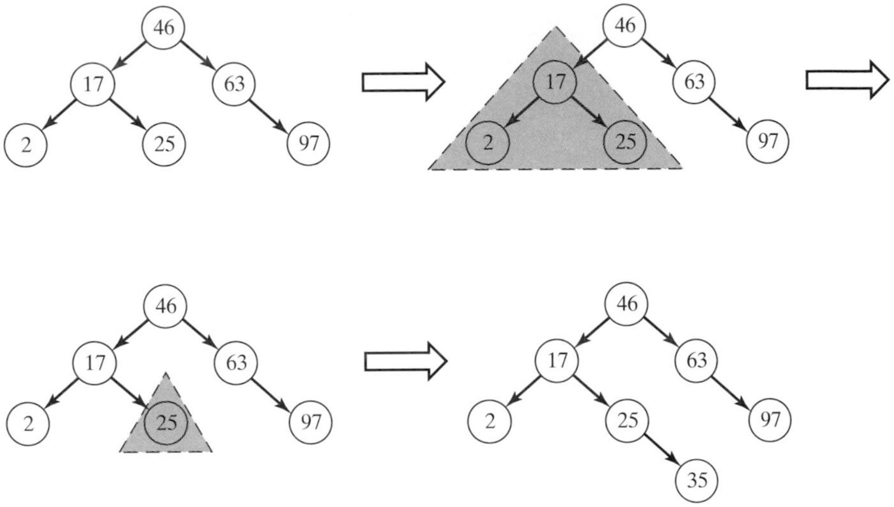

This completes our introduction to trees. The text's Web site provides a BST class that implements the preceding (and other) operations, and we invite the reader to experiment with it.

TREES IN STL

The Standard Template Library does not provide any templates with `Tree` in their name. However, some of its containers—the `set<T>`, `map<T1, T2>`, `multiset<T>`, and `multimap<T1, T2>` templates—are generally built using a special kind of *self-balancing binary search tree* called a *red–black tree*. A self-balancing BST ensures that the tree is always as balanced as possible, so that searches take $O(\log_2 n)$ time. The study of these trees is beyond the level of this text and is left to the sequel (see Footnote 6.) An introduction to the `set<T>` and `map<T1, T2>` templates is given on the text's Web site.

✔ Quick Quiz 15.4

1. A node that has no incoming links but from which every other node in the tree can be reached by following a unique sequence of consecutive links is called a(n) ________.
2. Nodes with no outgoing links are called ________.
3. Nodes that are directly accessible from a given node (by using only one link) are called the ________ of that node, which is said to be the ________ of these nodes.
4. Binary trees are trees in which each node has ________.

Questions 5–7 refer to the following binary search tree:

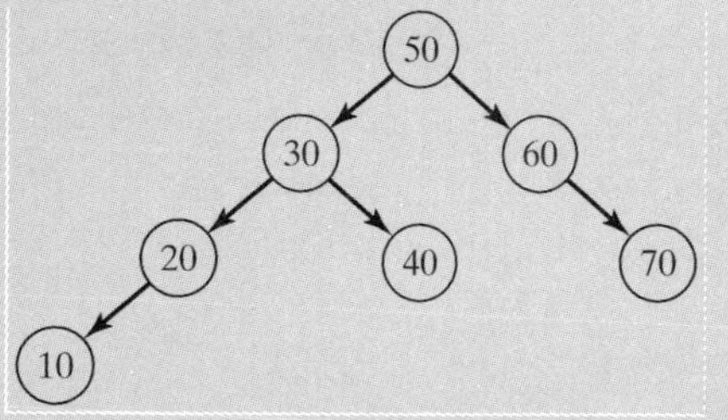

5. Which node is the root?
6. List all the leaves.
7. Draw the BST that results if 45, 55, and 65 are inserted.

For Questions 8–10, draw the BST that results when the C++ keywords are inserted in the order given, starting with an empty BST.

8. `if, do, for, case, switch, while, else`
9. `do, case, else, if, switch, while, for`
10. `while, switch, for, else, if, do, case`

Questions 11–13 refer to the following binary search tree:

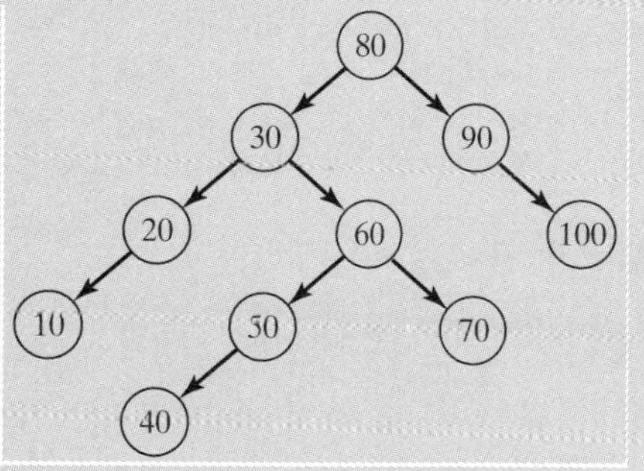

11. Perform an inorder traversal of this BST.
12. Perform a preorder traversal of this BST.
13. Perform a postorder traversal of this BST.

Exercises 15.4

For each of the lists of letters in Exercises 1–5, draw the BST that results when the letters are inserted in the order given, starting with an empty BST.

1. A, C, R, E, S
2. R, A, C, E, S
3. C, A, R, E, S
4. S, C, A, R, E
5. C, O, R, N, F, L, A, K, E, S

For each of the lists of C++ keywords in Exercises 6–10, draw the binary search tree that is constructed when the words are inserted in the order given, starting with an empty BST.

6. `new, float, short, if, main, break, for`
7. `break, long, return, char, else, switch, float`
8. `double, float, long, class, public, int, new`
9. `while, static, public, private, else, case`
10. `break, long, if, short, else, case, void, do, return, while, for, switch, double, true`

11–15. Perform inorder, preorder, and postorder traversals of the trees in Exercises 6–10, and show the sequence of words that results in each case.

Part of the Picture

Expert Systems

The game of animal is an old children's game. There are two participants in the game— the *player* and the *guesser*. The player is asked to think of an animal, which the guesser will try to guess. The guesser asks the player a series of yes-or-no questions, such as

Guesser: *Does it live on land?*

If the player answers 'yes,' then the guesser can eliminate from consideration those animals that do not live on land and use this information in formulating the next question, such as

Guesser: *Does it have four feet?*

Again, the answer to the question allows the user to eliminate from consideration either the animals with four feet or those that do not have four feet. Carefully formulating each question allows the guesser to eliminate a large group of animals from consideration, based on the player's response. Eventually, the guesser knows of only a single animal with the given characteristics:

Guesser: *Is it an elephant?*

If the guesser is correct, then he or she wins the game. Otherwise, the player wins the game, and the guesser asks the player:

Guesser: *What is your animal?*
Player: *An aardvark.*
Guesser: *How does an elephant differ from an aardvark?*
Player: *An elephant has a trunk, but an aardvark does not.*

By remembering the new animal and the difference between his or her animal and the new animal, the guesser learns to distinguish between the two animals.

A computer program that plays the animal game provides a classic example of a situation in which a program can seemingly *learn* and thus display **artificial intelligence**. The user of the program assumes the role of the player and the program assumes the role of the guesser.

The program maintains a knowledge base of questions, each of which allows it to eliminate animals from consideration. When the program has narrowed its search to a single animal, it guesses that animal. If the guess is correct, the program wins. Otherwise the program asks the player to name the animal of which he or she was thinking and then asks how to distinguish between this new animal and the animal it guessed. It then stores this question and the new animal in its knowledge base for the next time the game is played. The program thus exhibits some of the characteristics of learning each time it adds a new animal to its knowledge base.

As time passes and the program's knowledge base grows, it becomes more and more difficult for the player to think of animals that are not in the knowledge base—the program becomes an *expert* at guessing animals. Programs that exhibit expertise in some area through use of a knowledge base are known as **expert systems**, and the study of such systems is one of the branches of artificial intelligence. Examples of such systems range from welding experts that control welding robots on an automotive assembly line to legal experts that can help draw up standard legal documents.

Although most expert systems use fixed knowledge bases that the program is unable to modify, a program that plays the animal game is an example of a special *adaptive expert system*, because it adds new animals to its knowledge base as they are encountered. It is this ability to adapt its knowledge base that enables the animal program to simulate the process of learning.

Figure 15.9 presents a program that plays the animal game. For its knowledge base, it uses a special `DecisionTree` class that we have built specially for this purpose.

Fig. 15.8 Playing the animal game. (Part 1 of 3)

```
/* animal.cpp plays the game of 'animal', in which the player
 *  thinks of an animal, and the program tries to guess it.
 */

#include <iostream>
using namespace std;
#include "DecisionTree.h"

bool playMore();

int main()
{
   cout << "\nWelcome to the game of Animal!\n";

   DecisionTree dTree("animal.data"); // load knowledge base

   do
   {
      cout << "\nThink of an animal, and I will try to guess it...\n\n";
      int winner = dTree.descend();    // 0 == the person,
                                       // 1 == the program
```

Fig. 15.8 Playing the animal game. (Part 2 of 3)

```
        if (winner)
            cout << "\nHa! Even a computer program can beat you...\n";
        else
            cout << "\nYou were just lucky...\n";
    }
    while ( playMore() );
}  // knowledge base is auto-saved to file by DecisionTree destructor

bool playMore()
{
    char answer;
    cout << "\nDo you want to play again (y or n)? ";
    cin >> answer;
    return ((answer == 'y') || (answer == 'Y'));
}
```

Sample Run:

```
Welcome to the game of Animal!

Think of an animal, and I will try to guess it...

Does it live on land (y or n)? y

Does it have wings (y or n) ? n

Is it a(n) elephant (y or n)? y

Ha! Even a computer program can beat you...

Do you want to play again (y or n)? y

Think of an animal, and I will try to guess it...

Does it live on land (y or n)? n

Is it a(n) whale (y or n)? n

What animal are you thinking of? shark
```

Fig. 15.8 Playing the animal game. (Part 3 of 3)

```
Please enter a question, such that the answer is
 yes - for a(n) shark, and
 no - for a(n) whale
--> Is it cold-blooded

You were just lucky...

Think of an animal, and I will try to guess it...

Does it live on land (y or n)? n

Is it cold-blooded (y or n)? y

Is it a(n) shark (y or n)? n

What animal are you thinking of? electric eel

Please enter a question, such that the answer is
 yes - for a(n) shark, and
 no - for a(n) whale
--> Is meeting it a shocking experience

You were just lucky...

Do you want to play again (y or n)? n
```

The program plays the game by building a special tree to serve as its knowledge base, containing the questions and the animals it "knows." For example, when the program was first written, it "knew" only three animals: a duck, an elephant, and a whale. Its knowledge base was initially structured as follows:

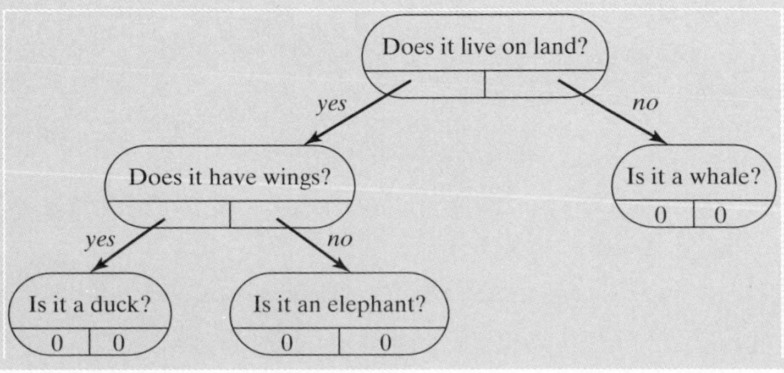

Such a structure is called a **decision tree**—each node in the tree contains the information needed to make a yes-or-no decision between its two subtrees. The guesser begins by asking the topmost question and, based on the player's response, follows the *yes* branch or the *no* branch to the next question. The guesser continues this process, descending through the tree until it reaches a leaf node (i.e., the end of a line of questioning), in which case it asks its final question and guesses the animal stored in that node.

By implementing such a tree as a linked structure, new nodes can be easily inserted (or deleted). Thus, in the first game listed in Figure 15.9, the program "got lucky" because it happened that the animal the player was thinking of (an elephant) was one of the three it knew about. However in the second game, the user was thinking of a shark—an animal the program did not know about. Using the information supplied by the player, the program learned to distinguish between a whale and a shark by creating and inserting the nodes that will allow it to distinguish between the two animals:

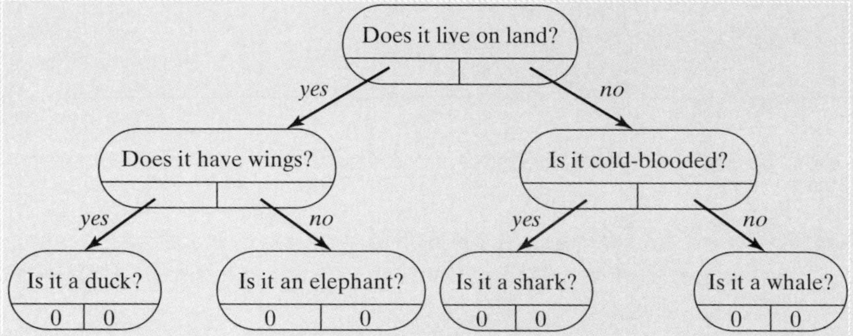

Similarly, in the next game, the program learned to distinguish between a shark and an electric eel:

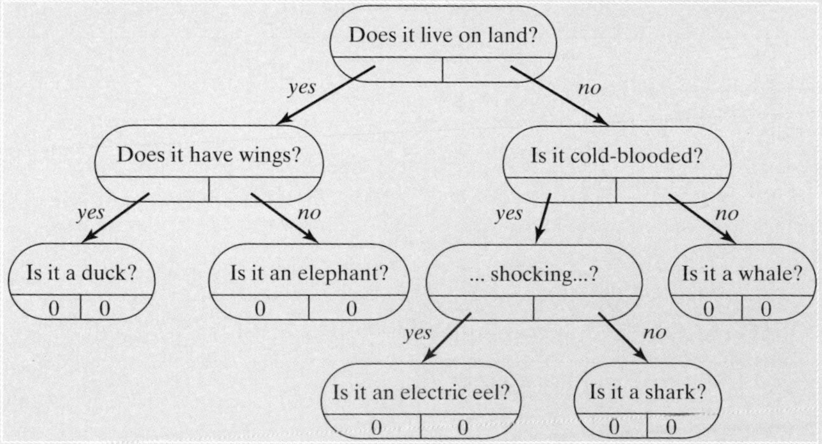

The program thus "learns" by expanding its decision tree each time it encounters an animal that is not already there.

To avoid "forgetting" what it has "learned," the `DecisionTree` destructor writes the tree's data to a file when the program terminates, and the `DecisionTree` constructor reads from this same file to initialize the `DecisionTree` when the program is run again. This simple mechanism allows the program to "remember" what it has "learned" in previous games. Over the course of time, such a program can become quite adept at identifying animals, based on the characteristics it is taught. The source code for the `DecisionTree` class is available on the text's Web site, and we invite the interested reader to study it further.

CHAPTER SUMMARY

Key Terms & Notes

activation record
adapter
artificial intelligence
back of a queue
binary search
binary search tree (BST)
binary tree
buffer
children
container
data structure
decision tree
deque
`deque<T>`
expert system
expression tree
First-In-First-Out (FIFO)
front of a queue
head of a queue
infix
inorder
input/output buffer
Last-In-First-Out (LIFO)
leaf node
linear search
linked list
`list<T>`
node
parent
pop
postfix
postorder
prefix
preorder
priority queue
push
push-down stack
queue
`queue<T>`
rear of a queue
recursion
Reverse Polish Notation
root
run-time stack
sibling
singly-linked list
spool queue
stack
`stack<T>`
subtree
tail of a queue
top of a stack
traversal
tree
`vector<T>`

- Containers (or data structures) are structures that store groups of values.

- A stack has LIFO (Last-In-First-Out) behavior. A queue has FIFO (First-In-First-Out) behavior.
- The STL containers stack<T>, queue<T>, and priority_queue<T> are adapters that wrap some other container to give it a new interface. The internal container may be a vector<T>, list<T>, or deque<T> for stack<T>; a list<T> or deque<T> for queue<T>; and a vector<T> or deque<T> for priority_queue<T>.
- Whenever a function is called, an activation record is pushed onto a run-time stack. Whenever a function terminates, the run-time stack is popped and control returns to the function whose activation record is uncovered.
- A tree consists of a finite collection of nodes linked together in such a way that if the tree is not empty, then one of the nodes, called the root, has no incoming links, but every other node in the tree can be reached from the root by following a unique sequence of consecutive links.
- A binary tree is a tree in which each node has at most two children.
- In a binary search tree, for each node, all of the values in its left subtree are smaller than the value in this node, which is less than all values in its right subtree.
- Inorder traversal visits the nodes in a BST in ascending order.
- STL uses self-balancing binary search trees called *red–black trees* to implement its set<T>, multiset<T>, map<T1, T2>, and multimap<T1, T2> containers. set<T> containers may not contain duplicate values, but multiset<T>s may. map<T1, T2> containers (as well as multimap<T1, T2>s) are useful in problems where an arbitrary type T1 must be mapped to another arbitrary type T2.

Programming Pointers

Program Style and Design

1. *If a problem solution requires that values stored more recently will be needed before the values stored less recently, then a stack is the appropriate structure for storing these values.* Stacks are LIFO (Last-In-First-Out) lists, since the operation to remove a value will always retrieve the value that was inserted most recently.
2. *If a problem solution requires that values will be needed in the order in which they were stored, then a queue is the appropriate structure for storing these values.* Queues are FIFO (First-In-First-Out) lists, since the operation to remove a value from the queue will always retrieve the value that was inserted least recently.
3. *If a problem solution requires access, insertion, and deletion only at the ends of a list, a deque is an appropriate structure for storing these values.* Deques are double-ended queues.
4. *If a problem solution requires fast access to arbitrary elements, but also requires that the collection be allowed to grow and shrink due to frequent insertions and deletions, then a binary search tree (BST) may be the appropriate structure to use.* BSTs are linked structures and thus can grow and shrink without excessive memory waste. And they can be searched in a binary search manner, which (except when the tree becomes lopsided) is more efficient ($O(\log_2 n)$) than a linear search ($O(n)$).

Potential Pitfalls

1. *STL's* `queue<T>` *container may wrap a* `deque<T>` *or a* `list<T>`, *but not a* `vector<T>`.Removing an element at the front of a `vector<T>` is too inefficient.
2. *STL's* `priority_queue<T>` *container may wrap a* `deque<T>` *or a* `vector<T>`, *but not a* `list<T>`. It needs direct access to its elements.

Programming Problems

Section 15.1

1. Write a program that reads a string, one character at a time, and determines whether the string contains balanced parentheses, that is, for each left parenthesis (if there are any) there is exactly one matching right parenthesis later in the string. (*Hint*: Store the left parentheses in a stack.)
2. Problem 1 can be solved without using a stack; in fact, a simple integer variable can be used. Describe how this can be done, and write a program that uses your method to solve the problem.
3. For a given integer $n > 1$, the smallest integer $d > 1$ that divides n is a prime factor. We can find the *prime factorization* of n if we find d and then replace n by the quotient of n divided by d, repeating this until n becomes 1. Write a program that determines the prime factorization of n in this manner, but that displays the prime factors in descending order. For example, for $n = 3960$, your program should produce

   11*5*3*3*2*2*2
4. A program is to be written to find a path from one point in a maze to another.
   a) Describe how a two-dimensional array could be used to model the maze.
   b) Describe how a stack could be used in an algorithm for finding a path.
   c) Write the program.

Section 15.2

5. Write a program that generates a random sequence of letters and digits, displays them to the user one at a time for a second or so, and then asks the user to reproduce the sequence. Use a queue to store the sequence of characters.
6. Write a "quiz-tutor" program, perhaps on a topic from one of the earlier chapters, or some other topic about which you are knowledgeable. The program should read a question and its answer from a file, display the question, and accept an answer from the user. If the answer is correct, the program should go on to the next question. If it is not correct, store the question in a queue. When the file of questions is exhausted, the questions that were missed should be displayed again (in their original order). Keep a count of the correct answers, and display the final count. Also, display the correct answer when necessary in the second round of questioning.
7. Write a program that reads a string of characters, pushing each character onto a stack as it is read and simultaneously adding it to a queue. When the end of the string is encountered, the program should use the basic stack and queue operations to determine if the string is a *palindrome* (a string that reads the same from left to right as from right to left).
8. Proceed as in Problem 7, but use a single deque to store the characters instead of a stack and a queue.

9. In text-editing and word-processing applications, one formatting convention sometimes used to indicate that a piece of text is a footnote or an endnote is to mark it with some special delimiters such as { and }. When the text is formatted for output, these notes are not printed as normal text, but are stored in a queue for later output. Write a program that reads a document containing endnotes indicated in this manner, collects them in a queue, and displays them at the end of the document. Number the endnotes, and in the text where the endnote occurred, put its number enclosed in brackets [ ].

10. Suppose that jobs entering a computer system are assigned a job number and a priority from 0 through 9. The numbers of jobs awaiting execution by the system are kept in a priority queue. Write a program that reads one of the letters `R` (remove), `A` (add), or `L` (list). For `R`, remove a job from the priority, queue and display the job number; for `A`, read a job number and priority and then add it to the priority queue in the manner just described; and for `L`, list all the job numbers in the queue.

11. (Project) Suppose that a certain airport has one runway, that each airplane takes `landingTime` minutes to land and `takeOffTime` minutes to take off, and that on the average, `takeOffRate` planes take off and `landingRate` planes land each hour. Assume that the planes arrive at random instants of time. (Delays make the assumption of randomness quite reasonable.) There are two types of queues: a queue of airplanes waiting to land and a queue of airplanes waiting to take off. Because it is more expensive to keep a plane airborne than to have one waiting on the ground, we assume that the airplanes in the landing queue have priority over those in the takeoff queue.

    Write a program to simulate this airport's operation. You might assume a simulated clock that advances in one-minute intervals. For each minute, generate two random numbers: If the first is less than `landingRate` / 60, a "landing arrival" has occurred and is added to the landing queue; and if the second is less than `takeOffRate` / 60, a "takeoff arrival" has occurred and is added to the takeoff queue. Next, check whether the runway is free. If it is, first check whether the landing queue is nonempty, and if so, allow the first airplane to land; otherwise, consider the takeoff queue. Have the program calculate the average queue length and the average time that an airplane spends in a queue. You might also investigate the effect of varying arrival and departure rates to simulate the prime and slack times of day, or what happens if the amount of time to land or take off is increased or decreased.

Section 15.4

12. Write a spell checker, that is, a program that reads the words in a piece of text and looks up each of them in a dictionary to check its spelling. Use a BST to store this dictionary, reading the list of words from a file. While checking the spelling of words in a piece of text, the program should print a list of all words not found in the dictionary.

13. Write a program to construct a text concordance, which is an alphabetical listing of all the distinct words in a piece of text. It should read a piece of text; construct a concordance that contains the distinct words that appear in the text and for each word, the line (or page) number of its first occurrence; and then allow the user to search this concordance. Use an array or vector of 26 BSTs, one for each letter of the alphabet, to store the concordance.

14. Extend the program in Problem 13, so that a (linked) list of all occurrences of each word is stored. When the concordance is searched for a particular word, the program should display the line (or page) numbers of all occurrences of this word. The data structure used for the concordance is thus an array or vector of binary search trees, each of whose nodes stores an object containing a string and an ordered linked list of integers.

A

ASCII Character Set

ASCII codes of characters

Decimal	Octal	Character	Decimal	Octal	Character
0	000	NUL (Null)	25	031	EM (End of medium)
1	001	SOH (Start of heading)	26	032	SUB (Substitute)
2	002	STX (Start of text)	27	033	ESC (Escape)
3	003	ETX (End of text)	28	034	FS (File separator)
4	004	EOT (End of transmission)	29	035	GS (Group separator)
5	005	ENQ (Enquiry)	30	036	RS (Record separator)
6	006	ACK (Acknowledge)	31	037	US (Unit separator)
7	007	BEL (Ring bell)	32	040	SP (Space)
8	010	BS (Backspace)	33	041	!
9	011	HT (Horizontal tab)	34	042	"
10	012	LF (Line feed)	35	043	#
11	013	VT (Vertical tab)	36	044	$
12	014	FF (Form feed)	37	045	%
13	015	CR (Carriage return)	38	046	&
14	016	SO (Shift out)	39	047	' (Single quote)
15	017	SI (Shift in)	40	050	(
16	020	DLE (Data link escape)	41	051	)
17	021	DC1 (Device control 1)	42	052	*
18	022	DC2 (Device control 2)	43	053	+
19	023	DC3 (Device control 3)	44	054	, (Comma)
20	024	DC4 (Device control 4)	45	055	- (Hyphen)
21	025	NAK (Negative ACK)	46	056	. (Period)
22	026	SYN (Synchronous)	47	057	/
23	027	ETB (EOT block)	48	060	0
24	030	CAN (Cancel)	49	061	1

Decimal	Octal	Character	Decimal	Octal	Character
50	062	2	79	117	O
51	063	3	80	120	P
52	064	4	81	121	Q
53	065	5	82	122	R
54	066	6	83	123	S
55	067	7	84	124	T
56	070	8	85	125	U
57	071	9	86	126	V
58	072	:	87	127	W
59	073	;	88	130	X
60	074	<	89	131	Y
61	075	=	90	132	Z
62	076	>	91	133	[
63	077	?	92	134	\
64	100	@	93	135	]
65	101	A	94	136	^
66	102	B	95	137	_ (Underscore)
67	103	C	96	140	`
68	104	D	97	141	a
69	105	E	98	142	b
70	106	F	99	143	c
71	107	G	100	144	d
72	110	H	101	145	e
73	111	I	102	146	f
74	112	J	103	147	g
75	113	K	104	150	h
76	114	L	105	151	i
77	115	M	106	152	j
78	116	N	107	153	k

Decimal	Octal	Character	Decimal	Octal	Character
108	154	l	118	166	v
109	155	m	119	167	w
110	156	n	120	170	x
111	157	o	121	171	y
112	160	p	122	172	z
113	161	q	123	173	{
114	162	r	124	174	|
115	163	s	125	175	}
116	164	t	126	176	~
117	165	u	127	177	DEL

B

C++ Keywords

The following table lists all of the keywords in C++, together with a brief description of the context in which they usually appear.

Keyword	Contextual Description
`asm`	Used to declare that information is to be passed directly to the assembler
`auto`	Used to declare objects whose lifetime is the duration of control within their block
`bool`	Used to declare objects whose values are `true` or `false`
`break`	Used to terminate processing of a `switch` statement or loop
`case`	Used in a `switch` statement to specify a match for the statement's expression
`catch`	Used to specify the actions to be taken when an exception occurs (see `throw`, `try`)
`char`	Used to declare objects whose values are characters
`class`	Used to construct new types encapsulating data and operations (default `private`)
`const`	Used to declare objects whose values should not change during execution
`const_cast`	Used to add or remove the `const` or `volatile` property of a type
`continue`	Used in a loop statement to transfer control to the beginning of the loop
`default`	Used in a `switch` statement to handle expression values not specified using `case`
`delete`	Used to deallocate memory allocated at run time, returning it to the free store
`do`	Used to mark the beginning of a `do-while` statement, providing repetitive control
`double`	Used to declare objects whose values are (double precision) real numbers
`dynamic_cast`	Used to cast pointer or reference types in a class hierarchy
`else`	Used in an `if` statement to mark the section to be executed if the condition is false
`enum`	Used to declare a type whose values are programmer-specified identifiers
`explicit`	Used to prevent constructors from being called implicitly for conversion purposes
`extern`	Used to declare objects whose definitions are external to the local block
`false`	A `bool` value
`float`	Used to declare objects whose values are (single precision) real numbers
`for`	Used to mark the beginning of a `for` statement, providing repetitive control
`friend`	Used to declare class operations that are not member functions
`goto`	Used to transfer control to a label
`if`	Used to mark the beginning of an `if` statement, providing selective control
`inline`	Used to declare a function whose text is to be substituted for its call
`int`	Used to declare objects whose values are integer numbers
`long`	Used to declare 32-bit integer or extended double-precision real numbers
`mutable`	Used to declare class data member as modifiable even in a `const` object

Keyword	Contextual Description
`namespace`	Used to control the scope of global names (to avoid name conflicts)
`new`	Used to request memory allocation at run time
`operator`	Used to overload an operator with a new declaration
`private`	Used to declare class members that are inaccessible from outside of the class
`protected`	Used to declare class members that are `private`, except to derived classes
`public`	Used to declare class members that can be accessed outside of the class
`register`	Used to declare objects whose values are to be kept in registers
`reinterpret_cast`	Used to perform type conversions on unrelated types
`return`	Used to terminate a function, usually returning the value of some expression
`short`	Used to declare 16-bit integer numbers
`signed`	Used to declare an object in which the value's *sign* is stored in the high-order bit
`sizeof`	Used to find the size (in bytes) of an object or of the representation of a type
`static`	Used to declare objects whose lifetime is the duration of the program
`static_cast`	Used to convert one type to another type
`struct`	Used to construct new types encapsulating data and operations (default `public`)
`switch`	Used to mark the beginning of a switch statement, providing selective control
`template`	Used to declare type-independent classes or functions
`this`	A pointer within a class that stores the address of an instance of the class
`throw`	Used to generate an exception (see `catch`, `try`)
`true`	A `bool` value
`try`	Used to mark the beginning of a block containing exception handlers (see `catch`)
`typedef`	Used to declare a name as a synonym for an existing type
`typeid`	Used to obtain type information during run time
`typename`	Can be used instead of class in template parameter lists and to identify qualified names as types
`union`	Used to declare a structure, such that different objects can have different members
`unsigned`	Used to declare an object in which the high-order bit is used for data (see `signed`)
`using`	Used to access members of a namespace
`virtual`	Used to declare a base-class function that will be defined by a derived class
`void`	Used to indicate the absence of any type
`volatile`	Used to declare objects whose values may be modified by means undetectable to the compiler (such as shared-memory objects of concurrent processes)
`while`	Used to mark the beginning of a `while` statement, as well as the end of a `do-while` statement, each of which provides repetitive control

C

C++ Operators

The following table lists all of the operators available in C++, ordered by their precedence levels, from highest to lowest—higher precedence operators are applied before lower precedence operators. Operators in the same horizontal band of the table have equal precedence. The table also gives each operator's associativity—in an expression containing operators of equal precedence, associativity determines which is applied first—whether they can be overloaded, their arity (number of operands), and a brief description.

Operator	Associativity	Overloadable	Arity	Description
::	right	no	unary	global scope
::	left	no	binary	class scope
.	left	no	binary	direct member selection
->	left	yes	binary	indirect member selection
[]	left	yes	binary	subscript (array index)
()	left	yes	n/a	function call
()	left	yes	n/a	type construction
sizeof	right	n/a	unary	size (in bytes) of an object or type
++	right	yes	unary	increment
--	right	yes	unary	decrement
~	right	yes	unary	bitwise NOT
!	right	yes	unary	logical NOT
+	right	yes	unary	plus (sign)
-	right	yes	unary	minus (sign)
*	right	yes	unary	pointer dereferencing
&	right	yes	unary	get address of an object
new	right	yes	unary	memory allocation
delete	right	yes	unary	memory deallocation
()	right	yes	binary	type conversion (cast)
.	left	no	binary	direct member pointer selection
->	left	yes	binary	indirect member pointer selection
*	left	yes	binary	multiplication
/	left	yes	binary	division
%	left	yes	binary	modulus (remainder)
+	left	yes	binary	addition
-	left	yes	binary	subtraction
<<	left	yes	binary	bit-shift left
>>	left	yes	binary	bit-shift right

Operator	Associativity	Overloadable	Arity	Description
`<`	left	yes	binary	less-than
`<=`	left	yes	binary	less-than-or-equal
`>`	left	yes	binary	greater-than
`>=`	left	yes	binary	greater-than-or-equal
`==`	left	yes	binary	equality
`!=`	left	yes	binary	inequality
`&`	left	yes	binary	bitwise AND
`^`	left	yes	binary	bitwise XOR
`|`	left	yes	binary	bitwise OR
`&&`	left	yes	binary	logical AND
`||`	left	yes	binary	logical OR
`?:`	left	no	ternary	conditional expression
`=`	right	yes	binary	assignment
`+=`	right	yes	binary	addition-assignment shortcut
`-=`	right	yes	binary	subtraction-assignment shortcut
`*=`	right	yes	binary	multiplication-assignment shortcut
`/=`	right	yes	binary	division-assignment shortcut
`%=`	right	yes	binary	modulus-assignment shortcut
`&=`	right	yes	binary	bitwise-AND-assignment shortcut
`|=`	right	yes	binary	bitwise-OR-assignment shortcut
`^=`	right	yes	binary	bitwise-XOR-assignment shortcut
`<<=`	right	yes	binary	bitshift-left-assignment shortcut
`>>=`	right	yes	binary	bitshift-right-assignment shortcut
`throw`	right	yes	unary	throw an exception
`,`	left	yes	binary	expression separation

D

Libraries and Classes

C Libraries

Many of the C++ libraries were originally C libraries. The following describes some of the most useful items in the more commonly used libraries.

`cassert` (FORMERLY `assert.h`)

`void assert(bool expr)`	Tests the boolean expression `expr` and if it is true, allows execution to proceed. If it is false, execution is terminated and an error message is displayed.

`cctype` (FORMERLY `ctype.h`)

`int isalnum(int c)`	Returns true if `c` is a letter or a digit, false otherwise
`int isalpha(int c)`	Returns true if `c` is a letter, false otherwise
`int iscntrl(int c)`	Returns true if `c` is a control character, false otherwise
`int isdigit(int c)`	Returns true if `c` is a decimal digit, false otherwise
`int isgraph(int c)`	Returns true if `c` is a printing character except space, false otherwise
`int islower(int c)`	Returns true if `c` is lowercase, false otherwise
`int isprint(int c)`	Returns true if `c` is a printing character including space, false otherwise
`int ispunct(int c)`	Returns true if `c` is a punctuation character (not a space, an alphabetic character, or a digit), false otherwise
`int isspace(int c)`	Returns true if `c` is a white space character (space, `'\f'`, `'\n'`, `'\r'`, `'\t'`, or `'\v'`), false otherwise
`int isupper(int c)`	Returns true if `c` is uppercase, false otherwise
`int isxdigit(int c)`	Returns true if `c` is a hexadecimal digit, false otherwise
`int tolower(int c)`	Returns lowercase equivalent of `c` (if `c` is uppercase)
`int toupper(int c)`	Returns uppercase equivalent of `c` (if `c` is lowercase)

`cfloat` (FORMERLY `float.h`)

The following constants specify the minimum value in the specified floating-point type:

`FLT_MIN (≤ -1E+37)`	`float`
`DBL_MIN (≤ -1E+37)`	`double`
`LDBL_MIN (≤ -1E+37)`	`long double`

The following constants specify the maximum value in the specified floating-point type:

`FLT_MAX (≥ 1E+37)`	`float`
`DBL_MAX (≥ 1E+37)`	`double`
`LDBL_MAX (≥ 1E+37)`	`long double`

The following constants specify the smallest positive value representable in the specified floating-point type:

`FLT_EPSILON (≤ 1E-37)`	`float`
`DBL_EPSILON (≤ 1E-37)`	`double`
`LDBL_EPSILON (≤ 1E-37)`	`long double`

`climits` (FORMERLY `limits.h`)

The following constants specify the minimum and maximum values for the specified type:

`SCHAR_MIN` (≤ −127)	`signed char`
`SCHAR_MAX` (≥ 127)	`signed char`
`UCHAR_MAX` (≥ 255)	`unsigned char`
`CHAR_MIN` (0 or `SCHAR_MIN`)	`char`
`CHAR_MAX` (`SCHAR_MAX` or `USHRT_MAX`)	`char`
`SHRT_MIN` (≤ −32767)	`short int`
`SHRT_MAX` (≥ 32767)	`short int`
`USHRT_MAX` (≥ 65535)	`unsigned short int`
`INT_MIN` (≤ −32767)	`int`
`INT_MAX` (≥ 32767)	`int`
`UINT_MAX` (≥ 65535)	`unsigned int`
`LONG_MIN` (≤ −2147483647)	`long int`
`LONG_MAX` (≥ 2147483647)	`long int`
`ULONG_MAX` (≥ 4294967295)	`unsigned long int`

`cmath` (FORMERLY `math.h`)

`double acos(double x)`	Returns the angle in [0, π] (in radians) whose cosine is `x`
`double asin(double x)`	Returns the angle in [−π/2, π/2] (in radians) whose sine is `x`
`double atan(double x)`	Returns the angle in (−π/2, π/2) (in radians) whose tangent is `x`
`double atan2(double x, double y)`	Returns the angle in (−π, π] (in radians) whose tangent is `x/y`
`double ceil(double x)`	Returns the least integer ≥ `x`
`double cos(double x)`	Returns the cosine of `x` (radians)
`double cosh(double x)`	Returns the hyperbolic cosine of `x`
`double exp(double x)`	Returns e^{x}
`double fabs(double x)`	Returns the absolute value of `x`
`double floor(double x)`	Returns the greatest integer ≤ `x`
`double fmod(double x, double y)`	Returns the integer remainder of `x / y`
`double frexp(double x,int& ex)`	Returns value `v` in [1/2, 1] and sends back `ex` such that $x = v * 2^{ex}$
`double ldexp(double x, int ex)`	Returns $x * 2^{ex}$
`double log(double x)`	Returns natural logarithm of `x`
`double log10(double x)`	Returns base-ten logarithm of `x`
`double modf(double x, double& ip)`	Returns fractional part of `x` and sends back `ip` = the integer part of `x`
`double pow(double x, double y)`	Returns x^{y}
`double sin(double x)`	Returns the sine of `x` (radians)
`double sinh(double x)`	Returns the hyperbolic sine of `x`
`double sqrt(double x)`	Returns the square root of `x` (provided `x` ≥ 0)

`double tan(double x)`	Returns the tangent of `x` (radians)
`double tanh(double x)`	Returns the hyperbolic tangent of `x`

cstdlib (FORMERLY stdlib.h)

`int abs(int i)` `long abs(long li)`	`abs(i)` and `labs(li)` return the `int` and `long int` absolute value of `i` and `li`, respectively

`double strtod(char s[])`
`double atof(char s[])`
`int atoi(char s[])`
`long atol(char s[])`
	`strtod(s)` and `atof(s)` return the value obtained by converting the character string `s` to `double`; `atoi(s)` and `atol(s)` return the value obtained by converting the character string `s` to `int` and `long int`, respectively

`void exit(int status)`	Terminates program execution and returns control to the operating system; `status` = 0 signals successful termination and any nonzero value signals unsuccessful termination
`int rand()`	Returns a pseudorandom integer in the range 0 to `RAND_MAX`
`RAND_MAX`	An integer constant (≥ 32767) that is the maximum value returned by `rand()`
`void srand(int seed)`	Uses `seed` to initialize the sequence of pseudorandom numbers returned by `rand()`
`int system(char s[])`	Passes the string `s` to the operating system to be executed as a command and returns an implementation-dependent value

THE string CLASS

The `string` class, which was described in Chapter 5, is defined by

```
typedef basic_string<char> string;
```

The unsigned integer type `size_type` is defined in this class as is an integer constant `npos`, which is some integer that is either negative or greater than the number of characters in a string. The following is a list of the major operations defined on a `string` object `s`; `pos`, `pos1`, `pos2`, `n`, `n1`, and `n2` are of type `size_type`; `str`, `str1`, and `str2` are of type `string`; `charArray` is a character array; `ch` and `delim` are of type `char`; `istr` is an `istream`; `ostr` is an `ostream`; `it1` and `it2` are iterators; and `inpIt1` and `inpIt2` are input iterators. All of these operations except >>, <<, +, the relational operators, `getline()`, and the second version of `swap()` are methods.

Constructors:

`string s;`	This declaration invokes the default constructor to construct `s` as an empty string
`string s(charArray);`	This declaration initializes `s` to contain a copy of `charArray`
`string s(charArray, n);`	This declaration initializes `s` to contain a copy of the first `n` characters in `charArray`
`string s(str);`	This declaration initializes `s` to contain a copy of string `str`
`string s(str, pos, n);`	This declaration initializes `s` to contain a copy of the `n` characters in string `str`, starting at position `pos`; if `n` is too large, characters are copied only to the end of `str`
`string s(n, ch);`	This declaration initializes `s` to contain `n` copies of the character `ch`

`string s(inpIt1, inpIt2)`	This declaration initializes `s` to contain the characters in the range `[inpIt1, inpIt2)`
`getline(istr, s, delim)`	Extracts characters from `istr` and stores them in `s` until `s.max_size()` characters have been extracted, the end of file occurs, or `delim` is encountered, in which case `delim` is extracted from `istr` but is not stored in `s`
`getline(istr, s)`	Inputs a string value for `s` as in the preceding function with `delim = '\n'`
`istr >> s`	Extracts characters from `istr` and stores them in `s` until `s.max_size()` characters have been extracted, the end of file occurs, or a white-space character is encountered, in which case the white-space character is not removed from `istr`; returns `istr`
`ostr << s`	Inserts characters of `s` into `ostr`; returns `ostr`
`s = val`	Assigns a copy of `val` to `s`; `val` may be a string, a character array, or a character
`s += val`	Appends a copy of `val` to `s`; `val` may be a string, a character array, or a character
`s[pos]`	Returns a reference to the character stored in `s` at position `pos`, provided `pos < s.length()`
`s + t` `t + s`	Returns the result of concatenating `s` and `t`; `t` may be a string, a character array, or a character.

`s < t, t < s`
`s <= t, t <= s`
`s > t, t > s`
`s >= t, t >= s`
`s == t, t == s`
`s != t, t != s`
	Returns `true` or `false` as determined by the relational operator; `t` may be a string or a character array

`s.append(str)`	Appends string `str` at the end of `s`; returns `s`
`s.append(str, pos, n)`	Appends at the end of `s` a copy of the `n` characters in `str`, starting at position `pos`; if `n` is too large, characters are copied only until the end of `str` is reached; returns `s`
`s.append(charArray)`	Appends `charArray` at the end of `s`; returns `s`
`s.append(charArray, n)`	Appends the first `n` characters in `charArray` at the end of `s`; returns `s`
`s.append(n, ch)`	Appends `n` copies of `ch` at the end of `s`; returns `s`
`s.append(inpIt1, inpIt2)`	Appends copies of the characters in the range `[inpIt1, inpIt2)` to `s`; returns `s`
`s.assign(str)`	Assigns a copy of `str` to `s`; returns `s`
`s.assign(str, pos, n)`	Assigns to `s` a copy of the `n` characters in `str`, starting at position `pos`; if `n` is too large, characters are copied only until the end of `str` is reached; returns `s`
`s.assign(charArray)`	Assigns to `s` a copy of `charArray`; returns `s`
`s.assign(charArray, n)`	Assigns to `s` a string consisting of the first `n` characters in `charArray`; returns `s`
`s.assign(n, ch)`	Assigns to `s` a string consisting of `n` copies of `ch`; returns `s`

`s.assign(inpIt1, inpIt2)`	Assigns to `s` a string consisting of the characters in the range `[inpIt1, inpIt2)`; returns `s`
`s.at(pos)`	Returns `s[pos]`
`s.begin()`	Returns an iterator positioned at the first character in `s`
`s.c_str()`	Returns (the base address of) a `char` array containing the characters stored in `s`, terminated by a null character
`s.capacity()`	Returns the size (of type `size_type`) of the storage allocated in `s`
`s.clear()`	Removes all the characters in `s`; return type is `void`
`s.compare(str)`	Returns a negative value, 0, or a positive value according as `s` is less than, equal to, or greater than `str`
`s.compare(charArray)`	Compares `s` and `charArray` as in the preceding method
`s.compare(pos, n, str)`	Compares strings `s` and `str` as before, but starts at position `pos` in `s` and compares only the next `n` characters
`s.compare(pos, n, charArray)`	Compares string `s` and `charArray` as in the preceding method
`s.compare(pos1, n1, str, pos2, n2)`	Compares `s` and `str` as before, but starts at position `pos1` in `s`, position `pos2` in `str`, and compares only the next `n1` characters in `s` and the next `n2` characters in `str`
`s.compare(pos1, n1, charArray, n2)`	Compares strings `s` and `charArray` as before, but using only the first `n2` characters in `charArray`
`s.copy(charArray, pos, n)`	Replaces the string in `s` with `n` characters in `charArray`, starting at position `pos` or at position 0, if `pos` is omitted; if `n` is too large, characters are copied only until the end of `charArray` is reached; returns the number (of type `size_type`) of characters copied
`s.data()`	Returns a `char` array containing the characters stored in `s`
`s.empty()`	Returns `true` if `s` contains no characters, `false` otherwise
`s.end()`	Returns an iterator positioned immediately after the last character in `s`
`s.erase(pos, n)`	Removes `n` characters from `s`, beginning at position `pos` (default value 0); if `n` is too large or is omitted, characters are erased only to the end of `s`; returns `s`
`s.erase(it)`	Removes the character at the position specified by `it`; returns an iterator positioned immediately after the erased character
`s.find(str, pos)`	Returns the first position ≥ `pos` such that the next `str.size()` characters of `s` match those in `str`; returns `npos` if there is no such position; 0 is the default value for `pos`
`s.find(ch, pos)`	Searches `s` as in the preceding method, but for `ch`
`s.find(charArray, pos)`	Searches `s` as in the preceding method, but for the characters in `charArray`
`s.find(charArray, pos, n)`	Searches `s` as in the preceding method, but for the first `n` characters in `charArray`; the value `pos` must be given
`s.find_first_not_of(str, pos)`	Returns the first position ≥ `pos` of a character in `s` that does not match any of the characters in `str`; returns `npos` if there is no such position; 0 is the default value for `pos`
`s.find_first_not_of(ch, pos)`	Searches `s` as in the preceding method, but for `ch`

`s.find_first_not_of(charArray, pos)`	Searches `s` as in the preceding method, but for the characters in `charArray`
`s.find_first_not_of(charArray, pos, n)`	Searches `s` as in the preceding method, but using the first `n` characters in `charArray`; the value `pos` must be given
`s.find_first_of(str, pos)`	Returns the first position ≥ `pos` of a character in `s` that matches any character in `str`; returns `npos` if there is no such position; 0 is the default value for `pos`
`s.find_first_of(ch, pos)`	Searches `s` as in the preceding method, but for `ch`
`s.find_first_of(charArray, pos)`	Searches `s` as in the preceding method, but for the characters in `charArray`
`s.find_first_of(charArray, pos, n)`	Searches `s` as in the preceding method, but using the first `n` characters in `charArray`; the value `pos` must be given
`s.find_last_not_of(str, pos)`	Returns the highest position ≤ `pos` of a character in `s` that does not match any character in `str`; returns `npos` if there is no such position; `npos` is the default value for `pos`
`s.find_last_not_of(ch, pos)`	Searches `s` as in the preceding method, but for `ch`
`s.find_last_not_of(charArray, pos)`	Searches `s` as in the preceding method, but using the characters in `charArray`
`s.find_last_not_of(charArray, pos, n)`	Searches `s` as in the preceding method, but using the first `n` characters in `charArray`; the value `pos` must be given
`s.find_last_of(str, pos)`	Returns the highest position ≤ `pos` of a character in `s` that matches any character in `str`; returns `npos` if there is no such position; `npos` is the default value for `pos`
`s.find_last_of(ch, pos)`	Searches `s` as in the preceding method, but for `ch`
`s.find_last_of(charArray, pos)`	Searches `s` as in the preceding method, but using the characters in `charArray`
`s.find_last_of(charArray, pos, n)`	Searches `s` as in the preceding method, but using the first `n` characters in `charArray`; the value `pos` must be given
`s.insert(pos, str)`	Inserts a copy of `str` into `s` at position `pos`; returns `s`
`s.insert(pos1, str, pos2, n)`	Inserts a copy of `n` characters of `str` starting at position `pos2` into `s` at position `pos`; if `n` is too large, characters are copied only until the end of `str` is reached; returns `s`
`s.insert(pos, charArray, n)`	Inserts a copy of the first `n` characters of `charArray` into `s` at position `pos`; inserts all of its characters if `n` is omitted; returns `s`
`s.insert(pos, n, ch)`	Inserts `n` copies of the character `ch` into `s` at position `pos`; returns `s`
`s.insert(it, ch)`	Inserts a copy of the character `ch` into `s` at the position specified by `it` and returns an iterator positioned at this copy
`s.insert(it, n, ch)`	Inserts `n` copies of the character `ch` into `s` at the position specified by `it`; return type is `void`
`s.insert(it, inpIt1, inpIt2)`	Inserts copies of the characters in the range `[inpIt1, inpIt2)` into `s` at the position specified by `it`; return type is `void`
`s.length()`	Returns the length (of type `size_type`) of `s`
`s.max_size()`	Returns the maximum length (of type `size_type`) of `s`
`s.rbegin()`	Returns a reverse iterator positioned at the last character in `s`

s.rend()	Returns a reverse iterator positioned immediately before the first character in s
s.replace(pos1, n1, str)	Replaces the substring of s of length n1 beginning at position pos1 with str; if n1 is too large, all characters to the end of s are replaced; returns s
s.replace(it1, it2, str)	Same as the preceding, but for the substring of s consisting of the characters in the range [it1, it2); returns s
s.replace(pos1, n1, str, pos2, n2)	Replaces a substring of s as in the preceding reference, but using n2 characters in str, beginning at position pos2; if n2 is too large, characters to the end of str are used; returns s
s.replace(pos1, n1, charArray, n2)	Replaces a substring of s as before, but with the first n2 characters in charArray; if n2 is too large, characters to the end of charArray are used; if n2 is omitted, all of charArray is used; returns s
s.replace(it1, it2, charArray, n2)	Same as the preceding, but for the substring of s consisting of the characters in the range [it1, it2); returns s
s.replace(pos1, n1, n2, ch)	Replaces a substring of s as before, but with n2 copies of ch
s.replace(it1, it2, n2, ch)	Same as the preceding, but for the substring of s consisting of the characters in the range [it1, it2); returns s
s.replace(it1, it2, inpIt1, inpIt2)	Same as the preceding, but replaces with copies of the characters in the range [inpIt1, inpIt2); returns s
s.reserve(n)	Changes the storage allocation for s so that s.capacity() ≥ n, 0 if n is omitted; return type is void
s.resize(n, ch)	If n ≤ s.size(), truncates rightmost characters in s to make it of size n; otherwise, adds copies of character ch to end of s to increase its size to n, or adds a default character value (usually a blank) if ch is omitted; return type is void
s.rfind(str, pos)	Returns the highest position ≤ pos such that the next str.size() characters of s match those in str; returns npos if there is no such position; npos is the default value for pos
s.rfind(ch, pos)	Searches s as in the preceding method, but for ch
s.rfind(charArray, pos)	Searches s as in the preceding method, but for the characters in charArray
s.rfind(charArray, pos, n)	Searches s as in the preceding method, but for the first n characters in charArray; the value pos must be given
s.size()	Returns the length (of type size_type) of s
s.substr(pos, n)	Returns a copy of the substring consisting of n characters from s, beginning at position pos (default value 0); if n is too large or is omitted, characters are copied only until the end of s is reached
s.swap(str)	Swaps the contents of s and str; return type is void
swap(str1, str2)	Swaps the contents of str1 and str2; return type is void

THE list<T> CLASS TEMPLATE

The list<T> class template from the Standard Template Library (STL) was introduced in Chapter 14. The following is a list of the operations defined on list<T> objects; n is of type size_type; l, l1, and l2 are of type list<T>; val, val1, and val2 are of type T; ptr1 and ptr2 are pointers to values of type T; it1 and it2 are iterators; and inpIt1 and inpIt2 are input iterators.

Constructors:

`list<T> l;`	This declaration invokes the default constructor to construct `l` as an empty list
`list<T> l(n);`	This declaration initializes `l` to contain `n` default values of type `T`
`list<T> l(n, val);`	This declaration initializes `l` to contain `n` copies of `val`
`list<T> l(ptr1, ptr2)`	This declaration initializes `s` to contain the copies of all the `T` values in the range [`ptr1, ptr2`)
`list<T> l(l1);`	This declaration initializes `l` to contain a copy of `l1`
`l = l1`	Assigns a copy of `l1` to `l`
`l1 == l2`	Returns `true` if `l` and `l2` contain the same values, and `false` otherwise
`l1 < l2`	Returns `true` if `l1` is lexicographically less than `l2`—`l1.size()` is less than `l2.size()` and all the elements of `l1` match the first elements of `l2`; or if `val1` and `val2` are the first elements of `l1` and `l2`, respectively, that are different, `val1` is less than `val2`—and it returns `false` otherwise
`l.assign(n, val)`	Erases `l` and then inserts `n` copies of `val` (default `T` value if omitted)
`l.assign(inpIt1, inpIt2)`	Erases `l` and then inserts copies of the `T` values in the range [`inpIt1, inpIt2`)
`l.back()`	Returns a reference to the last element of `l`
`l.begin()`	Returns an iterator positioned at the first element of `l`
`l.empty()`	Returns true if `l` contains no elements, `false` otherwise
`l.end()`	Returns an iterator positioned immediately after the last element of `l`
`l.erase(it)`	Removes from `l` the element at the position specified by `it`; return type is `void`
`l.erase(it1, it2)`	Removes from `l` the elements in the range [`it1, it2`); return type is `void`
`l.front()`	Returns a reference to the first element of `l`
`l.insert(it, val)`	Inserts a copy of `val` (default `T` value if omitted) into `l` at the position specified by `it` and returns an iterator positioned at this copy
`l.insert(it, n, val)`	Inserts `n` copies of `val` into `l` at the position specified by `it`; return type is `void`
`l.insert(it, inpIt1, inpIt2)`	Inserts copies of the `T` values in the range [`inpIt1, inpIt2`) into `l` at the position specified by `it`; return type is `void`
`l.insert(ptr1, ptr2)`	Inserts copies of all the `T` values in the range [`ptr1, ptr2`) at the position specified by `it`; return type is `void`
`l.max_size()`	Returns the maximum number (of type `size_type`) of values that `l` can contain
`l.merge(l1)`	Merges the elements of `l1` into `l` so that the resulting list is sorted; both `l` and `l1` must have been already sorted (using <); return type is `void`
`l.push_back(val)`	Adds a copy of `val` at the end of `l`; return type is `void`
`l.push_front(val)`	Adds a copy of `val` at the front of `l`; return type is `void`
`l.pop_back()`	Removes the last element of `l`; return type is `void`

`l.pop_front()`	Removes the first element of `l`; return type is `void`
`l.rbegin()`	Returns a reverse iterator positioned at the last element of `l`
`l.remove(val)`	Removes all occurrences of `val` from `l`, using == to compare elements; return type is `void`
`l.rend()`	Returns a reverse iterator positioned immediately before the first element of `l`
`l.resize(n, val)`	Sets the size of `l` to `n`; if `n` > `l.size()`, copies of `val` (default `T` value if omitted) are appended to `l`; if `n` < `l.size()`, the appropriate number of elements is removed from the end of `l`
`l.reverse()`	Reverses the order of the elements of `l`; return type is `void`
`l.size()`	Returns the number (of type `size_type`) of elements `l` contains
`l.sort()`	Sorts the elements of `l` using <; return type is `void`
`l.splice(it, l1)`	Removes the elements of `l1` and inserts them into `l` at the position specified by `it`; return type is `void`
`l.splice(it, l1, it1)`	Removes the element of `l1` at the position specified by `it1` and inserts it into `l` at the position specified by `it`; return type is `void`
`l.splice(it, l1, it1, it2)`	Removes the elements of `l1` in the range [`it1, it2`) and inserts them into `l` at the position specified by `it`; return type is `void`
`l.swap(l1)`	Swaps the contents of `l` and `l1`; return type is `void`
`l.unique()`	Replaces all repeating sequences of an element of `l` with a single occurrence of that element; return type is `void`

E

Answers to Quick Quizzes

Quick Quiz 1.2

1. program
2. comment
3. curly braces, main
4. `return`
5. Design
   Coding
   Testing, execution, and debugging
   Maintenance
6. State program's behavior
   Identify the objects
   Identify the operations
   Arrange operations in an algorithm
7. objects
8. operations
9. variables
10. `cout, ostream`
11. `cin, istream`
12. `<<, >>`
13. debugging
14. syntax errors and logic errors

Quick Quiz 1.4

1. reusable
2. class
3. space for storing an object's attributes and operations to manipulate the object
4. message
5. false

Quick Quiz 2.2

1. integers, integer variations, reals, characters, booleans
2. `short`, `int`, `unsigned`
3. `float`, `double`, `long double`
4. literal
5. false
6. true
7. true
8. single quotes (or apostrophes)
9. false
10. true
11. escape
12. double quotes
13. not legal—must begin with a letter
14. legal
15. not legal—identifiers may contain only letters, digits, and underscores
16. not legal—same reason as 15
17. integer
18. neither
19. real
20. real
21. neither
22. real
23. integer
24. integer

Quick Quiz 2.2 (Continued)

25. character
26. neither
27. string
28. string
29. character
30. character
31. character
32. neither
33. `const int GRAVITY = 32;`
34.
```
const double EARTH = 1.5E10,
             MARS  = 1.2E12;
```
35. `int distanceTraveled;`
36.
```
unsigned idNumber;
float salary;
char employeeCode;
```
37. `int distanceTraveled = 0;`
38.
```
unsigned idNumber = 9999;
float salary = 0;
char employeeCode = ' ';
```

Quick Quiz 2.3

1. attributes, operations
2. header
3. attribute
4. `public:`
5. instance, data members

Quick Quiz 3.2

1. 0
2. 2.6
3. 2
4. 5
5. 8
6. 3
7. 2
8. 36.0
9. 3.0
10. 8.0
11. 2.0
12. 3.0
13. 11.0
14. 1
15. 7.0
16. 5.1
17. 8.0
18. 10.0
19. 3.0
20. 32.0
21. `10 + 5 * B - 4 * A * C`
22. `sqrt(A + 3 * pow(B, 2))`

Quick Quiz 3.3

1. `false, true`
2. <, >, ==, <=, >=, !=
3. `!, &&, ||`
4. `false`

Quick Quiz 3.3 (Continued)

5. `true`
6. `false`
7. `false`
8. `true`
9. `true`
10. `true`
11. `true`
12. `true` (but probably should be written `0 <= count && count <= 2`, which would be false)
13. `true`
14. `x != 0`
15. `-10 < x && x < 10`
16. `(x > 0 && y > 0) || (x < 0 && y < 0)` or more simply, `x * y > 0`

Quick Quiz 3.4

1. single quotes
2. false
3. true
4. `assert('0' <= c && c <= '9');`
5. `assert(isdigit(c));`
6.
```
assert(c == 'a' || c = 'A' || c == 'e' || c = 'E' ||
       c == 'i' || c = 'I' || c == 'o' || c = 'O' ||
       c == 'u' || c = 'U');
```

Quick Quiz 3.5

1. valid
2. not valid—variable must be to left of assignment operator
3. valid
4. not valid—variable must be to left of assignment operator
5. valid
6. not valid—can't assign a string to an integer variable
7. valid
8. not valid—`'65'` is not a legal character constant
9. valid
10. valid
11. valid
12. valid
13. valid
14. valid
15. not valid—++ can only be used with integer variables
16. `xValue:` 3.5
17. `xValue:` 6.1
18. `jobId:` 6
19. `xValue:` 5.0
20. `jobId:` 1
21. `jobId:` 5
    `intFive1:` 6
22. `jobId:` 6
    `intFive2:` 6

Quick Quiz 3.5 (Continued)

23. `intEight:` 64

24. `letter:  a`

25. `check:  true`

26. `distance = rate * time;`

27. `c = sqrt(a*a + b*b);`

28.
```
++x;
x++;
x += 1;
x = x + 1;
```

Quick Quiz 3.7

1. streams

2. `true`

3. `cin`, `istream`

4. `cout`, `cerr`, `ostream`

5. `>>`

6. `<<`

7. `cin`

8. `cout`

9. right

10. format manipulators

11. `12323.4568`

12. `␣␣123124␣␣125127` ← blank line

13.
```
␣␣␣␣␣23.
␣␣␣␣23.5
␣␣␣23.46
␣␣␣23.46
23.5
```

14.
`number1:` 11
`number2:` 22
`number3:` 33

15.
`real1:` 1.1
`real2:` 2.0
`real3:` 33

16. `number1:` 1
Input error: attempting to read a period for integer variable

17.
`number1:` 1
`real1:` .1
`number2:` 2
`real2:` 3.3
`number3:` 4
`real3:` 5.5

Quick Quiz 3.8

1. constructor

2. default

3. false

4. true

5. scope, `::`

6. explicit

7. parameters

8. arguments

Quick Quiz 4.2

1. objects received from the calling function
   objects returned to the calling function
2. parameters
3. `double`
4. `void`
5. no statements
6. argument
7. 6
8. true
9. false
10. `int what(int n);`
11.
```
#include <cmath>
double func(double x)
{
   return x*x + sqrt(x);
}
```
12.
```
int average(int num1, int num2)
{
   return (num1 + num2)/ 2;
}
```
13.
```
void display(int num1, int num2, int num3)
{
   cout << num1 << "\n\n"
        << num2 << "\n\n"
        << num1 << endl;
}
```

Quick Quiz 4.3

1. `6`
2. `5`
3. `6`
4. `10`
5. `10`
6. `10`
7. `excellent`
8. `excellent`
9. `good`
10. `fair`
11. `bad`
12.
```
if (number < 0 || number > 100)
   cout << "Out of range\n";
```
13.
```
if (x <= 1.5)
   n = 1;
else if (x <= 2.5)
   n = 2;
else
   n = 3;
```

Quick Quiz 4.4

1.
```
Hello
Hello
Hello
Hello
Hello
```

2.
```
HelloHelloHello
```

3.
```
Hello
Hello
Hello
```

4.
```
1 2
2 3
3 4
4 5
5 6
6 7
```

5.
```

36


25


16


9


4


1
```

6.
```
Hello
```

7. No output produced.

8.
```
1
3
5
7
9
```

9.
```
10
```

Quick Quiz 4.6

1. false

2. header (or interface), implementation, and documentation

3.
1. Functions in a library are reusable.
2. They hide implementation details.
3. They make programs easier to maintain.

4. header (or interface)

Quick Quiz 4.6 (Continued)

4. They provide separate compilation.
5. The support independent coding.
6. They simplify testing.

5. implementation
6. header
7. public, private
8. `<lib>`
9. `"lib"`
10. compilation and linking
11. false
12. true
13. Information hiding

Quick Quiz 4.7

1. class, instance
2. Class methods are messages sent to a class; instance methods are messages sent to an object.
3. `C::m(a);`
4. `static`
5. true
6. scope, `::`
7. `static`
8. true
9. false
10. true

Quick Quiz 5.2

1. encapsulation
2. data, function
3. overloading
4. dot
5. `month`, `day`, `year`
6. `display()`
7. `birth.display();`

Quick Quiz 5.3

1. Bjarne Stroustrup
2. Jerry Schwarz
3. `istream` and `ostream`
4. stream
5. `istream`
6. `cin`
7. good, bad, and fail
8. `good()`
9. `clear()`
10. `ignore()`
11. true
12. false
13. `ostream`
14. `cout`, `cerr`
15. `endl`, `flush`
16. false
17. true

Quick Quiz 5.4

1. empty
2. `string label;`
3. `const string UNITS = "meters";`
4. `"ABC", "DEF"`
5. `'e'`
6. `8`
7. `0`
8. `false`
9. `true`
10. `true`
11. `false`
12. `"seashoreshell"`
13. `"she"`
14. `10`
15. `27`
16. `12`
17. `29`
18. `0`
19. `35`
20. `"bell"`
21. `"seal on the shore"`
22. `"She sells the seashore."`

Quick Quiz 5.6

1. objects
2. accessor
3. mutator
4. convertor
5. utility
6. false
7. `const`

Quick Quiz 6.4

1. `198`
2. `198`
`98`
`default`
3. `default`
4. `default`
5. `-2`
6. `-2`
`default`
7. `123`
8. `456`
9. no output produced
10. error—`x` must be integer (or integer compatible)

Quick Quiz 6.6

1. mutator
2. input
3. Validation
4. true
5. false

Quick Quiz 7.4

1. counting (or counter-controlled) loops, `for`

2. initialization expression, loop condition, step expression, loop body

3. `if-break` (or `if-return`)

4. pretest

5. posttest

6. posttest

7. pretest

8.
```
2*0 = 0
2*1 = 2
2*2 = 4
2*3 = 6
2*4 = 8
2*5 = 10
2*6 = 12
2*7 = 14
2*8 = 16
2*9 = 18
```

9.
```
1   3   5   7   9   11
```

10.
```
11
22
1
33
2
1
```

11.
```
000
112
228
18
```

12.
```
4
5
6
```

13.
```
3
2
1
0
-1

*****
```

14.
```
0 1
1 2
2 5
3 10
4 17
```

15.
```
4 12
3 5
2 0
1 -3
```

Quick Quiz 7.6

1. sentinel, counting, query-controlled
2. end-of-data flag, sentinel
3. true
4. end-of-file (or eof)
5. `eof()`
6. false
7. false
8. query

Quick Quiz 7.8

1. Inheritance
2. Inheritance
3. child (or sub-)
4. parent (or super- or base)
5. is a
6. `public`
7. override
8. A's
9. true
10. `B:m1()`
11. hierarchies

Quick Quiz 8.3

1. value
2. value
3. value
4. reference
5. ampersand (&)
6. false
7. true
8. false
9. false
10. false
11.
```
void f(const int & x, int & y, int & z)
{
   z = y = x * x + 1;
}
```
12. `String = batbatelk`

Quick Quiz 8.4

1. true
2. `inline`
3. That it replace each call to this function with the body of the function, with the arguments for that function call substituted for the function's parameters
4. `cout << number * (number + 1) / 2;`
5. header
6. true
7. false

Quick Quiz 8.5

1. scope
2. false
3. end of the block
4. the body of the function
5. a scope error message (perhaps a warning) indicating that `i` in the last line is not declared
6. signature
7. name
8. signature
9. template
10. type
11. Generate an instance of `print()` with type parameter `something` replaced everywhere by `int`.

Quick Quiz 8.6

1. recursion
2. 1. An anchor or base case that specifies the function's value for one or more values of the parameter(s)

   2. An inductive or recursive step that defines the function's value for the current values of the parameter(s) in terms of previously defined function and/or parameter values
3. true
4. 15
5. 0
6. 120
7. infinite recursion results

Quick Quiz 8.7

1. class
2. `static`
3. false
4. true
5. false
6. constructor
7. destructor
8. `C`
9. `~C`

Quick Quiz 9.2

1. `istream`, `cin`
2. `ostream`, `cout` (or `cerr`)
3. `istream`
4. `ostream`
5. `fstream`
6. false
7.
```
ifstream inputStream;
inputStream.open("EmployeeInfo");
```

Quick Quiz 9.2 (Continued)

8. `ifstream inputStream("EmployeeInfo");`

9.
```
ofstream outputStream;
outputStream.open("EmployeeReport");
```

10. `ofstream outputStream("EmployeeReport");`

11.
```
string inFileName, outFileName;
cout << "Name of input file? ";
cin >> inFileName;
ifstream inputStream;
inputStream.open(inFileName.data());
```
or replace the last two lines with
```
ifstream inputStream(inFileName.data());
```

12. false

13. true

14. `assert(inputStream.is_open());`

15. `get_line(inputStream, str);` where `str` is of type `string`

16.
```
if (inputSteam.eof())
   cout << "End of file\n";
```

17. `inputStream.close();`

Quick Quiz 9.4

1. false

2. true

3. random

4. `tellg()`, `seekg()`

5.
```
inputStream.seekg(3,
            ios::beg());
```

6.
```
inputStream.seekg(3,
            ios::cur());
```

7.
```
inputStream.seekg(0,
            ios::end());
```

8.
```
char ch;
inputStream.get(ch);
cout << ch;
```

9.
```
char ch;
inputStream.peek(ch);
cout << ch;
```
or
```
inputStream.get(ch);
cout << ch;
inputStream.putback(ch)
```

10. formatting manipulators

Quick Quiz 10.2

1. false

2. false (not necessarily)

3. true

4. false

5. true

6. false

Quick Quiz 10.2 (Continued)

7. false

8. 5

9. true

10. true

11. true

12. false

13. true

14. base

15. false

16. true

17. false

18. reference

19.
```
xValue[0]: 0.0
xValue[1]: 0.5
xValue[2]: 1.0
xValue[3]: 1.5
xValue[4]: 2.0
```

20.
```
number[0]: 0
number[1]: 3
number[2]: 4
number[3]: 7
number[4]: 8
```

21.
```
number[0]: 1
number[1]: 2
number[2]: 4
number[3]: 8
number[4]: 16
```

22.
```
number[0]: 0
number[1]: 0
number[2]: 0
number[3]: 0
number[4]: 0
```

Quick Quiz 10.3

1. For a list $x_1, x_2, \ldots, x_n$, simple selection sort makes a pass through the list to find the smallest element, swaps it with x_1; it then finds the smallest element in the sublist $x_2, \ldots, x_n$ and swaps it with x_2. It repeatedly does this until the sublist it is examining has only two elements.

2. For a list $x_1, x_2, \ldots, x_n$, linear insertion sort inserts x_2 into the already sorted one-element list x_1, then inserts x_2 into the already sorted two-element list x_1, x_2. It continues in this way until x_n is inserted into the already sorted $(n - 1)$-element list $x_1, x_2, \ldots, x_{n-1}$.

3. true

4. Quicksort selects one element called a pivot and correctly positions it so that all elements to its left are smaller and all elements to its right are larger. The two sublists then can be sorted independently using quicksort recursively.

5. pivot

Quick Quiz 10.6

1. `int`

2. 0, 0

3. 5, 5

4. 5, 5

5. 10, 7

6. `1 1`

7. `0 88`

8. true

Quick Quiz 10.6 (Continued)

9. false
10. true
11. `1 1 1 1 1`
12. `0 0 0 0 0 77`
13. 0
14. memory location after the last element
15. true
16. 0, 0, 0, 0, 0, 0, 0.5, 1.0, 1.5, 2.0
17. 1, 1, 1, 1, 1, 0, 3, 4, 7, 8
18. 1, 1, 1, 1, 1, 2, 2, 2, 2
19. 1, 1, 2, 2, 2
20. Alex Stepanov and Meng Lee
21. stack
22. queue

Quick Quiz 11.4

1. class, class library
2. operations
3. data
4. false
5. I-can-do-it-myself
6. encapsulation
7. to prevent programs from accessing the data
8. private
9. preprocessor
10. #
11. conditional-compilation
12. methods
13. false
14. name of the class, scope (::)
15. constant, `const`
16. `Employee`
17. default-value constructors, explicit-value constructors
18. public
19.
```
class Employee
{
 public:
   void print(ostream & out);
   void read(istream & in);
 private:
   int myID;
   string myName;
};
```

Quick Quiz 12.2

1. integer
2. false
3. true
4. false
5. 3
6. 3
7. 6
8. 0

Quick Quiz 12.2 (Continued)

9. 8
10. 4
11. `Nonsense`
12. enumerator
13. true
14. false
15. true
16. true
17.
```
enum WeekDays {Sunday = 1, Monday, Tuesday, Wednesday,
               Thursday, Friday, Saturday};
```
18. To store a type declaration and the operations on objects of that type

Quick Quiz 12.3

1. 1. Operations on a C-style enumeration cannot be defined as function members, and so C-style enumerations are not consistent with the I-can-do-it-myself principle.

2. Because there is no class invariant, operations on a C-style enumeration cannot assume that valid values will be passed to an enumeration parameter.

2. true
3. So that other operations that use the class's members can be assured that the invariant holds.
4. explicit-value
5. `(), (int)`

Quick Quiz 13.2

1. two-dimensional
2. three-dimensional
3. square
4. 82
5. 33
6. –1
7. 33
8. 12
9. 1, 2, 3, 4
10. 95
11. 999
12. 29
13. 1326
14. 1326
15. self-contained

Quick Quiz 13.3

1. true
2. true
3. 5, 4
4. `qqTab[1][3] = 1.1;`
5. 5
6. 4

Quick Quiz 13.3 (Continued)

7. `qqTab[1].push_back(99.9);`

8. `TableRow bottom(4, 0.0);`
   `qqTab.push_back(bottom);`

Quick Quiz 13.4

1. $m \times n$ matrix

2. 2, 2

3. $\begin{bmatrix} 5 & -2 \\ 8 & 8 \end{bmatrix}$

4. $\begin{bmatrix} 1 & 2 & 0 \\ -1 & 3 & -3 \\ 10 & 5 & 9 \end{bmatrix}$

5. Not defined—number of columns in $B \neq$ number of rows in C

6. Not defined—number of columns in $C \neq$ number of rows in B

7. $\begin{bmatrix} 4 & 2 \\ 3 & -1 \\ 0 & 1 \end{bmatrix}$

8. $\begin{bmatrix} -2 & -2 \\ 1 & -1 \\ 2 & 5 \end{bmatrix}$

Quick Quiz 14.1

1. address
2. `&`
3. `*`
4. `*`
5. `->`
6. address
7. `double` value
8. address
9. address
10. `double` value
11. `double` value
12. address
13. null
14. `1.1`
15. `3.3`
16. true
17. true
18. `012a50`

Quick Quiz 14.2

1. compile, run
2. `new`, null address, address, anonymous
3. `delete`
4. pointer variable
5. `66`

Quick Quiz 14.2 (Continued)

6. `C(const C& original);`
7. `~C();`
8. false
9. true
10. default, byte, byte
11. A class should have a copy constructor when the class allocates memory at run time. This is to ensure that a distinct copy of the run-time object is constructed.
12. memory leak
13. destructor
14. A class should have a destructor when the class allocates memory at run time. This is to ensure that such memory is not marooned.
15. A class should have an assignment operator when the class allocates memory at run time. This is to ensure that a distinct copy of the value being assigned is constructed.

Quick Quiz 15.1

1. 10011010010
2. 2322
3. 4D2
4. first, LIFO (last-in-first-out)
5. empty, push, top, pop
6. adapter
7. 123
8. 111, 111
9. 0, 2, 4

Quick Quiz 15.2

1. For a queue, elements are added at one end and removed at the other. For a stack, elements are added and removed at the same end.
2. last
3. FIFO
4. spool
5. buffers
6. deque
7. 789
8. 222, 111
9. 4, 6, 8

Quick Quiz 15.4

1. root
2. leaves
3. children, parent
4. at most two children
5. 50
6. 10, 40, 70

Quick Quiz 15.4 (Continued)

7.

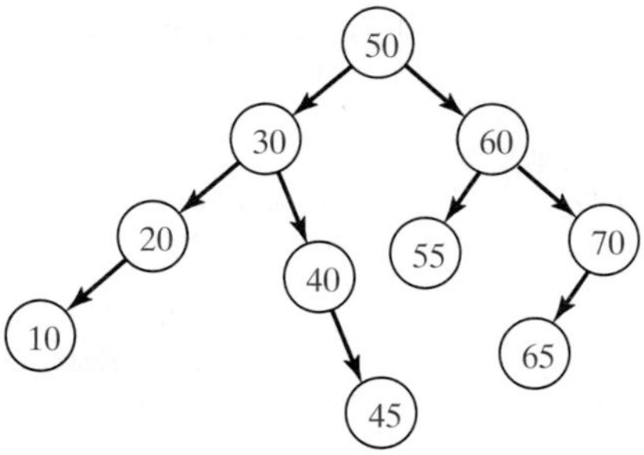

8.

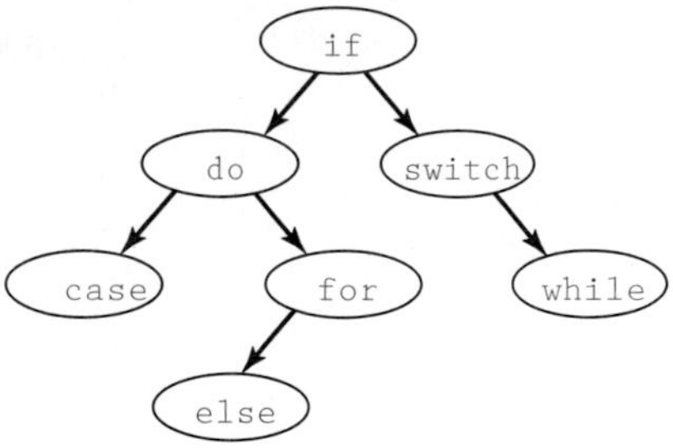

9.

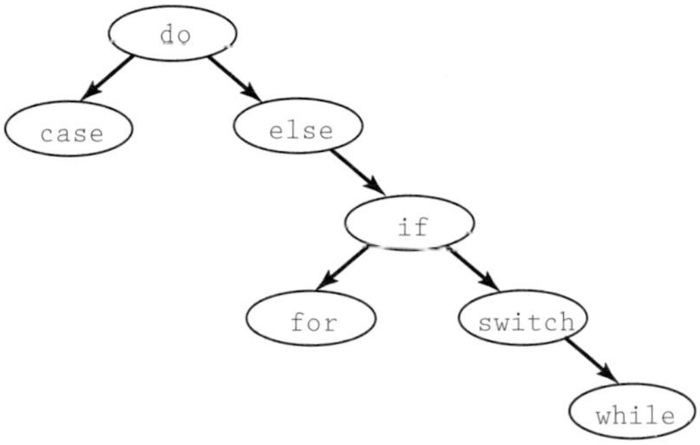

10.

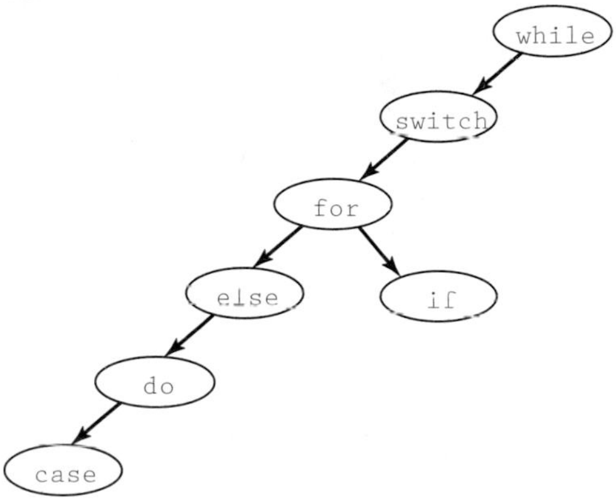

11. 10, 20, 30, 40, 50, 60, 70, 80, 90, 100

12. 80, 30, 20, 10, 60, 50, 40, 70, 90, 100

13. 10, 20, 40, 50, 70, 60, 30, 100, 90, 80

INDEX

G